Bhagavad-gītā As It Is

COMPLETE EDITION

*with original Sanskrit text,
Roman transliteration, English equivalents,
translation and elaborate purports*

His Divine Grace
A.C. Bhaktivedanta Swami Prabhupāda

Founder-Ācārya of the International Society for Krishna Consciousness

**The Macmillan Company, New York, New York
Collier-Macmillan Limited, London**

Bhagavad-gītā As It Is

is a reproduction of the book first published by
Collier Books and Macmillan Company in 1972

Krishna Books Inc is licensed by the Bhaktivedanta Book Trust
to print and publish the pre-1978 literary works of
His Divine Grace A.C. Bhaktivedanta Swami Prabhupāda.

Reader interested in obtaining other titles by the
author may contact Krishna Books Inc:

at: http://www.krishnabooks.org
email: info@krishnabooks.org

Krishna Books Inc
578 Washington Blvd. Suite 808
Marina del Rey, CA 90292 USA

Library of Congress Catalog Card Number: 72-79319
Complete 1972 English Edition Chapter 1-18;   ISBN: 978-1-60293-000-1

To further experience the bliss of chanting Hare Krishna
please visit an Iskcon Center near you: http://iskcon.org/

HARE KRISHNA HARE KRISHNA   KRISHNA KRISHNA HARE HARE
HARE RAMA HARE RAMA   RAMA RAMA HARE HARE

Reprints: 1999-2015

To
ŚRĪLA BALADEVA VIDYĀBHŪṢAṆA
who presented so nicely
the "*Govinda-bhāṣya*" commentary
on
Vedānta philosophy

BOOKS by

His Divine Grace

A.C. Bhaktivedanta Swami Prabhupāda

Published by Krishna Books Inc.

Bhagavad-gītā As It Is

Śrīmad Bhāgavatam, First Canto

Kṛṣṇa, the Supreme Personality of Godhead

Teachings of Lord Chaitanya

Śrī Īśopaniṣad

The Nectar of Devotion

The Science of Self-Realization

Rāja-vidyā: The King of Knowledge

Easy Journey to Other Planets

Kṛṣṇa, the Reservoir of Pleasure

The Perfection of Yoga

Beyond Birth and Death

On Chanting Hare Krishna

TABLE OF CONTENTS

Foreword VII

Preface IX

Introduction 1

CHAPTER ONE
**Observing the Armies on
the Battlefield of Kurukṣetra** 31

CHAPTER TWO
Contents of the Gītā Summarized 71

CHAPTER THREE
Karma-yoga 161

CHAPTER FOUR
Transcendental Knowledge 213

CHAPTER FIVE
**Karma-yoga–
Action in Kṛṣṇa Consciousness** 271

CHAPTER SIX
Sāṅkhya-yoga 307

CHAPTER SEVEN
Knowledge of the Absolute 361

CHAPTER EIGHT
Attaining the Supreme 409

CHAPTER NINE
The Most Confidential Knowledge 441

CHAPTER TEN
The Opulence of the Absolute 491

CHAPTER ELEVEN
The Universal Form 539

CHAPTER TWELVE
Devotional Service 595

CHAPTER THIRTEEN
**Nature, the Enjoyer,
and Consciousness** 619

CHAPTER FOURTEEN
The Three Modes of Material Nature 663

CHAPTER FIFTEEN
The Yoga of the Supreme Person 693

CHAPTER SIXTEEN
The Divine and Demoniac Natures 721

CHAPTER SEVENTEEN
The Divisions of Faith 751

CHAPTER EIGHTEEN
**Conclusion–
The Perfection of Renunciation** 779

Appendixes
Picture Index 851
References 859
Glossary 861
Sanskrit Pronunciation Guide 877
Index of Sanskrit Verses 879
General Index 895
Reviews 978

Foreword

The *Bhagavad-gītā* is the best known and the most frequently translated of Vedic religious texts. Why it should be so appealing to the Western mind is an interesting question. It has drama, for its setting is a scene of two great armies, banners flying, drawn up opposite one another on the field, poised for battle. It has ambiguity, and the fact that Arjuna and his charioteer Kṛṣṇa are carrying on their dialogue between the two armies suggests the indecision of Arjuna about the basic question: should he enter battle against and kill those who are friends and kinsmen? It has mystery, as Kṛṣṇa demonstrates to Arjuna His cosmic form. It has a properly complicated view of the ways of the religious life and treats of the paths of knowledge, works, discipline and faith and their inter-relationships, problems that have bothered adherents of other religions in other times and places. The devotion spoken of is a deliberate means of religious satisfaction, not a mere outpouring of poetic emotion. Next to the *Bhāgavata-purāṇa*, a long work from South India, the *Gītā* is the text most frequently quoted in the philosophical writings of the Gauḍīya Vaiṣṇava school, the school represented by Swami Bhaktivedanta as the latest in a long succession of teachers. It can be said that this school of Vaiṣṇavism was founded, or revived, by Śrī Kṛṣṇa-Caitanya Mahāprabhu (1486-1533) in Bengal, and that it is currently the strongest single religious force in the eastern part of the Indian subcontinent. The Gauḍīya Vaiṣṇava school, for whom Kṛṣṇa is Himself the Supreme God, and not merely an incarnation of another deity, sees *bhakti* as an immediate and powerful religious force, consisting of love between man and God. Its discipline consists of devoting all one's actions to the Deity, and one listens to the stories of Kṛṣṇa from the sacred texts, one chants Kṛṣṇa's name, washes, bathes, and dresses the *mūrti* of Kṛṣṇa, feeds Him and takes the remains of the food offered to Him, thus absorbing His grace; one does these things and many more, until one has been changed: the devotee has become transformed into one close to Kṛṣṇa, and sees the Lord face to face.

Swami Bhaktivedanta comments upon the *Gītā* from this point of view, and that is legitimate. More than that, in this translation the Western reader has the unique opportunity of seeing how a Kṛṣṇa devotee interprets his own texts. It is the Vedic exegetical tradition, justly famous, in action. This book is then a welcome addition from many points of view. It can serve as a valuable textbook for the college student. It allows us to listen to a skilled interpreter explicating a text which has profound religious meaning. It gives us insights into the original and highly convincing ideas of the Gauḍīya Vaiṣṇava school. In providing the Sanskrit in both Devanagari and transliteration, it offers the Sanskrit specialist the opportunity to re-interpret, or debate particular Sanskrit meanings—although I think there will be little disagreement about the quality of the Swami's Sanskrit scholarship. And finally, for the nonspecialist, there is readable English and a devotional attitude which cannot help but move the sensitive reader. And there are the paintings, which, incredibly as it may seem to those familiar with contemporary Indian religious art, were done by American devotees.

The scholar, the student of Gauḍīya Vaiṣṇavism, and the increasing number of Western readers interested in classical Vedic thought have been done a service by Swami Bhaktivedanta. By bringing us a new and living interpretation of a text already known to many, he has increased our understanding manyfold; and arguments for understanding, in these days of estrangement, need not be made.

Professor Edward C. Dimock, Jr.

Department of South Asian Languages and Civilization
University of Chicago

Preface

Originally I wrote *Bhagavad-gītā As It Is* in the form in which it is presented now. When this book was first published, the original manuscript was, unfortunately, cut short to less than 400 pages, without illustrations and without explanations for most of the original verses of the *Śrīmad Bhagavad-gītā*. In all of my other books—*Śrīmad Bhāgavatam, Śrī Īśopaniṣad*, etc.—the system is that I give the original verse, its English transliteration, word-for-word Sanskrit-English equivalents, translations and purports. This makes the book very authentic and scholarly and makes the meaning self-evident. I was not very happy, therefore, when I had to minimize my original manuscript. But later on, when the demand for *Bhagavad-gītā As It Is* considerably increased, I was requested by many scholars and devotees to present the book in its original form, and Messrs. Macmillan and Co. agreed to publish the complete edition. Thus the present attempt is to offer the original manuscript of this great book of knowledge with full *paramparā* explanation in order to establish the Kṛṣṇa consciousness movement more soundly and progressively.

Our Kṛṣṇa consciousness movement is genuine, historically authorized, natural and transcendental due to its being based on *Bhagavad-gītā As It Is*. It is gradually becoming the most popular movement in the entire world, especially amongst the younger generation. It is becoming more and more interesting to the older generation also. Older gentlemen are becoming interested, so much so that the fathers and grandfathers of my disciples are encouraging us by becoming life members of our great society, the International Society for Krishna Consciousness. In Los Angeles many fathers and mothers used to come to see me to express their feelings of gratitude for my leading the Kṛṣṇa consciousness movement throughout the entire world. Some of them said that it is greatly fortunate for the Americans that I have started the Kṛṣṇa consciousness movement in America. But actually the original father of this movement is Lord Kṛṣṇa Himself, since it was started a very long time ago but is coming down to human society by disciplic succession. If I have any credit in this connection, it does not belong to me personally, but it is due to my eternal spiritual master, His Divine Grace Oṁ Viṣṇupāda Paramahaṁsa Parivrā-jakācārya 108 Śrī Śrīmad Bhaktisiddhānta Sarasvatī Gosvāmī Mahārāja Prabhupāda.

If personally I have any credit in this matter, it is only that I have tried to present *Bhagavad-gītā* as it is, without adulteration. Before my presentation of *Bhagavad-gītā As It Is*, almost all the English editions of *Bhagavad-gītā* were introduced to fulfill someone's personal ambition. But our attempt, in presenting *Bhagavad-gītā As It Is*, is to present the mission of the Supreme Personality of Godhead, Kṛṣṇa. Our business is to present the will of Kṛṣṇa, not that of any mundane speculator like the politician, philosopher or scientist, for they have very little knowledge of Kṛṣṇa, despite all their other knowledge. When Kṛṣṇa says, *man-manā bhava mad-bhakto mad-yājī mām namaskuru*, etc., we, unlike the so-called scholars, do not say that Kṛṣṇa and His inner spirit are different. Kṛṣṇa is absolute, and there is no difference between Kṛṣṇa's name, Kṛṣṇa's form, Kṛṣṇa's quality, Kṛṣṇa's pastimes, etc. This absolute position of Kṛṣṇa is difficult to understand for any person who is not a devotee of Kṛṣṇa in the *paramparā* (disciplic succession) system. Generally the so-called scholars, politicians, philosophers, and *svāmīs*, without perfect knowledge of Kṛṣṇa, try to banish or kill Kṛṣṇa when writing commentary on *Bhagavad-gītā*. Such unauthorized commentary upon *Bhagavad-gītā* is known as *Māyāvādī-Bhāṣya*, and Lord Caitanya has warned us about these unauthorized men. Lord Caitanya clearly says that anyone who tries to understand *Bhagavad-gītā* from the Māyāvādī point of view will commit a great blunder. The result of such a blunder will be that the misguided student of *Bhagavad-gītā* will certainly be bewildered on the path of spiritual guidance and will not be able to go back home, back to Godhead.

Our only purpose is to present this *Bhagavad-gītā As It Is* in order to guide the conditioned student to the same purpose for which Kṛṣṇa descends to this planet once in a day of Brahmā, or every 8,600,000,000 years. This purpose is stated in *Bhagavad-gītā*, and we have to accept it as it is; otherwise there is no point in trying to understand the *Bhagavad-gītā* and its speaker, Lord Kṛṣṇa. Lord Kṛṣṇa first spoke *Bhagavad-gītā* to the sun-god some hundreds of millions of years ago. We have to accept this fact and thus understand the historical significance of *Bhagavad-gītā*, without misinterpretation, on the authority of Kṛṣṇa. To interpret *Bhagavad-gītā* without any reference to the will of Kṛṣṇa is the greatest offense. In order to save oneself from this offense, one has to understand the Lord as the Supreme Personality of Godhead, as He was directly understood by Arjuna, Lord Kṛṣṇa's first disciple. Such understanding of *Bhagavad-gītā* is really profitable and authorized for the welfare of human society in fulfilling the mission of life.

The Kṛṣṇa consciousness movement is essential in human society, for it offers the highest perfection of life. How this is so is explained fully in the

Bhagavad-gītā. Unfortunately, mundane wranglers have taken advantage of *Bhagavad-gītā* to push forward their demonic propensities and mislead people regarding right understanding of the simple principles of life. Everyone should know how God or Kṛṣṇa is great, and everyone should know the factual position of the living entities. Everyone should know that a living entity is eternally a servant and that unless one serves Kṛṣṇa one has to serve illusion in different varieties of the three modes of material nature, and thus perpetually one has to wander within the cycle of birth and death; even the so-called liberated Māyāvādī speculator has to undergo this process. This knowledge constitutes a great science, and each and every living being has to hear it for his own interest.

People in general, especially in this age of Kali, are enamored by the external energy of Kṛṣṇa, and they wrongly think that by advancement of material comforts every man will be happy. They have no knowledge that the material or external nature is very strong, for everyone is strongly bound by the stringent laws of material nature. A living entity is happily the part and parcel of the Lord, and thus his natural function is to render immediate service to the Lord. By the spell of illusion one tries to be happy by serving his personal sense gratification in different forms which will never make him happy. Instead of satisfying his own personal material senses, he has to satisfy the senses of the Lord. That is the highest perfection of life. The Lord wants this, and He demands it. One has to understand this central point of *Bhagavad-gītā.* Our Kṛṣṇa consciousness movement is teaching the whole world this central point, and because we are not polluting the theme of *Bhagavad-gītā As It Is,* anyone seriously interested in deriving benefit by studying the *Bhagavad-gītā* must take help from the Kṛṣṇa consciousness movement for practical understanding of *Bhagavad-gītā* under the direct guidance of the Lord. We hope, therefore, that people will derive the greatest benefit by studying *Bhagavad-gītā As It Is* as we have presented it here, and if even one man becomes a pure devotee of the Lord we shall consider our attempt a success.

12 May 1971
Sydney, Australia

INTRODUCTION

om ajñāna-timirāndhasya jñānāñjana-śalākayā
cakṣur unmīlitaṁ yena tasmai śrī-gurave namaḥ

śrī-caitanya-mano 'bhīṣṭaṁ sthāpitaṁ yena bhū-tale
svayaṁ rūpaḥ kadā mahyaṁ dadāti sva-padāntikam

I was born in the darkest ignorance, and my spiritual master opened my eyes with the torch of knowledge. I offer my respectful obeisances unto him.

When will Śrīla Rūpa Gosvāmī Prabhupāda, who has established within this material world the mission to fulfill the desire of Lord Caitanya, give me shelter under his lotus feet?

vande 'haṁ śrī-guroḥ śrī-yuta-pada-kamalaṁ śrī-gurun vaiṣṇavāṁś ca
śrī-rūpaṁ sāgrajātaṁ saha-gaṇa-raghunāthānvitaṁ taṁ sa-jīvam
sādvaitaṁ sāvadhūtaṁ parijana-sahitaṁ kṛṣṇa-caitanya-devaṁ
śrī-rādhā-kṛṣṇa-pādān saha-gaṇa-lalitā-śrī-viśākhānvitāṁś ca

I offer my respectful obeisances unto the lotus feet of my spiritual master and unto the feet of all Vaiṣṇavas. I offer my respectful obeisances unto the lotus feet of Śrīla Rūpa Gosvāmī along with his elder brother Sanātana Gosvāmī, as well as Raghunātha Dāsa and Raghunātha Bhaṭṭa, Gopāla Bhaṭṭa, and Śrīla Jīva Gosvāmī. I offer my respectful obeisances to Lord Kṛṣṇa Caitanya and Lord Nityānanda along with Advaita Ācārya,

1

Gadādhara, Śrīvāsa, and other associates. I offer my respectful obeisances to Śrīmatī Rādhārāṇī and Śrī Kṛṣṇa along with Their associates, Śrī Lalitā and Viśākhā.

> *he kṛṣṇa karuṇā-sindho dīna-bandho jagat-pate*
> *gopeśa gopikā-kānta rādhā-kānta namo 'stu te*

O my dear Kṛṣṇa, You are the friend of the distressed and the source of creation. You are the master of the *gopīs* and the lover of Rādhārāṇī. I offer my respectful obeisances unto You.

> *tapta-kāñcana-gaurāṅgi rādhe vṛndāvaneśvari*
> *vṛṣabhānu-sute devi praṇamāmi hari-priye*

I offer my respects to Rādhārāṇī whose bodily complexion is like molten gold and who is the Queen of Vṛndāvana. You are the daughter of King Vṛṣabhānu, and You are very dear to Lord Kṛṣṇa.

> *vāñchā-kalpatarubhyaś ca kṛpā-sindhubhya eva ca*
> *patitānāṁ pāvanebhyo vaiṣṇavebhyo namo namaḥ*

I offer my respectful obeisances unto all the Vaiṣṇava devotees of the Lord who can fulfill the desires of everyone, just like desire trees, and who are full of compassion for the fallen souls.

> *śrī kṛṣṇa caitanya prabhu nityānanda*
> *śrī advaita gadādhara śrīvāsādi-gaura-bhakta-vṛnda*

I offer my obeisances to Śrī Kṛṣṇa Caitanya, Prabhu Nityānanda, Śrī Advaita, Gadādhara, Śrīvāsa and all others in the line of devotion.

> *hare kṛṣṇa, hare kṛṣṇa, kṛṣṇa kṛṣṇa, hare hare*
> *hare rāma, hare rāma, rāma rāma, hare hare.*

Bhagavad-gītā is also known as *Gītopaniṣad*. It is the essence of Vedic knowledge and one of the most important *Upaniṣads* in Vedic literature. Of course there are many commentaries in English on the *Bhagavad-gītā*, and one may question the necessity for another one. This present edition can be explained in the following way. Recently an American lady asked me to recommend an English translation of *Bhagavad-gītā*. Of course in America there are so many editions of *Bhagavad-gītā* available in English, but as far as I have seen, not only in America but also in India, none of them can be strictly said to be authoritative because in almost every one of them the commentator has expressed his own opinions without touching the spirit of *Bhagavad-gītā* as it is.

The spirit of *Bhagavad-gītā* is mentioned in *Bhagavad-gītā* itself. It is just like this: if we want to take a particular medicine, then we have to follow the directions written on the label. We cannot take the medicine according to our own whim or the direction of a friend. It must be taken according to the directions on the label or the directions given by a physician. Similarly, *Bhagavad-gītā* should be taken or accepted as it is directed by the speaker himself. The speaker of *Bhagavad-gītā* is Lord Śrī Kṛṣṇa. He is mentioned on every page of *Bhagavad-gītā* as the Supreme Personality of Godhead, Bhagavān. Of course the word "*bhagavān*" sometimes refers to any powerful person or any powerful demigod, and certainly here Bhagavān designates Lord Śrī Kṛṣṇa as a great personality, but at the same time we should know that Lord Śrī Kṛṣṇa is the Supreme Personality of Godhead, as is confirmed by all great *ācāryas* (spiritual masters) like Śaṅkarācārya, Rāmānujācārya, Madhvācārya, Nimbārka Svāmī, Śrī Caitanya Mahāprabhu and many other authorities of Vedic knowledge in India. The Lord Himself also establishes Himself as the Supreme Personality of Godhead in the *Bhagavad-gītā*, and He is accepted as such in the *Brahma-saṁhitā* and all the *Purāṇas*, especially the *Śrīmad-Bhāgavatam*, known as the *Bhāgavata Purāṇa* (*Kṛṣṇas tu bhagavān svayam*). Therefore we should take *Bhagavad-gītā* as it is directed by the Personality of Godhead Himself.

In the Fourth Chapter of the *Gītā* the Lord says:

> (1) *imaṁ vivasvate yogaṁ proktavān aham avyayam*
> *vivasvān manave prāha manur ikṣvākave 'bravīt*

> (2) *evaṁ paramparā-prāptam imaṁ rājarṣayo viduḥ*
> *sa kāleneha mahatā yogo naṣṭaḥ parantapa*

> (3) *sa evāyaṁ mayā te 'dya yogaḥ proktaḥ purātanaḥ*
> *bhakto 'si me sakhā ceti rahasyaṁ hy etad uttamam*

Here the Lord informs Arjuna that this system of *yoga*, the *Bhagavad-gītā*, was first spoken to the sun-god, and the sun-god explained it to Manu, and Manu explained it to Ikṣvāku, and in that way, by disciplic succession, one speaker after another, this *yoga* system has been coming down. But in the course of time it has become lost. Consequently the Lord has to speak it again, this time to Arjuna on the Battlefield of Kurukṣetra.

He tells Arjuna that He is relating this supreme secret to him because he is His devotee and His friend. The purport of this is that *Bhagavad-gītā* is a treatise which is especially meant for the devotee of the Lord. There are three classes of transcendentalists, namely the *jñānī*, the *yogī* and the *bhakta*, or the impersonalist, the meditator and the devotee. Here the Lord clearly tells Arjuna that He is making him the first receiver of a new *paramparā* (disciplic succession) because the old succession was broken. It was the Lord's wish, therefore, to establish another *paramparā* in the same line of thought that was coming down from the sun-god to others, and it was His wish that His teaching be distributed anew by Arjuna. He wanted Arjuna to become the authority in understanding the *Bhagavad-gītā*. So we see that *Bhagavad-gītā* is instructed to Arjuna especially because Arjuna was a devotee of the Lord, a direct student of Kṛṣṇa, and His intimate friend. Therefore *Bhagavad-gītā* is best understood by a person who has qualities similar to Arjuna's. That is to say he must be a devotee in a direct relationship with the Lord. As soon as one becomes a devotee of the Lord, he also has a direct relationship with the Lord. That is a very elaborate subject matter, but briefly it can be stated that a devotee is in a relationship with the Supreme Personality of Godhead in one of five different ways:

1. One may be a devotee in a passive state;
2. One may be a devotee in an active state;
3. One may be a devotee as a friend;
4. One may be a devotee as a parent;
5. One may be a devotee as a conjugal lover.

Arjuna was in a relationship with the Lord as friend. Of course there is a gulf of difference between this friendship and the friendship found in the material world. This is transcendental friendship which cannot be had by everyone. Of course everyone has a particular relationship with the Lord, and that relationship is evoked by the perfection of devotional service. But in the present status of our life, we have not only forgotten the Supreme Lord, but we have forgotten our eternal relationship with the Lord. Every living being, out of many, many billions and trillions of living beings, has a particular relationship with the Lord eternally. That is called *svarūpa*. By the process of devotional service, one can revive that *svarūpa*, and that stage is called *svarūpa-siddhi*—perfection of one's constitutional position. So Arjuna was a devotee, and he was in touch with the Supreme Lord in friendship.

How Arjuna accepted this *Bhagavad-gītā* should be noted. His manner of acceptance is given in the Tenth Chapter.

> (12) *arjuna uvāca*
> *paraṁ brahma paraṁ dhāma pavitraṁ paramaṁ bhavān*
> *puruṣaṁ śāśvataṁ divyam ādi-devam ajaṁ vibhum*
>
> (13) *āhus tvām ṛṣayaḥ sarve devarṣir nāradas tathā*
> *asito devalo vyāsaḥ svayaṁ caiva bravīṣi me*
>
> (14) *sarvam etad ṛtaṁ manye yan māṁ vadasi keśava*
> *na hi te bhagavan vyaktiṁ vidur devā na dānavāḥ*

"Arjuna said: You are the Supreme Brahman, the ultimate, the supreme abode and purifier, the Absolute Truth and the eternal Divine Person. You are the primal God, transcendental and original, and You are the unborn and all-pervading beauty. All the great sages like Nārada, Asita, Devala, and Vyāsa proclaim this of You, and now You Yourself are declaring it to me. O Kṛṣṇa, I totally accept as truth all that You have told me. Neither the gods nor demons, O Lord, know Thy personality." (Bg. 10. 12-14).

After hearing *Bhagavad-gītā* from the Supreme Personality of Godhead, Arjuna accepted Kṛṣṇa as *Paraṁ Brahma*, the Supreme Brahman. Every living being is Brahman, but the supreme living being, or the Supreme Personality of Godhead, is the Supreme Brahman. *Paraṁ dhāma* means that He is the supreme rest or abode of everything, *pavitram* means that He is pure, untainted by material contamination, *puruṣam* means that He is the supreme enjoyer, *divyam*, transcendental, *ādi-devam*, the Supreme Personality of Godhead, *ajam*, the unborn, and *vibhum*, the greatest, the all-pervading.

Now one may think that because Kṛṣṇa was the friend of Arjuna, Arjuna was telling Him all this by way of flattery, but Arjuna, just to drive out this kind of doubt from the minds of the readers of *Bhagavad-gītā*, substantiates these praises in the next verse when he says that Kṛṣṇa is accepted as the Supreme Personality of Godhead not only by himself but by authorities like the sage Nārada, Asita, Devala, Vyāsadeva and so on. These are great personalities who distribute the Vedic knowledge as it is accepted by all ācāryas. Therefore Arjuna tells Kṛṣṇa that he accepts whatever He says to be completely perfect. *Sarvam etad ṛtaṁ manye*: "I accept everything You say to be true." Arjuna also says that the personality of the Lord is very difficult to understand and that He cannot be known even by the great demigods. This means that the Lord cannot even be known by personalities greater than human beings. So how can a human being understand Śrī Kṛṣṇa without becoming His devotee?

Therefore *Bhagavad-gītā* should be taken up in a spirit of devotion. One should not think that he is equal to Kṛṣṇa, nor should he think that Kṛṣṇa is an ordinary personality or even a very great personality. Lord Śrī Kṛṣṇa is the Supreme Personality of Godhead, at least theoretically, according to the statements of *Bhagavad-gītā* or the statements of Arjuna, the person who is trying to understand the *Bhagavad-gītā*. We should therefore at least theoretically accept Śrī Kṛṣṇa as the Supreme Personality of Godhead, and with that submissive spirit we can understand the *Bhagavad-gītā*. Unless one reads the *Bhagavad-gītā* in a submissive spirit, it is very difficult to understand *Bhagavad-gītā* because it is a great mystery.

Just what is the *Bhagavad-gītā*? The purpose of *Bhagavad-gītā* is to deliver mankind from the nescience of material existence. Every man is in difficulty in so many ways, as Arjuna also was in difficulty in having to fight the Battle of Kurukṣetra. Arjuna surrendered unto Śrī Kṛṣṇa, and consequently this *Bhagavad-gītā* was spoken. Not only Arjuna, but every one of us is full of anxieties because of this material existence. Our very existence is in the atmosphere of nonexistence. Actually we are not meant to be threatened by nonexistence. Our existence is eternal. But somehow or other we are put into *asat*. *Asat* refers to that which does not exist.

Out of so many human beings who are suffering, there are a few who are actually inquiring about their position, as to what they are, why they are put into this awkward position and so on. Unless one is awakened to this position of questioning his suffering, unless he realizes that he doesn't want suffering but rather wants to make a solution to all sufferings, then one is not to be considered a perfect human being. Humanity begins when this sort of inquiry is awakened in one's mind. In the *Brahma-sūtra* this inquiry is called "*brahma-jijñāsā*." Every activity of the human being is to be considered a failure unless he inquires about the nature of the Absolute. Therefore those who begin to question why they are suffering or where they came from and where they shall go after death are proper students for understanding *Bhagavad-gītā*. The sincere student should also have a firm respect for the Supreme Personality of Godhead. Such a student was Arjuna.

Lord Kṛṣṇa descends specifically to reestablish the real purpose of life when man forgets that purpose. Even then, out of many, many human beings who awaken, there may be one who actually enters the spirit of understanding his position, and for him this *Bhagavad-gītā* is spoken. Actually we are all followed by the tiger of nescience, but the Lord is very merciful upon living entities, especially human beings. To this end He spoke the *Bhagavad-gītā*, making His friend Arjuna His student.

Being an associate of Lord Kṛṣṇa, Arjuna was above all ignorance, but Arjuna was put into ignorance on the Battlefield of Kurukṣetra just to question Lord Kṛṣṇa about the problems of life so that the Lord could explain them for the benefit of future generations of human beings and chalk out the plan of life. Then man could act accordingly and perfect the mission of human life.

The subject of the *Bhagavad-gītā* entails the comprehension of five basic truths. First of all, the science of God is explained and then the constitutional position of the living entities, *jīvas*. There is *īśvara*, which means controller, and there are *jīvas*, the living entities which are controlled. If a living entity says that he is not controlled but that he is free, then he is insane. The living being is controlled in every respect, at least in his conditioned life. So in the *Bhagavad-gītā* the subject matter deals with the *īśvara*, the supreme controller, and the *jīvas*, the controlled living entities. *Prakṛti* (material nature) and time (the duration of existence of the whole universe or the manifestation of material nature) and *karma* (activity) are also discussed. The cosmic manifestation is full of different activities. All living entities are engaged in different activities. From *Bhagavad-gītā* we must learn what God is, what the living entities are, what *prakṛti* is, what the cosmic manifestation is and how it is controlled by time, and what the activities of the living entities are.

Out of these five basic subject matters in *Bhagavad-gītā* it is established that the Supreme Godhead, or Kṛṣṇa, or Brahman, or supreme controller, or Paramātmā—you may use whatever name you like—is the greatest of all. The living beings are in quality like the supreme controller. For instance, the Lord has control over the universal affairs, over material nature, etc., as will be explained in the later chapters of *Bhagavad-gītā*. Material nature is not independant. She is acting under the directions of the Supreme Lord. As Lord Kṛṣṇa says, "*Prakṛti* is working under My direction." When we see

wonderful things happening in the cosmic nature, we should know that
behind this cosmic manifestation there is a controller. Nothing could be
manifested without being controlled. It is childish not to consider the
controller. For instance, a child may think that an automobile is quite
wonderful to be able to run without a horse or other animal pulling it,
but a sane man knows the nature of the automobile's engineering arrangement. He always knows that behind the machinery there is a man, a driver.
Similarly, the Supreme Lord is a driver under whose direction everything
is working. Now the *jīvas*, or the living entities, have been accepted by the
Lord, as we will note in the later chapters, as His parts and parcels. A
particle of gold is also gold, a drop of water from the ocean is also salty,
and similarly, we the living entities, being part and parcel of the supreme
controller, *īśvara*, or Bhagavān, Lord Śrī Kṛṣṇa, have all the qualities of the
Supreme Lord in minute quantity because we are minute *īśvaras*, subordinate *īśvaras*. We are trying to control nature, as presently we are trying
to control space or planets, and this tendency to control is there because
it is in Kṛṣṇa. But although we have a tendency to lord it over material
nature, we should know that we are not the supreme controller. This is
explained in *Bhagavad-gītā*.

What is material nature? This is also explained in *Gītā* as inferior
prakṛti, inferior nature. The living entity is explained as the superior
prakṛti. *Prakṛti* is always under control, whether inferior or superior.
Prakṛti is female, and she is controlled by the Lord just as the activities of
a wife are controlled by the husband. *Prakṛti* is always subordinate,
predominated by the Lord, who is the predominator. The living entities
and material nature are both predominated, controlled by the Supreme
Lord. According to the *Gītā*, the living entities, although parts and parcels
of the Supreme Lord, are to be considered *prakṛti*. This is clearly mentioned
in the Seventh Chapter, fifth verse of *Bhagavad-gītā*: "*Apareyam itas tv
anyām.*" "This *prakṛti* is My lower nature." "*Prakṛtiṁ viddhi me parām
jīva-bhūtāṁ mahā-bāho yayedaṁ dhāryate jagat.*" And beyond this there
is another *prakṛti: jīva-bhūtām*, the living entity.

Prakṛti itself is constituted by three qualities: the mode of goodness, the
mode of passion and the mode of ignorance. Above these modes there is
eternal time, and by a combination of these modes of nature and under
the control and purview of eternal time there are activities which are called
karma. These activities are being carried out from time immemorial, and
we are suffering or enjoying the fruits of our activities. For instance,
suppose I am a businessman and have worked very hard with intelligence
and have amassed a great bank balance. Then I am an enjoyer. But then

say I have lost all my money in business; then I am a sufferer. Similarly, in every field of life we enjoy the results of our work, or we suffer the results. This is called *karma*.

Īśvara (the Supreme Lord), *jīva* (the living entity), *prakṛti* (nature), eternal time and *karma* (activity) are all explained in the *Bhagavad-gītā*. Out of these five, the Lord, the living entities, material nature and time are eternal. The manifestation of *prakṛti* may be temporary, but it is not false. Some philosophers say that the manifestation of material nature is false, but according to the philosophy of *Bhagavad-gītā* or according to the philosophy of the Vaiṣṇavas, this is not so. The manifestation of the world is not accepted as false; it is accepted as real, but temporary. It is likened unto a cloud which moves across the sky, or the coming of the rainy season which nourishes grains. As soon as the rainy season is over and as soon as the cloud goes away, all the crops which were nourished by the rain dry up. Similarly, this material manifestation takes place at a certain interval, stays for a while and then disappears. Such are the workings of *prakṛti* But this cycle is working eternally. Therefore *prakṛti* is eternal; it is not false. The Lord refers to this as "My *prakṛti*." This material nature is the separated energy of the Supreme Lord, and similarly the living entities are also the energy of the Supreme Lord, but they are not separated. They are eternally related. So the Lord, the living entity, material nature and time are all interrelated and are all eternal. However, the other item, *karma*, is not eternal. The effects of *karma* may be very old indeed. We are suffering or enjoying the results of our activities from time immemorial, but we can change the results of our *karma*, or our activity, and this change depends on the perfection of our knowledge. We are engaged in various activities. Undoubtedly we do not know what sort of activities we should adopt to gain relief from the actions and reactions of all these activities, but this is also explained in the *Bhagavad-gītā*.

The position of *īsvara* is that of supreme consciousness. The *jīvas*, or the living entities, being parts and parcels of the Supreme Lord, are also conscious. Both the living entity and material nature are explained as *prakṛti*, the energy of the Supreme Lord, but one of the two, the *jīva*, is conscious. The other *prakṛti* is not conscious. That is the difference. Therefore the *jīva-prakṛti* is called superior because the *jīva* has consciousness which is similar to the Lord's. The Lord's is supreme consciousness, however, and one should not claim that the *jīva*, the living entity, is also supremely conscious. The living being cannot be supremely conscious at any stage of his perfection, and the theory that he can be so is a misleading theory. Conscious he may be, but he is not perfectly or supremely conscious.

The distinction between the *jīva* and the *īśvara* will be explained in the Thirteenth Chapter of *Bhagavad-gītā*. The Lord is *kṣetra-jñaḥ*, conscious, as is the living being, but the living being is conscious of his particular body, whereas the Lord is conscious of all bodies. Because He lives in the heart of every living being, He is conscious of the psychic movements of the particular *jīvas*. We should not forget this. It is also explained that the *Paramātmā*, the Supreme Personality of Godhead, is living in everyone's heart as *īśvara*, as the controller, and that He is giving directions for the living entity to act as he desires. The living entity forgets what to do. First of all he makes a determination to act in a certain way, and then he is entangled in the acts and reactions of his own *karma*. After giving up one type of body, he enters another type of body, as we put on and take off old clothes. As the soul thus migrates, he suffers the actions and reactions of his past activities. These activities can be changed when the living being is in the mode of goodness, in sanity, and understands what sort of activities he should adopt. If he does so, then all the actions and reactions of his past activities can be changed. Consequently, *karma* is not eternal. Therefore we stated that of the five items (*īśvara*, *jīva*, *prakṛti* time and *karma*) four are eternal, whereas *karma* is not eternal.

The supreme conscious *īśvara* is similar to the living entity in this way: both the consciousness of the Lord and that of the living entity are transcendental. It is not that consciousness is generated by the association of matter. That is a mistaken idea. The theory that consciousness develops under certain circumstances of material combination is not accepted in the *Bhagavad-gītā*. Consciousness may be pervertedly reflected by the covering of material circumstances, just as light reflected through colored glass may appear to be a certain color, but the consciousness of the Lord is not materially affected. Lord Kṛṣṇa says, "*mayādhyakṣeṇa prakṛtiḥ*." When He descends into the material universe, His consciousness is not materially affected. If He were so affected, He would be unfit to speak on transcendental matters as He does in the *Bhagavad-gītā*. One cannot say anything about the transcendental world without being free from materially contaminated consciousness. So the Lord is not materially contaminated. Our consciousness, at the present moment, however, is materially contaminated. The *Bhagavad-gītā* teaches that we have to purify this materially contaminated consciousness. In pure consciousness, our actions will be dovetailed to the will of *īśvara*, and that will make us happy. It is not that we have to cease all activities. Rather, our activities are to be purified, and purified activities are called *bhakti*. Activities in *bhakti* appear to be like ordinary activities, but they are not contaminated. An ignorant person may see that a devotee is acting or working like an ordinary man, but such a person with a poor fund of knowledge does not know that the activities of the devotee or of the Lord are not contaminated by impure consciousness or matter. They are transcendental to the three modes of nature. We should know, however, that at this point our consciousness is contaminated.

When we are materially contaminated, we are called conditioned. False consciousness is exhibited under the impression that I am a product of material nature. This is called false ego. One who is absorbed in the thought of bodily conceptions cannot understand his situation. *Bhagavad-gītā* was spoken to liberate one from the bodily conception of life, and Arjuna put himself in this position in order to receive this information from the Lord. One must become free from the bodily conception of life; that is the preliminary activity for the transcendentalist. One who wants to become free, who wants to become liberated, must first of all learn that he is not this material body. *Mukti* or liberation means freedom from material consciousness. In the *Śrīmad-Bhāgavatam* also the definition of liberation is given: *Mukti* means liberation from the contaminated consciousness of this material world and situation in pure consciousness. All the instructions of *Bhagavad-gītā* are intended to awaken this pure consciousness, and therefore we find at the last stage of the *Gītā's* instructions that Kṛṣṇa is asking Arjuna whether he is now in purified consciousness. Purified consciousness means acting in accordance with the instructions of the Lord. This is the whole sum and substance of purified consciousness. Consciousness is already there because we are part and parcel of the Lord, but for us there is the affinity of being affected by the inferior modes. But the Lord, being the Supreme, is never affected. That is the difference between the Supreme Lord and the conditioned souls.

What is this consciousness? This consciousness is "I am." Then what am I? In contaminated consciousness "I am" means "I am the lord of all I survey. I am the enjoyer." The world revolves because every living being thinks that he is the lord and creator of the material world. Material consciousness has two psychic divisions. One is that I am the creator, and the other is that I am the enjoyer. But actually the Supreme Lord is both the creator and the enjoyer, and the living entity, being part and parcel of the Supreme Lord, is neither the creator nor the enjoyer, but a cooperator. He is the created and the enjoyed. For instance, a part of a machine cooperates with the whole machine; a part of the body cooperates with the whole body. The hands, feet, eyes, legs and so on are all parts of the body, but they are not actually the enjoyers. The stomach is the enjoyer. The legs move, the hands supply food, the teeth chew and all parts of the body are engaged in satisfying the stomach because the stomach is the principal factor that nourishes the body's organization. Therefore everything is given to the stomach. One nourishes the tree by watering its root, and one nourishes the body by feeding the stomach, for if the body is to be kept in a healthy state, then the parts of the body must cooperate to feed the stomach. Similarly, the Supreme Lord is the enjoyer and the creator, and we, as subordinate living beings, are meant to cooperate to satisfy Him. This cooperation will actually help us, just as food taken by the stomach will help all other parts of the body. If the fingers of the hand think that they should take the food themselves instead of giving it to the stomach, then they will be frustrated. The central figure of creation and of enjoyment is the Supreme Lord, and the living entities are cooperators. By cooperation they enjoy. The relation is also like that of the master and the servant. If the master is fully satisfied, then the servant is satisfied. Similarly, the Supreme Lord should be satisfied, although the tendency to become the creator and the tendency to enjoy the material world are there also in the living entities because these tendencies are there in the Supreme Lord who has created the manifested cosmic world.

We shall find, therefore, in this *Bhagavad-gītā* that the complete whole is comprised of the supreme controller, the controlled living entities, the cosmic manifestation, eternal time, and *karma*, or activities, and all of these are explained in this text. All of these taken completely form the complete whole, and the complete whole is called the Supreme Absolute Truth. The complete whole and the complete Absolute Truth are the Supreme Personality of Godhead, Śrī Kṛṣṇa. All manifestations are due to His different energies. He *is* the complete whole.

It is also explained in the *Gītā* that impersonal Brahman is also subordinate to the complete. Brahman is more explicitly explained in the *Brahma-sūtra* to be like the rays of the sunshine. The impersonal Brahman is the shining rays of the Supreme Personality of Godhead. Impersonal Brahman is incomplete realization of the absolute whole, and so also is the conception of Paramātmā in the Twelfth Chapter. There it shall be seen that the Supreme Personality of Godhead, Puruṣottama, is above both impersonal Brahman and the partial realization of Paramātmā. The Supreme Personality of Godhead is called *sac-cid-ānanda-vigraha*. The *Brahma-saṁhitā* begins in this way: *īśvaraḥ paramaḥ kṛṣṇaḥ sac-cid-ānanda-vigrahaḥ / anādir ādir govindaḥ sarva-kāraṇa-kāraṇam.* "Kṛṣṇa is the cause of all causes. He is the primal cause, and He is the very form of eternal being, knowledge and bliss." Impersonal Brahman realization is the realization of His *sat* (being) feature. Paramātmā realization is the realization of the *cit* (eternal knowledge) feature. But realization of the Personality of Godhead, Kṛṣṇa, is realization of all the transcendental features: *sat, cit* and *ānanda* (being, knowledge, bliss) in complete *vigraha* (form).

People with less intelligence consider the Supreme Truth to be impersonal, but He is a transcendental person, and this is confirmed in all Vedic literatures. *Nityo nityānāṁ cetanaś cetanānām.* As we are all individual living beings and have our individuality, the Supreme Absolute Truth is also, in the ultimate issue, a person, and realization of the Personality of Godhead is realization of all of the transcendental features. The complete whole is not formless. If He is formless, or if He is less than any other thing, then He cannot be the complete whole. The complete whole must have everything within our experience and beyond our experience, otherwise it cannot be complete. The complete whole, Personality of Godhead, has immense potencies.

How Kṛṣṇa is acting in different potencies is also explained in *Bhagavad-gītā*. This phenomenal world or material world in which we are placed is also complete in itself because the twenty-four elements of which this material universe is a temporary manifestation, according to Sāṅkhya philosophy, are completely adjusted to produce complete resources which are necessary for the maintenance and subsistence of this universe. There is nothing extraneous; nor is there anything needed. This manifestation has its own time fixed by the energy of the supreme whole, and when its time is complete, these temporary manifestations will be annihilated by the complete arrangement of the complete. There is complete facility for the small complete units, namely the living entities, to realize the complete, and all sorts of incompleteness are experienced due to incomplete knowledge of the complete. So *Bhagavad-gītā* contains the complete knowledge of Vedic wisdom.

All Vedic knowledge is infallible, and Hindus accept Vedic knowledge to be complete and infallible. For example, cow dung is the stool of an animal, and according to *smṛti* or Vedic injunction, if one touches the stool of an animal he has to take a bath to purify himself. But in the Vedic scriptures cow dung is considered to be a purifying agent. One might consider this to be contradictory, but it is accepted because it is Vedic injunction, and indeed by accepting this, one will not commit a mistake; subsequently it has been proved by modern science that cow dung contains all antiseptic properties. So Vedic knowledge is complete because it is above all doubts and mistakes, and *Bhagavad-gītā* is the essence of all Vedic knowledge.

Vedic knowledge is not a question of research. Our research work is imperfect because we are researching things with imperfect senses. We have to accept perfect knowledge which comes down, as is stated in *Bhagavad-gītā,* by the *paramparā* disciplic succession. We have to receive knowledge from the proper source in disciplic succession beginning with the supreme spiritual master, the Lord Himself, and handed down to a succession of spiritual masters. Arjuna, the student who took lessons from Lord Śrī Kṛṣṇa, accepts everything that He says without contradicting Him. One is not allowed to accept one portion of *Bhagavad-gītā* and not another. No. We must accept *Bhagavad-gītā* without interpretation, without deletion and without our own whimsical participation in the matter. The *Gītā* should be taken as the most perfect presentation of Vedic knowledge. Vedic knowledge is received from transcendental sources, and the first words were spoken by the Lord Himself. The words spoken by the Lord are different from words spoken by a person of the mundane world who is infected with four defects. A mundaner 1) is sure to commit mistakes, 2) is invariably illusioned, 3) has the tendency to cheat others and 4) is limited by imperfect senses. With these four imperfections, one cannot deliver perfect information of all-pervading knowledge.

Vedic knowledge is not imparted by such defective living entities. It was imparted unto the heart of Brahmā, the first created living being, and Brahmā in his turn disseminated this knowledge to his sons and disciples, as he originally received it from the Lord. The Lord is *pūrṇam,* all-perfect, and there is no possibility of His becoming subjected to the laws of material nature. One should therefore be intelligent enough to know that the Lord is the only proprietor of everything in the universe and that He is the original creator, the creator of Brahmā. In the Eleventh Chapter the Lord is addressed as *prapitāmaha* because Brahmā is addressed as *pitāmaha,* the grandfather, and He is the creator of the grandfather. So no one should claim to be the proprietor of anything; one should accept only things which are set aside for him by the Lord as his quota for his maintenance.

There are many examples given of how we are to utilize those things which are set aside for us by the Lord. This is also explained in *Bhagavad-gītā.* In the beginning, Arjuna decided that he should not fight in the Battle of Kurukṣetra. This was his own decision. Arjuna told the Lord that it was not possible for him to enjoy the kingdom after killing his own kinsmen. This decision was based on the body because he was thinking that the body was himself and that his bodily relations or expansions were his brothers, nephews, brothers-in-law, grandfathers and so on. He was thinking in this way to satisfy his bodily demands. *Bhagavad-gītā* was spoken by the Lord just to change this view, and at the end Arjuna decides to fight under the directions of the Lord when he says, "*kariṣye vacanaṁ tava.*" "I shall act according to Thy word."

In this world man is not meant to toil like hogs. He must be intelligent to realize the importance of human life and refuse to act like an ordinary animal. A human being should realize the aim of his life, and this direction is given in all Vedic literatures, and the essence is given in *Bhagavad-gītā*. Vedic literature is meant for human beings, not for animals. Animals can kill other living animals, and there is no question of sin on their part, but if a man kills an animal for the satisfaction of his uncontrolled taste, he must be responsible for breaking the laws of nature. In the *Bhagavad-gītā* it is clearly explained that there are three kinds of activities according to the different modes of nature: the activities of goodness, of passion and of ignorance. Similarly, there are three kinds of eatables also: eatables in goodness, passion and ignorance. All of this is clearly described, and if we properly utilize the instructions of *Bhagavad-gītā*, then our whole life will become purified, and ultimately we will be able to reach the destination which is beyond this material sky.

That destination is called the *sanātana* sky, the eternal spiritual sky. In this material world we find that everything is temporary. It comes into being, stays for some time, produces some by-products, dwindles and then vanishes. That is the law of the material world, whether we use as an example this body, or a piece of fruit or anything. But beyond this temporary world there is another world of which we have information. This world consists of another nature which is *sanātana*, eternal. *Jīva* is also described as *sanātana*, eternal, and the Lord is also described as *sanātana* in the Eleventh Chapter. We have an intimate relationship with the Lord, and because we are all qualitatively one—the *sanātana-dhāma*, or sky, the *sanātana* Supreme Personality and the *sanātana* living entities—the whole purpose of *Bhagavad-gītā* is to revive our *sanātana* occupation, or *sanātana-dharma*, which is the eternal occupation of the living entity. We are temporarily engaged in different activities, but all of these activities can be purified when we give up all these temporary activities and take up the activities which are prescribed by the Supreme Lord. That is called our pure life.

The Supreme Lord and His transcendental abode are both *sanātana*, as are the living entities, and the combined association of the Supreme Lord and the living entities in the *sanātana* abode is the perfection of human life. The Lord is very kind to the living entities because they are His sons. Lord Kṛṣṇa declares in *Bhagavad-gītā,* "*sarva-yoniṣu...ahaṁ bīja-pradaḥ pitā.*" "I am the father of all." Of course there are all types of living entities according to their various *karmas,* but here the Lord claims that He is the father of all of them. Therefore the Lord descends to reclaim all of these fallen, conditioned souls to call them back to the *sanātana* eternal sky so that the *sanātana* living entities may regain their eternal *sanātana* positions in eternal association with the Lord. The Lord comes Himself in different incarnations, or He sends His confidential servants as sons or His associates or *ācāryas* to reclaim the conditioned souls.

Therefore, *sanātana-dharma* does not refer to any sectarian process of religion. It is the eternal function of the eternal living entities in relationship with the eternal Supreme Lord. *Sanātana-dharma* refers, as stated previously, to the eternal occupation of the living entity. Rāmānujācārya has explained the word *sanātana* as "that which has neither beginning nor end," so when we speak of *sanātana-dharma,* we must take it for granted on the authority of Śrī Rāmānujācārya that it has neither beginning nor end.

The English word "religion" is a little different from *sanātana-dharma.* Religion conveys the idea of faith, and faith may change. One may have faith in a particular process, and he may change this faith and adopt another, but *sanātana-dharma* refers to that activity which cannot be changed. For instance, liquidity cannot be taken from water, nor can heat be taken from fire. Similarly, the eternal function of the eternal living entity cannot be taken from the living entity. *Sanātana-dharma* is eternally integral with the living entity. When we speak of *sanātana-dharma,* therefore, we must take it for granted on the authority of Śrī Rāmānujācārya that it has neither beginning nor end. That which has neither end nor beginning must not be sectarian, for it cannot be limited by any boundaries. Yet those belonging to some sectarian faith will wrongly consider that *sanātana-dharma* is also sectarian, but if we go deeply into the matter and consider it in the light of modern science, it is possible for us to see that *sanātana-dharma* is the business of all the people of the world—nay, of all the living entities of the universe.

Non-*sanātana* religious faith may have some beginning in the annals of human history, but there is no beginning to the history of *sanātana-dharma* because it remains eternally with the living entities. Insofar as the living entities are concerned, the authoritative *śāstras* state that the living entity has neither birth nor death. In the *Gītā* it is stated that the living entity is never born, and he never dies. He is eternal and indestructible, and he continues to live after the destruction of his temporary material body. In reference to the concept of *sanātana-dharma,* we must try to understand the concept of religion from the Sanskrit root meaning of the word. *Dharma* refers to that which is constantly existing with the particular object. We conclude that there is heat and light along with the fire; without heat and light, there is no meaning to the word fire. Similarly, we must discover the essential part of the living being, that part which is his constant companion. That constant companion is his eternal quality, and that eternal quality is his eternal religion.

When Sanātana Gosvāmī asked Śrī Caitanya Mahāprabhu about the *svarūpa* of every living being, 'the Lord replied that the *svarūpa* or constitutional position of the living being is the rendering of service to the Supreme Personality of Godhead. If we analyze this statement of Lord Caitanya, we can easily see that every living being is constantly engaged in rendering service to another living being. A living being serves other living beings in two capacities. By doing so, the living entity enjoys life. The lower animals serve human beings as servants serve their master. A serves B master, B serves C master and C serves D master and so on. Under these circumstances, we can see that one friend serves another friend, the mother serves the son, the wife serves the husband, the husband serves the wife and so on. If we go on searching in this spirit, it will be seen that there is no exception in the society of living beings to the activity of service. The politician presents his manifesto for the public to convince them of his capacity for service. The voters therefore give the politician their valuable votes, thinking that he will render valuable service to society. The shopkeeper serves the customer, and the artisan serves the capitalist. The capitalist serves the family, and the family serves the state in the terms of the eternal capacity of the eternal living being. In this way we can see that no living being is exempt from rendering service to other living beings, and therefore we can safely conclude that service is the constant companion of the living being and that the rendering of service is the eternal religion of the living being.

Yet man professes to belong to a particular type of faith with reference to particular time and circumstance and thus claims to be a Hindu, Muslim, Christian, Buddhist or any other sect. Such designations are non-*sanātana-dharma.* A Hindu may change his faith to become a Muslim, or a Muslim may change his faith to become a Hindu, or a Christian may change his faith and so on. But in all circumstances the change of religious faith does not effect the eternal occupation of rendering service to others. The Hindu, Muslim or Christian in all circumstances is servant of someone.

Thus, to profess a particular type of sect is not to profess one's *sanātana-dharma*. The rendering of service is *sanātana-dharma*.

Factually we are related to the Supreme Lord in service. The Supreme Lord is the supreme enjoyer, and we living entities are His servitors. We are created for His enjoyment, and if we participate in that eternal enjoyment with the Supreme Personality of Godhead, we become happy. We cannot become happy otherwise. It is not possible to be happy independantly, just as no one part of the body can be happy without cooperating with the stomach. It is not possible for the living entity to be happy without rendering transcendental loving service unto the Supreme Lord.

In the *Bhagavad-gītā*, worship of different demigods or rendering service to them is not approved. It is stated in the Seventh Chapter, twentieth verse:

> *kāmais tais tair hṛt-ajñānāḥ prapadyante 'nya-devatāḥ*
> *taṁ taṁ niyamam āsthāya prakṛtyā niyatāḥ svayā*

"Those whose minds are distorted by material desires surrender unto demigods and follow the particular rules and regulations of worship according to their own natures." (Bg. 7.20) Here it is plainly said that those who are directed by lust worship the demigods and not the Supreme Lord Kṛṣṇa. When we mention the name Kṛṣṇa, we do not refer to any sectarian name. Kṛṣṇa means the highest pleasure, and it is confirmed that the Supreme Lord is the reservoir or storehouse of all pleasure. We are all hankering after pleasure. *Ānandamayo 'bhyāsāt.* (Vs. 1.1.12) The living entities, like the Lord, are full of consciousness, and they are after happiness. The Lord is perpetually happy, and if the living entities associate with the Lord, cooperate with Him and take part in His association, then they also become happy.

The Lord descends to this mortal world to show His pastimes in Vṛndāvana, which are full of happiness. When Lord Śrī Kṛṣṇa was in Vṛndāvana, His activities with His cowherd boy friends, with His damsel friends, with the inhabitants of Vṛndāvana and with the cows were all full of happiness. The total population of Vṛndāvana knew nothing but Kṛṣṇa. But Lord Kṛṣṇa even discouraged His father Nanda Mahārāja from worshiping the demigod Indra because He wanted to establish the fact that people need not worship any demigod. They need only worship the Supreme Lord because their ultimate goal is to return to His abode.

The abode of Lord Śrī Kṛṣṇa is described in the *Bhagavad-gītā*, Fifteenth Chapter, sixth verse:

na tad bhāsayate sūryo na śaśāṅko na pāvakaḥ
yad gatvā na nivartante tad dhāma paramaṁ mama

"That abode of Mine is not illumined by the sun or moon, nor by electricity. And anyone who reaches it never comes back to this material world." (Bg. 15.6)

This verse gives a description of that eternal sky. Of course we have a material conception of the sky, and we think of it in relationship to the sun, moon, stars and so on, but in this verse the Lord states that in the eternal sky there is no need for the sun nor for the moon nor fire of any kind because the spiritual sky is already illuminated by the *brahmajyoti*, the rays emanating from the Supreme Lord. We are trying with difficulty to reach other planets, but it is not difficult to understand the abode of the Supreme Lord. This abode is referred to as Goloka. In the *Brahma-saṁhitā* it is beautifully described: *Goloka eva nivasaty akhilātma-bhūtaḥ*. The Lord resides eternally in His abode Goloka, yet He can be approached from this world, and to this end the Lord comes to manifest His real form, *sac-cid-ānanda-vigraha*. When He manifests this form, there is no need for our imagining what He looks like. To discourage such imaginative speculation, He descends and exhibits Himself as He is, as Śyāmasundara. Unfortunately, the less intelligent deride Him because He comes as one of us and plays with us as a human being. But because of this we should not consider that the Lord is one of us. It is by His potency that He presents Himself in His real form before us and displays His pastimes, which are prototypes of those pastimes found in His abode.

In the effulgent rays of the spiritual sky there are innumerable planets floating. The *brahmajyoti* emanates from the supreme abode, Kṛṣṇaloka, and the *ānandamaya-cinmaya* planets, which are not material, float in those rays. The Lord says, *na tad bhāsayate sūryo na śaśāṅko na pāvakaḥ yad gatvā na nivartante tad dhāma paramaṁ mama*. One who can approach that spiritual sky is not required to descend again to the material sky. In the material sky, even if we approach the highest planet (Brahmaloka), what to speak of the moon, we will find the same conditions of life, namely birth, death, disease and old age. No planet in the material universe is free from these four principles of material existence. Therefore the Lord says in *Bhagavad-gītā*, *ābrahma-bhuvanāl lokāḥ punar āvartino 'rjuna*. The living entities are traveling from one planet to another, not by mechanical arrangement but by a spiritual process. This is also mentioned: *yānti deva-vratā devān pitṝn yānti pitṛ-vratāḥ*. No mechanical arrangement is necessary if we want interplanetary travel. The *Gītā* instructs: *yānti deva-vratā devān*. The moon, the sun and higher planets are called *svargaloka*. There are three different statuses of planets: higher, middle and lower planetary systems. The earth belongs to the middle planetary system. *Bhagavad-gītā* informs us how to travel to the higher planetary systems (*devaloka*) with a very simple formula: *yānti deva-vratā devān*. One need only worship the particular demigod of that particular planet and in that way go to the moon, the sun or any of the higher planetary systems.

Yet *Bhagavad-gītā* does not advise us to go to any of the planets in this material world because even if we go to Brahmaloka, the highest planet, through some sort of mechanical contrivance by maybe traveling for forty thousand years (and who would live that long?), we will still find the material inconveniences of birth, death, disease and old age. But one who wants to approach the supreme planet, Kṛṣṇaloka, or any of the other planets within the spiritual sky, will not meet with these material inconveniences. Amongst all of the planets in the spiritual sky there is one supreme planet called Goloka Vṛndāvana, which is the original planet in the abode of the original Personality of Godhead Śrī Kṛṣṇa. All of this information is given in *Bhagavad-gītā*, and we are given through its instruction information how to leave the material world and begin a truly blissful life in the spiritual sky.

In the Fifteenth Chapter of the *Bhagavad-gītā*, the real picture of the material world is given. It is said there:

> *ūrdhva-mūlam adhaḥ-śākham aśvatthaṁ prāhur avyayam*
> *chandāṁsi yasya parṇāni yas taṁ veda sa veda-vit*

"The Supreme Lord said: There is a banyan tree which has its roots upward and its branches down, and the Vedic hymns are its leaves. One who knows this tree is the knower of the *Vedas*." (Bg. 15.1) Here the material world is described as a tree whose roots are upwards and branches are below. We have experience of a tree whose roots are upward: if one stands on the bank of a river or any reservoir of water, he can see that the trees reflected in the water are upside down. The branches go downward and the roots upward. Similarly, this material world is a reflection of the spiritual world. The material world is but a shadow of reality. In the shadow there is no reality or substantiality, but from the shadow we can understand that there is substance and reality. In the desert there is no water, but the mirage suggests that there is such a thing as water. In the material world there is no water, there is no happiness, but the real water of actual happiness is there in the spiritual world.

The Lord suggests that we attain the spiritual world in the following manner:

nirmāna-mohā jita-saṅga-doṣā
adhyātma-nityā vinivṛtta-kāmāḥ
dvandvair vimuktāḥ sukha-duḥkha-saṁjñair
gacchanty amūḍhāḥ padam avyayaṁ tat.

That *padam avyayam* or eternal kingdom can be reached by one who is *nirmāna-moha*. What does this mean? We are after designations. Someone wants to become a son, someone wants to become Lord, someone wants to become the president or a rich man or a king or something else. As long as we are attached to these designations, we are attached to the body because designations belong to the body. But we are not these bodies, and realizing this is the first stage in spiritual realization. We are associated with the three modes of material nature, but we must become detached through devotional service to the Lord. If we are not attached to devotional service to the Lord, then we cannot become detached from the modes of material nature. Designations and attachments are due to our lust and desire, our wanting to lord it over the material nature. As long as we do not give up this propensity of lording it over material nature, there is no possibility of returning to the kingdom of the Supreme, the *sanātana-dhāma*. That eternal kingdom, which is never destroyed, can be approached by one who is not bewildered by the attractions of false material enjoyments, who is situated in the service of the Supreme Lord. One so situated can easily approach that supreme abode.

Elsewhere in the *Gītā* it is stated:

avyakto 'kṣara ity uktas tam āhuḥ paramāṁ gatim
yaṁ prāpya na nivartante tad dhāma paramaṁ mama.

Avyakta means unmanifested. Not even all of the material world is manifested before us. Our senses are so imperfect that we cannot even see all of the stars within this material universe. In Vedic literature we can receive much information about all the planets, and we can believe it or not believe it. All of the important planets are described in Vedic literatures, especially *Śrīmad-Bhāgavatam*, and the spiritual world, which is beyond this material sky, is described as *avyakta*, unmanifested. One should desire and hanker after that supreme kingdom, for when one attains that kingdom, he does not have to return to this material world.

Next, one may raise the question of how one goes about approaching that abode of the Supreme Lord. Information of this is given in the Eighth Chapter. It is said there:

anta-kāle ca mām eva smaran muktvā kalevaram
yaḥ prayāti sa mad-bhāvaṁ yāti nāsty atra saṁśayaḥ

"Anyone who quits his body, at the end of life, remembering Me, attains immediately to My nature; and there is no doubt of this." (Bg. 8.5) One who thinks of Kṛṣṇa at the time of his death goes to Kṛṣṇa. One must remember the form of Kṛṣṇa; if he quits his body thinking of this form, he approaches the spiritual kingdom. *Mad-bhāvaṁ* refers to the supreme nature of the Supreme Being. The Supreme Being is *sac-cid-ānanda-vigraha*—eternal, full of knowledge and bliss. Our present body is not *sac-cid-ānanda*. It is *asat*, not *sat*. It is not eternal; it is perishable. It is not *cit*, full of knowledge, but it is full of ignorance. We have no knowledge of the spiritual kingdom, nor do we even have perfect knowledge of this material world where there are so many things unknown to us. The body is also *nirānanda;* instead of being full of bliss it is full of misery. All of the miseries we experience in the material world arise from the body, but one who leaves this body thinking of the Supreme Personality of Godhead at once attains a *sac-cid-ānanda* body, as is promised in this fifth verse of the Eighth Chapter where Lord Kṛṣṇa says, "He attains My nature."

The process of quitting this body and getting another body in the material world is also organized. A man dies after it has been decided what form of body he will have in the next life. Higher authorities, not the living entity himself, make this decision. According to our activities in this life, we either rise or sink. This life is a preparation for the next life. If we can prepare, therefore, in this life to get promotion to the kingdom of God, then surely, after quitting this material body, we will attain a spiritual body just like the Lord.

As explained before, there are different kinds of transcendentalists, the *brahmavādi paramātmāvādi* and the devotee, and, as mentioned, in the *brahmajyoti* (spiritual sky) there are innumerable spiritual planets. The number of these planets is far, far greater than all of the planets of this material world. This material world has been approximated as only one quarter of the creation. In this material segment there are millions and billions of universes with trillions of planets and suns, stars and moons. But this whole material creation is only a fragment of the total creation. Most of the creation is in the spiritual sky. One who desires to merge into the existence of the Supreme Brahman is at once transferred to the *brahmajyoti* of the Supreme Lord and thus attains the spiritual sky. The devotee, who wants to enjoy the association of the Lord, enters into the Vaikuṇṭha planets, which are innumerable, and the Supreme Lord by His plenary expansions as Nārāyaṇa with four hands and with different names like Pradyumna, Aniruddha, Govinda, etc., associates with him there. Therefore at the end of life the transcendentalists either think of the *brahmajyoti*, the Paramātmā or the Supreme Personality of Godhead Śrī Kṛṣṇa. In all cases they enter into the spiritual sky, but only the devotee, or he who is in personal touch with the Supreme Lord, enters into the Vaikuṇṭha planets. The Lord further adds that of this "there is no doubt." This must be believed firmly. We should not reject that which does not tally with our imagination; our attitude should be that of Arjuna: "I believe everything that You have said." Therefore when the Lord says that at the time of death whoever thinks of Him as Brahman or Paramātmā or as the Personality of Godhead certainly enters into the spiritual sky, there is no doubt about it. There is no question of disbelieving it.

The information on how to think of the Supreme Being at the time of death is also given in the *Gītā*:

> *yaṁ yaṁ vāpi smaran bhāvaṁ tyajaty ante kalevaram*
> *taṁ tam evaiti kaunteya sadā tad-bhāva-bhāvitaḥ*

"In whatever condition one quits his present body, in his next life he will attain to that state of being without fail." (Bg. 8.6) Material nature is a display of one of the energies of the Supreme Lord. In the *Viṣṇu Purāṇa* the total energies of the Supreme Lord as *Viṣṇu-śaktiḥ parā proktā*, etc., are delineated. The Supreme Lord has diverse and innumerable energies which are beyond our conception; however, great learned sages or liberated souls have studied these energies and have analyzed them into three parts. All of the energies are of *Viṣṇu-śakti*, that is to say they are different potencies of Lord Viṣṇu. That energy is *parā*, transcendental. Living entities also belong to the superior energy, as has already been explained. The other energies, or material energies, are in the mode of ignorance. At the time of death we can either remain in the inferior energy of this material world, or we can transfer to the energy of the spiritual world.

In life we are accustomed to thinking either of the material or the spiritual energy. There are so many literatures which fill our thoughts with the material energy—newspapers, novels, etc. Our thinking, which is

now absorbed in these literatures, must be transferred to the Vedic literatures. The great sages, therefore, have written so many Vedic literatures
such as the *Purāṇas*, etc. The *Purāṇas* are not imaginative; they are
historical records. In the *Caitanya-caritāmṛita* there is the following verse:

> *māyā mugdha jīver nāhi svataḥ kṛṣṇa-jñān*
> *jīvera kṛpāya kailā kṛṣṇa veda-purāṇa*
>
> (Cc. *Madhya* 20.122)

The forgetful living entities or conditioned souls have forgotten their
relationship with the Supreme Lord, and they are engrossed in thinking of
material activities. Just to transfer their thinking power to the spiritual sky,
Kṛṣṇa has given a great number of Vedic literatures. First He divided the
Vedas into four, then He explained them in the *Purāṇas*, and for less
capable people He wrote the *Mahābhārata*. In the *Mahābhārata* there is
given the *Bhagavad-gītā*. Then all Vedic literature is summarized in the
Vedānta-sūtra, and for future guidance He gave a natural commentation
on the *Vedānta-sutra*, called *Śrīmad-Bhāgavatam*. We must always engage
our minds in reading these Vedic literatures. Just as materialists engage
their minds in reading newspapers, magazines and so many materialistic
literatures, we must transfer our reading to these literatures which are
given to us by Vyāsadeva; in that way it will be possible for us to remember
the Supreme Lord at the time of death. That is the only way suggested by
the Lord, and He guarantees the result: "There is no doubt." (Bg. 8.7)

> *tasmāt sarveṣu kāleṣu mām anusmara yudhya ca*
> *mayy arpita-mano-buddhir mām evaiṣyasy asaṁśayaḥ*

"Therefore, Arjuna, you should always think of Me, and at the same time
you should continue your prescribed duty and fight. With your mind and
activities always fixed on Me, and everything engaged in Me, you will
attain to Me without any doubt."

He does not advise Arjuna to simply remember Him and give up his
occupation. No, the Lord never suggests anything impractical. In this
material world, in order to maintain the body one has to work. Human
society is divided, according to work, into four divisions of social order—
brāhmaṇa, kṣatriya, vaiśya, śūdra. The *brāhmaṇa* class or intelligent class is
working in one way, the *kṣatriya* or administrative class is working in
another way, and the mercantile class and the laborers are all tending to
their specific duties. In the human society, whether one is a laborer,
merchant, warrior, administrator, or farmer, or even if one belongs to the
highest class and is a literary man, a scientist or a theologian, he has to
work in order to maintain his existence. The Lord therefore tells Arjuna
that he need not give up his occupation, but while he is engaged in his

occupation he should remember Kṛṣṇa. If he doesn't practice remembering Kṛṣṇa while he is struggling for existence, then it will not be possible for him to remember Kṛṣṇa at the time of death. Lord Caitanya also advises this. He says that one should practice remembering the Lord by chanting the names of the Lord always. The names of the Lord and the Lord are nondifferent. So Lord Kṛṣṇa's instruction to Arjuna to "remember Me" and Lord Caitanya's injunction to always "chant the names of Lord Kṛṣṇa" are the same instruction. There is no difference, because Kṛṣṇa and Kṛṣṇa's name are nondifferent. In the absolute status there is no difference between reference and referent. Therefore we have to practice remembering the Lord always, twenty-four hours a day, by chanting His names and molding our life's activities in such a way that we can remember Him always.

How is this possible? The ācāryas give the following example. If a married woman is attached to another man, or if a man has an attachment for a woman other than his wife, then the attachment is to be considered very strong. One with such an attachment is always thinking of the loved one. The wife who is thinking of her lover is always thinking of meeting him, even while she is carrying out her household chores. In fact, she carries out her household work even more carefully so her husband will not suspect her attachment. Similarly, we should always remember the supreme lover, Śrī Kṛṣṇa, and at the same time perform our material duties very nicely. A strong sense of love is required here. If we have a strong sense of love for the Supreme Lord, then we can discharge our duty and at the same time remember Him. But we have to develop that sense of love. Arjuna, for instance, was always thinking of Kṛṣṇa; he was the constant companion of Kṛṣṇa, and at the same time he was a warrior. Kṛṣṇa did not advise him to give up fighting and go to the forest to meditate. When Lord Kṛṣṇa delineates the yoga system to Arjuna, Arjuna says that the practice of this system is not possible for him.

> arjuna uvāca
> yo 'yaṁ yogas tvayā proktaḥ sāmyena madhusūdana
> etasyāhaṁ na paśyāmi cañcalatvāt sthitiṁ sthirām

"Arjuna said, O Madhusūdana, the system of yoga which you have summarized appears impractical and unendurable to me, for the mind is restless and unsteady." (Bg. 6.33)

But the Lord says:

> yoginām api sarveṣāṁ mad-gatenāntarātmanā
> śraddhāvān bhajate yo māṁ sa me yuktatamo mataḥ

"Of all *yogīs,* he who always abides in Me with great faith, worshiping Me in transcendental loving service, is most intimately united with Me in *yoga,* and is the highest of all." (Bg. 6.47) So one who thinks of the Supreme Lord always is the greatest *yogī,* the supermost *jñānī,* and the greatest devotee at the same time. The Lord further tells Arjuna that as a *kṣatriya* he cannot give up his fighting, but if Arjuna fights remembering Kṛṣṇa, then he will be able to remember Him at the time of death. But one must be completely surrendered in the transcendental loving service of the Lord.

We work not with our body, actually, but with our mind and intelligence. So if the intelligence and the mind are always engaged in the thought of the Supreme Lord, then naturally the senses are also engaged in His service. Superficially, at least, the activities of the senses remain the same, but the consciousness is changed. The *Bhagavad-gītā* teaches one how to absorb the mind and intelligence in the thought of the Lord. Such absorption will enable one to transfer himself to the kingdom of the Lord. If the mind is engaged in Kṛṣṇa's service, then the senses are automatically engaged in His service. This is the art, and this is also the secret of *Bhagavad-gītā:* total absorption in the thought of Śrī Kṛṣṇa.

Modern man has struggled very hard to reach the moon, but he has not tried very hard to elevate himself spiritually. If one has fifty years of life ahead of him, he should engage that brief time in cultivating this practice of remembering the Supreme Personality of Godhead. This practice is the devotional process of:

śravaṇaṁ kīrtanaṁ viṣṇoḥ smaraṇaṁ pāda-sevanam
arcanaṁ vandanaṁ dāsyaṁ sakhyam ātma-nivedanam

These nine processes, of which the easiest is *śravaṇaṁ,* hearing *Bhagavad-gītā* from the realized person, will turn one to the thought of the Supreme Being. This will lead to *niścala,* remembering the Supreme Lord, and will enable one, upon leaving the body, to attain a spiritual body which is just fit for association with the Supreme Lord.

The Lord further says:

abhyāsa-yoga-yuktena cetasā nānya-gāminā
paramaṁ puruṣaṁ divyaṁ yāti pārthānucintayan

"By practicing this remembering, without being deviated, thinking ever of the Supreme Godhead, one is sure to achieve the planet of the Divine, the Supreme Personality, O son of Kuntī." (Bg. 8.8)

This is not a very difficult process. However, one must learn it from an experienced person, from one who is already in the practice. The mind is always flying to this and that, but one must always practice concentrating the mind on the form of the Supreme Lord Śrī Kṛṣṇa or on the sound of His name. The mind is naturally restless, going hither and thither, but it can rest in the sound vibration of Kṛṣṇa. One must thus meditate on *paramaṁ puruṣaṁ*, the Supreme Person; and thus attain Him. The ways and the means for ultimate realization, ultimate attainment, are stated in the *Bhagavad-gītā*, and the doors of this knowledge are open for everyone. No one is barred out. All classes of men can approach the Lord by thinking of Him, for hearing and thinking of Him is possible for everyone.

The Lord further says:

> *māṁ hi pārtha vyapāśritya ye 'pi syuḥ pāpa-yonayaḥ*
> *striyo vaiśyās tathā śūdrās te 'pi yānti parāṁ gatim*
>
> *kiṁ punar brāhmaṇāḥ puṇyā bhaktā rājarṣayas tathā*
> *anityam asukhaṁ lokam imaṁ prāpya bhajasva mām*

"O son of Pṛthā, anyone who will take shelter in Me, whether a woman, or a merchant, or one born in a low family, can yet approach the supreme destination. How much greater then are the *brāhmaṇas*, the righteous, the devotees, and saintly kings! In this miserable world, these are fixed in devotional service to the Lord." (Bg. 9.32-33)

Human beings even in the lower statuses of life (a merchant, a woman or a laborer) can attain the Supreme. One does not need highly developed intelligence. The point is that anyone who accepts the principle of *bhakti-yoga* and accepts the Supreme Lord as the *summum bonum* of life, as the highest target, the ultimate goal, can approach the Lord in the spiritual sky. If one adopts the principles enunciated in *Bhagavad-gītā*, he can make his life perfect and make a perfect solution to all the problems of life which arise out of the transient nature of material existence. This is the sum and substance of the entire *Bhagavad-gītā*.

In conclusion, *Bhagavad-gīta* is a transcendental literature which one should read very carefully. It is capable of saving one from all fear.

> *nehābhikrama-nāśo 'sti pratyavāyo na vidyate*
> *svalpam apy asya dharmasya trāyate mahato bhayāt*

"In this endeavor there is no loss or diminution, and a little advancement on this path can protect one from the most dangerous type of fear." (Bg.

2.40) If one reads *Bhagavad-gītā* sincerely and seriously, then all of the reactions of his past misdeeds will not react upon him. In the last portion of *Bhagavad-gītā*, Lord Śrī Kṛṣṇa proclaims:

> *sarva-dharmān parityajya mām ekaṁ śaraṇaṁ vraja*
> *ahaṁ tvāṁ sarva-pāpebhyo mokṣayiṣyāmi mā śucaḥ*

"Give up all varieties of religiousness, and just surrender unto Me; and in return I shall protect you from all sinful reactions. Therefore, you have nothing to fear." (Bg. 18.66) Thus the Lord takes all responsibility for one who surrenders unto Him, and He indemnifies all the reactions of sin.

One cleanses himself daily by taking a bath in water, but one who takes his bath only once in the sacred Ganges water of the *Bhagavad-gītā* cleanses away all the dirt of material life. Because *Bhagavad-gītā* is spoken by the Supreme Personality of Godhead, one need not read any other Vedic literature. One need only attentively and regularly hear and read *Bhagavad-gītā*. In the present age, mankind is so absorbed with mundane activities that it is not possible to read all of the Vedic literatures. But this is not necessary. This one book, *Bhagavad-gītā*, will suffice because it is the essence of all Vedic literatures and because it is spoken by the Supreme Personality of Godhead. It is said that one who drinks the water of the Ganges certainly gets salvation, but what to speak of one who drinks the waters of *Bhagavad-gītā*? *Gītā* is the very nectar of the *Mahābhārata* spoken by Viṣṇu Himself, for Lord Kṛṣṇa is the original Viṣṇu. It is nectar emanating from the mouth of the Supreme Personality of Godhead, and the Ganges is said to be emanating from the lotus feet of the Lord. Of course there is no difference between the mouth and the feet of the Supreme Lord, but in our position we can appreciate that the *Bhagavad-gītā* is even more important than the Ganges.

The *Bhagavad-gītā* is just like a cow, and Lord Kṛṣṇa, who is a cowherd boy, is milking this cow. The milk is the essence of the *Vedas*, and Arjuna is just like a calf. The wise men, the great sages and pure devotees, are to drink the nectarean milk of *Bhagavad-gītā*.

In this present day, man is very eager to have one scripture, one God, one religion, and one occupation. So let there be one common scripture for the whole world—*Bhagavad-gītā*. And let there be one God only for the whole world—Śrī Kṛṣṇa. And one *mantra* only—Hare Kṛṣṇa, Hare Kṛṣṇa, Kṛṣṇa Kṛṣṇa, Hare Hare/ Hare Rāma, Hare Rāma, Rāma Rāma, Hare Hare. And let there be one work only—the service of the Supreme Personality of Godhead.

THE DISCIPLIC SUCCESSION

Evaṁ paramparā-prāptam imaṁ rājarṣayo viduḥ. (*Bhagavad-gītā,* 4.2) This *Bhagavad-gītā As It Is* is received through this disciplic succession:

1) **Kṛṣṇa,** 2) Brahmā, 3) Nārada, 4) Vyāsa, 5) Madhva, 6) Padmanābha, 7) Nṛhari, 8) Mādhava, 9) Akṣobhya, 10) Jaya Tīrtha, 11) Jñānasindhu, 12) Dayānidhi, 13) Vidyānidhi, 14) Rājendra, 15) Jayadharma, 16) Puruṣottama, 17) Brahmaṇya Tīrtha, 18) Vyāsa Tīrtha, 19) Lakṣmīpati, 20) Mādhavendra Purī, 21) Īśvara Purī, (Nityānanda, Advaita), 22) **Lord Caitanya,** 23) Rūpa, (Svarūpa, Sanātana), 24) Raghunātha, Jīva, 25) Kṛṣṇadāsa, 26) Narottama, 27) Viśvanātha, 28) (Baladeva) Jagannātha, 29) Bhaktivinoda, 30) Gaurakiśora, 31) Bhaktisiddhānta Sarasvatī, 32) Bhaktivedanta Swami Prabhupāda

CHAPTER ONE

Observing the Armies on the Battlefield of Kurukṣetra

TEXT 1

धृतराष्ट्र उवाच ।
धर्मक्षेत्रे कुरुक्षेत्रे समवेता युयुत्सवः ।
मामकाः पाण्डवाश्चैव किमकुर्वत सञ्जय ॥ १ ॥

dhṛtarāṣṭra uvāca
dharma-kṣetre kuru-kṣetre
samavetā yuyutsavaḥ
māmakāḥ pāṇḍavāś caiva
kim akurvata sañjaya

dhṛtarāṣṭraḥ—King Dhṛtarāṣṭra; uvāca—said; dharma-kṣetre—in the place of pilgrimage; kuru-kṣetre—in the place named Kurukṣetra; samavetāḥ—assembled; yuyutsavaḥ—desiring to fight; māmakāḥ—my party (sons); pāṇḍavāḥ—the sons of Pāṇḍu; ca—and; eva-certainly; kim—what; akurvata—did they do; sañjaya—O Sañjaya.

31

TRANSLATION

Dhṛtarāṣṭra said: O Sañjaya, after assembling in the place of pilgrimage at Kurukṣetra, what did my sons and the sons of Pāṇḍu do, being desirous to fight?

PURPORT

Bhagavad-gītā is the widely read theistic science summarized in the *Gītā-māhātmya (Glorification of the Gītā)*. There it says that one should read *Bhagavad-gītā* very scrutinizingly with the help of a person who is a devotee of Śrī Kṛṣṇa and try to understand it without personally motivated interpretations. The example of clear understanding is there in the *Bhagavad-gītā* itself, in the way the teaching is understood by Arjuna, who heard the *Gītā* directly from the Lord. If someone is fortunate enough to understand *Bhagavad-gītā* in that line of disciplic succession, without motivated interpretation, then he surpasses all studies of Vedic wisdom, and all scriptures of the world. One will find in the *Bhagavad-gītā* all that is contained in other scriptures, but the reader will also find things which are not to be found elsewhere. That is the specific standard of the *Gītā*. It is the perfect theistic science because it is directly spoken by the Supreme Personality of Godhead, Lord Śrī Kṛṣṇa.

The topics discussed by Dhṛtarāṣṭra and Sañjaya, as described in the *Mahābhārata*, form the basic principle for this great philosophy. It is understood that this philosophy evolved on the Battlefield of Kurukṣetra, which is a sacred place of pilgrimage from the immemorial time of the Vedic age. It was spoken by the Lord when He was present personally on this planet for the guidance of mankind.

The word *dharma-kṣetra* (a place where religious rituals are performed) is significant because, on the Battlefield of Kurukṣetra, the Supreme Personality of Godhead was present on the side of Arjuna. Dhṛtarāṣṭra, the father of the Kurus, was highly doubtful about the possibility of his sons' ultimate victory. In his doubt, he inquired from his secretary Sañjaya, "What did my sons and the sons of Pāṇḍu do?" He was confident that both his sons and the sons of his younger brother Pāṇḍu were assembled in that Field of Kurukṣetra for a determined engagement of the war. Still, his inquiry is significant. He did not want a compromise between the cousins and brothers, and he wanted to be sure of the fate of his sons on the battlefield. Because the battle was arranged to be fought at Kurukṣetra, which is mentioned elsewhere in the *Vedas* as a place of worship—even for the denizens of heaven—Dhṛtarāṣṭra became very fearful about the influence of the holy place on the outcome of the battle. He knew very well that this would influence Arjuna and the sons of Pāṇḍu favorably, because by nature they were all virtuous. Sañjaya was a student of Vyāsa, and therefore, by the mercy of Vyāsa, Sañjaya was able to envision the Battlefield of Kurukṣetra even while he was in the room of Dhṛtarāṣṭra. And so, Dhṛtarāṣṭra asked him about the situation on the battlefield.

Both the Pāṇḍavas and the sons of Dhṛtarāṣṭra belong to the same family, but Dhṛtarāṣṭra's mind is disclosed herein. He deliberately claimed only his sons as Kurus, and he separated the sons of Pāṇḍu from the family heritage. One can thus understand the specific position of Dhṛtarāṣṭra in his relationship with his nephews, the sons of Pāṇḍu. As in the paddy field the unnecessary plants are taken out, so it is expected from the very beginning of these topics that in the religious field of Kurukṣetra where the father of religion, Śrī Kṛṣṇa, was present, the unwanted plants like Dhṛtarāṣṭra's son Duryodhana and others would be wiped out and the thoroughly religious persons, headed by Yudhiṣṭhira, would be established by the Lord. This is the significance of the words *dharma-kṣetre* and *kuru-kṣetre*, apart from their historical and Vedic importance.

TEXT 2

सञ्जय उवाच ।
दृष्ट्वा तु पाण्डवानीकं व्यूढं दुर्योधनस्तदा ।
आचार्यमुपसंगम्य राजा वचनमब्रवीत् ॥ २ ॥

> sañjaya uvāca
> dṛṣṭvā tu pāṇḍavānīkaṁ
> vyūḍhaṁ duryodhanas tadā
> ācāryam upasaṅgamya
> rājā vacanam abravīt

sañjayaḥ—Sañjaya; *uvāca*—said; *dṛṣṭvā*—after seeing; *tu*—but; *pāṇḍava-anīkam*—the soldiers of the Pāṇḍavas; *vyūḍham*—arranged in military phalanx; *duryodhanaḥ*—King Duryodhana; *tadā*—at that time; *ācāryam*—the teacher; *upasaṅgamya*—approaching nearby; *rājā*—the king; *vacanam*—words; *abravīt*—spoke.

TRANSLATION

Sañjaya said: O King, after looking over the army gathered by the sons of Pāṇḍu, King Duryodhana went to his teacher and began to speak the following words:

PURPORT

Dhṛtarāṣṭra was blind from birth. Unfortunately, he was also bereft of spiritual vision. He knew very well that his sons were equally blind in the matter of religion, and he was sure that they could never reach an understanding with the Pāṇḍavas, who were all pious since birth. Still he was doubtful about the influence of the place of pilgrimage, and Sañjaya could understand his motive in asking about the situation on the battlefield. He wanted, therefore, to encourage the despondent King, and thus he warned him that his sons were not going to make any sort of compromise under the influence of the holy place. Sañjaya therefore informed the King that his son, Duryodhana, after seeing the military force of the Pāṇḍavas, at once went to the commander-in-chief, Droṇācārya, to inform him of the real position. Although Duryodhana is mentioned as the king, he still had to go to the commander on account of the seriousness of the situation. He was therefore quite fit to be a politician. But Duryodhana's diplomatic veneer could not disguise the fear he felt when he saw the military arrangement of the Pāṇḍavas.

TEXT 3

पश्यैतां पाण्डुपुत्राणामाचार्य महतीं चमूम् ।
व्यूढां द्रुपदपुत्रेण तव शिष्येण धीमता ॥ ३ ॥

paśyaitāṁ pāṇḍu-putrāṇām
ācārya mahatīṁ camūm
vyūḍhāṁ drupada-putreṇa
tava śiṣyeṇa dhīmatā

paśya—behold; *etām*—this; *pāṇḍu-putrāṇām*—of the sons of Pāṇḍu; *ācārya*—O teacher; *mahatīm*—great; *camūm*—military force; *vyuḍham*—arranged; *drupada-putreṇa*—by the son of Drupada; *tava*—your; *śiṣyeṇa*—disciple; *dhīmatā*—very intelligent.

TRANSLATION

O my teacher, behold the great army of the sons of Pāṇḍu, so expertly arranged by your intelligent disciple, the son of Drupada.

PURPORT

Duryodhana, a great diplomat, wanted to point out the defects of Droṇācārya, the great *brāhmaṇa* commander-in-chief. Droṇācārya had some political quarrel with King Drupada, the father of Draupadī, who was Arjuna's wife. As a result of this quarrel, Drupada performed a great sacrifice, by which he received the benediction of having a son who would be able to kill Droṇācārya. Droṇācārya knew this perfectly well, and yet, as a liberal *brāhmaṇa*, he did not hesitate to impart all his military secrets when the son of Drupada, Dhṛṣṭadyumna, was entrusted to him for military education. Now, on the Battlefield of Kurukṣetra, Dhṛṣṭadyumna took the side of the Pāṇḍavas, and it was he who arranged for their military phalanx, after having learned the art from Droṇācārya. Duryodhana pointed out this mistake of Droṇācārya's so that he might be alert and uncompromising in the fighting. By this he wanted to point out also that he should not be similarly lenient in battle against the Pāṇḍavas, who were also Droṇācārya's affectionate students. Arjuna, especially, was his most affectionate and brilliant student. Duryodhana also warned that such leniency in the fight would lead to defeat.

TEXT 4

अत्र शूरा महेष्वासा भीमार्जुनसमा युधि ।
युयुधानो विराटश्च द्रुपदश्च महारथः ॥ ४ ॥

atra śūrā maheṣv-āsā
bhīmārjuna-samā yudhi
yuyudhāno virāṭaś ca
drupadaś ca mahā-rathaḥ

atra—here; *śūrāḥ*—heroes; *maheṣvāsāḥ*—mighty bowmen; *bhīma-arjuna*—Bhīma and Arjuna; *samāḥ*—equal; *yudhi*—in the fight; *yuyudhānaḥ*—Yuyudhāna; *virāṭaḥ*—Virāṭa; *ca*—also; *drupadaḥ*—Drupada; *ca*—also; *mahā-rathaḥ*—great fighter.

TRANSLATION

Here in this army there are many heroic bowmen equal in fighting to Bhīma and Arjuna; there are also great fighters like Yuyudhāna, Virāṭa and Drupada.

PURPORT

Even though Dhṛṣṭadyumna was not a very important obstacle in the face of Droṇācārya's very great power in the military art, there were many others who were the cause of fear. They are mentioned by Duryodhana as great stumbling blocks on the path of victory because each and every one of them was as formidable as Bhīma and Arjuna. He knew the strength of Bhīma and Arjuna, and thus he compared the others with them.

TEXT 5

धृष्टकेतुश्चेकितानः काशिराजश्च वीर्यवान् ।
पुरुजित्कुन्तिभोजश्च शैब्यश्च नरपुङ्गवः ॥ ५ ॥

dhṛṣṭaketuś cekitānaḥ
kāśirājaś ca vīryavān
purujit kuntibhojaś ca
śaibyaś ca nara-puṅgavaḥ

dhṛṣṭaketuḥ—Dhṛṣṭaketu; *cekitānaḥ*—Cekitāna; *kāśirājaḥ*—Kaśirāja; *ca*—also; *vīryavān*—very powerful; *purujit*—Purujit; *kuntibhojaḥ*—Kuntibhoja; *ca*—and; *śaibyaḥ*—Śaibya; *ca*—and; *nara-puṅgavaḥ*—heroes in human society.

TRANSLATION

There are also great, heroic, powerful fighters like Dhṛṣṭaketu, Cekitāna, Kāśirāja, Purujit, Kuntibhoja and Śaibya.

TEXT 6

युधामन्युश्च विक्रान्त उत्तमौजाश्च वीर्यवान् ।
सौभद्रो द्रौपदेयाश्च सर्व एव महारथाः ॥ ६ ॥

> yudhāmanyuś ca vikrānta
> uttamaujāś ca vīryavān
> saubhadro draupadeyāś ca
> sarva eva mahā-rathāḥ

yudhāmanyuḥ—Yudhāmanyu; *ca*—and; *vikrāntaḥ*—mighty; *uttamaujāḥ*—Uttamaujā; *ca*—and; *vīryavān*—very powerful; *saubhadraḥ*—the son of Subhadrā; *draupadeyāḥ*—the sons of Draupadī; *ca*—and; *sarve*—all; *eva*—certainly; *mahā-rathāḥ*—great chariot fighters.

TRANSLATION

There are the mighty Yudhāmanyu, the very powerful Uttamaujā, the son of Subhadrā and the sons of Draupadī. All these warriors are great chariot fighters.

TEXT 7

अस्माकं तु विशिष्टा ये तान्निबोध द्विजोत्तम ।
नायका मम सैन्यस्य संज्ञार्थं तान्ब्रवीमि ते ॥ ७ ॥

> asmākaṁ tu viśiṣṭā ye
> tān nibodha dvijottama
> nāyakā mama sainyasya
> saṁjñārthaṁ tān bravīmi te

asmākam—our; *tu*—but; *viśiṣṭāḥ*—especially powerful; *ye*—those; *tān*—them; *nibodha*—just take note, be informed; *dvijottama*—the best of the *brāhmaṇas*; *nāyakāḥ*—captains; *mama*—my; *sainyasya*—of the soldiers; *saṁjñā-artham*—for information; *tān*—them; *bravīmi*—I am speaking; *te*—your.

TRANSLATION

O best of the brāhmaṇas, for your information, let me tell you about the captains who are especially qualified to lead my military force.

TEXT 8

भवान्भीष्मश्च कर्णश्च कृपश्च समितिंजयः ।
अश्वत्थामा विकर्णश्च सौमदत्तिस्तथैव च ॥ ८ ॥

bhavān bhīṣmaś ca karṇaś ca
kṛpaś ca samitiṁ-jayaḥ
aśvatthāmā vikarṇaś ca
saumadattis tathaiva ca

bhavān—yourself; *bhīṣmaḥ*—Grandfather Bhīṣma; *ca*—also; *karṇaḥ*—Karṇa; *ca*—and; *kṛpaḥ*—Kṛpa; *ca*—and; *samitiñjayaḥ*—always victorious in battle; *aśvatthāmā*—Aśvatthāmā; *vikarṇaḥ*—Vikarṇa; *ca*—as well as; *saumadattiḥ*—the son of Somadatta; *tathā*—and as; *eva*—certainly; *ca*—and.

TRANSLATION

There are personalities like yourself, Bhīṣma, Karṇa, Kṛpa, Aśvatthāmā, Vikarṇa and the son of Somadatta called Bhuriśrava, who are always victorious in battle.

PURPORT

Duryodhana mentioned the exceptional heroes in the battle, all of whom are ever-victorious. Vikarṇa is the brother of Duryodhana, Aśvatthāmā is the son of Droṇācārya, and Saumadatti, or Bhūriśrava, is the son of the King of the Bāhlīkas. Karṇa is the half brother of Arjuna, as he was born of Kuntī before her marriage with King Pāṇḍu. Kṛpācārya married the twin sister of Droṇācārya.

TEXT 9

अन्ये च बहवः शूरा मदर्थे त्यक्तजीविताः ।
नानाशस्त्रप्रहरणाः सर्वे युद्धविशारदाः ॥ ९ ॥

anye ca bahavaḥ śūrā
mad-arthe tyakta-jīvitāḥ
nānā-śastra-praharaṇāḥ
sarve yuddha-viśāradāḥ

anye—many others; *ca*—also; *bahavaḥ*—in great numbers; *śūrāḥ*—heroes; mad-arthe-for my sake; *tyakta-jīvitāḥ*—prepared to risk life; *nānā*—many; śastra-weapons; *praharaṇāḥ*—equipped with; *sarve*—all of them; *yuddha*—battle; *viśāradāḥ*—experienced in military science.

TRANSLATION

There are many other heroes who are prepared to lay down their lives for my sake. All of them are well equipped with different kinds of weapons, and all are experienced in military science.

PURPORT

As far as the others are concerned—like Jayadratha, Kṛtavarmā, Śalya, etc. —all are determined to lay down their lives for Duryodhana's sake. In other words, it is already concluded that all of them would die in the Battle of Kurukṣetra for joining the party of the sinful Duryodhana. Duryodhana was, of course, confident of his victory on account of the above-mentioned combined strength of his friends.

TEXT 10

अपर्याप्तं तदस्माकं बलं भीष्माभिरक्षितम् ।
पर्याप्तं त्विदमेतेषां बलं भीमाभिरक्षितम् ॥ १० ॥

aparyāptaṁ tad asmākaṁ
balaṁ bhīṣmābhirakṣitam
paryāptaṁ tv idam eteṣāṁ
balaṁ bhīmābhirakṣitam

aparyāptam—immeasurable; *tat*—that; *asmākam*—of ours; *balam*—strength; *bhīṣma*—by Grandfather Bhīṣma; *abhirakṣitam*—perfectly protected; *paryāptam*—limited; *tu*—but; *idam*—all these; *eteṣām*—of the Pāṇḍavas; *balam*—strength; *bhīma*—by Bhīma; *abhirakṣitam*—carefully protected.

TRANSLATION

Our strength is immeasurable, and we are perfectly protected by Grandfather Bhīṣma, whereas the strength of the Pāṇḍavas, carefully protected by Bhīma, is limited.

PURPORT

Herein an estimation of comparative strength is made by Duryodhana. He thinks that the strength of his armed forces is immeasurable, being specifically protected by the most experienced general, Grandfather Bhīṣma. On the other hand, the forces of the Pāṇḍavas are limited, being protected by a less experienced general, Bhīma, who is like a fig in the presence of Bhīṣma. Duryodhana was always envious of Bhīma because he knew perfectly well that if he should die at all, he would only be killed by Bhīma. But at the same time, he was confident of his victory on account of the presence of Bhīṣma, who was a far superior general. His conclusion that he would come out of the battle victorious was well ascertained.

TEXT 11

अयनेषु च सर्वेषु यथाभागमवस्थिताः ।
भीष्ममेवाभिरक्षन्तु भवन्तः सर्व एव हि ॥ ११ ॥

ayaneṣu ca sarveṣu
yathā-bhāgam avasthitāḥ
bhīṣmam evābhirakṣantu
bhavantaḥ sarva eva hi

ayaneṣu—in the strategic points; *ca*—also; *sarveṣu*—everywhere; *yathā-bhāgam*—as they are differently arranged; *avasthitāḥ*—situated; *bhīṣmam*—unto Grandfather Bhīṣma; *eva*—certainly; *abhirakṣantu*—support may be given; *bhavantaḥ*—all of you; *sarve*—respectively; *eva*—certainly; *hi*—and exactly.

TRANSLATION

Now all of you must give full support to Grandfather Bhīṣma, standing at your respective strategic points in the phalanx of the army.

PURPORT

Duryodhana, after praising the prowess of Bhīṣma, further considered that others might think that they had been considered less important, so in his usual diplomatic way, he tried to adjust the situation in the above words. He emphasized that Bhīṣmadeva was undoubtedly the greatest hero, but he was an old man, so everyone must especially think of his protection from all sides. He might become engaged in the fight, and the enemy might take advantage of his full engagement on one side. Therefore, it was important that other heroes would not leave their strategic positions and allow the enemy to break the phalanx. Duryodhana clearly felt that the victory of the Kurus depended on the presence of Bhīṣmadeva. He was confident of the full support of Bhīṣmadeva and Droṇācārya in the battle because he well knew that they did not even speak a word when Arjuna's wife Draupadī, in her helpless condition, had appealed to them for justice while she was being forced to strip naked in the presence of all the great generals in the assembly. Although he knew that the two generals had some sort of affection for the Pāṇḍavas, he hoped that all such affection would now be completely given up by them, as was customary during the gambling performances.

TEXT 12

तस्य संजनयन्हर्षं कुरुवृद्धः पितामहः ।
सिंहनादं विनद्योच्चैः शङ्खं दध्मौ प्रतापवान् ॥ १२ ॥

tasya sañjanayan harṣaṁ
kuru-vṛddhaḥ pitāmahaḥ
siṁha-nādaṁ vinadyoccaiḥ
śaṅkhaṁ dadhmau pratāpavān

tasya—his; *sañjanayan*—increasing; *harṣam*—cheerfulness; *kuru-vṛddhaḥ*—the grandsire of the Kuru dynasty (Bhīṣma); *pitāmahaḥ*—the grandfather; *siṁha-nādam*—roaring sound, like a lion; *vinadya*—vibrating; *uccaiḥ*—very loudly; *śaṅkham*—conchshell; *dadhmau*—blew; *pratāpavān*—the valiant.

TRANSLATION

Then Bhīṣma, the great valiant grandsire of the Kuru dynasty, the grandfather of the fighters, blew his conchshell very loudly like the sound of a lion, giving Duryodhana joy.

PURPORT

The grandsire of the Kuru dynasty could understand the inner meaning of the heart of his grandson Duryodhana, and out of his natural compassion for him he tried to cheer him by blowing his conchshell very loudly, befitting his position as a lion. Indirectly, by the symbolism of the conchshell, he informed his depressed grandson Duryodhana that he had no chance of victory in the battle, because the Supreme Lord Kṛṣṇa was on the other side. But still, it was his duty to conduct the fight, and no pains would be spared in that connection.

TEXT 13

ततः शङ्खाश्च भेर्यश्च पणवानकगोमुखाः ।
सहसैवाभ्यहन्यन्त स शब्दस्तुमुलोऽभवत् ॥ १३ ॥

*tataḥ śaṅkhāś ca bheryaś ca
paṇavānaka-gomukhāḥ
sahasaivābhyahanyanta
sa śabdas tumulo 'bhavat*

tataḥ—thereafter; *śaṅkhāḥ*—conchshells; *ca*—also; *bheryaḥ*—bugles; *ca*—and; *paṇava-ānaka*—trumpets and drums; *go-mukhāḥ*—horns; *sahasā*—all of a sudden; *eva*—certainly; *abhyahanyanta*—being simultaneously sounded; *saḥ*—that; *śabdaḥ*—combined sound; *tumulaḥ*—tumultuous; *abhavat*—became.

TRANSLATION

After that, the conchshells, bugles, trumpets, drums and horns were all suddenly sounded, and the combined sound was tumultuous.

TEXT 14

ततः श्वेतैर्हयैर्युक्ते महति स्यन्दने स्थितौ ।
माधवः पाण्डवश्चैव दिव्यौ शङ्खौ प्रदध्मतुः ॥ १४ ॥

*tataḥ śvetair hayair yukte
mahati syandane sthitau
mādhavaḥ pāṇḍavaś caiva
divyau śaṅkhau pradadhmatuḥ*

tataḥ—thereafter; *śvetaiḥ*—by white; *hayaiḥ*—horses; *yukte*—being yoked with; *mahati*—in the great; *syandane*—chariot; *sthitau*—so situated;

mādhavaḥ—Kṛṣṇa (the husband of the goddess of fortune); *pāṇḍavaḥ*—Arjuna (the son of Pāṇḍu); *ca*—also; *eva*—certainly; *divyau*—transcendental; *śaṅkhau*—conchshells; *pradadhmatuḥ*—sounded.

TRANSLATION

On the other side, both Lord Kṛṣṇa and Arjuna, stationed on a great chariot drawn by white horses, sounded their transcendental conchshells.

PURPORT

In contrast with the conchshell blown by Bhīṣmadeva, the conchshells in the hands of Kṛṣṇa and Arjuna are described as transcendental. The sounding of the transcendental conchshells indicated that there was no hope of victory for the other side because Kṛṣṇa was on the side of the Pāṇḍavas. *Jayas tu pāṇḍu-putrāṇāṁ yeṣāṁ pakṣe janārdanaḥ.* Victory is always with persons like the sons of Pāṇḍu because Lord Kṛṣṇa is associated with them. And whenever and wherever the Lord is present, the goddess of fortune is also there because the goddess of fortune never lives alone without her husband. Therefore, victory and fortune were awaiting Arjuna, as indicated by the transcendental sound produced by the conchshell of Viṣṇu, or Lord Kṛṣṇa. Besides that, the chariot on which both the friends were seated was donated by Agni (the fire-god) to Arjuna, and this indicated that this chariot was capable of conquering all sides, wherever it was drawn over the three worlds.

TEXT 15

पाञ्चजन्यं हृषीकेशो देवदत्तं धनंजयः ।
पौण्ड्रं दध्मौ महाशङ्खं भीमकर्मा वृकोदरः ॥ १५ ॥

pāñcajanyaṁ hṛṣīkeśo
devadattaṁ dhanañjayaḥ
pauṇḍraṁ dadhmau mahā-śaṅkhaṁ
bhīma-karmā vṛkodaraḥ

pāñcajanyam—the conchshell named Pāñcajanya; *hṛṣīkeśaḥ*—Hṛṣīkeśa (Kṛṣṇa, the Lord who directs the senses of the devotees); *devadattam*—the conchshell named Devadatta; *dhanañjayaḥ*—Dhanañjaya (Arjuna, the winner of wealth); *pauṇḍram*—the conch named Pauṇḍram; *dadhmau*—blew; *mahā-śaṅkham*—the terrific conchshell; *bhīma-karmā*—one who performs Herculean tasks; *vṛkodaraḥ*—the voracious eater (Bhīma).

TRANSLATION

Then, Lord Kṛṣṇa blew His conchshell, called Pāñcajanya; Arjuna blew his, the Devadatta; and Bhīma, the voracious eater and performer of Herculean tasks, blew his terrific conchshell called Pauṇḍram.

PURPORT

Lord Kṛṣṇa is referred to as Hṛṣīkeśa in this verse because He is the owner of all senses The living entities are part and parcel of Him, and, therefore, the senses of the living entities are also part and parcel of His senses. The impersonalists cannot account for the senses of the living entities, and therefore they are always anxious to describe all living entities as sense-less, or impersonal. The Lord, situated in the hearts of all living entities, directs their senses. But, He directs in terms of the surrender of the living entity, and in the case of a pure devotee He directly controls the senses. Here on the Battlefield of Kurukṣetra the Lord directly controls the transcendental senses of Arjuna, and thus His particular name of Hṛṣīkeśa. The Lord has different names according to His different activities. For example, His name is Madhusūdana because He killed the demon of the name Madhu; His name is Govinda because He gives pleasure to the cows and to the senses; His name is Vāsudeva because He appeared as the son of Vasudeva; His name is Devakī-nandana because He accepted Devakī as His mother; His name is Yaśodā-nandana because He awarded His childhood pastimes to Yaśodā at Vṛndāvana; His name is Pārtha-sārathi because He worked as charioteer of His friend Arjuna. Similarly, His name is Hṛṣīkeśa because He gave direction to Arjuna on the Battlefield of Kurukṣetra.

Arjuna is referred to as Dhanañjaya in this verse because he helped his elder brother in fetching wealth when it was required by the King to make expenditures for different sacrifices. Similarly, Bhīma is known as Vṛkodara because he could eat as voraciously as he could perform Herculean tasks, such as killing the demon Hiḍimba. So, the particular types of conchshell blown by the different personalities on the side of the Pāṇḍavas, beginning with the Lord's, were all very encouraging to the fighting soldiers. On the other side there were no such credits, nor the presence of Lord

Kṛṣṇa, the supreme director, nor that of the goddess of fortune. So, they were predestined to lose the battle—and that was the message announced by the sounds of the conchshells.

TEXTS 16-18

अनन्तविजयं राजा कुन्तीपुत्रो युधिष्ठिरः ।
नकुलः सहदेवश्च सुघोषमणिपुष्पकौ ॥ १६ ॥

काश्यश्च परमेष्वासः शिखण्डी च महारथः ।
धृष्टद्युम्नो विराटश्च सात्यकिश्चापराजितः ॥ १७ ॥

द्रुपदो द्रौपदेयाश्च सर्वशः पृथिवीपते ।
सौभद्रश्च महाबाहुः शङ्खान्दध्मुः पृथक्पृथक् ॥ १८ ॥

> anantavijayaṁ rājā
> kuntī-putro yudhiṣṭhiraḥ
> nakulaḥ sahadevaś ca
> sughoṣa-maṇipuṣpakau
>
> kāśyaś ca parameṣv-āsaḥ
> śikhaṇḍī ca mahā-rathaḥ
> dhṛṣṭadyumno virāṭaś ca
> sātyakiś cāparājitaḥ
>
> drupado draupadeyāś ca
> sarvaśaḥ pṛthivī-pate
> saubhadraś ca mahā-bāhuḥ
> śaṅkhān dadhmuḥ pṛthak pṛthak

ananta-vijayam—the conch named Ananta-vijaya; *rājā*—the king; *kuntī-putraḥ*—the son of Kuntī; *yudhiṣṭhiraḥ*—Yudhiṣṭhira; *nakulaḥ*—Nakula; *sahadevaḥ*—Sahadeva; *ca*—and; *sughoṣa-maṇipuṣpakau*—the conches named Sughoṣa and Maṇipuṣpaka; *kāśyaḥ*—the King of Kāśī (Vārāṇasī); *ca*—and; *parama-iṣu-āsaḥ*—the great archer; *śikhaṇḍī*—Śikhaṇḍī; *ca*—also; *mahā-rathaḥ*—one who can fight alone against thousands; *dhṛṣṭadyumnaḥ*—Dhṛṣṭadyumna (the son of King Drupada); *virāṭaḥ*—Virāṭa (the prince who gave shelter to the Pāṇḍavas while they were in disguise); *ca*—also; *sātyakiḥ*—Sātyaki (the same as Yuyudhāna, the charioteer of Lord Kṛṣṇa); *ca*—and; *aparājitaḥ*—who had never been vanquished; *drupadaḥ*—Drupada, the King of Pāñcāla; *draupadeyāḥ*—the sons of Draupadī; *ca*—also; *sarvaśaḥ*—

all; *pṛthivī-pate*—O King; *saubhadraḥ*—Abhimanyu, the son of Subhadrā; *ca*—also; *mahā-bāhuḥ*—mighty-armed; *śaṅkhān*—conchshells; *dadhmuḥ*—blew; *pṛthak pṛthak*—each separately.

TRANSLATION

King Yudhiṣṭhira, the son of Kuntī, blew his conchshell, the Anantavijaya, and Nakula and Sahadeva blew the Sughoṣa and Maṇipuṣpaka. That great archer the King of Kāśī, the great fighter Śikhaṇḍī, Dhṛṣṭadyumna, Virāṭa and the unconquerable Sātyaki, Drupada, the sons of Draupadī, and the others, O King, such as the son of Subhadrā, greatly armed, all blew their respective conchshells.

PURPORT

Sañjaya informed King Dhṛtarāṣṭra very tactfully that his unwise policy of deceiving the sons of Pāṇḍu and endeavoring to enthrone his own sons on the seat of the kingdom was not very laudable. The signs already clearly indicated that the whole Kuru dynasty would be killed in that great battle. Beginning with the grandsire, Bhīṣma, down to the grandsons like Abhimanyu and others—including kings from many states of the world —all were present there, and all were doomed. The whole catastrophe was due to King Dhṛtarāṣṭra, because he encouraged the policy followed by his sons.

TEXT 19

स घोषो धार्तराष्ट्राणां हृदयानि व्यदारयत् ।
नभश्च पृथिवीं चैव तुमुलोऽभ्यनुनादयन् ॥ १९ ॥

sa ghoṣo dhārtarāṣṭrāṇāṁ
hṛdayāni vyadārayat
nabhaś ca pṛthivīṁ caiva
tumulo 'bhyanunādayan

saḥ—that; *ghoṣaḥ*—vibration; *dhārtarāṣṭrāṇām*—of the sons of Dhṛtarāṣṭra; *hṛdayāni*—hearts; *vyadārayat*—shattered; *nabhaḥ*—the sky; *ca*—also; *pṛthivīm*—the surface of the earth; *ca*—also; *eva*—certainly; *tumulaḥ*—uproarious; *abhyanunādayan*—by resounding.

TRANSLATION

The blowing of these different conchshells became uproarious, and thus, vibrating both in the sky and on the earth, it shattered the hearts of the sons of Dhṛtarāṣṭra.

PURPORT

When Bhīṣma and the others on the side of Duryodhana blew their respective conchshells, there was no heart-breaking on the part of the Pāṇḍavas. Such occurrences are not mentioned, but in this particular verse it is mentioned that the hearts of the sons of Dhṛtarāṣṭra were shattered by the sounds vibrated by the Pāṇḍavas' party. This is due to the Pāṇḍavas and their confidence in Lord Kṛṣṇa. One who takes shelter of the Supreme Lord has nothing to fear, even in the midst of the greatest calamity.

TEXT 20

अथ व्यवस्थितान्दृष्ट्वा धार्तराष्ट्रान्कपिध्वजः ।
प्रवृत्ते शस्त्रसम्पाते धनुरुद्यम्य पाण्डवः ।
हृषीकेशं तदा वाक्यमिदमाह महीपते ॥ २० ॥

atha vyavasthitān dṛṣṭvā
dhārtarāṣṭrān kapi-dhvajaḥ
pravṛtte śastra-sampāte
dhanur udyamya pāṇḍavaḥ
hṛṣīkeśaṁ tadā vākyam
idam āha mahī-pate

atha—thereupon; *vyavasthitān*—situated; *dṛṣṭvā*—looking on; *dhārta-rāṣṭrān*—the sons of Dhṛtarāṣṭra; *kapi-dhvajaḥ*—one whose flag is marked with Hanumān; *pravṛtte*—while about to be engaged; *śastra-sampāte*—the arrows released; *dhanuḥ*—bow; *udyamya*—after taking up; *pāṇḍavaḥ*—the son of Pāṇḍu (Arjuna); *hṛṣīkeśam*—unto Lord Kṛṣṇa; *tadā*—at that time; *vākyam*—words; *idam*—these; *āha*—said; *mahī-pate*—O King.

TRANSLATION

O King, at that time Arjuna, the son of Pāṇḍu, who was seated in his chariot, his flag marked with Hanumān, took up his bow and prepared to shoot his arrows, looking at the sons of Dhṛtarāṣṭra. O King, Arjuna then spoke to Hṛṣīkeśa [Kṛṣṇa] these words:

PURPORT

The battle was just about to begin. It is understood from the above statement that the sons of Dhṛtarāṣṭra were more or less disheartened by the unexpected arrangement of military force by the Pāṇḍavas, who were guided by the direct instructions of Lord Kṛṣṇa on the battlefield. The emblem of Hanumān on the flag of Arjuna is another sign of victory because Hanumān cooperated with Lord Rāma in the battle between Rāma and Rāvaṇa, and Lord Rāma emerged victorious. Now both Rāma and Hanumān were present on the chariot of Arjuna to help him. Lord Kṛṣṇa is Rāma Himself, and wherever Lord Rāma is, His eternal servitor Hanumān and His eternal consort Sītā, the goddess of fortune, are present. Therefore, Arjuna had no cause to fear any enemies whatsoever. And above all, the Lord of the senses, Lord Kṛṣṇa, was personally present to give him direction. Thus, all good counsel was available to Arjuna in the matter of executing the battle. In such auspicious conditions, arranged by the Lord for His eternal devotee, lay the signs of assured victory.

TEXTS 21-22

अर्जुन उवाच ।
सेनयोरुभयोर्मध्ये रथं स्थापय मेऽच्युत ।
यावदेतान्निरीक्षेऽहं योद्धुकामानवस्थितान् ॥ २१ ॥
कैर्मया सह योद्धव्यमस्मिन्रणसमुद्यमे ॥ २२ ॥

arjuna uvāca
senayor ubhayor madhye
ratham sthāpaya me 'cyuta
yāvad etān nirīkṣe 'ham
yoddhu-kāmān avasthitān
kair mayā saha yoddhavyam
asmin raṇa-samudyame

arjunaḥ—Arjuna; uvāca—said; senayoḥ—of the armies; ubhayoḥ—of both the parties; madhye—in between them; ratham—the chariot; sthāpaya—please keep; me—my; acyuta—O infallible one; yāvat—as long as; etān—all these; nirīkṣe—may look; aham—I; yoddhu-kāmān—desiring to fight;

avasthitān—arrayed on the battlefield; *kaiḥ*—with whom; *mayā*—by me; *saha*—with; *yoddhavyam*—to fight with; *asmin*—in this; *raṇa*—strife; *samudyame*—in the attempt.

TRANSLATION

Arjuna said: O infallible one, please draw my chariot between the two armies so that I may see who is present here, who is desirous of fighting, and with whom I must contend in this great battle attempt.

PURPORT

Although Lord Kṛṣṇa is the Supreme Personality of Godhead, out of His causeless mercy He was engaged in the service of His friend. He never fails in His affection for His devotees, and thus He is addressed herein as infallible. As charioteer, He had to carry out the orders of Arjuna, and since He did not hesitate to do so, He is addressed as infallible. Although He had accepted the position of a charioteer for His devotee, His supreme position was not challenged. In all circumstances, He is the Supreme Personality of Godhead, Hṛṣīkeśa, the Lord of the total senses. The relationship between the Lord and His servitor is very sweet and transcendental. The servitor is always ready to render a service to the Lord, and, similarly, the Lord is always seeking an opportunity to render some service to the devotee. He takes greater pleasure in His pure devotee's assuming the advantageous postion of ordering Him than He does in being the giver of orders. As master, everyone is under His orders, and no one is above Him to order Him. But when he finds that a pure devotee is ordering Him, He obtains transcendental pleasure, although He is the infallible master of all circumstances.

As a pure devotee of the Lord, Arjuna had no desire to fight with his cousins and brothers, but he was forced to come onto the battlefield by the obstinacy of Duryodhana, who was never agreeable to any peaceful negotiation. Therefore, he was very anxious to see who the leading persons present on the battlefield were. Although there was no question of a peacemaking endeavor on the battlefield, he wanted to see them again, and to see how much they were bent upon demanding an unwanted war.

TEXT 23

योत्स्यमानानवेक्षेऽहं य एतेऽत्र समागताः ।

धार्तराष्ट्रस्य दुर्बुद्धेर्युद्धे प्रियचिकीर्षवः ॥ २३ ॥

yotsyamānān avekṣe 'ham

ya ete 'tra samāgatāḥ

dhārtarāṣṭrasya durbuddher

yuddhe priya-cikīrṣavaḥ

yotsyamānān—those who will be fighting; *avekṣe*—let me see; *aham*—I; *ye*—who; *ete*—those; *atra*—here; *samāgatāḥ*—assembled; *dhārtarāṣṭrasya*—the son of Dhṛtarāṣṭra; *durbuddheḥ*—evil-minded; *yuddhe*—in the fight; *priya*—well; *cikīrṣavaḥ*—wishing.

TRANSLATION

Let me see those who have come here to fight, wishing to please the evil-minded son of Dhṛtarāṣṭra.

PURPORT

It was an open secret that Duryodhana wanted to usurp the kingdom of the Pāṇḍavas by evil plans, in collaboration with his father, Dhṛtarāṣṭra. Therefore, all persons who had joined the side of Duryodhana must have been birds of the same feather. Arjuna wanted to see them in the battlefield before the fight was begun, just to learn who they were, but he had no intention of proposing peace negotiations with them. It was also a fact that he wanted to see them to make an estimate of the strength which he had to face, although he was quite confident of victory because Kṛṣṇa was sitting by his side.

TEXT 24

सञ्जय उवाच ।

एवमुक्तो हृषीकेशो गुडाकेशेन भारत ।

सेनयोरुभयोर्मध्ये स्थापयित्वा रथोत्तमम् ॥ २४ ॥

sañjaya uvāca
evam ukto hṛṣīkeśo
guḍākeśena bhārata
senayor ubhayor madhye
sthāpayitvā rathottamam

sañjayaḥ—Sañjaya; *uvāca*—said; *evam*—thus; *uktaḥ*—addressed; *hṛṣīkeśaḥ*
—Lord Kṛṣṇa; *guḍākeśena*—by Arjuna; *bhārata*—O descendant of Bharata;
senayoḥ—of armies; *ubhayoḥ*—of both; *madhye*—in the midst of; *sthāpayitvā*
—by placing; *rathottamam*—the finest chariot.

TRANSLATION

Sañjaya said: O descendant of Bharata, being thus addressed by Arjuna,
Lord Kṛṣṇa drew up the fine chariot in the midst of the armies of both
parties.

PURPORT

In this verse Arjuna is referred to as Guḍākeśa. *Guḍāka* means sleep, and
one who conquers sleep is called *guḍākeśa*. Sleep also means ignorance. So
Arjuna conquered both sleep and ignorance because of his friendship with
Kṛṣṇa. As a great devotee of Kṛṣṇa, he could not forget Kṛṣṇa even for a
moment, because that is the nature of a devotee. Either in waking or in
sleep, a devotee of the Lord can never be free from thinking of Kṛṣṇa's
name, form, quality and pastimes. Thus a devotee of Kṛṣṇa can conquer
both sleep and ignorance simply by thinking of Kṛṣṇa constantly. This is
called Kṛṣṇa consciousness, or *samādhi*. As Hṛṣīkeśa, or the director of the
senses and mind of every living entity, Kṛṣṇa could understand Arjuna's
purpose in placing the chariot in the midst of the armies. Thus He did so,
and spoke as follows.

TEXT 25

भीष्मद्रोणप्रमुखतः सर्वेषां च महीक्षिताम् ।
उवाच पार्थ पश्यैतान्समवेतान्कुरूनिति ॥ २५ ॥

bhīṣma-droṇa-pramukhataḥ
sarveṣāṁ ca mahī-kṣitām
uvāca pārtha paśyaitān
samavetān kurūn iti

bhīṣma—Grandfather Bhīṣma; *droṇa*—the teacher Droṇa; *pramukhataḥ*—in the front of; *sarveṣām*—all; *ca*—also; *mahīkṣitām*—chiefs of the world; *uvāca*—said; *pārtha*—O Pārtha (son of Pṛthā); *paśya*—just behold; *etān*—all of them; *samavetān*—assembled; *kurūn*—all the members of the *Kuru* dynasty; *iti*—thus.

TRANSLATION

In the presence of Bhīṣma, Droṇa and all other chieftains of the world, Hṛṣīkeśa, the Lord, said, Just behold, Pārtha, all the Kurus who are assembled here.

PURPORT

As the Supersoul of all living entities, Lord Kṛṣṇa could understand what was going on in the mind of Arjuna. The use of the word Hṛṣīkeśa in this connection indicates that He knew everything. And the word Pārtha, or the son of Kuntī or Pṛthā, is also similarly significant in reference to Arjuna. As a friend, He wanted to inform Arjuna that because Arjuna was the son of Pṛthā, the sister of His own father Vasudeva, He had agreed to be the charioteer of Arjuna. Now what did Kṛṣṇa mean when He told Arjuna to "behold the Kurus"? Did Arjuna want to stop there and not fight? Kṛṣṇa never expected such things from the son of His aunt Pṛthā. The mind of Arjuna was thus predicated by the Lord in friendly joking.

TEXT 26

तत्रापश्यत्स्थितान्पार्थः पितॄनथ पितामहान् ।
आचार्यान्मातुलान्भ्रातॄन्पुत्रान्पौत्रान्सखींस्तथा ।
श्वशुरान्सुहृदश्चैव सेनयोरुभयोरपि ॥ २६ ॥

tatrāpaśyat sthitān pārthaḥ
pitṝn atha pitāmahān
ācāryān mātulān bhrātṝn
putrān pautrān sakhīṁs tathā
śvaśurān suhṛdaś caiva
senayor ubhayor api

tatra—there; *apaśyat*—he could see; *sthitān*—standing; *pārthaḥ*—Arjuna; *pitṛn*—fathers; *atha*—also; *pitāmahān*—grandfathers; *ācāryān*—teachers; *mātulān*—maternal uncles; *bhrātṛn*—brothers; *putrān*—sons; *pautrān*—grandsons; *sakhīn*—friends; *tathā*—too, *śvaśurān*—fathers-in-law; *suhṛdaḥ*—well-wishers; *ca*—also; *eva*—certainly; *senayoḥ*—of the armies; *ubhayoḥ*—of both parties; *api*—including.

TRANSLATION

There Arjuna could see, within the midst of the armies of both parties, his fathers, grandfathers, teachers, maternal uncles, brothers, sons, grandsons, friends, and also his father-in-law and well-wishers—all present there.

PURPORT

On the battlefield Arjuna could see all kinds of relatives. He could see persons like Bhūriśravā, who were his father's contemporaries, grandfathers Bhīṣma and Somadatta, teachers like Droṇācārya and Kṛpācārya, maternal uncles like Śalya and Śakuni, brothers like Duryodhana, sons like Lakṣmaṇa, friends like Aśvatthāmā, well-wishers like Kṛtavarmā, etc. He could see also the armies which contained many of his friends.

TEXT 27

तान्समीक्ष्य स कौन्तेयः सर्वान्बन्धूनवस्थितान् ।
कृपया परयाविष्टो विषीदन्निदमब्रवीत् ॥ २७ ॥

tān samīkṣya sa kaunteyaḥ
sarvān bandhūn avasthitān
kṛpayā parayāviṣṭo
viṣīdann idam abravīt

tān—all of them; *samīkṣya*—after seeing; *saḥ*—he; *kaunteyaḥ*—the son of Kuntī; *sarvān*—all kinds of; *bandhūn*—relatives; *avasthitān*—situated; *kṛpayā*—by compassion; *parayā*—of a high grade; *āviṣṭaḥ*—overwhelmed by; *viṣīdan*—while lamenting; *idam*—thus; *abravīt*—spoke.

TRANSLATION

When the son of Kuntī, Arjuna, saw all these different grades of friends and relatives, he became overwhelmed with compassion and spoke thus:

TEXT 28

अर्जुन उवाच ।
दृष्ट्वेमं स्वजनं कृष्ण युयुत्सुं समुपस्थितम् ।
सीदन्ति मम गात्राणि मुखं च परिशुष्यति ॥ २८ ॥

arjuna uvāca
dṛṣṭvemaṁ sva-janaṁ kṛṣṇa
yuyutsuṁ samupasthitam
sīdanti mama gātrāṇi
mukhaṁ ca pariśuṣyati

arjunaḥ—Arjuna; uvāca—said; dṛṣṭvā—after seeing; imam—all these; sva-janam—kinsmen; kṛṣṇa—O Kṛṣṇa; yuyutsum—all in fighting spirit; samu-pasthitam—all present; sīdanti—quivering; mama—my; gātrāṇi—limbs of the body; mukham—mouth; ca—also; pariśuṣyati—drying up.

TRANSLATION

Arjuna said: My dear Kṛṣṇa, seeing my friends and relatives present before me in such a fighting spirit, I feel the limbs of my body quivering and my mouth drying up.

PURPORT

Any man who has genuine devotion to the Lord has all the good qualities which are found in godly persons or in the demigods, whereas the nondevotee, however advanced he may be in material qualifications by education and culture, lacks in godly qualities. As such, Arjuna, just after seeing his kinsmen, friends and relatives on the battlefield, was at once overwhelmed by compassion for them who had so decided to fight amongst themselves. As far as his soldiers were concerned, he was sympathetic from the beginning, but he felt compassion even for the soldiers of the opposite party, foreseeing their imminent death. And so thinking, the limbs of his body began to quiver, and his mouth became dry. He was more or less astonished to see their fighting spirit. Practically the whole community, all blood relatives of Arjuna, had come to fight with him. This overwhelmed a kind devotee like Arjuna. Although it is not mentioned here, still one can easily imagine that not only were Arjuna's bodily limbs quivering and his mouth drying up, but that he was also crying out of compassion. Such symptoms in Arjuna were not due to weakness but to his softheartedness, a characteristic of a pure devotee of the Lord. It is said therefore:

> yasyāsti bhaktir bhagavaty akiñcanā
> sarvair guṇais tatra samāsate surāḥ
> harāv abhaktasya kuto mahad-guṇā
> mano-rathenāsati dhāvato bahiḥ

"One who has unflinching devotion for the Personality of Godhead has all the good qualities of the demigods. But one who is not a devotee of the Lord has only material qualifications that are of little value. This is because he is hovering on the mental plane and is certain to be attracted by the glaring material energy." (Bhāg. 5.18.12)

TEXT 29

वेपथुश्च शरीरे मे रोमहर्षश्च जायते ।
गाण्डीवं स्रंसते हस्तात्त्वक्चैव परिदह्यते ॥ २९ ॥

> vepathuś ca śarīre me
> roma-harṣaś ca jāyate
> gāṇḍīvaṁ sraṁsate hastāt
> tvak caiva paridahyate

vepathuḥ—trembling of the body; ca—also; śarīre—on the body; me—my; roma-harṣaḥ—standing of hair on end; ca—also; jāyate—is taking place; gāṇḍīvam—the bow of Arjuna; sraṁsate—is slipping; hastāt—from the hands; tvak—skin; ca—also; eva—certainly; paridahyate—burning.

TRANSLATION

My whole body is trembling, and my hair is standing on end. My bow Gāṇḍīva is slipping from my hand, and my skin is burning.

PURPORT

There are two kinds of trembling of the body, and two kinds of standings of the hair on end. Such phenomena occur either in great spiritual ecstasy or out of great fear under material conditions. There is no fear in transcendental realization. Arjuna's symptoms in this situation are out of material fear—namely, loss of life. This is evident from other symptoms also; he became so impatient that his famous bow Gāṇḍīva was slipping from his hands, and, because his heart was burning within him, he was feeling a burning sensation of the skin. All these are due to a material conception of life.

TEXT 30

न च शक्नोम्यवस्थातुं भ्रमतीव च मे मनः ।
निमित्तानि च पश्यामि विपरीतानि केशव ॥ ३० ॥

na ca śaknomy avasthātuṁ
bhramatīva ca me manaḥ
nimittāni ca paśyāmi
viparītāni keśava

na—nor; ca—also; śaknomi—am I able; avasthātum—to stay; bhramati—forgetting; iva—as; ca—and; me—my; manaḥ—mind; nimittāni—causes; ca—also; paśyāmi—I foresee; viparītāni—just the opposite; keśava—O killer of the demon Keśī (Kṛṣṇa).

TRANSLATION

I am now unable to stand here any longer. I am forgetting myself, and my mind is reeling. I foresee only evil, O killer of the Keśī demon.

PURPORT

Due to his impatience, Arjuna was unable to stay on the battlefield, and he was forgetting himself on account of the weakness of his mind. Excessive attachment for material things puts a man in a bewildering condition of existence. Bhayaṁ dvitīyābhiniveśataḥ: such fearfulness and loss of mental equilibrium take place in persons who are too affected by material conditions. Arjuna envisioned only unhappiness in the battle-field—he would not be happy even by gaining victory over the foe. The word *nimitta* is significant. When a man sees only frustration in his expectations, he thinks, "Why am I here?" Everyone is interested in himself and his own welfare. No one is interested in the Supreme Self. Arjuna is supposed to show disregard for self-interest by submission to the will of Kṛṣṇa, who is everyone's real self-interest. The conditioned soul forgets this, and therefore suffers material pains. Arjuna thought that his victory in the battle would only be a cause of lamentation for him.

TEXT 31

न च श्रेयोऽनुपश्यामि हत्वा स्वजनमाहवे ।
न काङ्क्षे विजयं कृष्ण न च राज्यं सुखानि च ॥ ३१ ॥

na ca śreyo 'nupaśyāmi
hatvā sva-janam āhave
na kāṅkṣe vijayaṁ kṛṣṇa
na ca rājyaṁ sukhāni ca

na—nor; *ca*—also; *śreyaḥ*—good; *anupaśyāmi*—do I foresee; *hatvā*—by killing; *svajanam*—own kinsmen; *āhave*—in the fight; *na*—nor; *kāṅkṣe*—do I desire; *vijayam*—victory; *kṛṣṇa*—O Kṛṣṇa; *na*—nor; *ca*—also; *rājyam*—kingdom; *sukhāni*—happiness thereof; *ca*—also.

TRANSLATION

I do not see how any good can come from killing my own kinsmen in this battle, nor can I, my dear Kṛṣṇa, desire any subsequent victory, kingdom, or happiness.

PURPORT

Without knowing that one's self-interest is in Viṣṇu (or Kṛṣṇa), conditioned souls are attracted by bodily relationships, hoping to be happy in such situations. Under delusion, they forget that Kṛṣṇa is also the cause of material happiness. Arjuna appears to have even forgotten the moral codes for a *kṣatriya*. It is said that two kinds of men, namely the *kṣatriya* who dies directly in front of the battlefield under Kṛṣṇa's personal orders and the person in the renounced order of life who is absolutely devoted to spiritual culture, are eligible to enter into the sun-globe, which is so powerful and dazzling. Arjuna is reluctant even to kill his enemies, let alone his relatives. He thought that by killing his kinsmen there would be no happiness in his life, and therefore he was not willing to fight, just as a person who does not feel hunger is not inclined to cook. He has now decided to go into the forest and live a secluded life in frustration. But as a kṣatriya, he requires a kingdom for his subsistence, because the kṣatriyas cannot engage themselves in any other occupation. But Arjuna has had no kingdom. Arjuna's sole opportunity for gaining a kingdom lay in fighting with his cousins and brothers and reclaiming the kingdom inherited from his father, which he does not like to do. Therefore he considers himself fit to go to the forest to live a secluded life of frustration.

TEXTS 32-35

किं नो राज्येन गोविन्द किं भोगैर्जीवितेन वा ।
येषामर्थे काङ्क्षितं नो राज्यं भोगाः सुखानि च ॥ ३२ ॥

त इमेऽवस्थिता युद्धे प्राणांस्त्यक्त्वा धनानि च ।
आचार्याः पितरः पुत्रास्तथैव च पितामहाः ॥ ३३ ॥

मातुलाः श्वशुराः पौत्राः श्यालाः सम्बन्धिनस्तथा ।
एतान्न हन्तुमिच्छामि घ्नतोऽपि मधुसूदन ॥ ३४ ॥

अपि त्रैलोक्यराज्यस्य हेतोः किं नु महीकृते ।
निहत्य धार्तराष्ट्रान्नः का प्रीतिः स्याज्जनार्दन ॥ ३५ ॥

kiṁ no rājyena govinda
kiṁ bhogair jīvitena vā
yeṣām arthe kāṅkṣitaṁ no
rājyaṁ bhogāḥ sukhāni ca

ta ime 'vasthitā yuddhe
prāṇāṁs tyaktvā dhanāni ca
ācāryāḥ pitaraḥ putrās
tathaiva ca pitāmahāḥ

mātulāḥ śvaśurāḥ pautrāḥ
śyālāḥ sambandhinas tathā
etān na hantum icchāmi
ghnato 'pi madhusūdana

api trailokya-rājyasya
hetoḥ kiṁ nu mahī-kṛte
nihatya dhārtarāṣṭrān naḥ
kā prītiḥ syāj janārdana

kim—what use; naḥ—to us; rājyena—is the kingdom; govinda—O Kṛṣṇa; kim—what; bhogaiḥ—enjoyment; jīvitena—by living; vā—either; yeṣām—for whom; arthe—for the matter of; kāṅkṣitam—desired; naḥ—our; rājyam—kingdom; bhogāḥ—material enjoyment; sukhāni—all happiness; ca —also; te—all of them; ime—these; avasthitāḥ—situated; yuddhe—in this battlefield; prāṇān—lives; tyaktvā—giving up; dhanāni—riches; ca—also; ācāryāḥ—teachers; pitaraḥ—fathers; putrāḥ—sons; tathā—as well as; eva— certainly; ca—also; pitāmahāḥ—grandfathers; mātulāḥ—maternal uncles; śvaśurāḥ—fathers-in-law; pautrāḥ—grandsons; śyālāḥ—brothers-in-law; sam-bandhinaḥ—relatives; tathā—as well as; etān—all these; na—never; hantum— for killing; icchāmi—do I wish; ghnataḥ—being killed; api—even; madhu-sūdana—O killer of the demon Madhu (Kṛṣṇa); api—even if; trailokya—of the three worlds; rājyasya—of the kingdoms; hetoḥ—in exchange; kim—what to speak of; nu—only; mahī-kṛte—for the sake of earth; nihatya—by killing; dhārtarāṣṭrān—the sons of Dhṛtarāṣṭra; naḥ—our; kā—what; prītiḥ— pleasure; syāt—will there be; janārdana—O maintainer of all living entities.

TRANSLATION

O Govinda, of what avail to us are kingdoms, happiness or even life itself when all those for whom we may desire them are now arrayed in this battlefield? O Madhusūdana, when teachers, fathers, sons, grand-fathers, maternal uncles, fathers-in-law, grandsons, brothers-in-law and all relatives are ready to give up their lives and properties and are standing before me, then why should I wish to kill them, though I may survive? O maintainer of all creatures, I am not prepared to fight with them even in exchange for the three worlds, let alone this earth.

PURPORT

Arjuna has addressed Lord Kṛṣṇa as Govinda because Kṛṣṇa is the object of all pleasures for cows and the senses. By using this significant word, Arjuna indicates what will satisfy his senses. Although Govinda is not meant for satisfying our senses, if we try to satisfy the senses of Govinda then automatically our own senses are satisfied. Materially, everyone wants to satisfy his senses, and he wants God to be the order supplier for such satisfaction. The Lord will satisfy the senses of the living entities as much as they deserve, but not to the extent that they may covet. But when one takes the opposite way—namely, when one tries to satisfy the senses of Govinda without desiring to satisfy one's own senses—then by the grace of Govinda all desires of the living entity are satisfied. Arjuna's deep affection for community and family members is exhibited here partly due to his natural compassion for them. He is therefore not prepared to fight. Everyone wants to show his opulence to friends and relatives, but Arjuna fears that all his relatives and friends will be killed in the battlefield, and he will be unable to share his opulence after victory. This is a typical calculation of material life. The transcendental life is, however, different. Since a devotee wants to satisfy the desires of the Lord, he can, Lord willing, accept all kinds of opulence for the service of the Lord, and if the Lord is not willing, he should not accept a farthing. Arjuna did not want to kill his relatives, and if there were any need to kill them, he desired that Kṛṣṇa kill them personally. At this point he did not know that Kṛṣṇa had already killed them before their coming into the battlefield and that he was only to become an instrument for Kṛṣṇa. This fact is disclosed in following chapters. As a natural devotee of the Lord, Arjuna did not like to retaliate against his miscreant cousins and brothers, but it was the Lord's plan that they should all be killed. The devotee of the Lord does not retaliate against the wrongdoer, but the Lord does not tolerate any mischief done to the devotee by the miscreants. The Lord can excuse a person on His own account, but He excuses no one who has done harm to His devotees. Therefore the Lord was determined to kill the miscreants, although Arjuna wanted to excuse them.

TEXT 36

पापमेवाश्रयेदस्मान्हत्वैतानाततायिनः ।
तस्मान्नार्हा वयं हन्तुं धार्तराष्ट्रान्स्वबान्धवान् ।
स्वजनं हि कथं हत्वा सुखिनः स्याम माधव ॥ ३६ ॥

pāpam evāśrayed asmān
hatvaitān ātatāyinaḥ
tasmān nārhā vayaṁ hantuṁ
dhārtarāṣṭrān sa-bāndhavān
sva-janaṁ hi kathaṁ hatvā
sukhinaḥ syāma mādhava

pāpam—vices; eva—certainly; āśrayet—must take upon; asmān—us; hatvā —by killing; etān—all these; ātatāyinaḥ—aggressors; tasmāt—therefore; na— never; arhāḥ—deserving; vayam—us; hantum—to kill; dhārtarāṣṭrān—the sons of Dhṛtarāṣṭra; svabāndhavān—along with friends; svajanam—kinsmen; hi—certainly; katham—how; hatvā—by killing; sukhinaḥ—happy; syāma— become; mādhava—O Kṛṣṇa, husband of the goddess of fortune.

TRANSLATION

Sin will overcome us if we slay such aggressors. Therefore it is not proper for us to kill the sons of Dhṛtarāṣṭra and our friends. What should we gain, O Kṛṣṇa, husband of the goddess of fortune, and how could we be happy by killing our own kinsmen?

PURPORT

According to Vedic injunctions there are six kinds of aggressors: 1) a poison giver, 2) one who sets fire to the house, 3) one who attacks with deadly weapons, 4) one who plunders riches, 5) one who occupies another's land, and 6) one who kidnaps a wife. Such aggressors are at once to be killed, and no sin is incurred by killing such aggressors. Such killing of aggressors is quite befitting for any ordinary man, but Arjuna was not an ordinary person. He was saintly by character, and therefore he wanted to deal with them in saintliness. This kind of saintliness, however, is not for a kṣatriya. Although a responsible man in the administration of a state is required to be saintly, he should not be cowardly. For example, Lord Rāma was so saintly that people were anxious to live in His kingdom, (Rāma-rājya), but Lord Rāma never showed any cowardice. Rāvaṇa was an aggressor against Rāma because he kidnapped Rāma's wife, Sītā, but Lord Rāma gave him sufficient lessons, unparalleled in the history of the world. In Arjuna's case, however, one should consider the special type of aggressors, namely his own grandfather, own teacher, friends, sons, grandsons, etc. Because of them, Arjuna thought that he should not take the severe steps necessary against ordinary aggressors. Besides that, saintly persons are advised to forgive. Such injunctions for saintly persons are more important than any political emergency. Arjuna considered that rather than kill his own kinsmen for political reasons, it would be better to forgive them on grounds of religion and saintly behavior. He did not, therefore, consider such killing profitable simply for the matter of temporary bodily happiness. After all, kingdoms and pleasures derived therefrom are not permanent, so why should he risk his life and eternal salvation by killing his own kinsmen? Arjuna's addressing of Kṛṣṇa as "Mādhava," or the husband of the goddess of fortune, is also significant in this connection. He wanted to point out to Kṛṣṇa that, as husband of the goddess of fortune, He should not have to induce Arjuna to take up a matter which would ultimately bring about misfortune. Kṛṣṇa, however, never brings misfortune to anyone, to say nothing of His devotees.

TEXTS 37-38

यद्यप्येते न पश्यन्ति लोभोपहतचेतसः ।
कुलक्षयकृतं दोषं मित्रद्रोहे च पातकम् ॥ ३७ ॥
कथं न ज्ञेयमस्माभिः पापादस्मान्निवर्तितुम् ।
कुलक्षयकृतं दोषं प्रपश्यद्भिर्जनार्दन ॥ ३८ ॥

yady apy ete na paśyanti
lobhopahata-cetasaḥ
kula-kṣaya-kṛtaṁ doṣaṁ
mitra-drohe ca pātakam
kathaṁ na jñeyam asmābhiḥ
pāpād asmān nivartitum
kula-kṣaya-kṛtaṁ doṣaṁ
prapaśyadbhir janārdana

yadi—if; api—certainly; ete—they; na—do not; paśyanti—see; lobha—greed; upahata—overpowered; cetasaḥ—the hearts; kula-kṣaya—in killing the family; kṛtam—done; doṣam—fault; mitra-drohe—quarreling with friends; ca—also; pātakam—sinful reactions; katham—why; na—shall not; jñeyam—know this; asmābhiḥ—by us; pāpāt—from sins; asmāt—ourselves; nivartitum—to cease; kula-kṣaya—the destruction of a dynasty; kṛtam—by so doing; doṣam—crime; prapaśyadbhiḥ—by those who can see; janārdana—O Kṛṣṇa.

TRANSLATION

O Janārdana, although these men, overtaken by greed, see no fault in killing one's family or quarreling with friends, why should we, with knowledge of the sin, engage in these acts?

PURPORT

A *kṣatriya* is not supposed to refuse to battle or gamble when he is so invited by some rival party. Under such obligation, Arjuna could not refuse to fight because he was challenged by the party of Duryodhana. In this connection, Arjuna considered that the other party might be blind to the effects of such a challenge. Arjuna, however, could see the evil consequences and could not accept the challenge. Obligation is actually binding when the effect is good, but when the effect is otherwise, then no one can be bound. Considering all these pros and cons, Arjuna decided not to fight.

TEXT 39

कुलक्षये प्रणश्यन्ति कुलधर्माः सनातनाः ।
धर्मे नष्टे कुलं कृत्स्नमधर्मोऽभिभवत्युत ॥ ३९ ॥

kula-kṣaye praṇaśyanti
kula-dharmāḥ sanātanāḥ
dharme naṣṭe kulaṁ kṛtsnam
adharmo 'bhibhavaty uta

kula-kṣaye—in destroying the family; *praṇaśyanti*—becomes vanquished; *kula-dharmāḥ*—the family traditions; *sanātanāḥ*—eternal; *dharme*—in religion; *naṣṭe*—being destroyed; *kulam*—family; *kṛtsnam*—wholesale; *adharmaḥ*—irreligious; *abhibhavati*—transforms; *uta*—it is said.

TRANSLATION

With the destruction of dynasty, the eternal family tradition is vanquished, and thus the rest of the family becomes involved in irreligious practice.

PURPORT

In the system of the *varṇāśrama* institution there are many principles of religious traditions to help members of the family grow properly and attain spiritual values. The elder members are responsible for such purifying processes in the family, beginning from birth to death. But on the death of the elder members, such family traditions of purification may stop, and the remaining younger family members may develop irreligious habits and thereby lose their chance for spiritual salvation. Therefore, for no purpose should the elder members of the family be slain.

TEXT 40

अधर्माभिभवात्कृष्ण प्रदुष्यन्ति कुलस्त्रियः ।
स्त्रीषु दुष्टासु वार्ष्णेय जायते वर्णसङ्करः ॥ ४० ॥

adharmābhibhavāt kṛṣṇa
praduṣyanti kula-striyaḥ
strīṣu duṣṭāsu vārṣṇeya
jāyate varṇa-saṅkaraḥ

adharma—irreligion; *abhibhavāt*—having been predominant; *kṛṣṇa*—
O Kṛṣṇa; *praduṣyanti*—become polluted; *kula-striyaḥ*—family ladies; *strīṣu*
—of the womanhood; *duṣṭāsu*—being so polluted; *vārṣṇeya*—O descendant
of Vṛṣṇi; *jāyate*—it so becomes; *varṇa-saṅkaraḥ*—unwanted progeny.

TRANSLATION

When irreligion is prominent in the family, O Kṛṣṇa, the women of the
family become corrupt, and from the degradation of womanhood, O
descendant of Vṛṣṇi, comes unwanted progeny.

PURPORT

Good population in human society is the basic principle for peace,
prosperity and spiritual progress in life. The *varṇāśrama* religion's principles
were so designed that the good population would prevail in society for the
general spiritual progress of state and community. Such population
depends on the chastity and faithfulness of its womanhood. As children
are very prone to be misled, women are similarly very prone to degradation.
Therefore, both children and women require protection by the elder
members of the family. By being engaged in various religious practices,
women will not be misled into adultery. According to Cāṇakya Paṇḍit,
women are generally not very intelligent and therefore not trustworthy.
So, the different family traditions of religious activities should always
engage them, and thus their chastity and devotion will give birth to a good
population eligible for participating in the *varṇāśrama* system. On the
failure of such *varṇāśrama-dharma*, naturally the women become free to
act and mix with men, and thus adultery is indulged in at the risk of
unwanted population. Irresponsible men also provoke adultery in society,
and thus unwanted children flood the human race at the risk of war and
pestilence.

TEXT 41

सङ्करो नरकायैव कुलघ्नानां कुलस्य च ।
पतन्ति पितरो ह्येषां लुप्तपिण्डोदकक्रियाः ॥ ४१ ॥

saṅkaro narakāyaiva
kula-ghnānāṁ kulasya ca
patanti pitaro hy eṣāṁ
lupta-piṇḍodaka-kriyāḥ

saṅkaraḥ—such unwanted children; *narakāya*—for hellish life; *eva*—
certainly; *kula-ghnānām*—of those who are killers of the family; *kulasya*—
of the family; *ca*—also; *patanti*—fall down; *pitaraḥ*—forefathers; *hi*—
certainly; *eṣām*—of them; *lupta*—stopped; *piṇḍa*—offerings; *udaka*—water;
kriyāḥ— performance.

TRANSLATION

When there is increase of unwanted population, a hellish situation is
created both for the family and for those who destroy the family tradition.
In such corrupt families, there is no offering of oblations of food and
water to the ancestors.

PURPORT

According to the rules and regulations of fruitive activities, there is a
need to offer periodical food and water to the forefathers of the family.
This offering is performed by worship of Viṣṇu, because eating the
remnants of food offered to Viṣṇu can deliver one from all kinds of sinful
actions. Sometimes the forefathers may be suffering from various types
of sinful reactions, and sometimes some of them cannot even acquire a
gross material body and are forced to remain in subtle bodies as ghosts.
Thus, when remnants of *prasādam* food are offered to forefathers by
descendants, the forefathers are released from ghostly or other kinds of
miserable life. Such help rendered to forefathers is a family tradition, and
those who are not in devotional life are required to perform such rituals.
One who is engaged in the devotional life is not required to perform such
actions. Simply by performing devotional service, one can deliver hundreds

and thousands of forefathers from all kinds of misery. It is stated in the *Bhāgavatam*:

> *devarṣi-bhūtāpta-nṛnāṁ pitṝṇāṁ*
> *na kiṅkaro nāyamṛṇī ca rājan*
> *sarvātmanā yaḥ śaraṇaṁ śaraṇyaṁ*
> *gato mukundaṁ parihṛtya kartam*

"Anyone who has taken shelter of the lotus feet of Mukunda, the giver of liberation, giving up all kinds of obligation, and has taken to the path in all seriousness, owes neither duties nor obligations to the demigods, sages, general living entities, family members, humankind or forefathers." (*Bhāg.* 11.5.41) Such obligations are automatically fulfilled by performance of devotional service to the Supreme Personality of Godhead.

TEXT 42

दोषैरेतैः कुलघ्नानां वर्णसङ्करकारकैः ।
उत्साद्यन्ते जातिधर्माः कुलधर्माश्च शाश्वताः ॥ ४२ ॥

> *doṣair etaiḥ kula-ghnānām*
> *varṇa-saṅkara-kārakaiḥ*
> *utsādyante jāti-dharmāḥ*
> *kula-dharmāś ca śāśvatāḥ*

doṣaiḥ—by such faults; *etaiḥ*—all these; *kula-ghnānām*—of the destroyer of a family; *varṇa-saṅkara*—unwanted children; *kārakaiḥ*—by the doers; *utsādyante*—causes devastation; *jāti-dharmāḥ*—community project; *kula-dharmāḥ*—family tradition; *ca*—also; *śāśvatāḥ*—eternal.

TRANSLATION

Due to the evil deeds of the destroyers of family tradition, all kinds of community projects and family welfare activities are devastated.

PURPORT

The four orders of human society, combined with family welfare activities as they are set forth by the institution of the *sanātana-dharma* or *varṇāśrama-dharma*, are designed to enable the human being to attain his ultimate salvation. Therefore, the breaking of the *sanātana-dharma* tradition by irresponsible leaders of society brings about chaos in that society, and consequently people forget the aim of life—Viṣṇu. Such leaders are called blind, and persons who follow such leaders are sure to be led into chaos.

TEXT 43

उत्सन्नकुलधर्माणां मनुष्याणां जनार्दन ।
नरके नियतं वासो भवतीत्यनुशुश्रुम ॥ ४३ ॥

utsanna-kula-dharmāṇām
manuṣyāṇāṁ janārdana
narake niyataṁ vāso
bhavatīty anuśuśruma

utsanna—spoiled; *kula-dharmāṇām*—of those who have the family traditions; *manuṣyāṇām*—of such men; *janārdana*—O Kṛṣṇa; *narake*—in hell; *niyatam*—always; *vāsaḥ*—residence; *bhavati*—it so becomes; *iti*—thus; *anuśuśruma*—I have heard by disciplic succession.

TRANSLATION

O Kṛṣṇa, maintainer of the people, I have heard by disciplic succession that those who destroy family traditions dwell always in hell.

PURPORT

Arjuna bases his argument not on his own personal experience, but on what he has heard from the authorities. That is the way of receiving real knowledge. One cannot reach the real point of factual knowledge without being helped by the right person who is already established in that knowledge. There is a system in the *varṇāśrama* institution by which one has to undergo the process of ablution before death for his sinful activities. One who is always engaged in sinful activities must utilize the process of ablution called the *prāyaścitta*. Without doing so, one surely will be transferred to hellish planets to undergo miserable lives as the result of sinful activities.

TEXT 44

अहो बत महत्पापं कर्तुं व्यवसिता वयम् ।
यद्राज्यसुखलोभेन हन्तुं स्वजनमुद्यताः ॥ ४४ ॥

*aho bata mahat pāpaṁ
kartuṁ vyavasitā vayam
yad rājya-sukha-lobhena
hantuṁ sva-janam udyatāḥ*

ahaḥ—alas; *bata*—how strange it is; *mahat*—great; *pāpam*—sins; *kartum*—to perform; *vyavasitāḥ*—decided; *vayam*—we; *yat*—so that; *rājya*—kingdom; *sukha-lobhena*—driven by greed for royal happiness; *hantum*—to kill; *svajanam*—kinsmen; *udyatāḥ*—trying for.

TRANSLATION

Alas, how strange it is that we are preparing to commit greatly sinful acts, driven by the desire to enjoy royal happiness.

PURPORT

Driven by selfish motives, one may be inclined to such sinful acts as the killing of one's own brother, father, or mother. There are many such instances in the history of the world. But Arjuna, being a saintly devotee of the Lord, is always conscious of moral principles and therefore takes care to avoid such activities.

TEXT 45

यदि मामप्रतीकारमशस्त्रं शस्त्रपाणयः ।
धार्तराष्ट्रा रणे हन्युस्तन्मे क्षेमतरं भवेत् ॥ ४५ ॥

*yadi mām apratīkāram
aśastraṁ śastra-pāṇayaḥ
dhārtarāṣṭrā raṇe hanyus
tan me kṣemataraṁ bhavet*

yadi—even if; *mām*—unto me; *apratīkāram*—without being resistant; *aśastram*—without being fully equipped; *śastra-pāṇayaḥ*—those with weapons in hand; *dhārtarāṣṭrāḥ*—the sons of Dhṛtarāṣṭra; *raṇe*—in the battlefield; *hanyuḥ*—may kill; *tat*—that; *me*—mine; *kṣemataram*—better; *bhavet*—become.

TRANSLATION

I would consider it better for the sons of Dhṛtarāṣṭra to kill me unarmed and unresisting, rather than fight with them.

PURPORT

It is the custom—according to *kṣatriya* fighting principles—that an un-armed and unwilling foe should not be attacked. Arjuna, however, in such an enigmatic position, decided he would not fight if he were attacked by the enemy. He did not consider how much the other party was bent upon fighting. All these symptoms are due to softheartedness resulting from his being a great devotee of the Lord.

TEXT 46

सञ्जय उवाच ।
एवमुक्त्वार्जुनः सङ्ख्ये रथोपस्थ उपाविशत् ।
विसृज्य सशरं चापं शोकसंविग्नमानसः ॥ ४६ ॥

> *sañjaya uvāca*
> *evam uktvārjunaḥ saṅkhye*
> *rathopastha upāviśat*
> *visṛjya sa-śaraṁ cāpaṁ*
> *śoka-saṁvigna-mānasaḥ*

sañjayaḥ—Sañjaya; *uvāca*—said; *evam*—thus; *uktvā*—saying; *arjunaḥ*—Arjuna; *saṅkhye*—in the battlefield; *ratha*—chariot; *upasthaḥ*—situated on; *upāviśat*—sat down again; *visṛjya*—keeping aside; *sa-śaram*—along with arrows; *cāpam*—the bow; *śoka*—lamentation; *saṁvigna*—distressed; *mānasaḥ*—within the mind.

TRANSLATION

Sañjaya said: Arjuna, having thus spoken on the battlefield, cast aside his bow and arrows and sat down on the chariot, his mind overwhelmed with grief.

PURPORT

While observing the situation of his enemy, Arjuna stood up on the chariot, but he was so afflicted with lamentation that he sat down again, setting aside his bow and arrows. Such a kind and softhearted person, in the devotional service of the Lord, is fit to receive self-knowledge.

Thus end the Bhaktivedanta Purports to the First Chapter of the Śrīmad-Bhagavad-gītā in the matter of Observing the Armies on the Battlefield of Kurukṣetra.

CHAPTER TWO

Contents of the Gītā Summarized

TEXT 1

सञ्जय उवाच ।
तं तथा कृपयाविष्टमश्रुपूर्णाकुलेक्षणम् ।
विषीदन्तमिदं वाक्यमुवाच मधुसूदनः ॥ १ ॥

sañjaya uvāca
taṁ tathā kṛpayāviṣṭam
aśru-pūrṇākulekṣaṇam
viṣīdantam idaṁ vākyam
uvāca madhusūdanaḥ

sañjayaḥ uvāca—Sañjaya said; *tam*—unto Arjuna; *tathā*—thus; *kṛpayā*—by compassion; *āviṣṭam*—overwhelmed; *aśru-pūrṇa*—full of tears; *ākula*—depressed; *īkṣaṇam*—eyes; *viṣīdantam*—lamenting; *idam*—this; *vākyam*—words; *uvāca*—said; *madhusūdanaḥ*—the killer of Madhu.

TRANSLATION

Sañjaya said: Seeing Arjuna full of compassion and very sorrowful, his eyes brimming with tears, Madhusūdana, Kṛṣṇa, spoke the following words.

PURPORT

Material compassion, lamentation and tears are all signs of ignorance of the real self. Compassion for the eternal soul is self-realization. The word "Madhusūdana" is significant in this verse. Lord Kṛṣṇa killed the demon Madhu, and now Arjuna wanted Kṛṣṇa to kill the demon of misunderstanding that had overtaken him in the discharge of his duty. No one knows where compassion should be applied. Compassion for the dress of a drowning man is senseless. A man fallen in the ocean of nescience cannot be saved simply by rescuing his outward dress—the gross material body. One who does not know this and laments for the outward dress is called a *śūdra*, or one who laments unnecessarily. Arjuna was a *kṣatriya*, and this conduct was not expected from him. Lord Kṛṣṇa, however, can dissipate the lamentation of the ignorant man, and for this purpose the *Bhagavad-gītā* was sung by Him. This chapter instructs us in self-realization by an analytical study of the material body and the spirit soul, as explained by the supreme authority, Lord Śrī Kṛṣṇa. This realization is made possible by working with the fruitive being situated in the fixed conception of the real self.

TEXT 2

श्रीभगवानुवाच ।
कुतस्त्वा कश्मलमिदं विषमे समुपस्थितम् ।
अनार्यजुष्टमस्वर्ग्यमकीर्तिकरमर्जुन ॥ २ ॥

*śrī-bhagavān uvāca
kutas tvā kaśmalam idaṁ
viṣame samupasthitam
anārya-juṣṭam asvargyam
akīrti-karam arjuna*

śrī bhagavān uvāca—the Supreme Personality of Godhead said; *kutaḥ*—wherefrom; *tvā*—unto you; *kaśmalam*—dirtiness; *idam*—this lamentation;

viṣame—this hour of crisis; *samupasthitam*—arrived; *anārya*—persons who do not know the value of life; *juṣṭam*—practiced by; *asvargyam*—that which does not lead to higher planets; *akīrti*—infamy; *karam*—the cause of; *arjuna*—O Arjuna.

TRANSLATION

The Supreme Person [Bhagavān] said: My dear Arjuna, how have these impurities come upon you? They are not at all befitting a man who knows the progressive values of life. They do not lead to higher planets, but to infamy.

PURPORT

Kṛṣṇa and the Supreme Personality of Godhead are identical. Therefore Lord Kṛṣṇa is referred to as "Bhagavān" throughout the *Gītā*. Bhagavān is the ultimate in the Absolute Truth. Absolute Truth is realized in three phases of understanding, namely Brahman or the impersonal all-pervasive spirit; Paramātmā, or the localized aspect of the Supreme within the heart of all living entities; and Bhagavān, or the Supreme Personality of Godhead, Lord Kṛṣṇa. In the *Śrīmad-Bhāgavatam* this conception of the Absolute Truth is explained thus:

> *vadanti tat tattva-vidas tattvaṁ yaj jñānam advayam*
> *brahmeti paramātmeti bhagavān iti śabdyate.*

"The Absolute Truth is realized in three phases of understanding by the knower of the Absolute Truth, and all of them are identical. Such phases of the Absolute Truth are expressed as Brahman, Paramātmā, and Bhagavān." (*Bhāg.* 1.2.11) These three divine aspects can be explained by the example of the sun, which also has three different aspects, namely the sunshine, the sun's surface and the sun planet itself. One who studies the sunshine only is the preliminary student. One who understands the sun's surface is further advanced. And one who can enter into the sun planet is the highest. Ordinary students who are satisfied by simply understanding the sunshine-its universal pervasiveness and the glaring effulgence of its impersonal nature-may be compared to those who can realize only the Brahman feature of the Absolute Truth. The student who has advanced still further can know the sun disc, which is compared to knowledge of the Paramātmā feature of the Absolute Truth. And the student who can enter into the heart of the sun planet is compared to those who realize the personal features of the Supreme Absolute Truth. Therefore, the *bhaktas*, or the transcendentalists who have realized the Bhagavān feature of the Absolute Truth, are the topmost transcendentalists, although all students who are engaged in the study of the Absolute Truth are engaged in the same subject matter. The sunshine, the sun disc and the inner affairs of the sun planet cannot be separated from one another, and yet the students of the three different phases are not in the same category.

The Sanskrit word *Bhagavān* is explained by the great authority, Parāśara Muni, the father of Vyāsadeva. The Supreme Personality who possesses all riches, all strength, all fame, all beauty, all knowledge and all renunciation is called Bhagavān. There are many persons who are very rich, very powerful, very beautiful, very famous, very learned, and very much detached, but no one can claim that he possesses all riches, all strength, etc., entirely. Only Kṛṣṇa can claim this because He is the Supreme Personality of Godhead. No living entity, including Brahmā, Lord Śiva, or Nārāyaṇa, can possess opulences as fully as Kṛṣṇa. Therefore it is concluded in the *Brahma-saṁhitā* by Lord Brahmā himself that Lord Kṛṣṇa is the Supreme Personality of Godhead. No one is equal to or above Him. He is the primeval Lord, or Bhagavān, known as Govinda, and He is the supreme cause of all causes.

> *īśvaraḥ paramaḥ kṛṣṇaḥ sac-cid-ānanda-vigrahaḥ*
> *anādir ādir govindaḥ sarua-kāraṇa-kāraṇam*

"There are many personalities possessing the qualities of Bhagavān, but Kṛṣṇa is the supreme because none can excel Him. He is the Supreme Person, and His body is eternal, full of knowledge and bliss. He is the primeval Lord Govinda and the cause of all causes." (*Brahma-saṁhitā* 5.1)

In the *Bhāgavatam* also there is a list of many incarnations of the Supreme Personality of Godhead, but Kṛṣṇa is described as the original Personality of Godhead, from whom many, many incarnations and Personalities of Godhead expand:

> *ete cāṁśa-kalāḥ puṁsaḥ kṛṣṇas tu bhagavān svayam*
> *indrāri-vyākulaṁ lokaṁ mṛḍayanti yuge yuge*

"All the lists of the incarnations of Godhead submitted herewith are either plenary expansions or parts of the plenary expansions of the Supreme Godhead, but Kṛṣṇa is the Supreme Personality of Godhead Himself." (Bhag. 1.3.28)

Therefore, Kṛṣṇa is the original Supreme Personality of Godhead, the Absolute Truth, the source of both the Supersoul and the impersonal Brahman.

In the presence of the Supreme Personality of Godhead, Arjuna's lamentation for his kinsmen is certainly unbecoming, and therefore Kṛṣṇa expressed His surprise with the word *kutas,* "wherefrom." Such unmanly sentiments were never expected from a person belonging to the civilized class of men known as *Āryans.* The word *āryan* is applicable to persons who know the value of life and have a civilization based on spiritual realization. Persons who are led by the material conception of life do not know that the aim of life is realization of the Absolute Truth, Viṣṇu, or Bhagavān, and they are captivated by the external features of the material world, and therefore they do not know what liberation is. Persons who have no knowledge of liberation from material bondage are called non-Āryans. Although Arjuna was a *kṣatriya,* he was deviating from his prescribed duties by declining to fight. This act of cowardice is described as befitting the non-Āryans. Such deviation from duty does not help one in the progress of spiritual life, nor does it even give one the opportunity to become famous in this world. Lord Kṛṣṇa did not approve of the so-called compassion of Arjuna for his kinsmen.

TEXT 3

कैब्यं मा स्म गमः पार्थ नैतत्त्वय्युपपद्यते ।
क्षुद्रं हृदयदौर्बल्यं त्यक्त्वोत्तिष्ठ परन्तप ॥ ३ ॥

klaibyaṁ mā sma gamaḥ pārtha
naitat tvayy upapadyate
kṣudraṁ hṛdaya-daurbalyaṁ
tyaktvottiṣṭha parantapa

klaibyam—impotence; *mā*—do not; *sma*—take it; *gamaḥ*—go in; *pārtha*—O son of Pṛthā; *na*—never; *etat*—like this; *tvayi*—unto you; *upapadyate*—is befitting; *kṣudram*—very little; *hṛdaya*—heart; *daurbalyam*—weakness; *tyaktvā*—giving up; *uttiṣṭha*—get up; *parantapa*—O chastiser of the enemies.

TRANSLATION

O son of Pṛthā, do not yield to this degrading impotence. It does not become you. Give up such petty weakness of heart and arise, O chastiser of the enemy.

PURPORT

Arjuna was addressed as the "son of Pṛthā," who happened to be the sister of Kṛṣṇa's father Vasudeva. Therefore Arjuna had a blood relationship with Kṛṣṇa. If the son of a kṣatriya declines to fight, he is a kṣatriya in name only, and if the son of a brāhmaṇa acts impiously, he is a brāhmaṇa in name only. Such kṣatriyas and brāhmaṇas are unworthy sons of their fathers; therefore, Kṛṣṇa did not want Arjuna to become an unworthy son of a kṣatriya. Arjuna was the most intimate friend of Kṛṣṇa, and Kṛṣṇa was directly guiding him on the chariot; but in spite of all these credits, if Arjuna abandoned the battle, he would be committing an infamous act; therefore Kṛṣṇa said that such an attitude in Arjuna did not fit his personality. Arjuna might argue that he would give up the battle on the grounds of his magnanimous attitude for the most respectable Bhīṣma and his relatives, but Kṛṣṇa considered that sort of magnanimity not approved by authority. Therefore, such magnanimity or so-called nonviolence should be given up by persons like Arjuna under the direct guidance of Kṛṣṇa.

TEXT 4

अर्जुन उवाच ।
कथं भीष्ममहं सङ्ख्ये द्रोणं च मधुसूदन ।
इषुभिः प्रतियोत्स्यामि पूजार्हावरिसूदन ॥ ४ ॥

arjuna uvāca
katham bhīṣmam aham saṅkhye
droṇam ca madhusūdana
iṣubhiḥ pratiyotsyāmi
pūjārhāv ari-sūdana

arjunaḥ uvāca—Arjuna said; katham—how; bhīṣmam—unto Bhīṣma; aham—I; saṅkhye—in the fight; droṇam—unto Droṇa; ca—also, madhu-sūdana—O killer of Madhu; iṣubhiḥ—with arrows; pratiyotsyāmi—shall counterattack; pūjā-arhau—those who are worshipable; arisūdana—O killer of the enemies.

TRANSLATION

Arjuna said: O killer of Madhu [Kṛṣṇa], how can I counterattack with arrows in battle men like Bhīṣma and Droṇa, who are worthy of my worship?

PURPORT

Respectable superiors like Bhīṣma the grandfather and Droṇācārya the teacher are always worshipable. Even if they attack, they should not be counterattacked. It is general etiquette that superiors are not to be offered even a verbal fight. Even if they are sometimes harsh in behavior, they should not be harshly treated. Then, how is it possible for Arjuna to counterattack them? Would Kṛṣṇa ever attack His own grandfather, Ugrasena, or His teacher, Sāndīpani Muni? These were some of the arguments by Arjuna to Kṛṣṇa.

TEXT 5

गुरूनहत्वा हि महानुभावान्
श्रेयो भोक्तुं भैक्ष्यमपीह लोके ।
हत्वार्थकामांस्तु गुरूनिहैव
भुञ्जीय भोगान्रुधिरप्रदिग्धान् ॥ ५ ॥

gurūn ahatvā hi mahānubhāvān
śreyo bhoktuṁ bhaikṣyam apīha loke
hatvārtha-kāmāṁs tu gurūn ihaiva
bhuñjīya bhogān rudhira-pradigdhān

gurūn—the superiors; *ahatvā*—by killing; *hi*—certainly; *mahā-anubhāvān*—great souls; *śreyaḥ*—it is better; *bhoktum*—to enjoy life; *bhaikṣyam*—begging; *api*—even; *iha*—in this life; *loke*—in this world; *hatvā*—killing; *artha*—gain; *kāmān*—so desiring; *tu*—but; *gurūn*—superiors; *iha*—in this world; *eva*—certainly; *bhuñjīya*—has to enjoy; *bhogān*—enjoyable things; *rudhira*—blood; *pradigdhān*—tainted with.

TRANSLATION

It is better to live in this world by begging than to live at the cost of the lives of great souls who are my teachers. Even though they are avaricious, they are nonetheless superiors. If they are killed, our spoils will be tainted with blood.

PURPORT

According to scriptural codes, a teacher who engages in an abominable action and has lost his sense of discrimination is fit to be abandoned. Bhīṣma and Droṇa were obliged to take the side of Duryodhana because of his financial assistance, although they should not have accepted such a position simply on financial considerations. Under the circumstances, they have lost the respectability of teachers. But Arjuna thinks that nevertheless they remain his superiors, and therefore to enjoy material profits after killing them would mean to enjoy spoils tainted with blood.

TEXT 6

न चैतद्विद्मः कतरन्नो गरीयो
यद्वा जयेम यदि वा नो जयेयुः ।
यानेव हत्वा न जिजीविषाम-
स्तेऽवस्थिताः प्रमुखे धार्तराष्ट्राः ॥ ६ ॥

na caitad vidmaḥ kataran no garīyo
yad vā jayema yadi vā no jayeyuḥ
yān eva hatvā na jijīviṣāmas
te 'vasthitāḥ pramukhe dhārtarāṣṭrāḥ

na—nor; *ca*—also; *etat*—this; *vidmaḥ*—do know; *katarat*—which; *naḥ*—us; *garīyaḥ*—better; *yat*—what; *vā*—either; *jayema*—conquer us; *yadi*—if; *vā*—or; *naḥ*—us; *jayeyuḥ*—conquer; *yān*—those; *eva*—certainly; *hatvā*—by killing; *na*—never; *jijīviṣāmaḥ*—want to live; *te*—all of them; *avasthitāḥ*—are situated; *pramukhe*—in the front; *dhārtarāṣṭrāḥ*—the sons of Dhṛtarāṣṭra.

TRANSLATION

Nor do we know which is better—conquering them or being conquered by them. The sons of Dhṛtarāṣṭra, whom if we killed we should not care to live, are now standing before us on this battlefield.

PURPORT

Arjuna did not know whether he should fight and risk unnecessary violence, although fighting is the duty of the *kṣatriyas,* or whether he should refrain and live by begging. If he did not conquer the enemy, begging would be his only means of subsistence. Nor was there certainty of victory, because either side might emerge victorious. Even if victory awaited them (and their cause was justified), still, if the sons of

Dhṛtarāṣṭra died in battle, it would be very difficult to live in their absence. Under the circumstances, that would be another kind of defeat for them. All these considerations by Arjuna definitely prove that he was not only a great devotee of the Lord but that he was also highly enlightened and had complete control over his mind and senses. His desire to live by begging, although he was born in the royal household, is another sign of detachment. He was truly virtuous, as these qualities, combined with his faith in the words of instruction of Śrī Kṛṣṇa (his spiritual master), indicate. It is concluded that Arjuna was quite fit for liberation. Unless the senses are controlled, there is no chance of elevation to the platform of knowledge, and without knowledge and devotion there is no chance of liberation. Arjuna was competent in all these attributes, over and above his enormous attributes in his material relationships.

TEXT 7

कार्पण्यदोषोपहतस्वभावः
पृच्छामि त्वां धर्मसम्मूढचेताः ।
यच्छ्रेयः स्यान्निश्चितं ब्रूहि तन्मे
शिष्यस्तेऽहं शाधि मां त्वां प्रपन्नम् ॥ ७ ॥

kārpaṇya-doṣopahata-svabhāvaḥ
pṛcchāmi tvāṁ dharma-sammūḍha-cetāḥ
yac chreyaḥ syān niścitaṁ brūhi tan me
śiṣyas te 'haṁ śādhi māṁ tvāṁ prapannam

kārpaṇya—miserly; *doṣa*—weakness; *upahata*—being inflicted by; *sva-bhāvaḥ*—characteristics; *pṛcchāmi*—I am asking; *tvām*—unto You; *dharma*—religion; *sammūḍha*—bewildered; *cetāḥ*—in heart; *yat*—what; *śreyaḥ*—all-good; *syāt*—may be; *niścitam*—confidently; *brūhi*—tell; *tat*—that; *me*—unto me; *śiṣyaḥ*—disciple; *te*—Your; *aham*—I am; *śādhi*—just instruct; *mām*—me; *tvām*—unto You; *prapannam*—surrendered.

TRANSLATION

Now I am confused about my duty and have lost all composure because of weakness. In this condition I am asking You to tell me clearly what is best for me. Now I am Your disciple, and a soul surrendered unto You. Please instruct me.

PURPORT

By nature's own way the complete system of material activities is a source of perplexity for everyone. In every step there is perplexity, and therefore it behooves one to approach a bona fide spiritual master who can give one proper guidance for executing the purpose of life. All Vedic literatures advise us to approach a bona fide spiritual master to get free from the perplexities of life which happen without our desire. They are like a forest fire that somehow blazes without being set by anyone. Similarly, the world situation is such that perplexities of life automatically appear, without our wanting such confusion. No one wants fire, and yet it takes place, and we become perplexed. The Vedic wisdom therefore advises that in order to solve the perplexities of life and to understand the science of the solution, one must approach a spiritual master who is in the disciplic succession. A person with a bona fide spiritual master is supposed to know everything. One should not, therefore, remain in material perplexities but should approach a spiritual master. This is the purport of this verse.

Who is the man in material perplexities? It is he who does not understand the problems of life. In the *Garga Upaniṣad* the perplexed man is described as follows:

yo vā etad akṣaraṁ gārgy aviditvāsmāl lokāt praiti sa kṛpaṇaḥ

"He is a miserly man who does not solve the problems of life as a human and who thus quits this world like the cats and dogs, without understanding the science of self-realization." This human form of life is a most valuable asset for the living entity who can ultilize it for solving the problems of life; therefore, one who does not utilize this opportunity properly is a miser. On the other hand, there is the *brāhmaṇa*, or he who is intelligent enough to utilize this body to solve all the problems of life.

The *kṛpaṇas*, or miserly persons, waste their time in being overly affectionate for family, society, country, etc., in the material conception of life. One is often attached to family life, namely to wife, children and other members, on the basis of "skin disease." The *kṛpaṇa* thinks that he is able to protect his family members from death; or the *kṛpaṇa* thinks that his family or society can save him from the verge of death. Such family attachment can be found even in the lower animals who take care of children also. Being intelligent, Arjuna could understand that his affection for family members and his wish to protect them from death were the causes of his perplexities. Although he could understand that his duty to fight was awaiting him, still, on account of miserly weakness, he could not discharge the duties. He is therefore asking Lord Kṛṣṇa, the supreme spiritual master, to make a definite solution. He offers himself to Kṛṣṇa as a disciple. He wants to stop friendly talks. Talks between the master and the disciple are serious, and now Arjuna wants to talk very seriously before the recognized spiritual master. Kṛṣṇa is therefore the original spiritual master of the science of *Bhagavad-gītā*, and Arjuna is the first disciple for understanding the *Gītā*. How Arjuna understands the *Bhagavad-gītā* is stated in the *Gītā* itself. And yet foolish mundane scholars explain that one need not submit to Kṛṣṇa as a person, but to "the unborn within Kṛṣṇa." There is no difference between Kṛṣṇa's within and without. And one who has no sense of this understanding is the greatest fool in trying to understand *Bhagavad-gītā*.

TEXT 8

न हि प्रपश्यामि ममापनुद्या-
द्यच्छोकमुच्छोषणमिन्द्रियाणाम् ।
अवाप्य भूमावसपत्नमृद्धं
राज्यं सुराणामपि चाधिपत्यम् ॥ ८ ॥

na hi prapaśyāmi mamāpanudyād
yac chokam ucchoṣaṇam indriyāṇām
avāpya bhūmāv asapatnam ṛddham
rājyaṁ surāṇām api cādhipatyam

na—do not; *hi*—certainly; *prapaśyāmi*—I see; *mama*—my; *apanudyāt*—they can drive away; *yat*—that; *śokam*—lamentation; *ucchoṣaṇam*—drying up; *indriyāṇām*—of the senses; *avāpya*—achieving; *bhūmau*—on the earth; *asapatnam*—without rival; *ṛddham*—prosperous; *rājyam*—kingdom; *surāṇām*—of the demigods; *api*—even; *ca*—also; *ādhipatyam*—supremacy.

TRANSLATION

I can find no means to drive away this grief which is drying up my senses. I will not be able to destroy it even if I win an unrivalled kingdom on the earth with sovereignty like that of the demigods in heaven.

PURPORT

Although Arjuna was putting forward so many arguments based on knowledge of the principles of religion and moral codes, it appears that he was unable to solve his real problem without the help of the spiritual master, Lord Śrī Kṛṣṇa. He could understand that his so-called knowledge was useless in driving away his problems, which were drying up his whole existence; and it was impossible for him to solve such perplexities without the help of a spiritual master like Lord Kṛṣṇa. Academic knowledge, scholarship, high position, etc., are all useless in solving the problems of life; help can only be given by a spiritual master like Kṛṣṇa. Therefore, the conclusion is that a spiritual master who is one hundred percent Kṛṣṇa conscious is the bona fide spiritual master, for he can solve the problems of life. Lord Caitanya said that one who is master in the science of Kṛṣṇa consciousness, regardless of his social position, is the real spiritual master.

> *kibā vipra, kibā nyāsī, śūdra kene naya*
> *yei kṛṣṇa-tattva-vettā, sei 'guru' haya.*
> (*Caitanya-caritāmṛta*, Madhya 8.127)

"It does not matter whether a person is a *vipra* [learned scholar in Vedic wisdom] or is born in a lower family, or is in the renounced order of life—if he is master in the science of Kṛṣṇa, he is the perfect and bona fide spiritual master." So without being a master in the science of Kṛṣṇa consciousness, no one is a bona fide spiritual master. It is also said in Vedic literatures:

> *ṣaṭ-karma-nipuṇo vipro mantra-tantra-viśāradaḥ*
> *avaiṣṇavo gurur na syād vaiṣṇavaḥ śvapaco guruḥ*

"A scholarly *brāhmaṇa*, expert in all subjects of Vedic knowledge, is unfit to become a spiritual master without being a Vaiṣṇava, or expert in the science of Kṛṣṇa consciousness. But a person born in a family of a lower caste can become a spiritual master if he is a Vaiṣṇava, or Kṛṣṇa conscious."

The problems of material existence—birth, old age, disease and death—cannot be counteracted by accumulation of wealth and economic development. In many parts of the world there are states which are replete with all facilities of life, which are full of wealth, and economically developed, yet the problems of material existence are still present. They are seeking peace in different ways, but they ean achieve real happiness only if they consult Kṛṣṇa, or the *Bhagavad-gītā* and *Śrīmad-Bhāgavatam*—which constitute the science of Kṛṣṇa—or the bona fide representative of Kṛṣṇa, the man in Kṛṣṇa consciousness.

If economic development and material comforts could drive away one's lamentations for family, social, national or international inebrieties, then Arjuna would not have said that even an unrivalled kingdom on earth or supremacy like that of the demigods in the heavenly planets would not be able to drive away his lamentations. He sought, therefore, refuge in Kṛṣṇa consciousness, and that is the right path for peace and harmony. Economic development or supremacy over the world can be finished at any moment by the cataclysms of material nature. Even elevation into a higher planetary situation, as men are now seeking a place on the moon planet, can also be finished at one stroke. The *Bhagavad-gītā* confirms this: *kṣīṇe puṇye martyalokaṁ viśanti* "When the results of pious activities are finished, one falls down again from the peak of happiness to the lowest status of life." Many politicians of the world have fallen down in that way. Such downfalls only constitute more causes for lamentation.

Therefore, if we want to curb lamentation for good, then we have to take shelter of Kṛṣṇa, as Arjuna is seeking to do. So Arjuna asked Kṛṣṇa to solve his problem definitely, and that is the way of Kṛṣṇa consciousness.

TEXT 9

सञ्जय उवाच ।
एवमुक्त्वा हृषीकेशं गुडाकेशः परन्तपः ।
न योत्स्य इति गोविन्दमुक्त्वा तूष्णीं बभूव ह ॥ ९ ॥

sañjaya uvāca
evam uktvā hṛṣīkeśaṁ
guḍākeśaḥ parantapaḥ
na yotsya iti govindam
uktvā tūṣṇīṁ babhūva ha

sañjayaḥ uvāca—Sañjaya said; *evam*—thus; *uktvā*—speaking; *hṛṣīkeśam*—unto Kṛṣṇa, the master of the senses; *guḍākeśaḥ*—Arjuna, the master at curbing ignorance; *parantapaḥ*—the chastiser of the enemies; *na yotsye*—I shall not fight; *iti*—thus; *govindam*—unto Kṛṣṇa, the giver of pleasure; *uktvā*—saying; *tūṣṇīm*—silent; *babhūva*—became; *ha*—certainly.

TRANSLATION

Sañjaya said: Having spoken thus, Arjuna, chastiser of enemies, told Kṛṣṇa, "Govinda, I shall not fight," and fell silent.

PURPORT

Dhṛtarāṣṭra must have been very glad to understand that Arjuna was not going to fight and was instead leaving the battlefield for the begging profession. But Sañjaya disappointed him again in relating that Arjuna was competent to kill his enemies (*parantapaḥ*). Although Arjuna was for the time being overwhelmed with false grief due to family affection, he surrendered unto Kṛṣṇa, the supreme spiritual master, as a disciple. This indicated that he would soon be free from the false lamentation resulting from family affection and would be enlightened with perfect knowledge of self-realization, or Kṛṣṇa consciousness, and would then surely fight. Thus Dhṛtarāṣṭra's joy would be frustrated, since Arjuna would be enlightened. by Kṛṣṇa and would fight to the end.

TEXT 10

तमुवाच हृषीकेशः प्रहसन्निव भारत ।
सेनयोरुभयोर्मध्ये विषीदन्तमिदं वचः ॥ १० ॥

tam uvāca hṛṣīkeśaḥ
prahasann iva bhārata
senayor ubhayor madhye
viṣīdantam idaṁ vacaḥ

tam—unto him; *uvāca*—said; *hṛṣīkeśaḥ*—the master of the senses, Kṛṣṇa; *prahasan*—smiling; *iva*—like that; *bhārata*—O Dhṛtarāṣṭra, descendant of Bharata; *senayoḥ*—of the armies; *ubhayoḥ*—of both parties; *madhye*—between; *viṣīdantam*—unto the lamenting one; *idam*—the following; *vacaḥ*—words.

TRANSLATION

O descendant of Bharata, at that time Kṛṣṇa, smiling, in the midst of both the armies, spoke the following words to the grief-stricken Arjuna.

PURPORT

The talk was going on between intimate friends, namely the Hṛṣīkeśa and the Guḍākeśa. As friends, both of them were on the same level, but one of them voluntarily became a student of the other. Kṛṣṇa was smiling because a friend had chosen to become a disciple. As Lord of all, He is always in the superior position as the master of everyone, and yet the Lord accepts one who wishes to be a friend, a son, a lover or a devotee, or who wants Him in such a role. But when He was accepted as the master, He at once assumed the role and talked with the disciple like the master—with gravity, as it is required. It appears that the talk between the master and the disciple was openly exchanged in the presence of both armies so that all were benefitted. So the talks of *Bhagavad-gītā* are not for any particular person, society, or community, but they are for all, and friends or enemies are equally entitled to hear them.

TEXT 11

श्रीभगवानुवाच ।
अशोच्यानन्वशोचस्त्वं प्रज्ञावादांश्च भाषसे ।
गतासूनगतासूंश्च नानुशोचन्ति पण्डिताः ॥ ११ ॥

*śrī-bhagavān uvāca
aśocyān anvaśocas tvaṁ
    prajñā-vādāṁś ca bhāṣase
gatāsūn agatāsūṁś ca
    nānuśocanti paṇḍitāḥ*

śrī bhagavān uvāca—the Supreme Personality of Godhead said; *aśocyān*—that which is not worthy of lamentation; *anvaśocaḥ*—you are lamenting; *tvam*—you; *prajñā-vādāḥ*—learned talks; *ca*—also; *bhāṣase*—speaking; *gata*—lost; *asūn*—life; *agata*—not past; *asūn*—life; *ca*—also; *na*—never; *anuśocanti*—lament; *paṇḍitāḥ*—the learned.

TRANSLATION

The Blessed Lord said: While speaking learned words, you are mourning for what is not worthy of grief. Those who are wise lament neither for the living nor the dead.

PURPORT

The Lord at once took the position of the teacher and chastised the student, calling him, indirectly, a fool. The Lord said, you are talking like a learned man, but you do not know that one who is learned—one who knows what is body and what is soul—does not lament for any stage of the body, neither in the living nor in the dead condition. As it will be explained in later chapters, it will be clear that knowledge means to know matter and spirit and the controller of both. Arjuna argued that religious principles should be given more importance than politics or sociology, but he did not know that knowledge of matter, soul and the Supreme is even more important than religious formularies. And, because he was lacking in that knowledge, he should not have posed himself as a very learned man. As he did not happen to be a very learned man, he was consequently lamenting for something which was unworthy of lamentation. The body is born and is destined to be vanquished today or tomorrow; therefore the body is not as important as the soul. One who knows this is actually learned, and for him there is no cause for lamentation, regardless of the condition of the material body.

TEXT 12

नत्वेवाहं जातु नासं न त्वं नेमे जनाधिपाः ।
न चैव नभविष्यामः सर्वे वयमतः परम् ॥ १२ ॥

na tv evāham jātu nāsam
na tvam neme janādhipāḥ
na caiva na bhaviṣyāmaḥ
sarve vayam ataḥ param

na—never; *tu*—but; *eva*—certainly; *aham*—I; *jātu*—become; *na*—never; *āsam*—existed; *na*—it is not so; *tvam*—yourself; *na*—not; *ime*—all these; *janādhipāḥ*—kings; *na*—never; *ca*—also; *eva*—certainly; *na*—not like that; *bhaviṣyāmaḥ*—shall exist; *sarve*—all of us; *vayam*—we; *ataḥ param*—hereafter.

TRANSLATION

Never was there a time when I did not exist, nor you, nor all these kings; nor in the future shall any of us cease to be.

PURPORT

In the *Vedas*, in the *Kaṭha Upaniṣad* as well as in the *Śvetāśvatara Upaniṣad*, it is said that the Supreme Personality of Godhead is the maintainer of innumerable living entities, in terms of their different situations according to individual work and reaction of work. That Supreme Personality of Godhead is also, by His plenary portions, alive in the heart of every living entity. Only saintly persons who can see, within and without, the same Supreme Lord, can actually attain to perfect and eternal peace.

> *nityo nityānāṁ cetanaś cetanānām*
> *eko bahūnāṁ yo vidadhāti kāmān*
> *tam ātmasthaṁ ye 'nupaśyanti dhīrās*
> *teṣāṁ śāntiḥ śāśvatī netareṣām.*
>
> (*Kaṭha 2.2.13*)

The same Vedic truth given to Arjuna is given to all persons in the world who pose themselves as very learned but factually have but a poor fund of knowledge. The Lord says clearly that He Himself, Arjuna, and all the kings who are assembled on the battlefield, are eternally individual beings and that the Lord is eternally the maintainer of the individual living entities both in their conditioned as well as in their liberated situations. The Supreme Personality of Godhead is the supreme individual person, and Arjuna, the Lord's eternal associate, and all the kings assembled there are individual, eternal persons. It is not that they did not exist as individuals in the past, and it is not that they will not remain eternal persons. Their individuality existed in the past, and their individuality will continue in the future without interruption. Therefore, there is no cause for lamentation for anyone.

The Māyāvādī theory that after liberation the individual soul, separated by the covering of māyā or illusion, will merge into the impersonal Brahman and lose its individual existence is not supported herein by Lord Kṛṣṇa, the supreme authority. Nor is the theory that we only think of individuality in the conditioned state supported herein. Kṛṣṇa clearly says herein that in the future also the individuality of the Lord and others, as it is confirmed in the *Upaniṣads*, will continue eternally. This statement of Kṛṣṇa is authoritative because Kṛṣṇa cannot be subject to illusion. If individuality is not a fact, then Kṛṣṇa would not have stressed it so much —even for the future. The Māyāvādī may argue that the individuality spoken of by Kṛṣṇa is not spiritual, but material. Even accepting the argument that the individuality is material, then how can one distinguish Kṛṣṇa's individuality? Kṛṣṇa affirms His individuality in the past and confirms His individuality in the future also. He has confirmed His individuality in many ways, and impersonal Brahman has been declared to be subordinate to Him. Kṛṣṇa has maintained spiritual individuality all along; if He is accepted as an ordinary conditioned soul in individual consciousness, then His *Bhagavad-gītā* has no value as authoritative scripture. A common man with all the four defects of human frailty is unable to teach that which is worth hearing. The *Gītā* is above such literature. No mundane book compares with the *Bhagavad-gītā*. When one accepts Kṛṣṇa as an ordinary man, the *Gītā* loses all importance. The Māyāvādī argues that the plurality mentioned in this verse is conventional and that it refers to the body. But previous to this verse such a bodily conception is already condemned. After condemning the bodily conception of the living entities, how was it possible for Kṛṣṇa to place a conventional proposition on the body again? Therefore, individuality is maintained on spiritual grounds and is thus confirmed by great *ācāryas* like Śrī Rāmānuja and others. It is clearly mentioned in many places in the *Gītā* that this spiritual individuality is understood by those who are devotees of the Lord. Those who are envious of Kṛṣṇa as the Supreme Personality of Godhead have no bona fide access to the great literature. The nondevotee's approach to the teachings of the *Gīta* is something like bees licking on a bottle of honey. One cannot have a taste of honey unless one opens the bottle. Similarly, the mysticism of the *Bhagavad-gītā* can be understood only by devotees, and no one else can taste it, as it is stated in the Fourth Chapter of the book. Nor can the *Gītā* be touched by persons who envy the very existence of the Lord. Therefore, the Māyāvādī explanation of the *Gītā* is a most misleading presentation of the whole truth. Lord Caitanya has forbidden us to read commentations made by the Māyāvādīs and warns that one who takes to such an understanding of the Māyāvādī philosophy loses all power to understand the real mystery of the *Gītā*. If individuality refers to the empirical universe, then there is no need of teaching by the Lord. The plurality of the individual soul and of the Lord is an eternal fact, and it is confirmed by the *Vedas* as above mentioned.

TEXT 13

देहिनोऽस्मिन्यथा देहे कौमारं यौवनं जरा ।
तथा देहान्तरप्राप्तिर्धीरस्तत्र न मुह्यति ॥ १३ ॥

dehino 'smin yathā dehe
kaumāraṁ yauvanaṁ jarā
tathā dehāntara-prāptir
dhīras tatra na muhyati

dehinaḥ—of the embodied; *asmin*—in this; *yathā*—as; *dehe*—in the body; *kaumāram*—boyhood; *yauvanam*—youth; *jarā*—old age; *tathā*—similarly; *dehāntara*—transference of the body; *prāptiḥ*—achievement; *dhīraḥ*—the sober; *tatra*—thereupon; *na*—never; *muhyati*—deluded.

TRANSLATION

As the embodied soul continually passes, in this body, from boyhood to youth to old age, the soul similarly passes into another body at death. The self-realized soul is not bewildered by such a change.

PURPORT

Since every living entity is an individual soul, each is changing his body every moment, manifesting sometimes as a child, sometimes as a youth, and sometimes as an old man. Yet the same spirit soul is there and does not undergo any change. This individual soul finally changes the body at death and transmigrates to another body; and since it is sure to have another body in the next birth—either material or spiritual—there was no cause for lamentation by Arjuna on account of death, neither for Bhīṣma nor for Droṇa, for whom he was so much concerned. Rather, he should rejoice for their changing bodies from old to new ones, thereby rejuvenating their energy. Such changes of body account for varieties of enjoyment or suffering, according to one's work in life. So Bhīṣma and Droṇa, being noble souls, were surely going to have either spiritual bodies in the next life, or at least life in heavenly bodies for superior enjoyment of material existence. So, in either case, there was no cause of lamentation.

Any man who has perfect knowledge of the constitution of the individual soul, the Supersoul, and nature—both material and spiritual—is called a *dhīra* or a most sober man. Such a man is never deluded by the change of bodies. The Māyāvādī theory of oneness of the spirit soul cannot be entertained on the ground that spirit soul cannot be cut into pieces as a fragmental portion. Such cutting into different individual souls would make the Supreme cleavable or changeable, against the principle of the Supreme Soul being unchangeable.

As confirmed in the *Gītā*, the fragmental portions of the Supreme exist eternally (*sanātana*) and are called *kṣara*; that is, they have a tendency to fall down into material nature. These fragmental portions are eternally so, and even after liberation, the individual soul remains the same—fragmental. But once liberated, he lives an eternal life in bliss and knowledge with the Personality of Godhead. The theory of reflection can be applied to the Supersoul who is present in each and every individual body and is known as the Paramātmā, who is different from the individual living entity. When the sky is reflected in water, the reflections represent both the sun and the moon and the stars also. The stars can be compared to the living entities and the sun or the moon to the Supreme Lord. The individual fragmental spirit soul is represented by Arjuna, and the Supreme Soul is the Personality of Godhead Śrī Kṛṣṇa. They are not on the same level, as it will be apparent in the beginning of the Fourth Chapter. If Arjuna is on the same level with Kṛṣṇa, and Kṛṣṇa is not superior to Arjuna, then their relationship of instructor and instructed becomes meaningless. If both of them are deluded by the illusory energy (māyā), then there is no need of one being the instructor and the other the instructed. Such instruction would be useless because, in the clutches of māyā, no one can be an authoritative instructor. Under the circumstances, it is admitted that Lord Kṛṣṇa is the Supreme Lord, superior in position to the living entity, Arjuna, who is a forgotten soul deluded by māyā.

TEXT 14

मात्रास्पर्शास्तु कौन्तेय शीतोष्णसुखदुःखदाः ।
आगमापायिनोऽनित्यास्तांस्तितिक्षस्व भारत ॥ १४ ॥

mātrā-sparśās tu kaunteya
śītoṣṇa-sukha-duḥkha-dāḥ
āgamāpāyino 'nityās
tāṁs titikṣasva bhārata

mātrā—sensuous; *sparśāḥ*—perception; *tu*—only; *kaunteya*—O son of Kuntī; *śīta*—winter; *uṣṇa*—summer; *sukha*—happiness; *duḥkha-daḥ*—giving pain; *āgama*—appearing; *apāyinaḥ*—disappearing; *anityāḥ*—nonpermanent; *tān*—all of them; *titikṣasva*—just try to tolerate; *bhārata*—O descendant of the Bhārata dynasty.

TRANSLATION

O son of Kuntī, the nonpermanent appearance of happiness and distress, and their disappearance in due course, are like the appearance and disappearance of winter and summer seasons. They arise from sense perception, O scion of Bharata, and one must learn to tolerate them without being disturbed.

PURPORT

In the proper discharge of duty, one has to learn to tolerate nonpermanent appearances and disappearances of happiness and distress. According to Vedic injunction, one has to take his bath early in the morning even during the month of *Māgha* (January-February). It is very cold at that time, but in spite of that a man who abides by the religious principles does not hesitate to take his bath. Similarly, a woman does not hesitate to cook in the kitchen in the months of May and June, the hottest part of the summer season. One has to execute his duty in spite of climatic inconveniences. Similarly, to fight is the religious principle of the *kṣatriyas*, and although one has to fight with some friend or relative, one should not deviate from his prescribed duty. One has to follow the prescribed rules and regulations of religious principles in order to rise up to the platform of knowledge because by knowledge and devotion only can one liberate himself from the clutches of *māyā* (illusion).

The two different names of address given to Arjuna are also significant. To address him as Kaunteya signifies his great blood relations from his mother's side; and to address him as Bhārata signifies his greatness from his father's side. From both sides he is supposed to have a great heritage. A great heritage brings responsibility in the matter of proper discharge of duties; therefore, he cannot avoid fighting.

TEXT 15

यं हि न व्यथयन्त्येते पुरुषं पुरुषर्षभ ।
समदुःखसुखं धीरं सोऽमृतत्वाय कल्पते ॥ १५ ॥

yaṁ hi na vyathayanty ete
puruṣaṁ puruṣarṣabha
sama-duḥkha-sukhaṁ dhīraṁ
so 'mṛtatvāya kalpate

yam—one who; *hi*—certainly; *na*—never; *vyathayanti*—are distressing; *ete*—all these; *puruṣam*—to a person; *puruṣarṣabha*—is best among men; *sama*—unaltered; *duḥkha*—distress; *sukham*—happiness; *dhīram*—patient; *saḥ*—he; *amṛtatvāya*—for liberation; *kalpate*—is considered eligible.

TRANSLATION

O best among men [Arjuna], the person who is not disturbed by happiness and distress and is steady in both is certainly eligible for liberation.

PURPORT

Anyone who is steady in his determination for the advanced stage of spiritual realization and can equally tolerate the onslaughts of distress and happiness is certainly a person eligible for liberation. In the *varṇāśrama* institution, the fourth stage of life, namely the renounced order (*sannyāsa*) is a painstaking situation. But one who is serious about making his life perfect surely adopts the *sannyāsa* order of life in spite of all difficulties. The difficulties usually arise from having to sever family relationships, to give up the connection of wife and children. But if anyone is able to tolerate such difficulties, surely his path to spiritual realization is complete. Similarly, in Arjuna's discharge of duties as a *kṣatriya*, he is advised to persevere, even if it is difficult to fight with his family members or similarly beloved persons. Lord Caitanya took *sannyāsa* at the age of twenty-four, and His dependants, young wife as well as old mother, had no one else to look after them. Yet for a higher cause He took *sannyāsa* and was steady in the discharge of higher duties. That is the way of achieving liberation from material bondage.

TEXT 16

नासतो विद्यते भावो नाभावो विद्यते सतः ।
उभयोरपि दृष्टोऽन्तस्त्वनयोस्तत्त्वदर्शिभिः ॥ १६ ॥

> *nāsato vidyate bhāvo*
> *nābhāvo vidyate sataḥ*
> *ubhayor api dṛṣṭo 'ntas*
> *tv anayos tattva-darśibhiḥ*

na—never; *asataḥ*—of the nonexistent; *vidyate*—there is; *bhāvaḥ*—endurance; *na*—never; *abhāvaḥ*—changing quality; *vidyate*—there is; *sataḥ*—of the eternal; *ubhayoḥ*—of the two; *api*—verily; *dṛṣṭaḥ*—observed; *antaḥ*—conclusion; *tu*—but; *anayoḥ*—of them; *tattva*—truth; *darśibhiḥ*—by the seers.

TRANSLATION

Those who are seers of the truth have concluded that of the nonexistent there is no endurance, and of the existent there is no cessation. This seers have concluded by studying the nature of both.

PURPORT

There is no endurance of the changing body. That the body is changing every moment by the actions and reactions of the different cells is admitted by modern medical science; and thus growth and old age are taking place in the body. But the spirit soul exists permanently, remaining the same despite all changes of the body and the mind. That is the difference between matter and spirit. By nature, the body is ever changing, and the soul is eternal. This conclusion is established by all classes of seers of the truth, both impersonalist and personalist. In the *Viṣṇu Purāṇa* it is stated that Viṣṇu and His abodes all have self-illuminated spiritual existence. "*Jyotīṁṣi viṣṇur bhavanāni viṣṇuḥ.*" The words existent and nonexistent refer only to spirit and matter. That is the version of all seers of truth.

This is the beginning of the instruction by the Lord to the living entities who are bewildered by the influence of ignorance. Removal of ignorance involves the reestablishment of the eternal relationship between the worshiper and the worshipable and the consequent understanding of the difference between the part and parcel living entities and the Supreme Personality of Godhead. One can understand the nature of the Supreme by thorough study of oneself, the difference between oneself and the Supreme being understood as the relationship between the part and the whole. In the *Vedānta-sūtras*, as well as in the *Śrīmad-Bhāgavatam*, the Supreme has been accepted as the origin of all emanations. Such emanations are experienced by superior and inferior natural sequences. The living entities belong to the superior nature, as it will be revealed in the Seventh Chapter. Although there is no difference between the energy and the energetic, the energetic is accepted as the Supreme, and energy or nature is accepted as the subordinate. The living entities, therefore, are always subordinate to the Supreme Lord, as in the case of the master and the servant, or the teacher and the taught. Such clear knowledge is impossible to understand under the spell of ignorance, and to drive away such ignorance the Lord teaches the *Bhagavad-gītā* for the enlightenment of all living entities for all time.

TEXT 17

अविनाशि तु तद्विद्धि येन सर्वमिदं ततम् ।
विनाशमव्ययस्यास्य न कश्चित्कर्तुमर्हति ॥ १७ ॥

*avināśi tu tad viddhi
    yena sarvam idaṁ tatam
vināśam avyayasyāsya
    na kaścit kartum arhati*

avināśi—imperishable; *tu*—but; *tat*—that; *viddhi*—know it; *yena*—by whom; *sarvam*—all of the body; *idam*—this; *tatam*—widespread; *vināśam*—destruction; *avyayasya*—of the imperishable; *asya*—of it; *na kaścit*—no one; *kartum*—to do; *arhati*—able.

TRANSLATION

Know that which pervades the entire body is indestructible. No one is able to destroy the imperishable soul.

PURPORT

This verse more clearly explains the real nature of the soul, which is spread all over the body. Anyone can understand what is spread all over the body: it is consciousness. Everyone is conscious of the pains and pleasures of the body in part or as a whole. This spreading of consciousness is limited within one's own body. The pains and pleasures of one body are unknown to another. Therefore, each and every body is the embodiment of an individual soul, and the symptom of the soul's presence is perceived as individual consciousness. This soul is described as one ten-thousandth part of the upper portion of the hair point in size. The *Śvetāśvatara Upaniṣad* confirms this:

*bālāgra-śata-bhāgasya śatadhā kalpitasya ca
bhāgo jīvaḥ sa vijñeyaḥ sa cānantyāya kalpate.*

"When the upper point of a hair is divided into one hundred parts and again each of such parts is further divided into one hundred parts, each such part is the measurement of the dimension of the spirit soul." (*Svet.* 5.9) Similarly, in the *Bhāgavatam* the same version is stated:

> keśāgra-śata-bhāgasya śatāṁśaḥ sādṛśātmakaḥ
> jīvaḥ sūkṣma-svarupo 'yaṁ saṅkhyātīto hi cit-kaṇaḥ

"There are innumerable particles of spiritual atoms, which are measured as one ten-thousandth of the upper portion of the hair."

Therefore, the individual particle of spirit soul is a spiritual atom smaller than the material atoms, and such atoms are innumerable. This very small spiritual spark is the basic principle of the material body, and the influence of such a spiritual spark is spread all over the body as the influence of the active principle of some medicine spreads throughout the body. This current of the spirit soul is felt all over the body as consciousness, and that is the proof of the presence of the soul. Any layman can understand that the material body minus consciousness is a dead body, and this consciousness cannot be revived in the body by any means of material administration. Therefore, consciousness is not due to any amount of material combination, but to the spirit soul. In the *Muṇḍaka Upaniṣad* the measurement of the atomic spirit soul is further explained:

> eṣo 'ṇurātmā cetasā veditavyo
> yasmin prāṇaḥ pañcadhā saṁviveśa
> prāṇaiś cittaṁ sarvam otaṁ prajānāṁ
> yasmin viśuddhe vibhavaty eṣa ātmā.

"The soul is atomic in size and can be perceived by perfect intelligence. This atomic soul is floating in the five kinds of air [*prāṇa, apāna, vyāna, samāna* and *udāna*], is situated within the heart, and spreads its influence all over the body of the embodied living entities. When the soul is purified from the contamination of the five kinds of material air, its spiritual influence is exhibited." (*Muṇḍ.* 3.1.9)

The *haṭha-yoga* system is meant for controlling the five kinds of air encircling the pure soul by different kinds of sitting postures—not for any material profit, but for liberation of the minute soul from the entanglement of the material atmosphere.

So the constitution of the atomic soul is admitted in all Vedic literatures, and it is also actually felt in the practical experience of any sane man. Only the insane man can think of this atomic soul as all-pervading *Viṣṇu-tattva*.

The influence of the atomic soul can be spread all over a particular body. According to the *Muṇḍaka Upaniṣad*, this atomic soul is situated in the heart of every living entity, and because the measurement of the atomic soul is beyond the power of appreciation of the material scientists, some of them assert foolishly that there is no soul. The individual atomic soul is definitely there in the heart along with the Supersoul, and thus all the energies of bodily movement are emanating from this part of the body. The corpuscles which carry the oxygen from the lungs gather energy from the soul. When the soul passes away from this position, activity of the blood, generating fusion, ceases. Medical science accepts the importance of the red corpuscles, but it cannot ascertain that the source of the energy is the soul. Medical science, however, does admit that the heart is the seat of all energies of the body.

Such atomic particles of the spirit whole are compared to the sunshine molecules. In the sunshine there are innumerable radiant molecules. Similarly, the fragmental parts of the Supreme Lord are atomic sparks of the rays of the Supreme Lord, called by the name *prabhā* or superior energy. Neither Vedic knowledge nor modern science denies the existence of the spirit soul in the body, and the science of the soul is explicitly described in the *Bhagavad-gītā* by the Personality of Godhead Himself.

TEXT 18

अन्तवन्त इमे देहा नित्यस्योक्ताः शरीरिणः ।
अनाशिनोऽप्रमेयस्य तस्माद्युध्यस्व भारत ॥ १८ ॥

*antavanta ime dehā
nityasyoktāḥ śarīriṇaḥ
anāśino 'prameyasya
tasmād yudhyasva bhārata*

antavantaḥ—perishable; *ime*—all these; *dehāḥ*—material bodies; *nityasya*—eternal in existence; *uktāḥ*—it is so said; *śarīriṇaḥ*—the embodied souls; *anāśinaḥ*—never to be destroyed; *aprameyasya*—immeasurable; *tasmāt*—therefore; *yudhyasva*—fight; *bhārata*—O descendant of Bharata.

TRANSLATION

Only the material body of the indestructible, immeasurable and eternal living entity is subject to destruction; therefore, fight, O descendant of Bharata.

PURPORT

The material body is perishable by nature. It may perish immediately, or it may do so after a hundred years. It is a question of time only. There is no chance of maintaining it indefinitely. But the spirit soul is so minute that it cannot even be seen by an enemy, to say nothing of being killed. As mentioned in the previous verse, it is so small that no one can have any idea how to measure its dimension. So from both viewpoints there is no cause of lamentation because the living entity can neither be killed as he is, nor can the material body, which cannot be saved for any length of time, be permanently protected. The minute particle of the whole spirit acquires this material body according to his work, and therefore observance of religious principles should be utilized. In the *Vedānta-sūtras* the living entity is qualified as light because he is part and parcel of the supreme light. As sunlight maintains the entire universe, so the light of the soul maintains this material body. As soon as the spirit soul is out of this material body, the body begins to decompose; therefore it is the spirit soul which maintains this body. The body itself is unimportant. Arjuna was advised to fight and sacrifice the material body for the cause of religion.

TEXT 19

य एनं वेत्ति हन्तारं यश्चैनं मन्यते हतम् ।
उभौ तौ न विजानीतो नायं हन्ति न हन्यते ॥ १९ ॥

ya enaṁ vetti hantāraṁ
yaś cainaṁ manyate hatam
ubhau tau na vijānīto
nāyaṁ hanti na hanyate

yaḥ—anyone; *enam*—this; *vetti*—knows; *hantāram*—the killer; *yaḥ*—anyone; *ca*—also; *enam*—this; *manyate*—thinks; *hatam*—killed; *ubhau*—both of them; *tau*—they; *na*—never; *vijānītaḥ*—in knowledge; *na*—never; *ayam*—this; *hanti*—kills; *na*—nor; *hanyate*—be killed.

TRANSLATION

He who thinks that the living entity is the slayer or that he is slain, does not understand. One who is in knowledge knows that the self slays not nor is slain.

PURPORT

When an embodied living entity is hurt by fatal weapons, it is to be
known that the living entity within the body is not killed. The spirit soul
is so small that it is impossible to kill him by any material weapon, as is
evident from the previous verses. Nor is the living entity killable because
of his spiritual constitution. What is killed, or is supposed to be killed,
is the body only. This, however, does not at all encourage killing of
the body. The Vedic injunction is, "*māhiṁsyāt sarva-bhūtāni*" never
commit violence to anyone. Nor does understanding that the living entity
is not killed encourage animal slaughter. Killing the body of anyone without authority is abominable and is punishable by the law of the state as
well as by the law of the Lord. Arjuna, however, is being engaged in killing
for the principle of religion, and not whimsically.

TEXT 20

न जायते म्रियते वा कदाचि-
न्नायं भूत्वा भविता वा न भूयः ।
अजो नित्यः शाश्वतोऽयं पुराणो
न हन्यते हन्यमाने शरीरे ॥ २० ॥

*na jāyate mriyate vā kadācin
nāyaṁ bhūtvā bhavitā vā na bhūyaḥ
ajo nityaḥ śāśvato 'yaṁ purāṇo
na hanyate hanyamāne śarīre*

na—never; *jāyate*—takes birth; *mriyate*—never dies; *vā*—either; *kadācit*—
at any time (past, present or future); *na*—never; *ayam*—this; *bhūtvā*—came
into being; *bhavitā*—will come to be; *vā*—or; *na*—not; *bhūyaḥ*—or has come
to be; *ajaḥ*—unborn; *nityaḥ*—eternal; *śāśvataḥ*—permanent; *ayam*—this;
purāṇaḥ—the oldest; *na*—never; *hanyate*—is killed; *hanyamāne*—being
killed; *śarīre*—by the body.

TRANSLATION

For the soul there is never birth nor death. Nor, having once been,
does he ever cease to be. He is unborn, eternal, ever-existing, undying
and primeval. He is not slain when the body is slain.

PURPORT

Qualitatively, the small atomic fragmental part of the Supreme Spirit is one with the Supreme. He undergoes no changes like the body. Sometimes the soul is called the steady, or *kūṭastha*. The body is subject to six kinds of transformations. It takes its birth in the womb of the mother's body, remains for some time, grows, produces some effects, gradually dwindles, and at last vanishes into oblivion. The soul, however, does not go through such changes. The soul is not born, but, because he takes on a material body, the body takes its birth. The soul does not take birth there, and the soul does not die. Anything which has birth also has death. And because the soul has no birth, he therefore has no past, present or future. He is eternal, ever-existing, and primeval—that is, there is no trace in history of his coming into being. Under the impression of the body, we seek the history of birth, etc., of the soul. The soul does not at any time become old, as the body does. The so-called old man, therefore, feels himself to be in the same spirit as in his childhood or youth. The changes of the body do not affect the soul. The soul does not deteriorate like a tree, nor anything material. The soul has no by-product either. The by-products of the body, namely children, are also different individual souls; and, owing to the body, they appear as children of a particular man. The body develops because of the soul's presence, but the soul has neither offshoots nor change. Therefore, the soul is free from the six changes of the body.

In the *Kaṭha Upaniṣad* also we find a similar passage which reads:

> *na jāyate mriyate vā vipaścin*
> *nāyaṁ kutaścin na vibhūva kaścit*
> *ajo nityaḥ śāśvato 'yaṁ purāṇo*
> *na hanyate hanyamāne śarīre.*
>
> (Kaṭha 1.2.18)

The meaning and purport of this verse is the same as in the *Bhagavad-gītā*, but here in this verse there is one special word, *vipaścit*, which means learned or with knowledge.

The soul is full of knowledge, or full always with consciousness. Therefore, consciousness is the symptom of the soul. Even if one does not find the soul within the heart, where he is situated, one can still understand the presence of the soul simply by the presence of consciousness. Sometimes we do not find the sun in the sky owing to clouds, or for some other reason, but the light of the sun is always there, and we are convinced that it is therefore daytime. As soon as there is a little light in the sky early in the morning, we can understand that the sun is in the sky. Similarly, since there is some consciousness in all bodies—whether man or animal—we can understand the presence of the soul. This consciousness of the soul is, however, different from the consciousness of the Supreme because the supreme consciousness is all-knowledge—past, present and future. The consciousness of the individual soul is prone to be forgetful. When he is forgetful of his real nature, he obtains education and enlightenment from the superior lessons of Kṛṣṇa. But Kṛṣṇa is not like the forgetful soul. If so, Kṛṣṇa's teachings of Bhagavad-gītā would be useless.

There are two kinds of souls—namely the minute particle soul (aṇu-ātmā) and the Supersoul (the vibhu-ātmā). This is also confirmed in the Kaṭha Upaniṣad in this way:

> aṇor aṇīyān mahato mahīyān
> ātmāsya jantor nihito guhāyām
> tam akratuḥ paśyati vīta-śoko
> dhātuḥ prasādān mahimānam ātmanaḥ
> (Kaṭha 1.2.20)

"Both the Supersoul [Paramātmā] and the atomic soul [jīvātmā] are situated on the same tree of the body within the same heart of the living being, and only one who has become free from all material desires as well as lamentations can, by the grace of the Supreme, understand the glories of the soul." Kṛṣṇa is the fountainhead of the Supersoul also, as it will be disclosed in the following chapters, and Arjuna is the atomic soul, forgetful of his real nature; therefore he requires to be enlightened by Kṛṣṇa, or by His bona fide representative (the spiritual master).

TEXT 21

वेदाविनाशिनं नित्यं य एनमजमव्ययम् ।
कथं स पुरुषः पार्थ कं घातयति हन्ति कम् ॥ २१ ॥

> vedāvināśinaṁ nityaṁ
> ya enam ajam avyayam
> kathaṁ sa puruṣaḥ pārtha
> kaṁ ghātayati hanti kam

veda—in knowledge; avināśinam—indestructible; nityam—always; yaḥ—one who; enam—this (soul); ajam—unborn; avyayam—immutable; katham—

how; *saḥ*—he; *puruṣaḥ*—person; *pārtha*—O Pārtha (Arjuna); *kam*—whom; *ghātayati*—hurts; *hanti*—kills; *kam*—whom.

TRANSLATION

O Pārtha, how can a person who knows that the soul is indestructible, unborn, eternal and immutable, kill anyone or cause anyone to kill?

PURPORT

Everything has its proper utility, and a man who is situated in complete knowledge knows how and where to apply a thing for its proper utility. Similarly, violence also has its utility, and how to apply violence rests with the person in knowledge. Although the justice of the peace awards capital punishment to a person condemned for murder, the justice of the peace cannot be blamed because he orders violence to another person according to the codes of justice. In *Manu-saṁhitā*, the lawbook for mankind, it is supported that a murderer should be condemned to death so that in his next life he will not have to suffer for the great sin he has committed. Therefore, the king's punishment of hanging a murderer is actually beneficial. Similarly, when Kṛṣṇa orders fighting, it must be concluded that violence is for supreme justice, and, as such, Arjuna should follow the instruction, knowing well that such violence, committed in the act of fighting for Kṛṣṇa, is not violence at all because, at any rate, the man, or rather the soul, cannot be killed; so for the administration of justice, so-called violence is permitted. A surgical operation is not meant to kill the patient, but to cure him. Therefore the fighting to be executed by Arjuna at the instruction of Kṛṣṇa is with full knowledge, so there is no possibility of sinful reaction.

TEXT 22

वासांसि जीर्णानि यथा विहाय
नवानि गृह्णाति नरोऽपराणि ।
तथा शरीराणि विहाय जीर्णा-
न्यन्यानि संयाति नवानि देही ॥ २२ ॥

vāsāṁsi jīrṇāni yathā vihāya
navāni gṛhṇāti naro 'parāṇi
tathā śarīrāṇi vihāya jīrṇāny
anyāni saṁyāti navāni dehī

vāsāṁsi—garments; *jīrṇāni*—old and worn out; *yathā*—as it is; *vihāya*—giving up; *navāni*—new garments; *gṛhṇāti*—does accept; *naraḥ*—a man; *aparāṇi*—other; *tathā*—in the same way; *śarīrāṇi*—bodies; *vihāya*—giving up; *jīrṇāni*—old and useless; *anyāni*—different; *saṁyāti*—verily accepts; *navāni*—new sets; *dehī*—the embodied.

TRANSLATION

As a person puts on new garments, giving up old ones, similarly, the soul accepts new material bodies, giving up the old and useless ones.

PURPORT

Change of body by the atomic individual soul is an accepted fact. Even some of the modern scientists who do not believe in the existence of the soul, but at the same time cannot explain the source of energy from the heart, have to accept continuous changes of body which appear from childhood to boyhood and from boyhood to youth and again from youth to old age. From old age, the change is transferred to another body. This has already been explained in the previous verse.

Transference of the atomic individual soul to another body is made possible by the grace of the Supersoul. The Supersoul fulfills the desire of the atomic soul as one friend fulfills the desire of another. The *Vedas*, like the *Muṇḍaka Upaniṣad*, as well as the *Śvetāśvatara Upaniṣad*, compare the soul and the Supersoul to two friendly birds sitting on the same tree. One of the birds (the individual atomic soul) is eating the fruit of the tree, and the other bird (Kṛṣṇa) is simply watching His friend. Of these two birds—although they are the same in quality—one is captivated by the fruits of the material tree, while the other is simply witnessing the activities of His friend. Kṛṣṇa is the witnessing bird, and Arjuna is the eating bird. Although they are friends, one is still the master and the other is the servant. Forgetfulness of this relationship by the atomic soul is the cause of one's changing his position from one tree to another or from one body to another. The *jīva* soul is struggling very hard on the tree of the material body, but as soon as he agrees to accept the other bird as the supreme spiritual master—as Arjuna agreed to do by voluntary surrender unto Kṛṣṇa for instruction—the subordinate bird immediately becomes free from all lamentations. Both the *Kaṭha Upaniṣad* and *Śvetāśvatara Upaniṣad* confirm this:

> samāne vṛkṣe puruṣo nimagno
> 'nīśayā śocati muhyamānaḥ
> juṣṭaṁ yadā paśyaty anyam īśam asya
> mahimānam iti vīta-śokaḥ

"Although the two birds are in the same tree, the eating bird is fully engrossed with anxiety and moroseness as the enjoyer of the fruits of the tree. But if in some way or other he turns his face to his friend who is the Lord and knows His glories—at once the suffering bird becomes free from all anxieties." Arjuna has now turned his face towards his eternal friend, Kṛṣṇa, and is understanding the *Bhagavad-gītā* from Him. And thus, hearing from Kṛṣṇa, he can understand the supreme glories of the Lord and be free from lamentation.

Arjuna is advised herewith by the Lord not to lament for the bodily change of his old grandfather and his teacher. He should rather be happy to kill their bodies in the righteous fight so that they may be cleansed at once of all reactions from various bodily activities. One who lays down his life on the sacrificial altar, or in the proper battlefield, is at once cleansed of bodily reactions and promoted to a higher status of life. So there was no cause for Arjuna's lamentation.

TEXT 23

नैनं छिन्दन्ति शस्त्राणि नैनं दहति पावकः ।
न चैनं क्लेदयन्त्यापो न शोषयति मारुतः ॥ २३ ॥

> nainaṁ chindanti śastrāṇi
> nainaṁ dahati pāvakaḥ
> na cainaṁ kledayanty āpo
> na śoṣayati mārutaḥ

na—never; *enam*—unto this soul; *chindanti*—can cut into pieces; *śastrāṇi*—all weapons; *na*—never; *enam*—unto this soul; *dahati*—burns; *pāvakaḥ*—fire; *na*—never; *ca*—also; *enam*—unto this soul; *kledayanti*—moistens; *āpaḥ*—water; *na*—never; *śoṣayati*—dries; *mārutaḥ*—wind.

TRANSLATION

The soul can never be cut into pieces by any weapon, nor can he be burned by fire, nor moistened by water, nor withered by the wind.

PURPORT

All kinds of weapons, swords, flames, rains, tornadoes, etc., are unable to kill the spirit soul. It appears that there were many kinds of weapons made of earth, water, air, ether, etc., in addition to the modern weapons of fire. Even the nuclear weapons of the modern age are classified as fire weapons, but formerly there were other weapons made of all different types of material elements. Firearms were counteracted by water weapons, which are now unknown to modern science. Nor do modern scientists have knowledge of tornado weapons. Nonetheless, the soul can never be cut into pieces, nor annihilated by any number of weapons, regardless of scientific devices.

Nor was it ever possible to cut the individual souls from the original Soul. The Māyāvādī, however, cannot describe how the individual soul evolved from ignorance and consequently became covered by illusory energy. Because they are atomic individual souls (sanātana) eternally, they are prone to be covered by the illusory energy, and thus they become separated from the association of the Supreme Lord, just as the sparks of the fire, although one in quality with the fire, are prone to be extinguished when out of the fire. In the Varāha Purāṇa, the living entities are described as separated parts and parcels of the Supreme. They are eternally so, according to the Bhagavad-gītā also. So, even after being liberated from illusion, the living entity remains a separate identity, as is evident from the teachings of the Lord to Arjuna. Arjuna became liberated by the knowledge received from Kṛṣṇa, but he never became one with Kṛṣṇa.

TEXT 24

अच्छेद्योऽयमदाह्योऽयमक्लेद्योऽशोष्य एव च ।
नित्यः सर्वगतः स्थाणुरचलोऽयं सनातनः ॥ २४ ॥

acchedyo 'yam adāhyo 'yam
akledyo 'śoṣya eva ca
nityaḥ sarva-gataḥ sthāṇur
acalo 'yaṁ sanātanaḥ

acchedyaḥ—unbreakable; *ayam*—this soul; *adāhyaḥ*—cannot be burned; *ayam*—this soul; *akledyaḥ*—insoluble; *aśoṣyaḥ*—cannot be dried; *eva*—certainly; *ca*—and; *nityaḥ*—everlasting; *sarva-gataḥ*—all-pervading; *sthāṇuḥ*—unchangeable; *acalaḥ*—immovable; *ayam*—this soul; *sanātanaḥ*—eternally the same.

TRANSLATION

This individual soul is unbreakable and insoluble, and can be neither burned nor dried. He is everlasting, all-pervading, unchangeable, immovable and eternally the same.

PURPORT

All these qualifications of the atomic soul definitely prove that the individual soul is eternally the atomic particle of the spirit whole, and he remains the same atom eternally, without change. The theory of monism is very difficult to apply in this case, because the individual soul is never expected to become one homogeneously. After liberation from material contamination, the atomic soul may prefer to remain as a spiritual spark in the effulgent rays of the Supreme Personality of Godhead, but the intelligent souls enter into the spiritual planets to associate with the Personality of Godhead.

The word *sarva-gataḥ* (all-pervading) is significant because there is no doubt that living entities are all over God's creation. They live on the land, in the water, in the air, within the earth and even within fire. The belief that they are sterilized in fire is not acceptable, because it is clearly stated here that the soul cannot be burned by fire. Therefore, there is no doubt that there are living entities also in the sun planet with suitable bodies to live there. If the sun globe is uninhabited, then the word *sarva-gataḥ*—living everywhere—becomes meaningless.

TEXT 25

अव्यक्तोऽयमचिन्त्योऽयमविकार्योऽयमुच्यते ।
तस्मादेवं विदित्वैनं नानुशोचितुमर्हसि ॥ २५ ॥

avyakto 'yam acintyo 'yam
avikāryo 'yam ucyate
tasmād evaṁ viditvainaṁ
nānuśocitum arhasi

avyaktaḥ—invisible; *ayam*—this soul; *acintyaḥ*—inconceivable; *ayam*—this soul; *avikāryaḥ*—unchangeable; *ayam*—this soul; *ucyate*—is said; *tasmāt*—therefore; *evam*—like this; *viditvā*—knowing it well; *enam*—this soul; *na*—do not; *anuśocitum*—may lament over; *arhasi*—you deserve.

TRANSLATION

It is said that the soul is invisible, inconceivable, immutable, and unchangeable. Knowing this, you should not grieve for the body.

PURPORT

As described previously, the magnitude of the soul is so small for our material calculation that he cannot be seen even by the most powerful microscope; therefore, he is invisible. As far as the soul's existence is concerned, no one can establish his existence experimentally beyond the proof of *śruti* or Vedic wisdom. We have to accept this truth, because there is no other source of understanding the existence of the soul, although it is a fact by perception. There are many things we have to accept solely on grounds of superior authority. No one can deny the existence of his father, based upon the authority of his mother. There is no other source of understanding the identity of the father except by the authority of the mother. Similarly, there is no other source of understanding the soul except by studying the *Vedas*. In other words, the soul is inconceivable by human experimental knowledge. The soul is consciousness and conscious—that also is the statement of the *Vedas*, and we have to accept that. Unlike the bodily changes, there is no change in the soul. As eternally unchangeable, the soul remains atomic in comparison to the infinite Supreme Soul. The Supreme Soul is infinite, and the atomic soul is infinitesimal. Therefore, the infinitesimal soul, being unchangeable, can never become equal to the infinite soul, or the Supreme Personality of Godhead. This concept is repeated in the *Vedas* in different ways just to confirm the stability of the conception of the soul. Repetition of something is necessary in order that we understand the matter thoroughly without error.

TEXT 26

अथ चैनं नित्यजातं नित्यं वा मन्यसे मृतम् ।
तथापि त्वं महाबाहो नैनं शोचितुमर्हसि ॥ २६ ॥

atha cainaṁ nitya-jātaṁ
nityaṁ vā manyase mṛtam
tathāpi tvaṁ mahā-bāho
nainaṁ śocitum arhasi

atha—if, however; ca—also; enam—this soul; nitya-jātam—always born; nityam—forever; vā—either; manyase—so think; mṛtam—dead; tathāpi—still; tvam—you; mahā-bāho—O mighty-armed one; na—never; enam—about the soul; śocitum—to lament; arhasi—deserve.

TRANSLATION

If, however, you think that the soul is perpetually born and always dies, still you have no reason to lament, O mighty-armed.

PURPORT

There is always a class of philosophers, almost akin to the Buddhists, who do not believe in the separate existence of the soul beyond the body. When Lord Kṛṣṇa spoke the Bhagavad-gītā, it appears that such philosophers existed, and they were known as the Lokāyatikas and Vaibhāṣikas. These philosophers maintained that life symptoms, or soul, takes place at a certain mature condition of material combination. The modern material scientist and materialist philosophers also think similarly. According to them, the body is a combination of physical elements, and at a certain stage the life symptoms develop by interaction of the physical and chemical elements. The science of anthropology is based on this philosophy. Currently, many pseudo-religions—now becoming fashionable in America—are also adhering to this philosophy, as well as to the nihilistic nondevotional Buddhist sects.

Even if Arjuna did not believe in the existence of the soul—as in the Vaibhāṣika philosophy—there would still have been no cause for lamentation. No one laments the loss of a certain bulk of chemicals and stops discharging his prescribed duty. On the other hand, in modern science and scientific warfare, so many tons of chemicals are wasted for achieving victory over the enemy. According to the Vaibhāṣika philosophy, the so-called soul or ātmā vanishes along with the deterioration of the body. So, in any case, whether Arjuna accepted the Vedic conclusion that there is an atomic soul, or whether he did not believe in the existence of the soul, he had no reason to lament. According to this theory, since there are so many living entities generating out of matter every moment, and so many of them are being vanquished every moment, there is no need to grieve for such an incidence. However, since he was not risking rebirth of the soul, Arjuna had no reason to be afraid of being affected with sinful reactions due to his killing his grandfather and teacher. But at the same time, Kṛṣṇa sarcastically addressed Arjuna as *mahā-bāhu*, mighty-armed, because He, at least, did not accept the theory of the *Vaibhāṣikas*, which leaves aside the Vedic wisdom. As a *kṣatriya*, Arjuna belonged to the Vedic culture, and it behooved him to continue to follow its principles.

TEXT 27

जातस्य हि ध्रुवो मृत्युर्ध्रुवं जन्म मृतस्य च ।
तस्मादपरिहार्येऽर्थे न त्वं शोचितुमर्हसि ॥ २७ ॥

*jātasya hi dhruvo mṛtyur
dhruvaṁ janma mṛtasya ca
tasmād aparihārye 'rthe
na tvaṁ śocitum arhasi*

jātasya—one who has taken his birth; *hi*—certainly; *dhruvaḥ*—a fact; *mṛtyuḥ*—death; *dhruvam*—it is also a fact; *janma*—birth; *mṛtasya*—of the dead; *ca*—also; *tasmāt*—therefore; *aparihārye*—for that which is unavoidable; *arthe*—in the matter of; *na*—do not; *tvam*—you; *śocitum*—to lament; *arhasi*—deserve.

TRANSLATION

For one who has taken his birth, death is certain; and for one who is dead, birth is certain. Therefore, in the unavoidable discharge of your duty, you should not lament.

PURPORT

One has to take birth according to one's activities of life. And, after finishing one term of activities, one has to die to take birth for the next. In this way the cycle of birth and death is revolving, one after the other without liberation. This cycle of birth and death does not, however, support unnecessary murder, slaughter and war. But at the same time, violence and war are inevitable factors in human society for keeping law and order.

The Battle of Kurukṣetra, being the will of the Supreme, was an inevitable event, and to fight for the right cause is the duty of a kṣatriya. Why should he be afraid of or aggrieved at the death of his relatives since he was discharging his proper duty? He did not deserve to break the law, thereby becoming subjected to the reactions of sinful acts, of which he was so afraid. By avoiding the discharge of his proper duty, he would not be able to stop the death of his relatives, and he would be degraded due to his selection of the wrong path of action.

TEXT 28

अव्यक्तादीनि भूतानि व्यक्तमध्यानि भारत ।
अव्यक्तनिधनान्येव तत्र का परिदेवना ॥ २८ ॥

avyaktādīni bhūtāni
vyakta-madhyāni bhārata
avyakta-nidhanāny eva
tatra kā paridevanā

avyaktādīni—in the beginning unmanifested; *bhūtāni*—all that are created; *vyakta*—manifested; *madhyāni*—in the middle; *bhārata*—O descendant of Bharata; *avyakta*—nonmanifested; *nidhanāni*—all that are vanquished; *eva*—it is all like that; *tatra*—therefore; *kā*-what; *paridevanā*—lamentation.

TRANSLATION

All created beings are unmanifest in their beginning, manifest in their interim state, and unmanifest again when they are annihilated. So what need is there for lamentation?

PURPORT

Accepting that there are two classes of philosophers, one believing in the existence of soul and the other not believing in the existence of the soul, there is no cause for lamentation in either case. Nonbelievers in the existence of the soul are called atheists by followers of Vedic wisdom. Yet even if, for argument's sake, we accept the atheistic theory, there is still no cause for lamentation. Apart from the separate existence of the soul, the material elements remain unmanifested before creation. From this subtle state of unmanifestation comes manifestation, just as from ether, air is generated; from air, fire is generated; from fire, water is generated; and from water, earth becomes manifested. From the earth, many varieties of manifestations take place. Take, for example, a big skyscraper manifested from the earth. When it is dismantled, the manifestation becomes again unmanifested and remains as atoms in the ultimate stage. The law of conservation of energy remains, but in course of time things are manifested and unmanifested—that is the difference. Then what cause is there for lamentation either in the stage of manifestation or unmanifestation? Somehow or other, even in the unmanifested stage, things are not lost. Both at the beginning and at the end, all elements remain unmanifested, and only in the middle are they manifested, and this does not make any real material difference.

And if we accept the Vedic conclusion as stated in the *Bhagavad-gītā* (*antavanta ime dehāḥ*) that these material bodies are perishable in due course of time (*nityasyoktāḥ śarīriṇaḥ*) but that soul is eternal, then we must remember always that the body is like a dress; therefore why lament the changing of a dress? The material body has no factual existence in relation to the eternal soul. It is something like a dream. In a dream we may think of flying in the sky, or sitting on a chariot as a king, but when we wake up we can see that we are neither in the sky nor seated on the chariot. The Vedic wisdom encourages self-realization on the basis of the nonexistence of the material body. Therefore, in either case, whether one believes in the existence of the soul, or one does not believe in the existence of the soul, there is no cause for lamentation for loss of the body.

TEXT 29

आश्चर्यवत्पश्यति कश्चिदेन-
माश्चर्यवद्वदति तथैव चान्यः ।
आश्चर्यवच्चैनमन्यः शृणोति
श्रुत्वाप्येनं वेद न चैव कश्चित् ॥ २९ ॥

āścarya-vat paśyati kaścid enam
āścarya-vad vadati tathaiva cānyaḥ
āścarya-vac cainam anyaḥ śṛṇoti
śrutvāpy enaṁ veda na caiva kaścit

āścaryavat—amazing; *paśyati*—see; *kaścit*—some; *enam*—this soul; *āścar-yavat*—amazing; *vadati*—speak; *tathā*—there; *eva*—certainly; *ca*—also; *anyaḥ*—others; *āścaryavat*—similarly amazing; *ca*—also; *enam*—this soul; *anyaḥ*—others; *śṛṇoti*—hear; *śrutvā*—having heard; *api*—even; *enam*—this soul; *veda*—do know; *na*—never; *ca*—and; *eva*—certainly; *kaścit*—anyone.

TRANSLATION

Some look on the soul as amazing, some describe him as amazing, and some hear of him as amazing, while others, even after hearing about him, cannot understand him at all.

PURPORT

Since *Gītopaniṣad* is largely based on the principles of the *Upaniṣads*, it is not surprising to also find this passage in the *Kaṭha Upaniṣad*.

> *śravaṇāyāpi bahubhir yo na labhyaḥ*
> *śṛṇvanto 'pi bahavo yaḥ na vidyuḥ*
> *āścaryo vaktā kuśalo 'sya labdhā*
> *āścaryo jñātā kuśalānuśiṣṭaḥ.*

The fact that the atomic soul is within the body of a gigantic animal, in the body of a gigantic banyan tree, and also in the microbic germs, millions and billions of which occupy only an inch of space, is certainly very amazing. Men with a poor fund of knowledge and men who are not austere cannot understand the wonders of the individual atomic spark of spirit, even though it is explained by the greatest authority of knowledge, who imparted lessons even to Brahmā, the first living being in the universe. Owing to a gross material conception of things, most men in this age cannot imagine how such a small particle can become both so great and so small. So men look at the soul proper as wonderful either by constitution or by description. Illusioned by the material energy, people are so engrossed in subject matter for sense gratification that they have very little time to understand the question of self-understanding, even though it is a fact that without this self-understanding all activities result in ultimate defeat in the struggle for existence. Perhaps one has no idea that one must think of the soul, and also make a solution of the material miseries.

Some people who are inclined to hear about the soul may be attending lectures, in good association, but sometimes, owing to ignorance, they are misguided by acceptance of the Supersoul and the atomic soul as one without distinction of magnitude. It is very difficult to find a man who perfectly understands the position of the soul, the Supersoul, the atomic soul, their respective functions, relationships and all other major and minor details. And it is still more difficult to find a man who has actually derived full benefit from knowledge of the soul, and who is able to describe the position of the soul in different aspects. But if, somehow or other, one is able to understand the subject matter of the soul, then one's life is successful. The easiest process for understanding the subject matter of self, however, is to accept the statements of the *Bhagavad-gītā* spoken by the greatest authority, Lord Kṛṣṇa, without being deviated by other theories. But it also requires a great deal of penance and sacrifice, either in this life or in the previous ones, before one is able to accept Kṛṣṇa as the Supreme Personality of Godhead. Kṛṣṇa can, however, be known as such by the causeless mercy of the pure devotee and by no other way.

TEXT 30

देही नित्यमवध्योऽयं देहे सर्वस्य भारत ।
तस्मात्सर्वाणि भूतानि न त्वं शोचितुमर्हसि ॥ ३० ॥

dehī nityam avadhyo 'yaṁ
dehe sarvasya bhārata
tasmāt sarvāṇi bhūtāni
na tvaṁ śocitum arhasi

dehī—the owner of the material body; *nityam*—eternally; *avadhyaḥ*—cannot be killed; *ayam*—this soul; *dehe*—in the body; *sarvasya*—of everyone; *bhārata*—O descendant of Bharata; *tasmāt*—therefore; *sarvāṇi*—all; *bhūtāni*—living entities (that are born); *na*—never; *tvam*—yourself; *śocitum*—to lament; *arhasi*—deserve.

TRANSLATION

O descendant of Bharata, he who dwells in the body is eternal and can never be slain. Therefore you need not grieve for any creature.

PURPORT

The Lord now concludes the chapter of instruction on the immutable spirit soul. In describing the immortal soul in various ways, Lord Kṛṣṇa establishes that the soul is immortal and the body is temporary. Therefore Arjuna as a kṣatriya should not abandon his duty out of fear that his grandfather and teacher—Bhīṣma and Droṇa—will die in the battle. On the authority of Śrī Kṛṣṇa, one has to believe that there is a soul different from the material body, not that there is no such thing as soul, or that living symptoms develop at a certain stage of material maturity resulting from the interaction of chemicals. Though the soul is immortal, violence is not encouraged, but at the time of war it is not discouraged when there is actual need for it. That need must be justified in terms of the sanction of the Lord, and not capriciously.

TEXT 31

स्वधर्ममपि चावेक्ष्य न विकम्पितुमर्हसि ।
धर्म्याद्धि युद्धाच्छ्रेयोऽन्यत्क्षत्रियस्य न विद्यते ॥ ३१ ॥

sva-dharmam api cāvekṣya
na vikampitum arhasi
dharmyād dhi yuddhāc chreyo 'nyat
kṣatriyasya na vidyate

svadharmam—one's own religious principles; api—also; ca—indeed; avekṣya—considering; na—never; vikampitum—to hesitate; arhasi—you deserve; dharmyāt—from religious principles; hi—indeed; yuddhāt—of fighting; śreyaḥ—better engagements; anyat—anything else; kṣatriyasya—of the kṣatriya; na—does not; vidyate—exist.

TRANSLATION

Considering your specific duty as a kṣatriya, you should know that there is no better engagement for you than fighting on religious principles; and so there is no need for hesitation.

PURPORT

Out of the four orders of social administration, the second order, for the matter of good administration, is called kṣatriya. Kṣat means hurt. One who gives protection from harm is called kṣatriya (trayate—to give protection). The kṣatriyas are trained for killing in the forest. A kṣatriya would go into the forest and challenge a tiger face to face and fight with the tiger with his sword. When the tiger was killed, it would be offered the royal order of cremation. This system is being followed even up to the present day by the kṣatriya kings of Jaipur state. The kṣatriyas are specially trained for challenging and killing because religious violence is sometimes a necessary factor. Therefore, kṣatriyas are never meant for accepting directly the order of sannyāsa or renunciation. Nonviolence in politics may be a diplomacy, but it is never a factor or principle. In the religious law books it is stated:

> āhaveṣu mitho 'nyonyaṁ jighāṁsanto mahīkṣitaḥ
>   yuddhamānāḥ paraṁ śaktyā svargaṁ yānty aparāṅmukhāḥ
> yajñeṣu paśavo brahman hanyante satataṁ dvijaiḥ
>   saṁskṛtāḥ kila mantraiś ca te 'pi svargam avāpnuvan.

"In the battlefield, a king or kṣatriya, while fighting another king envious of him, is eligible for achieving heavenly planets after death, as the brāhmaṇas also attain the heavenly planets by sacrificing animals in the sacrificial fire." Therefore, killing on the battle on the religious principle and the killing of animals in the sacrificial fire are not at all considered to be acts of violence, because everyone is benefitted by the religious principles involved. The animal sacrificed gets a human life immediately without undergoing the gradual evolutionary process from one form to another, and the kṣatriyas killed in the battlefield also attain the heavenly planets as do the brāhmaṇas who attain them by offering sacrifice.

There are two kinds of svadharmas, specific duties. As long as one is not liberated, one has to perform the duties of that particular body in accordance with religious principles in order to achieve liberation. When one is liberated, one's svadharma—specific duty—becomes spiritual and is not in the material bodily concept. In the bodily conception of life there are specific duties for the brāhmaṇas and kṣatriyas respectively, and such duties are unavoidable. Svadharma is ordained by the Lord, and this will be clarified in the Fourth Chapter. On the bodily plane svadharma is called varṇāśrama-dharma, or man's steppingstone for spiritual understanding. Human civilization begins from the stage of varṇāśrama-dharma, or specific duties in terms of the specific modes of nature of the body obtained. Discharging one's specific duty in any field of action in accordance with varṇāśrama-dharma serves to elevate one to a higher status of life.

TEXT 32

यदृच्छया चोपपन्नं स्वर्गद्वारमपावृतम् ।
सुखिनः क्षत्रियाः पार्थ लभन्ते युद्धमीदृशम् ॥ ३२ ॥

yadṛcchayā copapannaṁ
svarga-dvāram apāvṛtam
sukhinaḥ kṣatriyāḥ pārtha
labhante yuddham īdṛśam

yadṛcchayā—by its own accord; *ca*—also; *upapannam*—arrived at; *svarga*—heavenly planet; *dvāram*—door; *apāvṛtam*—wide open; *sukhinaḥ*—very happy; *kṣatriyāḥ*—the members of the royal order; *pārtha*—O son of Pṛthā; *labhante*—do achieve; *yuddham*—war; *īdṛśam*—like this.

TRANSLATION

O Pārtha, happy are the kṣatriyas to whom such fighting opportunities come unsought, opening for them the doors of the heavenly planets.

PURPORT

As supreme teacher of the world, Lord Kṛṣṇa condemns the attitude of Arjuna who said, "I do not find any good in this fighting. It will cause perpetual habitation in hell." Such statements by Arjuna were due to ignorance only. He wanted to become nonviolent in the discharge of his specific duty. For a *kṣatriya* to be in the battlefield and to become nonviolent is the philosophy of fools. In the *Parāśara-smṛti* or religious codes made by Parāśara, the great sage and father of Vyāsadeva, it is stated:

kṣatriyo hi prajā rakṣan śastra-pāṇiḥ pradaṇḍayan
nirjitya parasainyādi kṣitiṁ dharmeṇa pālayet.

"The *kṣatriya's* duty is to protect the citizens from all kinds of difficulties, and for that reason he has to apply violence in suitable cases for law and order. Therefore he has to conquer the soldiers of inimical kings, and thus, with *religious principles*, he should rule over the world."

Considering all aspects, Arjuna had no reason to refrain from fighting. If he should conquer his enemies, he would enjoy the kingdom; and if he should die in the battle, he would be elevated to the heavenly planets whose doors were wide open to him. Fighting would be for his benefit in either case.

TEXT 33

अथ चेत्त्वमिमं धर्म्यं संग्रामं न करिष्यसि ।
ततः स्वधर्मं कीर्तिं च हित्वा पापमवाप्स्यसि ॥ ३३ ॥

atha cet tvam imaṁ dharmyaṁ
saṅgrāmaṁ na kariṣyasi
tataḥ sva-dharmaṁ kīrtiṁ ca
hitvā pāpam avāpsyasi

atha—therefore; *cet*—if; *tvam*—you; *imam*—this; *dharmyam*—religious duty; *saṅgrāmam*—fighting; *na*—do not; *kariṣyasi*—perform; *tataḥ*—then; *svadharmam*—your religious duty; *kīrtim*—reputation; *ca*—also; *hitvā*—losing; *pāpam*—sinful reaction; *avāpsyasi*—do gain.

TRANSLATION

If, however, you do not fight this religious war, then you will certainly incur sins for neglecting your duties and thus lose your reputation as a fighter.

PURPORT

Arjuna was a famous fighter, and he attained fame by fighting many great demigods, including even Lord Śiva. After fighting and defeating Lord Śiva in the dress of a hunter, Arjuna pleased the Lord and received as a reward a weapon called *pāśupata-astra*. Everyone knew that he was a great warrior. Even Droṇācārya gave him benediction and awarded him the special weapon by which he could kill even his teacher. So he was credited with so many military certificates from many authorities, including his adopted father Indra, the heavenly king. But if he abandoned the battle, he would not only neglect his specific duty as a *kṣatriya*, but he would lose all his fame and good name and thus prepare his royal road to hell. In other words, he would go to hell, not by fighting, but by withdrawing from battle.

TEXT 34

अकीर्तिं चापि भूतानि कथयिष्यन्ति तेऽव्ययाम् ।
संभावितस्य चाकीर्तिर्मरणादतिरिच्यते ॥ ३४ ॥

akīrtiṁ cāpi bhūtāni
kathayiṣyanti te 'vyayām
sambhāvitasya cākīrtir
maraṇād atiricyate

akīrtim—infamy; *ca*—also; *api*—over and above; *bhūtāni*—all people; *kathayiṣyanti*—will speak; *te*-of you; *avyayām*—forever; *sambhāvitasya*—for a respectable man; *ca*—also; *akīrtiḥ*—ill fame; *maraṇāt*—than death; *atiricyate*—becomes more than.

TRANSLATION

People will always speak of your infamy, and for one who has been honored, dishonor is worse than death.

PURPORT

Both as friend and philosopher to Arjuna, Lord Kṛṣṇa now gives His final judgement regarding Arjuna's refusal to fight. The Lord says, "Arjuna, if you leave the battlefield, people will call you a coward even before your actual flight. And if you think that people may call you bad names but that you will save your life by fleeing the battlefield, then My advice is that you'd do better to die in the battle. For a respectable man like you, ill fame is worse than death. So, you should not flee for fear of your life; better to die in the battle. That will save you from the ill fame of misusing My friendship and from losing your prestige in society."

So, the final judgement of the Lord was for Arjuna to die in the battle and not withdraw.

TEXT 35

भयाद्रणादुपरतं मंस्यन्ते त्वां महारथाः ।
येषां च त्वं बहुमतो भूत्वा यास्यसि लाघवम् ॥ ३५ ॥

bhayād raṇād uparataṁ
maṁsyante tvāṁ mahā-rathāḥ
yeṣāṁ ca tvaṁ bahu-mato
bhūtvā yāsyasi lāghavam

bhayāt—out of fear; *raṇāt*—from the battlefield; *uparatam*—ceased; *maṁsyante*—will consider; *tvām*—unto you; *mahā-rathāḥ*—the great generals;

yeṣām—of those who; *ca*—also; *tvam*—you; *bahu-mataḥ*—in great estimation; *bhūtvā*—will become; *yāsyasi*—will go; *lāghavam*—decreased in value.

TRANSLATION

The great generals who have highly esteemed your name and fame will think that you have left the battlefield out of fear only, and thus they will consider you a coward.

PURPORT

Lord Kṛṣṇa continued to give His verdict to Arjuna: "Do not think that the great generals like Duryodhana, Karṇa, and other contemporaries will think that you have left the battlefield out of compassion for your brothers and grandfather. They will think that you have left out of fear for your life. And thus their high estimation of your personality will go to hell."

TEXT 36

अवाच्यवादांश्च बहून्वदिष्यन्ति तवाहिताः ।
निन्दन्तस्तव सामर्थ्यं ततो दुःखतरं नु किम् ॥ ३६ ॥

avācya-vādāṁś ca bahūn
vadiṣyanti tavāhitāḥ
nindantas tava sāmarthyaṁ
tato duḥkhataraṁ nu kim

avācya—unkind; *vādān*—fabricated words; *ca*—also; *bahūn*—many; *vadiṣyanti*—will say; *tava*—your; *ahitāḥ*—enemies; *nindantaḥ*—while vilifying; *tava*—your; *sāmarthyam*—ability; *tataḥ*—thereafter; *duḥkhataram*—more painful; *nu*—of course; *kim*—what is there.

TRANSLATION

Your enemies will describe you in many unkind words and scorn your ability. What could be more painful for you?

PURPORT

Lord Kṛṣṇa was astonished in the beginning at Arjuna's uncalled-for plea for compassion, and He described his compassion as befitting the non-

Aryans. Now in so many words, He has proved His statements against
Arjuna's so-called compassion.

TEXT 37

हतो वा प्राप्स्यसि स्वर्गं जित्वा वा भोक्ष्यसे महीम् ।
तस्मादुत्तिष्ठ कौन्तेय युद्धाय कृतनिश्चयः ॥ ३७ ॥

hato vā prāpsyasi svargaṁ
jitvā vā bhokṣyase mahīm
tasmād uttiṣṭha kaunteya
yuddhāya kṛta-niścayaḥ

hataḥ—being killed; vā—either; prāpsyasi—you gain; svargam—the
heavenly kingdom; jitvā—by conquering; vā—or; bhokṣyase—you enjoy;
mahīm—the world; tasmāt—therefore; uttiṣṭha—get up; kaunteya—O son of
Kuntī; yuddhāya—to fight; kṛta—determination; niścayaḥ—uncertainty.

TRANSLATION

O son of Kuntī, either you will be killed on the battlefield and attain
the heavenly planets, or you will conquer and enjoy the earthly kingdom.
Therefore get up and fight with determination.

PURPORT

Even though there was no certainty of victory for Arjuna's side, he still
had to fight; for, even being killed there, he could be elevated into the
heavenly planets.

TEXT 38

सुखदुःखे समे कृत्वा लाभालाभौ जयाजयौ ।
ततो युद्धाय युज्यस्व नैवं पापमवाप्स्यसि ॥ ३८ ॥

sukha-duḥkhe same kṛtvā
lābhālābhau jayājayau
tato yuddhāya yujyasva
naivaṁ pāpam avāpsyasi

sukha—happiness; *duḥkhe*—in distress; *same*—in equanimity; *kṛtvā*—doing so; *lābhālābhau*—both in loss and profit; *jayājayau*—both in defeat and victory; *tataḥ*—thereafter; *yuddhāya*—for the sake of fighting; *yujyasva*—do fight; *na*—never; *evam*—in this way; *pāpam*—sinful reaction; *avāpsyasi*—you will gain.

TRANSLATION

Do thou fight for the sake of fighting, without considering happiness or distress, loss or gain, victory or defeat—and, by so doing, you shall never incur sin.

PURPORT

Lord Kṛṣṇa now directly says that Arjuna should fight for the sake of fighting because He desires the battle. There is no consideration of happiness or distress, profit or gain, victory or defeat in the activities of Kṛṣṇa consciousness. That everything should be performed for the sake of Kṛṣṇa is transcendental consciousness; so there is no reaction to material activities. He who acts for his own sense gratification, either in goodness or in passion, is subject to the reaction, good or bad. But he who has completely surrendered himself in the activities of Kṛṣṇa consciousness is no longer obliged to anyone, nor is he a debtor to anyone, as one is in the ordinary course of activities. It is said:

> *devarṣi-bhutāpta-nṛṇāṁ pitṝṇāṁ*
> *na kiṅkaro nāyamṛṇī ca rājan*
> *sarvātmanā yaḥ śaraṇaṁ śaraṇyaṁ*
> *gato mukundaṁ parihṛtya kartam*
> (Bhag. 11.5.41)

"Anyone who has completely surrendered unto Kṛṣṇa, Mukunda, giving up all other duties, is no longer a debtor, nor is he obliged to anyone—not the demigods, nor the sages, nor the people in general, nor kinsmen, nor humanity, nor forefathers." That is the indirect hint given by Kṛṣṇa to Arjuna in this verse, and the matter will be more clearly explained in the following verses.

TEXT 39

एषा तेऽभिहिता साङ्ख्ये बुद्धिर्योगे त्विमां शृणु ।
बुद्ध्या युक्तो यया पार्थ कर्मबन्धं प्रहास्यसि ॥ ३९ ॥

eṣā te 'bhihitā sāṅkhye
buddhir yoge tv imāṁ śṛṇu
buddhyā yukto yayā pārtha
karma-bandhaṁ prahāsyasi

eṣā—all these; *te*—unto you; *abhihitā*—described; *sāṅkhye*—by analytical study; *buddhiḥ*—intelligence; *yoge*—work without fruitive result; *tu*—but; *imām*-this; *śṛṇu*—just hear; *buddhyā*—by intelligence; *yuktaḥ*—dovetailed; *yayā*—by which; *pārtha*—O son of Pṛthā; *karma-bandham*—bondage of reaction; *prahāsyasi*—you can be released from.

TRANSLATION

Thus far I have declared to you the analytical knowledge of sāṅkhya philosophy. Now listen to the knowledge of yoga whereby one works without fruitive result. O son of Pṛthā, when you act by such intelligence, you can free yourself from the bondage of works.

PURPORT

According to the *Nirukti*, or the Vedic dictionary, *saṅkhya* means that which describes phenomena in detail, and *saṅkhya* refers to that philosophy which describes the real nature of the soul. And *yoga* involves controlling the senses. Arjuna's proposal not to fight was based on sense gratification. Forgetting his prime duty, he wanted to cease fighting because he thought that by not killing his relatives and kinsmen he would be happier than by enjoying the kingdom by conquering his cousins and brothers, the sons of Dhṛtarāṣṭra. In both ways, the basic principles were for sense gratification. Happiness derived from conquering them and happiness derived by seeing kinsmen alive are both on the basis of personal sense gratification, for there is a sacrifice of wisdom and duty. Kṛṣṇa, therefore, wanted to explain to Arjuna that by killing the body of his grandfather he would not be killing the soul proper, and He explained that all individual persons, including the Lord Himself, are eternal individuals; they were individuals in the past, they are individuals in the present, and they will continue to remain individuals in the future, because all of us are individual souls eternally, and we simply change our bodily dress in different manners. But, actually, we keep our individuality even after liberation from the bondage of material dress. An analytical study of the soul and the body has been very graphically explained by Lord Kṛṣṇa. And this descriptive knowledge of the soul and the body from different angles of vision has been described here as *sāṅkhya*, in terms of the *Nirukti* dictionary. This *sāṅkhya* has nothing to do with the *sāṅkhya* philosophy of the atheist Kapila. Long before the imposter Kapila's *sāṅkhya*, the *sāṅkhya* philosophy was expounded in the *Śrīmad-Bhāgavatam* by the true Lord Kapila, the incarnation of Lord Kṛṣṇa, who explained it to His mother, Devahūti. It is clearly explained by Him that the *Puruṣa*, or the Supreme Lord, is active and that He creates by looking over the *prakṛti*. This is accepted in the *Vedas* and in the *Gītā*. The description in the *Vedas* indicates that the Lord glanced over the *prakṛti*, or nature, and impregnated it with atomic individuals souls. All these individuals are working in the material world for sense gratification, and under the spell of material energy they are thinking of being enjoyers. This mentality is dragged to the last point of liberation when the living entity wants to become one with the Lord. This is the last snare of *māyā* or sense gratificatory illusion, and it is only after many, many births of such sense gratificatory activities that a great soul surrenders unto Vāsudeva, Lord Kṛṣṇa, thereby fulfilling the search after the ultimate truth.

Arjuna has already accepted Kṛṣṇa as his spiritual master by surrendering himself unto Him: *śiṣyas te 'haṁ śādhi māṁ tvāṁ prapannam.* Consequently, Kṛṣṇa will now tell him about the working process in *buddhi-yoga*, or *karma-yoga*, or in other words, the practice of devotional service only for the sense gratification of the Lord. This *buddhi-yoga* is clearly explained in Chapter Ten, verse ten, as being direct communion with the Lord, who is sitting as Paramātmā in everyone's heart. But such communion does not take place without devotional service. One who is therefore situated in devotional or transcendental loving service to the Lord, or, in other words, in Kṛṣṇa consciousness, attains to this stage of *buddhi-yoga* by the special grace of the Lord. The Lord says, therefore, that only to those who are always engaged in devotional service out of transcendental love does He award the pure knowledge of devotion in love. In that way the devotee can reach Him easily in the ever-blissful kingdom of God.

Thus the *buddhi-yoga* mentioned in this verse is the devotional service of the Lord, and the word *sāṅkhya* mentioned herein has nothing to do with the atheistic *sāṅkhya-yoga* enunciated by the impostor Kapila. One should not, therefore, misunderstand that the *sāṅkhya-yoga* mentioned herein has any connection with the atheistic *sāṅkhya*. Nor did that philosophy have any influence during that time; nor would Lord Kṛṣṇa care to mention such godless philosophical speculations. Real *sāṅkhya* philosophy is described by Lord Kapila in the *Śrīmad-Bhāgavatam*, but even that sāṅkhya has nothing to do with the current topics. Here, sāṅkhya means analytical description of the body and the soul. Lord Kṛṣṇa made an analytical description of the soul just to bring Arjuna to the point of buddhi-yoga, or bhakti-yoga. Therefore, Lord Kṛṣṇa's sāṅkhya and Lord Kapila's sāṅkhya, as described in the Bhāgavatam, are one and the same. They are all bhakti-yoga. He said, therefore, that only the less intelligent class of men make a distinction between sāṅkhya-yoga and bhakti-yoga.

Of course, atheistic sāṅkhya-yoga has nothing to do with bhakti-yoga, yet the unintelligent claim that the atheistic sāṅkhya-yoga is referred to in the Bhagavad-gītā.

One should therefore understand that buddhi-yoga means to work in Kṛṣṇa consciousness, in the full bliss and knowledge of devotional service. One who works for the satisfaction of the Lord only, however difficult such work may be, is working under the principles of buddhi-yoga and finds himself always in transcendental bliss. By such transcendental engagement, one achieves all transcendental qualities automatically, by the grace of the Lord, and thus his liberation is complete in itself, without his making extraneous endeavors to acquire knowledge. There is much difference between work in Kṛṣṇa consciousness and work for fruitive results, especially in the matter of sense gratification for achieving results in terms of family or material happiness. Buddhi-yoga is therefore the transcendental quality of the work that we perform.

TEXT 40

नेहाभिक्रमनाशोऽस्ति प्रत्यवायो न विद्यते ।
स्वल्पमप्यस्य धर्मस्य त्रायते महतो भयात् ॥ ४० ॥

nehābhikrama-nāśo 'sti
pratyavāyo na vidyate
sv-alpam apy asya dharmasya
trāyate mahato bhayāt

na—there is not; iha—in this world; abhikrama—endeavoring; nāśaḥ—loss; asti—there is; pratyavāyaḥ—diminution; na—never; vidyate—there is; svalpam—little; api—although; asya—of this; dharmasya—of this occupation; trāyate—releases; mahataḥ—of very great; bhayāt—from danger.

TRANSLATION

In this endeavor there is no loss or diminution, and a little advancement on this path can protect one from the most dangerous type of fear.

PURPORT

Activity in Kṛṣṇa consciousness, or acting for the benefit of Kṛṣṇa without expectation of sense gratification, is the highest transcendental quality of work. Even a small beginning of such activity finds no impediment, nor can that small beginning be lost at any stage. Any work begun on the material plane has to be completed, otherwise the whole attempt becomes a failure. But any work begun in Kṛṣṇa consciousness has a permanent effect, even though not finished. The performer of such work is therefore not at a loss even if his work in Kṛṣṇa consciousness is incomplete. One percent done in Kṛṣṇa consciousness bears permanent results, so that the next beginning is from the point of two percent; whereas, in material activity, without a hundred percent success, there is no profit. Ajāmila performed his duty in some percentage of Kṛṣṇa consciousness, but the result he enjoyed at the end was a hundred percent, by the grace of the Lord. There is a nice verse in this connection in Śrīmad-Bhāgavatam:

> tyaktvā sva-dharmaṁ caraṇāmbujaṁ harer
> bhajan na pakko 'tha patet tato yadi
> yatra kva vābhadram abhūd amuṣya kiṁ
> ko vārtha āpto 'bhajatāṁ sva-dharmataḥ

"If someone gives up self-gratificatory pursuits and works in Kṛṣṇa consciousness and then falls down on account of not completing his work, what loss is there on his part? And, what can one gain if one performs his material activities perfectly?" (Bhāg. 1.5.17) Or, as the Christians say, "What profiteth a man if he gain the whole world yet suffers the loss of his eternal soul?"

Material activities and their results end with the body. But work in Kṛṣṇa consciousness carries the person again to Kṛṣṇa consciousness, even after the loss of the body. At least one is sure to have a chance in the next life of being born again as a human being, either in the family of a great cultured brāhmaṇa or in a rich aristocratic family that will give one a further chance for elevation. That is the unique quality of work done in Kṛṣṇa consciousness.

TEXT 41

व्यवसायात्मिका बुद्धिरेकेह कुरुनन्दन ।
बहुशाखा ह्यनन्ताश्च बुद्धयोऽव्यवसायिनाम् ॥ ४१ ॥

vyavasāyātmikā buddhir
ekeha kuru-nandana
bahu-śākhā hy anantāś ca
buddhayo 'vyavasāyinām

vyavasāyātmikā—resolute Kṛṣṇa consciousness; *buddhiḥ*—intelligence; *ekā*—only one; *iha*—in this world; *kuru-nandana*—O beloved child of the Kurus; *bahu-śākhāḥ*—various branches; *hi*—indeed; *anantāḥ*—unlimited; *ca*—also; *buddhayaḥ*—intelligence; *avyavasāyinām*—of those who are not in Kṛṣṇa consciousness.

TRANSLATION

Those who are on this path are resolute in purpose, and their aim is one. O beloved child of the Kurus, the intelligence of those who are irresolute is many-branched.

PURPORT

A strong faith in Kṛṣṇa consciousness that one should be elevated to the highest perfection of life is called *vyavasāyātmikā* intelligence. The *Caitanya-caritāmṛta* states:

'śraddhā'-śabde viśvāsa kahe sudṛḍha niścaya
kṛṣṇe bhakti kaile sarva-karma kṛta haya

Faith means unflinching trust in something sublime. When one is engaged in the duties of Kṛṣṇa consciousness, he need not act in relationship to the material world with obligations to family traditions, humanity, or nationality. Fruitive activities are the engagements of one's reactions from past good or bad deeds. When one is awake in Kṛṣṇa consciousness, he need no longer endeavor for good results in his activities. When one is situated in Kṛṣṇa consciousness, all activities are on the absolute plane, for they are no longer subject to dualities like good and bad. The highest perfection of Kṛṣṇa consciousness is renunciation of the material conception of life. This state is automatically achieved by progressive Kṛṣṇa consciousness. The resolute purpose of a person in Kṛṣṇa consciousness is based on knowledge ("*Vāsudevaḥ sarvam iti sa mahātmā sudurlabhaḥ*") by which one comes to know perfectly that Vāsudeva, or Kṛṣṇa, is the root of all manifested causes. As water on the root of a tree is automatically distributed to the leaves and branches, in Kṛṣṇa consciousness, one can render the highest service to everyone—namely self, family, society, country, humanity, etc. If Kṛṣṇa is satisfied by one's actions, then everyone will be satisfied.

Service in Kṛṣṇa consciousness is, however, best practiced under the able guidance of a spiritual master who is a bona fide representative of Kṛṣṇa, who knows the nature of the student and who can guide him to act in Kṛṣṇa consciousness. As such, to be well-versed in Kṛṣṇa consciousness one has to act firmly and obey the representative of Kṛṣṇa, and one should accept the instruction of the bona fide spiritual master as one's mission in life. Śrīla Viśvanātha Cakravartī Ṭhākur instructs us, in his famous prayers for the spiritual master, as follows:

> *yasya prasādād bhagavat-prasādo*
> *yasyāprasādānna gatiḥ kuto 'pi*
> *dhyāyaṁ stuvaṁs tasya yaśas tri-sandhyaṁ*
> *vande guroḥ śrī-caraṇāravindam.*

"By satisfaction of the spiritual master, the Supreme Personality of Godhead becomes satisfied. And by not satisfying the spiritual master, there is no chance of being promoted to the plane of Kṛṣṇa consciousness. I should, therefore, meditate and pray for his mercy three times a day, and offer my respectful obeisances unto him, my spiritual master."

The whole process, however, depends on perfect knowledge of the soul beyond the conception of the body—not theoretically but practically, when there is no longer chance for sense gratification manifested in fruitive activities. One who is not firmly fixed in mind is diverted by various types of fruitive acts.

TEXTS 42-43

यामिमां पुष्पितां वाचं प्रवदन्त्यविपश्चितः ।
वेदवादरताः पार्थ नान्यदस्तीति वादिनः ॥ ४२ ॥

कामात्मानः स्वर्गपरा जन्मकर्मफलप्रदाम् ।
क्रियाविशेषबहुलां भोगैश्वर्यगतिं प्रति ॥ ४३ ॥

> *yām imāṁ puṣpitāṁ vācam*
> *pravadanty avipaścitaḥ*
> *veda-vāda-ratāḥ pārtha*
> *nānyad astīti vādinaḥ*
>
> *kāmātmānaḥ svarga-parā*
> *janma-karma-phala-pradām*
> *kriyā-viśeṣa-bahulāṁ*
> *bhogaiśvarya-gatiṁ prati*

yām imām—all these; *puṣpitām*—flowery; *vācam*—words; *pravadanti*—say; *avipaścitaḥ*—men with a poor fund of knowledge; *veda-vāda-ratāḥ*—supposed followers of the Vedas; *pārtha*—O son of Pṛthā; *na*—never; *anyat*—anything else; *asti*—there is; *iti*—this; *vādinaḥ*—advocates; *kāma-ātmānaḥ*—desirous of sense gratification; *svarga-parāḥ*—aiming to achieve heavenly planets; *janma-karma-phala-pradām*—resulting in fruitive action, good birth, etc.; *kriyā-viśeṣa*—pompous ceremonies; *bahulām*—various; *bhoga*—sense enjoyment; *aiśvarya*—opulence; *gatim*—progress; *prati*—towards.

TRANSLATION

Men of small knowledge are very much attached to the flowery words of the Vedas, which recommend various fruitive activities for elevation to heavenly planets, resultant good birth, power, and so forth. Being desirous of sense gratification and opulent life, they say that there is nothing more than this.

PURPORT

People in general are not very intelligent, and due to their ignorance they are most attached to the fruitive activities recommended in the *karma-kāṇḍa* portions of the Vedas. They do not want anything more than sense gratificatory proposals for enjoying life in heaven, where wine and women are available and material opulence is very common. In the Vedas many sacrifices are recommended for elevation to the heavenly planets, especially the *jyotiṣṭoma* sacrifices. In fact, it is stated that anyone desiring elevation to heavenly planets must perform these sacrifices, and men with a poor fund of knowledge think that this is the whole purpose of Vedic wisdom. It is very difficult for such inexperienced persons to be situated in the determined action of Kṛṣṇa consciousness. As fools are attached to the flowers of poisonous trees without knowing the results of such attractions, similarly unenlightened men are attracted by such heavenly opulence and the sense enjoyment thereof.

In the karma-kāṇḍa section of the Vedas it is said that those who perform the four monthly penances become eligible to drink the somarasa beverages to become immortal and happy forever. Even on this earth some are very eager to have somarasa to become strong and fit to enjoy sense gratifications. Such persons have no faith in liberation from material bondage, and they are very much attached to the pompous ceremonies of Vedic sacrifices. They are generally sensual, and they do not want anything other than the heavenly pleasures of life. It is understood that there are gardens called nandana-kānana in which there is good opportunity for association with angelic, beautiful women and having a profuse supply of somarasa wine. Such bodily happiness is certainly sensual; therefore there are those who are purely attached to material, temporary happiness, as lords of the material world.

TEXT 44

भोगैश्वर्यप्रसक्तानां तयापहृतचेतसाम् ।
व्यवसायात्मिका बुद्धिः समाधौ न विधीयते ॥ ४४ ॥

bhogaiśvarya-prasaktānāṁ
tayāpahṛta-cetasām
vyavasāyātmikā buddhiḥ
samādhau na vidhīyate

bhoga—material enjoyment; aiśvarya—opulence; prasaktānām—those who are so attached; tayā—by such things; apahṛta-cetasām—bewildered in mind; vyavasāyātmikā—fixed determination; buddhiḥ—devotional service of the Lord; samādhau—in the controlled mind; na—never; vidhīyate—does take place.

TRANSLATION

In the minds of those who are too attached to sense enjoyment and material opulence, and who are bewildered by such things, the resolute determination of devotional service to the Supreme Lord does not take place.

PURPORT

Samādhi means "fixed mind." The Vedic dictionary, the Nirukti, says, samyag ādhīyate 'sminn ātmatattva-yāthātmyam: "When the mind is fixed for understanding the self, it is called *samādhi*. "*Samādhi* is never possible for persons interested in material sense enjoyment, nor for those who are bewildered by such temporary things. They are more or less condemned by the process of material energy.

TEXT 45

त्रैगुण्यविषया वेदा निस्त्रैगुण्यो भवार्जुन ।
निर्द्वन्द्वो नित्यसत्त्वस्थो निर्योगक्षेम आत्मवान् ॥ ४५ ॥

trai-guṇya-viṣayā vedā
nistrai-guṇyo bhavārjuna
nirdvandvo nitya-sattva-stho
niryoga-kṣema ātmavān

traiguṇya—pertaining to the three modes of material nature; *viṣayāḥ*—on the subject matter; *vedāḥ*—Vedic literatures; *nistraiguṇyaḥ*—in a pure state of spiritual existence; *bhava*—be; *arjuna*-O Arjuna; *nirdvandvaḥ*—free from the pains of opposites; *nitya-sattva-sthaḥ*—ever remaining in *sattva* (goodness); *niryoga-kṣemaḥ*—free from (the thought of) acquisition and preservation; *ātmavān*—established in the Self.

TRANSLATION

The Vedas mainly deal with the subject of the three modes of material nature. Rise above these modes, O Arjuna. Be transcendental to all of them. Be free from all dualities and from all anxieties for gain and safety, and be established in the Self.

PURPORT

All material activities involve actions and reactions in the three modes of material nature. They are meant for fruitive results, which cause bondage in the material world. The *Vedas* deal mostly with fruitive activities to gradually elevate the general public from the field of sense gratification to a position on the transcendental plane. Arjuna, as a student and friend of Lord Kṛṣṇa, is advised to raise himself to the transcendental position of *Vedānta* philosophy where, in the beginning, there is *brahma-jijñāsā*, or questions on the Supreme Transcendence. All the living entities who are in the material world are struggling very hard for existence. For them the

Lord, after creation of the material world, gave the Vedic wisdom advising how to live and get rid of the material entanglement. When the activities for sense gratification, namely the *karma-kāṇḍa* chapter, are finished, then the chance for spiritual realization is offered in the form of the *Upaniṣads,* which are part of different *Vedas,* as the *Bhagavad-gītā* is a part of the fifth *Veda,* namely the *Mahābhārata.* The *Upaniṣads* mark the beginning of transcendental life.

As long as the material body exists, there are actions and reactions in the material modes. One has to learn tolerance in the face of dualities such as happiness and distress, or cold and warmth, and by tolerating such dualities become free from anxieties regarding gain and loss. This transcendental position is achieved in full Kṛṣṇa consciousness when one is fully dependant on the good will of Kṛṣṇa

TEXT 46

यावानर्थ उदपाने सर्वतः सम्प्लुतोदके ।
तावान्सर्वेषु वेदेषु ब्राह्मणस्य विजानतः ॥ ४६ ॥

yāvān artha udapāne
sarvataḥ samplutodake
tāvān sarveṣu vedeṣu
brāhmaṇasya vijānataḥ

yāvān—all that; *arthaḥ*—is meant; *udapāne*—in a well of water; *sarvataḥ*—in all respects; *sampluta-udake*—in a great reservoir of water; *tāvān*—similarly; *sarveṣu*—in all; *vedeṣu*—Vedic literatures; *brāhmaṇasya*—of the man who knows the Supreme Brahman; *vijānataḥ*—of one who is in complete knowledge.

TRANSLATION

All purposes that are served by the small pond can at once be served by the great reservoirs of water. Similarly, all the purposes of the Vedas can be served to one who knows the purpose behind them.

PURPORT

The rituals and sacrifices mentioned in the *karma-kāṇḍa* division of the Vedic literature are to encourage gradual development of self-realization.

And the purpose of self-realization is clearly stated in the Fifteenth Chapter of the *Bhagavad-gītā* (15.15): the purpose of studying the *Vedas* is to know Lord Kṛṣṇa, the primeval cause of everything. So, self-realization means understanding Kṛṣṇa and one's eternal relationship with Him. The relationship of the living entities with Kṛṣṇa is also mentioned in the Fifteenth Chapter of *Bhagavad-gītā*. The living entities are parts and parcels of Kṛṣṇa; therefore, revival of Kṛṣṇa consciousness by the individual living entity is the highest perfectional stage of Vedic knowledge. This is confirmed in the *Śrīmad-Bhāgavatam* (3.33.7) as follows:

> aho bata śvapaco'to garīyān
> yaj-jihvāgre vartate nāma tubhyam
> tepus tapas te juhuvuḥ sasnur āryā
> brahmānūcur nāma gṛṇanti ye te.

"O my Lord, a person who is chanting Your holy name, although born of a low family like that of a *cāṇḍāla* [dog eater], is situated on the highest platform of self-realization. Such a person must have performed all kinds of penances and sacrifices according to Vedic rituals and studied the Vedic literatures many, many times after taking his bath in all the holy places of pilgrimage. Such a person is considered to be the best of the Āryan family." So one must be intelligent enough to understand the purpose of the *Vedas*, without being attached to the rituals only, and must not desire to be elevated to the heavenly kingdoms for a better quality of sense gratification. It is not possible for the common man in this age to follow all the rules and regulations of the Vedic rituals and the injunctions of the *Vedāntas* and the *Upaniṣads*. It requires much time, energy, knowledge and resources to execute the purposes of the *Vedas*. This is hardly possible in this age. The best purpose of Vedic culture is served, however, by chanting the holy name of the Lord, as recommended by Lord Caitanya, the deliverer of all fallen souls. When Lord Caitanya was asked by a great Vedic scholar, Prakāśānanda Sarasvatī, why He, the Lord, was chanting the holy name of the Lord like a sentimentalist instead of studying *Vedānta* philosophy, the Lord replied that His spiritual master found Him to be a great fool, and thus he asked Him to chant the holy name of Lord Kṛṣṇa. He did so, and became ecstatic like a madman. In this age of Kali, most of the population is foolish and not adequately educated to understand *Vedānta* philosophy; the best purpose of *Vedānta* philosophy is served by inoffensively chanting the holy name of the Lord. *Vedānta* is the last word in Vedic wisdom, and the author and knower of the *Vedānta* philosophy is Lord Kṛṣṇa; and the highest Vedantist is the great soul who takes pleasure in chanting the holy name of the Lord. That is the ultimate purpose of all Vedic mysticism.

TEXT 47

कर्मण्येवाधिकारस्ते मा फलेषु कदाचन ।
मा कर्मफलहेतुर्भूर्मा ते सङ्गोऽस्त्वकर्मणि ॥ ४७ ॥

karmaṇy evādhikāras te
mā phaleṣu kadācana
mā karma-phala-hetur bhūr
mā te saṅgo 'stv akarmaṇi

karmaṇi—prescribed duties; *eva*—certainly; *adhikāraḥ*—right; *te*—of you; *mā*—never; *phaleṣu*—in the fruits; *kadācana*—at any time; *mā*—never; *karma-phala*—in the result of the work; *hetuḥ*—cause; *bhūḥ*—become; *mā*—never; *te*—of you; *saṅgaḥ*—attachment; *astu*—be there; *akarmaṇi*—in not doing.

TRANSLATION

You have a right to perform your prescribed duty, but you are not entitled to the fruits of action. Never consider yourself to be the cause of the results of your activities, and never be attached to not doing your duty.

PURPORT

There are three considerations here: prescribed duties, capricious work, and inaction. Prescribed duties refer to activities performed while one is in the modes of material nature. Capricious work means actions without the sanction of authority, and inaction means not performing one's prescribed duties. The Lord advised that Arjuna not be inactive, but that he perform his prescribed duty without being attached to the result. One who is attached to the result of his work is also the cause of the action. Thus he is the enjoyer or sufferer of the result of such actions.

As far as prescribed duties are concerned, they can be fitted into three subdivisions, namely routine work, emergency work and desired activities. Routine work, in terms of the scriptural injunctions, is done without desire for results. As one has to do it, obligatory work is action in the mode of goodness. Work with results becomes the cause of bondage; therefore such work is not auspicious. Everyone has his proprietory right in regard to prescribed duties, but should act without attachment to the result; such disinterested obligatory duties doubtlessly lead one to the path of liberation.

Arjuna was therefore advised by the Lord to fight as a matter of duty without attachment to the result. His nonparticipation in the battle is another side of attachment. Such attachment never leads one to the path of salvation. Any attachment, positive or negative, is cause for bondage. Inaction is sinful. Therefore, fighting as a matter of duty was the only auspicious path of salvation for Arjuna.

TEXT 48

योगस्थः कुरु कर्माणि सङ्गं त्यक्त्वा धनंजय ।
सिद्ध्यसिद्ध्योः समो भूत्वा समत्वं योग उच्यते ॥ ४८ ॥

yoga-sthaḥ kuru karmāṇi
saṅgaṁ tyaktvā dhanañjaya
siddhy-asiddhyoḥ samo bhūtvā
samatvaṁ yoga ucyate

yoga-sthaḥ—steadfast in *yoga; kuru*—perform; *karmāṇi*—your duty; *saṅgam*—attachment; *tyaktvā*—having abandoned; *dhanañjaya*—O Dhanañjaya; *siddhi-asiddhyoḥ*—in success and failure; *samaḥ*—the same; *bhūtvā*—having become; *samatvam*—evenness of mind; *yogaḥ-yoga; ucyate*—is called.

TRANSLATION

Be steadfast in yoga, O Arjuna. Perform your duty and abandon all attachment to success or failure. Such evenness of mind is called yoga.

PURPORT

Kṛṣṇa tells Arjuna that he should act in *yoga.* And what is that *yoga? Yoga* means to concentrate the mind upon the Supreme by controlling the ever-disturbing senses. And who is the Supreme? The Supreme is the Lord. And because He Himself is telling Arjuna to fight, Arjuna has nothing to do with the results of the fight. Gain or victory are Kṛṣṇa's concern; Arjuna is simply advised to act according to the dictation of Kṛṣṇa. The following of Kṛṣṇa's dictation is real *yoga,* and this is practiced in the process called Kṛṣṇa consciousness. By Kṛṣṇa consciousness only can one give up the sense of proprietorship. One has to become the servant of Kṛṣṇa, or the servant of the servant of Kṛṣṇa. That is the right way to discharge duty in Kṛṣṇa consciousness, which alone can help one to act in *yoga*.

Arjuna is a *kṣatriya*, and as such he is participating in the *varṇāśrama-dharma* institution. It is said in the *Viṣṇu Purāṇa* that in the *varṇāśrama-dharma*, the whole aim is to satisfy Viṣṇu. No one should satisfy himself, as is the rule in the material world, but one should satisfy Kṛṣṇa. So, unless one satisfies Kṛṣṇa, one cannot correctly observe the principles of *varṇāśrama-dharma*. Indirectly, Arjuna was advised to act as Kṛṣṇa told him.

TEXT 49

दूरेण ह्यवरं कर्म बुद्धियोगाद्धनंजय ।
बुद्धौ शरणमन्विच्छ कृपणाः फलहेतवः ॥ ४९ ॥

dūreṇa hy avaraṁ karma
buddhi-yogād dhanañjaya
buddhau śaraṇam anviccha
kṛpaṇāḥ phala-hetavaḥ

dūreṇa—by discarding it at a long distance; *hi*—certainly; *avaram*—abominable; *karma*—activities; *buddhi-yogāt*—on the strength of Kṛṣṇa consciousness; *dhanañjaya*—O conqueror of wealth; *buddhau*—in such consciousness; *śaraṇam*—full surrender; *anviccha*—desire; *kṛpaṇāḥ*—the misers; *phala-hetavaḥ*—those desiring fruitive action.

TRANSLATION

O Dhanañjaya, rid yourself of all fruitive activities by devotional service, and surrender fully to that consciousness. Those who want to enjoy the fruits of their work are misers.

PURPORT

One who has actually come to understand one's constitutional position as the eternal servitor of the Lord gives up all engagements save working in Kṛṣṇa consciousness. As already explained, *buddhi-yoga* means transcendental loving service to the Lord. Such devotional service is the right course of action for the living entity. Only misers desire to enjoy the fruit of their own work just to be further entangled in material bondage. Except for work in Kṛṣṇa consciousness, all activities are abominable because they continually bind the worker to the cycle of birth and death. One should therefore never desire to be the cause of work. Everything should be done in Kṛṣṇa consciousness for the satisfaction of Kṛṣṇa. Misers do not know how to utilize the assets of riches which they acquire by good fortune or by hard labor. One should spend all energies working in Kṛṣṇa consciousness, and that will make one's life successful. Like the misers, unfortunate persons do not employ their human energy in the service of the Lord.

TEXT 50

बुद्धियुक्तो जहातीह उभे सुकृतदुष्कृते ।
तस्माद्योगाय युज्यस्व योगः कर्मसु कौशलम् ॥ ५० ॥

buddhi-yukto jahātīha
ubhe sukṛta-duṣkṛte
tasmād yogāya yujyasva
yogaḥ karmasu kauśalam

buddhi-yuktaḥ—one who is engaged in devotional service; *jahāti*—can get rid of; *iha*—in this life; *ubhe*—in both; *sukṛta-duṣkṛte*—in good and bad results; *tasmāt*—therefore; *yogāya*—for the sake of devotional service; *yujyasva*—be so engaged; *yogaḥ*—Kṛṣṇa consciousness; *karmasu*—in all activities; *kauśalam*—art.

TRANSLATION

A man engaged in devotional service rids himself of both good and bad actions even in this life. Therefore strive for yoga, O Arjuna, which is the art of all work.

PURPORT

Since time immemorial each living entity has accumulated the various reactions of his good and bad work. As such, he is continuously ignorant of his real constitutional position. One's ignorance can be removed by the instruction of the *Bhagavad-gītā* which teaches one to surrender unto Lord Śrī Kṛṣṇa in all respects and become liberated from the chained victimization of action and reaction, birth after birth. Arjuna is therefore advised to act in Kṛṣṇa consciousness, the purifying process of resultant action.

TEXT 51

कर्मजं बुद्धियुक्ता हि फलं त्यक्त्वा मनीषिणः ।
जन्मबन्धविनिर्मुक्ताः पदं गच्छन्त्यनामयम् ॥ ५१ ॥

karma-jaṁ buddhi-yuktā hi
phalaṁ tyaktvā manīṣiṇaḥ
janma-bandha-vinirmuktāḥ
padaṁ gacchanty anāmayam

karma-jam—because of fruitive activities; *buddhi-yuktāḥ*—being done in devotional service; *hi*—certainly; *phalam*—results; *tyaktvā*—giving up; *manīṣiṇaḥ*—devotees who are great sages; *janma-bandha*—the bondage of birth and death; *vinirmuktāḥ*—liberated souls; *padam*—position; *gacchanti* —reach; *anāmayam*—without miseries.

TRANSLATION

The wise, engaged in devotional service, take refuge in the Lord, and free themselves from the cycle of birth and death by renouncing the fruits of action in the material world. In this way they can attain that state beyond all miseries.

PURPORT

The liberated living entities seek that place where there are no material miseries. The *Bhāgavatam* says:

samāśritā ye padapallava-plavaṁ
mahat-padaṁ puṇya-yaśo murāreḥ
bhāvāmbudhir vatsa-padaṁ paraṁ padaṁ
paraṁ padaṁ yad vipadāṁ na teṣām
(Bhāg. 10.14.58)

"For one who has accepted the boat of the lotus feet of the Lord, who is the shelter of the cosmic manifestation and is famous as Mukunda or the giver of *mukti*, the ocean of the material world is like the water contained in a calf's hoofprint. *Param padam*, or the place where there are no material miseries, or Vaikuṇṭha, is his goal, not the place where there is danger in every step of life."

Owing to ignorance, one does not know that this material world is a miserable place where there are dangers at every step. Out of ignorance only, less intelligent persons try to adjust to the situation by fruitive activities, thinking that resultant actions will make them happy. They do not know that no kind of material body anywhere within the universe can give life without miseries. The miseries of life, namely birth, death, old age and diseases, are present everywhere within the material world. But one who understands his real constitutional position as the eternal servitor of the Lord, and thus knows the position of the Personality of Godhead, engages himself in the transcendental loving service of the Lord. Consequently he becomes qualified to enter into the Vaikuṇṭha planets, where there is neither material, miserable life, nor the influence of time and death. To know one's constitutional position means to know also the sublime position of the Lord. One who wrongly thinks that the living entity's position and the Lord's position are on the same level is to be understood to be in darkness and therefore unable to engage himself in the devotional service of the Lord. He becomes a lord himself and thus paves the way for the repetition of birth and death. But one who, understanding that his position is to serve, transfers himself to the service of the Lord, at once becomes eligible for Vaikuṇṭhaloka. Service for the cause of the Lord is called *karma-yoga* or *buddhi-yoga*, or in plain words, devotional service to the Lord.

TEXT 52

यदा ते मोहकलिलं बुद्धिर्व्यतितरिष्यति ।
तदा गन्तासि निर्वेदं श्रोतव्यस्य श्रुतस्य च ॥ ५२ ॥

yadā te moha-kalilaṁ
buddhir vyatitariṣyati
tadā gantāsi nirvedaṁ
śrotavyasya śrutasya ca

yadā—when; *te*—your; *moha*—illusory; *kalilam*—dense forest; *buddhiḥ*—transcendental service with intelligence; *vyatitariṣyati*—surpasses; *tadā*—at that time; *gantāsi*—you shall go; *nirvedam*—callousness; *śrotavyasya*—all that is to be heard; *śrutasya*—all that is already heard; *ca*—also.

TRANSLATION

When your intelligence has passed out of the dense forest of delusion, you shall become indifferent to all that has been heard and all that is to be heard.

PURPORT

There are many good examples in the lives of the great devotees of the Lord of those who became indifferent to the rituals of the *Vedas* simply by devotional service to the Lord. When a person factually understands Kṛṣṇa and his relationship with Kṛṣṇa, he naturally becomes completely indifferent to the rituals of fruitive activities, even though an experienced *brāhmaṇa*. Śrī Mādhavendra Purī, a great devotee and *ācārya* in the line of the devotees, says:

sandhyā-vandana bhadram astu bhavato bhoḥ snāna tubhyaṁ namo
bho devāḥ pitaraś ca tarpaṇa-vidhau nāhaṁ kṣamaḥ kṣamyatām
yatra kvāpi niṣadya yādava-kulottamasya kaṁsa-dviṣaḥ
smāraṁ smāram aghaṁ harāmi tad alaṁ manye kim anyena me.

"O Lord, in my prayers three times a day, all glory to You. Bathing, I offer my obeisances unto You. O demigods! O forefathers! Please excuse me for my inability to offer you my respects. Now wherever I sit, I can remember the great descendant of the Yadu dynasty [Kṛṣṇa], the enemy of Kaṁsa, and thereby I can free myself from all sinful bondage. I think this is sufficient for me."

The Vedic rites and rituals are imperative for neophytes: comprehending all kinds of prayer three times a day, taking a bath early in the morning, offering respects to the forefathers, etc. But, when one is fully in Kṛṣṇa consciousness and is engaged in His transcendental loving service, one becomes indifferent to all these regulative principles because he has already attained perfection. If one can reach the platform of understanding by service to the Supreme Lord Kṛṣṇa, he has no longer to execute different types of penances and sacrifices as recommended in revealed scriptures. And, similarly, if one has not understood that the purpose of the *Vedas* is to reach Kṛṣṇa and simply engages in the rituals, etc., then he is uselessly wasting time in such engagements. Persons in Kṛṣṇa consciousness transcend the limit of *śabda-brahma*, or the range of the *Vedas* and *Upaniṣads*.

TEXT 53

श्रुतिविप्रतिपन्ना ते यदा स्थास्यति निश्चला ।
समाधावचला बुद्धिस्तदा योगमवाप्स्यसि ॥ ५३ ॥

śruti-vipratipannā te
yadā sthāsyati niścalā
samādhāv acalā buddhis
tadā yogam avāpsyasi

śruti—Vedic revelation; *vipratipannā*—without being influenced by the fruitive results of the *Vedas*; *te*—your; *yadā*—when; *sthāsyati*—remains; *niścalā*—unmoved; *samādhau*—in transcendental consciousness, or Kṛṣṇa consciousness; *acalā*—unflinching; *buddhiḥ*—intelligence; *tadā*—at that time; *yogam*—self-realization; *avāpsyasi*—you will achieve.

TRANSLATION

When your mind is no longer disturbed by the flowery language of the Vedas, and when it remains fixed in the trance of self-realization, then you will have attained the Divine consciousness.

PURPORT

To say that one is in *samādhi* is to say that one has fully realized Kṛṣṇa consciousness; that is, one in full *samādhi* has realized Brahman, Paramātmā and Bhagavān. The highest perfection of self-realization is to understand that one is eternally the servitor of Kṛṣṇa and that one's only business is to discharge one's duties in Kṛṣṇa consciousness. A Kṛṣṇa conscious person, or unflinching devotee of the Lord, should not be disturbed by the flowery language of the *Vedas* nor be engaged in fruitive activities for promotion to the heavenly kingdom. In Kṛṣṇa consciousness, one comes directly into communion with Kṛṣṇa, and thus all directions from Kṛṣṇa may be understood in that transcendental state. One is sure to achieve results by such activities and attain conclusive knowledge. One has only to carry out the orders of Kṛṣṇa or His representative, the spiritual master.

TEXT 54

अर्जुन उवाच ।
स्थितप्रज्ञस्य का भाषा समाधिस्थस्य केशव ।
स्थितधीः किं प्रभाषेत किमासीत व्रजेत किं ॥ ५४ ॥

arjuna uvāca
sthita-prajñasya kā bhāṣā
samādhi-sthasya keśava
sthita-dhīḥ kiṁ prabhāṣeta
kim āsīta vrajeta kim

arjuna uvāca—Arjuna said; *sthita-prajñasya*—of one who is situated in fixed Kṛṣṇa consciousness; *kā*—what; *bhāṣā*—language; *samādhi-sthasya*—of one situated in trance; *keśava*—O Kṛṣṇa; *sthita-dhīḥ*—one fixed in Kṛṣṇa consciousness; *kim*—what; *prabhāṣeta*—speak; *kim*—how; *āsīta*—does remain; *vrajeta*—walk; *kim*—how.

TRANSLATION

Arjuna said: What are the symptoms of one whose consciousness is thus merged in Transcendence? How does he speak, and what is his language? How does he sit, and how does he walk?

PURPORT

As there are symptoms for each and every man, in terms of his particular situation, similarly one who is Kṛṣṇa conscious has his particular nature—talking, walking, thinking, feeling, etc. As a rich man has his symptoms by which he is known as a rich man, as a diseased man has his symptoms, by which he is known as diseased, or as a learned man has his symptoms, so a man in transcendental consciousness of Kṛṣṇa has specific symptoms in various dealings. One can know his specific symptoms from the *Bhagavad-gītā*. Most important is how the man in Kṛṣṇa consciousness speaks, for speech is the most important quality of any man. It is said that a fool is undiscovered as long as he does not speak, and certainly a well-dressed fool cannot be identified unless he speaks, but as soon as he speaks, he reveals himself at once. The immediate symptom of a Kṛṣṇa conscious man is that he speaks only of Kṛṣṇa and of matters relating to Him. Other symptoms then automatically follow, as stated below.

TEXT 55

श्रीभगवानुवाच
प्रजहाति यदा कामान्सर्वान्पार्थ मनोगतान् ।
आत्मन्येवात्मना तुष्टः स्थितप्रज्ञस्तदोच्यते ॥ ५५ ॥

śrī-bhagavān uvāca
prajahāti yadā kāmān
    sarvān pārtha mano-gatān
ātmany evātmanā tuṣṭaḥ
    sthita-prajñas tadocyate

śrī bhagavān uvāca—the Supreme Personality of Godhead said; prajahāti—gives up; yadā—when; kāmān—desires for sense gratification; sarvān—of all varieties; pārtha—O son of Pṛthā; manaḥ-gatān—of mental concoction; ātmani—in the pure state of the soul; eva—certainly; ātmanā—by the purified mind; tuṣṭaḥ—satisfied; sthita-prajñaḥ—transcendentally situated; tadā—at that time; ucyate—is said.

TRANSLATION

The Blessed Lord said: O Pārtha, when a man gives up all varieties of sense desire which arise from mental concoction, and when his mind finds satisfaction in the self alone, then he is said to be in pure transcendental consciousness.

PURPORT

The *Bhāgavatam* affirms that any person who is fully in Kṛṣṇa consciousness, or devotional service of the Lord, has all the good qualities of the great sages, whereas a person who is not so transcendentally situated has no good qualifications, because he is sure to be taking refuge in his own mental concoctions. Consequently, it is rightly said herein that one has to give up all kinds of sense desire manufactured by mental concoction. Artificially, such sense desires cannot be stopped. But if one is engaged in Kṛṣṇa consciousness, then, automatically, sense desires subside without extraneous efforts. Therefore, one has to engage himself in Kṛṣṇa consciousness without hesitation, for this devotional service will instantly help one on to the platform of transcendental consciousness. The highly developed soul always remains satisfied in himself by realizing himself as the eternal servitor of the Supreme Lord. Such a transcendentally situated person has no sense desires resulting from petty materialism; rather, he remains always happy in his natural position of eternally serving the Supreme Lord.

TEXT 56

दुःखेष्वनुद्विग्नमनाः सुखेषु विगतस्पृहः ।
वीतरागभयक्रोधः स्थितधीर्मुनिरुच्यते ॥ ५६ ॥

duḥkheṣv anudvigna-manāḥ
sukheṣu vigata-spṛhaḥ
vīta-rāga-bhaya-krodhaḥ
sthita-dhīr munir ucyate

duḥkheṣu—in the threefold miseries; *anudvigna-manāḥ*—without being agitated in mind; *sukheṣu*—in happiness; *vigata-spṛhaḥ*—without being too interested; *vīta*—free from; *rāga*—attachment; *bhaya*—fear; *krodhaḥ*—anger; *sthita-dhīḥ*—one who is steady; *muniḥ*—sage; *ucyate*—is called.

TRANSLATION

One who is not disturbed in spite of the threefold miseries, who is not elated when there is happiness, and who is free from attachment, fear and anger, is called a sage of steady mind.

PURPORT

The word *muni* means one who can agitate his mind in various ways for mental speculation without coming to a factual conclusion. It is said that every *muni* has a different angle of vision, and unless a *muni* differs from other *munis*, he cannot be called a *muni* in the strict sense of the term. *Nāsau munir yasya matam na binnam.* But a *sthita-dhī-muni* as mentioned herein by the Lord, is different from an ordinary *muni* The *sthita-dhī-muni* is always in Kṛṣṇa consciousness, for he has exhausted all his business of creative speculation. He has surpassed the stage of mental speculations and has come to the conclusion that Lord Śrī Kṛṣṇa, or Vāsudeva, is everything. He is called a *muni* fixed in mind. Such a fully Kṛṣṇa conscious person is not at all disturbed by the onslaughts of the threefold miseries, for he accepts all miseries as the mercy of the Lord, thinking himself only worthy of more trouble due to his past misdeeds; and he sees that his miseries, by the grace of the Lord, are minimized to the lowest. Similarly, when he is happy he gives credit to the Lord, thinking himself unworthy of the happiness; he realizes that it is due only to the Lord's grace that he is in such a comfortable condition and able to render better service to the Lord. And, for the service of the Lord, he is always daring and active and is not influenced by attachment or aversion. Attachment means accepting things for one's own sense gratification, and detachment is the absence of such sensual attachment. But one fixed in Kṛṣṇa consciousness has neither attachment nor detachment because his life is dedicated in the service of the Lord. Consequently he is not at all angry even when his attempts are unsuccessful. A Kṛṣṇa conscious person is always steady in his determination.

TEXT 57

यः सर्वत्रानभिस्नेहस्तत्तत्प्राप्य शुभाशुभम् ।
नाभिनन्दति न द्वेष्टि तस्य प्रज्ञा प्रतिष्ठिता ॥ ५७ ॥

yaḥ sarvatrānabhisnehas
tat tat prāpya śubhāśubham
nābhinandati na dveṣṭi
tasya prajñā pratiṣṭhitā

yaḥ—one who; *sarvatra*—everywhere; *anabhisnehaḥ*—without affection; *tat*—that; *tat*—that; *prāpya*—achieving; *śubha*—good; *aśubham*—evil; *na*—never; *abhinandati*—prays; *na*—never; *dveṣṭi*—envies; *tasya*—his; *prajñā*—perfect knowledge; *pratiṣṭhita*—fixed.

TRANSLATION

He who is without attachment, who does not rejoice when he obtains good, nor lament when he obtains evil, is firmly fixed in perfect knowledge.

PURPORT

There is always some upheaval in the material world which may be good or evil. One who is not agitated by such material upheavals, who is unaffected by good and evil, is to be understood to be fixed in Kṛṣṇa consciousness. As long as one is in the material world there is always the possibility of good and evil because this world is full of duality. But one who is fixed in Kṛṣṇa consciousness is not affected by good and evil because he is simply concerned with Kṛṣṇa, who is all good absolute. Such consciousness in Kṛṣṇa situates one in a perfect transcendental position called, technically, *samādhi*.

TEXT 58

यदा संहरते चायं कूर्मोऽङ्गानीव सर्वशः ।
इन्द्रियाणीन्द्रियार्थेभ्यस्तस्य प्रज्ञा प्रतिष्ठिता ॥ ५८ ॥

yadā saṁharate cāyaṁ
kūrmo 'ṅgānīva sarvaśaḥ
indriyāṇīndriyārthebhyas
tasya prajñā pratiṣṭhitā

yadā—when; *saṁharate*—winds up; *ca*—also; *ayam*—all these; *kūrmaḥ*—tortoise; *aṅgāni*—limbs; *iva*—like; *sarvaśaḥ*—altogether; *indriyāṇi*—senses; *indriya-arthebhyaḥ*—from the sense objects; *tasya*—his; *prajñā*—consciousness; *pratiṣṭhitā*—fixed up.

TRANSLATION

One who is able to withdraw his senses from sense objects, as the tortoise draws his limbs within the shell, is to be understood as truly situated in knowledge.

PURPORT

The test of a *yogī*, devotee, or self-realized soul is that he is able to control the senses according to his plan. Most people, however, are servants of the senses and are thus directed by the dictation of the senses. That is the answer to the question as to how the *yogī* is situated. The senses are compared to venomous serpents. They want to act very loosely and without restriction. The *yogī*, or the devotee, must be very strong to control the serpents—like a snake charmer. He never allows them to act independently. There are many injunctions in the revealed scriptures; some of them are do-not's, and some of them are do's. Unless one is able to follow the do's and the do-not's, restricting oneself from sense enjoyment, it is not possible to be firmly fixed in Kṛṣṇa consciousness. The best example, set herein, is the tortoise. The tortoise can at any moment wind up his senses and exhibit them again at any time for particular purposes. Similarly, the senses of the Kṛṣṇa conscious persons are used only for some particular purpose in the service of the Lord and are withdrawn otherwise. Keeping the senses always in the service of the Lord is the example set by the analogy of the tortoise, who keeps the senses within.

TEXT 59

विषया विनिवर्तन्ते निराहारस्य देहिनः ।
रसवर्जं रसोऽप्यस्य परं दृष्ट्वा निवर्तते ॥ ५९ ॥

viṣayā vinivartante
nirāhārasya dehinaḥ
rasa-varjaṁ raso 'py asya
paraṁ dṛṣṭvā nivartate

viṣayāḥ—objects for sense enjoyment; *vinivartante*—are practiced to be refrained from; *nirāhārasya*—by negative restrictions; *dehinaḥ*—for the embodied; *rasa-varjam*—giving up the taste; *rasaḥ*—sense of enjoyment; *api*—although there is; *asya*—his; *param*—far superior things; *dṛṣṭvā*—by experiencing; *nivartate*—ceases from.

TRANSLATION

The embodied soul may be restricted from sense enjoyment, though the taste for sense objects remains. But, ceasing such engagements by experiencing a higher taste, he is fixed in consciousness.

PURPORT

Unless one is transcendentally situated, it is not possible to cease from sense enjoyment. The process of restriction from sense enjoyment by rules and regulations is something like restricting a diseased person from certain types of eatables. The patient, however, neither likes such restrictions, nor loses his taste for eatables. Similarly, sense restriction by some spiritual process like *aṣṭāṅga-yoga*, in the matter of *yama, niyama, āsana, prāṇā-yāma, pratyāhāra, dhāraṇā, dhyāna*, etc., is recommended for less intelligent persons who have no better knowledge. But one who has tasted the beauty of the Supreme Lord Kṛṣṇa, in the course of his advancement in Kṛṣṇa consciousness, no longer has a taste for dead material things. Therefore, restrictions are there for the less intelligent neophytes in the spiritual advancement of life, but such restrictions are only good if one actually has a taste for Kṛṣṇa consciousness. When one is actually Kṛṣṇa conscious, he automatically loses his taste for pale things.

TEXT 60

यततो ह्यपि कौन्तेय पुरुषस्य विपश्चितः ।
इन्द्रियाणि प्रमाथीनि हरन्ति प्रसभं मनः ॥ ६० ॥

yatato hy api kaunteya
puruṣasya vipaścitaḥ
indriyāṇi pramāthīni
haranti prasabhaṁ manaḥ

yatataḥ—while endeavoring; *hi*—certainly; *api*—in spite of; *kaunteya*—O son of Kuntī; *puruṣasya*—of the man; *vipaścitaḥ*—full of discriminating knowledge; *indriyāṇi*—the senses; *pramāthīni*—stimulated; *haranti*—throws forcefully; *prasabham*—by force; *manaḥ*—the mind.

TRANSLATION

The senses are so strong and impetuous, O Arjuna, that they forcibly carry away the mind even of a man of discrimination who is endeavoring to control them.

PURPORT

There are many learned sages, philosophers and transcendentalists who try to conquer the senses, but in spite of their endeavors, even the greatest of them sometimes fall victim to material sense enjoyment due to the agitated mind. Even Viśvāmitra, a great sage and perfect *yogī*, was misled by Menakā into sex enjoyment, although the *yogī* was endeavoring for sense control with severe types of penance and *yoga* practice. And, of course, there are so many similar instances in the history of the world. Therefore, it is very difficult to control the mind and the senses without being fully Kṛṣṇa conscious. Without engaging the mind in Kṛṣṇa, one cannot cease such material engagements. A practical example is given by Śrī Yāmunā-cārya, a great saint and devotee, who says: "Since my mind has been engaged in the service of the lotus feet of Lord Kṛṣṇa, and I have been enjoying an ever new transcendental humor, whenever I think of sex life with a woman, my face at once turns from it, and I spit at the thought."

Kṛṣṇa consciousness is such a transcendentally nice thing that automatically material enjoyment becomes distasteful. It is as if a hungry man had satisfied his hunger by a sufficient quantity of nutritious eatables. Mahārāja Ambarīṣa also conquered a great *yogī*, Durvāsā Muni, simply because his mind was engaged in Kṛṣṇa consciousness.

TEXT 61

तानि सर्वाणि संयम्य युक्त आसीत मत्परः ।
वशे हि यस्येन्द्रियाणि तस्य प्रज्ञा प्रतिष्ठिता ॥ ६१ ॥

tāni sarvāṇi saṁyamya
yukta āsīta mat-paraḥ
vaśe hi yasyendriyāṇi
tasya prajñā pratiṣṭhitā

tāni—those senses; *sarvāṇi*—all; *saṁyamya*—keeping under control; *yuktaḥ*—being engaged; *āsīta*—being so situated; *mat-paraḥ*—in relationship with Me; *vaśe*—in full subjugation; *hi*—certainly; *yasya*—one whose; *indriyāṇi*—senses; *tasya*—his; *prajñā*—consciousness; *pratiṣṭhitā*—fixed.

TRANSLATION

One who restrains his senses and fixes his consciousness upon Me is known as a man of steady intelligence.

PURPORT

That the highest conception of *yoga* perfection is Kṛṣṇa consciousness is clearly explained in this verse. And, unless one is Kṛṣṇa conscious, it is not at all possible to control the senses. As cited above, the great sage Durvāsā Muni picked a quarrel with Mahārāja Ambarīṣa, and Durvāsā Muni unnecessarily became angry out of pride and therefore could not check his senses. On the other hand, the King, although not as powerful a *yogī* as the sage, but a devotee of the Lord, silently tolerated all the sage's injustices and thereby emerged victorious. The King was able to control his senses because of the following qualifications, as mentioned in the *Śrīmad-Bhāgavatam*:

sa vai manaḥ kṛṣṇa-padāravindayor
vacāṁsi vaikuṇṭha-guṇānavarṇane
karau harer mandira-mārjanādiṣu
śrutiṁ cakārācyuta-sat-kathodaye

mukunda-liṅgālaya-darśane dṛśau
tad-bhṛtya-gātra-sparśe'ṅga-saṅgamam
ghrāṇaṁ ca tat-pāda-saroja-saurabhe
śrīmat-tulasyā rasanāṁ tad-arpite

pādau hareḥ kṣetra-padānusarpaṇe
śiro hṛṣīkeśa-padābhivandane
kāmaṁ ca dāsye na tu kāma-kāmyayā
yathottamaśloka-janāśrayā ratiḥ

"King Ambarīṣa fixed his mind on the lotus feet of Lord Kṛṣṇa, engaged his words in describing the abode of the Lord, his hands in cleansing the temple of the Lord, his ears in hearing the pastimes of the Lord, his eyes in seeing the form of the Lord, his body in touching the body of the devotee, his nostrils in smelling the flavor of the flowers offered to the lotus feet of the Lord, his tongue in tasting the *tulasī* leaves offered to Him, his legs in traveling to the holy place where His temple is situated, his head in offering obeisances unto the Lord, and his desires in fulfilling the desires of the Lord ... and all these qualifications made him fit to become a *mat-paraḥ* devotee of the Lord." (*Bhāg.* 9.4.18-20)

The word *mat-paraḥ* is most significant in this connection. How one can become a *mat-paraḥ* is described in the life of Mahārāja Ambarīṣa. Śrīla Baladeva Vidyābhūṣaṇa, a great scholar and *ācārya* in the line of the *mat-paraḥ*, remarks: "*mad-bhakti-prabhāveṇa sarvendriya-vijaya-pūrvikā svātma dṛṣṭiḥ sulabheti bhāvaḥ.*" "The senses can be completely controlled only by the strength of devotional service to Kṛṣṇa." Also the example of fire is sometimes given: "As the small flames within burn everything within the room, similarly Lord Viṣṇu, situated in the heart of the *yogī*, burns up all kinds of impurities." The *Yoga-sūtra* also prescribes meditation on Viṣṇu, and not meditation on the void. The so-called *yogīs* who meditate on something which is not the Viṣṇu form simply waste their time in a vain search after some phantasmagoria. We have to be Kṛṣṇa conscious—devoted to the Personality of Godhead. This is the aim of the real *yoga*.

TEXT 62

ध्यायतो विषयान्पुंसः सङ्गस्तेषूपजायते ।
सङ्गात्संजायते कामः कामात्क्रोधोऽभिजायते ॥ ६२ ॥

dhyāyato viṣayān puṁsaḥ
saṅgas teṣūpajāyate
saṅgāt sañjāyate kāmaḥ
kāmāt krodho 'bhijāyate

His Divine Grace A.C. Bhaktivedanta Swami Prabhupāda
the Founder-*Ācārya* of ISKCON and greatest exponent of
Kṛṣṇa consciousness in the western world.

Śrīla Bhaktisiddhānta Sarasvatī Gosvāmī Mahārājā
the spiritual master of
His Divine Grace A.C. Bhaktivedanta Swami Prabhupāda
and foremost scholar and devotee in the recent age.

Śrīla Gaura Kiśora Dās Bābājī Mahārāja
the spiritual master of
Śrīla Bhaktisiddhānta Sarasvatī Gosvāmī and
intimate student of Śrīla Ṭhākur Bhaktivinode

Śrīla Ṭhākur Bhaktivinode
the pioneer of the program to benedict
the entire world with Kṛṣṇa consciousness

Plate 1. Dhṛtarāṣṭra inquires from Sañjaya
about the events of the battle. (p. 32)

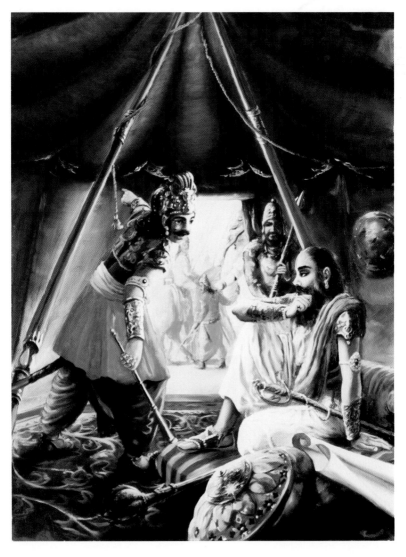

Plate 2. "O my teacher, behold the great army of the sons of Pāṇḍu." (*p. 35*)

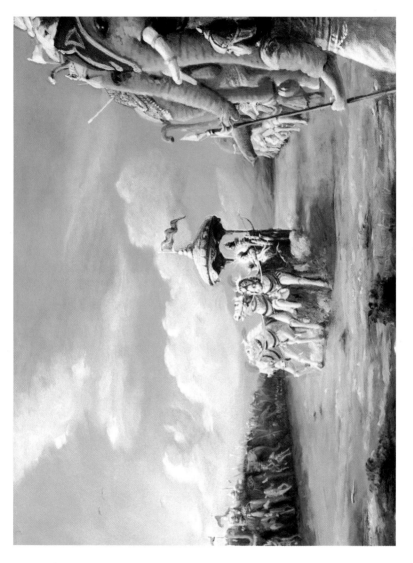

Plate 3. Kṛṣṇa and Arjuna in the midst of the two armies. (*p. 35*)

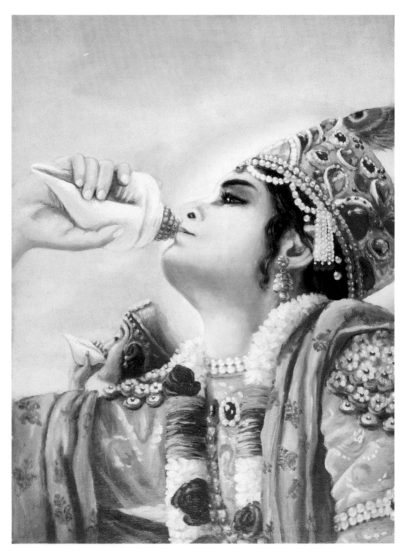

Plate 4. Kṛṣṇa and Arjuna sounded their transcendental conchshells. *(p. 43)*

Plate 5. When Arjuna saw all different grades of friends and relatives, he became overwhelmed with compassion. *(p. 53)*

Plate 6. The insulting of Draupadī. (*p. 41*)

Plate 7. The Blessed Lord said: The wise lament neither
for the living nor the dead. (*p. 85*)

Plate 8. The soul changes bodies as a person changes garments. (*p. 89*)

Plate 9. The body changes but the soul remains the same. (*p. 83-84*)

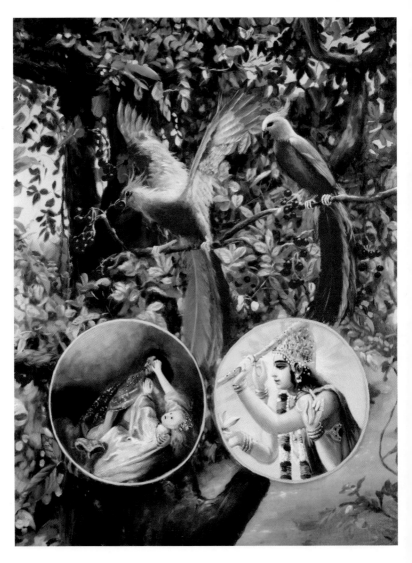

Plate 10. Kṛṣṇa and the living entity are seated
on the tree of the body. *(p. 102)*

Plate 11. While contemplating the objects of the senses, a person develops attachment for them. *(p. 149)*

Plate 12. "Be thou happy by this sacrifice because its performance
will bestow upon you all desirable things." (*p. 172*)

dhyayataḥ—while contemplating; *viṣayān*—sense objects; *puṁsaḥ*—of the person; *saṅgaḥ*—attachment; *teṣu*—in the sense objects; *upajāyate*—develops; *saṅgāt*—attachment; *sañjāyate*—develops; *kāmaḥ*—desire; *kāmāt*—from desire; *krodhaḥ*—anger; *abhijāyate*—becomes manifest.

TRANSLATION

While contemplating the objects of the senses, a person develops attachment for them, and from such attachment lust develops, and from lust anger arises.

PURPORT

One who is not Kṛṣṇa conscious is subjected to material desires while contemplating the objects of senses. The senses require real engagements, and if they are not engaged in the transcendental loving service of the Lord, they will certainly seek engagement in the service of materialism. In the material world everyone, including Lord Śiva and Lord Brahmā—to say nothing of other demigods in the heavenly planets—is subjected to the influence of sense objects, and the only method to get out of this puzzle of material existence is to become Kṛṣṇa conscious. Lord Śiva was deep in meditation, but when Pārvatī agitated him for sense pleasure, he agreed to the proposal, and as a result Kārtikeya was born. When Haridāsa Ṭhākur was a young devotee of the Lord, he was similarly allured by the incarnation of Māyā Devī, but Haridāsa easily passed the test because of his unalloyed devotion to Lord Kṛṣṇa. As illustrated in the above-mentioned verse of Śrī Yāmunācārya, a sincere devotee of the Lord shuns all material sense enjoyment due to his higher taste for spiritual enjoyment in the association of the Lord. That is the secret of success. One who is not, therefore, in Kṛṣṇa consciousness, however powerful he may be in controlling the senses by artificial repression, is sure ultimately to fail, for the slightest thought of sense pleasure will agitate him to gratify his desires.

TEXT 63

क्रोधाद्भवति सम्मोहः सम्मोहात्स्मृतिविभ्रमः ।
स्मृतिभ्रंशाद्बुद्धिनाशो बुद्धिनाशात्प्रणश्यति ॥ ६३ ॥

krodhād bhavati sammohaḥ
sammohāt smṛti-vibhramaḥ
smṛti-bhraṁśād buddhi-nāśo
buddhi-nāśāt praṇaśyati

krodhāt—from anger; *bhavati*—takes place; *sammohaḥ*—perfect illusion; *sammohāt*—from illusion; *smṛti*—of memory; *vibhramaḥ*—bewilderment; *smṛti-bhraṁśāt*—after bewilderment of memory; *buddhi-nāśaḥ*—loss of intelligence; *buddhi-nāśāt*—and from loss of intelligence; *praṇaśyati*—falls down.

TRANSLATION

From anger, delusion arises, and from delusion bewilderment of memory. When memory is bewildered, intelligence is lost, and when intelligence is lost, one falls down again into the material pool.

PURPORT

By development of Kṛṣṇa consciousness one can know that everything has its use in the service of the Lord. Those who are without knowledge of Kṛṣṇa consciousness artificially try to avoid material objects, and as a result, although they desire liberation from material bondage, they do not attain to the perfect stage of renunciation. On the other hand, a person in Kṛṣṇa consciousness knows how to use everything in the service of the Lord; therefore he does not become a victim of material consciousness. For example, for an impersonalist, the Lord, or the Absolute, being impersonal, cannot eat. Whereas an impersonalist tries to avoid good eatables, a devotee knows that Kṛṣṇa is the supreme enjoyer and that He eats all that is offered to Him in devotion. So, after offering good eatables to the Lord, the devotee takes the remnants, called *prasādam*. Thus everything becomes spiritualized and there is no danger of a downfall. The devotee takes *prasādam* in Kṛṣṇa consciousness, whereas the nondevotee rejects it as material. The impersonalist, therefore, cannot enjoy life due to his artificial renunciation; and for this reason, a slight agitation of the mind pulls him down again into the pool of material existence. It is said that such a soul, even though rising up to the point of liberation, falls down again due to his not having support in devotional service.

TEXT 64

रागद्वेषविमुक्तैस्तु विषयानिन्द्रियैश्चरन् ।
आत्मवश्यैर्विधेयात्मा प्रसादमधिगच्छति ॥ ६४ ॥

rāga-dveṣa-vimuktais tu
viṣayān indriyaiś caran
ātma-vaśyair vidheyātmā
prasādam adhigacchati

rāga—attachment; dveṣa—detachment; vimuktaiḥ—by one who has been free from such things; tu—but; viṣayān—sense objects; indriyaiḥ—by the senses; caran—acting; ātma-vaśyaiḥ—one who has control over; vidheyātmā—one who follows regulated freedom; prasādam—the mercy of the Lord; adhigacchati—attains.

TRANSLATION

One who can control his senses by practicing the regulated principles of freedom can obtain the complete mercy of the Lord and thus become free from all attachment and aversion.

PURPORT

It is already explained that one may externally control the senses by some artificial process, but unless the senses are engaged in the transcendental service of the Lord, there is every chance of a fall. Although the person in full Kṛṣṇa consciousness may apparently be on the sensual plane, because of his being Kṛṣṇa conscious, he has no attachment to sensual activities. The Kṛṣṇa conscious person is concerned only with the satisfaction of Kṛṣṇa, and nothing else. Therefore he is transcendental to all attachment. If Kṛṣṇa wants, the devotee can do anything which is ordinarily undesirable; and if Kṛṣṇa does not want, he shall not do that which he would have ordinarily done for his own satisfaction. Therefore to act or not to act is within his control because he acts only under the direction of Kṛṣṇa. This consciousness is the causeless mercy of the Lord, which the devotee can achieve in spite of his being attached to the sensual platform.

TEXT 65

प्रसादे सर्वदुःखानां हानिरस्योपजायते ।
प्रसन्नचेतसो ह्याशु बुद्धिः पर्यवतिष्ठते ॥ ६५ ॥

prasāde sarva-duḥkhānāṁ
hānir asyopajāyate
prasanna-cetaso hy āśu
buddhiḥ paryavatiṣṭhate

prasāde—on achievement of the causeless mercy of the Lord; *sarva*—all; *duḥkhānām*—material miseries; *hāniḥ*—destruction; *asya*—his; *upajāyate*—takes place; *prasanna-cetasaḥ*—of the happy-minded; *hi*—certainly; *āśu*—very soon; *buddhiḥ*—intelligence; *pari*—sufficiently; *avatiṣṭhate*—established.

TRANSLATION

For one who is so situated in the Divine consciousness, the threefold miseries of material existence exist no longer; in such a happy state, one's intelligence soon becomes steady.

TEXT 66

नास्ति बुद्धिरयुक्तस्य न चायुक्तस्य भावना ।
न चाभावयतः शान्तिरशान्तस्य कुतः सुखम् ॥ ६६ ॥

nāsti buddhir ayuktasya
na cāyuktasya bhāvanā
na cābhāvayataḥ śāntir
aśāntasya kutaḥ sukham

na asti—there cannot be; *buddhiḥ*—transcendental intelligence; *ayuktasya*—of one who is not connected (with Kṛṣṇa consciousness); *na*—neither; *ca*—and; *ayuktasya*—of one devoid of Kṛṣṇa consciousness; *bhāvanā*—mind fixed in happiness; *na*—neither; *ca*—and; *abhāvayataḥ*—one who is not fixed; *śāntiḥ*—peace; *aśāntasya*—of the unpeaceful; *kutaḥ*—where is; *sukham*—happiness.

TRANSLATION

One who is not in transcendental consciousness can have neither a controlled mind nor steady intelligence, without which there is no possibility of peace. And how can there be any happiness without peace?

PURPORT

Unless one is in Kṛṣṇa consciousness, there is no possibility of peace. So it is confirmed in the Fifth Chapter (5.29) that when one understands that Kṛṣṇa is the only enjoyer of all the good results of sacrifice and penance, and that He is the proprietor of all universal manifestations, that He is the real friend of all living entities, then only can one have real peace. Therefore, if one is not in Kṛṣṇa consciousness, there cannot be a final goal for the mind. Disturbance is due to want of an ultimate goal, and when one is certain that Kṛṣṇa is the enjoyer, proprietor and friend of everyone and everything, then one can, with a steady mind, bring about peace. Therefore, one who is engaged without a relationship with Kṛṣṇa is certainly always in distress and is without peace, however much one may make a show of peace and spiritual advancement in life. Kṛṣṇa consciousness is a self-manifested peaceful condition which can be achieved only in relationship with Kṛṣṇa.

TEXT 67

इन्द्रियाणां हि चरतां यन्मनोऽनुविधीयते ।
तदस्य हरति प्रज्ञां वायुर्नावमिवाम्भसि ॥ ६७ ॥

indriyāṇāṁ hi caratāṁ
yan mano 'nuvidhīyate
tad asya harati prajñāṁ
vāyur nāvam ivāmbhasi

indriyāṇām—of the senses; hi—certainly; caratām—while herding over; yat—that; manaḥ—mind; anuvidhīyate—becomes constantly engaged; tat—that; asya—his; harati—takes away; prajñām—intelligence; vāyuḥ—wind; nāvam—a boat; iva—like; ambhasi—on the water.

TRANSLATION

As a boat on the water is swept away by a strong wind, even one of the senses on which the mind focuses can carry away a man's intelligence.

PURPORT

Unless all of the senses are engaged in the service of the Lord, even one of them engaged in sense gratification can deviate the devotee from the path of transcendental advancement. As mentioned in the life of Mahārāja Ambarīṣa, all of the senses must be engaged in Kṛṣṇa consciousness, for that is the correct technique for controlling the mind.

TEXT 68

तस्माद्यस्य महाबाहो निगृहीतानि सर्वशः ।
इन्द्रियाणीन्द्रियार्थेभ्यस्तस्य प्रज्ञा प्रतिष्ठिता ॥ ६८ ॥

tasmād yasya mahā-bāho
nigṛhītāni sarvaśaḥ
indriyāṇīndriyārthebhyas
tasya prajñā pratiṣṭhitā

tasmāt—therefore; *yasya*—of one's; *mahā-bāho*—O mighty-armed one; *nigṛhītāni*—so curbed down; *sarvaśaḥ*—all around; *indriyāṇi*—the senses; *indriya-arthebhyaḥ*—for the sake of sense objects; *tasya*—his; *prajñā*—intelligence; *pratiṣṭhitā*—fixed.

TRANSLATION

Therefore, O mighty-armed, one whose senses are restrained from their objects is certainly of steady intelligence.

PURPORT

As enemies are curbed by superior force, similarly, the senses can be curbed not by any human endeavor, but only by keeping them engaged in the service of the Lord. One who has understood this—that only by Kṛṣṇa consciousness is one really established in intelligence and that one should practice this art under the guidance of a bona fide spiritual master—is called *sādhaka*, or a suitable candidate for liberation.

TEXT 69

या निशा सर्वभूतानां तस्यां जागर्ति संयमी ।
यस्यां जाग्रति भूतानि सा निशा पश्यतो मुनेः ॥ ६९ ॥

yā niśā sarva-bhūtānāṁ
tasyāṁ jāgarti saṁyamī
yasyāṁ jāgrati bhūtāni
sā niśā paśyato muneḥ

yā—what; niśā—is night; sarva—all; bhūtānām—of living entities; tasyām—in that; jāgarti—wakeful; saṁyamī—the self-controlled; yasyām—in which; jāgrati—awake; bhūtāni—all beings; sā—that is; niśā—night; paśyataḥ—for the introspective; muneḥ—sage.

TRANSLATION

What is night for all beings is the time of awakening for the self-controlled; and the time of awakening for all beings is night for the introspective sage.

PURPORT

There are two classes of intelligent men. The one is intelligent in material activities for sense gratification, and the other is introspective and awake to the cultivation of self-realization. Activities of the introspective sage, or thoughtful man, are night for persons materially absorbed. Materialistic persons remain asleep in such a night due to their ignorance of self-realization. The introspective sage remains alert in the "night" of the materialistic men. The sage feels transcendental pleasure in the gradual advancement of spiritual culture, whereas the man in materialistic activities, being asleep to self-realization, dreams of varieties of sense pleasure, feeling sometimes happy and sometimes distressed in his sleeping condition. The introspective man is always indifferent to materialistic happiness and distress. He goes on with his self-realization activities undisturbed by material reaction.

TEXT 70

आपूर्यमाणमचलप्रतिष्ठं
समुद्रमापः प्रविशन्ति यद्वत् ।
तद्वत्कामा यं प्रविशन्ति सर्वे
स शान्तिमाप्नोति न कामकामी ॥ ७० ॥

āpūryamāṇam acala-pratiṣṭhaṁ
samudram āpaḥ praviśanti yadvat
tadvat kāmā yaṁ praviśanti sarve
sa śāntim āpnoti na kāma-kāmī

āpūryamāṇam—always filled; *acala-pratiṣṭham*—steadily situated; *samudram*—the ocean; *āpaḥ*—water; *praviśanti*—enter; *yadvat*—as; *tadvat*—so; *kāmāḥ*—desires; *yam*—unto one; *praviśanti*—enter; *sarve*—all; *saḥ*—that person; *śāntim*—peace; *āpnoti*—achieves; *na*—not; *kāma-kāmī*—one who desires to fulfill desires.

TRANSLATION

A person who is not disturbed by the incessant flow of desires—that enter like rivers into the ocean which is ever being filled but is always still—can alone achieve peace, and not the man who strives to satisfy such desires.

PURPORT

Although the vast ocean is always filled with water, it is always, especially during the rainy season, being filled with much more water. But the ocean remains the same—steady; it is not agitated, nor does it cross beyond the limit of its brink. That is also true of a person fixed in Kṛṣṇa consciousness. As long as one has the material body, the demands of the body for sense gratification will continue. The devotee, however, is not disturbed by such desires because of his fullness. A Kṛṣṇa conscious man is not in need of anything because the Lord fulfills all his material necessities. Therefore he is like the ocean—always full in himself. Desires may come to him like the waters of the rivers that flow into the ocean, but he is steady in his activities, and he is not even slightly disturbed by desires for sense gratification. That is the proof of a Kṛṣṇa conscious man—one who has lost all inclinations for material sense gratification, although the desires are present. Because he remains satisfied in the transcendental loving service of the Lord, he can remain steady, like the ocean, and therefore enjoy full peace. Others, however, who fulfill desires even up to the limit of liberation, what to speak of material success, never attain peace. The fruitive workers, the salvationists, and also the *yogīs* who are after mystic powers, are all unhappy because of unfulfilled desires. But the person in Kṛṣṇa consciousness is happy in the service of the Lord, and he has no desires to be fulfilled. In fact, he does not even desire liberation from the so-called material bondage. The devotees of Kṛṣṇa have no material desires, and therefore they are in perfect peace.

TEXT 71

विहाय कामान्यः सर्वान्पुमांश्चरति निःस्पृहः ।
निर्ममो निरहंक्रारः स शान्तिमधिगच्छति ॥ ७१ ॥

*vihāya kāmān yaḥ sarvān
pumāṁś carati niḥspṛhaḥ
nirmamo nirahaṅkāraḥ
sa śāntim adhigacchati*

vihāya—after giving up; *kāmān*—all material desires for sense gratification; *yaḥ*—the person; *sarvān*—all; *pumān*—a person; *carati*—lives; *niḥspṛhaḥ*—desireless; *nirmamaḥ*—without a sense of proprietorship; *nirahaṅkāraḥ*—without false ego; *saḥ*—all; *śāntim*—perfect peace; *adhigacchati*—attains.

TRANSLATION

A person who has given up all desires for sense gratification, who lives free from desires, who has given up all sense of proprietorship and is devoid of false ego—he alone can attain real peace.

PURPORT

To become desireless means not to desire anything for sense gratification. In other words, desire for becoming Kṛṣṇa conscious is actually desirelessness. To understand one's actual position as the eternal servitor of Kṛṣṇa, without falsely claiming this material body to be oneself and without falsely claiming proprietorship over anything in the world, is the perfect stage of Kṛṣṇa consciousness. One who is situated in this perfect stage knows that because Kṛṣṇa is the proprietor of everything, therefore everything must be used for the satisfaction of Kṛṣṇa. Arjuna did not want to fight for his own sense satisfaction, but when he became fully Kṛṣṇa conscious he fought because Kṛṣṇa wanted him to fight. For himself there was no desire to fight, but for Kṛṣṇa the same Arjuna fought to his best ability. Desire for the satisfaction of Kṛṣṇa is really desirelessness; it is not an artificial attempt to abolish desires. The living entity cannot be desireless or senseless, but he does have to change the quality of the desires. A materially desireless person certainly knows that everything belongs to Kṛṣṇa (*īśāvāsyam idaṁ sarvam*), and therefore he does not falsely claim proprietorship over anything. This transcendental knowledge is based on self-realization—namely, knowing perfectly well that every living entity is the eternal part and parcel of Kṛṣṇa in spiritual identity. and therefore the eternal position of the living entity is never on the level of Kṛṣṇa or greater than Him. This understanding of Kṛṣṇa consciousness is the basic principle of real peace.

TEXT 72

एषा ब्राह्मी स्थितिः पार्थ नैनां प्राप्य विमुह्यति ।
स्थित्वास्यामन्तकालेऽपि ब्रह्मनिर्वाणमृच्छति ॥ ७२ ॥

eṣā brāhmī sthitiḥ pārtha
naināṁ prāpya vimuhyati
sthitvāsyām anta-kāle 'pi
brahma-nirvāṇam ṛcchati

eṣā—this; *brāhmī*—spiritual; *sthitiḥ*—situation; *pārtha*—O son of Pṛthā; *na*—never; *enām*—this; *prāpya*—achieving; *vimuhyati*—bewilders; *sthitvā*—being so situated; *asyām*—being so; *anta-kāle*—at the end of life; *api*—also; *brahma-nirvāṇam*—spiritual (kingdom of God); *ṛcchati*—attains.

TRANSLATION

That is the way of the spiritual and godly life, after attaining which a man is not bewildered. Being so situated, even at the hour of death, one can enter into the kingdom of God.

PURPORT

One can attain Kṛṣṇa consciousness or divine life at once, within a second-or one may not attain such a state of life even after millions of births. It is only a matter of understanding and accepting the fact. Khaṭvāṅga Mahārāja attained this state of life just a few minutes before his death, by surrendering unto Kṛṣṇa. *Nirvāṇa* means ending the process of materialistic life. According to Buddhist philosophy, there is only void after the completion of this material life, but *Bhagavad-gītā* teaches differently. Actual life begins after the completion of this material life. For the gross materialist it is sufficient to know that one has to end this materialistic way of life, but for persons who are spiritually advanced, there is another life after this materialistic life. Before ending this life, if one fortunately becomes Kṛṣṇa conscious, he at once attains the stage of *Brahma-nirvāṇa*. There is no difference between the kingdom of God and the devotional service of the Lord. Since both of them are on the absolute plane, to be engaged in the transcendental loving service of the Lord is to have attained the spiritual kingdom. In the material world there are activities of sense gratification, whereas in the spiritual world there are activities of Kṛṣṇa consciousness. Attainment of Kṛṣṇa consciousness even during this life is immediate attainment of Brahman, and one who is situated in Kṛṣṇa consciousness has certainly already entered into the kingdom of God.

Brahman is just the opposite of matter. Therefore *brāhmī sthitiḥ* means "not on the platform of material activities." Devotional service of the Lord is accepted in the *Bhagavad-gītā* as the liberated stage. Therefore, *brāhmī-sthitiḥ* is liberation from material bondage.

Śrīla Bhaktivinode Ṭhākur has summarized this Second Chapter of the *Bhagavad-gītā* as being the contents for the whole text. In the *Bhagavad-gītā*, the subject matters are *karma-yoga*, *jñāna-yoga*, and *bhakti-yoga*. In the Second Chapter *karma-yoga* and *jñāna-yoga* have been clearly discussed, and a glimpse of *bhakti-yoga* has also been given, as the contents for the complete text.

Thus end the Bhaktivedanta Purports to the Second Chapter of the Śrīmad-Bhagavad-gītā in the matter of its Contents.

CHAPTER THREE

Karma-yoga

TEXT 1

अर्जुन उवाच ।
ज्यायसी चेत्कर्मणस्ते मता बुद्धिर्जनार्दन ।
तत्किं कर्मणि घोरे मां नियोजयसि केशव ॥ १ ॥

arjuna uvāca
jyāyasī cet karmaṇas te
matā buddhir janārdana
tat kiṁ karmaṇi ghore mām
niyojayasi keśava

arjunaḥ—Arjuna; *uvāca*—said; *jyāyasī*—speaking very highly; *cet*—although; *karmaṇaḥ*—than fruitive action; *te*—your; *matā*—opinion; *buddhiḥ*—intelligence; *janārdana*—O Kṛṣṇa; *tat*—therefore; *kim*—why; *karmaṇi*—in action; *ghore*—ghastly; *mām*—me; *niyojayasi*—engaging me; *keśava*—O Kṛṣṇa.

TRANSLATION

Arjuna said: O Janārdana, O Keśava, why do You urge me to engage in this ghastly warfare, if You think that intelligence is better than fruitive work?

PURPORT

The Supreme Personality of Godhead Śrī Kṛṣṇa has very elaborately described the constitution of the soul in the previous chapter, with a view to deliver His intimate friend Arjuna from the ocean of material grief. And the path of realization has been recommended: *buddhi-yoga*, or Kṛṣṇa consciousness. Sometimes Kṛṣṇa consciousness is misunderstood to be inertia, and one with such a misunderstanding often withdraws to a secluded place to become fully Kṛṣṇa conscious by chanting the holy name of Lord Kṛṣṇa. But without being trained in the philosophy of Kṛṣṇa consciousness, it is not advisable to chant the holy name of Kṛṣṇa in a secluded place where one may acquire only cheap adoration from the innocent public. Arjuna also thought of Kṛṣṇa consciousness or *buddhi -yoga*, or intelligence in spiritual advancement of knowledge, as something like retirement from active life and the practice of penance and austerity at a secluded place. In other words, he wanted to skillfully avoid the fighting by using Kṛṣṇa consciousness as an excuse. But as a sincere student, he placed the matter before his master and questioned Kṛṣṇa as to his best course of action. In answer, Lord Kṛṣṇa elaborately explained *karma-yoga*, or work in Kṛṣṇa consciousness, in this Third Chapter.

TEXT 2

व्यामिश्रेणेव वाक्येन बुद्धिं मोहयसीव मे ।
तदेकं वद निश्चित्य येन श्रेयोऽहमाप्नुयाम् ॥ २ ॥

vyāmiśreṇeva vākyena
buddhiṁ mohayasīva me
tad ekaṁ vada niścitya
yena śreyo 'ham āpnuyām

vyāmiśreṇa—by equivocal; *iva*—as; *vākyena*—words; *buddhim*—intelligence; *mohayasi*—bewildering; *iva*—as; *me*—my; *tat*—therefore; *ekam*—only one; *vada*—please tell; *niścitya*—ascertaining; *yena*—by which; *śreyaḥ*—real benefit; *aham*—I; *āpnuyām*—may have it.

TRANSLATION

My intelligence is bewildered by Your equivocal instructions. Therefore, please tell me decisively what is most beneficial for me.

PURPORT

In the previous chapter, as a prelude to the *Bhagavad-gītā*, many different paths were explained, such as *sāṅkhya-yoga, buddhi-yoga*, control of the senses by intelligence, work without fruitive desire, and the position of the neophyte. This was all presented unsystematically. A more organized outline of the path would be necessary for action and understanding. Arjuna, therefore, wanted to clear up these apparently confusing matters so that any common man could accept them without misinterpretation. Although Kṛṣṇa had no intention of confusing Arjuna by any jugglery of words, Arjuna could not follow the process of Kṛṣṇa consciousness—either by inertia or active service. In other words, by his questions he is clearing the path of Kṛṣṇa consciousness for all students who seriously want to understand the mystery of the *Bhagavad-gītā*.

TEXT 3

श्रीभगवानुवाच ।
लोकेऽस्मिन्द्विविधा निष्ठा पुरा प्रोक्ता मयानघ ।
ज्ञानयोगेन साङ्ख्यानां कर्मयोगेन योगिनाम् ॥ ३ ॥

śrī-bhagavān uvāca
loke 'smin dvi-vidhā niṣṭhā
purā proktā mayānagha
jñāna-yogena sāṅkhyānām
karma-yogena yoginām

śrī bhagavān uvāca—the Supreme Personality of Godhead said; *loke*—in the world; *asmin*—this; *dvi-vidhā*—two kinds of; *niṣṭhā*—faith; *purā*—formerly; *proktā*—was said; *mayā*—by Me; *anagha*—O sinless one; *jñāna-*

yogena—by the linking process of knowledge; *sāṅkhyānām*—of the empiric philosophers; *karma-yogena*—by the linking process of devotion; *yogīnām* —of the devotees.

TRANSLATION

The Blessed Lord said: O sinless Arjuna, I have already explained that there are two classes of men who realize the Self. Some are inclined to understand Him by empirical, philosophical speculation, and others are inclined to know Him by devotional work.

PURPORT

In the Second Chapter, verse 39, the Lord explained two kinds of procedures—namely *sāṅkhya-yoga* and *karma-yoga*, or *buddhi-yoga*. In this verse, the Lord explains the same more clearly. *Sāṅkhya-yoga*, or the analytical study of the nature of spirit and matter, is the subject matter for persons who are inclined to speculate and understand things by experimental knowledge and philosophy. The other class of men work in Kṛṣṇa consciousness, as it is explained in the 61st verse of the Second Chapter. The Lord has explained, also in the 39th verse, that by working by the principles of *buddhi-yoga*, or Kṛṣṇa consciousness, one can be relieved from the bonds of action; and, furthermore, there is no flaw in the process. The same principle is more clearly explained in the 61st verse—that this *buddhi-yoga* is to depend entirely on the Supreme (or more specifically, on Kṛṣṇa), and in this way all the senses can be brought under control very easily. Therefore, both the *yogas* are interdependant, as religion and philosophy. Religion without philosophy is sentiment, or sometimes fanaticism, while philosophy without religion is mental speculation. The ultimate goal is Kṛṣṇa, because the philosophers who are also sincerely searching after the Absolute Truth come in the end to Kṛṣṇa consciousness. This is also stated in the *Bhagavad-gītā*. The whole process is to understand the real position of the self in relation to the Superself. The indirect process is philosophical speculation, by which, gradually, one may come to the point of Kṛṣṇa consciousness; and the other process is directly connecting with everything in Kṛṣṇa consciousness. Of these two, the path of Kṛṣṇa consciousness is better because it does not depend on purifying the senses by a philosophical process. Kṛṣṇa consciousness is itself the purifying process, and by the direct method of devotional service it is simultaneously easy and sublime.

TEXT 4

न कर्मणामनारम्भान्नैष्कर्म्यं पुरुषोऽश्नुते ।
न च संन्यसनादेव सिद्धिं समधिगच्छति ॥ ४ ॥

na karmaṇām anārambhān
naiṣkarmyaṁ puruṣo 'śnute
na ca sannyasanād eva
siddhiṁ samadhigacchati

na—without; *karmaṇām*—of the prescribed duties; *anārambhāt*—non-performance; *naiṣkarmyam*—freedom from reaction; *puruṣah*—man; *aśnute*—achieve; *na*—nor; *ca*—also; *sannyasanāt*—by renunciation; *eva*—simply; *siddhim*—success; *samadhigacchati*—attain.

TRANSLATION

Not by merely abstaining from work can one achieve freedom from reaction, nor by renunciation alone can one attain perfection.

PURPORT

The renounced order of life can be accepted upon being purified by the discharge of the prescribed form of duties which are laid down just to purify the heart of materialistic men. Without purification, one cannot attain success by abruptly adopting the fourth order of life (*sannyāsa*). According to the empirical philosophers, simply by adopting *sannyāsa*, or retiring from fruitive activities, one at once becomes as good as Nārāyaṇa. But Lord Kṛṣṇa does not approve this principle. Without purification of heart, *sannyāsa* is simply a disturbance to the social order. On the other hand, if someone takes to the transcendental service of the Lord, even without discharging his prescribed duties, whatever he may be able to advance in the cause is accepted by the Lord (*buddhi-yoga*). *Svalpam apy asya dharmasya trāyate mahato bhayāt.* Even a slight performance of such a principle enables one to overcome great difficulties.

TEXT 5

न हि कश्चित्क्षणमपि जातु तिष्ठत्यकर्मकृत् ।
कार्यते ह्यवशः कर्म सर्वः प्रकृतिजैर्गुणैः ॥ ५ ॥

> na hi kaścit kṣaṇam api
> jātu tiṣṭhaty akarma-kṛt
> kāryate hy avaśaḥ karma
> sarvaḥ prakṛti-jair guṇaiḥ

na—nor; hi—certainly; kaścit—anyone; kṣaṇam—even a moment; api—also; jātu—even; tiṣṭhati—stands; akarma-kṛt—without doing something; kāryate—is forced to do; hi—certainly; avaśaḥ—helplessly; karma—work; sarvaḥ—everything; prakṛti-jaiḥ—out of the modes of material nature; guṇaiḥ—by the qualities.

TRANSLATION

All men are forced to act helplessly according to the impulses born of the modes of material nature; therefore no one can refrain from doing something, not even for a moment.

PURPORT

It is not a question of embodied life, but it is the nature of the soul to be always active. Without the presence of the spirit soul, the material body cannot move. The body is only a dead vehicle to be worked by the spirit soul, which is always active and cannot stop even for a moment. As such, the spirit soul has to be engaged in the good work of Kṛṣṇa consciousness, otherwise it will be engaged in occupations dictated by illusory energy. In contact with material energy, the spirit soul acquires material modes, and to purify the soul from such affinities it is necessary to engage in the prescribed duties enjoined in the śāstras. But if the soul is engaged in his natural function of Kṛṣṇa consciousness, whatever he is able to do is good for him. The Śrīmad-Bhāgavatam affirms this:

> tyaktvā sva-dharmaṁ caraṇāmbujaṁ harer
> bhajann apakvo 'tha patet tato yadi
> yatra kva vābhadram abhūd amuṣya kiṁ
> ko vārtha āpto 'bhajatāṁ sva-dharmataḥ.

"If someone takes to Kṛṣṇa consciousness, even though he may not follow the prescribed duties in the śāstras nor execute the devotional service properly, and even though he may fall down from the standard, there is no loss or evil for him. But if he carries out all the injunctions for purification in the śāstras, what does it avail him if he is not Kṛṣṇa conscious?" (Bhāg.

1.5.17) So the purificatory process is necessary for reaching this point of
Kṛṣṇa consciousness. Therefore, sannyāsa, or any purificatory process, is to
help reach the ultimate goal of becoming Kṛṣṇa conscious, without which
everything is considered a failure.

TEXT 6

कर्मेन्द्रियाणि संयम्य य आस्ते मनसा स्मरन् ।
इन्द्रियार्थान्विमूढात्मा मिथ्याचारः स उच्यते ॥ ६ ॥

*karmendriyāṇi saṁyamya
ya āste manasā smaran
indriyārthān vimūḍhātmā
mithyācāraḥ sa ucyate*

karma-indriyāṇi—the five working sense organs; *saṁyamya*—controlling;
yaḥ—anyone who; *āste*—remains; *manasā*—by mind; *smaran*—thinking;
indriya-arthān—sense objects; *vimūḍha*—foolish; *ātmā*—soul; *mithyā-ācāraḥ*
—pretender; *saḥ*—he; *ucyate*—is called.

TRANSLATION

One who restrains the senses and organs of action, but whose mind
dwells on sense objects, certainly deludes himself and is called a pretender.

PURPORT

There are many pretenders who refuse to work in Kṛṣṇa consciousness
but make a show of meditation, while actually dwelling within the mind
upon sense enjoyment. Such pretenders may also speak on dry philosophy
in order to bluff sophisticated followers, but according to this verse these
are the greatest cheaters. For sense enjoyment one can act in any capacity
of the social order, but if one follows the rules and regulations of his
particular status, he can make gradual progress in purifying his existence.
But he who makes a show of being a *yogī*, while actually searching for the
objects of sense gratification, must be called the greatest cheater, even though
he sometimes speaks of philosophy. His knowledge has no value because
the effects of such a sinful man's knowledge are taken away by the illusory
energy of the Lord. Such a pretender's mind is always impure, and therefore his show of yogic meditation has no value whatsoever.

TEXT 7

यस्त्विन्द्रियाणि मनसा नियम्यारभतेऽर्जुन ।
कर्मेन्द्रियैः कर्मयोगमसक्तः स विशिष्यते ॥ ७ ॥

*yas tv indriyāṇi manasā
niyamyārabhate 'rjuna
karmendriyaiḥ karma-yogam
asaktaḥ sa viśiṣyate*

yaḥ—one who; *tu*—but; *indriyāṇi*—senses; *manasā*—by the mind; *niyamya*—regulating; *ārabhate*—begins; *arjuna*—O Arjuna; *karma-indriyaiḥ*—by the active sense organs; *karma-yogam*—devotion; *asaktaḥ*—without attachment; *saḥ*—he; *viśiṣyate*—by far the better.

TRANSLATION

On the other hand, he who controls the senses by the mind and engages his active organs in works of devotion, without attachment, is by far superior.

PURPORT

Instead of becoming a pseudo-transcendentalist for the sake of wanton living and sense enjoyment, it is far better to remain in one's own business and execute the purpose of life, which is to get free from material bondage and enter into the kingdom of God. The prime *svārtha-gati*, or goal of self-interest, is to reach Viṣṇu. The whole institution of *varṇa* and *āśrama* is designed to help us reach this goal of life. A householder can also reach this destination by regulated service in Kṛṣṇa consciousness. For self-realization, one can live a controlled life, as prescribed in the *śāstras*, and continue carrying out his business without attachment, and in that way make progress. Such a sincere person who follows this method is far better situated than the false pretender who adopts show-bottle spiritualism to cheat the innocent public. A sincere sweeper in the street is far better than the charlatan meditator who meditates only for the sake of making a living.

TEXT 8

नियतं कुरु कर्म त्वं कर्म ज्यायो ह्यकर्मणः ।
शरीरयात्रापि च ते न प्रसिद्ध्येदकर्मणः ॥ ८ ॥

niyataṁ kuru karma tvaṁ
karma jyāyo hy akarmaṇaḥ
śarīra-yātrāpi ca te
na prasiddhyed akarmaṇaḥ

niyatam—prescribed; *kuru*—do; *karma*—duties; *tvam*—you; *karma*—work; *jyāyaḥ*—better; *hi*—than; *akarmaṇaḥ*—without work; *śarīra*—bodily; *yātrā*—maintenance; *api*—even; *ca*—also; *te*—your; *na*—never; *prasiddhyet*—effected; *akarmaṇaḥ*—without work.

TRANSLATION

Perform your prescribed duty, for action is better than inaction. A man cannot even maintain his physical body without work.

PURPORT

There are many pseudo-meditators who misrepresent themselves as belonging to high parentage, and great professional men who falsely pose that they have sacrificed everything for the sake of advancement in spiritual life. Lord Kṛṣṇa did not want Arjuna to become a pretender, but that he perform his prescribed duties as set forth for kṣatriyas. Arjuna was a householder and a military general, and therefore it was better for him to remain as such and perform his religious duties as prescribed for the householder kṣatriya. Such activities gradually cleanse the heart of a mundane man and free him from material contamination. So-called renunciation for the purpose of maintenance is never approved by the Lord, nor by any religious scripture. After all, one has to maintain one's body and soul together by some work. Work should not be given up capriciously, without purification of materialistic propensities. Anyone who is in the material world is certainly possessed of the impure propensity for lording it over material nature, or, in other words, for sense gratification. Such polluted propensities have to be cleared. Without doing so, through prescribed duties, one should never attempt to become a so-called transcendentalist, renouncing work and living at the cost of others.

TEXT 9

यज्ञार्थात्कर्मणोऽन्यत्र लोकोऽयं कर्मबन्धनः ।
तदर्थं कर्म कौन्तेय मुक्तसङ्गः समाचर ॥ ९ ॥

yajñārthāt karmaṇo 'nyatra
loko 'yaṁ karma-bandhanaḥ
tad-arthaṁ karma kaunteya
mukta-saṅgaḥ samācara

yajña-arthāt—only for the sake of Yajña, or Viṣṇu; *karmaṇaḥ*—work done; *anyatra*—otherwise; *lokaḥ*—this world; *ayam*—this; *karma-bandhanaḥ* —bondage by work; *tat*—Him; *artham*—for the sake of; *karma*—work; *kaunteya*—O son of Kuntī; *mukta-saṅgaḥ*—liberated from association; *samācara*—do it perfectly.

TRANSLATION

Work done as a sacrifice for Viṣṇu has to be performed, otherwise work binds one to this material world. Therefore, O son of Kuntī, perform your prescribed duties for His satisfaction, and in that way you will always remain unattached and free from bondage.

PURPORT

Since one has to work even for the simple maintenance of the body, the prescribed duties for a particular social position and quality are so made that that purpose can be fulfilled. *Yajña* means Lord Viṣṇu, or sacrificial performances. All sacrificial performances also are meant for the satisfaction of Lord Viṣṇu. The *Vedas* enjoin: *yajño vai viṣṇuḥ*. In other words, the same purpose is served whether one performs prescribed *yajñas* or directly serves Lord Viṣṇu. Kṛṣṇa consciousness is therefore performance of *yajña* as it is prescribed in this verse. The *varṇāśrama* institution also aims at this for satisfying Lord Viṣṇu. "*Varṇāśramācāra-vatā puruṣeṇa paraḥ pumān/viṣṇur ārādhyate...*" (*Viṣṇu Purāṇa* 3.8.8) Therefore one has to work for the satisfaction of Viṣṇu. Any other work done in this material world will be a cause of bondage, for both good and evil work have their reactions, and any reaction binds the performer. Therefore, one has to work in Kṛṣṇa consciousness to satisfy Kṛṣṇa (or Viṣṇu); and while performing such activities one is in a liberated stage. This is the great art of doing work, and in the beginning this process requires very expert guidance. One should therefore act very diligently, under the expert guidance of a devotee of Lord Kṛṣṇa, or under the direct instruction of Lord Kṛṣṇa Himself (under whom Arjuna had the opportunity to work). Nothing should be performed for sense gratification, but everything should be done for the satisfaction of Kṛṣṇa. This practice will not only save one from the reaction of work, but will also gradually elevate one to transcendental loving service of the Lord, which alone can raise one to the kingdom of God.

TEXT 10

सहयज्ञाः प्रजाः सृष्ट्वा पुरोवाच प्रजापतिः ।
अनेन प्रसविष्यध्वमेष वोऽस्त्विष्टकामधुक् ॥ १० ॥

saha-yajñāḥ prajāḥ sṛṣṭvā
purovāca prajāpatiḥ
anena prasaviṣyadhvam
eṣa vo 'stv iṣṭa-kāma-dhuk

saha—along with; *yajñāḥ*—sacrifices; *prajāḥ*—generations; *sṛṣṭvā*—by creating; *purā*—anciently; *uvāca*—said; *prajā-patiḥ*—the Lord of creatures; *anena*—by this; *prasaviṣyadhvam*—be more and more prosperous; *eṣaḥ*—certainly; *vaḥ*—your; *astu*—let it be; *iṣṭa*—all desirable; *kāma-dhuk*—bestower.

TRANSLATION

In the beginning of creation, the Lord of all creatures sent forth generations of men and demigods, along with sacrifices for Viṣṇu, and blessed them by saying, "Be thou happy by this *yajña* [sacrifice] because its performance will bestow upon you all desirable things."

PURPORT

The material creation by the Lord of creatures (Viṣṇu) is a chance offered to the conditioned souls to come back home-back to Godhead. All living entities within the material creation are conditioned by material nature because of their forgetfulness of their relationship to Kṛṣṇa, the Supreme Personality of Godhead. The Vedic principles are to help us understand this eternal relation as it is stated in the *Bhagavad-gītā: vedaiś ca sarvair aham eva vedyaḥ.* The Lord says that the purpose of the *Vedas* is to understand Him. In the Vedic hymns it is said: *patiṁ viśvasyātmeśvaram.* Therefore, the Lord of the living entities is the Supreme Personality of Godhead, Viṣṇu. In the *Śrīmad-Bhāgavatam* also Śrīla Śukadeva Gosvāmī describes the Lord as *pati* in so many ways:

śriyaḥ-patir yajña-patiḥ prajā-patir
dhiyāṁ patir loka-patir dharā-patiḥ
patir gatiś cāndhaka-vṛṣṇi-sātvatāṁ
prasīdatāṁ me bhagavān satāṁ patiḥ
(Bhāg. 2.4.20)

The *prajā-pati* is Lord Viṣṇu, and He is the Lord of all living creatures, all worlds, and all beauties, and the protector of everyone. The Lord created this material world for the conditioned souls to learn how to perform *yajñas* (sacrifice) for the satisfaction of Viṣṇu, so that while in the material world they can live very comfortably without anxiety. Then after finishing the present material body, they can enter into the kingdom of God. That is the whole program for the conditioned soul. By performance of *yajña*, the conditioned souls gradually become Kṛṣṇa conscious and become godly in all respects. In this age of Kali, the *saṅkīrtana-yajña* (the chanting of the names of God) is recommended by the Vedic scriptures, and this transcendental system was introduced by Lord Caitanya for the deliverance of all men in this age. *Saṅkīrtana-yajña* and Kṛṣṇa consciousness go well together. Lord Kṛṣṇa in His devotional form (as Lord Caitanya) is mentioned in the *Śrīmad-Bhāgavatam* as follows, with special reference to the *saṅkīrtana-yajña:*

kṛṣṇa-varṇaṁ tviṣākṛṣṇāṁ sāṅgopāṅgāstra-pārṣadam
yajñaiḥ saṅkīrtana-prāyair yajanti hi su-medhasaḥ

"In this age of Kali, people who are endowed with sufficient intelligence

will worship the Lord, who is accompanied by His associates, by performance of saṅkīrtana-yajña." (Bhāg. 11.5.29) Other yajñas prescribed in the
Vedic literatures are not easy to perform in this age of Kali, but the
saṅkīrtana-yajña is easy and sublime for all purposes.

TEXT 11

देवान्भावयतानेन ते देवा भावयन्तु वः ।
परस्परं भावयन्तः श्रेयः परमवाप्स्यथ ॥ ११ ॥

devān bhāvayatānena
te devā bhāvayantu vaḥ
parasparaṁ bhāvayantaḥ
śreyaḥ param avāpsyatha

devān—demigods; bhāvayata—having been pleased; anena—by this
sacrifice; te—those; devāḥ—the demigods; bhāvayantu—will please; vaḥ—you;
parasparam—mutual; bhāvayantaḥ—pleasing one another; sreyaḥ—benediction; param—the supreme; avāpsyatha—do you achieve.

TRANSLATION

**The demigods, being pleased by sacrifices, will also please you; thus
nourishing one another, there will reign general prosperity for all.**

PURPORT

The demigods are empowered administrators of material affairs. The
supply of air, light, water and all other benedictions for maintaining the
body and soul of every living entity are entrusted to the demigods, who are
innumerable assistants in different parts of the body of the Supreme
Personality of Godhead. Their pleasures and displeasures are dependant
on the performance of yajñas by the human being. Some of the yajñas are
meant to satisfy particular demigods; but even in so doing, Lord Viṣṇu is
worshiped in all yajñas as the chief beneficiary. It is stated also in the
Bhagavad-gītā that Kṛṣṇa Himself is the beneficiary of all kinds of yajñas:
bhoktāraṁ yajña-tapasām. Therefore, ultimate satisfaction of the yajñapati
is the chief purpose of all yajñas. When these yajñas are perfectly

performed, naturally the demigods in charge of the different departments of supply are pleased, and there is no scarcity in the supply of natural products.

Performance of *yajñas* has many side benefits, ultimately leading to liberation from the material bondage. By performance of *yajñas*, all activities become purified, as it is stated in the *Vedas*:

> *āhāra-śuddhau sattva-śuddhiḥ sattva-śuddhau*
> *dhruvā smṛtiḥ smṛti-lambhe sarva-granthīnāṁ vipra-mokṣaḥ*

As it will be explained in the following verse, by performance of *yajña*, one's eatables become sanctified, and by eating sanctified foodstuffs, one's very existence becomes purified; by the purification of existence, finer tissues in the memory become sanctified, and when memory is sanctified, one can think of the path of liberation, and all these combined together lead to Kṛṣṇa consciousness, the great necessity of present-day society.

TEXT 12

इष्टान्भोगान्हि वो देवा दास्यन्ते यज्ञभाविताः ।
तैर्दत्तानप्रदायैभ्यो यो भुङ्क्ते स्तेन एव सः ॥ १२ ॥

> *iṣṭān bhogān hi vo devā*
> *dāsyante yajña-bhāvitāḥ*
> *tair dattān apradāyaibhyo*
> *yo bhuṅkte stena eva saḥ*

iṣṭān—desired; *bhogān*—necessities of life; *hi*—certainly; *vaḥ*—unto you; *devāḥ*—the demigods; *dāsyante*—award; *yajña-bhāvitāḥ*—being satisfied by the performance of sacrifices; *taiḥ*—by them; *dattān*—things given; *apradāya*—without offering; *ebhyaḥ*—to the demigods; *yaḥ*—he who; *bhuṅkte*—enjoys; *stenaḥ*—thief; *eva*—certainly; *saḥ*—is he.

TRANSLATION

In charge of the various necessities of life, the demigods, being satisfied by the performance of yajña [sacrifice], supply all necessities to man. But he who enjoys these gifts, without offering them to the demigods in return, is certainly a thief.

PURPORT

The demigods are authorized supplying agents on behalf of the Supreme Personality of Godhead, Viṣṇu. Therefore, they must be satisfied by the performance of prescribed yajñas. In the Vedas, there are different kinds of yajñas prescribed for different kinds of demigods, but all are ultimately offered to the Supreme Personality of Godhead. For one who cannot understand what the Personality of Godhead is, sacrifice to the demigods is recommended. According to the different material qualities of the persons concerned, different types of yajñas are recommended in the Vedas. Worship of different demigods is also on the same basis—namely, according to different qualities. For example, the meat-eaters are recommended to worship the goddess Kālī, the ghastly form of material nature, and before the goddess the sacrifice of animals is recommended. But for those who are in the mode of goodness, the transcendental worship of Viṣṇu is recommended. But ultimately, all yajñas are meant for gradual promotion to the transcendental position. For ordinary men, at least five yajñas, known as pañca-mahāyajña, are necessary.

One should know, however, that all the necessities of life that the human society requires are supplied by the demigod agents of the Lord. No one can manufacture anything. Take, for example, all the eatables of human society. These eatables include grains, fruits, vegetables, milk, sugar, etc., for the persons in the mode of goodness, and also eatables for the non-vegetarians, like meats, etc., none of which can be manufactured by men. Then again, take for example heat, light, water, air, etc., which are also necessities of life—none of them can be manufactured by the human society. Without the Supreme Lord, there can be no profuse sunlight, moonlight, rainfall, breeze, etc., without which no one can live. Obviously, our life is dependant on supplies from the Lord. Even for our manufacturing enterprises, we require so many raw materials like metal, sulphur, mercury, manganese, and so many essentials—all of which are supplied by the agents of the Lord, with the purpose that we should make proper use of them to keep ourselves fit and healthy for the purpose of self-realization, leading to the ultimate goal of life, namely, liberation from the material struggle for existence. This aim of life is attained by performance of yajñas. If we forget the purpose of human life and simply take supplies from the agents of the Lord for sense gratification and become more and more entangled in material existence, which is not the purpose of creation, certainly we become thieves, and therefore we are punished by the laws of material nature. A society of thieves can never be happy because they have no aim in life. The gross materialist thieves have no ultimate goal of life. They are simply directed to sense gratification; nor do they have knowledge of how to perform yajñas. Lord Caitanya, however, inaugurated the easiest performance of yajña, namely the saṅkīrtana-yajña, which can be performed by anyone in the world who accepts the principles of Kṛṣṇa consciousness.

TEXT 13

यज्ञशिष्टाशिनः सन्तो मुच्यन्ते सर्वकिल्बिषैः ।
भुञ्जते ते त्वघं पापा ये पचन्त्यात्मकारणात् ॥ १३ ॥

yajña-śiṣṭāśinaḥ santo
mucyante sarva-kilbiṣaiḥ
bhuñjate te tv aghaṁ pāpā
ye pacanty ātma-kāraṇāt

yajña-śiṣṭa—food taken after performance of yajña; aśinaḥ—eaters; santaḥ—the devotees; mucyante—get relief from; sarva—all kinds of; kilbiṣaiḥ—sins; bhuñjate—enjoy; te—they; tu—but; agham—grievous sins; pāpāḥ—sinners; ye—those; pacanti—prepare food; ātma-kāraṇāt—for sense enjoyment.

TRANSLATION

The devotees of the Lord are released from all kinds of sins because they eat food which is offered first for sacrifice. Others, who prepare food for personal sense enjoyment, verily eat only sin.

PURPORT

The devotees of the Supreme Lord, or the persons who are in Kṛṣṇa consciousness, are called santas, and they are always in love with the Lord as it is described in the Brahma-saṁhitā: premāñjana-cchurita-bhakti-vilocanena santaḥ sadaiva hṛdayeṣu vilokayanti. The santas, being always in a compact of love with the Supreme Personality of Godhead, Govinda (the giver of all pleasures), or Mukunda (the giver of liberation), or Kṛṣṇa (the all-attractive person), cannot accept anything without first offering it to the Supreme Person. Therefore, such devotees always perform yajñas in different modes of devotional service, such as *śravaṇam, kīrtanam, smaraṇam, arcanam,* etc., and these performances of *yajñas* keep them always aloof from all kinds of contamination of sinful association in the material world. Others, who prepare food for self or sense gratification, are not only thieves, but are also the eaters of all kinds of sins. How can a person be happy if he is both a thief and sinful? It is not possible. Therefore, in order for people to become happy in all respects, they must be taught to perform the easy process of *saṅkīrtana-yajña,* in full Kṛṣṇa consciousness. Otherwise, there can be no peace or happiness in the world.

TEXT 14

अन्नाद्भवन्ति भूतानि पर्जन्यादन्नसम्भवः ।
यज्ञाद्भवति पर्जन्यो यज्ञः कर्मसमुद्भवः ॥ १४ ॥

annād bhavanti bhūtāni
parjanyād anna-sambhavaḥ
yajñād bhavati parjanyo
yajñaḥ karma-samudbhavaḥ

annāt—from grains; *bhavanti*—grow; *bhūtāni*—the material bodies; *parjanyāt*—from rains; *anna*—food grains; *sambhavaḥ*—are made possible; *yajñāt*—from the performance of sacrifice; *bhavati*—becomes possible; *parjanyaḥ*—rains; *yajñaḥ*—performance of *yajña*; *karma*—prescribed duties; *samudbhavaḥ*—born of.

TRANSLATION

All living bodies subsist on food grains, which are produced from rain. Rains are produced by performance of yajña [sacrifice], and yajña is born of prescribed duties.

PURPORT

Śrīla Baladeva Vidyābhūṣaṇa, a great commentator on the *Bhagavad-gītā,* writes as follows: *ye indrādy-aṅga-tayāvasthitaṁ yajñaṁ sarveśvaraṁ viṣṇum abhyarccya taccheṣam aśnanti tena taddeha-yāntrāṁ sampādayanti te santaḥ sarveśvarasya bhaktāḥ sarva-kilviṣair anādi-kāla-vivṛddhair ātmānubhava-pratibandhakair nikhilaiḥ pāpair vimucyante.* The Supreme

Lord, who is known as the *yajña-puruṣaḥ*, or the personal beneficiary of all sacrifices, is the master of all demigods who serve Him as the different limbs of the body serve the whole. Demigods like Indra, Candra, Varuṇa, etc., are appointed officers who manage material affairs, and the Vedas direct sacrifices to satisfy these demigods so that they may be pleased to supply air, light and water sufficiently to produce food grains. When Lord Kṛṣṇa is worshiped, the demigods, who are different limbs of the Lord, are also automatically worshiped; therefore there is no separate need to worship the demigods. For this reason, the devotees of the Lord, who are in Kṛṣṇa consciousness, offer food to Kṛṣṇa and then eat—a process which nourishes the body spiritually. By such action not only are past sinful reactions in the body vanquished, but the body becomes immunized to all contamination of material nature. When there is an epidemic disease, an antiseptic vaccine protects a person from the attack of such an epidemic. Similarly, food offered to Lord Viṣṇu and then taken by us makes us sufficiently resistant to material affection, and one who is accustomed to this practice is called a devotee of the Lord. Therefore, a person in Kṛṣṇa consciousness, who eats only food offered to Kṛṣṇa, can counteract all reactions of past material infections, which are impediments to the progress of self-realization. On the other hand, one who does not do so continues to increase the volume of sinful action, and this prepares the next body to resemble hogs and dogs, to suffer the resultant reactions of all sins. The material world is full of contaminations, and one who is immunized by accepting *prasādam* of the Lord (food offered to Viṣṇu) is saved from the attack, whereas one who does not do so becomes subjected to contamination.

Food grains or vegetables are factually eatables. The human being eats different kinds of food grains, vegetables, fruits, etc., and the animals eat the refuse of the food grains and vegetables, grass, plants, etc. Human beings who are accustomed to eating meat and flesh must also depend on the production of vegetation in order to eat the animals. Therefore, ultimately, we have to depend on the production of the field and not on the production of big factories. The field production is due to sufficient rain from the sky, and such rains are controlled by demigods like Indra, sun, moon, etc., and they are all servants of the Lord. The Lord can be satisfied by sacrifices; therefore, one who cannot perform them will find himself in scarcity—that is the law of nature. *Yajña*, specifically the *saṅkīrtana-yajña* prescribed for this age, must therefore be performed to save us at least from scarcity of food supply.

TEXT 15

कर्म ब्रह्मोद्भवं विद्धि ब्रह्माक्षरसमुद्भवम् ।
तस्मात्सर्वगतं ब्रह्म नित्यं यज्ञे प्रतिष्ठितम् ॥ १५ ॥

karma brahmodbhavaṁ viddhi
brahmākṣara-samudbhavam
tasmāt sarva-gataṁ brahma
nityaṁ yajñe pratiṣṭhitam

karma—work; *brahma*-Vedas; *udbhavam*—produced from; *viddhi*—one should know; *brahma*—the Vedas; *akṣara*—the Supreme Brahman (Personality of Godhead); *samudbhavam*; directly manifested; *tasmāt*—therefore; *sarva-gatam*—all-pervading; *brahma*—Transcendence; *nityam*—eternally; *yajñe*—in sacrifice; *pratiṣṭhitam*—situated.

TRANSLATION

Regulated activities are prescribed in the Vedas, and the Vedas are directly manifested from the Supreme Personality of Godhead. Consequently the all-pervading Transcendence is eternally situated in acts of sacrifice.

PURPORT

Yajñārtha karma, or the necessity of work for the satisfaction of Kṛṣṇa only, is more expressly stated in this verse. If we have to work for the satisfaction of the *yajña-puruṣa*, Viṣṇu, then we must find out the direction of work in Brahman, or the transcendental *Vedas*. The *Vedas* are therefore codes of working directions. Anything performed without the direction of the *Vedas* is called *vikarma*, or unauthorized or sinful work. Therefore, one should always take direction from the *Vedas* to be saved from the reaction of work. As one has to work in ordinary life by the direction of the state, similarly, one has to work under direction of the supreme state of the Lord. Such directions in the *Vedas* are directly manifested from the breathing of the Supreme Personality of Godhead. It is said: *asya mahato bhūtasya naśvasitam etad yad ṛg-vedo yajur-vedaḥ sāma-vedo 'tharvāṅ girasaḥ*. "The four *Vedas*—namely the Ṛg-veda, Yajur-veda, Sāma-veda and Atharva-veda—are all emanations from the breathing of the great Personality of Godhead." The Lord, being omnipotent, can speak by breathing air, as it is confirmed in the *Brahma-saṁhitā*, for the Lord has the omnipotence to perform through each of His senses the actions of all other senses. In other words, the Lord can speak through His breathing, and He can impregnate by His eyes. In fact, it is said that He glanced over material nature and thus fathered all living entities. After creating or impregnating the conditioned souls into the womb of material nature, He gave His directions in the Vedic wisdom as to how such conditioned souls can return home, back to Godhead. We should always remember that the conditioned souls in material nature are all eager for material enjoyment. But the Vedic directions are so made that one can satisfy one's perverted desires, then return to Godhead, having finished his so-called enjoyment. It is a chance for the conditioned souls to attain liberation; therefore the conditioned souls must try to follow the process of *yajña* by becoming Kṛṣṇa conscious. Even those who cannot follow the Vedic injunctions may adopt the principles of Kṛṣṇa consciousness, and that will take the place of performance of Vedic *yajñas*, or *karmas*.

TEXT 16

एवं प्रवर्तितं चक्रं नानुवर्तयतीह यः ।
अघायुरिन्द्रियारामो मोघं पार्थ स जीवति ॥ १६ ॥

evaṁ pravartitaṁ cakraṁ
nānuvartayatīha yaḥ
aghāyur indriyārāmo
moghaṁ pārtha sa jīvati

evam—thus prescribed; *pravartitam*—established by the *Vedas*; *cakram*—cycle; *na*—does not; *anuvartayati*—adopt; *iha*—in this life; *yaḥ*—one who; *aghāyuḥ*—life full of sins; *indriya-ārāmaḥ*—satisfied in sense gratification; *mogham*—useless; *pārtha*—O son of Pṛthā (Arjuna); *saḥ*—one who does so; *jīvati*—lives.

TRANSLATION

My dear Arjuna, a man who does not follow this prescribed Vedic system of sacrifice certainly leads a life of sin, for a person delighting only in the senses lives in vain.

PURPORT

The mammonist philosophy of work very hard and enjoy sense gratification is condemned herein by the Lord. Therefore, for those who want to enjoy this material world, the above-mentioned cycle of performing *yajñas* is absolutely necessary. One who does not follow such regulations is living a very risky life, being condemned more and more. By nature's law, this human form of life is specifically meant for self-realization, in either of the three ways—namely *karma-yoga*, *jñāna-yoga*, or *bhakti-yoga*. There is no necessity of rigidly following the performances of the prescribed *yajñas* for the transcendentalists who are above vice and virtue; but those who are engaged in sense gratification require purification by the above-mentioned cycle of *yajña* performances. There are different kinds of activities. Those who are not Kṛṣṇa conscious are certainly engaged in sensory consciousness; therefore they need to execute pious work. The *yajña* system is planned in such a way that sensory conscious persons may satisfy their desires without becoming entangled in the reaction of sense-gratificatory work. The prosperity of the world depends not on our own efforts but on the background arrangement of the Supreme Lord, directly carried out by the demigods. Therefore, the *yajñas* are directly aimed at the particular demigod mentioned in the *Vedas*. Indirectly, it is the practice of Kṛṣṇa consciousness, because when one masters the performance of *yajñas*, one is sure to become Kṛṣṇa conscious. But if by performing *yajñas* one does not become Kṛṣṇa conscious, such principles are counted as only moral codes. One should not, therefore, limit his progress only to the point of moral codes, but should transcend them, to attain Kṛṣṇa consciousness.

TEXT 17

यस्त्वात्मरतिरेव स्यादात्मतृप्तश्च मानवः ।
आत्मन्येव च सन्तुष्टस्तस्य कार्यं न विद्यते ॥ १७ ॥

yas tv ātma-ratir eva syād
ātma-tṛptaś ca mānavaḥ
ātmany eva ca santuṣṭas
tasya kāryaṁ na vidyate

yaḥ—one who; *tu*—but; *ātma-ratiḥ*—takes pleasure; *eva*—certainly; *syāt*—remains; *ātma-tṛptaḥ*—self-illuminated; *ca*—and; *mānavaḥ*—a man; *ātmani*—

in himself; *eva*—only; *ca*—and; *santuṣṭaḥ*—perfectly satiated; *tasya*—his; *kāryam*—duty; *na*—does not; *vidyate*—exist.

TRANSLATION

One who is, however, taking pleasure in the self, who is illumined in the self, who rejoices in and is satisfied with the self only, fully satiated—for him there is no duty.

PURPORT

A person who is *fully* Kṛṣṇa conscious, and is fully satisfied by his acts in Kṛṣṇa consciousness, no longer has any duty to perform. Due to his being Kṛṣṇa conscious, all impiety within is instantly cleansed, an effect of many, many thousands of *yajña* performances. By such clearing of consciousness, one becomes fully confident of his eternal position in relationship with the Supreme. His duty thus becomes self-illuminated by the grace of the Lord, and therefore he no longer has any obligations to the Vedic injunctions. Such a Kṛṣṇa conscious person is no longer interested in material activities and no longer takes pleasure in material arrangements like wine, women and similar infatuations.

TEXT 18

नैव तस्य कृतेनार्थो नाकृतेनेह कश्चन ।
न चास्य सर्वभूतेषु कश्चिदर्थव्यपाश्रयः ॥ १८ ॥

naiva tasya kṛtenārtho
nākṛteneha kaścana
na cāsya sarva-bhūteṣu
kaścid artha-vyapāśrayaḥ

na—never; *eva*—certainly; *tasya*—his; *kṛtena*—by discharge of duty; *arthaḥ*—purpose; *na*—nor; *akṛtena*—without discharge of duty; *iha*—in this world; *kaścana*—whatever; *na*—never; *ca*—and; *asya*—of him; *sarva-bhūteṣu*—in all living beings; *kaścit*—any; *artha*—purpose; *vyapa-āśrayaḥ*—taking shelter of.

TRANSLATION

A self-realized man has no purpose to fulfill in the discharge of his prescribed duties, nor has he any reason not to perform such work. Nor has he any need to depend on any other living being.

PURPORT

A self-realized man is no longer obliged to perform any prescribed duty, save and except activities in Kṛṣṇa consciousness. Kṛṣṇa consciousness is not inactivity either, as will be explained in the following verses. A Kṛṣṇa conscious man does not take shelter of any person—man or demigod. Whatever he does in Kṛṣṇa consciousness is sufficient in the discharge of his obligation.

TEXT 19

तस्मादसक्तः सततं कार्यं कर्म समाचर ।
असक्तो ह्याचरन्कर्म परमाप्नोति पूरुषः ॥ १९ ॥

tasmād asaktaḥ satatam
kāryaṁ karma samācara
asakto hy ācaran karma
param āpnoti pūruṣaḥ

tasmāt—therefore; asaktaḥ—without attachment; satatam—constantly; kāryam—as duty; karma—work; samācara—perform; asaktaḥ—nonattachment; hi—certainly; ācaran—performing; karma—work; param—the Supreme; āpnoti—achieves; pūruṣaḥ—a man.

TRANSLATION

Therefore, without being attached to the fruits of activities, one should act as a matter of duty; for by working without attachment, one attains the Supreme.

PURPORT

The Supreme is the Personality of Godhead for the devotees, and liberation for the impersonalist. A person, therefore, acting for Kṛṣṇa, or in

Kṛṣṇa consciousness, under proper guidance and without attachment to the result of the work, is certainly making progress toward the supreme goal of life. Arjuna is told that he should fight in the Battle of Kurukṣetra for the interest of Kṛṣṇa because Kṛṣṇa wanted him to fight. To be a good man or a nonviolent man is a personal attachment, but to act on behalf of the Supreme is to act without attachment for the result. That is perfect action of the highest degree, recommended by the Supreme Personality of Godhead, Śrī Kṛṣṇa. Vedic rituals, like prescribed sacrifices, are performed for purification of impious activities that were performed in the field of sense gratification. But action in Kṛṣṇa consciousness is transcendental to the reactions of good or evil work. A Kṛṣṇa conscious person has no attachment for the result but acts on behalf of Kṛṣṇa alone. He engages in all kinds of activities, but is completely nonattached.

TEXT 20

कर्मणैव हि संसिद्धिमास्थिता जनकादयः ।
लोकसंग्रहमेवापि सम्पश्यन्कर्तुमर्हसि ॥ २० ॥

*karmaṇaiva hi saṁsiddhim
āsthitā janakādayaḥ
loka-saṅgraham evāpi
sampaśyan kartum arhasi*

karmaṇā—by work; *eva*—even; *hi*—certainly; *saṁsiddhim*—perfection; *āsthitāḥ*—situated; *janaka-ādayaḥ*—kings like Janaka and others; *loka-saṅgraham*—educating the people in general; *eva*—also; *api*—for the sake of; *sampaśyan*—by considering; *kartum*—to act; *arhasi*—deserve.

TRANSLATION

Even kings like Janaka and others attained the perfectional stage by performance of prescribed duties. Therefore, just for the sake of educating the people in general, you should perform your work.

PURPORT

Kings like Janaka and others were all self-realized souls; consequently they had no obligation to perform the prescribed duties in the *Vedas*.

Nonetheless they performed all prescribed activities just to set examples
for the people in general. Janaka was the father of Sītā, and father-in-law
of Lord Śrī Rāma. Being a great devotee of the Lord, he was transcendentally situated, but because he was the King of Mithila (a subdivision of
Behar province in India), he had to teach his subjects how to fight right-
eously in battle. He and his subjects fought to teach people in general that
violence is also necessary in a situation where good arguments fail. Before
the Battle of Kurukṣetra, every effort was made to avoid the war, even by
the Supreme Personality of Godhead, but the other party was determined
to fight. So for such a right cause, there is a necessity for fighting.
Although one who is situated in Kṛṣṇa consciousness may not have any
interest in the world, he still works to teach the public how to live and
how to act. Experienced persons in Kṛṣṇa consciousness can act in such a
way that others will follow, and this is explained in the following verse.

TEXT 21

यद्यदाचरति श्रेष्ठस्तत्तदेवेतरो जनः ।
स यत्प्रमाणं कुरुते लोकस्तदनुवर्तते ॥ २१ ॥

yad yad ācarati śreṣṭhas
tat tad evetaro janaḥ
sa yat pramāṇaṁ kurute
lokas tad anuvartate

yat—whatever; *yat*—and whichever; *ācarati*—does he act; *śreṣṭhaḥ*—
respectable leader; *tat*—that; *tat*—and that alone; *eva*—certainly; *itaraḥ*—
common; *janaḥ*—person; *saḥ*—he; *yat*—whichever; *pramāṇam*—evidence;
kurute—does perform; *lokaḥ*—all the world; *tat*—that; *anuvartate*—follow in
the footsteps.

TRANSLATION

**Whatever action is performed by a great man, common men follow in
his footsteps. And whatever standards he sets by exemplary acts, all the
world pursues.**

PURPORT

People in general always require a leader who can teach the public by
practical behavior. A leader cannot teach the public to stop smoking if he

himself smokes. Lord Caitanya said that a teacher should behave properly even before he begins teaching. One who teaches in that way is called ācārya, or the ideal teacher. Therefore, a teacher must follow the principles of śāstra (scripture) to reach the common man. The teacher cannot manufacture rules against the principles of revealed scriptures. The revealed scriptures, like Manu-saṁhitā and similar others, are considered the standard books to be followed by human society. Thus the leader's teaching should be based on the principles of the standard rules as they are practiced by the great teachers. The Śrīmad-Bhāgavatam also affirms that one should follow in the footsteps of great devotees, and that is the way of progress on the path of spiritual realization. The king or the executive head of a state, the father and the school teacher are all considered to be natural leaders of the innocent people in general. All such natural leaders have a great responsibility to their dependants; therefore they must be conversant with standard books of moral and spiritual codes.

TEXT 22

न मे पार्थास्ति कर्तव्यं त्रिषु लोकेषु किञ्चन ।
नानवाप्तमवाप्तव्यं वर्त एव च कर्मणि ॥ २२ ॥

na me pārthāsti kartavyaṁ
triṣu lokeṣu kiñcana
nānavāptam avāptavyaṁ
varta eva ca karmaṇi

na—none; me—Mine; pārtha—O son of Pṛthā; asti—there is; kartavyam—any prescribed duty; triṣu—in the three; lokeṣu—planetary systems; kiñcana—anything; na—no; anavāptam—in want; avāptavyam—to be gained; varte—engaged; eva—certainly; ca—also; karmaṇi—in one's prescribed duty.

TRANSLATION

O son of Pṛthā, there is no work prescribed for Me within all the three planetary systems. Nor am I in want of anything, nor have I need to obtain anything—and yet I am engaged in work.

PURPORT

The Supreme Personality of Godhead is described in the Vedic literatures as follows:

> *tam īśvarāṇāṁ paramaṁ maheśvaram*
> *taṁ devatānāṁ paramaṁ ca daivatam*
> *patiṁ patīnāṁ paramaṁ parastād*
> *vidāma devaṁ bhuvaneśam īḍyam*

> *na tasya kāryaṁ karaṇaṁ ca vidyate*
> *na tat-samaś cābhyadhikaś ca dṛśyate*
> *parāsya śaktir vividhaiva śrūyate*
> *svā-bhāvikī jñāna-bala-kriyā ca.*

"The Supreme Lord is the controller of all other controllers, and He is the greatest of all the diverse planetary leaders. Everyone is under His control. All entities are delegated with particular power only by the Supreme Lord; they are not supreme themselves. He is also worshipable by all demigods and is the supreme director of all directors. Therefore, He is transcendental to all kinds of material leaders and controllers and is worshipable by all. There is no one greater than Him, and He is the supreme cause of all causes.

"He does not possess bodily form like that of an ordinary living entity. There is no difference between His body and His soul. He is absolute. All His senses are transcendental. Any one of His senses can perform the action of any other sense. Therefore, no one is greater than Him or equal to Him. His potencies are multifarious, and thus His deeds are automatically performed as a natural sequence." (*Śvetāśvatara Upaniṣad* 6.7-8)

Since everything is in full opulence in the Personality of Godhead and is existing in full truth, there is no duty for the Supreme Personality of Godhead to perform. One who must receive the results of work has some designated duty, but one who has nothing to achieve within the three planetary systems certainly has no duty. And yet Lord Kṛṣṇa is engaged on the Battlefield of Kurukṣetra as the leader of the *kṣatriyas* because the *kṣatriyas* are duty-bound to give protection to the distressed. Although He is above all the regulations of the revealed scriptures, He does not do anything that violates the revealed scriptures.

TEXT 23

यदि ह्यहं न वर्तेयं जातु कर्मण्यतन्द्रितः ।

मम वर्त्मानुवर्तन्ते मनुष्याः पार्थ सर्वशः ॥ २३ ॥

yadi hy ahaṁ na varteyaṁ
jātu karmaṇy atandritaḥ
mama vartmānuvartante
manuṣyāḥ pārtha sarvaśaḥ

yadi—if; *hi*—certainly; *aham*—I; *na*—do not; *varteyam*—thus engage; *jātu*—ever; *karmaṇi*—in the performance of prescribed duties; *atandritaḥ*—with great care; *mama*—My; *vartma*—path; *anuvartante*—would follow; *manuṣyāḥ*—all men; *pārtha*—O son of Pṛthā; *sarvaśaḥ*—in all respects.

TRANSLATION

For, if I did not engage in work, O Pārtha, certainly all men would follow My path.

PURPORT

In order to keep the balance of social tranquility for progress in spiritual life, there are traditional family usages meant for every civilized man. Although such rules and regulations are for the conditioned souls and not Lord Kṛṣṇa, because He descended to establish the principles of religion, He followed the prescribed rules. Otherwise, common men would follow in His footsteps because He is the greatest authority. From the *Śrīmad-Bhāgavatam* it is understood that Lord Kṛṣṇa was performing all the religious duties at home and out of home, as required of a householder.

TEXT 24

उत्सीदेयुरिमे लोका न कुर्यां कर्म चेदहम् ।

संकरस्य च कर्ता स्यामुपहन्यामिमाः प्रजाः ॥ २४ ॥

utsīdeyur ime lokā
na kuryāṁ karma ced aham
saṅkarasya ca kartā syām
upahanyām imāḥ prajāḥ

utsīdeyuḥ—put into ruin; *ime*—all these; *lokāḥ*—worlds; *na*—do not; *kuryām*—perform; *karma*—prescribed duties; *cet*—if; *aham*—I; *saṅkarasya*—of unwanted population; *ca*—and; *kartā*—creator; *syām*—shall be; *upahanyām*—destroy; *imāḥ*—all these; *prajāḥ*—living entities.

TRANSLATION

If I should cease to work, then all these worlds would be put to ruination. I would also be the cause of creating unwanted population, and I would thereby destroy the peace of all sentient beings.

PURPORT

Varṇa-saṅkara is unwanted population which disturbs the peace of the general society. In order to check this social disturbance, there are prescribed rules and regulations by which the population can automatically become peaceful and organized for spiritual progress in life. When Lord Kṛṣṇa descends, naturally He deals with such rules and regulations in order to maintain the prestige and necessity of such important performances. The Lord is the father of all living entities, and if the living entities are misguided, indirectly the responsibility goes to the Lord. Therefore, whenever there is general disregard of regulative principles, the Lord Himself descends and corrects the society. We should, however, note carefully that although we have to follow in the footsteps of the Lord, we still have to remember that we cannot imitate Him. Following and imitating are not on the same level. We cannot imitate the Lord by lifting Govardhana Hill, as the Lord did in His childhood. It is impossible for any human being. We have to follow His instructions, but we may not imitate Him at any time. The *Śrīmad-Bhāgavatam* affirms:

> *naitat samācarej jātu manasāpi hy anīśvaraḥ*
> *vinaśyaty ācaran mauḍhyād yathā 'rudro 'bdhijaṁ viṣam*

> *īśvarāṇāṁ vacaḥ satyaṁ tathaivācaritaṁ kvacit*
> *teṣāṁ yat sva-vaco yuktaṁ buddhimāṁs tat samācaret*

"One should simply follow the instructions of the Lord and His empowered servants. Their instructions are all good for us, and any intelligent person will perform them as instructed. However, one should guard against trying to imitate their actions. One should not try to drink the ocean of poison in imitation of Lord Śiva." (*Bhāg.* 10.33.30)

We should always consider the position of the *īśvaras*, or those who can actually control the movements of the sun and moon, as superior. Without such power, one cannot imitate the *īśvaras*, who are superpowerful. Lord Śiva drank poison to the extent of swallowing an ocean, but if any common man tries to drink even a fragment of such poison, he will be killed. There are many psuedo-devotees of Lord Śiva who want to indulge in smoking gāñjā (marijuana) and similar intoxicating drugs, forgetting that by so imitating the acts of Lord Śiva they are calling death very near. Similarly, there are some psuedo-devotees of Lord Kṛṣṇa who prefer to imitate the Lord in His *rāsa-līlā*, or dance of love, forgetting their inability to lift Govardhana Hill. It is best, therefore, that one not try to imitate the powerful, but simply follow their instructions; nor should one try to occupy their posts without qualification. There are so many "incarnations" of God without the power of the Supreme Godhead.

TEXT 25

सक्ताः कर्मण्यविद्वांसो यथा कुर्वन्ति भारत ।
कुर्याद्विद्वांस्तथासक्तश्चिकीर्षुर्लोकसंग्रहम् ॥ २५ ॥

saktāḥ karmaṇy avidvāṁso
yathā kurvanti bhārata
kuryād vidvāṁs tathāsaktaś
cikīrṣur loka-saṅgraham

saktāḥ—being attached; *karmaṇi*—prescribed duties; *avidvāṁsaḥ*—the ignorant; *yathā*—as much as; *kurvanti*—do it; *bhārata*—O descendant of Bharata; *kuryāt*—must do; *vidvān*—the learned; *tathā*—thus; *asaktaḥ*—without attachment; *cikīrṣuḥ*—desiring to; *loka-saṅgraham*—leading the people in general.

TRANSLATION

As the ignorant perform their duties with attachment to results, similarly the learned may also act, but without attachment, for the sake of leading people on the right path.

PURPORT

A person in Kṛṣṇa consciousness and a person not in Kṛṣṇa consciousness are differentiated by different desires. A Kṛṣṇa conscious person does not do anything which is not conducive to development of Kṛṣṇa consciousness. He may even act exactly like the ignorant person, who is too much attached to material activities, but one is engaged in such activities for the satisfaction of his sense gratification, whereas the other is engaged for the satisfaction of Kṛṣṇa. Therefore, the Kṛṣṇa conscious person is required to show the people how to act and how to engage the results of action for the purpose of Kṛṣṇa consciousness.

TEXT 26

न बुद्धिभेदं जनयेदज्ञानां कर्मसङ्गिनाम् ।
जोषयेत्सर्वकर्माणि विद्वान्युक्तः समाचरन् ॥ २६ ॥

na buddhi-bhedaṁ janayed
ajñānāṁ karma-saṅginām
joṣayet sarva-karmāṇi
vidvān yuktaḥ samācaran

na—do not; buddhi-bhedam—disrupt the intelligence; janayet—do; ajñānām—of the foolish; karma-saṅginām—attached to fruitive work; joṣayet—dovetailed; sarva—all; karmāṇi—work; vidvān—learned; yuktaḥ—all engaged; samācaran—practicing.

TRANSLATION

Let not the wise disrupt the minds of the ignorant who are attached to fruitive action. They should not be encouraged to refrain from work, but to engage in work in the spirit of devotion.

PURPORT

Vedaiś ca sarvair aham eva vedyaḥ: that is the end of all Vedic rituals. All rituals, all performances of sacrifices, and everything that is put into the Vedas, including all directions for material activities, are meant for understanding Kṛṣṇa, who is the ultimate goal of life. But because the conditioned souls do not know anything beyond sense gratification, they study the *Vedas* to that end. Through sense regulations, however, one is gradually elevated to Kṛṣṇa consciousness. Therefore a realized soul in Kṛṣṇa consciousness should not disturb others in their activities or understanding, but he should act by showing how the results of all work can be dedicated to the service of Kṛṣṇa. The learned Kṛṣṇa conscious person may act in such a way that the ignorant person working for sense gratification may learn how to act and how to behave. Although the ignorant man is not to be disturbed in his activities, still, a slightly developed Kṛṣṇa conscious person may directly be engaged in the service of the Lord without waiting for other Vedic formulas. For this fortunate man there is no need to follow the Vedic rituals, because in direct Kṛṣṇa consciousness one can have all the results simply by following the prescribed duties of a particular person.

TEXT 27

प्रकृतेः क्रियमाणानि गुणैः कर्माणि सर्वशः ।
अहङ्कारविमूढात्मा कर्ताहमिति मन्यते ॥ २७ ॥

prakṛteḥ kriyamāṇāni
guṇaiḥ karmāṇi sarvaśaḥ
ahaṅkāra-vimūḍhātmā
kartāham iti manyate

prakṛteḥ—of material nature; *kriyamāṇāni*—all being done; *guṇaiḥ*—by the modes; *karmāṇi*—activities; *sarvaśaḥ*—all kinds of; *ahaṅkāra-vimūḍha*—bewildered by false ego; *ātmā*—the spirit soul; *kartā*—doer; *aham*—I; *iti*—thus; *manyate*—thinks.

TRANSLATION

The bewildered spirit soul, under the influence of the three modes of material nature, thinks himself to be the doer of activities, which are in actuality carried out by nature.

PURPORT

Two persons, one in Kṛṣṇa consciousness and the other in material consciousness, working on the same level, may appear to be working on the same platform, but there is a wide gulf of difference in their respective positions. The person in material consciousness is convinced by false ego that he is the doer of everything. He does not know that the mechanism of the body is produced by material nature, which works under the supervision of the Supreme Lord. The materialistic person has no knowledge that ultimately he is under the control of Kṛṣṇa. The person in false ego takes all credit for doing everything independently, and that is the symptom of his nescience. He does not know that this gross and subtle body is the creation of material nature, under the order of the Supreme Personality of Godhead, and as such his bodily and mental activities should be engaged in the service of Kṛṣṇa, in Kṛṣṇa consciousness. The ignorant man forgets that the Supreme Personality of Godhead is known as Hṛṣīkeśa, or the master of the senses of the material body, for due to his long misuse of the senses in sense gratification, he is factually bewildered by the false ego, which makes him forget his eternal relationship with Kṛṣṇa.

TEXT 28

तत्त्वविन्तु महाबाहो गुणकर्मविभागयोः ।
गुणा गुणेषु वर्तन्त इति मत्वा न सज्जते ॥ २८ ॥

tattva-vit tu mahā-bāho
guṇa-karma-vibhāgayoḥ
guṇā guṇeṣu vartanta
iti matvā na sajjate

tattvavit—the knower of the Absolute Truth; *tu*—but; *mahā-bāho*—O mighty-armed one; *guṇa-karma*—works under material influence; *vibhā-gayoḥ*—differences; *guṇāḥ*—senses; *guṇeṣu*—in sense gratification; *vartante*—being engaged; *iti*—thus; *matvā*—thinking; *na*—never; *sajjate*—becomes attached.

TRANSLATION

One who is in knowledge of the Absolute Truth, O mighty-armed, does not engage himself in the senses and sense gratification, knowing well the differences between work in devotion and work for fruitive results.

PURPORT

The knower of the Absolute Truth is convinced of his awkward position in material association. He knows that he is part and parcel of the Supreme Personality of Godhead, Kṛṣṇa, and that his position should not be in the material creation. He knows his real identity as part and parcel of the Supreme, who is eternal bliss and knowledge, and he realizes that somehow or other he is entrapped in the material conception of life. In his pure state of existence he is meant to dovetail his activities in devotional service to the Supreme Personality of Godhead, Kṛṣṇa. He therefore engages himself in the activities of Kṛṣṇa consciousness and becomes naturally unattached to the activities of the material senses, which are all circumstantial and temporary. He knows that his material condition of life is under the supreme control of the Lord; consequently he is not disturbed by all kinds of material reactions, which he considers to be the mercy of the Lord. According to Śrīmad-Bhāgavatam, one who knows the Absolute Truth in three different features—namely Brahman, Paramātmā, and the Supreme Personality of Godhead—is called tattvavit, for he knows also his own factual position in relationship with the Supreme.

TEXT 29

प्रकृतेर्गुणसम्मूढाः सज्जन्ते गुणकर्मसु ।
तानकृत्स्नविदो मन्दान्कृत्स्नविन्न विचालयेत् ॥ २९ ॥

prakṛter guṇa-sammūḍhāḥ
sajjante guṇa-karmasu
tān akṛtsna-vido mandān
kṛtsna-vin na vicālayet

prakṛteḥ—impelled by the material modes; *guṇa-sammūḍhāḥ*—befooled by material identification; *sajjante*—become engaged; *guṇa-karmasu*—in material activities; *tān*—all those; *akṛtsna-vidaḥ*—persons with a poor fund of knowledge; *mandān*—lazy to understand self-realization; *kṛtsna-vit*—one who is in factual knowledge; *na*—may not; *vicālayet*—try to agitate.

TRANSLATION

Bewildered by the modes of material nature, the ignorant fully engage themselves in material activities and become attached. But the wise should not unsettle them, although these duties are inferior due to the performers' lack of knowledge.

PURPORT

Persons who are unknowledgeable falsely identify with gross material consciousness and are full of material designations. This body is a gift of the material nature, and one who is too much attached to the bodily consciousness is called *mandān*, or a lazy person without understanding of spirit soul. Ignorant men think of the body as the self; bodily connections with others are accepted as kinsmanship; the land in which the body is obtained is the object of worship; and the formalities of religious rituals are considered ends in themselves. Social work, nationalism, and altruism are some of the activities for such materially designated persons. Under the spell of such designations, they are always busy in the material field; for them spiritual realization is a myth, and so they are not interested. Such bewildered persons may even be engaged in such primary moral principles of life as nonviolence and similar materially benevolent work. Those who are, however, enlightened in spiritual life, should not try to agitate such materially engrossed persons. Better to prosecute one's own spiritual activities silently.

Men who are ignorant cannot appreciate activities in Kṛṣṇa consciousness, and therefore Lord Kṛṣṇa advises us not to disturb them and simply waste valuable time. But the devotees of the Lord are more kind than the Lord because they understand the purpose of the Lord. Consequently they undertake all kinds of risks, even to the point of approaching ignorant men to try to engage them in the acts of Kṛṣṇa consciousness, which are absolutely necessary for the human being.

TEXT 30

मयि सर्वाणि कर्माणि संन्यस्याध्यात्मचेतसा ।
निराशीर्निर्ममो भूत्वा युध्यस्व विगतज्वरः ॥ ३० ॥

mayi sarvāṇi karmāṇi
sannyasyādhyātma-cetasā
nirāśīr nirmamo bhūtvā
yudhyasva vigata-jvaraḥ

mayi—unto Me; *sarvāṇi*—all sorts of; *karmāṇi*—activities; *sannyasya*—giving up completely; *adhyātma*—with full knowledge of the self; *cetasā*—consciousness; *nirāśīḥ*—without desire for profit; *nirmamaḥ*—without ownership; *bhūtvā*—so being; *yudhyasva*—fight; *vigata-jvaraḥ*—without being lethargic.

TRANSLATION

Therefore, O Arjuna, surrendering all your works unto Me, with mind intent on Me, and without desire for gain and free from egoism and lethargy, fight.

PURPORT

This verse clearly indicates the purpose of the *Bhagavad-gītā*. The Lord instructs that one has to become fully Kṛṣṇa conscious to discharge duties, as if in military discipline. Such an injunction may make things a little difficult; nevertheless duties must be carried out, with dependence on Kṛṣṇa, because that is the constitutional position of the living entity. The living entity cannot be happy independant of the cooperation of the Supreme Lord because the eternal constitutional position of the living entity is to become subordinate to the desires of the Lord. Arjuna was, therefore, ordered by Śrī Kṛṣṇa to fight as if the Lord were his military commander. One has to sacrifice everything for the good will of the Supreme Lord, and at the same time discharge prescribed duties without claiming proprietorship. Arjuna did not have to consider the order of the Lord; he had only to execute His order. The Supreme Lord is the Soul of all souls; therefore, one who depends solely and wholly on the Supreme Soul without personal consideration, or in other words, one who is fully Kṛṣṇa conscious, is called *adhyātma-cetasā*. *Nirāśīḥ* means that one has to act on the order of the master. Nor should one ever expect fruitive results. The cashier may count millions of dollars for his employer, but he does not claim a cent for himself. Similarly, one has to realize that nothing in the world belongs to any individual person, but that everything belongs to the Supreme Lord. That is the real purport of *mayi*, or unto Me. And when one acts in such Kṛṣṇa consciousness, certainly he does not claim proprietorship over anything. This consciousness is called *nirmama*, or nothing is mine. And, if there is any reluctance to execute such a stern order which is without consideration of so-called kinsmen in the bodily relationship, that reluctance should be thrown off; in this way one may become *vigata-jvara*, or without feverish mentality or lethargy. Everyone, according to his quality and position, has a particular type of work to discharge, and all such duties may be discharged in Kṛṣṇa consciousness, as described above. That will lead one to the path of liberation.

TEXT 31

ये मे मतमिदं नित्यमनुतिष्ठन्ति मानवाः ।
श्रद्धावन्तोऽनसूयन्तो मुच्यन्ते तेऽपि कर्मभिः ॥ ३१ ॥

ye me matam idaṁ nityam
anutiṣṭhanti mānavāḥ
śraddhāvanto 'nasūyanto
mucyante te 'pi karmabhiḥ

ye—those; *me*—My; *matam*—injunctions; *idam*—this; *nityam*—eternal function; *anutiṣṭhanti*—execute regularly; *mānavāḥ*—humankind; *śraddhā-vantaḥ*—with faith and devotion; *anasūyantaḥ*—without envy; *mucyante*—become free; *te*—all of them; *api*—even; *karmabhiḥ*—from the bondage of the law of fruitive action.

TRANSLATION

One who executes his duties according to My injunctions and who follows this teaching faithfully, without envy, becomes free from the bondage of fruitive actions.

PURPORT

The injunction of the Supreme Personality of Godhead, Kṛṣṇa, is the essence of all Vedic wisdom, and therefore is eternally true without exception. As the *Vedas* are eternal, so this truth of Kṛṣṇa consciousness is also eternal. One should have firm faith in this injunction, without envying the Lord. There are many philosophers who write comments on the *Bhagavad-gītā* but have no faith in Kṛṣṇa. They will never be liberated from the bondage of fruitive action. But an ordinary man with firm faith in the eternal injunctions of the Lord, even though unable to execute such orders, becomes liberated from the bondage of the law of *karma*. In the beginning of Kṛṣṇa consciousness, one may not fully discharge the injunctions of the Lord, but because one is not resentful of this principle and works sincerely without consideration of defeat and hopelessness, he will surely be promoted to the stage of pure Kṛṣṇa consciousness.

TEXT 32

ये त्वेतदभ्यसूयन्तो नानुतिष्ठन्ति मे मतम् ।
सर्वज्ञानविमूढांस्तान्विद्धि नष्टानचेतसः ॥ ३२ ॥

ye tv etad abhyasūyanto
nānutiṣṭhanti me matam
sarva-jñāna-vimūḍhāṁs tān
viddhi naṣṭān acetasaḥ

ye—those; *tu*—however; *etat*—this; *abhyasūyantaḥ*—out of envy; *na*—do not; *anutiṣṭhanti*—regularly perform; *me*—My; *matam*—injunction; *sarva-jñāna*—all sorts of knowledge; *vimūḍhān*—perfectly befooled; *tān*—they are; *viddhi*—know it well; *naṣṭān*—all ruined; *acetasaḥ*—without Kṛṣṇa consciousness.

TRANSLATION

But those who, out of envy, disregard these teachings and do not practice them regularly, are to be considered bereft of all knowledge, befooled, and doomed to ignorance and bondage.

PURPORT

The flaw of not being Kṛṣṇa conscious is clearly stated herein. As there is punishment for disobedience to the order of the supreme executive head, so there is certainly punishment for the disobedience of the order of the Supreme Personality of Godhead. A disobedient person, however great he may be, is ignorant of his own self, of the Supreme Brahman, and Paramātmā and the Personality of Godhead, due to a vacant heart. Therefore there is no hope of perfection of life for him.

TEXT 33

सदृशं चेष्टते स्वस्याः प्रकृतेर्ज्ञानवानपि ।
प्रकृतिं यान्ति भूतानि निग्रहः किं करिष्यति ॥ ३३ ॥

sadṛśaṁ ceṣṭate svasyāḥ
prakṛter jñānavān api
prakṛtiṁ yānti bhūtāni
nigrahaḥ kiṁ kariṣyati

sadṛśam—accordingly; *ceṣṭate*—tries; *svasyāḥ*—in one's own nature; *prakṛteḥ*—modes; *jñānavān*—the learned; *api*—although; *prakṛtim*—nature; *yānti*—undergo; *bhūtāni*—all living entities; *nigrahaḥ*—suppression; *kim*—what; *kariṣyati*—can do.

TRANSLATION

Even a man of knowledge acts according to his own nature, for everyone follows his nature. What can repression accomplish?

PURPORT

Unless one is situated on the transcendental platform of Kṛṣṇa consciousness, he cannot get free from the influence of the modes of material nature, as it is confirmed by the Lord in the Seventh Chapter (7.14). Therefore, even for the most highly educated person on the mundane plane, it is impossible to get out of the entanglement of *māyā* simply by theoretical knowledge, or by separating the soul from the body. There are many so-called spiritualists who outwardly pose to be advanced in the science, but inwardly or privately are completely under the particular modes of nature which they are unable to surpass. Academically, one may be very learned, but because of his long association with material nature, he is in bondage. Kṛṣṇa consciousness helps one to get out of the material entanglement, even though one may be engaged in his prescribed duties. Therefore, without being fully in Kṛṣṇa consciousness, no one should suddenly give up his prescribed duties and become a so-called *yogī* or transcendentalist artificially. It is better to be situated in one's position and to try to attain Kṛṣṇa consciousness under superior training. Thus one may be freed from the clutches of *māyā*.

TEXT 34

इन्द्रियस्येन्द्रियस्यार्थे रागद्वेषौ व्यवस्थितौ ।
तयोर्न वशमागच्छेत्तौ ह्यस्य परिपन्थिनौ ॥ ३४ ॥

indriyasyendriyasyārthe
rāga-dveṣau vyavasthitau
tayor na vaśam āgacchet
tau hy asya paripanthinau

indriyasya—of the senses; *indriyasya arthe*—in the sense objects; *rāga*—attachment; *dveṣau*—also in detachment; *vyavasthitau*—put under regulations; *tayoḥ*—of them; *na*—never; *vaśam*—control; *āgacchet*—one should come; *tau*—those; *hi*—certainly are; *asya*—his; *paripanthinau*—stumbling blocks.

TRANSLATION

Attraction and repulsion for sense objects are felt by embodied beings, but one should not fall under the control of senses and sense objects because they are stumbling blocks on the path of self-realization.

PURPORT

Those who are in Kṛṣṇa consciousness are naturally reluctant to engage in material sense gratifications. But those who are not in such consciousness should follow the rules and regulations of the revealed scriptures. Unrestricted sense enjoyment is the cause of material encagement, but one who follows the rules and regulations of the revealed scriptures does not become entangled by the sense objects. For example, sex enjoyment is a necessity for the conditioned soul, and sex enjoyment is allowed under the license of marriage ties. For example, according to scriptural injunctions, one is forbidden to engage in sex relationships with any women other than one's wife. All other women are to be considered as one's mother. But, in spite of such injunctions, a man is still inclined to have sex relationships with other women. These propensities are to be curbed; otherwise they will be stumbling blocks on the path of self-realization. As long as the material body is there, the necessities of the material body are allowed, but under rules and regulations. And yet, we should not rely upon the control of such allowances. One has to follow those rules and regulations, un-attached to them, because practice of sense gratifications under regulations may also lead one to go astray-as much as there is always the chance of an accident, even on the royal roads. Although they may be very carefully maintained, no one can guarantee that there will be no danger even on the safest road. The sense enjoyment spirit has been current a very long, long time, owing to material association. Therefore, in spite of regulated sense enjoyment, there is every chance of falling down; therefore any attachment for regulated sense enjoyment must also be avoided by all means. But action in the loving service of Kṛṣṇa detaches one from all kinds of sensory activities. Therefore, no one should try to be detached from Kṛṣṇa consciousness at any stage of life. The whole purpose of detachment from all kinds of sense attachment is ultimately to become situated on the platform of Kṛṣṇa consciousness.

TEXT 35

श्रेयान्स्वधर्मो विगुणः परधर्मात्स्वनुष्ठितात् ।
स्वधर्मे निधनं श्रेयः परधर्मो भयावहः ॥ ३५ ॥

śreyān sva-dharmo viguṇaḥ
para-dharmāt sv-anuṣṭhitāt
sva-dharme nidhanaṁ śreyaḥ
para-dharmo bhayāvahaḥ

śreyān—far better; sva-dharmaḥ—one's prescribed duties; viguṇaḥ—even faulty; para-dharmāt—from duties mentioned for others; svanuṣṭhitāt—than perfectly done; sva-dharme—in one's prescribed duties; nidhanam—destruction; śreyaḥ—better; para-dharmaḥ—duties prescribed for others; bhaya-āvahaḥ—dangerous.

TRANSLATION

It is far better to discharge one's prescribed duties, even though they may be faulty, than another's duties. Destruction in the course of performing one's own duty is better than engaging in another's duties, for to follow another's path is dangerous.

PURPORT

One should therefore discharge his prescribed duties in full Kṛṣṇa consciousness rather than those prescribed for others. Prescribed duties complement one's psychophysical condition, under the spell of the modes of material nature. Spiritual duties are as ordered by the spiritual master, for the transcendental service of Kṛṣṇa. But both materially or spiritually, one should stick to his prescribed duties even up to death, rather than imitate another's prescribed duties. Duties on the spiritual platform and duties on the material platform may be different, but the principle of following the authorized direction is always good for the performer. When one is under the spell of the modes of material nature, one should follow the prescribed rules for particular situations and should not imitate others. For example, a *brāhmaṇa*, who is in the mode of goodness, is nonviolent, whereas a *kṣatriya*, who is in the mode of passion, is allowed to be violent. As such, for a *kṣatriya* it is better to be vanquished following the rules of violence than to imitate a *brāhmaṇa* who follows the principles of nonviolence. Everyone has to cleanse his heart by a gradual process, not abruptly. However, when one transcends the modes of material nature and is fully situated in Kṛṣṇa consciousness, he can perform anything and everything under the direction of the bona fide spiritual master. In that complete stage of Kṛṣṇa consciousness, the *kṣatriya* may act as a *brāhmaṇa*, or a *brāhmaṇa* may act as a *kṣatriya*. In the transcendental stage, the distinctions of the material world do not apply. For example, Viśvāmitra was originally a *kṣatriya*, but later on he acted as a *brāhmaṇa*, whereas Paraśurāma was a *brāhmaṇa*, but later on he acted as a *kṣatriya*. Being transcendentally situated, they could do so; but as long as one is on the material platform, he must perform his duties according to the modes of material nature. At the same time, he must have a full sense of Kṛṣṇa consciousness.

TEXT 36

अर्जुन उवाच ।
अथ केन प्रयुक्तोऽयं पापं चरति पूरुषः ।
अनिच्छन्नपि वार्ष्णेय बलादिव नियोजितः ॥ ३६ ॥

arjuna uvāca
atha kena prayukto 'yaṁ
pāpaṁ carati pūruṣaḥ
anicchann api vārṣṇeya
balād iva niyojitaḥ

arjunaḥ uvāca—Arjuna said; *atha*—hereafter; *kena*—by what; *prayuktaḥ*—impelled; *ayam*—one; *pāpam*—sins; *carati*—acts; *pūruṣaḥ*—a man; *anicchan*—

without desiring; *api*—although; *vārṣṇeya*—O descendant of Vṛṣṇi; *balāt*—by force; *iva*—as if; *niyojitaḥ*—engaged.

TRANSLATION

Arjuna said: O descendant of Vṛṣṇi, by what is one impelled to sinful acts, even unwillingly, as if engaged by force?

PURPORT

A living entity, as part and parcel of the Supreme, is originally spiritual, pure, and free from all material contaminations. Therefore, by nature he is not subjected to the sins of the material world. But when he is in contact with the material nature, he acts in many sinful ways without hesitation, and sometimes even against his will. As such, Arjuna's question to Kṛṣṇa is very sanguine, as to the perverted nature of the living entities. Although the living entity sometimes does not want to act in sin, he is still forced to act. Sinful actions are not, however, impelled by the Supersoul within, but are due to another cause, as the Lord explains in the next verse.

TEXT 37

श्रीभगवानुवाच
काम एष क्रोध एष रजोगुणसमुद्भवः ।
महाशनो महापाप्मा विद्ध्येनमिह वैरिणम् ॥ ३७ ॥

*śrī-bhagavān uvāca
kāma eṣa krodha eṣa
rajo-guṇa-samudbhavaḥ
mahāśano mahā-pāpmā
viddhy enam iha vairiṇam*

śrī bhagavān uvāca—the Personality of Godhead said; *kāmaḥ*—lust; *eṣaḥ*—all these; *krodhaḥ*—wrath; *eṣaḥ*—all these; *rajo-guṇa*—the mode of passion; *samudbhavaḥ*—born of; *mahā-śanaḥ*—all-devouring; *mahā-pāpmā*—greatly sinful; *viddhi*—know; *enam*—this; *iha*—in the material world; *vairiṇam*—greatest enemy.

TRANSLATION

The Blessed Lord said: It is lust only, Arjuna, which is born of contact
with the material modes of passion and later transformed into wrath, and
which is the all-devouring, sinful enemy of this world.

PURPORT

When a living entity comes in contact with the material creation, his
eternal love for Kṛṣṇa is transformed into lust, in association with the mode
of passion. Or, in other words, the sense of love of God becomes transformed into lust, as milk in contact with sour tamarind is transformed into
yogurt. Then again, when lust is unsatisfied, it turns into wrath; wrath is
transformed into illusion, and illusion continues the material existence.
Therefore, lust is the greatest enemy of the living entity, and it is lust only
which induces the pure living entity to remain entangled in the material
world. Wrath is the manifestation of the mode of ignorance; these modes
exhibit themselves as wrath and other corollaries. If, therefore, the modes
of passion, instead of being degraded into the modes of ignorance, are
elevated to the modes of goodness by the prescribed method of living and
acting, then one can be saved from the degradation of wrath by spiritual
attachment.

The Supreme Personality of Godhead expanded Himself into many for
His ever-increasing spiritual bliss, and the living entities are parts and parcels
of this spiritual bliss. They also have partial independence, but by misuse
of their independence, when the service attitude is transformed into the
propensity for sense enjoyment, they come under the sway of lust. This
material creation is created by the Lord to give a facility to the conditioned
souls to fulfill these lustful propensities, and when they are completely
baffled by prolonged lustful activities, the living entities begin to inquire
about their real position.

This inquiry is the beginning of the Vedānta-sūtras, wherein it is said,
athāto brahma-jijñāsā: one should inquire into the Supreme. And the
Supreme is defined in Śrīmad-Bhāgavatam as janmādyasya yato 'nvayād
itarataś ca, or, "The origin of everything is the Supreme Brahman."
Therefore, the origin of lust is also in the Supreme. If, therefore, lust is
transformed into love for the Supreme, or transformed into Kṛṣṇa consciousness—or, in other words, desiring everything for Kṛṣṇa—then both
lust and wrath can be spiritualized. Hanumān, the great servitor of Lord
Rama, engaged his wrath upon his enemies for the satisfaction of the Lord.

Therefore, lust and wrath, when they are employed in Kṛṣṇa consciousness, become our friends instead of our enemies.

TEXT 38

धूमेनात्रियते वह्निर्यथादर्शो मलेन च ।
यथोल्बेनावृतो गर्भस्तथा तेनेदमावृतम् ॥ ३८ ॥

dhūmenāvriyate vahnir
yathādarśo malena ca
yatholbenāvṛto garbhas
tathā tenedam āvṛtam

dhūmena—by smoke; *āvriyate*—covered; *vahniḥ*—fire; *yathā*—just as; *ādarśaḥ*—mirror; *malena*—by dust; *ca*—also; *yathā*—just as; *ulbena*—by the womb; *āvṛtaḥ*—is covered; *garbhaḥ*—embryo; *tathā-so; *tena*—by that lust; *idam*—this; *āvṛtam*—is covered.

TRANSLATION

As fire is covered by smoke, as a mirror is covered by dust, or as the embryo is covered by the womb, similarly, the living entity is covered by different degrees of this lust.

PURPORT

There are three degrees of covering of the living entity by which his pure consciousness is obscured. This covering is but lust under different manifestations like smoke in the fire, dust on the mirror, and the womb about the embryo. When lust is compared to smoke, it is understood that the fire of the living spark can be a little perceived. In other words, when the living entity exhibits his Kṛṣṇa consciousness slightly, he may be likened to the fire covered by smoke. Although fire is necessary where there is smoke, there is no overt manifestation of fire in the early stage. This stage is like the beginning of Kṛṣṇa consciousness. The dust on the mirror refers to a cleansing process of the mirror of the mind by so many spiritual methods. The best process is to chant the holy names of the Lord. The embryo covered by the womb is an analogy illustrating a helpless position, for the child in the womb is so helpless that he cannot even move. This stage of living condition can be compared to that of the trees. The trees are also living entities, but they have been put in such a condition of life by such a great exhibition of lust that they are almost void of all consciousness. The covered mirror is compared to the birds and beasts, and the smoke covered fire is compared to the human being. In the form of a human being, the living entity may revive a little Kṛṣṇa consciousness, and, if he makes further development, the fire of spiritual life can be kindled in the human form of life. By careful handling of the smoke in the fire, the fire can be made to blaze. Therefore the human form of life is a chance for the living entity to escape the entanglement of material existence. In the human form of life, one can conquer the enemy, lust, by cultivation of Kṛṣṇa consciousness under able guidance.

TEXT 39

आवृतं ज्ञानमेतेन ज्ञानिनो नित्यवैरिणा ।
कामरूपेण कौन्तेय दुष्पूरेणानलेन च ॥ ३९ ॥

āvṛtaṁ jñānam etena
jñānino nitya-vairiṇā
kāma-rūpeṇa kaunteya
duṣpūreṇānalena ca

āvṛtam—covered; jñānam—pure consciousness; etena—by this; jñāninaḥ—of the knower; nitya-vairiṇā—eternal enemy; kāma-rūpeṇa—in the form of lust; kaunteya—O son of Kuntī; duṣpūreṇa—never to be satisfied; analena—by the fire; ca—also.

TRANSLATION

Thus, a man's pure consciousness is covered by his eternal enemy in the form of lust, which is never satisfied and which burns like fire.

PURPORT

It is said in the Manu-smṛti that lust cannot be satisfied by any amount of sense enjoyment, just as fire is never extinguished by a constant supply of fuel. In the material world, the center of all activities is sex, and thus this material world is called *maithunya-āgāra,* or the shackles of sex life. In the ordinary prison house, criminals are kept within bars; similarly, the criminals who are disobedient to the laws of the Lord are shackled by sex life. Advancement of material civilization on the basis of sense gratification means increasing the duration of the material existence of a living entity. Therefore, this lust is the symbol of ignorance by which the living entity is kept within the material world. While one enjoys sense gratification, it may be that there is some feeling of happiness, but actually that so-called feeling of happiness is the ultimate enemy of the sense enjoyer.

TEXT 40

इन्द्रियाणि मनो बुद्धिरस्याधिष्ठानमुच्यते ।
एतैर्विमोहयत्येष ज्ञानमावृत्य देहिनम् ॥ ४० ॥

indriyāṇi mano buddhir
asyādhiṣṭhānam ucyate
etair vimohayaty eṣa
jñānam āvṛtya dehinam

indriyāṇi—the senses; *manaḥ*—the mind; *buddhiḥ*—the intelligence; *asya* —of the lust; *adhiṣṭhānam*—sitting place; *ucyate*—called; *etaiḥ*—by all these; *vimohayati*—bewilders; *eṣaḥ*—of this; *jñānam*—knowledge; *āvṛtya*—covering; *dehinam*—the embodied.

TRANSLATION

The senses, the mind and the intelligence are the sitting places of this lust, which veils the real knowledge of the living entity and bewilders him.

PURPORT

The enemy has captured different strategic positions in the body of the conditioned soul, and therefore Lord Kṛṣṇa is giving hints of those places, so that one who wants to conquer the enemy may know where he can be found. Mind is the center of all the activities of the senses, and thus the mind is the reservoir of all ideas of sense gratification; and, as a result, the mind and the senses become the repositories of lust. Next, the intelligence department becomes the capital of such lustful propensities. Intelligence is the immediate next-door neighbor of the spirit soul. Lusty intelligence influences the spirit soul to acquire the false ego and identify itself with matter, and thus with the mind and senses. The spirit soul becomes addicted to enjoying the material senses and mistakes this as true happiness. This false identification of the spirit soul is very nicely explained in the *Śrīmad-Bhāgavatam*:

> *yasyātma-buddhiḥ kuṇape tri-dhātuke*
> *sva-dhīḥ kalatrādiṣu bhauma idyadhīḥ*
> *yat-tīrtha-buddhiḥ salile na karhicij*
> *janeṣv abhijñeṣu sa eva gokharaḥ.*

"A human being who identifies this body made of three elements with his self, who considers the by-products of the body to be his kinsmen, who considers the land of birth as worshipable, and who goes to the place of pilgrimage simply to take a bath rather than meet men of transcendental knowledge there, is to be considered as an ass or a cow."

TEXT 41

तस्मात्त्वमिन्द्रियाण्यादौ नियम्य भरतर्षभ ।
पाप्मानं प्रजहि ह्येनं ज्ञानविज्ञाननाशनम् ॥ ४१ ॥

tasmāt tvam indriyāṇy ādau
niyamya bharatarṣabha
pāpmānaṁ prajahi hy enaṁ
jñāna-vijñāna-nāśanam

tasmāt—therefore; *tvam*-you; *indriyāṇi*—senses; *ādau*—in the beginning; *niyamya*—by regulating; *bharatarṣabha*—O chief amongst the descendants of Bharata; *pāpmānam*—the great symbol of sin; *prajahi*—curb; *hi*—certainly; *enam*—this; *jñāna*—knowledge; *vijñāna*—scientific knowledge of the pure soul; *nāśanam*—destroyer.

TRANSLATION

Therefore, O Arjuna, best of the Bhāratas, in the very beginning curb this great symbol of sin [lust] by regulating the senses, and slay this destroyer of knowledge and self-realization.

PURPORT

The Lord advised Arjuna to regulate the senses from the very beginning so that he could curb the greatest sinful enemy, lust, which destroys the urge for self-realization, and specifically, knowledge of the self. *Jñānam* refers to knowledge of self as distinguished from non-self, or, in other words, knowledge that the spirit soul is not the body. *Vijñānam* refers to specific knowledge of the spirit soul and knowledge of one's constitutional position and his relationship to the Supreme Soul. It is explained thus in the *Śrīmad-Bhāgavatam: jñānaṁ parama-guhyaṁ me yad-vijñāna-samanvitam / sarahasyaṁ tad-aṅgaṁ ca gṛhāṇa gaditaṁ mayā:* "The knowledge of the self and the Supreme Self is very confidential and mysterious, being veiled by *māyā*, but such knowledge and specific realization can be understood if it is explained by the Lord Himself." *Bhagavad-gītā* gives us that knowledge, specifically knowledge of the self. The living entities are parts and parcels of the Lord, and therefore they are simply meant to serve the Lord. This consciousness is called Kṛṣṇa consciousness. So, from the very beginning of life one has to learn this Kṛṣṇa consciousness, and thereby one may become fully Kṛṣṇa conscious and act accordingly.

Lust is only the perverted reflection of the love of God which is natural for every living entity. But if one is educated in Kṛṣṇa consciousness from the very beginning, that natural love of God cannot deteriorate into lust. When love of God deteriorates into lust, it is very difficult to return to the normal condition. Nonetheless, Kṛṣṇa consciousness is so powerful that even a late beginner can become a lover of God by following the regulative principles of devotional service. So, from any stage of life, or from the time of understanding its urgency, one can begin regulating the senses in Kṛṣṇa consciousness, devotional service of the Lord, and turn the lust into love of Godhead—the highest perfectional stage of human life.

TEXT 42

इन्द्रियाणि पराण्याहुरिन्द्रियेभ्यः परं मनः ।
मनसस्तु परा बुद्धियों बुद्धेः परतस्तु सः ॥ ४२ ॥

*indriyāṇi parāṇy āhur
indriyebhyaḥ paraṁ manaḥ
manasas tu parā buddhir
yo buddheḥ paratas tu saḥ*

indriyāṇi—senses; *parāṇi*—superior; *āhuḥ*—is said; *indriyebhyaḥ*—more than the senses; *param*—superior; *manaḥ*—the mind; *manasaḥ*—more than the mind; *tu*—also; *parā*—superior; *buddhiḥ*—intelligence; *yaḥ*—one which; *buddheḥ*—more than the intelligence; *parataḥ*—superior; *tu*—but; *saḥ*—he.

TRANSLATION

The working senses are superior to dull matter; mind is higher than the senses; intelligence is still higher than the mind; and he [the soul] is even higher than the intelligence.

PURPORT

The senses are different outlets for the activities of lust. Lust is reserved within the body, but it is given vent through the senses. Therefore, the senses are superior to the body as a whole. These outlets are not in use when there is superior consciousness, or Kṛṣṇa consciousness. In Kṛṣṇa consciousness the soul makes direct connection with the Supreme Personality of Godhead; therefore the bodily functions, as described here, ultimately end in the Supreme Soul. Bodily action means the functions of the senses, and stopping the senses means stopping all bodily actions. But since the mind is active, then, even though the body may be silent and at rest, the mind will act—as it does during dreaming. But, above the mind there is the determination of the intelligence, and above the intelligence is the soul proper. If, therefore, the soul is directly engaged with the Supreme, naturally all other subordinates, namely, the intelligence, mind and the senses, will be automatically engaged. In the *Kaṭha Upaniṣad* there is a passage in which it is said that the objects of sense gratification are superior to the senses, and mind is superior to the sense objects. If, therefore, the mind is directly engaged in the service of the Lord constantly, then there is no chance of the senses becoming engaged in other ways. This mental attitude has already been explained. If the mind is engaged in the transcendental service of the Lord, there is no chance of its being engaged in the lower propensities. In the *Kaṭha Upaniṣad* the soul has been described as *mahān*, the great. Therefore the soul is above all—namely, the sense objects, the senses, the mind and the intelligence. Therefore, directly understanding the constitutional position of the soul is the solution of the whole problem.

With intelligence one has to seek out the constitutional position of the soul and then engage the mind always in Kṛṣṇa consciousness. That solves the whole problem. A neophyte spiritualist is generally advised to keep aloof from the objects of senses. One has to strengthen the mind by use of intelligence. If by intelligence one engages one's mind in Kṛṣṇa consciousness, by complete surrender unto the Supreme Personality of Godhead, then, automatically, the mind becomes stronger, and even though the senses are very strong, like serpents, they will be no more effective than serpents with broken fangs. But even though the soul is the master of intelligence and mind, and the senses also, still, unless it is strengthened by association with Kṛṣṇa in Kṛṣṇa consciousness, there is every chance of falling down due to the agitated mind.

TEXT 43

एवं बुद्धेः परं बुद्ध्वा संस्तभ्यात्मानमात्मना ।
जहि शत्रुं महाबाहो कामरूपं दुरासदम् ॥ ४३ ॥

evaṁ buddheḥ paraṁ buddhvā
saṁstabhyātmānam ātmanā
jahi śatruṁ mahā-bāho
kāma-rūpaṁ durāsadam

evam—thus; *buddheḥ*—of intelligence; *param*—superior; *buddhvā*—so knowing; *saṁstabhya*—by steadying; *ātmānam*—the mind; *ātmanā*—by deliberate intelligence; *jahi*—conquer; *śatrum*—the enemy; *mahā-bāho*—O mighty-armed one; *kāma-rūpam*—the form of lust; *durāsadam*—formidable.

TRANSLATION

Thus knowing oneself to be transcendental to material senses, mind and intelligence, one should control the lower self by the higher self and thus—by spiritual strength—conquer this insatiable enemy known as lust.

PURPORT

This Third Chapter of the *Bhagavad-gītā* is conclusively directive to Kṛṣṇa consciousness by knowing oneself as the eternal servitor of the Supreme Personality of Godhead, without considering impersonal voidness as the ultimate end. In the material existence of life, one is certainly influenced by propensities for lust and desire for dominating the resources of material nature. Desire for overlording and sense gratification are the greatest enemies of the conditioned soul; but by the strength of Kṛṣṇa consciousness, one can control the material senses, the mind and the intelligence. One may not give up work and prescribed duties all of a sudden; but by gradually developing Kṛṣṇa consciousness, one can be situated in a transcendental position without being influenced by the material senses and the mind—by steady intelligence directed toward one's pure identity. This is the sum total of this chapter. In the immature stage of material existence, philosophical speculations and artificial attempts to control the senses by the so-called practice of yogic postures can never help a man toward spiritual life. He must be trained in Kṛṣṇa consciousness by higher intelligence.

Thus end the Bhaktivedanta Purports to the Third Chapter of the Śrīmad-Bhagavad-gītā in the matter of Karma-yoga, or the Discharge of One's Prescribed Duty in Kṛṣṇa Consciousness.

CHAPTER FOUR

Transcendental Knowledge

TEXT 1

श्रीभगवानुवाच ।
इमं विवस्वते योगं प्रोक्तवानहमव्ययम् ।
विवस्वान्मनवे प्राह मनुरिक्ष्वाकवेऽब्रवीत् ॥ १ ॥

śrī-bhagavān uvāca
imaṁ vivasvate yogaṁ
proktavān aham avyayam
vivasvān manave prāha
manur ikṣvākave 'bravīt

śrī bhagavān uvāca—the Supreme Personality of Godhead said; *imam*—this; *vivasvate*—unto the sun-god; *yogam*—the science of one's relationship to the Supreme; *proktavān*—instructed; *aham*—I; *avyayam*—imperishable; *vivasvān*—Vivasvān (the sun-god's name); *manave*—unto the father of mankind (of the name Vaivasvata); *prāha*—told; *manuḥ*—the father of mankind; *ikṣvākave*—unto King Ikṣvāku; *abravīt*—said.

213

TRANSLATION

The Blessed Lord said: I instructed this imperishable science of yoga to the sun-god, Vivasvān, and Vivasvān instructed it to Manu, the father of mankind, and Manu in turn instructed it to Ikṣvāku.

PURPORT

Herein we find the history of the *Bhagavad-gītā* traced from a remote time when it was delivered to the royal order, the kings of all planets. This science is especially meant for the protection of the inhabitants and therefore the royal order should understand it in order to be able to rule the citizens and protect them from the material bondage to lust. Human life is meant for cultivation of spiritual knowledge, in eternal relationship with the Supreme Personality of Godhead, and the executive heads of all states and all planets are obliged to impart this lesson to the citizens by education, culture and devotion. In other words, the executive heads of all states are intended to spread the science of Kṛṣṇa consciousness so that the people may take advantage of this great science and pursue a successful path, utilizing the opportunity of the human form of life.

In this millennium, the sun-god is known as Vivasvān, the king of the sun, which is the origin of all planets within the solar system. In the *Brahma-saṁhitā* it is stated:

> *yac-cakṣur eṣa savitā sakala-grahāṇāṁ*
> *rājā samasta-sura-mūrttir aśeṣa-tejāḥ*
> *yasyājñayā bhramati sambhṛta-kālacakro*
> *govindam ādi-puruṣaṁ tam ahaṁ bhajāmi*

"Let me worship," Lord Brahmā said, "the Supreme Personality of Godhead, Govinda [Kṛṣṇa], who is the original person and under whose order the sun, which is the king of all planets, is assuming immense power and heat. The sun represents the eye of the Lord and traverses its orbit in obedience to His order."

The sun is the king of the planets, and the sun-god (at present of the name Vivasvān) rules the sun planet, which is controlling all other planets by supplying heat and light. He is rotating under the order of Kṛṣṇa, and Lord Kṛṣṇa originally made Vivasvān His first disciple to understand the science of *Bhagavad-gītā*. The *Gītā* is not, therefore, a speculative treatise for the insignificant mundane scholar but is a standard book of knowledge coming down from time immemorial. In the *Mahābhārata* (*Śānti-parva* 348.51-52) we can trace out the history of the *Gītā* as follows:

> *tretā-yugādau ca tato vivasvān manave dadau*
> *manuś ca loka-bhṛty-artham sutāyekṣvākave dadau*
> *ikṣvākuṇā ca kathito vyāpya lokān avasthitāḥ*

"In the beginning of the Tretā-yuga [millennium] this science of the relationship with the Supreme was delivered by Vivasvān to Manu. Manu, being the father of mankind, gave it to his son Mahārāja Ikṣvāku, the King of this earth planet and forefather of the Raghu dynasty in which Lord Rāmacandra appeared. Therefore, *Bhagavad-gītā* existed in the human society from the time of Mahārāja Ikṣvāku."

At the present moment we have just passed through five thousand years of the Kali-yuga, which lasts 432,000 years. Before this there was Dvāpara-yuga (800,000 years), and before that there was Tretā-yuga (1,200,000 years). Thus, some 2,005,000 years ago, Manu spoke the *Bhagavad-gītā* to his disciple and son Mahārāja Ikṣvāku, the King of this planet earth. The age of the current Manu is calculated to last some 305,300,000 years, of which 120,400,000 have passed. Accepting that before the birth of Manu, the *Gītā* was spoken by the Lord to His disciple, the sun-god Vivasvān, a rough estimate is that the *Gītā* was spoken at least 120,400,000 years ago; and in human society it has been extant for two million years. It was respoken by the Lord again to Arjuna about five thousand years ago. That is the rough estimate of the history of the *Gīta*, according to the *Gītā* itself and according to the version of the speaker, Lord Śrī Kṛṣṇa. It was spoken to the sun-god Vivasvān because he is also a *kṣatriya* and is the father of all *kṣatriyas* who are descendants of the sun-god, or the *sūrya-vaṁśa kṣatriyas*. Because *Bhagavad-gītā* is as good as the *Vedas*, being spoken by the Supreme Personality of Godhead, this knowledge is *apauruṣeya*, super-human. Since the Vedic instructions are accepted as they are, without human interpretation, the *Gītā* must therefore be accepted without mundane interpretation. The mundane wranglers may speculate on the *Gītā* in their own ways, but that is not *Bhagavad-gītā* as it is. Therefore, *Bhagavad-gītā* has to be accepted as it is, from the disciplic succession, and it is described herein that the Lord spoke to the sun-god, the sun-god spoke to his son Manu, and Manu spoke to his son Ikṣvāku.

TEXT 2

एवं परम्पराप्राप्तमिमं राजर्षयो विदुः ।
स कालेनेह महता योगो नष्टः परन्तप ॥ २ ॥

*evaṁ paramparā-prāptam
imaṁ rājarṣayo viduḥ
sa kāleneha mahatā
yogo naṣṭaḥ parantapa*

evam—thus; *paramparā*—disciplic succession; *prāptam*—received; *imam*—this science; *rājarṣayaḥ*—the saintly kings; *viduḥ*—understood; *saḥ*—that knowledge; *kālena*—in the course of time; *iha*—in this world; *mahatā*—by great; *yogaḥ*—the science of one's relationship with the Supreme; *naṣṭaḥ*—scattered; *parantapa*—O Arjuna, subduer of the enemies.

TRANSLATION

This supreme science was thus received through the chain of disciplic succession, and the saintly kings understood it in that way. But in course of time the succession was broken, and therefore the science as it is appears to be lost.

PURPORT

It is clearly stated that the *Gītā* was especially meant for the saintly kings because they were to execute its purpose in ruling over the citizens. Certainly *Bhagavad-gītā* was never meant for the demonic persons, who would dissipate its value for no one's benefit and would devise all types of interpretations according to personal whims. As soon as the original purpose was scattered by the motives of the unscrupulous commentators, there arose the need to reestablish the disciplic succession. Five thousand years ago it was detected by the Lord Himself that the disciplic succession was broken, and therefore He declared that the purpose of the *Gītā* appeared to be lost. In the same way, at the present moment also there are so many editions of the *Gītā* (especially in English), but almost all of them are not according to authorized disciplic succession. There are innumerable interpretations rendered by different mundane scholars, but almost all of them do not accept the Supreme Personality of Godhead, Kṛṣṇa, although they make a good business on the words of Śrī Kṛṣṇa.

This spirit is demonic, because demons do not believe in God but simply enjoy the property of the Supreme. Since there is a great need of an edition of the *Gītā* in English, as it is received by the *paramparā* (disciplic succession) system, an attempt is made herewith to fulfill this great want. *Bhagavad-gītā*—accepted as it is—is a great boon to humanity; but if it is accepted as a treatise of philosophical speculations, it is simply a waste of time.

TEXT 3

स एवायं मया तेऽद्य योगः प्रोक्तः पुरातनः ।
भक्तोऽसि मे सखा चेति रहस्यं ह्येतदुत्तमम् ॥ ३ ॥

sa evāyaṁ mayā te 'dya
yogaḥ proktaḥ purātanaḥ
bhakto 'si me sakhā ceti
rahasyaṁ hy etad uttamam

saḥ—the same ancient; *eva*—certainly; *ayam*—this; *mayā*—by Me; *te*—unto you; *adya*—today; *yogaḥ*—the science of *yoga; proktaḥ*—spoken; *purātanaḥ*—very old; *bhaktaḥ*—devotee; *asi*—you are; *me*—My; *sakhā*—friend; *ca*—also; *iti*—therefore; *rahasyam*—mystery; *hi*—certainly; *etat*—this; *uttamam*—transcendental.

TRANSLATION

That very ancient science of the relationship with the Supreme is today told by Me to you because you are My devotee as well as My friend; therefore you can understand the transcendental mystery of this science.

PURPORT

There are two classes of men, namely the devotee and the demon. The Lord selected Arjuna as the recipient of this great science owing to his becoming the devotee of the Lord, but for the demon it is not possible to understand this great mysterious science. There are a number of editions of this great book of knowledge, and some of them have commentaries by the devotees, and some of them have commentaries by the demons.

Commentation by the devotees is real, whereas that of the demons is useless. Arjuna accepts Śrī Kṛṣṇa as the Supreme Personality of Godhead, and any commentary on the *Gītā* following in the footsteps of Arjuna is real devotional service to the cause of this great science. The demonic, however, concoct something about Kṛṣṇa and mislead the public and general readers from the path of Kṛṣṇa's instructions. One should try to follow the disciplic succession from Arjuna, and thus be benefitted.

TEXT 4

अर्जुन उवाच ।
अपरं भवतो जन्म परं जन्म विवस्वतः ।
कथमेतद्विजानीयां त्वमादौ प्रोक्तवानिति ॥ ४ ॥

*arjuna uvāca
aparaṁ bhavato janma
paraṁ janma vivasvataḥ
katham etad vijānīyāṁ
tvam ādau proktavān iti*

arjunaḥ uvāca—Arjuna said; aparam—junior; bhavataḥ—Your; janma—birth; param—superior; janma—birth; vivasvataḥ—of the sun-god; katham—how; etat—this; vijānīyām—shall I understand; tvam—You; ādau—in the beginning; proktavān—instructed; iti—thus.

TRANSLATION

Arjuna said: The sun-god Vivasvān is senior by birth to You. How am I to understand that in the beginning You instructed this science to him?

PURPORT

Arjuna is an accepted devotee of the Lord, so how could he not believe Kṛṣṇa's words? The fact is that Arjuna is not inquiring for himself but for those who do not believe in the Supreme Personality of Godhead or for the demons who do not like the idea that Kṛṣṇa should be accepted as the Supreme Personality of Godhead; for them only Arjuna inquires on this point, as if he were himself not aware of the Personality of Godhead, or Kṛṣṇa. As it will be evident from the Tenth Chapter, Arjuna knew perfectly well that Kṛṣṇa is the Supreme

Personality of Godhead, the fountainhead of everything and the last word in Transcendence. Of course, Kṛṣṇa also appeared as the son of Devakī on this earth. How Kṛṣṇa remained the same Supreme Personality of Godhead, the eternal, original person, is very difficult for an ordinary man to understand. Therefore, to clarify this point, Arjuna put this question before Kṛṣṇa so that He Himself could speak authoritatively. That Kṛṣṇa is the supreme authority is accepted by the whole world, not only at present, but from time immemorial, and the demons alone reject Him. Anyway, since Kṛṣṇa is the authority accepted by all, Arjuna put this question before Him in order that Kṛṣṇa would describe Himself without being depicted by the demons who always try to distort Him in a way understandable to the demons and their followers. It is necessary that everyone, for his own interest, know the science of Kṛṣṇa. Therefore, when Kṛṣṇa Himself speaks about Himself, it is auspicious for all the worlds. To the demons, such explanations by Kṛṣṇa Himself may appear to be strange because the demons always study Kṛṣṇa from their own standpoint, but those who are devotees heartily welcome the statements of Kṛṣṇa when they are spoken by Kṛṣṇa Himself. The devotees will always worship such authoritative statements of Kṛṣṇa because they are always eager to know more and more about Him. The atheists, who consider Kṛṣṇa an ordinary man, may in this way come to know that Kṛṣṇa is superhuman, that He is *sac-cid-ānanda-vigraha*—the eternal form of bliss and knowledge—that He is transcendental, and that He is above the domination of the modes of material nature and above the influence of time and space. A devotee of Kṛṣṇa's, like Arjuna, is undoubtedly above any misunderstanding of the transcendental position of Kṛṣṇa. Arjuna's putting this question before the Lord is simply an attempt by the devotee to defy the atheistic attitude of persons who consider Kṛṣṇa to be an ordinary human being subject to the modes of material nature.

TEXT 5

श्रीभगवानुवाच ।
बहूनि मे व्यतीतानि जन्मानि तव चार्जुन ।
तान्यहं वेद सर्वाणि न त्वं वेत्थ परन्तप ॥ ५ ॥

śrī-bhagavān uvāca
bahūni me vyatītāni
janmāni tava cārjuna

tāny aham veda sarvāṇi
na tvaṁ vettha parantapa

śrī bhagavān uvāca—the Personality of Godhead said; *bahūni*—many; *me*—of Mine; *vyatītāni*—have passed; *janmāni*—births; *tava*—of yours; *ca*— and also; *arjuna*—O Arjuna; *tāni*—all those; *aham*—I; *veda*—do know; *sarvāṇi*—all; *na*—not; *tvam*—yourself; *vettha*—know; *parantapa*—O subduer of the enemy.

TRANSLATION

The Blessed Lord said: Many, many births both you and I have passed. I can remember all of them, but you cannot, O subduer of the enemy!

PURPORT

In the *Brahma-saṁhitā* we have information of many, many incarnations of the Lord. It is stated there:

advaitam acyutam anādim ananta-rūpam
ādyaṁ purāṇa-puruṣaṁ nava-yauvanaṁ ca
vedeṣu durllabham adurllabham ātma-bhaktau
govindam ādi-puruṣaṁ tam ahaṁ bhajāmi.

(Bs. 5.33)

"I worship the Supreme Personality of Godhead, Govinda [Kṛṣṇa], who is the original person—absolute, infallible, without beginning, although expanded into unlimited forms, still the same original, the oldest, and the person always appearing as a fresh youth. Such eternal, blissful, all-knowing forms of the Lord are usually understood by the best Vedic scholars, but they are always manifest to pure, unalloyed devotees."

It is also stated in *Brahma-saṁhitā:*

rāmādi mūrttiṣu kalā-niyamena tiṣṭhan
nānāvatāram akarod bhuvaneṣu kintu
kṛṣṇaḥ svayaṁ samabhavat paramaḥ pumān yo
govindam ādi-puruṣaṁ tam ahaṁ bhajāmi

(Bs. 5.39)

"I worship the Supreme Personality of Godhead, Govinda [Kṛṣṇa], who is always situated in various incarnations such as Rāma, Nṛsiṁha and many sub-incarnations as well, but who is the original Personality of Godhead known as Kṛṣṇa, and who incarnates personally also."

In the *Vedas* also it is said that the Lord, although one without a second, nevertheless manifests Himself in innumerable forms. He is like the *vaidurya* stone, which changes color yet still remains one. All those multiforms are understood by the pure, unalloyed devotees, but not by a simple study of the *Vedas: vedeṣu durllabham adurllabham ātma-bhaktau*. Devotees like Arjuna are constant companions of the Lord, and whenever the Lord incarnates, the associate devotees also incarnate in order to serve the Lord in different capacities. Arjuna is one of these devotees, and in this verse it is understood that some millions of years ago when Lord Kṛṣṇa spoke the *Bhagavad-gītā* to the sun-god Vivasvān, Arjuna, in a different capacity, was also present. But the difference between the Lord and Arjuna is that the Lord remembered the incidence, whereas Arjuna could not remember. That is the difference between the part and parcel living entity and the Supreme Lord. Although Arjuna is addressed herein as the mighty hero who could subdue the enemies, he is unable to recall what had happened in his various past births. Therefore, a living entity, however great he may be in the material estimation, can never equal the Supreme Lord. Anyone who is a constant companion of the Lord is certainly a liberated person, but he cannot be equal to the Lord. The Lord is described in the *Brahma-saṁhitā* as infallible (*acyuta*), which means that He never forgets Himself, even though He is in material contact. Therefore, the Lord and the living entity can never be equal in all respects, even if the living entity is as liberated as Arjuna. Although Arjuna is a devotee of the Lord, he sometimes forgets the nature of the Lord, but by the divine grace a devotee can at once understand the infallible condition of the Lord, whereas a nondevotee or a demon cannot understand this transcendental nature. Consequently these descriptions in the *Gītā* cannot be understood by demonic brains. Kṛṣṇa remembered acts which were performed by Him millions of years before, but Arjuna could not, despite the fact that both Kṛṣṇa and Arjuna are eternal in nature. We may also note herein that a living entity forgets everything due to his change of body, but the Lord remembers because He does not change His *sac-cid-ānanda* body. He is *advaita*, which means there is no distinction between His body and Himself. Everything in relation to Him is spirit—whereas the conditioned soul is different from his material body. And, because the Lord's body and self are identical, His position is always different from the ordinary living entity, even when He descends to the material platform. The demons cannot adjust themselves to this transcendental nature of the Lord, as the Lord explains in the following verse.

TEXT 6

अजोऽपि सन्नव्ययात्मा भूतानामीश्वरोऽपि सन् ।
प्रकृतिं स्वामधिष्ठाय सम्भवाम्यात्ममायया ॥ ६ ॥

ajo 'pi sann avyayātmā
bhūtānām īśvaro 'pi san
prakṛtiṁ svām adhiṣṭhāya
sambhavāmy ātma-māyayā

ajah—unborn; *api*—although; *san*—being so; *avyaya*—without deterioration; *ātmā*—body; *bhūtānām*—all those who are born; *īśvaraḥ*—the Supreme Lord; *api*—although; *san*—being so; *prakṛtim*—transcendental form; *svām*—of Myself; *adhiṣṭhāya*—being so situated; *sambhavāmi*—I do incarnate; *ātma-māyayā*—by My internal energy.

TRANSLATION

Although I am unborn and My transcendental body never deteriorates, and although I am the Lord of all sentient beings, I still appear in every millennium in My original transcendental form.

PURPORT

The Lord has spoken about the peculiarity of His birth: although He may appear like an ordinary person, He remembers everything of His many, many past "births," whereas a common man cannot remember what he has done even a few hours before. If someone is asked what he did exactly at the same time one day earlier, it would be very difficult for a common man to answer immediately. He would surely have to dredge his memory to recall what he was doing exactly at the same time one day before. And yet, men often dare claim to be God, or Kṛṣṇa. One should not be misled by such meaningless claims. Then again, the Lord explains His *prakṛti* or His form. *Prakṛti* means nature as well as *svarūpa*, or one's own form. The Lord says that He appears in His own body. He does not change His body, as the common living entity changes from one body to another. The conditioned soul may have one kind of body in the present birth, but he has a different body in the next birth. In the material world, the living entity has no fixed body but transmigrates from one body to another. The Lord, however, does not do so. Whenever He appears, He does so in the same original body, by His internal potency. In other words,

Kṛṣṇa appears in this material world in His original eternal form, with two hands, holding a flute. He appears exactly in His eternal body, uncontaminated by this material world. Although He appears in the same transcendental body and is Lord of the universe, it still appears that He takes His birth like an ordinary living entity. Despite the fact Lord Kṛṣṇa grows from childhood to boyhood and from boyhood to youth, astonishingly enough He never ages beyond youth. At the time of the Battle of Kurukṣetra, He had many grandchildren at home; or, in other words, He had sufficiently aged by material calculations. Still He looked just like a young man twenty or twenty-five years old. We never see a picture of Kṛṣṇa in old age because He never grows old like us, although He is the oldest person in the whole creation—past, present, and future. Neither His body nor His intelligence ever deteriorates or changes. Therefore, it is clear that in spite of His being in the material world, He is the same unborn, eternal form of bliss and knowledge, changeless in His transcendental body and intelligence. Factually, His appearance and disappearance are like the sun's rising, moving before us, and then disappearing from our eyesight. When the sun is out of sight, we think that the sun is set, and when the sun is before our eyes, we think that the sun is on the horizon. Actually, the sun is always in its fixed position, but owing to our defective, insufficient senses, we calculate the appearance and disappearance of the sun in the sky. And, because His appearance and disappearance are completely different from that of any ordinary, common living entity, it is evident that He is eternal, blissful knowledge by His internal potency—and He is never contaminated by material nature. The *Vedas* also confirm that the Supreme Personality of Godhead is unborn, yet He still appears to take His birth in multi-manifestations. The Vedic supplementary literatures also confirm that even though the Lord appears to be taking His birth, He is still without change of body. In the *Bhāgavatam*, He appears before His mother as Nārāyaṇa, with four hands and the decorations of the six kinds of full opulences. His appearance in His original eternal form is His causeless mercy, according to the *Viśvakośa* dictionary. The Lord is conscious of all of His previous appearances and disappearances, but a common living entity forgets everything about his past body as soon as he gets another body. He is the Lord of all living entities because He performs wonderful and superhuman activities while He is on this earth. Therefore, the Lord is always the same Absolute Truth and is without differentiation between His form and self, or between His quality and body. A question may now be raised as to why the Lord appears and disappears in this world. This is explained in the next verse.

TEXT 7

यदा यदा हि धर्मस्य ग्लानिर्भवति भारत ।
अभ्युत्थानमधर्मस्य तदात्मानं सृजाम्यहम् ॥ ७ ॥

*yadā yadā hi dharmasya
glānir bhavati bhārata
abhyutthānam adharmasya
tadātmānaṁ sṛjāmy aham*

yadā—whenever; *yadā*—wherever; *hi*—certainly; *dharmasya*—of religion; *glāniḥ*—discrepancies; *bhavati*—manifested, becomes; *bhārata*—O descendant of Bharata; *abhyutthānam*—predominance; *adharmasya*—of irreligion; *tadā*—at that time; *ātmānam*—self; *sṛjāmi*—manifest; *aham*—I.

TRANSLATION

Whenever and wherever there is a decline in religious practice, O descendant of Bharata, and a predominant rise of irreligion—at that time I descend Myself.

PURPORT

The word *sṛjāmi* is significant herein. *Sṛjāmi* cannot be used in the sense of creation. because, according to the previous verse, there is no creation of the Lord's form or body, since all of the forms are eternally existent. Therefore *sṛjāmi* means that the Lord manifests Himself as He is. Although the Lord appears on schedule, namely at the end of Dvāpara-yuga of the twenty-eighth millennium of the eighth Manu, in one day of Brahmā, still He has no obligation to adhere to such rules and regulations because He is completely free to act in many ways at His will. He therefore appears by His own will whenever there is a predominance of irreligiosity and a disappearance of true religion. Principles of religion are laid down in the *Vedas*, and any discrepancy in the matter of properly executing the rules of the *Vedas* makes one irreligious. In the *Bhāgavatam* it is stated that such principles are the laws of the Lord. Only the Lord can manufacture a system of religion. The *Vedas* are also accepted as originally spoken by the Lord Himself to Brahmā, from within his heart. Therefore, the principles of *dharma*, or religion, are the direct orders of the Supreme Personality of Godhead (*dharmaṁ tu sākṣāt-bhagavat-praṇītam*). These principles are clearly indicated throughout the *Bhagavad-gītā*. The purpose of the *Vedas* is to establish such principles under the order of the Supreme Lord, and the Lord directly orders, at the end of the *Gītā*, that the highest principle of religion is to surrender unto Him only, and nothing more. The Vedic principles push one towards complete surrender unto Him; and, whenever such principles are disturbed by the demonic, the Lord appears. From the *Bhāgavatam* we understand that Lord Buddha is the incarnation of Kṛṣṇa who appeared when materialism was rampant and materialists were using the pretext of the authority of the *Vedas*. Although there are certain restrictive rules and regulations regarding animal sacrifice for particular purposes in the *Vedas*, people of demonic tendency still took to animal sacrifice without reference to the Vedic principles. Lord Buddha appeared to stop this nonsense and to establish the Vedic principles of nonviolence. Therefore each and every *avatāra*, or incarnation of the Lord, has a particular mission, and they are all described in the revealed scriptures. No one should be accepted as an *avatāra* unless he is referred to by scriptures. It is not a fact that the Lord appears only on Indian soil. He can advent Himself anywhere and every-where, and whenever He desires to appear. In each and every incarnation, He speaks as much about religion as can be understood by the particular people under their particular circumstances. But the mission is the same—to lead people to God consciousness and obedience to the principles of religion. Sometimes He descends personally, and sometimes He sends His bona fide representative in the form of His son, or servant, or Himself in some disguised form.

The principles of the *Bhagavad-gītā* were spoken to Arjuna, and, for that matter, to other highly elevated persons, because he was highly advanced compared to ordinary persons in other parts of the world. Two plus two equals four is a mathematical principle that is true both in the beginner's arithmetic class and in the advanced class as well. Still, there are higher and lower mathematics. In all incarnations of the Lord, therefore, the same principles are taught, but they appear to be higher and lower in varied circumstances. The higher principles of religion begin with the acceptance of the four orders and the four statuses of social life, as will be explained later. The whole purpose of the mission of incarnations is to arouse Kṛṣṇa consciousness everywhere. Such consciousness is manifest and nonmanifest only under different circumstances.

TEXT 8

परित्राणाय साधूनां विनाशाय च दुष्कृताम् ।
धर्मसंस्थापनार्थाय सम्भवामि युगे युगे ॥ ८ ॥

paritrāṇāya sādhūnāṁ
vināśāya ca duṣkṛtām
dharma-saṁsthāpanārthāya
sambhavāmi yuge yuge

paritrāṇāya—for the deliverance; *sādhūnām*—of the devotees; *vināśāya*—for the annihilation; *ca*—also; *duṣkṛtām*—of the miscreants; *dharma*—principles of religion; *saṁsthāpana-arthāya*—to reestablish; *sambhavāmi*—I do appear; *yuge*—millennium; *yuge*—after millennium.

TRANSLATION

In order to deliver the pious and to annihilate the miscreants, as well as to reestablish the principles of religion, I advent Myself millennium after millennium.

PURPORT

According to *Bhagavad-gītā*, a *sādhu* (holyman) is a man in Kṛṣṇa consciousness. A person may appear to be irreligious, but if he has the qualifications of Kṛṣṇa consciousness wholly and fully, he is to be understood to be a *sādhu*. And *duṣkṛtam* applies to one who doesn't care for Kṛṣṇa consciousness. Such miscreants, or *duṣkṛtam*, are described as foolish and the lowest of mankind, even though they may be decorated with mundane education; whereas another person, who is one hundred percent engaged in Kṛṣṇa consciousness, is accepted as *sādhu*, even though such a person may neither be learned nor well cultured. As far as the atheistic are concerned, it is not necessary for the Supreme Lord to appear as He is to destroy them, as He did with the demons Rāvaṇa and Kaṁsa. The Lord has many agents who are quite competent to vanquish demons. But the Lord especially descends to appease His unalloyed devotees, who are always harassed by the demonic. The demon harasses the devotee, even though the latter may happen to be his kin. Although Prahlāda Mahārāja was the son of Hiraṇyakaśipu, he was nonetheless persecuted by his father; although Devakī, the mother of Kṛṣṇa, was the sister of Kaṁsa, she and her husband Vasudeva were persecuted only because Kṛṣṇa was to be born of them. So Lord Kṛṣṇa appeared primarily to deliver Devakī, rather than kill Kaṁsa, but both were performed simultaneously. Therefore it is said here that to deliver the devotee and vanquish the demon miscreants, the Lord appears in different incarnations.

In the *Caitanya-caritāmṛta* of Kṛṣṇadāsa Kavirāja, the following verses summarize these principles of incarnation:

> *sṛṣṭi-hetu yei mūrti prapañce avatare*
> *sei īśvara-mūrti 'avatāra' nāma dhare*
> *māyātita paravyome savāra avasthāna*
> *viśve 'avatāri' dhare 'avatāra' nāma.*

"The *avatāra*, or incarnation of Godhead, descends from the kingdom of God for material manifestation. And the particular form of the Personality of Godhead who so descends is called an incarnation, or *avatāra*. Such incarnations are situated in the spiritual world, the kingdom of God. When they descend to the material creation, they assume the name *avatāra*."

There are various kinds of *avatāras*, such as *puruṣāvatāras*, *guṇāvatāras*, *līlāvatāras*, *śaktyāveśa avatāras*, *manvantara-avatāras* and *yugāvatāras*—all appearing on schedule all over the universe. But Lord Kṛṣṇa is the primeval Lord, the fountainhead of all *avatāras*. Lord Śrī Kṛṣṇa descends for the specific purposes of mitigating the anxieties of the pure devotees, who are very anxious to see Him in His original Vṛndāvana pastimes. Therefore, the prime purpose of the Kṛṣṇa *avatāra* is to satisfy His unalloyed devotees.

The Lord says that He incarnates Himself in every millennium. This indicates that He incarnates also in the age of Kali. As stated in the *Śrīmad-Bhāgavatam*, the incarnation in the age of Kali is Lord Caitanya Mahāprabhu, who spread the worship of Kṛṣṇa by the *saṅkīrtana* movement (congregational chanting of the holy names), and spread Kṛṣṇa consciousness throughout India. He predicted that this culture of *saṅkīrtana* would be broadcast all over the world, from town to town and village to village. Lord Caitanya as the incarnation of Kṛṣṇa, the Personality of Godhead, is described secretly but not directly in the confidential parts of the revealed scriptures, such as the *Upaniṣads*, *Mahābhārata*, *Bhāgavatam*, etc. The devotees of Lord Kṛṣṇa are much attracted by the *saṅkīrtana* movement of Lord Caitanya. This *avatāra* of the Lord does not kill the miscreants, but delivers them by the causeless mercy of the Lord.

TEXT 9

जन्म कर्म च मे दिव्यमेवं यो वेत्ति तत्त्वतः ।
त्यक्त्वा देहं पुनर्जन्म नैति मामेति सोऽर्जुन ॥ ९ ॥

> *janma karma ca me divyam*
> *evaṁ yo vetti tattvataḥ*
> *tyaktvā dehaṁ punar janma*
> *naiti mām eti so 'rjuna*

janma—birth; *karma*—work; *ca*—also; *me*—of Mine; *divyam*—transcendental; *evam*—like this; *yaḥ*—anyone who; *vetti*—knows; *tattvataḥ*—in reality;
tyaktvā—leaving aside; *deham*—this body; *punaḥ*—again; *janma*—birth;
na—never; *eti*—does attain; *mām*—unto Me; *eti*—does attain; *saḥ*—he;
arjuna—O Arjuna.

TRANSLATION

One who knows the transcendental nature of My appearance and activities does not, upon leaving the body, take his birth again in this material
world, but attains My eternal abode, O Arjuna.

PURPORT

The Lord's descent from His transcendental abode is already explained
in the 6th verse. One who can understand the truth of the appearance of
the Personality of Godhead is already liberated from material bondage, and
therefore he returns to the kingdom of God immediately after quitting
this present material body. Such liberation of the living entity from
material bondage is not at all easy. The impersonalists and the *yogīs* attain
liberation only after much trouble and many, many births. Even then, the
liberation they achieve—merging into the impersonal *brahmajyoti* of the
Lord—is only partial, and there is the risk of returning again to this material world. But the devotee, simply by understanding the transcendental
nature of the body and activities of the Lord, attains the abode of the
Lord after ending this body and does not run the risk of returning again to
this material world. In the *Brahma-saṁhitā* it is stated that the Lord has
many, many forms and incarnations: *advaitam acyutam anādim ananta-
rūpam.* Although there are many transcendental forms of the Lord, they
are still one and the same Supreme Personality of Godhead. One has to
understand this fact with conviction, although it is incomprehensible to
mundane scholars and empiric philosophers. As stated in the *Vedas:*

eko devo nitya-līlānurakto bhakta-vyāpī hṛdy antarātmā.

"The one Supreme Personality of Godhead is eternally engaged in many,
many transcendental forms in relationships with His unalloyed devotees."
This Vedic version is confirmed in this verse of the *Gītā* personally by the
Lord. He who accepts this truth on the strength of the authority of the
Vedas and of the Supreme Personality of Godhead and who does not waste
time in philosophical speculations attains the highest perfectional stage of
liberation. Simply by accepting this truth on faith, one can, without a
doubt, attain liberation. The Vedic version, *"tattvamasi,"* is actually applied

in this case. Anyone who understands Lord Kṛṣṇa to be the Supreme, or who says unto the Lord, "You are the same Supreme Brahman, the Personality of Godhead" is certainly liberated instantly, and consequently his entrance into the transcendental association of the Lord is guaranteed. In other words, such a faithful devotee of the Lord attains perfection, and this is confirmed by the following Vedic assertion:

tam eva viditvātimṛtyumeti nānyaḥ panthā vidyate ayanāya.

One can attain the perfect stage of liberation from birth and death simply by knowing the Lord, the Supreme Personality of Godhead. There is no alternative because anyone who does not understand Lord Kṛṣṇa as the Supreme Personality of Godhead is surely in the mode of ignorance. Consequently he will not attain salvation, simply, so to speak, by licking the outer surface of the bottle of honey, or by interpreting the *Bhagavad-gītā* according to mundane scholarship. Such empiric philosophers may assume very important roles in the material world, but they are not necessarily eligible for liberation. Such puffed up mundane scholars have to wait for the causeless mercy of the devotee of the Lord. One should therefore cultivate Kṛṣṇa consciousness with faith and knowledge, and in this way attain perfection.

TEXT 10

वीतरागभयक्रोधा मन्मया मामुपाश्रिताः ।
बहवो ज्ञानतपसा पूता मद्भावमागताः ॥ १० ॥

vīta-rāga-bhaya-krodhā
man-mayā mām upāśritāḥ
bahavo jñāna-tapasā
pūtā mad-bhāvam āgatāḥ

vīta—freed from; *rāga*—attachment; *bhaya*—fear; *krodhāḥ*—anger; *mat-mayā*—fully in Me; *mām*—unto Me; *upāśritāḥ*—being fully situated; *bahavaḥ*—many; *jñāna*—knowledge; *tapasā*—by penance; *pūtāḥ*—being purified; *mat-bhāvam*—transcendental love for Me; *āgatāḥ*—attained.

TRANSLATION

Being freed from attachment, fear and anger, being fully absorbed in Me and taking refuge in Me, many, many persons in the past became puri-

fled by knowledge of Me—and thus they all attained transcendental love
for Me.

PURPORT

As described above, it is very difficult for a person who is too materially
affected to understand the personal nature of the Supreme Absolute Truth.
Generally, people who are attached to the bodily conception of life are so
absorbed in materialism that it is almost impossible for them to understand
that there is a transcendental body which is imperishable, full of knowledge and eternally blissful. In the materialistic concept, the body is perishable, full of ignorance and completely miserable. Therefore, people in
general keep this same bodily idea in mind when they are informed of the
personal form of the Lord. For such materialistic men, the form of the
gigantic material manifestation is supreme. Consequently they consider the
Supreme to be impersonal. And because they are too materially absorbed,
the conception of retaining the personality after liberation from matter
frightens them. When they are informed that spiritual life is also individual
and personal, they become afraid of becoming persons again, and so they
naturally prefer a kind of merging into the impersonal void. Generally,
they compare the living entities to the bubbles of the ocean, which merge
into the ocean. That is the highest perfection of spiritual existence attainable without individual personality. This is a kind of fearful stage of life,
devoid of perfect knowledge of spiritual existence. Furthermore there are
many persons who cannot understand spiritual existence at all. Being
embarassed by so many theories and by contradictions of various types of
philosophical speculation, they become disgusted or angry and foolishly
conclude that there is no supreme cause and that everything is ultimately
void. Such people are in a diseased condition of life. Some people are too
materially attached and therefore do not give attention to spiritual life,
some of them want to merge into the supreme spiritual cause, and some of
them disbelieve in everything, being angry at all sorts of spiritual speculation out of hopelessness. This last class of men take to the shelter of some
kind of intoxication, and their affective hallucinations are sometimes
accepted as spiritual vision. One has to get rid of all three stages of attachment to the material world: negligence of spiritual life, fear of a spiritual
personal identity, and the conception of void that underlies the frustration
of life. To get free from these three stages of the material concept of life,
one has to take complete shelter of the Lord, guided by the bona fide
spiritual master, and follow the disciplines and regulative principles of

devotional life. The last stage of the devotional life is called *bhāva*, or transcendental love of Godhead.

According to *Bhakti-rasāmṛta-sindhu*, the science of devotional service:

> ādau śraddhā tataḥ sādhu-saṅgo 'tha bhajana-kriyā
> tato 'nartha-nivṛttiḥ syāt tato niṣṭhā rucis tataḥ
> athāsaktis tato bhāvas tataḥ premābhyudañcati
> sādhakānām ayaṁ premṇaḥ prādurbhāve bhavet kramaḥ.

"In the beginning one must have a preliminary desire for self-realization. This will bring one to the stage of trying to associate with persons who are spiritually elevated. In next stage one becomes initiated by an elevated spiritual master, and under his instruction the neophyte devotee begins the process of devotional service. By execution of devotional service under the guidance of the spiritual master, one becomes free from all material attachment, attains steadiness in self-realization, and acquires a taste for hearing about the Absolute Personality of Godhead, Śrī Kṛṣṇa. This taste leads one further forward to attachment for Kṛṣṇa consciousness, which is matured in *bhāva*, or the preliminary stage of transcendental love of God. Real love for God is called *premā*, the highest perfectional stage of life." In the *premā* stage there is constant engagement in the transcendental loving service of the Lord. So, by the slow process of devotional service, under the guidance of the bona fide spiritual master, one can attain the highest stage, being freed from all material attachment, from the fearfulness of one's individual spiritual personality, and from the frustrations resulting from void philosophy. Then one can ultimately attain to the abode of the Supreme Lord.

TEXT 11

ये यथा मां प्रपद्यन्ते तांस्तथैव भजाम्यहम् ।
मम वर्त्मानुवर्तन्ते मनुष्याः पार्थ सर्वशः ॥ ११ ॥

ye yathā māṁ prapadyante
tāṁs tathaiva bhajāmy aham
mama vartmānuvartante
manuṣyāḥ pārtha sarvaśaḥ

ye—all of them; *yathā*—as; *mām*—unto Me; *prapadyante*—surrender; *tān*—unto them; *tathā*—so; *eva*—certainly; *bhajāmi*—do I reward; *aham*—I;

mama—My; *vartma*—path; *anuvartante*—do follow; *manuṣyāḥ*—all men; *pārtha*—O son of Pṛthā; *sarvaśaḥ*—in all respects.

TRANSLATION

All of them—as they surrender unto Me—I reward accordingly. Everyone follows My path in all respects, O son of Pṛthā.

PURPORT

Eveyone is searching for Kṛṣṇa in the different aspects of His manifestations. Kṛṣṇa, the Supreme Personality of Godhead, is partially realized in His impersonal *brahmajyoti* effulgence and as the all-pervading Supersoul dwelling within everything, including the particles of atoms. But Kṛṣṇa is only fully realized by His pure devotees. Consequently, Kṛṣṇa is the object of everyone's realization, and thus anyone and everyone is satisfied according to one's desire to have Him. In the transcendental world also, Kṛṣṇa reciprocates with His pure devotees in the transcendental attitude, just as the devotee wants Him. One devotee may want Kṛṣṇa as supreme master, another as his personal friend, another as his son, and still another as his lover. Kṛṣṇa rewards all the devotees equally, according to their different intensities of love for Him. In the material world, the same reciprocations of feelings are there, and they are equally exchanged by the Lord with the different types of worshipers. The pure devotees both here and in the transcendental abode associate with Him in person and are able to render personal service to the Lord and thus derive transcendental bliss in His loving service. As for those who are impersonalists and who want to commit spiritual suicide by annihilating the individual existence of the living entity, Kṛṣṇa helps also by absorbing them into His effulgence. Such impersonalists do not agree to accept the eternal, blissful Personality of Godhead; consequently they cannot relish the bliss of transcendental personal service to the Lord, having extinguished their individuality. Some of them, who are not situated even in the impersonal existence, return to this material field to exhibit their dormant desires for activities. They are not admitted in the spiritual planets, but they are again given a chance to act on the material planets. For those who are fruitive workers, the Lord awards the desired results of their prescribed duties, as the *yajñeśvara*; and those who are *yogīs* seeking mystic powers are awarded such powers. In other words, everyone is dependant for success upon His mercy alone, and all kinds of spiritual processes are but different degrees of success on the same path. Unless, therefore, one comes to the highest perfection of Kṛṣṇa consciousness, all attempts remain imperfect, as is stated in the Śrīmad-Bhāgavatam:

akāmaḥ sarva-kāmo vā mokṣa-kāma udāradhīḥ
tīvreṇa bhakti-yogena yajeta puruṣam param

"Whether one is without desire [the condition of the devotees], or is desirous of all fruitive results, or is after liberation, one should with all efforts try to worship the Supreme Personality of Godhead for complete perfection, culminating in Kṛṣṇa consciousness." (*Bhāg.* 2.3.10)

TEXT 12

काङ्क्षन्तः कर्मणां सिद्धिं यजन्त इह देवताः ।
क्षिप्रं हि मानुषे लोके सिद्धिर्भवति कर्मजा ॥ १२ ॥

kāṅkṣantaḥ karmaṇām siddhim
yajanta iha devatāḥ
kṣipram hi mānuṣe loke
siddhir bhavati karma-jā

kāṅkṣantaḥ—desiring; *karmaṇām*—of fruitive activities; *siddhim*—perfection; *yajante*—worship by sacrifices; *iha*—in the material world; *devatāḥ*—the demigods; *kṣipram*—very quickly; *hi*—certainly; *mānuṣe*—in human society; *loke*—within this world; *siddhiḥ bhavati*—becomes successful; *karmajā*—the fruitive worker.

TRANSLATION

Men in this world desire success in fruitive activities, and therefore they worship the demigods. Quickly, of course, men get results from fruitive work in this world.

PURPORT

There is a great misconception about the gods or demigods of this material world, and men of less intelligence, although passing as great scholars, take these demigods to be various forms of the Supreme Lord. Actually, the demigods are not different forms of God, but they are God's different parts and parcels. God is one, and the parts and parcels are many. The *Vedas* say, *nityo nityānām:* God is one. *Īśvaraḥ paramaḥ kṛṣṇaḥ.* The Supreme God is one—Kṛṣṇa—and the demigods are delegated with powers to manage this material world. These demigods are all living entities *(nityānām)* with different grades of material power. They cannot be equal to the Supreme God—Nārāyaṇa, Viṣṇu, or Kṛṣṇa. Anyone who thinks that God and the demigods are on the same level is called an atheist, or *pāṣaṇḍī.* Even the great demigods like Brahmā and Śiva cannot be compared to the Supreme Lord. In fact, the Lord is worshiped by demigods such as Brahmā and Śiva *(śiva-viriñci-nutam).* Yet curiously enough there are many human leaders who are worshiped by foolish men under the misunderstanding of anthropomorphism or zoomorphism. *Iha devatāḥ* denotes a powerful man or demigod of this material world. But Nārāyaṇa, Viṣṇu or Kṛṣṇa, the Supreme Personality of Godhead, does not belong to this world. He is above, or transcendental to, material creation. Even Śrīpāda Śaṅkarācārya, the leader of the impersonalists, maintains that Nārāyaṇa, or Kṛṣṇa, is beyond this material creation. However, foolish people *(hṛt-añjana)* worship the demigods because they want immediate results. They get the results, but do not know that results so obtained are temporary and are meant for less intelligent persons. The intelligent person is in Kṛṣṇa consciousness, and he has no need to worship the paltry demigods for some immediate, temporary benefit. The demigods of this material world, as well as their worshipers, will vanish with the annihilation of this material world. The boons of the demigods are material and temporary. Both the material worlds and their inhabitants, including the demigods, and their worshipers, are bubbles in the cosmic ocean. In this world, however, human society is mad after temporary things such as the material opulence of possessing land, family and enjoyable paraphernalia. To achieve such temporary things, they worship the demigods or powerful men in human society. If a man gets some ministership in the government by worshiping a political leader, he considers that he has achieved a great boon. All of them are therefore kowtowing to the so-called leaders or "big guns" in order to achieve temporary boons, and they indeed achieve such things. Such foolish men are not interested in Kṛṣṇa consciousness for the permanent solution to the hardships of material existence. They are all after sense enjoyment, and to get a little facility for sense enjoyment they are attracted to worship empowered living entities known as demigods. This verse indicates that people are rarely interested in Kṛṣṇa consciousness. They are mostly interested in material enjoyment, and therefore they worship some powerful living entity.

TEXT 13

चातुर्वर्ण्यं मया सृष्टं गुणकर्मविभागशः ।
तस्य कर्तारमपि मां विद्ध्यकर्तारमव्ययम् ॥ १३ ॥

cātur-varṇyaṁ mayā sṛṣṭaṁ
guṇa-karma-vibhāgaśaḥ
tasya kartāram api māṁ
viddhy akartāram avyayam

cātur-varṇyam—the four divisions of human society; mayā—by Me; sṛṣṭam—created; guṇa—quality; karma—work; vibhāgaśaḥ—in terms of division; tasya—of that; kartāram—the father; api—although; mām—Me; viddhi—you may know; akartāram—as the non-doer; avyayam—being unchangeable.

TRANSLATION

According to the three modes of material nature and the work ascribed to them, the four divisions of human society were created by Me. And, although I am the creator of this system, you should know that I am yet the non-doer, being unchangeable.

PURPORT

The Lord is the creator of everything. Everything is born of Him, everything is sustained by Him, and everything, after annihilation, rests in Him. He is therefore the creator of the four divisions of the social order, beginning with the intelligent class of men, technically called brāhmaṇas due to their being situated in the mode of goodness. Next is the administrative class, technically called the kṣatriyas due to their being situated in the mode of passion. The mercantile men, called the vaiśyas, are situated in the mixed modes of passion and ignorance, and the śūdras, or laborer class, are situated in the ignorant mode of material nature. In spite of His creating the four divisions of human society, Lord Kṛṣṇa does not belong to any of these divisions, because He is not one of the conditioned souls, a section of whom form human society. Human society is similar to any other animal society, but to elevate men from the animal status, the above-mentioned divisions are created by the Lord for the systematic development of Kṛṣṇa consciousness. The tendency of a particular man toward work is determined by the modes of material nature which he has acquired.

Such symptoms of life, according to different modes of material nature, are described in the Eighteenth Chapter of this book. A person in Kṛṣṇa consciousness, however, is above even the *brāhmaṇas*, because a *brāhmaṇa* by quality is supposed to know about Brahman, the Supreme Absolute Truth. Most of them approach the impersonal Brahman manifestation of Lord Kṛṣṇa, but only a man who transcends the limited knowledge of a *brāhmaṇa* and reaches the knowledge of the Supreme Personality of Godhead, Lord Śrī Kṛṣṇa, becomes a person in Kṛṣṇa consciousness—or, in other words, a *Vaiṣṇava*. Kṛṣṇa consciousness includes knowledge of all different plenary expansions of Kṛṣṇa, namely Rāma, Nṛsiṁha, Varāha, etc. However, as Kṛṣṇa is transcendental to this system of the four divisions of human society, a person in Kṛṣṇa consciousness is also transcendental to all divisions of human society, whether we consider the divisions of community, nation or species.

TEXT 14

न मां कर्माणि लिम्पन्ति न मे कर्मफले स्पृहा ।
इति मां योऽभिजानाति कर्मभिर्न स बध्यते ॥ १४ ॥

na māṁ karmāṇi limpanti
na me karma-phale spṛhā
iti māṁ yo 'bhijānāti
karmabhir na sa badhyate

na—never; *mām*—unto Me; *karmāṇi*—all kinds of work; *limpanti*—do affect; *na*—nor; *me*—My; *karma-phale*—in fruitive action; *spṛhā*—aspiration; *iti*—thus; *mām*—unto Me; *yaḥ*—one who; *abhijānāti*—does know; *karmabhiḥ*—by the reaction of such work; *na*—never does; *saḥ*—he; *badhyate*—become entangled.

TRANSLATION

There is no work that affects Me; nor do I aspire for the fruits of action. One who understands this truth about Me also does not become entangled in the fruitive reactions of work.

PURPORT

As there are constitutional laws in the material world stating that the king can do no wrong, or that the king is not subject to the state laws, similarly the Lord, although He is the creator of this material world, is not affected by the activities of the material world. He creates and remains aloof from the creation, whereas the living entities are entangled in the fruitive results of material activities because of their propensity for lording it over material resources. The proprietor of an establishment is not responsible for the right and wrong activities of the workers, but the workers are themselves responsible. The living entities are engaged in their respective activities of sense gratification, and these activities are not ordained by the Lord. For advancement of sense gratification, the living entities are engaged in the work of this world, and they aspire to heavenly happiness after death. The Lord, being full in Himself, has no attraction for so-called heavenly happiness. The heavenly demigods are only His engaged servants. The proprietor never desires the low-grade happiness such as the workers may desire. He is aloof from the material actions and reactions. For example, the rains are not responsible for different types of vegetation that appear on the earth, although without such rains there is no possibility of vegetative growth. Vedic *smṛti* confirms this fact as follows:

> nimitta-mātram evāsau sṛjyānāṁ sarga-karmaṇi
> pradhāna-kāraṇī-bhūtā yato vai sṛjya-śaktayaḥ.

In the material creations, the Lord is only the supreme cause. The immediate cause is material nature by which the cosmic manifestation is visible. The created beings are of many varieties, such as the demigods, human beings and lower animals, and all of them are subject to the reactions of their past good or bad activities. The Lord only gives them the proper facilities for such activities and the regulations of the modes of nature, but He is never responsible for their past and present activities. In the *Vedānta-sūtras* it is confirmed that the Lord is never partial to any living entity. The living entity is responsible for his own acts. The Lord only gives him facilities, through the agency of material nature, the external energy. Anyone who is fully conversant with all the intricacies of this law of *karma*, or fruitive activities, does not become affected by the results of his activities. In other words, the person who understands this transcendental nature of the Lord is an experienced man in Kṛṣṇa consciousness, and thus he is never subjected to the laws of *karma*. One who does not know the transcendental nature of the Lord and who thinks that the activities of the Lord are aimed at fruitive results, as are the activities of the ordinary living entities, certainly becomes entangled himself in fruitive reaction. But one who knows the Supreme Truth is a liberated soul fixed in Kṛṣṇa consciousness.

TEXT 15

एवं ज्ञात्वा कृतं कर्म पूर्वैरपि मुमुक्षुभिः ।
कुरु कर्मैव तस्मात्त्वं पूर्वैः पूर्वतरं कृतम् ॥ १५ ॥

evaṁ jñātvā kṛtaṁ karma
pūrvair api mumukṣubhiḥ
kuru karmaiva tasmāt tvaṁ
pūrvaiḥ pūrvataraṁ kṛtam

evam—thus; *jñātvā*—knowing well; *kṛtam*—performed; *karma*—work; *pūrvaiḥ*—by past authorities; *api*—although; *mumukṣubhiḥ*—who attained liberation; *kuru*—just perform; *karma*—prescribed duty; *eva*—certainly; *tasmāt*—therefore; *tvam*—you; *pūrvaiḥ*—by the predecessors; *pūrvataram*—ancient predecessors; *kṛtam*—as performed.

TRANSLATION

All the liberated souls in ancient times acted with this understanding and so attained liberation. Therefore, as the ancients, you should perform your duty in this divine consciousness.

PURPORT

There are two classes of men. Some of them are full of polluted material things within their hearts, and some of them are materially free. Kṛṣṇa consciousness is equally beneficial for both of these persons. Those who are full of dirty things can take to the line of Kṛṣṇa consciousness for a gradual cleansing process, following the regulative principles of devotional service. Those who are already cleansed of the impurities may continue to act in the same Kṛṣṇa consciousness so that others may follow their exemplary activities and thereby be benefitted. Foolish persons or neophytes in Kṛṣṇa consciousness often want to retire from activities without having knowledge of Kṛṣṇa consciousness. Arjuna's desire to retire from activities on the battlefield was not approved by the Lord. One need only know how to act. To retire from the activities of Kṛṣṇa consciousness and to sit aloof making a show of Kṛṣṇa consciousness; is less important than actually engaging in the field of activities for the sake of Kṛṣṇa. Arjuna is here advised to act in Kṛṣṇa consciousness, following in the footsteps of the Lord's previous disciples, such as the sun-god Vivasvān, as mentioned hereinbefore. The Supreme Lord knows all His past activities, as well as those of persons who acted in Kṛṣṇa consciousness in the past. Therefore He recommends the acts of the sun-god, who learned this art from the Lord some millions of years before. All such students of Lord Kṛṣṇa are mentioned here as past liberated persons, engaged in the discharge of duties allotted by Kṛṣṇa.

TEXT 16

किं कर्म किमकर्मेति कवयोऽप्यत्र मोहिताः ।
तत्ते कर्म प्रवक्ष्यामि यज्ज्ञात्वा मोक्ष्यसेऽशुभात् ॥ १६ ॥

kiṁ karma kim akarmeti
kavayo 'py atra mohitāḥ
tat te karma pravakṣyāmi
yaj jñātvā mokṣyase 'śubhāt

kim—what is; *karma*—action; *kim*—what is; *akarma*—inaction; *iti*—thus; *kavayaḥ*—the intelligent; *api*—also; *atra*—in this matter; *mohitāḥ*—bewildered; *tat*—that; *te*—unto you; *karma*—work; *pravakṣyāmi*—I shall explain; *yat*—which; *jñātvā*—knowing; *mokṣyase*—be liberated; *aśubhāt*—from ill fortune.

TRANSLATION

Even the intelligent are bewildered in determining what is action and what is inaction. Now I shall explain to you what action is, knowing which you shall be liberated from all sins.

PURPORT

Action in Kṛṣṇa consciousness has to be executed in accord with the examples of previous bona fide devotees. This is recommended in the 15th verse. Why such action should not be independant will be explained in the text to follow.

To act in Kṛṣṇa consciousness, one has to follow the leadership of authorized persons who are in a line of disciplic succession as explained in the beginning of this chapter. The system of Kṛṣṇa consciousness was first narrated to the sun-god, the sun-god explained it to his son Manu, Manu explained it to his son Ikṣvāku, and the system is current on this earth from that very remote time. Therefore, one has to follow in the footsteps of previous authorities in the line of disciplic succession. Otherwise even the most intelligent men will be bewildered regarding the standard actions of Kṛṣṇa consciousness. For this reason, the Lord decided to instruct Arjuna in Kṛṣṇa consciousness directly. Because of the direct instruction of the Lord to Arjuna, anyone who follows in the footsteps of Arjuna is certainly not bewildered.

It is said that one cannot ascertain the ways of religion simply by imperfect experimental knowledge. Actually, the principles of religion can only be laid down by the Lord Himself. *Dharmaṁ hi sākṣāt-bhagavat-praṇītam.* No one can manufacture a religious principle by imperfect speculation. One must follow in the footsteps of great authorities like Brahmā, Śiva, Nārada, Manu, Kumāra, Kapila, Prahlāda, Bhīṣma, Śukadeva Gosvāmī, Yamarāja, Janaka, etc. By mental speculation one cannot ascertain what is religion or self-realization. Therefore, out of causeless mercy to His devotees, the Lord explains directly to Arjuna what action is and what inaction is. Only action performed in Kṛṣṇa consciousness can deliver a person from the entanglement of material existence.

TEXT 17

कर्मणो ह्यपि बोद्धव्यं बोद्धव्यं च विकर्मणः ।
अकर्मणश्च बोद्धव्यं गहना कर्मणो गतिः ॥ १७ ॥

karmaṇo hy api boddhavyaṁ
boddhavyaṁ ca vikarmaṇaḥ
akarmaṇaś ca boddhavyaṁ
gahanā karmaṇo gatiḥ

karmaṇaḥ—working order ; *hi*—certainly; *api*—also; *boddhavyam*—should be understood; *boddhavyam*—to be understood; *ca*—also; *vikarmaṇaḥ*—forbidden work; *akarmaṇaḥ*—inaction; *ca*—also; *boddhavyam*—should be understood; *gahanā*—very difficult; *karmaṇaḥ*—working order; *gatiḥ*—to enter into.

TRANSLATION

The intricacies of action are very hard to understand. Therefore one should know properly what action is, what forbidden action is, and what inaction is.

PURPORT

If one is serious about liberation from material bondage, one has to understand the distinctions between action, inaction and unauthorized actions. One has to apply oneself to such an analysis of action, reaction and perverted actions because it is a very difficult subject matter. To understand Kṛṣṇa consciousness and action according to the modes, one has to learn one's relationship with the Supreme; i.e., one who has learned perfectly knows that every living entity is the eternal servitor of the Lord and that consequently one has to act in Kṛṣṇa consciousness. The entire *Bhagavad-gītā* is directed toward this conclusion. Any other conclusions, against this consciousness and its attendant reactions, are *vikarmas*, or prohibitive actions. To understand all this one has to associate with authorities in Kṛṣṇa consciousness and learn the secret from them; this is as good as learning from the Lord directly. Otherwise, even the most intelligent person will be bewildered.

TEXT 18

कर्मण्यकर्म यः पश्येदकर्मणि च कर्म यः ।
सा बुद्धिमान्मनुष्येषु स युक्तः कृत्स्नकर्मकृत् ॥ १८ ॥

karmaṇy akarma yaḥ paśyed
akarmaṇi ca karma yaḥ
sa buddhimān manuṣyeṣu
sa yuktaḥ kṛtsna-karma-kṛt

karmaṇi—in action; *akarma*—inaction; *yaḥ*—one who; *paśyet*—observes; *akarmaṇi*—in inaction; *ca*—also; *karma*—fruitive action; *yaḥ*—one who; *saḥ*—he; *buddhimān*—is intelligent; *manuṣyeṣu*—in human society; *saḥ*—he; *yuktaḥ*—is in the transcendental position; *kṛtsna-karma-kṛt*—although engaged in all activities.

TRANSLATION

One who sees inaction in action, and action in inaction, is intelligent among men, and he is in the tranecendental position, although engaged in all sorts of activities.

PURPORT

A person acting in Kṛṣṇa consciousness is naturally free from the bonds of *karma*. His activities are all performed for Kṛṣṇa; therefore he does not enjoy or suffer any of the effects of work. Consequently he is intelligent in human society, even though he is engaged in all sorts of activities for Kṛṣṇa. *Akarma* means without reaction to work. The impersonalist ceases fruitive activities out of fear, so that the resultant action may not be a stumbling block on the path of self-realization, but the personalist knows rightly his position as the eternal servitor of the Supreme Personality of Godhead. Therefore he engages himself in the activities of Kṛṣṇa consciousness. Because everything is done for Kṛṣṇa, he enjoys only transcendental happiness in the discharge of this service. Those who are engaged in this process are known to be without desire for personal sense gratification. The sense of eternal servitorship to Kṛṣṇa makes one immune to all sorts of reactionary elements of work.

TEXT 19

यस्य सर्वे समारम्भाः कामसंकल्पवर्जिताः ।
ज्ञानाग्निदग्धकर्माणं तमाहुः पण्डितं बुधाः ॥ १९ ॥

yasya sarve samārambhāḥ
kāma-saṅkalpa-varjitāḥ
jñānāgni-dagdha-karmāṇaṁ
tam āhuḥ paṇḍitaṁ budhāḥ

yasya—one whose; *sarve*—all sorts of; *samārambhāḥ*—in all attempts; *kāma*—desire for sense gratification; *saṅkalpa*—determination; *varjitāḥ*—are devoid of; *jñāna*—of perfect knowledge; *agni*—fire; *dagdha*—being burnt by; *karmāṇam*—the performer; *tam*—him; *āhuḥ*—declare; *paṇḍitam*—learned; *budhāḥ*—those who know.

TRANSLATION

One is understood to be in full knowledge whose every act is devoid of desire for sense gratification. He is said by sages to be a worker whose fruitive action is burned up by the fire of perfect knowledge.

PURPORT

Only a person in full knowledge can understand the activities of a person in Kṛṣṇa consciousness. Because the person in Kṛṣṇa consciousness is devoid of all kinds of sense-gratificatory propensities, it is to be understood that he has burned up the reactions of his work by perfect knowledge of his constitutional position as the eternal servitor of the Supreme Personality of Godhead. He is actually learned who has attained to such perfection of knowledge. Development of this knowledge of the eternal servitorship of the Lord is compared to fire. Such a fire, once kindled, can burn up all kinds of reactions to work.

TEXT 20

त्यक्त्वा कर्मफलासङ्गं नित्यतृप्तो निराश्रयः ।
कर्मण्यभिप्रवृत्तोऽपि नैव किंचित्करोति सः ॥ २० ॥

tyaktvā karma-phalāsaṅgaṁ
nitya-tṛpto nirāśrayaḥ
karmaṇy abhipravṛtto 'pi
naiva kiñcit karoti saḥ

tyaktvā—having given up; *karma-phala-āsaṅgam*—attachment for fruitive results; *nitya*—always; *tṛptaḥ*—being satisfied; *nirāśrayaḥ*—without any center; *karmaṇi*—in activity; *abhipravṛttaḥ*—being fully engaged; *api*—in spite of; *na*—does not; *eva*—certainly; *kiñcit*—anything; *karoti*—do; *saḥ*—he.

TRANSLATION

Abandoning all attachment to the results of his activities, ever satisfied and independant, he performs no fruitive action, although engaged in all kinds of undertakings.

PURPORT

This freedom from the bondage of actions is possible only in Kṛṣṇa consciousness when one is doing everything for Kṛṣṇa. A Kṛṣṇa conscious person acts out of pure love for the Supreme Personality of Godhead, and therefore he has no attraction for the results of the action. He is not even attached to his personal maintenance, for everything is left to Kṛṣṇa. Nor is he anxious to secure things, nor to protect things already in his possession. He does his duty to his best ability and leaves everything to Kṛṣṇa. Such an unattached person is always free from the resultant reactions of good and bad; it is as though he were not doing anything. This is the sign of *akarma*, or actions without fruitive reactions. Any other action, therefore, devoid of Kṛṣṇa consciousness, is binding upon the worker, and that is the real aspect of *vikarma*, as explained hereinbefore.

TEXT 21

निराशीर्यतचित्तात्मा त्यक्तसर्वपरिग्रहः ।
शारीरं केवलं कर्म कुर्वन्नाप्नोति किल्बिषम् ॥ २१ ॥

*nirāśīr yata-cittātmā
tyakta-sarva-parigrahaḥ
śārīraṁ kevalaṁ karma
kurvan nāpnoti kilbiṣam*

nirāśīḥ—without desire for the results; *yata*—controlled; *citta-ātmā*—mind and intelligence; *tyakta*—giving up; *sarva*—all; *parigrahaḥ*—sense of proprietorship over all possessions; *śārīram*—in keeping body and soul together; *kevalam*—only; *karma*—work; *kurvan*—doing so; *na*—never; *āpnoti*—does not acquire; *kilbiṣam*—sinful reactions.

TRANSLATION

Such a man of understanding acts with mind and intelligence perfectly controlled, gives up all sense of proprietorship over his possessions and acts only for the bare necessities of life. Thus working, he is not affected by sinful reactions.

PURPORT

A Kṛṣṇa conscious person does not expect good or bad results in his activities. His mind and intelligence are fully controlled. He knows that he is part and parcel of the Supreme, and therefore the part played by him, as a part and parcel of the whole, is not his by choice but is chosen for him by the Supreme and is done only through His agency. When the hand moves, it does not move out of its own accord, but by the endeavor of the whole body. A Kṛṣṇa conscious person is always dovetailed with the supreme desire, for he has no desire for personal sense gratification. He moves exactly like a part of a machine. As a machine part requires oiling and cleaning for maintenance, similarly, a Kṛṣṇa conscious man maintains himself by his work just to remain fit for action in the transcendental loving service of the Lord. He is therefore immune to all the reactions of his endeavors. Like an animal, he has no proprietorship even over his own body. A cruel proprietor of an animal sometimes kills the animal in his possession, yet the animal does not protest. Nor does it have any real independence. A Kṛṣṇa conscious person, fully engaged in self-realization, has very little time to falsely possess any material object. For maintaining body and soul, he does not require unfair means of accumulating money. He does not, therefore, become contaminated by such material sins. He is free from all reactions to his actions.

TEXT 22

यदृच्छालाभसन्तुष्टो द्वन्द्वातीतो विमत्सरः ।
समः सिद्धावसिद्धौ च कृत्वापि न निबध्यते ॥ २२ ॥

yadṛcchā-lābha-santuṣṭo
dvandvātīto vimatsaraḥ
samaḥ siddhāv asiddhau ca
kṛtvāpi na nibadhyate

yadṛcchā—out of its own accord; lābha—gain; santuṣṭaḥ—satisfied; dvandva—duality; atītaḥ—surpassed; vimatsaraḥ—free from envy; samaḥ—steady; siddhau—in success; asiddhau—failure; ca—also; kṛtvā—doing; api—although; na—never; nibadhyate—is affected.

TRANSLATION

He who is satisfied with gain which comes of its own accord, who is free from duality and does not envy, who is steady both in success and failure, is never entangled, although performing actions.

PURPORT

A Kṛṣṇa conscious person does not make much endeavor even to maintain his body. He is satisfied with gains which are obtained of their own accord. He neither begs nor borrows, but he labors honestly as far as is in his power, and is satisfied with whatever is obtained by his own honest labor. He is therefore independent in his livelihood. He does not allow anyone's service to hamper his own service in Kṛṣṇa consciousness. However, for the service of the Lord he can participate in any kind of action without being disturbed by the duality of the material world. The duality of the material world is felt in terms of heat and cold, or misery and happiness. A Kṛṣṇa conscious person is above duality because he does not hesitate to act in any way for the satisfaction of Kṛṣṇa. Therefore he is steady both in success and in failure. These signs are visible when one is fully in transcendental knowledge.

TEXT 23

गतसङ्गस्य मुक्तस्य ज्ञानावस्थितचेतसः ।
यज्ञायाचरतः कर्म समग्रं प्रविलीयते ॥ २३ ॥

gata-saṅgasya muktasya
jñānāvasthita-cetasaḥ
yajñāyācarataḥ karma
samagraṁ pravilīyate

gata-saṅgasya—unattached to the modes of material nature; *muktasya*—of the liberated; *jñāna-avasthita*—situated in transcendence; *cetasaḥ*—of such wisdom; *yajñāya*—for the sake of Yajña (Kṛṣṇa); *ācarataḥ*—so acting; *karma*—work; *samagram*—in total; *pravilīyate*—merges entirely.

TRANSLATION

The work of a man who is unattached to the modes of material nature and who is fully situated in transcendental knowledge merges entirely into transcendence.

PURPORT

Becoming fully Kṛṣṇa conscious, one is freed from all dualities and thus is free from the contaminations of the material modes. He can become liberated because he knows his constitutional position in relationship with Kṛṣṇa; and thus his mind cannot be drawn from Kṛṣṇa consciousness.

Consequently, whatever he does, he does for Kṛṣṇa, who is the primeval Viṣṇu. Therefore, all his works are technically sacrifices because sacrifice involves satisfying the Supreme Person, Kṛṣṇa. The resultant reactions to all such work certainly merge into transcendence, and one does not suffer material effects.

TEXT 24

ब्रह्मार्पणं ब्रह्म हविर्ब्रह्माग्नौ ब्रह्मणा हुतम् ।
ब्रह्मैव तेन गन्तव्यं ब्रह्म कर्म समाधिना ॥ २४ ॥

brahmārpaṇaṁ brahma havir
brahmāgnau brahmaṇā hutam
brahmaiva tena gantavyaṁ
brahma-karma-samādhinā

brahma—spiritual nature; *arpaṇam*—contribution; *brahma*—the Supreme; *haviḥ*—butter; *brahma*—spiritual; *agnau*—in the fire of consummation; *brāhmaṇā*—by the spirit soul; *hutam*—offered; *brahma*—spiritual kingdom; *eva*—certainly; *tena*—by him; *gantavyam*—to be reached; *brahma*—spiritual; *karma*—activities; *samādhinā*—by complete absorption.

TRANSLATION

A person who is fully absorbed in Kṛṣṇa consciousness is sure to attain the spiritual kingdom because of his full contribution to spiritual activities, in which the consummation is absolute and that which is offered is of the same spiritual nature.

PURPORT

How activities in Kṛṣṇa consciousness can lead one ultimately to the spiritual goal is described here. There are various activities in Kṛṣṇa consciousness, and all of them will be described in the following verses. But, for the present, just the principle of Kṛṣṇa consciousness is described. A conditioned soul, entangled in material contamination, is sure to act in the material atmosphere, and yet he has to get out of such an environment. The process by which the conditioned soul can get out of the material atmosphere is Kṛṣṇa consciousness. For example, a patient who is suffering from a disorder of the bowels due to overindulgence in milk products is cured by another milk product, namely curds. The materially absorbed conditioned soul can be cured by Kṛṣṇa consciousness as set forth here in the Gītā. This process is generally known as yajña, or activities (sacrifices) simply meant for the satisfaction of Viṣṇu or Kṛṣṇa. The more the activities of the material world are performed in Kṛṣṇa consciousness, or for Viṣṇu only, the more the atmosphere becomes spiritualized by complete absorption. Brahman means spiritual. The Lord is spiritual, and the rays of His transcendental body are called brahmajyoti, His spiritual effulgence. Everything that exists is situated in that brahmajyoti, but when the jyoti is covered by illusion (māyā) or sense gratification, it is called material. This material veil can be removed at once by Kṛṣṇa consciousness; thus the offering for the sake of Kṛṣṇa consciousness, the consuming agent of such an offering or contribution; the process of consumption, the contributor, and the result are—all combined together—Brahman, or the Absolute Truth. The Absolute Truth covered by māyā is called matter. Matter dovetailed for the cause of the Absolute Truth regains its spiritual quality. Kṛṣṇa consciousness is the process of converting the illusory consciousness into Brahman, or the Supreme. When the mind is fully absorbed in Kṛṣṇa consciousness, it is said to be in samādhi, or trance. Anything done in such transcendental consciousness is called yajña, or sacrifice for the Absolute. In that condition of spiritual consciousness, the contributor, the contribution, the consumption, the performer or leader of the performance, and the result or ultimate gain—everything—becomes one in the Absolute, the Supreme Brahman. That is the method of Kṛṣṇa consciousness.

TEXT 25

दैवमेवापरे यज्ञं योगिनः पर्युपासते ।
ब्रह्माग्नावपरे यज्ञं यज्ञेनैवोपजुह्वति ॥ २५ ॥

daivam evāpare yajñaṁ
yoginaḥ paryupāsate
brahmāgnāv apare yajñaṁ
yajñenaivopajuhvati

daivam—in worshiping the demigods; *eva*—like this; *apare*—some; *yajñam* —sacrifices; *yoginaḥ*—the mystics; *paryupāsate*—worship perfectly; *brahma*

—the Absolute Truth; *agnau*—in the fire of; *apare*—others; *yajñam*—sacrifice; *yajñena*—by sacrifice; *eva*—thus; *upajuhvati*—worship.

TRANSLATION

Some yogīs perfectly worship the demigods by offering different sacrifices to them, and some of them offer sacrffices in the fire of the Supreme Brahman.

PURPORT

As described above, a person engaged in discharging duties in Kṛṣṇa consciousness is also called a perfect *yogī* or a first-class mystic. But there are others also, who perform similar sacrifices in the worship of demigods, and still others who sacrifice to the Supreme Brahman, or the impersonal feature of the Supreme Lord. So there are different kinds of sacrifices in terms of different categories. Such different categories of sacrifice by different types of performers only superficially demark varieties of sacrifice. Factual sacrifice means to satisfy the Supreme Lord, Viṣṇu, who is also known as *Yajña*. All the different varieties of sacrifice can be placed within two primary divisions: namely, sacrifice of worldly possessions and sacrifice in pursuit of transcendental knowledge. Those who are in Kṛṣṇa consciousness sacrifice all material possessions for the satisfaction of the Supreme Lord, while others, who want some temporary material happiness, sacrifice their material possessions to satisfy demigods such as Indra, the sun-god, etc. And others, who are impersonalists, sacrifice their identity by merging into the existence of impersonal Brahman. The demigods are powerful living entities appointed by the Supreme Lord for the maintenance and supervision of all material functions like the heating, watering and lighting of the universe. Those who are interested in material benefits worship the demigods by various sacrifices according to the Vedic rituals. They are called *bahv-īśvara-vādī*, or believers in many gods. But others, who worship the impersonal feature of the Absolute Truth and regard the forms of the demigods as temporary, sacrifice their individual selves in the supreme fire and thus end their individual existences by merging into the existence of the Supreme. Such impersonalists spend their time in philosophical speculation to understand the transcendental nature of the Supreme. In other words, the fruitive workers sacrifice their material possessions for material enjoyment, whereas the impersonalist sacrifices his material designations with a view to merging into the existence of the

Supreme. For the impersonalist, the fire altar of sacrifice is the Supreme Brahman, and the offering is the self being consumed by the fire of Brahman. The Kṛṣṇa conscious person, like Arjuna, however, sacrifices everything for the satisfaction of Kṛṣṇa, and thus all his material possessions as well as his own self—everything—is sacrificed for Kṛṣṇa. Thus, he is the first-class *yogī*; but he does not lose his individual existence.

TEXT 26

श्रोत्रादीनीन्द्रियाण्यन्ये संयमाग्निषु जुह्वति ।
शब्दादीन्विषयानन्य इन्द्रियाग्निषु जुह्वति ॥ २६ ॥

śrotrādīnīndriyāṇy anye
saṁyamāgniṣu juhvati
śabdādīn viṣayān anya
indriyāgniṣu juhvati

śrotra ādīni—hearing process; *indriyāṇi*—senses; *anye*—others; *saṁyama*—of restraint; *agniṣu*—in the fire; *juhvati*—offers; *śabda-ādīn*—sound vibration, etc.; *viṣayān*—objects of sense gratification; *anye*—others: *indriya*—of sense organs; *agniṣu*—in the fire; *juhvati*—sacrifice.

TRANSLATION

Some of them sacrifice the hearing process and the senses in the fire of the controlled mind, and others sacrifice the objects of the senses, such as sound, in the fire of sacrifice.

PURPORT

The four divisions of human life, namely the *brahmacārī*, the *gṛhastha*, the *vānaprastha*, and the *sannyāsī*, are all meant to help men become perfect *yogīs* or transcendentalists. Since human life is not meant for our enjoying sense gratification like the animals, the four orders of human life are so arranged that one may become perfect in spiritual life. The *brahmacārīs*, or students under the care of a bona fide spiritual master, control the mind by abstaining from sense gratification. They are referred to in this verse as sacrificing the hearing process and the senses in the fire of the controlled mind. A *brahmacārī* hears only words concerning Kṛṣṇa consciousness; hearing is the basic principle for understanding, and therefore the pure *brahmacārī* engages fully in *harer nāmānukīrtanam*—chanting and hearing the glories of the Lord. He restrains himself from the vibrations of material sounds, and his hearing is engaged in the transcendental sound vibration of Hare Kṛṣṇa, Hare Kṛṣṇa. Similarly, the householders, who have some license for sense gratification, perform such acts with great restraint. Sex life, intoxication and meat eating are general tendencies of human society, but a regulated householder does not indulge in unrestricted sex life and other sense gratifications. Marriage on principles of religious life is therefore current in all civilized human society because that is the way for restricted sex life. This restricted, unattached sex life is also a kind of *yajña* because the restricted householder sacrifices his general tendency toward sense gratification for higher transcendental life.

TEXT 27

सर्वाणीन्द्रियकर्माणि प्राणकर्माणि चापरे ।
आत्मसंयमयोगाग्नौ जुह्वति ज्ञानदीपिते ॥ २७ ॥

sarvāṇīndriya-karmāṇi
prāṇa-karmāṇi cāpare
ātma-saṁyama-yogāgnau
juhvati jñāna-dīpite

sarvāṇi—all; *indriya*—senses; *karmāṇi*—functions; *prāṇa-karmāṇi*—functions of the life breath; *ca*—also; *apare*—others; *ātma-saṁyama*—controlling the mind; *yoga*—linking process; *agnau*—in the fire of; *juhvati*—offers; *jñāna-dīpite*—because of the urge for self-realization.

TRANSLATION

Those who are interested in self-realization, in terms of mind and sense control, offer the functions of all the senses, as well as the vital force [breath], as oblations into the fire of the controlled mind.

PURPORT

The *yoga* system conceived by Patañjali is referred to herein. In the *Yoga-sūtra* of Patañjali, the soul is called *pratyag-ātmā* and *parag-ātmā*. As long as the soul is attached to sense enjoyment, it is called *parag-ātmā*. The soul is subjected to the functions of ten kinds of air at work within the body, and this is perceived through the breathing system. The Pātañjala system of *yoga* instructs one on how to control the functions of the body's air in a technical manner so that ultimately all the functions of the air within become favorable for purifying the soul of material attachment. According to this *yoga* system, *pratyag ātmā* is the ultimate goal. This *pratyag ātmā* is a withdrawal from activities in matter. The senses interact with the sense objects, like the ear for hearing, eyes for seeing, nose for smelling, tongue for tasting, hand for touching, and all of them are thus engaged in activities outside the self. They are called the functions of the *prāṇa-vāyu*. The *apāna-vāyu* goes downwards, *vyāna-vāyu* acts to shrink and expand, *samāna-vāyu* adjusts equilibrium, *udāna-vāyu* goes upwards— and when one is enlightened, one engages all these in searching for self-realization.

TEXT 28

द्रव्ययज्ञास्तपोयज्ञा योगयज्ञास्तथापरे ।
स्वाध्यायज्ञानयज्ञाश्च यतयः संशितव्रताः ॥ २८ ॥

dravya-yajñās tapo-yajñā
yoga-yajñās tathāpare
svādhyāya-jñāna-yajñāś ca
yatayaḥ saṁśita-vratāḥ

dravya-yajñāḥ—sacrificing one's possessions; *tapo-yajñāḥ*—sacrifice in austerities; *yoga-yajñāḥ*—sacrifice in eightfold mysticism; *tathā*—thus; *apare*—others; *svādhyāya*—sacrifice in the study of the *Vedas*; *jñāna-yajñāḥ*—sacrifice in advancement of transcendental knowledge; *ca*—also; *yatayaḥ*—enlightened; *saṁśita*—taken to strict; *vratāḥ*—vows.

TRANSLATION

There are others who, enlightened by sacrificing their material possessions in severe austerities, take strict vows and practice the yoga of eightfold mysticism, and others study the Vedas for the advancement of transcendental knowledge.

PURPORT

These sacrifices may be fitted into various divisions. There are persons who are sacrificing their possessions in the form of various kinds of charities. In India, the rich mercantile community or princely orders open various kinds of charitable institutions like *dharmaśālā, anna-kṣetra, atithi-śālā, anathalaya, vidyāpīṭha*, etc. In other countries, too, there are many hospitals, old age homes and similar charitable foundations meant for distributing food, education and medical treatment free to the poor. All these charitable activities are called *dravyamaya-yajña*. There are others who, for higher elevation in life or for promotion to higher planets within the universe, voluntarily accept many kinds of austerities such as *candrāyana* and *cāturmāsya*. These processes entail severe vows for conducting life under certain rigid rules. For example, under the *cāturmāsya* vow the candidate does not shave for four months during the year (July to October), he does not eat certain foods, does not eat twice in a day and does not leave home. Such sacrifice of the comforts of life is called *tapomaya-yajña*. There are still others who engage themselves in different kinds of mystic *yogas* like the Patañjali system (for merging into the existence of the Absolute), or *haṭha-yoga* or *aṣṭāṅga-yoga* (for particular perfections). And some travel to all the sanctified places of pilgrimage. All these practices are called *yoga-yajña*, sacrifice for a certain type of perfection in the material world. There are others who engage themselves in the studies of different Vedic literatures, specifically the *Upaniṣads* and *Vedānta-sūtras*, or the *sāṅkhya* philosophy. All of these are called *svādhyāya-yajña*, or engagement in the sacrifice of studies. All these *yogīs* are faithfully engaged in different types of sacrifice and are seeking a higher status of life. Krṣṇa consciousness, is, however, different from these because it is the direct service of the Supreme Lord. Kṛṣṇa consciousness cannot be attained by any one of the above-mentioned types of sacrifices but can be attained only by the mercy of the Lord and His bona fide devotee. Therefore, Kṛṣṇa consciousness is transcendental.

TEXT 29

अपाने जुह्वति प्राणं प्राणेऽपानं तथापरे ।
प्राणापानगती रुद्ध्वा प्राणायामपरायणाः ।
अपरे नियताहाराः प्राणान्प्राणेषु जुह्वति ॥ २९ ॥

apāne juhvati prāṇaṁ
prāṇe 'pānaṁ tathāpare
prāṇāpāna-gatī ruddhvā
prāṇāyāma-parāyaṇāḥ
apare niyatāhārāḥ
prāṇān prāṇeṣu juhvati

apāne—air which acts downward; juhvati—offers; prāṇam—air which acts outward; prāṇe—in the air going outward; apānam—air going downward; tathā—as also; apare—others; prāṇa—air going outward; apāna—air going downward; gatī—movement; ruddhvā—checking; prāṇāyāma—trance induced by stopping all breathing; parāyaṇāḥ—so inclined; apare—others; niyata—controlled; āhārāḥ—eating; prāṇān—outgoing air; prāṇeṣu—in the outgoing air; juhvati—sacrifices.

TRANSLATION

And there are even others who are inclined to the process of breath restraint to remain in trance, and they practice stopping the movement of the outgoing breath into the incoming, and incoming breath into the outgoing, and thus at last remain in trance, stopping all breathing. Some of them, curtailing the eating process, offer the outgoing breath into itself, as a sacrifice.

PURPORT

This system of yoga for controlling the breathing process is called prāṇā-yāma, and in the beginning it is practiced in the haṭha-yoga system through different sitting postures. All of these processes are recommended for controlling the senses and for advancement in spiritual realization. This practice involves controlling the air within the body to enable simultaneous passage in opposite directions. The apāna air goes downward, and the prāṇa air goes up. The prāṇāyāma yogī practices breathing the opposite way until the currents are neutralized into pūraka, equilibrium. Similarly, when the exhaled breathing is offered to inhaled breathing, it is called recaka. When both air currents are completely stopped, it is called kumbhaka-yoga. By practice of kumbhaka-yoga, the yogīs increase the duration of life by many, many years. A Kṛṣṇa conscious person, however, being always situated in the transcendental loving service of the Lord, automatically becomes the controller of the senses. His senses, being always engaged in the service of Kṛṣṇa, have no chance of becoming otherwise engaged. So at the end of life, he is naturally transferred to the transcendental plane of Lord Kṛṣṇa; consequently he makes no attempt to increase his longevity. He is at once raised to the platform of liberation. A Kṛṣṇa conscious person begins from the transcendental stage, and he is constantly in that consciousness. Therefore, there is no falling down, and ultimately he enters into the abode of the Lord without delay. The practice of reduced eating is automatically done when one eats only Kṛṣṇa prasādam, or food which is offered first to the Lord. Reducing the eating process is very helpful in the matter of sense control. And without sense control there is no possibility of getting out of the material entanglement.

TEXT 30

सर्वेऽप्येते यज्ञविदो यज्ञक्षपितकल्मषाः ।
यज्ञशिष्टामृतभुजो यान्ति ब्रह्म सनातनम् ॥ ३० ॥

sarve 'py ete yajña-vido
yajña-kṣapita-kalmaṣāḥ
yajña-śiṣṭāmṛta-bhujo
yānti brahma sanātanam

sarve—all; *api*—although apparently different; *ete*—all these; *yajña-vidaḥ*—conversant with the purpose of performing; *yajña*—sacrifices; *kṣapita*—being cleansed of the result of such performances; *kalmaṣāḥ*—sinful reactions; *yajña-śiṣṭa*—as a result of such performances of *yajña*; *amṛta-bhujaḥ*—those who have tasted such nectar; *yānti*—do approach; *brahma*—the supreme; *sanātanam*—eternal atmosphere.

TRANSLATION

All these performers who know the meaning of sacrifice become cleansed of sinful reaction, and, having tasted the nectar of the remnants of such sacrifice, they go to the supreme eternal atmosphere.

PURPORT

From the foregoing explanation of differents types of sacrifice (namely sacrifice of one's possessions, study of the *Vedas* or philosophical doctrines, and performance of the *yoga* system), it is found that the common aim of all is to control the senses. Sense gratification is the root cause of material existence; therefore, unless and until one is situated on a platform apart from sense gratification, there is no chance of being elevated to the eternal platform of full knowledge, full bliss and full life. This platform is in the eternal atmosphere, or Brahman atmosphere. All the above-mentioned sacrifices help one to become cleansed of the sinful reactions of material existence. By this advancement in life, one not only becomes happy and opulent in this life, but also, at the end, he enters into the eternal kingdom of God, either merging into the impersonal Brahman or associating with the Supreme Personality of Godhead, Kṛṣṇa.

TEXT 31

नायं लोकोऽस्त्ययज्ञस्य कुतोऽन्यः कुरुसत्तम ॥ ३१ ॥

nāyaṁ loko 'sty ayajñasya
kuto 'nyaḥ kuru-sattama

na—never; *ayam*—this; *lokaḥ*—planet; *asti*—there is; *ayajñasya*—of the foolish; *kutaḥ*—where is; *anyaḥ*—the other; *kuru-sattama*—O best amongst the Kurus.

TRANSLATION

O best of the Kuru dynasty, without sacrifice one can never live happily on this planet or in this life: what then of the next?

PURPORT

Whatever form of material existence one is in, one is invariably ignorant of his real situation. In other words, existence in the material world is due to the multiple reactions to our sinful lives. Ignorance is the cause of sinful life, and sinful life is the cause of one's dragging on in material existence. The human form of life is the only loophole by which one may get out of this entanglement. The *Vedas*, therefore, give us a chance for escape by pointing out the paths of religion, economic comfort, regulated sense gratification and, at last, the means to get out of the miserable condition entirely. The path of religion, or the different kinds of sacrifice recommended above, automatically solves our economic problems. By performance of *yajña* we can have enough food, enough milk, etc.—even if there is a so-called increase of population. When the body is fully supplied, naturally the next stage is to satisfy the senses. The *Vedas* prescribe, therefore, sacred marriage for regulated sense gratification. Thereby one is gradually elevated to the platform of release from material bondage, and the highest perfection of liberated life is to associate with the Supreme Lord. Perfection is achieved by performance of *yajña* (sacrifice), as described above. Now, if a person is not inclined to perform *yajña* according to the *Vedas*, how can he expect a happy life? There are different grades of material comforts in different heavenly planets, and in all cases there is immense happiness for persons engaged in different kinds of *yajña*. But the highest kind of happiness that a man can achieve is to be promoted to the spiritual planets by practice of Kṛṣṇa consciousness. A life of Kṛṣṇa consciousness is therefore the solution to all the problems of material existence.

TEXT 32

एवं बहुविधा यज्ञा वितता ब्रह्मणो मुखे ।
कर्मजान्विद्धि तान्सर्वानेवं ज्ञात्वा विमोक्ष्यसे ॥ ३२ ॥

evaṁ bahu-vidhā yajñā
vitatā brahmaṇo mukhe
karma-jān viddhi tān sarvān
evaṁ jñātvā vimokṣyase

evam—thus; *bahu-vidhāḥ*—various kinds of; *yajñāḥ*—sacrifices; *vitatāḥ*—widespread; *brahmaṇaḥ*—of the *Vedas*; *mukhe*—in the face of; *karma-jān*—born of work; *viddhi*—you should know; *tān*—them; *sarvān*—all; *evam*—thus; *jñātvā*—knowing; *vimokṣyase*—be liberated.

TRANSLATION

All these different types of sacrifice are approved by the Vedas, and all of them are born of different types of work. Knowing them as such, you will become liberated.

PURPORT

Different types of sacrifice, as discussed above, are mentioned in the *Vedas* to suit the different types of worker. Because men are so deeply

absorbed in the bodily concept, these sacrifices are so arranged that one
can work either with the body, the mind, or the intelligence. But all of
them are recommended for ultimately bringing about liberation from the
body. This is confirmed by the Lord herewith from His own mouth.

TEXT 33

श्रेयान्द्रव्यमयाद्यज्ञाज्ज्ञानयज्ञः परन्तप ।
सर्वं कर्माखिलं पार्थ ज्ञाने परिसमाप्यते ॥ ३३ ॥

śreyān dravya-mayād yajñāj
jñāna-yajñaḥ parantapa
sarvaṁ karmākhilaṁ pārtha
jñāne parisamāpyate

śreyān—greater; *dravyamayāt*—than the sacrifice of material possessions;
yajñāt—knowledge; *jñāna-yajñaḥ*—sacrifice in knowledge; *parantapa*—O
chastiser of the enemy; *sarvam*—all; *karma*—activities; *akhilam*—in totality;
pārtha—O son of Pṛthā; *jñāne*—in knowledge; *parisamāpyate*—ends in.

TRANSLATION

O chastiser of the enemy, the sacrifice of knowledge is greater than
the sacrifice of material possessions. O son of Pṛthā, after all, the sacrifice
of work culminates in transcendental knowledge.

PURPORT

The purpose of all sacrifices is to arrive at the status of complete
knowledge, then to gain release from material miseries, and, ultimately, to
engage in loving transcendental service to the Supreme Lord (Kṛṣṇa
consciousness). Nonetheless, there is a mystery about all these different
activities of sacrifice, and one should know this mystery. Sacrifices
sometimes take different forms according to the particular faith of the
performer. When one's faith reaches the stage of transcendental knowledge,
the performer of sacrifices should be considered more advanced than
those who simply sacrifice material possessions without such knowledge,
for without attainment of knowledge, sacrifices remain on the material
platform and bestow no spiritual benefit. Real knowledge culminates in

Kṛṣṇa consciousness, the highest stage of transcendental knowledge. Without the elevation of knowledge, sacrifices are simply material activities. When, however, they are elevated to the level of transcendental knowledge, all such activities enter onto the spiritual platform. Depending on differences in consciousness, sacrificial activities are sometimes called *karma-kāṇḍa*, fruitive activities, and sometimes *jñāna-kāṇḍa*, knowledge in the pursuit of truth. It is better when the end is knowledge.

TEXT 34

तद्विद्धि प्रणिपातेन परिप्रश्नेन सेवया ।
उपदेक्ष्यन्ति ते ज्ञानं ज्ञानिनस्तत्त्वदर्शिनः ॥ ३४ ॥

tad viddhi praṇipātena
paripraśnena sevayā
upadekṣyanti te jñānaṁ
jñāninas tattva-darśinaḥ

tat—that knowledge of different sacrifices; *viddhi*—try to understand; *praṇipātena*—by approaching a spiritual master; *paripraśnena*—by submissive inquiries; *sevayā*—by the rendering of service; *upadekṣyanti*—initiate; *te*—unto you; *jñānam*—knowledge; *jñāninaḥ*—the self-realized; *tattva*—truth; *darśinaḥ*—the seers.

TRANSLATION

Just try to learn the truth by approaching a spiritual master. Inquire from him submissively and render service unto him. The self-realized soul can impart knowledge unto you because he has seen the truth.

PURPORT

The path of spiritual realization is undoubtedly difficult. The Lord therefore advises us to approach a bona fide spiritual master in the line of disciplic succession from the Lord Himself. No one can be a bona fide spiritual master without following this principle of disciplic succession.

The Lord is the original spiritual master, and a person in the disciplic succession can convey the message of the Lord as it is to his disciple. No one can be spiritually realized by manufacturing his own process, as is the fashion of the foolish pretenders. The *Bhāgavatam* says: *dharmaṁ hi sākṣād-bhagavat-praṇītam*—the path of religion is directly enunciated by the Lord. Therefore, mental speculation or dry arguments cannot help one progress in spiritual life. One has to approach a bona fide spiritual master to receive the knowledge. Such a spiritual master should be accepted in full surrender, and one should serve the spiritual master like a menial servant, without false prestige. Satisfaction of the self-realized spiritual master is the secret of advancement in spiritual life. Inquiries and submission constitute the proper combination for spiritual understanding. Unless there is submission and service, inquiries from the learned spiritual master will not be effective. One must be able to pass the test of the spiritual master, and when he sees the genuine desire of the disciple, he automatically blesses the disciple with genuine spiritual understanding. In this verse, both blind following and absurd inquiries are condemned. One should not only hear submissively from the spiritual master, but one must also get a clear understanding from him, in submission and service and inquiries. A bona fide spiritual master is by nature very kind toward the disciple. Therefore when the student is submissive and is always ready to render service, the reciprocation of knowledge and inquiries becomes perfect.

TEXT 35

यज्ज्ञात्वा न पुनर्मोहमेवं यास्यसि पाण्डव ।
येन भूतान्यशेषाणि द्रक्ष्यस्यात्मन्यथो मयि ॥ ३५ ॥

yaj jñātvā na punar moham
evaṁ yāsyasi pāṇḍava
yena bhūtāny aśeṣāṇi
drakṣyasy ātmany atho mayi

yat—which; *jñātvā*—knowing; *na*—never; *punaḥ*—again; *moham*—illusion; *evam*—like this; *yāsyasi*—you shall go; *pāṇḍava*—O son of Pāṇḍu; *yena*—by which; *bhūtāni*—all living entities; *aśeṣāṇi*—totally; *drakṣyasi*—you will see; *ātmani*—in the Supreme Soul; *atho*—or in other words; *mayi*—in Me.

TRANSLATION

And when you have thus learned the truth, you will know that all living beings are but part of Me—and that they are in Me, and are Mine.

PURPORT

The result of receiving knowledge from a self-realized soul, or one who knows things as they are, is learning that all living beings are parts and parcels of the Supreme Personality of Godhead, Lord Śrī Kṛṣṇa. The sense of a separated existence from Kṛṣṇa is called māyā (mā—not, yā—this). Some think that we have nothing to do with Kṛṣṇa, that Kṛṣṇa is only a great historical personality and that the Absolute is the impersonal Brahman. Factually, as it is stated in the Bhagavad-gītā, this impersonal Brahman is the personal effulgence of Kṛṣṇa. Kṛṣṇa, as the Supreme Personality of Godhead, is the cause of everything. In the Brahma-saṁhitā it is clearly stated that Kṛṣṇa is the Supreme Personality of Godhead, the cause of all causes. Even the millions of incarnations are only His different expansions. Similarly, the living entities are also expansions of Kṛṣṇa. The Māyāvādī philosophers wrongly think that Kṛṣṇa loses His own separate existence in His many expansions. This thought is material in nature. We have experience in the material world that a thing, when fragmentally distributed, loses its own original identity. But the Māyāvādī philosophers fail to understand that Absolute means that one plus one is equal to one, and that one minus one is also equal to one. This is the case in the absolute world.

For want of sufficient knowledge in the absolute science, we are now covered with illusion, and therefore we think that we are separate from Kṛṣṇa. Although we are separated parts of Kṛṣṇa, we are nevertheless not different from Him. The bodily difference of the living entities is māyā, or not actual fact. We are all meant to satisfy Kṛṣṇa. By māyā alone Arjuna thought that the temporary bodily relationship with his kinsmen was more important than his eternal spiritual relationship with Kṛṣṇa. The whole teaching of the Gītā is targetted toward this end: that a living being, as His eternal servitor, cannot be separated from Kṛṣṇa, and his sense of being an identity apart from Kṛṣṇa is called māyā. The living entities, as separate parts and parcels of the Supreme, have a purpose to fulfill. Having forgotten that purpose, since time immemorial they are situated in different bodies, as men, animals, demigods, etc. Such bodily differences arise from forgetfulness of the transcendental service of the Lord. But when one is engaged in transcendental service through Kṛṣṇa consciousness, one becomes at once liberated from this illusion. One can acquire such pure knowledge only from the bona fide spiritual master and thereby avoid the delusion that the living entity is equal to Kṛṣṇa. Perfect knowledge is that the Supreme Soul, Kṛṣṇa, is the supreme shelter for all living entities, and giving up such shelter, the living entities are deluded by the material energy, imagining themselves to have a separate identity. Thus, under different standards of material identity, they become forgetful of Kṛṣṇa. When, however, such deluded living entities become situated in Kṛṣṇa consciousness, it is to be understood that they are on the path of liberation, as confirmed in the *Bhāgavatam*: *muktir hitvānyathā rūpaṁ svarūpeṇa vyavasthitiḥ*. Liberation means to be situated in one's constitutional position as the eternal servitor of Kṛṣṇa (Kṛṣṇa consciousness).

TEXT 36

अपि चेदसि पापेभ्यः सर्वेभ्यः पापकृत्तमः ।
सर्वं ज्ञानप्लवेनैव वृजिनं सन्तरिष्यसि ॥ ३६ ॥

api ced asi pāpebhyaḥ
sarvebhyaḥ pāpa-kṛt-tamaḥ
sarvaṁ jñāna-plavenaiva
vṛjinaṁ santariṣyasi

api—even; *cet*—if; *asi*—you are; *pāpebhyaḥ*—of sinners; *sarvebhyaḥ*—of all; *pāpa-kṛttamaḥ*—the greatest sinner; *sarvam*—all such sinful actions; *jñāna-plavena*—by the boat of transcendental knowledge; *eva*—certainly; *vṛjinam*—the ocean of miseries; *santariṣyasi*—you will cross completely.

TRANSLATION

Even if you are considered to be the most sinful of all sinners, when you are situated in the boat of transcendental knowledge, you will be able to cross over the ocean of miseries.

PURPORT

Proper understanding of one's constitutional position in relationship to Kṛṣṇa is so nice that it can at once lift one from the struggle for existence which goes on in the ocean of nescience. This material world is sometimes regarded as an ocean of nescience and sometimes as a blazing forest. In the ocean, however expert a swimmer one may be, the struggle for existence is very severe. If someone comes forward and lifts the struggling swimmer from the ocean, he is the greatest savior. Perfect knowledge, received from the Supreme Personality of Godhead, is the path of liberation. The boat of Kṛṣṇa consciousness is very simple, but at the same time the most sublime.

TEXT 37

यथैधांसि समिद्धोऽग्निर्भस्मसात्कुरुतेऽर्जुन ।
ज्ञानाग्निः सर्वकर्माणि भस्मसात्कुरुते तथा ॥ ३७ ॥

yathaidhāṁsi samiddho 'gnir
bhasma-sāt kurute 'rjuna
jñānāgniḥ sarva-karmāṇi
bhasma-sāt kurute tathā

yathā—just as; edhāṁsi—firewood; samiddhaḥ—blazing; agniḥ—fire; bhasmasāt—turns into ashes; kurute—so does; arjuna—O Arjuna; jñāna-agniḥ—the fire of knowledge; sarva-karmāṇi—all reactions to material activities; bhasmasāt—to ashes; kurute—it so does; tathā—similarly.

TRANSLATION

As the blazing fire turns firewood to ashes, O Arjuna, so does the fire of knowledge burn to ashes all reactions to material activities.

PURPORT

Perfect knowledge of self and Superself and of their relationship is compared herein to fire. This fire not only burns up all reactions to impious activities, but also all reactions to pious activities, turning them to ashes. There are many stages of reaction: reaction in the making, reaction fructifying, reaction already achieved, and reaction a priori. But knowledge of the constitutional position of the living entity burns everything to ashes. When one is in complete knowledge, all reactions, both a priori and a posteriori, are consumed. In the Vedas it is stated: ubhe uhaivaiṣa ete taraty *amṛtaḥ sādhv-asādhūnī:* "One overcomes both the pious and impious interactions of work."

TEXT 38

न हि ज्ञानेन सदृशं पवित्रमिह विद्यते ।
तत्स्वयं योगसंसिद्धः कालेनात्मनि विन्दति ॥ ३८ ॥

*na hi jñānena sadṛśaṁ
pavitram iha vidyate
tat svayaṁ yoga-saṁsiddhaḥ
kālenātmani vindati*

na—never; *hi*—certainly; *jñānena*—with knowledge; *sadṛśam*—in comparison; *pavitram*—sanctified; *iha*—in this world; *vidyate*—exists; *tat*—that; *svayam*—itself; *yoga*—devotion; *saṁsiddhaḥ*—matured; *kālena*—in course of time; *ātmani*—in himself; *vindati*—enjoys.

TRANSLATION

In this world, there is nothing so sublime and pure as transcendental knowledge. Such knowledge is the mature fruit of all mysticism. And one who has achieved this enjoys the self within himself in due course of time.

PURPORT

When we speak of transcendental knowledge, we do so in terms of spiritual understanding. As such, there is nothing so sublime and pure as transcendental knowledge. Ignorance is the cause of our bondage, and knowledge is the cause of our liberation. This knowledge is the mature fruit of devotional service, and when one is situated in transcendental knowledge, he need not search for peace elsewhere, for he enjoys peace within himself. In other words, this knowledge and peace are culminated in Kṛṣṇa consciousness. That is the last word in the *Bhagavad-gītā.*

TEXT 39

श्रद्धावाँल्लभते ज्ञानं तत्परः संयतेन्द्रियः ।
ज्ञानं लब्ध्वा परां शान्तिमचिरेणाधिगच्छति ॥ ३९ ॥

śraddhāvāl labhate jñānaṁ
tat-paraḥ saṁyatendriyaḥ
jñānaṁ labdhvā parāṁ śāntim
acireṇādhigacchati

śraddhāvān—a faithful man; labhate—achieves; jñānam—knowledge;
tat-paraḥ—very much attached to it; saṁyata—controlled; indriyaḥ—senses;
jñanam—knowledge; labdhvā—having achieved; parām—transcendental;
śāntim—peace; acireṇa—very soon; adhigacchati—attains.

TRANSLATION

**A faithful man who is absorbed in transcendental knowledge and who
subdues his senses quickly attains the supreme spiritual peace.**

PURPORT

Such knowledge in Kṛṣṇa consciousness can be achieved by a faithful
person who believes firmly in Kṛṣṇa. One is called a faithful man who
thinks that, simply by acting in Kṛṣṇa consciousness, he can attain the
highest perfection. This faith is attained by the discharge of devotional
service, and by chanting "Hare Kṛṣṇa, Hare Kṛṣṇa, Kṛṣṇa Kṛṣṇa, Hare
Hare/ Hare Rāma, Hare Rāma, Rāma Rāma, Hare Hare," which cleanses
one's heart of all material dirt. Over and above this, one should control the
senses. A person who is faithful to Kṛṣṇa and who controls the senses can
easily attain perfection in the knowledge of Kṛṣṇa consciousness without
delay.

TEXT 40

अज्ञश्चाश्रद्दधानश्च संशयात्मा विनश्यति ।
नायं लोकोऽस्ति न परो न सुखं संशयात्मनः ॥ ४० ॥

ajñaś cāśraddadhānaś ca
saṁśayātmā vinaśyati
nāyaṁ loko 'sti na paro
na sukhaṁ saṁśayātmanaḥ

ajñaḥ—fools who have no knowledge in standard scriptures; ca—and;
aśraddadhānaḥ—without faith in revealed scriptures; ca—also; saṁśaya—

doubts; *ātmā*—person; *vinaśyati*—falls back; *na*—never; *ayam*—this; *lokaḥ*—world; *asti*—there is; *na*—neither; *paraḥ*—next life; *na*—not; *sukham*—happiness; *saṁśaya*—doubtful; *ātmanaḥ*—of the person.

TRANSLATION

But ignorant and faithless persons who doubt the revealed scriptures do not attain God consciousness. For the doubting soul there is happiness neither in this world nor in the next.

PURPORT

Out of many standard and authoritative revealed scriptures, the *Bhagavad-gītā* is the best. Persons who are almost like animals have no faith in, or knowledge of, the standard revealed scriptures; and some, even though they have knowledge of, or can cite passages from, the revealed scriptures, have actually no faith in these words. And even though others may have faith in scriptures like *Bhagavad-gītā*, they do not believe in or worship the Personality of Godhead, Śrī Kṛṣṇa. Such persons cannot have any standing in Kṛṣṇa consciousness. They fall down. Out of all the above-mentioned persons, those who have no faith and are always doubtful make no progress at all. Men without faith in God and His revealed word find no good in this world, nor in the next. For them there is no happiness what-soever. One should therefore follow the principles of revealed scriptures with faith and thereby be raised to the platform of knowledge. Only this knowledge will help one become promoted to the transcendental platform of spiritual understanding. In other words, doubtful persons have no status whatsoever in spiritual emancipation. One should therefore follow in the footsteps of great *ācāryas* who are in the disciplic succession and thereby attain success.

TEXT 41

योगसन्न्यस्तकर्माणं ज्ञानसंछिन्नसंशयम् ।
आत्मवन्तं न कर्माणि निबध्नन्ति धनंजय ॥ ४१ ॥

yoga-sannyasta-karmāṇaṁ
jñāna-sañchinna-saṁśayam
ātmavantaṁ na karmāṇi
nibadhnanti dhanañjaya

yoga—devotional service in karma-yoga; sannyasta—renounced; karmā-ṇam—of the performers; jñāna—knowledge; sañchinna—cut by the advancement of knowledge; samsáyam—doubts; ātma-vantam—situated in the self; na—never; karmāṇi—work; nibadhnanti—do bind up; dhananjaya—O conquerer of riches.

TRANSLATION

Therefore, one who has renounced the fruits of his action, whose doubts are destroyed by transcendental knowledge, and who is situated firmly in the self, is not bound by works, O conqueror of riches.

PURPORT

One who follows the instruction of the Gītā, as it is imparted by the Lord, the Personality of Godhead Himself, becomes free from all doubts by the grace of transcendental knowledge. He, as a part and parcel of the Lord, in full Kṛṣṇa consciousness, is already established in self-knowledge. As such, he is undoubtedly above bondage to action.

TEXT 42

तस्मादज्ञानसम्भूतं हृत्स्थं ज्ञानासिनात्मनः ।
छित्त्वैनं संशयं योगमातिष्ठोत्तिष्ठ भारत ॥ ४२ ॥

tasmād ajñāna-sambhūtaṁ
hṛt-sthaṁ jñānāsinātmanaḥ
chittvainaṁ samsáyaṁ yogam
ātiṣṭhottiṣṭha bhārata

tasmāt—therefore; ajñāna-sambhūtam—outcome of ignorance; hṛt-sthaṁ—situated in the heart; jñāna—knowledge; asinā—by the weapon of; ātmanaḥ—of the self; chittvā—cutting off; enam—this; samsáyam—doubt; yogam—in yoga; ātiṣṭha—be situated; uttiṣṭha—stand up to fight; bhārata—O descendant of Bharata.

TRANSLATION

Therefore the doubts which have arisen in your heart out of ignorance should be slashed by the weapon of knowledge. Armed with yoga, O Bhārata, stand and fight.

PURPORT

The yoga system instructed in this chapter is called sanātana-yoga, or eternal activities performed by the living entity. This yoga has two divisions of sacrificial actions: one is called sacrifice of one's material possessions, and the other is called knowledge of self, which is pure spiritual activity. If sacrifice of one's material possessions is not dovetailed for spiritual realization, then such sacrifice becomes material. But one who performs such sacrifices with a spiritual objective, or in devotional service, makes a perfect sacrifice. When we come to spiritual activities, we find that these are also divided into two: namely, understanding of one's own self (or one's constitutional position), and the truth regarding the Supreme Personality of Godhead. One who follows the path of the Gītā as it is can very easily understand these two important divisions of spiritual knowledge. For him there is no difficulty in obtaining perfect knowledge of the self as part and parcel of the Lord. And such understanding is beneficial for such a person who easily understands the transcendental activities of the Lord. In the beginning of this chapter, the transcendental activities of the Lord were discussed by the Supreme Lord Himself. One who does not understand the instructions of the Gītā is faithless, and is to be considered to be misusing the fragmental independence awarded to him by the Lord. In spite of such instructions, one who does not understand the real nature of the Lord as the eternal, blissful, all-knowing Personality of Godhead, is certainly fool number one. Ignorance can be removed by gradual acceptance of the principles of Kṛṣṇa consciousness. Kṛṣṇa consciousness is awakened by different types of sacrifices to the demigods, sacrifice to Brahman, sacrifice in celibacy, in household life, in controlling the senses, in practicing mystic yoga, in penance, in foregoing material possessions, in studying the Vedas, and in partaking of the social institution called varṇāśrama-dharma. All of these are known as sacrifice, and all of them are based on regulated action. But within all these activities, the important factor is self-realization. One who seeks that objective is the real student of Bhagavad-gītā, but one who doubts the authority of Kṛṣṇa falls back. One is therefore advised to study Bhagavad-gītā, or any other scripture, under a bona fide spiritual master, with service and surrender. A bona fide spiritual master is in the disciplic succession from time eternal, and he does not deviate at all from the instructions of the Supreme Lord as they were imparted millions of years ago to the sun-god, from whom the instructions of Bhagavad-gītā have come down to the earthly kingdom. One should, therefore, follow the path of Bhagavad-gītā as it is expressed in the Gītā itself and beware of self-interested people after personal aggrandizement who deviate others from the actual path. The Lord is definitely the supreme person, and His activities are transcendental. One who understands this is a liberated person from the very beginning of his study of the *Gītā*.

Thus end the Bhaktivedanta Purports to the Fourth Chapter of the Śrīmad-Bhagavad-gītā *in the matter of Transcendental Knowledge.*

CHAPTER FIVE

Karma-yoga—
Action in Kṛṣṇa Consciousness

TEXT 1

अर्जुन उवाच ।
सन्न्यासं कर्मणां कृष्ण पुनर्योगं च शंससि ।
यच्छ्रेय एतयोरेकं तन्मे ब्रूहि सुनिश्चितम् ॥ १ ॥

arjuna uvāca
sannyāsaṁ karmaṇāṁ kṛṣṇa
punar yogaṁ ca śaṁsasi
yac chreya etayor ekaṁ
tan me brūhi su-niścitam

arjunaḥ uvāca—Arjuna said; *sannyāsam*—renunciation; *karmaṇām*—of
all activities; *kṛṣṇa*—O Kṛṣṇa; *punaḥ*—again; *yogam*—devotional service;
ca—also; *śaṁsasi*—You are praising; *yat*—which; *śreyaḥ*—is beneficial;
etayoḥ—of these two; *ekam*—one; *tat*—that; *me*—unto me; *brūhi*—please tell;
suniścitam—definitely.

271

TRANSLATION

Arjuna said: O Kṛṣṇa, first of all You ask me to renounce work, and then again You recommend work with devotion. Now will You kindly tell me definitely which of the two is more beneficial?

PURPORT

In this Fifth Chapter of the *Bhagavad-gītā*, the Lord says that work in devotional service is better than dry mental speculation. Devotional service is easier than the latter because, being transcendental in nature, it frees one from reaction. In the Second Chapter, preliminary knowledge of the soul and its entanglement in the material body were explained. How to get out of this material encagement by *buddhi-yoga*, or devotional service, was also explained therein. In the Third Chapter, it was explained that a person who is situated on the platform of knowledge no longer has any duties to perform. And, in the Fourth Chapter, the Lord told Arjuna that all kinds of sacrificial work culminate in knowledge. However, at the end of the Fourth Chapter, the Lord advised Arjuna to wake up and fight, being situated in perfect knowledge. Therefore, by simultaneously stressing the importance of both work in devotion and inaction in knowledge, Kṛṣṇa has perplexed Arjuna and confused his determination. Arjuna understands that renunciation in knowledge involves cessation of all kinds of work performed as sense activities. But if one performs work in devotional service, then how is work stopped? In other words, he thinks that *sannyāsam*, or renunciation in knowledge, should be altogether free from all kinds of activity because work and renunciation appear to him to be incompatible. He appears not to have understood that work in full knowledge is nonreactive and is therefore the same as inaction. He inquires, therefore, whether he should cease work altogether, or work with full knowledge.

TEXT 2

श्रीभगवानुवाच ।
सन्न्यासः कर्मयोगश्च निःश्रेयसकरावुभौ ।
तयोस्तु कर्मसन्न्यासात्कर्मयोगो विशिष्यते ॥ २ ॥

> śrī-bhagavān uvāca
> sannyāsaḥ karma-yogaś ca
> niḥśreyasa-karāv ubhau
> tayos tu karma-sannyāsāt
> karma-yogo viśiṣyate

śrī bhagavān uvāca—the Personality of Godhead said; sannyāsaḥ—renunciation of work; karma-yogaḥ—work in devotion; ca—also; niḥ-śreyasa-karau—all leading to the path of liberation; ubhau—both; tayoḥ—of the two; tu—but; karma-sannyāsāt—in comparison to the renunciation of fruitive work; karma-yogaḥ—work in devotion; viśiṣyate—is better.

TRANSLATION

The Blessed Lord said: The renunciation of work and work in devotion are both good for liberation. But, of the two, work in devotional service is better than renunciation of works.

PURPORT

Fruitive activities (seeking sense gratification) are cause for material bondage. As long as one is engaged in activities aimed at improving the standard of bodily comfort, one is sure to transmigrate to different types of bodies, thereby continuing material bondage perpetually. Śrīmad-Bhāgavatam confirms this as follows:

> nūnaṁ pramattaḥ kurute vikarma yad indriya-prītaya āpṛṇoti
> na sādhu manye yata ātmano 'yam asann api kleśada āsa dehaḥ
>
> parābhavas tāvad abodha-jāto yāvanna jijñāsata ātma-tattvam
> yāvat kriyās tāvad idaṁ mano vai karmātmakaṁ yena śarīra-bandhaḥ
>
> evaṁ manaḥ karma vaśaṁ prayuṅkte avidyayātmany upadhīyamāne
> prītir na yāvan mayi vāsudeve na mucyate deha-yogena tāvat

"People are mad after sense gratification, and they do not know that this present body, which is full of miseries, is a result of one's fruitive activities in the past. Although this body is temporary, it is always giving one trouble in many ways. Therefore, to act for sense gratification is not good. One is considered to be a failure in life as long as he makes no inquiry about the nature of work for fruitive results, for as long as one is engrossed in the consciousness of sense gratification, one has to transmigrate from one body to another. Although the mind may be engrossed in fruitive activities and influenced by ignorance, one must develop a love for devotional service to Vāsudeva. Only then can one have the opportunity to get out of the bondage of material existence." (*Bhāg.* 5.5.4-6)

Therefore, *jñāna* (or knowledge that one is not this material body but spirit soul) is not sufficient for liberation. One has to *act* in the status of spirit soul, otherwise there is no escape from material bondage. Action in Kṛṣṇa consciousness is not, however, action on the fruitive platform. Activities performed in full knowledge strengthen one's advancement in real knowledge. Without Kṛṣṇa consciousness, mere renunciation of fruitive activities does not actually purify the heart of a conditioned soul. As long as the heart is not purified, one has to work on the fruitive platform. But action in Kṛṣṇa consciousness automatically helps one escape the result of fruitive action so that one need not descend to the material platform. Therefore, action in Kṛṣṇa consciousness is always superior to renunciation, which always entails a risk of falling. Renunciation without Kṛṣṇa consciousness is incomplete, as is confirmed by Śrīla Rūpa Gosvāmī in his *Bhakti-rasāmṛta-sindhu.*

> *prāpañcikatayā buddhyā hari-sambandhi-vastunaḥ*
> *mumukṣubhiḥ parityāgo vairāgyaṁ phalgu kathyate.*

"Renunciation by persons eager to achieve liberation of things which are related to the Supreme Personality of Godhead, though they are material, is called incomplete renunciation." Renunciation is complete when it is in the knowledge that everything in existence belongs to the Lord and that no one should claim proprietorship over anything. One should understand that, factually, nothing belongs to anyone. Then where is the question of renunciation? One who knows that everything is Kṛṣṇa's property is always situated in renunciation. Since everything belongs to Kṛṣṇa, everything should be employed in the service of Kṛṣṇa. This perfect form of action in Kṛṣṇa consciousness is far better than any amount of artificial renunciation by a *sannyāsī* of the Māyāvādī school.

TEXT 3

ज्ञेयः स नित्यसन्न्यासी यो न द्वेष्टि न काङ्क्षति ।

निर्द्वन्द्वो हि महाबाहो सुखं बन्धात्प्रमुच्यते ॥ ३ ॥

jñeyaḥ sa nitya-sannyāsī
yo na dveṣṭi na kāṅkṣati
nirdvandvo hi mahā-bāho
sukhaṁ bandhāt pramucyate

jñeyaḥ—should be known; saḥ—he; nitya—always; sannyāsī—renouncer; yaḥ—who; na—never; dveṣṭi—abhors; na—nor; kāṅkṣati—desires; nirdvand-vaḥ—free from all dualities; hi—certainly; mahā-bāho—O mighty-armed one; sukham—happily; bandhāt—from bondage; pramucyate—completely liberated.

TRANSLATION

One who neither hates nor desires the fruits of his activities is known to be always renounced. Such a person, liberated from all dualities, easily overcomes material bondage and is completely liberated, O mighty-armed Arjuna.

PURPORT

One who is fully in Kṛṣṇa consciousness is always a renouncer because he feels neither hatred nor desire for the results of his actions. Such a renouncer, dedicated to the transcendental loving service of the Lord, is fully qualified in knowledge because he knows his constitutional position in his relationship with Kṛṣṇa. He knows fully well that Kṛṣṇa is the whole and that he is part and parcel of Kṛṣṇa. Such knowledge is perfect because it is qualitatively and quantitatively correct. The concept of oneness with Kṛṣṇa is incorrect because the part cannot be equal to the whole. Knowledge that one is one in quality yet different in quantity is correct transcendental knowledge leading one to become full in himself, having nothing to aspire to nor lament over. There is no duality in his mind because whatever he does, he does for Kṛṣṇa. Being thus freed from the platform of dualities, he is liberated—even in this material world.

TEXT 4

सांख्ययोगौ पृथग्बालाः प्रवदन्ति न पण्डिताः ।
एकमप्यास्थितः सम्यगुभयोर्विन्दते फलम् ॥ ४ ॥

sāṅkhya-yogau pṛthag bālāḥ
pravadanti na paṇḍitāḥ
ekam apy āsthitaḥ samyag
ubhayor vindate phalam

sāṅkhya—analytical study of the material world; *yogau*—work in devotional service; *pṛthak*—different; *bālāḥ*—less intelligent; *pravadanti*—do talk; *na*—never; *paṇḍitāḥ*—the learned; *ekam*—in one; *api*—even though; *āsthitaḥ*—being situated; *samyak*—complete; *ubhayoḥ*—of both; *vindate*—enjoys; *phalam*—result.

TRANSLATION

Only the ignorant speak of karma-yoga and devotional service as being different from the analytical study of the material world [sāṅkhya]. Those who are actually learned say that he who applies himself well to one of these paths achieves the results of both.

PURPORT

The aim of the analytical study of the material world is to find the soul of existence. The soul of the material world is Viṣṇu, or the Supersoul. Devotional service to the Lord entails service to the Supersoul. One process is to find the root of the tree, and next to water the root. The real student of *sāṅkhya* philosophy finds the root of the material world, Viṣṇu, and then, in perfect knowledge, engages himself in the service of the Lord. Therefore, in essence, there is no difference between the two because the aim of both is Viṣṇu. Those who do not know the ultimate end say that the purposes of *sāṅkhya* and *karma-yoga* are not the same, but one who is learned knows the unifying aim in these different processes.

TEXT 5

यत्साङ्ख्यैः प्राप्यते स्थानं तद्योगैरपि गम्यते ।
एकं साङ्ख्यं च योगं च यः पश्यति स पश्यति ॥ ५ ॥

yat sāṅkhyaiḥ prāpyate sthānaṁ
tad yogair api gamyate

ekaṁ sāṅkhyaṁ ca yogaṁ ca
yaḥ paśyati sa paśyati

yat—what; *sāṅkhyaiḥ*—by means of *sāṅkhya* philosophy; *prāpyate*—is achieved; *sthānam*—place; *tat*—that; *yogaiḥ*—by devotional service; *api*—also; *gamyate*—one can attain; *ekam*—one; *sāṅkhyam*—analytical study; *ca*—and; *yogam*—action in devotion; *ca*—and; *yaḥ*—one who; *paśyati*—sees; *saḥ*—he; *paśyati*—actually sees.

TRANSLATION

One who knows that the position reached by means of renunciation can also be attained by works in devotional service and who therefore sees that the path of works and the path of renunciation are one, sees things as they are.

PURPORT

The real purpose of philosophical research is to find the ultimate goal of life. Since the ultimate goal of life is self-realization, there is no difference between the conclusions reached by the two processes. By *sāṅkhya* philosophical research one comes to the conclusion that a living entity is not a part and parcel of the material world, but of the supreme spirit whole. Consequently, the spirit soul has nothing to do with the material world; his actions must be in some relation with the Supreme. When he acts in Kṛṣṇa consciousness, he is actually in his constitutional position. In the first process of *sāṅkhya*, one has to become detached from matter, and in the devotional *yoga* process one has to attach himself to the work of Kṛṣṇa. Factually, both processes are the same, although superficially one process appears to involve detachment and the other process appears to involve attachment. However, detachment from matter and attachment to Kṛṣṇa are one and the same. One who can see this sees things as they are.

TEXT 6

सन्न्यासस्तु महाबाहो दुःखमाप्तुमयोगतः ।
योगयुक्तो मुनिर्ब्रह्म नचिरेणाधिगच्छति ॥ ६ ॥

sannyāsas tu mahā-bāho
duḥkham āptum ayogataḥ

yoga-yukto munir brahma
na cireṇādhigacchati

sannyāsaḥ—the renounced order of life; *tu*—but; *mahā-bāho*—O mighty-armed one; *duḥkham*—distress; *āptum*—to be afflicted with; *ayogataḥ*—without devotional service; *yoga-yuktaḥ*—one engaged in devotional service; *muniḥ*—thinker;   *brahma*—Supreme;   *na*—without;   *cireṇa*—delay; *adhigacchati*—attains.

TRANSLATION

Unless one is engaged in the devotional service of the Lord, mere renunciation of activities cannot make one happy. The sages, purified by works of devotion, achieve the Supreme without delay.

PURPORT

There are two classes of *sannyāsīs*, or persons in the renounced order of life. The Māyāvādī *sannyāsīs* are engaged in the study of *sāṅkhya* philosophy, whereas the Vaiṣṇava *sannyāsīs* are engaged in the study of *Bhāgavatam* philosophy, which affords the proper commentary on the *Vedānta-sūtras*. The Māyāvādī *sannyāsīs* also study the *Vedānta-sūtras*, but use their own commentary, called *Śārīraka-bhāṣya*, written by Śaṅkarācārya. The students of the *Bhāgavata* school are engaged in devotional service of the Lord, according to *pāñcarātrikī* regulations, and therefore the Vaiṣṇava *sannyāsīs* have multiple engagements in the transcendental service of the Lord. The Vaiṣṇava *sannyāsīs* have nothing to do with material activities, and yet they perform various activities in their devotional service to the Lord. But the Māyāvādī *sannyāsīs*, engaged in the studies of *sāṅkhya* and *Vedānta* and speculation, cannot relish transcendental service of the Lord. Because their studies become very tedious, they sometimes become tired of Brahman speculation, and thus they take shelter of the *Bhāgavatam* without proper understanding. Consequently their study of the *Śrīmad-Bhāgavatam* becomes troublesome. Dry speculations and impersonal interpretations by artificial means are all useless for the Māyāvādī *sannyāsīs*. The Vaiṣṇava *sannyāsīs*, who are engaged in devotional service, are happy in the discharge of their transcendental duties, and they have the guarantee of ultimate entrance into the kingdom of God. The Māyāvādī *sannyāsīs* sometimes fall down from the path of self-realization and again enter into material activities of a philanthropic and altruistic nature, which are nothing but material engagements. Therefore, the conclusion is that those who are engaged in Kṛṣṇa consciousness are better situated than the *sannyāsīs* engaged in simple Brahman speculation, although they too come to Kṛṣṇa consciousness, after many births.

TEXT 7

योगयुक्तो विशुद्धात्मा विजितात्मा जितेन्द्रियः ।
सर्वभूतात्मभूतात्मा कुर्वन्नपि न लिप्यते ॥ ७ ॥

yoga-yukto viśuddhātmā
vijitātmā jitendriyaḥ
sarva-bhūtātma-bhūtātmā
kurvann api na lipyate

yoga-yuktaḥ—engaged in devotional service; *viśuddha-ātmā*—a purified soul; *vijita-ātmā*—self-controlled; *jita-indriyaḥ*—having conquered the senses; *sarvabhuta-ātmabhūta-ātmā*—compassionate to all living entities; *kurvan api*—although engaged in work; *na*—never; *lipyate*—is entangled.

TRANSLATION

One who works in devotion, who is a pure soul, and who controls his mind and senses, is dear to everyone, and everyone is dear to him. Though always working, such a man is never entangled.

PURPORT

One who is on the path of liberation by Kṛṣṇa consciousness is very dear to every living being, and every living being is dear to him. This is due to his Kṛṣṇa consciousness. Such a person cannot think of any living being as separate from Kṛṣṇa, just as the leaves and branches of a tree are not separate from the tree. He knows very well that by pouring water on the root of the tree, the water will be distributed to all the leaves and branches, or by supplying food to the stomach, the energy is automatically distributed throughout the body. Because one who works in Kṛṣṇa consciousness is servant to all, he is very dear to everyone. And, because everyone is satisfied by his work, he is pure in consciousness. Because he is pure in consciousness, his mind is completely controlled. And, because his mind is controlled, his senses are also controlled. Because his mind is always fixed on Kṛṣṇa, there is no chance of his being deviated from Kṛṣṇa. Nor is there a chance that he will engage his senses in matters other than the service of the Lord. He does not like to hear anything except topics relating to Kṛṣṇa; he does not like to eat anything which is not offered to Kṛṣṇa; and he does not wish to go anywhere if Kṛṣṇa is not involved. Therefore, his senses are controlled. A man of controlled senses cannot be offensive to anyone. One may ask, "Why then was Arjuna offensive (in battle) to others? Wasn't he in Kṛṣṇa consciousness?" Arjuna was only superficially offensive because (as has already been explained in the Second Chapter) all the assembled persons on the battlefield would continue to live individually, as the soul cannot be slain. So, spiritually, no one was killed on the Battlefield of Kurukṣetra. Only their dresses were changed by the order of Kṛṣṇa, who was personally present. Therefore Arjuna, while fighting on the Battlefield of Kurukṣetra, was not really fighting at all; he was simply carrying out the orders of Kṛṣṇa in full Kṛṣṇa consciousness. Such a person is never entangled in the reactions of work.

TEXTS 8-9

नैव किंचित्करोमीति युक्तो मन्येत तत्त्ववित् ।
पश्यञ्शृण्वन्स्पृशञ्जिघ्रन्नश्नन्गच्छन्स्वपन्श्वसन् ॥ ८ ॥

प्रलपन्विसृजन्गृह्णन्नुन्मिषन्निमिषन्नपि ।
इन्द्रियाणीन्द्रियार्थेषु वर्तन्त इति धारयन् ॥ ९ ॥

naiva kiñcit karomīti
yukto manyeta tattva-vit
paśyañ śṛṇvan spṛśañ jighrann
aśnan gacchan svapan śvasan
pralapan visṛjan gṛhṇann
unmiṣan nimiṣann api
indriyāṇīndriyārtheṣu
vartanta iti dhārayan

na—never; eva—certainly; kiñcit—anything; karomi—do I do; iti—thus; yuktaḥ—engaged in the divine consciousness; manyeta—thinks; tattvavit—

one who knows the truth; *paśyan*—by seeing; *śṛṇvan*—by hearing; *spṛśan*—by touching; *jighran*—by smelling; *aśnan*—by eating; *gacchan*—by going; *svapan*—by dreaming; *śvasan*—by breathing; *pralapan*—by talking; *visṛjan*—by giving up; *gṛhṇan*—by accepting; *unmiṣan*—opening; *nimiṣan*—closing; *api*—in spite of; *indriyāṇi*—the senses; *indriya-artheṣu*—in sense gratification; *vartante*—let them be so engaged; *iti*—thus; *dhārayan*—considering.

TRANSLATION

A person in the divine consciousness, although engaged in seeing, hearing, touching, smelling, eating, moving about, sleeping, and breathing, always knows within himself that he actually does nothing at all. Because while speaking, evacuating, receiving, opening or closing his eyes, he always knows that only the material senses are engaged with their objects and that he is aloof from them.

PURPORT

A person in Kṛṣṇa consciousness is pure in his existence, and consequently he has nothing to do with any work which depends upon five immediate and remote causes: the doer, the work, the situation, the endeavor and fortune. This is because he is engaged in the loving transcendental service of Kṛṣṇa. Although he appears to be acting with his body and senses, he is always conscious of his actual position, which is spiritual engagement. In material consciousness, the senses are engaged in sense gratification, but in Kṛṣṇa consciousness the senses are engaged in the satisfaction of Kṛṣṇa's senses. Therefore, the Kṛṣṇa conscious person is always free, even though he appears to be engaged in things of the senses. Activities such as seeing, hearing, speaking, evacuating, etc., are actions of the senses meant for work. A Kṛṣṇa consciousness person is never affected by the actions of the senses. He cannot perform any act except in the service of the Lord because he knows that he is the eternal servitor of the Lord.

TEXT 10

ब्रह्मण्याधाय कर्माणि सङ्गं त्यक्त्वा करोति यः ।
लिप्यते न स पापेन पद्मपत्रमिवाम्भसा ॥ १० ॥

brahmaṇy ādhāya karmāṇi
saṅgaṁ tyaktvā karoti yaḥ
lipyate na sa pāpena
padma-patram ivāmbhasā

brahmaṇi—the Supreme Personality of Godhead; *ādhāya*—resigning unto; *karmāṇi*—all works; *saṅgam*—attachment; *tyaktvā*—giving up; *karoti*—performs; *yaḥ*—who; *lipyate*—is affected; *na*—never; *saḥ*—he; *pāpena*—by sin; *padma-patram*—lotus leaf; *iva*—like; *ambhasā*—in the water.

TRANSLATION

One who performs his duty without attachment, surrendering the results unto the Supreme God, is not affected by sinful action, as the lotus leaf is untouched by water.

PURPORT

Here *brahmaṇi* means in Kṛṣṇa consciousness. The material world is a sum total manifestation of the three modes of material nature, technically called the *pradhāna*. The Vedic hymns, *sarvam etad brahma, tasmād etad brahma nāma-rūpam annaṁ ca jāyate,* and, in the *Bhagavad-gītā, mama yonir mahad brahma,* indicate that everything in the material world is the manifestation of Brahman; and, although the effects are differently manifested, they are nondifferent from the cause. In the *Īśopaniṣad* it is said that everything is related to the Supreme Brahman or Kṛṣṇa, and thus everything belongs to Him only. One who knows perfectly well that everything belongs to Kṛṣṇa, that He is the proprietor of everything and that, therefore, everything is engaged in the service of the Lord, naturally has nothing to do with the results of his activities, whether virtuous or sinful. Even one's material body, being a gift of the Lord for carrying out a particular type of action, can be engaged in Kṛṣṇa consciousness. It is beyond contamination by sinful reactions, exactly as the lotus leaf, though remaining in the water, is not wet. The Lord also says in the *Gītā: mayi sarvāṇi karmāṇi sannyasya:* "Resign all works unto Me [Kṛṣṇa]." The conclusion is that a person without Kṛṣṇa consciousness acts according to the concept of the material body and senses, but a person in Kṛṣṇa consciousness acts according to the knowledge that the body is the property of Kṛṣṇa and should therefore be engaged in the service of Kṛṣṇa.

TEXT 11

कायेन मनसा बुद्ध्या केवलैरिन्द्रियैरपि ।
योगिनः कर्म कुर्वन्ति सङ्गं त्यक्त्वात्मशुद्धये ॥ ११ ॥

*kāyena manasā buddhyā
kevalair indriyair api
yoginaḥ karma kurvanti
saṅgaṁ tyaktvātma-śuddhaye*

kāyena—with the body; *manasā*—with the mind; *buddhyā*—with the intelligence; *kevalaiḥ*—purified; *indriyaiḥ*—with the senses; *api*—even with; *yoginaḥ*—the Kṛṣṇa conscious persons; *karma*—actions; *kurvanti*—they act; *saṅgam*—attachment; *tyaktvā*—giving up; *ātma*—self; *śuddhaye*—for the purpose of purification.

TRANSLATION

The yogīs, abandoning attachment, act with body, mind, intelligence, and even with the senses, only for the purpose of purification.

PURPORT

By acting in Kṛṣṇa consciousness for the satisfaction of the senses of Kṛṣṇa, any action, whether of the body, mind, intelligence or even of the senses, is purified of material contamination. There are no material reactions resulting from the activities of a Kṛṣṇa conscious person. Therefore, purified activities, which are generally called *sadācāra*, can be easily performed by acting in Kṛṣṇa consciousness. Śrī Rūpa Gosvāmī in his *Bhakti-rasāmṛta-sindhu* describes this as follows:

*īhā yasya harer dāsye karmaṇā manasā girā
nikhilāsv apy avasthāsu jīvanmuktaḥ sa ucyate*

A person acting in Kṛṣṇa consciousness (or, in other words, in the service of Kṛṣṇa) with his body, mind, intelligence and words is a liberated person even within the material world, although he may be engaged in many so-called material activities. He has no false ego, nor does he believe that he is this material body, nor that he possesses the body. He knows that he is not this body and that this body does not belong to him. He himself belongs to Kṛṣṇa, and the body too belongs to Kṛṣṇa. When he applies everything produced of the body, mind, intelligence, words, life, wealth, etc.—whatever he may have within his possession—to Kṛṣṇa's service, he is at once dovetailed with Kṛṣṇa. He is one with Kṛṣṇa and is devoid of the false ego that leads one to believe that he is the body, etc. This is the perfect stage of Kṛṣṇa consciousness.

TEXT 12

युक्तः कर्मफलं त्यक्त्वा शान्तिमाप्नोति नैष्ठिकीम् ।
अयुक्तः कामकारेण फले सक्तो निबध्यते ॥ १२ ॥

yuktaḥ karma-phalaṁ tyaktvā
śāntim āpnoti naiṣṭhikīm
ayuktaḥ kāma-kāreṇa
phale sakto nibadhyate

yuktaḥ—one who is engaged in devotional service; *karma-phalam*—the results of all activities; *tyaktvā*—giving up; *śāntim*—perfect peace; *āpnoti*—achieves; *naiṣṭhikīm*—unflinching; *ayuktaḥ*—one who is not in Kṛṣṇa consciousness; *kāma-kāreṇa*—for enjoying the result of work; *phale*—in the result; *saktaḥ*—attached; *nibadhyate*—becomes entangled.

TRANSLATION

The steadily devoted soul attains unadulterated peace because he offers the result of all activities to Me; whereas a person who is not in union with the Divine, who is greedy for the fruits of his labor, becomes entangled.

PURPORT

The difference between a person in Kṛṣṇa consciousness and a person in bodily consciousness is that the former is attached to Kṛṣṇa, whereas the latter is attached to the results of his activities. The person who is attached to Kṛṣṇa and works for Him only is certainly a liberated person, and he is not anxious for fruitive rewards. In the *Bhāgavatam*, the cause of anxiety over the result of an activity is explained as being due to one's functioning in the conception of duality, that is, without knowledge of the Absolute Truth. Kṛṣṇa is the Supreme Absolute Truth, the Personality of Godhead. In Kṛṣṇa consciousness, there is no duality. All that exists is a product of Kṛṣṇa's energy, and Kṛṣṇa is all good. Therefore, activities in Kṛṣṇa consciousness are on the absolute plane; they are transcendental and have no material effect. One is, therefore, filled with peace in Kṛṣṇa consciousness. One who is, however, entangled in profit calculation for sense gratification cannot have that peace. This is the secret of Kṛṣṇa consciousness—realization that there is no existence besides Kṛṣṇa is the platform of peace and fearlessness.

TEXT 13

सर्वकर्माणि मनसा संन्यस्यास्ते सुखं वशी ।
नवद्वारे पुरे देही नैव कुर्वन्न कारयन् ॥ १३ ॥

sarva-karmāṇi manasā
sannyasyāste sukhaṁ vaśī
nava-dvāre pure dehī
naiva kurvan na kārayan

sarva—all; *karmāṇi*—activities; *manasā*—by the mind; *sannyasya*—giving up; *āste*—remains; *sukham*—in happiness; *vaśī*—one who is controlled; *nava-dvāre*—in the place where there are nine gates; *pure*—in the city; *dehī*—the embodied soul; *na*—never; *eva*—certainly; *kurvan*—doing anything; *na*—not; *kārayan*—causing to be done.

TRANSLATION

When the embodied living being controls his nature and mentally renounces all actions, he resides happily in the city of nine gates [the material body], neither working nor causing work to be done.

PURPORT

The embodied soul lives in the city of nine gates. The activities of the body, or the figurative city of body, are conducted automatically by the particular modes of nature. The soul, although subjecting himself to the conditions of the body, can be beyond those conditions, if he so desires. Owing only to forgetfulness of his superior nature, he identifies with the material body, and therefore suffers. By Kṛṣṇa consciousness, he can revive his real position and thus come out of his embodiment. Therefore, when one takes to Kṛṣṇa consciousness, one at once becomes completely aloof from bodily activities. In such a controlled life, in which his deliberations are changed, he lives happily within the city of nine gates. The nine gates are described as follows:

nava-dvāre pure dehī haṁso lelāyate bahiḥ
vaśī sarvasya lokasya sthāvarasya carasya ca.

"The Supreme Personality of Godhead, who is living within the body of a living entity, is the controller of all living entities all over the universe. The body consists of nine gates: two eyes, two nostrils, two ears, one mouth, the anus and the genital. The living entity in his conditioned stage identifies himself with the body, but when he identifies himself with the Lord within himself, he becomes just as free as the Lord, even while in the body." (Śvet. 3.18)

Therefore, a Kṛṣṇa conscious person is free from both the outer and inner activities of the material body.

TEXT 14

न कर्तृत्वं न कर्माणि लोकस्य सृजति प्रभुः ।
न कर्मफलसंयोगं स्वभावस्तु प्रवर्तते ॥ १४ ॥

na kartṛtvaṁ na karmāṇi
lokasya sṛjati prabhuḥ
na karma-phala-saṁyogaṁ
svabhāvas tu pravartate

na—never; *kartṛtvam*—proprietorship; *na*—nor; *karmāṇi*—activities; *lokasya*—of the people; *sṛjati*—creates; *prabhuḥ*—the master of the city of the body; *na*—nor; *karma-phala*—results of activities; *saṁyogam*—connection; *svabhāvaḥ*—modes of material nature; *tu*—but; *pravartate*—acts.

TRANSLATION

The embodied spirit, master of the city of his body, does not create activities, nor does he induce people to act, nor does he create the fruits of action. All this is enacted by the modes of material nature.

PURPORT

The living entity, as will be explained in the Seventh Chapter, is one in nature with the Supreme Lord, distinguished from matter, which is another nature—called inferior—of the Lord. Somehow, the superior nature, the living entity, has been in contact with material nature since time immemorial. The temporary body or material dwelling place which he obtains is the cause of varieties of activities and their resultant reactions. Living in such a conditional atmosphere, one suffers the results of the activities of the body by identifying himself (in ignorance) with the body. It is ignorance acquired from time immemorial that is the cause of bodily suffering and distress. As soon as the living entity becomes aloof from the activities of the body, he becomes free from the reactions as well. As long as he is in the city of body, he appears to be the master of it, but actually he is neither its proprietor nor controller of its actions and reactions. He is simply in the midst of the material ocean, struggling for existence. The waves of the ocean are tossing him, and he has no control over them. His best solution is to get out of the water by transcendental Kṛṣṇa consciousness. That alone will save him from all turmoil.

TEXT 15

नादत्ते कस्यचित्पापं न चैव सुकृतं विभुः ।
अज्ञानेनावृतं ज्ञानं तेन मुह्यन्ति जन्तवः ॥ १५ ॥

nādatte kasyacit pāpaṁ
na caiva sukṛtaṁ vibhuḥ
ajñānenāvṛtaṁ jñānaṁ
tena muhyanti jantavaḥ

na—never; *ādatte*—accepts; *kasyacit*—anyone's; *pāpam*—sin; *na*—nor; *ca*—also; *eva*—certainly; *sukṛtam*—pious activities; *vibhuḥ*—the Supreme Lord;

ajñānena—by ignorance; *āvṛtam*—covered; *jñānam*—knowledge; *tena*—by that; *muhyanti*—bewildered; *jantavaḥ*—the living entities.

TRANSLATION

Nor does the Supreme Spirit assume anyone's sinful or pious activities. Embodied beings, however, are bewildered because of the ignorance which covers their real knowledge.

PURPORT

The Sanskrit word *vibhuḥ* means the Supreme Lord who is full of unlimited knowledge, riches, strength, fame, beauty and renunciation. He is always satisfied in Himself, undisturbed by sinful or pious activities. He does not create a particular situation for any living entity, but the living entity, bewildered by ignorance, desires to be put into certain conditions of life, and thereby his chain of action and reaction begins. A living entity is, by superior nature, full of knowledge. Nevertheless, he is prone to be influenced by ignorance due to his limited power. The Lord is omnipotent, but the living entity is not. The Lord is *vibhu*, or omniscient, but the living entity is *aṇu*, or atomic. Because he is a living soul, he has the capacity to desire by his free will. Such desire is fulfilled only by the omnipotent Lord. And so, when the living entity is bewildered in his desires, the Lord allows him to fulfill those desires, but the Lord is never responsible for the actions and reactions of the particular situation which may be desired. Being in a bewildered condition, therefore, the embodied soul identifies himself with the circumstantial material body and becomes subjected to the temporary misery and happiness of life. The Lord is the constant companion of the living entity as Paramātmā, or the Supersoul, and therefore He can understand the desires of the individual soul, as one can smell the flavor of a flower by being near it. Desire is a subtle form of conditioning of the living entity. The Lord fulfills his desire as he deserves: Man proposes and God disposes. The individual is not, therefore, omnipotent in fulfilling his desires. The Lord, however, can fulfill all desires, and the Lord, being neutral to everyone, does not interfere with the desires of the minute independant living entities. However, when one desires Kṛṣṇa, the Lord takes special care and encourages one to desire in such a way that one can attain to Him and be eternally happy. The Vedic hymn therefore declares:

> *eṣa u hy eva sādhu karma kārayati taṁ yamebhyo lokebhya unninīṣate*
> *eṣa u evāsādhu karma kārayati yamadho ninīṣate.*

ajño jantur aniso 'yam ātmanaḥ sukha-duḥkhayoḥ
īśvara-prerito gacchet svargaṁ vāśvabhram eva ca.

"The Lord engages the living entity in pious activities so he may be elevated. The Lord engages him in impious activities so he may go to hell. The living entity is completely dependant in his distress and happiness. By the will of the Supreme he can go to heaven or hell, as a cloud is driven by the air."

Therefore the embodied soul, by his immemorial desire to avoid Kṛṣṇa consciousness, causes his own bewilderment. Consequently, although he is constitutionally eternal, blissful and cognizant, due to the littleness of his existence he forgets his constitutional position of service to the Lord and is thus entrapped by nescience. And, under the spell of ignorance, the living entity claims that the Lord is responsible for his conditional existence. The *Vedānta-sūtras* also confirm this:

vaiṣamya-nairghṛṇye na sāpekṣatvāt tathā hi darśayati.

"The Lord neither hates nor likes anyone, though He appears to."

TEXT 16

ज्ञानेन तु तदज्ञानं येषां नाशितमात्मनः ।
तेषामादित्यवज्ज्ञानं प्रकाशयति तत्परम् ॥ १६ ॥

jñānena tu tad ajñānaṁ
yeṣāṁ nāśitam ātmanaḥ
teṣām āditya-vaj jñānaṁ
prakāśayati tat param

jñānena—by knowledge; *tu*—but; *tat*—that; *ajñānam*—nescience; *yeṣām*—of those; *nāśitam*—is destroyed; *ātmanaḥ*—of the living entity; *teṣām*—of their; *ādityavat*—like the rising sun; *jñānam*—knowledge; *prakāśayati*—discloses; *tat param*—in Kṛṣṇa consciousness.

TRANSLATION

When, however, one is enlightened with the knowledge by which nescience is destroyed, then his knowledge reveals everything, as the sun lights up everything in the daytime.

PURPORT

Those who have forgotten Kṛṣṇa must certainly be bewildered, but those who are in Kṛṣṇa consciousness are not bewildered at all. It is stated in the *Bhagavad-gītā*, "*sarvaṁ jñāna-plavena*," "*jñānāgniḥ sarva karmāṇi*" and "*na hi jñānena sadṛśam*." Knowledge is always highly esteemed. And what is that knowledge? Perfect knowledge is achieved when one surrenders unto Kṛṣṇa, as is said in the Seventh Chapter, 19th verse: *bahūnāṁ janmanām ante jñānavān māṁ prapadyate*. After passing through many, many births, when one perfect in knowledge surrenders unto Kṛṣṇa, or when one attains Kṛṣṇa consciousness, then everything is revealed to him, as the sun reveals everything in the daytime. The living entity is bewildered in so many ways. For instance, when he thinks himself God, unceremoniously, he actually falls into the last snare of nescience. If a living entity is God, then how can he become bewildered by nescience? Does God become bewildered by nescience? If so, then nescience, or Satan, is greater than God. Real knowledge can be obtained from a person who is in perfect Kṛṣṇa consciousness. Therefore, one has to seek out such a bona fide spiritual master and, under him, learn what Kṛṣṇa consciousness is. The spiritual master can drive away all nescience, as the sun drives away darkness. Even though a person may be in full knowledge that he is not this body but is transcendental to the body, he still may not be able to discriminate between the soul and the Supersoul. However, he can know everything well if he cares to take shelter of the perfect, bona fide Kṛṣṇa conscious spiritual master. One can know God and one's relationship with God only when one actually meets a representative of God. A representative of God never claims that he is God, although he is paid all the respect ordinarily paid to God because he has knowledge of God. One has to learn the distinction between God and the living entity. Lord Śrī Kṛṣṇa therefore stated in the Second Chapter (2.12) that every living being is individual and that the Lord also is individual. They were all individuals in the past, they are individuals at present, and they will continue to be individuals in the future, even after liberation. At night we see everything as one in the darkness, but in day when the sun is up, we see everything in its real identity. Identity with individuality in spiritual life is real knowledge.

TEXT 17

तद्बुद्धयस्तदात्मानस्तन्निष्ठास्तत्परायणाः ।
गच्छन्त्यपुनरावृत्तिं ज्ञाननिर्धूतकल्मषाः ॥ १७ ॥

tad-buddhayas tad-ātmānas
tan-niṣṭhās tat-parāyaṇāḥ
gacchanty apunar-āvṛttiṁ
jñāna-nirdhūta-kalmaṣāḥ

tad-buddhayaḥ—one whose intelligence is always in the Supreme; tad-ātmānaḥ—one whose mind is always in the Supreme; tat-niṣṭhāḥ—whose mind is only meant for the Supreme; tat-parāyaṇāḥ—who has completely taken shelter of Him; gacchanti—goes; apunaḥ-āvṛttim—liberation; jñāna—knowledge; nirdhūta—cleanses; kalmaṣāḥ—misgivings.

TRANSLATION

When one's intelligence, mind, faith and refuge are all fixed in the Supreme, then one becomes fully cleansed of misgivings through complete knowledge and thus proceeds straight on the path of liberation.

PURPORT

The Supreme Transcendental Truth is Lord Kṛṣṇa. The whole *Bhagavad-gītā* centers around the declaration of Kṛṣṇa as the Supreme Personality of Godhead. That is the version of all Vedic literature. *Paratattva* means the Supreme Reality, who is understood by the knowers of the Supreme as Brahman, Paramātmā and Bhagavān. Bhagavān, or the Supreme Personality of Godhead, is the last word in the Absolute. There is nothing more than that. The Lord says, *mattaḥ parataraṁ nānyat kiñcit asti dhanañjaya.* Impersonal Brahman is also supported by Kṛṣṇa: *brahmaṇo pratiṣṭhāham.* Therefore in all ways Kṛṣṇa is the Supreme Reality. One whose mind, intelligence, faith and refuge are always in Kṛṣṇa, or, in other words, one who is fully in Kṛṣṇa consciousness, is undoubtedly washed clean of all misgivings and is in perfect knowledge in everything concerning transcendence. A Kṛṣṇa conscious person can thoroughly understand that there is duality (simultaneous identity and individuality) in Kṛṣṇa, and, equipped with such transcendental knowledge, one can make steady progress on the path of liberation.

TEXT 18

विद्याविनयसम्पन्ने ब्राह्मणे गवि हस्तिनि ।
शुनि चैव श्वपाके च पण्डिताः समदर्शिनः ॥ १८ ॥

vidyā-vinaya-sampanne
brāhmaṇe gavi hastini
śuni caiva śva-pāke ca
paṇḍitāḥ sama-darśinaḥ

vidyā—education; *vinaya*—gentleness; *sampanne*—fully equipped; *brāhmaṇe*—in the *brāhmaṇa*; *gavi*—in the cow; *hastini*—in the elephant; *śuni*—in the dog; *ca*—and; *eva*—certainly; *śvapāke*—in the dog-eater (the outcaste); *ca*—respectively; *paṇḍitāḥ*-those who are so wise; *sama-darśinaḥ* —do see with equal vision.

TRANSLATION

The humble sage, by virtue of true knowledge, sees with equal vision a learned and gentle brāhmaṇa, a cow, an elephant, a dog and a dog-eater [outcaste] .

PURPORT

A Kṛṣṇa conscious person does not make any distinction between species or castes. The *brāhmaṇa* and the outcaste may be different from the social point of view, or a dog, a cow, or an elephant may be different from the point of view of species, but these differences of body are meaningless from the viewpoint of a learned transcendentalist. This is due to their relationship to the Supreme, for the Supreme Lord, by His plenary portion as Paramātmā, is present in everyone's heart. Such an understanding of the Supreme is real knowledge. As far as the bodies are concerned in different castes or different species of life, the Lord is equally kind to everyone because He treats every living being as a friend yet maintains Himself as Paramātmā regardless of the circumstances of the living entities. The Lord as Paramātmā is present both in the outcaste and in the *brāhmaṇa*, although the body of a *brāhmaṇa* and that of an outcaste are not the same. The bodies are material productions of different modes of material nature, but the soul and the Supersoul within the body are of the same spiritual quality. The similarity in the quality of the soul and the Supersoul, however, does not make them equal in quantity, for the individual soul is present only in that particular body, whereas the Paramātmā is present in each and every body. A Kṛṣṇa conscious person has full knowledge of this, and therefore he is truly learned and has equal vision. The similar characteristics of the soul and Supersoul are that they are both conscious, eternal and blissful. But the difference is that the individual soul is conscious within the limited jurisdiction of the body, whereas the Supersoul is conscious of all bodies. The Supersoul is present in all bodies without distinction.

TEXT 19

इहैव तैर्जितः सर्गो येषां साम्ये स्थितं मनः ।
निर्दोषं हि समं ब्रह्म तस्माद्ब्रह्मणि ते स्थिताः ॥ १९ ॥

ihaiva tair jitaḥ sargo
yeṣāṁ sāmye sthitaṁ manaḥ
nirdoṣaṁ hi samaṁ brahma
tasmād brahmaṇi te sthitāḥ

iha—in this life; *eva*—certainly; *taiḥ*—by them; *jitaḥ*—conquered; *sargaḥ*—birth and death; *yeṣām*—of those; *sāmye*—in equanimity; *sthitam*—so situated; *manaḥ*—mind; *nirdoṣam*—flawless; *hi*—certainly; *samam*—in equanimity; *brahma*—the Supreme; *tasmāt*—therefore; *brahmaṇi*—in the Supreme; *te*—they; *sthitāḥ*—are situated.

TRANSLATION

Those whose minds are established in sameness and equanimity have already conquered the conditions of birth and death. They are flawless like Brahman, and thus they are already situated in Brahman.

PURPORT

Equanimity of mind, as mentioned above, is the sign of self-realization. Those who have actually attained to such a stage should be considered to have conquered material conditions, specifically birth and death. As long as one identifies with this body, he is considered a conditioned soul, but as soon as he is elevated to the stage of equanimity through realization of self, he is liberated from conditional life. In other words, he is no longer subject to take birth in the material world but can enter into the spiritual sky after his death. The Lord is flawless because He is without attraction or hatred. Similarly, when a living entity is without attraction or hatred, he also becomes flawless and eligible to enter into the spiritual sky. Such

persons are to be considered already liberated, and their symptoms are
described below.

TEXT 20

न प्रहृष्येत्प्रियं प्राप्य नोद्विजेत्प्राप्य चाप्रियम् ।
स्थिरबुद्धिरसम्मूढो ब्रह्मविद्ब्रह्मणि स्थितः ॥ २० ॥

na prahṛṣyet priyaṁ prāpya
nodvijet prāpya cāpriyam
sthira-buddhir asammūḍho
brahma-vid brahmaṇi sthitaḥ

na—never; *prahṛṣyet*—rejoice; *priyam*—pleasant; *prāpya*—achieving; *na*—
does not; *udvijet*—agitated; *prāpya*—obtaining; *ca*—also; *apriyam*—unpleasant; *sthira-buddhiḥ*—self-intelligent; *asammūḍhaḥ*—unbewildered; *brahmavit*—
one who knows the Supreme perfectly; *brahmaṇi*—in the Transcendence;
sthitaḥ—situated.

TRANSLATION

**A person who neither rejoices upon achieving something pleasant nor
laments upon obtaining something unpleasant, who is self-intelligent,
unbewildered, and who knows the science of God, is to be understood as
already situated in Transcendence.**

PURPORT

The symptoms of the self-realized person are given herein. The first
symptom is that he is not illusioned by the false identification of the body
with his true self. He knows perfectly well that he is not this body, but is
the fragmental portion of the Supreme Personality of Godhead. He is
therefore not joyful in achieving something, nor does he lament in losing
anything which is related to his body. This steadiness of mind is called
sthira-buddhi, or self-intelligence. He is therefore never bewildered by
mistaking the gross body for the soul, nor does he accept the body as
permanent and disregard the existence of the soul. This knowledge elevates
him to the station of knowing the complete science of the Absolute Truth,

namely Brahman, Paramātmā and Bhagavān. He thus knows his constitutional position perfectly well, without falsely trying to become one with the Supreme in all respects. This is called Brahman realization, or self-realization. Such steady consciousness is called Kṛṣṇa consciousness.

TEXT 21

बाह्यस्पर्शेष्वसक्तात्मा विन्दत्यात्मनि यत्सुखम् ।
स ब्रह्मयोगयुक्तात्मा सुखमक्षयमश्नुते ॥ २१ ॥

bāhya-sparśeṣv asaktātmā
vindaty ātmani yat sukham
sa brahma-yoga-yuktātmā
sukham akṣayam aśnute

bāhya-sparśeṣu—in external sense pleasure; *asakta-ātmā*—one who is not so attached; *vindati*—enjoys; *ātmani*—in the self; *yat*—that which; *sukham*—happiness; *saḥ*—that; *brahma-yoga*—concentrated in Brahman; *yukta-ātmā*—self-connected; *sukham*—happiness; *akṣayam*—unlimited; *aśnute*—enjoys.

TRANSLATION

Such a liberated person is not attracted to material sense pleasure or external objects but is always in trance, enjoying the pleasure within. In this way the self-realized person enjoys unlimited happiness, for he concentrates on the Supreme.

PURPORT

Śrī Yāmunācārya, a great devotee in Kṛṣṇa consciousness, said:

yadāvadhi mama cetaḥ kṛṣṇa-padāravinde
nava-nava-rasa-dhāmanudyata rantum āsīt
tadāvadhi bata nārī-saṅgame smaryamāne
bhavati mukha-vikāraḥ suṣṭu niṣṭhīvanaṁ ca

"Since I have been engaged in the transcendental loving service of Kṛṣṇa, realizing ever-new pleasure in Him, whenever I think of sex pleasure, I spit at the thought, and my lips curl with distaste." A person in *brahma-yoga*, or Kṛṣṇa consciousness, is so absorbed in the loving service of the Lord that he loses his taste for material sense pleasure altogether. The highest pleasure in terms of matter is sex pleasure. The whole world is moving under its spell, and a materialist cannot work at all without this motivation. But a person engaged in Kṛṣṇa consciousness can work with greater vigor without sex pleasure, which he avoids. That is the test in spiritual realization. Spiritual realization and sex pleasure go ill together. A Kṛṣṇa conscious person is not attracted to any kind of sense pleasure due to his being a liberated soul.

TEXT 22

ये हि संस्पर्शजा भोगा दुःखयोनय एव ते ।
आद्यन्तवन्तः कौन्तेय न तेषु रमते बुधः ॥ २२ ॥

ye hi saṁsparśa-jā bhogā
duḥkha-yonaya eva te
ādy-antavantaḥ kaunteya
na teṣu ramate budhaḥ

ye—those; *hi*—certainly; *saṁsparśajāḥ*—by contact with the material senses; *bhogāḥ*—enjoyment; *duḥkha*—distress; *yonayaḥ*—sources of; *eva*—certainly; *te*—they are; *ādi*—in the beginning; *antavantaḥ*—subject to; *kaunteya*—O son of Kuntī; *na*—never; *teṣu*—in those; *ramate*—take delight; *budhaḥ*—the intelligent.

TRANSLATION

An intelligent person does not take part in the sources of misery, which are due to contact with the material senses. O son of Kuntī, such pleasures have a beginning and an end, and so the wise man does not delight in them.

PURPORT

Material sense pleasures are due to the contact of the material senses, which are all temporary because the body itself is temporary. A liberated soul is not interested in anything which is temporary. Knowing well the joys of transcendental pleasures, how can a liberated soul agree to enjoy false pleasure? In the *Padma Purāṇa* it is said:

> ramante yogino 'nante satyānanda-cid-ātmani
> iti rāma-padenāsau paraṁ brahmābhidhīyate

"The mystics derive unlimited transcendental pleasures from the Absolute Truth, and therefore the Supreme Absolute Truth, the Personality of Godhead, is also known as Rāma."

In the *Śrīmad-Bhāgavatam* also it is said:

> nāyaṁ deho deha-bhājāṁ nṛ-loke
> kaṣṭān kāmān arhate viḍ-bhajāṁ ye
> tapo divyaṁ putrakā yena sattvaṁ
> śuddhyed yasmād brahma-saukhyaṁ tv anantam.

"My dear sons, there is no reason to labor very hard for sense pleasure while in this human form of life; such pleasures are available to the stool-eaters [hogs]. Rather, you should undergo penances in this life by which your existence will be purified, and, as a result, you will be able to enjoy unlimited transcendental bliss." (*Bhāg.* 5.5.1)

Therefore, those who are true *yogīs* or learned transcendentalists are not attracted by sense pleasures, which are the causes of continuous material existence. The more one is addicted to material pleasures, the more he is entrapped by material miseries.

TEXT 23

शक्नोतीहैव यः सोढुं प्राक्शरीरविमोक्षणात् ।
कामक्रोधोद्भवं वेगं स युक्तः स सुखी नरः ॥ २३ ॥

> śaknotīhaiva yaḥ soḍhuṁ
> prāk śarīra-vimokṣaṇāt
> kāma-krodhodbhavaṁ vegaṁ
> sa yuktaḥ sa sukhī naraḥ

śaknoti—able to do; iha eva—in the present body; yaḥ—one who; soḍhum—to tolerate; prāk—before; śarīra—body; vimokṣaṇāt—giving up;

kāma—desire; *krodha*—anger; *udbhavam*—generated from; *vegam*—urge; *sah*—he; *yuktah*—in trance; *sah*—he; *sukhī*—happy; *narah*—human being.

TRANSLATION

Before giving up this present body, if one is able to tolerate the urges of the material senses and check the force of desire and anger, he is a yogī and is happy in this world.

PURPORT

If one wants to make steady progress on the path of self-realization, he must try to control the forces of the material senses. There are the forces of talk, forces of anger, forces of mind, forces of the stomach, forces of the genitals, and forces of the tongue. One who is able to control the forces of all these different senses, and the mind, is called *gosvāmī*, or *svāmī*. Such *gosvāmīs* live strictly controlled lives, and forego altogether the forces of the senses. Material desires, when unsatiated, generate anger, and thus the mind, eyes and chest become agitated. Therefore, one must practice to control them before one gives up this material body. One who can do this is understood to be self-realized and is thus happy in the state of self-realization. It is the duty of the transcendentalist to try strenuously to control desire and anger.

TEXT 24

योऽन्तःसुखोऽन्तरारामस्तथान्तर्ज्योतिरेव यः ।
स योगी ब्रह्मनिर्वाणं ब्रह्मभूतोऽधिगच्छति ॥ २४ ॥

yo 'ntah-sukho 'ntar-ārāmas
tathāntar-jyotir eva yah
sa yogī brahma-nirvāṇam
brahma-bhūto 'dhigacchati

yah—one who; *antah-sukhah*—happy from within; *antah-ārāmah*—active within; *tathā*—as well as; *antah-jyotih*—aiming within; *eva*—certainly; *yah*—anyone; *sah*—he; *yogī*—mystic; *brahma-nirvāṇam*—liberated in the Supreme; *brahma-bhūtah*—self-realized; *adhigacchati*—attains.

TRANSLATION

One whose happiness is within, who is active within, who rejoices within and is illumined within, is actually the perfect mystic. He is liberated in the Supreme, and ultimately he attains the Supreme.

PURPORT

Unless one is able to relish happiness from within, how can one retire from the external engagements meant for deriving superficial happiness? A liberated person enjoys happiness by factual experience. He can, therefore, sit silently at any place and enjoy the activities of life from within. Such a liberated person no longer desires external material happiness. This state is called *brahma-bhūta*, attaining which one is assured of going back to Godhead, back to home.

TEXT 25

लभन्ते ब्रह्मनिर्वाणमृषयः क्षीणकल्मषाः ।
छिन्नद्वैधा यतात्मानः सर्वभूतहिते रताः ॥ २५ ॥

*labhante brahma-nirvāṇam
ṛṣayaḥ kṣīṇa-kalmaṣāḥ
chinna-dvaidhā yatātmānaḥ
sarva-bhūta-hite ratāḥ*

labhante—achieve; *brahma-nirvāṇam*—liberation in the Supreme; *ṛṣayaḥ*—those who are active within; *kṣīṇa-kalmaṣāḥ*—who are devoid of all sins; *chinna*—torn off; *dvaidhāḥ*—duality; *yata-ātmānaḥ*—engaged in self-realization; *sarva-bhūta*—in all living entities; *hite*—in welfare work; *ratāḥ*—engaged.

TRANSLATION

One who is beyond duality and doubt, whose mind is engaged within, who is always busy working for the welfare of all sentient beings, and who is free from all sins, achieves liberation in the Supreme.

PURPORT

Only a person who is fully in Kṛṣṇa consciousness can be said to be engaged in welfare work for all living entities. When a person is actually in the knowledge that Kṛṣṇa is the fountainhead of everything, then when he acts in that spirit he acts for everyone. The sufferings of humanity are due to forgetfulness of Kṛṣṇa as the supreme enjoyer, the supreme proprietor, and the supreme friend. Therefore, to act to revive this consciousness within the entire human society is the highest welfare work. One cannot be engaged in first-class welfare work without being liberated in the Supreme. A Kṛṣṇa conscious person has no doubt about the supremacy of Kṛṣṇa. He has no doubt because he is completely freed from all sins. This is the state of divine love.

A person engaged only in ministering to the physical welfare of human society cannot factually help anyone. Temporary relief of the external body and the mind is not satisfactory. The real cause of one's difficulties in the hard struggle for life may be found in one's forgetfulness of his relationship with the Supreme Lord. When a man is fully conscious of his relationship with Kṛṣṇa, he is actually a liberated soul, although he may be in the material tabernacle.

TEXT 26

कामक्रोधविमुक्तानां यतीनां यतचेतसाम् ।
अभितो ब्रह्मनिर्वाणं वर्तते विदितात्मनाम् ॥ २६ ॥

kāma-krodha-vimuktānāṁ
yatīnāṁ yata-cetasām
abhito brahma-nirvāṇaṁ
vartate viditātmanām

kāma—desires; *krodha*—anger; *vimuktānām*—of those who are so liberated; *yatīnām*—of the saintly persons; *yata-cetasām*—of persons who have full control over the mind; *abhitaḥ*—assured in the near future; *brahma-nirvāṇam*—liberation in the Supreme; *vartate*—is there; *vidita-ātmanām*—of those who are self-realized.

TRANSLATION

Those who are free from anger and all material desires, who are selfrealized, self-disciplined and constantly endeavoring for perfection, are assured of liberation in the Supreme in the very near future.

PURPORT

Of the saintly persons who are constantly engaged in striving toward salvation, one who is in Kṛṣṇa consciousness is the best of all. The *Bhāgavatam* confirms this fact as follows:

> yat-pāda-paṅkaja-palāśa-vilāsa-bhaktyā
> karmāśayaṁ grathitam udgrathayanti santaḥ
> tadvan na rikta-matayo yatayo 'pi ruddha-
> srotogaṇās tam araṇaṁ bhaja vāsudevam.

"Just try to worship, in devotional service, Vāsudeva, the Supreme Personality of Godhead. Even great sages are not able to control the forces of the senses as effectively as those who are engaged in transcendental bliss by serving the lotus feet of the Lord, uprooting the deep grown desire for fruitive activities." (*Bhāg.* 4.22.39)

In the conditioned soul the desire to enjoy the fruitive results of work is so deep-rooted that it is very difficult even for the great sages to control such desires, despite great endeavors. A devotee of the Lord, constantly engaged in devotional service in Kṛṣṇa consciousness, perfect in self-realization, very quickly attains liberation in the Supreme. Owing to his complete knowledge in self-realization, he always remains in trance. To cite an analagous example of this:

> darśana-dhyāna-saṁsparśair matsya-kūrma-vihaṅgamāḥ
> svānya patyāni puṣṇanti tathāham api padmaja.

"By vision, by meditation and by touch only do the fish, the tortoise and the birds maintain their offspring. Similarly do I also, O Padmaja!"

The fish brings up its offspring simply by looking at them. The tortoise brings up its offspring simply by meditation. The eggs of the tortoise are laid on land, and the tortoise meditates on the eggs while in the water. Similarly, a devotee in Kṛṣṇa consciousness, although far away from the Lord's abode, can elevate himself to that abode simply by thinking of Him constantly—by engagement in Kṛṣṇa consciousness. He does not feel the pangs of material miseries; this state of life is called *brahma-nirvāṇa*, or the absence of material miseries due to being constantly immersed in the Supreme.

TEXTS 27-28

स्पर्शान्कृत्वा बहिर्बाह्यांश्चक्षुश्चैवान्तरे भ्रुवोः ।
प्राणापानौ समौ कृत्वा नासाभ्यन्तरचारिणौ ॥ २७ ॥
यतेन्द्रियमनोबुद्धिर्मुनिर्मोक्षपरायणः ।
विगतेच्छाभयक्रोधो यः सदा मुक्त एव सः ॥ २८ ॥

sparśān kṛtvā bahir bāhyāṁś
cakṣuś caivāntare bhruvoḥ
prāṇāpānau samau kṛtvā
nāsābhyantara-cāriṇau
yatendriya-mano-buddhir
munir mokṣa-parāyaṇaḥ
vigatecchā-bhaya-krodho
yaḥ sadā mukta eva saḥ

sparśān—external sense objects, such as sound, etc.; *kṛtvā*—doing so; *bahiḥ*—external; *bāhyān*—unnecessary; *cakṣuḥ*—eyes; *ca*—also; *eva*—certainly; *antare*—within; *bhruvoḥ*—of the eyebrows; *prāṇa-apānau*—up-and-down-moving air; *samau*—in suspension; *kṛtvā*—doing so; *nāsā-abhyantara*—within the nostrils; *cāriṇau*—blowing; *yata*—controlled; *indriya*—senses; *manaḥ*—mind; *buddhiḥ*—intelligence; *muniḥ*—the transcendentalist; *mokṣa*—liberation; *parāyaṇaḥ*—being so destined; *vigata*—discarded; *icchā*—wishes; *bhaya*—fear; *krodhaḥ*—anger; *yaḥ*—one who; *sadā*—always; *muktaḥ*—liberated; *eva*—certainly; *saḥ*—he is.

TRANSLATION

Shutting out all external sense objects, keeping the eyes and vision concentrated between the two eyebrows, suspending the inward and outward breaths within the nostrils-thus controlling the mind, senses and intelligence, the tranecendentalist becomes free from desire, fear and anger. One who is always in this state is certainly liberated.

PURPORT

Being engaged in Kṛṣṇa consciousness, one can immediately understand one's spiritual identity, and then one can understand the Supreme Lord by means of devotional service. When he is well situated in devotional service, one comes to the transcendental position, qualified to feel the presence of the Lord in the sphere of one's activity. This particular position is called liberation in the Supreme.

After explaining the above principles of liberation in the Supreme, the Lord gives instruction to Arjuna as to how one can come to that position by the practice of mysticism or yoga, known as aṣṭāṅga-yoga, which is divisible into an eightfold procedure called yama, niyama, āsana, prāṇā-yāma, pratyāhāra, dhāraṇā, dhyāna, and samādhi. In the Sixth Chapter the subject of yoga is explicitly detailed, and at the end of the Fifth it is only preliminarily explained. One has to drive out the sense objects such as sound, touch, form, taste and smell by the pratyāhāra (breathing) process in yoga, and then keep the vision of the eyes between the two eyebrows and concentrate on the tip of the nose with half closed lids. There is no benefit in closing the eyes altogether, because then there is every chance of falling asleep. Nor is there benefit in opening the eyes completely, because then there is the hazard of being attracted by sense objects. The breathing movement is restrained within the nostrils by neutralizing the up- and down-moving air within the body. By practice of such yoga one is able to gain control over the senses, refrain from outward sense objects, and thus prepare oneself for liberation in the Supreme.

This yoga process helps one become free from all kinds of fear and anger and thus feel the presence of the Supersoul in the transcendental situation. In other words, Kṛṣṇa consciousness is the easiest process of executing yoga principles. This will be thoroughly explained in the next chapter. A Kṛṣṇa conscious person, however, being always engaged in devotional service, does not risk losing his senses to some other engagement. This is a better way of controlling the senses than by the aṣṭāṅga-yoga.

TEXT 29

भोक्तारं यज्ञतपसां सर्वलोकमहेश्वरम् ।
सुहृदं सर्वभूतानां ज्ञात्वा मां शान्तिमृच्छति ॥ २९ ॥

bhoktāraṁ yajña-tapasāṁ
sarva-loka-maheśvaram

suhṛdaṁ sarva-bhūtānāṁ
jñātvā māṁ śāntim ṛcchati

bhoktāram—beneficiary; *yajña*—sacrifices; *tapasām*—of penances and austerities; *sarva-loka*—all planets and the demigods thereof; *maheśvaram*—the Supreme Lord; *suhṛdam*—benefactor; *sarva*—all; *bhūtānām*—of the living entities; *jñātvā*—thus knowing; *mām*—Me (Lord Kṛṣṇa); *śāntim*—relief from material pangs; *ṛcchati*—achieves.

TRANSLATION

The sages, knowing Me as the ultimate purpose of all sacrifices and austerities, the Supreme Lord of all planets and demigods and the benefactor and well-wisher of all living entities, attain peace from the pangs of material miseries.

PURPORT

The conditioned souls within the clutches of illusory energy are all anxious to attain peace in the material world. But they do not know the formula for peace, which is explained in this part of the *Bhagavad-gītā*. The greatest peace formula is simply this: Lord Kṛṣṇa is the beneficiary in all human activities. Men should offer everything to the transcendental service of the Lord because He is the proprietor of all planets and the demigods thereon. No one is greater than He. He is greater than the greatest of the demigods, Lord Śiva and Lord Brahmā. In the *Vedas* the Supreme Lord is described as *tam īśvarāṇāṁ paramaṁ maheśvaram*. Under the spell of illusion, living entities are trying to be lords of all they survey, but actually they are dominated by the material energy of the Lord. The Lord is the master of material nature, and the conditioned souls are under the stringent rules of material nature. Unless one understands these bare facts, it is not possible to achieve peace in the world either individually or collectively. This is the sense of Kṛṣṇa consciousness: Lord Kṛṣṇa is the supreme predominator, and all living entities, including the great demigods, are His subordinates. One can attain perfect peace only in complete Kṛṣṇa consciousness.

This Fifth Chapter is a practical explanation of Kṛṣṇa consciousness, generally known as *karma-yoga*. The question of mental speculation as to how *karma-yoga* can give liberation is answered herewith. To work in Kṛṣṇa consciousness is to work with the complete knowledge of the Lord as the predominator. Such work is not different from transcendental knowledge. Direct Kṛṣṇa consciousness is *bhakti-yoga*, and *jñāna-yoga* is a path leading to *bhakti-yoga*. Kṛṣṇa consciousness means to work in full knowledge of one's relationship with the Supreme Absolute, and the perfection of this consciousness is full knowledge of Kṛṣṇa, or the Supreme Personality of Godhead. A pure soul is the eternal servant of God as His fragmental part and parcel. He comes into contact with *māyā* (illusion) due to the desire to lord it over *māyā*, and that is the cause of his many sufferings. As long as he is in contact with matter, he has to execute work in terms of material necessities. Kṛṣṇa consciousness, however, brings one into spiritual life even while one is within the jurisdiction of matter, for it is an arousing of spiritual existence by practice in the material world. The more one is advanced, the more he is freed from the clutches of matter. The Lord is not partial toward anyone. Everything depends on one's practical performance of duties in an effort to control the senses and conquer the influence of desire and anger. And, attaining Kṛṣṇa consciousness by controlling the above-mentioned passions, one remains factually in the transcendental stage, or *brahman-nirvāṇa*. The eightfold *yoga* mysticism is automatically practiced in Kṛṣṇa consciousness because the ultimate purpose is served. There is gradual process of elevation in the practice of *yama, niyama, āsana, pratyāhāra, dhyāna, dhāraṇā, prāṇāyāma*, and *samādhi*. But these only preface perfection by devotional service, which alone can award peace to the human being. It is the highest perfection of life.

Thus end the Bhaktivedanta Purports to the Fifth Chapter of the Śrīmad-Bhagavad-gītā *in the matter of Karma-yoga, or Action in Kṛṣṇa Consciousness.*

CHAPTER SIX

Sāṅkhya-yoga

TEXT 1

श्रीभगवानुवाच ।
अनाश्रितः कर्मफलं कार्यं कर्म करोति यः ।
स संन्यासी च योगी च न निरग्निर्न चाक्रियः ॥ १ ॥

śrī-bhagavān uvāca
anāśritaḥ karma-phalaṁ
kāryaṁ karma karoti yaḥ
sa sannyāsī ca yogī ca
na niragnir na cākriyaḥ

śrī bhagavān uvāca—the Lord said; *anāśritaḥ*—without shelter; *karma-phalam*—the result of work; *kāryam*—obligatory; *karma*—work; *karoti*—performs; *yaḥ*—one who; *saḥ*—he; *sannyāsī*—in the renounced order; *ca*—also; *yogī*—mystic; *ca*—also; *na*—not; *nir*—without; *agniḥ*—fire; *na*—nor; *ca*—also; *akriyaḥ*—without duty.

307

TRANSLATION

The Blessed Lord said: One who is unattached to the fruits of his work and who works as he is obligated is in the renounced order of life, and he is the true mystic: not he who lights no fire and performs no work.

PURPORT

In this chapter the Lord explains that the process of the eightfold *yoga* system is a means to control the mind and the senses. However, this is very difficult for people in general to perform, especially in the age of Kali. Although the eightfold *yoga* system is recommended in this chapter, the Lord emphasizes that the process of *karma-yoga*, or acting in Kṛṣṇa consciousness, is better. Everyone acts in this world to maintain his family and their paraphernalia, but no one is working without some self-interest, some personal gratification, be it concentrated or extended. The criterion of perfection is to act in Kṛṣṇa consciousness, and not with a view to enjoying the fruits of work. To act in Kṛṣṇa consciousness is the duty of every living entity because all are constitutionally parts and parcels of the Supreme. The parts of the body work for the satisfaction of the whole body. The limbs of the body do not act for self-satisfaction but for the satisfaction of the complete whole. Similarly, the living entity who acts for satisfaction of the supreme whole and not for personal satisfaction is the perfect *sannyāsī*, the perfect *yogī*.

The *sannyāsīs* sometimes artificially think that they have become liberated from all material duties, and therefore they cease to perform *agnihotra yajñas* (fire sacrifices), but actually they are self-interested because their goal is becoming one with the impersonal Brahman. Such a desire is greater than any material desire, but it is not without self-interest. Similarly, the mystic *yogī* who practices the *yoga* system with half-open eyes, ceasing all material activities, desires some satisfaction for his personal self. But a person acting in Kṛṣṇa consciousness works for the satisfaction of the whole, without self-interest. A Kṛṣṇa conscious person has no desire for self-satisfaction. His criterion of success is the satisfaction of Kṛṣṇa, and thus he is the perfect *sannyāsī*, or perfect *yogī*. Lord Caitanya, the highest perfectional symbol of renunciation, prays in this way:

> *na dhanaṁ na janaṁ na sundarīṁ kavitāṁ vā jagadīśa kāmaye.*
> *mama janmani janmanīśvare bhavatād bhaktir ahaitukī tvayi.*

"O Almighty Lord, I have no desire to accumulate wealth, nor to enjoy beautiful women. Nor do I want any number of followers. What I want only is the causeless mercy of Your devotional service in my life, birth after birth."

TEXT 2

यं संन्यासमिति प्राहुर्योगं तं विद्धि पाण्डव ।
न ह्यसंन्यस्तसंकल्पो योगी भवति कश्चन ॥ २ ॥

*yam sannyāsam iti prāhur
yogaṁ taṁ viddhi pāṇḍava
na hy asannyasta-saṅkalpo
yogī bhavati kaścana*

yam—what; *sannyāsam*—renunciation; *iti*—thus; *prāhuḥ*—they say; *yogam*—linking with the Supreme; *tam*—that; *viddhi*—you must know; *pāṇḍava*—O son of Pāṇḍu; *na*—never; *hi*—certainly; *asannyasta*—without giving up; *saṅkalpaḥ*—self-satisfaction; *yogī*—a mystic transcendentalist; *bhavati*—becomes; *kaścana*—anyone.

TRANSLATION

What is called renunciation is the same as yoga, or linking oneself with the Supreme, for no one can become a yogī unless he renounces the desire for sense gratification.

PURPORT

Real *sannyāsa-yoga* or *bhakti* means that one should know his constitutional position as the living entity, and act accordingly. The living entity has no separate independant identity. He is the marginal energy of the Supreme. When he is entrapped by material energy, he is conditioned, and when he is Kṛṣṇa conscious, or aware of the spiritual energy, then he is in his real and natural state of life. Therefore, when one is in complete knowledge, one ceases all material sense gratification, or renounces all kinds of sense gratificatory activities. This is practiced by the *yogīs* who restrain the senses from material attachment. But a person in Kṛṣṇa consciousness has no opportunity to engage his senses in anything which is not for the purpose of Kṛṣṇa. Therefore, a Kṛṣṇa conscious person is simultaneously a *sannyāsī* and a *yogī*. The purpose of knowledge and of restraining the senses, as prescribed in the *jñāna* and *yoga* processes, is automatically served in Kṛṣṇa consciousness. If one is unable to give up the activities of his selfish nature, then *jñāna* and *yoga* are of no avail. The real aim is for a living entity to give up all selfish satisfaction and to be prepared to satisfy the Supreme. A Kṛṣṇa conscious person has no desire for any kind of self-enjoyment. He is always engaged for the enjoyment of the Supreme. One who has no information of the Supreme must therefore be engaged in self-satisfaction because no one can stand on the platform of inactivity. All these purposes are perfectly served by the practice of Kṛṣṇa consciousness.

TEXT 3

आरुरुक्षोर्मुनेर्योगं कर्म कारणमुच्यते ।
योगारूढस्य तस्यैव शमः कारणमुच्यते ॥ ३ ॥

ārurukṣor muner yogaṁ
karma kāraṇam ucyate
yogārūḍhasya tasyaiva
śamaḥ kāraṇam ucyate

ārurukṣoḥ—of one who has just begun *yoga*; *muneḥ*—of the sage; *yogam* —the eightfold *yoga* system; *karma*—work; *kāraṇam*—the cause; *ucyate*—is said to be; *yoga*—eightfold *yoga*; *ārūḍhasya*—one who has attained; *tasya*— his; *eva*—certainly; *śamaḥ*—cessation of all material activities; *kāraṇam*—the cause; *ucyate*—is said to be.

TRANSLATION

For one who is a neophyte in the eightfold yoga system, work is said to be the means; and for one who has already attained to yoga, cessation of all material activities is said to be the means.

PURPORT

The process of linking oneself with the Supreme is called *yoga*, which may be compared to a ladder for attaining the topmost spiritual realization. This ladder begins from the lowest material condition of the living entity and rises up to perfect self-realization in pure spiritual life. According to various elevations, different parts of the ladder are known by different names. But all in all, the complete ladder is called *yoga* and may be divided into three parts, namely *jñāna-yoga*, *dhyāna-yoga* and *bhakti-yoga*. The beginning of the ladder is called the *yogārurukṣa* stage, and the highest rung is called *yogārūḍha*.

Concerning the eightfold *yoga* system, attempts in the beginning to enter into meditation through regulative principles of life and practice of different sitting postures (which are more or less bodily exercises) are considered fruitive material activities. All such activities lead to achieving perfect mental equilibrium to control the senses. When one is accomplished in the practice of meditation, he ceases all disturbing mental activities.

A Kṛṣṇa conscious person is, however, situated from the beginning on the platform of meditation because he always thinks of Kṛṣṇa. And, being constantly engaged in the service of Kṛṣṇa, he is considered to have ceased all material activities.

TEXT 4

यदा हि नेन्द्रियार्थेषु न कर्मस्वनुषज्जते ।
सर्वसंकल्पसंन्यासी योगारूढस्तदोच्यते ॥ ४ ॥

yadā hi nendriyārtheṣu
na karmasv anuṣajjate
sarva-saṅkalpa-sannyāsī
yogārūḍhas tadocyate

yadā—when; *hi*—certainly; *na*—not; *indriya-artheṣu*—in sense gratification; *na*—never; *karmasu*—in fruitive activities; *anuṣajjate*—does necessarily engage; *sarva-saṅkalpa*—all material desires; *sannyāsī*—renouncer; *yoga-ārūḍhaḥ*—elevated in *yoga*; *tadā*—at that time; *ucyate*—is said to be.

TRANSLATION

A person is said to have attained to yoga when, having renounced all material desires, he neither acts for sense gratification nor engages in fruitive activities.

PURPORT

When a person is fully engaged in the transcendental loving service of the Lord, he is pleased in himself, and thus he is no longer engaged in sense gratification or in fruitive activities. Otherwise, one must be engaged in sense gratification, since one cannot live without engagement. Without Kṛṣṇa consciousness, one must be always seeking self-centered or extended selfish activities. But a Kṛṣṇa conscious person can do everything for the satisfaction of Kṛṣṇa and thereby be perfectly detached from sense gratification. One who has no such realization must mechanically try to escape material desires before being elevated to the top rung of the yoga ladder.

TEXT 5

उद्धरेदात्मनात्मानं नात्मानमवसादयेत् ।
आत्मैव ह्यात्मनो बन्धुरात्मैव रिपुरात्मनः ॥ ५ ॥

uddhared ātmanātmānaṁ
nātmānam avasādayet
ātmaiva hy ātmano bandhur
ātmaiva ripur ātmanaḥ

uddharet—one must deliver; *ātmanā*—by the mind; *ātmānam*—the conditioned soul; *na*—never; *ātmānam*—the conditioned soul; *avasādayet*—put into degradation; *ātmā*—mind; *eva*—certainly; *hi*—indeed; *ātmanaḥ*—of the conditioned soul; *bandhuḥ*—friend; *ātmā*—mind; *eva*—certainly; *ripuḥ*—enemy; *ātmanaḥ*—of the conditioned soul.

TRANSLATION

A man must elevate himself by his own mind, not degrade himself. The mind is the friend of the conditioned soul, and his enemy as well.

PURPORT

The word *ātmā* denotes body, mind and soul—depending upon different circumstances. In the *yoga* system, the mind and the conditioned soul are especially important. Since the mind is the central point of *yoga* practice, *ātmā* refers here to the mind. The purpose of the *yoga* system is to control the mind and to draw it away from attachment to sense objects. It is stressed herein that the mind must be so trained that it can deliver the conditioned soul from the mire of nescience. In material existence one is subjected to the influence of the mind and the senses. In fact, the pure soul is entangled in the material world because of the mind's ego which desires to lord it over material nature. Therefore, the mind should be trained so that it will not be attracted by the glitter of material nature, and in this way the conditioned soul may be saved. One should not degrade oneself by attraction to sense objects. The more one is attracted by sense objects, the more one becomes entangled in material existence. The best way to disentangle oneself is to always engage the mind in Kṛṣṇa consciousness. The word *hi* is used for emphasizing this point, i.e., that one *must* do this. It is also said:

> *mana eva manuṣyāṇāṁ kāraṇaṁ bandha-mokṣayoḥ*
> *bandhāya viṣayāsaṅgo muktyai nirviṣayaṁ manaḥ.*

"For man, mind is the cause of bondage and mind is the cause of liberation. Mind absorbed in sense objects is the cause of bondage, and mind detached from the sense objects is the cause of liberation." Therefore, the mind which is always engaged in Kṛṣṇa consciousness is the cause of supreme liberation.

TEXT 6

बन्धुरात्मात्मनस्तस्य येनात्मैवात्मना जितः ।
अनात्मनस्तु शत्रुत्वे वर्तेतात्मैव शत्रुवत् ॥ ६ ॥

bandhur ātmātmanas tasya
yenātmaivātmanā jitaḥ
anātmanas tu śatrutve
vartetātmaiva śatru-vat

bandhuḥ—friend; *ātmā*—mind; *ātmanaḥ*—of the living entity; *tasya*—of him; *yena*—by whom; *ātmā*—mind; *eva*—certainly; *ātmanā*—by the living entity; *jitaḥ*—conquered; *anātmanaḥ*—of one who has failed to control the mind; *tu*—but; *śatrutve*—because of enmity; *varteta*—remains; *ātmā eva*—the very mind; *śatruvat*—as an enemy.

TRANSLATION

For him who has conquered the mind, the mind is the best of friends; but for one who has failed to do so, his very mind will be the greatest enemy.

PURPORT

The purpose of practicing eightfold *yoga* is to control the mind in order to make it a friend in discharging the human mission. Unless the mind is controlled, the practice of *yoga* (for show) is simply a waste of time. One who cannot control his mind lives always with the greatest enemy, and thus his life and its mission are spoiled. The constitutional position of the living entity is to carry out the order of the superior. As long as one's mind remains an unconquered enemy, one has to serve the dictations of lust, anger, avarice, illusion, etc. But when the mind is conquered, one voluntarily agrees to abide by the dictation of the Personality of Godhead, who is situated within the heart of everyone as Paramātmā. Real *yoga* practice entails meeting the Paramātmā within the heart and then following His dictation. For one who takes to Kṛṣṇa consciousness directly, perfect surrender to the dictation of the Lord follows automatically.

TEXT 7

जितात्मनः प्रशान्तस्य परमात्मा समाहितः ।
शीतोष्णसुखदुःखेषु तथा मानापमानयोः ॥ ७ ॥

jitātmanaḥ praśāntasya
paramātmā samāhitaḥ
śītoṣṇa-sukha-duḥkheṣu
tathā mānāpamānayoḥ

jita-ātmanaḥ—of one who has conquered his mind; *praśāntasya*—of one who has attained tranquility by such control over the mind; *paramātmā*—the Supersoul; *samāhitaḥ*—approached completely; *śīta*—cold; *uṣṇa*—heat; *sukha*—in happiness; *duḥkheṣu*—in distress; *tathā*—also; *māna*—honor; *apamānayoḥ*—in dishonor.

TRANSLATION

For one who has conquered the mind, the Supersoul is already reached, for he has attained tranquility. To such a man happiness and distress, heat and cold, honor and dishonor are all the same.

PURPORT

Actually, every living entity is intended to abide by the dictation of the Supreme Personality of Godhead, who is seated in everyone's heart as Paramātmā. When the mind is misled by the external illusory energy, one becomes entangled in material activities. Therefore, as soon as one's mind is controlled through one of the *yoga* systems, one is to be considered as having already reached the destination. One has to abide by superior dictation. When one's mind is fixed on the superior nature, he has no other alternative but to follow the dictation of the Supreme. The mind must admit some superior dictation and follow it. The effect of controlling the mind is that one automatically follows the dictation of the Paramātmā or Supersoul. Because this transcendental position is at once achieved by one who is in Kṛṣṇa consciousness, the devotee of the Lord is unaffected by the dualities of material existence, namely distress and happiness, cold and heat, etc. This state is practical *samādhi*, or absorption in the Supreme.

TEXT 8

ज्ञानविज्ञानतृप्तात्मा कूटस्थो विजितेन्द्रियः ।
युक्त इत्युच्यते योगी समलोष्ट्राश्मकाञ्चनः ॥ ८ ॥

jñāna-vijñāna-tṛptātmā
kūṭa-stho vijitendriyaḥ
yukta ity ucyate yogī
sama-loṣṭrāśma-kāñcanaḥ

jñāna—acquired knowledge; *vijñāna*—realized knowledge; *tṛpta*—satisfied; *ātmā*—living entity; *kūṭasthaḥ*—spiritually situated; *vijita-indriyaḥ*—sensually controlled; *yuktaḥ*—competent for self-realization; *iti*—thus; *ucyate*—is said; *yogī*—the mystic; *sama*—equiposed; *loṣṭra*—pebbles; *aśma*—stone; *kāñcanaḥ*—gold.

TRANSLATION

A person is said to be established in self-realization and is called a yogī [or mystic] when he is fully satisfied by virtue of acquired knowledge and realization. Such a person is situated in transcendence and is self-controlled. He sees everything—whether it be pebbles, stones or gold—as the same.

PURPORT

Book knowledge without realization of the Supreme Truth is useless. This is stated as follows:

> atah śrī-krsna-nāmādi na bhaved grāhyam indriyaih
> sevonmukhe hi jihvādau svayam eva sphuraty adah.

"No one can understand the transcendental nature of the name, form, quality and pastimes of Śrī Krṣṇa through his materially contaminated senses. Only when one becomes spiritually saturated by transcendental service to the Lord are the transcendental name, form, quality and pastimes of the Lord revealed to him." (*Padma Purāṇa*)

This *Bhagavad-gītā* is the science of Krṣṇa consciousness. No one can become Krṣṇa conscious simply by mundane scholarship. One must be fortunate enough to associate with a person who is in pure consciousness. A Krṣṇa conscious person has realized knowledge, by the grace of Krṣṇa, because he is satisfied with pure devotional service. By realized knowledge, one becomes perfect. By transcendental knowledge one can remain steady in his convictions, but by mere academic knowledge one can be easily deluded and confused by apparent contradictions. It is the realized soul who is actually self-controlled because he is surrendered to Krṣṇa. He is transcendental because he has nothing to do with mundane scholarship. For him mundane scholarship and mental speculation, which may be as good as gold to others, are of no greater value than pebbles or stones.

TEXT 9

सुहृन्मित्रार्युदासीनमध्यस्थद्वेष्यबन्धुषु ।
साधुष्वपि च पापेषु समबुद्धिर्विशिष्यते ॥ ९ ॥

suhṛn-mitrāry-udāsīna-
madhyastha-dveṣya-bandhuṣu
sādhuṣv api ca pāpeṣu
sama-buddhir viśiṣyate

suhṛt—by nature a well-wisher; *mitra*—benefactor with affection; *ari*—enemy; *udāsīna*—neutral between the belligerents; *madhyastha*—mediator between the belligerents; *dveṣya*—envious; *bandhuṣu*—among the relatives or well-wishers; *sādhuṣu*—unto the pious; *api*—as well as; *ca*—and; *pāpeṣu*—unto the sinners; *sama-buddhiḥ*—having equal intelligence; *viśiṣyate*—is far advanced.

TRANSLATION

A person is said to be still further advanced when he regards all—the honest well-wisher, friends and enemies, the envious, the pious, the sinner and those who are indifferent and impartial-with an equal mind.

TEXT 10

योगी युञ्जीत सततमात्मानं रहसि स्थितः ।
एकाकी यतचित्तात्मा निराशीरपरिग्रहः ॥ १० ॥

yogī yuñjīta satatam
ātmānaṁ rahasi sthitaḥ
ekākī yata-cittātmā
nirāśīr aparigrahaḥ

yogī—a transcendentalist; *yuñjīta*—must concentrate in Kṛṣṇa consciousness; *satatam*—constantly; *ātmānam*—himself (by the body, mind and self); *rahasi*—in a secluded place; *sthitaḥ*—being so situated; *ekākī*—alone; *yata-cittātmā*—always careful in mind; *nirāśīḥ*—without being attracted by anything else; *aparigrahaḥ*—free from the feeling of possessiveness.

TRANSLATION

A transcendentalist should always try to concentrate his mind on the Supreme Self; he should live alone in a secluded place and should always carefully control his mind. He should be free from desires and feelings of possessiveness.

PURPORT

Kṛṣṇa is realized in different degrees as Brahman, Paramātmā and the Supreme Personality of Godhead. Kṛṣṇa consciousness means, concisely, to be always engaged in the transcendental loving service of the Lord. But those who are attached to the impersonal Brahman or the localized Supersoul are also partially Kṛṣṇa conscious, because impersonal Brahman is the spiritual ray of Kṛṣṇa and Supersoul is the all-pervading partial expansion of Kṛṣṇa. Thus the impersonalist and the meditator are also indirectly Kṛṣṇa conscious. A directly Kṛṣṇa conscious person is the topmost transcendentalist because such a devotee knows what is meant by Brahman or Paramātmā. His knowledge of the Absolute Truth is perfect, whereas the impersonalist and the meditative yogī are imperfectly Kṛṣṇa conscious.

Nevertheless, all of these are instructed herewith to be constantly engaged in their particular pursuits so that they may come to the highest perfection sooner or later. The first business of a transcendentalist is to keep the mind always on Kṛṣṇa. One should always think of Kṛṣṇa and not forget Him even for a moment. Concentration of the mind on the Supreme is called *samādhi* or trance. In order to concentrate the mind, one should always remain in seclusion and avoid disturbance by external objects. He should be very careful to accept favorable and reject unfavorable conditions that affect his realization. And, in perfect determination, he should not hanker after unnecessary material things that entangle him by feelings of possessiveness.

All these perfections and precautions are perfectly executed when one is directly in Kṛṣṇa consciousness because direct Kṛṣṇa consciousness means self-abnegation, wherein there is very little chance for material possessiveness. Śrīla Rūpa Gosvāmī characterizes Kṛṣṇa consciousness in this way:

anāsaktasya viṣayān yathārham upayuñjataḥ
nirbandhaḥ kṛṣṇa-sambandhe yuktaṁ vairāgyam ucyate
prāpañcikatayā buddhyā hari-sambandhi-vastunaḥ
mumukṣubhiḥ parityāgo vairāgyaṁ phalgu kathyate.
(Bhakti-rasāmṛta-sindhu 2.255-256)

"When one is not attached to anything, but at the same time accepts everything in relation to Kṛṣṇa, one is rightly situated above possessiveness. On the other hand, one who rejects everything without knowledge of its relationship to Kṛṣṇa is not as complete in his renunciation."

A Kṛṣṇa conscious person well knows that everything belongs to Kṛṣṇa, and thus he is always free from feelings of personal possession. As such, he has no hankering for anything on his own personal account. He knows how to accept things in favor of Kṛṣṇa consciousness and how to reject things unfavorable to Kṛṣṇa consciousness. He is always aloof from material things because he is always transcendental, and he is always alone, having nothing to do with persons not in Kṛṣṇa consciousness. Therefore a person in Kṛṣṇa consciousness is the perfect yogī.

TEXTS 11-12

शुचौ देशे प्रतिष्ठाप्य स्थिरमासनमात्मनः ।
नात्युच्छ्रितं नातिनीचं चैलाजिनकुशोत्तरम् ॥ ११ ॥
तत्रैकाग्रं मनः कृत्वा यतचित्तेन्द्रियक्रियः ।
उपविश्यासने युञ्ज्याद्योगमात्मविशुद्धये ॥ १२ ॥

> śucau deśe pratiṣṭhāpya
> sthiram āsanam ātmanaḥ
> nāty-ucchritaṁ nāti-nīcaṁ
> cailājina-kuśottaram
> tatraikāgraṁ manaḥ kṛtvā
> yata-cittendriya-kriyaḥ
> upaviśyāsane yuñjyād
> yogam ātma-viśuddhaye

śucau—in sanctified; deśe—in the land; pratiṣṭhāpya—placing; sthiram—firm; āsanam—seat; ātmanaḥ—self-dependant; na—not; ati—too; ucchritam—high; na—nor; ati—too; nīcam—low; caila-ajna—soft cloth and deerskin; kuśottaram-kuśa grass; tatra—thereupon; ekāgram—one attention; manaḥ—mind; kṛtvā—doing so; yata-citta—controlling the mind; indriya—senses; kriyaḥ—activities; upaviśya—sitting on; āsane—on the seat; yuñjyāt—execute; yogam—yoga practice; ātma—heart; viśuddhaye—for clarifying.

TRANSLATION

To practice yoga, one should go to a secluded place and should lay kuśa-grass on the ground and then cover it with a deerskin and a soft cloth. The seat should neither be too high nor too low and should be situated in a sacred place. The yogī should then sit on it very firmly and should practice yoga by controlling the mind and the senses, purifying the heart and fixing the mind on one point.

PURPORT

"Sacred place" refers to places of pilgrimage. In India the *yogīs*, the transcendentalists or the devotees all leave home and reside in sacred places such as Prayāg, Mathurā, Vṛndāvana, Hṛṣīkeśa, and Hardwar and in solitude practice *yoga* where the sacred rivers like the Yamunā and the Ganges flow. But often this is not possible, especially for Westerners. The so-called *yoga* societies in big cities may be successful in earning material benefit, but they are not at all suitable for the actual practice of *yoga*. One who is not self-controlled and whose mind is not undisturbed cannot practice meditation. Therefore, in the *Bṛhan-Nāradīya Purāṇa* it is said that in the Kali-yuga (the present *yuga* or age) when people in general are short-lived, slow in spiritual realization and always disturbed by various anxieties, the best means of spiritual realization is chanting the holy name of the Lord.

> *harer nāma harer nāma harer nāmaiva kevalam*
> *kalau nāsty eva nāsty eva nāsty eva gatir anyathā.*

"In this age of quarrel and hypocrisy the only means of deliverance is chanting the holy name of the Lord. There is no other way. There is no other way. There is no other way."

TEXTS 13-14

समं कायशिरोग्रीवं धारयन्नचलं स्थिरः ।
संप्रेक्ष्य नासिकाग्रं स्वं दिशश्चानवलोकयन् ॥ १३ ॥
प्रशान्तात्मा विगतभीर्ब्रह्मचारिव्रते स्थितः ।
मनः संयम्य मच्चित्तो युक्त आसीत मत्परः ॥ १४ ॥

samaṁ kāya-śiro-grīvaṁ
dhārayann acalaṁ sthiraḥ
samprekṣya nāsikāgraṁ svam
diśaś cānavalokayan

prasāntātmā vigata-bhīr
brahmacāri-vrate sthitaḥ
manaḥ samyamya mac-citto
yukta āsīta mat-paraḥ

samam—straight; *kāya-śiraḥ*—body and head; *grīvam*—neck; *dhārayan*—holding; *acalam*—unmoved; *sthiraḥ*—still; *samprekṣya*—looking; *nāsikā*—nose; *agram*—tip; *svam*—own; *diśaḥ*—all sides; *ca*—also; *anavalokayan*—not seeing; *praśānta*—unagitated; *ātmā*—mind; *vigata-bhīḥ*—devoid of fear; *brahmacāri-vrate*—in the vow of celibacy; *sthitaḥ*—situated; *manaḥ*—mind; *samyamya*—completely subdued; *mat*—unto Me (Kṛṣṇa); *cittaḥ*—concentrated; *yuktaḥ*—actual yogī; *āsīta*—being so; *mat*—unto Me; *paraḥ*—ultimate goal.

TRANSLATION

One should hold one's body, neck and head erect in a straight line and stare steadily at the tip of the nose. Thus with an unagitated, subdued mind, devoid of fear, completely free from sex life, one should meditate upon Me within the heart and make Me the ultimate goal of life.

PURPORT

The goal of life is to know Kṛṣṇa, who is situated within the heart of every living being as Paramātmā, the four-handed Viṣṇu form. The yoga process is practiced in order to discover and see this localized form of Viṣṇu, and not for any other purpose. The localized Viṣṇu-mūrti is the plenary representation of Kṛṣṇa dwelling within one's heart. One who has no program to realize this Viṣṇu-mūrti is uselessly engaged in mock-yoga practice and is certainly wasting his time. Kṛṣṇā is the ultimate goal of life, and the Viṣṇu-mūrti situated in one's heart is the object of yoga practice. To realize this Viṣṇu-mūrti within the heart, one has to observe complete abstinence from sex life; therefore one has to leave home and live alone in a secluded place, remaining seated as mentioned above. One cannot enjoy sex life daily at home or elsewhere and attend a so-called yoga class and thus become a yogī. One has to practice controlling the mind and avoiding all kinds of sense gratification, of which sex life is the chief. In the rules of celibacy written by the great sage Yājñavalkya it is said:

karmaṇā manasā vācā sarvāvasthāsu sarvadā
sarvatra maithuna-tyāgo brahmacaryaṁ pracakṣate.

"The vow of *brahmacarya* is meant to help one completely abstain from sex indulgence in work, words and mind-at all times, under all circumstances, and in all places." No one can perform correct *yoga* practice through sex indulgence. *Brahmacarya* is taught, therefore, from childhood when one has no knowledge of sex life. Children at the age of five are sent to the *guru-kula*, or the place of the spiritual master, and the master trains the young boys in the strict discipline of becoming *brahmacārīs*. Without such practice, no one can make advancement in any *yoga*, whether it be *dhyāna*, *jñāna* or *bhakti*. One who, however, follows the rules and regulations of married life, having sexual relationship only with his wife (and that also under regulation), is also called *brahmacārī*. Such a restrained householder *brahmacārī* may be accepted in the *bhakti* school, but the *jñāna* and *dhyāna* schools do not admit even householder *brahmacārīs*. They require complete abstinence without compromise. In the *bhakti* school, a householder *brahmacārī* is allowed controlled sex life because the cult of *bhakti-yoga* is so powerful that one automatically loses sexual attraction, being engaged in the superior service of the Lord. In the *Bhagavad-gītā* it is said:

> *viṣayā vinivartante nirāhārasya dehinaḥ*
> *rasa-varjaṁ raso 'py asya paraṁ dṛṣṭvā nivartate*

Whereas others are forced to restrain themselves from sense gratification, a devotee of the Lord automatically refrains because of superior taste. Other than the devotee, no one has any information of that superior taste.

Vigatabhīḥ. One cannot be fearless unless one is fully in Kṛṣṇa consciousness. A conditioned soul is fearful due to his perverted memory, his forgetfulness of his eternal relationship with Kṛṣṇa. The *Bhāgavatam* says, *bhayaṁ dvitīyābhiniveśataḥ syād īśād apetasya viparyayo 'smṛtiḥ*: Kṛṣṇa consciousness is the only basis for fearlessness. Therefore, perfect practice is possible for a person who is Kṛṣṇa conscious. And since the ultimate goal of *yoga* practice is to see the Lord within, a Kṛṣṇa conscious person is already the best of all *yogīs*. The principles of the *yoga* system mentioned herein are different from those of the popular so-called *yoga* societies.

TEXT 15

युञ्जन्नेवं सदात्मानं योगी नियतमानसः ।
शान्तिं निर्वाणपरमां मत्संस्थामधिगच्छति ॥ १५ ॥

yuñjann evaṁ sadātmānaṁ
yogī niyata-mānasaḥ
śāntiṁ nirvāṇa-paramāṁ
mat-saṁsthām adhigacchati

yuñjan—practicing like this; evam—as mentioned above; sadā—constantly; ātmānam—body, mind and soul; yogī—the mystic transcendentalist; niyata-mānasaḥ—regulated mind; śāntim—peace; nirvāṇa-paramām—cessation of material existence; mat-saṁsthām—in the spiritual sky (the kingdom of God); adhigacchati—does attain.

TRANSLATION

Thus practicing control of the body, mind and activities, the mystic transcendentalist attains to the kingdom of God [or the abode of Kṛṣṇa] by cessation of material existence.

PURPORT

The ultimate goal in practicing yoga is now clearly explained. Yoga practice is not meant for attaining any kind of material facility; it is to enable the cessation of all material existence. One who seeks an improvement in health or aspires after material perfection is no yogī according to Bhagavad-gītā. Nor does cessation of material existence entail one's entering into "the void," which is only a myth. There is no void anywhere within the creation of the Lord. Rather, the cessation of material existence enables one to enter into the spiritual sky, the abode of the Lord. The abode of the Lord is also clearly described in the Bhagavad-gītā as that place where there is no need of sun, moon, nor electricity. All the planets in the spiritual kingdom are self-illuminated like the sun in the material sky. The kingdom of God is everywhere, but the spiritual sky and the planets thereof are called paraṁ dhāma, or superior abodes.

A consummate yogī, who is perfect in understanding Lord Kṛṣṇa, as is clearly stated herein (mat-cittaḥ, mat-paraḥ, mat-sthānam) by the Lord Himself, can attain real peace and can ultimately reach His supreme abode, the Kṛṣṇa-loka known as Goloka Vṛndāvana. In the Brahma-saṁhitā it is clearly stated (goloka eva nivasaty akhilātma-bhūtaḥ) that the Lord, although residing always in His abode called Goloka, is the all-pervading Brahman and the localized Paramātmā as well by dint of His superior spiritual energies. No one can reach the spiritual sky or enter into the eternal abode (Vaikuṇṭha Goloka Vṛndāvana) of the Lord without the proper understanding of Kṛṣṇa and His plenary expansion Viṣṇu. Therefore a person working in Kṛṣṇa consciousness is the perfect *yogī*, because his mind is always absorbed in Kṛṣṇa's activities. *Sa vai manaḥ kṛṣṇa-padāravindayoḥ.* In the *Vedas* also we learn: *tam eva viditvātimṛtyum eti:* "One can overcome the path of birth and death only by understanding the Supreme Personality of Godhead, Kṛṣṇa." In other words, perfection of the *yoga* system is the attainment of freedom from material existence and not some magical jugglery or gymnastic feats to befool innocent people.

TEXT 16

नात्यश्रतस्तु योगोऽस्ति न चैकान्तमनश्रतः ।
न चातिस्वप्नशीलस्य जाग्रतो नैव चार्जुन ॥ १६ ॥

nāty-aśnatas 'tu yogo 'sti
na caikāntam anaśnataḥ
na cāti-svapna-śīlasya
jāgrato naiva cārjuna

na—never; *ati*—too much; *aśnataḥ*—of one who eats so; *tu*—but; *yogaḥ*—linking with the Supreme; *asti*—there is; *na*—nor; *ca*—also; *ekāntam*—very low; *anaśnataḥ*—abstaining from eating; *na*—nor; *ca*—also; *ati*—too much; *svapna-śīlasya*—of one who sleeps too much; *jāgrataḥ*—or one who keeps night watch too much; *na*—not; *eva*—ever; *ca*—and; *arjuna*—O Arjuna.

TRANSLATION

There is no possibility of one's becoming a *yogī*, O Arjuna, if one eats too much, or eats too little, sleeps too much or does not sleep enough.

PURPORT

Regulation of diet and sleep is recommended herein for the *yogīs*. Too much eating means eating more than is required to keep the body and soul together. There is no need for men to eat animals because there is an ample supply of grains, vegetables, fruits and milk. Such simple foodstuff is considered to be in the mode of goodness according to the *Bhagavad-gītā*. Animal food is for those in the mode of ignorance. Therefore, those who indulge in animal food, drinking, smoking and eating food which is not first offered to Kṛṣṇa will suffer sinful reactions because of eating only polluted things. *Bhuñjate te tv aghaṁ pāpā ye pacanty ātma-kāraṇāt.* Anyone who eats for sense pleasure, or cooks for himself, not offering his food to Kṛṣṇa, eats only sin. One who eats sin and eats more than is allotted to him cannot execute perfect *yoga.* It is best that one eat only the remnants of foodstuff offered to Kṛṣṇa. A person in Kṛṣṇa consciousness does not eat anything which is not first offered to Kṛṣṇa. Therefore, only the Kṛṣṇa conscious person can attain perfection in *yoga* practice. Nor can one who artificially abstains from eating, manufacturing his own personal process of fasting, practice *yoga.* The Kṛṣṇa conscious person observes fasting as it is recommended in the scriptures. He does not fast or eat more than is required, and he is thus competent to perform *yoga* practice. One who eats more than required will dream very much while sleeping, and he must consequently sleep more than is required. One should not sleep more than six hours daily. One who sleeps more than six hours out of twenty-four is certainly influenced by the mode of ignorance. A person in the mode of ignorance is lazy and prone to sleep a great deal. Such a person cannot perform *yoga.*

TEXT 17

युक्ताहारविहारस्य युक्तचेष्टस्य कर्मसु ।
युक्तस्वप्नावबोधस्य योगो भवति दुःखहा ॥ १७ ॥

yuktāhāra-vihārasya
yukta-ceṣṭasya karmasu
yukta-svapnāvabodhasya
yogo bhavati duḥkha-hā

yukta—regulated; *āhāra*—eating; *vihārasya*—recreation; *yukta*—regulated; *ceṣṭasya*—of one who works for maintenance; *karmasu*—in discharging duties; *yukta*—regulated; *svapna-avabodhasya*—regulated sleep and wakefulness; *yogaḥ*—practice of *yoga*; *bhavati*—becomes; *duḥkha-hā*—diminishing pains.

TRANSLATION

He who is temperate in his habits of eating, sleeping, working and recreation can mitigate all material pains by practicing the yoga system.

PURPORT

Extravagance in the matter of eating, sleeping, defending and mating—which are demands of the body—can block advancement in the practice of *yoga*. As far as eating is concerned, it can be regulated only when one is practiced to take and accept *prasādam*, sanctified food. Lord Kṛṣṇa is offered, according to the *Bhagavad-gītā* (Bg. 9.26), vegetables, flowers, fruits, grains, milk, etc. In this way, a person in Kṛṣṇa consciousness becomes automatically trained not to accept food not meant for human consumption, or which is not in the category of goodness. As far as sleeping is concerned, a Kṛṣṇa conscious person is always alert in the discharge of his duties in Kṛṣṇa consciousness, and therefore any unnecessary time spent sleeping is considered a great loss. A Kṛṣṇa conscious person cannot bear to pass a minute of his life without being engaged in the service of the Lord. Therefore, his sleeping is kept to a minimum. His ideal in this respect is Śrīla Rūpa Gosvāmī, who was always engaged in the service of Kṛṣṇa and who could not sleep more than two hours a day, and sometimes not even that. Ṭhākura Haridāsa would not even accept *prasādam* nor even sleep for a moment without finishing his daily routine of chanting with his beads three hundred thousand names. As far as work is concerned, a Kṛṣṇa conscious person does not do anything which is not connected with Kṛṣṇa's interest, and thus his work is always regulated and is untainted by sense gratification. Since there is no question of sense gratification, there is no material leisure for a person in Kṛṣṇa consciousness. And because he is regulated in all his work, speech, sleep, wakefulness and all other bodily activities, there is no material misery for him.

TEXT 18

यदा विनियतं चित्तमात्मन्येवावतिष्ठते ।
निस्पृहः सर्वकामेभ्यो युक्त इत्युच्यते तदा ॥ १८ ॥

yadā viniyataṁ cittam
ātmany evāvatiṣṭhate
nispṛhaḥ sarva-kāmebhyo
yukta ity ucyate tadā

yadā—when; *viniyatam*—particularly disciplined; *cittam*—the mind and its activities; *ātmani*—in the Transcendence; *eva*—certainly; *avatiṣṭhate*—

becomes situated; *nispṛhaḥ*—devoid of; *sarva*—all kinds of; *kāmebhyaḥ*—material desires; *yuktaḥ*—well situated in *yoga; iti*—thus; *ucyate*—is said to be; *tadā*—at that time.

TRANSLATION

When the yogī, by practice of yoga, disciplines his mental activities and becomes situated in Transcendence-devoid of all material desires-he is said to have attained yoga.

PURPORT

The activities of the *yogī* are distinguished from those of an ordinary person by his characteristic cessation from all kinds of material desires—of which sex is the chief. A perfect *yogī* is so well disciplined in the activities of the mind that he can no longer be disturbed by any kind of material desire. This perfectional stage can automatically be attained by persons in Kṛṣṇa consciousness, as is stated in the *Śrīmad-Bhāgavatam* (9.4.18-20):

sa vai manaḥ kṛṣṇa-padāravindayor vacāṁsi vaikuṇṭha-guṇānuvarṇane
karau harer mandira-mārjanādiṣu śrutiṁ cakārācyuta-sat-kathodaye
mukunda-liṅgālaya-darśane dṛśau tad-bhṛtyagātra-sparśe 'ṅga-saṅgamam
ghrāṇaṁ ca tat-pāda-saroja-saurabhe śrīmat tulasyā rasanāṁ tad-arpite
pādau hareḥ kṣetra-padānusarpaṇe śiro hṛṣīkeśa-padābhivandane
kāmaṁ ca dāsye na tu kāma-kāmyayā yathottama-śloka-janāśrayā ratiḥ

"King Ambarīṣa first of all engaged his mind on the lotus feet of Lord Kṛṣṇa; then, one after another, he engaged his words in describing the transcendental qualities of the Lord, his hands in mopping the temple of the Lord, his ears in hearing of the activities of the Lord, his eyes in seeing the transcendental forms of the Lord, his body in touching the bodies of the devotees, his sense of smell in smelling the scents of the lotus flower offered to the Lord, his tongue in tasting the *tulasī* leaf offered at the lotus feet of the Lord, his legs in going to places of pilgrimage and the temple of the Lord, his head in offering obeisances unto the Lord and his desires in executing the mission of the Lord. All these transcendental activities are quite befitting a pure devotee."

This transcendental stage may be inexpressible subjectively by the followers of the impersonalist path, but it becomes very easy and practical for a person in Kṛṣṇa consciousness, as is apparent in the above description of the engagements of Mahārāja Ambarīṣa. Unless the mind is fixed on the lotus feet of the Lord by constant remembrance, such transcendental

engagements are not practical. In the devotional service of the Lord,
therefore, these prescribed activities are called *arcanā*, or engaging all the
senses in the service of the Lord. The senses and the mind require engagements. Simple abnegation is not practical. Therefore, for people in
general—especially those who are not in the renounced order of life—
transcendental engagement of the senses and the mind as described above
is the perfect process for transcendental achievement, which is called
yukta in the *Bhagavad-gītā*.

TEXT 19

यथा दीपो निवातस्थो नेङ्गते सोपमा स्मृता ।
योगिनो यतचित्तस्य युञ्जतो योगमात्मनः ॥ १९ ॥

yathā dīpo nivāta-stho
neṅgate sopamā smṛtā
yogino yata-cittasya
yuñjato yogam ātmanaḥ

yathā—as; *dīpaḥ*—a lamp; *nivātasthaḥ*—in a place without wind; *na*—does
not; *iṅgate*—waver; *sā upamā*—compared to that; *smṛtā*—likened; *yoginaḥ*—
of the *yogī*; *yata-cittasya*—whose mind is controlled; *yuñjataḥ*—constantly
engaged in; *yogam*—meditation; *ātmanaḥ*—on Transcendence.

TRANSLATION

**As a lamp in a windless place does not waver, so the transcendentalist,
whose mind is controlled, remains always steady in his meditation on the
transcendent Self.**

PURPORT

A truly Kṛṣṇa conscious person, always absorbed in Transcendence, in
constant undisturbed meditation on his worshipable Lord, is as steady as a
lamp in a windless place.

TEXTS 20-23

यत्रोपरमते चित्तं निरुद्धं योगसेवया ।
यत्र चैवात्मनात्मानं पश्यन्नात्मनि तुष्यति ॥ २० ॥

सुखमात्यन्तिकं यत्तद्बुद्धिग्राह्यमतीन्द्रियम् ।
वेत्ति यत्र न चैवायं स्थितश्चलति तत्त्वतः ॥ २१ ॥
यं लब्ध्वा चापरं लाभं मन्यते नाधिकं ततः ।
यस्मिन्स्थितो न दुःखेन गुरुणापि विचाल्यते ॥ २२ ॥
तं विद्याद्दुःखसंयोगवियोगं योगसंज्ञितम् ॥ २३ ॥

yatroparamate cittaṁ
niruddhaṁ yoga-sevayā
yatra caivātmanātmānaṁ
paśyann ātmani tuṣyati

sukham ātyantikaṁ yat tad
buddhi-grāhyam atīndriyam
vetti yatra na caivāyaṁ
sthitaś calati tattvataḥ

yaṁ labdhvā cāparaṁ lābhaṁ
manyate nādhikaṁ tataḥ
yasmin sthito na duḥkhena
guruṇāpi vicālyate

taṁ vidyād duḥkha-saṁyoga-
viyogaṁ yoga-saṁjñitam

yatra—in that state of affairs; *uparamate*—when one feels transcendental happiness; *cittam*—mental activities; *niruddham*—restrained from matter; *yoga-sevayā*—by performance of *yoga; yatra*—in that; *ca*—also; *eva*—certainly; *ātmanā*—by the pure mind; *ātmānam*—self; *paśyan*—realizing the position; *ātmani*—in the self; *tuṣyati*—becomes satisfied; *sukham*—happiness; *ātyantikam*—supreme; *yat*—in which; *tat*—that; *buddhi*—intelligence; *grāhyam*—acceptable; *atīndriyam*—transcendental; *vetti*—knows; *yatra*—wherein; *na*—never; *ca*—also; *eva*—certainly; *ayam*—in this; *sthitaḥ*—situated; *calati*—moves; *tattvataḥ*—from the truth; *yam*—that which; *labdhvā*—by attainment; *ca*—also; *aparam*—any other; *lābham*—gain; *manyate*—does not mind; *na*—never; *adhikam*—more than that; *tataḥ*—from that; *yasmin*—in which; *sthitaḥ*—being situated; *na*—never; *duḥkhena*—by miseries; *guruṇāpi* —even though very difficult; *vicālyate*—becomes shaken; *tam*—that; *vidyāt* —you must know; *duḥkha-saṁyoga*—miseries of material contact; *viyogam* —extermination; *yoga-saṁjñitam*—trance in *yoga*.

TRANSLATION

The stage of perfection is called trance, or samādhi, when one's mind is completely restrained from material mental activities by practice of yoga. This is characterized by one's ability to see the self by the pure mind and to relish and rejoice in the self. In that joyous state, one is situated in boundless transcendental happiness and enjoys himself through transcendental senses. Established thus, one never departs from the truth, and upon gaining this he thinks there is no greater gain. Being situated in such a position, one is never shaken, even in the midst of greatest difficulty. This indeed is actual freedom from all miseries arising from material contact.

PURPORT

By practice of yoga one becomes gradually detached from material concepts. This is the primary characteristic of the yoga principle. And after this, one becomes situated in trance, or samādhi which means that the yogī realizes the Supersoul through transcendental mind and intelligence, without any of the misgivings of identifying the self with the Superself. Yoga practice is more or less based on the principles of the Patañjali system. Some unauthorized commentators try to identify the individual soul with the Supersoul, and the monists think this to be liberation, but they do not understand the real purpose of the Patañjali system of yoga. There is an acceptance of transcendental pleasure in the Patañjali system, but the monists do not accept this transcendental pleasure out of fear of jeopardizing the theory of oneness. The duality of knowledge and knower is not accepted by the nondualist, but in this verse transcendental pleasure-realized through transcendental senses-is accepted. And this is corroborated by the Patañjali Muni, the famous exponent of the yoga system. The great sage declares in his Yoga-sūtras: puruṣārtha-śūnyānāṁ guṇānāṁ pratiprasavaḥ kaivalyaṁ svarūpa-pratiṣṭhā vā citi-śaktir iti.

This citi-śakti, or internal potency, is transcendental. Puruṣārtha means material religiosity, economic development, sense gratification and, at the end, the attempt to become one with the Supreme. This "oneness with the Supreme" is called kaivalyam by the monist. But according to Patañjali, this kaivalyam is an internal, or transcendental, potency by which the living entity becomes aware of his constitutional position. In the words of Lord Caitanya, this state of affairs is called ceto-darpaṇa-mārjanam, or clearance of the impure mirror of the mind. This "clearance" is actually liberation, or *bhava-mahādāvāgni-nirvāpaṇam*. The theory of *nirvāṇa*—also preliminary—corresponds with this principle. In the *Bhāgavatam* this is called *svarūpeṇa vyavasthitiḥ*. The *Bhagavad-gītā* also confirms this situation in this verse.

After *nirvāṇa*, or material cessation, there is the manifestation of spiritual activities, or devotional service of the Lord, known as Kṛṣṇa consciousness. In the words of the *Bhāgavatam*, *svarūpeṇa vyavasthitiḥ*: this is the "real life of the living entity." *Māyā*, or illusion, is the condition of spiritual life contaminated by material infection. Liberation from this material infection does not mean destruction of the original eternal position of the living entity. Patañjali also accepts this by his words *kaivalyam svarūpa-pratiṣṭhā vā citi-śaktir iti*. This *citi-śakti* or transcendental pleasure, is real life. This is confirmed in the *Vedānta-sūtras* as *ānandamayo 'bhyāsāt*. This natural transcendental pleasure is the ultimate goal of *yoga* and is easily achieved by execution of devotional service, or *bhakti-yoga*. *Bhakti-yoga* will be vividly described in the Seventh Chapter of *Bhagavad-gītā*.

In the *yoga* system, as described in this chapter, there are two kinds of *samādhi*, called *samprajñāta-samādhi* and *asamprajñāta-samādhi*. When one becomes situated in the transcendental position by various philosophical researches, it is called *samprajñāta-samādhi*. In the *asamprajñāta-samādhi* there is no longer any connection with mundane pleasure, for one is then transcendental to all sorts of happiness derived from the senses. When the *yogī* is once situated in that transcendental position, he is never shaken from it. Unless the *yogī* is able to reach this position, he is unsuccessful. Today's so-called *yoga* practice, which involves various sense pleasures, is contradictory. A *yogī* indulging in sex and intoxication is a mockery. Even those *yogīs* who are attracted by the *siddhis* (perfections) in the process of *yoga* are not perfectly situated. If the *yogīs* are attracted by the by-products of *yoga*, then they cannot attain the stage of perfection, as is stated in this verse. Persons, therefore, indulging in the make-show practice of gymnastic feats or *siddhis* should know that the aim of *yoga* is lost in that way.

The best practice of *yoga* in this age is Kṛṣṇa consciousness, which is not baffling. A Kṛṣṇa conscious person is so happy in his occupation that he does not aspire after any other happiness. There are many impediments, especially in this age of hypocrisy, to practicing *haṭha-yoga*, *dhyāna-yoga*, and *jñāna-yoga*, but there is no such problem in executing *karma-yoga* or *bhakti-yoga*.

As long as the material body exists, one has to meet the demands of the body, namely eating, sleeping, defending and mating. But a person who is in pure *bhakti-yoga* or in Kṛṣṇa consciousness does not arouse the senses while meeting the demands of the body. Rather, he accepts the bare necessities of life, making the best use of a bad bargain, and enjoys transcendental happiness in Kṛṣṇa consciousness. He is callous toward incidental occurrences—such as accidents, disease, scarcity and even the death of a most dear relative—but he is always alert to execute his duties in Kṛṣṇa consciousness or *bhakti-yoga*. Accidents never deviate him from his duty. As stated in the *Bhagavad-gītā*, *āgamāpāyino 'nityās tāṁs titikṣasva bhārata*. He endures all such incidental occurences because he knows that they come and go and do not affect his duties. In this way he achieves the highest perfection in *yoga* practice.

TEXT 24

स निश्चयेन योक्तव्यो योगोऽनिर्विण्णचेतसा
संकल्पप्रभवान्कामांस्त्यक्त्वा सर्वानशेषतः ।
मनसैवेन्द्रियग्रामं विनियम्य समन्ततः ॥ २४ ॥

sa niścayena yoktavyo
yogo 'nirviṇṇa-cetasā
saṅkalpa-prabhavān kāmāṁs
tyaktvā sarvān aśeṣataḥ
manasaivendriya-grāmaṁ
viniyamya samantataḥ

saḥ—that *yoga* system; *niścayena*—with firm determination; *yoktavyaḥ*—must be practiced; *yogaḥ*—in such practice; *anirviṇṇa-cetasā*—without deviation; *saṅkalpa*—material desires; *prabhavān*—born of; *kāmān*—sense gratification; *tyaktvā*—giving up; *sarvān*—all; *aśeṣataḥ*—completely; *manasā*—by the mind; *eva*—certainly; *indriya-grāmam*—the full set of senses; *viniyamya*—regulating; *samantataḥ*—from all sides.

TRANSLATION

One should engage oneself in the practice of yoga with undeviating determination and faith. One should abandon, without exception, all material desires born of false ego and thus control all the senses on all sides by the mind.

PURPORT

The *yoga* practitioner should be determined and should patiently prosecute the practice without deviation. One should be sure of success at the end and pursue this course with great perserverance, not becoming discouraged if there is any delay in the attainment of success. Success is sure for the rigid practitioner. Regarding *bhakti-yoga*, Rupa Gosvāmī says:

utsāhān niścayād dhairyāt tat tat karma-pravartanāt
saṅga-tyāgāt satovṛtteḥ ṣaḍbhir bhaktiḥ prasidhyati

"The process of *bhakti-yoga* can be executed successfully with full-hearted enthusiasm, perseverance, and determination by following the prescribed duties in the association of devotees and by engaging completely in activities of goodness."

As for determination, one should follow the example of the sparrow who lost her eggs in the waves of the ocean. A sparrow laid her eggs on the shore of the ocean, but the big ocean carried away the eggs on its waves. The sparrow became very upset and asked the ocean to return her eggs. The ocean did not even consider her appeal. So the sparrow decided to dry up the ocean. She began to pick out the water in her small beak, and everyone laughed at her for her impossible determination. The news of her activity spread, and at last Garuḍa, the gigantic bird carrier of Lord Viṣṇu, heard it. He became compassionate toward his small sister bird, and so he came to see the sparrow. Garuḍa was very pleased by the determination of the small sparrow, and he promised to help. Thus Garuḍa at once asked the ocean to return her eggs lest he himself take up the work of the sparrow. The ocean was frightened at this, and returned the eggs. Thus the sparrow became happy by the grace of Garuḍa.

Similarly, the practice of *yoga*, especially *bhakti-yoga* in Kṛṣṇa consciousness, may appear to be a very difficult job. But if anyone follows the principles with great determination, the Lord will surely help, for God helps those who help themselves.

TEXT 25

शनैः शनैरुपरमेद्बुद्ध्या धृतिगृहीतया ।
आत्मसंस्थं मनः कृत्वा न किंचिदपि चिन्तयेत् ॥ २५ ॥

śanaiḥ śanair uparamed
buddhyā dhṛti-gṛhītayā
ātma-saṁsthaṁ manaḥ kṛtvā
na kiñcid api cintayet

śanaiḥ—gradually; śanaiḥ—step by step; uparamet—hesitated; buddhyā—by intelligence; dhṛti-gṛhītayā—carrying the conviction; ātma-saṁstham—placed in transcendence; manaḥ—mind; kṛtvā—doing so; na—nothing; kiñcit—anything else; api—even; cintayet—be thinking of.

TRANSLATION

Gradually, step by step, with full conviction, one should become situated in trance by means of intelligence, and thus the mind should be fixed on the Self alone and should think of nothing else.

PURPORT

By proper conviction and intelligence one should gradually cease sense activities. This is called pratyāhāra. The mind, being controlled by conviction, meditation, and cessation of the senses, should be situated in trance, or samādhi. At that time there is no longer any danger of becoming engaged in the material conception of life. In other words, although one is involved with matter as long as the material body exists, one should not think about sense gratification. One should think of no pleasure aside from the pleasure of the Supreme Self. This state is easily attained by directly practicing Kṛṣṇa consciousness.

TEXT 26

यतो यतो निश्चलति मनश्चञ्चलमस्थिरम् ।
ततस्ततो नियम्यैतदात्मन्येव वशं नयेत् ॥ २६ ॥

yato yato niścalati
manaś cañcalam asthiram
tatas tato niyamyaitad
ātmany eva vaśaṁ nayet

yataḥ—whatever; yataḥ—wherever; niścalati—verily agitated; manaḥ—the mind; cañcalam—flickering; asthiram—unsteady; tataḥ—from there; tataḥ—

and thereafter; *niyamya*—regulating; *etat*—this; *ātmani*—in the self; *eva*—certainly; *vaśam*—control; *nayet*—must bring in.

TRANSLATION

From whatever and wherever the mind wanders due to its flickering and unsteady nature, one must certainly withdraw it and bring it back under the control of the Self.

PURPORT

The nature of the mind is flickering and unsteady. But a self-realized *yogī* has to control the mind; the mind should not control him. One who controls the mind (and therefore the senses as well) is called *gosvāmī*, or *svāmī*, and one who is controlled by the mind is called *godāsa*, or the servant of the senses. A *gosvāmī* knows the standard of sense happiness. In transcendental sense happiness, the senses are engaged in the service of Hṛṣīkeśa or the supreme owner of the senses—Kṛṣṇa. Serving Kṛṣṇa with purified senses is called Kṛṣṇa consciousness. That is the way of bringing the senses under full control. What is more, that is the highest perfection of *yoga* practice.

TEXT 27

प्रशान्तमनसं ह्येनं योगिनं सुखमुत्तमम् ।
उपैति शान्तरजसं ब्रह्मभूतमकल्मषम् ॥ २७ ॥

praśānta-manasaṁ hy enaṁ
yoginaṁ sukham uttamam
upaiti śānta-rajasaṁ
brahma-bhūtam akalmaṣam

praśānta—mind fixed on the lotus feet of Kṛṣṇa; *manasam*—of one whose mind is so fixed; *hi*—certainly; *enam*—this; *yoginam*—the *yogī*; *sukham*—happiness; *uttamam*—the highest; *upaiti*—attains; *śānta-rajasam*—pacified passion; *brahma-bhūtam*—liberated by identification with the Absolute; *akalmaṣam*—freed from all past sinful reaction.

TRANSLATION

The yogī whose mind is fixed on Me verily attains the highest happiness. By virtue of his identity with Brahman, he is liberated; his mind is peaceful, his passions are quieted, and he is freed from sin.

PURPORT

Brahma-bhūta is the state of being free from material contamination and situated in the transcendental service of the Lord. *Mad-bhaktim labhate parām* (Bg. 18.54). One cannot remain in the quality of Brahman, the Absolute, until one's mind is fixed on the lotus feet of the Lord. *Sa vai manaḥ kṛṣṇa-padāravindayoḥ.* To be always engaged in the transcendental loving service of the Lord, or to remain in Kṛṣṇa consciousness, is to be factually liberated from the mode of passion and all material contamination.

TEXT 28

युञ्जन्नेवं सदात्मानं योगी विगतकल्मषः ।
सुखेन ब्रह्मसंस्पर्शमत्यन्तं सुखमश्नुते ॥ २८ ॥

yuñjann evaṁ sadātmānaṁ
yogī vigata-kalmaṣaḥ
sukhena brahma-saṁsparśam
atyantaṁ sukham aśnute

yuñjan—thus being engaged in *yoga* practice; *evam*—thus; *sadā*—always; *ātmānam*—self; *yogī*—one who is in touch with the Supreme Self; *vigata*—is freed from; *kalmaṣaḥ*—all material contamination; *sukhena*—in transcendental happiness; *brahma-saṁsparśam*—being in constant touch with the Supreme; *atyantam*—highest; *sukham*—happiness; *aśnute*—attains.

TRANSLATION

Steady in the Self, being freed from all material contamination, the yogī achieves the highest perfectional stage of happiness in touch with the Supreme Consciousness.

PURPORT

Self-realization means knowing one's constitutional position in relationship to the Supreme. The individual soul is part and parcel of the Supreme, and his position is to render transcendental service to the Lord. This transcendental contact with the Supreme is called *brahma-saṁsparśa.*

TEXT 29

सर्वभूतस्थमात्मानं सर्वभूतानि चात्मनि ।
ईक्षते योगयुक्तात्मा सर्वत्र समदर्शनः ॥ २९ ॥

sarva-bhūta-stham ātmānaṁ
sarva-bhūtāni cātmani
īkṣate yoga-yuktātmā
sarvatra sama-darśanaḥ

sarva-bhūta-stham—situated in all beings; *ātmānam*—the Supersoul; *sarva*—all; *bhūtāni*—entities; *ca*—also; *ātmani*—in the Self; *īkṣate*—does see; *yoga-yukta-ātmā*—one who is dovetailed in Kṛṣṇa consciousness; *sarvatra*—everywhere; *sama-darśanaḥ*—seeing equally.

TRANSLATION

A true yogī observes Me in all beings, and also sees every being in Me. Indeed, the self-realized man sees Me everywhere.

PURPORT

A Kṛṣṇa conscious *yogī* is the perfect seer because he sees Kṛṣṇa, the Supreme, situated in everyone's heart as Supersoul (Paramātmā). *Īśvaraḥ sarva-bhūtānāṁ hṛd-deśe 'rjuna tiṣṭhati.* The Lord in His Paramātmā feature is situated within both the heart of the dog and that of a *brāhmaṇa.* The perfect *yogī* knows that the Lord is eternally transcendental and is not materially affected by His presence in either a dog or a *brāhmaṇa.* That is the supreme neutrality of the Lord. The individual soul is also situated in the individual heart, but he is not present in all hearts. That is the distinction between the individual soul and the Supersoul. One who is not factually in the practice of *yoga* cannot see so clearly. A Kṛṣṇa conscious person can see Kṛṣṇa in the heart of both the believer and nonbeliever. In the *smṛti* this is confirmed as follows: *ātatatvāc ca mātṛtvād ātmā hi paramo hariḥ.*

The Lord, being the source of all beings, is like the mother and the maintainer. As the mother is neutral to all different kinds of children, the Supreme Father (or Mother) is also. Consequently the Supersoul is always in every living being. Outwardly, also, every living being is situated in the energy of the Lord. As will be explained in the Seventh Chapter, the Lord has, primarily, two energies-the spiritual (or superior) and the material (or inferior). The living entity, although part of the superior energy, is conditioned by the inferior energy; the living entity is always in the Lord's energy. Every living entity is situated in Him in one way or another. The *yogī* sees equally because he sees that all living entities, although in different situations according to the results of fruitive work, in all circumstances remain the servants of God. While in the material energy, the living entity serves the material senses; and while in spiritual energy, he serves the Supreme Lord directly. In either case the living entity is the servant of God. This vision of equality is perfect in a person in Kṛṣṇa consciousness.

TEXT 30

यो मां पश्यति सर्वत्र सर्वं च मयि पश्यति ।
तस्याहं न प्रणश्यामि स च मे न प्रणश्यति ॥ ३० ॥

yo māṁ paśyati sarvatra
sarvaṁ ca mayi paśyati
tasyāhaṁ na praṇaśyāmi
sa ca me na praṇaśyati

yaḥ—whoever; *mām*—Me; *paśyati*—sees; *sarvatra*—everywhere; *sarvam*— everything; *ca*—and; *mayi*—in Me; *paśyati*—he sees; *tasya*—his; *aham*—I; *na*—not; *praṇaśyāmi*—am lost; *saḥ*—he; *ca*—also; *me*—to Me; *na*—nor; *praṇaśyati*—is lost.

TRANSLATION

For one who sees Me everywhere and sees everything in Me, I am never lost, nor is he ever lost to Me.

PURPORT

A person in Kṛṣṇa consciousness certainly sees Lord Kṛṣṇa everywhere, and he sees everything in Kṛṣṇa. Such a person may appear to see all separate manifestations of the material nature, but in each and every instance he is conscious of Kṛṣṇa, knowing that everything is the manifestation of Kṛṣṇa's energy. Nothing can exist without Kṛṣṇa, and Kṛṣṇa is the Lord of everything—this is the basic principle of Kṛṣṇa consciousness.

Kṛṣṇa consciousness is the development of love of Kṛṣṇa—a position transcendental even to material liberation. It is the stage beyond self-realization at which the devotee becomes one with Kṛṣṇa in the sense that Kṛṣṇa becomes everything for the devotee, and the devotee becomes full in loving Kṛṣṇa. An intimate relationship between the Lord and the devotee then exists. In that stage, the living entity attains his immortality. Nor is the Personality of Godhead ever out of the sight of the devotee. To merge in Kṛṣṇa is spiritual annihilation. A devotee takes no such risk. It is stated in the *Brahma-saṁhitā*:

> premāñjana-cchurita-bhakti-vilocanena
> santaḥ sadaiva hṛdayeṣu vilokayanti
> yaṁ śyāmasundaram acintya-guṇa-svarūpaṁ
> govindam ādi-puruṣaṁ tam ahaṁ bhajāmi

"I worship the primeval Lord, Govinda, who is always seen by the devotee whose eyes are anointed with the pulp of love. He is seen in His eternal form of Śyāmasundara situated within the heart of the devotee." (Bs. 5.38)

At this stage, Lord Kṛṣṇa never disappears from the sight of the devotee, nor does the devotee ever lose sight of the Lord. In the case of a *yogī* who sees the Lord as Paramātmā within the heart, the same applies. Such a *yogī* turns into a pure devotee and cannot bear to live for a moment without seeing the Lord within himself.

TEXT 31

सर्वभूतस्थितं यो मां भजत्येकत्वमास्थितः ।
सर्वथा वर्तमानोऽपि स योगी मयि वर्तते ॥ ३१ ॥

> sarva-bhūta-sthitaṁ yo māṁ
> bhajaty ekatvam āsthitaḥ
> sarvathā vartamāno 'pi
> sa yogī mayi vartate

sarva-bhūta-sthitam—situated in everyone's heart; *yaḥ*—he who; *mām*—unto Me; *bhajati*—serves in devotional service; *ekatvam*—oneness; *āsthitaḥ*—thus situated; *sarvathā*—in all respects; *vartamānaḥ*—being situated; *api*—in spite of; *saḥ*—he; *yogī*—transcendentalist; *mayi*—unto Me; *vartate*—remains.

TRANSLATION

The yogī who knows that I and the Supersoul within all creatures are one worships Me and remains always in Me in all circumstances.

PURPORT

A *yogī* who is practicing meditation on the Supersoul sees within himself the plenary portion of Kṛṣṇa as Viṣṇu—with four hands, holding conchshell, wheel, club and lotus flower. The *yogī* should know that Viṣṇu is not different from Kṛṣṇa. Kṛṣṇa in this form of Supersoul is situated in everyone's heart. Furthermore, there is no difference between the innumerable Supersouls present in the innumerable hearts of living entities. Nor is there a difference between a Kṛṣṇa conscious person always engaged in the transcendental loving service of Kṛṣṇa and a perfect *yogī* engaged in meditation on the Supersoul. The *yogī* in Kṛṣṇa consciousness—even though he may be engaged in various activities while in material existence—remains always situated in Kṛṣṇa. This is confirmed in the *Bhakti-rasāmṛta-sindhu* of Śrīla Rūpa Gosvāmī: *nikhileṣu avasthāsu jīvanmukta sa ucyate.* A devotee of the Lord, always acting in Kṛṣṇa consciousness, is automatically liberated. In the *Nārada-pañcarātra* this is confirmed in this way:

> dik-kālādy-anavacchinne kṛṣṇe ceto vidhāya ca
> tanmayo bhavati kṣipraṁ jīvo brahmaṇi yojayet.

"By concentrating one's attention on the transcendental form of Kṛṣṇa, who is all-pervading and beyond time and space, one becomes absorbed in thinking of Kṛṣṇa and then attains the happy state of transcendental association with Him."

Kṛṣṇa consciousness is the highest stage of trance in *yoga* practice. This very understanding that Kṛṣṇa is present as Paramātmā in everyone's heart makes the *yogī* faultless. The *Vedas* confirm this inconceivable potency of the Lord as follows:

> eko 'pi san bahudhā yo 'vabhāti
> aiśvaryād rūpam ekaṁ ca sūryavad bahudheyate.

"Viṣṇu is one, and yet He is certainly all-pervading. By His inconceivable potency, in spite of His one form, He is present everywhere. As the sun, He appears in many places at once."

TEXT 32

आत्मौपम्येन सर्वत्र समं पश्यति योऽर्जुन ।
सुखं वा यदि वा दुःखं स योगी परमो मतः ॥ ३२ ॥

*ātmaupamyena sarvatra
samaṁ paśyati yo 'rjuna
sukhaṁ vā yadi vā duḥkhaṁ
sa yogī paramo mataḥ*

ātma—self; *aupamyena*—by comparison; *sarvatra*—everywhere; *samam*—equality; *paśyati*—sees; *yaḥ*—he who; *arjuna*—O Arjuna; *sukham*—happiness; *vā*—or; *yadi*—if; *vā*—or; *duḥkham*—distress; *saḥ*—such; *yogī*—transcendentalist; *paramaḥ*—perfect; *mataḥ*—considered.

TRANSLATION

He is a perfect yogī who, by comparison to his own self, sees the true equality of all beings, both in their happiness and distress, O Arjuna!

PURPORT

One who is Kṛṣṇa conscious is a perfect *yogī*; he is aware of everyone's happiness and distress by dint of his own personal experience. The cause of the distress of a living entity is forgetfulness of his relationship with God. And the cause of happiness is knowing Kṛṣṇa to be the supreme enjoyer of all the activities of the human being. Kṛṣṇa is the proprietor of all lands and planets. The perfect *yogī* is the sincerest friend of all living entities. He knows that the living being who is conditioned by the modes of material nature is subjected to the threefold material miseries due to forgetfulness of his relationship with Kṛṣṇa. Because one in Kṛṣṇa consciousness is happy, he tries to distribute the knowledge of Kṛṣṇa everywhere. Since the perfect *yogī* tries to broadcast the importance of becoming Kṛṣṇa conscious, he is the best philanthropist in the world, and he is the dearest servitor of the Lord. *Na tasmāt kaścid me priyakṛt tamaḥ.* In other words, a devotee of the Lord always looks to the welfare of all living entities, and in this way he is factually the friend of everyone. He is the best *yogī* because he does not desire perfection in *yoga* for his personal benefit, but tries for others also. He does not envy his fellow living entities. Here is a contrast between a pure devotee of the Lord and a yogī interested only in his personal elevation. The yogī who has withdrawn to a secluded place in order to meditate perfectly may not be as perfect as a devotee who is trying his best to turn every man toward Kṛṣṇa consciousness.

TEXT 33

अर्जुन उवाच ।
योऽयं योगस्त्वया प्रोक्तः साम्येन मधुसूदन ।
एतस्याहं न पश्यामि चञ्चलत्वात्स्थितिं स्थिराम् ॥ ३३ ॥

arjuna uvāca
yo 'yaṁ yogas tvayā proktaḥ
sāmyena madhusūdana
etasyāhaṁ na paśyāmi
cañcalatvāt sthitiṁ sthirām

arjunaḥ uvāca—Arjuna said; yaḥ—the system; ayam—this; yogaḥ—mysticism; tvayā—by You; proktaḥ—described; sāmyena—generally; madhusūdana—O killer of the demon Madhu; etasya—of this; aham—I; na—do not; paśyāmi—see; cañcalatvāt—due to being restless; sthitim—situation; sthirām—stable.

TRANSLATION

Arjuna said: O Madhusūdana, the system of yoga which you have summarized appears impractical and unendurable to me, for the mind is restless and unsteady.

PURPORT

The system of mysticism described by Lord Kṛṣṇa to Arjuna beginning with the words śucau deśe and ending with yogī paramaḥ is here being rejected by Arjuna out of a feeling of inability. It is not possible for an ordinary man to leave home and go to a secluded place in the mountains or jungles to practice yoga in this age of Kali. The present age is characterized by a bitter struggle for a life of short duration. People are not serious about self-realization even by simple, practical means, and what to speak of this difficult yoga system, which regulates the mode of living, the manner of sitting, selection of place, and detachment of the mind from material engagements. As a practical man, Arjuna thought it was impossible to follow this system of yoga, even though he was favorably endowed in many ways. He belonged to the royal family and was highly elevated in terms of numerous qualities; he was a great warrior, he had great longevity, and, above all, he was the most intimate friend of Lord Kṛṣṇa, the Supreme Personality of Godhead. Five thousand years ago, Arjuna had much better facilities then we do now, yet he refused to accept this system of yoga. In fact, we do not find any record in history of his practicing it at any time. Therefore this system must be considered generally impossible in this age of Kali. Of course it may be possible for some very few, rare men, but for the people in general it is an impossible proposal. If this were so five thousand years ago, then what of the present day? Those who are imitating this yoga system in different so-called schools and societies, although complacent, are certainly wasting their time. They are completely in ignorance of the desired goal.

TEXT 34

चञ्चलं हि मनः कृष्ण प्रमाथि बलवद्‌दृढम् ।
तस्याहं निग्रहं मन्ये वायोरिव सुदुष्करम् ॥ ३४ ॥

cañcalaṁ hi manaḥ kṛṣṇa
pramāthi balavad dṛḍham
tasyāhaṁ nigrahaṁ manye
vāyor iva su-duṣkaram

cañcalam—flickering; hi—certainly; manaḥ—mind; kṛṣṇa—O Kṛṣṇa; pramāthi—agitating; balavat—strong; dṛḍham—obstinate; tasya—its; aham—I; nigraham—subduing; manye—think; vāyoḥ—of the wind; iva—like; suduṣkaram—difficult.

TRANSLATION

For the mind is restless, turbulent, obstinate and very strong, O Kṛṣṇa, and to subdue it is, it seems to me, more difficult than controlling the wind.

PURPORT

The mind is so strong and obstinate that it sometimes overcomes the intelligence, although mind is supposed to be subservient to the intelligence. For a man in the practical world who has to fight so many opposing elements, it is certainly very difficult to control the mind. Artificially, one may establish a mental equilibrium toward both friend and enemy, but ultimately no worldly man can do so, for this is more difficult than controlling the raging wind. In the Vedic literatures it is said:

ātmānaṁ rathinaṁ viddhi śarīraṁ ratham eva ca
buddhintu sārathiṁ viddhi manaḥ pragraham eva ca
indriyāṇi hayānāhur viṣayāṁs teṣu gocarān
ātmendriya-mano-yukto bhoktety āhur manīṣiṇaḥ.

"The individual is the passenger in the car of the material body, and intelligence is the driver. Mind is the driving instrument, and the senses are the horses. The self is thus the enjoyer or sufferer in the association of the mind and senses. So it is understood by great thinkers." Intelligence is supposed to direct the mind, but the mind is so strong and obstinate that it often overcomes even one's own intelligence. Such a strong mind is supposed to be controlled by the practice of *yoga*, but such practice is never practical for a worldly person like Arjuna. And what can we say of modern man? The simile used here is appropriate: one cannot capture the blowing wind. And it is even more difficult to capture the turbulent mind. The easiest way to control the mind, as suggested by Lord Caitanya, is chanting "Hare Kṛṣṇa," the great *mantra* for deliverance, in all humility. The method prescribed is *sa vai manaḥ kṛṣṇa-padāravindayoḥ*: one must engage one's mind fully in Kṛṣṇa. Only then will there remain no other engagements to agitate the mind.

TEXT 35

श्रीभगवानुवाच ।
असंशयं महाबाहो मनो दुर्निग्रहं चलम् ।
अभ्यासेन तु कौन्तेय वैराग्येण च गृह्यते ॥ ३५ ॥

śrī-bhagavān uvāca
asaṁśayaṁ mahā-bāho
mano durnigrahaṁ calam
abhyāsena tu kaunteya
vairāgyeṇa ca gṛhyate

śrī bhagavān uvāca—the Personality of Godhead said; asaṁśayam—undoubtedly; mahā-bāho—O mighty-armed one; manaḥ—mind; durnigraham—difficult to curb; calam—flickering; abhyāsena—by practice; tu—but; kaunteya—O son of Kuntī; vairāgyeṇa—by detachment; ca—also; gṛhyate—can be so controlled.

TRANSLATION

The Blessed Lord said: O mighty-armed son of Kuntī, it is undoubtedly very difficult to curb the restless mind, but it is possible by constant practice and by detachment.

PURPORT

The difficulty of controlling the obstinate mind, as expressed by Arjuna, is accepted by the Personality of Godhead. But at the same time He suggests that by practice and detachment it is possible. What is that practice? In the present age no one can observe strict rules and regulations, such as placing oneself in a sacred place, focusing the mind on the Supersoul, restraining the senses and mind, observing celibacy, remaining alone, etc. By the practice of Kṛṣṇa consciousness, however, one engages in nine types of devotional service to the Lord. The first and foremost of such devotional engagements is hearing about Kṛṣṇa. This is a very powerful transcendental method for purging the mind of all misgivings. The more one hears about Kṛṣṇa, the more one becomes enlightened and detached from everything that draws the mind away from Kṛṣṇa. By detaching the mind from activities not devoted to the Lord, one can very easily learn vairāgya. Vairāgya means detachment from matter and engagement of the mind in spirit. Impersonal spiritual detachment is more difficult than attaching the mind to the activities of Kṛṣṇa. This is practical because by hearing about Kṛṣṇa one becomes automatically attached to the Supreme Spirit. This attachment is called pareśānubhūti spiritual satisfaction. It is just like the feeling of satisfaction a hungry man has for every morsel of food he eats. Similarly, by discharge of devotional service, one feels transcendental satisfaction as the mind becomes detached from material objectives. It is something like curing a disease by expert treatment and appropriate diet. Hearing of the transcendental activities of Lord Kṛṣṇa is therefore expert treatment for the mad mind, and eating the foodstuff offered to Kṛṣṇa is the appropriate diet for the suffering patient. This treatment is the process of Kṛṣṇa consciousness.

TEXT 36

असंयतात्मना योगो दुष्प्राप इति मे मतिः ।
वश्यात्मना तु यतता शक्योऽऽवाप्तुमुपायतः ॥ ३६ ॥

asaṁyatātmanā yogo
duṣprāpa iti me matiḥ
vaśyātmanā tu yatatā
śakyo 'vāptum upāyataḥ

asaṁyata—unbridled; ātmanā—by the mind; yogaḥ—self-realization; duṣprāpaḥ—difficult to obtain; iti—thus; me—My; matiḥ—opinion; vaśya—controlled; ātmanā—by the mind; tu—but; yatatā—while endeavoring; śakyaḥ—practical; avāptum—to achieve; upāyataḥ—appropriate means.

TRANSLATION

For one whose mind is unbridled, self-realization is difficult work. But he whose mind is controlled and who strives by right means is assured of success. That is My opinion.

PURPORT

The Supreme Personality of Godhead declares that one who does not accept the proper treatment to detach the mind from material engagement can hardly achieve success in self-realization. Trying to practice yoga while engaging the mind in material enjoyment is like trying to ignite a fire while pouring water on it. Similarly, yoga practice without mental control is a waste of time. Such a show of yoga practice may be materially lucrative, but it is useless as far as spiritual realization is concerned. Therefore, the mind must be controlled by engaging it constantly in the transcendental loving service of the Lord. Unless one is engaged in Kṛṣṇa consciousness, he cannot steadily control the mind. A Kṛṣṇa conscious person easily achieves the result of yoga practice without separate endeavor, but a yoga practitioner cannot achieve success without becoming Kṛṣṇa conscious.

TEXT 37

अर्जुन उवाच ।
अयतिः श्रद्धयोपेतो योगाच्चलितमानसः ।
अप्राप्य योगसंसिद्धिं कां गतिं कृष्ण गच्छति ॥ ३७ ॥

arjuna uvāca
ayatiḥ śraddhayopeto
yogāc calita-mānasaḥ
aprāpya yoga-saṁsiddhiṁ
kāṁ gatiṁ kṛṣṇa gacchati

arjunaḥ uvāca—Arjuna said; *ayatiḥ*—unsuccessful transcendentalist; *śraddhayā*—with faith; *upetaḥ*—engaged; *yogāt*—from the mystic link; *calita*—deviated; *mānasaḥ*—of one who has such a mind; *aprāpya*—failing; *yoga-saṁsiddhim*—highest perfection in mysticism; *kām*—which; *gatim*—destination; *kṛṣṇa*—O Kṛṣṇa; *gacchati*—achieves.

TRANSLATION

Arjuna said: What is the destination of the man of faith who does not persevere, who in the beginning takes to the process of self-realization but who later desists due to worldly-mindedness and thus does not attain perfection in mysticism?

PURPORT

The path of self-realization or mysticism is described in the *Bhagavad-gītā*. The basic principle of self-realization is knowledge that the living entity is not this material body but that he is different from it and that his happiness is in eternal life, bliss and knowledge. These are transcendental, beyond both body and mind. Self-realization is sought by the path of knowledge, the practice of the eightfold system or by *bhakti-yoga*. In each of these processes one has to realize the constitutional position of the living entity, his relationship with God, and the activities whereby he can reestablish the lost link and achieve the highest perfectional stage of Kṛṣṇa consciousness. Following any of the above-mentioned three methods, one is sure to reach the supreme goal sooner or later. This was asserted by the Lord in the Second Chapter: even a little endeavor on the transcendental path offers a great hope for deliverance. Out of these three methods, the path of *bhakti-yoga* is especially suitable for this age because it is the most direct method of God realization. To be doubly assured, Arjuna is asking Lord Kṛṣṇa to confirm His former statement. One may sincerely accept the path of self-realization, but the process of cultivation of knowledge and the practice of the eightfold *yoga* system are generally very difficult for this age. Therefore, despite constant endeavor, one may fail for many reasons. First of all, one may not be following the process. To pursue the transcendental path is more or less to declare war on illusory energy. Consequently, whenever a person tries to escape the clutches of the illusory energy, she tries to defeat the practitioner by various allurements. A conditioned soul is already allured by the modes of material energy, and there is every chance of being allured again, even while performing transcendental disciplines. This is called *yogāt calita-mānasaḥ*: deviation from the transcendental path. Arjuna is inquisitive to know the results of deviation from the path of self-realization.

TEXT 38

कच्चिन्नोभयविभ्रष्टश्छिन्नाभ्रमिव नश्यति ।
अप्रतिष्ठो महाबाहो विमूढो ब्रह्मणः पथि ॥ ३८ ॥

*kaccin nobhaya-vibhraṣṭaś
chinnābhram iva naśyati
apratiṣṭho mahā-bāho
vimūḍho brahmaṇaḥ pathi*

kaccit—whether; *na*—not; *ubhaya*—both; *vibhraṣṭaḥ*—deviated from; *chinna*—fallen; *abhram*—cloud; *iva*—likened; *naśyati*—perishes; *apratiṣṭhaḥ*—without any position; *mahā-bāho*—O mighty-armed Kṛṣṇa; *vimūḍhaḥ*—bewildered; *brahmaṇaḥ*—of Transcendence; *pathi*—on the path.

TRANSLATION

O mighty-armed Kṛṣṇa, does not such a man, being deviated from the path of Transcendence, perish like a riven cloud, with no position in any sphere?

PURPORT

There are two ways to progress. Those who are materialists have no interest in Transcendence; therefore they are more interested in material advancement by economic development, or in promotion to the higher planets by appropriate work. When one takes to the path of Transcendence, one has to cease all material activities and sacrifice all forms of so-called material happiness. If the aspiring transcendentalist fails, then he apparently loses both ways; in other words, he can enjoy neither material happiness nor spiritual success. He has no position; he is like a riven cloud. A cloud in the sky sometimes deviates from a small cloud and joins a big one. But if it cannot join a big one, then it is blown away by the wind and becomes a nonentity in the vast sky. The *brahmaṇaḥ pathi* is the path of transcendental realization through knowing oneself to be spiritual in essence, part and parcel of the Supreme Lord who is manifested as Brahman, Paramātmā and Bhagavān. Lord Śrī Kṛṣṇa is the fullest manifestation of the Supreme Absolute Truth, and therefore one who is surrendered to the Supreme Person is a successful transcendentalist. To reach this goal of life through Brahman and Paramātmā realization takes many, many births: *Bahūnāṁ janmanām ante.* Therefore the supermost of transcendental realization is *bhakti-yoga* or Kṛṣṇa consciousness, the direct method.

TEXT 39

एतन्मे संशयं कृष्ण छेत्तुमर्हस्यशेषतः ।
त्वदन्यः संशयस्यास्य छेत्ता न ह्युपपद्यते ॥ ३९ ॥

etan me saṁśayaṁ kṛṣṇa
chettum arhasy aśeṣataḥ
tvad-anyaḥ saṁśayasyāsya
chettā na hy upapadyate

etat—this is; *me*—my; *saṁśayam*—doubt; *kṛṣṇa*—O Kṛṣṇa; *chettum*—to dispel; *arhasi*—requested to do; *aśeṣataḥ*—completely; *tvat*—Yourself; *anyaḥ*—without; *saṁśayāsya*—of the doubt; *asya*—of this; *chettā*—remover; *na*—never; *hi*—certainly; *upapadyate*—to be found.

TRANSLATION

This is my doubt O Kṛṣṇa, and I ask You to dispel it completely. But for Yourself, no one is to be found who can destroy this doubt.

PURPORT

Kṛṣṇa is the perfect knower of past, present and future. In the beginning of the *Bhagavad-gītā,* the Lord said that all living entities exist individually in the past, that they exist now in the present, and that they continue to retain individual identity in the future, even after liberation from the material entanglement. So He has already cleared up the question of the future of the individual living entity. Now, Arjuna wants to know of the future of the unsuccessful transcendentalist. No one is equal to or above Kṛṣṇa, and certainly the so-called great sages and philosophers who are at the mercy of material nature cannot equal Him. Therefore the verdict of Kṛṣṇa is the final and complete answer to all doubts because He knows past, present and future perfectly—but no one knows Him. Kṛṣṇa and Kṛṣṇa conscious devotees alone can know what is what.

TEXT 40

श्रीभगवानुवाच
पार्थ नैवेह नामुत्र विनाशस्तस्य विद्यते ।
न हि कल्याणकृत्कश्चिद्दुर्गतिं तात गच्छति ॥ ४० ॥

śrī-bhagavān uvāca
pārtha naiveha nāmutra
vināśas tasya vidyate
na hi kalyāṇa-kṛt kaścid
durgatiṁ tāta gacchati

śrī bhagavān uvāca—the Supreme Personality of Godhead said; *pārtha*—O son of Pṛthā; *na eva*—never is it so; *iha*—in this material world; *na*—never; *amutra*—in the next life; *vināśaḥ*—destruction; *tasya*—his; *vidyate*—exists; *na*—never; *hi*—certainly; *kalyāṇa-kṛt*—one who is engaged in auspicious activities; *kaścit*—anyone; *durgatim*—degradation; *tāta*—thereafter; *gacchati*—going.

TRANSLATION

The Blessed Lord said: Son of Pṛthā, a transcendentalist engaged in auspicious activities does not meet with destruction either in this world or in the spiritual world; one who does good, My friend, is never overcome by evil.

PURPORT

In the *Śrīmad-Bhāgavatam* (1.5.17) Śrī Nārada Muni instructs Vyāsadeva as follows:

tyaktvā sva-dharmaṁ caraṇāmbujaṁ harer
bhajann apakko 'tha patet tato yadi
yatra kva vābhadram abhūd amuṣya kiṁ
ko vārtha āpto 'bhajatāṁ sva-dharmataḥ

"If someone gives up all material prospects and takes complete shelter of the Supreme Personality of Godhead, there is no loss or degradation in any way. On the other hand a nondevotee may fully engage in his occupational duties and yet not gain anything." For material prospects, there are many activities both scriptural and customary. A transcendentalist is supposed to give up all material activities for the sake of spiritual advancement in life, Kṛṣṇa consciousness. One may argue that by Kṛṣṇa consciousness one may attain the highest perfection if it is completed, but if one does not attain such a perfectional stage, then he loses both materially and spiritually. It is enjoined in the scriptures that one has to suffer the reaction of not executing prescribed duties; therefore one who fails to discharge transcendental activities properly becomes subjected to these reactions. The *Bhāgavatam* assures the unsuccessful transcendentalist that there need be no worries. Even though he may be subjected to the reaction of not perfectly executing prescribed duties, he is still not a loser, because auspicious Kṛṣṇa consciousness is never forgotten, and one so engaged will continue to be so even if he is lowborn in the next life. On the other hand, one who simply follows strictly the prescribed duties need not necessarily attain auspicious results if he is lacking in Kṛṣṇa consciousness.

The purport may be understood as follows: humanity may be divided into two sections, namely, the regulated and the nonregulated. Those who are engaged simply in bestial sense gratifications without knowledge of their next life or spiritual salvation belong to the nonregulated section. And those who follow the principles of prescribed duties in the scriptures are classified amongst the regulated section. The nonregulated section, both civilized and noncivilized, educated and noneducated, strong and weak, are full of animal propensities. Their activities are never auspicious because, enjoying the animal propensities of eating, sleeping, defending and mating, they perpetually remain in material existence, which is always miserable. On the other hand, those who are regulated by scriptural injunctions and thus gradually rise to Kṛṣṇa consciousness certainly progress in life.

Those who are then following the path of auspiciousness can be divided into three sections, namely, 1) the followers of scriptural rules and regulations who are enjoying material prosperity, 2) those who are trying to find out the ultimate liberation from material existence, and 3) those who are devotees in Kṛṣṇa consciousness. Those who are following the rules and regulations of the scriptures for material happiness may be further divided into two classes: those who are fruitive workers and those who desire no fruit for sense gratification. Those who are after fruitive results for sense gratification may be elevated to a higher standard of life—even to the higher planets; but still, because they are not free from material existence, they are not following the truly auspicious path. The only auspicious activities are those which lead one to liberation. Any activity which is not aimed at ultimate self-realization or liberation from the material bodily concept of life is not at all auspicious. Activity in Kṛṣṇa consciousness is the only auspicious activity, and anyone who voluntarily accepts all bodily discomforts for the sake of making progress on the path of Kṛṣṇa consciousness can be called a perfect transcendentalist under severe austerity. And because the eightfold yoga system is directed toward the ultimate realization of Kṛṣṇa consciousness, such practice is also auspicious, and no one who is trying his best in this matter need fear degradation.

TEXT 41

प्राप्य पुण्यकृतां लोकानुषित्वा शाश्वतीः समाः ।
शुचीनां श्रीमतां गेहे योगभ्रष्टोऽभिजायते ॥ ४१ ॥

prāpya puṇya-kṛtāṁ lokān
uṣitvā śāśvatīḥ samāḥ
śucīnāṁ śrīmatāṁ gehe
yoga-bhraṣṭo 'bhijāyate

prāpya—after achieving; *puṇya-kṛtām*—of those who performed pious activities; *lokān*—planets; *uṣitvā*—after dwelling; *śāśvatīḥ*—many; *samāḥ*—years; *śucīnām*—of the pious; *śrīmatām*—of the prosperous; *gehe*—in the house of; *yoga-bhraṣṭaḥ*—one who is fallen from the path of self-realization; *abhijāyate*—takes his birth.

TRANSLATION

The unsuccessful yogī, after many, many years of enjoyment on the planets of the pious living entities, is born into a family of righteous people, or into a family of rich aristocracy.

PURPORT

The unsuccessful *yogīs* are divided into two classes: one is fallen after very little progress, and one is fallen after long practice of *yoga*. The *yogī* who falls after a short period of practice goes to the higher planets where pious living entities are allowed to enter. After prolonged life there, he is sent back again to this planet, to take birth in the family of a righteous *brāhmaṇa vaiṣṇava* or of aristocratic merchants.

The real purpose of *yoga* practice is to achieve the highest perfection of Kṛṣṇa consciousness. But those who do not persevere to such an extent and fail due to material allurements are allowed, by the grace of the Lord, to make full utilization of their material propensities. And after that, they are given opportunities to live prosperous lives in righteous or aristocratic families. Those who are born in such families may take advantage of the facilities and try to elevate themselves to full Kṛṣṇa consciousness.

TEXT 42

अथवा योगिनामेव कुले भवति धीमताम् ।
एतद्धि दुर्लभतरं लोके जन्म यदीदृशम् ॥ ४२ ॥

atha vā yoginām eva
kule bhavati dhīmatām
etad dhi durlabhataraṁ
loke janma yad īdṛśam

athavā—or; *yoginām*—of learned transcendentalists; *eva*—certainly; *kule*—in the family of; *bhavati*—takes birth; *dhīmatām*—of those who are endowed with great wisdom; *etat*—this; *hi*—certainly; *durlabhataram*—very rare; *loke*—in this world; *janma*—birth; *yat*—that which; *īdṛśam*—like this.

TRANSLATION

Or he takes his birth in a family of transcendentalists who are surely great in wisdom. Verily, such a birth is rare in this world.

PURPORT

Birth in a family of *yogīs* or transcendentalists—those with great wisdom —is praised herein because the child born in such a family receives

spiritual impetus from the very beginning of his life. It is especially the
case in the ācārya or gosvāmī families. Such families are very learned and
devoted by tradition and training, and thus they become spiritual masters.
In India there are many such ācārya families, but they have now degenerated
due to insufficient education and training. By the grace of the Lord, there
are still families that foster transcendentalists generation after generation.
It is certainly very fortunate to take birth in such families. Fortunately,
both our spiritual master, Oṁ Viṣṇupāda Śrī Śrīmad Bhaktisiddhānta
Sarasvatī Gosvāmī Mahārāja, and our humble self, had the opportunity to
take birth in such families, by the grace of the Lord, and both of us were
trained in the devotional service of the Lord from the very beginning of
our lives. Later on we met by the order of the transcendental system.

TEXT 43

तत्र तं बुद्धिसंयोगं लभते पौर्वदेहिकम् ।
यतते च ततो भूयः संसिद्धौ कुरुनन्दन ॥ ४३ ॥

*tatra taṁ buddhi-saṁyogaṁ
labhate paurva-dehikam
yatate ca tato bhūyaḥ
saṁsiddhau kuru-nandana*

tatra—thereupon; *tam*—that; *buddhi-saṁyogam*—revival of such consciousness; *labhate*—regains; *paurva*—previous; *dehikam*—bodily consciousness; *yatate*—endeavors; *ca*—also; *tataḥ*—thereafter; *bhūyaḥ*—again;
saṁsiddhau—for perfection; *kuru-nandana*—O son of Kuru.

TRANSLATION

On taking such a birth, he again revives the divine consciousness of his
previous life, and he tries to make further progress in order to achieve complete success, O son of Kuru.

PURPORT

King Bharata, who took his third birth in the family of a good *brāhmaṇa*,
is an example of good birth for the revival of previous transcendental consciousness. King Bharata was the Emperor of the world, and since his time
this planet is known among the demigods as Bhāratavarṣa. Formerly it was
known as Ilāvartavarṣa. The Emperor, at an early age, retired for spiritual

perfection but failed to achieve success. In his next life he took birth in the family of a good *brāhmaṇa* and was known as Jaḍabharata because he always remained secluded and did not talk to anyone. And later on, he was discovered as the greatest transcendentalist by King Rahūgaṇa. From his life it is understood that transcendental endeavors, or the practice of *yoga*, never go in vain. By the grace of the Lord the transcendentalist gets repeated opportunities for complete perfection in Kṛṣṇa consciousness.

TEXT 44

पूर्वाभ्यासेन तेनैव ह्रियते ह्यवशोऽपि सः ।
जिज्ञासुरपि योगस्य शब्दब्रह्मातिवर्तते ॥ ४४ ॥

pūrvābhyāsena tenaiva
hriyate hy avaśo 'pi saḥ
jijñāsur api yogasya
śabda-brahmātivartate

pūrva—previous; *abhyāsena*—practice; *tena*—by the influence of that; *eva*—certainly; *hriyate*—is attracted; *hi*—surely; *avaśaḥ*—helpless; *api*—also; *saḥ*—he; *jijñāsuḥ*—willing to know; *api*—so; *yogasya*—of *yoga*; *śabda-brahma*—ritualistic principles of scripture; *ativartate*—transcends.

TRANSLATION

By virtue of the divine consciousness of his previous life, he automatically becomes attracted to the yogic principles-even without seeking them. Such an inquisitive transcendentalist, striving for yoga, stands always above the ritualistic principles of the scriptures.

PURPORT

Advanced *yogīs* are not very much attracted to the rituals of the scriptures, but they automatically become attracted to the *yoga* principles, which can elevate them to complete Kṛṣṇa consciousness, the highest *yoga* perfection. In the *Śrīmad-Bhāgavatam* (3.33.8), such disregard of Vedic rituals by the advanced transcendentalists is explained as follows:

aho bata śvapaco 'to garīyān
yajjihvāgre vartate nāma tubhyam

tepus tapas te juhuvuḥ sasnur āryā
brahmānūcur nāma gṛṇanti ye te.

"O my Lord! Persons who chant the holy names of Your Lordship are far, far advanced in spiritual life, even if born in families of dog-eaters. Such chanters have undoubtedly performed all kinds of austerities and sacrifices, bathed in all sacred places, and finished all scriptural studies."

The famous example of this was presented by Lord Caitanya, who accepted Ṭhākur Haridāsa as one of His most important disciples. Although Ṭhākur Haridāsa happened to take his birth in a Moslem family, he was elevated to the post of *nāmācārya* by Lord Caitanya due to his rigidly attended principle of chanting three hundred thousand holy names of the Lord daily: Hare Kṛṣṇa, Hare Kṛṣṇa, Kṛṣṇa Kṛṣṇa, Hare Hare/ Hare Rāma, Hare Rāma, Rāma Rāma, Hare Hare. And because he chanted the holy name of the Lord constantly, it is understood that in his previous life he must have passed through all the ritualistic methods of the *Vedas*, known as *śabda-brahman*. Unless, therefore, one is purified, one cannot take to the principle of Kṛṣṇa consciousness nor become engaged in chanting the holy name of the Lord, Hare Kṛṣṇa.

TEXT 45

प्रयत्नाद्यतमानस्तु योगी संशुद्धकिल्बिषः ।
अनेकजन्मसंसिद्धस्ततो याति परां गतिम् ॥ ४५ ॥

prayatnād yatamānas tu
yogī saṁśuddha-kilbiṣaḥ
aneka-janma-saṁsiddhas
tato yāti parāṁ gatim

prayatnāt—by rigid practice; *yatamānaḥ*—one who endeavors; *tu*—but; *yogī*—such a transcendentalist; *saṁśuddha*—washed off; *kilbiṣaḥ*—all kinds of sins; *aneka*—many, many; *janma*—births; *saṁsiddhaḥ*—so achieved perfection; *tataḥ*—thereafter; *yāti*—attains; *parām*—highest; *gatim*—destination.

TRANSLATION

But when the yogī engages himself with sincere endeavor in making further progress, being washed of all contaminations, then ultimately, after many, many births of practice, he attains the supreme goal.

PURPORT

A person born in a particularly righteous, aristocratic or sacred family becomes conscious of his favorable condition for executing *yoga* practice. With determination, therefore, he begins his unfinished task, and thus he completely cleanses himself of all material contaminations. When he is finally free from all contaminations, he attains the supreme perfection—Kṛṣṇa consciousness. Kṛṣṇa consciousness is the perfect stage of being freed of all contaminations. This is confirmed in the *Bhagavad-gītā*:

yeṣāṁ tvanta-gataṁ pāpaṁ janānāṁ puṇya-karmaṇām
te dvandva-moha-nirmuktā bhajante māṁ dṛḍha-vratāḥ

"After many, many births of executing pious activities, when one is completely freed from all contaminations, and from all illusory dualities, one then becomes engaged in the transcendental loving service of the Lord."

TEXT 46

तपस्विभ्योऽधिको योगी ज्ञानिभ्योऽपि मतोऽधिकः ।
कर्मिभ्यश्चाधिको योगी तस्माद्योगी भवार्जुन ॥ ४६ ॥

tapasvibhyo 'dhiko yogī
jñānibhyo 'pi mato 'dhikaḥ
karmibhyaś cādhiko yogī
tasmād yogī bhavārjuna

tapasvibhyaḥ—than the ascetic; *adhikaḥ*—greater; *yogī*—the *yogī*; *jñānibhyaḥ*—than the wise; *api*—also; *mataḥ*—considered; *adhikaḥ*—greater than; *karmibhyaḥ*—than the fruitive worker; *ca*—also; *adhikaḥ*—greater than; *yogī*—the *yogī*; *tasmāt*—therefore; *yogī*—a transcendentalist; *bhava*—just become; *arjuna*—O Arjuna.

TRANSLATION

A yogī is greater than the ascetic, greater than the empiricist and greater than the fruitive worker. Therefore, O Arjuna, in all circumstances, be a yogī.

PURPORT

When we speak of *yoga* we refer to linking up our consciousness with the Supreme Absolute Truth. Such a process is named differently by various practitioners in terms of the particular method adopted. When the linking up process is predominantly in fruitive activities, it is called *karma-yoga*, when it is predominantly empirical, it is called *jñāna-yoga*, and when it is predominantly in a devotional relationship with the Supreme Lord, it is called *bhakti-yoga*. *Bhakti-yoga* or Kṛṣṇa consciousness is the ultimate perfection of all *yogas*, as will be explained in the next verse. The Lord has confirmed herein the superiority of *yoga*, but He has not mentioned that it is better than *bhakti-yoga*. *Bhakti-yoga* is full spiritual knowledge, and as such, nothing can excel it. Asceticism without self-knowledge is imperfect. Empiric knowledge without surrender to the Supreme Lord is also imperfect. And fruitive work without Kṛṣṇa consciousness is a waste of time. Therefore, the most highly praised form of *yoga* performance mentioned here is *bhakti-yoga*, and this is still more clearly explained in the next verse.

TEXT 47

योगिनामपि सर्वेषां मद्गतेनान्तरात्मना ।
श्रद्धावान्भजते यो मां स मे युक्ततमो मतः ॥ ४७ ॥

yoginām api sarveṣāṁ
mad-gatenāntar-ātmanā
śraddhāvān bhajate yo māṁ
sa me yuktatamo mataḥ

yoginām—of all *yogīs*; *api*—also; *sarveṣām*—all types of; *mat-gatena*—abiding in Me; *antaḥ-ātmanā*—always thinking of Me within; *śraddhāvān*—in full faith; *bhajate*—renders transcendental loving service; *yaḥ*—one who; *mām*—Me (the Supreme Lord); *saḥ*—he; *me*—Mine; *yuktatamaḥ*—the greatest *yogī*; *mataḥ*—is considered.

TRANSLATION

And of all *yogīs*, he who always abides in Me with great faith, worshiping Me in transcendental loving service, is most intimately united with Me in yoga and is the highest of all.

PURPORT

The word *bhajete* is significant here. *Bhajete* has its root in the verb *bhaj*, which is used when there is need of service. The English word "worship" cannot be used in the same sense as *bhaja*. Worship means to adore, or to show respect and honor to the worthy one. But service with love and faith is especially meant for the Supreme Personality of Godhead. One can avoid worshiping a respectable man or a demigod and may be called discourteous, but one cannot avoid serving the Supreme Lord without being thoroughly condemned. Every living entity is part and parcel of the Supreme Personality of Godhead, and thus every living entity is intended to serve the Supreme Lord by his own constitution. Failing to do this, he falls down. The *Bhāgavatam* confirms this as follows:

> *ya eṣāṁ puruṣaṁ sākṣād ātma-prabhavam īśvaram*
> *na bhajanty avajānanti sthānād bhraṣṭā patanty adhaḥ*

"Anyone who does not render service and neglects his duty unto the Primeval Lord, who is the source of all living entities, will certainly fall down from his constitutional position."

In this verse also the word *bhajanti* is used. Therefore, *bhajanti* is applicable to the Supreme Lord only, whereas the word "worship" can be applied to demigods or to any other common living entity. The word *avajānanti*, used in this verse of *Śrīmad-Bhāgavatam*, is also found in the *Bhagavad-gītā*: *avajānanti māṁ mūḍhāḥ*: "Only the fools and rascals deride the Supreme Personality of Godhead Lord Kṛṣṇa." Such fools take it upon themselves to write commentaries on the *Bhagavad-gītā* without an attitude of service to the Lord. Consequently they cannot properly distinguish between the word *bhajanti* and the word "worship."

The culmination of all kinds of *yoga* practices lies in *bhakti-yoga*. All other *yogas* are but means to come to the point of *bhakti* in *bhakti-yoga*. *Yoga* actually means *bhakti-yoga*; all other *yogas* are progressions toward the destination of *bhakti-yoga*. From the beginning of *karma-yoga* to the end of *bhakti-yoga* is a long way to self-realization. *Karma-yoga*, without fruitive results, is the beginning of this path. When *karma-yoga* increases in knowledge and renunciation, the stage is called *jñāna-yoga*. When *jñāna-yoga* increases in meditation on the Supersoul by different physical processes, and the mind is on Him, it is called *aṣṭāṅga-yoga*. And, when one surpasses the *aṣṭāṅga-yoga* and comes to the point of the Supreme Personality of Godhead Kṛṣṇa, it is called *bhakti-yoga*, the culmination. Factually, *bhakti-yoga* is the ultimate goal, but to analyze *bhakti-yoga* minutely one has to understand these other *yogas*. The *yogī* who is progressive is therefore on the true path of eternal good fortune. One who sticks to a particular point and does not make further progress is called by that particular name: *karma-yogī, jñāna-yogī* or *dhyāna-yogī, rāja-yogī, haṭha-yogī*, etc.

If one is fortunate enough to come to the point of *bhakti-yoga*, it is to be understood that he has surpassed all the other *yogas*. Therefore, to become Kṛṣṇa conscious is the highest stage of *yoga*, just as, when we speak of Himalayan, we refer to the world's highest mountains, of which the highest peak, Mount Everest, is considered to be the culmination.

It is by great fortune that one comes to Kṛṣṇa consciousness on the path of *bhakti-yoga* to become well situated according to the Vedic direction. The ideal *yogī* concentrates his attention on Kṛṣṇa, who is called Śyāmasundara, who is as beautifully colored as a cloud, whose lotus-like face is as effulgent as the sun, whose dress is brilliant with jewels and whose body is flower garlanded. Illuminating all sides is His gorgeous luster, which is called the *brahmajyoti*. He incarnates in different forms such as Rāma, Nṛsiṁha, Varāha and Kṛṣṇa, the Supreme Personality of Godhead, and He descends like a human being, as the son of Mother Yaśodā, and He is known as Kṛṣṇa, Govinda and Vāsudeva. He is the perfect child, husband, friend and master, and He is full with all opulences and transcendental qualities. If one remains fully conscious of these features of the Lord, he is called the highest *yogī*.

This stage of highest perfection in *yoga* can be attained only by *bhakti-yoga*, as is confirmed in all Vedic literature:

> yasya deve parā bhaktir yathā deve tathā gurau.
> tasyaite kathitā hy arthāḥ prakāśante mahātmanaḥ.

"Only unto those great souls who have implicit faith in both the Lord and the spiritual master are all the imports of Vedic knowledge automatically revealed."

Bhaktir asya bhajanaṁ tadihāmutropādhi nairāsyenāmuṣmin manaḥ kalpanam; etad eva naiṣkarmyam. "*Bhakti* means devotional service to the Lord which is free from desire for material profit, either in this life or in the next. Devoid of such inclinations, one should fully absorb the mind in the Supreme. That is the purpose of *naiṣkarmya*."

These are some of the means for performance of *bhakti* or Kṛṣṇa consciousness, the highest perfectional stage of the *yoga* system.

Thus end the Bhaktivedanta Purports to the Sixth Chapter of the Śrīmad-Bhagavad-gītā in the matter of Sāṅkhya-yoga Brahma-vidyā.

CHAPTER SEVEN

Knowledge of the Absolute

TEXT 1

श्रीभगवानुवाच ।
मय्यासक्तमनाः पार्थ योगं युञ्जन्मदाश्रयः ।
असंशयं समग्रं मां यथा ज्ञास्यसि तच्छृणु ॥ १ ॥

śrī-bhagavān uvāca
mayy āsakta-manāḥ pārtha
yogaṁ yuñjan mad-āśrayaḥ
asaṁśayaṁ samagraṁ māṁ
yathā jñāsyasi tac chṛṇu

śrī bhagavān uvāca—the Supreme Lord said; *mayi*—unto Me; *āsakta-manāḥ*—mind attached; *pārtha*—O son of Pṛthā; *yogam*—self-realization; *yuñjan*—so practicing; *mat-āśrayaḥ*—in consciousness of Me (Kṛṣṇa consciousness); *asaṁśayam*—without doubt; *samagram*—completely; *mām*—unto Me; *yathā*—as much as; *jñāsyasi*—you can know; *tat*—that; *śṛnu*—try to hear.

TRANSLATION

Now hear, O son of Pṛthā [Arjuna], how by practicing yoga in full consciousness of Me, with mind attached to Me, you can know Me in full, free from doubt.

PURPORT

In this Seventh Chapter of *Bhagavad-gītā*, the nature of Kṛṣṇa consciousness is fully described. Kṛṣṇa is full in all opulences, and how He manifests such opulences is described herein. Also, four kinds of fortunate people who become attached to Kṛṣṇa, and four kinds of unfortunate people who never take to Kṛṣṇa are described in this chapter.

In the first six chapters of *Bhagavad-gītā*, the living entity has been described as nonmaterial spirit soul which is capable of elevating himself to self-realization by different types of *yogas*. At the end of the Sixth Chapter, it has been clearly stated that the steady concentration of the mind upon Kṛṣṇa, or in other words Kṛṣṇa consciousness, is the highest form of all *yoga*. By concentrating one's mind upon Kṛṣṇa, one is able to know the Absolute Truth completely, but not otherwise. Impersonal *brahmajyoti* or localized Paramātmā realization is not perfect knowledge of the Absolute Truth because it is partial. Full and scientific knowledge is Kṛṣṇa, and everything is revealed to the person in Kṛṣṇa consciousness. In complete Kṛṣṇa consciousness one knows that Kṛṣṇa is ultimate knowledge beyond any doubts. Different types of *yoga* are only steppingstones on the path of Kṛṣṇa consciousness. One who takes directly to Kṛṣṇa consciousness automatically knows about *brahmajyoti* and Paramātmā in full. By practice of Kṛṣṇa consciousness *yoga*, one can know everything in full—namely the Absolute Truth, the living entities, the material nature, and their manifestations with paraphernalia.

One should therefore begin *yoga* practice as directed in the last verse of the Sixth Chapter. Concentration of the mind upon Kṛṣṇa the Supreme is made possible by prescribed devotional service in nine different forms, of which *śravaṇam* is the first and most important. The Lord therefore says to Arjuna, "*tat śṛṇu*," or "Hear from Me." No one can be a greater authority than Kṛṣṇa, and therefore by hearing from Him one receives the greatest opportunity for progress in Kṛṣṇa consciousness. One has therefore to learn from Kṛṣṇa directly or from a pure devotee of Kṛṣṇa—and not from a nondevotee upstart, puffed up with academic education.

In the *Śrīmad-Bhāgavatam* this process of understanding Kṛṣṇa, the

Supreme Personality of Godhead, the Absolute Truth, is described in the Second Chapter of the First Canto as follows:

> śṛṇvatāṁ sva-kathāṁ kṛṣṇaḥ puṇya-śravaṇa-kīrtanaḥ
> hṛdyantaḥstho hy abhadrāṇi vidbunoti suhṛt satām.

> naṣṭa-prāyeṣv abhadreṣu nityaṁ bhāgavata-sevayā
> bhagavaty uttama-śloke bhaktir bhavati naiṣṭhikī.

> tadā rajas-tamo-bhāvāḥ kāma-lobhadayaś ca ye
> ceta etair anāviddhaṁ sthitaṁ sattve prasīdati.

> evam prasanna-manaso bhagavad-bhakti-yogataḥ
> bhagavat-tattva-vijñānaṁ mukta-saṅgasya jāyate.

> bhidyate hṛdaya-granthiś chidyante sarva-saṁśayāḥ
> kṣīyante cāsya karmāṇi dṛṣṭa evātmanīśvare.

"To hear about Kṛṣṇa from Vedic literatures, or to hear from Him directly through the *Bhagavad-gītā*, is itself righteous activity. And for one who hears about Kṛṣṇa, Lord Kṛṣṇa, who is dwelling in everyone's heart, acts as a best-wishing friend and purifies the devotee who constantly engages in hearing of Him. In this way, a devotee naturally develops his dormant transcendental knowledge. As he hears more about Kṛṣṇa from the *Bhāgavatam* and from the devotees, he becomes fixed in the devotional service of the Lord. By development of devotional service one becomes freed from the modes of passion and ignorance, and thus material lusts and avarice are diminished. When these impurities are wiped away, the candidate remains steady in his position of pure goodness, becomes enlivened by devotional service and understands the science of God perfectly. Thus *bhakti-yoga* severs the hard knot of material affection and enables one to come at once to the stage of '*asaṁśayaṁ samagram*,' understanding of the Supreme Absolute Truth Personality of Godhead." (*Bhāg.* 1.2.17-21)

Therefore only by hearing from Kṛṣṇa or from His devotee in Kṛṣṇa consciousness can one understand the science of Kṛṣṇa.

TEXT 2

ज्ञानं तेऽहं सविज्ञानमिदं वक्ष्याम्यशेषतः ।
यज्ज्ञात्वा नेह भूयोऽन्यज्ज्ञातव्यमवशिष्यते ॥ २ ॥

jñānaṁ te 'haṁ sa-vijñānam
idaṁ vakṣyāmy aśeṣataḥ
yaj jñātvā neha bhūyo 'nyaj
jñātavyam avaśiṣyate

jñānam—phenomenal knowledge; *te*—unto you; *aham*—I; *sa*—with; *vijñānam*—noumenal knowledge; *idam*—this; *vakṣyāmi*—shall explain; *aśeṣataḥ*—in full; *yat*—which; *jñātvā*—knowing; *na*—not; *iha*—in this world; *bhūyaḥ*—further; *anyat*—anything more; *jñātavyam*—knowable; *avaśiṣyate*—remains to be known.

TRANSLATION

I shall now declare unto you in full this knowledge both phenomenal and noumenal, by knowing which there shall remain nothing further to be known.

PURPORT

Complete knowledge includes knowledge of the phenomenal world and the spirit behind it. The source of both of them is transcendental knowledge. The Lord wants to explain the above-mentioned system of knowledge because Arjuna is Kṛṣṇa's confidential devotee and friend. In the beginning of the Fourth Chapter this explanation was given by the Lord, and it is again confirmed here: complete knowledge can be achieved only by the devotee of the Lord directly from the Lord in disciplic succession. Therefore one should be intelligent enough to know the source of all knowledge, who is the cause of all causes and the only object for meditation in all types of *yoga* practices. When the cause of all causes becomes known, then everything knowable becomes known, and nothing remains unknown. The *Vedas* say, "*yasmin vijñāte sarvam eva vijñatam bhavanti.*"

TEXT 3

मनुष्याणां सहस्रेषु कश्चिद्यतति सिद्धये ।
यततामपि सिद्धानां कश्चिन्मां वेत्ति तत्त्वतः ॥ ३ ॥

manuṣyāṇāṁ sahasreṣu
kaścid yatati siddhaye
yatatām api siddhānāṁ
kaścin māṁ vetti tattvataḥ

manuṣyāṇām—of men; *sahasreṣu*—out of many thousands; *kaścit*—some-one; *yatati*—endeavors; *siddhaye*—for perfection; *yatatām*—of those so endeavoring; *api*—indeed; *siddhānām*—of those who have achieved perfec-tion; *kaścit*—someone; *mām*—Me; *vetti*—does know; *tattvataḥ*—in fact.

TRANSLATION

Out of many thousands among men, one may endeavor for perfection, and of those who have achieved perfection, hardly one knows Me in truth.

PURPORT

There are various grades of men, and out of many thousands one may be sufficiently interested in transcendental realization to try to know what is the self, what is the body, and what is the Absolute Truth. Generally mankind is simply engaged in the animal propensities, namely eating, sleeping, defending and mating, and hardly anyone is interested in tran-scendental knowledge. The first six chapters of the *Gītā* are meant for those who are interested in transcendental knowledge, in understanding the self, the Superself and the process of realization by *jñāna-yoga*, *dhyāna-yoga*, and discrimination of the self from matter. However, Kṛṣṇa can only be known by persons who are in Kṛṣṇa consciousness. Other transcendental-ists may achieve impersonal Brahman realization, for this is easier than understanding Kṛṣṇa. Kṛṣṇa is the Supreme Person, but at the same time He is beyond the knowledge of Brahman and Paramātmā. The *yogīs* and *jñānīs* are confused in their attempts to understand Kṛṣṇa, although the greatest of the impersonalists, Śrīpāda Śaṅkarācārya, has admitted in his *Gītā* commentary that Kṛṣṇa is the Supreme Personality of Godhead. But his followers do not accept Kṛṣṇa as such, for it is very difficult to know Kṛṣṇa, even though one has transcendental realization of impersonal Brahman.

Kṛṣṇa is the Supreme Personality of Godhead, the cause of all causes, the primeval Lord Govinda. *Īśvaraḥ paramaḥ kṛṣṇaḥ sac-cid-ānanda-vigrahaḥ anādir ādir govindaḥ sarva-kāraṇa-kāraṇam.* It is very difficult for the nondevotees to know Him. Although nondevotees declare that the path of *bhakti* or devotional service is very easy, they cannot practice it. If the path of *bhakti* is so easy, as the nondevotee class of men proclaim, then why do they take up the difficult path? Actually the path of *bhakti* is not easy. The so-called path of *bhakti* practiced by unauthorized persons without knowledge of *bhakti* may be easy, but when it is practiced factually according to the rules and regulations, the speculative scholars and philosophers fall away from the path. Śrīla Rūpa Gosvāmī writes in his *Bhakti-rasāmṛta-sindhu*:

> *śruti-smṛti-purāṇādi-pañcarātra-vidhiṁ vinā*
> *aikāntikī harer bhaktir utpātāyaiva kalpate.*

"Devotional service of the Lord that ignores the authorized Vedic literatures like the *Upaniṣads*, *Purāṇas*, *Nārada-pañcarātra*, etc., is simply an unnecessary disturbance in society."

It is not possible for the Brahman realized impersonalist or the Paramātmā realized *yogī* to understand Kṛṣṇa, the Supreme Personality of Godhead as the son of mother Yaśodā or the charioteer of Arjuna. Even the great demigods are sometimes confused about Kṛṣṇa: "*muhyanti yat sūrayaḥ,*" "*māṁ tu veda na kaścana.*" "No one knows Me as I am," the Lord says. And if one does know Him, then "*sa mahātmā sudurlabhaḥ.*" "Such a great soul is very rare." Therefore unless one practices devotional service to the Lord, he cannot know Kṛṣṇa as He is (*tattvataḥ*), even though one is a great scholar or philosopher. Only the pure devotees can know something of the inconceivable transcendental qualities in Kṛṣṇa, in the cause of all causes, in His omnipotence and opulence, and in His wealth, fame, strength, beauty, knowledge and renunciation, because Kṛṣṇa is benevolently inclined to His devotees. He is the last word in Brahman realization, and the devotees alone can realize Him as He is. Therefore it is said:

> *ataḥ śrī-kṛṣṇa-nāmādi na bhaved grāhyam indriyaiḥ*
> *sevonmukhe hi jihvādau svayam eva sphuraty adaḥ*

"No one can understand Kṛṣṇa as He is by the blunt material senses. But He reveals Himself to the devotees, being pleased with them for their transcendental loving service unto Him." (*Padma Purāṇa*)

TEXT 4

भूमिरापोऽनलो वायुः खं मनो बुद्धिरेव च ।
अहंकार इतीयं मे भिन्ना प्रकृतिरष्टधा ॥ ४ ॥

> *bhūmir āpo 'nalo vāyuḥ*
> *kham mano buddhir eva ca*
> *ahaṅkāra itīyam me*
> *bhinnā prakṛtir aṣṭadhā*

bhūmiḥ—earth; *āpaḥ*—water; *analaḥ*—fire; *vāyuḥ*—air; *kham*—ether; *manaḥ*—mind; *buddhiḥ*—intelligence; *eva*—certainly; *ca*—and; *ahaṅkāraḥ*—false ego; *iti*—thus; *iyam*—all these; *me*—My; *bhinnā*—separated; *prakṛtiḥ*—energies; *aṣṭadhā*—total eight.

TRANSLATION

Earth, water, fire, air, ether, mind, intelligence and false ego—altogether these eight comprise My separated material energies.

PURPORT

The science of God analyzes the constitutional position of God and His diverse energies. Material nature is called *prakṛti*, or the energy of the Lord in His different *puruṣa* incarnations (expansions) as described in the *Svatvata Tantra*:

> *viṣṇos tu trīṇi rūpāṇi puruṣākhyāny atho viduḥ*
> *ekantu mahataḥ srasṭr dvitīyam tv aṇḍa-samsthitam*
> *tṛtīyam sarvabhūta-sthaṁ tāni jñātvā vimucyate*

"For material creation, Lord Kṛṣṇa's plenary expansion assumes three Viṣṇus. The first one, Mahā-Viṣṇu, creates the total material energy, known as *mahat-tattva*. The second, Garbhodakaśāyī Viṣṇu, enters into all the universes to create diversities in each of them. The third, Kṣīrodakaśāyī Viṣṇu, is diffused as the all-pervading Supersoul in all the universes and is known as Paramātmā, who is present even within the atoms. Anyone who knows these three Viṣṇu can be liberated from material entanglement."

This material world is a temporary manifestation of one of the energies of the Lord. All the activities of the material world are directed by these three Viṣṇu expansions of Lord Kṛṣṇa. These *Puruṣas* are called incarnations. Generally one who does not know the science of God (Kṛṣṇa) assumes that this material world is for the enjoyment of the living entities and that the living entities are the causes (*Puruṣas*), controllers and enjoyers of the material energy. According to *Bhagavad-gītā* this atheistic conclusion is false. In the verse under discussion it is stated that Kṛṣṇa is the original cause of the material manifestation. *Śrīmad-Bhāgavatam* also confirms this. The ingredients of the material manifestation are separated energies of the Lord. Even the *brahmajyoti*, which is the ultimate goal of the impersonalists, is a spiritual energy manifested in the spiritual sky. There are no spiritual diversities in *brahmajyoti* as there are in the Vaikuṇṭhalokas, and the impersonalist accepts this *brahmajyoti* as the ultimate eternal goal. The Paramātmā manifestation is also a temporary all-pervasive aspect of the Kṣīrodakaśāyī Viṣṇu. The Paramātmā manifestation is not eternal in the spiritual world. Therefore the factual Absolute Truth is the Supreme Personality of Godhead Kṛṣṇa. He is the complete energetic person, and He possesses different separated and internal energies.

In the material energy, the principal manifestations are eight, as above mentioned. Out of these, the first five manifestations, namely earth, water, fire, air and sky, are called the five gigantic creations or the gross creations, within which the five sense objects are included. They are the manifestations of physical sound, touch, form, taste and smell. Material science comprises these ten items and nothing more. But the other three items, namely mind, intelligence and false ego, are neglected by the materialists. Philosophers who deal with mental activities are also not perfect in knowledge because they do not know the ultimate source, Kṛṣṇa. The false ego—"I am," and "It is mine," which constitute the basic principle of material existence—includes ten sense organs for material activities. Intelligence refers to the total material creation, called the *mahat-tattva*. Therefore from the eight separated energies of the Lord are manifest the twenty-four elements of the material world, which are the subject matter of *sāṅkhya* atheistic philosophy; they are originally offshoots from Kṛṣṇa's energies and are separated from Him, but atheistic *sāṅkhya* philosophers with a poor fund of knowledge do not know Kṛṣṇa as the cause of all causes. The subject matter for discussion in the *sāṅkhya* philosophy is only the manifestation of the external energy of Kṛṣṇa, as it is described in the *Bhagavad-gītā*.

TEXT 5

अपरेयमितस्त्वन्यां प्रकृतिं विद्धि मे पराम् ।
जीवभूतां महाबाहो ययेदं धार्यते जगत् ॥ ५ ॥

apareyam itas tv anyāṁ
prakṛtiṁ viddhi me parām
jīva-bhūtāṁ mahā-bāho
yayedaṁ dhāryate jagat

aparā—inferior; *iyam*—this; *itaḥ*—besides this; *tu*—but; *anyām*—another; *prakṛtim*—energy; *viddhi*—just try to understand; *me*—My; *parām*—superior; *jīva-bhūtām*—the living entities; *mahā-bāho*—O mighty-armed one; *yayā*—by whom; *idam*—this; *dhāryate*—being utilized or exploited; *jagat*—the material world.

TRANSLATION

Besides this inferior nature, O mighty-armed Arjuna, there is a superior energy of Mine, which are all living entities who are struggling with material nature and are sustaining the universe.

PURPORT

Here it is clearly mentioned that living entities belong to the superior nature (or energy) of the Supreme Lord. The inferior energy is matter manifested in different elements, namely earth, water, fire, air, ether, mind, intelligence and false ego. Both forms of material nature, namely gross (earth, etc.) and subtle (mind, etc.), are products of the inferior energy. The living entities, who are exploiting these inferior energies for different purposes, are the superior energy of the Supreme Lord, and it is due to this energy that the entire material world functions. The cosmic manifestation has no power to act unless it is moved by the superior energy, the living entity. Energies are always controlled by the energetic, and therefore living entities are always controlled by the Lord—they have no independent existence. They are never equally powerful, as unintelligent men think. The distinction between the living entities and the Lord is described in *Śrīmad-Bhāgavatam* as follows (10.87.30):

> *aparimitā dhruvās tanubhṛto yadi sarva-gatās*
> *tarhiṁ na śāsyateti niyamo dhruva netarathā*
> *ajani ca yanmayaṁ tad avimucya niyantṛ*
> *bhavet samam anujānatāṁ yad-amataṁ mata-duṣṭatayā*

"O Supreme Eternal! If the embodied living entities were eternal and all-pervading like You, then they would not be under Your control. But if the living entities are accepted as minute energies of Your Lordship, then they are at once subject to Your supreme control. Therefore real liberation entails surrender by the living entities to Your control, and that surrender will make them happy. In that constitutional position only can they be controllers. Therefore, men with limited knowledge who advocate the monistic theory that God and the living entities are equal in all respects are actually misleading themselves and others."

The Supreme Lord Kṛṣṇa is the only controller, and all living entities are controlled by Him. These living entities are His superior energy because the quality of their existence is one and the same with the Supreme, but they are never equal to the Lord in quantity of power. While exploiting the gross and subtle inferior energy (matter), the superior energy (the living entity) forgets his real spiritual mind and intelligence. This forgetfulness is due to the influence of matter upon the living entity. But when the living entity becomes free from the influence of the illusory material energy, he attains the stage called *mukti*, or liberation. The false ego, under the influence of material illusion, thinks, "I am matter, and material acquisitions are mine." His actual position is realized when he is liberated from all material ideas, including the conception of his becoming one in all respects with God. Therefore one may conclude that the *Gītā* confirms the living entity to be only one of the multi-energies of Kṛṣṇa; and when this energy is freed from material contamination, it becomes fully Kṛṣṇa conscious, or liberated.

TEXT 6

एतद्योनीनि भूतानि सर्वाणीत्युपधारय ।
अहं कृत्स्नस्य जगतः प्रभवः प्रलयस्तथा ॥ ६ ॥

etad-yonīni bhūtāni
sarvāṇīty upadhāraya
ahaṁ kṛtsnasya jagataḥ
prabhavaḥ pralayas tathā

etat—these two natures; yonīni—source of birth; bhūtāni—everything created; sarvāṇi—all; iti—thus; upadhāraya—know; aham—I; kṛtsnasya—all-inclusive; jagataḥ—of the world; prabhavaḥ—source of manifestation; pralayaḥ—annihilation; tathā—as well as.

TRANSLATION

Of all that is material and all that is spiritual in this world, know for certain that I am both its origin and dissolution.

PURPORT

Everything that exists is a product of matter and spirit. Spirit is the basic field of creation, and matter is created by spirit. Spirit is not created at a certain stage of material development. Rather, this material world is manifested only on the basis of spiritual energy. This material body is developed because spirit is present within matter; a child grows gradually to boyhood and then to manhood because of that superior energy, spirit soul, being present. Similarly, the entire cosmic manifestation of the gigantic universe is developed because of the presence of the Supersoul, Viṣṇu. Therefore spirit and matter, which combine together to manifest this gigantic universal form, are originally two energies of the Lord, and consequently the Lord is the original cause of everything. A fragmental part and parcel of the Lord, namely, the living entity, may by manipulation of material energy construct a skyscraper, factory or city, but he cannot create matter out of nothing, and he certainly cannot construct a planet or a universe. The cause of the universe is the Supersoul, Kṛṣṇa, the supreme creator of all individual souls and the original cause of all causes, as the *Kaṭha Upaniṣad* confirms: *nityo nityānāṁ cetanaś cetanānām.*

TEXT 7

मत्तः परतरं नान्यत्किंचिदस्ति धनंजय ।
मयि सर्वमिदं प्रोतं सूत्रे मणिगणा इव ॥ ७ ॥

mattaḥ parataraṁ nānyat
kiñcid asti dhanañjaya
mayi sarvam idaṁ protaṁ
sūtre maṇi-gaṇā iva

mattaḥ—beyond Myself; *parataram*—superior; *na*—not; *anyat*—anything else; *kiñcit*—something; *asti*—there is; *dhanañjaya*—O conqueror of wealth; *mayi*—in Me; *sarvam*—all that be; *idam*—which we see; *protam*—strung; *sūtre*—on a thread; *maṇi-gaṇāḥ*—pearls; *iva*—likened.

TRANSLATION

O conqueror of wealth [Arjuna], there is no Truth superior to Me. Everything rests upon Me, as pearls are strung on a thread.

PURPORT

There is a common controversy over whether the Supreme Absolute Truth is personal or impersonal. As far as *Bhagavad-gītā* is concerned, the Absolute Truth is the Personality of Godhead Śrī Kṛṣṇa, and this is confirmed in every step. In this verse, in particular, it is stressed that the Absolute Truth is a person. That the Personality of Godhead is the Supreme Absolute Truth is also the affirmation of the *Brahma-saṁhitā*: *īśvaraḥ paramaḥ kṛṣṇaḥ sac-cid-ānanda-vigrahaḥ;* that is, the Supreme Absolute Truth Personality of Godhead is Lord Kṛṣṇa, who is the primeval Lord, the reservoir of all pleasure, Govinda, and the eternal form of complete bliss and knowledge. These authorities leave no doubt that the Absolute Truth is the Supreme Person, the cause of all causes. The impersonalist, however, argues on the strength of the Vedic version given in the *Śvetāśvatara Upaniṣad: tato yad uttarataraṁ tad arūpam anāmayaṁ ya etad vidur amṛtās te bhavanti athetare duḥkham evāpi yanti.* "In the material world Brahmā, the primeval living entity within the universe, is understood to be the supreme amongst the demigods, human beings and lower animals. But beyond Brahmā there is the Transcendence who has no material form and is free from all material contaminations. Anyone who can know Him also becomes transcendental, but those who do not know Him suffer the miseries of the material world."

The impersonalist puts more stress on the word *arūpam.* But this *arūpam* is not impersonal. It indicates the transcendental form of eternity, bliss and knowledge as described in the *Brahma-saṁhitā* quoted above. Other verses in the *Śvetāśvatara Upaniṣad* substantiate this as follows:

vedāham etaṁ puruṣaṁ mahāntam āditya-varṇaṁ tamasaḥ parastāt
tam eva vidvān amṛta iha bhavati nānyaḥ panthā vidyate ayanāya
yasmāt param nāparam asti kiñcid yasmānnāṇīyo na jyāyo 'sti kiñcit

"I know that Supreme Personality of Godhead who is transcendental to all material conceptions of darkness. Only he who knows Him can transcend the bonds of birth and death. There is no way for liberation other than this knowledge of that Supreme Person.

"There is no truth superior to that Supreme Person because He is the supermost. He is smaller than the smallest, and He is greater than the greatest. He is situated as a silent tree, and He illumines the transcendental sky, and as a tree spreads its roots, He spreads His extensive energies."

From these verses one concludes that the Supreme Absolute Truth is the Supreme Personality of Godhead who is all-pervading by His multi-energies, both material and spiritual.

TEXT 8

रसोऽहमप्सु कौन्तेय प्रभास्मि शशिसूर्ययोः ।
प्रणवः सर्ववेदेषु शब्दः खे पौरुषं नृषु ॥ ८ ॥

raso 'ham apsu kaunteya
prabhāsmi śaśi-sūryayoḥ
praṇavaḥ sarva-vedeṣu
śabdaḥ khe pauruṣaṁ nṛṣu

rasaḥ—taste; *aham*—I; *apsu*—in water; *kaunteya*—O son of Kuntī; *prabhā asmi*—I am the light; *śaśi-sūryayoḥ*—in the sun and the moon; *praṇavaḥ*—the three letters A.U.M.; *sarva*—in all; *vedeṣu*—in the *Vedas*; *śabdaḥ*—sound vibration; *khe*—in the ether; *pauruṣam*—ability; *nṛṣu*—in man.

TRANSLATION

O son of Kuntī [Arjuna], I am the taste of water, the light of the sun and the moon, the syllable om in the Vedic mantras; I am the sound in ether and ability in man.

PURPORT

This verse explains how the Lord is all-pervasive by His diverse material and spiritual energies. The Supreme Lord can be preliminarily perceived by His different energies, and in this way He is realized impersonally. As the demigod in the sun is a person and is perceived by his all-pervading energy, the sunshine, similarly, the Lord, although in His eternal abode, is perceived by His all-pervading, diffusive energies. The taste of water is the active principle of water. No one likes to drink sea water because the pure taste of water is mixed with salt. Attraction for water depends on the purity of the taste, and this pure taste is one of the energies of the Lord. The impersonalist perceives the presence of the Lord in water by its taste, and the personalist also glorifies the Lord for His kindly supplying water to quench man's thirst. That is the way of perceiving the Supreme. Practically speaking, there is no conflict between personalism and impersonalism. One who knows God knows that the impersonal conception and personal conception are simultaneously present in everything and that there is no contradiction. Therefore Lord Caitanya established His sublime doctrine: *acintya-bheda* and *abheda-tattvam*-simultaneously one and different.

The light of the sun and the moon is also originally emanating from the *brahmajyoti*, which is the impersonal effulgence of the Lord. Similarly *praṇava* or the *omkāra* transcendental sound used in the beginning of every Vedic hymn to address the Supreme Lord also emanates from Him. Because the impersonalists are very much afraid of addressing the Supreme Lord Kṛṣṇa by His innumerable names, they prefer to vibrate the transcendental sound *omkāra*. But they do not realize that *omkāra* is the sound representation of Kṛṣṇa. The jurisdiction of Kṛṣṇa consciousness extends everywhere, and one who knows Kṛṣṇa consciousness is blessed. Those who do not know Kṛṣṇa are in illusion, and so knowledge of Kṛṣṇa is liberation, and ignorance of Him is bondage.

TEXT 9

पुण्यो गन्धः पृथिव्यां च तेजश्चास्मि विभावसौ ।
जीवनं सर्वभूतेषु तपश्चास्मि तपस्विषु ॥ ९ ॥

puṇyo gandhaḥ pṛthivyāṁ ca
tejaś cāsmi vibhāvasau
jīvanaṁ sarva-bhūteṣu
tapaś cāsmi tapasviṣu

puṇyaḥ—original; *gandhaḥ*—fragrance; *pṛthivyām*—in the earth; *ca*—also; *tejaḥ*—temperature; *ca*—also; *asmi*—I am; *vibhāvasau*—in the fire; *jīvanam*—life; *sarva*—all; *bhūteṣu*—living entities; *tapaḥ*—penance; *ca*—also; *asmi*—I am; *tapasviṣu*—in those who practice penance.

TRANSLATION

I am the original fragrance of the earth, and I am the heat in fire. I am the life of all that lives, and I am the penances of all ascetics.

PURPORT

Punya means that which is not decomposed; *punya* is original. Everything in the material world has a certain flavor or fragrance, as the flavor and fragrance in a flower, or in the earth, in water, in fire, in air, etc. The uncontaminated flavor, the original flavor, which permeates everything, is Kṛṣṇa. Similarly, everything has a particular original taste, and this taste can be changed by the mixture of chemicals. So everything original has some smell, some fragrance, and some taste. *Vibhāva* means fire. Without fire we cannot run factories, we cannot cook, etc., and that fire is Kṛṣṇa. The heat in the fire is Kṛṣṇa. According to Vedic medicine, indigestion is due to a low temperature in the belly. So even for digestion fire is needed. In Kṛṣṇa consciousness we become aware that earth, water, fire, air and every active principle, all chemicals and all material elements are due to Kṛṣṇa. The duration of man's life is also due to Kṛṣṇa. Therefore by the grace of Kṛṣṇa, man can prolong his life or diminish it. So Kṛṣṇa consciousness is active in every sphere.

TEXT 10

बीजं मां सर्वभूतानां विद्धि पार्थ सनातनम् ।
बुद्धिर्बुद्धिमतामस्मि तेजस्तेजस्विनामहम् ॥ १० ॥

bījaṁ māṁ sarva-bhūtānāṁ
viddhi pārtha sanātanam
buddhir buddhimatām asmi
tejas tejasvinām aham

bījam—seed; *mām*—unto Me; *sarva-bhūtānām*—of all living entities; *viddhi*—try to understand; *pārtha*—O son of Pṛthā; *sanātanam*—original, eternal; *buddhiḥ*—intelligence; *buddhimatām*—of the intelligent; *asmi*—I am; *tejaḥ*—prowess; *tejasvinām*—of the powerful; *aham*—I am.

TRANSLATION

O son of Pṛthā, know that I am the original seed of all existences, the intelligence of the intelligent, and the prowess of all powerful men.

PURPORT

Bījam means seed; Kṛṣṇa is the seed of everything. In contact with material nature, the seed fructifies into various living entities, movable and inert. Birds, beasts, men and many other living creatures are moving living entities; trees and plants, however, are inert-they cannot move, but only stand. Every entity is contained within the scope of 8,400,000 species of life; some of them are moving and some of them are inert. In all cases, however, the seed of their life is Kṛṣṇa. As stated in Vedic literature, Brahman, or the Supreme Absolute Truth, is that from which everything is emanating. Kṛṣṇa is Parabrahman, the Supreme Spirit. Brahman is impersonal and Parabrahman is personal. Impersonal Brahman is situated in the personal aspect-that is stated in *Bhagavad-gītā*. Therefore, originally, Kṛṣṇa is the source of everything. He is the root. As the root of a tree maintains the whole tree, Kṛṣṇa, being the original root of all things, maintains everything in this material manifestation. This is also confirmed in the Vedic literature. *Yato vā imāni bhūtāni jāyante.* "The Supreme Absolute Truth is that from which everything is born." He is the prime eternal among all eternals. He is the supreme living entity of all living entities, and He alone is maintaining all life. Kṛṣṇa also says that He is the root of all intelligence. Unless a person is intelligent he cannot understand the Supreme Personality of Godhead, Kṛṣṇa.

TEXT 11

बलं बलवतां चाहं कामरागविवर्जितम् ।
धर्माविरुद्धो भूतेषु कामोऽस्मि भरतर्षभ ॥ ११ ॥

balaṁ balavatāṁ cāhaṁ
kāma-rāga-vivarjitam
dharmāviruddho bhūteṣu
kāmo 'smi bharatarṣabha

balam—strength; *balavatām*—of the strong; *ca*—and; *aham*—I am; *kāma*—passion; *rāga*—attachment; *vivarjitam*—devoid of; *dharma-aviruddha*—not against the religious principles; *bhūteṣu*—in all beings; *kāmaḥ*—sex-life; *asmi*—I am; *bharatarṣabha*—O lord of the Bhāratas.

TRANSLATION

I am the strength of the strong, devoid of passion and desire. I am sex life which is not contrary to religious principles, O Lord of the Bhāratas [Arjuna].

PURPORT

The strong man's strength should be applied to protect the weak, not for personal aggression. Similarly, sex life, according to religious principles (dharma), should be for the propagation of children, not otherwise. The responsibility of parents is then to make their offspring Kṛṣṇa conscious.

TEXT 12

ये चैव सात्त्विका भावा राजसास्तामसाश्च ये ।
मत्त एवेति तान्विद्धि न त्वहं तेषु ते मयि ॥ १२ ॥

ye caiva sāttvikā bhāvā
rājasās tāmasāś ca ye
matta eveti tān viddhi
na tv ahaṁ teṣu te mayi

ye—all those; ca—and; eva—certainly; sāttvikāḥ—in goodness; bhāvāḥ—states of being; rājasāḥ—mode of passion; tāmasāḥ—mode of ignorance; ca—also; ye—although; mattaḥ—from Me; eva—certainly; iti—thus; tān—those; viddhi—try to know; na—not; tu—but; aham—I; teṣu—in those; te—they; mayi—unto Me.

TRANSLATION

All states of being—be they of goodness, passion or ignorance—are manifested by My energy. I am, in one sense, everything—but I am independent. I am not under the modes of this material nature.

PURPORT

All material activities in the world are being conducted under the three modes of material nature. Although these material modes of nature are emanations from the Supreme Lord, Kṛṣṇa, He is not subject to them. For instance, under the state laws one may be punished, but the king, the lawmaker, is not subject to that law. Similarly, all the modes of material nature—goodness, passion and ignorance—are emanations from the Supreme Lord Kṛṣṇa, but Kṛṣṇa is not subject to material nature. Therefore He is *nirguṇa*, which means that these *guṇas*, or modes, although issuing from Him, do not affect Him. That is one of the special characteristics of Bhagavān, or the Supreme Personality of Godhead.

TEXT 13

त्रिभिर्गुणमयैर्भावैरेभिः सर्वमिदं जगत् ।
मोहितं नाभिजानाति मामेभ्यः परमव्ययम् ॥ १३ ॥

tribhir guṇa-mayair bhāvair
ebhiḥ sarvam idaṁ jagat
mohitaṁ nābhijānāti
mām ebhyaḥ param avyayam

tribhiḥ—three; *guṇamayaiḥ*—by the three *guṇas*; *bhāvaiḥ*—state of being; *ebhiḥ*—all this; *sarvam*—the whole world; *idam*—in this world; *jagat*—universe; *mohitam*—deluded; *na abhijānāti*—do not know; *mām*—unto Me; *ebhyaḥ*—above these; *param*—the Supreme; *avyayam*—inexhaustible.

TRANSLATION

Deluded by the three modes [goodness, passion and ignorance], the whole world does not know Me who am above the modes and inexhaustible.

PURPORT

The whole world is enchanted by three modes of material nature. Those who are bewildered by these three modes cannot understand that transcendental to this material nature is the Supreme Lord, Kṛṣṇa. In this material world everyone is under the influence of these three *guṇas* and is thus bewildered.

By nature living entities have particular types of body and particular types of psychic and biological activities accordingly. There are four classes of men functioning in the three material modes of nature. Those who are purely in the mode of goodness are called *brāhmaṇas*. Those who are purely in the mode of passion are called *kṣatriyas*. Those who are in the modes of both passion and ignorance are called *vaiśyas*. Those who are completely in ignorance are called *śūdras*. And those who are less than that are animals or animal life. However, these designations are not permanent. I may either be a *brāhmaṇa, kṣatriya, vaiśya* or whatever-in any case, this life is temporary. But although life is temporary and we do not know what we are going to be in the next life, still, by the spell of this illusory energy, we consider ourselves in the light of this bodily conception of life, and we thus think that we are American, Indian, Russian or *brāhmaṇa*, Hindu, Muslim, etc. And if we become entangled with the modes of material nature, then we forget the Supreme Personality of Godhead who is behind all these modes. So Lord Kṛṣṇa says that men, deluded by these three modes of nature, do not understand that behind the material background is the Supreme Godhead.

There are many different kinds of living entities-human beings, demigods, animals, etc.-and each and every one of them is under the influence of material nature, and all of them have forgotten the transcendent Personality of Godhead. Those who are in the modes of passion and ignorance, and even those who are in the mode of goodness, cannot go beyond the impersonal Brahman conception of the Absolute Truth. They are bewildered before the Supreme Lord in His personal feature, which possesses all beauty, opulence, knowledge, strength, fame and renunciation. When even those who are in goodness cannot understand, what hope is there for those in passion and ignorance? Kṛṣṇa consciousness is transcendental to all these three modes of material nature, and those who are truly established in Kṛṣṇa consciousness are actually liberated.

TEXT 14

दैवी ह्येषा गुणमयी मम माया दुरत्यया ।
मामेव ये प्रपद्यन्ते मायामेतां तरन्ति ते ॥ १४ ॥

daivī hy eṣā guṇa-mayī
mama māyā duratyayā
mām eva ye prapadyante
māyām etāṁ taranti te

daivī—transcendental; *hi*—certainly; *eṣā*—this; *guṇamayī*—consisting of the three modes of material nature; *mama*—My; *māyā*—energy; *duratyayā*—very difficult to overcome; *mām*—unto Me; *eva*—certainly; *ye*—those; *prapadyante*—surrender; *māyām etām*—this illusory energy; *taranti*—overcome; *te*—they.

TRANSLATION

This divine energy of Mine, consisting of the three modes of material nature, is difficult to overcome. But those who have surrendered unto Me can easily cross beyond it.

PURPORT

The Supreme Personality of Godhead has innumerable energies, and all these energies are divine. Although the living entities are part of His energies and are therefore divine, due to contact with material energy, their original superior power is covered. Being thus covered by material energy, one cannot possibly overcome its influence. As previously stated, both the material and spiritual natures, being emanations from the Supreme Personality of Godhead, are eternal. The living entities belong to the eternal superior nature of the Lord, but due to contamination by the inferior nature, matter, their illusion is also eternal. The conditioned soul is therefore called *nitya-baddha*, or eternally conditioned. No one can trace out the history of his becoming conditioned at a certain date in material history. Consequently, his release from the clutches of material nature is very difficult, even though that material nature is an inferior energy, because material energy is ultimately conducted by the supreme will, which the living entity cannot overcome. Inferior material nature is defined herein as divine nature due to its divine connection and movement by the divine will. Being conducted by divine will, material nature, although inferior, acts so wonderfully in the construction and destruction of the cosmic manifestation. The *Vedas* confirm this as follows:

māyāṁ tu prakṛtiṁ vidyān māyinaṁ tu maheśvaram.

"Although *māyā* [illusion] is false or temporary, the background of *māyā* is the supreme magician, the Personality of Godhead, who is Maheśvara, the supreme controller."

Another meaning of *guṇa* is rope; it is to be understood that the conditioned soul is tightly tied by the ropes of illusion. A man bound by the hands and feet cannot free himself-he must be helped by a person who is unbound. Because the bound cannot help the bound, the rescuer must be liberated. Therefore, only Lord Kṛṣṇa, or His bona fide representative the spiritual master, can release the conditioned soul. Without such superior help, one cannot be freed from the bondage of material nature. Devotional service, or Kṛṣṇa consciousness, can help one gain such release. Kṛṣṇa, being the Lord of illusory energy, can order this insurmountable energy to release the conditioned soul. He orders this release out of His causeless mercy on the surrendered soul and out of His paternal affection for the living entity who is originally a beloved son of the Lord. Therefore surrender unto the lotus feet of the Lord is the only means to get free from the clutches of the stringent material nature.

The words *mām eva* are also significant. *Mām* means unto Kṛṣṇa (Viṣṇu) only, and not Brahmā or Śiva. Although Brahmā and Śiva are greatly elevated and are almost on the level of Viṣṇu, it is not possible for such incarnations of *rājo-guṇa* (passion) and *tamo-guṇa* (ignorance) to release the conditioned soul from the clutches of *māyā*. In other words, both Brahmā and Śiva are also under the influence of *māyā*. Only Viṣṇu is the master of *māyā*; therefore He can alone give release to the conditioned soul. The *Vedas* confirm this in the phrase *tvam eva viditvā* or "Freedom is possible only by understanding Kṛṣṇa." Even Lord Śiva affirms that liberation can be achieved only by the mercy of Viṣṇu. Lord Śiva says:

mukti-pradātā sarveṣāṁ viṣṇur eva na saṁśayaḥ.

"There is no doubt that Viṣṇu is the deliverer of liberation for everyone.

TEXT 15

न मां दुष्कृतिनो मूढाः प्रपद्यन्ते नराधमाः ।
माययापहृतज्ञाना आसुरं भावमाश्रिताः ॥ १५ ॥

*na māṁ duṣkṛtino mūḍhāḥ
prapadyante narādhamāḥ
māyayāpahṛta-jñānā
āsuraṁ bhāvam āśritāḥ*

na—not; *mām*—unto Me; *duṣkṛtinaḥ*—miscreants; *mūḍhāḥ*—foolish; *prapadyante*—surrender; *narādhamāḥ*—lowest among mankind; *māyayā*—

by the illusory energy; *apahṛta*—stolen by illusion; *jñānāḥ*—knowledge; *asuram*—demonic; *bhāvam*—nature; *āśritāḥ*—accepting.

TRANSLATION

Those miscreants who are grossly foolish, lowest among mankind, whose knowledge is stolen by illusion, and who partake of the atheistic nature of demons, do not surrender unto Me.

PURPORT

It is said in *Bhagavad-gītā* that simply by surrendering oneself unto the lotus feet of the Supreme Personality Kṛṣṇa, one can surmount the stringent laws of material nature. At this point a question arises: How is it that educated philosophers, scientists, businessmen, administrators and all the leaders of ordinary men do not surrender to the lotus feet of Śrī Kṛṣṇa, the all-powerful Personality of Godhead? *Mukti*, or liberation from the laws of material nature, is sought by the leaders of mankind in different ways and with great plans and perseverance for a great many years and births. But if that liberation is possible by simply surrendering unto the lotus feet of the Supreme Personality of Godhead, then why don't these intelligent and hard-working leaders adopt this simple method?

The *Gītā* answers this question very frankly. Those really learned leaders of society like Brahmā, Śiva, Kapila, the Kumāras, Manu, Vyāsa, Devala, Asita, Janaka, Prahlāda, Bali, and later on Madhvācārya, Rāmānujācārya, Śrī Caitanya and many others—who are faithful philosophers, politicians, educators, scientists, etc.—surrender to the lotus feet of the Supreme Person, the all-powerful authority. Those who are not actually philosophers, scientists, educators, administrators, etc., but who pose themselves as such for material gain, do not accept the plan or path of the Supreme Lord. They have no idea of God; they simply manufacture their own worldly plans and consequently complicate the problems of material existence in their vain attempts to solve them. Because material energy (nature) is so powerful, it can resist the unauthorized plans of the atheists and baffle the knowledge of "planning commissions."

The atheistic plan-makers are described herein by the word *duṣkṛtina*, or "miscreants." *Kṛtina* means one who has performed meritorious work. The atheist planmaker is sometimes very intelligent and meritorious also, because any gigantic plan, good or bad, must take intelligence to execute. But because the atheist's brain is improperly utilized in opposing the plan of the Supreme Lord, the atheistic planmaker is called *duṣkṛtina*, which indicates that his intelligence and efforts are misdirected.

In the *Gītā* it is clearly mentioned that material energy works fully under the direction of the Supreme Lord. It has no independant authority. It works as the shadow moves, in accordance with the movements of the object. But still material energy is very powerful, and the atheist, due to his godless temperament, cannot know how it works; nor can he know the plan of the Supreme Lord. Under illusion and the modes of passion and ignorance, all his plans are baffled, as in the case of Hiraṇyakaśipu and Rāvaṇa, whose plans were smashed to dust although they were both materially learned as scientists, philosophers, administrators and educators. These *duṣkṛtinas*, or miscreants, are of four different patterns, as outlined below:

(1) The *mūḍhas* are those who are grossly foolish, like hard-working beasts of burden. They want to enjoy the fruits of their labor by themselves, and so do not want to part with them for the Supreme. The typical example of the beast of burden is the ass. This humble beast is made to work very hard by his master. The ass does not really know for whom he works so hard day and night. He remains satisfied by filling his stomach with a bundle of grass, sleeping for a while under fear of being beaten by his master, and satisfying his sex appetite at the risk of being repeatedly kicked by the opposite party. The ass sings poetry and philosophy sometimes, but this braying only disturbs others. This is the position of the foolish fruitive worker who does not know for whom he should work. He does not know that *karma* (action) is meant for *yajña* (sacrifice).

Most often, those who work very hard day and night to clear the burden of self-created duties say that they have no time to hear of the immortality of the living being. To such *mūḍhas*, material gains, which are destructible, are life's all in all-despite the fact that the *mūḍhas* enjoy only a very small fraction of the fruit of labor. Sometimes they spend sleepless days and nights for fruitive gain, and although they may have ulcers or indigestion, they are satisfied with practically no food; they are simply absorbed in working hard day and night for the benefit of illusory masters. Ignorant of their real master, the foolish workers waste their valuable time serving mammon. Unfortunately, they never surrender to the supreme master of all masters, nor do they take time to hear of Him from the proper sources. The swine who eat the soil do not care to accept sweetmeats made of sugar and ghee. Similarly, the foolish worker will untiringly continue to hear of the sense-enjoyable tidings of the flickering mundane force that moves the material world.

(2) Another class of *duṣkṛtina*, or miscreant, is called the *narādhama*, or the lowest of mankind. *Nara* means human being, and *adhama* means the lowest. Out of the 8,400,000 different species of living beings, there are 400,000 human species. Out of these there are numerous lower forms of human life that are mostly uncivilized. The civilized human beings are those who have regulated principles of social, political and religious life. Those who are socially and politically developed, but who have no religious principles, must be considered *narādhamas*. Nor is religion without God religion, because the purpose of following religious principles is to know the Supreme Truth and man's relation with Him. In the *Gītā* the Personality of Godhead clearly states that there is no authority above Him and that He is the Supreme Truth. The civilized form of human life is meant for man's *reviving the lost consciousness* of his eternal relation with the Supreme Truth, the Personality of Godhead Śrī Kṛṣṇa, who is all-powerful. Whoever loses this chance is classified as a *narādhama*. We get information from revealed scriptures that when the baby is in the mother's womb (an extremely uncomfortable situation) he prays to God for deliverance and promises to worship Him alone as soon as he gets out. To pray to God when he is in difficulty is a natural instinct in every living being because he is eternally related with God. But after his deliverance, the child forgets the difficulties of birth and forgets his deliverer also, being influenced by *māyā*, the illusory energy.

It is the duty of the guardians of children to revive the divine consciousness dormant in them. The ten processes of reformatory ceremonies, as enjoined in the *Manu-smṛti*, which is the guide to religious principles, are meant for reviving God consciousness in the system of *varṇāśrama*. However, no process is strictly followed now in any part of the world, and therefore 99.9 percent of the population is *narādhama*.

When the whole population becomes *narādhama*, naturally all their so-called education is made null and void by the all-powerful energy of physical nature. According to the standard of the *Gītā*, a learned man is he who sees on equal terms the learned *brāhmaṇa*, the dog, the cow, the elephant and the dog-eater. That is the vision of a true devotee. Śrī Nityānanda Prabhu, who is the incarnation of Godhead as divine master, delivered the typical *narādhamas*, the brothers Jagai and Madhai, and showed how the mercy of a real devotee is bestowed upon the lowest of mankind. So the *narādhama* who is condemned by the Personality of Godhead can again revive his spiritual consciousness only by the mercy of a devotee.

Śrī Caitanya Mahāprabhu, in propagating the *bhāgavata-dharma* or activities of the devotees, has recommended that people submissively hear the message of the Personality of Godhead. The essence of this message is *Bhagavad-gītā*. The lowest amongst human beings can be delivered by this submissive hearing process only, but unfortunately they even deny giving an aural reception to these messages, and what to speak of surrendering to the will of the Supreme Lord? *Narādhamas*, or the lowest of mankind, willfully neglect the prime duty of the human being.

(3) The next class of *duṣkṛtina* is called *māyayāpahṛta-jñāna*, or those persons whose erudite knowledge has been nullified by the influence of illusory material energy. They are mostly very learned fellows—great philosophers, poets, literati, scientists, etc.—but the illusory energy misguides them, and therefore they disobey the Supreme Lord.

There are a great number of *māyayāpahṛta-jñānas* at the present moment, even amongst the scholars of the *Gītā*. In the *Gītā*, in plain and simple language, it is stated that Śrī Kṛṣṇa is the Supreme Personality of Godhead. There is none equal to or greater than Him. He is mentioned as the father of Brahmā, the original father of all human beings. In fact, Śrī Kṛṣṇa is said to be not only the father of Brahmā but also the father of all species of life. He is the root of the impersonal Brahman and Paramātmā; the Supersoul in every entity is His plenary portion. He is the fountainhead of everything, and everyone is advised to surrender unto His lotus feet. Despite all these clear statements, the *māyayāpahṛta-jñāna* deride the Personality of the Supreme Lord and consider Him merely another human being. They do not know that the blessed form of human life is designed after the eternal and transcendental feature of the Supreme Lord.

All the unauthorized interpretations of the *Gītā* by the class of *māyayāpahṛta-jñāna*, outside the purview of the *paramparā* system, are so many stumbling blocks in the path of spiritual understanding. The deluded interpreters do not surrender unto the lotus feet of Śrī Kṛṣṇa, nor do they teach others to follow this principle.

(4) The last class of *duṣkṛtina* is called *āsuraṁ bhāvam āśrita*, or those of demonic principles. This class is openly atheistic. Some of them argue that the Supreme Lord can never descend upon this material world, but they are unable to give any tangible reasons as to why not. There are others who make Him subordinate to the impersonal feature, although the opposite is declared in the *Gītā*. Envious of the Supreme Personality of Godhead, the atheist will present a number of illicit incarnations manufactured in the factory of his brain. Such persons whose very principle of life is to decry the Personality of Godhead cannot surrender unto the lotus feet of Śrī Kṛṣṇa.

Śrī Yāmunācārya Albandru of South India said, "O my Lord! You are unknowable to persons involved with atheistic principles despite Your uncommon qualities, features, and activities and despite Your personality being confirmed by all the revealed scriptures in the quality of goodness, and despite Your being acknowledged by the famous authorities renowned for their depth of knowledge in the transcendental science and situated in the godly qualities."

Therefore, (1) grossly foolish persons, (2) the lowest of mankind, (3) the deluded speculators, and (4) the professed atheists, as above mentioned, never surrender unto the lotus feet of the Personality of Godhead in spite of all scriptural and authoritative advice.

TEXT 16

चतुर्विधा भजन्ते मां जनाः सुकृतिनोऽर्जुन ।
आर्तो जिज्ञासुरर्थार्थी ज्ञानी च भरतर्षभ ॥ १६ ॥

catur-vidhā bhajante mām
janāḥ sukṛtino 'rjuna
ārto jijñāsur arthārthī
jñānī ca bharatarṣabha

catur-vidhāḥ—four kinds of; *bhajante*—render services; *mām*—unto Me; *janāḥ*—persons; *sukṛtinaḥ*—those who are pious; *arjuna*—O Arjuna; *ārtaḥ*—the distressed; *jijñāsuḥ*—the inquisitive; *artha-arthī*—one who desires material gain; *jñānī*—one who knows things as they are; *ca*—also; *bharatarṣabha*—O great one amongst the descendants of Bharata.

TRANSLATION

O best among the Bhāratas [Arjuna], four kinds of pious men render devotional service unto Me—the distressed, the desirer of wealth, the inquisitive, and he who is searching for knowledge of the Absolute.

PURPORT

Unlike the miscreants, these are adherents of the regulative principles of the scriptures, and they are called *sukṛtina*, or those who obey the rules and regulations of scriptures, the moral and social laws, and are, more or less, devoted to the Supreme Lord. Out of these there are four classes of men—those who are sometimes distressed, those who are in need of money, those who are sometimes inquisitive, and those who are sometimes searching after knowledge of the Absolute Truth. These persons come to the Supreme Lord for devotional service under different conditions. These are not pure devotees because they have some aspiration to fulfill in exchange for devotional service. Pure devotional service is without aspiration and without desire for material profit. The *Bhakti-rasāmṛta-sindhu* defines pure devotion thus:

*anyābhilāṣitāśūnyaṁ jñāna-karmādy-anāvṛtam
ānukūlyena kṛṣṇānuśīlanaṁ bhaktir uttamā.*

"One should render transcendental loving service to the Supreme Lord Kṛṣṇa favorably and without desire for material profit or gain through fruitive activities or philosophical speculation. That is called pure devotional service."

When these four kinds of persons come to the Supreme Lord for devotional service and are completely purified by the association of a pure devotee, they also become pure devotees. As far as the miscreants are concerned, for them devotional service is very difficult because their lives are selfish, irregular and without spiritual goals. But even some of them, by chance, when they come in contact with a pure devotee, also become pure devotees.

Those who are always busy with fruitive activities come to the Lord in material distress and at that time associate with pure devotees and become, in their distress, devotees of the Lord. Those who are simply frustrated also come sometimes to associate with the pure devotees and become inquisitive to know about God. Similarly, when the dry philosophers are frustrated in every field of knowledge, they sometimes want to learn of God, and they come to the Supreme Lord to render devotional service and thus transcend knowledge of the impersonal Brahman and the localized Paramātmā and come to the personal conception of Godhead by the grace of the Supreme Lord or His pure devotee. On the whole, when the distressed, the inquisitive, the seekers of knowledge, and those who are in need of money are free from all material desires, and when they fully understand that material remuneration has nothing to do with spiritual improvement, they become pure devotees. As long as such a purified stage is not attained, devotees in transcendental service to the Lord are tainted with fruitive activities, and they search after mundane knowledge, etc. So one has to transcend all this before one can come to the stage of pure devotional service.

TEXT 17

तेषां ज्ञानी नित्ययुक्त एकभक्तिर्विशिष्यते ।
प्रियो हि ज्ञानिनोऽत्यर्थमहं स च मम प्रियः ॥ १७ ॥

teṣāṁ jñānī nitya-yukta
eka-bhaktir viśiṣyate
priyo hi jñānino 'tyartham
ahaṁ sa ca mama priyaḥ

teṣām—out of them; *jñānī*—one in full knowledge; *nitya-yuktaḥ*—always engaged; *eka*—only one; *bhaktiḥ*—devotional service; *viśiṣyate*—especially; *priyaḥ*—very dear; *hi*—certainly; *jñāninaḥ*—person in knowledge; *atyartham*—highly; *aham*—I am; *saḥ*—he; *ca*—also; *mama*—Mine; *priyaḥ*—dear.

TRANSLATION

Of these, the wise one who is in full knowledge in union with Me through pure devotional service is the best. For I am very dear to him, and he is dear to Me.

PURPORT

Free from all contaminations of material desires, the distressed, the inquisitive, the penniless, and the seeker after supreme knowledge can all become pure devotees. But out of them, he who is in knowledge of the Absolute Truth and free from all material desires becomes a really pure devotee of the Lord. And of the four orders, the devotee who is in full knowledge and is at the same time engaged in devotional service is, the Lord says, the best. By searching after knowledge one realizes that his self is different from his material body, and when further advanced he comes to the knowledge of impersonal Brahman and Paramātmā. When one is fully purified, he realizes that his constitutional position is to be the eternal servant of God. So by association with pure devotees, the inquisitive, the distressed, the seeker after material amelioration and the man in knowledge all become themselves pure. But in the preparatory stage, the man who is in full knowledge of the Supreme Lord and is at the same time executing devotional service is very dear to the Lord. He who is situated in pure knowledge of the transcendence of the Supreme Personality of God is so protected in devotional service that material contaminations cannot touch him.

TEXT 18

उदाराः सर्व एवैते ज्ञानी त्वात्मैव मे मतम् ।
आस्थितः स हि युक्तात्मा मामेवानुत्तमां गतिम् ॥ १८ ॥

udārāḥ sarva evaite
jñānī tv ātmaiva me matam
āsthitaḥ sa hi yuktātmā
mām evānuttamāṁ gatim

udārāḥ—magnanimous; *sarve*—all; *eva*—certainly; *ete*—these; *jñānī*—one who is in knowledge; *tu*—but; *ātmā eva*—just like Myself; *me*—Mine; *matam*—opinion; *āsthitaḥ*—situated; *saḥ*—he; *hi*—certainly; *yukta-ātmā*—engaged in devotional service; *mām*—unto Me; *eva*—certainly; *anuttamām*—the highest goal; *gatim*—destination.

TRANSLATION

All these devotees are undoubtedly magnanimous souls, but he who is situated in knowledge of Me I consider verily to dwell in Me. Being engaged in My transcendental service, he attains Me.

PURPORT

It is not that other devotees who are less complete in knowledge are not dear to the Lord. The Lord says that all are magnanimous because anyone who comes to the Lord for any purpose is called a *mahātmā* or great soul. The devotees who want some benefit out of devotional service are accepted by the Lord because there is an exchange of affection. Out of affection they ask the Lord for some material benefit, and when they get it they become so satisfied that they also advance in devotional service. But the devotee in full knowledge is considered to be very dear to the Lord because his only purpose is to serve the Supreme Lord with love and devotion. Such a devotee cannot live a second without contacting or serving the Supreme Lord. Similarly, the Supreme Lord is very fond of His devotee and cannot be separated from him.

In the *Śrīmad-Bhāgavatam* (9.4.57), the Lord says:

> *ahaṁ bhakta-parādhīno hy asvatantra iva dvija*
> *sādhubhir grasta-hṛdayo bhaktair bhakta-jana-priyaḥ*

"The devotees are always in My heart, and I am always in the heart of the devotees. The devotee does not know anything beyond Me, and I also cannot forget the devotee. There is a very intimate relationship between Me and the pure devotees. Pure devotees in full knowledge are never out of spiritual touch, and therefore they are very much dear to Me."

TEXT 19

बहूनां जन्मनामन्ते ज्ञानवान्मां प्रपद्यते ।
वासुदेवः सर्वमिति स महात्मा सुदुर्लभः ॥ १९ ॥

> *bahūnāṁ janmanām ante*
> *jñānavān māṁ prapadyate*
> *vāsudevaḥ sarvam iti*
> *sa mahātmā su-durlabhaḥ*

bahūnām—many; *janmanām*—births; *ante*—after; *jñānavān*—he possessing knowledge; *mām*—unto Me; *prapadyate*—surrenders; *vāsudevaḥ*—cause of all causes; *sarvam*—all; *iti*—thus; *saḥ*—such; *mahātmā*—great soul; *sudurlabhaḥ*—very rare.

TRANSLATION

After many births and deaths, he who is actually in knowledge surrenders unto Me, knowing Me to be the cause of all causes and all that is. Such a great soul is very rare.

PURPORT

The living entity, while executing devotional service or transcendental rituals after many, many births, may actually become situated in transcendental pure knowledge that the Supreme Personality of Godhead is the ultimate goal of spiritual realization. In the beginning of spiritual realization, while one is trying to give up one's attachment to materialism, there is some leaning towards impersonalism, but when one is further advanced he can understand that there are activities in the spiritual life and that these activities constitute devotional service. Realizing this, he becomes attached to the Supreme Personality of Godhead and surrenders to Him. At such a time one can understand that Lord Śrī Kṛṣṇa's mercy is everything, that He is the cause of all causes and that this material manifestation is not independent from Him. He realizes the material world to be a perverted reflection of spiritual variegatedness and realizes that in everything there is a relationship with the Supreme Lord Kṛṣṇa. Thus he thinks of everything in relation to Vāsudeva, or Śrī Kṛṣṇa. Such a universal vision of Vāsudeva precipitates one's full surrender to the Supreme Lord Śrī Kṛṣṇa as the highest goal. Such surrendered great souls are very rare.

This verse is very nicely explained in the Third Chapter of Śvetāśvatara Upaniṣad: "In this body there are powers of speaking, of seeing, of hearing, of mental activities, etc. But these are not important if not related to the Supreme Lord. And because Vāsudeva is all-pervading and everything is Vāsudeva, the devotee surrenders in full knowledge." (Cf. Bhagavad-gītā 7.17 and 11.40)

TEXT 20

कामैस्तैस्तैर्हृतज्ञानाः प्रपद्यन्तेऽन्यदेवताः ।
तं तं नियममास्थाय प्रकृत्या नियताः स्वया ॥ २० ॥

kāmais tais tair hṛta-jñānāḥ
prapadyante 'nya-devatāḥ
taṁ taṁ niyamam āsthāya
prakṛtyā niyatāḥ svayā

kāmaiḥ—by desires; taiḥ—by those; taiḥ—by those; hṛta—distorted; jñānāḥ—knowledge; prapadyante—surrender; anya—other; devatāḥ—demigods; tam—that; tam—that; niyamam—rules; āsthāya—following; prakṛtyā—by nature; niyatāḥ—controlled; svayā—by their own.

TRANSLATION

Those whose minds are distorted by material desires surrender unto demigods and follow the particular rules and regulations of worship according to their own natures.

PURPORT

Those who are freed from all material contaminations surrender unto the Supreme Lord and engage in His devotional service. As long as the material contamination is not completely washed off, they are by nature nondevotees. But even those who have material desires and who resort to the Supreme Lord are not so much attracted by external nature; because of approaching the right goal, they soon become free from all material lust. In the *Śrīmad-Bhāgavatam* it is recommended that whether one is free from all material desires, or is full of material desires, or desires liberation from material contamination, or is a pure devotee and has no desire for material sense gratification, he should in all cases surrender to Vāsudeva and worship Him.

It is said in the *Bhāgavatam* that less intelligent people who have lost their spiritual sense take shelter of demigods for immediate fulfillment of material desires. Generally, such people do not go to the Supreme Personality of Godhead, because they are in particular modes of nature (ignorance and passion) and therefore worship various demigods. Following the rules and regulations of worship, they are satisfied. The worshipers of demigods are motivated by small desires and do not know how to reach the supreme goal, but a devotee of the Supreme Lord is not misguided. Because in Vedic literature there are recommendations for worshiping different gods for different purposes (e.g., a diseased man is recommended to worship the sun), those who are not devotees of the Lord think that for certain purposes demigods are better than the Supreme Lord. But a pure devotee knows that the Supreme Lord Kṛṣṇa is the master of all. In the *Caitanya-caritāmṛta* it is said that only the Supreme Personality of Godhead, Kṛṣṇa, is master and all others are servants. Therefore a pure devotee never goes to demigods for satisfaction of his material needs. He depends on the Supreme Lord. And the pure devotee is satisfied with whatever He gives.

TEXT 21

यो यो यां यां तनुं भक्तः श्रद्धयार्चितुमिच्छति ।
तस्य तस्याचलां श्रद्धां तामेव विदधाम्यहम् ॥ २१ ॥

yo yo yāṁ yāṁ tanuṁ bhaktaḥ
śraddhayārcitum icchati
tasya tasyācalāṁ śraddhāṁ
tām eva vidadhāmy aham

yaḥ—that; *yaḥ*—that; *yām*—which; *yām*—which; *tanum*—form of the demigods; *bhaktaḥ*—devotee; *śraddhayā*—with faith; *arcitum*—to worship; *icchati*—desires; *tasya*—of that; *tasya*—of that; *acalām*—steady; *śraddhām*—faith; *tam*—him; *eva*—surely; *vidadhāmi*—give; *aham*—I.

TRANSLATION

I am in everyone's heart as the Supersoul. As soon as one desires to worship the demigods, I make his faith steady so that he can devote himself to some particular deity.

PURPORT

God has given independence to everyone; therefore, if a person desires to material enjoyment and wants very sincerely to have such facilities from the material demigods, the Supreme Lord, as Supersoul in everyone's heart, understands and gives facilities to such persons. As the supreme father of all living entities, He does not interfere with their independence, but gives all facilities so that they can fulfill their material desires. Some may ask why the all-powerful God gives facilities to the living entities for enjoying this material world and so lets them fall into the trap of the illusory energy. The answer is that if the Supreme Lord as Supersoul does not give such facilities, then there is no meaning to independence. Therefore He gives everyone full independence—whatever one likes—but His ultimate instruction we find in the *Bhagavad-gītā*: man should give up all other engagements and fully surrender unto Him. That will make man happy.

Both the living entity and the demigods are subordinate to the will of the Supreme Personality of Godhead; therefore the living entity cannot worship the demigod by his own desire, nor can the demigod bestow any benediction without the supreme will. As it is said, not a blade of grass moves without the will of the Supreme Personality of Godhead. Generally, persons who are distressed in the material world go to the demigods, as they are advised in the Vedic literature. A person wanting some particular thing may worship such and such a demigod. For example, a diseased person is recommended to worship the sun-god; a person wanting education may worship the goddess of learning, Sarasvatī; and a person wanting a beautiful wife may worship the goddess Umā, the wife of Lord Śiva. In this way there are recommendations in the *śāstras* (Vedic scriptures) for different modes of worship of different demigods. And because a particular living entity wants to enjoy a particular material facility, the Lord inspires him with a strong desire to achieve that benediction from that particular demigod, and so he successfully receives the benediction. The particular mode of the devotional attitude of the living entity toward a particular type of demigod is also arranged by the Supreme Lord. The demigods cannot infuse the living entities with such an affinity, but because He is the Supreme Lord or the Supersoul who is present in the heart of all living entities, Kṛṣṇa gives impetus to man to worship certain demigods. The demigods are actually different parts of the universal body of the Supreme Lord; therefore they have no independence. In the Vedic literature (*Taittirīya Upaniṣad*, First *Anuvāka*) it is stated: "The Supreme Personality of Godhead as Supersoul is also present within the heart of the demigod; therefore He arranges through the demigod to fulfill the desire of the living entity. But both the demigod and the living entity are dependent on the supreme will. They are not independent."

TEXT 22

स तया श्रद्धया युक्तस्तस्याराधनमीहते ।
लभते च ततः कामान्मयैव विहितान्हितान् ॥ २२ ॥

sa tayā śraddhayā yuktas
tasyārādhanam īhate
labhate ca tataḥ kāmān
mayaiva vihitān hi tān

saḥ—he; *tayā*—with that; *śraddhayā*—with faith; *yuktaḥ*—endowed; *tasya*—his; *ārādhanam*—worship; *īhate*—seeks; *labhate*—obtains; *ca*—and; *tataḥ*—from which; *kāmān*—desires; *mayā*—by Me; *eva*—alone; *vihitān*—regulated; *hi*—for; *tān*—those.

TRANSLATION

Endowed with such a faith, he seeks favors of a particular demigod and obtains his desires. But in actuality these benefits are bestowed by Me alone.

PURPORT

The demigods cannot award benediction to the devotees without the permission of the Supreme Lord. The living entity may forget that everything is the property of the Supreme Lord, but the demigods do not forget. So the worship of demigods and achievement of desired results are not due to the demigods but to the Supreme Personality of Godhead, by arrangement. The less intelligent living entity does not know this, and therefore he foolishly goes to the demigods for some benefit. But the pure devotee, when in need of something, prays only to the Supreme Lord. Asking for material benefit, however, is not a sign of a pure devotee. A living entity goes to the demigods usually because he is mad to fulfill his lust. This happens when something undue is desired by the living entity, and the Lord Himself does not fulfill the desire. In the *Caitanya-caritāmṛta* it is said that one who worships the Supreme Lord and at the same time desires material enjoyment is contradictory in his desires. Devotional service of the Supreme Lord and the worship of a demigod cannot be on the same platform because worship of a demigod is material and devotional service to the Supreme Lord is completely spiritual.

For the living entity who desires to return to Godhead, material desires are impediments. A pure devotee of the Lord is therefore not awarded the material benefits desired by less intelligent living entities who prefer to worship demigods of the material world rather than engage in devotional service of the Supreme Lord.

TEXT 23

अन्तवत्तु फलं तेषां तद्भवत्यल्पमेधसाम् ।
देवान्देवयजो यान्ति मद्भक्ता यान्ति मामपि ॥ २३ ॥

*antavat tu phalaṁ teṣāṁ
tad bhavaty alpa-medhasām
devān deva-yajo yānti
mad-bhaktā yānti mām api*

antavat tu—limited and temporary; *phalam*—fruits; *teṣām*—their; *tat*—that; *bhavati*—becomes; *alpa-medhasām*—of those of small intelligence; *devān*—demigods' planets; *deva-yajaḥ*—worshipers of demigods; *yānti*—achieve; *mat*—My; *bhaktāḥ*—devotees; *yānti*—attain; *mām*—unto Me; *api*—surely.

TRANSLATION

Men of small intelligence worship the demigods, and their fruits are limited and temporary. Those who worship the demigods go to the planets of the demigods, but My devotees ultimately reach My supreme planet.

PURPORT

Some commentators on the *Gītā* say that one who worships a demigod can reach the Supreme Lord, but here it is clearly stated that the worshipers of demigods go to the different planetary systems where various demigods are situated, just as a worshiper of the sun achieves the sun or a worshiper of the demigod of the moon achieves the moon. Similarly, if anyone wants to worship a demigod like Indra, he can attain that particular god's planet. It is not that everyone, regardless of whatever demigod is worshiped, will reach the Supreme Personality of Godhead. That is denied here, for it is clearly stated that the worshipers of demigods go to different planets in the material world, but the devotee of the Supreme Lord goes directly to the supreme planet of the Personality of Godhead.

Here the point may be raised that if the demigods are different parts of the body of the Supreme Lord, then the same end should be achieved by worshiping them. However, worshipers of the demigods are less intelligent because they don't know to what part of the body food must be supplied. Some of them are so foolish that they claim that there are many parts and many ways to supply food. This isn't very sanguine. Can anyone supply food to the body through the ears or eyes? They do not know that these demigods are different parts of the universal body of the Supreme Lord, and in their ignorance they believe that each and every demigod is a separate God and a competitor of the Supreme Lord.

Not only are demigods parts of the Supreme Lord, but ordinary living entities are also. In the *Śrīmad-Bhāgavatam* it is stated that the *brāhmaṇas* are the head of the Supreme Lord, the *kṣatriyas* are the arms, etc., and that all serve different functions. Regardless of the situation, if one knows that both the demigods and himself are part and parcel of the Supreme Lord, his knowledge is perfect. But if he does not understand this, he achieves different planets where the demigods reside. This is not the same destination the devotee reaches.

The results achieved by the demigods' benedictions are perishable because within this material world the planets, the demigods and their worshipers are all perishable. Therefore it is clearly stated in this verse that all results achieved by worshiping demigods are perishable, and therefore such worship is performed by the less intelligent living entity. Because the pure devotee engaged in Kṛṣṇa consciousness in devotional service of the Supreme Lord achieves eternal blissful existence that is full of knowledge, his achievements and those of the common worshiper of the demigods are different. The Supreme Lord is unlimited; His favor is unlimited; His mercy

is unlimited. Therefore the mercy of the Supreme Lord upon His pure
devotees is unlimited.

TEXT 24

अव्यक्तं व्यक्तिमापन्नं मन्यन्ते मामबुद्धयः ।
परं भावमजानन्तो ममाव्ययमनुत्तमम् ॥ २४ ॥

*avyaktaṁ vyaktim āpannaṁ
manyante mām abuddhayaḥ
paraṁ bhāvam ajānanto
mamāvyayam anuttamam*

avyaktam—nonmanifested; *vyaktim*—personality; *āpannam*—achieved;
manyante—think; *mām*—unto Me; *abuddhayaḥ*—less intelligent persons;
param—supreme; *bhāvam*—state of being; *ajānantaḥ*—without knowing;
mama—My; *avyayam*—imperishable; *anuttamam*—the finest.

TRANSLATION

**Unintelligent men, who know Me not, think that I have assumed this
form and personality. Due to their small knowledge, they do not know
My higher nature, which is changeless and supreme.**

PURPORT

Those who are worshipers of demigods have been described as less intelligent persons, and here the impersonalists are similarly described. Lord
Kṛṣṇa in His personal form is here speaking before Arjuna, and still, due to
ignorance, impersonalists argue that the Supreme Lord ultimately has no
form. Yāmunācārya, a great devotee of the Lord in the disciplic succession
from Rāmānujācārya, has written two very appropriate verses in this connection. He says, "My dear Lord, devotees like Vyāsadeva and Nārada
know You to be the Personality of Godhead. By understanding different
Vedic literatures, one can come to know Your characteristics, Your form
and Your activities, and one can thus understand that You are the Supreme
Personality of Godhead. But those who are in the modes of passion and
ignorance, the demons, the nondevotees, cannot understand You. They

are unable to understand You. However expert such nondevotees may be in discussing *Vedānta* and the *Upaniṣads* and other Vedic literatures, it is not possible for them to understand the Personality of Godhead."

In the *Brahma-saṁhitā* it is stated that the Personality of Godhead cannot be understood simply by study of the *Vedānta* literature. Only by the mercy of the Supreme Lord can the Personality of the Supreme be known. Therefore in this verse it is clearly stated that not only the worshipers of the demigods are less intelligent, but those nondevotees who are engaged in *Vedānta* and speculation on Vedic literature without any tinge of true Kṛṣṇa consciousness are also less intelligent, and for them it is not possible to understand God's personal nature. Persons who are under the impression that the Absolute Truth is impersonal are described as *asuras*, which means one who does not know the ultimate feature of the Absolute Truth. In the *Śrīmad-Bhāgavatam* it is stated that supreme realization begins from the impersonal Brahman and then rises to the localized Supersoul—but the ultimate word in the Absolute Truth is the Personality of Godhead. Modern impersonalists are still less intelligent, for they do not even follow their great predecessor, Śaṅkarācārya, who has specifically stated that Kṛṣṇa is the Supreme Personality of Godhead. Impersonalists, therefore, not knowing the Supreme Truth, think Kṛṣṇa to be only the son of Devakī and Vasudeva, or a prince, or a powerful living entity. This is also condemned in *Bhagavad-gītā*: "Only the fools regard Me as an ordinary person." The fact is that no one can understand Kṛṣṇa without rendering devotional service and without developing Kṛṣṇa consciousness. The *Gītā* confirms this.

One cannot understand the Supreme Personality of Godhead, Kṛṣṇa, or His form, quality or name simply by mental speculation or by discussing Vedic literature. One must understand Him by devotional service. When one is fully engaged in Kṛṣṇa consciousness, beginning by chanting the *mahāmantra*-Hare Kṛṣṇa, Hare Kṛṣṇa, Kṛṣṇa Kṛṣṇa, Hare Hare/Hare Rāma, Hare Rāma, Rāma Rāma, Hare Hare-then only can one understand the Supreme Personality of Godhead. Nondevotee impersonalists think that Kṛṣṇa has a body made of this material nature and that all His activities, His form and everything, are *māyā*. These impersonalists are known as Māyāvādī. They do not know the ultimate truth.

The twentieth verse clearly states: "Those who are blinded by lusty desires surrender unto the different demigods." It is accepted that besides the Supreme Personality of Godhead, there are demigods who have their different planets (Bg. 7.23), and the Lord also has a planet. It is also stated that the worshipers of the demigods go to the different planets of the demigods, and those who are devotees of Lord Kṛṣṇa go to the Kṛṣṇaloka planet. Although this is clearly stated, the foolish impersonalists still maintain that the Lord is formless and that these forms are impositions. From the study of the *Gītā* does it appear that the demigods and their abodes are impersonal? Clearly, neither the demigods nor Kṛṣṇa, the Supreme Personality of Godhead, are impersonal. They are all persons; Lord Kṛṣṇa is the Supreme Personality of Godhead, and He has His own planet, and the demigods have theirs.

Therefore the monistic contention that ultimate truth is formless and that form is imposed does not hold true. It is clearly stated here that it is not imposed. From the *Gītā* we can clearly understand that the forms of the demigods and the form of the Supreme Lord are simultaneously existing and that Lord Kṛṣṇa is *sac-cid-ānanda*, eternal blissful knowledge. The *Vedas* also confirm that the Supreme Absolute Truth is *ānandamaya*, or full of blissful pleasure, and that He is *abhyāsāt*, by nature the reservoir of unlimited auspicious qualities. And in the *Gītā* the Lord says that although He is *aja* (unborn), He still appears. These are the facts that we should understand from the *Gītā*. We cannot understand how the Supreme Personality of Godhead can be impersonal; the imposition theory of the impersonalist monist is false as far as the statements of the *Gītā* are concerned. It is clear herein that the Supreme Absolute Truth, Lord Kṛṣṇa, has both form and personality.

TEXT 25

नाहं प्रकाशः सर्वस्य योगमायासमावृतः ।
मूढोऽयं नाभिजानाति लोको मामजमव्ययम् ॥ २५ ॥

nāhaṁ prakāśaḥ sarvasya
yoga-māyā-samāvṛtaḥ
mūḍho 'yaṁ nābhijānāti
loko māṁ ajam avyayam

na—nor; *aham*—I; *prakāśaḥ*—manifest; *sarvasya*—to everyone; *yoga-māyā*—internal potency; *samāvṛtaḥ*—covered; *mūḍhaḥ*—foolish; *ayam*—this; *na*—not; *abhijānāti*—can understand; *lokaḥ*—such less intelligent persons; *mām*—Me; *ajam*—unborn; *avyayam*—inexhaustible.

TRANSLATION

I am never manifest to the foolish and unintelligent. For them I am covered by My eternal creative potency [yoga-māyā]; and so the deluded world knows Me not, who am unborn and infallible.

PURPORT

It may be argued that since Kṛṣṇa was present on this earth and was visible to everyone, then why isn't He manifest to everyone now? But actually He was not manifest to everyone. When Kṛṣṇa was present there were only a few people who could understand Him to be the Supreme Personality of Godhead. In the assembly of Kurus, when Śiśupāla spoke against Kṛṣṇa being elected president of the assembly, Bhīṣma supported Him and proclaimed Him to be the Supreme God. Similarly, the Pāṇḍavas and a few others knew that He was the Supreme, but not everyone. He was not revealed to the nondevotees and the common man. Therefore in the Gītā Kṛṣṇa says that but for His pure devotees, all men consider Him to be like themselves. He was manifest only to His devotees as the reservoir of all pleasure. But to others, to unintelligent nondevotees, He was covered by His eternal potency.

In the prayers of Kuntī in the Śrīmad-Bhāgavatam (1.8.18), it is said that the Lord is covered by the curtain of yoga-māyā and thus ordinary people cannot understand Him. Kuntī prays: "O my Lord, You are the maintainer of the entire universe, and devotional service to You is the highest religious principle. Therefore, I pray that You will also maintain me. Your transcendental form is covered by the yoga-māyā. The brahma-jyoti is the covering of the internal potency. May You kindly remove this glowing effulgence that impedes my seeing Your sac-cid-ānanda-vigraha, Your eternal form of bliss and knowledge."

This yoga-māyā curtain is also mentioned in the Fifteenth Chapter of the Gītā. The Supreme Personality of Godhead in His transcendental form of bliss and knowledge is covered by the eternal potency of brahmajyoti and the less intelligent impersonalists cannot see the Supreme on this account. Also in the Śrīmad-Bhāgavatam (10.14.7) there is this prayer by Brahmā: "O Supreme Personality of Godhead, O Supersoul, O master of all mystery, who can calculate Your potency and pastimes in this world? You are always expanding Your eternal potency, and therefore no one can understand You. Learned scientists and learned scholars can examine the atomic constitution of the material world or even the planets, but still they are unable to calculate Your energy and potency, although You are present before them." The Supreme Personality of Godhead, Lord Kṛṣṇa, is not only unborn, but He is *avyaya*, inexhaustible. His eternal form is bliss and knowledge, and His energies are all inexhaustible.

TEXT 26

वेदाहं समतीतानि वर्तमानानि चार्जुन ।
भविष्याणि च भूतानि मां तु वेद न कश्चन ॥ २६ ॥

vedāham samatītāni
vartamānāni cārjuna
bhaviṣyāṇi ca bhūtāni
mām tu veda na kaścana

veda—know; *aham*—I; *sama*—equally; *atītāni*—past; *vartamānāni*—present; *ca*—and; *arjuna*—O Arjuna; *bhaviṣyāṇi*—future; *ca*—also; *bhūtāni*—living entities; *mām*—Me; *tu*—but; *veda*—knows; *na*—not; *kaścana*—anyone.

TRANSLATION

O Arjuna, as the Supreme Personality of Godhead, I know everything that has happened in the past, all that is happening in the present, and all things that are yet to come. I also know all living entities; but Me no one knows.

PURPORT

Here the question of personality and impersonality is clearly stated. If Kṛṣṇa, the form of the Supreme Personality of Godhead, is considered by the impersonalists to be *māyā*, to be material, then He would, like the living entity, change His body and forget everything in His past life. Anyone with a material body cannot remember his past life, nor can he foretell his future life, nor can he predict the outcome of his present life; therefore he cannot know what is happening in past, present and future. Unless one is liberated from material contamination, he cannot know past, present and future.

Unlike the ordinary human being, Lord Kṛṣṇa clearly says that He completely knows what happened in the past, what is happening in the present, and what will happen in the future. In the Fourth Chapter we have seen that Lord Kṛṣṇa remembers instructing Vivasvān, the sun-god, millions of years ago. Kṛṣṇa knows every living entity because He is situated in every living being's heart as the Supreme Soul. But despite His presence in every living entity as Supersoul and His presence beyond the material sky, as the Supreme Personality of Godhead, the less intelligent cannot realize Him as the Supreme Person. Certainly the transcendental body of Śrī Kṛṣṇa is not perishable. He is just like the sun, and *maya* is like the cloud. In the material world we can see that there is the sun and that there are clouds and different stars and planets. The clouds may cover all these in the sky temporarily, but this covering is only apparent to our limited vision. The sun, moon and stars are not actually covered. Similarly, *maya* cannot cover the Supreme Lord. By His internal potency He is not manifest to the less intelligent class of men. As it is stated in the third verse of this chapter, out of millions and millions of men, some try to become perfect in this human form of life, and out of thousands and thousands of such perfected men, hardly one can understand what Lord Kṛṣṇa is. Even if one is perfected by realization of impersonal Brahman or localized Paramātmā, he cannot possibly understand the Supreme Personality of Godhead, Śrī Kṛṣṇa, without being in Kṛṣṇa consciousness.

TEXT 27

इच्छाद्वेषसमुत्थेन द्वन्द्वमोहेन भारत ।
सर्वभूतानि संमोहं सर्गे यान्ति परन्तप ॥ २७ ॥

icchā-dveṣa-samutthena
dvandva-mohena bhārata
sarva-bhūtāni sammohaṁ
sarge yānti parantapa

icchā—desire; *dveṣa*—hate; *samutthena*—born; *dvandva*—duality; *mohena*—overcome; *bhārata*—O scion of Bharata; *sarva*—all; *bhūtāni*—living entities; *sammoham*—into delusion; *sarge*—in creation; *yānti*—go; *parantapa*—O conquerer of enemies.

TRANSLATION

O scion of Bharata [Arjuna], O conquerer of the foe, all living entities are born into delusion, overcome by the dualities of desire and hate.

PURPORT

The real constitutional position of the living entity is that of subordination to the Supreme Lord, who is pure knowledge. When one is deluded into separation from this pure knowledge, he becomes controlled by illusory energy and cannot understand the Supreme Personality of Godhead. The illusory energy is manifested in the duality of desire and hate. Due to desire and hate, the ignorant person wants to become one with the Supreme Lord and envies Kṛṣṇa as the Supreme Personality of Godhead. Pure devotees, who are not so deluded or contaminated by desire and hate, can understand that Lord Śrī Kṛṣṇa appears by His internal potencies, but those who are deluded by duality and nescience think that the Supreme Personality of Godhead is created by material energies. This is their misfortune. Such deluded persons, symptomatically, dwell in dualities of dishonor and honor, misery and happiness, woman and man, good and bad, pleasure and pain, etc., thinking, "This is my wife; this is my house; I am the master of this house; I am the husband of this wife." These are the dualities of delusion. Those who are so deluded by dualities are completely foolish and therefore cannot understand the Supreme Personality of Godhead.

TEXT 28

येषां त्वन्तगतं पापं जनानां पुण्यकर्मणाम् ।
ते द्वन्द्वमोहनिर्मुक्का भजन्ते मां दृढव्रताः ॥ २८ ॥

yeṣāṁ tv anta-gataṁ pāpaṁ
janānāṁ puṇya-karmaṇām
te dvandva-moha-nirmuktā
bhajante māṁ dṛḍha-vratāḥ

yeṣām—whose; tu—but; anta-gatam—completely eradicated; pāpam—sin; janānām—of the persons; puṇya—pious; karmaṇām—previous activities;

te—they; *dvandva*—duality; *moha*—delusion; *nirmuktāḥ*—free from; *bhajante*—worship; *mām*—Me; *dṛḍha-vratāḥ*—with determination.

TRANSLATION

Persons who have acted piously in previous lives and in this life, whose sinful actions are completely eradicated and who are freed from the duality of delusion, engage themselves in My service with determination.

PURPORT

Those eligible for elevation to the transcendental position are mentioned in this verse. For those who are sinful, atheistic, foolish and deceitful, it is very difficult to transcend the duality of desire and hate. Only those who have passed their lives in practicing the regulative principles of religion, who have acted piously and have conquered sinful reactions can accept devotional service and gradually rise to the pure knowledge of the Supreme Personality of Godhead. Then, gradually, they can meditate in trance on the Supreme Personality of Godhead. That is the process of being situated on the spiritual platform. This elevation is possible in Kṛṣṇa consciousness in the association of pure devotees who can deliver one from delusion.

It is stated in the *Śrīmad-Bhāgavatam* that if one actually wants to be liberated he must render service to the devotees; but one who associates with materialistic people is on the path leading to the darkest region of existence. All the devotees of the Lord traverse this earth just to recover the conditioned souls from their delusion. The impersonalists do not know that forgetting their constitutional position as subordinate to the Supreme Lord is the greatest violation of God's law. Unless one is reinstated in his own constitutional position, it is not possible to understand the Supreme Personality or to be fully engaged in His transcendental loving service with determination.

TEXT 29

जरामरणमोक्षाय मामाश्रित्य यतन्ति ये ।
ते ब्रह्म तद्विदुः कृत्स्नमध्यात्मं कर्म चाखिलम् ॥ २९ ॥

jarā-maraṇa-mokṣāya
mām āśritya yatanti ye
te brahma tad viduḥ kṛtsnam
adhyātmaṁ karma cākhilam

jarā—old age; *maraṇa*—death; *mokṣāya*—for the purpose of liberation; *mām*—unto Me; *āśritya*—taking shelter of; *yatanti*—endeavor; *ye*—all those; *te*—such persons; *brahma*—Brahman; *tat*—actually that; *viduḥ*—they know; *kṛtsnam*—everything; *adhyātmam*—transcendental; *karma*—fruitive activities; *ca*—also; *akhilam*—entirely.

TRANSLATION

Intelligent persons who are endeavoring for liberation from old age and death take refuge in Me in devotional service. They are actually Brahman because they entirely know everything about transcendental and fruitive activities.

PURPORT

Birth, death, old age and diseases affect this material body, but not the spiritual body. There is no birth, death, old age and disease for the spiritual body, so one who attains a spiritual body, becomes one of the associates of the Supreme Personality of Godhead and engages in eternal devotional service, is really liberated. *Aham brahmāsmi:* I am spirit. It is said that one should understand that he is Brahman-spirit soul. This Brahman conception of life is also in devotional service, as described in this verse. The pure devotees are transcendentally situated on the Brahman platform, and they know everything about transcendental and material activities.

Four kinds of impure devotees who engage themselves in the transcendental service of the Lord achieve their respective goals, and by the grace of the Supreme Lord, when they are fully Kṛṣṇa conscious, they actually enjoy spiritual association with the Supreme Lord. But those who are worshipers of demigods never reach the Supreme Lord in His supreme planet. Even the less intelligent Brahman-realized persons cannot reach the supreme planet of Kṛṣṇa known as Goloka Vṛndāvana. Only persons who perform activities in Kṛṣṇa consciousness (*mām āśritya*) are actually entitled to be called Brahman, because they are actually endeavoring to reach the Kṛṣṇa planet. Such persons have no misgivings about Kṛṣṇa, and thus they are factually Brahman.

Those who are engaged in worshiping the form or *arcā* of the Lord or who are engaged in meditation on the Lord simply for liberation from material bondage, also know, by the grace of the Lord, the purports of Brahman, *adhibhūta*, etc., as explained by the Lord in the next chapter.

TEXT 30

साधिभूताधिदैवं मां साधियज्ञं च ये विदुः ।
प्रयाणकालेऽपि च मां ते विदुर्युक्तचेतसः ॥ ३० ॥

sādhibhūtādhidaivaṁ māṁ
sādhiyajñaṁ ca ye viduḥ
prayāṇa-kāle 'pi ca māṁ
te vidur yukta-cetasaḥ

sa-adhibhūta—the governing principle of the material manifestation; *adhidaivam*—underlying all the demigods; *mām*—Me; *sa-adhiyajñam*—sustaining all sacrifices; *ca*—and; *ye*—those; *viduḥ*—know; *prayāṇa*—of death; *kāle*—at the time; *api*—even; *ca*—and; *mām*—Me; *te*—they; *viduḥ*—know; *yukta-cetasaḥ*—with steadfast mind.

TRANSLATION

Those who know Me as the Supreme Lord, as the governing principle of the material manifestation, who know Me as the one underlying all the demigods and as the one sustaining all sacrifices, can, with steadfast mind, understand and know Me even at the time of death.

PURPORT

Persons acting in Kṛṣṇa consciousness are never entirely deviated from the path of understanding the Supreme Personality of Godhead. In the transcendental association of Kṛṣṇa consciousness, one can understand how the Supreme Lord is the governing principle of the material manifestation and even of the demigods. Gradually, by such transcendental association, one becomes convinced of the Supreme Personality of Godhead Himself, and at the time of death such a Kṛṣṇa conscious person can never forget Kṛṣṇa. Naturally he is thus promoted to the planet of the Supreme Lord, Goloka Vṛndāvana.

This Seventh Chapter particularly explains how one can become a fully Kṛṣṇa conscious person. The beginning of Kṛṣṇa consciousness is association of persons who are Kṛṣṇa conscious. Such association is spiritual and puts one directly in touch with the Supreme Lord, and, by His grace, one can understand Kṛṣṇa to be the Supreme God. At the same time one can really understand the constitutional position of the living entity and how the living entity forgets Kṛṣṇa and becomes entangled in material activities. By gradual development of Kṛṣṇa consciousness in good association, the living entity can understand that due to forgetfulness of Kṛṣṇa he has become conditioned by the laws of material nature. He can also understand that this human form of life is an opportunity to regain Kṛṣṇa consciousness and that it should be fully utilized to attain the causeless mercy of the Supreme Lord.

Many subjects have been discussed in this chapter: the man in distress, the inquisitive man, the man in want of material necessities, knowledge of Brahman, knowledge of Paramātmā, liberation from birth, death and diseases, and worship of the Supreme Lord. However, he who is actually elevated in Kṛṣṇa consciousness does not care for the different processes. He simply directly engages himself in activities of Kṛṣṇa consciousness and thereby factually attains his constitutional position as eternal servitor of Lord Kṛṣṇa. In such a situation he takes pleasure in hearing and glorifying the Supreme Lord in pure devotional service. He is convinced that by doing so, all his objectives will be fulfilled. This determined faith is called dṛḍha-vrata, and it is the beginning of bhakti-yoga or transcendental loving service. That is the verdict of all scriptures. This Seventh Chapter of the Gītā is the substance of that conviction.

Thus end the Bhaktivedanta Purports to the Seventh Chapter of the Śrīmad-Bhagavad-gītā *in the matter of Knowledge of the Absolute.*

CHAPTER EIGHT

Attaining the Supreme

TEXT 1

अर्जुन उवाच ।
किं तद्ब्रह्म किमध्यात्मं किं कर्म पुरुषोत्तम ।
अधिभूतं च किं प्रोक्तमधिदैवं किमुच्यते ॥ १ ॥

> *arjuna uvāca*
> *kiṁ tad brahma kim adhyātmaṁ*
> *kiṁ karma puruṣottama*
> *adhibhūtaṁ ca kiṁ proktam*
> *adhidaivaṁ kim ucyate*

arjunaḥ uvāca—Arjuna said; *kim*—what; *tat*—that; *brahma*—Brahman; *kim*—what; *adhyātmam*—the self; *kim*—what; *karma*—fruitive activities; *puruṣottama*—O Supreme Person; *adhibhūtam*—the material manifestation; *ca*—and; *kim*—what; *proktam*—is called; *adhidaivam*—the demigods; *kim*—what; *ucyate*—is called.

409

TRANSLATION

Arjuna inquired: O my Lord, O Supreme Person, what is Brahman? What is the self? What are fruitive activities? What is this material manifestation? And what are the demigods? Please explain this to me.

PURPORT

In this chapter Lord Kṛṣṇa answers these different questions of Arjuna beginning with, "What is Brahman?" The Lord also explains karma, fruitive activities, devotional service and yoga principles, and devotional service in its pure form. The Śrīmad-Bhāgavatam explains that the Supreme Absolute Truth is known as Brahman, Paramātmā, and Bhagavān. In addition, the living entity, individual soul, is also called Brahman. Arjuna also inquires about ātmā, which refers to body, soul and mind. According to the Vedic dictionary, ātmā refers to the mind, soul, body and senses also.

Arjuna has addressed the Supreme Lord as Puruṣottama, Supreme Person, which means that he was putting these questions not simply to a friend but to the Supreme Person, knowing Him to be the supreme authority able to give definitive answers.

TEXT 2

अधियज्ञः कथं कोऽत्र देहेऽस्मिन्मधुसूदन ।
प्रयाणकाले च कथं ज्ञेयोऽसि नियतात्मभिः ॥ २ ॥

adhiyajñaḥ katham ko 'tra
dehe 'smin madhusūdana
prayāṇa-kāle ca katham
jñeyo 'si niyatātmabhiḥ

adhiyajñaḥ—the Lord of sacrifice; katham—how; kaḥ—who; atra—here; dehe—in the body; asmin—in this; madhusūdana—O Madhusūdana; prayāṇa-kāle—at the time of death; ca—and; katham—how; jñeyaḥ—be known; asi—You can; niyata-ātmabhiḥ—by the self-controlled.

TRANSLATION

How does this Lord of sacrifice live in the body, and in which part does He live, O Madhusūdana? And how can those engaged in devotional service know You at the time of death?

PURPORT

The Lord of sacrifice accepts Indra and Viṣṇu. Viṣṇu is the chief of the primal demigods, including Brahmā and Śiva, and Indra is the chief of the administrative demigods. Both Indra and Viṣṇu are worshiped by *yajña* performances. But here Arjuna asks who is actually the Lord of *yajña* (sacrifice), and how is the Lord residing within the body of the living entity.

Arjuna addresses the Lord as Madhusūdana because Kṛṣṇa once killed a demon named Madhu. Actually these questions, which are of the nature of doubts, should not have arisen in the mind of Arjuna because Arjuna is a Kṛṣṇa conscious devotee. Therefore these doubts are like demons. Since Kṛṣṇa is so expert in killing demons, Arjuna here addresses Him as Madhu-sūdana so that Kṛṣṇa might kill the demonic doubts that arise in Arjuna's mind.

Now the word *prayāṇa-kāle* in this verse is very significant because whatever we do in life will be tested at the time of death. Arjuna fears that at the time of death, those who are in Kṛṣṇa consciousness will forget the Supreme Lord because at such a time body functions are disrupted and the mind may be in a panic-stricken state. Therefore Mahārāja Kulaśekhara, a great devotee, prays, "My dear Lord, may I die immediately now that I'm healthy so that the swan of my mind may enter into the stem of Thy lotus feet." This metaphor is used because the swan often takes pleasure in entering the stem of the lotus flower-similarly, the mind of the pure devotee is drawn to the lotus feet of the Lord. Mahārāja Kulaśekhara fears that at the moment of death his throat will be so choked up that he will not be able to chant the holy names, so it is better to "die immediately." Arjuna questions how one's mind can remain fixed on Kṛṣṇa's lotus feet at such times.

TEXT 3

श्रीभगवानुवाच ।
अक्षरं ब्रह्म परमं स्वभावोऽध्यात्ममुच्यते ।
भूतभावोद्भवकरो विसर्गः कर्मसंज्ञितः ॥ ३ ॥

śrī-bhagavān uvāca
akṣaraṁ brahma paramaṁ
svabhāvo 'dhyātmam ucyate
bhūta-bhāvodbhava-karo
visargaḥ karma-saṁjñitaḥ

śrī bhagavān uvāca—the Supreme Personality of Godhead said; akṣaram—indestructible; brahma—Brahman; paramam—transcendental; svabhāvaḥ—eternal nature; adhyātmam—the self; ucyate—is called; bhūta-bhāva-udbhava-karaḥ—action producing the material bodies of the living entities; visargaḥ—creation; karma—fruitive activities; saṁjñitaḥ—is called.

TRANSLATION

The Supreme Lord said, The indestructible, transcendental living entity is called Brahman, and his eternal nature is called the self. Action pertaining to the development of these material bodies is called karma, or fruitive activities.

PURPORT

Brahman is indestructible and eternally existing, and its constitution is not changed at any time. But beyond Brahman there is Parabrahman. Brahman refers to the living entity, and Parabrahman refers to the Supreme Personality of Godhead. The constitutional position of the living entity is different from the position he takes in the material world. In material consciousness, his nature is to try to be the lord of matter, but in spiritual (Kṛṣṇa) consciousness, his position is to serve the Supreme. When the living entity is in material consciousness, he has to take on various bodies in the material world. That is called karma, or varied creation by the force of material consciousness.

In Vedic literature the living entity is called jīvātmā and Brahman, but he is never called Parabrahman. The living entity (jīvātmā) takes different positions—sometimes he merges into the dark material nature and identifies himself with matter, and sometimes he identifies himself with the superior spiritual nature. Therefore he is called the Supreme Lord's marginal energy. According to his identification with material or spiritual nature, he receives a material or spiritual body. In material nature he may take a body from any of the 8,400,000 species of life, but in spiritual nature he has only one body. In material nature he is sometimes manifested as a man, demigod, an animal, a beast, bird, etc., according to his karma. To attain material heavenly planets and enjoy their facilities, he sometimes performs sacrifices (yajña), but when his merit is exhausted, he returns to earth again in the form of a man.

In the process of sacrifice, the living entity makes specific sacrifices to attain specific heavenly planets and consequently reaches them. When the merit of sacrifice is exhausted, then the living entity descends to earth in the form of rain, then takes on the form of grains, and the grains are eaten by man and transformed into semen, which impregnates a woman, and thus the living entity once again attains the human form to perform sacrifice and so repeat the same cycle. In this way, the living entity perpetually comes and goes on the material path. The Kṛṣṇa conscious person, however, avoids such sacrifices. He takes directly to Kṛṣṇa consciousness and thereby prepares himself to return to Godhead.

Impersonalist commentators on the Gītā unreasonably assume that Brahman takes the form of jīva in the material world, and to substantiate this they refer to Chapter Fifteen, verse 7, of the Gītā. But this verse also speaks of the living entity as "an eternal fragment of Myself." The fragment of God, the living entity, may fall down into the material world, but the Supreme Lord (Acyuta) never falls down. Therefore this assumption that the Supreme Brahman assumes the form of jīva is not acceptable. It is important to remember that in Vedic literature Brahman (the living entity) is distinguished from Parabrahman (the Supreme Lord).

TEXT 4

अधिभूतं क्षरो भावः पुरुषश्चाधिदैवतम् ।
अधियज्ञोऽहमेवात्र देहे देहभृतां वर ॥ ४ ॥

adhibhūtaṁ kṣaro bhāvaḥ
puruṣaś cādhidaivatam
adhiyajño 'ham evātra
dehe deha-bhṛtāṁ vara

adhibhūtam—the physical manifestation; kṣaraḥ—constantly changing; bhāvaḥ—nature; puruṣaḥ—the universal form; ca—and; adhidaivatam—including all demigods like the sun and moon; adhiyajñaḥ—the Supersoul; aham—I (Kṛṣṇa); eva—certainly; atra—in this; dehe—body; deha-bhṛtām—of the embodied; vara—the Supreme.

TRANSLATION

Physical nature is known to be endlessly mutable. The universe is the cosmic form of the Supreme Lord, and I am that Lord represented as the Supersoul, dwelling in the heart of every embodied being.

PURPORT

The physical nature is constantly changing. Material bodies generally pass through six stages: they are born, they grow, they remain for some duration, they produce some by-products, they dwindle, and then they vanish. This physical nature is called *adhibhūtam*. Because it is created at a certain point and will be annihilated at a certain point, the conception of the universal form of the Supreme Lord that includes all the demigods and their different planets is called *adhidaivatam*. The individual soul (*jīva*) accompanies the body. The Supersoul, a plenary representation of Lord Kṛṣṇa, is called the Paramātmā or *adhiyajña* and is situated in the heart. The word *eva* is particularly important in the context of this verse because by this word the Lord stresses that the Paramātmā is not different from Him. The Supersoul, the Supreme Personality of Godhead, seated beside the individual soul, is the witness of the individual soul's activities and is the source of consciousness. The Supersoul gives the *jīva* an opportunity to act freely, and He witnesses his activities. The functions of all these different manifestations of the Supreme Lord automatically become clarified for the pure Kṛṣṇa conscious devotee engaged in transcendental service of the Lord. The gigantic universal form of the Lord called *adhidaivatam* is contemplated by the neophyte who cannot approach the Supreme Lord in His manifestation as Supersoul. The neophyte is advised to contemplate the universal form whose legs are considered the lowet planets and whose eyes are considered the sun and moon, and whose head is considered the upper planetary system.

TEXT 5

अन्तकाले च मामेव स्मरन्मुक्त्वा कलेवरम् ।
यः प्रयाति स मद्भावं याति नास्त्यत्र संशयः ॥ ५ ॥

anta-kāle ca mām eva
smaran muktvā kalevaram
yaḥ prayāti sa mad-bhāvaṁ
yāti nāsty atra saṁśayaḥ

anta-kāle—at the end of life; *ca*—also; *mām*—unto Me; *eva*—certainly; *smaran*—remembering; *muktvā*—quitting; *kalevaram*—the body; *yaḥ*—he who; *prayāti*—goes; *saḥ*—he; *mad-bhāvam*—My nature; *yāti*—achieves; *na*—not; *asti*—there is; *atra*—here; *saṁśayaḥ*—doubt.

TRANSLATION

And whoever, at the time of death, quits his body, remembering Me alone, at once attains My nature. Of this there is no doubt.

PURPORT

In this verse the importance of Kṛṣṇa consciousness is stressed. Anyone who quits his body in Kṛṣṇa consciousness is at once transferred to the transcendental abode of the Supreme Lord. The word *smaran* (remembering) is important. Remembrance of Kṛṣṇa is not possible for the impure soul who has not practiced Kṛṣṇa consciousness in devotional service. To remember Kṛṣṇa one should chant the *mahāmantra,* Hare Kṛṣṇa, Hare Kṛṣṇa, Kṛṣṇa Kṛṣṇa, Hare Hare/ Hare Rāma, Hare Rāma, Rāma Rāma, Hare Hare, incessantly, following in the footsteps of Lord Caitanya, being more tolerant than the tree, humbler than the grass and offering all respect to others without requiring respect in return. In such a way one will be able to depart from the body successfully remembering Kṛṣṇa and so attain the supreme goal.

TEXT 6

यं यं वापि स्मरन्भावं त्यजत्यन्ते कलेवरम् ।
तं तमेवैति कौन्तेय सदा तद्भावभावितः ॥ ६ ॥

yaṁ yaṁ vāpi smaran bhāvaṁ
tyajaty ante kalevaram
taṁ tam evaiti kaunteya
sadā tad-bhāva-bhāvitaḥ

yaṁ yam—whatever; *vā*—either; *api*—also; *smaran*—remembering; *bhāvam*—nature; *tyajati*—give up; *ante*—at the end; *kalevaram*—this body; *tam tam*—similar; *eva*—certainly; *eti*—gets; *kaunteya*—O son of Kuntī; *sadā*—always; *tat*—that; *bhāva*—state of being; *bhāvitaḥ*—remembering.

TRANSLATION

Whatever state of being one remembers when he quits his body, that state he will attain without fail.

PURPORT

The process of changing one's nature at the critical moment of death is here explained. How can one die in the proper state of mind? Mahārāja Bharata thought of a deer at the time of death and so was transferred to that form of life. However, as a deer, Mahārāja Bharata could remember his past activities. Of course the cumulative effect of the thoughts and actions of one's life influences one's thoughts at the moment of death; therefore the actions of this life determine one's future state of being. If one is transcendentally absorbed in Kṛṣṇa's service, then his next body will be transcendental (spiritual), not physical. Therefore the chanting of Hare Kṛṣṇa is the best process for successfully changing one's state of being to transcendental life.

TEXT 7

तस्मात्सर्वेषु कालेषु मामनुस्मर युध्य च ।
मय्यर्पितमनोबुद्धिर्मामेवैष्यस्यसंशयः ॥ ७ ॥

tasmāt sarveṣu kāleṣu
mām anusmara yudhya ca
mayy arpita-mano-buddhir
mām evaiṣyasy asaṁśayaḥ

tasmāt—therefore; *sarveṣu*—always; *kāleṣu*—time; *mām*—unto Me; *anusmara*—go on remembering; *yudhya*—fight; *ca*—also; *mayi*—unto Me; *arpita*—surrender; *manaḥ*—mind; *buddhiḥ*—intellect; *mām*—unto Me; *eva*—surely; *eṣyasi*—will attain; *asaṁśayaḥ*—beyond a doubt.

TRANSLATION

Therefore, Arjuna, you should always think of Me in the form of Kṛṣṇa and at the same time carry out your prescribed duty of fighting. With your activities dedicated to Me and your mind and intelligence fixed on Me, you will attain Me without doubt.

PURPORT

This instruction to Arjuna is very important for all men engaged in material activities. The Lord does not say that one should give up his prescribed duties or engagements. One can continue them and at the same time think of Kṛṣṇa by chanting Hare Kṛṣṇa. This will free one from material contamination and engage the mind and intelligence in Kṛṣṇa. By chanting Kṛṣṇa's names, one will be transferred to the supreme planet, Kṛṣṇaloka, without a doubt.

TEXT 8

अभ्यासयोगयुक्तेन चेतसा नान्यगामिना ।
परमं पुरुषं दिव्यं याति पार्थानुचिन्तयन् ॥ ८ ॥

abhyāsa-yoga-yuktena
cetasā nānya-gāminā
paramaṁ puruṣaṁ divyaṁ
yāti pārthānucintayan

abhyāsa—practice; *yoga-yuktena*—being engaged in meditation; *cetasā*—by the mind and intelligence; *na anya-gāminā*—without being deviated; *paramam*—the Supreme; *puruṣam*—Personality of Godhead; *divyam*—transcendental; *yāti*—achieves; *pārtha*—O son of Pṛthā; *anucintayan*—constantly thinking of.

TRANSLATION

He who meditates on the Supreme Personality of Godhead, his mind constantly engaged in remembering Me, undeviated from the path, he, O Pārtha [Arjuna], is sure to reach Me.

PURPORT

In this verse Lord Kṛṣṇa stresses the importance of remembering Him. One's memory of Kṛṣṇa is revived by chanting the *mahāmantra*, Hare Kṛṣṇa. By this practice of chanting and hearing the sound vibration of the Supreme Lord, one's ear, tongue and mind are engaged. This mystic meditation is very easy to practice, and it helps one attain the Supreme Lord. *Puruṣam* means enjoyer. Although living entities belong to the marginal energy of the Supreme Lord, they are in material contamination. They think themselves enjoyers, but they are not the supreme enjoyer. Here it is clearly stated that the supreme enjoyer is the Supreme Personality of Godhead in His different manifestations and plenary expansions as Nārāyaṇa, Vāsudeva, etc.

The devotees can constantly think of the object of worship, the Supreme Lord, in any of His features, Nārāyaṇa, Kṛṣṇa, Rāma, etc., by chanting Hare Kṛṣṇa. This practice will purify him, and at the end of his life, due to his constant chanting, he will be transferred to the kingdom of God. *Yoga* practice is meditation on the Supersoul within; similarly, by chanting Hare Kṛṣṇa one fixes his mind always on the Supreme Lord. The mind is fickle, and therefore it is necessary to engage the mind by force to think of Kṛṣṇa. One example often given is that of the caterpillar that thinks of becoming a butterfly and so is transformed into a butterfly in the same life. Similarly, if we constantly think of Kṛṣṇa, it is certain that at the end of our lives we shall have the same bodily constitution as Kṛṣṇa.

TEXT 9

कविं पुराणमनुशासितार-
मणोरणीयांसमनुस्मरेद्यः ।
सर्वस्य धातारमचिन्त्यरूप-
मादित्यवर्णं तमसः परस्तात् ॥ ९ ॥

kaviṁ purāṇam anuśāsitāram
aṇor aṇīyāṁsam anusmared yaḥ
sarvasya dhātāram acintya-rūpam
āditya-varṇaṁ tamasaḥ parastāt

kavim—one who knows everything; *purāṇam*—the oldest; *anuśāsitāram*—the controller; *aṇoḥ*—of the atom; *aṇīyāṁsam*—smaller than; *anusmaret*—always thinking; *yaḥ*—one who; *sarvasya*—of everything; *dhātāram*—maintainer; *acintya*—inconceivable; *rūpam*—form; *āditya-varṇam*—illuminated like the sun; *tamasaḥ*—of the darkness; *parastāt*—transcendental.

TRANSLATION

One should meditate upon the Supreme Person as the one who knows everything, as He who is the oldest, who is the controller, who is smaller than the smallest, who is the maintainer of everything, who is beyond all material conception, who is inconceivable, and who is always a person. He is luminous like the sun and, being transcendental, is beyond this material nature.

PURPORT

The process of thinking of the Supreme is mentioned in this verse. The foremost point is that He is not impersonal or void. One cannot meditate on something impersonal or void. That is very difficult. The process of thinking of Kṛṣṇa, however, is very easy and is factually stated herein. First of all, He is *puruṣa,* spiritual, Rāma and Kṛṣṇa, and is described herein as *kavim;* that is, He knows past, present and future and therefore knows everything. He is the oldest personality because He is the origin of everything; everything is born out of Him. He is also the supreme controller of the universe, maintainer and instructor of humanity. He is smaller than the smallest. The living entity is one 10,000th part of the tip of a hair, but the Lord is so inconceivably small that He enters into the heart of this particle. Therefore He is called smaller than the smallest. As the Supreme, He can enter into the atom and into the heart of the smallest and control him as the Supersoul. Although so small, He is still all-pervading and is maintaining everything. By Him all these planetary systems are sustained. We often wonder how these big planets are floating in the air. It is stated here that the Supreme Lord, by His inconceivable energy, is sustaining all these big planets and systems of galaxies. The word *acintya* (inconceivable) is very significant in this connection. God's energy is beyond our conception, beyond our thinking jurisdiction, and is therefore called inconceivable *(acintya).* Who can argue this point? He pervades this material world and yet is beyond it. We cannot even comprehend this material world, which is insignificant compared to the spiritual world—so how can we comprehend what is beyond? *Acintya* means that which is beyond this material world, that which our argument, logic and philosophical speculation cannot touch, that which is inconceivable. Therefore intelligent persons, avoiding useless argument and speculation, should accept what is stated in scriptures like the *Vedas, Gītā,* and *Śrīmad-Bhāgavatam* and follow the principles they set down. This will lead one to understanding.

TEXT 10

प्रयाणकाले मनसाऽचलेन
भक्तचा युक्तो योगबलेन चैव ।
भ्रुवोर्मध्ये प्राणमावेश्य सम्य-
क्स तं परं पुरुषमुपैति दिव्यम् ॥ १० ॥

*prayāṇa-kāle manasācalena
bhaktyā yukto yoga-balena caiva
bhruvor madhye prāṇam āveśya samyak
sa taṁ paraṁ puruṣam upaiti divyam*

prayāṇa-kāle—at the time of death; *manasā*—by the mind; *acalena*—without being deviated; *bhaktyā*—in full devotion; *yuktaḥ*—engaged; *yoga-balena*—by the power of mystic *yoga*; *ca*—also; *eva*—certainly; *bhruvoḥ*—between the two eyebrows; *madhye*—in; *prāṇam*—the life air; *āveśya*—establishing; *samyak*—completely; *saḥ*—he; *tam*—that; *param*—transcendental; *puruṣam*—Personality of Godhead; *upaiti*—achieves; *divyam*—in the spiritual kingdom.

TRANSLATION

One who, at the time of death, fixes his life air between the eyebrows and in full devotion engages himself in remembering the Supreme Lord, will certainly attain to the Supreme Personality of Godhead.

PURPORT

In this verse it is clearly stated that at the time of death the mind must be fixed in devotion on the Supreme Godhead. For those practiced in *yoga*, it is recommended that they raise the life force between the eyebrows, but for a pure devotee who does not practice such *yoga*, the mind should always be engaged in Kṛṣṇa consciousness so that at death he can remember the Supreme by His grace. This is explained in verse fourteen.

The particular use of the word *yoga-balena* is significant in this verse because without practice of *yoga* one cannot come to this transcendental state of being at the time of death. One cannot suddenly remember the Supreme Lord at death unless he is practiced in some *yoga* system, especially the system of *bhakti-yoga*. Since one's mind at death is very disturbed, one should practice transcendence through *yoga* during one's life.

TEXT 11

यदक्षरं वेदविदो वदन्ति
विशन्ति यद्यतयो वीतरागाः ।
यदिच्छन्तो ब्रह्मचर्यं चरन्ति
तत्ते पदं संग्रहेण प्रवक्ष्ये ॥ ११ ॥

yad akṣaraṁ veda-vido vadanti
viśanti yad yatayo vīta-rāgāḥ
yad icchanto brahmacaryaṁ caranti
tat te padaṁ saṅgraheṇa pravakṣye

yat—that which; akṣaram—inexhaustible; veda-vidaḥ—a person conversant with the Vedas; vadanti—say; viśanti—enters; yat—in which;
yatayaḥ—great sages; vīta-rāgāḥ—in the renounced order of life; yat—that
which; icchantaḥ—desiring; brahmacaryam—celibacy; caranti—practices;
tat—that; te—unto you; padam—situation; saṅgraheṇa—in summary;
pravakṣye—I shall explain.

TRANSLATION

**Persons learned in the Vedas, who utter omkāra and who are great
sages in the renounced order, enter into Brahman. Desiring such perfection, one practices celibacy. I shall now explain to you this process by
which one may attain salvation.**

PURPORT

Lord Kṛṣṇa explains that Brahman, although one without a second, has
different manifestations and features. For the impersonalists, the syllable
om is identical with Brahman. Kṛṣṇa here explains the impersonal
Brahman in which the renounced order of sages enter.

In the Vedic system of knowledge, students, from the very beginning,
are taught to vibrate om and learn of the ultimate impersonal Brahman by
living with the spiritual master in complete celibacy. In this way they
realize two of Brahman's features. This practice is very essential for the
student's advancement in spiritual life, but at the moment such brahmacārī
(unmarried celibate) life is not at all possible. The social construction of
the world has changed so much that there is no possibility of one's
practicing celibacy from the beginning of student life. Throughout the
world there are many institutions for different departments of knowledge,

but there is no recognized institution where students can be educated in the *brahmacārī* principles. Unless one practices celibacy, advancement in spiritual life is very difficult. Therefore Lord Caitanya has announced, according to the scriptural injunctions for this age of Kali, that no process of realizing the Supreme is possible except the chanting of the holy name of Lord Kṛṣṇa: Hare Kṛṣṇa, Hare Kṛṣṇa, Kṛṣṇa Kṛṣṇa, Hare Hare/ Hare Rāma, Hare Rāma, Rāma Rāma, Hare Hare.

TEXT 12

सर्वद्वाराणि संयम्य मनो हृदि निरुध्य च ।
मूर्ध्यधायात्मनः प्राणमास्थितो योगधारणाम् ॥ १२ ॥

*sarva-dvārāṇi saṁyamya
mano hṛdi nirudhya ca
mūrdhny ādhāyātmanaḥ prāṇam
āsthito yoga-dhāraṇām*

sarva-dvārāṇi—all the doors of the body; *saṁyamya*—controlling; *manaḥ* —mind; *hṛdi*—in the heart; *nirudhya*—confined; *ca*—also; *mūrdhni*—on the head; *ādhāya*—fixed; *ātmanaḥ*—soul; *prāṇam*—the life air; *āsthitaḥ*—situated; *yoga-dhāraṇām*—the yogic situation.

TRANSLATION

The yogic situation is that of detachment from all sensual engagements. Closing all the doors of the senses and fixing the mind on the heart and the life air at the top of the head, one establishes himself in yoga.

PURPORT

To practice *yoga*, as suggested here, one first has to close the door of all sense enjoyment. This practice is called *pratyāhāra*, or withdrawing the senses from the sense objects. Sense organs for acquiring knowledge, such as the eyes, ears, nose, tongue and touch, should be fully controlled and should not be allowed to engage in self-gratification. In this way the mind focuses on the Supersoul in the heart and the life force is raised to the top of the head. In the Sixth Chapter this process is described in detail. But as mentioned before, this practice is not practical in this age. The best process is Kṛṣṇa consciousness. If one is always able to fix his mind on

Kṛṣṇa in devotional service, it is very easy for him to remain in an undisturbed transcendental trance, or in samādhi.

TEXT 13

ओमित्येकाक्षरं ब्रह्म व्याहरन्मामनुस्मरन् ।
यः प्रयाति त्यजन्देहं स याति परमां गतिम् ॥ १३ ॥

om ity ekākṣaraṁ brahma
vyāharan mām anusmaran
yaḥ prayāti tyajan dehaṁ
sa yāti paramāṁ gatim

om—the combination of letters, *omkāra*; *iti*—thus; *eka-akṣaram*—supreme, indestructible; *brahma*—absolute; *vyāharan*—vibrating; *mām*—Me (Kṛṣṇa); *anusmaran*—remembering; *yaḥ*—anyone; *prayāti*—leaves; *tyajan*—quitting; *deham*—this body; *saḥ*—he; *yāti*—achieves; *paramām*—supreme; *gatim*—destination.

TRANSLATION

After being situated in this yoga practice and vibrating the sacred syllable om, the supreme combination of letters, if one thinks of the Supreme Personality of Godhead and quits his body, he will certainly reach the spiritual planets.

PURPORT

It is clearly stated here that *om*, Brahman, and Lord Kṛṣṇa are not different. The impersonal sound of Kṛṣṇa is *om*, but the sound Hare Kṛṣṇa contains *om*. It is clearly recommended in this age that if one quits his body at the end of this life chanting the *mahāmantra*, Hare Kṛṣṇa, he will reach the spiritual planets. Similarly, those who are devotees of Kṛṣṇa enter the Kṛṣṇa planet or Goloka Vṛndāvana, whereas the impersonalists remain in the *brahmajyoti*. The personalists also enter many innumerable planets in the spiritual sky known as Vaikuṇṭhas.

TEXT 14

अनन्यचेताः सततं यो मां स्मरति नित्यशः ।
तस्याहं सुलभः पार्थ नित्ययुक्तस्य योगिनः ॥ १४ ॥

ananya-cetāḥ satataṁ
yo māṁ smarati nityaśaḥ
tasyāhaṁ sulabhaḥ pārtha
nitya-yuktasya yoginaḥ

ananya-cetāḥ—without deviation; *satatam*—always; *yaḥ*—anyone; *mām*—Me (Kṛṣṇa); *smarati*—remembers; *nityaśaḥ*—regularly; *tasya*—to him; *aham*—I am; *sulabhaḥ*—very easy to achieve; *pārtha*—O son of Pṛthā; *nitya*—regularly; *yuktasya*—engaged; *yoginaḥ*—of the devotee.

TRANSLATION

For one who remembers Me without deviation, I am easy to obtain, O son of Pṛthā, because of his constant engagement in devotional service.

PURPORT

In this verse the *bhakti-yoga* of the unalloyed devotees of the Supreme Godhead is described. The preceeding verses mention four different kinds of devotees—the distressed, the inquisitive, those who seek material gain, and the speculative philosophers. Different processes of liberation from material entanglement have also been described: *karma-yoga, jñāna-yoga,* and *haṭha-yoga.* But here *bhakti-yoga,* without any mixture of these, is mentioned. In *bhakti-yoga* the devotees desire nothing but Kṛṣṇa. The pure *bhakti* devotee does not desire promotion to heavenly planets, nor does he seek salvation or liberation from material entanglement. A pure devotee does not desire anything. In the *Caitanya-caritāmṛta* the pure devotee is called *niṣkāma,* which means he has no desire for self-interest. Perfect peace belongs to him alone, not to them who strive for personal gain. The pure devotee only wants to please the Supreme Lord, and so the Lord says that for anyone who is unflinchingly devoted to Him, He is easy to attain. The devotee can render service to any of the transcendental forms of the Supreme Lord, and he meets with none of the problems that plague the practitioners of other *yogas. Bhakti-yoga* is very simple and pure and easy to perform. One can begin by simply chanting Hare Kṛṣṇa. Kṛṣṇa is very merciful to those who engage in His service, and He helps in various ways that devotee who is fully surrendered to Him so he can understand Him as He is. The Lord gives such a devotee sufficient intelligence so that ultimately the devotee can attain Him in His spiritual kingdom.

The special qualification of the pure devotee is that he is always thinking of Kṛṣṇa without considering the time or place. There should be no impediments. He should be able to carry out his service anywhere and at any time. Some say that the devotee should remain in holy places like Vṛndāvana or some holy town where the Lord lived, but a pure devotee can live anywhere and create the atmosphere of Vṛndāvana by his devotional service. It was Śrī Advaita who told Lord Caitanya, "Wherever You are, O Lord—*there* is Vṛndāvana."

A pure devotee constantly remembers Kṛṣṇa and meditates upon Him. These are qualifications of the pure devotee for whom the Lord is most easily attainable. *Bhakti-yoga* is the system that the *Gītā* recommends above all others. Generally, the *bhakti-yogīs* are engaged in five different ways: 1) *śānta-bhakta*, engaged in devotional service in neutrality; 2) *dāsya-bhakta*, engaged in devotional service as servant; 3) *sākhya-bhakta*, engaged as friend; 4) *vātsalya-bhakta*, engaged as parent; and 5) *mādhurya-bhakta*, engaged as conjugal lover of the Supreme Lord. In any of these ways, the pure devotee is always constantly engaged in the transcendental loving service of the Supreme Lord and cannot forget the Supreme Lord, and so for him the Lord is easily attained. A pure devotee cannot forget the Supreme Lord for a moment, and similarly, the Supreme Lord cannot forget His pure devotee for a moment. This is the great blessing of the Kṛṣṇa conscious process of chanting the *mahāmantra*, Hare Kṛṣṇa.

TEXT 15

मामुपेत्य पुनर्जन्म दुःखालयमशाश्वतम् ।
नाप्नुवन्ति महात्मानः संसिद्धिं परमां गताः ॥ १५ ॥

mām upetya punar janma
duḥkhālayam aśāśvatam
nāpnuvanti mahātmānaḥ
saṁsiddhiṁ paramāṁ gatāḥ

mām—unto Me; *upetya*—achieving; *punaḥ*—again; *janma*—birth; *duḥkha-ālayam*—place of miseries; *aśāśvatam*—temporary; *na*—never; *āpnuvanti*—attain; *mahātmānaḥ*—the great souls; *saṁsiddhim*—perfection; *paramām*—ultimate; *gatāḥ*—achieved.

TRANSLATION

After attaining Me, the great souls, who are yogīs in devotion, never return to this temporary world, which is full of miseries, because they have attained the highest perfection.

PURPORT

Since this temporary material world is full of the miseries of birth, old age, disease and death, naturally he who achieves the highest perfection and attains the supreme planet, Kṛṣṇaloka, Goloka Vṛndāvana, does not wish to return. The supreme planet is described in Vedic literature as beyond our material vision, and it is considered the highest goal. The *mahātmās* (great souls) receive transcendental messages from the realized devotees and thus gradually develop devotional service in Kṛṣṇa consciousness and become so absorbed in transcendental service that they no longer desire elevation to any of the material planets, nor do they even want to be transferred to any spiritual planet. They only want Kṛṣṇa's association and nothing else. Such great souls in Kṛṣṇa consciousness attain the highest perfection of life. In other words, they are the supreme souls.

TEXT 16

आब्रह्मभुवनाल्लोकाः पुनरावर्तिनोऽर्जुन ।
मामुपेत्य तु कौन्तेय पुनर्जन्म न विद्यते ॥ १६ ॥

ā-brahma-bhuvanāl lokāḥ
punar āvartino 'rjuna
mām upetya tu kaunteya
punar janma na vidyate

ābrahma—up to the Brahmaloka planet; *bhuvanāt*—from the planetary systems; *lokāḥ*—planets; *punaḥ*—again; *āvartinaḥ*—returning; *arjuna*—O Arjuna; *mām*—unto Me; *upetya*—arriving; *tu*—but; *kaunteya*—O son of Kuntī; *punaḥ janma*—rebirth; *na*—never; *vidyate*—takes to.

TRANSLATION

From the highest planet in the material world down to the lowest, all are places of misery wherein repeated birth and death take place.

But one who attains to My abode, O son of Kuntī, never takes birth again.

PURPORT

All kinds of yogīs-karma, jñāna, haṭha, etc.—eventually have to attain devotional perfection in bhakti-yoga, or Kṛṣṇa consciousness, before they can go to Kṛṣṇa's transcendental abode and never return. Those who attain the highest material planets or the planets of the demigods are again subjected to repeated birth and death. As persons on earth are elevated to higher planets, people in higher planets such as Brahmaloka, Candraloka and Indraloka fall down to earth. The practice of sacrifice called pañcāgni-vidyā, recommended in the Kaṭha Upaniṣad, enables one to achieve Brahmaloka, but if, in Brahmaloka, one does not cultivate Kṛṣṇa consciousness, then he must return to earth. Those who progress in Kṛṣṇa consciousness in the higher planets are gradually elevated to higher and higher planets and at the time of universal devastation are transferred to the eternal spiritual kingdom. When there is devastation of this material universe, Brahmā and his devotees, who are constantly engaged in Kṛṣṇa consciousness, are all transferred to the spiritual universe and to specific spiritual planets according to their desires.

TEXT 17

सहस्रयुगपर्यन्तमहर्यद्ब्रह्मणो विदुः ।
रात्रिं युगसहस्रान्तां तेऽहोरात्रविदो जनाः ॥ १७ ॥

sahasra-yuga-paryantam
ahar yad brahmaṇo viduḥ
rātriṁ yuga-sahasrāntāṁ
te 'ho-rātra-vido janāḥ

sahasra—thousand; yuga—millenniums; prayantam—including; ahaḥ—day; yat—that; brahmaṇaḥ—of Brahmā; viduḥ—know it; rātrim—night; yuga—millenniums; sahasra-antām—similarly, at the end of one thousand; te—that; ahaḥ-rātra—day and night; vidaḥ—understand; janāḥ—people.

TRANSLATION

By human calculation, a thousand ages taken together is the duration of Brahmā's one day. And such also is the duration of his night.

PURPORT

The duration of the material universe is limited. It is manifested in cycles of *kalpas*. A *kalpa* is a day of Brahmā, and one day of Brahmā consists of a thousand cycles of four *yugas* or ages: Satya, Tretā, Dvāpara, and Kali. The cycle of Satya is characterized by virtue, wisdom and religion, there being practically no ignorance and vice, and the *yuga* lasts 1,728,000 years. In the Tretā-yuga vice is introduced, and this *yuga* lasts 1,296,000 years. In the Dvāpara-yuga there is an even greater decline in virtue and religion, vice increasing, and this *yuga* lasts 864,000 years. And finally in Kali-yuga (the *yuga* we have now been experiencing over the past 5,000 years) there is an abundance of strife, ignorance, irreligion and vice, true virtue being practically nonexistent, and this *yuga* lasts 432,000 years. In Kali-yuga vice increases to such a point that at the termination of the *yuga* the Supreme Lord Himself appears as the Kalki *avatara*, vanquishes the demons, saves His devotees, and commences another Satya-yuga. Then the process is set rolling again. These four *yugas*, rotating a thousand times, comprise one day of Brahmā, the creator god, and the same number comprise one night. Brahmā lives one hundred of such "years" and then dies. These "hundred years" by earth calculations total to 311 trillion and 40 million earth years. By these calculations the life of Brahmā seems fantastic and interminable, but from the viewpoint of eternity it is as brief as a lightning flash. In the causal ocean there are innumerable Brahmās rising and disappearing like bubbles in the Atlantic. Brahmā and his creation are all part of the material universe, and therefore they are in constant flux.

In the material universe not even Brahmā is free from the process of birth, old age, disease and death. Brahmā, however, is directly engaged in the service of the Supreme Lord in the management of this universe—therefore he at once attains liberation. Elevated *sannyāsīs* are promoted to Brahmā's particular planet, Brahmaloka, which is the highest planet in the material universe and which survives all the heavenly planets in the upper strata of the planetary system, but in due course Brahmā and all inhabitants of Brahmaloka are subject to death, according to the law of material nature.

TEXT 18

अव्यक्ताद्व्यक्तयः सर्वाः प्रभवन्त्यहरागमे ।
रात्र्यागमे प्रलीयन्ते तत्रैवाव्यक्तसंज्ञके ॥ १८ ॥

avyaktād vyaktayaḥ sarvāḥ
prabhavanty ahar-āgame
rātry-āgame pralīyante
tatraivāvyakta-saṁjñake

avyaktāt—from the unmanifest; *vyaktayaḥ*—living entities; *sarvāḥ*—all; *prabhavanti*—come into being; *ahaḥ-āgame*—at the beginning of the day; *rātri-āgame*—at the fall of night; *pralīyante*—are annihilated; *tatra*—there; *eva*—certainly; *avyakta*—the unmanifest; *saṁjñake*—called.

TRANSLATION

When Brahmā's day is manifest, this multitude of living entities comes into being, and at the arrival of Brahmā's night they are all annihilated.

PURPORT

The less intelligent *jīvas* try to remain within this material world and are accordingly elevated and degraded in the various planetary systems. During the daytime of Brahmā they exhibit their activities, and at the coming of Brahmā's night they are annihilated. In the day they receive various bodies for material activities, and at night these bodies perish. The *jīvas* (individual souls) remain compact in the body of Viṣṇu and again and again are manifest at the arrival of Brahmā's day. When Brahmā's life is finally finished, they are all annihilated and remain unmanifest for millions and millions of years. Finally, when Brahmā is born again in another millennium, they are again manifest. In this way the *jīvas* are captivated by the material world. However, those intelligent beings who take to Kṛṣṇa consciousness and chant Hare Kṛṣṇa, Hare Rāma in devotional service transfer themselves, even in this life, to the spiritual planet of Kṛṣṇa and become eternally blissful there, not being subject to such rebirths.

TEXT 19

भूतग्रामः स एवायं भूत्वा भूत्वा प्रलीयते ।
रात्र्यागमेऽवशः पार्थ प्रभवत्यहरागमे ॥ १९ ॥

bhūta-grāmaḥ sa evāyaṁ
bhūtvā bhūtvā pralīyate
rātry-āgame 'vaśaḥ pārtha
prabhavaty ahar-āgame

bhūta-grāmaḥ—the aggregate of all living entities; *saḥ*—they; *eva*—certainly; *ayam*—this; *bhūtvā bhūtvā*—taking birth; *pralīyate*—annihilate; *rātri*—night; *āgame*—on arrival; *avaśaḥ*—automatically; *pārtha*—O son of Pṛthā; *prabhavanti*—manifest; *ahaḥ*—during daytime; *āgame*—on arrival.

TRANSLATION

Again and again the day comes, and this host of beings is active; and again the night falls, O Pārtha, and they are helplessly dissolved.

TEXT 20

परस्तस्मात्तु भावोऽन्योऽव्यक्तोऽव्यक्तात्सनातनः ।
यः स सर्वेषु भूतेषु नश्यत्सु न विनश्यति ॥ २० ॥

*paras tasmāt tu bhāvo 'nyo
'vyakto 'vyaktāt sanātanaḥ
yaḥ sa sarveṣu bhūteṣu
naśyatsu na vinaśyati*

paraḥ—transcendental; *tasmāt*—from that; *tu*—but; *bhāvaḥ*—nature; *anyaḥ*—another; *avyaktaḥ*—unmanifest; *avyaktāt*—from the unmanifest; *sanātanaḥ*—eternal; *yaḥ*—that; *saḥ*—which; *sarveṣu*—all; *bhūteṣu*—manifestation; *naśyatsu*—being annihilated; *na*—never; *vinaśyati*—annihilated.

TRANSLATION

Yet there is another nature, which is eternal and is transcendental to this manifested and unmanifested matter. It is supreme and is never annihilated. When all in this world is annihilated, that part remains as it is.

PURPORT

Kṛṣṇa's superior spiritual energy is transcendental and eternal. It is beyond all the changes of material nature, which is manifest and annihilated during the days and nights of Brahmā. Kṛṣṇa's superior energy is completely opposite in quality to material nature. Superior and inferior nature are explained in the Seventh Chapter.

TEXT 21

अव्यक्तोऽक्षर इत्युक्तस्तमाहुः परमां गतिम् ।
यं प्राप्य न निवर्तन्ते तद्धाम परमं मम ॥ २१ ॥

*avyakto 'kṣara ity uktas
tam āhuḥ paramāṁ gatim
yaṁ prāpya na nivartante
tad dhāma paramaṁ mama*

avyaktaḥ—unmanifested; *akṣaraḥ*—infallible; *iti*—thus; *uktaḥ*—said; *tam*—that which; *āhuḥ*—is known; *paramām*—ultimate; *gatim*—destination; *yam*—that which; *prāpya*—gaining; *na*—never; *nivartante*—comes back; *tat-dhāma*—that abode; *paramam*—supreme; *mama*—Mine.

TRANSLATION

That supreme abode is called unmanifested and infallible, and it is the supreme destination. When one goes there, he never comes back. That is My supreme abode.

PURPORT

The supreme abode of the Personality of Godhead, Kṛṣṇa, is described in the *Brahma-saṁhitā* as *cintāmaṇi-dhāma*, a place where all desires are fulfilled. The supreme abode of Lord Kṛṣṇa known as Goloka Vṛndāvana is full of palaces made of touchstone. There are also trees which are called "desire trees" that supply any type of eatable upon demand, and there are cows known as *surabhi* cows which supply a limitless supply of milk. In this abode, the Lord is served by hundreds of thousands of goddesses of fortune (Lakṣmīs), and He is called Govinda, the primal Lord and the cause of all causes. The Lord is accustomed to blow His flute (*veṇuṁ kvaṇantam*). His transcendental form is the most attractive in all the worlds-His eyes are like the lotus petals and the color of His body like clouds. He is so attractive that His beauty excels that of thousands of cupids. He wears saffron cloth, a garland around His neck and a peacock feather in His hair. In the *Gītā* Lord Kṛṣṇa gives only a small hint of His personal abode (Goloka Vṛndāvana) which is the supermost planet in the spiritual kingdom. A vivid description is given in the *Brahma-saṁhitā*. Vedic literature states that there is nothing superior to the abode of the Supreme Godhead, and that that abode is the ultimate destination. When one attains to it, he never returns to the material world. Kṛṣṇa's supreme abode and Kṛṣṇa Himself are nondifferent, being of the same quality. On this earth, Vṛndāvana, ninety miles southeast of Delhi, is a replica of that supreme Goloka Vṛndāvana located in the spiritual sky. When Kṛṣṇa descended on this earth, He sported on that particular tract of land known as Vṛndāvana in the district of Mathurā, India.

TEXT 22

पुरुषः स परः पार्थ भक्त्या लभ्यस्त्वनन्यया ।
यस्यान्तःस्थानि भूतानि येन सर्वमिदं ततम् ॥ २२ ॥

*purusaḥ sa paraḥ pārtha
bhaktyā labhyas tv ananyayā
yasyāntaḥ-sthāni bhūtāni
yena sarvam idaṁ tatam*

puruṣaḥ—the Supreme Personality; *saḥ*—He; *paraḥ*—the Supreme, than whom no one is greater; *pārtha*—O son of Pṛthā; *bhaktyā*—by devotional service; *labhyaḥ*—can be achieved; *tu*—but; *ananyayā*—unalloyed, undeviating devotion; *yasya*—His; *antaḥsthāni*—within; *bhūtāni*—all this material manifestation; *yena*—by whom; *sarvam*—all; *idam*—whatever we can see; *tatam*—distributed.

TRANSLATION

The Supreme Personality of Godhead, who is greater than all, is attainable by unalloyed devotion. Although He is present in His abode, He is all-pervading, and everything is situated within Him.

PURPORT

It is here clearly stated that the supreme destination from which there is no return is the abode of Kṛṣṇa, the Supreme Person. The *Brahma-saṁhitā* describes this supreme abode as *ānanda-cinmaya-rasa*, a place where everything is full of spiritual bliss. Whatever variegatedness is manifest there is all of the quality of spiritual bliss—there is nothing material. All variegatedness is expanded as the spiritual expansion of the Supreme Godhead Himself, for the manifestation there is totally of the spiritual energy, as explained in Chapter Seven. As far as this material world is concerned, although the Lord is always in His supreme abode, He is nonetheless all-pervading by His material energy. So by His spiritual and material energies He is present everywhere—both in the material and in the spiritual universes. *Yasyāntaḥsthāni* means that everything is sustained by Him, whether it be spiritual or material energy.

It is clearly stated here that only by *bhakti*, or devotional service, can one enter into the Vaikuṇṭha (spiritual) planetary system. In all the Vaikuṇṭhas there is only one Supreme Godhead, Kṛṣṇa, who has expanded Himself into millions and millions of plenary expansions. These plenary expansions are four-armed, and they preside over the innumerable spiritual planets. They are known by a variety of names—Puruṣottama, Trivikrama, Keśava, Mādhava, Aniruddha, Hṛṣīkeśa, Saṅkarṣaṇa, Pradyumna, Śrīdhara, Vāsudeva, Dāmodara, Janārdana, Nārāyaṇa, Vāmana, Padmanābha, etc. These plenary expansions are likened unto the leaves of a tree, and the main tree is likened to Kṛṣṇa. Kṛṣṇa, dwelling in Goloka Vṛndāvana, His supreme abode, systematically conducts all affairs of both universes (material and spiritual) without a flaw by power of His all-pervasiveness.

TEXT 23

यत्र काले त्वनावृत्तिमावृत्तिं चैव योगिनः ।
प्रयाता यान्ति तं कालं वक्ष्यामि भरतर्षभ ॥ २३ ॥

*yatra kāle tv anāvṛttim
āvṛttiṁ caiva yoginaḥ
prayātā yānti taṁ kālaṁ
vakṣyāmi bharatarṣabha*

yatra—in that; *kāle*—time; *tu*—but; *anāvṛttim*—no return; *āvṛttim*—return; *ca*—also; *eva*—certainly; *yoginaḥ*—of different kinds of mystics; *prayātāḥ*—one who goes; *yānti*—departs; *tam*—that; *kālam*—time; *vakṣyāmi*—describing; *bharatarṣabha*—O best of the Bhāratas.

TRANSLATION

O best of the Bhāratas, I shall now explain to you the different times at which, passing away from this world, one does or does not come back.

PURPORT

The unalloyed devotees of the Supreme Lord who are totally surrendered souls do not care when they leave their bodies or by what method. They leave everything in Kṛṣṇa's hands and so easily and happily return to Godhead. But those who are not unalloyed devotees and who depend instead on such methods of spiritual realization as *karma-yoga*, *jñāna-yoga*, *haṭha-yoga*, etc., must leave the body at a suitable time and thereby be assured whether or not they will return to the world of birth and death.

If the *yogī* is perfect, he can select the time and place for leaving this material world, but if he is not so perfect, then he has to leave at nature's will. The most suitable time to leave the body and not return is being explained by the Lord in these verses. According to Ācārya Baladeva Vidyābhūṣaṇa, the Sanskrit word *kāla* used herein refers to the presiding deity of time.

TEXT 24

अग्निर्ज्योतिरहः शुक्लः षण्मासा उत्तरायणम् ।
तत्र प्रयाता गच्छन्ति ब्रह्म ब्रह्मविदो जनाः ॥ २४ ॥

agnir jyotir ahaḥ śuklaḥ
ṣaṇ-māsā uttarāyaṇam
tatra prayātā gacchanti
brahma brahma-vido janāḥ

agniḥ—fire; *jyotiḥ*—light; *ahaḥ*—day; *śuklaḥ*—white; *ṣaṭ-māsāḥ*—six months; *uttarāyaṇam*—when the sun passes on the northern side; *tatra*—there; *prayātāḥ*—one who goes; *gacchanti*—passes away; *brahma*—the Absolute; *brahma-vidaḥ*—one who knows the Absolute; *janāḥ*—person.

TRANSLATION

Those who know the Supreme Brahman pass away from the world during the influence of the fiery god, in the light, at an auspicious moment, during the fortnight of the moon and the six months when the sun travels in the north.

PURPORT

When fire, light, day and moon are mentioned, it is to be understood that over all of them there are various presiding deities who make arrangements for the passage of the soul. At the time of death, the *jīva* sets forth on the path to a new life. If one leaves the body at the time designated above, either accidently or by arrangement, it is possible for him to attain the impersonal *brahmajyoti*. Mystics who are advanced in *yoga* practice can arrange the time and place to leave the body. Others have no control—if by accident they leave at an auspicious moment, then they will not return to the cycle of birth and death, but if not, then there is every possibility that they will have to return. However, for the pure devotee in Kṛṣṇa consciousness, there is no fear of returning, whether he leaves the body at an auspicious or inauspicious moment, by accident or arrangement.

TEXT 25

धूमो रात्रिस्तथा कृष्णः षण्मासा दक्षिणायनम् ।
तत्र चान्द्रमसं ज्योतिर्योगी प्राप्य निवर्तते ॥ २५ ॥

dhūmo rātris tathā kṛṣṇaḥ
ṣaṇ-māsā dakṣiṇāyanam
tatra cāndramasaṁ jyotir
yogī prāpya nivartate

dhūmaḥ—smoke; *rātriḥ*—night; *tathā*—also; *kṛṣṇaḥ*—the fortnight of the dark moon; *ṣaṭ-māsāḥ*—the six months; *dakṣiṇa-ayanam*—when the sun passes on the southern side; *tatra*—there; *cāndramasam*—the moon planet; *jyotiḥ*—light, *yogī*—the mystic; *prāpya*—achieves; *nivartate*—comes back.

TRANSLATION

The mystic who passes away from this world during the smoke, the night, the moonlight fortnight, or in the six months when the sun passes to the south, or who reaches the moon planet, again comes back.

PURPORT

In the Third Canto of *Śrīmad-Bhāgavatam* we are informed that those who are expert in fruitive activities and sacrificial methods on earth attain to the moon at death. These elevated souls live on the moon for about 10,000 years (by demigod calculations) and enjoy life by drinking soma-rasa. They eventually return to earth. This means that on the moon there are higher classes of living beings, though they may not be perceived by the gross senses.

TEXT 26

शुक्लकृष्णे गती ह्येते जगतः शाश्वते मते ।
एकया यात्यनावृत्तिमन्ययावर्तते पुनः ॥ २६ ॥

śukla-kṛṣṇe gatī hy ete
jagataḥ śāśvate mate
ekayā yāty anāvṛttim
anyayāvartate punaḥ

śukla—light; *kṛṣṇe*—darkness; *gatī*—passing away; *hi*—certainly; *ete*—all these; *jagataḥ*—of the material world; *śāśvate*—the Vedas; *mate*—in the opinion; *ekayā*—by one; *yāti*—goes; *anāvṛttim*—no return; *anyayā*—by the other; *āvartate*—comes back; *punaḥ*—again.

TRANSLATION

According to the Vedas, there are two ways of passing from this world— one in light and one in darkness. When one passes in light, he does not come back; but when one passes in darkness, he returns.

PURPORT

The same description of departure and return is quoted by Ācārya Baladeva Vidyābhūṣaṇa from the *Chāndogya Upaniṣad*. In such a way, those who are fruitive laborers and philosophical speculators from time immemorial are constantly going and coming. Actually they do not attain ultimate salvation, for they do not surrender to Kṛṣṇa.

TEXT 27

नैते सृती पार्थ जानन्योगी मुह्यति कश्चन ।
तस्मात्सर्वेषु कालेषु योगयुक्तो भवार्जुन ॥ २७ ॥

naite srtī pārtha jānan
yogī muhyati kaścana
tasmāt sarveṣu kāleṣu
yoga-yukto bhavārjuna

na—never; *ete*—all these; *srtī*—different paths; *pārtha*—O son of Pṛthā; *jānan*—even if they know; *yogī*—the devotees of the Lord; *muhyati*—bewildered; *kaścana*—anyone; *tasmāt*—therefore; *sarveṣu kāleṣu*—always; *yoga-yuktaḥ*—being engaged in Kṛṣṇa consciousness; *bhava*—just become; *arjuna*—O Arjuna.

TRANSLATION

The devotees who know these two paths, O Arjuna, are never bewildered. Therefore be always fixed in devotion.

PURPORT

Kṛṣṇa is here advising Arjuna that he should not be disturbed by the different paths the soul can take when leaving the material world. A devotee of the Supreme Lord should not worry whether he will depart either by arrangement or by accident. The devotee should be firmly established in Kṛṣṇa consciousness and chant Hare Kṛṣṇa. He should know that concern over either of these two paths is troublesome. The best way to be absorbed in Kṛṣṇa consciousness is to be always dovetailed in His service, and this will make one's path to the spiritual kingdom safe, certain, and direct. The word *yoga-yukta* is especially significant in this verse. One who is firm in *yoga* is constantly engaged in Kṛṣṇa consciousness in all his activities. Śrī Rūpa Gosvāmī advises that one should be unattached in the material world and that all affairs should be steeped in Kṛṣṇa consciousness. In this way one attains perfection. Therefore the devotee is not disturbed by these descriptions because he knows that his passage to the supreme abode is guaranteed by devotional service.

TEXT 28

वेदेषु यज्ञेषु तपःसु चैव
दानेषु यत्पुण्यफलं प्रदिष्टम् ।
अत्येति तत्सर्वमिदं विदित्वा
योगी परं स्थानमुपैति चाद्यम् ॥ २८ ॥

vedeṣu yajñeṣu tapaḥsu caiva
dāneṣu yat puṇya-phalaṁ pradiṣṭam
atyeti tat sarvam idaṁ viditvā
yogī paraṁ sthānam upaiti cādyam

vedeṣu—in the study of the Vedas; *yajñeṣu*—in the performances of *yajña*, sacrifice; *tapaḥsu*—undergoing different types of austerities; *ca*—also; *eva*—certainly; *dāneṣu*—in giving charities; *yat*—that which; *puṇya-phalam*—the result of pious work; *pradiṣṭam*—directed; *atyeti*—surpasses; *tat*—all those; *sarvam idam*—all those described above; *viditvā*—knowing; *yogī*—the devotee; *param*—supreme; *sthānam*—abode; *upaiti*—achieved peace; *ca*—also; *ādyam*—original.

TRANSLATION

A person who accepts the path of devotional service is not bereft of the results derived from studying the Vedas, performing austere sacrifices, giving charity or pursuing philosophical and fruitive activities. At the end he reaches the supreme abode.

PURPORT

This verse is the summation of the Seventh and Eighth Chapters, particularly as the chapters deal with Kṛṣṇa consciousness and devotional service. One has to study the Vedas under the guidance of the spiritual master and undergo many austerities and penances while living under his care. A *brahmacārī* has to live in the home of the spiritual master just like a servant, and he must beg alms from door to door and bring them to the spiritual master. He takes food only under the master's order, and if the master neglects to call the student for food that day, the student fasts. These are some of the Vedic principles for observing *brahmacarya*.

After the student studies the Vedas under the master for a period from five to twenty years, he may become a man of perfect character. Study of the Vedas is not meant for the recreation of armchair speculators, but for the formation of character. After this training, the *brahmacārī* is allowed to enter into household life and marry. When he is a householder, he also has to perform many sacrifices and strive for further enlightenment. Then after retiring from household life, upon accepting the order of *vānaprastha*, he undergoes severe penances, such as living in forests, dressing with tree bark, not shaving, etc. By carrying out the orders of *brahmacārī*, householder, *vānaprastha* and finally *sannyāsa*, one becomes elevated to the perfectional stage of life. Some are then elevated to the heavenly kingdoms, and when they become even more advanced they are liberated in the spiritual sky, either in the impersonal *brahmajyoti* or in the Vaikuṇṭha planets or Kṛṣṇaloka. This is the path outlined by Vedic literatures.

The beauty of Kṛṣṇa consciousness, however, is that by one stroke, by engaging in devotional service, one can surpass all rituals of the different orders of life.

One should try to understand the Seventh and Eighth Chapters of the *Gītā* not by scholarship or mental speculation, but by hearing them in association with pure devotees. Chapters Six through Twelve are the essence of the *Gītā*. If one is fortunate to understand the *Gītā*—especially these middle six chapters—in the association of devotees, then his life at once becomes glorified beyond all penances, sacrifices, charities, speculations, etc. One should hear the *Gītā* from the devotee because at the beginning of the Fourth Chapter it is stated that the *Gīta* can only be perfectly understood by devotees. Hearing the *Gītā* from devotees, not from mental speculators, is called faith. Through association of devotees, one is placed in devotional service, and by this service Kṛṣṇa's activities, form, pastimes, name, etc., become clear, and all misgivings are dispelled. Then once doubts are removed, the study of the *Gītā* becomes extremely pleasurable, and one develops a taste and feeling for Kṛṣṇa consciousness. In the advanced stage, one falls completely in love with Kṛṣṇa, and that is the beginning of the highest perfectional stage of life which prepares the devotee's transferral to Kṛṣṇa's abode in the spiritual sky, Goloka Vṛndāvana, where the devotee enters into eternal happiness.

Thus end the Bhaktivedanta Purports to the Eighth Chapter of the Śrīmad-Bhagavad-gītā in the matter of Attaining the Supreme.

CHAPTER NINE

The Most Confidential Knowledge

TEXT 1

श्रीभगवानुवाच ।
इदं तु ते गुह्यतमं प्रवक्ष्याम्यनसूयवे ।
ज्ञानं विज्ञानसहितं यज्ज्ञात्वा मोक्ष्यसेऽशुभात् ॥ १ ॥

*śrī-bhagavān uvāca
idaṁ tu te guhyatamaṁ
pravakṣyāmy anasūyave
jñānaṁ vijñāna-sahitaṁ
yaj jñātvā mokṣyase 'śubhāt*

śrī bhagavān uvāca—the Supreme Personality of Godhead said; *idam*—this; *tu*—but; *te*—unto you; *guhyatamam*—most confidential; *pravakṣ-yāmi*—I am speaking; *anasūyave*—to the nonenvious; *jñānam*—knowledge; *vijñāna*—realized knowledge; *sahitam*—with; *yat*—which; *jñātvā*—knowing; *mokṣyase*—be released; *aśubhāt*—from this miserable material existence.

441

TRANSLATION

The Supreme Lord said: My dear Arjuna, because you are never envious of Me, I shall impart to you this most secret wisdom, knowing which you shall be relieved of the miseries of material existence.

PURPORT

As a devotee hears more and more about the Supreme Lord, he becomes enlightened. This hearing process is recommended in the Śrīmad-Bhāgavatam: "The messages of the Supreme Personality of Godhead are full of potencies, and these potencies can be realized if topics regarding the Supreme Godhead are discussed amongst devotees. This cannot be achieved by the association of mental speculators or academic scholars, for it is realized knowledge."

The devotees are constantly engaged in the Supreme Lord's service. The Lord understands the mentality and sincerity of a particular living entity who is engaged in Kṛṣṇa consciousness and gives him the intelligence to understand the science of Kṛṣṇa in the association of the devotees. Discussion of Kṛṣṇa is very potent, and if a fortunate person has such association and tries to assimilate the knowledge, then he will surely make advancement toward spiritual realization. Lord Kṛṣṇa, in order to encourage Arjuna to higher and higher elevation in His potent service, describes in this Ninth Chapter matters more confidential than any He has already disclosed.

The very beginning of Bhagavad-gītā, the First Chapter, is more or less an introduction to the rest of the book; and in the Second and Third Chapters, the spiritual knowledge described is called confidential. Topics discussed in the Seventh and Eighth Chapters are specifically related to devotional service, and because they bring enlightenment in Kṛṣṇa consciousness, they are called more confidential. But the matters which are described in the Ninth Chapter deal with unalloyed, pure devotion. Therefore this is called the most confidential. One who is situated in the most confidential knowledge of Kṛṣṇa is naturally transcendental; he therefore has no material pangs, although he is in the material world. In the Bhakti-rasāmṛta-sindhu it is said that although one who has a sincere desire to render loving service to the Supreme Lord is situated in the conditional state of material existence, he is to be considered liberated. Similarly, we shall find in the Bhagavad-gītā, Tenth Chapter, that anyone who is engaged in that way is a liberated person.

Now this first verse has specific significance. Knowledge (*idaṁ jñānam*) refers to pure devotional service, which consists of nine different activities: hearing, chanting, remembering, serving, worshiping, praying, obeying, maintaining friendship and surrendering everything. By the practice of these nine elements of devotional service one is elevated to spiritual consciousness, Kṛṣṇa consciousness. At the time when one's heart is cleared of the material contamination, one can understand this science of Kṛṣṇa. Simply to understand that a living entity is not material is not sufficient. That may be the beginning of spiritual realization, but one should recognize the difference between activities of the body and spiritual activities by which one understands that he is not the body.

In the Seventh Chapter we have already discussed the opulent potency of the Supreme Personality of Godhead, His different energies, the inferior and superior natures, and all this material manifestation. Now in Chapters Nine and Ten the glories of the Lord will be delineated.

The Sanskrit word *anasūyave* in this verse is also very significant. Generally the commentators, even if they are highly scholarly, are all envious of Kṛṣṇa, the Supreme Personality of Godhead. Even the most erudite scholars write on *Bhagavad-gītā* very inaccurately. Because they are envious of Kṛṣṇa, their commentaries are useless. The commentaries given by devotees of the Lord are bona fide. No one can explain *Bhagavad-gītā*, or give perfect knowledge of Kṛṣṇa if he is envious. One who criticizes the character of Kṛṣṇa without knowing Him is a fool. So such commentaries should be very carefully avoided. For one who understands that Kṛṣṇa is the Supreme Personality of Godhead, the pure and transcendental Personality, these chapters will be very beneficial.

TEXT 2

राजविद्या राजगुह्यं पवित्रमिदमुत्तमम् ।
प्रत्यक्षावगमं धर्म्यं सुसुखं कर्तुमव्ययम् ॥ २ ॥

rāja-vidyā rāja-guhyaṁ
pavitram idam uttamam
pratyakṣāvagamaṁ dharmyaṁ
su-sukhaṁ kartum avyayam

rāja-vidyā—the king of education; *rāja-guhyam*—the king of confidential knowledge; *pavitram*—the purest; *idam*—this; *uttamam*—transcendental;

pratyakṣa—directly experienced; *avagamam*—understood; *dharmyam*—the principle of religion; *susukham*—very happy; *kartum*—to execute; *avyayam* —everlasting.

TRANSLATION

This knowledge is the king of education, the most secret of all secrets. It is the purest knowledge, and because it gives direct perception of the self by realization, it is the perfection of religion. It is everlasting, and it is joyfully performed.

PURPORT

This chapter of *Bhagavad-gītā* is called the king of education because it is the essence of all doctrines and philosophies explained before. There are seven principal philosophers in India: Gautama, Kaṇāda, Kapila, Yājña-valkya, Śāṇḍilya, Vaiśvānara, and, finally, Vyāsadeva, the author of the *Vedānta-sūtra*. So there is no dearth of knowledge in the field of philosophy or transcendental knowledge. Now the Lord says that this Ninth Chapter is the king of all such knowledge, the essence of all knowledge that can be derived from the study of the *Vedas* and different kinds of philosophy. It is the most confidential because confidential or transcendental knowledge involves understanding the difference between the soul and the body. And the king of all confidential knowledge culminates in devotional service.

Generally, people are not educated in this confidential knowledge; they are educated in external knowledge. As far as ordinary education is concerned, people are involved with so many departments: politics, sociology, physics, chemistry, mathematics, astronomy, engineering, etc. There are so many departments of knowledge all over the world and many huge universities, but there is, unfortunately, no university or educational institution where the science of the spirit soul is instructed. Yet the soul is the most important part of this body; without the presence of the soul, the body has no value. Still people are placing great stress on the bodily necessities of life, not caring for the vital soul.

The *Bhagavad-gītā*, especially from the Second Chapter on, stresses the importance of the soul. In the very beginning, the Lord says that this body is perishable and that the soul is not perishable. That is a confidential part of knowledge: simply knowing that spirit soul is different from this body and that its nature is immutable, indestructible and eternal. But that gives no positive information about the soul. Sometimes people are under the impression that the soul is different from the body and that when the body is finished, or one is liberated from the body, the soul remains in a void and becomes impersonal. But actually that is not the fact. How can the soul, which is so active within this body, be inactive after being liberated from the body? It is always active. If it is eternal, then it is eternally active, and its activities in the spiritual kingdom are the most confidential part of spiritual knowledge. These activities of the spirit soul are therefore indicated here as constituting the king of all knowledge, the most confidential part of all knowledge.

This knowledge is the purest form of all activities, as is explained in Vedic literature. In the *Padma Purāṇa*, man's sinful activities have been analyzed and are shown to be the results of sin after sin. Those who are engaged in fruitive activities are entangled in different stages and forms of sinful reactions. For instance, when the seed of a particular tree is sown, the tree does not appear immediately to grow; it takes some time. It is first a small, sprouting plant, then it assumes the form of a tree, then it flowers, bears fruit, and, when it is complete, the flowers and fruits are enjoyed by persons who have sown the seed of the tree. Similarly, a man performs a sinful act, and like a seed it takes time to fructify. There are different stages. The sinful action may have already stopped within the individual, but the results or the fruit of that sinful action are still enjoyed. There are sins which are still in the form of a seed, and there are others which are already fructified and are giving us fruit, which we are enjoying as distress and pain, as explained in the twentieth verse of the Seventh Chapter.

A person who has completely ended the reactions of all sinful activities and who is fully engaged in pious activities, being freed from the duality of this material world, becomes engaged in devotional service to the Supreme Personality of Godhead, Kṛṣṇa. In other words, those who are actually engaged in the devotional service of the Supreme Lord are already freed from all reactions. For those who are engaged in the devotional service of the Supreme Personality of Godhead, all sinful reactions, whether fructified, in the stock, or in the form of a seed, gradually vanish. Therefore the purifying potency of devotional service is very strong, and it is called *pavitram uttamam*, the purest. *Uttamam* means transcendental. *Tamas* means this material world or darkness, and *uttamam* means that which is transcendental to material activities. Devotional activities are never to be considered material, although sometimes it appears that devotees are engaged just like ordinary men. One who can see and is familiar with devotional service, however, will know that they are not material activities. They are all spiritual and devotional, uncontaminated by the material modes of nature.

It is said that the execution of devotional service is so perfect that one can perceive the results directly. This direct result is actually perceived, and we have practical experience that any person who is chanting the holy names of Kṛṣṇa (Hare Kṛṣṇa, Hare Kṛṣṇa, Kṛṣṇa Kṛṣṇa, Hare Hare/ Hare Rāma, Hare Rāma, Rāma Rāma, Hare Hare) in course of time feels some transcendental pleasure and very quickly becomes purified of all material contamination. This is actually seen. Furthermore, if one engages not only in hearing but in trying to broadcast the message of devotional activities as well, or if he engages himself in helping the missionary activities of Kṛṣṇa consciousness, he gradually feels spiritual progress. This advancement in spiritual life does not depend on any kind of previous education or qualification. The method itself is so pure that by simply engaging in it one becomes pure.

In the *Vedānta-sūtra* this is also described in the following words: *prakāśaś ca karmaṇy abhyāsāt.* "Devotional service is so potent that simply by engaging in the activities of devotional service, one becomes enlightened without a doubt." Nārada, who happened to be the son of a maidservant, had no education, nor was he born into a high family. But when his mother was engaged in serving great devotees, Nārada also became engaged, and sometimes, in the absence of his mother, he would serve the great devotees himself. Nārada personally says, "Once only, by their permission, I took the remnants of their food, and by so doing all my sins were at once eradicated. Thus being engaged, I became purified in heart, and at that time the very nature of the transcendentalist became attractive to me." (*Bhāg.* 1.5.25) Nārada tells his disciple Vyāsadeva that in a previous life he was engaged as a boy servant of purified devotees during four months of their stay and that he was intimately associating with them. Sometimes those sages left remnants of food on their dishes, and the boy, who would wash their dishes, wanted to taste the remnants. So he asked the great devotees whether he could eat them, and they gave their permission. Nārada then ate those remnants and consequently became freed from all sinful reactions. As he went on eating, he gradually became as purehearted as the sages, and he gradually developed the same taste. The great devotees relished the taste of unceasing devotional service of the Lord, hearing, chanting, etc., and by developing the same taste, Nārada wanted also to hear and chant the glories of the Lord. Thus by associating with the sages, he developed a great desire for devotional service. Therefore he quotes from the *Vedānta-sūtra* (*prakāśaś ca karmaṇy abhyāsāt*): If one is engaged simply in the acts of devotional service, everything is revealed to him automatically, and he can understand. This is called *prakāśaḥ*, directly perceived.

Nārada was actually a son of a maidservant. He had no opportunity to go to school. He was simply assisting his mother, and fortunately his mother rendered some service to the devotees. The child Nārada also got the opportunity and simply by association achieved the highest goal of all religions, devotional service. In the *Śrīmad-Bhāgavatam* it is said that religious people generally do not know that the highest perfection of religion is the attainment of the stage of devotional service. Generally Vedic knowledge is required for the understanding of the path of self-realization. But here, although he was not educated in the Vedic principle, Nārada acquired the highest results of Vedic study. This process is so potent that even without performing the religious process regularly, one can be raised to the highest perfection. How is this possible? This is also confirmed in Vedic literature: *ācāryavān puruṣo veda.* One who is in association with great *ācāryas*, even if he is not educated or has not studied the *Vedas*, can become familiar with all the knowledge necessary for realization.

The process of devotional service is a very happy one. Why? Devotional service consists of *śravaṇaṁ kīrtanaṁ viṣṇoḥ*, so one can simply hear the chanting of the glories of the Lord or can attend philosophical lectures on transcendental knowledge given by authorized *ācāryas*. Simply by sitting, one can learn; then one can eat the remnants of the food offered to God, nice palatable dishes. In every state devotional service is joyful. One can execute devotional service even in the most poverty-stricken condition. The Lord says, *patraṁ puṣpaṁ phalam:* He is ready to accept from the devotee any kind of offering, never mind what. Even a leaf, a flower, a bit of fruit, or a little water, which are all available in every part of the world, can be offered by *any* person, regardless of social position, and will be accepted if offered with love. There are many instances in history. Simply by tasting the *tulasī* leaves offered to the lotus feet of the Lord, great sages like Sanatkumāra became great devotees. Therefore the devotional process is very nice, and it can be executed in a happy mood. God accepts only the love with which things are offered to Him.

It is said here that this devotional service is eternally existing. It is not as the Māyāvādī philosophers claim. They sometimes take to so-called devotional service, and as long as they are not liberated they continue their devotional service, but at the end, when they become liberated, they "become one with God." Such temporary time-serving devotional service is not accepted as pure devotional service. Actual devotional service continues even after liberation. When the devotee goes to the spiritual planet in the kingdom of God, he is also engaged there in serving the Supreme Lord. He does not try to become one with the Supreme Lord.

As it will be seen, actual devotional service begins after liberation. So in *Bhagavad-gītā* it is said, *brahma-bhūta*. After being liberated, or being situated in the Brahman position, one's devotional service begins. By executing devotional service, one can understand the Supreme Lord. No one can understand the Supreme Personality of Godhead by executing *karma-yoga, jñāna,* or *aṣṭāṅga-yoga* or any other *yoga* independantly. Without coming to the stage of devotional service, one cannot understand what is the Personality of Godhead. In the *Śrīmad-Bhāgavatam* it is also confirmed that when one becomes purified by executing the process of devotional service, especially by hearing *Śrīmad-Bhāgavatam* or *Bhagavad-gītā* from realized souls, then he can understand the science of Kṛṣṇa or the science of God. *Evaṁ prasanna-manaso bhagavad-bhakti-yogataḥ.* When one's heart is cleared of all nonsense, then one can understand what God is. Thus the process of devotional service, of Kṛṣṇa consciousness, is the king of all education and the king of all confidential knowledge. It is the purest form of religion, and it can be executed joyfully without difficulty. Therefore one should adopt it.

TEXT 3

अश्रद्दधानाः पुरुषा धर्मस्यास्य परन्तप ।
अप्राप्य मां निवर्तन्ते मृत्युसंसारवर्त्मनि ॥ ३ ॥

*aśraddadhānāḥ puruṣā
dharmasyāsya parantapa
aprāpya māṁ nivartante
mṛtyu-saṁsāra-vartmani*

aśraddadhānāḥ—those who are faithless; *puruṣāḥ*—such persons; *dharmasya*—of this process of religion; *asya*—of it; *parantapa*—O killer of the enemies; *aprāpya*—without obtaining; *mām*—Me; *nivartante*—come back; *mṛtyu*—death; *saṁsāra*—material existence; *vartmani*—on the path of.

TRANSLATION

Those who are not faithful on the path of devotional service cannot attain Me, O conqueror of foes, but return to birth and death in this material world.

PURPORT

The faithless cannot accomplish this process of devotional service; that is the purport of this verse. Faith is created by association with devotees. Unfortunate people, even after hearing all the evidence of Vedic literature from great personalities, still have no faith in God. They are hesitant and cannot stay fixed in the devotional service of the Lord. Thus faith is a most important factor for progress in Kṛṣṇa consciousness. In the *Caitanya-caritāmṛta* it is said that one should have complete conviction that simply by serving the Supreme Lord Śrī Kṛṣṇa he can achieve all perfection. That is called real faith. In the *Śrīmad-Bhāgavatam* (3.4.12) it is stated that by giving water to the root of a tree, its branches, twigs and leaves become satisfied, and by supplying food to the stomach all the senses of the body become satisfied, and, similarly, by engaging in the transcendental service of the Supreme Lord, all the demigods and all the living entities automatically become satisfied.

After reading *Bhagavad-gītā* one should promptly come to the conclusion of *Bhagavad-gītā:* one should give up all other engagements and adopt the service of the Supreme Lord, Kṛṣṇa, the Personality of Godhead. If one is convinced of this philosophy of life, that is faith. Now the development of that faith is the process of Kṛṣṇa consciousness.

There are three divisions of Kṛṣṇa conscious men. In the third class are those who have no faith. If they are engaged in devotional service officially, for some ulterior purpose, they cannot achieve the highest perfectional stage. Most probably they will slip, after some time. They may become engaged, but because they haven't complete conviction and faith, it is very difficult for them to continue in Kṛṣṇa consciousness. We have practical experience in discharging our missionary activity that some people come and apply themselves to the Kṛṣṇa consciousness with some hidden motive, and as soon as they are economically a little well-situated, they give up this process and take to their old ways again. It is only by faith that one can advance in Kṛṣṇa consciousness. As far as the development of faith is concerned, one who is well versed in the literatures of devotional service and has attained the stage of firm faith is called a first-class person in Kṛṣṇa consciousness. And in the second class are those who are not very advanced in understanding the devotional scriptures but who automatically have firm faith that Kṛṣṇa *bhakti* or service to Kṛṣṇa is the best course and so in good faith have taken it up. Thus they are superior to the third class who have neither perfect knowledge of the scriptures nor good faith but by association and simplicity are trying to follow. The third-class person in

Kṛṣṇa consciousness may fall down, but when one is in the second class or first class, he does not fall down. One in the first class will surely make progress and achieve the result at the end. As far as the third-class person in Kṛṣṇa consciousness is concerned, although he has faith in the conviction that devotional service to Kṛṣṇa is very good, he has no knowledge of Kṛṣṇa through the scriptures like Śrīmad-Bhāgavatam and Bhagavad-gītā. Sometimes these third-class persons in Kṛṣṇa consciousness have some tendency toward karma-yoga and jñāna-yoga, and sometimes they are disturbed, but as soon as the infection of karma-yoga or jñāna-yoga is vanquished, they become second-class or first-class persons in Kṛṣṇa consciousness. Faith in Kṛṣṇa is also divided into three stages and described in Śrīmad-Bhāgavatam. First-class attachment, second-class attachment, and third-class attachment are also explained in Śrīmad-Bhāgavatam in the Eleventh Canto. Those who have no faith even after hearing about Kṛṣṇa and the excellence of devotional service, who think that it is simply eulogy, find the path very difficult, even if they are supposedly engaged in devotional service. For them there is very little hope in gaining perfection. Thus faith is very important in the discharge of devotional service.

TEXT 4

मया ततमिदं सर्वं जगदव्यक्तमूर्तिना ।
मत्स्थानि सर्वभूतानि न चाहं तेष्ववस्थितः ॥ ४ ॥

mayā tatam idaṁ sarvaṁ
jagad avyakta-mūrtinā
mat-sthāni sarva-bhūtāni
na cāhaṁ teṣv avasthitaḥ

mayā—by Me; tatam—spread; idam—all these manifestations; sarvam—all; jagat—cosmic manifestation; avyakta-mūrtinā—unmanifested form; mat-sthāni—unto Me; sarva-bhūtāni—all living entities; na—not; ca—also; aham—I; teṣu—in them; avasthitaḥ—situated.

TRANSLATION

By Me, in My unmanifested form, this entire universe is pervaded. All beings are in Me, but I am not in them.

PURPORT

The Supreme Personality of Godhead is not perceivable through the gross material senses. It is said that Lord Śrī Kṛṣṇa's name, fame, pastimes, etc., cannot be understood by material senses. Only to one who is engaged in pure devotional service under proper guidance is He revealed. In the *Brahma-saṁhitā* it is stated, *premāñjanacchurita....* One can see the Supreme Personality of Godhead, Govinda, always within himself and outside himself if he has developed the transcendental loving attitude towards Him. Thus for people in general He is not visible. Here it is said that although He is all-pervading, everywhere present, He is yet not conceivable by the material senses. But actually, although we cannot see Him, everything is resting in Him. As we have discussed in the Seventh Chapter, the entire material cosmic manifestation is only a combination of His two different energies, the superior spiritual energy and the inferior material energy. Just as the sunshine is spread all over the universe, the energy of the Lord is spread all over the creation, and everything is resting in that energy.

Yet one should not conclude that because He is spread all over He has lost His personal existence. To refute such argument the Lord says, "I am everywhere, and everything is in Me, but still I am aloof." For example, a king heads a government which is but the manifestation of the king's energy; the different governmental departments are nothing but the energies of the king, and each department is resting on the king's power. But still one cannot expect the king to be present in every department personally. That is a crude example. Similarly, all the manifestations that we see, and everything that exists both in this material world and in the spiritual world, are resting on the energy of the Supreme Personality of Godhead. The creation takes place by the diffusion of His different energies, and, as is stated in the *Bhagavad-gītā*, He is everywhere present by His personal representation, the diffusion of His different energies.

TEXT 5

न च मत्स्थानि भूतानि पश्य मे योगमैश्वरम् ।
भूतभृन्न च भूतस्थो ममात्मा भूतभावनः ॥ ५ ॥

na ca mat-sthāni bhūtāni
paśya me yogam aiśvaram
bhūta-bhṛn na ca bhūta-stho
mamātmā bhūta-bhāvanaḥ

na—never; ca—also; mat-sthāni—situated in Me; bhūtāni—all creation; paśya—just see; me—My; yogam aiśvaram—inconceivable mystic power; bhūta-bhṛt—maintainer of all living entities; na—never; ca—also; bhūta-sthaḥ—in the cosmic manifestation; mama—My; ātmā—Self; bhūta-bhāvanaḥ—is the source of all manifestations.

TRANSLATION

And yet everything that is created does not rest in Me. Behold My mystic opulence! Although I am the maintainer of all living entities, and although I am everywhere, still My Self is the very source of creation.

PURPORT

The Lord says that everything is resting on Him. This should not be misunderstood. The Lord is not directly concerned with the maintenance and sustenance of this material manifestation. Sometimes we see a picture of Atlas holding the globe on his shoulders; he seems to be very tired, holding this great earthly planet. Such an image should not be entertained in connection with Kṛṣṇa's upholding this created universe. He says that although everything is resting on Him, still He is aloof. The planetary systems are floating in space, and this space is the energy of the Supreme Lord. But He is different from space. He is differently situated. Therefore the Lord says, "Although they are situated on My inconceivable energy, still, as the Supreme Personality of Godhead, I am aloof from them." This is the inconceivable opulence of the Lord.

In the Vedic dictionary it is said, "The Supreme Lord is performing inconceivably wonderful pastimes, displaying His energy. His person is full of different potent energies, and His determination is itself actual fact. In this way the Personality of Godhead is to be understood." We may think to do something, but there are so many impediments, and sometimes it is not possible to do as we like. But when Kṛṣṇa wants to do something, simply by His willing, everything is performed so perfectly that one cannot imagine how it is being done. The Lord explains this fact: although He is the maintainer and sustainer of all material manifestation, He does not touch this material manifestation. Simply by His supreme will everything is created, everything is sustained, everything is maintained, and everything is annihilated. There is no difference between His mind and Himself (as there is a difference between ourselves and our present material mind) because He is absolute spirit. Simultaneously the Lord is present in everything; yet the common man cannot understand how He is also present personally. He is different from this material manifestation, yet everything is resting on Him. This is explained here as *yogam aiśvaram*, the mystic power of the Supreme Personality of Godhead.

TEXT 6

यथाकाशस्थितो नित्यं वायुः सर्वत्रगो महान् ।
तथा सर्वाणि भूतानि मत्स्थानीत्युपधारय ॥ ६ ॥

yathākāśa-sthito nityaṁ
vāyuḥ sarvatra-go mahān
tathā sarvāṇi bhūtāni
mat-sthānīty upadhāraya

yathā—as much as; *ākāśa-sthitaḥ*—situated in space; *nityam*—always; *vāyuḥ*—wind; *sarvatra-gaḥ*—blowing everywhere; *mahān*—great; *tathā*—similarly; *sarvāṇi*—everything, *bhūtāni*—created beings; *mat-sthāni*—situated in Me; *iti*—thus; *upadhāraya*—try to understand.

TRANSLATION

As the mighty wind, blowing everywhere, always rests in ethereal space know that in the same manner all beings rest in Me.

PURPORT

For the ordinary person it is almost inconceivable how the huge material creation is resting in Him. But the Lord is giving an example which may help us to understand. Space is the biggest manifestation we can conceive. The cosmic manifestation rests in space. Space permits the movement of even the atoms and on up to the greatest planets, the sun and the moon. Although the sky (or wind or air) is great, still it is situated within space. Space is not beyond the sky.

Similarly, all the wonderful cosmic manifestations are existing by the supreme will of God, and all of them are subordinate to that supreme will. As we generally say, not a blade of grass moves without the will of the Supreme Personality of Godhead. Thus everything is moving under His will: by His will everything is being created, everything is being maintained, and everything is being annihilated. Still He is aloof from everything, as

space is always aloof from the activities of the atmosphere. In the
Upaniṣads, it is stated, "It is out of the fear of the Supreme Lord that the
wind is blowing." In the Garga Upaniṣad also it is stated, "By the supreme
order, under the superintendence of the Supreme Personality of Godhead,
the moon, the sun and the great planets are moving." In the Brahma-
saṁhitā this is also stated. There is also a description of the movement of
the sun, and it is said that the sun is considered to be one of the eyes of
the Supreme Lord and that it has immense potency to diffuse heat and
light. Still it is moving in its prescribed orbit by the order and the supreme
will of Govinda. So, from the Vedic literature we can find evidence that
this material manifestation, which appears to us to be very wonderful and
great, is under the complete control of the Supreme Personality of Godhead. This will be further explained in the later verses of this chapter.

TEXT 7

सर्वभूतानि कौन्तेय प्रकृतिं यान्ति मामिकाम् ।
कल्पक्षये पुनस्तानि कल्पादौ विसृजाम्यहम् ॥ ७ ॥

sarva-bhūtāni kaunteya
prakṛtiṁ yānti māmikām
kalpa-kṣaye punas tāni
kalpādau visṛjāmy aham

sarva-bhūtāni—all created entities; *kaunteya*—O son of Kuntī; *prakṛtim*—
nature; *yānti*—enter; *māmikām*—unto Me; *kalpa-kṣaye*—at the end of the
millennium; *punaḥ*—again; *tāni*—all those; *kalpa-ādau*—in the beginning of
the millennium; *visṛjāmi*—I create; *aham*—I.

TRANSLATION

O son of Kuntī, at the end of the millennium every material manifestation enters into My nature, and at the beginning of another millennium,
by My potency I again create.

PURPORT

The creation, maintenance and annihilation of this material cosmic
manifestation is completely dependant on the supreme will of the Person-

ality of Godhead. "At the end of the millennium" means at the death of Brahmā. Brahmā lives for one hundred years, and his one day is calculated at 4,300,000,000 of our earthly years. His night is of the same duration. His month consists of thirty such days and nights, and his year of twelve months. After one hundred such years, when Brahmā dies, the devastation or annihilation takes place; this means that the energy manifested by the Supreme Lord is again wound up in Himself. Then again, when there is need to manifest the cosmic world, it is done by His will: "Although I am one, I shall become many." This is the Vedic aphorism. He expands Himself in this material energy, and the whole cosmic manifestation again takes place.

TEXT 8

प्रकृतिं स्वामवष्टभ्य विसृजामि पुनः पुनः ।
भूतग्राममिमं कृत्स्नमवशं प्रकृतेर्वशात् ॥ ८ ॥

prakṛtiṁ svām avaṣṭabhya
visṛjāmi punaḥ punaḥ
bhūta-grāmam imaṁ kṛtsnam
avaśaṁ prakṛter vaśāt

prakṛtim—material nature; svām—of My personal self; avaṣṭabhya—enter in; visṛjāmi—create; punaḥ punaḥ—again, again; bhūta-grāmam—all these cosmic manifestations; imam—this; kṛtsnam—total; avaśam—automatically; prakṛteḥ—by the force of nature; vaśāt—under obligation.

TRANSLATION

The whole cosmic order is under Me. By My will it is manifested again and again, and by My will it is annihilated at the end.

PURPORT

This matter is the manifestation of the inferior energy of the Supreme Personality of Godhead. This has already been explained several times. At the creation, the material energy is let loose as mahat-tattva, into which the Lord as His first Puruṣa incarnation, Mahā-Viṣṇu, enters. He lies within the Causal Ocean and breathes out innumerable universes, and into each universe the Lord again enters as Garbhodakaśāyī Viṣṇu. Each universe is in that way created. He still further manifests Himself as Kṣīrodakaśāyī Viṣṇu, and that Viṣṇu enters into everything—even into the minute atom. This fact is explained here. He enters into everything.

Now, as far as the living entities are concerned, they are impregnated into this material nature, and as a result of their past deeds they take different positions. Thus the activities of this material world begin. The activities of the different species of living beings are begun from the very moment of the creation. It is not that all is evolved. The different species of life are created immediately along with the universe. Men, animals, beasts, birds—everything is simultaneously created, because whatever desires the living entities had at the last annihilation are again manifested. It is clearly stated here that the living entities have nothing to do with this process. The state of being in their past life in the past creation is simply manifested again, and all this is done simply by His will. This is the inconceivable potency of the Supreme Personality of God. And after creating different species of life, He has no connection with them. The creation takes place to accommodate the inclinations of the various living entities, and so the Lord does not become involved with it.

TEXT 9

न च मां तानि कर्माणि निबध्नन्ति धनंजय ।
उदासीनवदासीनमसक्तं तेषु कर्मसु ॥ ९ ॥

na ca māṁ tāni karmāṇi
nibadhnanti dhanañjaya
udāsīna-vad āsīnam
asaktaṁ teṣu karmasu

na—never; *ca*—also; *mām*—Me; *tāni*—all those; *karmāṇi*—activities; *nibadhnanti*—bind; *dhanañjaya*—O conqueror of riches; *udāsīnavat*—as neutral; *āsīnam*—situated; *asaktam*—without attraction; *teṣu*—in them; *karmasu*—in activities.

TRANSLATION

O Dhanañjaya, all this work cannot bind Me. I am ever detached, seated as though neutral.

PURPORT

One should not think, in this connection, that the Supreme Personality of Godhead has no engagement. In His spiritual world He is always engaged. In the *Brahma-saṁhitā* it is stated: "He is always involved in His eternal, blissful, spiritual activities, but He has nothing to do with these material activities." Material activities are being carried on by His different potencies. The Lord is always neutral in the material activities of the created world. This neutrality is explained here. Although He has control over every minute detail of matter, He is sitting as if neutral. The example can be given of a high court judge sitting on his bench. By his order so many things are happening: someone is being hanged, someone is being put into jail, someone is awarded a huge amount of wealth—but still he is neutral. He has nothing to do with all that gain and loss. Similarly, the Lord is always neutral, although He has His hand in every sphere of activity. In the *Vedānta-sūtra* it is stated that He is not situated in the dualities of this material world. He is transcendental to these dualities. Nor is He attached to the creation and annihilation of this material world. The living entities take their different forms in the various species of life according to their past deeds, and the Lord doesn't interfere with them.

TEXT 10

मयाध्यक्षेण प्रकृतिः सूयते सचराचरम् ।
हेतुनानेन कौन्तेय जगद्विपरिवर्तते ॥ १० ॥

*mayādhyakṣeṇa prakṛtiḥ
sūyate sa-carācaram
hetunānena kaunteya
jagad viparivartate*

mayā—by Me; *adhyakṣeṇa*—by superintendence; *prakṛtiḥ*—material nature; *sūyate*—manifest; *sa*—with; *carācaram*—moving and nonmoving; *hetunā*—for this reason; *anena*—this; *kaunteya*—O son of Kuntī; *jagat*—the cosmic manifestation; *viparivartate*—is working.

TRANSLATION

This material nature is working under My direction, O son of Kuntī, and it is producing all moving and unmoving beings. By its rule this manifestation is created and annihilated again and again.

PURPORT

It is clearly stated here that the Supreme Lord, although aloof from all the activities of the material world, remains the supreme director. The Supreme Lord is the supreme will and the background of this material manifestation, but the management is being conducted by material nature. Kṛṣṇa also states in *Bhagavad-gītā* that of all the living entities in different forms and species, "I am the Father." The father gives seeds to the womb of the mother for the child, and similarly the Supreme Lord by His mere glance injects all the living entities into the womb of material nature, and they come out in their different forms and species, according to their last desires and activities. All these living entities, although born under the glance of the Supreme Lord, still take their different bodies according to their past deeds and desires. So the Lord is not directly attached to this material creation. He simply glances over material nature; material nature is thus activated, and everything is created immediately. Because He glances over material nature, there is undoubtedly activity on the part of the Supreme Lord, but He has nothing to do with the manifestation of the material world directly. This example is given in the *smṛti*: when there is a fragrant flower before someone, the fragrance is touched by the smelling power of the person, yet the smelling and the flower are detached from one another. There is a similar connection between the material world and the Supreme Personality of Godhead; actually He has nothing to do with this material world, but He creates by His glance and ordains. In summary, material nature, without the superintendence of the Supreme Personality of Godhead, cannot do anything. Yet the Supreme Personality is detached from all material activities.

TEXT 11

अवजानन्ति मां मूढा मानुषीं तनुमाश्रितम् ।
परं भावमजानन्तो मम भूतमहेश्वरम् ॥ ११ ॥

avajānanti māṁ mūḍhā
mānuṣīṁ tanum āśritam
paraṁ bhāvam ajānanto
mama bhūta-maheśvaram

avajānanti—deride; *mām*—Me; *mūḍhāḥ*—foolish men; *mānuṣīm*—in a human form; *tanum*—body; *āśritam*—assuming; *param*—transcendental; *bhā-vam*—nature; *ajānantaḥ*—not knowing; *mama*—Mine; *bhūta*—everything that be; *maheśvaram*—supreme proprietor.

TRANSLATION

Fools deride Me when I descend in the human form. They do not know My transcendental nature and My supreme dominion over all that be.

PURPORT

From the other explanations of the previous verses in this chapter, it is clear that the Supreme Personality of Godhead, although appearing like a human being, is not a common man. The Personality of Godhead, who conducts the creation, maintenance and annihilation of the complete cosmic manifestation, cannot be a human being. Yet there are many foolish men who consider Kṛṣṇa to be merely a powerful man and nothing more. Actually, He is the original Supreme Personality, as is confirmed in the Brahma-saṁhitā (īśvaraḥ paramaḥ kṛṣṇaḥ); He is the Supreme Lord.

There are many īśvaras, controllers, and one appears greater than another. In the ordinary management of affairs in the material world, we find some official or director, and above him there is a secretary, and above him a minister, and above him a president. Each of them is a controller, but one is controlled by another. In the Brahma-saṁhitā it is said that Kṛṣṇa is the supreme controller; there are many controllers undoubtedly both in the material and spiritual world, but Kṛṣṇa is the supreme controller (īśvaraḥ paramaḥ kṛṣṇaḥ), and His body is sac-cid-ānanda, non-material.

Material bodies cannot perform the wonderful acts described in previous verses. His body is eternal, blissful and full of knowledge. Although He is not a common man, the foolish deride Him and consider Him to be a man. His body is called here mānuṣīm because He is acting just like a man, a friend of Arjuna's, a politician involved in the Battle of Kurukṣetra. In so many ways He is acting just like an ordinary man, but actually His body is sac-cid-ānanda-vigraha—eternal bliss and knowledge absolute. This is confirmed in the Vedic language also (sac-cid-ānanda-rūpāya kṛṣṇāya): "I offer my obeisances unto the Supreme Personality of Godhead, Kṛṣṇa, who is the eternal blissful form of knowledge." There are other descriptions in the Vedic language also. Tam ekaṁ govindam: "You are Govinda, the pleasure of the senses and the cows." Sac-cid-ānanda-vigraham: "And Your form is transcendental, full of knowledge, bliss and eternality."

Despite the transcendental qualities of Lord Kṛṣṇa's body, its full bliss and knowledge, there are many so-called scholars and commentators of *Bhagavad-gītā* who deride Kṛṣṇa as an ordinary man. The scholar may be born an extraordinary man due to his previous good work, but this conception of Śrī Kṛṣṇa is due to a poor fund of knowledge. Therefore he is called *mūḍha*, for only foolish persons consider Kṛṣṇa to be an ordinary human being because they do not know the confidential activities of the Supreme Lord and His different energies. They do not know that Kṛṣṇa's body is a symbol of complete knowledge and bliss, that He is the proprietor of everything that be and that He can award liberation to anyone. Because they do not know that Kṛṣṇa has so many transcendental qualifications, they deride Him.

Nor do they know that the appearance of the Supreme Personality of Godhead in this material world is a manifestation of His internal energy. He is the master of the material energy. As has been explained in several places (*mama māyā duratyayā*), He claims that the material energy, although very powerful, is under His control, and whoever surrenders unto Him can get out of the control of this material energy. If a soul surrendered to Kṛṣṇa can get out of the influence of material energy, then how can the Supreme Lord, who conducts the creation, maintenance and annihilation of the whole cosmic nature, have a material body like us? So this conception of Kṛṣṇa is complete foolishness. Foolish persons, however, cannot conceive that the Personality of Godhead, Kṛṣṇa, appearing just like an ordinary man, can be the controller of all the atoms and of the gigantic manifestation of the universal form. The biggest and the minutest are beyond their conception, so they cannot imagine that a form like that of a human being can simultaneously control the infinite and the minute. Actually although He is controlling the infinite and the finite, He is apart from all this manifestation. It is clearly stated concerning His *yogam aiśvaram*, His inconceivable transcendental energy, that He can control the infinite and the finite simultaneously and that He can remain aloof from them. Although the foolish cannot imagine how Kṛṣṇa, who appears just like a human being, can control the infinite and the finite, those who are pure devotees accept this, for they know that Kṛṣṇa is the Supreme Personality of Godhead. Therefore they completely surrender unto Him and engage in Kṛṣṇa consciousness, devotional service of the Lord.

There are many controversies amongst the impersonalists and the personalists about the Lord's appearance as a human being. But if we consult *Bhagavad-gītā* and *Śrīmad-Bhāgavatam*, the authoritative texts for understanding the science of Kṛṣṇa, then we can understand that Kṛṣṇa is the Supreme Personality of Godhead. He is not an ordinary man, although He appeared on this earth as an ordinary human. In the *Śrīmad-Bhāgavatam*,

First Canto, First Chapter, when the sages inquire about the activities of Kṛṣṇa, it is stated that His appearance as a man bewilders the foolish. No human being could perform the wonderful acts that Kṛṣṇa performed while He was present on this earth. When Kṛṣṇa appeared before His father and mother, Vasudeva and Devakī, He appeared with four hands, but after the prayers of the parents, He transformed Himself into an ordinary child. His appearance as an ordinary human being is one of the features of His transcendental body. In the Eleventh Chapter of the Gītā also it is stated, tenaiva rūpeṇa etc. Arjuna prayed to see again that form of four hands, and when Kṛṣṇa was thus petitioned by Arjuna, He again assumed His original form. All these different features of the Supreme Lord are certainly not those of an ordinary human being.

Some of those who deride Kṛṣṇa, who are infected with the Māyāvādī philosophy, quote the following verse from the Śrīmad-Bhāgavatam to prove that Kṛṣṇa is just an ordinary man: ahaṁ sarveṣu bhūteṣu bhūtātmāvasthitaḥ sadā: "The Supreme is present in every living entity." (Bhāg. 3.29.21) We should better take note of this particular verse from the Vaiṣṇava ācāryas like Jīva Gosvāmī instead of following the interpretation of unauthorized persons who deride Kṛṣṇa. Jīva Gosvāmī, commenting on this verse, says that Kṛṣṇa, in His plenary expansion as Paramātmā, is situated in the moving and the nonmoving entities as the Supersoul, so any neophyte devotee who simply gives his attention to the arca-mūrti, the form of the Supreme Lord in the temple, and does not respect other living entities is uselessly worshiping the form of the Lord in the temple. There are three kinds of devotees of the Lord, and the neophyte is in the lowest stage. The neophyte devotee gives more attention to the Deity in the temple than to other devotees, so Jīva Gosvāmī warns that this sort of mentality should be corrected. A devotee should see that Kṛṣṇa is present in everyone's heart as Paramātmā; therefore every body is the embodiment or the temple of the Supreme Lord, and as such, as one offers respect to the temple of the Lord, he should similarly properly respect each and every body in whom the Paramātmā dwells. Everyone should therefore be given proper respect and should not be neglected.

There are also many impersonalists who deride temple worship. They say that since God is everywhere, why should one restrict himself to temple worship? But if God is everywhere, is He not in the temple or in the Deity? Although the personalist and the impersonalist will fight with one another perpetually, a perfect devotee in Kṛṣṇa consciousness knows that although Kṛṣṇa is the Supreme Personality, He is all-pervading, as is confirmed in the Brahma-saṁhitā. Although His personal abode is Goloka

Vṛndāvana and He is always staying there, still, by His different manifestations of energy and by His plenary expansion, He is present everywhere in all parts of the material and spiritual creation.

TEXT 12

मोघाशा मोघकर्माणो मोघज्ञाना विचेतसः ।
राक्षसीमासुरीं चैव प्रकृतिं मोहिनीं श्रिताः ॥ १२ ॥

moghāśā mogha-karmāṇo
mogha-jñānā vicetasaḥ
rākṣasīm āsurīm caiva
prakṛtim mohinīm śritāḥ

moghāśāḥ—baffled hope; *mogha-karmāṇaḥ*—baffled in fruitive activities; *mogha-jñānāḥ*—baffled in knowledge; *vicetasaḥ*—bewildered; *rākṣasīm*—demonic; *āsurīm*—atheistic; *ca*—and; *eva*—certainly; *prakṛtim*—nature; *mohinīm*—bewildering; *śritāḥ*—taking shelter of.

TRANSLATION

Those who are thus bewildered are attracted by demonic and atheistic views. In that deluded condition, their hopes for liberation, their fruitive activities, and their culture of knowledge are all defeated.

PURPORT

There are many devotees who assume themselves to be in Kṛṣṇa consciousness and devotional service but at heart do not accept the Supreme Personality of Godhead, Kṛṣṇa, as the Absolute Truth. For them, the fruit of devotional service—going back to Godhead—will never be tasted. Similarly, those who are engaged in fruitive, pious activities and who are ultimately hoping to be liberated from this material entanglement will never be successful either because they deride the Supreme Personality of Godhead, Kṛṣṇa. In other words, persons who mock Kṛṣṇa are to be understood to be demonic or atheistic. As described in the Seventh Chapter of

Bhagavad-gītā, such demonic miscreants never surrender to Kṛṣṇa. Therefore their mental speculations to arrive at the Absolute Truth bring them to the false conclusion that the ordinary living entity and Kṛṣṇa are one and the same. With such a false conviction, they think that the body of any human being is now simply covered by material nature and that as soon as one is liberated from this material body there is no difference between God and himself. This attempt to become one with Kṛṣṇa will be baffled because of delusion. Such atheistic and demoniac cultivation of spiritual knowledge is always futile. That is the indication of this verse. For such persons, cultivation of the knowledge in the Vedic literature, like the *Vedānta-sūtra* and the *Upaniṣads,* is always baffled.

It is a great offense, therefore, to consider Kṛṣṇa, the Supreme Personality of Godhead, to be an ordinary man. Those who do so are certainly deluded because they cannot understand the eternal form of Kṛṣṇa. In the *Bṛhad-vaiṣṇava mantra* it is clearly stated that one who considers the body of Kṛṣṇa to be material should be driven out from all rituals and activities of the *śruti.* And if one by chance sees his face, he should at once take bath in the Ganges to rid himself of infection. People jeer at Kṛṣṇa because they are envious of the Supreme Personality of Godhead. Their destiny is certainly to take birth after birth in the species of atheistic and demoniac life. Perpetually, their real knowledge will remain under delusion, and gradually they will regress to the darkest region of creation.

TEXT 13

महात्मानस्तु मां पार्थ दैवीं प्रकृतिमाश्रिताः ।
भजन्त्यनन्यमनसो ज्ञात्वा भूतादिमव्ययम् ॥ १३ ॥

mahātmānas tu māṁ pārtha
daivīṁ prakṛtim āśritāḥ
bhajanty ananya-manaso
jñātvā bhūtādim avyayam

mahātmānaḥ—the great souls; *tu*—but; *mām*—unto Me; *pārtha*—O son of Pṛthā; *daivīm*—divine; *prakṛtim*—nature; *āśritāḥ*—taken shelter of; *bhajanti* —render service; *ananya-manasaḥ*—without deviation of the mind; *jñātvā* —knowing; *bhūta*—creation; *ādim*—original; *avyayam*—inexhaustible.

TRANSLATION

O son of Pṛthā, those who are not deluded, the great souls, are under the protection of the divine nature. They are fully engaged in devotional service because they know Me as the Supreme Personality of Godhead, original and inexhaustible.

PURPORT

In this verse the description of *mahātmā* is clearly given. The first sign of the *mahātmā* is that he is already situated in the divine nature. He is not under the control of material nature. And how is this effected? That is explained in the Seventh Chapter: one who surrenders unto the Supreme Personality of Godhead, Śrī Kṛṣṇa, at once becomes freed from the control of material nature. That is the qualification. One can become free from the control of material nature as soon as he surrenders his soul to the Supreme Personality of Godhead. That is the preliminary formula. Being marginal potency, as soon as the living entity is freed from the control of material nature, he is put under the guidance of the spiritual nature. The guidance of the spiritual nature is called *daivīṁ prakṛtim*, divine nature. So, when one is promoted in that way—by surrendering to the Supreme Personality of Godhead—one attains to the stage of great soul, *mahātmā*.

The *mahātmā* does not divert his attention to anything outside Kṛṣṇa because he knows perfectly well that Kṛṣṇa is the original Supreme Person, the cause of all causes. There is no doubt about it. Such a *mahātmā*, or great soul, develops through association with other *mahātmās*, pure devotees. Pure devotees are not even attracted by Kṛṣṇa's other features, such as the four-armed Mahā-Viṣṇu. They are simply attracted by the two-armed form of Kṛṣṇa. Since they are not attracted to other features of Kṛṣṇa (what to speak of the demigods), they are not concerned with any form of a demigod or of a human being. They only meditate upon Kṛṣṇa in Kṛṣṇa consciousness. They are always engaged in the unswerving service of the Lord in Kṛṣṇa consciousness.

TEXT 14

सततं कीर्तयन्तो मां यतन्तश्च दृढव्रताः ।
नमस्यन्तश्च मां भक्त्या नित्ययुक्ता उपासते ॥ १४ ॥

> *satataṁ kīrtayanto māṁ*
> *yatantaś ca dṛḍha-vratāḥ*
> *namasyantaś ca māṁ bhaktyā*
> *nitya-yuktā upāsate*

satatam—always; *kīrtayantaḥ*—chanting; *mām*—Me; *yatantaḥ ca*—fully endeavoring also; *dṛḍha-vratāḥ*—with determination; *namasyantaḥ ca*—offering obeisances; *mām*—unto Me; *bhaktyā*—in devotion; *nitya-yuktāḥ*—perpetually engaged; *upāsate*—worship.

TRANSLATION

Always chanting My glories, endeavoring with great determination, bowing down before Me, these great souls perpetually worship Me with devotion.

PURPORT

The *mahātmā* cannot be manufactured by rubber-stamping an ordinary man. His symptoms are described here: a *mahātmā* is always engaged in chanting the glories of the Supreme Lord Kṛṣṇa, the Personality of Godhead. He has no other business. He is always engaged in the glorification of the Lord. In other words, he is not an impersonalist. When the question of glorification is there, one has to glorify the Supreme Lord, praising His holy name, His eternal form, His transcendental qualities and His uncommon pastimes. One has to glorify all these things; therefore a *mahātmā* is attached to the Supreme Personality of Godhead.

One who is attached to the impersonal feature of the Supreme Lord, the *brahmajyoti*, is not described as *mahātmā* in the *Bhagavad-gītā*. He is described in a different way in the next verse. The *mahātmā* is always engaged in different activities of devotional service, as described in the *Śrīmad-Bhāgavatam*, hearing and chanting about Viṣṇu, not a demigod or human being. That is devotion: *śravaṇaṁ kīrtanaṁ viṣṇoḥ, smaraṇam*, and remembering Him. Such a *mahātmā* has firm determination to achieve at the ultimate end the association of the Supreme Lord in any one of the five transcendental *rasas*. To achieve that success, he engages all activities—mental, bodily and vocal, everything—in the service of the Supreme Lord, Śrī Kṛṣṇa. That is called full Kṛṣṇa consciousness.

In devotional service there are certain activities which are called determined, such as fasting on certain days, like the eleventh day of the moon,

Ekādaśī, and on the appearance day of the Lord, etc. All these rules and regulations are offered by the great ācāryas for those who are actually interested in getting admission into the association of the Supreme Personality of Godhead in the transcendental world. The mahātmās, great souls, strictly observe all these rules and regulations, and therefore they are sure to achieve the desired result.

As described in the second verse of this chapter, this devotional service is not only easy, but it can be performed in a happy mood. One does not need to undergo any severe penance and austerity. He can live this life in devotional service, guided by an expert spiritual master, and in any position, either as a householder or a sannyāsī, or a brahmacārī; in any position and anywhere in the world, he can perform this devotional service to the Supreme Personality of Godhead and thus become actually mahātmā, a great soul.

TEXT 15

ज्ञानयज्ञेन चाप्यन्ये यजन्तो मामुपासते ।
एकत्वेन पृथक्त्वेन बहुधा विश्वतोमुखम् ॥ १५ ॥

jñāna-yajñena cāpy anye
yajanto mām upāsate
ekatvena pṛthaktvena
bahudhā viśvato-mukham

jñāna-yajñena—by cultivation of knowledge; ca—also; api—certainly; anye—others; yajantaḥ—worshiping; mām—Me; upāsate—worship; ekatvena —in oneness; pṛthaktvena—in duality; bahudhā—diversity; viśvataḥ-mukham —in the universal form.

TRANSLATION

Others, who are engaged in the cultivation of knowledge, worship the Supreme Lord as the one without a second, diverse in many, and in the universal form.

PURPORT

This verse is the summary of the previous verses. The Lord tells Arjuna that those who are purely in Kṛṣṇa consciousness and do not know anything other than Kṛṣṇa are called mahātmā; yet there are other persons who are not exactly in the position of *mahātmā* but who worship Kṛṣṇa also, in different ways. Some of them are already described as the distressed, the financially destitute, the inquisitive, and those who are engaged in the cultivation of knowledge. But there are others who are still lower, and these are divided into three: 1) He who worships himself as one with the Supreme Lord, 2) He who concocts some form of the Supreme Lord and worships that, and 3) He who accepts the universal form, the *viśvarūpa* of the Supreme Personality of Godhead, and worships that. Out of the above three, the lowest, those who worship themselves as the Supreme Lord, thinking themselves to be monists, are most predominant. Such people think themselves to be the Supreme Lord, and in this mentality they worship themselves. This is also a type of God worship, for they can understand that they are not the material body but are actually spiritual soul; at least, such a sense is prominent. Generally the impersonalists worship the Supreme Lord in this way. The second class includes the worshipers of the demigods, those who by imagination consider any form to be the form of the Supreme Lord. And the third class includes those who cannot conceive of anything beyond the manifestation of this material universe. They consider the universe to be the supreme organism or entity and worship that. The universe is also a form of the Lord.

TEXT 16

अहं क्रतुरहं यज्ञः स्वधाहमहमौषधम् ।
मन्त्रोऽहमहमेवाज्यमहमग्निरहं हुतम् ॥ १६ ॥

aham kratur aham yajñaḥ
svadhāham aham auṣadham
mantro 'ham aham evājyam
aham agnir aham hutam

aham—I; *kratuḥ*—ritual; *aham*—I; *yajñaḥ*—sacrifice; *svadhā*—oblation; *aham*—I ; *aham*—I; *auṣadham*—healing herb ; *mantraḥ*—transcendental chant; *aham*—I; *aham*—I; *eva*—certainly; *ajyam*—melted butter; *aham*—I; *agniḥ*—fire; *aham*—I; *hutam*—offering.

TRANSLATION

But it is I who am the ritual, I the sacrifice, the offering to the ancestors, the healing herb, the transcendental chant. I am the butter and the fire and the offering.

PURPORT

The sacrifice known as *jyotiṣṭoma* is also Kṛṣṇa, and He is also the *mahā-yajña* The oblations offered to the Pitṛloka or the sacrifice performed to please the Pitṛloka, considered as a kind of drug in the form of clarified butter, is also Kṛṣṇa. The *mantras* chanted in this connection are also Kṛṣṇa. And many other commodities made with milk products for offering in the sacrifices are also Kṛṣṇa. The fire is also Kṛṣṇa because fire is one of the five material elements and is therefore claimed as the separated energy of Kṛṣṇa. In other words, the Vedic sacrifices recommended in the *karma-kāṇḍa* division of the *Vedas* are in total also Kṛṣṇa. Or, in other words, those who are engaged in rendering devotional service unto Kṛṣṇa are to be understood to have performed all the sacrifices recommended in the *Vedas*.

TEXT 17

पिताहमस्य जगतो माता धाता पितामहः ।
वेद्यं पवित्रम् ॐकार ऋक् साम यजुरेव च ॥ १७ ॥

pitāham asya jagato
mātā dhātā pitāmahaḥ
vedyaṁ pavitram oṁkāra
ṛk sāma yajur eva ca

pitā—father; *aham*—I; *asya*—of this; *jagataḥ*—of the universe; *mātā*—mother; *dhātā*—supporter; *pitāmahaḥ*—grandfather; *vedyam*—what is to be known; *pavitram*—that which purifies; *oṁkāraḥ*—the syllable *om*; *ṛk*—the Ṛg-veda; *sāma*—the Sāma-veda; *yajuḥ*—the Yajur-veda; *eva*—certainly; *ca*—and.

TRANSLATION

I am the father of this universe, the mother, the support, and the grandsire. I am the object of knowledge, the purifier and the syllable *om*. I am also the Ṛk, the Sāma, and the Yajur [Vedas].

PURPORT

The entire cosmic manifestations, moving and nonmoving, are manifested by different activities of Kṛṣṇa's energy. In the material existence

we create different relationships with different living entities who are
nothing but Kṛṣṇa's marginal energy, but under the creation of *prakṛti*
some of them appear as our father, mother, grandfather, creator, etc., but
actually they are parts and parcels of Kṛṣṇa. As such, these living entities
who appear to be our father, mother, etc., are nothing but Kṛṣṇa. In this
verse the word *dhātā* means creator. Not only are our father and mother
parts and parcels of Kṛṣṇa, but their creator, grandmother, and grandfather, etc., are also Kṛṣṇa. Actually any living entity, being part and
parcel of Kṛṣṇa, is Kṛṣṇa. All the *Vedas*, therefore, aim only toward Kṛṣṇa.
Whatever we want to know through the *Vedas* is but a progressive step to
understand Kṛṣṇa. That subject matter which helps us purify our constitutional position is especially Kṛṣṇa. Similarly, the living entity who is inquisitive to understand all Vedic principles is also part and parcel of Kṛṣṇa and
as such is also Kṛṣṇa. In all the Vedic *mantras* the word *om*, called
praṇava, is a transcendental sound vibration and is also Kṛṣṇa. And because
in all the hymns of the four *Vedas*, *Sāma*, *Yajur*, *Ṛg* and *Atharva*, the
praṇava or *omkāra* is very prominent, it is understood to be Kṛṣṇa.

TEXT 18

गतिर्भर्ता प्रभुः साक्षी निवासः शरणं सुहृत् ।
प्रभवः प्रलयः स्थानं निधानं बीजमव्ययम् ॥ १८ ॥

gatir bhartā prabhuḥ sākṣī
nivāsaḥ śaraṇaṁ suhṛt
prabhavaḥ pralayaḥ sthānaṁ
nidhānaṁ bījam avyayam

gatiḥ—goal; *bhartā*—sustainer; *prabhuḥ*—Lord; *sākṣī*—witness; *nivāsaḥ*—
abode; *śaraṇam*—refuge; *suhṛt*—most intimate friend; *prabhavaḥ*—creation;
pralayaḥ—dissolution; *sthānam*—ground; *nidhānam*—resting place; *bījam*—
seed; *avyayam*—imperishable.

TRANSLATION

I am the goal, the sustainer, the master, the witness, the abode, the
refuge and the most dear friend. I am the creation and the annihilation,
the basis of everything, the resting place and the eternal seed.

PURPORT

Gati means the destination where we want to go. But the ultimate goal is Kṛṣṇa, although people do not know it. One who does not know Kṛṣṇa is misled, and his so-called progressive march is either partial or hallucinatory. There are many who make as their destination different demigods, and by rigid performance of the strict respective methods they reach different planets known as Candraloka, Sūryaloka, Indraloka, Maharloka, etc. But all such *lokas* or planets, being creations of Kṛṣṇa, are simultaneously Kṛṣṇa and not Kṛṣṇa. Actually such planets, being the manifestations of Kṛṣṇa's energy, are also Kṛṣṇa, but actually they only serve as a step forward for realization of Kṛṣṇa. To approach the different energies of Kṛṣṇa is to approach Kṛṣṇa indirectly. One should directly approach Kṛṣṇa, for that will save time and energy. For example, if there is a possibility of going to the top of a building by the help of an elevator, why should one go by the staircase, step by step? Everything is resting on Kṛṣṇa's energy; therefore without Kṛṣṇa's shelter nothing can exist. Kṛṣṇa is the supreme ruler because everything belongs to Him and everything exists on His energy. Kṛṣṇa, being situated in everyone's heart, is the supreme witness. The residences, countries or planets on which we live are also Kṛṣṇa. Kṛṣṇa is the ultimate goal of shelter, and as such one should take shelter of Kṛṣṇa either for protection or for annihilation of his distressed condition. And whenever we have to take protection, we should know that our protection must be a living force. Thus Kṛṣṇa is the supreme living entity. Since Kṛṣṇa is the source of our generation, or the supreme father, no one can be a better friend than Kṛṣṇa, nor can anyone be a better well-wisher. Kṛṣṇa is the original source of creation and the ultimate rest after annihilation. Kṛṣṇa is therefore the eternal cause of all causes.

TEXT 19

तपाम्यहमहं वर्षं निगृह्णाम्युत्सृजामि च ।
अमृतं चैव मृत्युश्च सदसच्चाहमर्जुन ॥ १९ ॥

tapāmy aham ahaṁ varṣaṁ
nigṛhṇāmy utsṛjāmi ca
amṛtaṁ caiva mṛtyuś ca
sad asac cāham arjuna

tapāmi—give heat; *aham*—I; *aham*—I; *varṣam*—rain; *nigṛhṇāmi*—withold; *utsṛjāmi*—send forth; *ca*—and; *amṛtam*—immortality; *ca*—and; *eva*—certainly; *mṛtyuḥ*—death; *ca*—and; *sat*—being; *asat*—nonbeing; *ca*—and; *aham*—I; *arjuna*—O Arjuna.

TRANSLATION

O Arjuna, I control heat, the rain and the drought. I am immortality, and I am also death personified. Both being and nonbeing are in Me.

PURPORT

Kṛṣṇa, by His different energies, diffuses heat and light through the agency of electricity and the sun. During summer season it is Kṛṣṇa who checks rain from falling from the sky, and then, during the rainy season, He gives unceasing torrents of rain. The energy which sustains us by prolonging the duration of our life is Kṛṣṇa, and Kṛṣṇa meets us at the end as death. By analyzing all these different energies of Kṛṣṇa, one can acertain that for Kṛṣṇa there is no distinction between matter and spirit, or, in other words, He is both matter and spirit. In the advanced stage of Kṛṣṇa consciousness, one does not therefore make such distinctions. He sees Kṛṣṇa only in everything.

Since Kṛṣṇa is both matter and spirit, the gigantic universal form comprising all material manifestations is also Kṛṣṇa, and His pastimes in Vṛndāvana as two-handed Śyāmasundara, playing on a flute, are those of the Supreme Personality of Godhead.

TEXT 20

त्रैविद्या मां सोमपाः पूतपापा
यज्ञैरिष्ट्वा स्वर्गतिं प्रार्थयन्ते ।
ते पुण्यमासाद्य सुरेन्द्रलोक-
मश्नन्ति दिव्यान्दिवि देवभोगान् ॥ २० ॥

trai-vidyā māṁ soma-pāḥ pūta-pāpā
yajñair iṣṭvā svar-gatiṁ prārthayante
te puṇyam āsādya surendra-lokam
aśnanti divyān divi deva-bhogān

trai-vidyāḥ—the knowers of the three *Vedas; mām*—unto Me; *soma-pāḥ*—drinkers of *soma* juice; *pūta*—purified; *pāpāḥ*—sins; *yajñaiḥ*—with sacrifices; *iṣṭvā*—after worshiping; *svargatim*—passage to heaven; *prārthayante*—pray; *te*—they; *puṇyam*—virtue; *āsādya*—enjoying; *surendra*—of Indra; *lokam*—world; *aśnanti*—enjoy; *divyān*—celestial; *divi*—in heaven; *deva-bhogān*—pleasures of the gods.

TRANSLATION

Those who study the Vedas and drink the soma juice, seeking the heavenly planets, worship Me indirectly. They take birth on the planet of Indra, where they enjoy godly delights.

PURPORT

The word *trai-vidyāḥ* refers to the three *Vedas, Sāma, Yajur* and *Ṛg.* A *brāhmaṇa* who has studied these three *Vedas* is called a *tri-vedī.* Anyone who is very much attached to knowledge derived from these three *Vedas* is respected in society. Unfortunately, there are many great scholars of the *Vedas* who do not know the ultimate purport of studying them. Therefore Kṛṣṇa herein declares Himself to be the ultimate goal for the *tri-vedīs.* Actual *tri-vedīs* take shelter under the lotus feet of Kṛṣṇa and engage in pure devotional service to satisfy the Lord. Devotional service begins with the chanting of the Hare Kṛṣṇa *mantra* and side by side trying to understand Kṛṣṇa in truth. Unfortunately those who are simply official students of the *Vedas* become more interested in offering sacrifices to the different demigods like Indra, Candra, etc. By such endeavor, the worshipers of different demigods are certainly purified of the contamination of the lower qualities of nature and are thereby elevated to the higher planetary system or heavenly planets known as Maharloka, Janaloka, Tapoloka, etc. Once situated on those higher planetary systems, one can satisfy his senses hundreds of thousands of times better than on this planet.

TEXT 21

ते तं भुक्त्वा स्वर्गलोकं विशालं
क्षीणे पुण्ये मर्त्यलोकं विशन्ति ।
एवं त्रयीधर्ममनुप्रपन्ना
गतागतं कामकामा लभन्ते ॥ २१ ॥

te tam bhuktvā svarga-lokam viśālam
kṣīṇe puṇye martya-lokam viśanti
evam trayī-dharmam anuprapannā
gatāgatam kāma-kāmā labhante

te—they; *tam*—that; *bhuktvā*—enjoying; *svarga-lokam*—heaven; *viśālam*—vast; *kṣīṇe*—being exhausted; *puṇye*—merits; *martya-lokam*—mortal earth; *viśanti*—fall down; *evam*—thus; *trayī*—three *Vedas*; *dharmam*—doctrines; *anuprapannāḥ*—following; *gata-agatam*—death and birth; *kāma-kāmāḥ*—desiring sense enjoyments; *labhante*—attain.

TRANSLATION

When they have thus enjoyed heavenly sense pleasure, they return to this mortal planet again. Thus, through the Vedic principles, they achieve only flickering happiness.

PURPORT

One who is promoted to those higher planetary systems enjoys a longer duration of life and better facilities for sense enjoyment, yet one is not allowed to stay there forever. One is again sent back to this earthly planet upon finishing the resultant fruits of pious activities. He who has not attained perfection of knowledge, as indicated in the *Vedānta-sūtra* (*janmādy asya yataḥ*), or, in other words, he who fails to understand Kṛṣṇa, the cause of all causes, becomes baffled in achieving the ultimate goal of life and is thus subjected to the routine of being promoted to the higher planets and then again coming down, as if situated on a ferris wheel which sometimes goes up and sometimes comes down. The purport is that instead of being elevated to the spiritual world where there is no longer any possibility of coming down, one simply revolves in the cycle of birth and death on higher and lower planetary systems. One should better take to the spiritual world to enjoy eternal life full of bliss and knowledge and never return to this miserable material existence.

TEXT 22

अनन्याश्चिन्तयन्तो मां ये जनाः पर्युपासते ।
तेषां नित्याभियुक्तानां योगक्षेमं वहाम्यहम् ॥ २२ ॥

ananyāś cintayanto mām
ye janāḥ paryupāsate
teṣāṁ nityābhiyuktānāṁ
yoga-kṣemaṁ vahāmy aham

ananyāḥ—no other; *cintayantaḥ*—concentrating; *mām*—unto Me; *ye*—who; *janāḥ*—persons; *paryupāsate*—properly worship; *teṣām*—their; *nitya*—always *abhiyuktānām*—fixed in devotion; *yoga-kṣemam*—requirements; *vahāmi*—carry; *aham*—I.

TRANSLATION

But those who worship Me with devotion, meditating on My transcendental form-to them I carry what they lack and preserve what they have.

PURPORT

One who is unable to live for a moment without Kṛṣṇa consciousness cannot but think of Kṛṣṇa twenty-four hours, being engaged in devotional service by hearing, chanting, remembering, offering prayers, worshiping, serving the lotus feet of the Lord, rendering other services, cultivating friendship and surrendering fully to the Lord. Such activities are all auspicious and full of spiritual potencies; indeed, they make the devotee perfect in self-realization. Then his only desire is to achieve the association of the Supreme Personality of Godhead. This is called *yoga*. By the mercy of the Lord, such a devotee never comes back to this material condition of life. *Kṣema* refers to the merciful protection of the Lord. The Lord helps the devotee to achieve Kṛṣṇa consciousness by *yoga*, and when he becomes fully Kṛṣṇa conscious the Lord protects him from falling down to a miserable conditioned life.

TEXT 23

येऽप्यन्यदेवताभक्ता यजन्ते श्रद्धयान्विताः ।
तेऽपि मामेव कौन्तेय यजन्त्यविधिपूर्वकम् ॥ २३ ॥

ye 'py anya-devatā-bhaktā
yajante śraddhayānvitāḥ
te 'pi mām eva kaunteya
yajanty avidhi-pūrvakam

ye—those; *api*—also; *anya*—other; *devatā*—demigods; *bhaktāḥ*—devotees; *yajante*—worship; *śraddhaya-anvitāḥ*—with faith; *te*—they; *api*—also; *mām*—Me; *eva*—even; *kaunteya*-O son of Kuntī; *yajanti*—sacrifice; *avidhi-pūrvakam*—in a wrong way.

TRANSLATION

Whatever a man may sacrifice to other gods, O son of Kuntī, is really meant for Me alone, but it is offered without true understanding.

PURPORT

"Persons who are engaged in the worship of demigods are not very intelligent, although such worship is done to Me indirectly," Kṛṣṇa says. For example, when a man pours water on the leaves and branches of a tree without pouring water on the root, he does so without sufficient knowledge or without observing regulative principles. Similarly, the process of rendering service to different parts of the body is to supply food to the stomach. The demigods are, so to speak, different officers and directors in the government of the Supreme Lord. One has to follow the laws made by the government, not by the officers or directors. Similarly, everyone is to offer his worship to the Supreme Lord only. That will automatically satisfy the different officers and directors of the Lord. The officers and directors are engaged as representatives of the government, and to offer some bribe to the officers and directors is illegal. This is stated here as *avidhi-pūrvakam*. In other words, Kṛṣṇa does not approve the unnecessary worship of the demigods.

TEXT 24

अहं हि सर्वयज्ञानां भोक्ता च प्रभुरेव च ।
न तु मामभिजानन्ति तत्त्वेनातश्च्यवन्ति ते ॥ २४ ॥

aham hi sarva-yajñānām
bhoktā ca prabhur eva ca
na tu mām abhijānanti
tattvenātaś cyavanti te

aham—I; *hi*—surely; *sarva*—of all; *yajñānām*—sacrifices; *bhoktā*—enjoyer; *ca*—and; *prabhuḥ*—Lord; *eva*—also; *ca*—and; *na*—not; *tu*—but; *mām*—Me;

abhijānanti—know; *tattvena*—in reality; *ataḥ*—therefore; *cyavanti*—fall down; *te*—they.

TRANSLATION

I am the only enjoyer and the only object of sacrifice. Those who do not recognize My true transcendental nature fall down.

PURPORT

Here it is clearly stated that there are many types of *yajña* performances recommended in the Vedic literatures, but actually all of them are meant for satisfying the Supreme Lord. *Yajña* means Viṣṇu. In the Second Chapter of *Bhagavad-gītā* it is clearly stated that one should only work for satisfying *Yajña* or Viṣṇu. The perfectional form of human civilization, known as *varṇāśrama-dharma*, is specifically meant for satisfying Viṣṇu. Therefore, Kṛṣṇa says in this verse, "I am the enjoyer of all sacrifices because I am the supreme master." However, less intelligent persons, without knowing this fact, worship demigods for temporary benefit. Therefore they fall down to material existence and do not achieve the desired goal of life. If, however, anyone has any material desire to be fulfilled, he had better pray for it to the Supreme Lord (although that is not pure devotion), and he will thus achieve the desired result.

TEXT 25

यान्ति देवव्रता देवान्पितृन्यान्ति पितृव्रताः ।
भूतानि यान्ति भूतेज्या यान्ति मद्याजिनोऽपि माम् ॥ २५ ॥

*yānti deva-vratā devān
pitṝn yānti pitṛ-vratāḥ
bhūtāni yānti bhūtejyā
yānti mad-yājino 'pi mām*

yānti—achieve; *deva-vratāḥ*—worshipers of demigods; *devān*—to demigods; *pitṝn*—to ancestors; *yānti*—go; *pitṛ-vratāḥ*—worshipers of ancestors; *bhūtāni*—to ghosts and spirits; *yānti*—go; *bhūtejyāḥ*—worshipers of ghosts and spirits; *yānti*—go; *mat*—My; *yājinaḥ*—devotees; *api*—also; *mām*—unto Me.

TRANSLATION

Those who worship the demigods will take birth among the demigods; those who worship ghosts and spirits will take birth among such beings; those who worship ancestors go to the ancestors; and those who worship Me will live with Me.

PURPORT

If anyone has any desire to go to the moon, the sun, or any other planet, one can attain the desired destination by following specific Vedic principles recommended for that purpose. These are vividly described in the fruitive activities portion of the *Vedas*, technically known as *darśa-paurṇamāsī*, which recommends a specific worship of demigods situated on different heavenly planets. Similarly, one can attain the *pitā* planets by performing a specific *yajña*. Similarly, one can go to many ghostly planets and become a *yakṣa*, *rakṣa* or *piśāca*. *Piśāca* worship is called "black arts" or "black magic." There are many men who practice this black art, and they think that it is spiritualism, but such activities are completely materialistic. Similarly, a pure devotee, who worships the Supreme Personality of Godhead only, achieves the planets of Vaikuṇṭha and Kṛṣṇaloka without a doubt. It is very easy to understand through this important verse that if by simply worshiping the demigods one can achieve the heavenly planets, or by worshiping the *pitā* achieve the *pitā* planets, or by practicing the black arts achieve the ghostly planets, why can the pure devotee not achieve the planet of Kṛṣṇa or Viṣṇu? Unfortunately many people have no information of these sublime planets where Kṛṣṇa and Viṣṇu live, and because they do not know of them they fall down. Even the impersonalists fall down from the *brahmajyoti*. This Kṛṣṇa consciousness movement is therefore distributing sublime information to the entire human society to the effect that by simply chanting the Hare Kṛṣṇa *mantra* one can become perfect in this life and go back home, back to Godhead.

TEXT 26

पत्रं पुष्पं फलं तोयं यो मे भक्त्या प्रयच्छति ।
तदहं भक्त्युपहृतमश्नामि प्रयतात्मनः ॥ २६ ॥

patraṁ puṣpaṁ phalaṁ toyaṁ
yo me bhaktyā prayacchati
tad ahaṁ bhakty-upahṛtam
aśnāmi prayatātmanaḥ

patram—a leaf; *puṣpam*—a flower; *phalam*—a fruit; *toyam*—water; *yaḥ*—whoever; *me*—unto Me; *bhaktyā*—with devotion; *prayacchati*—offers; *tat*—that; *aham*—I; *bhakti-upahṛtam*—offered in devotion; *aśnāmi*—accept; *prayata-ātmanaḥ*—of one in pure consciousness.

TRANSLATION

If one offers Me with love and devotion a leaf, a flower, fruit or water, I will accept it.

PURPORT

Here Lord Kṛṣṇa, having established that He is the only enjoyer, the primeval Lord, and the real object of all sacrificial offerings, reveals what types of sacrifices He desires to be offered. If one wishes to engage in devotional service to the Supreme in order to be purified and to reach the goal of life-the transcendental loving service of God-then he should find out what the Lord desires of him. One who loves Kṛṣṇa will give Him whatever He wants, and he avoids offering anything which is undesirable or unasked for. Thus, meat, fish and eggs should not be offered to Kṛṣṇa. If He desired such things as offerings, He would have said so. Instead He clearly requests that a leaf, fruit, flowers and water be given to Him, and He says of this offering, "I will accept it." Therefore, we should understand that He will not accept meat, fish and eggs. Vegetables, grains, fruits, milk and water are the proper foods for human beings and are prescribed by Lord Kṛṣṇa Himself. Whatever else we eat cannot be offered to Him, since He will not accept it. Thus we cannot be acting on the level of loving devotion if we offer such foods.

In the Third Chapter, verse thirteen, Śrī Kṛṣṇa explains that only the remains of sacrifice are purified and fit for consumption by those who are seeking advancement in life and release from the clutches of the material entanglement. Those who do not make an offering of their food, He says in the same verse, are said to be eating only sin. In other words, their every mouthful is simply deepening their involvement in the complexities of material nature. But preparing nice, simple vegetable dishes, offering them before the picture or Deity of Lord Kṛṣṇa and bowing down and praying for Him to accept such a humble offering, enable one to advance steadily in life, to purify the body, and to create fine brain tissues which will lead to clear thinking. Above all, the offering should be made with an attitude of love. Kṛṣṇa has no need of food, since He already possesses everything that be, yet He will accept the offering of one who desires to please Him in that way. The important element, in preparation, in serving and in offering, is to act with love for Kṛṣṇa.

The impersonalist philosophers, who wish to maintain that the Absolute Truth is without senses, cannot comprehend this verse of *Bhagavad-gītā*. To them, it is either a metaphor or proof of the mundane character of Kṛṣṇa, the speaker of the *Gītā*. But, in actuality, Kṛṣṇa, the Supreme Godhead, has senses, and it is stated that His senses are interchangeable; in other words, one sense can perform the function of any other. This is what it means to say that Kṛṣṇa is absolute. Lacking senses, He could hardly be considered full in all opulences. In the Seventh Chapter, Kṛṣṇa has explained that He impregnates the living entities into material nature. This is done by His looking upon material nature. And so in this instance, Kṛṣṇa's hearing the devotee's words of love in offering foodstuffs is *wholly* identical with His eating and actually tasting. This point should be emphasized: because of His absolute position, His hearing is wholly identical with His eating and tasting. Only the devotee, who accepts Kṛṣṇa as He describes Himself, without interpretation, can understand that the Supreme Absolute Truth can eat food and enjoy it.

TEXT 27

यत्करोषि यदश्नासि यज्जुहोषि ददासि यत् ।
यत्तपस्यसि कौन्तेय तत्कुरुष्व मदर्पणम् ॥ २७ ॥

yat karoṣi yad aśnāsi
yaj juhoṣi dadāsi yat
yat tapasyasi kaunteya
tat kuruṣva mad-arpaṇam

yat—what; *karoṣi*—you do; *yat*—whatever; *aśnāsi*—you eat; *yat*—whatever; *juhoṣi*—you offer; *dadāsi*—you give away; *yat*—whatever; *yat*—whatever; *tapasyasi*—austerities you perform; *kaunteya*—O son of Kuntī; *tat*—that; *kuruṣva*—make; *mat*—unto Me; *arpaṇam*—offering.

TRANSLATION

O son of Kuntī, all that you do, all that you eat, all that you offer and give away, as well as all austerities that you may perform, should be done as an offering unto Me.

PURPORT

Thus, it is the duty of everyone to mold his life in such a way that he will not forget Kṛṣṇa in any circumstance. Everyone has to work for maintenance of his body and soul together, and Kṛṣṇa recommends herein that one should work for Him. Everyone has to eat something to live; therefore he should accept the remnants of foodstuffs offered to Kṛṣṇa. Any civilized man has to perform some religious ritualistic ceremonies; therefore Kṛṣṇa recommends, "Do it for Me," and this is called *arcanā*. Everyone has a tendency to give something in charity; Kṛṣṇa says, "Give it to Me," and this means that all surplus money accummulated should be utilized in furthering the Kṛṣṇa consciousness movement. Nowadays people are very much inclined to the meditational process, which is not practical in this age, but if anyone practices meditating on Kṛṣṇa twenty-four hours by chanting the Hare Kṛṣṇa *mantra* round his beads, he is surely the greatest *yogī*, as substantiated by the Sixth Chapter of *Bhagavad-gītā*.

TEXT 28

शुभाशुभफलैरेवं मोक्ष्यसे कर्मबन्धनैः ।
सन्न्यासयोगयुक्तात्मा विमुक्तो मामुपैष्यसि ॥ २८ ॥

śubhāśubha-phalair evaṁ
mokṣyase karma-bandhanaiḥ
sannyāsa-yoga-yuktātmā
vimukto mām upaiṣyasi

śubha—good; *aśubha*—evil; *phalaiḥ*—results; *evam*—thus; *mokṣyase*—free; *karma*—action; *bandhanaiḥ*—bondage; *sannyāsa*—of renunciation; *yoga*—the yoga; *yukta-ātmā*—having the mind firmly set on; *vimuktaḥ*—liberated; *mām*—to Me; *upaiṣyasi*—you will attain.

TRANSLATION

In this way you will be freed from all reactions to good and evil deeds, and by this principle of renunciation you will be liberated and come to Me.

PURPORT

One who acts in Kṛṣṇa consciousness under superior direction is called *yukta*. The technical term is *yukta-vairāgya*. This is further explained by Rūpa Gosvāmī as follows.

Rūpa Gosvāmī says that as long as we are in this material world we have to act; we cannot cease acting. Therefore if actions are performed and the fruits are given to Kṛṣṇa, then that is called *yukta-vairāgya*. Actually situated in renunciation, such activities clear the mirror of the mind, and as the actor gradually makes progress in spiritual realization he becomes completely surrendered to the Supreme Personality of Godhead. Therefore at the end he becomes liberated, and this liberation is also specified. By this liberation he does not become one with the *brahmajyoti* but rather enters into the planet of the Supreme Lord. It is clearly mentioned here: *mām upaiṣyasi*, "he comes to Me," back home, back to Godhead. There are five different stages of liberation, and here it is specified that the devotee who has always lived his lifetime here under the direction of the Supreme Lord, as stated, has evolved to the point where he can, after quitting this body, go back to Godhead and engage directly in the association of the Supreme Lord.

Anyone who has no other interest but to dedicate his life to the service of the Lord is actually a *sannyāsī* Such a person always thinks of himself as an eternal servant, dependant on the supreme will of the Lord. As such, whatever he does, he does it for the benefit of the Lord. Whatever action he performs, he performs it as service to the Lord. He does not give serious attention to the fruitive activities or prescribed duties mentioned in the *Vedas*. For ordinary persons it is obligatory to execute the prescribed duties mentioned in the *Vedas*, but although a pure devotee who is completely engaged in the service of the Lord may sometimes appear to go against the prescribed Vedic duties, actually it is not so.

It is said, therefore, by Vaiṣṇava authorities that even the most intelligent person cannot understand the plans and activities of a pure devotee. The exact words are *vaiṣṇavera kriyā mudrā vijñe nā bujhaya*. A person who is thus always engaged in the service of the Lord or is always thinking and planning how to serve the Lord is to be considered completely liberated at present and in the future. His going home, back to Godhead, is guaranteed. He is above all materialistic criticism, just as Kṛṣṇa is above all criticism.

TEXT 29

समोऽहं सर्वभूतेषु न मे द्वेष्योऽस्ति न प्रियः ।
ये भजन्ति तु मां भक्त्या मयि ते तेषु चाप्यहम् ॥ २९ ॥

samo 'haṁ sarva-bhūteṣu
na me dveṣyo 'sti na priyaḥ
ye bhajanti tu māṁ bhaktyā
mayi te teṣu cāpy aham

samaḥ—equally disposed; *aham*—I; *sarva-bhūteṣu*—to all living entities; *na*—no one; *me*—Mine; *dveṣyaḥ*—hateful; *asti*—is; *na*—nor; *priyaḥ*—dear; *ye*—those; *bhajanti*—render transcendental service; *tu*—yet; *mām*—unto Me; *bhaktyā*—in devotion; *mayi*—unto Me; *te*—such persons; *teṣu*—in them; *ca*—also; *api*—certainly; *aham*—I.

TRANSLATION

I envy no one, nor am I partial to anyone. I am equal to all. But whoever renders service unto Me in devotion is a friend, is in Me, and I am also a friend to him.

PURPORT

One may question here that if Kṛṣṇa is equal to everyone and no one is His special friend, then why does He take a special interest in the devotees who are always engaged in His transcendental service? But this is not discrimination; it is natural. Any man in this material world may be very charitably disposed, yet he has a special interest in his own children. The Lord claims that every living entity—in whatever form—is His son, and as such He provides everyone with a generous supply of the necessities of life. He is just like a cloud which pours rain all over, regardless whether it falls on rock or land or water. But for His devotees, He gives specific attention. Such devotees are mentioned here: they are always in Kṛṣṇa consciousness, and therefore they are always transcendentally situated in Kṛṣṇa. The very phrase Kṛṣṇa consciousness suggests that those who are in such consciousness are living transcendentalists, situated in Him. The Lord says here distinctly, *"mayi te,"* "in Me." Naturally, as a result, the Lord is also in them. This is reciprocal. This also explains the words: *asti na priyaḥ/ye bhajanti:* "Whoever surrenders unto Me, proportionately I take care of him." This transcendental reciprocation exists because both the Lord and the devotee are conscious. When a diamond is set in a golden ring, it looks very nice. The gold is glorified, and at the same time the diamond is glorified. The Lord and the living entity eternally glitter, and when a living entity becomes inclined to the service of the Supreme Lord, he looks like gold. The Lord is a diamond, and so this combination is very nice. Living entities in a pure state are called devotees. The Supreme Lord becomes the devotee of His devotees. If a reciprocal relationship is not present between the devotee and the Lord, then there is no personalist philosophy. In the impersonal philosophy there is no reciprocation between the Supreme and the living entity, but in the personalist philosophy there is.

The example is often given that the Lord is like a desire tree, and whatever one wants from this desire tree, the Lord supplies. But here the explanation is more complete. The Lord is here stated to be partial to the devotees. This is the manifestation of the Lord's special mercy to the devotees. The Lord's reciprocation should not be considered to be under the law of *karma*. It belongs to the transcendental situation in which the Lord and His devotees function. Devotional service of the Lord is not an activity of this material world; it is part of the spiritual world where eternity, bliss and knowledge predominate.

TEXT 30

अपि चेत्सुदुराचारो भजते मामनन्यभाक् ।
साधुरेव स मन्तव्यः सम्यग्व्यवसितो हि सः ॥ ३० ॥

api cet su-durācāro
bhajate mām ananya-bhāk
sādhur eva sa mantavyaḥ
samyag vyavasito hi saḥ

api—in spite of; *cet*—although; *sudurācāraḥ*—one committing the most abominable actions; *bhajate*—engaged in devotional service; *mām*—unto Me; *ananya-bhāk*—without deviation; *sādhuḥ*—saint; *eva*—certainly; *saḥ*—he; *mantavyaḥ*—to be considered; *samyak*—completely; *vyavasitaḥ*—situated; *hi*—certainly; *saḥ*—he.

TRANSLATION

Even if one commits the most abominable actions, if he is engaged in devotional service, he is to be considered saintly because he is properly situated.

PURPORT

The word *sudurācāro* used in this verse is very significant, and we should understand it properly. When a living entity is conditioned, he has two kinds of activities: one is conditional, and the other is constitutional. As for protecting the body or abiding by the rules of society and state, certainly there are different activities, even for the devotees, in connection with the conditional life, and such activities are called conditional. Besides these, the living entity who is fully conscious of his spiritual nature and is engaged in Kṛṣṇa consciousness, or the devotional service of the Lord, has activities which are called transcendental. Such activities are performed in his constitutional position, and they are technically called devotional service. Now, in the conditioned state, sometimes devotional service and the conditional service in relation to the body will parallel one another. But then again, sometimes these activities become opposed to one another. As far as possible, a devotee is very cautious so that he does not do anything that could disrupt his wholesome condition. He knows that perfection in his activities depends on his progressive realization of Kṛṣṇa consciousness. Sometimes, however, it may be seen that a person in Kṛṣṇa consciousness commits some act which may be taken as most abominable socially or politically. But such a temporary falldown does not disqualify him. In the *Śrīmad-Bhāgavatam* it is stated that if a person falls down, but is wholeheartedly engaged in the transcendental service of the Supreme Lord, the Lord, being situated within his heart, beautifies him and excuses him from that abomination. The material contamination is so strong that even a *yogī* fully engaged in the service of the Lord sometimes becomes ensnared; but Kṛṣṇa consciousness is so strong that such an occasional falldown is at once rectified. Therefore the process of devotional service is always a success. No one should deride a devotee for some accidental falldown from the ideal path, for, as is explained in the next verse, such occasional falldowns will be stopped in due course, as soon as a devotee is completely situated in Kṛṣṇa consciousness.

Therefore a person who is situated in Kṛṣṇa consciousness and is engaged with determination in the process of chanting Hare Kṛṣṇa, Hare Kṛṣṇa, Kṛṣṇa Kṛṣṇa, Hare Hare/Hare Rāma, Hare Rāma, Rāma Rāma, Hare Hare should be considered to be in the transcendental position, even if by chance or accident he is found to have fallen. The words *sādhur eva*, "he is saintly," are very emphatic. They are a warning to the nondevotees that because of an accidental falldown a devotee should not be derided; he should still be considered saintly even if he has fallen down accidentally. And the word *mantavyaḥ* is still more emphatic. If one does not follow this rule, and derides a devotee for his accidental falldown, then he is disobeying the order of the Supreme Lord. The only qualification of a devotee is to be unflinchingly and exclusively engaged in devotional service.

The mark of a spot which may be seen on the moon does not become an impediment to the moonlight. Similarly, the accidental falldown of a devotee from the path of a saintly character does not make him abominable. On the other hand, one should not misunderstand that a devotee in transcendental devotional service can act in all kinds of abominable ways; this verse only refers to an accident due to the strong power of material connections. Devotional service is more or less a declaration of war against the illusory energy. As long as one is not strong enough to fight the illusory energy, there may be accidental falldowns. But when one is strong enough, he is no longer subjected to such falldowns, as previously explained. No one should take advantage of this verse and commit nonsense and think that he is still a devotee. If he does not improve in his character by devotional service, then it is to be understood that he is not a high devotee.

TEXT 31

क्षिप्रं भवति धर्मात्मा शश्वच्छान्तिं निगच्छति ।
कौन्तेय प्रतिजानीहि न मे भक्तः प्रणश्यति ॥ ३१ ॥

ksipram bhavati dharmātmā
śaśvac-chāntim nigacchati
kaunteya pratijānīhi
na me bhaktah pranaśyati

ksipram—very soon; *bhavati*—becomes; *dharma-ātmā*—righteous; *śaśvat-śāntim*—lasting peace; *nigacchati*—attains; *kaunteya*—O son of Kunti; *pratijānīhi*—justly declare; *na*—never; *me*—Mine; *bhaktah*—devotee; *pranaśyati*—perishes.

TRANSLATION

He quickly becomes righteous and attains lasting peace. O son of Kunti, declare it boldly that My devotee never perishes.

PURPORT

This should not be misunderstood. In the Seventh Chapter the Lord says that one who is engaged in mischievous activities cannot become a devotee of the Lord. One who is not a devotee of the Lord has no good qualifications whatsoever. The question remains, then, how can a person engaged in abominable activities—either by accident or intention—be a pure devotee? This question may justly be raised. The miscreants, as stated in the Seventh Chapter, who never come to the devotional service of the Lord, have no good qualifications, as is stated in the Śrīmad-Bhāgavatam. Generally, a devotee who is engaged in the nine kinds of devotional activities is engaged in the process of cleansing all material contamination from the heart. He puts the Supreme Personality of Godhead within his heart, and all sinful contaminations are naturally washed away. Continuous thinking of the Supreme Lord makes him pure by nature. According to the Vedas, there is a certain regulation that if one falls down from his exalted position, he has to undergo certain ritualistic processes to purify himself. But here there is no such condition because the purifying process is already there in the heart of the devotee, due to his remembering the Supreme Personality of Godhead constantly. Therefore, the chanting of Hare Kṛṣṇa, Hare Kṛṣṇa, Kṛṣṇa Kṛṣṇa, Hare Hare/ Hare Rāma, Hare Rāma, Rāma Rāma, Hare Hare should be continued without stoppage. This will protect a devotee from all accidental falldowns. He will thus remain perpetually free from all material contaminations.

TEXT 32

मां हि पार्थ व्यपाश्रित्य येऽपि स्युः पापयोनयः ।
स्त्रियो वैश्यास्तथा शूद्रास्तेऽपि यान्ति परां गतिम् ॥ ३२ ॥

*mām hi pārtha vyapāśritya
ye 'pi syuḥ pāpa-yonayaḥ
striyo vaiśyās tathā śūdrās
te 'pi yānti parāṁ gatim*

mām—unto Me; *hi*—certainly; *pārtha*—O son of Pṛthā; *vyapāśritya*—particularly taking shelter; *ye*—anyone; *api*—also; *syuḥ*—becomes; *pāpa-yonayaḥ*—born of a lower family; *striyaḥ*—women; *vaiśyāḥ*—mercantile people; *tathā*—also; *śūdrāḥ*—lower class men; *te api*—even they; *yānti*—go; *parām*—supreme; *gatim*—destination.

TRANSLATION

O son of Pṛthā, those who take shelter in Me, though they be of lower birth—women, vaiśyas [merchants], as well as śūdras [workers]—can approach the supreme destination.

PURPORT

It is clearly declared here by the Supreme Lord that in devotional service there is no distinction between the lower or higher classes of people. In the material conception of life, there are such divisions, but for a person engaged in transcendental devotional service to the Lord, there are not. Everyone is eligible for the supreme destination. In the *Śrīmad-Bhāgavatam* it is stated that even the lowest, who are called *caṇḍālas* (dog-eaters), can be elevated by association with a pure devotee. Therefore devotional service and guidance of a pure devotee are so strong that there is no discrimination between the lower and higher classes of men; anyone can take to it. The most simple man taking center of the pure devotee can be purified by proper guidance. According to the different modes of material nature, men are classified in the mode of goodness (*brāhmaṇas*), the mode of passion (*kṣatriyas*, or administrators), the mixed modes of passion and ignorance (*vaiśyas*, or merchants), and the mode of ignorance (*śūdras*, or workers). Those lower than them are called *caṇḍālas*, and they are born in sinful families. Generally, those who are born in sinful families are not accepted by the higher classes. But the process of devotional service and the pure devotee of the Supreme God are so strong that all the lower classes can attain the highest perfection of life. This is possible only when one takes center of Kṛṣṇa. One has to take center completely of Kṛṣṇa. Then one can become much greater than great *jñānīs* and *yogīs*.

TEXT 33

किं पुनर्ब्राह्मणाः पुण्या भक्ता राजर्षयस्तथा ।
अनित्यमसुखं लोकमिमं प्राप्य भजस्व माम् ॥ ३३ ॥

kiṁ punar brāhmaṇāḥ puṇyā
bhaktā rājarṣayas tathā
anityam asukhaṁ lokam
imaṁ prāpya bhajasva mām

kim—how much; punaḥ—again; brāhmaṇāḥ-brāhmaṇas; puṇyāḥ—righteous; bhaktāḥ—devotees; rājarṣayaḥ—saintly kings; tathā—also; anityam—temporary; asukham—sorrowful; lokam—planets; imam—this; prāpya—gaining; bhajasva—are engaged in loving service; mām—unto Me.

TRANSLATION

How much greater then are the brāhmaṇas, the righteous, the devotees and saintly kings who in this temporary miserable world engage in loving service unto Me.

PURPORT

In this material world there are classifications of people, but, after all, this world is not a happy place for anyone. It is clearly stated here, *anityam asukham lokam:* this world is temporary and full of miseries, not habitable for any sane gentleman. This world is declared by the Supreme Personality of Godhead to be temporary and full of miseries. Some of the philosophers, especially the minor philosophers, say that this world is false, but we can understand from *Bhagavad-gītā* that the world is not false; it is temporary. There is a difference between temporary and false. This world is temporary, but there is another world which is eternal. This world is miserable, but the other world is eternal and blissful.

Arjuna was born in a saintly royal family. To him also the Lord says, "Take to My devotional service and come quickly back to Godhead, back home." No one should remain in this temporary world, full as it is with miseries. Everyone should attach himself to the bosom of the Supreme Personality of Godhead so that he can be eternally happy. The devotional service of the Supreme Lord is the only process by which all problems of all classes of men can be solved. Everyone should therefore take to Kṛṣṇa consciousness and make his life perfect.

TEXT 34

मन्मना भव मद्भक्तो मद्याजी मां नमस्कुरु ।
मामेवैष्यसि युक्त्वैवमात्मानं मत्परायणः ॥ ३४ ॥

man-manā bhava mad-bhakto
mad-yājī māṁ namaskuru
mām evaiṣyasi yuktvaivam
ātmānaṁ mat-parāyaṇaḥ

mat-manāḥ—always thinking of Me; *bhava*—become; *mat*—My; *bhaktaḥ*—devotee; *mat*—My; *yājī*—worshiper; *mām*—unto Me; *namaskuru*—offer obeisances; *mām*—unto Me; *eva*—completely; *eṣyasi*—come; *yuktvā evam*—being absorbed; *ātmānam*—your soul; *mat-parāyaṇaḥ*—devoted to Me.

TRANSLATION

Engage your mind always in thinking of Me, offer obeisances and worship Me. Being completely absorbed in Me, surely you will come to Me.

PURPORT

In this verse it is clearly indicated that Kṛṣṇa consciousness is the only means of being delivered from the clutches of this contaminated material world. Sometimes unscrupulous commentators distort the meaning of what is clearly stated here: that all devotional service should be offered to the Supreme Personality of Godhead, Kṛṣṇa. Unfortunately, unscrupulous commentators divert the mind of the reader to that which is not at all feasible. Such commentators do not know that there is no difference between Kṛṣṇa's mind and Kṛṣṇa. Kṛṣṇa is not an ordinary human being; He is Absolute Truth. His body, mind and He Himself are one and absolute. It is stated in the *Kūrma Purāṇa*. As it is quoted by Bhaktisiddhānta Sarasvatī Gosvāmī in his *Anubhāṣya* comments on *Caitanya-caritāmṛta*, Fifth Chapter, *Ādi-līlā*, verses 41-48, "*deha-dehi-vibhedo 'yaṁ neśvare vidyate kvacit*," which means that there is no difference in Kṛṣṇa, the Supreme Lord, between Himself and His body. But, because they do not know this science of Kṛṣṇa, the commentators hide Kṛṣṇa and divide His personality from His mind or from His body. Although this is sheer ignorance of the science of Kṛṣṇa, some men make profit out of misleading the people.

There are some who are demonic; they also think of Kṛṣṇa, but enviously, just like King Kaṁsa, Kṛṣṇa's uncle. He was also thinking of Kṛṣṇa always, but he thought of Kṛṣṇa as his enemy. He was always in anxiety, wondering when Kṛṣṇa would come to kill him. That kind of thinking will not help us. One should be thinking of Kṛṣṇa in devotional love. That is *bhakti*. One should cultivate the knowledge of Kṛṣṇa continually. What is that favorable cultivation? It is to learn from a bona fide teacher. Kṛṣṇa is the Supreme Personality of Godhead, and we have several times explained that His body is not material, but is eternal, blissful knowledge. This kind of talk about Kṛṣṇa will help one become a devotee. Otherwise, understanding Kṛṣṇa from the wrong source will prove fruitless.

One should therefore engage his mind in the eternal form, the primal form of Kṛṣṇa; with conviction in his heart that Kṛṣṇa is the Supreme, he should engage himself in worship. There are hundreds of thousands of temples in India for the worship of Kṛṣṇa, and devotional service is practiced there. When such practice is made, one has to offer obeisances to

Kṛṣṇa. One should lower his head before the Deity and engage his mind, his body, his activities—everything. That will make one fully absorbed in Kṛṣṇa without deviation. This will help one transfer into the Kṛṣṇaloka. One should not be deviated by unscrupulous commentators. One must engage in the nine different processes of devotional service, beginning with hearing and chanting about Kṛṣṇa. Pure devotional service is the highest achievement of human society.

In the Seventh and Eighth Chapters of *Bhagavad-gītā*, pure devotional service to the Lord has been explained, apart from the *yoga* of knowledge and mystic *yoga* or fruitive activities. Those who are not purely sanctified may be attracted by different features of the Lord, like the impersonal *brahmajyoti* and localized Paramātmā, but a pure devotee directly takes to the service of the Supreme Lord.

There is a beautiful poem about Kṛṣṇa in which it is clearly stated that any person who is engaged in the worship of demigods is most unintelligent and cannot achieve at any time the supreme award of Kṛṣṇa. The devotee, in the beginning, may sometimes fall from the standard, but still he should be considered superior to all other philosophers and *yogīs*. One who always engages in Kṛṣṇa consciousness should be understood to be the perfect saintly person. His accidental nondevotional activities will diminish, and he will soon be situated without any doubt in complete perfection. The pure devotee has no actual chance to fall down because the Supreme Godhead personally takes care of His pure devotees. Therefore, the intelligent person should take directly to this process of Kṛṣṇa consciousness and happily live in this material world. He will eventually receive the supreme award of Kṛṣṇa.

Thus end the Bhaktivedanta Purports to the Ninth Chapter of the Śrīmad-Bhagavad-gītā in the matter of the Most Confidential Knowledge.

CHAPTER TEN

The Opulence of the Absolute

TEXT 1

श्रीभगवानुवाच ।
भूय एव महाबाहो शृणु मे परमं वचः ।
यत्तेऽहं प्रीयमाणाय वक्ष्यामि हितकाम्यया ॥ १ ॥

śrī-bhagavān uvāca
bhūya eva mahā-bāho
śṛṇu me paramaṁ vacaḥ
yat te 'haṁ prīyamāṇāya
vakṣyāmi hita-kāmyayā

śrī bhagavān uvāca—the Supreme Personality of Godhead said;
bhūyaḥ—again; *eva*—certainly; *mahā-bāho*—O mighty-armed; *śṛṇu*—just
hear; *me*—My; *paramaṁ*—supreme; *vacaḥ*—information; *yat*—that which;
te—to you; *aham*—I; *prīyamāṇāya*—thinking you dear to Me; *vakṣyāmi*—say;
hita-kāmyayā—for your benefit.

TRANSLATION

The Supreme Lord said: My dear friend, mighty-armed Arjuna, listen again to My supreme word, which I shall impart to you for your benefit and which will give you great joy.

PURPORT

The word *paramam* is explained thus by Parāśara Muni: one who is full in six opulences, who has full strength, full fame, wealth, knowledge, beauty and renunciation, is *paramam*, or the Supreme Personality of Godhead. While Kṛṣṇa was present on this earth, He displayed all six opulences. Therefore great sages like Parāśara Muni have all accepted Kṛṣṇa as the Supreme Personality of Godhead. Now Kṛṣṇa is instructing Arjuna in more confidential knowledge of His opulences and His work. Previously, beginning with the Seventh Chapter, the Lord already explained His different energies and how they are acting. Now in this chapter He explains His specific opulences to Arjuna. In the previous chapter he has clearly explained His different energies to establish devotion in firm conviction. Again in this chapter He tells Arjuna about His manifestations and various opulences.

The more one hears about the Supreme God, the more one becomes fixed in devotional service. One should always hear about the Lord in the association of devotees; that will enhance one's devotional service. Discourses in the society of devotees can take place only among those who are really anxious to be in Kṛṣṇa consciousness. Others cannot take part in such discourses. The Lord clearly tells Arjuna that because he is very dear to Him, for his benefit such discourses are taking place.

TEXT 2

न मे विदुः सुरगणाः प्रभवं न महर्षयः ।
अहमादिर्हि देवानां महर्षीणां च सर्वशः ॥ २ ॥

na me viduḥ sura-gaṇāḥ
prabhavaṁ na maharṣayaḥ
aham ādir hi devānāṁ
maharṣīṇāṁ ca sarvaśaḥ

na—never; *me*—My; *viduḥ*—knows; *sura-gaṇāḥ*—demigods; *prabhavam*—opulences; *na*—never; *maharṣayaḥ*—great sages; *aham*—I am; *ādiḥ*—the origin; *hi*—certainly; *devānām*—of the demigods; *maharṣīṇām*—of the great sages; *ca*—also; *sarvaśaḥ*—in all respects.

TRANSLATION

Neither the hosts of demigods nor the great sages know My origin, for, in every respect, I am the source of the demigods and the sages.

PURPORT

As stated in the *Brahma-saṁhitā*, Lord Kṛṣṇa is the Supreme Lord. No one is greater than Him; He is the cause of all causes. Here it is also stated by the Lord personally that He is the cause of all the demigods and sages. Even the demigods and great sages cannot understand Kṛṣṇa; they can understand neither His name nor His personality, so what is the position of the so-called scholars of this tiny planet? No one can understand why this Supreme God comes to earth as an ordinary human being and executes such commonplace and yet wonderful activities. One should know, then, that scholarship is not the qualification necessary to understand Kṛṣṇa. Even the demigods and the great sages have tried to understand Kṛṣṇa by their mental speculation, and they have failed to do so. In the *Śrīmad-Bhāgavatam* also it is clearly said that even the great demigods are not able to understand the Supreme Personality of Godhead. They can speculate to the limits of their imperfect senses and can reach the opposite conclusion of impersonalism, of something not manifested by the three qualities of material nature, or they can imagine something by mental speculation, but it is not possible to understand Kṛṣṇa by such foolish speculation.

Here the Lord indirectly says that if anyone wants to know the Absolute Truth, "Here I am present as the Supreme Personality of Godhead. I am the Supreme." One should know this. Although one cannot understand the inconceivable Lord who is personally present, He nonetheless exists. We can actually understand Kṛṣṇa, who is eternal, full of bliss and knowledge, simply by studying His words in *Bhagavad-gītā* and *Śrīmad-Bhāgavatam*. The impersonal Brahman can be conceived by persons who are already in the inferior energy of the Lord, but the Personality of Godhead cannot be conceived unless one is in the transcendental position.

Because most men cannot understand Kṛṣṇa in His actual situation, out of His causeless mercy He descends to show favor to such speculators. Yet despite the Supreme Lord's uncommon activities, these speculators, due to contamination in the material energy, still think that the impersonal Brahman is the Supreme. Only the devotees who are fully surrendered unto the Supreme Lord can understand, by the grace of the Supreme Personality, that He is Kṛṣṇa. The devotees of the Lord do not bother about the impersonal Brahman conception of God; their faith and devotion bring them to surrender immediately unto the Supreme Lord, and out of the causeless mercy of Kṛṣṇa, they can understand Kṛṣṇa. No one else can understand Him. So even great sages agree: What is ātmā, what is the Supreme? It is He whom we have to worship.

TEXT 3

यो मामजमनादिं च वेत्ति लोकमहेश्वरम् ।
असम्मूढः स मर्त्येषु सर्वपापैः प्रमुच्यते ॥ ३ ॥

yo mām ajam anādiṁ ca
vetti loka-maheśvaram
asammūḍhaḥ sa martyeṣu
sarva-pāpaiḥ pramucyate

yaḥ—anyone; mām—unto Me; ajam—unborn; anādim—without beginning; ca—also; vetti—knows; loka—the planets; maheśvaram—supreme master; asammūḍhaḥ—without doubt; saḥ—he; martyeṣu—among those subject to death; sarva-pāpaiḥ—from all sinful reactions; pramucyate—is delivered.

TRANSLATION

He who knows Me as the unborn, as the beginningless, as the Supreme Lord of all the worlds-he, undeluded among men, is freed from all sins.

PURPORT

As stated in the Seventh Chapter, those who are trying to elevate themselves to the platform of spiritual realization are not ordinary men. They are superior to millions and millions of ordinary men who have no knowledge of spiritual realization, but out of those actually trying to understand their spiritual situation, one who can come to the understanding that Kṛṣṇa is the Supreme Personality of Godhead, the proprietor of everything, the unborn, is the most successful spiritually realized person. In that stage only, when one has fully understood Kṛṣṇa's supreme position, can one be free completely from all sinful reactions.

Here the word *ajam*, meaning unborn, should not be confused with the living entities, who are described in the Second Chapter as *ajam*. The Lord is different from the living entities who are taking birth and dying due to material attachment. The conditional souls are changing their bodies, but His body is not changeable. Even when He comes to this material world, He comes as the same unborn; therefore in the Fourth Chapter it is said that the Lord, by His internal potency, is not under the inferior material energy, but is always in the superior energy.

He was existing before the creation, and He is different from His creation. All the demigods were created within this material world, but as far as Kṛṣṇa is concerned, it is said that He is not created; therefore Kṛṣṇa is different even from the great demigods like Brahmā and Śiva. And because He is the creator of Brahmā, Śiva and all the other demigods, He is the Supreme Person of all planets.

Śrī Kṛṣṇa is therefore different from everything that is created, and anyone who knows Him as such immediately becomes liberated from all sinful reaction. One must be liberated from all sinful activities to be in the knowledge of the Supreme Lord. Only by devotional service can He be known and not by any other means, as stated in *Bhagavad-gītā*.

One should not try to understand Kṛṣṇa as a human being. As stated previously, only a foolish person thinks Him to be a human being. This is again expressed here in a different way. A man who is not foolish, who is intelligent enough to understand the constitutional position of the Godhead, is always free from all sinful reactions.

If Kṛṣṇa is known as the son of Devakī, then how can He be unborn? That is also explained in *Śrīmad-Bhāgavatam*: When He appeared before Devakī and Vasudeva, He was not born as an ordinary child; He appeared in His original form, and then He transformed Himself into an ordinary child.

Anything done under the direction of Kṛṣṇa is transcendental. It cannot be contaminated by the material reactions, which may be auspicious or inauspicious. The conception that there are things auspicious and inauspicious in the material world is more or less a mental concoction because there is nothing auspicious in the material world. Everything is inauspicious because the very material mask is inauspicious. We simply imagine it to be auspicious. Real auspiciousness depends on activities in Kṛṣṇa consciousness in full devotion and service. Therefore if we at all want our activities to be auspicious, then we should work under the directions of the Supreme Lord. Such directions are given in authoritative scriptures such as *Śrīmad-Bhāgavatam* and *Bhagavad-gītā*, or from a bona fide spiritual master. Because the spiritual master is the representative of the Supreme Lord, his direction is directly the direction of the Supreme Lord. The spiritual master, saintly persons and scriptures direct in the same way. There is no contradiction in these three sources. All actions done under such direction are free from the reactions of pious or impious activities of this material world. The transcendental attitude of the devotee in the performance of activities is actually that of renunciation, and this is called *sannyāsa*. Anyone acting under the direction of the Supreme Lord is actually a *sannyāsī* and a *yogī*, and not the man who has simply taken the dress of the *sannyāsī*, or a pseudo-*yogī*.

TEXTS 4-5

बुद्धिर्ज्ञानमसम्मोहः क्षमा सत्यं दमः शमः ।
सुखं दुःखं भवोऽभावो भयं चाभयमेव च ॥ ४ ॥
अहिंसा समता तुष्टिस्तपो दानं यशोऽयशः ।
भवन्ति भावा भूतानां मत्त एव पृथग्विधाः ॥ ५ ॥

*buddhir jñānam asammohaḥ
kṣamā satyaṁ damaḥ śamaḥ
sukhaṁ duḥkhaṁ bhavo 'bhāvo
bhayaṁ cābhayam eva ca*

*ahiṁsā samatā tuṣṭis
tapo dānaṁ yaśo 'yaśaḥ
bhavanti bhāvā bhūtānāṁ
matta eva pṛthag-vidhāḥ*

buddhiḥ—intelligence; *jñānam*—knowledge; *asam-mohaḥ*—freedom from doubt; *kṣamā*—forgiveness; *satyam*—truthfulness; *damaḥ*—control of the senses; *śamaḥ*—control of the mind; *sukham*—happiness; *duḥkham*—distress; *bhavaḥ*—birth; *abhāvaḥ*—death; *bhayam*—fear; *ca*—also; *abhayam*—without fear; *eva*—also; *ca*—and; *ahiṁsā*—nonviolence; *samatā*—equilibrium; *tuṣṭiḥ*—satisfaction; *tapaḥ*—penance; *dānam*—charity; *yaśaḥ*—fame; *ayaśaḥ*—

infamy; *bhavanti*—become; *bhāvāḥ*—natures; *bhūtānām*—of living entities; *mattaḥ*—from Me; *eva*—certainly; *pṛthak-vidhāḥ*—differently arranged.

TRANSLATION

Intelligence, knowledge, freedom from doubt and delusion, forgiveness, truthfulness, self-control and calmness, pleasure and pain, birth, death, fear, fearlessness, nonviolence, equanimity, satisfaction, austerity, charity, fame and infamy are created by Me alone.

PURPORT

The different qualities of living entities, be they good or bad, are all created by Kṛṣṇa, and they are described here.

Intelligence refers to the power of analyzing things in proper perspective, and knowledge refers to understanding what is spirit and what is matter. Ordinary knowledge obtained by a university education pertains only to matter, and it is not accepted here as knowledge. Knowledge means knowing the distinction between spirit and matter. In modern education there is no knowledge about the spirit; they are simply taking care of the material elements and bodily needs. Therefore academic knowledge is not complete.

Asammohaḥ, freedom from doubt and delusion, can be achieved when one is not hesitant and when he understands the transcendental philosophy. Slowly but surely he becomes free from bewilderment. Nothing should be accepted blindly; everything should be accepted with care and with caution. *Kṣamā*, forgiveness, should be practiced, and one should excuse the minor offenses of others. *Satyam*, truthfulness, means that facts should be presented as they are for the benefit of others. Facts should not be misrepresented. According to social conventions, it is said that one can speak the truth only when it is palatable to others. But that is not truthfulness. The truth should be spoken in a straight and forward way, so that others will understand actually what the facts are. If a man is a thief and if people are warned that he is a thief, that is truth. Although sometimes the truth is unpalatable, one should not refrain from speaking it. Truthfulness demands that the facts be presented as they are for the benefit of others. That is the definition of truth.

Self-control means that the senses should not be used for unnecessary personal enjoyment. There is no prohibition against meeting the proper needs of the senses, but unnecessary sense enjoyment is detrimental for spiritual advancement. Therefore the senses should be restrained from unnecessary use. Similarly, the mind should not indulge in unnecessary thoughts; that is called *śamaḥ*, or calmness. Nor should one spend one's time pondering over earning money. That is a misuse of the thinking power. The mind should be used to understand the prime necessity of human beings, and that should be presented authoritatively. The power of thought should be developed in association with persons who are authorities in the scriptures, saintly persons and spiritual masters and those whose thinking is highly developed. *Sukham*, pleasure or happiness, should always be in that which is favorable for the cultivation of the spiritual knowledge of Kṛṣṇa consciousness. And similarly, that which is painful or which causes distress is that which is unfavorable for the cultivation of Kṛṣṇa consciousness. Anything favorable for the development of Kṛṣṇa consciousness should be accepted, and anything unfavorable should be rejected.

Bhava, birth, should be understood to refer to the body. As far as the soul is concerned, there is neither birth nor death; that we have discussed in the beginning of *Bhagavad-gītā*. Birth and death apply to one's embodiment in the material world. Fear is due to worrying about the future. A person in Kṛṣṇa consciousness has no fear because by his activities he is sure to go back to the spiritual sky, back home, back to Godhead. Therefore his future is very bright. Others, however, do not know what their future holds; they have no knowledge of what the next life holds. So they are therefore in constant anxiety. If we want to get free from anxiety, then the best course is to understand Kṛṣṇa and be situated always in Kṛṣṇa consciousness. In that way we will be free from all fear. In the *Śrīmad-Bhāgavatam*. it is stated that fear is caused by our absorption in the illusory energy, but those who are free from the illusory energy, those who are confident that they are not the material body, that they are spiritual parts of the Supreme Personality of Godhead and are therefore engaged in the transcendental service of the Supreme Godhead, have nothing to fear. Their future is very bright. This fear is a condition of persons who are not in Kṛṣṇa consciousness. *Bhayam*, fearlessness, is only possible for one in Kṛṣṇa consciousness.

Ahiṁsā, nonviolence, means that one should not do anything which will put others into misery or confusion. Material activities that are promised by so many politicians, sociologists, philanthropists, etc., do not produce very good results because the politicians and philanthropists have no transcendental vision; they do not know what is actually beneficial for human society. *Ahiṁsā* means that people should be trained in such a way that the full utilization of the human body can be achieved. The human body is meant for spiritual realization, so any movement or any commissions which do not further that end commit violence on the human body. That which furthers the future spiritual happiness of the people in general is called nonviolence.

Samatā, equanimity, refers to freedom from attachment and aversion. To be very much attached or to be very much detached is not the best. This material world should be accepted without attachment or aversion. Similarly, that which is favorable for prosecuting Kṛṣṇa consciousness should be accepted; that which is unfavorable should be rejected. That is called *samatā*, equanimity. A person in Kṛṣṇa consciousness has nothing to reject and nothing to accept unless it is useful in the prosecution of Kṛṣṇa consciousness.

Tuṣṭiḥ, satisfaction, means that one should not be eager to gather more and more material goods by unnecessary activity. One should be satisfied with whatever is obtained by the grace of the Supreme Lord; that is called satisfaction. *Tapas* means austerity or penance. There are many rules and definitions in the *Vedas* which apply here, like rising early in the morning and taking a bath. Sometimes it is very troublesome to rise early in the morning, but whatever voluntary trouble one may suffer in this way is called penance. Similarly, there are prescriptions for fasting on certain days of the month. One may not be inclined to practice such fasting, but because of his determination to make advancement in the science of Kṛṣṇa consciousness, he should accept such bodily troubles which are recommended. However, one should not fast unnecessarily or against Vedic injunctions. One should not fast for some political purpose; that is described in *Bhagavad-gītā* as fasting in ignorance, and anything done in ignorance or passion does not lead to spiritual advancement. Everything done in the mode of goodness does advance one, however, and fasting done in terms of the Vedic injunctions enriches one in spiritual knowledge.

As far as charity is concerned, one should give fifty percent of his earnings to some good cause. And what is a good cause? It is that which is conducted in terms of Kṛṣṇa consciousness. That is not only a good cause, but it is the best cause. Because Kṛṣṇa is good, His cause is also good. Thus charity should be given to a person who is engaged in Kṛṣṇa consciousness. According to Vedic literature, it is enjoined that charity should be given to the *brāhmaṇas*. This practice is still followed, although not very nicely in terms of the Vedic injunction. But still the injunction is that charity should be given to the *brāhmaṇas*. Why? Because they are engaged in higher cultivation of spiritual knowledge. A *brāhmaṇa* is supposed to devote his whole life to understanding Brahman. A *brahma-jana* is one who knows Brahman; he is called a *brāhmaṇa*. Thus charity is offered to the *brāhmaṇas* because since they are always engaged in higher spiritual service, they have no time to earn their livelihood. In the Vedic literature, charity is also to be awarded to the renouncer of life, the *sannyāsī*. The *sannyāsīs* beg from door to door, not for money but for missionary purposes. The system is that they go from door to door to awaken the householders from the slumber of ignorance. Because the householders are engaged in family affairs and have forgotten their actual purpose in life—awakening their Kṛṣṇa consciousness—it is the business of the *sannyāsīs* to go as beggars to the householders and encourage them to be Kṛṣṇa conscious. As it is said in the *Vedas*, one should awake and achieve what is due him in this human form of life. This knowledge and method is distributed by the *sannyāsīs*; hence charity is to be given to the renouncer of life, to the *brāhmaṇas*, and similar good causes, not to any whimsical cause.

Yaśaḥ, fame, should be according to Lord Caitanya, who said that a man is famous when he is known as a great devotee. That is real fame. If one has become a great man in Kṛṣṇa consciousness and it is known, then he is truly famous. One who does not have such fame is infamous.

All these qualities are manifest throughout the universe in human society and in the society of the demigods. There are many forms of humanity on other planets, and these qualities are there. Now, for one who wants to advance in Kṛṣṇa consciousness, Kṛṣṇa creates all these qualities, but the person develops them himself from within. One who engages in the devotional service of the Supreme Lord develops all the good qualities, as arranged by the Supreme Lord.

Of whatever we find, good or bad, the origin is Kṛṣṇa. Nothing can manifest in this material world which is not in Kṛṣṇa. That is knowledge; although we know that things are differently situated, we should realize that everything flows from Kṛṣṇa.

TEXT 6

महर्षयः सप्त पूर्वे चत्वारो मनवस्तथा ।
मद्भावा मानसा जाता येषां लोक इमाः प्रजाः ॥ ६ ॥

maharṣayaḥ sapta pūrve
catvāro manavas tathā
mad-bhāvā mānasā jātā
yeṣāṁ loka imāḥ prajāḥ

Plate 13. The Demigods, being satisfied by the performance of sacrifice, supply all needs to man. *(p. 174)*

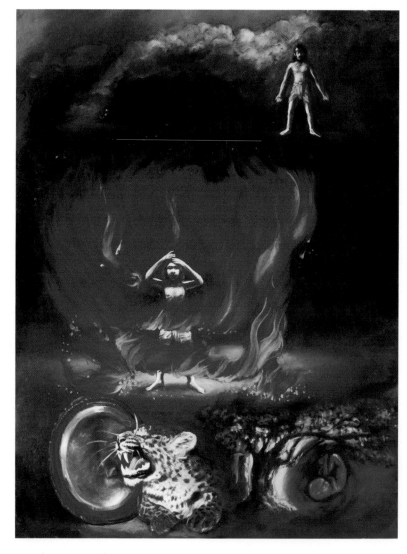

Plate 14. The living entity is covered by different degrees of lust. (*p. 205*)

Plate 15. The Blessed Lord first instructed this imperishable science of yoga to Vivasvān. *(p. 214)*

Plate 16. The Lord descends whenever there is a decline
in religious principles. *(p. 224)*

Plate 17. "In order to deliver the pious and
to annihilate the miscreants..." *(p. 226)*

Plate 18. "As they surrender to Me, I reward them accordingly." (*p. 232*)

Plate 19. He who applies himself well to one of these paths
achieves the results of both. (*p. 276*)

Plate 20. The humble sage sees with equal vision. *(p. 292)*

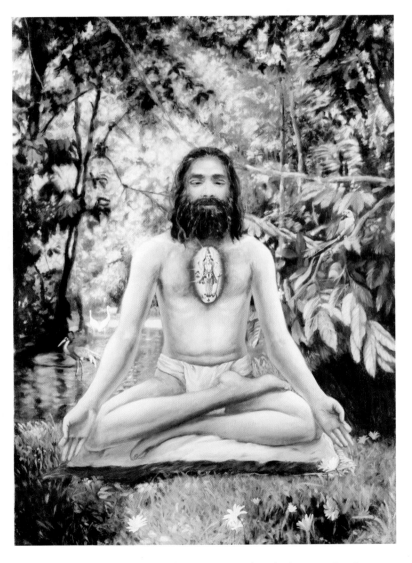

Plate 21. "One should meditate on Me within the heart and make Me the ultimate goal of life." (*p. 319*)

Plate 22. One should engage oneself in the practice of yoga with undeviating determination and faith. (*p. 333*)

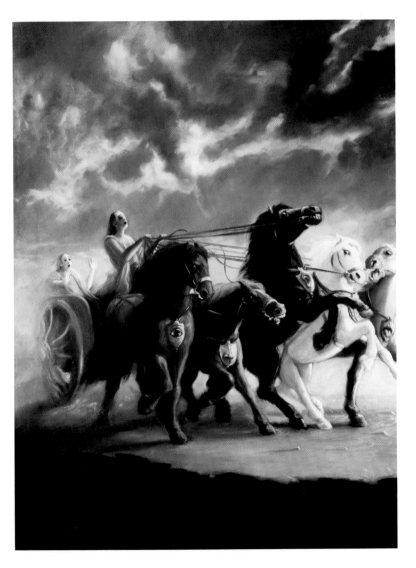

Plate 23. "The mind is restless, turbulent,
obstinate and very strong, O Kṛṣṇa." (*p. 343*)

Plate 24. "Of all yogīs, he who abides in Me
with great faith is the highest of all." (*p. 359*)

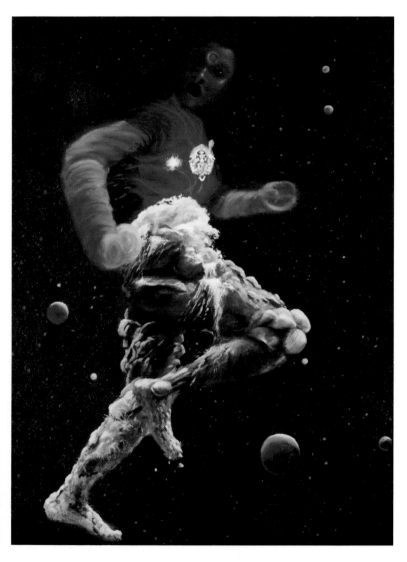

Plate 25. Kṛṣṇa's material and spiritual energies. *(p. 367)*

Plate 26. Four kinds of pious men surrender to Kṛṣṇa, and four kinds of impious men do not. (*p. 382*)

Plate 27. "When one goes there, he never comes back.
That is My supreme abode." (*p. 431*)

Plate 28. "Fools deride Me when I descend in the human form." (*p. 459*)

maharṣayaḥ—the great sages; *sapta*—seven; *pūrve*—before; *catvāraḥ*—four; *manavaḥ*—Manus; *tathā*—also; *mat-bhāvāḥ*—born of Me; *mānasāḥ*—from the mind; *jātāḥ*—born; *yeṣām*—of them; *loke*—the planets; *imāḥ*—all this; *prajāḥ*—population.

TRANSLATION

The seven great sages and before them the four other great sages and the Manus [progenitors of mankind] are born out of My mind, and all creatures in these planets descend from them.

PURPORT

The Lord is giving a genealogical synopsis of the universal population. Brahmā is the original creature born out of the energy of the Supreme Lord known as Hiraṇyagarbha. And from Brahmā all the seven great sages, and before them four other great sages, named Sanaka, Sananda, Sanātana, and Sanatkumāra, and the fourteen Manus, are manifest. All these twenty-five great sages are known as the patriarchs of the living entities all over the universe. There are innumerable universes and innumerable planets within each universe, and each planet is full of population of different varieties. All of them are born of these twenty-five patriarchs. Brahmā underwent penance for one thousand years of the demigods before he realized by the grace of Kṛṣṇa how to create. Then from Brahmā, Sanaka, Sananda, Sanātana, and Sanatkumāra came out, then Rudra, and then the seven sages, and in this way all the *brāhmaṇas* and *kṣatriyas* are born out of the energy of the Supreme Personality of Godhead. Brahmā is known as *pitāmaha*, the grandfather, and Kṛṣṇa is known as the *prapitāmaha*, the father of the grandfather. That is stated in the Eleventh Chapter of the *Bhagavad-gītā*. (Bg. 11.39)

TEXT 7

एतां विभूतिं योगं च मम यो वेत्ति तत्त्वतः ।
सोऽविकल्पेन योगेन युज्यते नात्र संशयः ॥ ७ ॥

etāṁ vibhūtiṁ yogaṁ ca
mama yo vetti tattvataḥ
so 'vikalpena yogena
yujyate nātra saṁśayaḥ

etām—all this; *vibhūtim*—opulence; *yogam ca*—also mystic power; *mama*—of Mine; *yaḥ*—anyone; *vetti*—knows; *tattvataḥ*—factually; *saḥ*—he; *avikalpena*—without division; *yogena*—in devotional service; *yujyate*—engaged; *na*—never; *atra*—here; *saṁśayaḥ*—doubt.

TRANSLATION

He who knows in truth this glory and power of Mine engages in unalloyed devotional service; of this there is no doubt.

PURPORT

The highest summit of spiritual perfection is knowledge of the Supreme Personality of Godhead. Unless one is firmly convinced of the different opulences of the Supreme Lord, he cannot engage in devotional service. Generally people know that God is great, but they do not know in detail how God is great. Here are the details. If one knows factually how God is great, then naturally he becomes a surrendered soul and engages himself in the devotional service of the Lord. When one factually knows the opulences of the Supreme, there is no alternative but to surrender to Him. This factual knowledge can be known from the descriptions in *Śrīmad-Bhāgavatam* and *Bhagavad-gītā* and similar literatures.

In the administration of this universe there are many demigods distributed throughout the planetary system, and the chief of them are Brahmā, Lord Śiva and the four great Kumāras and other patriarchs. There are many forefathers of the population of the universe, and all of them are born of the Supreme Lord Kṛṣṇa. The Supreme Personality of Godhead, Kṛṣṇa, is the original forefather of all forefathers.

These are some of the opulences of the Supreme Lord. When one is firmly convinced of them, he accepts Kṛṣṇa with great faith and without any doubt, and he engages in devotional service. All this particular knowledge is required in order to increase one's interest in the loving devotional service of the Lord. One should not neglect to understand fully how great Kṛṣṇa is, for by knowing the greatness of Kṛṣṇa one will be able to be fixed in sincere devotional service.

TEXT 8

अहं सर्वस्य प्रभवो मत्तः सर्वं प्रवर्तते ।
इति मत्वा भजन्ते मां बुधा भावसमन्विताः ॥ ८ ॥

aham sarvasya prabhavo
mattaḥ sarvam pravartate
iti matvā bhajante mām
budhā bhāva-samanvitāḥ

aham—I; sarvasya—of all; prabhavaḥ—source of generation; mattaḥ—from Me; sarvam—everything; pravartate—emanates; iti—thus; matvā—knowing; bhajante—becomes devoted; mām—unto Me; budhāḥ—learned; bhāva-samanvitāḥ—with great attention.

TRANSLATION

I am the source of all spiritual and material worlds. Everything emanates from Me. The wise who know this perfectly engage in My devotional service and worship Me with all their hearts.

PURPORT

A learned scholar who has studied the Vedas perfectly and has information from authorities like Lord Caitanya and who knows how to apply these teachings can understand that Kṛṣṇa is the origin of everything in both the material and spiritual worlds, and because he knows this perfectly he becomes firmly fixed in the devotional service of the Supreme Lord. He can never be deviated by any amount of nonsensical commentaries or by fools. All Vedic literature agrees that Kṛṣṇa is the source of Brahmā, Śiva and all other demigods. In the Atharva-veda it is said, "yo brahmāṇam vidadhāti: pūrvam yo vai vedāmś ca gāpayati sma kṛṣṇaḥ." "It was Kṛṣṇa who in the beginning instructed Brahmā in Vedic knowledge and who disseminated Vedic knowledge in the past." Then again it is said, "atha puruṣo ha vai nārāyaṇo 'kāmayata prajāḥ sṛjeya ity upakramya." "Then the Supreme Personality Nārāyaṇa desired to create living entities." Again it is said:

nārāyaṇād brahmā jāyate, nārāyaṇād prajāpatiḥ prajāyate, nārāyaṇād indro jāyate, nārāyaṇād aṣṭau vasavo jāyante, nārāyaṇād ekādaśa rudrā jāyante, nārāyaṇād dvādaśādityāḥ.

"From Nārāyaṇa, Brahmā is born, and from Nārāyaṇa, the patriarchs are also born. From Nārāyaṇa, Indra is born, from Nārāyaṇa the eight Vasus are born, from Nārāyaṇa the eleven Rudras are born, from Nārāyaṇa the twelve Ādityas are born."

It is said in the same *Vedas: brahmaṇyo devakī-putraḥ:* "The son of Devakī, Kṛṣṇa, is the Supreme Personality." Then it is said:

eko vai nārāyaṇa āsīn na brahmā na īśāno nāpo nāgni samau neme dyāv-āpṛthivī na nakṣatrāṇi na sūryaḥ sa ekākī na ramate tasya dhyānāntaḥ sthasya yatra chāndogaiḥ kriyamāṇāṣṭakādi-saṁjñakā stuti-stomaḥ stomam ucyate.

"In the beginning of the creation there was only the Supreme Personality Nārāyaṇa. There was no Brahmā, no Śiva, no fire, no moon, no stars in the sky, no sun. There was only Kṛṣṇa, who creates all and enjoys all."

In the many *Purāṇas* it is said that Lord Śiva was born from the highest, the Supreme Lord Kṛṣṇa, and the *Vedas* say that it is the Supreme Lord, the creator of Brahmā and Śiva, who is to be worshiped. In the *Mokṣadharma* Kṛṣṇa also says, *prajāpatiṁ ca rudraṁ cāpy aham eva sṛjāmi vai tau hi mām na vijānīto mama māyā-vimohitau.* "The patriarchs, Śiva and others are created by Me, though they do not know that they are created by Me because they are deluded by My illusory energy." In *Varāha Purāṇa* it is also said, *nārāyaṇaḥ paro devas tasmāj jātaś caturmukhaḥ tasmād rudro 'bhavad devaḥ sa ca sarvajñatāṁ gataḥ.* "Nārāyaṇa is the Supreme Personality of Godhead, and from Him Brahmā was born, from whom Śiva was born."

Lord Kṛṣṇa is the source of all generations, and He is called the most efficient cause of everything. He says that because "everything is born of Me, I am the original source of all. Everything is under Me; no one is above Me." There is no supreme controller other than Kṛṣṇa. One who understands Kṛṣṇa in such a way from a bona fide spiritual master and from Vedic literature, who engages all his energy in Kṛṣṇa consciousness, becomes a truly learned man. In comparison to him, all others, who do not know Kṛṣṇa properly, are but fools. Only a fool would consider Kṛṣṇa to be an ordinary man. A Kṛṣṇa conscious person should not be bewildered by fools; he should avoid all unauthorized commentaries and interpretations on *Bhagavad-gītā* and proceed in Kṛṣṇa consciousness with determination and firmness.

TEXT 9

मच्चित्ता मद्गतप्राणा बोधयन्तः परस्परम् ।
कथयन्तश्च मां नित्यं तुष्यन्ति च रमन्ति च ॥ ९ ॥

> mac-cittā mad-gata-prāṇā
> bodhayantaḥ parasparam
> kathayantaś ca māṁ nityaṁ
> tuṣyanti ca ramanti ca

mat-cittāḥ—minds fully engaged in Me; mat-gata-prāṇāḥ—lives devoted to the service of Kṛṣṇa; bodhayantaḥ—preaching; parasparam—among themselves; kathayantaḥ ca—talking also; mām—about Me; nityam—perpetually; tuṣyanti—are pleased; ca—also; ramanti—enjoy transcendental bliss; ca—also.

TRANSLATION

The thoughts of My pure devotees dwell in Me, their lives are surrendered to Me, and they derive great satisfaction and bliss enlightening one another and conversing about Me.

PURPORT

Pure devotees, whose characteristics are mentioned here, engage themselves fully in the transcendental loving service of the Lord. Their minds cannot be diverted from the lotus feet of Kṛṣṇa. Their talks are solely on the transcendental subjects. The symptoms of the pure devotees are described in this verse specifically. Devotees of the Supreme Lord are twenty-four hours daily engaged in glorifying the pastimes of the Supreme Lord. Their hearts and souls are constantly submerged in Kṛṣṇa, and they take pleasure in discussing Him with other devotees.

In the preliminary stage of devotional service they relish the transcendental pleasure from the service itself, and in the mature stage they are actually situated in love of God. Once situated in that transcendental position, they can relish the highest perfection which is exhibited by the Lord in His abode. Lord Caitanya likens transcendental devotional service to the sowing of a seed in the heart of the living entity. There are innumerable living entities traveling throughout the different planets of the universe, and out of them there are a few who are fortunate enough to meet a pure devotee and get the chance to understand devotional service. This devotional service is just like a seed, and if it is sown in the heart of a living entity, and if he goes on hearing and chanting, Hare Kṛṣṇa, Hare Kṛṣṇa, Kṛṣṇa Kṛṣṇa, Hare Hare/ Hare Rāma, Hare Rāma, Rāma Rāma, Hare Hare, that seed fructifies, just as the seed of a tree fructifies with regular watering. The spiritual plant of devotional service gradually grows and grows until it penetrates the covering of the material universe and enters into the *brahmajyoti* effulgence in the spiritual sky. In the spiritual sky also that plant grows more and more until it reaches the highest planet, which is called Goloka Vṛndāvana, the supreme planet of Kṛṣṇa. Ultimately, the plant takes shelter under the lotus feet of Kṛṣṇa and rests there. Gradually, as a plant grows fruits and flowers, that plant of devotional service also produces fruits, and the watering process in the form of chanting and hearing goes on. This plant of devotional service is fully described in the *Caitanya-caritāmṛta*. It is explained there that when the complete plant takes shelter under the lotus feet of the Supreme Lord, one becomes fully absorbed in love of God; then he cannot live even for a moment without being in contact with the Supreme Lord, just as a fish cannot live without water. In such a state, the devotee actually attains the transcendental qualities in contact with the Supreme Lord.

The *Śrīmad-Bhāgavatam* is also full of such narration about the relationship between the Supreme Lord and His devotees; therefore the *Śrīmad-Bhāgavatam* is very dear to the devotees. In this narration there is nothing about material activities, sense gratification or liberation. *Śrīmad-Bhāgavatam* is the only narration in which the transcendental nature of the Supreme Lord and His devotees is fully described. Thus the realized souls in Kṛṣṇa consciousness take continual pleasure in hearing such transcendental literatures, just as a young boy and girl take pleasure in association.

TEXT 10

तेषां सततयुक्तानां भजतां प्रीतिपूर्वकम् ।
ददामि बुद्धियोगं तं येन मामुपयान्ति ते ॥ १० ॥

teṣāṁ satata-yuktānāṁ
bhajatāṁ prīti-pūrvakam
dadāmi buddhi-yogaṁ taṁ
yena mām upayānti te

teṣām—unto them; *satata-yuktānām*—always engaged; *bhajatām*—in devotional service; *prīti-pūrvakam*—in loving ecstasy; *dadāmi*—I give; *buddhi-yogam*—real intelligence; *tam*—that; *yena*—by which; *mām*—unto Me; *upayānti*—come; *te*—they.

TRANSLATION

To those who are constantly devoted and worship Me with love, I give the understanding by which they can come to Me.

PURPORT

In this verse the word *buddhi-yogam* is very significant. We may remember that in the Second Chapter the Lord, instructing Arjuna, said that He had spoken to him of many things and that He would instruct him in the way of *buddhi-yoga*. Now *buddhi-yoga* is explained. *Buddhi-yogam* itself is action in Kṛṣṇa consciousness; that is the highest intelligence. *Buddhi* means intelligence, and *yogam* means mystic activities or mystic elevation. When one tries to go back home, back to Godhead, and takes fully to Kṛṣṇa consciousness in devotional service, his action is called *buddhi-yogam*. In other words, *buddhi-yogam* is the process by which one gets out of the entanglement of this material world. The ultimate goal of progress is Kṛṣṇa. People do not know this; therefore the association of devotees and a bona fide spiritual master are important. One should know that the goal is Kṛṣṇa, and when the goal is assigned, then the path is slowly but progressively traversed, and the ultimate goal is achieved.

When a person knows the goal of life but is addicted to the fruits of activities, he is acting in *karma-yoga*. When he knows that the goal is Kṛṣṇa, but he takes pleasure in mental speculations to understand Kṛṣṇa, he is acting in *jñāna-yoga*. And when he knows the goal and seeks Kṛṣṇa completely in Kṛṣṇa consciousness and devotional service, he is acting in *bhakti-yoga*, or *buddhi-yoga*, which is the complete *yoga*. This complete *yoga* is the highest perfectional stage of life.

A person may have a bona fide spiritual master and may be attached to a spiritual organization, but still, if he is not intelligent enough to make progress, then Kṛṣṇa from within gives him instructions so that he may ultimately come to Him without difficulty. The qualification is that a person always engage himself in Kṛṣṇa consciousness and with love and devotion render all kinds of services. He should perform some sort of work for Kṛṣṇa, and that work should be with love. If a devotee is intelligent enough, he will make progress on the path of self-realization. If one is sincere and devoted to the activities of devotional service, the Lord gives him a chance to make progress and ultimately attain to Him.

TEXT 11

तेषामेवानुकम्पार्थमहमज्ञानजं तमः ।
नाशयाम्यात्मभावस्थो ज्ञानदीपेन भास्वता ॥ ११ ॥

*teṣām evānukampārtham
aham ajñāna-jaṁ tamaḥ
nāśayāmy ātma-bhāva-stho
jñāna-dīpena bhāsvatā*

teṣām—for them; *eva*—certainly; *anukampā-artham*—to show special mercy; *aham*—I; *ajñāna-jam*—due to ignorance; *tamaḥ*—darkness; *nāśayāmi* —dispel; *ātma*—within; *bhāvasthaḥ*—themselves; *jñāna*—of knowledge; *dīpena*—with the lamp; *bhāsvatā*—glowing.

TRANSLATION

Out of compassion for them, I, dwelling in their hearts, destroy with the shining lamp of knowledge the darkness born of ignorance.

PURPORT

When Lord Caitanya was in Benares promulgating the chanting of Hare Kṛṣṇa, Hare Kṛṣṇa, Kṛṣṇa Kṛṣṇa, Hare Hare/ Hare Rāma, Hare Rāma, Rāma Rāma, Hare Hare, thousands of people were following Him. Prakāśānanda, a very influential and learned scholar in Benares at that time, derided Lord Caitanya for being a sentimentalist. Sometimes philosophers criticize the devotees because they think that most of the devotees are in the darkness of ignorance and are philosophically naive sentimentalists. Actually that is not the fact. There are very, very learned scholars who have put forward the philosophy of devotion, but even if a devotee does not take advantage of their literatures or of his spiritual master, if he is sincere in his devotional service he is helped by Kṛṣṇa Himself within his heart. So the sincere devotee engaged in Kṛṣṇa consciousness cannot be without knowledge. The only qualification is that one carry out devotional service in full Kṛṣṇa consciousness.

The modern philosophers think that without discriminating one cannot have pure knowledge. For them this answer is given by the Supreme Lord: those who are engaged in pure devotional service, even though they be without sufficient education and even without sufficient knowledge of the Vedic principles, are still helped by the Supreme God, as stated in this verse.

The Lord tells Arjuna that basically there is no possibility of understanding the Supreme Truth, the Absolute Truth, the Supreme Personality of Godhead, simply by speculating, for the Supreme Truth is so great that it is not possible to understand Him or to achieve Him simply by making a mental effort. Man can go on speculating for several millions of years, and if he is not devoted, if he is not a lover of the Supreme Truth, he will never understand Kṛṣṇa or the Supreme Truth. Only by devotional service is the Supreme Truth, Kṛṣṇa, pleased, and by His inconceivable energy He can reveal Himself to the heart of the pure devotee. The pure devotee always has Kṛṣṇa within his heart; therefore he is just like the sun that dissipates the darkness of ignorance. This is the special mercy rendered to the pure devotee by Kṛṣṇa.

Due to the contamination of material association, through many, many millions of births, one's heart is always covered with the dust of materialism, but when one engages in devotional service and constantly chants Hare Kṛṣṇa, the dust quickly clears, and one is elevated to the platform of pure knowledge. The ultimate goal of Viṣṇu can be attained only by this chant and by devotional service, and not by mental speculation or argument. The pure devotee does not have to worry about the necessities of life; he need not be anxious because when he removes the darkness from his heart, everything is provided automatically by the Supreme Lord, for He is pleased by the loving devotional service of the devotee. This is the essence of the *Gītā's* teachings. By studying *Bhagavad-gītā*, one can become a completely surrendered soul to the Supreme Lord and engage himself in pure devotional service. As the Lord takes charge, one becomes completely free from all kinds of materialistic endeavors.

TEXTS 12-13

अर्जुन उवाच ।
परं ब्रह्म परं धाम पवित्रं परमं भवान् ।
पुरुषं शाश्वतं दिव्यमादिदेवमजं विभुम् ॥ १२ ॥

आहुस्त्वामृषयः सर्वे देवर्षिर्नारदस्तथा ।
असितो देवलो व्यासः स्वयं चैव ब्रवीषि मे ॥ १३ ॥

arjuna uvāca
param brahma param dhāma
pavitram paramam bhavān
puruṣam śāśvatam divyam
ādi-devam ajam vibhum

āhus tvām ṛṣayaḥ sarve
devarṣir nāradas tathā
asito devalo vyāsaḥ
svayam caiva bravīṣi me

arjunaḥ uvāca—Arjuna said; *param*—supreme; *brahma*—truth; *param*—supreme; *dhāma*—sustenance; *pavitram*—purest; *paramam*—supreme; *bhavān*—Yourself; *puruṣam*—personality; *śāśvatam*—original; *divyam*—transcendental; *ādi-devam*—original Lord; *ajam*—unborn; *vibhum*—greatest; *āhuḥ*—say; *tvām*—unto You; *ṛṣayaḥ*—sages; *sarve*—all; *devarṣiḥ*—the sage among the demigods; *nāradaḥ*—Nārada; *tathā*—also; *asitaḥ*—Asita; *devalaḥ*—Devala; *vyāsaḥ*—Vyāsa; *svayam*—personally; *ca*—also; *eva*—certainly; *bravīṣi*—explaining; *me*—unto me.

TRANSLATION

Arjuna said: You are the Supreme Brahman, the ultimate, the supreme abode and purifier, the Absolute Truth and the eternal divine person. You are the primal God, transcendental and original, and You are the unborn and all-pervading beauty. All the great sages such as Nārada, Asita, Devala, and Vyāsa proclaim this of You, and now You Yourself are declaring it to me.

PURPORT

In these two verses the Supreme Lord gives a chance to the modern philosopher, for here it is clear that the Supreme is different from the individual soul. Arjuna, after hearing the essential four verses of *Bhagavad-gītā* in this chapter, became completely free from all doubts and accepted Kṛṣṇa as the Supreme Personality of Godhead. He at once boldly declares, "You are Parambrahma, the Supreme Personality of Godhead." And previously Kṛṣṇa states that He is the originator of everything and everyone. Every demigod and every human being is dependent on Him. Men and demigods, out of ignorance, think that they are absolute and independent of the Supreme Lord Kṛṣṇa. That ignorance is removed perfectly by the discharge of devotional service. This is already explained in the previous verse by the Lord. Now by His grace, Arjuna is accepting Him as the Supreme Truth, in concordance with the Vedic injunction. It is not because Kṛṣṇa is an intimate friend of Arjuna that he is flattering Him by calling Him the Supreme Personality of Godhead, the Absolute Truth. Whatever Arjuna says in these two verses is confirmed by Vedic truth. Vedic injunctions affirm that only one who takes to devotional service to the Supreme Lord can understand Him, whereas others cannot. Each and every word of this verse spoken by Arjuna is confirmed by Vedic injunction.

In the *Kena Upaniṣad* it is stated that the Supreme Brahman is the rest for everything, and Kṛṣṇa has already explained that everything is resting on Him. The *Muṇḍaka Upaniṣad* confirms that the Supreme Lord, in whom everything is resting, can be realized only by those who engage constantly in thinking of Him. This constant thinking of Kṛṣṇa is *smaraṇam*, one of the methods of devotional service. It is only by devotional service to Kṛṣṇa that one can understand his position and get rid of this material body.

In the *Vedas* the Supreme Lord is accepted as the purest of the pure. One who understands that Kṛṣṇa is the purest of the pure can become purified from all sinful activities. One cannot be disinfected from sinful activities unless he surrenders unto the Supreme Lord. Arjuna's acceptance of Kṛṣṇa as the supreme pure complies with the injunctions of Vedic literature. This is also confirmed by great personalities, of whom Nārada is the chief.

Kṛṣṇa is the Supreme Personality of Godhead, and one should always meditate upon Him and enjoy one's transcendental relationship with Him. He is the supreme existence. He is free from bodily needs, birth and death. Not only does Arjuna confirm this, but all the Vedic literatures, the *Purāṇas* and histories. In all Vedic literatures Kṛṣṇa is thus described, and the Supreme Lord Himself also says in the Fourth Chapter, "Although I am unborn, I appear on this earth to establish religious principles." He is the supreme origin; He has no cause, for He is the cause of all causes, and everything is emanating from Him. This perfect knowledge can be had by the grace of the Supreme Lord.

Here Arjuna expresses himself through the grace of Kṛṣṇa. If we want to understand *Bhagavad-gītā*, we should accept the statements in these two verses. This is called the *paramparā* system, acceptance of the disciplic succession. Unless one is in the disciplic succession, he cannot understand

Bhagavad-gītā. It is not possible by so-called academic education. Unfortunately those proud of their academic education, despite so much evidence in Vedic literatures, stick to their obstinate conviction that Kṛṣṇa is an ordinary person.

TEXT 14

सर्वमेतदृतं मन्ये यन्मां वदसि केशव ।
न हि ते भगवन्व्यक्तिं विदुर्देवा न दानवाः ॥ १४ ॥

sarvam etad ṛtaṁ manye
yan māṁ vadasi keśava
na hi te bhagavan vyaktiṁ
vidur devā na dānavāḥ

sarvam—all; *etat*—these; *ṛtam*—truths; *manye*—accept; *yat*—which; *mām*—unto me; *vadasi*—You tell; *keśava*—O Kṛṣṇa; *na*—never; *hi*—certainly; *te*—Your; *bhagavan*—O Personality of Godhead; *vyaktim*—revelation; *viduḥ*—can know; *devaḥ*—the demigods; *na*—nor; *dānavāḥ*—the demons.

TRANSLATION

O Kṛṣṇa, I totally accept as truth all that You have told me. Neither the gods nor demons, O Lord, know Thy personality.

PURPORT

Arjuna herein confirms that persons of faithless and demonic nature cannot understand Kṛṣṇa. He is not even known by the demigods, so what to speak of the so-called scholars of this modern world? By the grace of the Supreme Lord, Arjuna has understood that the Supreme Truth is Kṛṣṇa and that He is the perfect one. One should therefore follow the path of Arjuna. He received the authority of *Bhagavad-gītā*. As described in the Fourth Chapter, the *paramparā* system of disciplic succession for the understanding of *Bhagavad-gītā* was lost, and therefore Kṛṣṇa reestablished that disciplic succession with Arjuna because He considered Arjuna His intimate friend and a great devotee. Therefore, as stated in our Introduction to *Gītopaniṣad*, *Bhagavad-gītā* should be understood in the *paramparā* system. When the *paramparā* system was lost, Arjuna was again selected to rejuvenate it. The acceptance of Arjuna of all that Kṛṣṇa says should be emulated; then we can understand the essence of *Bhagavad-gītā*, and then only can we understand that Kṛṣṇa is the Supreme Personality of Godhead.

TEXT 15

स्वयमेवात्मनात्मानं वेत्थ त्वं पुरुषोत्तम ।
भूतभावन भूतेश देवदेव जगत्पते ॥ १५ ॥

svayam evātmanātmānaṁ
vettha tvaṁ puruṣottama
bhūta-bhāvana bhūteśa
deva-deva jagat-pate

svayam—personality; *eva*—certainly; *ātmanā*—by Yourself; *ātmānam*—Yourself; *vettha*—know; *tvam*—You; *puruṣottama*—O greatest of all persons; *bhūta-bhāvana*—O origin of everything; *bhūteśa*—O Lord of everything; *deva-deva*—O Lord of all demigods; *jagat-pate*—O Lord of the entire universe.

TRANSLATION

Indeed, You alone know Yourself by Your own potencies, O origin of all, Lord of all beings, God of gods, O Supreme Person, Lord of the universe!

PURPORT

The Supreme Lord Kṛṣṇa can be known by persons who are in a relationship with Him through the discharge of devotional service, like Arjuna and his successors. Persons of demonic or atheistic mentality cannot know Kṛṣṇa. Mental speculation that leads one away from the Supreme Lord is a serious sin, and one who does not know Kṛṣṇa should not try to comment on *Bhagavad-gītā*. *Bhagavad-gītā* is the statement of Kṛṣṇa, and since it is the science of Kṛṣṇa, it should be understood from Kṛṣṇa as Arjuna understood it. It should not be received from atheistic persons.

The Supreme Truth is realized in three aspects: as impersonal Brahman, localized Paramātmā and at last as the Supreme Personality of Godhead. So at the last stage of understanding the Absolute Truth, one comes to the

Supreme Personality of Godhead. A liberated man and even a common man may realize impersonal Brahman or localized Paramātmā, yet they may not understand God's personality from the verses of *Bhagavad-gītā*, which are being spoken by this person, Kṛṣṇa. Sometimes the impersonalists accept Kṛṣṇa as Bhagavan, or they accept His authority. Yet many liberated persons cannot understand Kṛṣṇa as Puruṣottama, the Supreme Person, the father of all living entities. Therefore Arjuna addresses Him as Puruṣottama. And if one comes to know Him as the father of all the living entities, still one may not know Him as the supreme controller; therefore He is addressed here as Bhūteśa, the supreme controller of everyone. And even if one knows Kṛṣṇa as the supreme controller of all living entities, still one may not know that He is the origin of all the demigods; therefore He is addressed herein as Devadeva, the worshipful God of all demigods. And even if one knows Him as the worshipful God of all demigods, one may not know that He is the supreme proprietor of everything; therefore He is addressed as Jagatpati. Thus the truth about Kṛṣṇa is established in this verse by the realization of Arjuna, and we should follow in the footsteps of Arjuna to understand Kṛṣṇa as He is.

TEXT 16

वक्तुमर्हस्यशेषेण दिव्या ह्यात्मविभूतयः ।
याभिर्विभूतिभिर्लोकानिमांस्त्वं व्याप्य तिष्ठसि ॥ १६ ॥

vaktum arhasy aśeṣeṇa
divyā hy ātma-vibhūtayaḥ
yābhir vibhūtibhir lokān
imāṁs tvaṁ vyāpya tiṣṭhasi

vaktum—to say; *arhasi*—deserve; *aśeṣeṇa*—in detail; *divyā*—divine; *hi*—certainly; *ātma*—Yourself; *vibhūtayaḥ*—opulences; *yābhiḥ*—by which; *vibhūtibhiḥ*—opulences; *lokān*—all the planets; *imān*—these; *tvam*—You; *vyāpya*—pervading; *tiṣṭhasi*—remain.

TRANSLATION

Please tell me in detail of Your divine powers by which You pervade all these worlds and abide in them.

PURPORT

In this verse it appears that Arjuna is already satisfied with his understanding of the Supreme Lord Kṛṣṇa. By Kṛṣṇa's grace, Arjuna has personal experience, intelligence and knowledge and whatever else a person may have through all these agencies, and he has understood Kṛṣṇa as the Supreme Personality of Godhead. For him there is no doubt, Yet he is asking Kṛṣṇa to explain His all-pervading nature so that in the future people will understand, especially the impersonalists, how He exists in His all-pervading aspect through His different energies. One should know that this is being asked by Arjuna on behalf of the common people.

TEXT 17

कथं विद्यामहं योगिंस्त्वां सदा परिचिन्तयन् ।
केषु केषु च भावेषु चिन्त्योऽसि भगवन्मया ॥ १७ ॥

katham vidyām aham yogims
tvām sadā paricintayan
keṣu keṣu ca bhāveṣu
cintyo 'si bhagavan mayā

katham—how; *vidyām aham*—shall I know; *yogin*—O supreme mystic; *tvām*—You; *sadā*—always; *paricintayan*—thinking; *keṣu*—in which; *keṣu*—in which; *ca*—also; *bhāveṣu*—nature; *cintyaḥ asi*—You are remembered; *bhagavan*—O Supreme; *mayā*—by me.

TRANSLATION

How should I meditate on You? In what various forms are You to be contemplated, O Blessed Lord?

PURPORT

As it is stated in the previous chapter, the Supreme Personality of Godhead is covered by His *yoga-māyā*. Only surrendered souls and devotees can see Him. Now Arjuna is convinced that His friend, Kṛṣṇa, is the Supreme Godhead, but he wants to know the general process by which the all-pervading Lord can be understood by the common man. No common man, including the demons and atheists, can know Kṛṣṇa because He is guarded by His *yoga-māyā* energy. Again, these questions are asked by Arjuna for their benefit. The superior devotee is not only concerned for his own understanding, but for the understanding of all mankind. Out of his mercy, because he is a Vaiṣṇava, a devotee, Arjuna is opening the understanding for the common man as far as the all-pervasiveness of the Supreme is concerned. He addresses Kṛṣṇa specifically as *yogin* because Śrī Kṛṣṇa is the master of the *yoga-māyā* energy by which He is covered and uncovered to the common man. The common man who has no love for Kṛṣṇa cannot always think of Kṛṣṇa; therefore he has to think materially. Arjuna is considering the mode of thinking of the materialistic persons of this world. Because materialists cannot understand Kṛṣṇa spiritually, they are advised to concentrate the mind on physical things and try to see how Kṛṣṇa is manifested by physical representations.

TEXT 18

विस्तरेणात्मनो योगं विभूतिं च जनार्दन ।
भूयः कथय तृप्तिर्हि शृण्वतो नास्ति मेऽमृतम् ॥ १८ ॥

vistareṇātmano yogaṁ
vibhūtiṁ ca janārdana
bhūyaḥ kathaya tṛptir hi
śṛṇvato nāsti me 'mṛtam

vistareṇa—in description; *ātmanaḥ*—of Yourself; *yogam*—mystic power; *vibhūtim*—opulences; *ca*—also; *janārdana*—O killer of the atheists; *bhūyaḥ* —again; *kathaya*—describe; *tṛptiḥ*—satisfaction; *hi*—certainly; *śṛṇvataḥ*— hearing; *na asti*—there is no; *me*—my; *amṛtam*—nectar.

TRANSLATION

Tell me again in detail, O Janārdana [Kṛṣṇa], of Your mighty potencies and glories, for I never tire of hearing Your ambrosial words.

PURPORT

A similar statement was made to Sūta Gosvāmī by the *ṛṣis* of Naimi-ṣāraṇya, headed by Śaunaka. That statement is:

vayaṁ tu na vitṛpyāma uttama-śloka-vikrame
yac chṛṇvatāṁ rasa-jñānāṁ svādu svādu pade pade

"One can never be satiated even though one continuously hears the transcendental pastimes of Kṛṣṇa, who is glorified by Vedic hymns. Those who have entered into a transcendental relationship with Kṛṣṇa relish in every step descriptions of the pastimes of the Lord." Thus Arjuna is interested to hear about Kṛṣṇa, specifically how He remains as the all-pervading Supreme Lord.

Now as far as amṛtam, nectar, is concerned, any narration or statement concerning Kṛṣṇa is just like nectar. And this nectar can be perceived by practical experience. Modern stories, fiction and histories are different from the transcendental pastimes of the Lord in that one will tire of hearing mundane stories, but one never tires of hearing about Kṛṣṇa. It is for this reason only that the history of the whole universe is replete with references to the pastimes of the incarnations of Godhead. For instance, the Purāṇas are histories of bygone ages that relate the pastimes of the various incarnations of the Lord. In this way the reading matter remains forever fresh, despite repeated readings.

TEXT 19

श्रीभगवानुवाच ।
हन्त ते कथयिष्यामि दिव्या ह्यात्मविभूतयः ।
प्राधान्यतः कुरुश्रेष्ठ नास्त्यन्तो विस्तरस्य मे ॥ १९ ॥

śrī-bhagavān uvāca
hanta te kathayiṣyāmi
divyā hy ātma-vibhūtayaḥ
prādhānyataḥ kuru-śreṣṭha
nāsty anto vistarasya me

śrī bhagavān uvāca—the Supreme Personality of Godhead said; *hanta*—yes; *te*—unto you; *kathayiṣyāmi*—I shall speak; *divyāḥ*—divine; *hi*—certainly; *ātma-vibhūtayaḥ*—personal opulences; *prādhānyataḥ*—principally; *kuru-śreṣṭha*—O best of the Kurus; *na asti*—there is no; *antaḥ*—limit; *vistarasya*—to the extent; *me*—My.

TRANSLATION

The Blessed Lord said: Yes, I will tell you of My splendorous manifestations, but only of those which are prominent, O Arjuna, for My opulence is limitless.

PURPORT

It is not possible to comprehend the greatness of Kṛṣṇa and His opulences. The senses of the individual soul are imperfect and do not permit him to understand the totality of Kṛṣṇa's affairs. Still the devotees try to understand Kṛṣṇa, but not on the principle that they will be able to understand Kṛṣṇa fully at any specific time or in any state of life. Rather, the very topics of Kṛṣṇa are so relishable that they appear to them as nectar. Thus they enjoy them. In discussing Kṛṣṇa's opulences and His diverse energies, the pure devotees take transcendental pleasure. Therefore they want to hear and discuss them. Kṛṣṇa knows that living entities do not understand the extent of His opulences; He therefore agrees to state only the principal manifestations of His different energies. The word *prādhān-yataḥ* (principal) is very important because we can understand only a few of the principal details of the Supreme Lord, for His features are unlimited. It is not possible to understand them all. And *vibhūti*, as used in this verse, refers to the opulences by which He controls the whole manifestation. In the *Amara-kośa* dictionary it is stated that *vibhūti* indicates an exceptional opulence.

The impersonalist or the pantheist cannot understand the exceptional opulences of the Supreme Lord nor the manifestations of His divine energy. Both in the material world and in the spiritual world His energies are distributed in every variety of manifestation. Now Kṛṣṇa is describing what can be directly perceived by the common man; thus part of His variegated energy is described in this way.

TEXT 20

अहमात्मा गुडाकेश सर्वभूताशयस्थितः ।
अहमादिश्च मध्यं च भूतानामन्त एव च ॥ २० ॥

aham ātmā guḍākeśa
sarva-bhūtāśaya-sthitaḥ
aham ādiś ca madhyaṁ ca
bhūtānām anta eva ca

aham—I; *ātmā*—soul; *guḍākeśa*—O Arjuna; *sarva-bhūta*—all living entities; *āśaya-sthitaḥ*—situated within; *aham*—I am; *ādiḥ*—origin; *ca*—also; *madhyam*—middle; *ca*—also; *bhūtānām*—all living entities; *antaḥ*—end; *eva*—certainly; *ca*—and.

TRANSLATION

I am the Self, O Guḍākeśa, seated in the hearts of all creatures. I am the beginning, the middle and the end of all beings.

PURPORT

In this verse Arjuna is addressed as Guḍākeśa, which means one who has conquered the darkness of sleep. For those who are sleeping in the darkness of ignorance, it is not possible to understand how the Supreme Godhead manifests Himself in the material and spiritual worlds. Thus this address by Kṛṣṇa to Arjuna is significant. Because Arjuna is above such darkness, the Personality of Godhead agrees to describe His various opulences.

Kṛṣṇa first informs Arjuna that He is the Self or soul of the entire cosmic manifestation by dint of His primary expansion. Before the material creation, the Supreme Lord, by His plenary expansion, accepts the Puruṣa incarnations, and from Him everything begins. Therefore He is ātmā, the soul of the mahat-tattva, the universal elements. The total material energy is not the cause of the creation, but actually the Mahā-Viṣṇu enters into the mahat-tattva, the total material energy. He is the soul. When Mahā-Viṣṇu enters into the manifested universes, He again manifests Himself as the Supersoul in each and every entity. We have experience that the personal body of the living entity exists due to the presence of the spiritual spark. Without the existence of the spiritual spark, the body cannot develop. Similarly, the material manifestation cannot develop unless the Supreme Soul of Kṛṣṇa enters.

The Supreme Personality of Godhead is existing as the Supersoul in all manifested universes. A description of the three puruṣa-avatāras is given in Śrīmad-Bhāgavatam. "The Supreme Personality of Godhead manifests three features, as Kāraṇodakaśāyī Viṣṇu, Garbhodakaśāyī Viṣṇu and Kṣīrodakaśāyī Viṣṇu, in this material manifestation." The Supreme Lord Kṛṣṇa, the cause of all causes, lies down in the cosmic ocean as Mahā-Viṣṇu or Kāraṇodakaśāyī Viṣṇu, and therefore Kṛṣṇa is the beginning of this universe, the maintainer of the universal manifestation, and the end of all the energy.

TEXT 21

आदित्यानामहं विष्णुर्ज्योतिषां रविरंशुमान् ।
मरीचिर्मरुतामस्मि नक्षत्राणामहं शशी ॥ २१ ॥

ādityānām aham viṣṇur
jyotiṣāṁ ravir aṁśumān
marīcir marutām asmi
nakṣatrāṇām aham śaśī

ādityānām—of the Ādityas; aham—I am; viṣṇuḥ—the Supreme Lord; jyotiṣām—of all luminaries; raviḥ—the sun; aṁśumān—radiant; marīciḥ—Marīci; marutām—of the Marutas; asmi—I am; nakṣatrāṇām—of stars; aham—I am; śaśī—the moon.

TRANSLATION

Of the Ādityas I am Viṣṇu, of lights I am the radiant sun, I am Marīci of the Maruts, and among the stars I am the moon.

PURPORT

There are twelve Ādityas, of which Kṛṣṇa is the principal. And among all the luminaries twinkling in the sky, the sun is the chief, and in the Brahma-saṁhitā the sun is accepted as the glowing effulgence of the Supreme Lord and is considered to be one of His eyes. Marīci is the controlling deity of the heavenly spaces. Among the stars, the moon is most prominent at night, and thus the moon represents Kṛṣṇa.

TEXT 22

वेदानां सामवेदोऽस्मि देवानामस्मि वासवः ।
इन्द्रियाणां मनश्चास्मि भूतानामस्मि चेतना ॥ २२ ॥

vedānāṁ sāma-vedo 'smi
devānām asmi vāsavaḥ
indriyāṇāṁ manaś cāsmi
bhūtānām asmi cetanā

vedānām—of all the Vedas; sāma-vedaḥ—the Sāma-veda; asmi—I am; devānām—of all the demigods; asmi—I am; vāsavaḥ—heavenly king; indriyāṇām—of all the senses; manaḥ—the mind; ca—also; asmi—I am; bhūtānām—of all living entities; asmi—I am; cetanā—the living force.

TRANSLATION

Of the Vedas I am the Sāma-veda; of the demigods I am Indra; of the senses I am the mind, and in living beings I am the living force [knowledge].

PURPORT

The difference between matter and spirit is that matter has no consciousness like the living entity; therefore this consciousness is supreme and eternal. Consciousness cannot be produced by a combination of matter.

TEXT 23

रुद्राणां शंकरश्चास्मि वित्तेशो यक्षरक्षसाम् ।
वसूनां पावकश्चास्मि मेरुः शिखरिणामहम् ॥ २३ ॥

rudrāṇāṁ śaṅkaraś cāsmi
vitteśo yakṣa-rakṣasām
vasūnāṁ pāvakaś cāsmi
meruḥ śikhariṇām aham

rudrāṇām—of all the Rudras; *śaṅkaraḥ*—Lord Śiva; *ca*—also; *asmi*—I am; *vitteśaḥ*—the lord of the treasury; *yakṣa-rakṣasām*—of the Yakṣas and Rākṣasas; *vasūnām*—of the Vasus; *pāvakaḥ*—fire; *ca*—also; *asmi*—I am; *meruḥ*—Meru; *śikhariṇām*—of all mountains; *aham*—I am.

TRANSLATION

Of all the Rudras I am Lord Śiva; of the Yakṣas and Rākṣasas I am the lord of wealth [Kuvera]; of the Vasus I am fire [Agni], and of the mountains I am Meru.

PURPORT

There are eleven Rudras, of whom Śaṅkara, Lord Śiva, is predominant. He is the incarnation of the Supreme Lord in charge of the modes of ignorance in the universe. Among the demigods Kuvera is the chief treasurer, and he is a representation of the Supreme Lord. Meru is a mountain famed for its rich natural resources.

TEXT 24

पुरोधसां च मुख्यं मां विद्धि पार्थ बृहस्पतिम् ।
सेनानीनामहं स्कन्दः सरसामस्मि सागरः ॥ २४ ॥

purodhasāṁ ca mukhyaṁ māṁ
viddhi pārtha bṛhaspatim
senānīnām ahaṁ skandaḥ
sarasām asmi sāgaraḥ

purodhasām—of all priests; *ca*—also; *mukhyam*—chief; *mām*—Me; *viddhi*
—understand; *pārtha*—O son of Pṛthā; *bṛhaspatim*—Bṛhaspati; *senānīnām*—
of all commanders; *aham*—I am; *skandaḥ*—Kārtikeya; *sarasām*—of all
reservoirs of water; *asmi*—I am; *sāgaraḥ*—the ocean.

TRANSLATION

Of priests, O Arjuna, know Me to be the chief, Bṛhaspati, the lord of devotion. Of generals I am Skanda, the lord of war; and of bodies of water I am the ocean.

PURPORT

Indra is the chief demigod of the heavenly planets and is known as the king of the heavens. The planet in which he reigns is called Indraloka. Bṛhaspati is Indra's priest, and since Indra is the chief of all kings, Bṛhaspati is the chief of all priests. And as Indra is the chief of all kings, similarly Skanda, the son of Pārvatī and Lord Śiva, is the chief of all military commanders. And of all bodies of water, the ocean is the greatest. These representations of Kṛṣṇa only give hints of His greatness.

TEXT 25

महर्षीणां भृगुरहं गिरामस्म्येकमक्षरम् ।
यज्ञानां जपयज्ञोऽस्मि स्थावराणां हिमालयः ॥ २५ ॥

maharṣīṇāṁ bhṛgur ahaṁ
girām asmy ekam akṣaram
yajñānāṁ japa-yajño 'smi
sthāvarāṇāṁ himālayaḥ

maharṣīṇām—among the great sages; *bhṛguḥ*—Bhṛgu; *aham*—I am; *girām* —of vibrations; *asmi*—I am; *ekam akṣaram-praṇava*; *yajñānām*—of sacrifices; *japa-yajñaḥ*—chanting; *asmi*—I am; *sthāvarāṇām*—of immovable things; *himālayaḥ*—the Himalayan mountains.

TRANSLATION

Of the great sages I am Bhṛgu; of vibrations I am the transcendental om. Of sacrifices I am the chanting of the holy names [japa], and of immovable things I am the Himalayas.

PURPORT

Brahmā, the first living creature within the universe, created several sons for the propagation of various kinds of species. The most powerful of his sons is Bhṛgu, who is also the greatest sage. Of all the transcendental vibrations, the "om" (*omkara*) represents the Supreme. Of all the sacrifices, the chanting of Hare Kṛṣṇa, Hare Kṛṣṇa, Kṛṣṇa Kṛṣṇa, Hare Hare/ Hare Rāma, Hare Rāma, Rāma Rāma, Hare Hare is the purest representation of Kṛṣṇa. Sometimes animal sacrifices are recommended, but in the sacrifice of Hare Kṛṣṇa, Hare Kṛṣṇa, there is no question of violence. It is the simplest and the purest. Whatever is sublime in the worlds is a representation of Kṛṣṇa. Therefore the Himalayas, the greatest mountains in the world, also represent Him. The mountain named Meru was mentioned in a previous verse, but Meru is sometimes movable, whereas the Himalayas are never movable. Thus the Himalayas are greater than Meru.

TEXT 26

अश्वत्थः सर्ववृक्षाणां देवर्षीणां च नारदः ।
गन्धर्वाणां चित्ररथः सिद्धानां कपिलो मुनिः ॥ २६ ॥

aśvatthaḥ sarva-vṛkṣāṇām
devarṣīṇāṁ ca nāradaḥ
gandharvāṇāṁ citrarathaḥ
siddhānāṁ kapilo muniḥ

aśvatthaḥ—the banyan tree; *sarva-vṛkṣāṇām*—of all trees; *devarṣīṇām*—of all the sages amongst the demigods; *ca*—and; *nāradaḥ*—Nārada; *gandharvā-*

nām—the citizens of the Gandharva planet; *citrarathaḥ*—Citraratha; *siddhānām*—of all those who are perfected; *kapilaḥ muniḥ*—Kapila Muni.

TRANSLATION

Of all trees I am the holy fig tree, and amongst sages and demigods I am Nārada. Of the singers of the gods [Gandharvas] I am Citraratha, and among perfected beings I am the sage Kapila.

PURPORT

The fig tree (*aśvattha*) is one of the most beautiful and highest trees, and people in India often worship it as one of their daily morning rituals. Amongst the demigods they also worship Nārada, who is considered the greatest devotee in the universe. Thus he is the representation of Kṛṣṇa as a devotee. The Gandharva planet is filled with entities who sing beautifully, and among them the best singer is Citraratha. Amongst the perpetually living entities, Kapila is considered an incarnation of Kṛṣṇa, and His philosophy is mentioned in the *Śrīmad-Bhāgavatam*. Later on another Kapila became famous, but his philosophy was atheistic. Thus there is a gulf of difference between them.

TEXT 27

उच्चैःश्रवसमश्वानां विद्धि माममृतोद्भवम् ।
ऐरावतं गजेन्द्राणां नराणां च नराधिपम् ॥ २७ ॥

uccaiḥśravasam aśvānāṁ
viddhi mām amṛtodbhavam
airāvataṁ gajendrāṇāṁ
narāṇāṁ ca narādhipam

uccaiḥśravasam—Uccaiḥśravā; *aśvānām*—among horses; *viddhi*—know; *mām*—Me; *amṛta-udbhavam*—produced from the churning of the ocean; *airāvatam*—Airāvata; *gajendrāṇām*—of elephants; *narāṇām*—among human beings; *ca*—and; *narādhipam*—the king.

TRANSLATION

Of horses know Me to be Uccaiḥśravā, who rose out of the ocean, born of the elixir of immortality; of lordly elephants I am Airāvata, and among men I am the monarch.

PURPORT

The devotee demigods and the demons (*asuras*) once took a sea journey. On this journey, nectar and poison were produced, and Lord Śiva drank the poison. From the nectar were produced many entities, of which there was a horse named Uccaiḥśrava. Another animal produced from the nectar was an elephant named Airāvata. Because these two animals were produced from nectar, they have special significance, and they are representatives of Kṛṣṇa.

Amongst the human beings, the king is the representative of Kṛṣṇa because Kṛṣṇa is the maintainer of the universe, and the kings, who are appointed on account of their godly qualifications, are maintainers of their kingdoms. Kings like Mahārāja Yudhiṣṭhira, Mahārāja Parīkṣit and Lord Rāma were all highly righteous kings who always thought of the citizens' welfare. In Vedic literature, the king is considered to be the representative of God. In this age, however, with the corruption of the principles of religion, monarchy decayed and is now finally abolished. It is to be understood that in the past, however, people were more happy under righteous kings.

TEXT 28

आयुधानामहं वज्रं धेनूनामस्मि कामधुक् ।
प्रजनश्चास्मि कन्दर्पः सर्पाणामस्मि वासुकिः ॥ २८ ॥

āyudhānām ahaṁ vajraṁ
dhenūnām asmi kāmadhuk
prajanaś cāsmi kandarpaḥ
sarpāṇām asmi vāsukiḥ

āyudhānām—of all weapons; *aham*—I am; *vajram*—the thunderbolt; *dhenūnām*—of cows; *asmi*—I am; *kāmadhuk*—the *surabhi* cows; *prajanaḥ*—for begetting children; *ca*—and; *asmi*—I am; *kandarpaḥ*—Cupid; *sarpāṇām*—of all snakes; *asmi*—I am; *vāsukiḥ*—Vāsuki.

TRANSLATION

Of weapons I am the thunderbolt; among cows I am the surabhi, givers of abundant milk. Of procreators I am Kandarpa, the god of love, and of serpents I am Vāsuki, the chief.

PURPORT

The thunderbolt, indeed a mighty weapon, represents Kṛṣṇa's power. In Kṛṣṇaloka in the spiritual sky there are cows which can be milked at any time, and they give as much milk as one likes. Of course such cows do not exist in this material world, but there is mention of them in Kṛṣṇaloka. The Lord keeps many such cows, which are called surabhi. It is stated that the Lord is engaged in herding the surabhi cows. Kandarpa is the sex desire for presenting good sons; therefore Kandarpa is the representative of Kṛṣṇa. Sometimes sex is engaged in only for sense gratification; such sex does not represent Kṛṣṇa. But sex for the generation of good children is called Kandarpa and represents Kṛṣṇa.

TEXT 29

अनन्तश्चास्मि नागानां वरुणो यादसामहम् ।
पितृणामर्यमा चास्मि यमः संयमतामहम् ॥ २९ ॥

anantaś cāsmi nāgānāṁ
varuṇo yādasām aham
pitṝṇām aryamā cāsmi
yamaḥ saṁyamatām aham

anantaḥ—Ananta; ca—also; asmi—I am; nāgānām—of all serpents; varuṇaḥ—the demigod controlling the water; yādasām—of all aquatics; aham—I am; pitṝṇām—of the ancestors; aryamā—Aryāma; ca—also; asmi—I am; yamaḥ—the controller of death; saṁyamatām—of all regulators; aham—I am.

TRANSLATION

Of the celestial Nāga snakes I am Ananta; of the aquatic deities I am Varuṇa. Of departed ancestors I am Aryamā, and among the dispensers of law I am Yama, lord of death.

PURPORT

Among the many celestial Naga serpents, Ananta is the greatest, as is Varuṇa among the aquatics. They both represent Kṛṣṇa. There is also a planet of trees presided over by Aryamā, who represents Kṛṣṇa. There are many living entities who give punishment to the miscreants, and among them Yama is the chief. Yama is situated in a planet near this earthly planet, and after death those who are very sinful are taken there, and Yama arranges different kinds of punishments for them.

TEXT 30

प्रह्लादश्चास्मि दैत्यानां कालः कलयतामहम् ।
मृगाणां च मृगेन्द्रोऽहं वैनतेयश्च पक्षिणाम् ॥ ३० ॥

prahlādaś cāsmi daityānāṁ
kālaḥ kalayatām aham
mṛgāṇāṁ ca mṛgendro 'haṁ
vainateyaś ca pakṣiṇām

prahlādaḥ—Prahlāda; *ca*—also; *asmi*—I am; *daityānām*—of the demons; *kālaḥ*—time; *kalayatām*—of subduers; *aham*—I am; *mṛgāṇām*—of animals; *ca*—and; *mṛgendraḥ*—the lion; *aham*—I am; *vainateyaḥ*—Garuḍa; *ca*—also; *pakṣiṇām*—of birds.

TRANSLATION

Among the Daitya demons I am the devoted Prahlāda; among subduers I am time; among the beasts I am the lion, and among birds I am Garuḍa, the feathered carrier of Viṣṇu.

PURPORT

Diti and Aditi are two sisters. The sons of Aditi are called Ādityas, and the sons of Diti are called Daityas. All the Ādityas are devotees of the Lord, and all the Daityas are atheistic. Although Prahlāda was born in the family of the Daityas, he was a great devotee from his childhood. Because of his devotional service and godly nature, he is considered to be a representative of Kṛṣṇa.

There are many subduing principles, but time wears down all things in the material universe and so represents Kṛṣṇa. Of the many animals, the lion is the most powerful and ferocious, and of the million varieties of birds, Garuḍa, the bearer of Lord Viṣṇu, is the greatest.

TEXT 31

पवनः पवतामस्मि रामः शस्त्रभृतामहम् ।
झषाणां मकरश्चास्मि स्रोतसामस्मि जाह्नवी ॥ ३१ ॥

pavanaḥ pavatām asmi
rāmaḥ śastra-bhṛtām aham
jhaṣāṇāṁ makaraś cāsmi
srotasām asmi jāhnavī

pavanaḥ—the wind; *pavatām*—of all that purifies; *asmi*—I am; *rāmaḥ*—Rāma; *śastra-bhṛtām*—of the carriers of weapons; *aham*—I am; *jhaṣāṇām*—of all aquatics; *makaraḥ*—shark; *ca asmi*—I am also; *srotasām*—of flowing rivers; *asmi*—I am; *jāhnavī*—the River Ganges.

TRANSLATION

Of purifiers I am the wind; of the wielders of weapons I am Rāma; of fishes I am the shark, and of flowing rivers I am the Ganges.

PURPORT

Of all the aquatics the shark is one of the biggest and is certainly the most dangerous to man. Thus the shark represents Kṛṣṇa. And of rivers, the greatest in India is the Mother Ganges. Lord Rāmacandra, of the *Rāmā-yaṇa*, an incarnation of Kṛṣṇa, is the mightest of warriors.

TEXT 32

सर्गाणामादिरन्तश्च मध्यं चैवाहमर्जुन ।
अध्यात्मविद्या विद्यानां वादः प्रवदतामहम् ॥ ३२ ॥

sargāṇām ādir antaś ca
madhyaṁ caivāham arjuna
adhyātma-vidyā vidyānāṁ
vādaḥ pravadatām aham

sargāṇām—of all creations; *ādiḥ*—beginning; *antaḥ*—end; *ca*—and; *madhyam*—middle; *ca*—also; *eva*—certainly; *aham*—I am; *arjuna*—O Arjuna;

adhyātma-vidyā—spiritual knowledge; *vidyānām*—of all education; *vādaḥ*—natural conclusion; *pravadatām*—of arguments; *aham*—I am.

TRANSLATION

Of all creations I am the beginning and the end and also the middle, O Arjuna. Of all sciences I am the spiritual science of the Self, and among logicians I am the conclusive truth.

PURPORT

Among created manifestations, the total material elements are first created by Mahā-Viṣṇu and are annihilated by Lord Śiva. Brahmā is the secondary creator. All these created elements are different incarnations of the material qualities of the Supreme Lord; therefore He is the beginning, the middle and the end of all creation.

Regarding the spiritual science of the Self, there are many literatures, such as the four *Vedas*, the *Vedānta-sūtra* and the *Purāṇas*, the *Śrīmad-Bhāgavatam* and the *Gītā*. These are all representatives of Kṛṣṇa. Among logicians there are different stages of argument. The presentation of evidence is called *japa*. The attempt to defeat one another is called *vitaṇḍa*, and the final conclusion is called *vāda*. The conclusive truth, the end of all reasoning processes, is Kṛṣṇa.

TEXT 33

अक्षराणामकारोऽस्मि द्वन्द्वः सामासिकस्य च ।
अहमेवाक्षयः कालो धाताहं विश्वतोमुखः ॥ ३३ ॥

akṣarāṇām akāro 'smi
dvandvaḥ sāmāsikasya ca
aham evākṣayaḥ kālo
dhātāhaṁ viśvato-mukhaḥ

akṣarāṇām—of letters; *akāraḥ*—the first; *asmi*—I am; *dvandvaḥ*—dual; *sāmāsikasya*—compounds; *ca*—and; *aham*—I am; *eva*—certainly; *akṣayaḥ*—eternal; *kālaḥ*—time; *dhātā*—creator; *aham*—I am; *viśvato-mukhaḥ*—Brahmā.

TRANSLATION

Of letters I am the letter A, and among compounds I am the dual word. I am also inexhaustable time, and of creators I am Brahmā, whose manifold faces turn everywhere.

PURPORT

Akāra, the first letter of the Sanskrit alphabet, is the beginning of the Vedic literature. Without akāra, nothing can be sounded; therefore it is the beginning of sound. In Sanskrit there are also many compound words, of which the dual word, like Rāma-kṛṣṇa, is called dvandvaḥ. For instance, Rāma and Kṛṣṇa have the same rhythm and therefore are called dual.

Among all kinds of killers, time is the ultimate because time kills everything. Time is the representative of Kṛṣṇa because in due course of time there will be a great fire and everything will be annihilated.

Among the creators and living entities, Brahmā is the chief. The various Brahmās exhibit four, eight, sixteen, etc., heads accordingly, and they are the chief creators in their respective universes. The Brahmās are representatives of Kṛṣṇa.

TEXT 34

मृत्युः सर्वहरश्चाहमुद्भवश्च भविष्यताम् ।
कीर्तिः श्रीर्वाक् च नारीणां स्मृतिर्मेधा धृतिः क्षमा ॥ ३४ ॥

mṛtyuḥ sarva-haraś cāham
udbhavaś ca bhaviṣyatām
kīrtiḥ śrīr vāk ca nārīṇāṁ
smṛtir medhā dhṛtiḥ kṣamā

mṛtyuḥ—death; sarva-haraḥ—all-devouring; ca—also; aham—I am; udbhavaḥ—generation; ca—also; bhaviṣyatām—of the future; kīrtiḥ—fame; śrīḥ vāk—beautiful speech; ca—also; nārīṇām—of women; smṛtiḥ—memory; medhā—intelligence; dhṛtiḥ—faithfulness; kṣamā—patience.

TRANSLATION

I am all-devouring death, and I am the generator of all things yet to be. Among women I am fame, fortune, speech, memory, intelligence, faithfulness and patience.

PURPORT

As soon as a man is born, he dies at every moment. Thus death is devouring every living entity at every moment, but the last stroke is called death itself. That death is Kṛṣṇa. All species of life undergo six basic changes. They are born, they grow, they remain for some time, they reproduce, they dwindle and finally vanish. Of these changes, the first is deliverance from the womb, and that is Kṛṣṇa. The first generation is the beginning of all future activities.

The six opulences listed are considered to be feminine. If a woman possesses all of them or some of them she becomes glorious. Sanskrit is a perfect language and is therefore very glorious. After studying, if one can remember the subject matter, he is gifted with good memory, or smṛti One need not read many books on different subject matters; the ability to remember a few and quote them when necessary is also another opulence.

TEXT 35

बृहत्साम तथा साम्नां गायत्री छन्दसामहम् ।
मासानां मार्गशीर्षोऽहमृतूनां कुसुमाकरः ॥ ३५ ॥

brhat-sāma tathā sāmnām
gāyatrī chandasām aham
māsānām mārga-śīrṣo 'ham
ṛtūnām kusumākaraḥ

brhat-sāma—the Brhat-sāma; tathā—also; sāmnām—of the Sāma-veda song; gāyatrī—the Gāyatrī hymns; chandasām—of all poetry; aham—I am; māsānām—of months; mārga-śīrṣo 'ham—the month of November-December; aham—I am; ṛtūnām—of all seasons; kusumākaraḥ—spring.

TRANSLATION

Of hymns I am the Brhat-sāma sung to the Lord Indra, and of poetry I am the Gāyatrī verse, sung daily by brāhmaṇas. Of months I am November and December, and of seasons I am flower-bearing spring.

PURPORT

It has already been explained by the Lord that amongst all the Vedas, the Sāma-veda is rich with beautiful songs played by the various demigods.

One of these songs is the *Bṛhat-sāma*, which has an exquisite melody and is sung at midnight.

In Sanskrit, there are definite rules that regulate poetry; rhyme and meter are not written whimsically, as in much modern poetry. Amongst the regulated poetry, the Gāyatrī *mantra*, which is chanted by the duly qualified *brāhmaṇas*, is the most prominent. The Gāyatrī *mantra* is mentioned in the *Śrīmad-Bhāgavatam*. Because the Gāyatrī *mantra* is especially meant for God realization, it represents the Supreme Lord. This *mantra* is meant for spiritually advanced people, and when one attains success in chanting it, he can enter into the transcendental position of the Lord. One must first acquire the qualities of the perfectly situated person, the qualities of goodness according to the laws of material nature, in order to chant the Gāyatrī *mantra*. The Gāyatrī *mantra* is very important in Vedic civilization and is considered to be the sound incarnation of Brahman. Brahmā is its initiator, and it is passed down from him in disciplic succession.

The months of November and December are considered the best of all months because in India grains are collected from the fields at this time, and the people become very happy. Of course spring is a season universally liked because it is neither too hot nor too cold, and the flowers and trees blossom and flourish. In spring there are also many ceremonies commemorating Kṛṣṇa's pastimes; therefore this is considered to be the most joyful of all seasons, and it is the representative of the Supreme Lord Kṛṣṇa.

TEXT 36

द्यूतं छलयतामस्मि तेजस्तेजस्विनामहम् ।
जयोऽस्मि व्यवसायोऽस्मि सत्त्वं सत्त्ववतामहम् ॥ ३६ ॥

dyūtaṁ chalayatām asmi
tejas tejasvinām aham
jayo 'smi vyavasāyo 'smi
sattvaṁ sattvavatām aham

dyūtam—gambling; *chalayatām*—of all cheats; *asmi*—I am; *tejaḥ*—splendid; *tejasvinām*—of everything splendid; *aham*—I am; *jayaḥ*—victory; *asmi*—I am; *vyavasāyaḥ*—adventure; *asmi*—I am; *sattvam*—strength; *sattvavatām*—of all the strong; *aham*—I am.

TRANSLATION

I am also the gambling of cheats, and of the splendid I am the splendor. I am victory, I am adventure, and I am the strength of the strong.

PURPORT

There are many kinds of cheaters all over the universe. Of all cheating processes, gambling stands supreme and therefore represents Kṛṣṇa. As the Supreme, Kṛṣṇa can be more deceitful than any mere man. If Kṛṣṇa chooses to deceive a person, no one can surpass Him in His deceit. His greatness is not simply one-sided—it is all-sided.

Among the victorious, He is victory. He is the splendor of the splendid. Among enterprising industrialists, He is the most enterprising. Among adventurers, He is the most adventurous, and among the strong, He is the strongest. When Kṛṣṇa was present on earth, no one could surpass Him in strength. Even in His childhood He lifted Govardhana Hill. No one can surpass Him in cheating, no one can surpass Him in splendor, no one can surpass Him in victory, no one can surpass Him in enterprise, and no one can surpass Him in strength.

TEXT 37

वृष्णीनां वासुदेवोऽस्मि पाण्डवानां धनञ्जयः ।
मुनीनामप्यहं व्यासः कवीनामुशना कविः ॥ ३७ ॥

vṛṣṇīnāṁ vāsudevo 'smi
pāṇḍavānāṁ dhanañjayaḥ
munīnām apy ahaṁ vyāsaḥ
kavīnām uśanā kaviḥ

vṛṣṇīnām—of the descendants of Vṛṣṇi; *vāsudevaḥ*—Kṛṣṇa in Dvāraka; *asmi*—I am; *pāṇḍavānām*—of the Pāṇḍavas; *dhanañjayaḥ*—Arjuna; *munīnām*—of the sages; *api*—also; *aham*—I am; *vyāsaḥ*—Vyāsa, the compiler of all Vedic literature; *kavīnām*—of all great thinkers; *uśanā*—Uśanā; *kaviḥ*—the thinker.

TRANSLATION

Of the descendants of Vṛṣṇi I am Vāsudeva, and of the Pāṇḍavas I am Arjuna. Of the sages I am Vyāsa, and among great thinkers I am Uśanā.

PURPORT

Kṛṣṇa is the original Supreme Personality of Godhead, and Vāsudeva is the immediate expansion of Kṛṣṇa. Both Lord Kṛṣṇa and Baladeva appear as the sons of Vasudeva. Amongst the sons of Pāṇḍu, Arjuna is famous and valiant. Indeed, he is the best of men and therefore represents Kṛṣṇa. Among the *munis,* or learned men conversant in Vedic knowledge, Vyāsa is the greatest because he explained Vedic knowledge in many different ways for the understanding of the common mass of people in this age of Kali. And Vyāsa is also known as an incarnation of Kṛṣṇa; therefore Vyāsa also represents Kṛṣṇa. *Kavis* are those who are capable of thinking thoroughly on any subject matter. Among the *kavis,* Uśanā was the spiritual master of the demons; he was extremely intelligent, far-seeing, political and spiritual in every way. Thus Uśanā is another representative of the opulence of Kṛṣṇa.

TEXT 38

दण्डो दमयतामस्मि नीतिरस्मि जिगीषताम् ।
मौनं चैवास्मि गुह्यानां ज्ञानं ज्ञानवतामहम् ॥ ३८ ॥

daṇḍo damayatām asmi
nītir asmi jigīṣatām
maunaṁ caivāsmi guhyānāṁ
jñānaṁ jñānavatām aham

daṇḍaḥ—punishment; *damayatām*—of all separation; *asmi*—I am; *nītiḥ*—morality; *asmi*—I am; *jigīṣatām*—of the victorious; *maunam*—silence; *ca*—and; *eva*—also; *asmi*—I am; *guhyānām*—of secrets; *jñānam*—knowledge; *jñānavatām*—of the wise; *aham*—I am.

TRANSLATION

Among punishments I am the rod of chastisement, and of those who seek victory, I am morality. Of secret things I am silence, and of the wise I am wisdom.

PURPORT

There are many suppressing agents, of which the most important are those that cut down the miscreants. When miscreants are punished, the rod of chastisement represents Kṛṣṇa. Among those who are trying to be victorious in some field of activity, the most victorious element is morality. Among the confidential activities of hearing, thinking and meditating, silence is most important because by silence one can make progress very quickly. The wise man is he who can discriminate between matter and spirit, between God's superior and inferior natures. Such knowledge is Kṛṣṇa Himself.

TEXT 39

यच्चापि सर्वभूतानां बीजं तदहमर्जुन ।
न तदस्ति विना यत्स्यान्मया भूतं चराचरम् ॥ ३९ ॥

yac cāpi sarva-bhūtānāṁ
bījaṁ tad aham arjuna
na tad asti vinā yat syān
mayā bhūtaṁ carācaram

yat—whatever; *ca*—also; *api*—may be; *sarva-bhūtānām*—of all creations; *bījam*—the seed; *tat*—that; *aham*—I am; *arjuna*—O Arjuna; *na*—not; *tat*—that; *asti*—there is; *vinā*—without; *yat*—that; *syāt*—exists; *mayā*—by Me; *bhūtam*—created; *carācaram*—moving and unmoving.

TRANSLATION

Furthermore, O Arjuna, I am the generating seed of all existences. There is no being-moving or unmoving-that can exist without Me.

PURPORT

Everything has a cause, and that cause or seed of manifestation is Kṛṣṇa. Without Kṛṣṇa's energy, nothing can exist; therefore He is called omnipotent. Without His potency, neither the movable nor the unmovable can exist. Whatever existence is not founded on the energy of Kṛṣṇa is called *māyā*, that which is not.

TEXT 40

नान्तोऽस्ति मम दिव्यानां विभूतीनां परन्तप ।
एष तूद्देशतः प्रोक्तो विभूतेर्विस्तरो मया ॥ ४० ॥

nānto 'sti mama divyānāṁ
vibhūtīnāṁ parantapa
eṣa tūddeśataḥ prokto
vibhūter vistaro mayā

na—nor; antaḥ—a limit; asti—is there; mama—of My; divyānām—divine;
vibhūtīnam—opulences; parantapa—O conquerer of the enemies; eṣaḥ—all
this; tu—that; uddeśataḥ—examples; proktaḥ—spoken; vibhūteḥ—opulences;
vistaraḥ—expanded; mayā—by Me.

TRANSLATION

O mighty conqueror of enemies, there is no end to My divine manifestations. What I have spoken to you is but a mere indication of My infinite
opulences.

PURPORT

As stated in the Vedic literature, although the opulences and energies
of the Supreme are understood in various ways, there is no limit to such
opulences; therefore not all the opulences and energies can be explained.
Simply a few examples are being described to Arjuna to pacify his
inquisitiveness.

TEXT 41

यद्यद्विभूतिमत्सत्त्वं श्रीमदूर्जितमेव वा ।
तत्तदेवावगच्छ त्वं मम तेजोंऽशसम्भवम् ॥ ४१ ॥

yad yad vibhūtimat sattvaṁ
śrīmad ūrjitam eva vā
tat tad evāvagaccha tvaṁ
mama tejo-'ṁśa-sambhavam

yat yat—whatever; vibhūti—opulences; mat—having; sattvam—existence;
śrīmat—beautiful; ūrjitam—glorious; eva—certainly; vā—or; tat tat—all
those; eva—certainly; avagaccha—you must know; tvam—you; mama—My;
tejaḥ—splendor; aṁśa—partly; sambhavam—born of.

TRANSLATION

Know that all beautiful, glorious, and mighty creations spring from but a spark of My splendor.

PURPORT

Any glorious or beautiful existence should be understood to be but a fragmental manifestation of Kṛṣṇa's opulence, whether it be in the spiritual or material world. Anything extraordinarily opulent should be considered to represent Kṛṣṇa's opulence.

TEXT 42

अथवा बहुनैतेन किं ज्ञातेन तवार्जुन ।
विष्टभ्याहमिदं कृत्स्नमेकांशेन स्थितो जगत् ॥ ४२ ॥

atha vā bahunaitena
kiṁ jñātena tavārjuna
viṣṭabhyāham idaṁ kṛtsnam
ekāṁśena sthito jagat

athavā—or; bahunā—many; etena—by this kind; kim—what; jñātena—knowing; tava—you; arjuna—O Arjuna; viṣṭabhya—entire; aham—I; idam—this; kṛtsnam—all manifestations; eka—one; aṁśena—part; sthithaḥ—situated; jagat—in the universe.

TRANSLATION

But what need is there, Arjuna, for all this detailed knowledge? With a single fragment of Myself I pervade and support this entire universe.

PURPORT

The Supreme Lord is represented throughout the entire material universes by His entering into all things as the Supersoul. The Lord here tells Arjuna that there is no point in understanding how things exist in their separate opulence and grandeur. He should know that all things are existing due to Kṛṣṇa's entering them as Supersoul. From Brahmā, the most gigantic entity, on down to the smallest ant, all are existing because the Lord has entered each and all and is sustaining them.

Worship of demigods is discouraged herein because even the greatest demigods like Brahmā and Śiva only represent part of the opulence of the Supreme Lord. He is the origin of everyone born, and no one is greater than Him. He is *samatā,* which means that no one is superior to Him and that no one is equal to Him. In the *Viṣṇu-mantra* it is said that one who considers the Supreme Lord Kṛṣṇa in the same category with demigods— be they even Brahmā or Śiva—becomes at once an atheist. If, however, one thoroughly studies the different descriptions of the opulences and expansions of Kṛṣṇa's energy, then one can understand without any doubt the position of Lord Śrī Kṛṣṇa and can fix his mind in the worship of Kṛṣṇa without deviation. The Lord is all-pervading by the expansion of His partial representation, the Supersoul, who enters into everything that is. Pure devotees, therefore, concentrate their minds in Kṛṣṇa consciousness in full devotional service; therefore they are always situated in the transcendental position. Devotional service and worship of Kṛṣṇa are very clearly indicated in this chapter in verses eight to eleven. That is the way of pure devotional service. How one can attain the highest devotional perfection of association with the Supreme Personality of Godhead has been thoroughly explained in this chapter.

Thus end the Bhaktivedanta Purports to the Tenth Chapter of the Śrīmad-Bhagavad-gītā in the matter of the Opulence of the Absolute.

CHAPTER ELEVEN

The Universal Form

TEXT 1

अर्जुन उवाच ।
मदनुग्रहाय परमं गुह्यमध्यात्मसंज्ञितम् ।
यत्त्वयोक्तं वचस्तेन मोहोऽयं विगतो मम ॥ १ ॥

arjuna uvāca
mad-anugrahāya paramaṁ
guhyam adhyātma-saṁjñitam
yat tvayoktaṁ vacas tena
moho 'yaṁ vigato mama

arjunaḥ uvāca—Arjuna said; *mat-anugrahāya*—just to show me favor; *paramam*—supreme; *guhyam*—confidential; *adhyātma*—spiritual; *saṁjñitam*—in the matter of; *yat*—what; *tvayā*—by You; *uktam*—said; *vacaḥ*—words; *tena*—by that; *mohaḥ*—illusion; *ayam*—this; *vigataḥ*—is educated; *mama*—my.

TRANSLATION

Arjuna said: I have heard Your instruction on confidential spiritual matters which You have so kindly delivered unto me, and my illusion is now dispelled.

PURPORT

This chapter reveals Kṛṣṇa as the cause of all causes. He is even the cause of the Mahā-Viṣṇu, and from Him the material universes emanate. Kṛṣṇa is not an incarnation; He is the source of all incarnations. That has been completely explained in the last chapter.

Now, as far as Arjuna is concerned, he says that his illusion is over. This means that Arjuna no longer thinks of Kṛṣṇa as a mere human being, as a friend of his, but as the source of everything. Arjuna is very enlightened and is glad that he has a great friend like Kṛṣṇa, but now he is thinking that although he may accept Kṛṣṇa as the source of everything, others may not. So in order to establish Kṛṣṇa's divinity for all, he is requesting Kṛṣṇa in this chapter to show His universal form. Actually when one sees the universal form of Kṛṣṇa one becomes frightened, like Arjuna, but Kṛṣṇa is so kind that after showing it He converts Himself again into His original form. Arjuna agrees to what Kṛṣṇa says several times. Kṛṣṇa is speaking to him just for his benefit, and Arjuna acknowledges that all this is happening to him by Kṛṣṇa's grace. He is now convinced that Kṛṣṇa is the cause of all causes and is present in everyone's heart as the Supersoul.

TEXT 2

भवाप्ययौ हि भूतानां श्रुतौ विस्तरशो मया ।
त्वत्तः कमलपत्राक्ष माहात्म्यमपि चाव्ययम् ॥ २ ॥

bhavāpyayau hi bhūtānāṁ
śrutau vistaraśo mayā
tvattaḥ kamala-patrākṣa
māhātmyam api cāvyayam

bhava—appearance; *apyayau*—disappearance; *hi*—certainly; *bhūtānām*—of all living entities; *śrutau*—have heard; *vistaraśaḥ*—detail; *mayā*—by me; *tvattaḥ*—from You; *kamala-patrākṣa*—O lotus-eyed one; *māhātmyam*—glories; *api*—also; *ca*—and; *avyayam*—inexhaustible.

TRANSLATION

O lotus-eyed one, I have heard from You in detail about the appearance and disappearance of every living entity, as realized through Your inexhaustible glories.

PURPORT

Arjuna addresses Lord Kṛṣṇa as "lotus-eyed" (Kṛṣṇa's eyes appear just like the petals of a lotus flower) out of his joy, for Kṛṣṇa has assured him, in the last verse of the previous chapter, that He sustains the entire universe with just a fragment of Himself. He is the source of everything in this material manifestation, and Arjuna has heard of this from the Lord in detail. Arjuna further knows that in spite of His being the source of all appearances and disappearances, He is aloof from them. His personality is not lost, although He is all-pervading. That is the inconceivable opulence of Kṛṣṇa which Arjuna admits that he has thoroughly understood.

TEXT 3

एवमेतद्यथात्थ त्वमात्मानं परमेश्वर ।
द्रष्टुमिच्छामि ते रूपमैश्वरं पुरुषोत्तम ॥ ३ ॥

evam etad yathāttha tvam
ātmānaṁ parameśvara
draṣṭum icchāmi te rūpam
aiśvaraṁ puruṣottama

evam—that; *etat*—this; *yathāttha*—as it is; *tvam*—You; *ātmānam*—the soul; *parameśvara*—the Supreme Lord; *draṣṭum*—to see; *icchāmi*—I wish; *te*—You; *rūpam*—form; *aiśvaram*—divine; *puruṣottama*—O best of personalities.

TRANSLATION

O greatest of all personalities, O supreme form, though I see here before me Your actual position, I yet wish to see how You have entered into this cosmic manifestation. I want to see that form of Yours.

PURPORT

The Lord said that because He entered into the material universe by His personal representation, the cosmic manifestation has been made possible and is going on. Now as far as Arjuna is concerned, he is inspired by the statements of Kṛṣṇa, but in order to convince others in the future who may think that Kṛṣṇa is an ordinary person, he desires to see Him actually in His universal form, to see how He is acting from within the universe, although He is apart from it. Arjuna's asking the Lord's permission is also significant. Since the Lord is the Supreme Personality of Godhead, He is present within Arjuna himself; therefore He knows the desire of Arjuna, and He can understand that Arjuna has no special desire to see Him in His universal form, for he is completely satisfied to see Him in His personal form of Kṛṣṇa. But He can understand also that Arjuna wants to see the universal form to convince others. He did not have any personal desire for confirmation. Kṛṣṇa also understands that Arjuna wants to see the universal form to set a criterion, for in the future there would be so many imposters who would pose themselves as incarnations of God. The people, therefore, should be careful; one who claims to be Kṛṣṇa should be prepared to show his universal form to confirm his claim to the people.

TEXT 4

मन्यसे यदि तच्छक्यं मया द्रष्टुमिति प्रभो ।
योगेश्वर ततो मे त्वं दर्शयात्मानमव्ययम् ॥ ४ ॥

manyase yadi tac chakyaṁ
mayā draṣṭum iti prabho
yogeśvara tato me tvaṁ
darśayātmānam avyayam

manyase—if You think; *yadi*—if; *tat*—that; *śakyam*—able to see; *mayā*—by me; *draṣṭum*—to see; *iti*—thus; *prabho*—O Lord; *yogeśvara*—the Lord of all mystic power; *tataḥ*—then; *me*—unto me; *tvam*—You; *darśaya*—show; *ātmānam*—Yourself; *avyayam*—eternal.

TRANSLATION

If You think that I am able to behold Your cosmic form, O my Lord, O master of all mystic power, then kindly show me that universal self.

PURPORT

It is said that one can neither see, hear, understand nor perceive the Supreme Lord, Kṛṣṇa, by the material senses. But if one is engaged in loving transcendental service to the Lord from the beginning, then one can see the Lord by revelation. Every living entity is only a spiritual spark; therefore it is not possible to see or to understand the Supreme Lord. Arjuna, as a devotee, does not depend on his speculative strength; rather, he admits his limitations as a living entity and acknowledges Kṛṣṇa's inestimable position. Arjuna could understand that for a living entity it is not possible to understand the unlimited infinite. If the infinite reveals Himself, then it is possible to understand the nature of the infinite by the grace of the infinite. The word *yogeśvara* is also very significant here because the Lord has inconceivable power. If He likes, He can reveal Himself by His grace, although He is unlimited. Therefore Arjuna pleads for the inconceivable grace of Kṛṣṇa. He does not give Kṛṣṇa orders. Kṛṣṇa is not obliged to reveal Himself to anyone unless one surrenders fully in Kṛṣṇa consciousness and engages in devotional service. Thus it is not possible for persons who depend on the strength of their mental speculations to see Kṛṣṇa.

TEXT 5

श्रीभगवानुवाच ।
पश्य मे पार्थ रूपाणि शतशोऽथ सहस्रशः ।
नानाविधानि दिव्यानि नानावर्णाकृतीनि च ॥ ५ ॥

*śrī-bhagavān uvāca
paśya me pārtha rūpāṇi
śataśo 'tha sahasraśaḥ
nānā-vidhāni divyāni
nānā-varṇākṛtīni ca*

śrī bhagavān uvāca—the Supreme Personality of Godhead said; *paśya*—just see; *me*—Mine; *pārtha*—O son of Pṛthā; *rūpāṇi*—forms; *śataśaḥ*—hundreds; *atha*—also; *sahasraśaḥ*—thousands; *nānā-vidhāni*—variegated; *divyāni*—divine; *nānā*—variegated; *varṇa*—colored; *akṛtīni*—forms; *ca*—also.

TRANSLATION

The Blessed Lord said: My dear Arjuna, O son of Pṛthā, behold now My opulences, hundreds of thousands of varied divine forms, multicolored like the sea.

PURPORT

Arjuna wanted to see Kṛṣṇa in His universal form, which, although a transcendental form, is just manifested for the cosmic manifestation and is therefore subject to the temporary time of this material nature. As the material nature is manifested and not manifested, similarly this universal form of Kṛṣṇa is manifested and unmanifested. It is not eternally situated in the spiritual sky like Kṛṣṇa's other forms. As far as a devotee is concerned, he is not eager to see the universal form, but because Arjuna wanted to see Kṛṣṇa in this way, Kṛṣṇa reveals this form. This universal form is not possible to be seen by any ordinary man. Kṛṣṇa must give one the power to see it.

TEXT 6

पश्यादित्यान्वसूनरुद्रानश्विनौ मरुतस्तथा ।
बहून्यदृष्टपूर्वाणि पश्याश्चर्याणि भारत ॥ ६ ॥

paśyādityān vasūn rudrān
aśvinau marutas tathā
bahūny adṛṣṭa-pūrvāṇi
paśyāścaryāṇi bhārata

paśya—see; *ādityān*—the twelve sons of Aditi; *vasūn*—the eight Vasus; *rudrān*—the eleven forms of Rudra; *aśvinau*—the two Asvins; *marutaḥ*—the forty-nine Maruts (demigods of the wind); *tathā*—also; *bahūni*—many; *adṛṣṭa*—that you have not heard or seen; *pūrvāṇi*—before; *paśya*—there see; *āścaryāṇi*—all the wonderful; *bhārata*—O best of the Bhāratas.

TRANSLATION

O best of the Bhāratas, see here the different manifestations of Ādityas, Rudras, and all the demigods. Behold the many things which no one has ever seen or heard before.

PURPORT

Even though Arjuna was a personal friend of Kṛṣṇa and the most advanced of learned men, it was still not possible for him to know everything about Kṛṣṇa. Here it is stated that humans have neither heard nor known of all these forms and manifestations. Now Kṛṣṇa reveals these wonderful forms.

TEXT 7

इहैकस्थं जगत्कृत्स्नं पश्याद्य सचराचरम् ।
मम देहे गुडाकेश यच्चान्यद्द्रष्टुमिच्छसि ॥ ७ ॥

ihaika-sthaṁ jagat kṛtsnaṁ
paśyādya sa-carācaram
mama dehe guḍākeśa
yac cānyad drastum icchasi

iha—in this; *ekastham*—in one; *jagat*—the universe; *kṛtsnam*—completely; *paśya*—see; *adya*—immediately; *sa*—with; *cara*—moving; *acaram*—not moving; *mama*—My; *dehe*—in this body; *guḍākeśa*—O Arjuna; *yat*—that; *ca*—also; *anyat*—other; *drastum*—to see; *icchasi*—you like.

TRANSLATION

Whatever you wish to see can be seen all at once in this body. This universal form can show you all that you now desire, as well as whatever you may desire in the future. Everything is here completely.

PURPORT

No one can see the entire universe sitting in one place. Even the most advanced scientist cannot see what is going on in other parts of the universe. Kṛṣṇa gives him the power to see anything he wants to see, past, present and future. Thus by the mercy of Kṛṣṇa, Arjuna is able to see everything.

TEXT 8

न तु मां शक्ष्यसे द्रष्टुमनेनैव स्वचक्षुषा ।
दिव्यं ददामि ते चक्षुः पश्य मे योगमैश्वरम् ॥ ८ ॥

na tu māṁ śakyase draṣṭum
anenaiva sva-cakṣuṣā
divyaṁ dadāmi te cakṣuḥ
paśya me yogam aiśvaram

na—never; tu—but; mām—Me; śakyase—able; draṣṭum—to see; anena—by this; eva—certainly; sva-cakṣuṣā—with your own eyes; divyam—divine; dadāmi—I give; te—you; cakṣuḥ—eyes; paśya—see; me—My; yogam aiśvaram—inconceivable mystic power.

TRANSLATION

But you cannot see Me with your present eyes. Therefore I give to you divine eyes by which you can behold My mystic opulence.

PURPORT

A pure devotee does not like to see Kṛṣṇa in any form except His form with two hands; a devotee must see His universal form by His grace, not with the mind but with spiritual eyes. To see the universal form of Kṛṣṇa, Arjuna is told not to change his mind but his vision. The universal form of Kṛṣṇa is not very important; that will be clear in the verses. Yet because Arjuna wanted to see it, the Lord gives him the particular vision required to see that universal form.

Devotees who are correctly situated in a transcendental relationship with Kṛṣṇa are attracted by loving features, not by a godless display of opulences. The playmates of Kṛṣṇa, the friends of Kṛṣṇa and the parents of Kṛṣṇa never want Kṛṣṇa to show His opulences. They are so immersed in pure love that they do not even know that Kṛṣṇa is the Supreme Personality of Godhead. In their loving exchange they forget that Kṛṣṇa is the Supreme Lord. In the Śrīmad-Bhāgavatam it is stated that the boys who play with Kṛṣṇa are all highly pious souls, and after many, many births they are able to play with Kṛṣṇa. Such boys do not know that Kṛṣṇa is the Supreme Personality of Godhead. They take Him as a personal friend. The Supreme Person is considered as the impersonal Brahman by great sages, as the Supreme Personality of Godhead by the devotees, and as a product of this material nature by ordinary men. The fact is that the devotee is not concerned to see the viśva-rūpa, the universal form, but Arjuna wanted to see it to substantiate Kṛṣṇa's statement so that in the future people could understand that Kṛṣṇa not only theoretically or philosophically presented

Himself as the Supreme but actually presented Himself as such to Arjuna. Arjuna must confirm this because Arjuna is the beginning of the *paramparā* system. Those who are actually interested to understand the Supreme Personality of Godhead, Kṛṣṇa, and who follow in the footsteps of Arjuna should understand that Kṛṣṇa not only theoretically presented Himself as the Supreme, but actually revealed Himself as the Supreme.

The Lord gave Arjuna the necessary power to see His universal form because He knew that Arjuna did not particularly want to see it, as we have already explained.

TEXT 9

सञ्जय उवाच ।
एवमुक्त्वा ततो राजन्महायोगेश्वरो हरिः ।
दर्शयामास पार्थाय परमं रूपमैश्वरम् ॥ ९ ॥

sañjaya uvāca
evam uktvā tato rājan
mahā-yogeśvaro hariḥ
darśayām āsa pārthāya
paramaṁ rūpam aiśvaram

sañjayaḥ uvāca—Sanjaya said; *evam*—thus; *uktvā*—saying; *tataḥ*—thereafter; *rājan*—O King; *mahā-yogeśvaraḥ*—the most powerful mystic; *hariḥ*—the Supreme Personality of Godhead, Kṛṣṇa; *darśayāmāsa*—showed; *pārthāya*—unto Arjuna; *paramam*—divine; *rūpam*—universal form; *aiśvaram*—opulences.

TRANSLATION

Sañjaya said: O King, speaking thus, the Supreme, the Lord of all mystic power, the Personality of Godhead, displayed His universal form to Arjuna.

TEXTS 10-11

अनेकवक्त्रनयनमनेकाद्भुतदर्शनम् ।
अनेकदिव्याभरणं दिव्यानेकोद्यतायुधम् ॥ १० ॥
दिव्यमाल्याम्बरधरं दिव्यगन्धानुलेपनम् ।
सर्वाश्चर्यमयं देवमनन्तं विश्वतोमुखम् ॥ ११ ॥

aneka-vaktra-nayanam
anekādbhuta-darśanam
aneka-divyābharaṇaṁ
divyānekodyatāyudham

divya-mālyāmbara-dharaṁ
divya-gandhānulepanam
sarvāścarya-mayaṁ devam
anantaṁ viśvato-mukham

aneka—various; *vaktra*—mouths; *nayanam*—eyes; *aneka*—various; *adbhuta*—wonderful; *darśanam*—sight; *aneka*—many; *divya*—divine; *ābharaṇam*—ornaments; *divya*—divine; *aneka*—various; *udyata*—uplifted; *āyudham*—weapons; *divya*—divine; *mālya*—garlands; *ambara-dharam*—covered with the dresses; *divya*—divine; *gandha*—fragrance; *anulepanam*—smeared; *sarva*—all; *aścaryamayam*—wonderful; *devam*—shining; *anantam*—unlimited; *viśvataḥ-mukham*—all-pervading.

TRANSLATION

Arjuna saw in that universal form unlimited mouths and unlimited eyes. It was all wondrous. The form was decorated with divine, dazzling ornaments and arrayed in many garbs. He was garlanded gloriously, and there were many scents smeared over His body. All was magnificent, all-expanding, unlimited. This was seen by Arjuna.

PURPORT

These two verses indicate that there is no limit to the hands, mouths, legs, etc., of the Lord. These manifestations are distributed throughout the universe and are unlimited. By the grace of the Lord, Arjuna could see them while sitting in one place. That is due to the inconceivable potency of Kṛṣṇa.

TEXT 12

दिवि सूर्यसहस्रस्य भवेद्युगपदुत्थिता ।
यदि भाः सदृशी सा स्याद्भासस्तस्य महात्मनः ॥ १२ ॥

divi sūrya-sahasrasya
bhaved yugapad utthitā

yadi bhāḥ sadṛśī sā syād
bhāsas tasya mahātmanaḥ

divi—in the sky; *sūrya*—sun; *sahasrasya*—of many thousands; *bhavet*—there were; *yugapat*—simultaneously; *utthitā*—present; *yadi*—if; *bhāḥ*—light; *sadṛśī*—like that; *sā*—that; *syāt*—may be; *bhāsaḥ*—effulgence; *tasya*—there is; *mahātmanaḥ*—of the great Lord.

TRANSLATION

If hundreds of thousands of suns rose up at once into the sky, they might resemble the effulgence of the Supreme Person in that universal form.

PURPORT

What Arjuna saw was indescribable, yet Sañjaya is trying to give a mental picture of that great revelation to Dhṛtarāṣṭra. Neither Sañjaya nor Dhṛtarāṣṭra were present, but Sañjaya, by the grace of Vyāsa, could see whatever happened. Thus he now compares the situation, as far as it can be understood, to an imaginable phenomenon (i.e. thousands of suns).

TEXT 13

तत्रैकस्थं जगत्कृत्स्नं प्रविभक्तमनेकधा ।
अपश्यद्देवदेवस्य शरीरे पाण्डवस्तदा ॥ १३ ॥

tatraika-sthaṁ jagat kṛtsnaṁ
pravibhaktam anekadhā
apaśyad deva-devasya
śarīre pāṇḍavas tadā

tatra—there; *ekastham*—one place; *jagat*—universe; *kṛtsnam*—completely; *pravibhaktam*—divided in; *anekadhā*—many kinds; *apaśyat*—could see; *deva-devasya*—of the Supreme Personality of Godhead; *śarīre*—in the universal form; *pāṇḍavaḥ*—Arjuna; *tadā*—at that time.

TRANSLATION

At that time Arjuna could see in the universal form of the Lord the unlimited expansions of the universe situated in one place although divided into many, many thousands.

PURPORT

The word *tatra* (there) is very significant. It indicates that both Arjuna and Kṛṣṇa were sitting on the chariot when Arjuna saw the universal form. Others on the battlefield could not see this form because Kṛṣṇa gave the vision only to Arjuna. Arjuna could see in the body of Kṛṣṇa many thousands of universes. As we learn from Vedic scriptures, there are many universes and many planets. Some of them are made of earth, some are made of gold, some are made of jewels, some are very great, some are not so great, etc. Sitting on his chariot, Arjuna could see all these universes. But no one could understand what was going on between Arjuna and Kṛṣṇa.

TEXT 14

ततः स विस्मयाविष्टो हृष्टरोमा धनञ्जयः ।
प्रणम्य शिरसा देवं कृताञ्जलिरभाषत ॥ १४ ॥

tataḥ sa vismayāviṣṭo
hṛṣṭa-romā dhanañjayaḥ
praṇamya śirasā devaṁ
kṛtāñjalir abhāṣata

tataḥ—thereafter; *saḥ*—he; *vismayāviṣṭaḥ*—being overwhelmed with wonder; *hṛṣṭa-romā*—with his bodily hairs standing on end due to his great ecstasy; *dhanañjayaḥ*—Arjuna ; *praṇamya*—offering obeisances; *śirasā*—with the head; *devam*—to the Supreme Personality of Godhead; *kṛtāñjaliḥ*—with folded hands; *abhāṣata*—began to say.

TRANSLATION

Then, bewildered and astonished, his hair standing on end, Arjuna began to pray with folded hands, offering obeisances to the Supreme Lord.

PURPORT

Once the divine vision is revealed, the relationship between Kṛṣṇa and Arjuna changes immediately. Before, Kṛṣṇa and Arjuna had a relationship based on friendship, but here, after the revelation, Arjuna is offering obeisances with great respect, and with folded hands he is praying to Kṛṣṇa. He is praising the universal form. Thus Arjuna's relationship becomes one of wonder rather than friendship. Great devotees see Kṛṣṇa as the reservoir of all relationships. In the scriptures there are twelve basic kinds of relationships mentioned, and all of them are present in Kṛṣṇa. It is said that He is the ocean of all the relationships exchanged between two living entities, between the gods, or between the Supreme Lord and His devotees.

It is said that Arjuna was inspired by the relationship of wonder, and in that wonder, although he was by nature very sober, calm and quiet, he became ecstatic, his hair stood up, and he began to offer his obeisances unto the Supreme Lord with folded hands. He was not, of course, afraid. He was affected by the wonders of the Supreme Lord. The immediate context is wonder; his natural loving friendship was overwhelmed by wonder, and thus he reacted in this way.

TEXT 15

अर्जुन उवाच ।
पश्यामि देवांस्तव देव देहे
सर्वांस्तथा भूतविशेषसङ्घान् ।
ब्रह्माणमीशं कमलासनस्थ-
मृषींश्च सर्वानुरगांश्च दिव्यान् ॥ १५ ॥

arjuna uvāca
paśyāmi devāṁs tava deva dehe
    sarvāṁs tathā bhūta-viśeṣa-saṅghān
brahmāṇam īśaṁ kamalāsana-stham
    ṛṣīṁś ca sarvān uragāṁś ca divyān

arjunaḥ uvāca—Arjuna said; *paśyāmi*—I see; *devān*—all the demigods; *tava*—Your; *deva*—O Lord; *dehe*—in the body; *sarvān*—all; *tathā*—also; *bhūta*—living entities; *viśeṣa-saṅghān*—specifically assembled; *brahmāṇam*— Lord Brahmā; *īśam*—Lord Śiva; *kamala-āsana-stham*—sitting on the lotus flower; *ṛṣīn*—great sages; *ca*—also; *sarvān*—all; *uragān*—serpents; *ca*—also; *divyān*—divine.

TRANSLATION

Arjuna said: My dear Lord Kṛṣṇa, I see assembled together in Your body all the demigods and various other living entities. I see Brahmā sitting on the lotus flower as well as Lord Śiva and many sages and divine serpents.

PURPORT

Arjuna sees everything in the universe; therefore he sees Brahmā, who is the first creature in the universe, and the celestial serpent upon which the Garbhodakaśāyī Viṣṇu lies in the lower regions of the universe. This snake bed is called Vāsuki. There are also other snakes known as Vāsuki. Arjuna can see from the Garbhodakaśāyī Viṣṇu up to the topmost part of the universe on the lotus-flower planet where Brahmā, the first creature of the universe, resides. That means that from the beginning to the end, everything could be seen by Arjuna sitting in one place on his chariot. This was possible by the grace of the Supreme Lord, Kṛṣṇa.

TEXT 16

अनेकबाहूदरवक्त्रनेत्रं
पश्यामि त्वां सर्वतोऽनन्तरूपम् ।
नान्तं न मध्यं न पुनस्तवादिं
पश्यामि विश्वेश्वर विश्वरूप ॥ १६ ॥

aneka-bāhūdara-vaktra-netram
paśyāmi tvāṁ sarvato 'nanta-rūpam
nāntaṁ na madhyaṁ na punas tavādiṁ
paśyāmi viśveśvara viśva-rūpa

aneka—many; *bāhū*—arms; *udara*—bellies; *vaktra*—mouths; *netram*—eyes; *paśyāmi*—I see; *tvām*—unto You; *sarvataḥ*—from all sides; *ananta-rūpam*—unlimited form; *na antam*—there is no end; *na madhyam*—there is no middle; *na punaḥ*—nor again; *tava*—Your; *ādim*—beginning; *paśyāmi*—I see; *viśveśvara*—O Lord of the universe; *viśva-rūpa*—in the form of the universe.

TRANSLATION

O Lord of the universe, I see in Your universal body many, many forms —bellies, mouths, eyes—expanded without limit. There is no end, there is no beginning, and there is no middle to all this.

PURPORT

Kṛṣṇa is the Supreme Personality of Godhead and is unlimited; thus through Him everything could be seen.

TEXT 17

किरीटिनं गदिनं चक्रिणं च
तेजोराशिं सर्वतो दीप्तिमन्तम् ।
पश्यामि त्वां दुर्निरीक्ष्यं समन्ता-
द्दीप्तानलार्कद्युतिमप्रमेयम् ॥ १७ ॥

kirīṭinaṁ gadinaṁ cakriṇaṁ ca
tejo-rāśiṁ sarvato dīptimantam
paśyāmi tvāṁ durnirīkṣyaṁ samantād
dīptānalārka-dyutim aprameyam

kirīṭinam—with helmets; *gadinam*—with maces; *cakriṇam*—with discs; *ca*—and; *tejorāśim*—effulgence; *sarvataḥ*—all sides; *dīptimantam*—glowing; *paśyāmi*—I see; *tvām*—You; *durnirīkṣyam*—difficult to see; *samantāt*—spreading; *dīpta-anala*—blazing fire; *arka*—sun; *dyutim*—sunshine; *aprameyam*—immeasurable.

TRANSLATION

Your form, adorned with various crowns, clubs and discs, is difficult to see because of its glaring effulgence, which is fiery and immeasurable like the sun.

TEXT 18

त्वमक्षरं परमं वेदितव्यं
त्वमस्य विश्वस्य परं निधानम् ।

त्वमव्ययः शाश्वतधर्मगोप्ता
सनातनस्त्वं पुरुषो मतो मे ॥ १८ ॥

tvam akṣaraṁ paramaṁ veditavyaṁ
tvam asya viśvasya paraṁ nidhānam
tvam avyayaḥ śāśvata-dharma-goptā
sanātanas tvaṁ puruṣo mato me

tvam—You; *akṣaram*—inexhaustible; *paramam*—supreme; *veditavyam*—to be understood; *tvam*—You; *asya*—of this; *viśvasya*—of the universe; *param*—supreme; *nidhānam*—basis; *tvam*—You are; *avyayaḥ*—inexhaustible; *śāśvata-dharma-goptā*—maintainer of the eternal religion; *sanātanaḥ*—eternal; *tvam*—You; *puruṣaḥ*—Supreme Personality; *mataḥ me*—is my opinion.

TRANSLATION

You are the supreme primal objective; You are the best in all the universes; You are inexhaustible, and You are the oldest; You are the maintainer of religion, the eternal Personality of Godhead.

TEXT 19

अनादिमध्यान्तमनन्तवीर्य-
मनन्तबाहुं शशिसूर्यनेत्रम् ।
पश्यामि त्वां दीप्तहुताशवक्त्रं
स्वतेजसा विश्वमिदं तपन्तम् ॥ १९ ॥

anādi-madhyāntam ananta-vīryam
ananta-bāhuṁ śaśi-sūrya-netram
paśyāmi tvāṁ dīpta-hutāśa-vaktram
sva-tejasā viśvam idaṁ tapantam

anādi—without beginning; *madhya*—without middle; *antam*—without end; *ananta*—unlimited; *vīryam*—glorious; *ananta*—unlimited; *bāhum*—arms; *śaśi*—moon; *sūrya*—sun; *netram*—eyes; *paśyāmi*—I see; *tvām*—You; *dīpta*—blazing; *hutāśa-vaktram*—fire coming out of Your mouth; *sva-tejasā*—by Your; *viśvam*—this universe; *idam*—this; *tapantam*—heating.

TRANSLATION

You are the origin without beginning, middle or end. You have numberless arms, and the sun and moon are among Your great unlimited eyes. By Your own radiance You are heating this entire universe.

PURPORT

There is no limit to the extent of the six opulences of the Supreme Personality of Godhead. Here and in many other places there is repetition, but according to the scriptures, repetition of the glories of Kṛṣṇa is not a literary weakness. It is said that at a time of bewilderment or wonder or of great ecstasy, statements are repeated over and over. That is not a flaw.

TEXT 20

द्यावापृथिव्योरिदमन्तरं हि
व्याप्तं त्वयैकेन दिशश्च सर्वाः ।
दृष्ट्वाद्भुतं रूपमुग्रं तवेदं
लोकत्रयं प्रव्यथितं महात्मन् ॥ २० ॥

dyāv āpṛthivyor idam antaraṁ hi
vyāptaṁ tvayaikena diśaś ca sarvāḥ
dṛṣṭvādbhutaṁ rūpam ugraṁ tavedaṁ
loka-trayaṁ pravyathitaṁ mahātman

dyau—in outer space; āpṛthivyoḥ—of the earth; idam—this; antaram—in between; hi—certainly; vyāptam—pervaded; tvayā—by You; ekena—by one; diśaḥ—directions; ca—and; sarvāḥ—all; dṛṣṭvā—by seeing; adbhutam—wonderful; rūpam—form; ugram—terrible; tava—Your; idam—this; loka—planetary system; trayam—three; pravyathitam—perturbed; mahātman—O great one.

TRANSLATION

Although You are one, You are spread throughout the sky and the planets and all space between. O great one, as I behold this terrible form, I see that all the planetary systems are perplexed.

PURPORT

Dyāv āpṛthivyoḥ (the space between heaven and earth) and *lokatrayam* (three worlds) are significant words in this verse because it appears that not only Arjuna saw this universal form of the Lord, but others in other planetary systems also saw it. The vision was not a dream. All who were spiritually awake with the divine vision saw it.

TEXT 21

अमी हि त्वां सुरसङ्घा विशन्ति
केचिद्भीताः प्राञ्जलयो गृणन्ति ।
स्वस्तीत्युक्त्वा महर्षिसिद्धसङ्घाः
स्तुवन्ति त्वां स्तुतिभिः पुष्कलाभिः ॥ २१ ॥

amī hi tvāṁ sura-saṅghā viśanti
kecid bhītāḥ prāñjalayo gṛṇanti
svastīty uktvā maharṣi-siddha-saṅghāḥ
stuvanti tvāṁ stutibhiḥ puṣkalābhiḥ

amī—all those; *hi*—certainly; *tvām*—unto You; *sura-saṅghāḥ*—groups of demigods; *viśanti*—entering; *kecit*—some of them; *bhītāḥ*—out of fear; *prāñjalayaḥ*—with folded hands; *gṛṇanti*—offering prayers unto; *svasti*—all peace; *iti*—thus; *uktvā*—speaking like that; *maharṣi*—great sages; *siddha-saṅghāḥ*—perfect sages; *stuvanti*—singing hymns; *tvām*—unto You; *stutibhiḥ*—with prayers; *puṣkalābhiḥ*—Vedic hymns.

TRANSLATION

All the demigods are surrendering and entering into You. They are very much afraid, and with folded hands they are singing the Vedic hymns.

PURPORT

The demigods in all the planetary systems feared the terrific manifestation of the universal form and its glowing effulgence and so prayed for protection.

TEXT 22

रुद्रादित्या वसवो ये च साध्या
विश्वेऽश्विनौ मरुतश्चोष्मपाश्च ।
गन्धर्वयक्षासुरसिद्धसङ्घा
वीक्षन्ते त्वां विस्मिताश्चैव सर्वे ॥ २२ ॥

rudrāditya vasavo ye ca sādhyā
viśve 'śvinau marutaś coṣmapāś ca
gandharva-yakṣāsura-siddha-saṅghā
vīkṣante tvāṁ vismitāś caiva sarve

rudra—manifestations of Lord Śiva; *ādityāḥ*—the Ādityas; *vasavaḥ*—the Vasus; *ye*—all those; *ca*—and; *sādhyāḥ*—the Sādhyas; *viśve*—the Viśvadevas; *aśvinau*—the Aśvinīkumāras; *marutaḥ*—the Maruts; *ca*—and; *uṣmapāḥ*—the forefathers; *ca*—and; *gandharva*—the Gandharvas; *yakṣa*—the Yakṣas; *asura-siddha*—the demons and the perfected demigods; *saṅghāḥ*—assemblies; *vīkṣante*—are seeing; *tvām*—You; *vismitāḥ*—in wonder; *ca*—also; *eva*—certainly; *sarve*—all.

TRANSLATION

The different manifestations of Lord Śiva, the Ādityas, the Vasus, the Sādhyas, the Viśvadevas, the two Aśvins, the Maruts, the forefathers and the Gandharvas, the Yakṣas, Asuras, and all perfected demigods are beholding You in wonder.

TEXT 23

रूपं महत्ते बहुवक्त्रनेत्रं
महाबाहो बहुबाहूरुपादम् ।
बहूदरं बहुदंष्ट्राकरालं
दृष्ट्वा लोकाः प्रव्यथितास्तथाहम् ॥ २३ ॥

rūpaṁ mahat te bahu-vaktra-netraṁ
mahā-bāho bahu-bāhūru-pādam
bahūdaraṁ bahu-daṁṣṭrā-karālaṁ
dṛṣṭvā lokāḥ pravyathitās tathāham

rūpam—form; *mahat*—very great; *te*—of You; *bahu*—many; *vaktra*—faces; *netram*—eyes; *mahā-bāho*—O mighty-armed one; *bahu*—many; *bāhu*—arms; *ūru*—thighs; *pādam*—legs; *bahu-udaram*—many bellies; *babu-daṁṣṭrā*—many teeth; *karālam*—horrible; *dṛṣṭvā*—seeing; *lokāḥ*—all the planets; *pravyathitāḥ*—perturbed; *tathā*—similarly; *aham*—I.

TRANSLATION

O mighty-armed one, all the planets with their demigods are disturbed at seeing Your many faces, eyes, arms, bellies and legs and Your terrible teeth, and as they are disturbed, so am I.

TEXT 24

नभःस्पृशं दीप्तमनेकवर्णं
व्यात्ताननं दीप्तविशालनेत्रम् ।
दृष्ट्वा हि त्वां प्रव्यथितान्तरात्मा
धृतिं न विन्दामि शमं च विष्णो ॥ २४ ॥

nabhaḥ-spṛśaṁ dīptam aneka-varṇaṁ
vyāttānanaṁ dīpta-viśāla-netram
dṛṣṭvā hi tvāṁ pravyathitāntar-ātmā
dhṛtiṁ na vindāmi śamaṁ ca viṣṇo

nabhaḥ spṛśam—touching the sky; *dīptam*—glowing; *aneka*—many; *varṇam*—color; *vyāttā*—open; *ānanam*—mouth; *dīpta*—glowing; *viśāla*—very great; *netram*—eyes; *dṛṣṭvā*—by seeing; *hi*—certainly; *tvām*—You; *pravyathitā*—perturbed; *antaḥ*—within; *ātmā*—soul; *dhṛtim*—steadiness; *na*—no; *vindāmi*—and have; *śamam*—mental tranquility; *ca*—also; *viṣṇo*—O Lord Viṣṇu.

TRANSLATION

O all-pervading Viṣṇu, I can no longer maintain my equilibrium. Seeing Your radiant colors fill the skies and beholding Your eyes and mouths, I am afraid.

TEXT 25

दंष्ट्राकरालानि च ते मुखानि
दृष्ट्वैव कालानलसन्निभानि ।

दिशो न जाने न लभे च शर्म
प्रसीद देवेश जगन्निवास ॥ २५ ॥

damṣṭrā-karālāni ca te mukhāni
dṛṣṭvaiva kālānala-sannibhāni
diśo na jāne na labhe ca śarma
prasīda deveśa jagan-nivāsa

damṣṭrā—teeth; *karālāni*—like that; *ca*—also; *te*—Your; *mukhāni*—faces; *dṛṣṭvā*—seeing; *eva*—thus; *kālānala*—the fire of death; *sannibhāni*—as if blazing; *diśaḥ*—directions; *na jāne*—do not know; *na labhe*—nor obtain; *ca śarma*—and grace; *prasīda*—be pleased; *deveśa*—O Lord of all lords; *jagat-nivāsa*—refuge of the worlds.

TRANSLATION

O Lord of lords, O refuge of the worlds, please be gracious to me. I cannot keep my balance seeing thus Your blazing deathlike faces and awful teeth. In all directions I am bewildered.

TEXTS 26-27

अमी च त्वां धृतराष्ट्रस्य पुत्राः
सर्वे सहैवावनिपालसङ्घैः ।
भीष्मो द्रोणः सूतपुत्रस्तथासौ
सहास्मदीयैरपि योधमुख्यैः ॥ २६ ॥
वक्त्राणि ते त्वरमाणा विशन्ति
दंष्ट्राकरालानि भयानकानि ।
केचिद्विलग्ना दशनान्तरेषु
सन्दृश्यन्ते चूर्णितैरुत्तमाङ्गैः ॥ २७ ॥

amī ca tvāṁ dhṛtarāṣṭrasya putrāḥ
sarve sahaivāvani-pāla-saṅghaiḥ
bhīṣmo droṇaḥ sūta-putras tathāsau
sahāsmadīyair api yodha-mukhyaiḥ

vaktrāṇi te tvaramāṇā viśanti
daṁṣṭrā-karālāni bhayānakāni

kecid vilagnā daśanāntareṣu
sandṛśyante cūrṇitair uttamāṅgaiḥ

amī—all those; *ca*—also; *tvām*—You; *dhṛtarāṣṭasya*—of Dhṛtarāṣṭra; *putrāḥ*—sons; *sarva*—all; *saha eva*—along with; *avanipāla*—warrior kings; *saṅghaiḥ*—with the groups; *bhīṣmaḥ*—Bhīṣmadeva; *droṇaḥ*—Droṇācārya; *sūta-putraḥ*—Karṇa; *tathā*—also; *asau*—that; *saha*—with; *asmadīyaiḥ*—our; *api*—also; *yodha-mukhyaiḥ*—chief among the warriors; *vaktrāṇi*—mouths; *te*—Your; *tvaramāṇāḥ*—fearful; *viśanti*—entering; *daṃṣṭrā*—teeth; *karālāni*—terrible; *bhayānakāni*—very fearful; *kecit*—some of them; *vilagnāḥ*—being attacked; *daśanāntareṣu*—between the teeth; *sandṛśyante*—being seen; *cūrṇitaiḥ*—smashed; *uttama-aṅgaiḥ*—by the head.

TRANSLATION

All the sons of Dhṛtarāṣṭra along with their allied kings, and Bhīṣma, Droṇa and Karṇa, and all our soldiers are rushing into Your mouths, their heads smashed by Your fearful teeth. I see that some are being crushed between Your teeth as well.

PURPORT

In a previous verse the Lord promised to show Arjuna things he would by very interested in seeing. Now Arjuna sees that the leaders of the opposite party (Bhīṣma, Droṇa, Karṇa and all the sons of Dhṛtarāṣṭra) and their soldiers and Arjuna's own soldiers are all being annihilated. This is an indication that Arjuna will emerge victorious in battle, despite heavy losses on both sides. It is also mentioned here that Bhīṣma, who is supposed to be unconquerable, will also be smashed. So also Karṇa. Not only will the great warriors of the other party like Bhīṣma be smashed, but some of the great warriors of Arjuna's side also.

TEXT 28

यथा नदीनां बहवोऽम्बुवेगाः
समुद्रमेवाभिमुखा   द्रवन्ति ।
तथा तवामी नरलोकवीरा
विशन्ति वक्त्राण्यभिविज्वलन्ति ॥ २८ ॥

> *yathā nadīnāṁ bahavo 'mbu-vegāḥ*
> *samudram evābhimukhā dravanti*
> *tathā tavāmī nara-loka-vīrā*
> *viśanti vaktrāṇy abhivijvalanti*

yathā—as; *nadīnām*—of the rivers; *bahavaḥ*—many; *ambu-vegāḥ*—waves of the waters; *samudram*—ocean; *eva*—certainly; *abhimukhāḥ*—towards; *dravanti*—gliding; *tathā*—similarly; *tava*—Your; *amī*—all those; *nara-loka-vīrāḥ*—the kings of human society; *viśanti*—entering; *vaktrāṇi*—into the mouths; *abhivijvalanti*—blazing.

TRANSLATION

As the rivers flow into the sea, so all these great warriors enter Your blazing mouths and perish.

TEXT 29

यथा प्रदीप्तं ज्वलनं पतङ्गा
विशन्ति नाशाय समृद्धवेगाः ।
तथैव नाशाय विशन्ति लोका-
स्तवापि वक्त्राणि समृद्धवेगाः ॥ २९ ॥

> *yathā pradīptaṁ jvalanaṁ pataṅgā*
> *viśanti nāśāya samṛddha-vegāḥ*
> *tathaiva nāśāya viśanti lokās*
> *tavāpi vaktrāṇi samṛddha-vegāḥ*

yathā—as; *pradīptam*—blazing; *jvalanam*—fire; *pataṅgāḥ*—moths; *viśanti*—enters; *nāśāya*—destruction; *samṛddha*—full; *vegāḥ*—speed; *tathā eva*—similarly; *nāśāya*—for destruction; *viśanti*—entering; *lokāḥ*—all people. *tava*—unto You; *api*—also; *vaktrāṇi*—in the mouths; *samṛddha-vegāḥ*—with full speed.

TRANSLATION

I see all people rushing with full speed into Your mouths as moths dash into a blazing fire.

TEXT 30

लेलिह्यसे ग्रसमानः समन्ता-
ल्लोकान्समग्रान्वदनैर्ज्वलद्भिः ।
तेजोभिरापूर्य जगत्समग्रं
भासस्तवोग्राः प्रतपन्ति विष्णो ॥ ३० ॥

lelihyase grasamānaḥ samantāl
lokān samagrān vadanair jvaladbhiḥ
tejobhir āpūrya jagat samagram
bhāsas tavogrāḥ pratapanti viṣṇo

lelihyase—licking; *grasamānaḥ*—devouring; *samantāt*—from all directions; *lokān*—people; *samagrān*—completely; *vadanaiḥ*—by the mouth; *jvaladbhiḥ*—with blazing; *tejobhiḥ*—by effulgence; *āpūrya*—covering; *jagat*—the universe; *samagram*—all; *bhāsaḥ*—illuminating; *tava*—Your; *ugrāḥ*—terrible; *pratapanti*—scorching; *viṣṇo*—O all-pervading Lord.

TRANSLATION

O Viṣṇu, I see You devouring all people in Your flaming mouths and covering the universe with Your immeasurable rays. Scorching the worlds, You are manifest.

TEXT 31

आख्याहि मे को भवानुग्ररूपो
नमोऽस्तु ते देववर प्रसीद ।
विज्ञातुमिच्छामि भवन्तमाद्यं
न हि प्रजानामि तव प्रवृत्तिम् ॥ ३१ ॥

ākhyāhi me ko bhavān ugra-rūpo
namo 'stu te deva-vara prasīda
vijñātum icchāmi bhavantam ādyaṁ
na hi prajānāmi tava pravṛttim

ākhyāhi—please explain; *me*—unto me; *kaḥ*—who; *bhavān*—You; *ugra-rūpaḥ*—fierce form; *namaḥ astu*—obeisances; *te*—unto You; *deva-vara*—the great one amongst the demigods; *prasīda*—be gracious; *vijñātum*—just to know; *icchāmi*—I wish; *bhavantam*—You; *ādyam*—the original; *na*—never; *hi*—certainly; *prajānāmi*—do I know; *tava*—Your; *pravṛttim*—mission.

TRANSLATION

O Lord of lords, so fierce of form, please tell me who You are. I offer my obeisances unto You; please be gracious to me. I do not know what Your mission is, and I desire to hear of it.

TEXT 32

श्रीभगवानुवाच ।
कालोऽस्मि लोकक्षयकृत्प्रवृद्धो
लोकान्समाहर्तुमिह प्रवृत्तः ।
ऋतेऽपि त्वां न भविष्यन्ति सर्वे
येऽवस्थिताः प्रत्यनीकेषु योधाः ॥ ३२ ॥

śrī-bhagavān uvāca
kālo 'smi loka-kṣaya-kṛt pravṛddho
lokān samāhartum iha pravṛttaḥ
ṛte 'pi tvāṁ na bhaviṣyanti sarve
ye 'vasthitāḥ pratyanīkeṣu yodhāḥ

śrī bhagavān uvāca—the Personality of Godhead said; *kālaḥ*—time; *asmi*—I am; *loka*—the worlds; *kṣaya-kṛt*—destroyer; *pravṛddhaḥ*—to engage; *lokān*—all people; *samāhartum*—to destroy; *iha*—in this world; *pravṛttaḥ*—to engage; *ṛte api*—without even; *tvām*—you; *na*—never; *bhaviṣyanti*—will be; *sarve*—all; *ye*—who; *avasthitāḥ*—situated; *pratyanīkeṣu*—on the opposite side; *yodhāḥ*—the soldiers.

TRANSLATION

The Blessed Lord said: Time I am, destroyer of the worlds, and I have come to engage all people. With the exception of you [the Pāṇḍavas], all the soldiers here on both sides will be slain.

PURPORT

Although Arjuna knew that Kṛṣṇa was his friend and the Supreme Personality of Godhead, he was nonetheless puzzled by the various forms exhibited by Kṛṣṇa. Therefore he asked further about the actual mission of this devastating force. It is written in the *Vedas* that the Supreme Truth destroys everything, even Brahmā. *Yasya brahme ca kṣatram ca ubhe bhavata odanaḥ/mṛtyur yasyopasecanaṁ ka itthā veda yatra saḥ.* Eventually all the *brāhmaṇas, kṣatriyas* and everyone else are devoured by the Supreme. This form of the Supreme Lord is an all-devouring giant, and here Kṛṣṇa presents Himself in that form of all-devouring time. Except for a few Pāṇḍavas, everyone who was present in that battlefield would be devoured by Him.

Arjuna was not in favor of the fight, and he thought it was better not to fight; then there would be no frustration. In reply, the Lord is saying that even if he did not fight, every one of them would be destroyed, for that is His plan. If he stopped fighting, they would die in another way. Death cannot be checked, even if he did not fight. In fact, they were already dead. Time is destruction, and all manifestations are to be vanquished by the desire of the Supreme Lord. That is the law of nature.

TEXT 33

तस्मात्त्वमुत्तिष्ठ यशो लभस्व
जित्वा शत्रून्भुङ्क्ष्व राज्यं समृद्धम् ।
मयैवैते निहताः पूर्वमेव
निमित्तमात्रं भव सव्यसाचिन् ॥ ३३ ॥

tasmāt tvam uttiṣṭha yaśo labhasva
jitvā śatrūn bhuṅkṣva rājyaṁ samṛddham
mayaivaite nihatāḥ pūrvam eva
nimitta-mātraṁ bhava savya-sācin

tasmāt—therefore; *tvām*—you; *uttiṣṭha*—get up; *yaśaḥ*—fame; *labhasva*—gain; *jitvā*—conquering; *śatrūn*—enemies; *bhuṅkṣva*—enjoy; *rājyam*—kingdom; *samṛddham*—flourishing; *mayā*—by Me; *eva*—certainly; *ete*—all these; *nihatāḥ*—already killed; *pūrvam eva*—by previous elements; *nimitta-mātram*—just become the cause; *bhava*—become; *savyasācin*—O Savyasācin.

TRANSLATION

Therefore get up and prepare to fight. After conquering your enemies you will enjoy a flourishing kingdom. They are already put to death by My arrangement, and you, O Savyasācin, can be but an instrument in the fight.

PURPORT

Savyasācin refers to one who can shoot arrows very expertly in the field; thus Arjuna is addressed as an expert warrior capable of delivering arrows to kill his enemies. "Just become an instrument": *nimitta-mātram*. This word is also very significant. The whole world is moving according to the plan of the Supreme Personality of Godhead. Foolish persons who do not have sufficient knowledge think that nature is moving without a plan and all manifestations are but accidental formations. There are many so-called scientists who suggest that perhaps it was like this, or maybe like that, but there is no question of "perhaps" and "maybe." There is a specific plan being carried out in this material world. What is this plan? This cosmic manifestation is a chance for the conditioned souls to go back to Godhead, back to home. As long they have the domineering mentality which makes them try to lord it over material nature, they are conditioned. But anyone who can understand the plan of the Supreme Lord and cultivate Kṛṣṇa consciousness is most intelligent. The creation and destruction of the cosmic manifestation are under the superior guidance of God. Thus the Battle of Kurukṣetra was fought according to the plan of God. Arjuna was refusing to fight, but he was told that he should fight and at the same time desire the Supreme Lord. Then he would be happy. If one is in full Kṛṣṇa consciousness and if his life is devoted to His transcendental service, he is perfect.

TEXT 34

द्रोणं च भीष्मं च जयद्रथं च
कर्णं तथान्यानपि योधवीरान् ।
मया हतांस्त्वं जहि माव्यथिष्ठा
युध्यस्व जेतासि रणे सपत्नान् ॥ ३४ ॥

droṇaṁ ca bhīṣmaṁ ca jayadrathaṁ ca
karṇaṁ tathānyān api yodha-vīrān
mayā hatāṁs tvaṁ jahi mā vyathiṣṭhā
yudhyasva jetāsi raṇe sapatnān

droṇam ca—also Droṇa; *bhīṣmam ca*—also Bhīṣma; *jayadratham ca*—also Jayadratha; *karṇam*—also Karṇa; *tathā*—also; *anyān*—others; *api*—certainly; *yodha-vīrān*—great warriors; *mayā*—by Me; *hatān*—already killed;

tvam—you; *jahi*—become victorious; *mā*—never; *vyathiṣṭhāḥ*—be disturbed; *yudhyasva*—just fight; *jetāsi*—just conquer; *raṇe*—in the fight; *sapatnān*—enemies.

TRANSLATION

The Blessed Lord said: All the great warriors—Droṇa, Bhīṣma, Jayadratha, Karṇa—are already destroyed. Simply fight, and you will vanquish your enemies.

PURPORT

Every plan is made by the Supreme Personality of Godhead, but He is so kind and merciful to His devotees that He wants to give the credit to His devotees who carry out His plan according to His desire. Life should therefore move in such a way that everyone acts in Kṛṣṇa consciousness and understands the Supreme Personality of Godhead through the medium of a spiritual master. The plans of the Supreme Personality of Godhead are understood by His mercy, and the plans of the devotees are as good as His plans. One should follow such plans and be victorious in the struggle for existence.

TEXT 35

सञ्जय उवाच ।
एतच्छ्रुत्वा वचनं केशवस्य
    कृताञ्जलिर्वेपमानः किरीती ।
नमस्कृत्वा भूय एवाह कृष्णं
    सगद्गदं भीतभीतः प्रणम्य ॥ ३५ ॥

sañjaya uvāca
etac chrutvā vacanaṁ keśavasya
    kṛtāñjalir vepamānaḥ kirītī
namaskṛtvā bhūya evāha kṛṣṇaṁ
    sa-gadgadaṁ bhīta-bhītaḥ praṇamya

sañjayaḥ uvāca—Sañjaya said; *etat*—thus; *śrutvā*—hearing; *vacanam*—speech; *keśavasya*—of Kṛṣṇa; *kṛtāñjaliḥ*—with folded hands; *vepamānaḥ*—

trembling; *kirītī*—Arjuna; *namaskṛtvā*—offering obeisances; *bhūyaḥ*—again; *eva*—also; *āha kṛṣṇam*—said unto Kṛṣṇa; *sa-gadgadam*—faltering; *bhīta-bhītaḥ*—fearful; *praṇamya*—offering obeisances.

TRANSLATION

Sañjaya said to Dhṛtarāṣṭra: O King, after hearing these words from the Supreme Personality of Godhead, Arjuna trembled, fearfully offered obeisances with folded hands and began, falteringly, to speak as follows:

PURPORT

As we have already explained, because of the situation created by the universal form of the Supreme Personality of Godhead, Arjuna became bewildered in wonder; thus he began to offer his respectful obeisances to Kṛṣṇa again and again, and with faltering voice he began to pray, not as a friend, but as a devotee in wonder.

TEXT 36

अर्जुन उवाच ।
स्थाने हृषीकेश तव प्रकीर्त्या
जगत्प्रहृष्यत्यनुरज्यते च ।
रक्षांसि भीतानि दिशो द्रवन्ति
सर्वे नमस्यन्ति च सिद्धसङ्घाः ॥ ३६ ॥

arjuna uvāca
sthāne hṛṣīkeśa tava prakīrtyā
jagat prahṛṣyaty anurajyate ca
rakṣāṁsi bhītāni diśo dravanti
sarve namasyanti ca siddha-saṅghāḥ

arjunaḥ uvāca—Arjuna said; *sthāne*—rightly; *hṛṣīkeśa*—O master of all senses; *tava*—Your; *prakīrtya*—glories; *jagat*—the entire world; *prahṛṣyati*—rejoicing; *anurajyate*—becoming attached; *rakṣāṁsi*—the demons; *bhītāni*—out of fear; *diśaḥ*—directions; *dravanti*—fleeing; *sarve*—all; *namasyanti*—offering respect; *ca*—also; *siddha-saṅghāḥ*—the perfect human beings.

TRANSLATION

O Hṛṣīkeśa, the world becomes joyful upon hearing Your name and thus everyone becomes attached to You. Although the perfected beings offer You their respectful homage, the demons are afraid, and they flee here and there. All this is rightly done.

PURPORT

Arjuna, after hearing from Kṛṣṇa about the outcome of the Battle of Kurukṣetra, became an enlightened devotee of the Supreme Lord. He admitted that everything done by Kṛṣṇa is quite fit. Arjuna confirmed that Kṛṣṇa is the maintainer and the object of worship for the devotees and the destroyer of the undesirables. His actions are equally good for all. Arjuna understood herein that when the Battle of Kurukṣetra was being concluded, in outer space there were present many demigods, *siddhas,* and the intelligentia of the higher planets, and they were observing the fight because Kṛṣṇa was present there. When Arjuna saw the universal form of the Lord, the demigods took pleasure in it, but others, who were demons and atheists, could not stand it when the Lord was praised. Out of their natural fear of the devastating form of the Supreme Personality of Godhead, they fled. Kṛṣṇa's treatment of the devotees and the atheists is praised by Arjuna. In all cases a devotee glorifies the Lord because he knows that whatever He does is good for all.

TEXT 37

कस्माच्च ते न नमेरन्महात्मन्
गरीयसे ब्रह्मणोऽप्यादिकर्त्रे ।
अनन्त देवेश जगन्निवास
त्वमक्षरं सदसत्तत्परं यत् ॥ ३७ ॥

*kasmāc ca te na nameran mahātman
garīyase brahmaṇo 'py ādi-kartre
ananta deveśa jagan-nivāsa
tvam akṣaraṁ sad-asat tat paraṁ yat*

kasmāt—why; *ca*—also; *te*—unto You; *na*—not; *nameran*—offer proper obeisances; *mahātman*—O great one; *garīyase*—You are better than;

brahmaṇaḥ—Brahmā; *api*—although; *ādi-kartre*—the supreme creator; *ananta*—unlimited; *deveśa*-God of the gods; *jagat-nivāsa*—O refuge of the universe; *tvam*—You are; *akṣaram*—imperishable; *sat-asat*—cause and effect; *tat-param*—transcendental; *yat*—because.

TRANSLATION

O great one, who stands above even Brahmā, You are the original master. Why should they not offer their homage up to You, O limitless one? O refuge of the universe, You are the invincible source, the cause of all causes, transcendental to this material manifestation.

PURPORT

By this offering of obeisances, Arjuna indicates that Kṛṣṇa is worshipable by everyone. He is all-pervading, and He is the Soul of every soul. Arjuna is addressing Kṛṣṇa as *mahātmā*, which means that He is most magnanimous and unlimited. *Ananta* indicates that there is nothing which is not covered by the influence and energy of the Supreme Lord, and *deveśa* means that He is the controller of all demigods and is above them all. He is the center of the whole universe. Arjuna also thought that it was fitting that all the perfect living entities and all powerful demigods offer their respectful obeisances unto Him because no one is greater than Him. He especially mentions that Kṛṣṇa is greater than Brahmā because Brahmā is created by Him. Brahmā is born out of the lotus stem grown from the navel abdomen of Garbhodakaśāyī Viṣṇu, who is Kṛṣṇa's plenary expansion; therefore Brahmā and Lord Śiva, who is born of Brahmā, and all other demigods must offer their respectful obeisances. Thus the Lord is respected by Lord Śiva and Brahmā and similar other demigods. The word *akṣaram* is very significant because this material creation is subject to destruction, but the Lord is above this material creation. He is the cause of all causes, and being so, He is superior to all the conditioned souls within this material nature as well as the material cosmic manifestation itself. He is therefore the all-great Supreme.

TEXT 38

त्वमादिदेवः पुरुषः पुराण-
स्त्वमस्य विश्वस्य परं निधानम् ।

वेत्तासि वेद्यं च परं च धाम
त्वया ततं विश्वमनन्तरूप ॥ ३८ ॥

tvam ādi-devaḥ puruṣaḥ purāṇas
tvam asya viśvasya paraṁ nidhānam
vettāsi vedyaṁ ca paraṁ ca dhāma
tvayā tataṁ viśvam ananta-rūpa

tvam—You; ādi-devaḥ—the original Supreme God; puruṣaḥ—personality; purāṇaḥ—old; tvam—You; asya—this; viśvasya—universe; param—transcendental; nidhānam—refuge; vettā—knower; asi—You are; vedyam ca—and the knowable; param ca—and transcendental; dhāma—refuge; tvayā—by You; tatam—pervaded; viśvam—universe; ananta-rūpa—unlimited form.

TRANSLATION

You are the original Personality, the Godhead. You are the only sanctuary of this manifested cosmic world. You know everything, and You are all that is knowable. You are above the material modes. O limitless form! This whole cosmic manifestation is pervaded by You!

PURPORT

Everything is resting on the Supreme Personality of Godhead; therefore He is the ultimate rest. Nidhānam means that everything, even the Brahman effulgence, rests on the Supreme Personality of Godhead Kṛṣṇa. He is the knower of everything that is happening in this world, and if knowledge has any end, He is the end of all knowledge; therefore He is the known and the knowable. He is the object of knowledge because He is all-pervading. Because He is the cause in the spiritual world, He is transcendental. He is also the chief personality in the transcendental world.

TEXT 39

वायुर्यमोऽग्निर्वरुणः शशाङ्कः
प्रजापतिस्त्वं प्रपितामहश्च ।
नमो नमस्तेऽस्तु सहस्रकृत्वः
पुनश्च भूयोऽपि नमो नमस्ते ॥ ३९ ॥

*vāyur yamo 'gnir varuṇaḥ śaśāṅkaḥ
prajāpatis tvaṁ prapitāmahaś ca
namo namas te 'stu sahasra-kṛtvaḥ
punaś ca bhūyo 'pi namo namas te*

vāyuḥ—air; *yamaḥ*—controller; *agniḥ*—fire; *varuṇaḥ*—water; *śaśāṅkaḥ*—moon; *prajāpatiḥ*—Brahmā; *tvam*—You; *prapitāmahaḥ*—grandfather; *ca*—also; *namaḥ*—offering respects; *namaḥ te*—again I offer my respects unto You; *astu*—are being; *sahasra-kṛtvaḥ*—a thousand times; *punaḥ ca*—and again; *bhūyaḥ*—again; *api*—also; *namaḥ*—offer my respects; *namaḥ te*—offering my respects unto You.

TRANSLATION

You are air, fire, water, and You are the moon! You are the supreme controller and the grandfather. Thus I offer my respectful obeisances unto You a thousand times, and again and yet again!

PURPORT

The Lord is addressed here as air because the air is the most important representation of all the demigods, being all-pervasive. Arjuna also addresses Kṛṣṇa as the grandfather because He is the father of Brahmā, the first living creature in the universe.

TEXT 40

नमः पुरस्तादथ पृष्ठतस्ते
नमोऽस्तु ते सर्वत एव सर्व ।
अनन्तवीर्यामितविक्रमस्त्वं
सर्वं समाप्नोषि ततोऽसि सर्वः ॥ ४० ॥

*namaḥ purastād atha pṛṣṭhatas te
namo 'stu te sarvata eva sarva
ananta-vīryāmita-vikramas tvaṁ
sarvaṁ samāpnoṣi tato 'si sarvaḥ*

namaḥ—offering obeisances; *purastāt*—from the front; *atha*—also; *pṛṣṭhataḥ*—from behind; *te*—You; *namaḥ astu*—offer my respects; *te*—unto You;

sarvataḥ—from all sides; *eva sarva*—because You are everything; *ananta-vīrya*—unlimited potency; *amita-vikramaḥ*—unlimited force; *tvam*—You; *sarvam*—everything; *samāpnoṣi*—cover; *tataḥ asi*—therefore You are; *sarvaḥ*—everything.

TRANSLATION

Obeisances from the front, from behind and from all sides! O unbounded power, You are the master of limitless, might! You are all-pervading, and thus You are everything!

PURPORT

Out of loving ecstasy for Kṛṣṇa, his friend, Arjuna is offering his respects from all sides. He is accepting that He is the master of all potencies and all prowess and far superior to all the great warriors assembled on the battlefield. It is said in the *Viṣṇu Purāṇa*: yo 'yaṁ tavāgato deva-samīpaṁ devatā-gaṇaḥ sa tvam eva jagat-sraṣṭā yataḥ sarva-gato bhavān. "Whoever comes before You, even if he be a demigod, is created by You, O Supreme Personality of Godhead."

TEXTS 41-42

सखेति मत्वा प्रसभं यदुक्तं
हे कृष्ण हे यादव हे सखेति ।
अजानता महिमानं तवेदं
मया प्रमादात्प्रणयेन वापि ॥ ४१ ॥

यच्चावहासार्थमसत्कृतोऽसि
विहारशय्यासनभोजनेषु ।
एकोऽथवाप्यच्युत तत्समक्षं
तत्क्षामये त्वामहमप्रमेयम् ॥ ४२ ॥

sakheti matvā prasabhaṁ yad uktaṁ
he kṛṣṇa he yādava he sakheti
ajānatā mahimānaṁ tavedaṁ
mayā pramādāt praṇayena vāpi

yac cāvahāsārtham asat-kṛto 'si
vihāra-śayyāsana-bhojaneṣu
eko 'tha vāpy acyuta tat-samakṣam
tat kṣāmaye tvām aham aprameyam

sakhā—friend; *iti*—thus; *matvā*—thinking; *prasabham*—temporary; *yat*—whatever; *uktam*—said; *he kṛṣṇa*—O Kṛṣṇa; *he yādava*—O Yādava; *he sakhā iti*—O my dear friend; *ajānatā*—without knowing; *mahimānam*—glories; *tava*—Your; *idam*—this; *mayā*—by me; *pramādāt*—out of foolishness; *praṇayena*—out of love; *vā api*—either; *yat*—whatever; *ca*—also; *avahāsārtham*—for joking; *asatkṛtaḥ*—dishonor; *asi*—have been done; *vihāra*—in relaxation; *śayyā*—in joking; *āsana*—in a resting place; *bhojaneṣu*—or while eating together; *ekaḥ*—alone; *athavā*—or; *api*—others; *acyuta*—O infallible one; *tat-samakṣam*—as Your competitor; *tat*—all those; *kṣāmaye*—excuse; *tvām*—You; *aham*—I; *aprameyam*—immeasurable.

TRANSLATION

I have in the past addressed You as "O Kṛṣṇa," "O Yādava," "O my friend," without knowing Your glories. Please forgive whatever I may have done in madness or in love. I have dishonored You many times while relaxing or while lying on the same bed or eating together, sometimes alone and sometimes in front of many friends. Please excuse me for all my offenses.

PURPORT

Although Kṛṣṇa is manifested before Arjuna in His universal form, Arjuna remembers his friendly relationship with Kṛṣṇa and is therefore asking pardon and requesting Him to excuse him for the many informal gestures which arise out of friendship. He is admitting that formerly he did not know that Kṛṣṇa could assume such a universal form, although He explained it as his intimate friend. Arjuna did not know how many times he may have dishonored Him by addressing Him as "O my friend, O Kṛṣṇa, O Yādava," etc., without acknowledging His opulence. But Kṛṣṇa is so kind and merciful that in spite of such opulence He played with Arjuna as a friend. Such is the transcendental loving reciprocation between the devotee and the Lord. The relationship between the living entity and Kṛṣṇa is fixed eternally; it cannot be forgotten, as we can see from the behavior of Arjuna. Although Arjuna has seen the opulence in the universal form, he could not forget his friendly relationship with Kṛṣṇa.

TEXT 43

पितासि लोकस्य चराचरस्य

त्वमस्य पूज्यश्च गुरुर्गरीयान् ।

न त्वत्समोऽस्त्यभ्यधिकः कुतोऽन्यो

लोकत्रयेऽप्यप्रतिमप्रभाव ॥ ४३ ॥

pitāsi lokasya carācarasya
tvam asya pūjyaś ca gurur garīyān
na tvat-samo 'sty abhyadhikaḥ kuto 'nyo
loka-traye 'py apratima-prabhāva

pitā—father; *asi*—You are; *lokasya*—of all the world; *cara*—moving; *acarasya*—nonmoving; *tvam*—You are; *asya*—of this; *pūjyaḥ*—worshipable; *ca*—also; *guruḥ*—master; *garīyān*—glorious; *na*—never; *tvat-samaḥ*—equal to You; *asti*—there is; *abhyadhikaḥ*—greater; *kutaḥ*—how is it possible; *anyaḥ*—other; *loka-traye*—in three planetary systems; *api*—also; *apratima*—immeasurable; *prabhāva*—power.

TRANSLATION

You are the father of this complete cosmic manifestation, the worshipable chief, the spiritual master. No one is equal to You, nor can anyone be one with You. Within the three worlds, You are immeasurable.

PURPORT

The Lord Kṛṣṇa is worshipable as a father is worshipable for his son. He is the spiritual master because He originally gave the Vedic instructions to Brahmā, and presently He is also instructing *Bhagavad-gītā* to Arjuna; therefore He is the original spiritual master, and any bona fide spiritual master at the present moment must be a descendant in the line of disciplic succession stemming from Kṛṣṇa. Without being a representative of Kṛṣṇa, one cannot become a teacher or spiritual master of transcendental subject matter.

The Lord is being paid obeisances in all respects. He is of immeasurable greatness. No one can be greater than the Supreme Personality of Godhead, Kṛṣṇa, because no one is equal to or higher than Kṛṣṇa within any manifestation, spiritual or material. Everyone is below Him. No one can excel Him.

The Supreme Lord Kṛṣṇa has senses and a body like the ordinary man, but for Him there is no difference between His senses, body, mind and Himself. Foolish persons who do not know Him perfectly say that Kṛṣṇa is different from His soul, mind, heart and everything else. Kṛṣṇa is absolute; therefore His activities and potencies are supreme. It is also stated that He does not have senses like ours. He can perform all sensual activities; therefore His senses are neither imperfect nor limited. No one can be greater than Him, no one can be equal to Him, and everyone is lower than Him.

Whoever knows His transcendental body, activities and perfection, after quitting his body, returns to Him and doesn't come back again to this miserable world. Therefore one should know that Kṛṣṇa's activities are different from others. The best policy is to follow the principles of Kṛṣṇa; that will make one perfect. It is also stated that there is no one who is master of Kṛṣṇa; everyone is His servant. Only Kṛṣṇa is God, and everyone is servant. Everyone is complying with His order. There is no one who can deny His order. Everyone is acting according to His direction, being under His superintendence. As stated in the *Brahma-saṁhitā*, He is the cause of all causes.

TEXT 44

तस्मात्प्रणम्य प्रणिधाय कायं
प्रसादये त्वामहमीशमीड्यम् ।
पितेव पुत्रस्य सखेव सख्युः
प्रियः प्रियायार्हसि देव सोढुम् ॥ ४४ ॥

tasmāt praṇamya praṇidhāya kāyaṁ
prasādaye tvām aham īśam īḍyam
piteva putrasya sakheva sakhyuḥ
priyaḥ priyāyārhasi deva soḍhum

tasmāt—therefore; *praṇamya*—after offering obeisances; *praṇidhāya*—laying down; *kāyam*—body; *prasādaye*—to beg mercy; *tvām*—unto you;

aham—I; *īśam*—unto the Supreme Lord; *īḍyam*—who is worshipable; *pitā iva*—like a father; *putrasya*—of a son; *sakhā iva*—like a friend; *sakhyuḥ*—of a friend; *priyaḥ*—lover; *priyāyāḥ*—of the dearmost; *arhasi*—You should; *deva*—my Lord; *soḍhum*—tolerate.

TRANSLATION

You are the Supreme Lord, to be worshiped by every living being. Thus I fall down to offer You my respects and ask Your mercy. Please tolerate the wrongs that I may have done to You and bear with me as a father with his son, or a friend with his friend, or a lover with his beloved.

PURPORT

Kṛṣṇa's devotees relate to Kṛṣṇa in various relationships; one might treat Kṛṣṇa as a son, one might treat Kṛṣṇa as a husband, as a friend, as a master, etc. Kṛṣṇa and Arjuna are related in friendship. As the father tolerates, or the husband or master tolerates, so Kṛṣṇa tolerates.

TEXT 45

अदृष्टपूर्वं हृषितोऽस्मि दृष्ट्वा
भयेन च प्रव्यथितं मनो मे ।
तदेव मे दर्शय देव रूपं
प्रसीद देवेश जगन्निवास ॥ ४५ ॥

adṛṣṭa-pūrvaṁ hṛṣito 'smi dṛṣṭvā
bhayena ca pravyathitaṁ mano me
tad eva me darśaya deva rūpaṁ
prasīda deveśa jagan-nivāsa

adṛṣṭa-pūrvam—never seen before; *hṛṣitaḥ*—gladdened; *asmi*—I am; *dṛṣṭvā*—by seeing; *bhayena*—out of fear; *ca*—also; *pravyathitam*—perturbed; *manaḥ*—mind; *me*—mine; *tat*—therefore; *eva*—certainly; *me*—unto me; *darśaya*—show; *deva*—O Lord; *rūpam*—the form; *prasīda*—just be gracious; *deveśa*—O Lord of lords; *jagat-nivāsa*—the refuge of the universe.

TRANSLATION

After seeing this universal form, which I have never seen before, I am gladdened, but at the same time my mind is disturbed with fear. Therefore please bestow Your grace upon me and reveal again Your form as the Personality of Godhead, O Lord of lords, O abode of the universe.

PURPORT

Arjuna is always in confidence with Kṛṣṇa because he is a very dear friend, and as a dear friend is gladdened by his friend's opulence, Arjuna is very joyful to see that his friend, Kṛṣṇa, is the Supreme Personality of Godhead and can show such a wonderful universal form. But at the same time, after seeing that universal form, he is afraid that he has committed so many offenses to Kṛṣṇa out of his unalloyed friendship. Thus his mind is disturbed out of fear, although he had no reason to fear. Arjuna therefore is asking Kṛṣṇa to show His Nārāyaṇa form because He can assume any form. This universal form is material and temporary, as the material world is temporary. But in the Vaikuṇṭha planets He has His transcendental form with four hands as Nārāyaṇa. There are innumerable planets in the spiritual sky, and in each of them Kṛṣṇa is present by His plenary manifesttations of different names. Thus Arjuna desired to see one of the forms manifest in the Vaikuṇṭha planets. Of course in each Vaikuṇṭha planet the form of Nārāyaṇa is four-handed, and the four hands hold different symbols, the conchshell, mace, lotus and disc. According to the different hands these four things are held in, the Nārāyaṇas are named. All of these forms are one and the same to Kṛṣṇa; therefore Arjuna requests to see His four-handed feature.

TEXT 46

किरीटिनं गदिनं चक्रहस्त-
मिच्छामि त्वां द्रष्टुमहं तथैव ।
तेनैव रूपेण चतुर्भुजेन
सहस्रबाहो भव विश्वमूर्ते ॥ ४६ ॥

kirīṭinaṁ gadinaṁ cakra-hastam
icchāmi tvāṁ draṣṭum ahaṁ tathaiva

tenaiva rūpeṇa catur-bhujena
sahasra-bāho bhava viśva-mūrte

kirīṭinam—with helmet; gadinam—with club; cakra-hastam—disc in hand; icchāmi—I wish; tvām—You; draṣṭum—to see; aham—I; tathā eva—in that position; tena eva—by that; rūpeṇa—with form; catur-bhujena—four-handed; sahasra-bāho—O thousand-handed one; bhava—just become; viśva-mūrte—O universal form.

TRANSLATION

O universal Lord, I wish to see You in Your four-armed form, with helmeted head and with club, wheel, conch and lotus flower in Your hands. I long to see You in that form.

PURPORT

In the *Brahmā-saṁhitā* it is stated that the Lord is eternally situated in hundreds and thousands of forms, and the main forms are those like Rāma, Nṛsiṁha, Nārāyaṇa, etc. There are innumerable forms. But Arjuna knew that Kṛṣṇa is the original Personality of Godhead assuming His temporary universal form. He is now asking to see the form of Nārāyaṇa, a spiritual form. This verse establishes without any doubt the statement of the *Śrīmad-Bhāgavatam* that Kṛṣṇa is the original Personality of Godhead and all other features originate from Him. He is not different from His plenary expansions, and He is God in any of His innumerable forms. In all of these forms He is fresh like a young man. That is the constant feature of the Supreme Personality of Godhead. One who knows Kṛṣṇa at once becomes free from all contamination of the material world.

TEXT 47

श्रीभगवानुवाच ।
मया प्रसन्नेन तवार्जुनेदं
रूपं परं दर्शितमात्मयोगात् ।
तेजोमयं विश्वमनन्तमाद्यं
यन्मे त्वदन्येन न दृष्टपूर्वम् ॥ ४७ ॥

śrī-bhagavān uvāca
mayā prasannena tavārjunedaṁ
rūpaṁ paraṁ darśitam ātma-yogāt
tejo-mayaṁ viśvam anantam ādyaṁ
yan me tvad anyena na dṛṣṭa-pūrvam

śrī bhagavān uvāca—the Supreme Personality of Godhead said; *mayā*—by Me; *prasannena*—happily; *tava*—unto you; *arjuna*—O Arjuna; *idam*—this; *rūpam*—form; *param*—transcendental; *darśitam*—shown; *ātma-yogāt*—by My internal potency; *tejomayam*—full of effulgence; *viśvam*—the entire universe; *anantam*—unlimited; *ādyam*—original; *yat me*—that which is Mine; *tvat-anyena*—besides you; *na dṛṣṭa-pūrvam*—no one has previously seen.

TRANSLATION

The Blessed Lord said: My dear Arjuna, happily do I show you this universal form within the material world by My internal potency. No one before you has ever seen this unlimited and glaringly effulgent form.

PURPORT

Arjuna wanted to see the universal form of the Supreme Lord, so out of His mercy upon His devotee Arjuna, Lord Kṛṣṇa showed His universal form full of effulgence and opulence. This form was glaring like the sun, and its many faces were rapidly changing. Kṛṣṇa showed this form just to satisfy the desire of His friend Arjuna. This form was manifested by Kṛṣṇa through His internal potency, which is inconceivable by human speculation. No one had seen this universal form of the Lord before Arjuna, but because the form was shown to Arjuna, other devotees in the heavenly planets and in other planets in outer space could also see it. They did not see it before, but because of Arjuna they were also able to see it. In other words, all the disciplic devotees of the Lord could see the universal form which was shown to Arjuna by the mercy of Kṛṣṇa. Someone commented that this form was shown to Duryodhana also when Kṛṣṇa went to Duryodhana to negotiate for peace. Unfortunately, Duryodhana did not accept the peace offer, but at that time Kṛṣṇa manifested some of His universal forms. But those forms are different from this one shown to Arjuna. It is clearly said that no one has ever seen this form before.

TEXT 48

न वेदयज्ञाध्ययनैर्न दानै-
र्न च क्रियाभिर्न तपोभिरुग्रैः ।
एवंरूपः शक्य अहं नृलोके
द्रष्टुं त्वदन्येन कुरुप्रवीर ॥ ४८ ॥

na veda-yajñādhyayanair na dānair
na ca kriyābhir na tapobhir ugraiḥ
evaṁ-rūpaḥ śakya ahaṁ nṛ-loke
draṣṭuṁ tvad anyena kuru-pravīra

na—never; veda—Vedic study; yajña—sacrifice; adhyayanaiḥ—studying; na dānaiḥ—by charity; na—never; ca—also; kriyābhiḥ—by pious activities; na tapobhiḥ—by serious penances; ugraiḥ—severe; evam—thus; rūpaḥ—form; śakyaḥ—can be seen; aham—I; nṛloke—in this material world; draṣṭum—to see; tvat—you; anyena—by another; kuru-pravīra—O best among the Kuru warriors.

TRANSLATION

O best of the Kuru warriors, no one before you has ever seen this universal form of Mine, for neither by studying the Vedas, nor by performing sacrifices, nor by charities or similar activities can this form be seen. Only you have seen this.

PURPORT

The divine vision in this connection should be clearly understood. Who can have divine vision? Divine means godly. Unless one attains the status of divinity as a demigod, he cannot have divine vision. And what is a demigod? It is stated in the Vedic scriptures that those who are devotees of Lord Viṣṇu are demigods. Those who are atheistic, i.e., who do not believe in Viṣṇu, or who only recognize the impersonal part of Kṛṣṇa as the Supreme, cannot have the divine vision. It is not possible to decry Kṛṣṇa and at the same time have the divine vision. One cannot have the divine vision without becoming divine. In other words, those who have divine vision can also see like Arjuna.

The *Bhagavad-gītā* gives the description of the universal form, and this description was unknown to everyone before Arjuna. Now one can have some idea of the *viśva-rūpa* after this incidence; those who are actually divine can see the universal form of the Lord. But one cannot be divine without being a pure devotee of Kṛṣṇa. The devotees, however, who are actually in the divine nature and who have divine vision, are not very much interested to see the universal form of the Lord. As described in the previous verse, Arjuna desired to see the four-handed form of Lord Kṛṣṇa as Viṣṇu, and he was actually afraid of the universal form.

In this verse there are some significant words, just like *veda-yajñādhya-yanaiḥ*, which refers to studying Vedic literature and the subject matter of sacrificial regulations. *Veda* refers to all kinds of Vedic literature, namely the four *Vedas* (*Ṛk, Yajus, Sāma* and *Atharva*) and the eighteen *Purāṇas* and *Upaniṣads*, and *Vedānta-sūtra*. One can study these at home or anywhere else. Similarly, there are *sūtras, Kalpa-sūtras* and *Mīmāṁsā-sūtras*, for studying the method of sacrifice. *Dānaiḥ* refers to charity which is offered to a suitable party. such as those who are engaged in the transcendental loving service of the Lord, the *brāhmaṇas* and the *Vaiṣṇavas*. Similarly, pious activities refer to the *agni-hotra*, etc., the prescribed duties of the different castes. Pious activities and the voluntary acceptance of some bodily pains are called *tapasya*. So one can perform all these, can accept bodily penances, give charity, study the *Vedas*, etc., but unless he is a devotee like Arjuna, it is not possible to see that universal form. Those who are impersonalists are also imagining that they are seeing the universal form of the Lord, but from *Bhagavad-gītā* we understand that the impersonalists are not devotees. Therefore they are unable to see the universal form of the Lord.

There are many persons who create incarnations. They falsely claim an ordinary human to be an incarnation, but this is all foolishness. We should follow the principles of *Bhagavad-gītā*, otherwise there is no possibility of attaining perfect spiritual knowledge. Although *Bhagavad-gītā* is considered the preliminary study of the science of God, still it is so perfect that one can distinguish what is what. The followers of a pseudo incarnation may say that they have also seen the transcendental incarnation of God, the universal form, but that is not acceptable because it is clearly stated here that unless one becomes a devotee of Kṛṣṇa, one cannot see the universal form of God. So one first of all has to become a pure devotee of Kṛṣṇa; then he can claim that he can show the universal form of what he has seen. A devotee of Kṛṣṇa cannot accept false incarnations or followers of false incarnations.

TEXT 49

मा ते व्यथा मा च विमूढभावो
दृष्ट्वा रूपं घोरमीदृङ्ममेदम् ।
व्यपेतभीः प्रीतमनाः पुनस्त्वं
तदेव मे रूपमिदं प्रपश्य ॥ ४९ ॥

mā te vyathā mā ca vimūḍha-bhāvo
dṛṣṭvā rūpaṁ ghoram īdṛṅ mamedam
vyapeta-bhīḥ prīta-manāḥ punas tvaṁ
tad eva me rūpam idaṁ prapaśya

mā—let it not be; te—unto you; vyathā—trouble; mā—let it not be; ca—also; vimūḍha-bhāvaḥ—bewilderment; dṛṣṭvā—by seeing; rūpam—form; ghoram—horrible; īdṛk—like this; mama—My; idam—as it is; vyapetabhīḥ—just become free from all fear; prīta-manāḥ—be pleased in mind; punaḥ—again; tvam—you; tat—that; eva—thus; me—My; rūpam—form; idam—this; prapaśya—just see.

TRANSLATION

Your mind has been perturbed upon seeing this horrible feature of Mine. Now let it be finished. My devotee, be free from all disturbance. With a peaceful mind you can now see the form you desire.

PURPORT

In the beginning of *Bhagavad-gītā* Arjuna was worried about killing Bhīṣma and Droṇa, his worshipful grandfathers and masters. But Kṛṣṇa said that he need not be afraid of killing his grandfather. When they tried to disrobe Draupadī in the assembly, Bhīṣma and Droṇa were silent, and for such negligence of duty they should be killed. Kṛṣṇa showed His universal form to Arjuna just to show him that these people were already killed for their unlawful action. That scene was shown to Arjuna because devotees are always peaceful, and they cannot perform such horrible actions. The purpose of the revelation of the universal form was shown; now Arjuna wanted to see the four-armed form, and Kṛṣṇa showed him. A devotee is not much interested in the universal form, for it does not enable one to reciprocate loving feelings. A devotee wants to offer his respectful worshiping feelings; thus he wants to see the two-handed or four-handed Kṛṣṇa form so he can reciprocate in loving service with the Supreme Personality of Godhead.

TEXT 50

सञ्जय उवाच ।
इत्यर्जुनं वासुदेवस्तथोक्ता
स्वकं रूपं दर्शयामास भूयः ।
आश्वासयामास च भीतमेनं
भूत्वा पुनः सौम्यवपुर्महात्मा ॥ ५० ॥

sañjaya uvāca
ity arjunaṁ vāsudevas tathoktvā
svakaṁ rūpaṁ darśayām āsa bhūyaḥ
āśvāsayām āsa ca bhītam enaṁ
bhūtvā punaḥ saumya-vapur mahātmā

sañjayaḥ uvāca—Sañjaya said; iti—thus; arjunam—unto Arjuna; vāsudevaḥ—Kṛṣṇa; tathā—that way; uktvā—saying; svakam—His own; rūpam—form; darśayāmāsa—showed; bhūyaḥ—again; āśvāsayāmāsa—also convinced him; ca—also; bhītam—fearful; enam—him; bhūtvā punaḥ—becoming again; saumya-vapuḥ—beautiful form; mahātmā—the great one.

TRANSLATION

Sañjaya said to Dhṛtarāṣṭra: The Supreme Personality of Godhead, Kṛṣṇa, while speaking thus to Arjuna, displayed His real four-armed form, and at last He showed him His two-armed form, thus encouraging the fearful Arjuna.

PURPORT

When Kṛṣṇa appeared as the son of Vasudeva and Devakī, He first of all appeared as four-armed Nārāyaṇa, but when He was requested by His parents, He transformed Himself into an ordinary child in appearance. Similarly, Kṛṣṇa knew that Arjuna was not interested in seeing a four-handed form of Kṛṣṇa, but since he asked to see this four-handed form,

He also showed him this form again and then showed Himself in His two-handed form. The word *saumya-vapuḥ* is very significant. *Saumya-vapu* is a very beautiful form; it is known as the most beautiful form. When He was present, everyone was attracted simply by Kṛṣṇa's form, and because Kṛṣṇa is director of the universe, He just banished the fear of Arjuna, His devotee, and showed him again His beautiful form of Kṛṣṇa. In the *Brahma-saṁhitā* it is stated that only a person whose eyes are smeared with the ointment of love can see the beautiful form of Śrī Kṛṣṇa.

TEXT 51

अर्जुन उवाच ।
दृष्ट्वेदं मानुषं रूपं तव सौम्यं जनार्दन ।
इदानीमस्मि संवृत्तः सचेताः प्रकृतिं गतः ॥ ५१ ॥

*arjuna uvāca
dṛṣṭvedaṁ mānuṣaṁ rūpaṁ
tava saumyaṁ janārdana
idānīm asmi saṁvṛttaḥ
sa-cetāḥ prakṛtiṁ gataḥ*

arjunaḥ uvāca—Arjuna said; *dṛṣṭvā*—seeing; *idam*—this; *mānuṣam*—human being; *rūpam*—form; *tava*—Your; *saumyam*—very beautiful; *janārdana*—O chastiser of the enemies; *idānīm*—just now; *asmi*—I am; *saṁvṛttaḥ*—settled; *sa-cetāḥ*—in my consciousness; *prakṛtim*—my own; *gataḥ*—I am.

TRANSLATION

When Arjuna thus saw Kṛṣṇa in His original form, he said: Seeing this humanlike form, so very beautiful, my mind is now pacified, and I am restored to my original nature.

PURPORT

Here the words *mānuṣam rūpam* clearly indicate the Supreme Personality of Godhead to be originally two-handed. Those who deride Kṛṣṇa to be an ordinary person are shown here to be ignorant of His divine nature. If Kṛṣṇa is like an ordinary human being, then how is it possible for Him to show the universal form and again to show the four-handed Nārāyaṇa form? So it is very clearly stated in *Bhagavad-gītā* that one who thinks that Kṛṣṇa is an ordinary person and misguides the reader by claiming that it is the impersonal Brahman within Kṛṣṇa speaking, is doing the greatest injustice. Kṛṣṇa has actually shown His universal form and His fourhanded Viṣṇu form. So how can He be an ordinary human being? A pure devotee is not confused by misguiding commentaries on *Bhagavad-gītā* because he knows what is what. The original verses of *Bhagavad-gītā* are as clear as the sun; they do not require lamplight from foolish commentators.

TEXT 52

श्रीभगवानुवाच ।
सुदुर्दर्शमिदं रूपं दृष्टवानसि यन्मम ।
देवा अप्यस्य रूपस्य नित्यं दर्शनकाङ्क्षिणः ॥ ५२ ॥

śrī-bhagavān uvāca
su-durdarśam idaṁ rūpaṁ
dṛṣṭavān asi yan mama
devā apy asya rūpasya
nityaṁ darśana-kāṅkṣiṇaḥ

śrī bhagavān uvāca—the Supreme Personality of Godhead said; *sudurdarśana*— very difficult to be seen; *idam*—this; *rūpam*—form; *dṛṣṭavān asi*—as you have seen; *yat*—which; *mama*—of Mine; *devāḥ*—the demigods; *api asya*—also this; *rūpasya*—of the form; *nityam*—eternally; *darśana-kāṅkṣiṇaḥ*—always aspire to see.

TRANSLATION

The Blessed Lord said: My dear Arjuna, the form which you are now seeing is very difficult to behold. Even the demigods are ever seeking the opportunity to see this form which is so dear.

PURPORT

In the forty-eighth verse of this chapter Lord Kṛṣṇa concluded revealing His universal form and informed Arjuna that this form is not possible to be seen by so many activities, sacrifices, etc. Now here the word *sudurdarśam* is used, indicating that Kṛṣṇa's two-handed form is still more confidential. One may be able to see the universal form of Kṛṣṇa by adding a little tinge of devotional service to various activities like penance, Vedic study and philosophical speculation, etc. It may be possible, but without a tinge of *bhakti*, one cannot see; that has already been explained. Still, beyond that universal form, the form of Kṛṣṇa as a two-handed man is still more difficult to see, even for demigods like Brahmā and Lord Śiva. They desire to see Him, and we have evidences in the *Śrīmad-Bhāgavatam* that when He was supposed to be in the womb of His mother, Devakī, all the demigods from heaven came to see the marvel of Kṛṣṇa. They even waited to see Him. A foolish person may deride Him, but that is an ordinary person. Kṛṣṇa is actually desired to be seen by demigods like Brahmā and Śiva in His two-armed form.

In *Bhagavad-gītā* it is also confirmed that He is not visible to the foolish persons who deride Him. Kṛṣṇa's body, as confirmed by *Brahmā-samhitā* and confirmed by Himself in *Bhagavad-gītā*, is completely spiritual and full of bliss and eternality. His body is never like a material body. But for some who make a study of Kṛṣṇa by reading *Bhagavad-gītā* or similar Vedic scriptures, Kṛṣṇa is a problem. For one using a material process, Kṛṣṇa is considered to be a great historical personality and very learned philosopher. But He isn't an ordinary man. But some think that even though He was so powerful, He had to accept a material body. Ultimately they think that the Absolute Truth is impersonal; therefore they think that from His impersonal feature He assumed a personal feature attached to material nature. This is a materialistic calculation of the Supreme Lord. Another calculation is speculative. Those who are in search of knowledge also speculate on Kṛṣṇa and consider Him to be less important than the universal form of the Supreme. Thus some think that the universal form of Kṛṣṇa which was manifested to Arjuna is more important than His personal form. According to them, the personal form of the Supreme is something imaginary. They believe that in the ultimate issue, the Absolute Truth is not a person. But the transcendental process is described in *Bhagavad-gītā*, Chapter Two: to hear about Kṛṣṇa from authorities. That is the actual Vedic process, and those who are actually in the Vedic line hear about Kṛṣṇa from authority, and by repeated hearing about Him, Kṛṣṇa becomes dear. As we have several times discussed, Kṛṣṇa is covered by His *yoga-māyā* potency. He is not to be seen or revealed to anyone and everyone. Only by one to whom He reveals Himself can He be seen. This is confirmed in Vedic literature; for one who is a surrendered soul, the

Absolute Truth can actually be understood. The transcendentalist, by continuous Kṛṣṇa consciousness and by devotional service to Kṛṣṇa, can have his spiritual eyes opened and can see Kṛṣṇa by revelation. Such a revelation is not possible even for the demigods; therefore it is difficult even for the demigods to understand Kṛṣṇa, and the advanced demigods are always in hope of seeing Kṛṣṇa in His two-handed form. The conclusion is that although to see the universal form of Kṛṣṇa is very, very difficult and not possible for anyone and everyone, it is still more difficult to understand His personal form as Śyāmasundara.

TEXT 53

नाहं वेदैर्न तपसा न दानेन न चेज्यया ।
शक्य एवंविधो द्रष्टुं दृष्टवानसि मां यथा ॥ ५३ ॥

nāhaṁ vedair na tapasā
na dānena na cejyayā
śakya evaṁ-vidho draṣṭuṁ
dṛṣṭavān asi māṁ yathā

na—never; *aham*—I; *vedaiḥ*—by study of the Vedas; *na*—never; *tapasā*—by serious penances; *na*—never; *dānena*—by charity; *na*—never; *ca*—also; *ijyayā*—by worship; *śakyaḥ*—is it possible; *evam-vidhaḥ*—like this; *draṣṭum*—to see; *dṛṣṭavān*—seeing; *asi*—you are; *mām*—Me; *yathā*—as.

TRANSLATION

The form which you are seeing with your transcendental eyes cannot be understood simply by studying the Vedas, nor by undergoing serious penances, nor by charity, nor by worship. It is not by these means that one can see Me as I am.

PURPORT

Kṛṣṇa first appeared before His parents Devakī and Vasudeva in a four-handed form, and then He transformed Himself into the two-handed form. This mystery is very difficult to understand for those who are atheists or who are devoid of devotional service. For scholars who have simply studied Vedic literature by way of speculation or out of mere academic interest, Kṛṣṇa is not easy to understand. Nor is He to he understood by persons who officially go to the temple to offer worship. They make their visit, but they cannot understand Kṛṣṇa as He is. Kṛṣṇa can be understood only through the path of devotional service, as explained by Kṛṣṇa Himself in the next verse.

TEXT 54

भक्त्या त्वनन्यया शक्य अहमेवंविधोऽर्जुन ।
ज्ञातुं द्रष्टुं च तत्त्वेन प्रवेष्टुं च परन्तप ॥ ५४ ॥

*bhaktyā tv ananyayā śakya
aham evaṁ-vidho 'rjuna
jñātuṁ draṣṭuṁ ca tattvena
praveṣṭuṁ ca parantapa*

bhaktyā—by devotional service; *tu*—but; *ananyayā*—without being mixed with fruitive activities or speculative knowledge; *śakyaḥ*—possible; *aham*—I; *evam-vidhaḥ*—like this; *arjuna*—O Arjuna; *jñātum*—to know; *draṣṭum*—to see; *tattvena*—in fact; *praveṣṭum*—and to enter into; *ca*—also; *parantapa*—O mighty-armed one.

TRANSLATION

My dear Arjuna, only by undivided devotional service can I be understood as I am, standing before you, and can thus be seen directly. Only in this way can you enter into the mysteries of My understanding.

PURPORT

Kṛṣṇa can be understood only by the process of undivided devotional service. He explicitly explains this in this verse so unauthorized commentators, who try to understand *Bhagavad-gītā* by the speculative process, will know that they are simply wasting their time. No one can understand Kṛṣṇa or how He came from parents in a four-handed form and at once changed Himself into a two-handed form. It is clearly stated here that no one can see Him. Those who, however, are very experienced students of Vedic literature can learn about Him from the Vedic literature in so many ways. There are so many rules and regulations, and if one at all wants to understand Kṛṣṇa, he must follow the regulative principles described in the authoritative literature. One can perform penance in accordance with those principles. As far as charity is concerned, it is plain that charity should be given to the devotees of Kṛṣṇa who are engaged in His devotional service to spread the Kṛṣṇa philosophy or Kṛṣṇa consciousness throughout the world. Kṛṣṇa consciousness is a benediction to humanity. Lord Caitanya was appreciated by Rūpa Gosvāmī as the most munificent man of charity because love of Kṛṣṇa, which is very difficult to achieve, was distributed freely by Him. And if one worships as prescribed in the temple (in the temples in India there is always some statue, usually of Viṣṇu or Kṛṣṇa), that is a chance to progress. For the beginners in devotional service to the Lord, temple worship is very essential, and this is confirmed in the Vedic literature.

One who has unflinching devotion for the Supreme Lord and is directed by the spiritual master can see the Supreme Personality of Godhead by revelation. For one who does not take personal training under the guidance of a bona fide spiritual master, it is impossible to even begin to understand Kṛṣṇa. The word *tu* is specifically used here to indicate that no other process can be used, can be recommended, or can be successful in understanding Kṛṣṇa.

The personal forms of Kṛṣṇa, the two-handed form and the four-handed, are completely different from the temporary universal form shown to Arjuna. The four-handed form is Nārāyaṇa, and the two-handed form is Kṛṣṇa; they are eternal and transcendental, whereas the universal form exhibited to Arjuna is temporary. The very word *sudurdarśam*, meaning difficult to see, suggests that no one saw that universal form. It also suggests that amongst the devotees there was no necessity of showing it. That form was exhibited by Kṛṣṇa at the request of Arjuna because in the future, when one represents himself as an incarnation of God, people can ask to see his universal form.

Kṛṣṇa changes from the universal form to the four-handed form of Nārāyaṇa and then to His own natural form of two hands. This indicates that the four-handed forms and other forms mentioned in Vedic literature are all emanations of the original two-handed Kṛṣṇa. He is the origin of all emanations. Kṛṣṇa is distinct even from these forms, not to speak of the impersonal conception. As far as the four-handed forms of Kṛṣṇa are concerned, it is stated clearly that even the most identical four-handed form of Kṛṣṇa (which is known as Mahā-Viṣṇu, who is lying on the cosmic ocean and from whose breathing so many innumerable universes are passing out and entering) is also an expansion of the Supreme Lord. Therefore one should conclusively worship the personal form of Kṛṣṇa as the Supreme

Personality of Godhead who is eternity, bliss and knowledge. He is the source of all forms of Viṣṇu, He is the source of all forms of incarnation, and He is the original Supreme Personality, as confirmed in *Bhagavad-gītā*.

In the Vedic literature it is stated that the Supreme Absolute Truth is a person. His name is Kṛṣṇa, and He sometimes descends on this earth. Similarly, in *Śrīmad-Bhāgavatam* there is a description of all kinds of incarnations of the Supreme Personality of Godhead, and there it is said that Kṛṣṇa is not an incarnation of God but is the original Supreme Personality of Godhead Himself. *Kṛṣṇas tu bhagavān svayam.* Similarly, in *Bhagavad-gītā* the Lord says, *mattaḥ parataram nānyāt:* "There is nothing superior to My form as the Personality of Godhead Kṛṣṇa." He also says elsewhere in *Bhagavad-gītā*, *aham ādir hi devānām:* "I am the origin of all the demigods." And after understanding *Bhagavad-gītā* from Kṛṣṇa, Arjuna also confirms this in the following words: *param brahma param dhāma pavitram paramam bhavān:* "I now fully understand that You are the Supreme Personality of Godhead, the Absolute Truth, and that You are the refuge of everything." Therefore the universal form which Kṛṣṇa showed to Arjuna is not the original form of God. The original is the Kṛṣṇa form. The universal form, with its thousands and thousands of heads and hands, is manifest just to draw the attention of those who have no love for God. It is not God's original form.

The universal form is not attractive for pure devotees, who are in love with the Lord in different transcendental relationships. The Supreme Godhead exchanges transcendental love in His original form of Kṛṣṇa. Therefore to Arjuna, who was so intimately related with Kṛṣṇa in friendship, this form of the universal manifestation was not pleasing; rather, it was fearful. Arjuna, who is a constant companion of Kṛṣṇa's, must have had transcendental eyes; he was not an ordinary man. Therefore he was not captivated by the universal form. This form may seem wonderful to persons who are involved in elevating themselves by fruitive activities, but to persons who are engaged in devotional service, the two-handed form of Kṛṣṇa is the most dear.

TEXT 55

मत्कर्मकृन्मत्परमो मद्भक्तः स्रावर्जितः ।
निर्वैरः सर्वभूतेषु यः स मामेति पाण्डव ॥ ५५ ॥

mat-karma-kṛn mat-paramo
mad-bhaktaḥ saṅga-varjitaḥ

nirvairaḥ sarva-bhūteṣu
yaḥ sa mām eti pāṇḍava

mat-karma-kṛt—engaged in doing My work; *mat-paramaḥ*—concerning Me, the Supreme; *mat-bhaktaḥ*—engaged in My devotional service; *saṅga-varjitaḥ*—freed from the contamination of previous activities and mental speculation; *nirvairaḥ*—without an enemy; *sarva-bhūteṣu*—to every living entity; *yaḥ*—one who; *saḥ*—he; *mām*—unto Me; *eti*—comes; *pāṇḍava*—O son of Pāṇḍu.

TRANSLATION

My dear Arjuna, one who is engaged in My pure devotional service, free from the contaminations of previous activities and from mental specula-tion, who is friendly to every living entity, certainly comes to Me.

PURPORT

Anyone who wants to approach the Supreme of all the Personalities of Godhead, on the Kṛṣṇaloka planet in the spiritual sky, and be intimately connected with the Supreme Personality, Kṛṣṇa, must take this formula, as is stated by the Supreme Himself. Therefore, this verse is considered to be the essence of *Bhagavad-gītā*. The *Bhagavad-gītā* is a book directed to the conditioned souls, who are engaged in the material world with the purpose of lording it over nature and who do not know of the real, spiritual life. The *Bhagavad-gītā* is meant to show how one can understand his spiritual existence and his eternal relationship with the Supreme Spiritual Person-ality and to teach one how to go back home, back to Godhead. Now here is the verse which clearly explains the process by which one can attain suc-cess in his spiritual activity: devotional service. As far as work is concerned, one should transfer his energy entirely to Kṛṣṇa conscious activities. No work should be done by any man except in relationship to Kṛṣṇa. This called Kṛṣṇa-*karma*. One may be engaged in various activities, but one should not be attached to the result of his work, but the result should be done for Him. For example, one may be engaged in business, but to trans-form that activity into Kṛṣṇa consciousness, one has to do business for Kṛṣṇa. If Kṛṣṇa is the proprietor of the business, then Kṛṣṇa should enjoy the profit of the business. If a businessman is in possession of thousands and thousands of dollars, and if he has to offer all this to Kṛṣṇa, he can do it. This is work for Kṛṣṇa. Instead of constructing a big building for his sense gratification, he can construct a nice temple for Kṛṣṇa, and he can install the Deity of Kṛṣṇa and arrange for the Deity's service, as is outlined in the authorized books of devotional service. This is all Kṛṣṇa-*karma*. One should not be attached to the result of his work, but the result should be offered to Kṛṣṇa. One should also accept as *prasādam*, food, the remnants of offerings to Kṛṣṇa. If, however, one is not able to construct a temple for Kṛṣṇa, one can engage himself in cleansing the temple of Kṛṣṇa; that is also Kṛṣṇa-*karma*. One can cultivate a garden. Anyone who has land—in India, at least, any poor man has a certain amount of land—can utilize that for Kṛṣṇa by growing flowers to offer Him. He can sow *tulasī* plants because *tulasī* leaves are very important, and Kṛṣṇa has recommended this in *Bhagavad-gītā*. Kṛṣṇa desires that one offer Him either a leaf, or a flower, or a little water-and He is satisfied. This leaf especially refers to the *tulasī* So one can sow *tulasī* leaves and pour water on the plant. Thus, even the poorest man can engage in the service of Kṛṣṇa. These are some of the examples of how one can engage in working for Kṛṣṇa.

The word *mat-paramaḥ* refers to one who considers the association of Kṛṣṇa in His supreme abode to be the highest perfection of life. Such a person does not wish to be elevated to the higher planets such as the moon or sun or heavenly planets, or even the highest planet of this universe, Brahmaloka. He has no attraction for that. He is only attracted to being transferred to the spiritual sky. And even in the spiritual sky he is not satisfied with merging into the glowing *brahmajyoti* effulgence, for he wants to enter the highest spiritual planet, namely Kṛṣṇaloka, Goloka Vṛndāvana. He has full knowledge of that planet, and therefore he is not interested in any other. As indicated by the word *mad-bhaktaḥ*, he fully engages in devotional service, specifically in the nine processes of devotional engagement: hearing, chanting, remembering, worshiping, serving the lotus feet of the Lord, offering prayers, carrying out the orders of the Lord, making friends with Him, and surrendering everything to Him. One can engage in all nine devotional processes, or eight, or seven, or at least in one, and that will surely make one perfect.

The term *saṅga-varjitaḥ* is very significant. One should disassociate himself from persons who are against Kṛṣṇa. Not only are the atheistic persons against Kṛṣṇa, but also those who are attracted to fruitive activities and mental speculation. Therefore the pure form of devotional service is described in *Bhakti-rasāmṛta-sindhu* as follows: *anyābhilāṣitā-śūnyaṁ jñāna-karmādy-anāvṛtam ānukūlyena kṛṣṇānuśīlanaṁ bhaktir uttamā*. In this verse Śrīla Rūpa Gosvāmī clearly states that if anyone wants to execute unalloyed devotional service, he must be freed from all kinds of material contamination. He must be freed from the association of persons who are addicted to fruitive activities and mental speculation. When, freed from such unwanted association and from the contamination of material desires, one favorably cultivates knowledge of Kṛṣṇa, that is called pure devotional service. *Ānukūlyasya saṅkaplaḥ prātikūlyasya varjanam.* One should think of Kṛṣṇa and act for Kṛṣṇa favorably, not unfavorably. Kaṁsa was an enemy of Kṛṣṇa's. From the very beginning of Kṛṣṇa's birth, he planned in so many ways to kill Him, and because he was always unsuccessful, he was always thinking of Kṛṣṇa. Thus while working, while eating and while sleeping, he was always Kṛṣṇa conscious in every respect, but that Kṛṣṇa consciousness was not favorable, and therefore in spite of his always thinking of Kṛṣṇa twenty-four hours a day, he was considered a demon, and Kṛṣṇa at last killed him. Of course anyone who is killed by Kṛṣṇa attains salvation immediately, but that is not the aim of the pure devotee. The pure devotee does not even want salvation. He does not want to be transferred even to the highest planet, Goloka Vṛndāvana. His only objective is to serve Kṛṣṇa wherever he may be.

A devotee of Kṛṣṇa is friendly to everyone. Therefore it is said here that he has no enemy. How is this? A devotee situated in Kṛṣṇa consciousness knows that only devotional service to Kṛṣṇa can relieve a person from all the problems of life. He has personal experience of this, and therefore he wants to introduce this system, Kṛṣṇa consciousness, into human society. There are many examples in history of devotees of the Lord risking their lives for the spreading of God consciousness. The favorite example is Lord Jesus Christ. He was crucified by the nondevotees, but He sacrificed His life for spreading God consciousness. Of course, it would be superficial to understand that He was killed. Similarly, in India also there are many examples, such as Ṭhākur Haridāsa. Why such risk? Because they wanted to spread Kṛṣṇa consciousness, and it is difficult. A Kṛṣṇa conscious person knows that if a man is suffering, it is due to his forgetfulness of his eternal relationship with Kṛṣṇa. Therefore, the highest benefit one can render to human society is relieving one's neighbor from all material problems. In such a way, a pure devotee is engaged in the service of the Lord. Now, we can imagine how merciful Kṛṣṇa is to those engaged in His service, risking everything for Him. Therefore it is certain that such persons must reach the supreme planet after leaving the body.

In summary, the universal form of Kṛṣṇa, which is a temporary manifestation, and the form of time which devours everything, and even the form of Viṣṇu, four-handed, have all been exhibited by Kṛṣṇa. Thus Kṛṣṇa is the origin of all these manifestations. It is not that Kṛṣṇa is a manifestation of the original *viśva-rūpa*, or Viṣṇu. Kṛṣṇa is the origin of all forms. There are hundreds and thousands of Viṣṇus, but for a devotee, no form of Kṛṣṇa is important but the original form, two-handed Śyāmasundara. In the *Brahmā-saṁhitā* it is stated that those who are attached to the Śyāmasundara form of Kṛṣṇa in love and devotion can see Him always within the heart and cannot see anything else. One should understand, therefore, that the purport of this Eleventh Chapter is that the form of Kṛṣṇa is essential and supreme.

Thus end the Bhaktivedanta Purports to the Eleventh Chapter of the Śrīmad-Bhagavad-gītā *in the matter of the Universal Form.*

CHAPTER TWELVE

Devotional Service

TEXT 1

अर्जुन उवाच ।
एवं सततयुक्ता ये भक्तास्त्वां पर्युपासते ।
ये चाप्यक्षरमव्यक्तं तेषां के योगवित्तमाः ॥ १ ॥

arjuna uvāca
evaṁ satata-yuktā ye
bhaktās tvāṁ paryupāsate
ye cāpy akṣaram avyaktaṁ
teṣāṁ ke yoga-vittamāḥ

arjunaḥ uvāca—Arjuna said; *evam*—thus; *satata*—always; *yuktāḥ*—engaged;
ye—those; *bhaktāḥ*—devotees; *tvām*—unto You; *paryupāsate*—properly
worship; *ye*—those; *ca*—also; *api*—again; *akṣaram*—beyond the senses;
avyaktam—unmanifested; *teṣām*—of them; *ke*—who; *yoga-vittamāḥ*—the
most perfect.

TRANSLATION

Arjuna inquired: Which is considered to be more perfect: those who are properly engaged in Your devotional service, or those who worship the impersonal Brahman, the unmanifested?

PURPORT

Kṛṣṇa has now explained about the personal, the impersonal and the universal and has described all kinds of devotees and yogīs. Generally, the transcendentalists can be divided into two classes. One is the impersonalist, and the other is the personalist. The personalist devotee engages himself with all energy in the service of the Supreme Lord. The impersonalist engages himself not directly in the service of Kṛṣṇa but in meditation on the impersonal Brahman, the unmanifested.

We find in this chapter that of the different processes for realization of the Absolute Truth, bhakti-yoga, devotional service, is the highest. If one at all desires to have the association of the Supreme Personality of Godhead, then he must take to devotional service.

Those who worship the Supreme Lord directly by devotional service are called personalists. Those who engage themselves in meditation on the impersonal Brahman are called impersonalists. Arjuna is here questioning which position is better. There are different ways to realize the Absolute Truth, but Kṛṣṇa indicates in this chapter that bhakti-yoga, or devotional service to Him, is highest of all. It is the most direct, and it is the easiest means for association with the Godhead.

In the Second Chapter the Lord explains that a living entity is not the material body but is a spiritual spark, a part of the Absolute Truth. In the Seventh Chapter He speaks of the living entity as part and parcel of the supreme whole and recommends that he transfer his attention fully to the whole. In the Eighth Chapter it is stated that whoever thinks of Kṛṣṇa at the moment of death is at once transferred to the spiritual sky, Kṛṣṇa's abode. And at the end of the Sixth Chapter the Lord says that out of all the yogīs, he who thinks of Kṛṣṇa within himself is considered to be the most perfect. So throughout the Gītā personal devotion to Kṛṣṇa is recommended as the highest form of spiritual realization. Yet there are those who are still attracted to Kṛṣṇa's impersonal brahmajyoti effulgence, which is the all-pervasive aspect of the Absolute Truth and which is unmanifest and beyond the reach of the senses. Arjuna would like to know which of these two types of transcendentalists is more perfect in knowledge. In other words, he is clarifying his own position because he is attached to the personal form of Kṛṣṇa. He is not attached to the impersonal Brahman. He wants to know whether his position is secure. The impersonal manifestation, either in this material world or in the spiritual world of the Supreme Lord, is a problem for meditation. Actually, one cannot perfectly conceive of the impersonal feature of the Absolute Truth. Therefore Arjuna wants to say, "What is the use of such a waste of time?" Arjuna experienced in the Eleventh Chapter that to be attached to the personal form of Kṛṣṇa is best because he could thus understand all other forms at the same time and there was no disturbance to his love for Kṛṣṇa. This important question asked of Kṛṣṇa by Arjuna will clarify the distinction between the impersonal and personal conceptions of the Absolute Truth.

TEXT 2

श्रीभगवानुवाच ।
मय्यावेश्य मनो ये मां नित्ययुक्ता उपासते ।
श्रद्धया परयोपेतास्ते मे युक्ततमा मताः ॥ २ ॥

śrī-bhagavān uvāca
mayy āveśya mano ye māṁ
nitya-yuktā upāsate
śraddhayā parayopetās
te me yuktatamā matāḥ

śrī bhagavān uvāca—the Supreme Personality of Godhead said; *mayi*—unto Me; *āveśya*—fixing; *manaḥ*—mind; *ye*—one who; *mām*—unto Me; *nitya*—always; *yuktāḥ*—engaged; *upāsate*—worships; *śraddhayā*—with faith; *parayā*—transcendental; *upetāḥ*—engages; *te*—they; *me*—Mine; *yuktatamāḥ*—most perfect; *matāḥ*—I consider.

TRANSLATION

The Blessed Lord said: He whose mind is fixed on My personal form, always engaged in worshiping Me with great and transcendental faith, is considered by Me to be most perfect.

PURPORT

In answer to Arjuna's question, Kṛṣṇa clearly says that he who concentrates upon His personal form and who worships Him with faith and devotion is to be considered most perfect in *yoga*. For one in such Kṛṣṇa consciousness there are no material activities because everything is done by Kṛṣṇa. A pure devotee is constantly engaged—sometimes he chants, sometimes he hears or reads books about Kṛṣṇa, or sometimes he cooks *prasādam* or goes to the marketplace to purchase something for Kṛṣṇa, or sometimes he washes the temple or the dishes—whatever he does, he does not let a single moment pass without devoting his activities to Kṛṣṇa. Such action is in full *samādhi*.

TEXTS 3-4

ये त्वक्षरमनिर्देश्यमव्यक्तं पर्युपासते ।
सर्वत्रगमचिन्त्यं च कूटस्थमचलं ध्रुवम् ॥ ३ ॥
संनियम्येन्द्रियग्रामं सर्वत्र समबुद्धयः ।
ते प्राप्नुवन्ति मामेव सर्वभूतहिते रताः ॥ ४ ॥

ye tv akṣaram anirdeśyam
avyaktaṁ paryupāsate
sarvatra-gam acintyaṁ ca
kūṭa-stham acalaṁ dhruvam

sanniyamyendriya-grāmaṁ
sarvatra sama-buddhayaḥ
te prāpnuvanti mām eva
sarva-bhūta-hite ratāḥ

ye—those; *tu*—but; *akṣaram*—which is beyond the perception of the senses; *anirdeśyam*—indefinite; *avyaktam*—unmanifested; *paryupāsate*—completely engages; *sarvatra-gam*—all-pervading; *acintyam*—inconceivable; *ca*—also; *kūṭastham*—in the center; *acalam*—immovable; *dhruvam*—fixed; *sanniyamya*—controlling; *indriya-grāmam*—all the senses; *sarvatra*—everywhere; *sama-buddhayaḥ*—equally disposed; *te*—they; *prāpnuvanti*—achieve; *mām*—unto Me; *eva*—certainly; *sarva-bhūta-hite*—all living entities' welfare; *ratāḥ*—engaged.

TRANSLATION

But those who fully worship the unmanifested, that which lies beyond the perception of the senses, the all-pervading, inconceivable, fixed, and immovable—the impersonal conception of the Absolute Truth—by controlling the various senses and being equally disposed to everyone, such persons, engaged in the welfare of all, at last achieve Me.

PURPORT

Those who do not directly worship the Supreme Godhead, Kṛṣṇa, but who attempt to achieve the same goal by an indirect process, also ultimately achieve the supreme goal, Śrī Kṛṣṇa, as is stated, "After many births the man of wisdom seeks refuge in Me, knowing Vāsudeva is all." When a person comes to full knowledge after many births, he surrenders unto Lord Kṛṣṇa. If one approaches the Godhead by the method mentioned in this verse, he has to control the senses, render service to everyone and engage in the welfare of all beings. It is inferred that one has to approach Lord Kṛṣṇa, otherwise there is no perfect realization. Often there is much penance involved before one fully surrenders unto Him.

In order to perceive the Supersoul within the individual soul, one has to cease the sensual activities of seeing, hearing, tasting, working, etc. Then one comes to understand that the Supreme Soul is present everywhere. Realizing this, one envies no living entity—he sees no difference between man and animal because he sees soul only, not the outer covering. But for the common man, this method of impersonal realization is very difficult.

TEXT 5

केशोऽधिकतरस्तेषामव्यक्तासक्तचेतसाम् ।
अव्यक्ता हि गतिर्दुःखं देहवद्भिरवाप्यते ॥ ५ ॥

*kleśo 'dhikataras teṣām
avyaktāsakta-cetasām
avyaktā hi gatir duḥkhaṁ
dehavadbhir avāpyate*

kleśaḥ—trouble; *adhikataraḥ*—more troublesome; *teṣām*—of them; *avyakta*—unmanifested; *āsakta*—being attached; *cetasām*—of those whose minds; *avyaktā*—unmanifested; *hi*—certainly; *gatiḥ duḥkham*—progress is troublesome; *dehavadbhiḥ*—of the embodiments; *avāpyate*—achieve.

TRANSLATION

For those whose minds are attached to the unmanifested, impersonal feature of the Supreme, advancement is very troublesome. To make progress in that discipline is always difficult for those who are embodied.

PURPORT

The group of transcendentalists who follow the path of the inconceivable, unmanifested, impersonal feature of the Supreme Lord are called *jñāna-yogīs*, and persons who are in full Kṛṣṇa consciousness, engaged in devotional service to the Lord, are called *bhakti-yogīs*. Now, here the difference between *jñāna-yoga* and *bhakti-yoga* is definitely expressed. The process of *jñāna-yoga*, although ultimately bringing one to the same goal, is very troublesome, whereas the path of *bhakti-yoga*, the process of being in direct service to the Supreme Personality of Godhead, is easier and is natural for the embodied soul. The individual soul is embodied since time immemorial. It is very difficult for him to simply theoretically understand that he is not the body. Therefore, the *bhakti-yogī* accepts the Deity of Kṛṣṇa as worshipable because there is some bodily conception fixed in the mind, which can thus be applied. Of course, worship of the Supreme Personality of Godhead in His form within the temple is not idol worship. There is evidence in the Vedic literature that worship may be *saguṇa* and *nirguṇa*—of the Supreme possessing or not possessing attributes. Worship of the Deity in the temple is *saguṇa* worship, for the Lord is represented by material qualities. But the form of the Lord, though represented by material qualities such as stone, wood, or oil paint, is not actually material. That is the absolute nature of the Supreme Lord.

A crude example may be given here. We may find some mailboxes on the street, and if we post our letters in those boxes, they will naturally go to their destination without difficulty. But any old box, or an imitation, which we may find somewhere, which is not authorized by the post office, will not do the work. Similarly, God has an authorized representation in the Deity form, which is called *arca-vigraha*. This *arca-vigraha* is an incarnation of the Supreme Lord. God will accept service through that form. The Lord is omnipotent and all-powerful; therefore, by His incarnation as *arca-vigraha*, He can accept the services of the devotee, just to make it convenient for the man in conditioned life.

So, for a devotee, there is no difficulty in approaching the Supreme immediately and directly, but for those who are following the impersonal way to spiritual realization, the path is difficult. They have to understand the unmanifested representation of the Supreme through such Vedic literatures as the *Upaniṣads*, and they have to learn the language, understand the nonperceptual feelings, and they have to realize all these processes. This is not very easy for a common man. A person in Kṛṣṇa consciousness, engaged in devotional service, simply by the guidance of the bona fide spiritual master, simply by offering regulative obeisances unto the Deity, simply by hearing the glories of the Lord, and simply by eating the remnants of foodstuffs offered to the Lord, realizes the Supreme Personality of Godhead very easily. There is no doubt that the impersonalists are unnecessarily taking a troublesome path with the risk of not realizing the Absolute Truth at the ultimate end. But the personalist, without any risk, trouble, or difficulty, approaches the Supreme Personality directly. A similar passage appears in *Śrīmad-Bhāgavatam*. It is stated there that if one has to ultimately surrender unto the Supreme Personality of Godhead (This surrendering process is called *bhakti*.), but instead takes the trouble to understand what is Brahman and what is not Brahman and spends his whole life in that way, the result is simply troublesome. Therefore it is advised here that one should not take up this troublesome path of self-realization because there is uncertainty in the ultimate result.

A living entity is eternally an individual soul, and if he wants to merge into the spiritual whole, he may accomplish the realization of the eternal and knowledgeable aspects of his original nature, but the blissful portion is not realized. By the grace of some devotee, such a transcendentalist, highly learned in the process of *jñāna-yoga*, may come to the point of *bhakti-yoga*, or devotional service. At that time, long practice in impersonalism also becomes a source of trouble, because he cannot give up the idea. Therefore an embodied soul is always in difficulty with the unmanifest, both at the time of practice and at the time of realization. Every living soul is partially independent, and one should know for certain that this unmanifested realization is against the nature of his spiritual blissful self. One should not take up this process. For every individual living entity the process of Kṛṣṇa consciousness, which entails full engagement in devotional service, is the best way. If one wants to ignore this devotional service, there is the danger of turning to atheism. Thus this process of centering attention on the unmanifested, the inconceivable, which is beyond the approach of the senses, as already expressed in this verse, should never be encouraged at any time, especially in this age. It is not advised by Lord Kṛṣṇa.

TEXTS 6-7

ये तु सर्वाणि कर्माणि मयि संन्यस्य मत्पराः ।
अनन्येनैव योगेन मां ध्यायन्त उपासते ॥ ६ ॥

तेषामहं समुद्धर्ता मृत्युसंसारसागरात् ।
भवामि न चिरात्पार्थ मय्यावेशितचेतसाम् ॥ ७ ॥

ye tu sarvāṇi karmāṇi
  mayi sannyasya mat-parāḥ
ananyenaiva yogena
  māṁ dhyāyanta upāsate

teṣām ahaṁ samuddhartā
  mṛtyu-saṁsāra-sāgarāt
bhavāmi na cirāt pārtha
  mayy āveśita-cetasām

ye—one who; tu—but; sarvāṇi—everything; karmāṇi—activities; mayi—
unto Me; sannyasya—giving up; mat-parāḥ—being attached to Me; ananyena
—without division; eva—certainly; yogena—by practice of such bhakti-yoga;
mām—unto Me; dhyāyantaḥ—meditating; upāsate—worship; teṣām—of
them; aham—I; samuddhartā—deliverer; mṛtyu—that; saṁsāra—material
existence; sāgarāt—from the ocean; bhavāmi—become; na cirāt—not a long
time; pārtha—O son of Pṛthā; mayi—unto Me; āveśita—fixed; cetasām—of
those whose minds are like that.

TRANSLATION

For one who worships Me, giving up all his activities unto Me and
being devoted to Me without deviation, engaged in devotional service and
always meditating upon Me, who has fixed his mind upon Me, O son of
Pṛthā, for him I am the swift deliverer from the ocean of birth and death.

PURPORT

It is explicitly stated here that the devotees are very fortunate to be
delivered very soon from material existence by the Lord. In pure devotional service one comes to the realization that God is great and that the
individual soul is subordinate to Him. His duty is to render service to the
Lord—if not, then he will render service to māyā.

As stated before, the Supreme Lord can only be appreciated by devotional service. Therefore, one should be fully devoted. One should fix his mind
fully on Kṛṣṇa in order to achieve Him. One should work only for Kṛṣṇa.
It does not matter in what kind of work one engages, but that work should
be done only for Kṛṣṇa. That is the standard of devotional service. The

devotee does not desire any achievement other than pleasing the Supreme Personality of Godhead. His life's mission is to please Kṛṣṇa, and he can sacrifice everything for Kṛṣṇa's satisfaction, just as Arjuna did in the Battle of Kurukṣetra. The process is very simple: one can devote himself in his occupation and engage at the same time in chanting Hare Kṛṣṇa, Hare Kṛṣṇa, Kṛṣṇa Kṛṣṇa, Hare Hare/ Hare Rāma, Hare Rāma, Rāma Rāma, Hare Hare. Such transcendental chanting attracts the devotee to the Personality of Godhead.

The Supreme Lord herein promises that He will without delay deliver a pure devotee thus engaged from the ocean of material existence. Those who are advanced in *yoga* practice can willfully transfer the soul to whatever planet they like by the *yoga* process, and others take the opportunity in various ways, but as far as the devotee is concerned, it is clearly stated here that the Lord Himself takes him. He does not need to wait to become very experienced in order to transfer himself to the spiritual sky.

In the *Varāha Purāṇa* this verse appears:

> *nayāmi paramaṁ sthānam arcirādi-gatiṁ vinā*
> *garuḍa-skandham āropya yatheccham anivāritaḥ*

The purport of this verse is that a devotee does not need to practice *aṣṭāṅga-yoga* in order to transfer his soul to the spiritual planets. The responsibility is taken by the Supreme Lord Himself. He clearly states here that He Himself becomes the deliverer. A child is completely cared for by his parents, and thus his position is secure. Similarly, a devotee does not need to endeavor to transfer himself by *yoga* practice to other planets. Rather, the Supreme Lord, by His great mercy, comes at once, riding on His bird carrier Garuḍa, and at once delivers the devotee from this material existence. Although a man who has fallen in the ocean may struggle very hard and may be very expert in swimming, he cannot save himself. But if someone comes and picks him up from the water, then he is easily rescued. Similarly, the Lord picks up the devotee from this material existence. One simply has to practice the easy process of Kṛṣṇa consciousness and fully engage himself in devotional service. Any intelligent man should always prefer the process of devotional service to all other paths. In the *Nārāyaṇīya* this is confirmed as follows:

> *yā vai sādhana-sampatti-puruṣārtha-catuṣṭaye*
> *tayā vinā tad-āpnoti naro nārāyaṇāśrayaḥ*

The purport of this verse is that one should not engage in the different processes of fruitive activity or cultivate knowledge by the mental speculative process. One who is devoted to the Supreme Personality can attain all the benefits derived from other yogic processes, speculation, rituals, sacrifices, charities, etc. That is the specific benediction of devotional service.

Simply by chanting the holy name of Kṛṣṇa—Hare Kṛṣṇa, Hare Kṛṣṇa, Kṛṣṇa Kṛṣṇa, Hare Hare / Hare Rāma, Hare Rāma, Rāma Rāma, Hare Hare—a devotee of the Lord can approach the supreme destination easily and happily, but this destination cannot be approached by any other process of religion.

The conclusion of *Bhagavad-gītā* is stated in the Eighteenth Chapter:

> *sarva-dharmān parityajya mām ekaṁ śaraṇaṁ vraja*
> *ahaṁ tvāṁ sarva-pāpebhyo mokṣayiṣyāmi mā śucaḥ.*

One should give up all other processes of self-realization and simply execute devotional service in Kṛṣṇa consciousness. That will enable one to reach the highest perfection of life. There is no need for one to consider the sinful actions of his past life because the Supreme Lord fully takes charge of him. Therefore one should not futilely try to deliver himself in spiritual realization. Let everyone take shelter of the supreme omnipotent Godhead Kṛṣṇa. That is the highest perfection of life.

TEXT 8

मय्येव मन आधत्स्व मयि बुद्धिं निवेशय ।
निवसिष्यसि मय्येव अत ऊर्ध्वं न संशयः ॥ ८ ॥

> *mayy eva mana ādhatsva*
> *mayi buddhiṁ niveśaya*
> *nivasiṣyasi mayy eva*
> *ata ūrdhvaṁ na saṁśayaḥ*

mayi—unto Me; *eva*—certainly; *manaḥ*—mind; *ādhatsva*—fix; *mayi*—upon Me; *buddhim*—intelligence; *niveśaya*—apply; *nivasiṣyasi*—you lead; *mayi*—unto Me; *eva*—certainly; *ataḥ*—therefore; *ūrdhvam*—up; *na*—never; *saṁśayaḥ*—doubt.

TRANSLATION

Just fix your mind upon Me, the Supreme Personality of Godhead, and engage all your intelligence in Me. Thus you will live in Me always, without a doubt.

PURPORT

One who is engaged in Lord Kṛṣṇa's devotional service lives in a direct relationship with the Supreme Lord, so there is no doubt that his position is transcendental from the very beginning. A devotee does not live on the material plane—he lives in Kṛṣṇa. The holy name of the Lord and the Lord are nondifferent; therefore when a devotee chants Hare Kṛṣṇa, Kṛṣṇa and His internal potency are dancing on the tongue of the devotee. When he offers Kṛṣṇa food, Kṛṣṇa directly accepts these eatables, and the devotee becomes Kṛṣṇa-ized by eating the remnants. One who does not engage in such service cannot understand how this is so, although this is a process recommended in the Gītā and in other Vedic literatures.

TEXT 9

अथ चित्तं समाधातुं न शक्नोषि मयि स्थिरम् ।
अभ्यासयोगेन ततो मामिच्छाप्तुं धनंजय ॥ ९ ॥

atha cittaṁ samādhātuṁ
na śaknoṣi mayi sthiram
abhyāsa-yogena tato
mām icchāptuṁ dhanañjaya

atha—if, therefore; *cittam*—mind; *samādhātam*—fixing; *na*—not; *śaknoṣi* —able; *mayi*—upon Me; *sthiram*—fixed; *abhyāsa*—practice; *yogena*—by devotional service; *tataḥ*—therefore; *mām*—Me; *icchā*—desire; *āptum*—to get; *dhanañjaya*—O Arjuna.

TRANSLATION

My dear Arjuna, O winner of wealth, if you cannot fix your mind upon Me without deviation, then follow the regulated principles of bhakti-yoga. In this way you will develop a desire to attain to Me.

PURPORT

In this verse, two different processes of *bhakti-yoga* are indicated. The first applies to one who has actually developed an attachment for Kṛṣṇa, the Supreme Personality of Godhead, by transcendental love. And the other is for one who has not developed an attachment for the Supreme Person by transcendental love. For this second class there are different prescribed rules and regulations, which one can follow to be ultimately elevated to the stage of attachment to Kṛṣṇa.

Bhakti-yoga is the purification of the senses. At the present moment in material existence the senses are always impure, being engaged in sense gratification. But, by the practice of *bhakti-yoga* these senses can become purified, and in the purified state they come directly in contact with the Supreme Lord. In this material existence, I may be engaged in some service to some master, but I don't really lovingly serve my master. I simply serve to get some money. And the master also is not in love; he takes service from me and pays me. So there is no question of love. But for spiritual life, one must be elevated to the pure stage of love. That stage of love can be achieved by practice of devotional service, performed with the present senses.

This love of God is now in a dormant state in everyone's heart. And, there, love of God is manifested in different ways, but it is contaminated by the material association. Now the material association has to be purified, and that dormant, natural love for Kṛṣṇa has to be revived. That is the whole process.

To practice the regulative principles of *bhakti-yoga* one should, under the guidance of an expert spiritual master, follow certain principles: one should rise early in the morning, take bath, enter the temple and offer prayers and chant Hare Kṛṣṇa, then collect flowers to offer to the Deity, cook foodstuffs to offer to the Deity, take *prasādam*, and so on. There are various rules and regulations which one should follow. And one should constantly hear *Bhagavad-gītā* and *Śrīmad-Bhāgavatam* from pure devotees. This practice can help anyone to rise to the level of love of God, and then he is sure of his progress into the spiritual kingdom of God. This practice of *bhakti-yoga*, under the rules and regulations, with the direction of a spiritual master, will surely bring one to the stage of love of God.

TEXT 10

अभ्यासेऽप्यसमर्थोऽसि मत्कर्मपरमो भव ।
मदर्थमपि कर्माणि कुर्वन्सिद्धिमवाप्स्यसि ॥ १० ॥

abhyāse 'py asamartho 'si
mat-karma-paramo bhava
mad-artham api karmāṇi
kurvan siddhim avāpsyasi

abhyāse—in the practice of; *api*—even; *asamarthaḥ*—unable; *asi*—you are; *mat-karma*—My work; *paramaḥ*—supreme; *bhava*—you become; *mat-artham*—for My sake; *api*—even though; *karmāṇi*—what; *kurvan*—performing; *siddhim*—perfection; *avāpsyasi*—achieve.

TRANSLATION

If you cannot practice the regulations of bhakti-yoga, then just try to work for Me, because by working for Me you will come to the perfect stage.

PURPORT

One who is not able even to practice the regulative principles of *bhakti-yoga*, under the guidance of a spiritual master, can still be drawn to this perfectional stage by working for the Supreme Lord. How to do this work has already been explained in the fifty-fifth verse of the Eleventh Chapter. One should be sympathetic to the propagation of Kṛṣṇa consciousness. There are many devotees who are engaged in the propagation of Kṛṣṇa consciousness, and they require help. So, even if one cannot directly practice the regulated principles of *bhakti-yoga*, he can try to help such work. Every endeavor requires land, capital, organization, and labor. Just as, in business, one requires a place to stay, some capital to use, some labor, and some organization to expand, so the same is required in the service of Kṛṣṇa. The only difference is that in materialism one works for sense gratification. The same work, however, can be performed for the satisfaction of Kṛṣṇa, and that is spiritual activity. If one has sufficient money, he can help in building an office or temple for propagating Kṛṣṇa consciousness. Or he can help with publications. There are various fields of activity, and one should be interested in such activities. If one cannot sacrifice the result of such activities, the same person can still sacrifice some percentage to propagate Kṛṣṇa consciousness. This voluntary service to the cause of Kṛṣṇa consciousness will help one to rise to a higher state of love for God, whereupon one becomes perfect.

TEXT 11

अथैतदप्यशक्तोऽसि कर्तुं मद्योगमाश्रितः ।
सर्वकर्मफलत्यागं ततः कुरु यतात्मवान् ॥ ११ ॥

athaitad apy aśakto 'si
kartuṁ mad-yogam āśritaḥ
sarva-karma-phala-tyāgaṁ
tataḥ kuru yatātmavān

atha—even though; *etat*—this; *api*—also; *aśaktaḥ*—unable; *asi*—you are; *kartum*—to perform; *mat*—unto Me; *yogam*—devotional service; *āśritaḥ*—refuge; *sarva-karma*—all activities; *phala*—result; *tyāgam*—for renunciation; *tataḥ*—therefore; *kuru*—do; *yata-ātmavan*—self-situated.

TRANSLATION

If, however, you are unable to work in this consciousness, then try to act giving up all results of your work and try to be self-situated.

PURPORT

It may be that one is unable to even sympathize with the activities of Kṛṣṇa consciousness because of social, familial or religious considerations or because of some other impediments. If one attaches himself directly to the activities of Kṛṣṇa consciousness, there may be objection from family members, or so many other difficulties. For one who has such a problem, it is advised that he sacrifice the accumulated result of his activities to some good cause. Such procedures are described in the Vedic rules. There are many descriptions of sacrifices and special functions of the *pumundi,* or special work in which the result of one's previous action may be applied. Thus one may gradually become elevated to the state of knowledge. It is also found that when one who is not even interested in the activities of Kṛṣṇa consciousness gives charity to some hospital or some other social institution, he gives up the hard-earned results of his activities. That is also recommended here because by the practice of giving up the fruits of one's activities one is sure to purify his mind gradually, and in that purified stage of mind one becomes able to understand Kṛṣṇa consciousness. Of course Kṛṣṇa consciousness is not dependent on any other experience because Kṛṣṇa consciousness itself can purify one's mind, but if there are impediments to Kṛṣṇa consciousness, one may try to give up the result of his action. In that respect, social service, community service, national service, sacrifice for one's country, etc., may be accepted so that some day one may come to the stage of pure devotional service to the Supreme Lord. In *Bhagavad-gītā* we find it is stated: *yataḥ pravṛttir bhūtānām:* If one decides to sacrifice for the supreme cause, even if he does not know that the supreme cause is Kṛṣṇa, he will come gradually to understand that Kṛṣṇa is the supreme cause by the sacrificial method.

TEXT 12

श्रेयो हि ज्ञानमभ्यासाज्ज्ञानाद्ध्यानं विशिष्यते ।
ध्यानात्कर्मफलत्यागस्त्यागाच्छान्तिरनन्तरम् ॥ १२ ॥

śreyo hi jñānam abhyāsāj
jñānād dhyānaṁ viśiṣyate
dhyānāt karma-phala-tyāgas
tyāgāc chāntir anantaram

śreyaḥ—better; *hi*—certainly; *jñānam*—knowledge; *abhyāsāt*—by practice; *jnānāt*—better than knowledge; *dhyānam*—meditation; *viśiṣyate*—especially considered; *dhyānāt*—from meditation; *karma-phala-tyāgaḥ*—renunciation of the results of fruitive action; *tyāgāt*—by such renunciation; *śāntiḥ*—peace; *anantaram*—thereafter.

TRANSLATION

If you cannot take to this practice, then engage yourself in the cultivation of knowledge. Better than knowledge, however, is meditation, and better than meditation is renunciation of the fruits of action, for by such renunciation one can attain peace of mind.

PURPORT

As mentioned in the previous verses, there are two kinds of devotional service: the way of regulated principles, and the way of full attachment in love to the Supreme Personality of Godhead. For those who are actually not able to follow the principles of Kṛṣṇa consciousness, it is better to cultivate knowledge because by knowledge one can be able to understand his real position. Gradually knowledge will develop to the point of meditation. By meditation one can be able to understand the Supreme Personality of Godhead by a gradual process. There are processes which make one understand that one himself is the Supreme, and that sort of meditation is preferred if one is unable to engage in devotional service. If one is not able to meditate in such a way, then there are prescribed duties, as enjoined in the Vedic literature, for the *brāhmaṇas, vaiśyas,* and *śūdras,* which we shall find in a later chapter of *Bhagavad-gītā.* But in all cases, one should give up the result or fruits of labor; this means to employ the result of *karma* for some good cause. In summary, to reach the Supreme Personality of Godhead, the highest goal, there are two processes: one process is by gradual development, and the other process is direct. Devotional service in Kṛṣṇa consciousness is the direct method, and the other method involves renouncing the fruits of one's activities. Then one can come to the stage of knowledge, then to the stage of meditation, then to the stage of understanding the Supersoul, and then to the stage of the Supreme Personality of Godhead. One may either take the step by step process or the direct path. The direct process is not possible for everyone; therefore the indirect process is also good. It is, however, to be understood that the indirect process is not recommended for Arjuna because he is already at the stage of loving devotional service to the Supreme Lord. It is for others who are not at this state; for them the gradual process of renunciation, knowledge, meditation and realization of the Supersoul and Brahman should be followed. But as far as *Bhagavad-gītā* is concerned, it is the direct method that is stressed. Everyone is advised to take to the direct method and surrender unto the Supreme Personality of Godhead, Kṛṣṇa.

TEXTS 13-14

अद्वेष्टा सर्वभूतानां मैत्रः करुण एव च ।
निर्ममो निरहंकारः समदुःखसुखः क्षमी ॥ १३ ॥

सन्तुष्टः सततं योगी यतात्मा दृढनिश्चयः ।
मय्यर्पितमनोबुद्धिर्यो मद्भक्तः स मे प्रियः ॥ १४ ॥

advesṭā sarva-bhūtānām
maitraḥ karuṇa eva ca
nirmamo nirahaṅkāraḥ
sama-duḥkha-sukhaḥ kṣamī

santuṣṭaḥ satataṁ yogī
yatātmā dṛḍha-niścayaḥ
mayy arpita-mano-buddhir
yo mad-bhaktaḥ sa me priyaḥ

adveṣṭā—not envious; *sarva-bhūtānām*—for all living entities; *maitraḥ*—friendly; *karuṇaḥ*—kindly; *eva*—certainly; *ca*—also; *nirmamaḥ*—with no sense of proprietorship; *nirahaṅkāraḥ*—without false ego; *sama*—equally; *duḥkhaḥ*—distress; *sukhaḥ*—happiness; *kṣamī*—forgiving; *santuṣṭaḥ*—satisfied; *satatam*—satisfied; *yogī*—engaged in devotion; *yatā-ātmā*—endeavoring; *dṛḍhaniścayaḥ*—with determination; *mayi*—upon Me; *arpita*—engaged; *manaḥ*—mind; *buddhiḥ*—intelligent; *yaḥ*—one who; *mat-bhaktaḥ*—My devotee; *saḥ me priyaḥ*—he is dear to Me.

TRANSLATION

One who is not envious but who is a kind friend to all living entities, who does not think himself a proprietor, who is free from false ego and equal both in happiness and distress, who is always satisfied and engaged in devotional service with determination and whose mind and intelligence are in agreement with Me—he is very dear to Me.

PURPORT

Coming again to the point of pure devotional service, the Lord is describing the transcendental qualifications of a pure devotee in these two verses. A pure devotee is never disturbed in any circumstances. Nor is he envious of anyone. Nor does a devotee become his enemy's enemy; he thinks that one is acting as his enemy due to his own past misdeeds. Thus it is better to suffer than to protest. In the *Śrīmad-Bhāgavatam* it is stated: *tat te 'nukampāṁ su-samīkṣyamāṇo.* Whenever a devotee is in distress or has fallen into difficulty, he thinks that it is the Lord's mercy upon him. He thinks: "Thanks to my past misdeeds I should suffer far, far greater than I am suffering now. So it is by the mercy of the Supreme Lord that I am not getting all the punishment I am due. I am just getting a little, by the mercy of the Supreme Personality of Godhead." Therefore he is always calm, quiet and patient, despite many distressful conditions. A devotee is also always kind to everyone, even to his enemy. *Nirmama* means that a devotee does not attach much importance to the peace and trouble pertaining to the body because he knows perfectly well that he is not the material body. He does not identify with the body; therefore he is freed from the conception of false ego and is equiposed both in happiness and distress. He is tolerant, and he is satisfied with whatever comes by the grace of the Supreme Lord. He does not endeavor much to achieve something with great difficulty; therefore he is always joyful. He is a completely perfect mystic because he is fixed in the instructions received from the spiritual master, and because his senses are controlled, he is determined. He is not swayed by false argument because no one can lead him from the fixed determination of devotional service. He is fully conscious that Kṛṣṇa is the eternal Lord, so no one can disturb him. All his qualifications enable him to depend entirely on the Supreme Lord. Such a standard of devotional service is undoubtably very rare, but a devotee becomes situated in that stage by following the regulative principles of devotional service. Furthermore, the Lord says that such a devotee is very dear to Him, for the Lord is always pleased with all his activities in full Kṛṣṇa consciousness.

TEXT 15

यस्मान्नोद्विजते लोको लोकान्नोद्विजते च यः ।
हर्षामर्षभयोद्वेगैर्मुक्तो यः स च मे प्रियः ॥ १५ ॥

yasmān nodvijate loko
lokān nodvijate ca yaḥ
harṣāmarṣa-bhayodvegair
mukto yaḥ sa ca me priyaḥ

yasmāt—from whom; na—never; udvijate—agitates; lokaḥ—persons; lokāt—persons; na—never; advijate—disturbed; ca—also; yaḥ—anyone; harṣa—happiness; amarṣa—distress; bhaya—fearfulness; udvegaiḥ—with anxiety; muktaḥ—freed; yaḥ—who; saḥ—anyone; ca—also; me—My; priyaḥ—very dear.

TRANSLATION

He for whom no one is put into difficulty and who is not dirturbed by anxiety, who is steady in happiness and distress, is very dear to Me.

PURPORT

A few of a devotee's qualifications are further being described. No one is put into difficulty, anxiety, fearfulness, or dissatisfaction by such a devotee. Since a devotee is kind to everyone, he does not act in such a way to put others into anxiety. At the same time, if others try to put a devotee into anxiety, he is not disturbed. It is by the grace of the Lord that he is so practiced that he is not disturbed by any outward disturbance. Actually because a devotee is always engrossed in Kṛṣṇa consciousness and engaged in devotional service, all such material circumstances cannot woo him. Generally a materialistic person becomes very happy when there is something for his sense gratification and his body, but when he sees that others have something for their sense gratification and he hasn't, he is sorry and envious. When he is expecting some retaliation from an enemy, he is in a state of fear, and when he cannot successfully execute something he becomes dejected. But a devotee is always transcendental to all these disturbances; therefore he is very dear to Kṛṣṇa.

TEXT 16

अनपेक्षः शुचिर्दक्ष उदासीनो गतव्यथः ।
सर्वारम्भपरित्यागी यो मद्भक्तः स मे प्रियः ॥ १६ ॥

anapekṣaḥ śucir dakṣa
udāsīno gata-vyathaḥ
sarvārambha-parityāgī
yo mad-bhaktaḥ sa me priyaḥ

anapekṣaḥ—neutral; *śuciḥ*—pure; *dakṣaḥ*—expert; *udāsīnaḥ*—free from care; *gata-vyathaḥ*—freed from all distress; *sarva-ārambha*—all endeavors; *parityāgī*—renouncer; *yaḥ*—anyone; *mat-bhaktaḥ*—My devotee; *saḥ*—he; *me*—Me; *priyaḥ*—very dear

TRANSLATION

A devotee who is not dependent on the ordinary course of activities, who is pure, expert, without cares, free from all pains, and who does not strive for some result, is very dear to Me.

PURPORT

Money may be offered to a devotee, but he should not struggle to acquire it. If automatically, by the grace of the Supreme, money comes to him, he is not agitated. Naturally a devotee takes bath at least twice in a day and rises early in the morning for devotional service. Thus he is naturally clean both inwardly and outwardly. A devotee is always expert because he fully knows the sense of all activities of life, and he is convinced of the authoritative scriptures. A devotee never takes the part of a particular party; therefore he is carefree. He is never pained because he is free from all designations; he knows that his body is a designation, so if there are some bodily pains, he is free. The pure devotee does not endeavor for anything which is against the principles of devotional service. For example, constructing a big building requires great energy, and a devotee does not take to such business if it does not benefit him by advancing his devotional service. He may construct a temple for the Lord, and for that he may take all kinds of anxiety, but he does not construct a big house for his personal relations.

TEXT 17

यो न हृष्यति न द्वेष्टि न शोचति न काङ्क्षति ।
शुभाशुभपरित्यागी भक्तिमान्यः स मे प्रियः ॥ १७ ॥

yo na hṛṣyati na dveṣṭi
na śocati na kāṅkṣati
śubhāśubha-parityāgī
bhaktimān yaḥ sa me priyaḥ

yaḥ—one who; *na*—never; *hṛṣyati*—takes pleasure; *na*—never; *dveṣṭi*—grieves; *na*—never; *śocati*—laments; *na*—never; *kāṅkṣati*—desires; *śubha*—auspicious; *aśubha*—inauspicious; *parityāgī*—renouncer; *bhaktimān*—devotee; *yaḥ*—one who; *saḥ*—he is; *me*—My; *priyaḥ*—dear.

TRANSLATION

One who neither grasps pleasure or grief, who neither laments nor desires, and who renounces both auspicious and inauspicious things, is very dear to Me.

PURPORT

A pure devotee is neither happy nor distressed over material gain and loss, nor is he very much anxious to get a son or disciple, nor is he distressed by not getting them. If he loses anything which is very dear to him, he does not lament. Similarly, if he does not get what he desires, he is not distressed. He is transcendental in the face of all kinds of auspicious, in-auspicious and sinful activities. He is prepared to accept all kinds of risks for the satisfaction of the Supreme Lord. Nothing is an impediment in the discharge of his devotional service. Such a devotee is very dear to Kṛṣṇa.

TEXTS 18-19

समः शत्रौ च मित्रे च तथा मानापमानयोः ।
शीतोष्णसुखदुःखेषु समः सङ्गविवर्जितः ॥ १८ ॥

तुल्यनिन्दास्तुतिर्मौनी संतुष्टो येन केन चित् ।
अनिकेतः स्थिरमतिर्भक्तिमान्मे प्रियो नरः ॥ १९ ॥

samaḥ śatrau ca mitre ca
tathā mānāpamānayoḥ
śītoṣṇa-sukha-duḥkheṣu
samaḥ saṅga-vivarjitaḥ

tulya-nindā-stutir maunī
santuṣṭo yena kenacit
aniketaḥ sthira-matir
bhaktimān me priyo naraḥ

samaḥ—equal; śatrau—to the enemy; ca—also; mitre—to friends; ca—also; tatha—so; māna—honor; apamānayoḥ—dishonor; śīta—cold; uṣṇa—heat; sukha—happiness; duḥkheṣu—distress; samaḥ—equiposed; saṅga-vivarjitaḥ—free from all association; tulya—equal; nindā—defamation; stutiḥ—repute; maunī—silent; santuṣṭaḥ—satisfied; yena—somehow; kena—or other; cit—if; aniketaḥ—having no residence; sthira—fixed; matiḥ—determination; bhaktimān—engaged in devotion; me—My; priyaḥ—dear; naraḥ—a man.

TRANSLATION

One who is equal to friends and enemies, who is equiposed in honor and dishonor, heat and cold, happiness and distress, fame and infamy, who is always free from contamination, always silent and satisfied with any-thing, who doesn't care for any residence, who is fixed in knowledge and engaged in devotional service, is very dear to Me.

PURPORT

A devotee is always free from all bad association. Sometimes one is praised and sometimes one is defamed; that is the nature of human society. But a devotee is always transcendental to artificial fame and infamy, distress or happiness. He is very patient. He does not speak of anything but the topics about Kṛṣṇa; therefore he is called silent. Silent does not mean that one should not speak; silent means that one should not speak nonsense. One should speak only of essentials, and the most essential speech for the devotee is to speak of the Supreme Lord. He is happy in all conditions; sometimes he may get very palatable foodstuffs, sometimes not, but he is satisfied. Nor does he care for any residential facility. He may sometimes live underneath a tree, and he may sometimes live in a very palatial building; he is attracted to neither. He is called fixed because he is fixed in his determination and knowledge. We may find some repetition in the descriptions of the qualifications of a devotee, but this is just to give an illustration of the fact that a devotee must acquire all these qualifications. Without good qualifications, one cannot be a pure devotee. One who is not a devotee has no good qualification. One who wants to be recognized as a devotee should develop the good qualifications. Of course he does not extraneously endeavor to acquire these qualifications, but engagement in Kṛṣṇa consciousness and devotional service automatically helps him develop them.

TEXT 20

ये तु धर्म्यामृतमिदं यथोक्तं पर्युपासते ।
श्रद्दधाना मत्परमा भक्तास्तेऽतीव मे प्रियाः ॥ २० ॥

ye tu dharmāmṛtam idaṁ
yathoktaṁ paryupāsate
śraddadhānā mat-paramā
bhaktās te 'tīva me priyāḥ

ye—one who; *tu*—but; *dharmya*—generosity; *amṛtam*—understanding; *idam*—this; *yathā*—as; *uktam*—said; *paryupāsate*—completely engages; *sraddadhānāḥ*—with faith; *mat-paramāḥ*—taking the Supreme Lord as everything; *bhaktāḥ*—devotees; *te*—such persons; *atīva*—very, very; *me*—Me; *priyāḥ*—dear.

TRANSLATION

He who follows this imperishable path of devotional service and who completely engages himself with faith, making Me the supreme goal, is very, very dear to Me.

PURPORT

In this chapter the religion of eternal engagement, the explanation of the process of transcendental service for approaching the Supreme Lord, is given. This process is very dear to the Lord, and He accepts a person who is engaged in such a process. The question who is better—one who is engaged in the path of impersonal Brahman or one who is engaged in the personal service of the Supreme Personality of Godhead—was raised by Arjuna, and the Lord replied to him so explicitly that there is no doubt that devotional service to the Personality of Godhead is the best of all processes of spiritual rea.lization. In other words, in this chapter it is decided that through good association, one develops attachment for pure devotional service and thereby accepts a bona fide spiritual master and from him begins to hear and chant and observe the regulative principles of devotional service with faith, attachment and devotion and thus becomes engaged in the transcendental service of the Lord. This path is recommended in this chapter; therefore there is no doubt that devotional service is the only absolute path for self-realization, for the attainment of the Supreme Personality of Godhead. The impersonal conception of the Supreme Absolute Truth, as described in this chapter, is recommended only up to the time one surrenders himself for self-realization. In other words, as long as one does not have the chance to associate with a pure devotee, the impersonal conception may be beneficial. In the impersonal conception of the Absolute Truth one works without fruitive result, meditates and cultivates knowledge to understand spirit and matter. This is necessary as long as one is not in the association of a pure devotee. Fortunately, if one develops directly a desire to engage in Kṛṣṇa consciousness in pure devotional service, he does not need to undergo step by step improvements in spiritual realization. Devotional service, as described in the middle six chapters of *Bhagavad-gītā,* is more congenial. One need not bother about materials to keep body and soul together because by the grace of the Lord everything is carried out automatically.

Thus end the Bhaktivedanta Purports to the Twelfth Chapter of the Śrīmad-Bhagavad-gītā *in the matter of Devotional Service.*

CHAPTER THIRTEEN

Nature, the Enjoyer, and Consciousness

TEXTS 1-2

अर्जुन उवाच ।
प्रकृतिं पुरुषं चैव क्षेत्रं क्षेत्रज्ञमेव च ।
एतद्वेदितुमिच्छामि ज्ञानं ज्ञेयं च केशव ॥ १ ॥

श्रीभगवानुवाच ।
इदं शरीरं कौन्तेय क्षेत्रमित्यभिधीयते ।
एतद्यो वेत्ति तं प्राहुः क्षेत्रज्ञ इति तद्विदः ॥ २ ॥

arjuna uvāca
prakṛtiṁ puruṣaṁ caiva
  kṣetraṁ kṣetra-jñam eva ca
etad veditum icchāmi
  jñānaṁ jñeyaṁ ca keśava

śrī-bhagavān uvāca
idaṁ śarīraṁ kaunteya
  kṣetram ity abhidhīyate

619

etad yo vetti taṁ prāhuḥ
kṣetra-jña iti tad-vidaḥ

arjunaḥ uvāca—Arjuna said; *prakṛtim*—nature; *puruṣam*—the enjoyer; *ca*—also; *eva*—certainly; *kṣetram*—body; *kṣetrajñam*—knower of the body; *eva*—certainly; *ca*—also; *etat*—all this; *veditum*—to understand; *icchāmi*—I wish; *jñānam*—knowledge; *jñeyam*—the object of knowledge; *ca*—also; *keśava*—O Kṛṣṇa; *śrī bhagavān uvāca*—the Personality of Godhead said; *idam*—this; *śarīram*—body; *kaunteya*—O son of Kuntī; *kṣetram*—the field; *iti*—thus; *abhidhīyate*—is called; *etat*—this; *yaḥ*—anyone; *vetti*—knows; *tam* —him; *prāhuḥ*—is called; *kṣetrajñaḥ*—knower of the body; *iti*—thus; *tat-vidaḥ*—one who knows.

TRANSLATION

Arjuna said: O my dear Kṛṣṇti, I wish to know about prakṛti [nature], Puruṣa [the enjoyer], and the field and the knower of the field, and of knowledge and the end of knowledge. The Blessed Lord then said: This body, O son of Kuntī, is called the field, and one who knows this body is called the knower of the field.

PURPORT

Arjuna was inquisitive about *prakṛti* or nature, *puruṣa*, the enjoyer, *kṣetra*, the field, *kṣetrajña*, its knower, and of knowledge and the object of knowledge. When he inquired about all these, Kṛṣṇa said that this body is called the field and that one who knows this body is called the knower of the field. This body is the field of activity for the conditioned soul. The conditioned soul is entrapped in material existence, and he attempts to lord over material nature. And so, according to his capacity to dominate material nature, he gets a field of activity. That field of activity is the body. And what is the body? The body is made of senses. The conditioned soul wants to enjoy sense gratification, and, according to his capacity to enjoy sense gratification, he is offered a body, or field of activity. Therefore the body is called *kṣetra,* or the field of activity for the conditioned soul. Now, the person who does not identify himself with the body is called *kṣetrajña,* the knower of the field. It is not very difficult to understand the difference between the field and its knower, the body and the knower of the body. Any person can consider that from childhood to old age he undergoes so many changes of body and yet is still one person, remaining. Thus there is a difference between the knower of the field of activities and the actual field of activities. A living conditioned soul can thus understand that he is different from the body. It is described in the beginning—*dehe 'smin*—that the living entity is within the body and that the body is changing from childhood to boyhood and from boyhood to youth and from youth to old age, and the person who owns the body knows that the body is changing. The owner is distinctly *kṣetrajña*. Sometimes we understand that I am happy, I am mad, I am a woman, I am a dog, I am a cat: these are the knowers. The knower is different from the field. Although we use many articles—our clothes, etc.—we know that we are different from the things used. Similarly, we also understand by a little contemplation that we are different from the body.

In the first six chapters of *Bhagavad-gītā*, the knower of the body, the living entity, and the position by which he can understand the Supreme Lord are described. In the middle six chapters of the *Gītā*, the Supreme Personality of Godhead and the relationship between the individual soul and the Supersoul in regard to devotional service are described. The superior position of the Supreme Personality of Godhead and the subordinate position of the individual soul are definitely defined in these chapters. The living entities are subordinate under all circumstances, but in their forgetfulness they are suffering. When enlightened by pious activities, they approach the Supreme Lord in different capacities—as the distressed, those in want of money, the inquisitive, and those in search of knowledge. That is also described. Now, starting with the Thirteenth Chapter, how the living entity comes into contact with material nature, how he is delivered by the Supreme Lord through the different methods of fruitive activities, cultivation of knowledge, and the discharge of devotional service are explained. Although the living entity is completely different from the material body, he somehow becomes related. This also is explained.

TEXT 3

क्षेत्रज्ञं चापि मां विद्धि सर्वक्षेत्रेषु भारत ।
क्षेत्रक्षेत्रज्ञयोर्ज्ञानं यत्तज्ज्ञानं मतं मम ॥ ३ ॥

kṣetra-jñaṁ cāpi māṁ viddhi
sarva-kṣetreṣu bhārata
kṣetra-kṣetrajñayor jñānaṁ
yat taj jñānaṁ mataṁ mama

kṣetrajñam—the knower; *ca*—also; *api*—certainly; *mām*—Me; *viddhi*—
know; *sarva*—all; *kṣetreṣu*—in bodily fields; *bhārata*—O son of Bharata;
kṣetra—field of activities (the body); *kṣetrajñayoḥ*—the knower of the
field; *jñānam*—knowledge; *yat*—that which is taught; *tat*—that; *jñānam*—
knowledge; *matam*—opinion; *mama*—that.

TRANSLATION

O scion of Bharata, you should understand that I am also the knower
in all bodies, and to understand this body and its owner is called
knowledge. That is My opinion.

PURPORT

While discussing the subject of this body and the owner of the body,
the soul and the Supersoul, we shall find three different topics of study:
the Lord, the living entity, and matter. In every field of activities, in every
body, there are two souls: the individual soul and the Supersoul. Because
the Supersoul is the plenary expansion of the Supreme Personality of Godhead, Kṛṣṇa, Kṛṣṇa says, "I am also the knower, but I am not the individual
owner of the body. I am the superknower. I am present in every body as
the Paramātmā, or Supersoul."

One who studies the subject matter of the field of activity and the
knower of the field very minutely, in terms of this *Bhagavad-gītā,* can
attain to knowledge.

The Lord says: "I am the knower of the field of activities in every
individual body." The individual may be the knower of his own body, but
he is not in knowledge of other bodies. The Supreme Personality of Godhead, who is present as the Supersoul in all bodies, knows everything
about all bodies. He knows all the different bodies of all the various species
of life. A citizen may know everything about his patch of land, but the
king knows not only his palace but all the properties possessed by the
individual citizens. Similarly, one may be the proprietor of the body
individually, but the Supreme Lord is the proprietor of all bodies. The
king is the original proprietor of the kingdom, and the citizen is the
secondary proprietor. Similarly, the Supreme Lord is the supreme proprietor of all bodies.

The body consists of the senses. The Supreme Lord is Hṛṣīkeśa, which
means controller of the senses. He is the original controller of the senses,
just as the king is the original controller of all the activities of the state,

and the citizens are secondary controllers. The Lord also says: "I am also the knower." This means that He is the superknower; the individual soul knows only his particular body. In the Vedic literature, it is stated as follows:

> kṣetrāṇi hi śarīrāṇi bījaṁ cāpi śubhāśubhe
> tāni vetti sa yogātmā tataḥ kṣetrajña ucyate.

This body is called the *kṣetra*, and within it dwells the owner of the body and the Supreme Lord who knows both the body and the owner of the body. Therefore He is called the knower of all fields. The distinction between the field of activities, the owner of activities and the supreme owner of activities is described as follows. Perfect knowledge of the constitution of the body, the constitution of the individual soul, and the constitution of the Supersoul is known in terms of Vedic literature as *jñānam*. That is the opinion of Kṛṣṇa. To understand both the soul and the Supersoul as one yet distinct is knowledge. One who does not understand the field of activity and the knower of activity is not in perfect knowledge. One has to understand the position of *prakṛti*, nature, and *puruṣa*, the enjoyer of the nature, and *īśvara*, the knower who dominates or controls nature and the individual soul. One should not confuse the three in their different capacities. One should not confuse the painter, the painting and the easel. This material world, which is the field of activities, is nature, and the enjoyer of nature is the living entity, and above them both is the supreme controller, the Personality of Godhead. It is stated in the Vedic language: "*bhoktā bhogyaṁ preritāraṁ ca matvā sarvaṁ proktaṁ tri-vidhaṁ brahmam etat.*" There are three Brahman conceptions: *prakṛti* is Brahman as the field of activities, and the *jīva* (individual soul) is also Brahman and is trying to control material nature, and the controller of both of them is also Brahman, but He is the factual controller.

In this chapter it will be also explained that out of the two knowers, one is fallible and the other is infallible. One is superior and the other is subordinate. One who understands the two knowers of the field to be one and the same contradicts the Supreme Personality of Godhead who states here very clearly that "I am also the knower of the field of activity." One who misunderstands a rope to be a serpent is not in knowledge. There are different kinds of bodies, and there are different owners of the bodies. Because each individual soul has his individual capacity of lording it over material nature, there are different bodies. But the Supreme also is present in them as the controller. The word *ca* is significant, for it indicates the total number of bodies. That is the opinion of Śrīla Baladeva Vidyābhūṣaṇa: Kṛṣṇa is the Supersoul present in each and every body apart from the individual soul. And Kṛṣṇa explicitly says here that the Supersoul is the controller of both the field of activities and the finite enjoyer.

TEXT 4

तत्क्षेत्रं यच्च यादृक् च यद्विकारि यतश्च यत् ।
स च यो यत्प्रभावश्च तत्समासेन मे शृणु ॥ ४ ॥

tat kṣetraṁ yac ca yādṛk ca
yad-vikāri yataś ca yat
sa ca yo yat-prabhāvaś ca
tat samāsena me śṛṇu

tat—that; kṣetram—field of activities; yat—as; ca—also; yādṛk—as it is; ca—also; yat—what is; vikāri—changes; yataḥ—from which; ca—also; yat—one; saḥ—he; ca—also; yaḥ—one; yat—which; prabhāvaḥ ca—influence also; tat—that; samāsena—in detail; me—from Me; śṛṇu—understand.

TRANSLATION

Now please hear My brief description of this field of activity and how it is constituted, what its changes are, whence it is produced, who that knower of the field of activities is, and what his influences are.

PURPORT

The Lord is describing the field of activities and the knower of the field of activities in their constitutional positions. One has to know how this body is constituted, the materials of which this body is made, under whose control this body is working, how the changes are taking place, wherefrom the changes are coming, what the causes are, what the reasons are, what the ultimate goal of the individual is, and what the actual form of the individual soul is. One should also know the distinction between the individual living soul and the Supersoul, the different influences, their potentials, etc. One just has to understand this Bhagavad-gītā directly from the description given by the Supreme Personality of Godhead, and all this will be clarified. But one should be careful not to consider the Supreme Personality of Godhead in every body and individual soul to be the *jīva*. This is something like equalizing the potent and the impotent.

TEXT 5

ऋषिभिर्बहुधा गीतं छन्दोभिर्विविधैः पृथक् ।
ब्रह्मसूत्रपदैश्चैव हेतुमद्भिर्विनिश्चितैः ॥ ५ ॥

> *ṛṣibhir bahudhā gītam*
> *chandobhir vividhaiḥ pṛthak*
> *brahma-sūtra-padais caiva*
> *hetumadbhir viniścitaiḥ*

ṛṣibhiḥ—by the wise sages; *bahudhā*—in many ways; *gītam*—described; *chandobhiḥ*—Vedic hymns; *vividhaiḥ*—in various; *pṛthak*—variously; *brahma-sūtra*—the Vedānta; *padaiḥ*—aphorism; *ca*—also; *eva*—certainly; *hetumadbhiḥ*—with cause and effect; *viniścitaiḥ*—ascertain.

TRANSLATION

That knowledge of the field of activities and of the knower of activities is described by various sages in various Vedic writings—especially in the Vedānta-sūtra—and is presented with all reasoning as to cause and effect.

PURPORT

The Supreme Personality of Godhead, Kṛṣṇa, is the highest authority in explaining this knowledge. Still, as a matter of course, learned scholars and standard authorities always give evidence from previous authorities. Kṛṣṇa is explaining this most controversial point regarding the duality and non-duality of the soul and the Supersoul by referring to Scriptures, the *Vedānta*, which are accepted as authority. First, He says, this is according to different sages. As far as the sages are concerned, besides Himself, Vyāsadeva, the author of the *Vedānta-sūtra*, is a great sage, and in the *Vedānta-sūtra* duality is perfectly explained. And Vyāsadeva's father, Parāśara, was also a great sage, and he writes in his books of religiosity: "*aham tvaṁ ca athānye...*" "We—you, I and various other living entities—are all transcendental, although in material bodies. Now we are fallen into the ways of the three modes of material nature according to our different *karma*. As such, some are on higher levels, and some are in the lower nature. The higher and lower natures exist due to ignorance and are being manifested in an infinite number of living entities. But the Supersoul, which is infallible, is uncontaminated by the three qualities of nature and is transcendental." Similarly, in the original *Vedas*, a distinction between the soul, the Supersoul and the body is made, especially in the *Kaṭha Upaniṣad*.

There is a manifestation of the Supreme Lord's energy known as *annamaya* by which one depends simply upon food for existence. This is a materialistic realization of the Supreme. Then there is *prāṇamaya*; this means that after realizing the Supreme Absolute Truth in foodstuff, one can realize the Absolute Truth in the living symptoms, or life forms. In *jñānamaya* the living symptom develops to the point of thinking, feeling, and willing. Then there is Brahman realization and the realization called *vijñānamaya* by which the living entity's mind and life symptoms are distinguished from the living entity himself. The next and supreme stage is *ānandamaya*, realization of the all-blissful nature. Thus there are five stages of Brahman realization, which is called *brahma puccham*. Out of these the first three—*annamaya*, *prāṇamaya*, and *jñānamaya*—involve the fields of activities of the living entities. Transcendental to all these fields of activities is the Supreme Lord, who is called *ānandamaya*. In the *Vedānta-sūtra* also the Supreme is called *ānandamayo 'bhyāsāt*. The Supreme Personality of Godhead is by nature full of joy, and to enjoy His transcendental bliss, He expands into *vijñānamaya, prāṇamaya, jñānamaya*, and *annamaya*. In this field of activities the living entity is considered to be the enjoyer, and different from him is the *ānandamaya*. That means that if the living entity decides to enjoy, in dovetailing himself with the *ānandamaya*, then he becomes perfect. This is the real picture of the Supreme Lord, as supreme knower of the field, the living entity, as subordinate knower, and the nature of the field of activities.

TEXTS 6-7

महाभूतान्यहङ्कारो बुद्धिरव्यक्तमेव च ।
इन्द्रियाणि दशैकं च पञ्च चेन्द्रियगोचराः ॥ ६ ॥

इच्छा द्वेषः सुखं दुःखं सङ्घातश्चेतना धृतिः ।
एतत्क्षेत्रं समासेन सविकारमुदाहृतम् ॥ ७ ॥

mahā-bhūtāny ahaṅkāro
buddhir avyaktam eva ca
indriyāṇi daśaikaṁ ca
pañca cendriya-gocarāḥ

icchā dveṣaḥ sukhaṁ duḥkhaṁ
saṅghātaś cetanā dhṛtiḥ
etat kṣetraṁ samāsena
sa-vikāram udāhṛtam

mahā-bhūtāni—great elements; ahaṅkāraḥ—false ego; buddhiḥ—intelligence; avyaktam—the unmanifested; eva—certainly; ca—also; indriyāṇi—senses ; daśa ekam—eleven; ca—also; pañca—five; ca—also; indriya-gocarāḥ—objects of the senses; icchā—desire; dveṣaḥ—hatred; sukham—happiness; duḥkham—distress; saṅghataḥ—the aggregate; cetanā—living symptoms; dhṛtiḥ—conviction; etat—all this; kṣetram—field of activities; samāsena—in summary; sa-vikāram—interaction; udāhṛtam—exemplified.

TRANSLATION

The five great elements, false ego, intelligence, the unmanifested, the ten senses, the mind, the five sense objects, desire, hatred, happiness, distress, the aggregate, the life symptoms, and convictions—all these are considered, in summary, to be the field of activities and its interactions.

PURPORT

From all the authoritative statements of the great sages, the Vedic hymns and the aphorisms of the Vedānta-sūtra, the components of this world are earth, water, fire, air and ether. These are the five great elements (mahābhūta). Then there are false ego, intelligence and the unmanifested stage of the three modes of nature. Then there are five senses for acquiring knowledge: the eyes, ears, nose, tongue and touch. Then five working senses: voice, legs, hands, the anus and the genitals. Then, above the senses, there is the mind, which is within and which can be called the sense within. Therefore, including the mind, there are eleven senses altogether. Then there are the five objects of the senses: smell, taste, warmth, touch and sound. Now the aggregate of these twenty-four elements is called the field of activity. If one makes an analytical study of these twenty-four subjects, then he can very well understand the field of activity. Then there is desire, hatred, pleasure and pain, which are interactions, representations of the five great elements in the gross body. The living symptoms, represented by consciousness and conviction, are the manifestation of the subtle body—mind, ego and intelligence. These subtle elements are included within the field of activities.

The five great elements are a gross representation of the subtle false ego. They are a representation in the material conception. Consciousness is represented by intelligence, of which the unmanifested stage is the three modes of material nature. The unmanifested three modes of material nature is called *pradhāna*.

One who desires to know the twenty-four elements in detail along with their interactions should study the philosophy in more detail. In *Bhagavad-gītā*, a summary only is given.

The body is the representation of all these factors, and there are changes of the body, which are six in number: the body is born, it grows, it stays, it produces by-products, then begins to decay, and at the last stage it vanishes. Therefore the field is a nonpermanent material thing. However, the *kṣetrajña*, the knower of the field, its proprietor, is different.

TEXTS 8-12

अमानित्वमदम्भित्वमहिंसा क्षान्तिरार्जवम् ।
आचार्योपासनं शौचं स्थैर्यमात्मविनिग्रहः ॥ ८ ॥

इन्द्रियार्थेषु वैराग्यमनहङ्कार एव च ।
जन्ममृत्युजराव्याधिदुःखदोषानुदर्शनम् ॥ ९ ॥

असक्तिरनभिष्वङ्गः पुत्रदारगृहादिषु ।
नित्यं च समचित्तत्वमिष्टानिष्टोपपत्तिषु ॥ १० ॥

मयि चानन्ययोगेन भक्तिरव्यभिचारिणी ।
विविक्तदेशसेवित्वमरतिर्जनसंसदि ॥ ११ ॥

अध्यात्मज्ञाननित्यत्वं तत्त्वज्ञानार्थदर्शनम् ।
एतज्ज्ञानमिति प्रोक्तमज्ञानं यदतोऽन्यथा ॥ १२ ॥

amānitvam adambhitvam
ahimsā kṣāntir ārjavam
ācāryopāsanaṁ śaucaṁ
sthairyam ātma-vinigrahaḥ

indriyārtheṣu vairāgyam
anahaṅkāra eva ca
janma-mṛtyu-jarā-vyādhi-
duḥkha-doṣānudarśanam

asaktir anabhiṣvaṅgaḥ
putra-dāra-gṛhādiṣu
nityaṁ ca sama-cittatvam
iṣṭāniṣṭopapattiṣu

mayi cānanya-yogena
bhaktir avyabhicāriṇī
vivikta-deśa-sevitvam
aratir jana-saṁsadi

adhyātma-jñāna-nityatvaṁ
tattva-jñānārtha-darśanam
etaj jñānam iti proktam
ajñānaṁ yad ato 'nyathā

amānitvam—humility; adambhitvam—pridelessness; ahiṁsā—nonviolence; kṣāntiḥ—tolerance; ārjavam—simplicity; ācārya-upāsanam—approaching a bona fide spiritual master; śaucam—cleanliness; sthairyam—steadfastness; ātma-vinigrahaḥ—control; indriya-artheṣu—in the matter of the senses; vairāgyam—renunciation; anahaṅkāraḥ—being without false egoism; eva—certainly; ca—also; janma—birth; mṛtyu—death; jarā—old age; vyādhi—disease; duḥkha—distress; doṣa—fault; anudarśanam—observing; asaktiḥ—without attachment; anabhiṣvaṅgaḥ—without association; putra—son; dāra—wife; gṛha-ādiṣu—home, etc.; nityam—eternal; ca—also; sama-cittatvam—equilibrium; iṣṭa—desirable; aniṣṭaḥ—undesirable; upapattiṣu—having obtained; mayi—unto Me; ca—also; ananya-yogena—by devotional service; bhaktiḥ—devotion; avyabhicāriṇī—constant, unalloyed; vivikta—solitary; deśa—place; sevitvam—aspiring; aratiḥ—without attachment; jana—people in general; saṁsadi—mass; adhyātma—pertaining to the self; jñāna—knowledge; nityatvam—eternity; tattva-jñāna—knowledge of the truth; artha—the object; darśanam—philosophy; etat—all this; jñānam—knowledge; iti—thus; proktam—declared; ajñānam—ignorance; yat—that which; ataḥ—from this; anyathā—others.

TRANSLATION

Humility, pridelessness, nonviolence, tolerance, simplicity, approaching a bona fide spiritual master, cleanliness, steadiness and self-control;

renunciation of the objects of sense gratification, absence of false ego, the perception of the evil of birth, death, old age and disease; nonattachment to children, wife, home and the rest, and evenmindedness amid pleasant and unpleasant events; constant and unalloyed devotion to Me, resorting to solitary places, detachment from the general mass of people; accepting the importance of self-realization, and philosophical search for the Absolute Truth—all these I thus declare to be knowledge, and what is contrary to these is ignorance.

PURPORT

This process of knowledge is sometimes misunderstood by less intelligent men as being the interaction of the field of activity. But actually this is the real process of knowledge. If one accepts this process, then the possibility of approaching the Absolute Truth exists. This is not the interaction of the tenfold elements, as described before, This is actually the means to get out of it. Of all the descriptions of the process of knowledge, the most important point is described in the first line of the tenth verse: The process of knowledge terminates in unalloyed devotional service to the Lord. So, if one does not approach, or is not able to approach, the transcendental service of the Lord, then the other nineteen items are of no particular value. But, if one takes to devotional service in full Kṛṣṇa consciousness, the other nineteen items automatically develop within him. The principle of accepting a spiritual master, as mentioned in the seventh verse, is essential. Even for one who takes to devotional service, it is most important. Transcendental life begins when one accepts a bona fide spiritual master. The Supreme Personality of Godhead, Śrī Kṛṣṇa, clearly states here that this process of knowledge is the actual path. Anything speculated beyond this is nonsense.

As for the knowledge outlined here, the items may be analyzed as follows: Humility means that one should not be anxious to have the satisfaction of being honored by others. The material conception of life makes us very eager to receive honor from others, but from the point of view of a man in perfect knowledge—who knows that he is not this body—anything, honor or dishonor, pertaining to this body is useless. One should not be hankering after this material deception. People are very anxious to be famous for their religion, and consequently sometimes it is found that without understanding the principles of religion, one enters into some group, which is not actually following religious principles, and then wants to advertise himself as a religious mentor. As for actual advancement in spiritual science, one should have a test to see how far he is progressing. He can judge by these items.

Nonviolence is generally taken to mean not killing or destroying the body, but actually nonviolence means not to put others into distress. People in general are trapped by ignorance in the material concept of life, and they perpetually suffer material pains. So, unless one elevates people to spiritual knowledge, one is practicing violence. One should try his best to distribute real knowledge to the people, so that they may become enlightened and leave this material entanglement. That is nonviolence.

Tolerance means that one should be practiced to bear insult and dishonor from others. If one is engaged in the advancement of spiritual knowledge, there will be so many insults and much dishonor from others. This is expected because material nature is so constituted. Even a boy like Prahlāda, who, only five years old, was engaged in the cultivation of spiritual knowledge, was endangered when his father became antagonistic to his devotion. The father tried to kill him in so many ways, but Prahlāda tolerated him. So, for making advancement in spiritual knowledge, there may be many impediments, but we should be tolerant and continue our progress with determination.

Simplicity means that without diplomacy one should be so straightforward that he can disclose the real truth even to an enemy. As for acceptance of the spiritual master, that is essential, because without the instruction of a bona fide spiritual master, one cannot progress in the spiritual science. One should approach the spiritual master with all humility and offer him all services so that he will be pleased to bestow his blessings upon the disciple. Because a bona fide spiritual master is a representative of Kṛṣṇa, if he bestows any blessings upon his disciple, that will make the disciple immediately advanced without the disciple's following the regulated principles. Or, the regulated principles will be easier for one who has served the spiritual master without reservation.

Cleanliness is essential for making advancement in spiritual life. There are two kinds of cleanliness: external and internal. External cleanliness means taking a bath, but for internal cleanliness, one has to think of Kṛṣṇa always and chant Hare Kṛṣṇa, Hare Kṛṣṇa, Kṛṣṇa Kṛṣṇa, Hare Hare/Hare Rāma, Hare Rāma, Rāma Rāma, Hare Hare. This process cleans the accumulated dust of past karma from the mind.

Steadiness means that one should be very determined to make progress in spiritual life. Without such determination, one cannot make tangible progress. And self-control means that one should not accept anything which is detrimental to the path of spiritual progress. One should become accustomed to this and reject anything which is against the path of spiritual progress. This is real renunciation. The senses are so strong that they are always anxious to have sense gratification. One should not cater to these demands, which are not necessary. The senses should only be gratified to keep the body fit so that one can discharge his duty in advancing in spiritual life. The most important and uncontrollable sense is the tongue. If one can control the tongue, then there is every possibility of controlling the other senses. The function of the tongue is to taste and to vibrate. Therefore, by systematic regulation, the tongue should always be engaged in tasting the remnants of foodstuffs offered to Kṛṣṇa and chanting Hare Kṛṣṇa. As far as the eyes are concerned, they should not be allowed to see anything but the beautiful form of Kṛṣṇa. That will control the eyes. Similarly, the ears should be engaged in hearing about Kṛṣṇa and the nose in smelling the flowers offered to Kṛṣṇa. This is the process of devotional service, and it is understood here that *Bhagavad-gītā* is simply expounding the science of devotional service. Devotional service is the main and sole objective. Unintelligent commentators on the *Gītā* try to divert the mind of the reader to other subjects, but there is no other subject in *Bhagavad-gītā* but devotional service.

False ego means accepting this body as oneself. When one understands that he is not his body and is spirit soul, that is real ego. Ego is there. False ego is condemned, but not real ego. In the Vedic literature, it is said: *ahaṁ brahmāsmi.* I am Brahman, I am spirit. This "I am," the sense of self, also exists in the liberated stage of self-realization. This sense of "I am" is ego, but when the sense of "I am" is applied to this false body, it is false ego. When the sense of self is applied to reality, that is real ego. There are some philosophers who say we should give up our ego, but we cannot give up our ego because ego means identity. We ought, of course, to give up the false identification with the body.

One should try to understand the distress of accepting birth, death, old age and disease. There are descriptions in various Vedic literatures of birth. In the *Śrīmad-Bhāgavatam* the world of the unborn, the child's stay in the womb of the mother, its suffering, etc., are all very graphically described. It should be thoroughly understood that birth is distressful. Because we forget how much distress we have suffered within the womb of the mother, we do not make any solution to the repetition of birth and death. Similarly at the time of death, there are all kinds of sufferings, and they are also mentioned in the authoritative scriptures. These should be discussed. And as far as disease and old age are concerned, everyone gets practical experience. No one wants to be diseased, and no one wants to become old, but there is no avoiding these. Unless we have a pessimistic view of this material life, considering the distresses of birth, death, old age and disease, there is no impetus for our making advancement in spiritual life.

As for detachment from children, wife and home, it is not meant that one should have no feeling for these. They are natural objects of affection, but when they are not favorable to spiritual progress, then one should not be attached to them. The best process for making the home pleasant is Kṛṣṇa consciousness. If one is in full Kṛṣṇa consciousness, he can make his home very happy because this process of Kṛṣṇa consciousness is very easy. One need only chant Hare Kṛṣṇa, Hare Kṛṣṇa, Kṛṣṇa Kṛṣṇa, Hare Hare/Hare Rāma, Hare Rāma, Rāma Rāma, Hare Hare, accept the remnants of foodstuffs offered to Kṛṣṇa, have some discussion on books like *Bhagavad-gītā* and *Śrīmad-Bhāgavatam*, and engage oneself in Deity worship. These four will make one happy. One should train the members of his family in this way. The family members can sit down morning and evening and chant together Hare Kṛṣṇa, Hare Kṛṣṇa, Kṛṣṇa Kṛṣṇa, Hare Hare/Hare Rāma, Hare Rāma, Rāma Rāma, Hare Hare. If one can mold his family life in this way to develop Kṛṣṇa consciousness, following these four principles, then there is no need to change from family life to renounced life. But if it is not congenial, not favorable for spiritual advancement, then family life should be abandoned. One must sacrifice everything to realize or serve Kṛṣṇa, just as Arjuna did. Arjuna did not want to kill his family members, but when he understood that these family members were impediments to his Kṛṣṇa realization, he accepted the instruction of Kṛṣṇa and fought and killed them. In all cases, one should be detached from the happiness and distress of family life because in this world one can never be fully happy or fully miserable. Happiness and distress are concommitant factors of material life. One should learn to tolerate, as advised in *Bhagavad-gītā*. One can never restrict the coming and going of happiness and distress, so one should be detached from the materialistic way of life and be automatically equiposed in both cases. Generally, when we get something desirable, we are very happy, and when we get something undesirable, we are distressed. But if we are actually in the spiritual position, these things will not agitate us. To reach that stage, we have to practice unbreakable devotional service; devotional service to Kṛṣṇa without deviation means engaging oneself in the nine processes of devotional service, chanting, hearing, worshiping, offering respect, etc., as described in the last verse of the Ninth Chapter. That process should be followed. Naturally, when one is adapted to the spiritual way of life, he will not want to mix with materialistic men. That would go against his grain. One may test himself by seeing how far he is inclined to live in a solitary place without unwanted association.

Naturally a devotee has no taste for unnecessary sporting or cinema-going or enjoying some social function, because he understands that these are simply a waste of time. There are many research scholars and philosophers who study sex life or some other subject, but according to Bhagavad-gītā, such research work and philosophical speculation have no value. That is more or less nonsensical. According to Bhagavad-gītā, one should make research by philosophical discretion into the nature of the soul. One should make research to understand with what the self is concerned. That is recommended here.

As far as self-realization is concerned, it is clearly stated here that bhakti-yoga is especially practical. As soon as there is a question of devotion, one must consider the relationship between the Supersoul and the individual soul. The individual soul and the Supersoul cannot be one, at least not in the bhakti conception, the devotional conception of life. This service of the individual soul to the Supreme Soul is eternal, nityam, as is clearly stated. So bhakti or devotional service is eternal. One should be established in that philosophical conviction, otherwise it is only a waste of time, ignorance.

In the Śrīmad-Bhāgavatam, this is explained; vadanti tat tattva-vidas tattvaṁ yaj jñānam advayam. "Those who are actually knowers of the Absolute Truth know that the Self is realized in three different phases as Brahman, Paramātmā and Bhagavān." (Bhāg. 1.2.11) Bhagavān is the last word in the realization of the Absolute Truth; therefore one should reach up to that platform of understanding the Supreme Personality of Godhead and thus engage in the devotional service of the Lord. That is perfection of knowledge.

Beginning from practicing humility up to the point of realization of the Supreme Truth, the Absolute Personality of Godhead, this process is just like a staircase beginning from the ground floor up to the top floor. Now on this staircase there are so many people who have reached the first floor, the second or third floor, etc., but unless one reaches the top floor, which is the understanding of Kṛṣṇa, he is at a lower stage of knowledge. If anyone wants to compete with God and at the same time make advancement in spiritual knowledge, he will be frustrated. It is clearly stated that without humility understanding is harmful. To think oneself God is most puffed up. Although the living entity is always being kicked by the stringent laws of material nature, still he thinks, "I am God" because of ignorance. One should be humble and know that he is subordinate to the Supreme Lord. Due to rebellion against the Supreme Lord, one becomes subordinate to material nature. One must know and be convinced of this truth.

TEXT 13

ज्ञेयं यत्तत्प्रवक्ष्यामि यज्ज्ञात्वाऽमृतमश्नुते ।
अनादिमत्परं ब्रह्म न सत्तन्नासदुच्यते ॥ १३ ॥

jñeyaṁ yat tat pravakṣyāmi
yaj jñātvāmṛtam aśnute
anādi mat-paraṁ brahma
na sat tan nāsad ucyate

jñeyam—knowable; *yat*—that; *tat*—which; *pravakṣyāmi*—I shall now explain; *yat*—which; *jñātvā*—knowing; *amṛtam*—nectar; *aśnute*—taste; *anādi*—beginningless; *mat-param*—subordinate to Me; *brahma*—spirit; *na*—neither; *sat*—cause; *tat*—that; *na*—nor; *asat*—effect; *ucyate*—is called.

TRANSLATION

I shall now explain the knowable, knowing which you will taste the eternal. This is beginningless, and it is subordinate to Me. It is called Brahman, the spirit, and it lies beyond the cause and effect of this material world.

PURPORT

The Lord has explained the field of activities and the knower of the field. He has also explained the process of knowing the knower of the field of activities. Now He is explaining the knowable, both the soul and the Supersoul respectively. By knowledge of the knower, both the soul and the Supersoul, one can relish the nectar of life. As explained in the Second Chapter, the living entity is eternal. This is also confirmed here. There is no specific date at which the *jīva* was born. Nor can anyone trace out the history of *jīvātmā's* manifestation from the Supreme Lord. Therefore it is beginningless. The Vedic literature confirms this: *na jāyate mṛjayate vā vipaścit.* The knower of the body is never born and never dies, and he is full of knowledge. The Supreme Lord is also stated in the Vedic literature as *pradhāna-kṣetrajña-patir guṇeśaḥ.* The Supreme Lord as the Supersoul is the chief knower of the body, and He is the master of the three modes of material nature. In the *smṛti* it is said: *dāsa-bhūto harer eva nānyasvaiva kadācana.* The living entities are eternally in the service of the Supreme Lord. This is also confirmed by Lord Caitanya in His teaching; therefore the description of Brahman mentioned in this verse is in relation to the individual soul, and when the word Brahman is applied to the living entity, it is to be understood that he is *vijñānaṁ brahma* as opposed to *ananta-brahma*. *Ananta-brahma* is the Supreme Brahman Personality of Godhead.

TEXT 14

सर्वतः पाणिपादं तत्सर्वतोऽक्षिशिरोमुखम् ।
सर्वतः श्रुतिमल्लोके सर्वमावृत्य तिष्ठति ॥ १४ ॥

sarvataḥ pāṇi-pādaṁ tat
sarvato 'kṣi-śiro-mukham
sarvataḥ śrutimal loke
sarvam āvṛtya tiṣṭhati

sarvataḥ—everywhere; *pāṇi*—hands; *pādam*—legs; *tat*—that; *sarvataḥ*—everywhere; *akṣi*—eyes; *śiraḥ*—head; *mukham*—face; *sarvataḥ*—everywhere; *śrutimat*—hearing; *loke*—in the world; *sarvam*—everywhere, *āvṛtya*—covering; *tiṣṭhati*—exists.

TRANSLATION

Everywhere are His hands and legs, His eyes and faces, and He hears everything. In this way the Supersoul exists.

PURPORT

As the sun exists diffusing its unlimited rays, so does the Supersoul, or Supreme Personality of Godhead. He exists in His all-pervading form, and in Him exist all the individual living entities, beginning from the first great teacher, Brahmā, down to the small ants. There are unlimited heads, legs, hands and eyes, and unlimited living entities. All are existing in and on the Supersoul. Therefore the Supersoul is all-pervading. The individual soul, however, cannot say that he has his hands, legs and eyes everywhere. That is not possible. If he thinks that although under ignorance he is not conscious that his hands and legs are diffused all over, but when he attains to proper knowledge he will come to that stage, his thinking is contradictory. This means that the individual soul, having become conditioned by material nature, is not supreme. The Supreme is different from the individual soul. The Supreme Lord can extend His hand without limit; the individual soul cannot. In *Bhagavad-gītā* the Lord says that if anyone offers Him a flower, or a fruit, or a little water, He accepts. If the Lord is a far distance away, how can He accept things? This is the omnipotence of the Lord: even though He is situated in His own abode, far, far away from earth, He can extend His hand to accept what anyone offers. That is His potency. In the *Brahmā-samhitā* it is stated, *goloka eva nivasati:* although He is always engaged in pastimes in His transcendental planet, He is all-pervading. The individual soul cannot claim that he is all-pervading. Therefore this verse describes the Supreme Soul, the Personality of Godhead, not the individual soul.

TEXT 15

सर्वेन्द्रियगुणाभासं सर्वेन्द्रियविवर्जितम् ।
असक्तं सर्वभृच्चैव निर्गुणं गुणभोक्तृ च ॥ १५ ॥

sarvendriya-guṇābhāsaṁ
sarvendriya-vivarjitam
asaktaṁ sarva-bhṛc caiva
nirguṇaṁ guṇa-bhoktṛ ca

sarve—all; *indriya*—senses; *guṇa*—qualities; *ābhāsam*—original source; *sarva*—all; *indriya*—senses; *vivarjitam*—being without; *asaktam*—without attachment; *sarva-bhṛt*—maintainer of everyone; *ca*—also; *eva*—certainly; *nirguṇam*—without material qualities; *guṇa-bhoktṛ*—simultaneously master of the *guṇas*; *ca*—also.

TRANSLATION

The Supersoul is the original source of all senses, yet He is without senses. He is unattached, although He is the maintainer of all living beings. He transcends the modes of nature, and at the same time He is the master of all modes of material nature.

PURPORT

The Supreme Lord, although the source of all the senses of the living entities, doesn't have material senses like they have. Actually, the individual souls have spiritual senses, but in conditioned life they are covered with the material elements, and therefore the sense activities are exhibited through matter. The Supreme Lord's senses are not so covered. His senses are transcendental and are therefore called *nirguṇa*. *Guṇa* means the material modes, but His senses are without material covering. It should be understood that His senses are not exactly like ours. Although He is the source of all our sensual activities, He has His transcendental senses which are uncontaminated. This is very nicely explained in the *Śvetāśvatara Upaniṣad* in the verse: *sarvataḥ pāṇi-pādam.* The Supreme Personality of Godhead has no hands which are materially contaminated, but He has His hands and accepts whatever sacrifice is offered to Him. That is the distinction between the conditioned soul and the Supersoul. He has no material eyes, but He has eyes—otherwise how could He see? He sees everything, past, present and future. He lives within the heart of the living being, and He knows what we have done in the past, what we are doing now, and what is awaiting us in the future. This is also confirmed in *Bhagavad-gītā:* He knows everything, but no one knows Him. It is said that the Supreme Lord has no legs like us, but He can travel throughout space because He has spiritual legs. In other words, the Lord is not impersonal; He has His eyes, legs, hands and everything else, and because we are part and parcel of the Supreme Lord we also have these things. But His hands, legs, eyes and senses are not contaminated by material nature.

Bhagavad-gītā also confirms that when the Lord appears He appears as He is by His internal potency. He is not contaminated by the material energy because He is the Lord of material energy. In the Vedic literature we find that His whole embodiment is spiritual. He has His eternal form called *sac-cid-ānanda-vigraha*. He is full of all opulence. He is the proprietor of all wealth and the owner of all energy. He is the most intelligent and is full of knowledge. These are some of the symptoms of the Supreme Personality of Godhead. He is maintainer of all living entities and the witness of all activities. As far as we can understand from Vedic literature, the Supreme Lord is always transcendental. Although we do not see His head, face, hands, or legs, He has them, and when we are elevated to the transcendental situation then we can see the Lord's form. Due to materially contaminated senses, we cannot see His form. Therefore the impersonalists who are still materially affected cannot understand the Personality of Godhead.

TEXT 16

बहिरन्तश्च भूतानामचरं चरमेव च ।
सूक्ष्मत्वात्तदविज्ञेयं दूरस्थं चान्तिके च तत् ॥ १६ ॥

*bahir antaś ca bhūtānām
acaraṁ caram eva ca
sūkṣmatvāt tad avijñeyaṁ
dūra-sthaṁ cāntike ca tat*

bahiḥ—outside; *antaḥ*—inside; *ca*—also; *bhūtānām*—of all living entities; *acaram*—not moving; *caram*—moving; *eva*—also; *ca*—and; *sūkṣmatvāt*—on account of being subtle; *tat*—that; *avijñeyam*—unknowable; *dūrastham*—far away; *ca antike*—near also; *ca*—and; *tat*—that.

TRANSLATION

The Supreme Truth exists both internally and externally, in the moving and nonmoving. He is beyond the power of the material senses to see or to know. Although far, far away, He is also near to all.

PURPORT

In Vedic literature we understand that Nārāyaṇa, the Supreme Person, is residing both outside and inside of every living entity. He is present both in the spiritual and material world. Although He is far, far away, still He is near to us. These are the statements of Vedic literature. *Āsīno dūraṁ vrajati śayāno yāti sarvataḥ*. And, because He is always engaged in transcendental bliss, we cannot understand how He is enjoying His full opulence. We cannot see or understand with these material senses. Therefore in the Vedic language it is said that to understand Him our material mind and senses cannot act. But one who has purified his mind and senses by practicing Kṛṣṇa consciousness in devotional service can see Him constantly. It is confirmed in *Brahma-saṁhitā* that the devotee who has developed love for the Supreme God can see Him always, without cessation. And it is confirmed in *Bhagavad-gītā* (11.54) that He can be seen and understood only by devotional service. *Bhaktyā tvananyayā śakyaḥ*.

TEXT 17

अविभक्तं च भूतेषु विभक्तमिव च स्थितम् ।
भूतभर्तृ च तज्ज्ञेयं ग्रसिष्णु प्रभविष्णु च ॥ १७ ॥

avibhaktaṁ ca bhūteṣu
vibhaktam iva ca sthitam
bhūta-bhartṛ ca taj jñeyaṁ
grasiṣṇu prabhaviṣṇu ca

avibhaktam—without division; *ca*—also; *bhūteṣu*—in every living being; *vibhaktam*—divided; *iva*—as if; *ca*—also; *sthitam*—situated; *bhūta-bhartṛ*—maintainer of all living entities; *ca*—also; *tat*—that; *jñeyam*—to be understood; *grasiṣṇu*—devours; *prabhaviṣṇu*—develops; *ca*—also.

TRANSLATION

Although the Supersoul appears to be divided, He is never divided. He is situated as one. Although He is the maintainer of every living entity, it is to be understood that He devours and develops all.

PURPORT

The Lord is situated in everyone's heart as the Supersoul. Does that mean that He has become divided? No. Actually, He is one. The example is given of the sun: the sun, at the meridian, is situated in his place. But if one goes for five thousand miles in all directions and asks, "Where is the sun?" everyone will say that it is shining on his head. In the Vedic literature this example is given to show that although He is undivided, He is situated as if divided. Also it is said in Vedic literature that one Viṣṇu is present everywhere by His omnipotence, just as the sun appears in many places to many persons. And the Supreme Lord, although the maintainer of every living entity, devours everything at the time of annihilation. This was confirmed in the Eleventh Chapter when the Lord said that He has come to devour all the warriors assembled at Kurukṣetra. He also mentions that in the form of time He devours also. He is the annihilator, the killer of all. When there is creation, He develops all from their original state, and at the time of annihilation He devours them. The Vedic hymns confirm the fact that He is the origin of all living entities and the rest of all. After creation, everything rests in His omnipotence, and after annihilation, everything again returns to rest in Him. These are the confirmations of Vedic hymns. *Yato vā imāni bhūtāni jāyante yena jātāni jīvanti yat prayanty abhisaṁviśanti tad brahma tad vijijñāsasva.* (*Taittirīya Upaniṣad*, 3.1)

TEXT 18

ज्योतिषामपि तज्ज्योतिस्तमसः परमुच्यते ।
ज्ञानं ज्ञेयं ज्ञानगम्यं हृदि सर्वस्य विष्ठितम् ॥ १८ ॥

jyotiṣām api taj jyotis
tamasaḥ param ucyate
jñānaṁ jñeyaṁ jñāna-gamyaṁ
hṛdi sarvasya viṣṭhitam

jyotiṣām—in all luminous objects; *api*—also; *tat*—that; *jyotiḥ*—source of light; *tamasaḥ*—of the darkness; *param*—beyond; *ucyate*—is said; *jñānam*—knowledge; *jñeyam*—to be known; *jñāna-gamyam*—to be approached by knowledge; *hṛdi*—in the heart; *sarvasya*—of everyone; *viṣṭhitam*—situated.

TRANSLATION

He is the source of light in all luminous objects. He is beyond the darkness of matter and is unmanifested. He is knowledge, He is the object of knowledge, and He is the goal of knowledge. He is situated in everyone's heart.

PURPORT

The Supersoul, the Supreme Personality of Godhead, is the source of light in all luminous objects like the sun, moon, stars, etc. In the Vedic literature we find that in the spiritual kingdom there is no need of sun or moon because the effulgence of the Supreme Lord is there. In the material world that *brahmajyoti*, the Lord's spiritual effulgence, is covered by the *mahat-tattva*, the material elements; therefore in this material world we require the assistance of sun, moon, electricity, etc., for light. But in the spiritual world there is no need of such things. It is clearly stated in the Vedic literature that because of His luminous effulgence, everything is illuminated. It is clear, therefore, that His situation is not in the material world. He is situated in the spiritual world which is far, far away in the spiritual sky. That is also confirmed in the Vedic literature. *Āditya-varṇam tamasaḥ parastāt.* He is just like the sun, eternally luminous, but He is far, far beyond the darkness of this material world. His knowledge is transcendental. The Vedic literature confirms that Brahman is concentrated transcendental knowledge. To one who is anxious to be transferred to that spiritual world, knowledge is given by the Supreme Lord who is situated in everyone's heart.

One Vedic *mantra* says: *taṁ ha devam ātma-buddhi-prakāśaṁ mumukṣur vai śaraṇam aham prapadye.* One must surrender unto the Supreme Personality of Godhead if he at all wants liberation. As far as the goal of ultimate knowledge is concerned, it is also confirmed in Vedic literature: *tam eva viditvātimṛtyum eti.* "Only by knowing You can one surpass the boundary of birth and death." He is situated in everyone's heart as the supreme controller. The Supreme has legs and hands distributed everywhere, and this cannot be said of the individual soul. Therefore that there are two knowers of the field of activity, the individual soul and the Supersoul, must be admitted. One's hands and legs are distributed locally, but Kṛṣṇa's hands and legs are distributed everywhere. This is confirmed in the *Śvetāśvatara Upaniṣad: sarvasya prabhum īśānaṁ sarvasya śaraṇaṁ bṛhat.* That Supreme Personality of Godhead, Supersoul, is the *prabhu* or master of all living entities; therefore He is the ultimate center of all living entities. So there is no denying the fact that the Supreme Supersoul and the individual soul are always different.

TEXT 19

इति क्षेत्रं तथा ज्ञानं ज्ञेयं चोक्तं समासतः ।
मद्भक्त एतद्विज्ञाय मद्भावायोपपद्यते ॥ १९ ॥

iti kṣetraṁ tathā jñānaṁ
jñeyaṁ coktaṁ samāsataḥ
mad-bhakta etad vijñāya
mad-bhāvāyopapadyate

iti—thus; *kṣetram*—field of activities (the body); *tathā*—also; *jñānam*—knowledge; *jñeyam*—knowable; *ca*—also; *uktam*—describe; *samāsataḥ*—in summary; *mat-bhaktaḥ*—My devotee; *etat*—all this; *vijñāya*—after understanding; *mat-bhāvāya*—My nature; *upapadyate*—attains.

TRANSLATION

Thus the field of activities [the body], knowledge, and the knowable have been summarily described by Me. Only My devotees can understand this thoroughly and thus attain to My nature.

PURPORT

The Lord has described in summary the body, knowledge and the knowable. This knowledge is of three things: the knower, the knowable and the process of knowing. Combined, these are called *vijñānam,* or the science of knowledge. Perfect knowledge can be understood by the unalloyed devotees of the Lord directly. Others are unable to understand. The monists say that at the ultimate stage these three items become one, but the devotees do not accept this. Knowledge and development of knowledge mean understanding oneself in Kṛṣṇa consciousness. We are being led by material consciousness, but as soon as we transfer all consciousness to Kṛṣṇa's activities and realize that Kṛṣṇa is everything, then we attain real knowledge. In other words, knowledge is nothing but the preliminary stage of understanding devotional service perfectly.

TEXT 20

प्रकृतिं पुरुषं चैव विद्ध्यनादी उभावपि ।
विकारांश्च गुणांश्चैव विद्धि प्रकृतिसंभवान् ॥ २० ॥

prakṛtiṁ puruṣaṁ caiva
viddhy anādī ubhāv api
vikārāṁś ca guṇāṁś caiva
viddhi prakṛti-sambhavān

prakṛtim—material nature; *puruṣam*—living entities; *ca*—also; *eva*—certainly; *viddhi*—must know; *anādī*—without beginning; *ubhau*—both; *api*—also; *vikārān*—transformation; *ca*—also; *guṇān*—three modes of nature; *ca*—also; *eva*—certainly; *viddhi*—know; *prakṛti*—material nature; *sambhavān*—produced of.

TRANSLATION

Material nature and the living entities should be understood to be beginningless. Their transformations and the modes of matter are products of material nature.

PURPORT

By this knowledge, the body, the field of activities and the knowers of the body (both the individual soul and the Supersoul) can be known. The body is the field of activity and is composed of material nature. It is the individual soul which is embodied. Enjoying the activities of the body is the *puruṣa*, or the living entity. He is one knower, and the other is the Supersoul. Of course, it is to be understood that both the Supersoul and the individual entity are different manifestations of the Supreme Personality of Godhead. The living entity is in the category of His energy, and the Supersoul is in the category of His personal expansion.

Both material nature and the living entity are eternal. That is to say that they existed before the creation. The material manifestation is from the energy of the Supreme Lord and so also are the living entities, but they are of the superior energy. Both of them existed before this cosmos was manifested. Material nature was absorbed in the Supreme Personality of Godhead, Mahā-Viṣṇu, and when it was required, it was manifested by the agency of *mahat-tattva*. Similarly, the living entities are also in Him, and because they are conditioned, they are adverse to serving the Supreme Lord. Thus they are not allowed to enter into the spiritual sky. After the winding up of material nature, these living entities are again given a chance to act in the material world and prepare themselves to enter into the spiritual world. That is the mystery of this material creation. Actually the living entity is originally the spiritual part and parcel of the Supreme Lord, but due to his rebellious nature, he is conditioned within material nature. It really does not matter how these living entities or superior entities of the Supreme Lord have come in contact with material nature. The Supreme Personality of Godhead knows, however, how and why this actually took place. In the scriptures the Lord says that those attracted by this material nature are undergoing a hard struggle for existence. But we should know it with certainty from the descriptions of these few verses that all the transformations and influences of material nature by the three modes are also productions of material nature. All transformations and variety in respect to living entities are due to the body. As far as spirit is concerned, living entities are all the same.

TEXT 21

कार्यकारणकर्तृत्वे हेतुः प्रकृतिरुच्यते ।
पुरुषः सुखदुःखानां भोक्तृत्वे हेतुरुच्यते ॥ २१ ॥

kārya-kāraṇa-kartṛtve
hetuḥ prakṛtir ucyate
puruṣaḥ sukha-duḥkhānāṁ
bhoktṛtve hetur ucyate

kārya—effect; *kāraṇa*—cause; *kartṛtve*—in the matter of creation; *hetuḥ*—instrument; *prakṛtiḥ*—material nature; *ucyate*—is said to be; *puruṣaḥ*—the living entities; *sukha*—happiness; *duḥkhānām*—of distresses; *bhoktṛtve*—in enjoyment; *hetuḥ*—instrument; *ucyate*—is said to be.

TRANSLATION

Nature is said to be the cause of all material activities and effects, whereas the living entity is the cause of the various sufferings and enjoyments in this world.

PURPORT

The different manifestations of body and senses among the living entities are due to material nature. There are 8,400,000 different species of life, and these varieties are the creation of the material nature. They arise from the different sensual pleasures of the living entity, who thus desires to live in this body or that. When he is put into different bodies, he enjoys different kinds of happiness and distress. His material happiness and distress are due to his body, and not to himself as he is. In his original state there is no doubt of enjoyment; therefore that is his real state. Because of the desire to lord it over material nature, he is in the material world. In the spiritual world there is no such thing. The spiritual world is pure, but in the material world everyone is struggling hard to acquire victims who present different pleasures to the body. It might be more clear to state that this body is the effect of the senses. The senses are instruments for gratifying desire. Now, the sum total—body and instrument senses—are offered by material nature, and, as will be clear in the next verse, the living entity is blessed or damned with circumstances according to his past desire and activity. According to one's desires and activities, material nature places one in various residential quarters. The being himself is the cause of his attaining such residential quarters and his attendant enjoyment or suffering. Once placed in some particular kind of body, he comes under the control of nature because the body, being matter, acts according to the laws of nature. At that time, the living entity has no power to change that law. Suppose an entity is put into the body of a dog. As soon as he is put into the body of a dog, he must act like a dog. He cannot act otherwise. And if the living entity is put into the body of a hog, then he is forced to eat stool and act like a hog. Similarly, if the living entity is put into the body of a demigod, he must act according to his body. This is the law of nature. But in all circumstances, the Supersoul is with the individual soul. That is explained in the *Vedas* as follows: *dvā suparṇā sayujā sakhāyā*. The Supreme Lord is so kind upon the living entity that He always accompanies the individual soul and in all circumstances is present as the Supersoul or Paramātmā.

TEXT 22

पुरुषः प्रकृतिस्थो हि भुङ्क्ते प्रकृतिजान्गुणान् ।
कारणं गुणसङ्गोऽस्य सदसद्योनिजन्मसु ॥ २२ ॥

> *puruṣaḥ prakṛti-stho hi*
> *bhuṅkte prakṛti-jān guṇān*
> *kāraṇaṁ guṇa-saṅgo 'sya*
> *sad-asad-yoni-janmasu*

puruṣaḥ—the living entity; *prakṛti-sthaḥ*—being situated in the material energy; *hi*—certainly; *bhuṅkte*—enjoys; *prakṛti-jān*—produced by the material nature; *guṇān*—modes of nature; *kāraṇam*—cause; *guṇa-saṅgaḥ*—

association with the modes of nature; *asya*—of the living entity; *sat-asat*—good and bad; *yoni*—species of life; *janmasu*—birth.

TRANSLATION

The living entity in material nature thus follows the ways of life, enjoying the three modes of nature. This is due to his association with that material nature. Thus he meets with good and evil amongst various species.

PURPORT

This verse is very important for an understanding of how the living entities transmigrate from one body to another. It is explained in the Second Chapter that the living entity is transmigrating from one body to another just as one changes dress. This change of dress is due to his attachment to material existence. As long as he is captivated by this false manifestation, he has to continue transmigrating from one body to another. Due to his desire to lord it over material nature, he is put into such undesirable circumstances. Under the influence of material desire, the entity is born sometimes as a demigod, sometimes as a man, sometimes as a beast, as a bird, as a worm, as an aquatic, as a saintly man, as a bug. This is going on. And in all cases the living entity thinks himself to be the master of his circumstances, yet he is under the influence of material nature.

How he is put into such different bodies is explained here. It is due to association with the different modes of nature. One has to rise, therefore, above the three material modes and become situated in the transcendental position. That is called Kṛṣṇa consciousness. Unless one is situated in Kṛṣṇa consciousness, his material consciousness will oblige him to transfer from one body to another because he has material desires since time immemorial. But he has to change that conception. That change can be effected only by hearing from authoritative sources. The best example is here: Arjuna is hearing the science of God from Kṛṣṇa. The living entity, if he submits to this hearing process, will lose his long-cherished desire to dominate material nature, and gradually and proportionately, as he reduces his long desire to dominate, he comes to enjoy spiritual happiness. In a Vedic *mantra* it is said that as he becomes learned in association with the Supreme Personality of Godhead, he proportionately relishes his eternal blissful life.

TEXT 23

उपद्रष्टानुमन्ता च भर्ता भोक्ता महेश्वरः ।
परमात्मेति चाप्युक्तो देहेऽस्मिन्पुरुषः परः ॥ २३ ॥

*upadraṣṭānumantā ca
bhartā bhoktā maheśvaraḥ
paramātmeti cāpy ukto
dehe 'smin puruṣaḥ paraḥ*

upadraṣṭā—overseer; *anumantā*—permitter; *ca*—also; *bhartā*—master; *bhoktā*—supreme enjoyer; *maheśvaraḥ*—the Supreme Lord; *paramātmā*—Supersoul; *iti*—also; *ca*—and; *api uktaḥ*—is said; *dehe*—in this body; *asmin*—this; *puruṣaḥ*—enjoyer; *paraḥ*—transcendental.

TRANSLATION

Yet in this body there is another, a transcendental enjoyer who is the Lord, the supreme proprietor, who exists as the overseer and permitter, and who is known as the Supersoul.

PURPORT

It is stated here that the Supersoul, who is always with the individual soul, is the representation of the Supreme Lord. He is not an ordinary living entity. Because the monist philosophers take the knower of the body to be one, they think that there is no difference between the Supersoul and the individual soul. To clarify this, the Lord says that He is the representation of Paramātmā in every body. He is different from the individual soul; He is *paraḥ*, transcendental. The individual soul enjoys the activities of a particular field, but the Supersoul is present not as finite enjoyer nor as one taking part in bodily activities, but as the witness, overseer, permitter and supreme enjoyer. His name is Paramātmā, not *ātmā*, and He is transcendental. It is distinctly clear that the *ātmā* and Paramātmā are different. The Supersoul, the Paramātmā, has legs and hands everywhere, but the individual soul does not. And because He is the Supreme Lord, He is present within to sanction the individual soul's desiring material enjoyment. Without the sanction of the Supreme Soul, the individual soul cannot do anything. The individual is *bhakta* or the sustained, and He is *bhukta* or the maintainer. There are innumerable living entities, and He is staying in them as a friend.

The fact is that individual living entities are eternally part and parcel of the Supreme Lord, and both of them are very intimately related as friends. But the living entity has the tendency to reject the sanction of the Supreme Lord and act independently in an attempt to dominate the supreme nature, and because he has this tendency, he is called the marginal energy of the Supreme Lord. The living entity can be situated either in the material energy or the spiritual energy. As long as he is conditioned by the material energy, the Supreme Lord, as his friend, the Supersoul, stays with him just to get him to return to the spiritual energy. The Lord is always eager to take him back to the spiritual energy, but due to his minute independence, the individual entity is continually rejecting the association of spiritual light. This misuse of independence is the cause of his material strife in the conditioned nature. The Lord, therefore, is always giving instruction from within and from without. From without He gives instructions as stated in *Bhagavad-gītā*, and from within He tries to convince him that his activities in the material field are not conducive to real happiness. "Just give it up and turn your faith toward Me. Then you will be happy," He says. Thus the intelligent person who places his faith in the Paramātmā or the Supreme Personality of Godhead begins to advance toward a blissful eternal life of knowledge

TEXT 24

य एवं वेत्ति पुरुषं प्रकृतिं च गुणैः सह ।
सर्वथा वर्तमानोऽपि न स भूयोऽभिजायते ॥ २४ ॥

ya evaṁ vetti puruṣaṁ
prakṛtiṁ ca guṇaiḥ saha
sarvathā vartamāno 'pi
na sa bhūyo 'bhijāyate

yaḥ—anyone; *evam*—thus; *vetti*—understands; *puruṣam*—the living entities; *prakṛtim*—material nature; *ca*—and; *guṇaiḥ*—modes of material nature; *saha*—with; *sarvathā*—by all means; *vartamānaḥ*—situated; *api*—in spite of; *na*—never; *saḥ*—he; *bhūyaḥ*—again; *abhijāyate*—takes his birth.

TRANSLATION

One who understands this philosophy concerning material nature, the living entity and the interaction of the modes of nature is sure to attain liberation. He will not take birth here again, regardless of his present position.

PURPORT

Clear understanding of material nature, the Supersoul, the individual soul and their interrelation makes one eligible to become liberated and turn to the spiritual atmosphere without being forced to return to this material nature. This is the result of knowledge. The purpose of knowledge is to understand distinctly that the living entity has by chance fallen into this material existence. By his personal endeavor in association with authorities, saintly persons and a spiritual master, he has to understand his position and then revert to spiritual consciousness or Kṛṣṇa consciousness by understanding *Bhagavad-gītā* as it is explained by the Personality of Godhead. Then it is certain that he will never come again into this material existence; he will be transferred into the spiritual world for a blissful eternal life of knowledge.

TEXT 25

ध्यानेनात्मनि पश्यन्ति केचिदात्मानमात्मना ।
अन्ये साङ्ख्येन योगेन कर्मयोगेन चापरे ॥ २५ ॥

dhyānenātmani paśyanti
kecid ātmānam ātmanā
anye sāṅkhyena yogena
karma-yogena cāpare

dhyānena—by meditation; *ātmani*—self; *paśyanti*—see; *kecit*—one; *ātmānam*—Supersoul; *ātmanā*—by the mind; *anye*—others; *sāṅkhyena*—by philosophical discussion; *yogena*—by the yoga system; *karma-yogena*—by activities without fruitive desire; *ca*—also; *apare*—others.

TRANSLATION

That Supersoul is perceived by some through meditation, by some through the cultivation of knowledge, and by others through working without fruitive desire.

PURPORT

The Lord informs Arjuna that the conditioned soul can be divided into two classes as far as man's search for self-realization is concerned. Those who are atheists, agnostics and skeptics are beyond the sense of spiritual understanding. But there are others who are faithful in their understanding of spiritual life, and they are called workers who have renounced fruitive results. Those who always try to establish the doctrine of monism are also counted among the atheists and agnostics. In other words, only the devotees of the Supreme Personality of Godhead are really capable of spiritual understanding because they understand that beyond this material nature there is the spiritual world and the Supreme Personality of Godhead who is expanded as the Paramātmā, the Supersoul in everyone, the all-pervading Godhead. Of course there are those who try to understand the Supreme Absolute Truth by cultivation of knowledge, and they can be counted in the second class. The atheistic philosophers analyze this material world into twenty-four elements, and they place the individual soul as the twenty-fifth item. When they are able to understand the nature of the individual soul to be transcendental to the material elements, they are able to understand also that above the individual soul there is the Supreme Personality of Godhead. He is the twenty-sixth element. Thus gradually they also come to the standard of devotional service in Kṛṣṇa consciousness. Those who work without fruitive results are also perfect in their attitude. They are given a chance to advance to the platform of devotional service in Kṛṣṇa consciousness. Here it is stated that there are some people who are pure in consciousness and who try to find out the Supersoul by meditation, and when they discover the Supersoul within themselves, they become transcendentally situated. Similarly, there are others who also try to understand the Supreme Soul by cultivation of knowledge, and there are others who cultivate the *haṭha-yoga* system and who try to satisfy the Supreme Personality of Godhead by childish activities.

TEXT 26

अन्ये त्वेवमजानन्तः श्रुत्वान्येभ्य उपासते ।
तेऽपि चातितरन्त्येव मृत्युं श्रुतिपरायणाः ॥ २६ ॥

anye tv evam ajānantaḥ
śrutvānyebhya upāsate
te 'pi cātitaranty eva
mṛtyuṁ śruti-parāyaṇāḥ

anye—others; *tu*—but; *evam*—this; *ajānantaḥ*—without spiritual knowledge; *śrutvā*—by hearing; *anyebhyaḥ*—from others; *upāsate*—begin to worship; *te*—they; *api*—also; *ca*—and; *atitaranti*—transcend; *eva*—certainly; *mṛtyum*—the path of death; *śruti-parāyaṇāḥ*—inclined to the process of hearing.

TRANSLATION

Again there are those who, although not conversant in spiritual knowledge, begin to worship the Supreme Person upon hearing about Him from others. Because of their tendency to hear from authorities, they also transcend the path of birth and death.

PURPORT

This verse is particularly applicable to modern society because in modern society there is practically no education in spiritual matters. Some of the people may appear to be atheistic or agnostic or philosophical, but actually there is no knowledge of philosophy. As for the common man, if he is a good soul, then there is a chance for advancement by hearing. This hearing process is very important. Lord Caitanya, who preached Kṛṣṇa consciousness in the modern world, gave great stress to hearing because if the common man simply hears from authoritative sources, he can progress, especially, according to Lord Caitanya, if he hears the transcendental vibration Hare Kṛṣṇa, Hare Kṛṣṇa, Kṛṣṇa Kṛṣṇa, Hare Hare/Hare Rāma, Hare Rāma, Rāma Rāma, Hare Hare. It is stated, therefore, that all men should take advantage of hearing from realized souls and gradually become able to understand everything. The worship of the Supreme Lord will then undoubtedly take place. Lord Caitanya has said that in this age no one needs to change his position, but one should give up the endeavor to understand the Absolute Truth by speculative reasoning. One should learn to become the servant of those who are in knowledge of the Supreme Lord. If one is fortunate enough to take shelter of a pure devotee, hear from him about self-realization and follow in his footsteps, he will be gradually elevated to the position of a pure devotee. In this verse particularly the process of hearing is strongly recommended, and this is very appropriate. Although the common man is often not as capable as so-called philosophers, faithful hearing from an authoritative person will help one transcend this material existence and go back to Godhead, back to home.

TEXT 27

यावत्संजायते किंचित्सत्त्वं स्थावरजङ्गमम् ।
क्षेत्रक्षेत्रज्ञसंयोगात्तद्विद्धि भरतर्षभ ॥ २७ ॥

yāvat sañjāyate kiñcit
sattvaṁ sthāvara-jaṅgamam
kṣetra-kṣetrajña-saṁyogāt
tad viddhi bharatarṣabha

yāvat—whatever; *saṁjāyate*—takes place; *kiñcit*—anything; *sattvam*—existence; *sthāvara*—not moving; *jaṅgamam*—moving; *kṣetra*—the body; *kṣetrajña*—knower of the body; *saṁyogāt*—union between; *tat viddhi*—you must know it; *bharatarṣabha*—O chief of the Bhāratas.

TRANSLATION

O chief of the Bhāratas, whatever you see in existence, both moving and unmoving, is only the combination of the field of activities and the knower of the field.

PURPORT

Both material nature and the living entity, which were existing before the creation of the cosmos, are explained in this verse. Whatever is created is but a combination of the living entity and material nature. There are many manifestations like trees, mountains and hills, which are not moving, and there are many existences which are moving, and all of them are but combinations of material nature and superior nature, the living entity. Without the touch of the superior nature, the living entity, nothing can grow. Therefore the relationship between matter and nature is eternally going on, and this combination is effected by the Supreme Lord; therefore He is the controller of both the superior and inferior natures. The material nature is created by Him, and the superior nature is placed in this material nature, and thus all these activities and manifestations take place.

TEXT 28

समं सर्वेषु भूतेषु तिष्ठन्तं परमेश्वरम् ।
विनश्यत्स्वविनश्यन्तं यः पश्यति स पश्यति ॥ २८ ॥

samaṁ sarveṣu bhūteṣu
tiṣṭhantaṁ parameśvaram
vinaśyatsv avinaśyantaṁ
yaḥ paśyati sa paśyati

samam—equally; *sarveṣu*—in all; *bhūteṣu*—living entities; *tiṣṭhantam*—residing; *parameśvaram*—the Supersoul; *vinaśyatsu*—in the destructible; *avinaśyantam*—not destroyed; *yaḥ*—anyone; *paśyati*—see; *saḥ*—he; *paśyati*—actually sees.

TRANSLATION

One who sees the Supersoul accompanying the individual soul in all bodies and who understands that neither the soul nor the Supersoul is ever destroyed, actually sees.

PURPORT

Anyone who can see three things—the body, the proprietor of the body, or individual soul, and the friend of the individual soul, combined together by good association—is actually in knowledge. Those who are not associated with the soul's friend are ignorant; they simply see the body, and when the body is destroyed they think that everything is finished, but actually it is not so. After the destruction of the body, both the soul and the Supersoul exist, and they go on eternally in many various moving and unmoving forms. The Sanskrit word *parameśvaram* is sometimes translated as the individual soul because the soul is the master of the body, and after the destruction of the body he transfers to another form. In that way he is master. But there are others who interpret this *parameśvaram* to be the Supersoul. In either case, both the Supersoul and the individual soul continue. They are not destroyed. One who can see in this way can actually see what is happening.

TEXT 29

समं पश्यन्हि सर्वत्र समवस्थितमीश्वरम् ।
न हिनस्त्यात्मनात्मानं ततो याति परां गतिम् ॥ २९ ॥

samaṁ paśyan hi sarvatra
samavasthitam īśvaram
na hinasty ātmanātmānaṁ
tato yāti parāṁ gatim

samam—equally; paśyan—seeing; hi—certainly; sarvatra—everywhere; samavasthitam—equally situated; īśvaram—Supersoul; na—does not; hinasti—degrade; ātmanā—by the mind; ātmānam—the soul; tataḥ yāti—then reaches; param—the transcendental; gatim—destination.

TRANSLATION

One who sees the Supersoul in every living being and equal everywhere does not degrade himself by his mind. Thus he approaches the transcendental destination.

PURPORT

The living entity, by accepting his material existence as just so much suffering, can become situated in his spiritual existence. If one understands that the Supreme is situated in His Paramātmā manifestation everywhere, that is, if one can see the presence of the Supreme Personality of Godhead in every living thing, he does not degrade himself, and he therefore gradually advances in the spiritual world. The mind is generally addicted to self-centered processes; but when the mind turns to the Supersoul, one becomes advanced in spiritual understanding.

TEXT 30

प्रकृत्यैव च कर्माणि क्रियमाणानि सर्वशः ।
यः पश्यति तथात्मानमकर्तारं स पश्यति ॥ ३० ॥

prakṛtyaiva ca karmāṇi
kriyamāṇāni sarvaśaḥ
yaḥ paśyati tathātmānam
akartāraṁ sa paśyati

prakṛtyā—material nature; *eva*—certainly; *ca*—also; *karmāṇi*—activities; *kriyamāṇāni*—engaged in performing; *sarvaśaḥ*—in all respects; *yaḥ*—anyone who; *paśyati*—sees; *tathā*—also; *ātmānam*—himself; *akartāram*—non-doer; *saḥ*—he; *paśyati*—sees perfectly.

TRANSLATION

One who can see that all activities are performed by the body, which is created of material nature, and sees that the self does nothing, actually sees.

PURPORT

This body is made by material nature under the direction of the Supersoul, and whatever activities are going on in respect to one's body are not his doing. Whatever one is supposed to do, either for happiness or for distress, one is forced to do because of the bodily constitution. The self, however, is outside all these bodily activities. This body is given according to one's past desires. To fulfill desires, one is given the body, with which he acts accordingly. Practically speaking, the body is a machine, designed by the Supreme Lord, to fulfill desires. Because of desires, one is put into difficult circumstances to suffer or to enjoy. This transcendental vision of the living entity, when developed, makes one separate from bodily activities. One who has such a vision is an actual seer.

TEXT 31

यदा भूतपृथग्भावमेकस्थमनुपश्यति ।
तत एव च विस्तारं ब्रह्म संपद्यते तदा ॥ ३१ ॥

yadā bhūta-pṛthag-bhāvam
eka-stham anupaśyati
tata eva ca vistāraṁ
brahma sampadyate tadā

yadā—when; *bhūta*—living entities; *pṛthak-bhāvam*—separated entities; *eka-stham*—situated in one; *anupaśyati*—tries to see through authority; *tataḥ eva*—thereafter; *ca*—also; *vistāram*—expanded; *brahma*—the Absolute; *sampadyate*—attains; *tadā*—at that time.

TRANSLATION

When a sensible man ceases to see different identities, which are due to different material bodies, he attains to the Brahman conception. Thus he sees that beings are expanded everywhere.

PURPORT

When one can see that the various bodies of living entities arise due to the different desires of the individual soul and do not actually belong to the soul itself, one actually sees. In the material conception of life, we find someone a demigod, someone a human being, a dog, a cat, etc. This is material vision, not actual vision. This material differentiation is due to a material conception of life. After the destruction of the material body, this spirit soul is one. The spirit soul, due to contact with material nature, gets different types of bodies. When one can see this, he attains spiritual vision; thus being freed from differentiations like man, animal, big, low, etc., one becomes beautified in his consciousness and able to develop Kṛṣṇa consciousness in his spiritual identity. How he then sees things will be explained in the next verse.

TEXT 32

अनादित्वान्निर्गुणत्वात्परमात्मायमव्ययः ।
शरीरस्थोऽपि कौन्तेय न करोति न लिप्यते ॥ ३२ ॥

anāditvān nirguṇatvāt
paramātmāyam avyayaḥ
śarīra-stho 'pi kaunteya
na karoti na lipyate

anāditvāt—due to eternity; *nirguṇatvāt*—due to transcendental; *param*—beyond material nature; *ātmā*—spirit; *ayam*—this; *avyayaḥ*—inexhaustable; *śarīra-sthaḥ api*—though dwelling in the body; *kaunteya*—O son of Kuntī; *na karoti*—never does anything; *na lipyate*—nor is he entangled.

TRANSLATION

Those with the vision of eternity can see that the soul is transcendental, eternal, and beyond the modes of nature. Despite contact with the material body, O Arjuna, the soul neither does anything nor is entangled.

PURPORT

A living entity appears to be born because of the birth of the material body, but actually the living entity is eternal; he is not born, and in spite of his being situated in a material body, he is transcendental and eternal. Thus he cannot be destroyed. By nature he is full of bliss. He does not engage himself in any material activities; therefore the activities performed due to his contact with material bodies do not entangle him.

TEXT 33

यथा सर्वगतं सौक्ष्म्यादाकाशं नोपलिप्यते ।
सर्वत्रावस्थितो देहे तथात्मा नोपलिप्यते ॥ ३३ ॥

yathā sarva-gataṁ saukṣmyād
ākāśaṁ nopalipyate
sarvatrāvasthito dehe
tathātmā nopalipyate

yathā—as; *sarva-gatam*—all-pervading; *saukṣmyāt*—due to being subtle; *ākāśam*—the sky; *na*—never; *upalipyate*—mixes; *sarvatra*—everywhere; *avasthitaḥ*—situated; *dehe*—in the body; *tathā*—such; *ātmā*—the self; *na*—never; *upalipyate*—mixes.

TRANSLATION

The sky, due to its subtle nature, does not mix with anything, although it is all-pervading. Similarly, the soul, situated in Brahman vision, does not mix with the body, though situated in that body.

PURPORT

The air enters into water, mud, stool and whatever else is there; still it does not mix with anything. Similarly, the living entity, even though situated in varieties of bodies, is aloof from them due to his subtle nature. Therefore it is impossible to see with the material eyes how the living entity is in contact with this body and how he is out of it after the destruction of the body. No one in science can ascertain this.

TEXT 34

यथा प्रकाशयत्येकः कृत्स्नं लोकमिमं रविः ।
क्षेत्रं क्षेत्री तथा कृत्स्नं प्रकाशयति भारत ॥ ३४ ॥

yathā prakāśayaty ekaḥ
kṛtsnaṁ lokam imaṁ raviḥ
kṣetraṁ kṣetrī tathā kṛtsnaṁ
prakāśayati bhārata

yathā—as; *prakāśayati*—illuminates; *ekaḥ*—one; *kṛtsnam*—the whole; *lokam*—universe; *imam*—this; *raviḥ*—the sun, *kṣetram*—this body; *kṣetrī*—the soul; *tathā*—similarly; *kṛtsnam*—all; *prakāśayati*—illuminates; *bhārata*—O son of Bharata.

TRANSLATION

O son of Bharata, as the sun alone illuminates all this universe, so does the living entity, one within the body, illuminate the entire body by consciousness.

PURPORT

There are various theories regarding consciousness. Here in *Bhagavad-gītā* the example of the sun and the sunshine is given. As the sun is situated in one place, but is illuminating the whole universe, so a small particle of spirit soul, although situated in the heart of this body, is illuminating the whole body by consciousness. Thus consciousness is the proof of the presence of the soul, as sunshine or light is the proof of the presence of the sun.

When the soul is present in the body, there is consciousness all over the body, and as soon as the soul has passed from the body, there is no more consciousness. This can be easily understood by any intelligent man. Therefore consciousness is not a production of the combinations of matter. It is the symptom of the living entity. The consciousness of the living entity, although qualitatively one with the supreme consciousness, is not supreme because the consciousness of one particular body does not share that of another body. But the Supersoul, which is situated in all bodies as the friend of the individual soul, is conscious of all bodies. That is the difference between supreme consciousness and individual consciousness.

TEXT 35

क्षेत्रक्षेत्रज्ञयोरेवमन्तरं ज्ञानचक्षुषा ।
भूतप्रकृतिमोक्षं च ये विदुर्यान्ति ते परम् ॥ ३५ ॥

*kṣetra-kṣetrajñayor evam
antaraṁ jñāna-cakṣuṣā
bhūta-prakṛti-mokṣaṁ ca
ye vidur yānti te param*

kṣetra—body; kṣetrajñayoḥ—of the proprietor of the body; evam—that; antaram—difference; jñāna-cakṣuṣā—by vision of knowledge; bhūta —living entity; prakṛti—material nature; mokṣam—liberation; ca—also; ye—one who; viduḥ—knows; yānti—approaches; te—they; param—Supreme.

TRANSLATION

One who knowingly sees this difference between the body and the owner of the body and can understand the process of liberation from this bondage, also attains to the supreme goal.

PURPORT

The purport of this Thirteenth Chapter is that one should know the distinction between the body, the owner of the body, and the Supersoul. A faithful person should at first have some good association to hear of God and thus gradually become enlightened. If one accepts a spiritual master, he can learn to distinguish between matter and spirit, and that becomes the steppingstone for further spiritual realization. A spiritual master teaches his students to get free from the material concept of life by various instructions. For instance, in *Bhagavad-gītā* we find Kṛṣṇa instructing Arjuna to free him from materialistic considerations.

One can understand that this body is matter; it can be analyzed with its twenty-four elements. That is the gross manifestation. And the subtle manifestation is the mind and psychological effects. And the symptoms of life are the interaction of these features. But over and above this, there is the soul, and there is also the Supersoul. The soul and the Supersoul are two. This material world is working by the conjunction of the soul and the twenty-four material elements. One who can see the constitution of the whole material manifestation as this combination of the soul and material elements and also can see the situation of the Supreme Soul becomes eligible for transfer to the spiritual world. These things are meant for contemplation and for realization, and one should have a complete understanding of this chapter with the help of the spiritual master.

Thus end the Bhaktivedanta Purports to the Thirteenth Chapter of the Śrīmad-Bhagavad-gītā *in the matter of Nature, the Enjoyer, and Consciousness.*

CHAPTER FOURTEEN

The Three Modes of Material Nature

TEXT 1

श्रीभगवानुवाच ।
परं भूयः प्रवक्ष्यामि ज्ञानानां ज्ञानमुत्तमम् ।
यज्ज्ञात्वा मुनयः सर्वे परां सिद्धिमितो गताः ॥ १ ॥

śrī bhagavān uvāca
param bhūyaḥ pravakṣyāmi
jñānānāṁ jñānam uttamam
yaj jñātvā munayaḥ sarve
param siddhim ito gatāḥ

śrī bhagavān uvāca—the Supreme Personality of Godhead said; *param*—transcendental; *bhūyaḥ*—again; *pravakṣyāmi*—I shall speak; *jñānānām*—of all knowledge; *jñānam*—knowledge; *uttamam*—the supreme; *yat*—which; *jñātvā*—knowing; *munayaḥ*—the sages; *sarve*—all; *parām*—transcendental; *siddhim*—perfection; *itaḥ*—from this world; *gatāḥ*—attain.

TRANSLATION

The Blessed Lord said: Again I shall declare to you this supreme wisdom, the best of all knowledge, knowing which all the sages have attained to supreme perfection.

PURPORT

From the Seventh Chapter to the end of the Twelfth Chapter, Śrī Kṛṣṇa in detail reveals the Absolute Truth, the Supreme Personality of Godhead. Now, the Lord Himself is further enlightening Arjuna. If one understands this chapter through the process of philosophical speculation, he will come to an understanding of devotional service. In the Thirteenth Chapter, it was clearly explained that by humbly developing knowledge one may possibly be freed from material entanglement. It has also been explained that it is due to association with the modes of nature that the living entity is entangled in this material world. Now, in this chapter, the Supreme Personality explains what those modes of nature are, how they act, how they bind and how they give liberation. The knowledge explained in this chapter is proclaimed by the Supreme Lord to be superior to the knowledge given so far in other chapters. By understanding this knowledge, various great sages attain perfection and transfer to the spiritual world. The Lord now explains the same knowledge in a better way. This knowledge is far, far superior to all other processes of knowledge thus far explained, and knowing this many attain perfection. Thus it is expected that one who understands this Fourteenth Chapter will attain perfection.

TEXT 2

इदं ज्ञानमुपाश्रित्य मम साधर्म्यमागताः ।
सर्गेऽपि नोपजायन्ते प्रलये न व्यथन्ति च ॥ २ ॥

idaṁ jñānam upāśritya
mama sādharmyam āgatāḥ
sarge 'pi nopajāyante
pralaye na vyathanti ca

idam—this; *jñānam*—knowledge; *upāśritya*—taking shelter of; *mama*—My; *sādharmyam*—nature; *āgatāḥ*—attain; *sarge api*—even in the creation; *na*—never; *upajāyante*—comes in; *pralaye*—in the annihilation; *na*—nor; *vyathanti*—disturbed; *ca*—also.

TRANSLATION

By becoming fixed in this knowledge, one can attain to the transcendental nature, which is like My own nature. Thus established, one is not born at the time of creation nor disturbed at the time of dissolution.

PURPORT

After acquiring perfect transcendental knowledge, one acquires qualitative equality with the Supreme Personality of Godhead, becoming free from the repetition of birth and death. One does not, however, lose his identity as an individual soul. It is understood from Vedic literature that the liberated souls who have reached the transcendental planets of the spiritual sky always look to the lotus feet of the Supreme Lord, being engaged in His transcendental loving service. So, even after liberation, the devotees do not lose their individual identities.

Generally, in the material world, whatever knowledge we get is contaminated by the three modes of material nature. But knowledge which is not contaminated by the three modes of nature is called transcendental knowledge. As soon as one is situated in that transcendental knowledge, he is on the same platform as that of the Supreme Person. Those who have no knowledge of the spiritual sky hold that after being freed from the material activities of the material form, this spiritual identity becomes formless, without any variegatedness. However, just as there is material variegatedness in this world, so, in the spiritual world, there is also variegatedness. Those in ignorance of this think that spiritual existence is opposed to material variety. But actually, in the spiritual sky, one attains spiritual form. There are spiritual activities, and the spiritual situation is called devotional life. That atmosphere is said to be uncontaminated, and there one is equal in quality with the Supreme Lord. To obtain such knowledge, one must develop all the spiritual qualities. One who thus develops the spiritual qualities is not affected either by the creation or the destruction of the material world.

TEXT 3

मम योनिर्महद्ब्रह्म तस्मिन्गर्भं दधाम्यहम् ।
सम्भवः सर्वभूतानां ततो भवति भारत ॥ ३ ॥

mama yonir mahad brahma
tasmin garbhaṁ dadhāmy aham
sambhavaḥ sarva-bhūtānām
tato bhavati bhārata

mama—My; yoniḥ—source of birth; mahat—the total material existence; brahma—supreme; tasmin—in that; garbham—pregnancy; dadhāmi—create; aham—I; sambhavaḥ—possibility; sarva-bhūtānām—of all living entities; tataḥ—thereafter; bhavati—becomes; bhārata—O son of Bharata.

TRANSLATION

The total material substance, called Brahman, is the source of birth, and it is that Brahman that I impregnate, making possible the births of all living beings, O son of Bharata.

PURPORT

This is an explanation of the world: everything that takes place is due to the combination of kṣetra and kṣetrajña, the body and the spirit soul. This combination of material nature and the living entity is made possible by the Supreme God Himself. The mahat-tattva is the total cause of the total cosmic manifestation, and because in the total substance of the material cause there are three modes of nature, it is sometimes called Brahman. The Supreme Personality impregnates that total substance, and thus innumerable universes become possible. This total material substance, the mahat-tattva, is described as Brahman in the Vedic literature: tasmād etad brahma nāma-rūpam annaṁ ca jāyate. Into that Brahman the seeds of the living entities are impregnated by the Supreme Person. The twenty-four elements, beginning from earth, water, fire and air, are all material energy, called Mahā-brahman, or the great Brahman, the material nature. As is explained in the Seventh Chapter, beyond this there is another, superior nature—the living entity. In material nature the superior nature is mixed by the will of the Supreme Personality of Godhead, and thereafter all living entities are born of this material nature.

The scorpion lays its eggs in piles of rice, and sometimes it is said that the scorpion is born out of rice. But the rice is not the cause of the scorpion. Actually, the eggs were laid by the mother. Similarly, material nature is not the cause of the birth of the living entities. The seed is given by the Supreme Personality of Godhead, and they only seem to come out as products of material nature. Thus every living entity, according to his past activities, has a different body, created by this material nature, and the entity can enjoy or suffer according to his past deeds. The Lord is the cause of all the manifestations of living entities in this material world.

TEXT 4

सर्वयोनिषु कौन्तेय मूर्तयः संभवन्ति याः ।
तासां ब्रह्म महद्योनिरहं बीजप्रदः पिता ॥ ४ ॥

sarva-yoniṣu kaunteya
mūrtayaḥ sambhavanti yāḥ
tāsāṁ brahma mahad yonir
ahaṁ bīja-pradaḥ pitā

sarva-yoniṣu—in all species of life; *kaunteya*—O son of Kuntī; *mūrtayaḥ*—forms; *sambhavanti*—as they appear; *yāḥ*—which; *tāsām*—all of them; *brahma*—supreme; *mahat yoniḥ*—the source of birth in the material substance; *aham*—Myself; *bīja-pradaḥ*—seed-giving; *pitā*—father.

TRANSLATION

It should be understood that all species of life, O son of Kuntī, are made possible by birth in this material nature, and that I am the seed-giving father.

PURPORT

In this verse it is clearly explained that the Supreme Personality of Godhead, Kṛṣṇa, is the original father of all living entities. The living entities are combinations of the material nature and the spiritual nature. Such living entities are seen not only on this planet, but in every planet, even in the highest where Brahmā is situated. Everywhere there are living entities; within the earth there are living entities, even within water and within fire. All these appearances are due to the mother, material nature, and Kṛṣṇa's seed-giving process. The purport is that the living entities, being impregnated in the material world, come out and form at the time of creation according to their past deeds.

TEXT 5

सत्त्वं रजस्तम इति गुणाः प्रकृतिसंभवाः ।
निबध्नन्ति महाबाहो देहे देहिनमव्ययम् ॥ ५ ॥

sattvaṁ rajas tama iti
guṇāḥ prakṛti-sambhavāḥ
nibadhnanti mahā-bāho
dehe dehinam avyayam

sattvam—mode of goodness; rajaḥ—mode of passion; tamaḥ—mode of ignorance; iti—thus; guṇāḥ—qualities; prakṛti—material nature; sambhavāḥ—produced of; nibadhnanti—does condition; mahā-bāho—O mighty-armed one; dehe—in this body; dehinam—the living entity; avyayam—eternal.

TRANSLATION

Material nature consists of the three modes—goodness, passion and ignorance. When the living entity comes in contact with nature, he becomes conditioned by these modes.

PURPORT

The living entity, because he is transcendental, has nothing to do with this material nature. Still, because he has become conditioned by the material world, he is acting under the spell of the three modes of material nature. Because living entities have different kinds of bodies, in terms of the different aspects of nature, they are induced to act according to that nature. This is the cause of the varieties of happiness and distress.

TEXT 6

तत्र सत्त्वं निर्मलत्वात्प्रकाशकमनामयम् ।
सुखसङ्गेन बध्नाति ज्ञानसङ्गेन चानघ ॥ ६ ॥

tatra sattvaṁ nirmalatvāt
prakāśakam anāmayam
sukha-saṅgena badhnāti
jñāna-saṅgena cānagha

tatra—thereafter; *sattvam*—mode of goodness; *nirmalatvāt*—being purest in the material world; *prakāśakam*—illuminating; *anāmayam*—without any sinful reachon; *sukha*—happiness; *saṅgena*—association; *badhnāti*—conditions; *jñāna*—knowledge; *saṅgena*—association; *ca*—also; *anagha*—O sinless one.

TRANSLATION

O sinless one, the mode of goodness, being purer than the others, is illuminating, and it frees one from all sinful reactions. Those situated in that mode develop knowledge, but they become conditioned by the concept of happiness.

PURPORT

The living entities conditioned by material nature are of various types. One is happy, another is very active, and another is helpless. All these types of psychological manifestations are causes of the entities' conditioned status in nature. How they are differently conditioned is explained in this section of *Bhagavad-gītā*. The mode of goodness is first considered. The effect of developing the mode of goodness in the material world is that one becomes wiser than those otherwise conditioned. A man in the mode of goodness is not so much affected by material miseries, and he has a sense of advancement in material knowledge. The representative type is the *brāhmaṇa*, who is supposed to be situated in the mode of goodness. This sense of happiness is due to understanding that, in the mode of goodness, one is more or less free from sinful reactions. Actually, in the Vedic literature it is said that the mode of goodness means greater knowledge and a greater sense of happiness.

The difficulty here is that when a living entity is situated in the mode of goodness, he becomes conditioned to feel that he is advanced in knowledge and is better than others. In this way he becomes conditioned. The best examples are the scientist and philosopher: each is very proud of his knowledge, and because they generally improve their living conditions, they feel a sort of material happiness. This sense of advanced happiness in conditioned life makes them bound by the mode of goodness of material nature. As such, they are attracted toward working in the mode of goodness, and, as long as they have an attraction for working in that way, they have to take some type of body in the modes of nature. Thus there is no likelihood of liberation, or of being transferred to the spiritual world. Repeatedly, one may become a philosopher, a scientist, or a poet, and, repeatedly, become entangled in the same disadvantages of birth and death. But, due to the illusion of the material energy, one thinks that that sort of life is pleasant.

TEXT 7

रजो रागात्मकं विद्धि तृष्णासङ्गसमुद्भवम् ।
तन्निबध्नाति कौन्तेय कर्मसङ्गेन देहिनम् ॥ ७ ॥

rajo rāgātmakaṁ viddhi
tṛṣṇā-saṅga-samudbhavam
tan nibadhnāti kaunteya
karma-saṅgena dehinam

rajaḥ—mode of passion; *rāga-ātmakam*—born of desire or lust; *viddhi*—know; *tṛṣṇā*—hankering; *saṅga*—association; *samudbhavam*—produced of; *tat*—that; *nibadhnāti*—is bound; *kaunteya*—O son of Kuntī; *karma-saṅgena*—association with fruitive activity; *dehinam*—of the embodied.

TRANSLATION

The mode of passion is born of unlimited desires and longings, O son of Kuntī, and because of this one is bound to material fruitive activities.

PURPORT

The mode of passion is characterized by the attraction between man and woman. Woman has attraction for man, and man has attraction for woman.

This is called the mode of passion. And, when the mode of passion is increased, one develops the hankering for material enjoyment. He wants to enjoy sense gratification. For sense gratification, a man in the mode of passion wants some honor in society, or in the nation, and he wants to have a happy family, with nice children, wife, and house. These are the products of the mode of passion. As long as one is hankering after these things, he has to work very hard. Therefore it is clearly stated here that he becomes associated with the fruits of his activities and thus becomes bound by such activities. In order to please his wife, children and society and to keep up his prestige, one has to work. Therefore, the whole material world is more or less in the mode of passion. Modern civilization is considered to be advanced in the standards of the mode of passion. Formerly, the advanced condition was considered to be in the mode of goodness. If there is no liberation for those in the mode of goodness, what of those who are entangled in the mode of passion?

TEXT 8

तमस्त्वज्ञानजं विद्धि मोहनं सर्वदेहिनाम् ।
प्रमादालस्यनिद्राभिस्तन्निबध्नाति भारत ॥ ८ ॥

tamas tv ajñāna-jaṁ viddhi
mohanaṁ sarva-dehinām
pramādālasya-nidrābhis
tan nibadhnāti bhārata

tamaḥ—mode of ignorance; *tu*—but; *ajñāna-jam*—products of ignorance; *viddhi*—knowing; *mohanam*—delusion; *sarva-dehinām*—of all embodied beings; *pramāda*—madness; *ālasya*—indolence; *nidrābhiḥ*—sleep; *tat*—that; *nibadhnāti*—binds; *bhārata*—O son of Bharata.

TRANSLATION

O son of Bharata, the mode of ignorance causes the delusion of all living entities. The result of this mode is madness, indolence and sleep, which bind the conditioned soul.

PURPORT

In this verse the specific application of the word *tu* is very significant. This means that the mode of ignorance is a very peculiar qualification of the embodied soul. This mode of ignorance is just the opposite of the mode of goodness. In the mode of goodness, by development of knowledge, one can understand what is what, but the mode of ignorance is just the opposite. Everyone under the spell of the mode of ignorance becomes mad, and a madman cannot understand what is what. Instead of making advancement, one becomes degraded. The definition of the mode of ignorance is stated in the Vedic literature: under the spell of ignorance, one cannot understand the thing as it is. For example, everyone can see that his grandfather has died, and therefore he will also die; man is mortal. The children that he conceives will also die. So death is sure. Still, people are madly accumulating money and working very hard all day and night, not caring for the eternal spirit. This is madness. In their madness, they are very reluctant to make advancement in spiritual understanding. Such people are very lazy. When they are invited to associate for spiritual understanding, they are not much interested. They are not even active like the man who is controlled by the mode of passion. Thus another symptom of one embedded in the mode of ignorance is that he sleeps more than is required. Six hours of sleep is sufficient, but a man in the mode of ignorance sleeps at least ten or twelve hours a day. Such a man appears to be always dejected, and is addicted to intoxicants and sleeping. These are the symptoms of a person conditioned by the mode of ignorance.

TEXT 9

सत्त्वं सुखे संजयति रजः कर्मणि भारत ।
ज्ञानमावृत्य तु तमः प्रमादे संजयत्युत ॥ ९ ॥

sattvaṁ sukhe sañjayati
rajaḥ karmaṇi bhārata
jñānam āvṛtya tu tamaḥ
pramāde sañjayaty uta

sattvam—mode of goodness; *sukhe*—in happiness; *sañjayati*—develops; *rajaḥ*—mode of passion; *karmaṇi*—fruits of activities; *bhārata*—O son of Bharata; *jñānam*—knowledge; *āvṛtya*—covering; *tu*—but; *tamaḥ*—the mode of ignorance; *pramāde*—in madness; *sañjayati*—develops; *uta*—it is said.

TRANSLATION

The mode of goodness conditions one to happiness, passion conditions him to the fruits of action, and ignorance to madness.

PURPORT

A person in the mode of goodness is satisfied by his work or intellectual pursuit, just as a philosopher, scientist, or educator may be engaged in a particular field of knowledge and may be satisfied in that way. A man in the modes of passion and goodness may be engaged in fruitive activity; he owns as much as he can and spends for good causes. Sometimes he tries to open hospitals, give to charity institutions, etc. These are the signs of one in the mode of passion. And the mode of ignorance covers knowledge. In the mode of ignorance, whatever one does is neither good for him nor for anyone.

TEXT 10

रजस्तमश्चाभिभूय सत्त्वं भवति भारत ।
रजः सत्त्वं तमश्चैव तमः सत्त्वं रजस्तथा ॥ १० ॥

rajas tamaś cābhibhūya
sattvaṁ bhavati bhārata
rajaḥ sattvaṁ tamaś caiva
tamaḥ sattvaṁ rajas tathā

rajaḥ—mode of passion; *tamaḥ*—mode of ignorance; *ca*—also; *abhibhūya*—also surpassing; *sattvam*—mode of goodness; *bhavati*—becomes prominent; *bhārata*—O son of Bharata; *rajaḥ*—mode of passion; *sattvam*—mode of goodness; *tamaḥ*—mode of ignorance; *ca*—also; *eva*—like that; *tamaḥ*—mode of ignorance; *sattvam*—mode of goodness; *rajaḥ*—mode of passion; *tathā*—as in this.

TRANSLATION

Sometimes the mode of passion becomes prominent, defeating the mode of goodness, O son of Bharata. And sometimes the mode of goodness defeats passion, and at other times the mode of ignorance defeats goodness and passion. In this way there is always competition for supremacy.

PURPORT

When the mode of passion is prominent, the modes of goodness and ignorance are defeated. When the mode of goodness is prominent, passion and ignorance are defeated. And, when the mode of ignorance is prominent, passion and goodness are defeated. This competition is always going on. Therefore, one who is actually intent on advancing in Kṛṣṇa consciousness has to transcend these three modes. The prominence of some certain mode of nature is manifested in one's dealings, in his activities, in eating, etc. All this will be explained in later chapters. But if one wants, he can develop, by practice, the mode of goodness and thus defeat the modes of ignorance and passion. One can similarly develop the mode of passion and defeat goodness and ignorance. Or, one can develop the mode of ignorance and defeat goodness and passion. Although there are these three modes of material nature, if one is determined, he can be blessed by the mode of goodness, and, by transcending the mode of goodness, he can be situated in pure goodness, which is called the *vāsudeva* state, a state in which one can understand the science of God. By the manifestation of particular activities, it can be understood in what mode of nature one is situated.

TEXT 11

सर्वद्वारेषु देहेऽस्मिन्प्रकाश उपजायते ।
ज्ञानं यदा तदा विद्याद्विवृद्धं सत्त्वमित्युत ॥ ११ ॥

sarva-dvāreṣu dehe 'smin
prakāśa upajāyate
jñānaṁ yadā tadā vidyād
vivṛddhaṁ sattvam ity uta

sarva-dvāreṣu—all the gates; *dehe asmin*—in this body; *prakāśaḥ*—quality of illumination; *upajāyate*—develops; *jñānam*—knowledge; *yadā*—when; *tadā*—at that time; *vidyāt*—must know; *vivṛddham*—increased; *sattvam*—mode of goodness; *iti*—thus; *uta*—said.

TRANSLATION

The manifestations of the mode of goodness can be experienced when all the gates of the body are illuminated by knowledge.

PURPORT

There are nine gates in the body: two eyes, two ears, two nostrils, the mouth, the genital and the anus. In every gate, when the symptom of goodness is illuminated, it should be understood that one has developed the mode of goodness. In the mode of goodness, one can see things in the right position, one can hear things in the right position, and one can taste things in the right position. One becomes cleansed inside and outside. In every gate there is development of the symptoms of happiness, and that is the position of goodness.

TEXT 12

लोभः प्रवृत्तिरारम्भः कर्मणामशमः स्पृहा ।
रजस्येतानि जायन्ते विवृद्धे भरतर्षभ ॥ १२ ॥

lobhaḥ pravṛttir ārambhaḥ
karmaṇām aśamaḥ spṛhā
rajasy etāni jāyante
vivṛddhe bharatarṣabha

lobhaḥ—greed; *pravṛttiḥ*—hankering; *ārambhaḥ*—endeavor; *karmaṇām*—of activities; *aśamaḥ*—uncontrollable; *spṛhā*—desire; *rajasi*—in the mode of passion; *etāni*—all this; *jāyante*—develop; *vivṛddhe*—when there is excess; *bharatarṣabha*—O chief of the descendants of Bharata.

TRANSLATION

O chief of the Bhāratas, when there is an increase in the mode of passion, the symptoms of great attachment, uncontrollable desire, hankering, and intense endeavor develop.

PURPORT

One in the mode of passion is never satisfied with the position he has already acquired; he hankers to increase his position. If he wants to construct a residential house, he tries his best to have a palatial house, as if he would be able to reside in that house eternally. And he develops a great hankering for sense gratification. There is no end to sense gratification. He always wants to remain with his family and in his house and to continue the process of sense gratification. There is no cessation of this. All these symptoms should be understood as characteristic of the mode of passion.

TEXT 13

अप्रकाशोऽप्रवृत्तिश्च प्रमादो मोह एव च ।
तमस्येतानि जायन्ते विवृद्धे कुरुनन्दन ॥ १३ ॥

aprakāśo 'pravṛttiś ca
pramādo moha eva ca
tamasy etāni jāyante
vivṛddhe kuru-nandana

aprakāśaḥ—darkness; *apravṛttiḥ*—inactivity; *ca*—and; *pramādaḥ*—madness; *mohaḥ*—illusion; *eva*—certainly; *ca*—also; *tamasi*—of the mode of ignorance; *etāni*—these; *jāyante*—are manifested; *vivṛddhe*—is developed; *kuru-nandana*—O son of Kuru.

TRANSLATION

O son of Kuru, when there is an increase in the mode of ignorance madness, illusion, inertia and darkness are manifested.

PURPORT

When there is no illumination, knowledge is absent. One in the mode of ignorance does not work by a regulative principle; he wants to act whimsically for no purpose. Even though he has the capacity to work, he makes no endeavor. This is called illusion. Although consciousness is going on, life is inactive. These are the symptoms of one in the mode of ignorance.

TEXT 14

यदा सत्त्वे प्रवृद्धे तु प्रलयं याति देहभृत् ।
तदोत्तमविदां लोकानमलान्प्रतिपद्यते ॥ १४ ॥

yadā sattve pravṛddhe tu
pralayaṁ yāti deha-bhṛt
tadottama-vidāṁ lokān
amalān pratipadyate

yadā—when; *sattve*—mode of goodness; *pravṛddhe*—in development; *tu*—but; *pralayam*—dissolution; *yāti*—goes; *deha-bhṛt*—embodied; *tadā*—at that time; *uttama-vidām*—of the great sages; *lokān*—the planets; *amalān*—pure; *pratipadyate*—attains.

TRANSLATION

When one dies in the mode of goodness, he attains to the pure higher planets.

PURPORT

One in goodness attains higher planetary systems, like Brahmaloka or Janaloka, and there enjoys godly happiness. The word *amalān* is significant; it means free from the modes of passion and ignorance. There are impurities in the material world, but the mode of goodness is the purest form of existence in the material world. There are different kinds of planets for different kinds of living entities. Those who die in the mode of goodness are elevated to the planets where great sages and great devotees live.

TEXT 15

रजसि प्रलयं गत्वा कर्मसङ्गिषु जायते ।
तथा प्रलीनस्तमसि मूढयोनिषु जायते ॥ १५ ॥

rajasi pralayaṁ gatvā
karma-saṅgiṣu jāyate
tathā pralīnas tamasi
mūḍha-yoniṣu jāyate

rajasi—in passion; *pralayam*—dissolution; *gatvā*—attaining; *karma-saṅgiṣu* —in the association of fruitive activities; *jāyate*—takes birth; *tathā*—thereafter; *pralīnaḥ*—being dissolved; *tamasi*—in ignorance; *mūḍha*—animal; *yoniṣu*—species; *jāyate*—take birth.

TRANSLATION

When one dies in the mode of passion, he takes birth among those engaged in fruitive activities; and when he dies in the mode of ignorance, he takes birth in the animal kingdom.

PURPORT

Some people have the impression that when the soul reaches the platform of human life, it never goes down again. This is incorrect. According to this verse, if one develops the mode of ignorance, after his death he is degraded to the animal form of life. From there one has to again elevate himself, by evolutionary process, to come again to the human form of life. Therefore, those who are actually serious about human life should take to the mode of goodness and in good association transcend the modes and become situated in Kṛṣṇa consciousness. This is the aim of human life. Otherwise, there is no guarantee that the human being will again attain to the human status.

TEXT 16

कर्मणः सुकृतस्याहुः सात्त्विकं निर्मलं फलम् ।
रजसस्तु फलं दुःखमज्ञानं तमसः फलम् ॥ १६ ॥

karmaṇaḥ sukṛtasyāhuḥ
sāttvikaṁ nirmalaṁ phalam
rajasas tu phalaṁ duḥkham
ajñānaṁ tamasaḥ phalam

karmaṇaḥ—of work; sukṛtasya—in the mode of goodness; āhuḥ—said; sāttvikam—mode of goodness; nirmalam—purified; phalam—result; rajasaḥ—of the mode of passion; tu—but; phalam—result; duḥkham—misery; ajñānam—nonsense; tamasaḥ—of the mode of ignorance; phalam—result.

TRANSLATION

By acting in the mode of goodness, one becomes purified. Works done in the mode of passion result in distress, and actions performed in the mode of ignorance result in foolishness.

PURPORT

By pious activities in the mode of goodness one is purified; therefore the sages, who are free from all illusion, are situated in happiness. Similarly, activities in the mode of passion are simply miserable. Any activity for material happiness is bound to be defeated. If, for example, one wants to have a skyscraper, so much human misery has to be undergone before a big skyscraper can be built. The financier has to take much trouble to earn a mass of wealth, and those who are slaving to construct the building have to render physical toil. The miseries are there. Thus *Bhagavad-gītā* says that in any activity performed under the spell of the mode of passion, there is definitely great misery. There may be a little so-called mental happiness— "I have this house or this money" —but this is not actual happiness. As far as the mode of ignorance is concerned, the performer is without knowledge, and therefore all his activities result in present misery, and afterwards he will go on toward animal life. Animal life is always miserable, although, under the spell of the illusory energy, *māyā*, the animals do not understand this. Slaughtering poor animals is also due to the mode of ignorance. The animal killers do not know that in the future the animal will have a body suitable to kill them. That is the law of nature. In human society, if one kills a man he has to be hanged. That is the law of the state. Because of ignorance, people do not perceive that there is a complete state controlled by the Supreme Lord. Every living creature is the son of the Supreme Lord, and He does not tolerate even an ant's being killed. One has to pay for it. So, indulgence in animal killing for the taste of the tongue is the grossest kind of ignorance. A human being has no need to kill animals because God has supplied so many nice things. If one indulges in meat-eating anyway, it is to be understood that he is acting in ignorance and is making his future very dark. Of all kinds of animal killing, the killing of cows is most vicious because the cow gives us all kinds of pleasure by supplying milk. Cow slaughter is an act of the grossest type of ignorance. In the Vedic literature the words *gobhiḥ prīṇita-matsaram* indicate that one who, being fully satisfied by milk, is desirous of killing the cow, is in the grossest ignorance. There is also a prayer in the Vedic literature that states:

> *namo brahmaṇya-devāya go-brāhmaṇa-hitāya ca*
> *jagaddhitāya kṛṣṇāya govindāya namo namaḥ*

"My Lord, You are the well-wisher of the cows and the *brāhmaṇas*, and You are the well-wisher of the entire human society and world." The purport is that special mention is given in that prayer for the protection of the cows and the *brāhmaṇas*. *Brāhmaṇas* are the symbol of spiritual education, and cows are the symbol of the most valuable food; these two living creatures, the *brāhmaṇas* and the cows, must be given all protection—that is real advancement of civilization. In modern human society, spiritual knowledge is neglected, and cow killing is encouraged. It is to be understood, then, that human society is advancing in the wrong direction and is clearing the path to its own condemnation. A civilization which guides the citizens to become animals in their next lives is certainly not a human civilization. The present human civilization is, of course, grossly misled by the modes of passion and ignorance. It is a very dangerous age, and all nations should take care to provide the easiest process, Kṛṣṇa consciousness, to save humanity from the greatest danger.

TEXT 17

सत्त्वात्संजायते ज्ञानं रजसो लोभ एव च ।
प्रमादमोहौ तमसो भवतोऽज्ञानमेव च ॥ १७ ॥

sattvāt sañjāyate jñānaṁ
rajaso lobha eva ca
pramāda-mohau tamaso
bhavato 'jñānam eva ca

sattvāt—from the mode of goodness; *sañjāyate*—develops; *jñānam*—knowledge; *rajasaḥ*—from the mode of passion; *lobhaḥ*—greed; *eva*—certainly; *ca*—also; *pramāda*—madness; *mohau*—illusion; *tamasaḥ*—from the mode of ignorance; *bhavataḥ*—develops; *ajñānam*—nonsense; *eva*—certainly; *ca*—also.

TRANSLATION

From the mode of goodness, real knowledge develops; from the mode of passion, grief develops; and from the mode of ignorance, foolishness, madness and illusion develop.

PURPORT

Since the present civilization is not very congenial to the living entities, Kṛṣṇa consciousness is recommended. Through Kṛṣṇa consciousness, society will develop the mode of goodness. When the mode of goodness is developed, people will see things as they are. In the mode of ignorance, people are just like animals and cannot see things clearly. In the mode of ignorance, for example, they do not see that by killing one animal they are taking a chance of being killed by the same animal in the next life. Because people have no education in actual knowledge, they become irresponsible. To stop this irresponsibility, education for developing the mode of goodness of the people in general must be there. When they are actually educated in the mode of goodness, they will become sober, in full knowledge of things as they are. Then people will be happy and prosperous. Even if the majority of the people aren't happy and prosperous, if a certain percentage of the population develops Kṛṣṇa consciousness and becomes situated in the mode of goodness, then there is the possibility for peace and prosperity all over the world. Otherwise, if the world is devoted to the modes of passion and ignorance, there can be no peace or prosperity. In the mode of passion, people become greedy, and their hankering for sense enjoyment has no limit. One can see that even if one has enough money and adequate arrangement for sense gratification, there is neither happiness nor peace of mind. That is not possible because one is situated in the mode of passion. If one wants happiness at all, his money will not help him; he has to elevate himself to the mode of goodness by practicing Kṛṣṇa consciousness. One engaged in the mode of passion is not only mentally unhappy, but his profession and occupation are also very troublesome. He has to devise so many plans and schemes to acquire enough money to maintain his status quo. This is all miserable. In the mode of ignorance, people become mad. Being distressed by their circumstances, they take shelter of intoxication, and thus they sink further into ignorance. Their future in life is very dark.

TEXT 18

ऊर्ध्वं गच्छन्ति सत्त्वस्था मध्ये तिष्ठन्ति राजसाः ।
जघन्यगुणवृत्तिस्था अधो गच्छन्ति तामसाः ॥ १८ ॥

ūrdhvaṁ gacchanti sattva-sthā
madhye tiṣṭhanti rājasāḥ
jaghanya-guṇa-vṛtti-sthā
adho gacchanti tāmasāḥ

ūrdhvam—upwards; *gacchanti*—goes; *sattva-sthāḥ*—one who is situated in the mode of goodness; *madhye*—in the middle; *tiṣṭhanti*—dwell; *rājasāḥ*—those who are situated in the mode of passion; *jaghanya*—abominable; *guṇa*—quality; *vṛtti-sthāḥ*—occupation; *adhaḥ*—down; *gacchanti*—go; *tāmasāḥ*—persons in the mode of ignorance.

TRANSLATION

Those situated in the mode of goodness gradually go upward to the higher planets; those in the mode of passion live on the earthly planets; and those in the mode of ignorance go down to the hellish worlds.

PURPORT

In this verse the results of actions in the three modes of nature are more explicitly set forth. There is an upper planetary system, consisting of the heavenly planets, where everyone is highly elevated. According to the degree of development of the mode of goodness, the living entity can be transferred to various planets in this system. The highest planet is Satyaloka, or Brahmaloka, where the prime person of this universe, Lord Brahmā, resides. We have seen already that we can hardly calculate the wondrous condition of life in Brahmaloka, but the highest condition of life, the mode of goodness, can bring us to this.

The mode of passion is mixed. It is in the middle, between the modes of goodness and ignorance. A person is not always pure, but even if he should be purely in the mode of passion, he will simply remain on this earth as a king or a rich man. But because there are mixtures, one can also go down. People on this earth, in the modes of passion or ignorance, cannot forcibly approach the higher planets by machine. In the mode of passion, there is also the chance of becoming mad in the next life.

The lowest quality, the mode of ignorance, is described here as abominable. The result of developing ignorance is very, very risky. It is the lowest quality in material nature. Beneath the human level there are eight million species of life: birds, beasts, reptiles, trees, etc., and, according to the development of the mode of ignorance, people are brought down to these abominable conditions. The word tāmasāḥ is very significant here. Tāmasāḥ indicates those who stay continually in the mode of ignorance without rising to a higher mode. Their future is very dark.

There is opportunity for men in the modes of ignorance and passion to be elevated to the mode of goodness, and that system is called Kṛṣṇa consciousness. But one who does not take advantage of this opportunity certainly will continue in the lower modes.

TEXT 19

नान्यं गुणेभ्यः कर्तारं यदा द्रष्टानुपश्यति ।
गुणेभ्यश्च परं वेत्ति मद्भावं सोऽधिगच्छति ॥ १९ ॥

nānyaṁ guṇebhyaḥ kartāraṁ
yadā draṣṭānupaśyati
guṇebhyaś ca paraṁ vetti
mad-bhāvaṁ so 'dhigacchati

na—never; *anyam*—other than; *guṇebhyaḥ*—from the qualities; *kartāram* —the performer; *yadā*—when; *draṣṭā anupaśyati*—he who sees properly; *guṇebhyaḥ ca*—from the modes of nature; *param*—transcendental; *vetti*— know; *mat-bhāvam*—My spiritual nature; *saḥ*—he; *adhigacchati*—is promoted.

TRANSLATION

When you see that there is nothing beyond these modes of nature in all activities and that the Supreme Lord is transcendental to all these modes, then you can know My spiritual nature.

PURPORT

One can transcend all the activities of the modes of material nature simply by understanding them properly by learning from the proper souls. The real spiritual master is Kṛṣṇa, and He is imparting this spiritual knowledge to Arjuna. Similarly, it is from those who are fully in Kṛṣṇa consciousness that one has to learn this science of activities in terms of the modes of nature. Otherwise, one's life will be misdirected. By the instruction of a bona fide spiritual master, a living entity can know of his spiritual position, his material body, his senses, how he is entrapped, and how he is under the spell of the material modes of nature. He is helpless, being in the grip of these modes, but when he can see his real position, then he can attain to the transcendental platform, having the scope for spiritual life. Actually, the living entity is not the performer of different activities. He is forced to act because he is situated in a particular type of body, conducted by some particular mode of material nature. Unless one has the help of spiritual authority, he cannot understand in what position he is actually situated. With the association of a bona fide spiritual master, he can see his real position, and, by such an understanding, he can become fixed in full Kṛṣṇa consciousness. A man in Kṛṣṇa consciousness is not controlled by the spell of the material modes of nature. It has already been stated in the Seventh Chapter that one who has surrendered to Kṛṣṇa is relieved from the activities of material nature. Therefore for one who is able to see things as they are, the influence of material nature gradually ceases.

TEXT 20

गुणानेतानतीत्य त्रीन्देही देहसमुद्भवान् ।
जन्ममृत्युजरादुःखैर्विमुक्तोऽमृतमश्नुते ॥ २० ॥

guṇān etān atītya trīn
dehī deha-samudbhavān
janma-mṛtyu-jarā-duḥkhair
vimukto 'mṛtam aśnute

guṇān—qualities; *etān*—all these; *atītya*—transcending; *trīn*—three; *dehī*—body; *deha*—body; *samudbhavān*—produced of; *janma*—birth; *mṛtyu*—death; *jarā*—old age; *duḥkhaiḥ*—distresses; *vimuktaḥ*—being freed from; *amṛtam*—nectar; *aśnute*—enjoys.

TRANSLATION

When the embodied being is able to transcend these three modes, he can become free from birth, death, old age and their distresses and can enjoy nectar even in this life.

PURPORT

How one can stay in the transcendental position, even in this body, in full Kṛṣṇa consciousness, is explained in this verse. The Sanskrit word *dehī* means embodied. Although one is within this material body, by his advancement in spiritual knowledge he can be free from the influence of the modes of nature. He can enjoy the happiness of spiritual life even in this body because, after leaving this body, he is certainly going to the spiritual sky. But even in this body he can enjoy spiritual happiness. In other words, devotional service in Kṛṣṇa consciousness is the sign of liberation from this material entanglement, and this will be explained in the Eighteenth Chapter. When one is freed from the influence of the modes of material nature, he enters into devotional service.

TEXT 21

अर्जुन उवाच ।
कैर्लिङ्गैस्त्रीन्गुणानेतानतीतो भवति प्रभो ।
किमाचारः कथं चैतांस्त्रीन्गुणानतिवर्तते ॥ २१ ॥

arjuna uvāca
kair liṅgais trīn guṇān etān
atīto bhavati prabho
kim ācāraḥ katham caitāṁs
trīn guṇān ativartate

arjunaḥ uvāca—Arjuna said; *kaiḥ*—by which; *liṅgaiḥ*—symptoms; *trīn*—three; *guṇān*—qualities; *etān*—all this; *atītaḥ*—transcend; *bhavati*—become; *prabho*—my Lord; *kim*—what; *ācāraḥ*—behavior; *katham*—what; *ca*—also; *etān*—these; *trīn*—three; *guṇān*—qualities; *ativartate*—transcend.

TRANSLATION

Arjuna inquired: O my dear Lord, by what symptoms is one known who is transcendental to those modes? What is his behavior? And how does he transcend the modes of nature?

PURPORT

In this verse, Arjuna's questions are very appropriate. He wants to know the symptoms of a person who has already transcended the material modes. He first inquires of the symptoms of such a transcendental person. How can one understand that he has already transcended the influence of the modes of material nature? The second question asks how he lives and what his activities are. Are they regulated or nonregulated? Then Arjuna inquires of the means by which he can attain the transcendental nature. That is very important. Unless one knows the direct means by which one can be situated always transcendentally, there is no possibility of showing the symptoms. So all these questions put by Arjuna are very important, and the Lord answers them.

TEXTS 22-25

श्रीभगवानुवाच ।
प्रकाशं च प्रवृत्तिं च मोहमेव च पाण्डव ।
न द्वेष्टि संप्रवृत्तानि न निवृत्तानि काङ्क्षति ॥ २२ ॥

उदासीनवदासीनो गुणैर्यो न विचाल्यते ।
गुणा वर्तन्त इत्येव योऽवतिष्ठति नेङ्गते ॥ २३ ॥

समदुःखसुखः स्वस्थः समलोष्टाश्मकाञ्चनः ।
तुल्यप्रियाप्रियो धीरस्तुल्यनिन्दात्मसंस्तुतिः ॥ २४ ॥

मानापमानयोस्तुल्यस्तुल्यो मित्रारिपक्षयोः ।
सर्वारम्भपरित्यागी गुणातीतः स उच्यते ॥ २५ ॥

śrī-bhagavān uvāca
prakāśaṁ ca pravṛttiṁ ca
moham eva ca pāṇḍava
na dveṣṭi sampravṛttāni
na nivṛttāni kāṅkṣati

udāsīna-vad āsīno
guṇair yo na vicālyate
guṇā vartanta ity evaṁ
yo 'vatiṣṭhati neṅgate

sama-duḥkha-sukhaḥ sva-sthaḥ
sama-loṣṭāśma-kāñcanaḥ
tulya-priyāpriyo dhīras
tulya-nindātma-saṁstutiḥ

mānāpamānayos tulyas
tulyo mitrāri-pakṣayoḥ
sarvārambha-parityāgī
guṇātītaḥ sa ucyate

śrī bhagavān uvāca—the Supreme Personality of Godhead said; prakāśam ca—and illumination; pravṛttim ca—and attachment; moham—illusion; eva ca—also; pāṇḍava—O son of Pāṇḍu; na dveṣṭi—does not hate; sampravṛttāni—although developed; na nivṛttāni—nor stop development; kāṅkṣati—desires; udāsīnavat—as if neutral; āsīnaḥ—situated; guṇaiḥ—by the qualities; yaḥ—one who; na—never; vicālyate—is agitated; guṇāḥ—the qualities; vartante—is situated; iti evam—knowing thus; yaḥ—one who; avatiṣṭhati—remains; na—never; iṅgate—flickering; sama—equally; duḥkha—in distress; sukhaḥ—in happiness; svasthaḥ—being situated himself; sama—equally; loṣṭa—a lump of earth; aśma—stone; kāñcanaḥ—gold; tulya—equally disposed; priya—dear; apriyaḥ—undesirable; dhīraḥ—steadily; tulya—equally; nindā—in defamation; ātma-saṁstutiḥ—in praise of himself; māna—honor; apamānayoḥ—dishonor; tulyaḥ—equally; tulyaḥ—equally; mitra—friend; ari—enemy; pakṣayoḥ—in party; sarva—all; ārambhaḥ—endeavor; parityāgī—renouncer; guṇa-atītaḥ—transcendental to the material modes of nature; saḥ—he; ucyate—is said to be.

TRANSLATION

The Blessed Lord said: He who does not hate illumination, attachment and delusion when they are present, nor longs for them when they disappear; who is seated like one unconcerned, being situated beyond these material reactions of the modes of nature, who remains firm, knowing that the modes alone are active; who regards alike pleasure and pain, and looks on a clod, a stone and a piece of gold with an equal eye; who is wise and holds praise and blame to be the same; who is unchanged in honor and dishonor, who treats friend and foe alike, who has abandoned all fruitive undertakings—such a man is said to have transcended the modes of nature.

PURPORT

Arjuna submitted the three different questions, and the Lord answers them one after another. In these verses, Kṛṣṇa first indicates that a person transcendentally situated neither envies anyone nor hankers for anything. When a living entity stays in this material world embodied by the material body, it is to be understood that he is under the control of one of the three modes of material nature. When he is actually out of the body, then he is out of the clutches of the material modes of nature. But as long as he is not out of the material body, he should be neutral. He should engage himself in the devotional service of the Lord so that his identity with the material body will automatically be forgotten. When one is conscious of the material body, he acts only for sense gratification, but when one transfers the consciousness to Kṛṣṇa, sense gratification automatically stops. One does not need this material body, and he does not need to accept the dictations of the material body. The qualities of the material modes in the body will act, but as spirit soul the self is aloof from such activities. How does he become aloof? He does not desire to enjoy the body, nor does he desire to get out of it. Thus transcendentally situated, the devotee becomes automatically free. He need not try to become free from the influence of the modes of material nature.

The next question concerns the dealings of a transcendentally situated person. The materially situated person is affected by so-called honor and dishonor offered to the body, but the transcendentally situated person is not affected by such false honor and dishonor. He performs his duty in Kṛṣṇa consciousness and does not mind whether a man honors or dishonors him. He accepts things that are favorable for his duty in Kṛṣṇa conscious-ness, otherwise he has no necessity of anything material, either a stone or gold. He takes everyone as his dear friend who helps him in his execution of Kṛṣṇa consciousness, and he does not hate his so-called enemy. He is equally disposed and sees everything on an equal level because he knows perfectly well that he has nothing to do with material existence. Social and political issues do not affect him because he knows the situation of temporary upheavals and disturbances. He does not attempt anything for his own sake. He can attempt anything for Kṛṣṇa, but for his personal self he does not attain anything. By such behavior one becomes actually transcendentally situated.

TEXT 26

मां च योऽव्यभिचारेण भक्तियोगेन सेवते ।
स गुणान्समतीत्यैतान्ब्रह्मभूयाय कल्पते ॥ २६ ॥

mām ca yo 'vyabhicāreṇa
bhakti-yogena sevate
sa guṇān samatītyaitān
brahma-bhūyāya kalpate

mām—unto Me; ca—also; yaḥ—person; avyabhicāreṇa—without fail; bhakti-yogena—by devotional service; sevate—renders service; saḥ—he; guṇān—all the modes of material nature; samatītya—transcending; etān—all this; brahma-bhūyāya—to be elevated on the Brahman platform; kalpate—is considered.

TRANSLATION

One who engages in full devotional service, who does not fall down in any circumstance, at once transcends the modes of material nature and thus comes to the level of Brahman.

PURPORT

This verse is a reply to Arjuna's third question: What is the means of attaining to the transcendental position? As explained before, the material world is acting under the spell of the modes of material nature. One should not be disturbed by the activities of the modes of nature;

instead of putting his consciousness into such activities, he may transfer his consciousness to Kṛṣṇa activities. Kṛṣṇa activities are known as *bhakti-yoga*—always acting for Kṛṣṇa. This includes not only Kṛṣṇa, but His different plenary expansions such as Rāma and Nārāyaṇa. He has innumerable expansions. One who is engaged in the service of any of the forms of Kṛṣṇa, or of His plenary expansions, is considered to be transcendentally situated. One should also note that all the forms of Kṛṣṇa are fully transcendental, blissful, full of knowledge and eternal. Such personalities of Godhead are omnipotent and omniscient, and they possess all transcendental qualities. So, if one engages himself in the service of Kṛṣṇa or His plenary expansions with unfailing determination, although these modes of material nature are very difficult to overcome, he can overcome them easily. This is already explained in the Seventh Chapter. One who surrenders unto Kṛṣṇa at once surmounts the influence of the modes of material nature. To be in Kṛṣṇa consciousness or in devotional service means to acquire the equality of Kṛṣṇa. The Lord says that His nature is eternal, blissful and full of knowledge, and the living entities are part and parcel of the Supreme, as gold particles are part of a gold mine. Thus the living entity's spiritual position is as good as gold, as good as Kṛṣṇa in quality. The difference of individuality continues, otherwise there is no question of *bhakti-yoga*. *Bhakti-yoga* means that the Lord is there, the devotee is there and the activity of exchange of love between the Lord and the devotee is there. Therefore the individuality of two persons is present in the Supreme Personality of Godhead and the individual person, otherwise there is no meaning to *bhakti-yoga*. If one is not situated in the same transcendental position with the Lord, one cannot serve the Supreme Lord. To be a personal assistant to a king, one must acquire the qualifications. Thus the qualification is to become Brahman, or freed from all material contamination. It is said in the Vedic literature: *brahmaiva san brahmāpyeti*. One can attain the Supreme Brahman by becoming Brahman. This means that one must qualitatively become one with Brahman. By attainment of Brahman, one does not lose his eternal Brahman identity as individual soul.

TEXT 27

ब्रह्मणो हि प्रतिष्ठाहममृतस्याव्ययस्य च ।
शाश्वतस्य च धर्मस्य सुखस्यैकान्तिकस्य च ॥ २७ ॥

brahmaṇo hi pratiṣṭhāham
amṛtasyāvyayasya ca
śāśvatasya ca dharmasya
sukhasyaikāntikasya ca

brahmaṇaḥ—of the impersonal *brahmajyoti; hi*—certainly; *pratiṣṭhā*—the rest; *aham*—I am; *amṛtasya*—of the imperishable; *avyayasya*—immortal; *ca*—also; *śāśvatasya*—of eternal; *ca*—and; *dharmasya*—of the constitutional position; *sukhasya*—happiness; *aikāntikasya*—ultimate; *ca*—also.

TRANSLATION

And I am the basis of the impersonal Brahman, which is the constitutional position of ultimate happiness, and which is immortal, imperishable and eternal.

PURPORT

The constitution of Brahman is immortality, imperishability, eternity, and happiness. Brahman is the beginning of transcendental realization. Paramātmā, the Supersoul, is the middle, the second stage in transcendental realization, and the Supreme Personality of Godhead is the ultimate realization of the Absolute Truth. Therefore, both Paramātmā and the impersonal Brahman are within the Supreme Person. It is explained in the Seventh Chapter that material nature is the manifestation of the inferior energy of the Supreme Lord. The Lord impregnates the inferior material nature with the fragments of the superior nature, and that is the spiritual touch in the material nature. When a living entity conditioned by this material nature begins the cultivation of spiritual knowledge, he elevates himself from the position of material existence and gradually rises up to the Brahman conception of the Supreme. This attainment of the Brahman conception of life is the first stage in self-realization. At this stage the Brahman realized person is transcendental to the material position, but he is not actually perfect in Brahman realization. If he wants, he can continue to stay in the Brahman position and then gradually rise up to Paramātmā realization and then to the realization of the Supreme Personality of Godhead. There are many examples of this in Vedic literature. The four Kumāras were situated first in the impersonal Brahman conception of truth, but then they gradually rose to the platform of devotional service. One who cannot elevate himself beyond the impersonal conception of Brahman runs the risk of falling down. In Śrīmad-Bhāgavatam it is stated that although a person may rise to the stage of impersonal Brahman, without going farther, with no information of the Supreme Person, his intelligence is not perfectly clear. Therefore, in spite of being raised to the Brahman platform, there is the chance of falling down if one is not engaged in the devotional service of the Lord. In the Vedic language it is also said: *raso vai saḥ; rasaṁ hy evāyaṁ labdhvānandī bhavati.* "When one understands the Personality of God, the reservoir of pleasure, Kṛṣṇa, he actually becomes transcendentally blissful." The Supreme Lord is full in six opulences, and when a devotee approaches Him, there is an exchange of these six opulences. The servant of the king enjoys on an almost equal level with the king. And so, eternal happiness, imperishable happiness, eternal life accompany devotional service. Therefore, realization of Brahman, or eternity, or imperishability is included in devotional service. This is already possessed by a person who is engaged in devotional service.

The living entity, although Brahman by nature, has the desire to lord it over the material world, and due to this he falls down. In his constitutional position, a living entity is above the three modes of material nature, but association with material nature entangles him in the different modes of material nature, goodness, passion and ignorance. Due to the association of these three modes, his desire to dominate the material world is there. By engagement in devotional service in full Kṛṣṇa consciousness, he is immediately situated in the transcendental position, and his unlawful desire to control material nature is removed. Therefore the process of devotional service beginning with hearing, chanting, remembering—the prescribed nine methods for realizing devotional service—should be practiced in the association of devotees. Gradually, by such association, by the influence of the spiritual master, one's material desire to dominate is removed, and one becomes firmly situated in the Lord's transcendental loving service. This method is prescribed from the twenty-second to the last verse of this chapter. Devotional service to the Lord is very simple: one should always engage in the service of the Lord, should eat the remnants of foodstuffs offered to the Deity, smell the flowers offered to the lotus feet of the Lord, see the places where the Lord had His transcendental pastimes, read of the different activities of the Lord, His reciprocation of love with His devotees, chant always the transcendental vibration Hare Kṛṣṇa, Hare Kṛṣṇa, Kṛṣṇa Kṛṣṇa, Hare Hare/ Hare Rāma, Hare Rāma, Rāma Rāma, Hare Hare, and observe the fasting days commemorating the appearances and disappearances of the Lord and His devotees. By following such a process one becomes completely detached from all material activities. One who can thus situate himself in the *brahmajyoti* is equal to the Supreme Personality of Godhead in quality.

Thus end the Bhaktivedanta Purports to the Fourteenth Chapter of the Śrīmad-Bhagavad-gītā in the matter of the Three Modes of Material Nature.

CHAPTER FIFTEEN

The Yoga of the Supreme Person

TEXT 1

श्रीभगवानुवाच ।
ऊर्ध्वमूलमधःशाखमश्वत्थं प्राहुरव्ययम् ।
छन्दांसि यस्य पर्णानि यस्तं वेद स वेदवित् ॥ १ ॥

śrī bhagavān uvāca
ūrdhva-mūlam adhaḥ-śākham
aśvatthaṁ prāhur avyayam
chandāṁsi yasya parṇāni
yas taṁ veda sa veda-vit

śrī bhagavān uvāca—the Supreme Personality of Godhead said; *ūrdhva-mūlam*—with roots above; *adhaḥ*—downwards; *śākham*—branches; *aśvattham*—banyan tree; *prāhuḥ*—said; *avyayam*—eternal; *chandāṁsi*—Vedic hymns; *yasya*—of which; *parṇāni*—the leaves; *yaḥ*—anyone; *tam*—that; *veda*—knows; *saḥ*—he; *veda-vit*—the knower of the Vedas.

TRANSLATION

The Blessed Lord said: There is a banyan tree which has its roots upward and its branches down and whose leaves are the Vedic hymns. One who knows this tree is the knower of the Vedas.

PURPORT

After the discussion of the importance of *bhakti-yoga*, one may question, "What about the *Vedas*?" It is explained in this chapter that the purpose of Vedic study is to understand Kṛṣṇa. Therefore one who is in Kṛṣṇa consciousness, who is engaged in devotional service, already knows the *Vedas*.

The entanglement of this material world is compared here to a banyan tree. For one who is engaged in fruitive activities, there is no end to the banyan tree. He wanders from one branch to another, to another, to another. The tree of this material world has no end, and for one who is attached to this tree, there is no possibility of liberation. The Vedic hymns, meant for elevating oneself, are called the leaves of this tree. This tree's roots grow upward because they begin from where Brahmā is located, the topmost planet of this universe. If one can understand this indestructible tree of illusion, then one can get out of it.

This process of extrication should be understood. In the previous chapters it has been explained that there are many processes by which to get out of the material entanglement. And, up to the Thirteenth Chapter, we have seen that devotional service to the Supreme Lord is the best way. Now, the basic principle of devotional service is detachment from material activities and attachment to the transcendental service of the Lord. The process of breaking attachment to the material world is discussed in the beginning of this chapter. The root of this material existence grows upward. This means that it begins from the total material substance, from the topmost planet of the universe. From there, the whole universe is expanded, with so many branches, representing the various planetary systems. The fruits represent the results of the living entities' activities, namely, religion, economic development, sense gratification and liberation.

Now, there is no ready experience in this world of a tree situated with its branches down and its roots upward, but there is such a thing. That tree can be found beside a reservoir of water. We can see that the trees on the bank reflect upon the water with their branches down and roots up. In other words, the tree of this material world is only a reflection of the real tree of the spiritual world. This reflection of the spiritual world is situated on desire, just as the tree's reflection is situated on water. Desire is the cause of things' being situated in this reflected material light. One who wants to get out of this material existence must know this tree thoroughly through analytical study. Then he can cut off his relationship with it.

This tree, being the reflection of the real tree, is an exact replica. Everything is there in the spiritual world. The impersonalists take Brahmā to be the root of this material tree, and from the root, according to *sāṅkhya* philosophy, come *prakṛti, puruṣa,* then the three *guṇas,* then the five gross elements (*pañca-mahābhūta*), then the ten senses (*daśendriya*), mind, etc. In this way they divide up the whole material world. If Brahmā is the center of all manifestations, then this material world is a manifestation of the center by 180 degrees, and the other 180 degrees constitute the spiritual world. The material world is the perverted reflection, so the spiritual world must have the same variegatedness, but in reality. The *prakṛti* is the external energy of the Supreme Lord, and the *puruṣa* is the Supreme Lord Himself, and that is explained in *Bhagavad-gītā.* Since this manifestation is material, it is temporary. A reflection is temporary, for it is sometimes seen and sometimes not seen. But the origin from whence the reflection is reflected is eternal. The material reflection of the real tree has to be cut off. When it is said that a person knows the *Vedas,* it is assumed that he knows how to cut off attachment to this material world. If one knows that process, he actually knows the *Vedas.* One who is attracted by the ritualistic formulas of the *Vedas* is attracted by the beautiful green leaves of the tree. He does not exactly know the purpose of the *Vedas.* The purpose of the *Vedas,* as disclosed by the Personality of Godhead Himself, is to cut down this reflected tree and attain the real tree of the spiritual world.

TEXT 2

अधश्चोर्ध्वं प्रसृतास्तस्य शाखा
गुणप्रवृद्धा विषयप्रवालाः ।
अधश्च मूलान्यनुसंततानि
कर्मानुबन्धीनि मनुष्यलोके ॥ २ ॥

adhaś cordhvaṁ prasṛtās tasya śākhā
guṇa-pravṛddhā viṣaya-pravālāḥ
adhaś ca mūlāny anusantatāni
karmānubandhīni manuṣya-loke

adhaḥ—downward; *ca*—and; *ūrdhvam*—upward; *prasṛtāḥ*—extended; *tasya*—its; *śākhāḥ*—branches; *guṇa*—modes of material nature; *pravṛddhāḥ*—developed; *viṣaya*—sense objects; *pravālāḥ*—twigs; *adhaḥ*—downward; *ca*—and; *mūlāni*—roots; *anusantatāni*—extended; *karma*—according to work; *anubandhīni*—bound; *manuṣya-loke*—in the world of human society.

TRANSLATION

The branches of this tree extend downward and upward, nourished by the three modes of material nature. The twigs are the objects of the senses. This tree also has roots going down, and these are bound to the fruitive actions of human society.

PURPORT

The description of the banyan tree is further explained here. Its branches are spread in all directions. In the lower parts, there are variegated manifestations of living entities, such as human beings, animals, horses, cows, dogs, cats, etc. These are situated on the lower parts of the branches, whereas on the upper parts are higher forms of living entities: the demigods, Gandharvas (fairies), and many other higher species of life. As a tree is nourished by water, so this tree is nourished by the three modes of material nature. Sometimes we find that a tract of land is barren for want of sufficient water, and sometimes a tract is very green; similarly, where the modes of material nature are proportionately greater in quantity, the different species of life are manifested in that proportion.

The twigs of the tree are considered to be the sense objects. By development of the different modes of nature, we develop different senses, and, by the senses, we enjoy different varieties of sense objects. The source of the senses—the ears, the nose, eyes, etc. —is considered to be the upper twigs, tuned to the enjoyment of different sense objects. The leaves are sound, form, touch—the sense objects. The roots, which are subsidiary, are the by-products of different varieties of suffering and sense enjoyment. Thus we develop attachment and aversion. The tendencies toward piety and impiety are considered to be the secondary roots, spreading in all directions. The real root is from Brahmaloka, and the other roots are in the human planetary systems. After one enjoys the results of virtuous activities in the upper planetary systems, he comes down to this earth and renews his *karma* or fruitive activities for promotion. This planet of human beings is considered the field of activities.

TEXTS 3-4

न रूपमस्येह तथोपलभ्यते
नान्तो न चादिर्न च संप्रतिष्ठा ।
अश्वत्थमेनं सुविरूढमूल-
मसङ्गशस्त्रेण दृढेन छित्त्वा ॥ ३ ॥

ततः पदं तत्परिमार्गितव्यं
यस्मिन्गता न निवर्तन्ति भूयः ।
तमेव चाद्यं पुरुषं प्रपद्ये
यतः प्रवृत्तिः प्रसृता पुराणी ॥ ४ ॥

na rūpam asyeha tathopalabhyate
nānto na cādir na ca sampratiṣṭhā
aśvattham enaṁ su-virūḍha-mūlam
asaṅga-śastreṇa dṛḍhena chittvā

tataḥ padaṁ tat parimārgitavyaṁ
yasmin gatā na nivartanti bhūyaḥ
tam eva cādyaṁ puruṣaṁ prapadye
yataḥ pravṛttiḥ prasṛtā purāṇī

na—not; *rūpam*—form; *asya*—of this tree; *iha*—in this; *tathā*—also; *upalabhyate*—can be perceived; *na*—never; *antaḥ*—end; *na*—never; *ca*—also; *ādiḥ*—beginning; *na*—never; *ca*—also; *sampratiṣṭhā*—the foundation; *aśvattham*—banyan tree; *enam*—this; *suvirūḍha*—strongly; *mūlam*—rooted; *asaṅga-śastreṇa*—by the weapon of detachment; *dṛḍhena*—strong; *chittvā*—by cutting; *tataḥ*—thereafter; *padam*—situation; *tat*—that; *parimārgitavyam*—has to be searched out; *yasmin*—where; *gatāḥ*—going; *na*—never; *nivartanti*—comes back; *bhūyaḥ*—again; *tam*—to him; *eva*—certainly; *ca*—also; *ādyam*—original; *puruṣam*—the Personality of Godhead; *prapadye*—surrender; *yataḥ*—from whom; *pravṛttiḥ*—beginning; *prasṛtā*—extension; *purāṇī*—very old.

TRANSLATION

The real form of this tree cannot be perceived in this world. No one can understand where it ends, where it begins, or where its foundation is. But with determination one must cut down this tree with the weapon of detachment. So doing, one must seek that place from which, having once gone, one never returns, and there surrender to that Supreme Personality of Godhead from whom everything has begun and in whom everything is abiding since time immemorial.

PURPORT

It is now clearly stated that the real form of this banyan tree cannot be understood in this material world. Since the root is upwards, the extension of the real tree is at the other end. No one can see how far the tree extends, nor can one see the beginning of this tree. Yet one has to find out the cause. "I am the son of my father, my father is the son of such and such a person, etc." By searching in this way, one comes to Brahmā, who is generated by the Garbhodakaśāyī Viṣṇu. Finally, in this way, when one reaches to the Supreme Personality of Godhead, that is the end of research work. One has to search out that origin of this tree, the Supreme Personality of Godhead, through the association of persons who are in the knowledge of that Supreme Personality of Godhead. Then by understanding one becomes gradually detached from this false reflection of reality, and by knowledge one can cut off the connection and actually become situated in the real tree.

The word *asaṅga* is very important in this connection because the attachment for sense enjoyment and lording it over the material nature is very strong. Therefore one must learn detachment by discussion of spiritual science based on authoritative scriptures, and one must hear from persons who are actually in knowledge. As a result of such discussion in the association of devotees, one comes to the Supreme Personality of Godhead. Then the first thing one must do is surrender to Him. The description of that place whence going no one returns to this false reflected tree is given here. The Supreme Personality of Godhead, Kṛṣṇa, is the original root from whom everything has emanated. To gain favor of that Personality of Godhead, one has only to surrender, and this is a result of performing devotional service by hearing, chanting, etc. He is the cause of this extension of this material world. This is already explained by the Lord Himself: *ahaṁ sarvasya prabhavaḥ.* "I am the origin of everything."

Therefore to get out of the entanglement of this strong banyan tree of material life, one must surrender to Kṛṣṇa. As soon as one surrenders unto Kṛṣṇa, he becomes detached automatically from this material extension.

TEXT 5

निर्मानमोहा जितसङ्गदोषा
अध्यात्मनित्या विनिवृत्तकामाः ।
द्वन्द्वैर्विमुक्ताः सुखदुःखसंज्ञै-
र्गच्छन्त्यमूढाः पदमव्ययं तत् ॥ ५ ॥

*nirmāna-mohā jita-saṅga-doṣā
adhyātma-nityā vinivṛtta-kāmāḥ
dvandvair vimuktāḥ sukha-duḥkha-saṁjñair
gacchanty amūḍhāḥ padam avyayaṁ tat*

nir—without; *māna*—respect; *mohāḥ*—illusion; *jita*—having conquered; *saṅga*—association; *doṣāḥ*—faulty; *adhyātma*—spiritual; *nityāḥ*—eternity; *vinivṛtta*—associated; *kāmāḥ*—lusts; *dvandvaiḥ*—with duality; *vimuktāḥ*—liberated; *sukha-duḥkha*—happiness and distress; *saṁjñaiḥ*—named; *gacchanti*—attains; *amūḍhāḥ*—unbewildered; *padam*—situation; *avyayam*—eternal; *tat*—that.

TRANSLATION

One who is free from illusion, false prestige, and false association, who understands the eternal, who is done with material lust and is freed from the duality of happiness and distress, and who knows how to surrender unto the Supreme Person, attains to that eternal kingdom.

PURPORT

The surrendering process is described here very nicely. The first qualification is that one should not be deluded by pride. Because the conditioned soul is puffed up, thinking himself the lord of material nature, it is very difficult for him to surrender unto the Supreme Personality of Godhead. One should know by the cultivation of real knowledge that he is not lord of material nature; the Supreme Personality of Godhead is the Lord. When one is free from delusion caused by pride, he can begin the process of surrender. For one who is always expecting some honor in this material world, it is not possible to surrender to the Supreme Person. Pride is due to illusion, for although one comes here, stays for a brief time and then goes away, he has the foolish notion that he is the lord of the world. He thus makes all things complicated, and he is always in trouble. The whole world moves under this impression. People are considering that the land, this earth, belongs to human society, and they have divided the land under the false impression that they are the proprietors. One has to get out of this false notion that human society is the proprietor of this world. When one is freed from such a false notion, he becomes free from all the false associations caused by familial, social, and national affections. These fake associations bind one to this material world. After this stage, one has to develop spiritual knowledge. One has to cultivate knowledge of what is actually his own and what is actually not his own. And, when one has an understanding of things as they are, he becomes free from all dual conceptions such as happiness and distress, pleasure and pain. He becomes full in knowledge; then it is possible for him to surrender to the Supreme Personality of Godhead.

TEXT 6

न तद्भासयते सूर्यो न शशाङ्को न पावकः ।
यद्गत्वा न निवर्तन्ते तद्धाम परमं मम ॥ ६ ॥

na tad bhāsayate sūryo
na śaśāṅko na pāvakaḥ
yad gatvā na nivartante
tad dhāma paramaṁ mama

na—not; tat—that; bhāsayate—illuminates; sūryaḥ—sun; na—nor; śaśāṅkaḥ—the moon; na—nor; pāvakaḥ—fire, electricity; yat—where; gatvā—going; na—never; nivartante—comes back; tat dhāma—that abode; paramam—supreme; mama—My.

TRANSLATION

That abode of Mine is not illumined by the sun or moon, nor by electricity. One who reaches it never returns to this material world.

PURPORT

The spiritual world, the abode of the Supreme Personality of Godhead, Kṛṣṇa—which is known as Kṛṣṇaloka, Goloka Vṛndāvana—is described here. In the spiritual sky there is no need of sunshine, moonshine, fire or electricity, because all the planets are self-luminous. We have only one planet in this universe, the sun, which is self-luminous, but all the planets in the spiritual sky are self-luminous. The shining effulgence of all those planets (called Vaikuṇṭhas) constitutes the shining sky known as the *brahmajyoti*. Actually, the effulgence is emanating from the planet of Kṛṣṇa, Goloka Vṛndāvana. Part of that shining effulgence is covered by the *mahat-tattva*, the material world. Other than this, the major portion of that shining sky is full of spiritual planets, which are called Vaikuṇṭhas, chief of which is Goloka Vṛndāvana.

As long as a living entity is in this dark material world, he is in conditional life, but as soon as he reaches the spiritual sky, by cutting through the false, perverted tree of this material world, he becomes liberated. Then there is no chance of his coming back here. In his conditional life, the living entity considers himself to be the lord of this material world, but in his liberated state he enters into the spiritual kingdom and becomes the associate of the Supreme Lord. There he enjoys eternal bliss, eternal life, and full knowledge.

One should be captivated by this information. He should desire to transfer himself to that eternal world and extricate himself from this false reflection of reality. For one who is too much attached to this material world, it is very difficult to cut that attachment, but if he takes to Kṛṣṇa consciousness, there is a chance of gradually becoming detached. One has to associate himself with devotees, those who are in Kṛṣṇa consciousness. One should search out a society dedicated to Kṛṣṇa consciousness and learn how to discharge devotional service. In this way he can cut off his attachment to the material world. One cannot become detached from the attraction of the material world simply by dressing himself in saffron cloth. He must become attached to the devotional service of the Lord. Therefore one should take it very seriously that devotional service as described in the Twelfth Chapter is the only way to get out of this false representation of the real tree. In Chapter Fourteen the contamination of all kinds of processes by material nature is described. Only devotional service is described as purely transcendental.

The words *paramaṁ mama* are very important here. Actually every nook and corner is the property of the Supreme Lord, but the spiritual world is *paramam*, full of six opulences. In the *Upaniṣads* it is also confirmed that in the spiritual world there is no need of sunshine or moonshine, for the whole spiritual sky is illuminated by the internal potency of the Supreme Lord. That supreme abode can be achieved only by surrender and by no other means.

TEXT 7

ममैवांशो जीवलोके जीवभूतः सनातनः ।
मनःषष्ठानीन्द्रियाणि प्रकृतिस्थानि कर्षति ॥ ७ ॥

mamaivāṁśo jīva-loke
jīva-bhūtaḥ sanātanaḥ
manaḥ-ṣaṣṭhānīndriyāṇi
prakṛti-sthāni karṣati

mama—My; *eva*—certainly; *aṁśaḥ*—fragmental particles; *jīva-loke*—world of conditional life; *jīva-bhūtaḥ*—the conditioned living entities; *sanātanaḥ*—eternal; *manaḥ*—mind; *ṣaṣṭhāni*—six; *indriyāṇi*—senses; *prakṛti*—material nature; *sthāni*—situated; *karṣati*—struggling hard.

TRANSLATION

The living entities in this conditioned world are My eternal, fragmental parts. Due to conditioned life, they are struggling very hard with the six senses, which include the mind.

PURPORT

In this verse the identity of the living being is clearly given. The living entity is the fragmental part and parcel of the Supreme Lord—eternally. It is not that he assumes individuality in his conditional life and in his liberated state becomes one with the Supreme Lord. He is eternally fragmented. It is clearly said, *sanātanaḥ*. According to the Vedic version, the Supreme Lord manifests and expands Himself in innumerable expansions, of which the primary expansions are called *Viṣṇu-tattva*, and the secondary expansions are called the living entities. In other words, the *Viṣṇu-tattva* is the personal expansion, and the living entities are separated expansions. By His personal expansion, He is manifested in various forms like Lord Rāma, Nṛsiṁhadeva, Viṣṇumūrti and all the predominating Deities in the

Vaikuṇṭha planets. The separated expansions, the living entities, are eternally servitors. The personal expansions of the Supreme Personality of Godhead, the individual identities of the Godhead, are always present. Similarly, the separated expansions of living entities have their identities. As fragmental parts and parcels of the Supreme Lord, the living entities have also fragmental qualities, of which independence is one. Every living entity has an individual soul, his personal individuality and a minute form of independence. By misuse of that independence, one becomes a conditioned soul, and by proper use of independence he is always liberated. In either case, he is qualititatively eternal, as the Supreme Lord is. In his liberated state he is freed from this material condition, and he is under the engagement of transcendental service unto the Lord; in his conditioned life he is dominated by the material modes of nature, and he forgets the transcendental loving service of the Lord. As a result, he has to struggle very hard to maintain his existence in the material world.

The living entities, not only the human beings and the cats and dogs, but even the greater controllers of the material world—Brahmā, Lord Śiva, and even Viṣṇu—are all parts and parcels of the Supreme Lord. They are all eternal, not temporary manifestations. The word karṣati (struggling or grappling hard) is very significant. The conditioned soul is bound up, as though shackled by iron chains. He is bound up by the false ego, and the mind is the chief agent which is driving him in this material existence. When the mind is in the mode of goodness, his activities are good; when the mind is in the mode of passion, his activities are troublesome; and when the mind is in the mode of ignorance, he travels in the lower species of life. It is clear, however, in this verse, that the conditioned soul is covered by the material body, with the mind and the senses, and when he is liberated this material covering perishes, but his spiritual body manifests in its individual capacity. The following information is there in the Mādhyandi-nāyana-śruti: sa vā eṣa brahma-niṣṭha idaṁ sarīraṁ marttyam atisṛjya brahmābhisampadya brahmaṇā paśyati brahmaṇā śṛṇoti brahmaṇaivedaṁ sarvam anubhavati. It is stated here that when a living entity gives up this material embodiment and enters into the spiritual world, he revives his spiritual body, and in his spiritual body he can see the Supreme Personality of Godhead face to face. He can hear and speak to Him face to face, and he can understand the Supreme Personality as He is. In smṛti also it is understood that in the spiritual planets everyone lives in bodies featured like the Supreme Personality of Godhead's. As far as bodily construction is concerned, there is no difference between the part and parcel living entities and the expansions of Viṣṇumūrti. In other words, at liberation the living entity gets a spiritual body by the grace of the Supreme Personality of Godhead.

The word mamaivāṁśaḥ (fragmental parts and parcels of the Supreme Lord) is also very significant. The fragmental portion of the Supreme Lord is not like some material broken part. We have already understood in the Second Chapter that the spirit cannot be cut into pieces. This fragment is not materially conceived. It is not like matter which can be cut into pieces and joined together again. That conception is not applicable here because the Sanskrit word sanātana (eternal) is used. The fragmental portion is eternal. It is also stated in the beginning of the Second Chapter that (dehino 'smin yathā) in each and every individual body, the fragmental portion of the Supreme Lord is present. That fragmental portion, when liberated from the bodily entanglement, revives its original spiritual body in the spiritual sky in a spiritual planet and enjoys association with the Supreme Lord. It is, however, understood here that the living entity, being the fragmental part and parcel of the Supreme Lord, is qualitatively one, just as the parts and parcels of gold are also gold.

TEXT 8

शरीरं यदवाप्रोति यच्चाप्युत्क्रामतीश्वरः ।
गृहीत्वैतानि संयाति वायुर्गन्धानिवाशयात् ॥ ८ ॥

śarīraṁ yad avāpnoti
yac cāpy utkrāmatīśvaraḥ
gṛhītvaitāni saṁyāti
vāyur gandhān ivāśayāt

śarīram—body; yat—as much as; avāpnoti—gets; yat—that which; ca—also; api—virtually; utkrāmati—gives up; īśvaraḥ—the lord of the body; gṛhītvā—taking; etāni—all these; saṁyāti—goes away; vāyuḥ—air; gandhān—smell; iva—like; āśayāt—from the flower.

TRANSLATION

The living entity in the material world carries his different conceptions of life from one body to another as the air carries aromas.

PURPORT

Here the living entity is described as *īśvara*, the controller of his own body. If he likes, he can change his body to a higher grade, and if he likes he can move to a lower class. Minute independence is there. The change his body undergoes depends upon him. At the time of death, the consciousness he has created will carry him on to the next type of body. If he has made his consciousness like that of a cat or dog, he is sure to change to a cat's or dog's body. And, if he has fixed his consciousness on godly qualities, he will change into the form of a demigod. And, if he is in Kṛṣṇa consciousness, he will be transferred to Kṛṣṇaloka in the spiritual world and will associate with Kṛṣṇa. It is a false claim that after the annihilation of this body everything is finished. The individual soul is transmigrating from one body to another, and his present body and present activities are the background of his next body. One gets a different body according to *karma*, and he has to quit this body in due course. It is stated here that the subtle body, which carries the conception of the next body, develops another body in the next life. This process of transmigrating from one body to another and struggling while in the body is called *karṣati* or struggle for existence.

TEXT 9

श्रोत्रं चक्षुः स्पर्शनं च रसनं घ्राणमेव च ।
अधिष्ठाय मनश्चायं विषयानुपसेवते ॥ ९ ॥

śrotraṁ cakṣuḥ sparśanaṁ ca
rasanaṁ ghrāṇam eva ca
adhiṣṭhāya manaś cāyaṁ
viṣayān upasevate

śrotram—ears; *cakṣuḥ*—eyes; *sparśanam*—touch; *ca*—also; *rasanam*—tongue; *ghrāṇam*—smelling power; *eva*—also; *ca*—and; *adhiṣṭhāya*—being situated; *manaḥ*—mind; *ca*—also; *ayam*—this; *viṣayān*—sense objects; *upasevate*—enjoys.

TRANSLATION

The living entity, thus taking another gross body, obtains a certain type of ear, tongue, and nose and sense of touch, which are grouped about the mind. He thus enjoys a particular set of sense objects.

PURPORT

In other words, if the living entity adulterates his consciousness with the qualities of cats and dogs, in his next life he gets a cat or dog body and enjoys. Consciousness is originally pure, like water. But if we mix water with a certain color, it changes. Similarly, consciousness is pure, for the spirit soul is pure. But consciousness is changed according to the association of the material qualities. Real consciousness is Kṛṣṇa consciousness. When, therefore, one is situated in Kṛṣṇa consciousness, he is in his pure life. But if his consciousness is adulterated by some type of material mentality, in the next life he gets a corresponding body. He does not necessarily get a human body again; he can get the body of a cat, dog, hog, demigod or one of many other forms, for there are 8,400,000 species.

TEXT 10

उत्क्रामन्तं स्थितं वाऽपि भुञ्जानं वा गुणान्वितम् ।
विमूढा नानुपश्यन्ति पश्यन्ति ज्ञानचक्षुषः ॥ १० ॥

utkrāmantaṁ sthitaṁ vāpi
bhuñjānaṁ vā guṇānvitam
vimūḍhā nānupaśyanti
paśyanti jñāna-cakṣuṣaḥ

utkrāmantam—quitting the body; *sthitam*—situated in the body; *vāpi*—either; *bhuñjānam*—enjoying; *vā*—or; *guṇa-anvitam*—under the spell of the modes of material nature; *vimūḍhāḥ*—foolish persons; *na*—never; *anupaśyanti*—can see; *paśyanti*—one can see; *jñāna-cakṣuṣaḥ*—one who has the eyes of knowledge.

TRANSLATION

The foolish cannot understand how a living entity can quit his body, nor can they understand what sort of body he enjoys under the spell of the modes of nature. But one whose eyes are trained in knowledge can see all this.

PURPORT

The word *jñāna-cakṣuṣaḥ* is very significant. Without knowledge, one cannot understand how a living entity leaves his present body, nor what form of body he is going to take in the next life, nor even why he is living in a particular type of body. This requires a great amount of knowledge understood from *Bhagavad-gītā* and similar literatures heard from a bona fide spiritual master. One who is trained to perceive all these things is fortunate. Every living entity is quitting his body under certain circumstances; he is living under certain circumstances and enjoying under certain circumstances under the spell of material nature. As a result, he is suffering different kinds of happiness and distress, under the illusion of sense enjoyment. Persons who are everlastingly fooled by lust and desire lose all power of understanding their change of body and their stay in a particular body. They cannot comprehend it. Those who have developed spiritual knowledge, however, can see that the spirit is different from the body and is changing its body and enjoying in different ways. A person in such knowledge can understand how the conditioned living entity is suffering in this material existence. Therefore those who are highly developed in Kṛṣṇa consciousness try their best to give this knowledge to the people in general, for their conditional life is very much troublesome. They should come out of it and be Kṛṣṇa conscious and liberate themselves to transfer to the spiritual world.

TEXT 11

यतन्तो योगिनश्चैनं पश्यन्त्यात्मन्यवस्थितम् ।
यतन्तोऽप्यकृतात्मानो नैनं पश्यन्त्यचेतसः ॥ ११ ॥

yatanto yoginaś cainaṁ
paśyanty ātmany avasthitam
yatanto 'py akṛtātmāno
nainaṁ paśyanty acetasaḥ

yatantaḥ—endeavoring; *yoginaḥ*—transcendentalists; *ca*—also; *enam*—this; *paśyanti*—can see; *ātmani*—in the self; *avasthitam*—situated; *yatantaḥ*—although endeavoring; *api*—although; *akṛta-ātmānaḥ*—without self-realization; *na*—does not; *enam*—this; *paśyanti*—can see; *acetasaḥ*—undeveloped mind.

TRANSLATION

The endeavoring transcendentalist, who is situated in self-realization, can see all this clearly. But those who are not situated in self-realization cannot see what is taking place, though they may try to.

PURPORT

There are many transcendentalists in the path of spiritual self-realization, but one who is not situated in self-realization cannot see how things are changing in the body of the living entity. The word *yoginaḥ* is significant in this connection. In the present day there are many so-called *yogīs*, and there are many so-called associations of *yogīs*, but they are actually blind in the matter of self-realization. They are simply addicted to some sort of gymnastic exercise and are satisfied if the body is well-built and healthy. They have no other information. They are called *yatanto'py akṛtātmānaḥ*. Even though they are endeavoring in a so-called *yoga* system, they are not self-realized. Such people cannot understand the process of the transmigration of the soul. Only those who are actually in the *yoga* system and have realized the self, the world, and the Supreme Lord, in other words, the *bhakti-yogīs*, those engaged in pure devotional service in Kṛṣṇa consciousness, can understand how things are taking place.

TEXT 12

यदादित्यगतं तेजो जगद्भासयतेऽखिलम् ।
यच्चन्द्रमसि यच्चाग्नौ तत्तेजो विद्धि मामकम् ॥ १२ ॥

yad āditya-gataṁ tejo
jagad bhāsayate 'khilam
yac candramasi yac cāgnau
tat tejo viddhi māmakam

yat—that which; *āditya-gatam*—in the sunshine; *tejaḥ*—splendor; *jagat*—the whole world; *bhāsayate*—illuminates; *akhilam*—entirely; *yat*—that which; *candramasi*—in the moon; *yat*—that which; *ca*—also; *agnau*—in the fire; *tat*—that; *tejaḥ*—splendor; *viddhi*—understand; *māmakam*—from Me.

TRANSLATION

The splendor of the sun, which dissipates the darkness of this whole world, comes from Me. And the splendor of the moon and the splendor of fire are also from Me.

PURPORT

The unintelligent cannot understand how things are taking place. The beginning of knowledge can be established by understanding what the Lord explains here. Everyone sees the sun, moon, fire and electricity. One should simply try to understand that the splendor of the sun, the splendor of the moon, and splendor of electricity or fire are coming from the Supreme Personality of Godhead. In such a conception of life, the beginning of Kṛṣṇa consciousness, lies a great deal of advancement for the conditioned soul in this material world. The living entities are essentially the parts and parcels of the Supreme Lord, and He is giving herewith the hint how they can come back to Godhead, back to home. From this verse we can understand that the sun is illuminating the whole solar system. There are different universes and solar systems, and there are different suns, moons and planets also. Sunlight is due to the spiritual effulgence in the spiritual sky of the Supreme Lord. With the rise of the sun, the activities of human beings are set up. They set fire to prepare their foodstuff; they set fire to start the factories, etc. So many things are done with the help of fire. Therefore sunrise, fire and moonlight are so pleasing to the living entities. Without their help no living entity can live. So if one can understand that the light and splendor of the sun, moon and fire are emanating from the Supreme Personality of Godhead, Kṛṣṇa, then one's Kṛṣṇa consciousness will begin. By the moonshine, all the vegetables are nourished. The moonshine is so pleasing that people can easily understand that they are living by the mercy of the Supreme Personality of Godhead Kṛṣṇa. Without His mercy there cannot be sun, without His mercy there cannot be moon, and without His mercy there cannot be fire, and without the help of sun, moon and fire, no one can live. These are some thoughts to provoke Kṛṣṇa consciousness in the conditioned soul.

TEXT 13

गामाविश्य च भूतानि धारयाम्यहमोजसा ।
पुष्णामि चौषधीः सर्वाः सोमो भूत्वा रसात्मकः ॥ १३ ॥

gām āviśya ca bhūtāni
dhārayāmy aham ojasā
puṣṇāmi cauṣadhīḥ sarvāḥ
somo bhūtvā rasātmakaḥ

gām—the planets; āviśya—entering; ca—also; bhūtāni—living entities;
dhārayāmi—sustaining; aham—I; ojasā—by My energy; puṣṇāmi—nourishing;
ca—and; auṣadhīḥ—all vegetables; sarvāḥ—all; somaḥ—the moon; bhūtvā—
becoming; rasa-ātmakaḥ—supplying the juice.

TRANSLATION

I enter into each planet, and by My energy they stay in orbit. I become
the moon and thereby supply the juice of life to all vegetables.

PURPORT

It is understood that all the planets are floating in the air only by the
energy of the Lord. The Lord enters into every atom, every planet, and
every living being. That is discussed in the Brahma-saṁhitā. It is said
there that one plenary portion of the Supreme Personality of Godhead,
Paramātmā, enters into the planets, the universe, the living entity, and
even into the atom. So due to His entrance, everything is appropriately
manifested. When the spirit soul is there, a living man can float on the
water, but when the living spark is out of the body and the body is dead,
it sinks. Of course when it is decomposed it floats just like straw and
other things, but as soon as the man is dead, he at once sinks in the water.
Similarly, all these planets are floating in space, and this is due to the
entrance of the supreme energy of the Supreme Personality of Godhead.
His energy is sustaining each planet, just like a handful of dust. If someone
holds a handful of dust, there is no possibility of the dust falling, but if
one throws it in the air, it will fall down. Similarly, these planets, which
are floating in air, are actually held in the fist of the universal form of the
Supreme Lord. By His strength and energy, all moving and unmoving
things stay in their place. It is said that because of the Supreme Personality

of Godhead, the sun is shining and the planets are steadily moving. Were it not for Him, all the planets would scatter, like dust in air, and perish. Similarly, it is due to the Supreme Personality of Godhead that the moon nourishes all vegetables. Due to the moon's influence, the vegetables become delicious. Without the moonshine, the vegetables can neither grow nor taste succulent. Human society is working, living comfortably and enjoying food due to the supply from the Supreme Lord. Otherwise, mankind could not survive. The word *rasātmakaḥ* is very significant. Everything becomes palatable by the agency of the Supreme Lord through the influence of the moon.

TEXT 14

अहं वैश्वानरो भूत्वा प्राणिनां देहमाश्रितः ।
प्राणापानसमायुक्तः पचाम्यन्नं चतुर्विधम् ॥ १४ ॥

aham vaiśvānaro bhūtvā
prāṇināṁ deham āśritaḥ
prāṇāpāna-samāyuktaḥ
pacāmy annaṁ catur-vidham

aham—I; *vaiśvānaraḥ*—by My plenary portion as the digesting fire; *bhūtvā*—becoming; *prāṇinām*—of all living entities; *deham*—body; *āśritaḥ*—situated; *prāṇa*—outgoing air; *apāna*—downgoing air; *samāyuktaḥ*—keep balance; *pacāmi*—digest; *annam*—foodstuff; *catur-vidham*—four kinds of.

TRANSLATION

I am the fire of digestion in every living body, and I am the air of life, outgoing and incoming, by which I digest the four kinds of foodstuff.

PURPORT

According to *Āyur-vedic śāstra*, we understand that there is a fire in the stomach which digests all food sent there. When the fire is not blazing, there is no hunger, and when the fire is in order, we become hungry. Sometimes when the fire is not going nicely, treatment is required. In any case, this fire is representative of the Supreme Personality of Godhead. Vedic *mantras* also confirm that the Supreme Lord or

Brahman is situated in the form of fire within the stomach and is digesting all kinds of foodstuff. Therefore since He is helping the digestion of all kinds of foodstuff, the living entity is not independent in the eating process. Unless the Supreme Lord helps him in digesting, there is no possibility of eating. He thus produces and digests foodstuff, and, by His grace, we are enjoying life. In the *Vedānta-sūtra* this is also confirmed: *śabdādibhyo 'ntaḥ pratiṣṭhānāc ca.* The Lord is situated within sound and within the body, within the air and even within the stomach as the digestive force. There are four kinds of foodstuff: some are swallowed, some are chewed, some are licked up, and some are sucked, and He is the digestive force for all of them.

TEXT 15

सर्वस्य चाहं हृदि सन्निविष्टो
मत्तः स्मृतिर्ज्ञानमपोहनं च ।
वेदैश्च सर्वैरहमेव वेद्यो
वेदान्तकृद्वेदविदेव चाहम् ॥ १५ ॥

sarvasya cāhaṁ hṛdi sanniviṣṭo
mattaḥ smṛtir jñānam apohanaṁ ca
vedaiś ca sarvair aham eva vedyo
vedānta-kṛd veda-vid eva cāham

sarvasya—of all living beings; *ca*—and; *aham*—I; *hṛdi*—in the heart; *sanniviṣṭaḥ*—being situated; *mattaḥ*—from Me; *smṛtiḥ*—remembrance; *jñānam*—knowledge; *apohanam ca*—and forgetfulness; *vedaiḥ*—by the *Vedas*; *ca*—also; *sarvaiḥ*—all; *aham*—I am; *eva*—certainly; *vedyaḥ*—knowable; *vedānta-kṛt*—the compiler of the *Vedānta*; *veda-vit*—the knower of the *Vedas*; *eva*—certainly; *ca*—and; *aham*—I.

TRANSLATION

I am seated in everyone's heart, and from Me come remembrance, knowledge and forgetfulness. By all the Vedas am I to be known; indeed I am the compiler of Vedānta, and I am the knower of the Vedas.

PURPORT

The Supreme Lord is situated as Paramātmā in everyone's heart, and it is from Him that all activities are initiated. The living entity forgets everything of his past life, but he has to act according to the direction of the Supreme Lord, who is witness to all his work. Therefore he begins his work according to his past deeds. Required knowledge is supplied to him, and remembrance is given to him, and he forgets, also, about his past life. Thus, the Lord is not only all-pervading; He is also localized in every individual heart. He awards the different fruitive results. He is not only worshipable as the impersonal Brahman, the Supreme Personality of Godhead, and the localized Paramātmā, but as the form of the incarnation of the *Vedas* as well. The *Vedas* give the right direction to the people so that they can properly mold their lives and come back to Godhead, back to home. The *Vedas* offer knowledge of the Supreme Personality of Godhead, Kṛṣṇa, and Kṛṣṇa in His incarnation as Vyāsadeva is the compiler of the *Vedānta-sūtra*. The commentation on the *Vedānta-sūtra* by Vyāsadeva in the *Śrīmad-Bhāgavatam* gives the real understanding of *Vedānta-sūtra*. The Supreme Lord is so full that for the deliverance of the conditioned soul He is the supplier and digester of foodstuff, the witness of his activity, the giver of knowledge in the form of *Vedas* and as the Supreme Personality of Godhead, Śrī Kṛṣṇa, the teacher of the *Bhagavad-gītā*. He is worshipable by the conditioned soul. Thus God is all-good; God is all-merciful.

Antaḥpraviṣṭaḥ śāstā janānām. The living entity forgets as soon as he quits his present body, but he begins his work again, initiated by the Supreme Lord. Although he forgets, the Lord gives him the intelligence to renew his work where he ended his last life. So not only does a living entity enjoy or suffer in this world according to the dictation from the Supreme Lord situated locally in the heart, but he receives the opportunity to understand *Vedas* from Him. If one is serious to understand the Vedic knowledge, then Kṛṣṇa gives the required intelligence. Why does He present the Vedic knowledge for understanding? Because a living entity individually needs to understand Kṛṣṇa. Vedic literature confirms this: *yo 'sau sarvair vedair gīyate.* In all Vedic literature, beginning from the four *Vedas*, *Vedānta-sūtra* and the *Upaniṣads* and *Purāṇas*, the glories of the Supreme Lord are celebrated. By performing Vedic rituals, discussing the Vedic philosophy and worshiping the Lord in devotional service, He is attained. Therefore the purpose of the *Vedas* is to understand Kṛṣṇa. The *Vedas* give us direction to understand Kṛṣṇa and the process of understanding. The ultimate goal is the Supreme Personality of Godhead. *Vedānta-sūtra* confirms this in the following words: *tat tu samanvayāt.* One can attain perfection by understanding Vedic literature, and one can understand his relationship with the Supreme Personality of Godhead by performing the different processes. Thus one can approach Him and at the end attain the supreme goal, who is no other than the Supreme Personality of Godhead. In this verse, however, the purpose of the *Vedas*, the understanding of the *Vedas* and the goal of *Vedas* are clearly defined.

TEXT 16

द्वाविमौ पुरुषौ लोके क्षराक्षर एव च ।
क्षरः सर्वाणि भूतानि कूटस्थोऽक्षर उच्यते ॥ १६ ॥

*dvāv imau puruṣau loke
kṣaraś cākṣara eva ca
kṣaraḥ sarvāṇi bhūtāni
kūṭa-stho 'kṣara ucyate*

dvau—two; *imau*—in this (world); *puruṣau*—living entities; *loke*—in the world; *kṣaraḥ*—fallible; *ca*—and; *akṣaraḥ*—infallible; *eva*—certainly; *ca*—and; *kṣaraḥ*—the fallible; *sarvāṇi*—all; *bhūtāni*—living entities; *kūṭasthaḥ*—in oneness; *akṣaraḥ*—infallible; *ucyate*—is said.

TRANSLATION

There are two classes of beings, the fallible and the infallible. In the material world every entity is fallible, and in the spiritual world every entity is called infallible.

PURPORT

As already explained, the Lord in His incarnation as Vyāsadeva compiled the *Vedānta-sutra*. Here the Lord is giving, in summary, the contents of the *Vedānta-sūtra*: He says that the living entities, who are innumerable, can be divided into two classes—the fallible and the infallible. The living entities are eternally separated parts and parcels of the Supreme Personality of Godhead. When they are in contact with the material world, they are called *jīva-bhūtāḥ*, and the Sanskrit words given here, *sarvāṇi bhūtāni*, mean that they are fallible. Those who are in oneness with the Supreme Personality of Godhead, however, are called infallible. Oneness does not mean that they have no individuality, but that there is no disunity. They are all agreeable to the purpose of the creation. Of course, in the spiritual world, there is no such thing as creation, but since the Supreme Personality of Godhead has stated in the *Vedānta-sūtra* that He is the source of all emanations, that conception is explained.

According to the statement of the Supreme Personality of Godhead, Lord Kṛṣṇa, there are two classes of men. The *Vedas* give evidence of this, so there is no doubt about it. The living entities, who are struggling in this world with the mind and five senses, have their material bodies which are changing as long as the living entities are conditioned. One's body changes due to contact with matter; matter is changing, so the living entity appears to be changing. But in the spiritual world the body is not made of matter; therefore there is no change. In the material world the living entity undergoes six changes—birth, growth, duration, reproduction, then dwindling and vanishing. These are the changes of the material body. But in the spiritual world the body does not change; there is no old age, there is no birth, there is no death. There all exists in oneness. It is more clearly explained as *sarvāṇi bhūtāni*: any living entity who has come in contact with matter, beginning from the first created being, Brahmā, down to a small ant, is changing its body; therefore they are all fallible. In the spiritual world, however, they are always liberated in oneness.

TEXT 17

उत्तमः पुरुषस्त्वन्यः परमात्मेत्युदाहृतः ।
यो लोकत्रयमाविश्य बिभर्त्यव्यय ईश्वरः ॥ १७ ॥

uttamaḥ puruṣas tv anyaḥ
paramātmety udāhṛtaḥ
yo loka-trayam āviśya
bibharty avyaya īśvaraḥ

uttamaḥ—the best; *puruṣaḥ*—personality; *tu*—but; *anyaḥ*—another; *param*—the Supreme; *ātmā*—Self; *iti*—thus; *udāhṛtaḥ*—said; *yaḥ*—one who; *loka*—of the universe; *trayam*—the three divisions; *āviśya*—entering; *bibharti*—maintaining; *avyayaḥ*—inexhaustible; *īśvaraḥ*—the Lord.

TRANSLATION

Besides these two, there is the greatest living personality, the Lord Himself, who has entered into these worlds and is maintaining them.

PURPORT

This verse is very nicely expressed in the *Kaṭha Upaniṣad* and *Śvetāśvatara Upaniṣad*. It is clearly stated there that above the innumerable living entities, some of whom are conditioned and some of whom are liberated, there is the Supreme Personality who is Paramātmā. The Upaniṣadic verse runs as follows: *nityo nityānāṁ cetanaś cetanānām.* The purport is that amongst all the living entities, both conditioned and liberated, there is one supreme living personality, the Supreme Personality of Godhead, who maintains them and gives them all the facility of enjoyment according to different work. That Supreme Personality of Godhead is situated in everyone's heart as Paramātmā. A wise man who can understand Him is eligible to attain the perfect peace, not others.

It is incorrect to think of the Supreme Lord and the living entities as being on the same level or equal in all respects. There is always the question of superiority and inferiority in their personalities. This particular word *uttama* is very significant. No one can surpass the Supreme Personality of Godhead. *Loke* is also significant because in the *Pauruṣa*, a Vedic literature, it is stated: *lokyate vedārtho'nena.* This Supreme Lord in His localized aspect as Paramātmā explains the purpose of the *Vedas.* The following verse also appears in the *Vedas*:

> *tāvad eṣa samprasādo 'smāc*
> *charīrāt samutthāya param*
> *jyoti-rūpaṁ sampadya svena*
> *rūpeṇābhiniṣpadyate sa uttamaḥ puruṣaḥ*

"The Supersoul coming out of the body enters the impersonal *brahma-jyoti;* then in His form He remains in His spiritual identity. That Supreme is called the Supreme Personality." This means that the Supreme Personality is exhibiting and diffusing His spiritual effulgence, which is the ultimate illumination. That Supreme Personality also has a localized aspect as Paramātmā. By incarnating Himself as the son of Satyavatī and Parāśara, He explains the Vedic knowledge as Vyāsadeva.

TEXT 18

यस्मात्क्षरमतीतोऽहमक्षरादपि चोत्तमः ।
अतोऽस्मि लोके वेदे च प्रथितः पुरुषोत्तमः ॥ १८ ॥

> yasmāt kṣaram atīto 'ham
> akṣarād api cottamaḥ
> ato 'smi loke vede ca
> prathitaḥ puruṣottamaḥ

yasmāt—because; *kṣaram*—the fallible; *atītaḥ*—transcendental; *aham*—I; *akṣarāt*—from the infallible; *api*—better than that; *ca*—and; *uttamaḥ*—the best; *ataḥ*—therefore; *asmi*—I am; *loke*—in the world; *vede*—in the Vedic literature; *ca*—and; *prathitaḥ*—celebrated; *puruṣottamaḥ*—as the Supreme Personality.

TRANSLATION

Because I am transcendental, beyond both the fallible and the infallible, and because I am the greatest, I am celebrated both in the world and in the Vedas as that Supreme Person.

PURPORT

No one can surpass the Supreme Personality of Godhead, Kṛṣṇa—neither the conditioned soul nor the liberated soul. He is, therefore, the greatest of personalities. Now it is clear here that the living entities and the Supreme Personality of Godhead are individuals. The difference is that the living entities, either in the conditioned state or in the liberated state, cannot surpass in quantity the inconceivable potencies of the Supreme Personality of Godhead.

TEXT 19

यो मामेवमसंमूढो जानाति पुरुषोत्तमम् ।
स सर्वविद्भजति मां सर्वभावेन भारत ॥ १९ ॥

> yo mām evam asammūḍho
> jānāti puruṣottamam
> sa sarva-vid bhajati māṁ
> sarva-bhāvena bhārata

yaḥ—anyone; *mām*—unto Me; *evam*—certainly; *asammūḍhaḥ*—without a doubt; *jānāti*—knows; *puruṣottamam*—the Supreme Personality of

Godhead; *saḥ*—he; *sarva-vit*—knower of everything; *bhajati*—renders devotional service; *mām*—unto Me; *sarva-bhāvena*—in all respects; *bhārata*—O son of Bharata.

TRANSLATION

Whoever knows Me as the Supreme Personality of Godhead, without doubting, is to be understood as the knower of everything, and he therefore engages himself in full devotional service, O son of Bharata

PURPORT

There are many philosophical speculations about the constitutional position of the living entities and the Supreme Absolute Truth. Now in this verse the Supreme Personality of Godhead clearly explains that anyone who knows Lord Kṛṣṇa as the Supreme Person is actually the knower of everything. The imperfect knower goes on simply speculating about the Absolute Truth, but the perfect knower, without wasting his valuable time, engages directly in Kṛṣṇa consciousness, the devotional service of the Supreme Lord. Throughout the whole of *Bhagavad-gītā*, this fact is being stressed at every step. And still there are so many stubborn commentators on *Bhagavad-gītā* who consider the Supreme Absolute Truth and the living entities to be one and the same.

Vedic knowledge is called *śruti*, learning by aural reception. One should actually receive the Vedic message from authorities like Kṛṣṇa and His representatives. Here Kṛṣṇa distinguishes everything very nicely, and one should hear from this source. Simply to hear like the hogs is not sufficient; one must be able to understand from the authorities. It is not that one should simply speculate academically. One should submissively hear from *Bhagavad-gītā* that these living entities are always subordinate to the Supreme Personality of Godhead. Anyone who is able to understand this, according to the Supreme Personality of Godhead, Śrī Kṛṣṇa, knows the purpose of the *Vedas*; no one else knows the purpose of the *Vedas*.

The word *bhajate* is very significant. In many places the word *bhajate* is expressed in relationship with the service of the Supreme Lord. If a person is engaged in full Kṛṣṇa consciousness in devotional service of the Lord, it is to be understood that he has understood all the Vedic knowledge. In the Vaiṣṇava *paramparā* it is said that if one is engaged in the devotional service of Kṛṣṇa, then there is no need for a spiritual process to understand the Supreme Absolute Truth. He has already come to the post because he is engaged in the devotional service of the Lord. He has ended all preliminary processes of understanding; similarly, if anyone, after speculating for hundreds of thousands of lives, does not come to the point that Kṛṣṇa is the Supreme Personality of Godhead and that one has to surrender there, all his speculation for so many years and lives is a useless waste of time.

TEXT 20

इति गुह्यतमं शास्त्रमिदमुक्तं मयाऽनघ ।
एतद्बुद्ध्वा बुद्धिमान्स्यात्कृतकृत्यश्च भारत ॥ २० ॥

*iti guhyatamaṁ śāstram
idam uktaṁ mayānagha
etad buddhvā buddhimān syāt
kṛta-kṛtyaś ca bhārata*

iti—thus; *guhyatamam*—the most confidential; *śāstram*—revealed scriptures; *idam*—this; *uktam*—disclosed; *mayā*—by Me; *anagha*—O sinless one; *etat*—this; *buddhvā*—understanding; *buddhimān*—intelligent; *syāt*—one becomes; *kṛta-kṛtyaḥ*—the most perfect; *ca*—and; *bhārata*—O son of Bharata.

TRANSLATION

This is the most confidential part of the Vedic scriptures, O sinless one, and it is disclosed now by Me. Whoever understands this will become wise, and his endeavors will know perfection.

PURPORT

The Lord clearly explains here that this is the substance of all revealed scriptures. And one should understand this as it is given by the Supreme Personality of Godhead. Thus one will become intelligent and perfect in transcendental knowledge. In other words, by understanding this philosophy of the Supreme Personality of Godhead and engaging in His transcendental service, everyone can become freed from all contaminations of the modes of material nature. Devotional service is a process of spiritual understanding. Wherever devotional service exists, the material contamination cannot coexist. Devotional service to the Lord and the Lord Himself are one and the same because they are spiritual—the internal energy of the Supreme Lord. The Lord is said to be the sun, and ignorance is called darkness. Where the sun is present, there is no question of darkness. Therefore, whenever devotional service is present under the proper guidance of a bona fide spiritual master, there is no question of ignorance.

Everyone must take to this consciousness of Kṛṣṇa and engage in devotional service to become intelligent and purified. Unless one comes to this position of understanding Kṛṣṇa and engages in devotional service, however intelligent he may be in the estimation of some common man, he is not perfectly intelligent.

The word anagha, by which Arjuna is addressed, is significant. Anagha, O sinless one, means that unless one is free from all sinful reactions, it is very difficult to understand Kṛṣṇa. One has to become free from all contamination, all sinful activities; then he can understand. But devotional service is so pure and potent that once one is engaged in devotional service he automatically comes to the stage of sinlessness.

While performing devotional service in the association of pure devotees in full Kṛṣṇa consciousness, there are certain things which require to be vanquished altogether. The most important thing one has to surmount is weakness of the heart. The first falldown is caused by the desire to lord it over material nature. Thus one gives up the transcendental loving service of the Supreme Lord. The second weakness of the heart is that as one increases the propensity of lording it over material nature, he becomes attached to matter and the possession of matter. The problems of material existence are due to these weaknesses of the heart.

Thus end the Bhaktivedanta Purports to the Fifteenth Chapter of the Śrīmad-Bhagavad-gītā in the matter of Puruṣottama-yoga, the Yoga of the Supreme Person.

CHAPTER SIXTEEN

The Divine and Demoniac Natures

TEXTS 1-3

श्रीभगवानुवाच ।
अभयं सत्त्वसंशुद्धिर्ज्ञानयोगव्यवस्थितिः ।
दानं दमश्च यज्ञश्च स्वाध्यायस्तप आर्जवम् ॥ १ ॥
अहिंसा सत्यमक्रोधस्त्यागः शान्तिरपैशुनम् ।
दया भूतेष्वलोलुप्त्वं मार्दवं ह्रीरचापलम् ॥ २ ॥
तेजः क्षमा धृतिः शौचमद्रोहो नातिमानिता ।
भवन्ति संपदं दैवीमभिजातस्य भारत ॥ ३ ॥

śrī-bhagavān uvāca
abhayaṁ sattva-saṁśuddhir
jñāna-yoga-vyavasthitiḥ
dānaṁ damaś ca yajñaś ca
svādhyāyas tapa ārjavam

ahiṁsā satyam akrodhas
tyāgaḥ śāntir apaiśunam

dayā bhūteṣv aloluptvaṁ
mārdavaṁ hrīr acāpalam

tejaḥ kṣamā dhṛtiḥ śaucam
adroho nāti-mānitā
bhavanti sampadaṁ daivīm
abhijātasya bhārata

śrī bhagavān uvāca—the Supreme Personality of Godhead said; *abhayam*—fearlessness; *sattva-saṁśuddhiḥ*—purification of one's existence; *jñāna*—knowledge; *yoga*—of linking up; *vyavasthitiḥ*—the situation; *dānam*—charity; *damaḥ ca*—and controlling the mind; *yajñaḥ ca*—and performance of sacrifice; *svādhyāyaḥ*—study of Vedic literature; *tapaḥ*—austerity; *ārjavam*—simplicity; *ahiṁsā*—nonviolence; *satyam*—truthfulness; *akrodhaḥ*—freedom from anger; *tyāgaḥ*—renunciation; *śāntiḥ*—tranquility; *apaiśunam*—aversion to faultfinding; *dayā*—mercy; *bhūteṣu*—towards all living entities; *aloluptvam*—freedom from greed; *mārdavam*—gentleness; *hrīḥ*—modesty; *acāpalam*—determination; *tejaḥ*—vigor ; *kṣamā*—forgiveness; *dhṛtiḥ*—fortitude; *śaucam*—cleanliness; *adrohaḥ*—freedom from envy; *na*—not; *atimānitā*—expectation of honor; *bhavanti*—become; *sampadam*—qualities; *daivīm*—transcendental; *abhijātasya*—one who is born of; *bhārata*—O son of Bharata.

TRANSLATION

The Blessed Lord said: Fearlessness, purification of one's existence, cultivation of spiritual knowledge, charity, self-control, performance of sacrifice, study of the Vedas, austerity and simplicity; nonviolence, truthfulness, freedom from anger; renunciation, tranquility, aversion to faultfinding, compassion and freedom from covetousness; gentleness, modesty and steady determination; vigor, forgiveness, fortitude, cleanliness, freedom from envy and the passion for honor—these transcendental qualities, O son of Bharata, belong to godly men endowed with divine nature.

PURPORT

In the beginning of the Fifteenth Chapter, the banyan tree of this material world was explained. The extra roots coming out of it were compared to the activities of the living entities, some auspicious, some inauspicious. In the Ninth Chapter, also, the *devas*, or godly, and the *asuras*, the ungodly, or demons, were explained. Now, according to Vedic rites, activities in the mode of goodness are considered auspicious for progress on the path of liberation, and such activities are known as *deva-*

prakṛti, transcendental by nature. Those who are situated in the transcendental nature make progress on the path of liberation. For those who are acting in the modes of passion and ignorance, on the other hand, there is no possibility of liberation. Either they will have to remain in this material world as human beings, or they will descend among the species of animals or even lower life forms. In this Sixteenth Chapter the Lord explains both the transcendental nature and its attendant qualities, as well as the demoniac nature and its qualities. He also explains the advantages and disadvantages of these qualities.

The word *abhijātasya* in reference to one born of transcendental qualities or godly tendencies is very significant. To beget a child in a godly atmosphere is known in the Vedic scriptures as *Garbhādhāna-saṁskāra.* If the parents want a child in the godly qualities they should follow the ten principles of the human being. In *Bhagavad-gītā* we have studied also before that sex life for begetting a good child is Kṛṣṇa Himself. Sex life is not condemned provided the process is used in Kṛṣṇa consciousness. Those who are in Kṛṣṇa consciousness at least should not beget children like cats and dogs but should beget them so they may become Kṛṣṇa conscious after birth. That should be the advantage of children born of a father or mother absorbed in Kṛṣṇa consciousness.

The social institution known as *varṇāśrama-dharma*—the institution dividing society into four divisions or castes—is not meant to divide human society according to birth. Such divisions are in terms of educational qualifications. They are to keep the society in a state of peace and prosperity. The qualities mentioned herein are explained as transcendental qualities meant for making a person progress in spiritual understanding so he can get liberated from the material world. In the *varṇāśrama* institution the *sannyāsī,* or the person in the renounced order of life, is considered to be the head or the spiritual master of all the social statuses and orders. A *brāhmaṇa* is considered to be the spiritual master of the three other sections of a society, namely, the *kṣatriyas,* the *vaiśyas* and the *śūdras,* but a *sannyāsī,* who is on the top of the institution, is considered to be the spiritual master of the *brāhmaṇas* also. For a *sannyāsī,* the first qualification should be fearlessness. Because a *sannyāsī* has to be alone without any support or guarantee of support, he has simply to depend on the mercy of the Supreme Personality of Godhead. If he thinks, "After leaving my connections, who will protect me?" he should not accept the renounced order of life. One must be fully convinced that Kṛṣṇa or the Supreme Personality of Godhead in His localized aspect as Paramātmā is always within, that He is seeing everything and He always knows what one intends to do. One must thus have firm conviction that Kṛṣṇa as Paramātmā will take care of a soul surrendered to Him. "I shall never be alone," one should think. "Even if I live in the darkest regions of a forest I shall be accompanied by Kṛṣṇa, and He will give me all protection." That conviction is called *abhayam*, without fear. This state of mind is necessary for a person in the renounced order of life. Then he has to purify his existence. There are so many rules and regulations to be followed in the renounced order of life. Most important of all, a *sannyāsī* is strictly forbidden to have any intimate relationship with a woman. He is even forbidden to talk with a woman in a secluded place. Lord Caitanya was an ideal *sannyāsī*, and when He was at Purī His feminine devotees could not even come near to offer their respects. They were advised to bow down from a distant place. This is not a sign of hatred for women as a class, but it is a stricture imposed on the *sannyāsī* not to have close connections with women. One has to follow the rules and regulations of a particular status of life in order to purify his existence. For a *sannyāsī*, intimate relations with women and possessions of wealth for sense gratification are strictly forbidden. The ideal *sannyāsī* was Lord Caitanya Himself, and we can learn from His life that He was very strict in regards to women. Although He is considered to be the most liberal incarnation of Godhead, accepting the most fallen conditioned souls, He strictly followed the rules and regulations of the *sannyāsa* order of the life in connection with association with woman. One of His personal associates, namely Choṭa Haridāsa, was personally associated with Lord Caitanya, along with His other confidential personal associates, but somehow or other this Choṭa Haridāsa looked lustily on a young woman, and Lord Caitanya was so strict that He at once rejected him from the society of His personal associates. Lord Caitanya said, "For a *sannyāsī* or anyone who is aspiring to get out of the clutches of material nature and trying to elevate himself to the spiritual nature and go back to home, back to Godhead, for him, looking toward material possessions and women for sense gratification—not even enjoying them, but just looking toward them with such a propensity—is so condemned that he had better commit suicide before experiencing such illicit desires." So these are the processes for purification.

The next item is *jñāna-yoga-vyavasthitiḥ*: being engaged in the cultivation of knowledge. *Sannyāsī* life is meant for distributing knowledge to the householders and others who have forgotten their real life of spiritual advancement. A *sannyāsī* is supposed to beg from door to door for his livelihood, but this does not mean that he is a beggar. Humility is also one of the qualifications of a transcendentally situated person, and out of sheer humility the *sannyāsī* goes from door to door, not exactly for the purpose of begging, but to see the householders and awaken them to Kṛṣṇa consciousness. This is the duty of a *sannyāsī*. If he is actually advanced and so ordered by his spiritual master, he should preach Kṛṣṇa consciousness with logic and understanding, and if he is not so advanced he should not accept the renounced order of life. But even if he has accepted the renounced order of life without sufficient knowledge, he should engage himself fully in hearing from a bona fide spiritual master to cultivate knowledge. A *sannyāsī* or one in the renounced order of life must be situated in fearlessness, *sattva-saṁśuddhiḥ* (purity) and *jñāna-yoga* (knowledge).

The next item is charity. Charity is meant for the householders. The householders should earn a livelihood by an honorable means and spend fifty percent of their income to propagate Kṛṣṇa consciousness all over the world. Thus a householder should give in charity to such institutional societies that are engaged in that way. Charity should be given to the right receiver. There are different kinds of charities, as will be explained later on, charity in the modes of goodness, passion and ignorance. Charity in the mode of goodness is recommended by the scriptures, but charity in the modes of passion and ignorance is not recommended because it is simply a waste of money. Charity should be given only to propagate Kṛṣṇa consciousness all over the world. That is charity in the mode of goodness.

Then as far as *damaḥ* (self-control) is concerned, it is not only meant for other orders of religious society, but it is especially meant for the householder. Although he has a wife, a householder should not use his senses for sex life unnecessarily. There are restrictions for the householders even in sex life, which should only be engaged in for the propagation of children. If he does not require children, he should not enjoy sex life with his wife. Modern society enjoys sex life with contraceptive methods or more abominable methods to avoid the responsibility of children. This is not in the transcendental quality but is demoniac. If anyone, even if he is a householder, wants to make progress in spiritual life, he must control his sex life and should not beget a child without the purpose of serving Kṛṣṇa. If he is able to beget children who will be in Kṛṣṇa consciousness, one can produce hundreds of children, but without this capacity one should not indulge only for sense pleasure.

Sacrifice is another item to be performed by the householders because sacrifices require a large amount of money. Other orders of life, namely the *brahmacarya,* the *vānaprastha* and *sannyāsa,* have no money; they live by begging. So performance of different types of sacrifice is meant for the householder. They should perform *agni-hotra* sacrifices as enjoined in the Vedic literature, but such sacrifices at the present moment are very expensive, and it is not possible for any householder to perform them. The best sacrifice recommended in this age is called *saṅkīrtana-yajña,* the chanting of Hare Kṛṣṇa, Hare Kṛṣṇa, Kṛṣṇa Kṛṣṇa, Hare Hare/Hare Rāma, Hare Rāma, Rāma Rāma, Hare Hare. This is the best and most inexpensive sacrifice; everyone can adopt it and derive benefit. So these three items, namely charity, sense control and performance of sacrifice, are meant for the householder.

Then *svādhyāyaḥ,* Vedic study, and *tapas,* austerity, and *ārjavam,* gentleness or simplicity, are meant for the *brahmacarya* or student life. *Brahmacārīs* should have no connection with women; they should live a life of celibacy and engage the mind in the study of Vedic literature for cultivation of spiritual knowledge. This is called *svādhyāyaḥ. Tapas* or austerity is especially meant for the retired life. One should not remain a householder throughout his whole life; he must always remember that there are four divisions of life, *brahmacarya, gṛhastha, vānaprastha* and *sannyāsa.* So after *gṛhastha,* householder life, one should retire. If one lives for a hundred years, he should spend twenty-five years in student life, twenty-five in householder life, twenty-five in retired life and twenty-five in the renounced order of life. These are the regulations of the Vedic religious discipline. A man retired from household life must practice austerities of the body, mind and tongue. That is *tapasyā.* The entire *varṇāśrama-dharma* society is meant for *tapasyā.* Without *tapasyā* or austerity no human being can get liberation. The theory that there is no need of austerity in life, that one can go on speculating and everything will be nice, is neither recommended in the Vedic literature nor in *Bhagavad-gītā.* Such theories are manufactured by showbottle spiritualists who are trying to gather more followers. If there are restrictions, rules and regulations, people will not become attracted. Therefore those who want followers in the name of religion, just to have a show only, don't restrict the lives of their students nor their own lives. But that method is not approved by the *Vedas.*

As far as simplicity is concerned, not only should a particular order of life follow this principle, but every member, be he in the *brahmacarya-*

āśrama, or *gṛhastha-āśrama* or *vānaprastha-āśrama.* One must live very simply.

Ahiṁsā means not arresting the progressive life of any living entity. One should not think that since the spirit spark is never killed even after the killing of the body there is no harm in killing animals for sense gratification. People are now addicted to eating animals, in spite of having an ample supply of grains, fruits and milk. There is no necessity for animal killing. This injunction is for everyone. When there is no other alternative, one may kill an animal, but it should be offered in sacrifice. At any rate, when there is an ample food supply for humanity, persons who are desiring to make advancement in spiritual realization should not commit violence to animals. Real *ahiṁsā* means not checking anyone's progressive life. The animals are also making progress in their evolutionary life by transmigrating from one category of animal life to another. If a particular animal is killed, then his progress is checked. If an animal is staying in a particular body for so many days or so many years and is untimely killed, then he has to come back again in that form of life to complete the remaining days in order to be promoted to another species of life. So their progress should not be checked simply to satisfy one's palate. This is called *ahiṁsā.*

Satyam. This word means that one should not distort the truth for some personal interest. In Vedic literature there are some difficult passages, but the meaning or the purpose should be learned from a bona fide spiritual master. That is the process for understanding *Vedas. Śruti* means that one should hear from the authority. One should not construe some interpretation for his personal interest. There are so many commentaries on *Bhagavad-gītā* that misinterpret the original text. The real import of the word should be presented, and that should be learned from a bona fide spiritual master.

Akrodhaḥ means to check anger. Even if there is provocation one should be tolerant, for once one becomes angry his whole body becomes polluted. Anger is the product of the modes of passion and lust, so one who is transcendentally situated should check himself from anger. *Apaiśunam* means that one should not find fault with others or correct them unnecessarily. Of course to call a thief a thief is not faultfinding, but to call an honest person a thief is very much offensive for one who is making advancement in spiritual life. *Hrīḥ* means that one should be very modest and must not perform some act which is abominable. *Acāpalam,* determination, means that one should not be agitated or frustrated in some attempt. There may be failure in some attempt, but one should not be sorry for that; he should make progress with patience and determination. The word *tejaḥ* used here is meant for the *kṣatriyas*. The *kṣatriyas* should always be very strong to be able to give protection to the weak. They should not pose themselves as nonviolent. If violence is required, they must exhibit it.

Śaucam means cleanliness, not only in mind and body but in one's dealings also. It is especially meant for the mercantile people, who should not deal in the black market. *Nātimānitā*, not expecting honor, applies to the *śūdras*, the worker class, which are considered, according to Vedic injunctions, to be the lowest of the four classes. They should not be puffed up with unnecessary prestige or honor and should remain in their own status. It is the duty of the *śūdras* to offer respect to the higher class for the upkeep of the social order.

All these sixteen qualifications mentioned are transcendental qualities. They should be cultivated according to the different statuses of the social order. The purport is that even though material conditions are miserable, if these qualities are developed by practice, by all classes of men, then gradually it is possible to rise to the highest platform of transcendental realization.

TEXT 4

दम्भो दर्पोऽभिमानश्च क्रोधः पारुष्यमेव च ।
अज्ञानं चाभिजातस्य पार्थ संपदमासुरीम् ॥ ४ ॥

dambho darpo 'bhimānaś ca
krodhaḥ pāruṣyam eva ca
ajñānaṁ cābhijātasya
pārtha sampadam āsurīm

dambhaḥ—pride; *darpaḥ*—arrogance; *abhimānaḥ*—conceit; *ca*—and; *krodhaḥ*—anger; *pāruṣyam*—harshness; *eva*—certainly; *ca*—and; *ajñānam*—ignorance; *ca*—and; *abhijātasya*—one who is born; *pārtha*—O son of Pṛthā; *sampadam*—nature; *āsurīm*—demoniac.

TRANSLATION

Arrogance, pride, anger, conceit, harshness and ignorance—these qualities belong to those of demonic nature, O son of Pṛthā.

PURPORT

In this verse, the royal road to hell is described. The demoniac want to make a show of religion and advancement in spiritual science, although they do not follow the principles. They are always arrogant or proud in possessing some type of education or so much wealth. They desire to be worshiped by others, and demand respectability, although they do not command respect. Over trifles they become very angry and speak harshly, not gently. They do not know what should be done and what should not be done. They do everything whimsically, according to their own desire, and they do not recognize any authority. These demoniac qualities are taken on by them from the beginning of their bodies in the wombs of their mothers, and as they grow they manifest all these inauspicious qualities.

TEXT 5

दैवी संपद्विमोक्षाय निबन्धायासुरी मता ।
मा शुचः संपदं दैवीमभिजातोऽसि पाण्डव ॥ ५ ॥

daivī sampad vimokṣāya
nibandhāyāsurī matā
mā śucaḥ sampadaṁ daivīm
abhijāto 'si pāṇḍava

daivī—transcendental; *sampat*—nature; *vimokṣāya*—meant for liberation; *nibandhāya*—for bondage; *āsurī*—demoniac qualities; *matā*—it is considered; *mā*—do not; *śucaḥ*—worry; *sampadam*—nature; *daivīm*—transcendental; *abhijātaḥ*—born; *asi*—you are; *pāṇḍava*—O son of Pāṇḍu.

TRANSLATION

The transcendental qualities are conducive to liberation, whereas the demonic qualities make for bondage. Do not worry, O son of Pāṇḍu, for you are born with the divine qualities.

PURPORT

Lord Kṛṣṇa encouraged Arjuna by telling him that he was not born with demoniac qualities. His involvement in the fight was not demoniac because he was considering the pro's and con's. He was considering whether respectable persons such as Bhīṣma and Droṇa should be killed or not, so he was not acting under the influence of anger, false prestige, or harshness. Therefore he was not of the quality of the demons. For a *kṣatriya,* a military man, shooting arrows at the enemy is considered transcendental, and refraining from such a duty is demoniac. Therefore, there was no cause for Arjuna to lament. Anyone who performs the regulated principles of the different orders of life is transcendentally situated.

TEXT 6

द्रौ भूतसर्गौ लोकेऽस्मिन्दैव आसुर एव च ।
दैवो विस्तरशः प्रोक्त आसुरं पार्थ मे शृणु ॥ ६ ॥

*dvau bhūta-sargau loke 'smin
daiva āsura eva ca
daivo vistaraśaḥ proktā
āsuraṁ pārtha me śṛṇu*

dvau—two; *bhūta-sargau*—created living beings; *loke*—in this world; *asmin*—this; *daivaḥ*—godly; *āsuraḥ*—demoniac; *eva*—certainly; *ca*—and; *daivaḥ*—divine; *vistaraśaḥ*—at great length; *proktaḥ*—said; *asuram*—demoniac; *pārtha*—O son of Pṛthā; *me*—from Me; *śṛṇu*—just hear.

TRANSLATION

O son of Pṛthā, in this world there are two kinds of created beings. One is called the divine and the other demonic. I have already explained to you at length the divine qualities. Now hear from Me of the demoniac.

PURPORT

Lord Kṛṣṇa, having assured Arjuna that he was born with the divine qualities, is now describing the demoniac way. The conditioned living entities are divided into two classes in this world. Those who are born with divine qualities follow a regulated life; that is to say they abide by the injunctions in scriptures and by the authorities. One should perform duties in the light of authoritative scripture. This mentality is called divine. One who does not follow the regulative principles as they are laid down in the scriptures and who acts according to his whims is called demoniac or asuric. There is no other criterion but obedience to the regulative principles of scriptures. It is mentioned in Vedic literature that both the demigods and the demons are born of the Prajāpati; the only difference is that one class obeys the Vedic injunctions and the other does not.

TEXT 7

प्रवृत्तिं च निवृत्तिं च जना न विदुरासुराः ।
न शौचं नापि चाचारो न सत्यं तेषु विद्यते ॥ ७ ॥

*pravṛttiṁ ca nivṛttiṁ ca
janā na vidur āsurāḥ
na śaucaṁ nāpi cācāro
na satyaṁ teṣu vidyate*

pravṛttim—proper action; *ca*—also; *nivṛttim*—improper action; *ca*—and; *janāḥ*—persons; *na*—never; *viduḥ*—know; *āsurāḥ*—in demoniac quality; *na*—never; *śaucam*—cleanliness; *na*—nor; *api*—also; *ca*—and; *ācāraḥ*—behavior; *na*—never; *satyam*—truth; *teṣu*—in them; *vidyate*—there is.

TRANSLATION

Those who are demoniac do not know what is to be done and what is not to be done. Neither cleanliness nor proper behavior nor truth is found in them.

PURPORT

In every civilized human society there is some set of scriptural rules and regulations which are followed from the beginning, especially among the Āryans, those who adopt the Vedic civilization and who are known as the most advanced civilized peoples. Those who do not follow the scriptural injunctions are supposed to be demons. Therefore it is stated here that the demons do not know the scriptural rules, nor do they have any inclination to follow them. Most of them do not know them, and even if some of them know, they have not the tendency to follow them. They have no faith, nor are they willing to act in terms of the Vedic injunctions. The demons are not clean, either externally or internally.

One should always be careful to keep his body clean by bathing, brushing teeth, changing clothes, etc. As far as internal cleanliness is concerned, one should always remember the holy names of God and chant Hare Kṛṣṇa, Hare Kṛṣṇa, Kṛṣṇa Kṛṣṇa, Hare Hare/Hare Rāma, Hare Rāma, Rāma Rāma, Hare Hare. The demons neither like nor follow all these rules for external and internal cleanliness.

As for behavior, there are many rules and regulations guiding human behavior, such as the *Manu-samhitā*, which is the law of the human race. Even up to today, those who are Hindu follow the *Manu-samhitā*. Laws of inheritance and other legalities are derived from this book. Now, in the *Manu-samhitā*, it is clearly stated that a woman should not be given freedom. That does not mean that women are to be kept as slaves, but they are like children. Children are not given freedom, but that does not mean that they are kept as slaves. The demons have now neglected such injunctions, and they think that women should be given as much freedom as men. However, this has not improved the social condition of the world. Actually, a woman should be given protection at every stage of life. She should be given protection by the father in her younger days, by the husband in her youth, and by the grownup sons in her old age. This is proper social behavior according to the *Manu-samhitā*. But modern education has artificially devised a puffed up concept of womanly life, and therefore marriage is practically now an imagination in human society. Nor is the moral condition of woman very good now. The demons, therefore, do not accept any instruction which is good for society, and because they do not follow the experience of great sages and the rules and regulations laid down by the sages, the social condition of the demoniac people is very miserable.

TEXT 8

असत्यमप्रतिष्ठं ते जगदाहुरनीश्वरम् ।
अपरस्परसंभूतं किमन्यत्कामहैतुकम् ॥ ८ ॥

*asatyam apratiṣṭham te
jagad āhur anīśvaram
aparaspara-sambhūtam
kim anyat kāma-haitukam*

asatyam—unreal; *apratiṣṭham*—without foundation; *te*—they; *jagat*—the cosmic manifestation; *āhuḥ*—is said; *anīśvaram*—with no controller;

aparaspara—by mutual lust; *sambhūtam*—caused; *kim anyat*—there is no other cause; *kāma-haitukam*—it is due to lust only.

TRANSLATION

They say that this world is unreal, that there is no foundation and that there is no God in control. It is produced of sex desire, and has no cause other than lust.

PURPORT

The demoniac conclude that the world is phantasmagoria. There is no cause, no effect, no controller, no purpose: everything is unreal. They say that this cosmic manifestation arises due to chance material actions and reactions. They do not think that the world was created by God for a certain purpose. They have their own theory: that the world has come about in its own way and that there is no reason to believe that there is a God behind it. For them there is no difference between spirit and matter, and they do not accept the Supreme Spirit. Everything is matter only, and the whole cosmos is supposed to be a mass of ignorance. According to them, everything is void, and whatever manifestation exists is due to our ignorance in perception. They take it for granted that all manifestation of diversity is a display of ignorance. Just as in a dream we may create so many things, which actually have no existence, so when we are awake we shall see that everything is simply a dream. But factually, although the demons say that life is a dream, they are very expert in enjoying this dream. And so, instead of acquiring knowledge, they become more and more implicated in their dreamland. They conclude that as a child is simply the result of sexual intercourse between man and woman, this world is born without any soul. For them it is only a combination of matter that has produced the living entities, and there is no question of the existence of the soul. As many living creatures come out from perspiration and from a dead body without any cause, similarly, the whole living world has come out of the material combinations of the cosmic manifestation. Therefore material nature is the cause of this manifestation, and there is no other cause. They do not believe in the words of Kṛṣṇa in *Bhagavad-gītā: mayādhyakṣeṇa prakṛtiḥ sūyate sa-carācaram.* "Under My direction the whole material world is moving." In other words, amongst the demons there is no perfect knowledge of the creation of this world; every one of them has some particular theory of his own. According to them, one interpretation of the scriptures is as good as another, for they do not believe in a standard understanding of the scriptural injunctions.

TEXT 9

एतां दृष्टिमवष्टभ्य नष्टात्मानोऽल्पबुद्धयः ।
प्रभवन्त्युग्रकर्माणः क्षयाय जगतोऽहिताः ॥ ९ ॥

etāṁ dṛṣṭim avaṣṭabhya
naṣṭātmāno 'lpa-buddhayaḥ
prabhavanty ugra-karmāṇaḥ
kṣayāya jagato 'hitāḥ

etām—thus; dṛṣṭim—vision; avaṣṭabhya—accepting; naṣṭa—lost; ātmānaḥ—self; alpa-buddhayaḥ—less intelligent; prabhavanti—flourish; ugra-karmāṇaḥ—in painful activities; kṣayāya—for destruction; jagataḥ—of the world; ahitāḥ—unbeneficial.

TRANSLATION

Following such conclusions, the demoniac, who are lost to themselves and who have no intelligence, engage in unbeneficial, horrible works meant to destroy the world.

PURPORT

The demoniac are engaged in activities that will lead the world to destruction. The Lord states here that they are less intelligent. The materialists, who have no concept of God, think that they are advancing. But, according to Bhagavad-gītā, they are unintelligent and devoid of all sense. They try to enjoy this material world to the utmost limit and therefore always engage in inventing something for sense gratification. Such materialistic inventions are considered to be advancement of human civilization, but the result is that people grow more and more violent and more and more cruel, cruel to animals and cruel to other human beings. They have no idea how to behave toward one another. Animal killing is very prominent amongst demoniac people. Such people are considered the enemies of the world because ultimately they will invent or create something which will bring destruction to all. Indirectly, this verse anticipates the invention of nuclear weapons, of which the whole world is today very proud. At any moment war may take place, and these atomic weapons may create havoc. Such things are created solely for the destruction of the world, and this is indicated here. Due to godlessness, such weapons are invented in human society; they are not meant for the peace and prosperity of the world.

TEXT 10

काममाश्रित्य दुष्पूरं दम्भमानमदान्विताः ।
मोहाद्गृहीत्वासद्ग्राहान्प्रवर्तन्तेऽशुचिव्रताः ॥ १० ॥

kāmam āśritya duṣpūraṁ
dambha-māna-madānvitāḥ
mohād gṛhītvāsad-grāhān
pravartante 'śuci-vratāḥ

kāmam—lust; *āśritya*—taking shelter of; *duṣpūram*—insatiable; *dambha*—pride; *māna*—false prestige; *mada-anvitāḥ*—absorbed in conceit; *mohāt*—by illusion; *gṛhītvā*—taking; *asat*—nonpermanent; *grāhān*—things; *pravartante*—flourish; *aśuci*—unclean; *vratāḥ*—avowed.

TRANSLATION

The demoniac, taking shelter of insatiable lust, pride and false prestige, and being thus illusioned, are always sworn to unclean work, attracted by the impermanent.

PURPORT

The demoniac mentality is described here. The demons' lust is never satiated. They will go on increasing and increasing their insatiable desires for material enjoyment. Although they are always full of anxieties on account of accepting nonpermanent things, they still continue to engage in such activities out of illusion. They have no knowledge and cannot tell that they are heading the wrong way. Accepting nonpermanent things, such demoniac people create their own God, create their own hymns and chant accordingly. The result is that they become more and more attracted to two things—sex enjoyment and accumulation of material wealth. The word *aśuci-vratāḥ,* unclean vow, is very significant in this connection. Such demoniac people are only attracted by wine, women, gambling and meat eating; those are their *aśuci,* unclean habits. Induced by pride and false prestige, they create some principles of religion which are not approved by the Vedic injunctions. Although such demoniac people are most abominable in the world, still, by artificial means, the world creates a false honor for them. Although they are gliding toward hell, they consider themselves very much advanced.

TEXTS 11-12

चिन्तामपरिमेयां च प्रलयान्तामुपाश्रिताः ।
कामोपभोगपरमा एतावदिति निश्चिताः ॥ ११ ॥

आशापाशशतैर्बद्धाः कामक्रोधपरायणाः ।
ईहन्ते कामभोगार्थमन्यायेनार्थसंचयान् ॥ १२ ॥

cintām aparimeyāṁ ca
pralayāntām upāśritāḥ
kāmopabhoga-paramā
etāvad iti niścitāḥ

āśā-pāśa-śatair baddhāḥ
kāma-krodha-parāyaṇāḥ
īhante kāma-bhogārtham
anyāyenārtha-sañcayān

cintām—fears and anxieties; *aparimeyām*—unmeasurable; *ca*—and; *pralaya-antām*—unto the point of death; *upāśritāḥ*—having taken shelter of them; *kāma-upabhoga*—sense gratification; *paramāḥ*—the highest goal of life; *etāvat*—thus; *iti*—in this way; *niścitāḥ*—ascertain; *āśā-pāśa*—entanglement in the network of hope; *śataiḥ*—by hundreds; *baddhāḥ*—being bound; *kāma*—lust; *krodha*—anger; *parāyaṇāḥ*—always situated in that mentality; *īhante*—desire; *kāma*—lust; *bhoga*—sense enjoyment; *artham*—for that purpose; *anyāyena*—illegally; *artha*—wealth; *sañcayān*—accumulate.

TRANSLATION

They believe that to gratify the senses unto the end of life is the prime necessity of human civilization. Thus there is no end to their anxiety.

Being bound by hundreds and thousands of desires, by lust and anger, they secure money by illegal means for sense gratification.

PURPORT

The demoniac accept that the enjoyment of the senses is the ultimate goal of life, and this concept they maintain until death. They do not believe in life after death, and they do not believe that one takes on different types of bodies according to one's *karma*, or activities in this world. Their plans for life are never finished, and they go on preparing plan after plan, all of which are never finished. We have personal experience of a person of such demoniac mentality, who, even at the point of death, was requesting the physician to prolong his life for four years more because his plans were not yet complete. Such foolish people do not know that a physician cannot prolong life even for a moment. When the notice is there, there is no consideration of the man's desire. The laws of nature do not allow a second beyond what one is destined to enjoy.

The demoniac person, who has no faith in God or the Supersoul within himself, performs all kinds of sinful activities simply for sense gratification. He does not know that there is a witness sitting within his heart. The Supersoul is observing the activities of the individual soul. As it is stated in the Vedic literature, the *Upaniṣads*, there are two birds sitting in one tree; the one is acting and enjoying or suffering the fruits of the branches, and the other is witnessing. But one who is demoniac has no knowledge of Vedic scripture, nor has he any faith; therefore he feels free to do anything for sense enjoyment, regardless of the consequences.

TEXTS 13-15

इदमद्य मया लब्धमिमं प्राप्स्ये मनोरथम् ।
इदमस्तीदमपि मे भविष्यति पुनर्धनम् ॥ १३ ॥

असौ मया हतः शत्रुर्हनिष्ये चापरानपि ।
ईश्वरोऽहमहं भोगी सिद्धोऽहं बलवान्सुखी ॥ १४ ॥

आढ्योऽभिजनवानस्मि कोऽन्योऽस्ति सदृशो मया ।
यक्ष्ये दास्यामि मोदिष्य इत्यज्ञानविमोहिताः ॥ १५ ॥

*idam adya mayā labdham
   imaṁ prāpsye manoratham
idam astīdam api me
   bhaviṣyati punar dhanam*

*asau mayā hataḥ śatrur
   haniṣye cāparān api
īśvaro 'ham ahaṁ bhogī
   siddho 'haṁ balavān sukhī*

*ādhyo 'bhijanavān asmi
   ko 'nyo 'sti sadṛśo mayā
yakṣye dāsyāmi modiṣya
   ity ajñāna-vimohitāḥ*

idam—this; adya—today; mayā—by me; labdham—gained; imam—this; prāpsye—I shall gain; manoratham—according to my desires; idam—this; asti—there is; idam—this; api—also; me—mine; bhaviṣyati—will increase in the future; punaḥ—again; dhanam—wealth; asau—that; mayā—by me; hataḥ—has been killed; śatruḥ—enemy; haniṣye—I shall kill; ca—also; aparān—others; api—certainly; īśvaraḥ—the lord; aham—I am; aham—I am; bhogī—the enjoyer; siddhaḥ—perfect; aham—I am; balavān—powerful; sukhī—happy; ādhyaḥ—wealthy; abhijanavān—surrounded by aristocratic relatives; asmi—I am; kaḥ—who else; anyaḥ—other; asti—there is; sadṛśaḥ—like; mayā—me; yakṣye—I shall sacrifice; dāsyāmi—I shall give in charity; modiṣye—I shall rejoice; iti—thus; ajñāna—ignorance; vimohitāḥ—deluded by.

TRANSLATION

The demoniac person thinks: "So much wealth do I have today, and I will gain more according to my schemes. So much is mine now, and it will increase in the future, more and more. He is my enemy, and I have killed him; and my other enemy will also be killed. I am the lord of everything, I am the enjoyer, I am perfect, powerful and happy. I am the richest man, surrounded by aristocratic relatives. There is none so powerful and happy as I am. I shall perform sacrifices, I shall give some charity, and thus I shall rejoice." In this way, such persons are deluded by ignorance.

TEXT 16

अनेकचित्तविभ्रान्ता मोहजालसमावृताः ।
प्रसक्ताः कामभोगेषु पतन्ति नरकेऽशुचौ ॥ १६ ॥

*aneka-citta-vibhrāntā
moha-jāla-samāvṛtāḥ
prasaktāḥ kāma-bhogeṣu
patanti narake 'śucau*

aneka—numerous; *citta-vibhrāntāḥ*—perplexed by anxieties; *moha*—of illusions; *jāla*—by a network; *samāvṛtāḥ*—surrounded; *prasaktāḥ*—attached; *kāma*—lust; *bhogeṣu*—sense gratification; *patanti*—glides down; *narake*—into hell; *aśucau*—unclean.

TRANSLATION

Thus perplexed by various anxieties and bound by a network of illusions, one becomes too strongly attached to sense enjoyment and falls down into hell.

PURPORT

The demoniac man knows no limit to his desire to acquire money. That is unlimited. He only thinks how much assessment he has just now and schemes to engage that stock of wealth farther and farther. For that reason, he does not hesitate to act in any sinful way and so deals in the black market for illegal gratification. He is enamoured by the possessions he has already, such as land, family, house and bank balance, and he is always planning to improve them. He believes in his own strength, and he does not know that whatever he is gaining is due to his past good deeds. He is given an opportunity to accumulate such things, but he has no conception of past causes. He simply thinks that all his mass of wealth is due to his own endeavor. A demoniac person believes in the strength of his personal work, not in the law of *karma*. According to the law of *karma*, a man takes his birth in a high family, or becomes rich, or very well educated, or very beautiful because of good work in the past. The demoniac thinks that all these things are accidental and due to the strength of his personal ability. He does not sense any arrangement behind all the varieties of people, beauty, and education. Anyone who comes into competition with such a demoniac man is his enemy. There are many demoniac people, and each is enemy to the others. This enmity becomes more and more deep—between persons, then between families, then between societies, and at last between nations. Therefore there is constant strife, war and enmity all over the world.

Each demoniac person thinks that he can live at the sacrifice of all others. Generally, a demoniac person thinks of himself as the Supreme God, and a demoniac preacher tells his followers: "Why are you seeking God elsewhere? You are all yourselves God! Whatever you like, you can do. Don't believe in God. Throw away God. God is dead." These are the demoniac's preachings.

Although the demoniac person sees others equally rich and influential, or even more so, he thinks that no one is richer than him and that no one is more influential than him. As far as promotion to the higher planetary system is concerned, he does not believe in performing *yajñas* or sacrifices. Demons think that they will manufacture their own process of *yajña* and prepare some machine, by which they will be able to reach any higher planet. The best example of such a demoniac man was Rāvaṇa. He offered a program to the people by which he would prepare a staircase so that anyone could reach the heavenly planets without performing sacrifices, such as are prescribed in the *Vedas*. Similarly, in the present age such demoniac men are striving to reach the higher planetary systems by mechanical arrangement. These are examples of bewilderment. The result is that, without their knowledge, they are gliding toward hell. Here the Sanskrit word *moha-jāla* is very significant. *Jāla* means net; like fishes caught in a net, they have no way to come out.

TEXT 17

आत्मसंभाविताः स्तब्धा धनमानमदान्विताः ।
यजन्ते नामयज्ञैस्ते दम्भेनाविधिपूर्वकम् ॥ १७ ॥

ātma-sambhāvitāḥ stabdhā
dhana-māna-madānvitāḥ
yajante nāma-yajñais te
dambhenāvidhi-pūrvakam

ātma-sambhāvitāḥ—self-complacent; *stabdhāḥ*—impudent; *dhana-māna*—wealth and false prestige; *mada-anvitāḥ*—absorbed in pride; *yajante*—perform sacrifices; *nāma*—in name only; *yajñaiḥ*—with such a sacrifice; *te*—they;

dambhena—out of pride; *avidhi-pūrvakam*—without following any rules and regulations.

TRANSLATION

Self-complacent and always impudent, deluded by wealth and false prestige, they sometimes perform sacrifices in name only without following any rules or regulations.

PURPORT

Thinking themselves all in all, not caring for any authority or scripture, the demoniac sometimes perform so-called religious or sacrificial rites. And since they do not believe in authority, they are very impudent. This is due to illusion caused by accumulating some wealth and false prestige. Sometimes such demons take up the role of preacher, mislead the people, and become known as religious reformers or as incarnations of God. They make a show of performing sacrifices, or they worship the demigods, or manufacture their own God. Common men advertise them as God and worship them, and by the foolish they are considered advanced in the principles of religion, or in the principles of spiritual knowledge. They take the dress of the renounced order of life and engage in all nonsense in that dress. Actually there are so many restrictions for one who has renounced this world. The demons, however, do not care for such restrictions. They think that whatever path one can create is one's own path; there is no such thing as a standard path one has to follow. The word *avidhi-pūrvakam*, meaning disregard for the rules and regulations, is especially stressed here. These things are always due to ignorance and illusion.

TEXT 18

अहङ्कारं बलं दर्पं कामं क्रोधं च संश्रिताः ।
मामात्मपरदेहेषु प्रद्विषन्तोऽभ्यसूयकाः ॥ १८ ॥

ahaṅkāraṁ balaṁ darpaṁ
kāmaṁ krodhaṁ ca saṁśritāḥ
mām ātma-para-deheṣu
pradviṣanto 'bhyasūyakāḥ

ahaṅkāram—false ego; *balam*—strength; *darpam*—pride; *kāmam*—lust; *krodham*—anger; *ca*—also; *saṁśritāḥ*—having taken shelter of; *mām*—Me;

ātma—one's own; *para-deheṣu*—in other bodies; *pradviṣantaḥ*—blasphemes; *abhyasūyakāḥ*—envious.

TRANSLATION

Bewildered by false ego, strength, pride, lust and anger, the demon becomes envious of the Supreme Personality of Godhead, who is situated in his own body and in the bodies of others, and blasphemes against the real religion.

PURPORT

A demoniac person, being always against God's supremacy, does not like to believe in the scriptures. He is envious of both the scriptures and of the existence of the Supreme Personality of Godhead. This is caused by his so-called prestige and his accumulation of wealth and strength. He does not know that the present life is a preparation for the next life. Not knowing this, he is actually envious of his own self, as well as of others. He commits violence on other bodies and on his own. He does not care for the supreme control of the Personality of Godhead because he has no knowledge. Being envious of the scriptures and the Supreme Personality of Godhead, he puts forward false arguments against the existence of God and refutes the scriptural authority. He thinks himself independent and powerful in every action. He thinks that since no one can equal him in strength, power, or in wealth, he can act in any way and no one can stop him. If he has an enemy who might check the advancement of his sensual activities, he makes plans to cut him down by his own power.

TEXT 19

तानहं द्विषतः क्रूरान्संसारेषु नराधमान् ।
क्षिपाम्यजस्रमशुभानासुरीष्वेव योनिषु ॥ १९ ॥

*tān ahaṁ dviṣataḥ krūrān
saṁsāreṣu narādhamān
kṣipāmy ajasram aśubhān
āsurīṣv eva yoniṣu*

tān—those; *aham*—I; *dviṣataḥ*—envious; *krūrān*—mischievous; *saṁsāreṣu*—into the ocean of material existence; *narādhamān*—the lowest of mankind;

kṣipāmi—put; ajasram—innumerable; aśubhān—inauspicious; āsurīṣu—demoniac; eva—certainly; yoniṣu—in the wombs.

TRANSLATION

Those who are envious and mischievous, who are the lowest among men, are cast by Me into the ocean of material existence, into various demoniac species of life.

PURPORT

In this verse it is clearly indicated that the placing of a particular individual soul in a particular body is the prerogative of the supreme will. The demoniac person may not agree to accept the supremacy of the Lord, and it is a fact that he may act according to his own whims, but his next birth will depend upon the decision of the Supreme Personality of Godhead and not on himself. In the Śrīmad-Bhāgavatam, Third Canto, it is stated that an individual soul, after his death, is put into the womb of a mother where he gets a particular type of body under the supervision of superior power. Therefore in the material existence we find so many species of life—animals, insects, men, and so on. All are arranged by the superior power. They are not accidental. As for the demoniac, it is clearly said here that they are perpetually put into the wombs of demons, and thus they continue to be envious, the lowest of mankind. Such demoniac species of life are held to be always full of lust, always violent and hateful and always unclean. They are just like so many beasts in a jungle.

TEXT 20

आसुरीं योनिमापन्ना मूढा जन्मनिजन्मनि ।
मामप्राप्यैव कौन्तेय ततो यान्त्यधमां गतिम् ॥ २० ॥

āsurīṁ yonim āpannā
mūḍhā janmani janmani
mām aprāpyaiva kaunteya
tato yānty adhamāṁ gatim

āsurīm—demoniac; yonim—species; āpannāḥ—gaining; mūḍhāḥ—the foolish; janmani janmani—in birth after birth; mām—unto Me; aprāpya—

without achieving; *eva*—certainly; *kaunteya*—O son of Kuntī; *tataḥ*—thereafter; *yānti*—goes; *adhamām*—condemned; *gatim*—destination.

TRANSLATION

Attaining repeated birth amongst the species of demoniac life, such persons can never approach Me. Gradually they sink down to the most abominable type of existence.

PURPORT

It is known that God is all-merciful, but here we find that God is never merciful to the demoniac. It is clearly stated that the demoniac people, life after life, are put into the wombs of similar demons, and, not achieving the mercy of the Supreme Lord, they go down and down, so that at last they achieve bodies like those of cats, dogs and hogs. It is clearly stated that such demons have practically no chance of receiving the mercy of God at any stage of later life. In the *Vedas* also it is stated that such persons gradually sink to become dogs and hogs. It may be then argued in this connection that God should not be advertised as all-merciful if He is not merciful to such demons. In answer to this question, in the *Vedānta-sūtra* we find that the Supreme Lord has no hatred for anyone. The placing of the *asuras*, the demons, in the lowest status of life is simply another feature of His mercy. Sometimes the *asuras* are killed by the Supreme Lord, but this killing is also good for them, for in Vedic literature we find that anyone who is killed by the Supreme Lord becomes liberated. There are instances in history of many *asuras*—Rāvaṇa, Kaṁsa, Hiraṇyakaśipu—to whom the Lord appeared in various incarnations just to kill. Therefore God's mercy is shown to the *asuras* if they are fortunate enough to be killed by Him.

TEXT 21

त्रिविधं नरकस्येदं द्वारं नाशनमात्मनः ।
कामः क्रोधस्तथा लोभस्तस्मादेतत्त्रयं त्यजेत् ॥ २१ ॥

tri-vidhaṁ narakasyedaṁ
dvāraṁ nāśanam ātmanaḥ
kāmaḥ krodhas tathā lobhas
tasmād etat trayaṁ tyajet

tri-vidham—three kinds of; *narakasya*—hellish; *idam*—this; *dvāram*—gate; *nāśanam*—destructive; *ātmanaḥ*—of the self; *kāmaḥ*—lust; *krodhaḥ*—anger; *tathā*—as well as; *lobhaḥ*—greed; *tasmāt*—therefore; *etat*—these; *trayam*—three; *tyajet*—must give up.

TRANSLATION

There are three gates leading to this hell—lust, anger, and greed. Every sane man should give these up, for they lead to the degradation of the soul.

PURPORT

The beginning of demoniac life is described herein. One tries to satisfy his lust, and when he cannot, anger and greed arise. A sane man who does not want to glide down to the species of demoniac life must try to give up these three enemies which can kill the self to such an extent that there will be no possibility of liberation from this material entanglement.

TEXT 22

एतैर्विमुक्तः कौन्तेय तमोद्वारैस्त्रिभिर्नरः ।
आचरत्यात्मनः श्रेयस्ततो याति परां गतिम् ॥ २२ ॥

etair vimuktaḥ kaunteya
tamo-dvārais tribhir naraḥ
ācaraty ātmanaḥ śreyas
tato yāti parāṁ gatim

etaiḥ—by these; *vimuktaḥ*—being liberated; *kaunteya*—O son of Kuntī; *tamaḥ-dvāraiḥ*—the gates of ignorance; *tribhiḥ*—three kinds of; *naraḥ*—a person; *ācarati*—performs; *ātmanaḥ*—self; *śreyaḥ*—benediction; *tataḥ*—thereafter; *yāti*—goes; *parām*—supreme; *gatim*—destination.

TRANSLATION

The man who has escaped these three gates of hell, O son of Kuntī, performs acts conducive to self-realization and thus gradually attains the supreme destination.

PURPORT

One should be very careful of these three enemies to human life: lust, anger, and greed. The more a person is freed from lust, anger and greed, the more his existence becomes pure. Then he can follow the rules and regulations enjoined in the Vedic literature. By following the regulative principles of human life, one gradually raises himself to the platform of spiritual realization. If one is so fortunate, by such practice, to rise to the platform of Kṛṣṇa consciousness, then success is guaranteed for him. In the Vedic literature, the ways of action and reaction are prescribed to enable one to come to the stage of purification. The whole method is based on giving up lust, greed and anger. By cultivating knowledge of this process, one can be elevated to the highest position of self-realization; this self-realization is perfected in devotional service. In that devotional service, the liberation of the conditioned soul is guaranteed. Therefore, according to the Vedic system, there are instituted the four orders of life and the four statuses of life, called the caste system and the spiritual order system. There are different rules and regulations for different castes or divisions of society, and if a person is able to follow them, he will be automatically raised to the highest platform of spiritual realization. Then he can have liberation without a doubt.

TEXT 23

यः शास्त्रविधिमुत्सृज्य वर्तते कामकारतः ।
न स सिद्धिमवाप्नोति न सुखं न परां गतिम् ॥ २३ ॥

yaḥ śāstra-vidhim utsṛjya
vartate kāma-kārataḥ
na sa siddhim avāpnoti
na sukhaṁ na parāṁ gatim

yaḥ—anyone; śāstra-vidhim—the regulations of the scriptures; utsṛjya—giving up; vartate—remains; kāma-kārataḥ—acting whimsically in lust; na—never; saḥ—he; siddhim—perfection; avāpnoti—achieves; na—never; sukham—happiness; na—never; parām—the supreme; gatim—perfectional stage.

TRANSLATION

But he who discards scriptural injunctions and acts according to his own whims attains neither perfection, nor happiness, nor the supreme destination.

PURPORT

As described before, the *śāstra-vidhim*, or the direction of the *śāstra*, is given to the different castes and orders of human society. Everyone is expected to follow these rules and regulations. If one does not follow them and acts whimsically according to his lust, greed and desire, then he never will be perfect in his life. In other words, a man may theoretically know all these things, but if he does not apply them in his own life, then he is to be known as the lowest of mankind. In the human form of life, a living entity is expected to be sane and to follow the regulations given for elevating his life to the highest platform, but if he does not follow them, then he degrades himself. But even if he follows the rules and regulations and moral principles and ultimately does not come to the stage of understanding the Supreme Lord, then all his knowledge becomes spoiled. Therefore one should gradually raise himself to the platform of Kṛṣṇa consciousness and devotional service; it is then and there that he can attain the highest perfectional stage, not otherwise.

The word *kāma-cārataḥ* is very significant. A person who knowingly violates the rules acts in lust. He knows that this is forbidden, still he acts. This is called acting whimsically. He knows that this should be done, but still he does not do it; therefore he is called whimsical. Such persons are destined to be condemned by the Supreme Lord. Such persons cannot have the perfection which is meant for the human life. The human life is especially meant for purifying one's existence, and one who does not follow the rules and regulations cannot purify himself, nor can he attain the real stage of happiness.

TEXT 24

तस्माच्छास्त्रं प्रमाणं ते कार्याकार्यव्यवस्थितौ ।
ज्ञात्वा शास्त्रविधानोक्तं कर्म कर्तुमिहार्हसि ॥ २४ ॥

tasmāc chāstraṁ pramāṇaṁ te
kāryākārya-vyavasthitau
jñātvā śāstra-vidhānoktaṁ
karma kartum ihārhasi

tasmāt—therefore; *śāstram*—scriptures; *pramāṇam*—evidence; *te*—your; *kārya*—duty; *akārya*—forbidden activities; *vyavasthitau*—in determining;

jñātvā—knowing; *śāstra*—of scripture; *vidhāna*—regulations; *uktam*—as declared; *karma*—work; *kartum*—to do; *iha arhasi*—you should do it.

TRANSLATION

One should understand what is duty and what is not duty by the regulations of the scriptures. Knowing such rules and regulations, one should act so that he may gradually be elevated.

PURPORT

As stated in the Fifteenth Chapter, all the rules and regulations of the *Vedas* are meant for knowing Kṛṣṇa. If one understands Kṛṣṇa from the *Bhagavad-gītā* and becomes situated in Kṛṣṇa consciousness, engaging himself in devotional service, he has reached the highest perfection of knowledge offered by the Vedic literature. Lord Caitanya Mahāprabhu made this process very easy: He asked people simply to chant Hare Kṛṣṇa, Hare Kṛṣṇa, Kṛṣṇa Kṛṣṇa, Hare Hare/ Hare Rāma, Hare Rāma, Rāma Rāma, Hare Hare and to engage in the devotional service of the Lord and eat the remnants of foodstuff offered to the Deity. One who is directly engaged in all these devotional activities is to be understood as having studied all Vedic literature. He has come to the conclusion perfectly. Of course, for the ordinary persons who are not in Kṛṣṇa consciousness or who are not engaged in devotional service, what is to be done and what is not to be done must be decided by the injunctions of the *Vedas*. One should act accordingly, without argument. That is called following the principles of *śāstra*, or scripture. *Śāstra* is without the four principal defects that are visible in the conditioned soul: imperfect senses, the propensity for cheating, certainty of committing mistakes, and certainty of being illusioned. These four principal defects in conditioned life disqualify one from putting forth rules and regulations. Therefore, the rules and regulations as described in the *śāstra*—being above these defects—are accepted without alteration by all great saints, *ācāryas*, and great souls.

In India there are many parties of spiritual understanding, generally classified as two: the impersonalist and the personalist. Both of them, however, lead their lives according to the principles of the *Vedas*. Without following the principles of the scriptures, one cannot elevate himself to the perfectional stage. One who actually, therefore, understands the purport of the *śāstras* is considered fortunate.

In human society, aversion to the principles of understanding the Supreme Personality of Godhead is the cause of all falldowns. That is the greatest offense of human life. Therefore, *māyā*, the material energy of the Supreme Personality of Godhead, is always giving us trouble in the shape of the threefold miseries. This material energy is constituted of the three modes of material nature. One has to raise himself at least to the mode of goodness before the path to understanding the Supreme Lord can be opened. Without raising oneself to the standard of the mode of goodness, one remains in ignorance and passion, which are the cause of demoniac life. Those in the modes of passion and ignorance deride the scriptures, deride the holy man, and deride the proper understanding of the spiritual master, and they do not care for the regulations of the scriptures. In spite of hearing the glories of devotional service, they are not attracted. Thus they manufacture their own way of elevation. These are some of the defects of human society, which lead to the demoniac status of life. If, however, one is able to be guided by a proper and bona fide spiritual master, who can lead one to the path of elevation, to the higher stage, then one's life becomes successful.

Thus end the Bhaktivedanta Purports to the Sixteenth Chapter of the Śrīmad-Bhagavad-gītā in the matter of the Divine and Demoniac Natures.

CHAPTER SEVENTEEN

The Divisions of Faith

TEXT 1

अर्जुन उवाच ।
ये शास्त्रविधिमुत्सृज्य यजन्ते श्रद्धयान्विताः ।
तेषां निष्ठा तु का कृष्ण सत्त्वमाहो रजस्तमः ॥ १ ॥

arjuna uvāca
ye śāstra-vidhim utsṛjya
yajante śraddhayānvitāḥ
teṣāṁ niṣṭhā tu kā kṛṣṇa
sattvam āho rajas tamaḥ

arjunaḥ uvāca—Arjuna said; *ye*—those; *śāstra-vidhim*—the regulations of scripture; *utsṛjya*—giving up; *yajante*—worships; *śraddhayā*—full faith; *anvitāḥ*—possessed of; *teṣām*—of them; *niṣṭhā*—faith; *tu*—but; *kā*—what is that; *kṛṣṇa*—O Kṛṣṇa; *sattvam*—in goodness; *āho*—said; *rajaḥ*—in passion; *tamaḥ*—in ignorance.

TRANSLATION

Arjuna said, O Kṛṣṇa, what is the situation of one who does not follow the principles of scripture but worships according to his own imagination? Is he in goodness, in passion or in ignorance?

PURPORT

In the Fourth Chapter, thirty-ninth verse, it is said that a person faithful to a particular type of worship gradually becomes elevated to the stage of knowledge and attains the highest perfectional stage of peace and prosperity. In the Sixteenth Chapter, it is concluded that one who does not follow the principles laid down in the scriptures is called an *asura*, demon, and one who follows the scriptural injunctions faithfully is called a *deva*, or demigod. Now, if one, with faith, follows some rules which are not mentioned in the scriptural injunctions, what is his position? This doubt of Arjuna is to be cleared by Kṛṣṇa. Are those who create some sort of God by selecting a human being and placing their faith in him worshiping in goodness, passion or ignorance? Do such persons attain the perfectional stage of life? Is it possible for them to be situated in real knowledge and elevate themselves to the highest perfectional stage? Do those who do not follow the rules and regulations of the scriptures but who have faith in something and worship gods and demigods and men attain success in their effort? Arjuna is putting these questions to Kṛṣṇa.

TEXT 2

श्रीभगवानुवाच ।
त्रिविधा भवति श्रद्धा देहिनां सा स्वभावजा ।
सात्त्विकी राजसी चैव तामसी चेति तां शृणु ॥ २ ॥

śrī bhagavān uvāca
tri-vidhā bhavati śraddhā
dehināṁ sā svabhāva-jā
sāttvikī rājasī caiva
tāmasī ceti tāṁ śṛṇu

śrī bhagavān uvāca—the Supreme Personality of Godhead said; *tri-vidhā*—three kinds; *bhavati*—become; *śraddhā*—faith; *dehinām*—of the embodied; *sā*—that; *sva-bhāva-jā*—according to his mode of material nature; *sāttvikī*—

mode of goodness; *rājasī*—mode of passion; *ca*—also; *eva*—certainly; *tāmasī*—mode of ignorance; *ca*—and; *iti*—thus; *tām*—that; *sṛṇu*—hear from Me.

TRANSLATION

The Supreme Lord said, according to the modes of nature acquired by the embodied soul, one's faith can be of three kinds—goodness, passion or ignorance. Now hear about these.

PURPORT

Those who know the rules and regulations of the scriptures, but, out of laziness or indolence, give up following these rules and regulations, are governed by the modes of material nature. According to their previous activities in the modes of goodness, passion or ignorance, they acquire a nature which is of a specific quality. The association of the living entity with the different modes of nature has been going on perpetually since the living entity is in contact with material nature. Thus he acquires different types of mentality according to his association with the material modes. But this nature can be changed if one associates with a bona fide spiritual master and abides by his rules and the scriptures. Gradually, one can change his position from ignorance to goodness, or from passion to goodness. The conclusion is that blind faith in a particular mode of nature cannot help a person become elevated to the perfectional stage. One has to consider things carefully, with intelligence, in the association of a bona fide spiritual master. Thus one can change his position to a higher mode of nature.

TEXT 3

सत्त्वानुरूपा सर्वस्य श्रद्धा भवति भारत ।
श्रद्धामयोऽयं पुरुषो यो यच्छ्रद्धः स एव सः ॥ ३ ॥

sattvānurūpā sarvasya
śraddhā bhavati bhārata
śraddhā-mayo 'yaṁ puruṣo
yo yac-chraddhaḥ sa eva saḥ

sattva-anurūpā—according to the existence; *sarvasya*—of everyone; *śraddhā*—faith; *bhavati*—becomes; *bhārata*—O son of Bhārata; *śraddhā*—faith; *mayaḥ*—full; *ayam*—this; *puruṣaḥ*—living entity; *yaḥ*—anyone; *yat*—that; *śraddhaḥ*—faith; *saḥ*—that; *eva*—certainly; *saḥ*—he.

TRANSLATION

According to one's existence under the various modes of nature, one evolves a particular kind of faith. The living being is said to be of a particular faith according to the modes he has acquired.

PURPORT

Everyone has a particular type of faith, regardless of what he is. But his faith is considered good, passionate or ignorant according to the nature he has acquired. Thus, according to his particular type of faith, one associates with certain persons. Now the real fact is that every living being, as is stated in the Fifteenth Chapter, is originally the fragmental part and parcel of the Supreme Lord. Therefore one is originally transcendental to all the modes of material nature. But when one forgets his relationship with the Supreme Personality of Godhead and comes into contact with the material nature in conditional life, he generates his own position by association with the different varieties of material nature. The resultant artificial faith and existence are only material. Although one may be conducted by some impression, or some conception of life, still, originally, he is *nirguṇa*, or transcendental. Therefore one has to become cleansed of the material contamination that he has acquired in order to regain his relationship with the Supreme Lord. That is the only path back without fear: Kṛṣṇa consciousness. If one is situated in Kṛṣṇa consciousness, then that path is guaranteed for his elevation to the perfectional stage. If one does not take to this path of self-realization, then he is surely to be conducted by the influence of the modes of nature.

The word *sattva*, or faith, is very significant in this verse. *Sattva* or faith always comes out of the works of goodness. One's faith may be in a demigod or some created God or some mental concoction. It is supposed to be one's strong faith in something that is productive of the works of material goodness. But in material conditional life, no works of material nature are completely purified. They are mixed. They are not in pure goodness. Pure goodness is transcendental; in purified goodness one can understand the real nature of the Supreme Personality of Godhead. As long as one's faith is not completely in purified goodness, the faith is subject to contamination by any of the modes of material nature. The contaminated modes of material nature expand to the heart. Therefore according to the position of the heart in contact with a particular mode of material nature, one's faith is established. It should be understood, that if one's heart is in the mode of goodness, his faith is also in the mode of goodness. If his heart is in the mode of passion, his faith is also in the mode of passion. And if his heart is in the mode of darkness, illusion, his faith is also thus contaminated. Thus we find different types of faith in this world, and there are different types of religions due to different types of faith. The real principle of religious faith is situated in the mode of pure goodness, but because the heart is tainted, we find different types of religious principles. Thus according to different types of faith, there are different kinds of worship.

TEXT 4

यजन्ते सात्त्विका देवान्यक्षरक्षांसि राजसाः ।
प्रेतान्भूतगणांश्चान्ये यजन्ते तामसा जनाः ॥ ४ ॥

yajante sāttvikā devān
yakṣa-rakṣāṁsi rājasāḥ
pretān bhūta-gaṇāṁś cānye
yajante tāmasā janāḥ

yajante—worship; *sāttvikāḥ*—those who are in the mode of goodness; *devān*—demigods; *yakṣa-rakṣāṁsi rājasāḥ*—those who are in the mode of passion worship demons; *pretān*—dead spirits; *bhūta-gaṇān*—ghosts; *ca anye* —and others; *yajante*—worship; *tāmasāḥ*—in the mode of ignorance; *janāḥ* —people.

TRANSLATION

Men in the mode of goodness worship the demigods; those in the mode of passion worship the demons; and those in the mode of ignorance worship ghosts and spirits.

PURPORT

In this verse the Supreme Personality of Godhead describes different kinds of worshipers according to their external activities. According to scriptural injunction, only the Supreme Personality of Godhead is worshipable, but those who are not very conversant with, or faithful to, the scriptural injunctions worship different objects, according to their specific situations in the modes of material nature. Those who are situated in goodness generally worship the demigods. The demigods include Brahmā, Śiva and others such as Indra, Candra and the sun-god. There are various demigods. Those in goodness worship a particular demigod for a particular purpose. Similarly, those who are in the mode of passion worship the demons. We recall that during the Second World War, a man in Calcutta worshiped Hitler because thanks to that war he had amassed a large amount of wealth by dealing in the black market. Similarly, those in the modes of passion and ignorance generally select a powerful man to be God. They think that anyone can be worshiped as God and that the same results will be obtained.

Now, it is clearly described here that those who are in the mode of passion worship and create such gods, and those who are in the mode of ignorance, in darkness, worship dead spirits. Sometimes people worship at the tomb of some dead man. Sexual service is also considered to be in the mode of darkness. Similarly, in remote villages in India there are worshipers of ghosts. We have seen that in India the lower class people sometimes go to the forest, and if they have knowledge that a ghost lives in a tree, they worship that tree and offer sacrifices. These different kinds of worship are not actually God worship. God worship is for persons who are transcendentally situated in pure goodness. In the *Śrīmad-Bhāgavatam* it is said, *sattvaṁ viśuddham vāsudeva-śabditam.* "When a man is situated in pure goodness, he worships Vāsudeva." The purport is that those who are completely purified of the material modes of nature and who are transcendentally situated can worship the Supreme Personality of Godhead.

The impersonalists are supposed to be situated in the mode of goodness, and they worship five kinds of demigods. They worship the impersonal Viṣṇu, or Viṣṇu form in the material world, which is known as philosophized Viṣṇu. Viṣṇu is the expansion of the Supreme Personality of Godhead, but the impersonalists, because they do not ultimately believe in the Supreme Personality of Godhead, imagine that the Viṣṇu form is just another aspect of the impersonal Brahman; similarly, they imagine that Lord Brahmā is the impersonal form in the material mode of passion. Thus they sometimes describe five kinds of gods that are worshipable, but because they think that the actual truth is impersonal Brahman, they dispose of all worshipable objects at the ultimate end. In conclusion, the different qualities of the material modes of nature can be purified through association with persons who are of transcendental nature.

TEXTS 5-6

अशास्त्रविहितं घोरं तप्यन्ते ये तपो जनाः ।
दम्भाहङ्कारसंयुक्ताः कामरागबलान्विताः ॥ ५ ॥
कर्षयन्तः शरीरस्थं भूतग्राममचेतसः ।
मां चैवान्तः शरीरस्थं तान्विद्ध्यासुरनिश्चयान् ॥ ६ ॥

asāstra-vihitaṁ ghoram
tapyante ye tapo janāḥ
dambhāhaṅkāra-saṁyuktāḥ
kāma-rāga-balānvitāḥ

karṣayantaḥ śarīra-sthaṁ
bhūta-grāmam acetasaḥ
māṁ caivāntaḥ śarīra-sthaṁ
tān viddhy āsura-niścayān

asāstra—not mentioned in the scriptures; vihitam—directed; ghoram—harmful to others; tapyante—undergo penances; ye—those; tapaḥ—austerities; janāḥ—persons; dambha—pride; ahaṅkāra—egotism; saṁyuktāḥ—engaged; kāma—lust; rāga—attachment; bala—force; anvitāḥ—impelled by; karṣayantaḥ—tormenting; śarīra-stham—situated within the body; bhūta-grāmam—combination of material elements; acetasaḥ—by such a misled mentality; mām—to Me; ca—also; eva—certainly; antaḥ—within; śarīra-stham—situated in the body; tān—them; viddhi—understand; āsura—demons; niścayān—certainly.

TRANSLATION

Those who undergo severe austerities and penances not recommended in the scriptures, performing them out of pride, egotism, lust and attachment, who are impelled by passion and who torture their bodily organs as well as the Supersoul dwelling within are to be known as demons.

PURPORT

There are persons who manufacture modes of austerity and penances which are not mentioned in the scriptural injunctions. For instance, fasting for some ulterior purpose, such as to promote a purely political end, is not mentioned in the scriptural directions. The scriptures recommend fasting for spiritual advancement, not for some political end or social purpose. Persons who take to such austerities are, according to *Bhagavad-gītā*, certainly demoniac. Their acts are against the scriptural injunction and are not beneficial for the people in general. Actually, they act out of pride, false ego, lust and attachment for material enjoyment. By such activities, not only are the combination of material elements of which the body is constructed disturbed, but also the Supreme Personality of Godhead Himself living within the body. Such unauthorized fasting or austerities for some political end are certainly very disturbing to others. They are not mentioned in the Vedic literature. A demoniac person may think that he can force his enemy or other parties to comply with his desire by this method, but sometimes one dies by such fasting. These acts are not approved by the Supreme Personality of Godhead, and He says that those who engage in them are demons. Such demonstrations are insults to the Supreme Personality of Godhead because they are enacted in disobedience to the Vedic scriptural injunctions. The word *acetasaḥ* is significant in this connection—persons of normal mental condition must obey the scriptural injunctions. Those who are not in such a position neglect and disobey the scriptures and manufacture their own way of austerities and penances. One should always remember the ultimate end of the demoniac people, as described in the previous chapter. The Lord forces them to take birth in the womb of demoniac persons. Consequently they will live by demoniac principles life after life without knowing their relationship with the Supreme Personality of Godhead. If, however, such persons are fortunate enough to be guided by a spiritual master who can direct them to the path of Vedic wisdom, they can get out of this entanglement and ultimately achieve the supreme goal.

TEXT 7

आहारस्त्वपि सर्वस्य त्रिविधो भवति प्रियः ।
यज्ञस्तपस्तथा दानं तेषां भेदमिमं शृणु ॥ ७ ॥

āhāras tv api sarvasya
tri-vidho bhavati priyaḥ
yajñas tapas tathā dānaṁ
teṣāṁ bhedam imaṁ śṛṇu

āhāraḥ—eating; *tu*—certainly; *api*—also; *sarvasya*—of everyone; *trividhaḥ*—three kinds; *bhavati*—there are; *priyaḥ*—dear; *yajñaḥ*—sacrifice; *tapaḥ*—austerity; *tathā*—also; *dānam*—charity; *teṣām*—of them; *bhedam*—differences; *imam*—thus; *śṛṇu*—hear.

TRANSLATION

Even food of which all partake is of three kinds, according to the three modes of material nature. The same is true of sacrifices, austerities and charity. Listen, and I shall tell you of the distinctions of these.

PURPORT

In terms of different situations and the modes of material nature, there are differences in the manner of eating, performing sacrifices, austerities and charities. They are not all conducted on the same level. Those who can understand analytically what kind of performances are in what modes of material nature are actually wise; those who consider all kinds of sacrifice or foods or charity to be the same cannot discriminate, and they are foolish. There are missionary workers who advocate that one can do whatever he likes and attain perfection. But these foolish guides are not acting according to the direction of the scripture. They are manufacturing ways and misleading the people in general.

TEXT 8-10

आयुःसत्त्वबलारोग्यसुखप्रीतिविवर्धनाः ।
रस्याः स्निग्धाः स्थिरा हृद्या आहाराः सात्त्विकप्रियाः ॥ ८ ॥
कट्वम्ललवणात्युष्णतीक्ष्णरूक्षविदाहिनः ।
आहारा राजसस्येष्टा दुःखशोकामयप्रदाः ॥ ९ ॥
यातयामं गतरसं पूति पर्युषितं च यत् ।
उच्छिष्टमपि चामेध्यं भोजनं तामसप्रियम् ॥ १० ॥

āyuḥ-sattva-balārogya-
  sukha-prīti-vivardhanāḥ
rasyāḥ snigdhāḥ sthirā hṛdyā
  āhārāḥ sāttvika-priyāḥ

katv-amla-lavaṇāty-uṣṇa-
tīkṣṇa-rūkṣa-vidāhinaḥ
āhārā rājasasyeṣṭā
duḥkha-śokāmaya-pradāḥ

yāta-yāmaṁ gata-rasaṁ
pūti paryuṣitaṁ ca yat
ucchiṣṭam api cāmedhyaṁ
bhojanaṁ tāmasa-priyam

āyuḥ—duration of life; *sattva*—existence; *bala*—strength; *ārogya*—health; *sukha*—happiness; *prīti*—and satisfaction; *vivardhanāḥ*—increasing; *rasyāḥ*—juicy; *snigdhāḥ*—fatty; *sthirāḥ*—enduring; *hṛdyāḥ*—pleasing to the heart; *āhārāḥ*—food; *sāttvika*—goodness; *priyāḥ*—palatable; *kaṭu*—bitter; *amla*—sour; *lavaṇa*—salty; *ati-uṣṇa*—very hot; *tīkṣṇa*—pungent; *rūkṣa*—dry; *vidāhinaḥ*—burning; *āhārāḥ*—food; *rājasasya*—to one in the mode of passion; *iṣṭāḥ*—palatable; *duḥkha*—distress; *śoka*—misery; *āmaya-pradāḥ*—causing disease;; *yāta-yāmam*—food cooked three hours before being eaten; *gata-rasam*—tasteless; *pūti*—bad-smelling; *paryuṣitam*—decomposed; *ca*—also; *yat*—that which; *ucchiṣṭam*—remnants of food eaten by others; *api*—also; *ca*—and; *amedhyam*—untouchable; *bhojanam*—eating; *tāmasa*—to one in the mode of darkness; *priyam*—dear.

TRANSLATION

Foods in the mode of goodness increase the duration of life, purify one's existence and give strength, health, happiness and satisfaction. Such nourishing foods are sweet, juicy, fattening and palatable. Foods that are too bitter, too sour, salty, pungent, dry and hot, are liked by people in the modes of passion. Such foods cause pain, distress, and disease. Food cooked more than three hours before being eaten, which is tasteless, stale, putrid, decomposed and unclean, is food liked by people in the mode of ignorance.

PURPORT

The purpose of food is to increase the duration of life, purify the mind and aid bodily strength. This is its only purpose. In the past, great authorities selected those foods that best aid health and increase life's duration, such as milk products, sugar, rice, wheat, fruits and vegetables. These foods are very dear to those in the mode of goodness. Some other foods, such as baked corn and molasses, while not very palatable in themselves, can be made pleasant when mixed with milk or other foods. They are then in the mode of goodness. All these foods are pure by nature. They are quite distinct from untouchable things like meat and liquor. Fatty foods, as mentioned in the eighth verse, have no connection with animal fat obtained by slaughter. Animal fat is available in the form of milk, which is the most wonderful of all foods. Milk, butter, cheese and similar products give animal fat in a form which rules out any need for the killing of innocent creatures. It is only through brute mentality that this killing goes on. The civilized method of obtaining needed fat is by milk. Slaughter is the way of subhumans. Protein is amply available through split peas, *dhall*, whole wheat, etc.

Foods in the mode of passion, which are bitter, too salty, or too hot or overly mixed with red pepper, cause misery by producing mucous in the stomach, leading to disease. Foods in the mode of ignorance or darkness are essentially those that are not fresh. Any food cooked more than three hours before it is eaten (except *prasādam*, food offered to the Lord) is considered to be in the mode of darkness. Because they are decomposing, such foods give a bad odor, which often attracts people in this mode but repulses those in the mode of goodness.

Remnants of food may be eaten only when they are part of a meal that was first offered to the Supreme Lord or first eaten by saintly persons, especially the spiritual master. Otherwise the remnants of food are considered to be in the mode of darkness, and they increase infection or disease. Such foodstuffs, although very palatable to persons in the mode of darkness, are neither liked nor even touched by those in the mode of goodness. The best food is the remnant of what is offered to the Supreme Personality of Godhead. In *Bhagavad-gītā* the Supreme Lord says that He accepts preparations of vegetables, flour and milk when offered with devotion. *Patraṁ puṣpaṁ phalaṁ toyam*. Of course, devotion and love are the chief things which the Supreme Personality of Godhead accepts. But it is also mentioned that the *prasādam* should be prepared in a particular way. Any food prepared by the injunction of the scripture offered to the Supreme Personality of Godhead can be taken even if prepared long, long ago, because such food is transcendental. Therefore to make food antiseptic, eatable and palatable for all persons, one should offer food to the Supreme Personality of Godhead.

TEXT 11

अफलाकाङ्क्षिभिर्यज्ञो विधिदिष्टो य इज्यते ।
यष्टव्यमेवेति मनः समाधाय स सात्त्विकः ॥ ११ ॥

*aphalākāṅkṣibhir yajño
vidhi-diṣṭo ya ijyate
yaṣṭavyam eveti manaḥ
samādhāya sa sāttvikaḥ*

aphala-kāṅkṣibhiḥ—devoid of desire for result; *yajñaḥ*—sacrifice; *vidhi*—accordingly; *dṛṣṭaḥ*—direction; *yaḥ*—anyone; *ijyate*—performs; *yaṣṭavyam*—must be performed; *eva*—certainly; *iti*—thus; *manaḥ*—mind; *samādhāya*—fixed in; *saḥ*—he; *sāttvikaḥ*—is in the mode of goodness.

TRANSLATION

Of sacrifices, that sacrifice performed according to duty and to scriptural rules, and with no expectation of reward, is of the nature of goodness.

PURPORT

The general tendency is to offer sacrifice with some purpose in mind, but here it is stated that sacrifice should be performed without any such desire. It should be done as a matter of duty. Take, for example, the performance of rituals in temples or in churches. Generally they are performed with the purpose of material benefit, but that is not in the mode of goodness. One should go to a temple or church as a matter of duty, offer respect to the Supreme Personality of Godhead and offer flowers and eatables. Everyone thinks that there is no use in going to the temple just to worship God. But worship for economic benefit is not recommended in the scriptural injunction. One should go simply to offer respect to the Deity. That will place one in the mode of goodness. It is the duty of every civilized man to obey the injunctions of the scriptures and offer respect to the Supreme Personality of Godhead.

TEXT 12

अभिसंधाय तु फलं दम्भार्थमपि चैव यत् ।
इज्यते भरतश्रेष्ठ तं यज्ञं विद्धि राजसम् ॥ १२ ॥

> *abhisandhāya tu phalaṁ*
> *dambhārtham api caiva yat*
> *ijyate bharata-śreṣṭha*
> *taṁ yajñaṁ viddhi rājasam*

abhisandhāya—desiring; *tu*—but; *phalam*—the result; *dambha*—pride; *artham*—material benefits; *api*—also; *ca*—and; *eva*—certainly; *yat*—that which; *ijyate*—worship; *bharata-śreṣṭha*—O chief of the Bhāratas; *tam*—that; *yajñam*—sacrifice; *viddhi*—know; *rājasam*—in the mode of passion.

TRANSLATION

But that sacrifice performed for some material end or benefit or performed ostentatiously, out of pride, is of the nature of passion, O chief of the Bhāratas.

PURPORT

Sometimes sacrifices and rituals are performed for elevation to the heavenly kingdom or for some material benefits in this world. Such sacrifices or ritualistic performances are considered to be in the mode of passion.

TEXT 13

विधिहीनमसृष्टान्नं मन्त्रहीनमदक्षिणम् ।
श्रद्धाविरहितं यज्ञं तामसं परिचक्षते ॥ १३ ॥

> *vidhi-hīnam asṛṣṭānnaṁ*
> *mantra-hīnam adakṣiṇam*
> *śraddhā-virahitaṁ yajñaṁ*
> *tāmasaṁ paricakṣate*

vidhi-hīnam—without scriptural direction; *asṛṣṭa-annam*—without distribution of *prasādam*; *mantra-hīnam*—with no chanting of the Vedic hymns; *adakṣiṇam*—with no remunerations to the priests; *śraddhā*—faith; *virahitam*—without; *yajñam*—sacrifice; *tāmasam*—in the mode of ignorance; *paricakṣate*—is to be considered.

TRANSLATION

And that sacrifice performed in defiance of scriptural injunctions, in which no spiritual food is distributed, no hymns are chanted and no remunerations are made to the priests, and which is faithless—that sacrifice is of the nature of ignorance.

PURPORT

Faith in the mode of darkness or ignorance is actually faithlessness. Sometimes people worship some demigod just to make money and then spend the money for recreation, ignoring the scriptural injunctions. Such ceremonial shows of religiosity are not accepted as genuine. They are all in the mode of darkness; they produce a demoniac mentality and do not benefit human society.

TEXT 14

देवद्विजगुरुप्राज्ञपूजनं शौचमार्जवम् ।
ब्रह्मचर्यमहिंसा च शारीरं तप उच्यते ॥ १४ ॥

deva-dvija-guru-prājña-
pūjanaṁ śaucam ārjavam
brahmacaryam ahiṁsā ca
śārīraṁ tapa ucyate

deva—the Supreme Lord; *dvija*—the *brāhmaṇa*; *guru*—the spiritual master; *prājña*—worshipable personalities; *pūjanam*—worship; *śaucam*—cleanliness; *ārjavam*—simplicity; *brahma-caryam*—celibacy; *ahiṁsā*—nonviolence; *ca*—also; *śārīram*—pertaining to the body; *tapaḥ*—austerity; *ucyate*—is said to be.

TRANSLATION

The austerity of the body consists in this: worship of the Supreme Lord, the brāhmaṇas, the spiritual master, and superiors like the father and mother. Cleanliness, simplicity, celibacy and nonviolence are also austerities of the body.

PURPORT

The Supreme Godhead here explains the different kinds of austerity and penance. First He explains the austerities and penances practiced by the body. One should offer, or learn to offer, respect to God or to the demigods, the perfect, qualified *brāhmaṇas* and the spiritual master and superiors like father, mother or any person who is conversant with Vedic knowledge. These should be given proper respect. One should practice cleansing oneself externally and internally, and he should learn to become simple in behavior. He should not do anything which is not sanctioned by the scriptural injunction. He should not indulge in sex outside of married life, for sex is sanctioned in the scripture only in marriage, not otherwise. This is called celibacy. These are penances and austerities as far as the body is concerned.

TEXT 15

अनुद्वेगकरं वाक्यं सत्यं प्रियहितं च यत् ।
स्वाध्यायाभ्यसनं चैव वाङ्मयं तप उच्यते ॥ १५ ॥

anudvega-karaṁ vākyaṁ
satyaṁ priya-hitaṁ ca yat
svādhyāyābhyasanaṁ caiva
vāṅ-mayaṁ tapa ucyate

anudvega—not agitating; *karam*—producing; *vākyam*—words; *satyam*—truthful; *priya*—dear; *hitam*—beneficial; *ca*—also; *yat*—which; *svādhyāya*—Vedic study; *abhyasanam*—practice; *ca*—also; *eva*—certainly; *vāṅmayam*—of the voice; *tapaḥ*—austerity; *ucyate*—is said to be.

TRANSLATION

Austerity of speech consists in speaking truthfully and beneficially and in avoiding speech that offends. One should also recite the Vedas regularly.

PURPORT

One should not speak in such a way as to agitate the minds of others. Of course, when a teacher speaks, he can speak the truth for the instruction of his students, but such a teacher should not speak to others who are not his students if he will agitate their minds. This is penance as far as talking is concerned. Besides that, one should not talk nonsense. When speaking in spiritual circles, one's statements must be upheld by the scriptures. One should at once quote from scriptural authority to back up what he is saying. At the same time, such talk should be very pleasurable to the ear. By such discussions, one may derive the highest benefit and elevate human society. There is a limitless stock of Vedic literature, and one should study this. This is called penance of speech.

TEXT 16

मनःप्रसादः सौम्यत्वं मौनमात्मविनिग्रहः ।
भावसंशुद्धिरित्येतत्तपो मानसमुच्यते ॥ १६ ॥

*manaḥ-prasādaḥ saumyatvaṁ
maunam ātma-vinigrahaḥ
bhāva-saṁśuddhir ity etat
tapo mānasam ucyate*

manaḥ-prasādaḥ—satisfaction of the mind; *saumyatvam*—without duplicity towards others; *maunam*—gravity; *ātma*—self; *vinigrahaḥ*—control; *bhāva*—nature; *saṁśuddhiḥ*—purification; *iti*—thus; *etat*—that is; *tapaḥ*—austerity; *mānasam*—of the mind; *ucyate*—is said to be.

TRANSLATION

And serenity, simplicity, gravity, self-control and purity of thought are the austerities of the mind.

PURPORT

To make the mind austere is to detach it from sense gratification. It should be so trained that it can be always thinking of doing good for others. The best training for the mind is gravity in thought. One should not deviate from Kṛṣṇa consciousness and must always avoid sense gratification. To purify one's nature is to become Kṛṣṇa conscious. Satisfaction of the mind can be obtained only by taking the mind away from thoughts of sense enjoyment. The more we think of sense enjoyment, the more the mind becomes dissatisfied. In the present age we unnecessarily engage the mind in so many different ways for sense gratification, and so there is no possibility of the mind's becoming satisfied. The best course is to divert the mind to the Vedic literature, which is full of satisfying stories, as in the *Purāṇas* and the *Mahābhārata*. One can take advantage of this knowledge and thus become purified. The mind should be devoid of duplicity, and one should think of the welfare of all. Silence means that one is always thinking of self-realization. The person in Kṛṣṇa consciousness observes perfect silence in this sense. Control of the mind means detaching the mind from sense enjoyment. One should be straightforward in his dealing and thereby purify his existence. All these qualities together constitute austerity in mental activities.

TEXT 17

श्रद्धया परया तप्तं तपस्तत्त्रिविधं नरैः ।
अफलाकाङ्क्षिभिर्युक्तैः सात्त्विकं परिचक्षते ॥ १७ ॥

śraddhayā parayā taptaṁ
tapas tat tri-vidhaṁ naraiḥ
aphalākāṅkṣibhir yuktaiḥ
sāttvikaṁ paricakṣate

śraddhayā—with faith; *parayā*—transcendental; *taptam*—executed; *tapaḥ* —austerity; *tat*—that; *tri-vidham*—three kinds; *naraiḥ*—by men; *aphala-ākāṅkṣibhiḥ*—without desires for fruits; *yuktaiḥ*—engaged; *sāttvikam*—in the mode of goodness; *pari-cakṣate*—is called.

TRANSLATION

This threefold austerity, practiced by men whose aim is not to benefit themselves materially but to please the Supreme, is of the nature of goodness.

TEXT 18

सत्कारमानपूजार्थं तपो दम्भेन चैव यत् ।
क्रियते तदिह प्रोक्तं राजसं चलमध्रुवम् ॥ १८ ॥

satkāra-māna-pūjārthaṁ
tapo dambhena caiva yat
kriyate tad iha proktaṁ
rājasaṁ calam adhruvam

satkāra—respect; *māna*—honor; *pūjā-artham*—for worship; *tapaḥ*—austerity; *dambhena*—with pride; *ca*—also; *eva*—certainly; *yat*—which is; *kriyate*—
performed; *tat*—that; *iha*—in this world; *proktam*—is said; *rājasam*—in the
mode of passion; *calam*—flickering; *adhruvam*—temporary.

TRANSLATION

**Those ostentatious penances and austerities which are performed in order
to gain respect, honor and reverence are said to be in the mode of passion.
They are neither stable nor permanent.**

PURPORT

Sometimes penance and austerity are executed to attract people and
receive honor, respect and worship from others. Persons in the mode of
passion arrange to be worshiped by subordinates and let them wash their
feet and offer riches. Such arrangements artificially made by the
performance of penances are considered to be in the mode of passion.
The results are temporary; they can be continued for some time, but they
are not permanent.

TEXT 19

मूढग्राहेणात्मनो यत्पीडया क्रियते तपः ।
परस्योत्सादनार्थं वा तत्तामसमुदाहृतम् ॥ १९ ॥

mūḍha-grāheṇātmano yat
pīḍayā kriyate tapaḥ
parasyotsādanārthaṁ vā
tat tāmasam udāhṛtam

mūḍha—foolish; *grāheṇa*—with endeavor; *ātmanaḥ*—of one's own self;
yat—which; *pīḍayā*—by torture; *kriyate*—is performed; *tapaḥ*—penance;
parasya—to others; *utsādanārtham*—causing annihilation; *vā*—or; *tat*—that;
tāmasam—in the mode of darkness; *udāhṛtam*—is said to be.

TRANSLATION

And those penances and austerities which are performed foolishly by means of obstinant self-torture, or to destroy or injure others, are said to be in the mode of ignorance.

PURPORT

There are instances of foolish penance undertaken by demons like Hiraṇyakaśipu, who performed austere penances to become immortal and kill the demigods. He prayed to Brahmā for such things, but ultimately he was killed by the Supreme Personality of Godhead. To undergo penances for something which is impossible is certainly in the mode of ignorance.

TEXT 20

दातव्यमिति यद्दानं दीयतेऽनुपकारिणे ।
देशे काले च पात्रे च तद्दानं सात्त्विकं स्मृतम् ॥ २० ॥

dātavyam iti yad dānaṁ
dīyate 'nupakāriṇe
deśe kāle ca pātre ca
tad dānaṁ sāttvikaṁ smṛtam

dātavyam—worth giving; iti—thus; yat—that which; dānam—charity; dīyate—given; anupakāriṇe—to any person irrespective of doing good; deśe—in place; kāle—in time; ca—also; pātre—suitable person; ca—and; tat—that; dānam—charity; sāttvikam—in the mode of goodness; smṛtam—consider.

TRANSLATION

That gift which is given out of duty, at the proper time and place, to a worthy person, and without expectation of return, is considered to be charity in the mode of goodness.

PURPORT

In the Vedic literature, charity given to a person engaged in spiritual activities is recommended. There is no recommendation for giving charity indiscriminately. Spiritual perfection is always a consideration. Therefore charity is recommended to be given at a place of pilgrimage and at lunar or solar eclipses or at the end of the month or to a qualified *brāhmaṇa* or a Vaiṣṇava (devotee) or in temples. Such charities should be given without any consideration of return. Charity to the poor is sometimes given out of compassion, but if a poor man is not worth giving charity to, then there is no spiritual advancement. In other words, indiscriminate charity is not recommended in the Vedic literature.

TEXT 21

यत्तु प्रत्युपकारार्थं फलमुद्दिश्य वा पुनः ।
दीयते च परिक्लिष्टं तद्दानं राजसं स्मृतम् ॥ २१ ॥

*yat tu pratyupakārārtham
phalam uddiśya vā punaḥ
dīyate ca parikliṣṭaṁ
tad dānaṁ rājasaṁ smṛtam*

yat—that which; *tu*—but; *prati-upakāra-artham*—for the sake of getting some return; *phalam*—result; *uddiśya*—desiring; *vā*—or; *punaḥ*—again; *dīyate*—is given in charity; *ca*—also; *parikliṣṭam*—grudgingly; *tat*—that; *dānam*—charity; *rājasam*—in the mode of passion; *smṛtam*—is understood to be.

TRANSLATION

But charity performed with the expectation of some return, or with a desire for fruitive results, or in a grudging mood, is said to be charity in the mode of passion.

PURPORT

Charity is sometimes performed for elevation to the heavenly kingdom and sometimes with great trouble and with repentance afterwards. "Why have I spent so much in this way?" Charity is also sometimes made under some obligation, at the request of a superior. These kinds of charity are said to be made in the mode of passion.

There are many charitable foundations which offer their gifts to institutions where sense gratification goes on. Such charities are not recommended in the Vedic scripture. Only charity in the mode of goodness is recommended.

TEXT 22

अदेशकाले यद्दानमपात्रेभ्यश्च दीयते ।
असत्कृतमवज्ञातं तत्तामसमुदाहृतम् ॥ २२ ॥

adeśa-kāle yad dānam
apātrebhyaś ca dīyate
asat-kṛtam avajñātaṁ
tat tāmasam udāhṛtam

adeśa—unpurified place; *kāle*—unpurified time; *yat*—that which is; *dānam* —charity; *apātrebhyaḥ*—to unworthy persons; *ca*—also; *dīyate*—is given; *asatkṛtam*—without respect; *avajñātam*—without proper attention; *tat*— that; *tāmasam*—in the mode of darkness; *udāhṛtam*—is said to be.

TRANSLATION

And charity performed at an improper place and time and given to unworthy persons without respect and with contempt is charity in the mode of ignorance.

PURPORT

Contributions for indulgence in intoxication and gambling are not encouraged here. That sort of contribution is in the mode of ignorance. Such charity is not beneficial; rather, sinful persons are encouraged. Similarly, if a person gives charity to a suitable person without respect and without attention, that sort of charity is also said to be in the mode of darkness.

TEXT 23

ओंतत्सदिति निर्देशो ब्रह्मणस्त्रिविधः स्मृतः ।
ब्राह्मणास्तेन वेदाश्च यज्ञाश्च विहिताः पुरा ॥ २३ ॥

om tat sad iti nirdeśo
brahmaṇas tri-vidhaḥ smṛtaḥ
brāhmaṇās tena vedāś ca
yajñāś ca vihitāḥ purā

om—indication of the Supreme; tat—that; sat—eternal; iti—that; nirdeśaḥ—indication; brāhmaṇāḥ—of the Supreme; tri-vidhaḥ—three kinds; smṛtaḥ—consider; brahmaṇaḥ—the brāhmaṇas; tena—therefore; vedāḥ— the Vedic literature; ca—also; yajñāḥ—sacrifice; ca—also; vihitāḥ—sacrifice; purā—formerly.

TRANSLATION

From the beginning of creation, the three syllables—om tat sat—have been used to indicate the Supreme Absolute Truth [Brahman]. They were uttered by brāhmaṇas while chanting Vedic hymns and during sacrifices, for the satisfaction of the Supreme.

PURPORT

It has been explained that penance, sacrifice, charity and foods are divided into three categories: the modes of goodness, passion and ignorance. But whether first class, second class or third class, they are all conditioned, contaminated by the material modes of nature. When they are aimed at the Supreme—om tat sat, the Supreme Personality of Godhead, the eternal—they become means for spiritual elevation. In the scriptural injunctions such an objective is indicated. These three words, om tat sat, particularly indicate the Absolute Truth, the Supreme Personality of Godhead. In the Vedic hymns, the word om is always found.

One who acts without following the regulations of the scriptures will not attain the Absolute Truth. He will get some temporary result, but not the ultimate end of life. The conclusion is that the performance of charities, sacrifice and penance must be done in the mode of goodness. Performed in the modes of passion or ignorance, they are certainly inferior in quality. The three words om tat sat are uttered in conjunction with the holy name of the Supreme Lord, e.g., om tad viṣṇoḥ. Whenever a Vedic hymn or the holy name of the Supreme Lord is uttered, om is added. This is the indication of Vedic literature. These three words are taken from Vedic hymns. Om ity etad brahmaṇo nediṣṭaṁ nāma indicates the first goal. Then *tattvamasi* indicates the second goal. And *sad eva saumya* indicates the third goal. Combined they become *om tat sat*. Formerly when Brahmā, the first created living entity, performed sacrifices, he spoke these three names of the Supreme Personality of Godhead. The same principle holds by disciplic succession. So this hymn has great significance. *Bhagavad-gītā* recommends, therefore, that any work done should be done for *om tat sat*, or for the Supreme Personality of Godhead. When one performs penance, charity, and sacrifice with these three words, he is acting in Kṛṣṇa consciousness. Kṛṣṇa consciousness is a scientific execution of transcendental activities which enables one to return home, back to Godhead. There is no loss of energy in acting in such a transcendental way.

TEXT 24

तस्मादोमित्युदाहृत्य यज्ञदानतपःक्रियाः ।
प्रवर्तन्ते विधानोक्ताः सततं ब्रह्मवादिनाम् ॥ २४ ॥

tasmād om ity udāhṛtya
yajña-dāna-tapaḥ-kriyāḥ
pravartante vidhānoktāḥ
satataṁ brahma-vādinām

tasmāt—therefore; *om*—beginning with *om*; *iti*—thus; *udāhṛtya*—indicating; *yajña*—sacrifice; *dāna*—charity; *tapaḥ*—penance; *kriyāḥ*—performances; *pravartante*—begins; *vidhāna-uktāḥ*—according to scriptural regulation; *satatam*—always; *brahma-vādinām*—of the transcendentalists.

TRANSLATION

Thus the transcendentalists undertake sacrifices, charities, and penances, beginning always with om, to attain the Supreme.

PURPORT

Om tad viṣṇoḥ paramaṁ padam. The lotus feet of Viṣṇu are the supreme devotional platform. The performance of everything on behalf of the Supreme Personality of Godhead assures the perfection of all activity.

TEXT 25

तदित्यनभिसंधाय फलं यज्ञतपःक्रियाः ।
दानक्रियाश्च विविधाः क्रियन्ते मोक्षकाङ्क्षिभिः ॥ २५ ॥

tad ity anabhisandhāya
phalaṁ yajña-tapaḥ-kriyāḥ
dāna-kriyāś ca vividhāḥ
kriyante mokṣa-kāṅkṣibhiḥ

tat—that; *iti*—they; *anabhisandhāya*—without fruitive result; *phalam*—result of sacrifice; *yajña*—sacrifice; *tapaḥ*—penance; *kriyāḥ*—activities; *dāna*—charity; *kriyāḥ*—activities; *ca*—also; *vividhāḥ*—varieties; *kriyante*—done; *mokṣa-kāṅkṣibhiḥ*—those who actually desire liberation.

TRANSLATION

One should perform sacrifice, penance and charity with the word *tat.* The purpose of such transcendental activities is to get free from the material entanglement.

PURPORT

To be elevated to the spiritual position, one should not act for any material gain. Acts should be performed for the ultimate gain of being transferred to the spiritual kingdom, back to home, back to Godhead.

TEXTS 26-27

सद्भावे साधुभावे च सदित्येतत्प्रयुज्यते ।
प्रशस्ते कर्मणि तथा सच्छब्दः पार्थ युज्यते ॥ २६ ॥
यज्ञे तपसि दाने च स्थितिः सदिति चोच्यते ।
कर्म चैव तदर्थीयं सदित्येवाभिधीयते ॥ २७ ॥

sad-bhāve sādhu-bhāve ca
sad ity etat prayujyate
praśaste karmaṇi tathā
sac-chabdaḥ pārtha yujyate

yajñe tapasi dāne ca
sthitiḥ sad iti cocyate
karma caiva tad-arthīyaṁ
sad ity evābhidhīyate

sat-bhāve—in the sense of the nature of the Supreme; *sādhu-bhāve*—in the sense of the nature of devotion; *ca*—also; *sat*—the Supreme; *iti*—thus; *etat*—this; *prayujyate*—is used; *praśaste*—bona fide; *karmaṇi*—activities; *tathā*—also; *sat-śabdaḥ*—sound; *pārtha*—O son of Pṛthā; *yujyate*—is used; *yajñe*—sacrifice; *tapasi*—in penance; *dāne*—charity; *ca*—also; *sthitiḥ*—situated; *sat*—the Supreme; *iti*—thus; *ca*—and; *ucyate*—pronounced; *karma*—work; *ca*—also; *eva*—certainly; *tat*—that; *arthīyam*—are meant; *sat*—Supreme; *iti*—thus; *eva*—certainly; *abhidhīyate*—is practiced.

TRANSLATION

The Absolute Truth is the objective of devotional sacrifice, and it is indicated by the word *sat*. These works of sacrifice, of penance and of charity, true to the absolute nature, are performed to please the Supreme Person, O son of Pṛthā.

PURPORT

The words *praśaste karmaṇi*, or prescribed duties, indicate that there are many activities prescribed in the Vedic literature which are purificatory processes beginning from parental care up to the end of one's life. Such purificatory processes are adopted for the ultimate liberation of the living entity. In all such activities it is recommended that one should vibrate *om tat sat*. The words *sad-bhāve* and *sādhu-bhāve* indicate the transcendental situation. One who is acting in Kṛṣṇa consciousness is called *sattva*, and one who is fully conscious of activities in Kṛṣṇa consciousness is called *svarūpa*. In the Śrīmad-Bhāgavatam it is said that the transcendental subject matter becomes clear in the association of the devotees. Without good association, one cannot achieve transcendental knowledge. When initiating a person or offering the sacred thread, one vibrates the words *om tat sat*. Similarly, in all kinds of yogic performances, the supreme object, *om tat sat* is invoked. These words *om tat sat* are used to perfect all activities. This supreme *om tat sat* makes everything complete.

TEXT 28

अश्रद्धया हुतं दत्तं तपस्तप्तं कृतं च यत् ।
असदित्युच्यते पार्थ न च तत्प्रेत्य नो इह ॥ २८ ॥

aśraddhayā hutaṁ dattaṁ
tapas taptaṁ kṛtaṁ ca yat
asad ity ucyate pārtha
na ca tat pretya no iha

aśraddhayā—without faith; *hutam*—performed; *dattam*—given; *tapaḥ*—penance; *taptam*—executed; *kṛtam*—performed; *ca*—also; *yat*—that which; *asat*—falls; *iti*—thus; *ucyate*—is said to be; *pārtha*—O son of Pṛthā; *na*—never; *ca*—also; *tat*—that; *pretya*—after death; *no*—nor; *iha*—in this life.

TRANSLATION

But sacrifices, austerities and charities performed without faith in the Supreme are nonpermanent, O son of Pṛthā, regardless of whatever rites are performed. They are called asat and are useless both in this life and the next.

PURPORT

Anything done without the transcendental objective—whether it be sacrifice, charity or penance—is useless. Therefore, in this verse, it is declared that such activities are abominable. Everything should be done for the Supreme in Kṛṣṇa consciousness. Without such faith, and without the proper guidance, there can never be any fruit. In all the Vedic scriptures, faith in the Supreme is advised. In the pursuit of all Vedic instructions, the ultimate goal is the understanding of Kṛṣṇa. No one can obtain success without following this principle. Therefore, the best course is to work from the very beginning in Kṛṣṇa consciousness under the guidance of a bona fide spiritual master. That is the way to make everything successful.

In the conditional state, people are attracted to worship demigods, ghosts, or Yakṣas like Kuvera. The mode of goodness is better than the modes of passion and ignorance, but one who takes directly to Kṛṣṇa consciousness is transcendental to all three modes of material nature. Although there is a process of gradual elevation, if one, by the association of pure devotees, takes directly to Kṛṣṇa consciousness, that is the best way. And that is recommended in this chapter. To achieve success in this way, one must first find the proper spiritual master and receive training under his direction. Then one can achieve faith in the Supreme. When that faith matures, in course of time, it is called love of God. This love is the ultimate goal of the living entities. One should, therefore, take to Kṛṣṇa consciousness directly. That is the message of this Seventeenth Chapter.

Thus end the Bhaktivedanta Purports to the Seventeenth Chapter of the Śrīmad-Bhagavad-gītā in the matter of the Divisions of Faith.

CHAPTER EIGHTEEN

Conclusion—
The Perfection of Renunciation

TEXT 1

अर्जुन उवाच ।
संन्यासस्य महाबाहो तत्त्वमिच्छामि वेदितुम् ।
त्यागस्य च हृषीकेश पृथक्केशिनिषूदन ॥ १ ॥

arjuna uvāca
sannyāsasya mahā-bāho
tattvam icchāmi veditum
tyāgasya ca hṛṣīkeśa
pṛthak keśi-niṣūdana

arjunaḥ uvāca—Arjuna said; *sannyāsasya*—renunciation; *mahā-bāho*—O
mighty-armed one; *tattvam*—truth; *icchāmi*—I wish; *veditum*—to understand;
tyāgasya—of renunciation; *ca*—also; *hṛṣīkeśa*—O master of the senses;
pṛthak—differently; *keśi-niṣūdana*—O killer of the Keśī demon.

779

TRANSLATION

Arjuna said, O mighty-armed one, I wish to understand the purpose of renunciation [tyāga] and of the renounced order of life [sannyāsa], O killer of the Keśī demon, Hṛṣīkeśa.

PURPORT

Actually the *Bhagavad-gītā* is finished in seventeen chapters. The Eighteenth Chapter is a supplementary summarization of the topics discussed before. In every chapter of *Bhagavad-gītā*, Lord Kṛṣṇa stresses that devotional service unto the Supreme Personality of Godhead is the ultimate goal of life. This same point is summarized in the Eighteenth Chapter as the most confidential path of knowledge. In the first six chapters, stress was given to devotional service: *yoginām api sarveṣām...* "Of all *yogīs* or transcendentalists, one who always thinks of Me within himself is best." In the next six chapters, pure devotional service and its nature and activity were discussed. In the third six chapters, knowledge, renunciation, the activities of material nature and transcendental nature, and devotional service were described. It was concluded that all acts should be performed in conjunction with the Supreme Lord, summarized by the words *om tat sat*, which indicate Viṣṇu, the Supreme Person. In the third part of *Bhagavad-gītā*, devotional service was established by the example of past *ācāryas* and the *Brahma-sūtra*, the *Vedānta-sūtra*, which cites that devotional service is the ultimate purpose of life and nothing else. Certain impersonalists consider themselves monopolizers of the knowledge of *Vedānta-sūtra*, but actually the *Vedānta-sūtra* is meant for understanding devotional service, for the Lord Himself is the composer of the *Vedānta-sūtra*, and He is its knower. That is described in the Fifteenth Chapter. In every scripture, every *Veda*, devotional service is the objective. That is explained in *Bhagavad-gītā*.

As in the Second Chapter a synopsis of the whole subject matter was described, similarly, in the Eighteenth Chapter also the summary of all instruction is given. The purpose of life is indicated to be renunciation and attainment of the transcendental position above the three material modes of nature. Arjuna wants to clarify the two distinct subject matters of *Bhagavad-gītā*, namely renunciation (*tyāga*) and the renounced order of life (*sannyāsa*). Thus he is asking the meaning of these two words.

Two words used in this verse to address the Supreme Lord—Hṛṣīkeśa and Keśinisūdana—are significant. Hṛṣīkeśa is Kṛṣṇa, the master of all senses, who can always help us attain mental serenity. Arjuna requests Him to summarize everything in such a way that he can remain equiposed. Yet he has some doubts, and doubts are always compared to demons. He therefore addresses Kṛṣṇa as Keśinisūdana. Keśī was a most formidable demon who was killed by the Lord; now Arjuna is expecting Kṛṣṇa to kill the demon of doubt.

TEXT 2

श्रीभगवानुवाच ।
काम्यानां कर्मणां न्यासं संन्यासं कवयो विदुः ।
सर्वकर्मफलत्यागं प्राहुस्त्यागं विचक्षणाः ॥ २ ॥

śrī-bhagavān uvāca
kāmyānāṁ karmaṇāṁ nyāsaṁ
sannyāsaṁ kavayo viduḥ
sarva-karma-phala-tyāgaṁ
prāhus tyāgaṁ vicakṣaṇāḥ

śrī bhagavān uvāca—the Supreme Personality of Godhead said; *kāmyānām*—with desire; *karmaṇām*—activities; *nyāsam*—renunciation; *sannyāsam*— renounced order of life; *kavayaḥ*—the learned; *viduḥ*—know; *sarva*—all; *karma*—activities; *phala*—of results; *tyāgam*—renunciation; *prāhuḥ*—call; *tyāgam*—renunciation; *vicakṣaṇāḥ*—the experienced.

TRANSLATION

The Supreme Lord said, To give up the results of all activities is called renunciation [tyāga] by the wise. And that state is called the renounced order of life [sannyāsa] by great learned men.

PURPORT

The performance of activities for results has to be given up. This is the instruction of *Bhagavad-gītā*. But activities leading to advanced spiritual knowledge are not to be given up. This will be made clear in the next verse. There are many prescriptions of methods for performing sacrifice for some particular purpose in the Vedic literatures. There are certain sacrifices to perform to attain a good son or to attain elevation to the higher planets, but sacrifices prompted by desires should be stopped. However, sacrifice for the purification of one's heart or for advancement in the spiritual science should not be given up.

TEXT 3

त्याज्यं दोषवदित्येके कर्म प्राहुर्मनीषिणः ।
यज्ञदानतपःकर्म न त्याज्यमिति चापरे ॥ ३ ॥

*tyājyaṁ doṣa-vad ity eke
karma prāhur manīṣiṇaḥ
yajña-dāna-tapaḥ-karma
na tyājyam iti cāpare*

tyājyam—must be given up; *doṣavat*—as an evil; *iti*—thus; *eke*—one group; *karma*—work; *prāhuḥ*—said; *manīṣiṇaḥ*—of great thinkers; *yajña*—sacrifice; *dāna*—charity; *tapaḥ*—penance; *karma*—work; *na*—never; *tyājyam*—is to be given up; *iti*—thus; *ca*—certainly; *apare*—others.

TRANSLATION

Some learned men declare that all kinds of fruitive activities should be given up, but there are yet other sages who maintain that acts of sacrifice, charity and penance should never be abandoned.

PURPORT

There are many activities in the Vedic literatures which are subjects of contention. For instance, it is said that an animal can be killed in a sacrifice, yet some maintain animal killing is completely abominable. Although animal killing in a sacrifice is recommended in the Vedic literature, the animal is not considered to be killed. The sacrifice is to give a new life to the animal. Sometimes the animal is given a new animal life after being killed in the sacrifice, and sometimes the animal is promoted immediately to the human form of life. But there are different opinions among the sages. Some say that animal killing should always be avoided, and others say that for a specific sacrifice it is good. All these different opinions on sacrificial activity are now being clarified by the Lord Himself.

TEXT 4

निश्चयं शृणु मे तत्र त्यागे भरतसत्तम ।
त्यागो हि पुरुषव्याघ्र त्रिविधः संप्रकीर्तितः ॥ ४ ॥

niścayaṁ śṛṇu me tatra
tyāge bharata-sattama
tyāgo hi puruṣa-vyāghra
tri-vidhaḥ samprakīrtitaḥ

niścayam—certainly; *śṛṇu*—hear; *me*—from Me; *tatra*—there; *tyāge*—in the matter of renunciation; *bharata-sattama*—O best of the Bhāratas; *tyāgaḥ*—renunciation; *hi*—certainly; *puruṣa-vyāghra*—O tiger among human beings; *tri-vidhaḥ*—three kinds; *samprakīrtitaḥ*—is declared.

TRANSLATION

O best of the Bhāratas, hear from Me now about renunciation. O tiger among men, there are three kinds of renunciation declared in the scriptures.

PURPORT

Although there are differences of opinion about renunciation, here the Supreme Personality of Godhead, Śrī Kṛṣṇa, gives His judgment, which should be taken as final. After all, the *Vedas* are different laws given by the Lord. Here the Lord is personally present, and His word should be taken as final. The Lord says that the process of renunciation should be considered in terms of the modes of material nature in which they are performed.

TEXT 5

यज्ञदानतपःकर्म न त्याज्यं कार्यमेव तत् ।
यज्ञो दानं तपश्चैव पावनानि मनीषिणाम् ॥ ५ ॥

yajña-dāna-tapaḥ-karma
na tyājyaṁ kāryam eva tat
yajño dānaṁ tapaś caiva
pāvanāni manīṣiṇām

yajña—sacrifice; *dāna*—charity; *tapaḥ*—penance; *karma*—activities; *na*—never; *tyājyam*—to be given up; *kāryam*—must be done; *eva*—certainly; *tat*—that; *yajñaḥ*—sacrifice; *dānam*—charity; *tapaḥ*—penance; *ca*—also; *eva*—certainly; *pāvanāni*—purifying; *manīṣiṇām*—even of the great souls.

TRANSLATION

Acts of sacrifice, charity and penance are not to be given up but should be performed. Indeed, sacrifice, charity and penance purify even the great souls.

PURPORT

The *yogīs* should perform acts for the advancement of human society. There are many purificatory processes for advancing a human being to spiritual life. The marriage ceremony, for example, is considered to be one of these sacrifices. It is called *vivāha-yajña*. Should a *sannyāsī*, who is in the renounced order of life and who has given up his family relations, encourage the marriage ceremony? The Lord says here that any sacrifice which is meant for human welfare should never be given up. *Vivāha-yajña*, the marriage ceremony, is meant to regulate the human mind to become peaceful for spiritual advancement. For most men, this *vivāha-yajña* should be encouraged even by persons in the renounced order of life. *Sannyasīs* should never associate with women, but that does not mean that one who is in the lower stages of life, a young man, should not accept a wife in the marriage ceremony. All prescribed sacrifices are meant for achieving the Supreme Lord. Therefore, in the lower stages, they should not be given up. Similarly, charity is for the purification of the heart. If charity is given to suitable persons, as described previously, it leads one to advanced spiritual life.

TEXT 6

एतान्यपि तु कर्माणि सङ्गं त्यक्त्वा फलानि च ।
कर्तव्यानीति मे पार्थ निश्चितं मतमुत्तमम् ॥ ६ ॥

etāny api tu karmāṇi
saṅgaṁ tyaktvā phalāni ca
kartavyānīti me pārtha
niścitaṁ matam uttamam

etāni—all this; *api*—certainly; *tu*—must; *karmāṇi*—activities; *saṅgam*—association; *tyaktvā*—renouncing; *phalāni*—results; *ca*—also; *kartavyāni*—as duty; *iti*—thus; *me*—My; *pārtha*—O son of Pṛthā; *niścitam*—definite; *matam*—opinion; *uttamam*—the best.

TRANSLATION

All these activities should be performed without any expectation of result. They should be performed as a matter of duty, O son of Pṛthā. That is My final opinion.

PURPORT

Although all sacrifices are purifying, one should not expect any result by such performances. In other words, all sacrifices which are meant for material advancement in life should be given up, but sacrifices that purify one's existence and elevate one to the spiritual plane should not be stopped. Everything that leads to Kṛṣṇa consciousness must be encouraged. In the *Śrīmad-Bhāgavatam* also it is said that any activity which leads to devotional service to the Lord should be accepted. That is the highest criterion of religion. A devotee of the Lord should accept any kind of work, sacrifice, or charity which will help him in the discharge of devotional service to the Lord

TEXT 7

नियतस्य तु संन्यासः कर्मणो नोपपद्यते ।
मोहात्तस्य परित्यागस्तामसः परिकीर्तितः ॥ ७ ॥

niyatasya tu sannyāsaḥ
karmaṇo nopapadyate
mohāt tasya parityāgas
tāmasaḥ parikīrtitaḥ

niyatasya—prescribed duties; *tu*—but; *sannyāsaḥ*—renunciation; *karmaṇaḥ*—activities; *na*—never; *upapadyate*—is deserved; *mohāt*—by illusion; *tasya*—of which; *parityāgaḥ*—renunciation; *tāmasaḥ*—in the mode of ignorance; *parikīrtitaḥ*—declared.

TRANSLATION

Prescribed duties should never be renounced. If, by illusion, one gives up his prescribed duties, such renunciation is said to be in the mode of ignorance.

PURPORT

Work for material satisfaction must be given up, but activities which promote one to spiritual activity, like cooking for the Supreme Lord and offering the food to the Lord and then accepting the food, are recommended. It is said that a person in the renounced order of life should not cook for himself. Cooking for oneself is prohibited, but cooking for the Supreme Lord is not prohibited. Similarly, a *sannyāsī* may perform a marriage ceremony to help his disciple in the advancement of Kṛṣṇa consciousness. If one renounces such activities, it is to be understood that he is acting in the mode of darkness.

TEXT 8

दुःखमित्येव यत्कर्म कायक्लेशभयात्त्यजेत् ।
स कृत्वा राजसं त्यागं नैव त्यागफलं लभेत् ॥ ८ ॥

duḥkham ity eva yat karma
kāya-kleśa-bhayāt tyajet
sa kṛtvā rājasaṁ tyāgaṁ
naiva tyāga-phalaṁ labhet

duḥkham—unhappy; *iti*—thus; *eva*—certainly; *yat*—that which; *karma*—work; *kāya*—body; *kleśa*—troublesome; *bhayāt*—out of; *tyajet*—fear; *saḥ*—that; *kṛtvā*—after doing; *rājasam*—in the mode of passion; *tyāgam*—renunciation; *na eva*—certainly not; *tyāga*—renounced; *phalam*—results; *labhet*—gain.

TRANSLATION

Anyone who gives up prescribed duties as troublesome, or out of fear, is said to be in the mode of passion. Such action never leads to the elevation of renunciation.

PURPORT

One who is in Kṛṣṇa consciousness should not give up earning money out of fear that he is performing fruitive activities. If by working one can engage his money in Kṛṣṇa consciousness, or if by rising early in the morning one can advance his transcendental Kṛṣṇa consciousness, one should not desist out of fear or because such activities are considered troublesome. Such renunciation is in the mode of passion. The result of passionate work is always miserable. Even if a person renounces work in that spirit, he never gets the result of renunciation.

TEXT 9

कार्यमित्येव यत्कर्म नियतं क्रियतेऽर्जुन ।
सङ्गं त्यक्त्वा फलं चैव स त्यागः सात्त्विको मतः ॥ ९ ॥

kāryam ity eva yat karma
niyataṁ kriyate 'rjuna
saṅgaṁ tyaktvā phalaṁ caiva
sa tyāgaḥ sāttviko mataḥ

kāryam—must be done; *iti*—thus; *eva*—thus; *yat*—that which; *karma*—work; *niyatam*—prescribed; *kriyate*—performed; *arjuna*—O Arjuna; *saṅgam*—association; *tyaktvā*—giving up; *phalam*—result; *ca*—also; *eva*—certainly; *saḥ*—that; *tyāgaḥ*—renunciation; *sāttvikaḥ*—in the mode of goodness; *mataḥ*—in My opinion.

TRANSLATION

But he who performs his prescribed duty only because it ought to be done, and renounces all attachment to the fruit—his renunciation is of the nature of goodness, O Arjuna.

PURPORT

Prescribed duties must be performed with this mentality. One should act without attachment for the result; he should be disassociated from the modes of work. A man working in Kṛṣṇa consciousness in a factory does not associate himself with the work of the factory, nor with the workers of the factory. He simply works for Kṛṣṇa. And when he gives up the result for Kṛṣṇa, he is acting transcendentally.

TEXT 10

न द्वेष्ट्यकुशलं कर्म कुशले नानुषज्जते ।
त्यागी सत्त्वसमाविष्टो मेधावी छिन्नसंशयः ॥ १० ॥

na dveṣṭy akuśalaṁ karma
kuśale nānuṣajjate
tyāgī sattva-samāviṣṭo
medhāvī chinna-saṁśayaḥ

na—never; *dveṣṭi*—hates; *akuśalam*—inauspicious; *karma*—work; *kuśale*—in auspicious; *na*—nor; *anuṣajjate*—becomes attached; *tyāgī*—the renouncer; *sattva*—goodness; *samāviṣṭaḥ*—absorbed in; *medhāvī*—intelligent; *chinna*—cut up; *saṁśayaḥ*—all doubts.

TRANSLATION

Those who are situated in the mode of goodness, who neither hate inauspicious work nor are attached to auspicious work, have no doubts about work.

PURPORT

It is said in *Bhagavad-gītā* that one can never give up work at any time. Therefore he who works for Kṛṣṇa and does not enjoy the fruitive results, who offers everything to Kṛṣṇa, is actually a renouncer. There are many members of the International Society for Krishna Consciousness who work very hard in their office or in the factory or some other place, and whatever they earn they give to the Society. Such highly elevated souls are actually *sannyāsīs* and are situated in the renounced order of life. It is clearly outlined here how to renounce the fruits of work and for what purpose fruits should be renounced.

TEXT 11

न हि देहभृता शक्यं त्यक्तुं कर्माण्यशेषतः ।
यस्तु कर्मफलत्यागी स त्यागीत्यभिधीयते ॥ ११ ॥

> na hi deha-bhṛtā śakyaṁ
>   tyaktuṁ karmāṇy aśeṣataḥ
> yas tu karma-phala-tyāgī
>   sa tyāgīty abhidhīyate

na—never; *hi*—certainly; *deha-bhṛtā*—of the embodied; *śakyam*—possible; *tyaktum*—to renounce; *karmāṇi*—activities of; *aśeṣataḥ*—altogether; *yaḥ tu*—anyone who; *karma*—work; *phala*—result; *tyāgī*—renouncer; *saḥ*—he; *tyāgī*—the renouncer; *iti*—thus; *abhidhīyate*—it is said.

TRANSLATION

It is indeed impossible for an embodied being to give up all activities. Therefore it is said that he who renounces the fruits of action is one who has truly renounced.

PURPORT

A person in Kṛṣṇa consciousness acting in knowledge of his relationship with Kṛṣṇa is always liberated. Therefore he does not have to enjoy or suffer the results of his acts after death.

TEXT 12

अनिष्टमिष्टं मिश्रं च त्रिविधं कर्मणः फलम् ।
भवत्यत्यागिनां प्रेत्य न तु संन्यासिनां कचित् ॥ १२ ॥

> aniṣṭam iṣṭaṁ miśraṁ ca
>   tri-vidhaṁ karmaṇaḥ phalam
> bhavaty atyāginām pretya
>   na tu sannyāsinām kvacit

aniṣṭam—leading to hell; *iṣṭam*—leading to heaven; *miśram ca*—or mixture; *tri-vidham*—three kinds; *karmaṇaḥ*—work; *phalam*—result; *bhavati*—becomes; *atyāginām*—of the renouncer; *pretya*—after death; *na tu*—but not; *sannyāsinām*—of the renounced order; *kvacit*—at any time.

TRANSLATION

For one who is not renounced, the threefold fruits of action—desirable, undesirable and mixed—accrue after death. But those who are in the renounced order of life have no such results to suffer or enjoy.

PURPORT

A person in Kṛṣṇa consciousness or in the mode of goodness does not hate anyone or anything which troubles his body. He does work in the proper place and at the proper time without fearing the troublesome effects of his duty. Such a person situated in transcendence should be understood to be most intelligent and beyond all doubts in his activities.

TEXTS 13-14

पञ्चैतानि महाबाहो कारणानि निबोध मे ।
साङ्ख्ये कृतान्ते प्रोक्तानि सिद्धये सर्वकर्मणाम् ॥ १३ ॥

अधिष्ठानं तथा कर्ता करणं च पृथग्विधम् ।
विविधाश्च पृथक्चेष्टा दैवं चैवात्र पञ्चमम् ॥ १४ ॥

pañcaitāni mahā-bāho
kāraṇāni nibodha me
sāṅkhye kṛtānte proktāni
siddhaye sarva-karmaṇām

adhiṣṭhānaṁ tathā kartā
karaṇaṁ ca pṛthag-vidham
vividhāś ca pṛthak ceṣṭā
daivaṁ caivātra pañcamam

pañca—five; *etāni*—all these; *mahā-bāho*—O mighty-armed one; *kāraṇāni*—cause; *nibodha*—just understand; *me*—from Me; *sāṅkhye*—in the *Vedas*; *kṛtānte*—after performance; *proktāni*—said; *siddhaye*—perfection; *sarva*—all; *karmaṇām*—actuated; *adhiṣṭhānam*—place; *tathā*—also; *kartā*—worker; *karaṇam ca*—and instruments; *pṛthak-vidham*—different kinds; *vividhāḥ ca*—varieties; *pṛthak*—separately; *ceṣṭāḥ*—endeavor; *daivam*—the Supreme; *ca*—also; *eva*—certainly; *atra*—here; *pañcamam*—five.

TRANSLATION

O mighty-armed Arjuna, learn from Me of the five factors which bring about the accomplishment of all action. These are declared in sāṅkhya philosophy to be the place of action, the performer, the senses, the endeavor, and ultimately the Supersoul.

PURPORT

A question may be raised that since any activity performed must have some reaction, how is it that the person in Kṛṣṇa consciousness does not suffer or enjoy the reactions of work? The Lord is citing *Vedānta* philosophy to show how this is possible. He says that there are five causes for all activities and for success in all activity, and one should know these five causes. *Sāṅkhya* means the stalk of knowledge, and *Vedānta* is the final stalk of knowledge accepted by all leading *ācāryas*. Even Śaṅkara accepts *Vedānta-sūtra* as such. Therefore such authority should be consulted.

The ultimate will is invested in the Supersoul, as it is stated in the *Gītā*, "*sarvasya cāhaṁ hṛdi.*" He is engaging everyone in certain activities. Acts done under His direction from within yield no reaction, either in this life or in the life after death.

The instruments of action are the senses, and by senses the soul acts in various ways, and for each and every action there is a different endeavor. But all one's activities depend on the will of the Supersoul, who is seated within the heart as a friend. The Supreme Lord is the super cause. Under these circumstances, he who is acting in Kṛṣṇa consciousness under the direction of the Supersoul situated within the heart is naturally not bound by any activity. Those in complete Kṛṣṇa consciousness are not ultimately responsible for their actions. Everything is dependant on the supreme will, the Supersoul, the Supreme Personality of Godhead.

TEXT 15

शरीरवाङ्मनोभिर्यत्कर्म प्रारभते नरः ।
न्याय्यं वा विपरीतं वा पञ्चैते तस्य हेतवः ॥ १५ ॥

śarīra-vāṅ-manobhir yat
karma prārabhate naraḥ
nyāyyaṁ vā viparītaṁ vā
pañcaite tasya hetavaḥ

śarīra—body; *vāk*—speech; *manobhiḥ*—by the mind; *yat*—anything; *karma*—work; *prārabhate*—begins; *naraḥ*—a person; *nyāyyam*—right; *vā*—or;

viparītam—the opposite; *vā*—or; *pañca*—five; *ete*—all these; *tasya*—its; *hetavaḥ*—causes.

TRANSLATION

Whatever right or wrong action a man performs by body, mind or speech is caused by these five factors.

PURPORT

The words "right" and "wrong" are very significant in this verse. Right work is work done in terms of the prescribed directions in the scriptures, and wrong work is work done against the principles of the scriptural injunctions. But whatever is done requires these five factors for its complete performance.

TEXT 16

तत्रैवं सति कर्तारमात्मानं केवलं तु यः ।
पश्यत्यकृतबुद्धित्वान्न स पश्यति दुर्मतिः ॥ १६ ॥

tatraivaṁ sati kartāram
ātmānaṁ kevalaṁ tu yaḥ
paśyaty akṛta-buddhitvān
na sa paśyati durmatiḥ

tatra—there; *evam*—certainly; *sati*—being thus; *kartāram*—of the worker; *ātmānam*—the soul; *kevalam*—only; *tu*—but; *yaḥ*—anyone; *paśyati*—sees; *akṛta-buddhitvāt*—due to unintelligence; *na*—never; *saḥ*—he; *paśyati*—sees; *durmatiḥ*—foolish.

TRANSLATION

Therefore one who thinks himself the only doer, not considering the five factors, is certainly not very intelligent and cannot see things as they are.

PURPORT

A foolish person cannot understand that the Supersoul is sitting as a friend within and conducting his actions. Although the material causes are the place, the worker, the endeavor and the senses, the final cause is the Supreme, the Personality of Godhead. Therefore, one should see not only the four material causes, but the supreme efficient cause as well. One who does not see the Supreme thinks himself to be the instrument.

TEXT 17

यस्य नाहंकृतो भावो बुद्धिर्यस्य न लिप्यते ।
हत्वाऽपि स इमाँल्लोकान्न हन्ति न निबध्यते ॥ १७ ॥

yasya nāhaṅkṛto bhāvo
buddhir yasya na lipyate
hatvāpi sa imāl lokān
na hanti na nibadhyate

yasya—of one who; *na*—never; *ahaṅkṛtaḥ*—false ego; *bhāvaḥ*—nature; *buddhiḥ*—intelligence; *yasya*—one who; *na*—never; *lipyate*—is attached; *hatvā api*—even killing; *saḥ*—he; *imān*—this; *lokān*—world; *na*—never; *hanti* —kills; *na*—never; *nibadhyate*—becomes entangled.

TRANSLATION

One who is not motivated by false ego, whose intelligence is not entangled, though he kills men in this world, is not the slayer. Nor is he bound by his actions.

PURPORT

In this verse the Lord informs Arjuna that the desire not to fight arises from false ego. Arjuna thought himself to be the doer of action, but he did not consider the Supreme sanction within and without. If one does not know that a super sanction is there, why should he act? But one who knows the instrument of work, himself as the worker, and the Supreme Lord as the supreme sanctioner, is perfect in doing everything. Such a person is never in illusion. Personal activity and responsibility arise from false ego and godlessness, or a lack of Kṛṣṇa consciousness. Anyone who is acting in Kṛṣṇa consciousness under the direction of the Supersoul or the Supreme Personality of Godhead, even though killing, does not kill. Nor is he ever affected with the reaction of such killing. When a soldier kills under the command of a superior officer, he is not subject to be judged. But if a soldier kills on his own personal account, then he is certainly judged by a court of law.

TEXT 18

ज्ञानं ज्ञेयं परिज्ञाता त्रिविधा कर्मचोदना ।
करणं कर्म कर्तेति त्रिविधः कर्मसंग्रहः ॥ १८ ॥

jñānaṁ jñeyaṁ parijñātā
tri-vidhā karma-codanā
karaṇaṁ karma karteti
tri-vidhaḥ karma-saṅgrahaḥ

jñānam—knowledge; *jñeyam*—objective; *parijñātā*—the knower; *tri-vidhā*—three kinds; *karma*—work; *codanā*—impetus; *karaṇam*—the senses; *karma*—work; *kartā*—the doer; *iti*—thus; *tri-vidhaḥ*—three kinds; *karma*—work; *saṅgrahaḥ*—accumulation.

TRANSLATION

Knowledge, the object of knowledge and the knower are the three factors which motivate action; the senses, the work and the doer comprise the threefold basis of action.

PURPORT

There are three kinds of impetus for daily work: knowledge, the object of knowledge and the knower. The instruments of work, the work itself and the worker are called the constituents of work. Any work done by any human being has these elements. Before one acts, there is some impetus, which is called inspiration. Any solution arrived at before work is actualized is a subtle form of work. Then work takes the form of action. First one has to undergo the psychological processes of thinking, feeling and willing, and that is called impetus. Actually the faith to perform acts is called knowledge. The inspiration to work is the same if it comes from the scripture or from the instruction of the spiritual master. When the inspiration is there and the worker is there, then actual activity takes place by the help of the senses. The mind is the center of all senses, and the object is work itself. These are the different phases of work as described in *Bhagavad-gītā*. The sum total of all activities is called accumulation of work.

TEXT 19

ज्ञानं कर्म च कर्ता च त्रिधैव गुणभेदतः ।
प्रोच्यते गुणसंख्याने यथावच्छृणु तान्यपि ॥ १९ ॥

> *jñānaṁ karma ca kartā ca*
> *tridhaiva guṇa-bhedataḥ*
> *procyate guṇa-saṅkhyāne*
> *yathāvac chṛṇu tāny api*

jñānam—knowledge; karma—work; ca—also; kartā—worker; ca—also; tridhā—three kinds; eva—certainly; guṇa-bhedataḥ—in terms of different modes of material nature; procyate—is said; guṇa-saṅkhyāne—in terms of different modes; yathāvat—as they act; śṛṇu—hear; tāni—all of them; api—also.

TRANSLATION

In accordance with the three modes of material nature, there are three kinds of knowledge, action, and performers of action. Listen as I describe them.

PURPORT

In the Fourteenth Chapter the three divisions of the modes of material nature were elaborately described. In that chapter it was said that the mode of goodness is illuminating, the mode of passion materialistic, and the mode of ignorance conducive to laziness and indolence. All the modes of material nature are binding; they are not sources of liberation. Even in the mode of goodness one is conditioned. In the Seventeenth Chapter, the different types of worship by different types of men in different modes of material nature were described. In this verse, the Lord wishes to speak about the different types of knowledge, workers, and work itself according to the three material modes.

TEXT 20

सर्वभूतेषु येनैकं भावमव्ययमीक्षते ।
अविभक्तं विभक्तेषु तज्ज्ञानं विद्धि सात्त्विकम् ॥ २० ॥

> *sarva-bhūteṣu yenaikaṁ*
> *bhāvam avyayam īkṣate*
> *avibhaktaṁ vibhakteṣu*
> *taj jñānaṁ viddhi sāttvikam*

sarva-bhūteṣu—in all living entities; *yena*—by whom; *ekam*—one; *bhāvam*—situation; *avyayam*—imperishable; *īkṣate*—does see; *avibhaktam*—undivided; *vibhakteṣu*—in the numberless divided; *tat*—that; *jñānam*—knowledge; *viddhi*—knows; *sāttvikam*—in the mode of goodness.

TRANSLATION

That knowledge by which one undivided spiritual nature is seen in all existences, undivided in the divided, is knowledge in the mode of goodness.

PURPORT

A person who sees one spirit soul in every living being, whether a demigod, human being, animal, bird, beast, aquatic or plant, possesses knowledge in the mode of goodness. In all living entities, one spirit soul is there, although they have different bodies in terms of their previous work. As described in the Seventh Chapter, the manifestation of the living force in every body is due to the superior nature of the Supreme Lord. Thus to see that one superior nature, that living force, in every body is to see in the mode of goodness. That living energy is imperishable, although the bodies are perishable. The difference is perceived in terms of the body because there are many forms of material existence in conditional life; therefore they appear to be divided. Such impersonal knowledge finally leads to self-realization.

TEXT 21

पृथक्त्वेन तु यज्ज्ञानं नानाभावान्पृथग्विधान् ।
वेत्ति सर्वेषु भूतेषु तज्ज्ञानं विद्धि राजसम् ॥ २१ ॥

pṛthaktvena tu yaj jñānaṁ
nānā-bhāvān pṛthag-vidhān
vetti sarveṣu bhūteṣu
taj jñānaṁ viddhi rājasam

pṛthaktvena—because of division; *tu*—but; *yat jñānam*—which knowledge; *nānā-bhāvān*—multifarious situations; *pṛthak-vidhān*—differently; *vetti*—one who knows; *sarveṣu*—in all; *bhūteṣu*—living entities; *tat jñānam*—that knowledge; *viddhi*—must be known; *rājasam*—in terms of passion.

TRANSLATION

That knowledge by which a different type of living entity is seen to be dwelling in different bodies is knowledge in the mode of passion.

PURPORT

The concept that the material body is the living entity and that with the destruction of the body the consciousness is also destroyed is called knowledge in the mode of passion. According to that knowledge, bodies differ from one another because of the development of different types of consciousness, otherwise there is no separate soul which manifests consciousness. The body is itself the soul, and there is no separate soul beyond this body. According to such knowledge, consciousness is temporary. Or else there are no individual souls, but there is an all-pervading soul, which is full of knowledge, and this body is a manifestation of temporary ignorance. Or beyond this body there is no special individual or Supreme Soul. All such conceptions are considered products of the mode of passion.

TEXT 22

यत्तु कृत्स्नवदेकस्मिन्कार्ये सक्तमहैतुकम् ।
अतत्त्वार्थवदल्पं च तत्तामसमुदाहृतम् ॥ २२ ॥

yat tu kṛtsna-vad ekasmin
kārye saktam ahaitukam
atattvārtha-vad alpaṁ ca
tat tāmasam udāhṛtam

yat—that which; tu—but; kṛtsnavat—all in all; ekasmin—in one; kārye—work; saktam—attached; ahaitukam—without cause; atattva-arthavat—without reality; alpam ca—and very meager; tat—that; tāmasam—in the mode of darkness; udāhṛtam—is spoken.

TRANSLATION

And that knowledge by which one is attached to one kind of work as the all in all, without knowledge of the truth, and which is very meager, is said to be in the mode of darkness.

PURPORT

The "knowledge" of the common man is always in the mode of darkness or ignorance because every living entity in conditional life is born into the mode of ignorance. One who does not develop knowledge through the authorities or scriptural injunctions has knowledge that is limited to the body. He is not concerned about acting in terms of the directions of scripture. For him God is money, and knowledge means the satisfaction of bodily demands. Such knowledge has no connection with the Absolute Truth. It is more or less like the knowledge of the ordinary animals: the knowledge of eating, sleeping, defending and mating. Such knowledge is described here as the product of the mode of darkness. In other words, knowledge concerning the spirit soul beyond this body is called knowledge in the mode of goodness, and knowledge producing many theories and doctrines by dint of mundane logic and mental speculation is the product of the mode of passion, and knowledge concerned with only keeping the body comfortable is said to be in the mode of ignorance.

TEXT 23

नियतं सङ्गरहितमरागद्वेषतः कृतम् ।
अफलप्रेप्सुना कर्म यत्तत्सात्त्विकमुच्यते ॥ २३ ॥

niyataṁ saṅga-rahitam
arāga-dveṣataḥ kṛtam
aphala-prepsunā karma
yat tat sāttvikam ucyate

niyatam—regulative; *saṅga-rahitam*—without attachment; *arāga-dveṣataḥ* —without love or hatred; *kṛtam*—done; *aphala-prepsunā*—without fruitive result; *karma*—acts; *yat*—that which; *tat*—that; *sāttvikam*—in the mode of goodness; *ucyate*—is called.

TRANSLATION

As for actions, that action in accordance with duty, which is performed without attachment, without love or hate, by one who has renounced fruitive results, is called action in the mode of goodness.

PURPORT

Regulated occupational duties, as prescribed in the scriptures in terms of the different orders and divisions of society, performed without attachment or proprietary rights and therefore without any love or hatred and performed in Kṛṣṇa consciousness for the satisfaction of the Supreme, without self-satisfaction or self-gratification, are called actions in the mode of goodness.

TEXT 24

यत्तु कामेप्सुना कर्म साहङ्कारेण वा पुनः ।
क्रियते बहुलायासं तद्राजसमुदाहृतम् ॥ २४ ॥

yat tu kāmepsunā karma
sāhaṅkāreṇa vā punaḥ
kriyate bahulāyāsaṁ
tad rājasam udāhṛtam

yat—that which; tu—but; kāma-īpsunā—with fruitive result; karma—work; sāhaṅkāreṇa—with ego; vā—or; punaḥ—again; kriyate—performed; bahula-āyāsam—with great labor; tat—that; rājasam—in the mode of passion; udāhṛtam—is said to be.

TRANSLATION

But action performed with great effort by one seeking to gratify his desires, and which is enacted from a sense of false ego, is called action in the mode of passion.

TEXT 25

अनुबन्धं क्षयं हिंसामनपेक्ष्य च पौरुषम् ।
मोहादारभ्यते कर्म यत्तत्तामसमुच्यते ॥ २५ ॥

anubandhaṁ kṣayaṁ hiṁsām
anapekṣya ca pauruṣam
mohād ārabhyate karma
yat tat tāmasam ucyate

anubandham—future bondage; *kṣayam*—distracted; *hiṁsām*—violence; *anapekṣya*—without consideration of consequences; *ca*—also; *pauruṣam*—distressing to others; *mohāt*—by illusion; *ārabhyate*—begun; *karma*—work; *yat*—that; *tat*—which; *tāmasam*—in the mode of ignorance; *ucyate*—is said to be.

TRANSLATION

And that action performed in ignorance and delusion without consideration of future bondage or consequences, which inflicts injury and is impractical, is said to be action in the mode of ignorance.

PURPORT

One has to give account of one's actions to the state or to the agents of the Supreme Lord called the Yamadūtas. Irresponsible work is distraction because it destroys the regulative principles of scriptural injunction. It is often based on violence and is distressing to other living entities. Such irresponsible work is carried out in the light of one's personal experience. This is called illusion. And all such illusory work is a product of the mode of ignorance.

TEXT 26

मुक्तसङ्गोनहंवादी धृत्युत्साहसमन्वितः ।
सिद्ध्यसिद्ध्योर्निर्विकारः कर्ता सात्त्विक उच्यते ॥ २६ ॥

mukta-saṅgo 'nahaṁ-vādī
dhṛty-utsāha-samanvitaḥ
siddhy-asiddhyor nirvikāraḥ
kartā sāttvika ucyate

mukta-saṅgaḥ—liberated from all material association; *anaham-vādī*—without false ego; *dhṛti-utsāha*—with great enthusiasm; *samanvitaḥ*—qualified in that way; *siddhi*—perfection; *asiddhyoḥ*—failure; *nirvikāraḥ*—without change; *kartā*—worker; *sāttvikaḥ*—in the mode of goodness; *ucyate*—is said to be.

TRANSLATION

The worker who is free from all material attachments and false ego, who is enthusiastic and resolute and who is indifferent to success or failure, is a worker in the mode of goodness.

PURPORT

A person in Kṛṣṇa consciousness is always transcendental to the material modes of nature. He has no expectations for the result of the work entrusted to him because he is above false ego and pride. Still, he is always enthusiastic till the completion of such work. He does not worry about the distress undertaken; he is always enthusiastic. He does not care for success or failure; he is equal both in distress or happiness. Such a worker is situated in the mode of goodness.

TEXT 27

रागी कर्मफलप्रेप्सुर्लुब्धो हिंसात्मकोऽशुचिः ।
हर्षशोकान्वितः कर्ता राजसः परिकीर्तितः ॥ २७ ॥

rāgī karma-phala-prepsur
lubdho hiṁsātmako 'śuciḥ
harṣa-śokānvitaḥ kartā
rājasaḥ parikīrtitaḥ

rāgī—very much attached; *karma-phala*—to the fruit of the work; *prepsuḥ*—desiring; *lubdhaḥ*—greedy; *hiṁsā-ātmakaḥ*—and always envious; *aśuciḥ*—unclean; *harṣa-śoka-anvitaḥ*—complicated, with joy and sorrow; *kartā*—such a worker; *rājasaḥ*—in the mode of passion; *parikīrtitaḥ*—is declared.

TRANSLATION

But that worker who is attached to the fruits of his labor and who passionately wants to enjoy them, who is greedy, envious and impure and moved by happiness and distress, is a worker in the mode of passion.

PURPORT

A person is too much attached to certain kind of work or to the result because he has too much attachment for materialism or hearth and home, wife and children. Such a person has no desire for higher elevation of life. He is simply concerned with making this world as materially comfortable as possible. He is generally very greedy, and he thinks that anything attained by him is permanent and never to be lost. Such a person is envious of others and prepared to do anything wrong for sense gratification. Therefore such a person is unclean, and he does not care whether his earning is pure or impure. He is very happy if his work is successful and very much distressed when his work is not successful. Such is a man in the mode of passion.

TEXT 28

अयुक्तः प्राकृतः स्तब्धः शठो नैष्कृतिकोऽलसः ।
विषादी दीर्घसूत्री च कर्ता तामस उच्यते ॥ २८ ॥

ayuktaḥ prākṛtaḥ stabdhaḥ
śaṭho naiṣkṛtiko 'lasaḥ
viṣādī dīrgha-sūtrī ca
kartā tāmasa ucyate

ayuktaḥ—without reference to the scriptural injunctions; *prākṛtaḥ*—materialistic; *stabdhaḥ*—obstinate; *śaṭhaḥ*—deceitful; *naiṣkṛtikaḥ*—expert in insulting others; *alasaḥ*—lazy; *viṣādī*—morose; *dīrgha-sūtrī*—procrastinating; *ca*—also; *kartā*—worker; *tāmasaḥ*—in the mode of ignorance; *ucyate*—is said to be.

TRANSLATION

And that worker who is always engaged in work against the injunction of the scripture, who is materialistic, obstinate, cheating and expert in insulting others, who is lazy, always morose and procrastinating, is a worker in the mode of ignorance.

PURPORT

In the scriptural injunctions we find what sort of work should be performed and what sort of work should not be performed. Those who do not care for those injunctions engage in work not to be done, and such persons are generally materialistic. They work according to the modes of nature, not according to the injunctions of the scripture. Such workers are not very gentle, and generally they are always cunning and expert in insulting others. They are very lazy; even though they have some duty, they do not do it properly, and they put it aside to be done later on. Therefore they appear to be morose. They procrastinate; anything which can be done in an hour they drag on for years. Such workers are situated in the mode of ignorance.

TEXT 29

बुद्धेर्भेदं धृतेश्चैव गुणतस्त्रिविधं शृणु ।
प्रोच्यमानमशेषेण पृथक्त्वेन धनंजय ॥ २९ ॥

buddher bhedaṁ dhṛteś caiva
guṇatas tri-vidhaṁ śṛṇu
procyamānam aśeṣeṇa
pṛthaktvena dhanañjaya

buddheḥ—of intelligence; *bhedam*—differences; *dhṛteḥ*—of steadiness; *ca*—also; *eva*—certainly; *guṇataḥ*—by the modes of material nature; *tri-vidham*—the three kinds of; *śṛṇu*—just hear; *procyamānam*—as described by Me; *aśeṣeṇa*—in detail; *pṛthaktvena*—differently; *dhanañjaya*—O winner of wealth.

TRANSLATION

Now, O winner of wealth, please listen as I tell you in detail of the three kinds of understanding and determination according to the three modes of nature.

PURPORT

Now after explaining knowledge, the object of knowledge and the knower, in three different divisions according to modes of material nature, the Lord is explaining the intelligence and determination of the worker in the same way.

TEXT 30

प्रवृत्तिं च निवृत्तिं च कार्याकार्ये भयाभये ।
बन्धं मोक्षं च या वेत्ति बुद्धिः सा पार्थ सात्त्विकी ॥ ३० ॥

pravṛttiṁ ca nivṛttiṁ ca
kāryākārye bhayābhaye
bandhaṁ mokṣaṁ ca yā vetti
buddhiḥ sā pārtha sāttvikī

pravṛttim—deserving; *ca*—also; *nivṛttim*—not deserving; *kārya*—work; *akārye*—reaction; *bhaya*—fearful; *abhaye*—fearlessness; *bandham*—obligation; *mokṣam ca*—and liberation; *yā*—that which; *vetti*—knows; *buddhiḥ*—understanding; *sā*—that; *pārtha*—O son of Pṛthā; *sāttvikī*—in the mode of goodness.

TRANSLATION

O son of Pṛthā, that understanding by which one knows what ought to be done and what ought not to be done, what is to be feared and what is not to be feared, what is binding and what is liberating, that understanding is established in the mode of goodness.

PURPORT

Actions which are performed in terms of the directions of the scriptures are called *pravṛtti*, or actions that deserve to be performed, and actions which are not so directed are not to be performed. One who does not know the scriptural directions becomes entangled in the actions and reactions of work. Understanding which discriminates by intelligence is situated in the mode of goodness.

TEXT 31

यया धर्ममधर्मं च कार्यं चाकार्यमेव च ।
अयथावत्प्रजानाति बुद्धिः सा पार्थ राजसी ॥ ३१ ॥

yayā dharmam adharmaṁ ca
kāryaṁ cākāryam eva ca
ayathāvat prajānāti
buddhiḥ sā pārtha rājasī

yayā—by which; *dharmam*—principles of religion; *adharmam ca*—and irreligion; *kāryam*—work; *ca*—also; *akāryam*—what ought not to be done; *eva*—certainly; *ca*—also; *ayathāvat*—not perfectly; *prajānāti*—knows;

buddhiḥ—intelligence; *sā*—that; *pārtha*—O son of Pṛthā; *rājasī*—in the mode of passion.

TRANSLATION

And that understanding which cannot distinguish between the religious way of life and the irreligious, between action that should be done and action that should not be done, that imperfect understanding, O son of Pṛthā, is in the mode of passion.

PURPORT

Intelligence in the mode of passion is always working perversely. It accepts religions which are not actually religions and rejects actual religion. All views and activities are misguided. Men of passionate intelligence understand a great soul to be a common man and accept a common man as a great soul. They think truth to be untruth and accept untruth as truth. In all activities they simply take the wrong path; therefore their intelligence is in the mode of passion.

TEXT 32

अधर्मं धर्ममिति या मन्यते तमसावृता ।
सर्वार्थान्विपरीतांश्च बुद्धिः सा पार्थ तामसी ॥ ३२ ॥

adharmaṁ dharmam iti yā
manyate tamasāvṛtā
sarvārthān viparītāṁś ca
buddhiḥ sā pārtha tāmasī

adharmam—irreligion; *dharmam*—religion; *iti*—thus; *yā*—which; *manyate*—thinks; *tamasā*—by illusion; *āvṛtā*—covered; *sarva-arthān*—all things; *viparītān*—the wrong direction; *ca*—also; *buddhiḥ*—intelligence; *sa*—that; *pārtha*—O son of Pṛthā; *tāmasī*—the mode of ignorance.

TRANSLATION

That understanding which considers irreligion to be religion and religion to be irreligion, under the spell of illusion and darkness, and strives always in the wrong direction, O Pārtha, is in the mode of ignorance.

TEXT 33

धृत्या यया धारयते मनःप्राणेन्द्रियक्रियाः ।
योगेनाव्यभिचारिण्या धृतिः सा पार्थ सात्त्विकी ॥ ३३ ॥

dhṛtyā yayā dhārayate
manaḥ-prāṇendriya-kriyāḥ
yogenāvyabhicāriṇyā
dhṛtiḥ sā pārtha sāttvikī

dhṛtyā—determination; *yayā*—by which; *dhārayate*—is sustained; *manaḥ*—mind; *prāṇa*—life; *indriya*—senses; *kriyāḥ*—activities; *yogena*—by yoga practice; *avyabhicāriṇyā*—without any break; *dhṛtiḥ*—such determination; *sā*—that; *pārtha*—O son of Pṛthā; *sāttvikī*—in the mode of goodness.

TRANSLATION

O son of Pṛthā, that determination which is unbreakable, which is sustained with steadfastness by yoga practice, and thus controls the mind, life, and the acts of the senses, is in the mode of goodness.

PURPORT

Yoga is a means to understand the Supreme Soul. One who is steadily fixed in the Supreme Soul with determination, concentrating one's mind, life and sensual activities on the Supreme, engages in Kṛṣṇa consciousness. That sort of determination is in the mode of goodness. The word *avyabhicāriṇya* is very significant, for it refers to persons who are engaged in Kṛṣṇa consciousness and are never deviated by any other activity.

TEXT 34

यया तु धर्मकामार्थान्धृत्या धारयतेऽर्जुन ।
प्रसङ्गेन फलाकाङ्क्षी धृतिः सा पार्थ राजसी ॥ ३४ ॥

yayā tu dharma-kāmārthān
dhṛtyā dhārayate 'rjuna
prasaṅgena phalākāṅkṣī
dhṛtiḥ sā pārtha rājasī

yayā—by which; *tu*—but; *dharma-kāma-arthān*—for religiosity and economic development; *dhṛtyā*—by determination; *dhārayate*—in such terms; *arjuna*—O Arjuna; *prasaṅgena*—for that; *phala-ākāṅkṣī*—desiring fruitive result; *dhṛtiḥ*—determination; *sā*—that; *pārtha*—O son of Pṛthā; *rājasī*—in the mode of passion.

TRANSLATION

And that determination by which one holds fast to fruitive result in religion, economic development and sense gratification is of the nature of passion, O Arjuna.

PURPORT

Any person who is always desirous of fruitive results in religious or economic activities, whose only desire is sense gratification, and whose mind, life and senses are thus engaged, is in the mode of passion.

TEXT 35

यया स्वप्नं भयं शोकं विषादं मदमेव च ।
न विमुञ्चति दुर्मेधा धृतिः सा पार्थ तामसी ॥ ३५ ॥

yayā svapnaṁ bhayaṁ śokaṁ
viṣādaṁ madam eva ca
na vimuñcati durmedhā
dhṛtiḥ sā pārtha tāmasī

yayā—by which; *svapnam*—dream; *bhayam*—fearfulness; *śokam*—lamentation; *viṣādam*—moroseness; *madam*—illusion; *eva*—certainly; *ca*—also; *na*—never; *vimuñcati*—is liberated; *durmedhāḥ*—unintelligent; *dhṛtiḥ*—determination; *sā*—that; *pārtha*—O son of Pṛthā; *tāmasī*—in the mode of ignorance.

TRANSLATION

And that determination which cannot go beyond dreaming, fearfulness, lamentation, moroseness, and illusion—such unintelligent determination is in the mode of darkness.

PURPORT

It should not be concluded that a person in the mode of goodness does not dream. Here dream means too much sleep. Dream is always present; either in the mode of goodness, passion or ignorance, dream is a natural occurrence. But those who cannot avoid oversleeping, who cannot avoid the pride of enjoying material objects and who are always dreaming of lording it over the material world, whose life, mind, and senses are thus engaged, are considered to be in the mode of ignorance.

TEXTS 36-37

सुखं त्विदानीं त्रिविधं शृणु मे भरतर्षभ ।
अभ्यासाद्रमते यत्र दुःखान्तं च निगच्छति ॥ ३६ ॥
यत्तदग्रे विषमिव परिणामेऽमृतोपमम् ।
तत्सुखं सात्त्विकं प्रोक्तमात्मबुद्धिप्रसादजम् ॥ ३७ ॥

> sukhaṁ tv idānīṁ tri-vidhaṁ
> śṛṇu me bharatarṣabha
> abhyāsād ramate yatra
> duḥkhāntaṁ ca nigacchati
>
> yat tad agre viṣam iva
> pariṇāme 'mṛtopamam
> tat sukhaṁ sāttvikaṁ proktam
> ātma-buddhi-prasāda-jam

sukham—happiness; tu—but; idānīm—now; tri-vidham—three kinds; śṛṇu—hear; me—from Me; bharatarṣabha—O best amongst the Bhāratas; abhyāsāt—by practice; ramate—enjoyer; yatra—where; duḥkha—distress; antam—end; ca—also; nigacchati—gains; yat—that which; tat—that; agre—in the beginning; viṣam iva—like poison; pariṇāme—at the end; amṛta—nectar; upamam—compared to; tat—that; sukham—happiness; sāttvikam—in the mode of goodness; proktam—is said; ātma—self; buddhi—intelligence; prasāda-jam—satisfactory.

TRANSLATION

O best of the Bhāratas, now please hear from Me about the three kinds of happiness which the conditioned soul enjoys, and by which he sometimes comes to the end of all distress. That which in the beginning may be just like poison but at the end is just like nectar and which awakens one to self-realization is said to be happiness in the mode of goodness.

PURPORT

A conditioned soul tries to enjoy material happiness again and again. Thus he chews the chewed, but, sometimes, in the course of such enjoyment, he becomes relieved from material entanglement by association with a great soul. In other words, a conditioned soul is always engaged in some type of sense gratification, but when he understands by good association that it is only a repetition of the same thing, and he is awakened to his real Kṛṣṇa consciousness, he is sometimes relieved from such repetitive so-called happiness.

In the pursuit of self-realization, one has to follow many rules and regulations to control the mind and the senses and to concentrate the mind on the Self. All these procedures are very difficult, bitter like poison, but if one is successful in following the regulations and comes to the transcendental position, he begins to drink real nectar, and he enjoys life.

TEXT 38

विषयेन्द्रियसंयोगाद्यत्तदग्रेऽमृतोपमम् ।
परिणामे विषमिव तत्सुखं राजसं स्मृतम् ॥ ३८ ॥

*viṣayendriya-saṁyogād
yat tad agre 'mṛtopamam
pariṇāme viṣam iva
tat sukhaṁ rājasaṁ smṛtam*

viṣaya—objects of sense; *indriya*—senses; *saṁyogāt*—combination; *yat*—that; *tat*—which; *agre*—in the beginning; *amṛta-upamam*—just like nectar; *pariṇāme*—at the end; *viṣam iva*—like poison; *tat*—that; *sukham*—happiness; *rājasam*—in the mode of passion; *smṛtam*—is considered.

TRANSLATION

That happiness which is derived from contact of the senses with their objects and which appears like nectar at first but poison at the end is said to be of the nature of passion.

PURPORT

A young man and a young woman meet, and the senses drive the young man to see her, to touch her and to have sexual intercourse. In the beginning this may be very pleasing to the senses, but at the end, or after some time, it becomes just like poison. They are separated or there is divorce, there is lamentation, there is sorrow, etc. Such happiness is always in the mode of passion. Happiness derived from a combination of the senses and the sense objects is always a cause of distress and should be avoided by all means.

TEXT 39

यदग्रे चानुबन्धे च सुखं मोहनमात्मनः ।
निद्रालस्यप्रमादोत्थं तत्तामसमुदाहृतम् ॥ ३९ ॥

yad agre cānubandhe ca
sukhaṁ mohanam ātmanaḥ
nidrālasya-pramādottham
tat tāmasam udāhṛtam

yat—that which; agre—in the beginning; ca—also; anubandhe—by binding; ca—also; sukham—happiness; mohanam—illusion; ātmanaḥ—of the self; nidrā—sleeping; ālasya—laziness; pramāda—illusion; uttham—produced of; tat—that; tāmasam—in the mode of ignorance; udāhṛtam—is said to be.

TRANSLATION

And that happiness which is blind to self-realization, which is delusion from beginning to end and which arises from sleep, laziness and illusion is said to be of the nature of ignorance.

PURPORT

One who takes pleasure in laziness and in sleep is certainly in the mode of darkness, and one who has no idea how to act and how not to act is also in the mode of ignorance. For the person in the mode of ignorance, everything is illusion. There is no happiness either in the beginning or the end. For the person in the mode of passion there might be some kind of ephemeral happiness in the beginning and at the end distress, but for the person in the mode of ignorance there is only distress both in the beginning and at the end.

TEXT 40

न तदस्ति पृथिव्यां वा दिवि देवेषु वा पुनः ।
सत्त्वं प्रकृतिजैर्मुक्तं यदेभिः स्यात्त्रिभिर्गुणैः ॥ ४० ॥

na tad asti pṛthivyāṁ vā
divi deveṣu vā punaḥ
sattvaṁ prakṛti-jair muktaṁ
yad ebhiḥ syāt tribhir guṇaiḥ

na—not; *tat*—that; *asti*—there is; *pṛthivyām*—within the universe; *vā*—or; *divi*—in the higher planetary system; *deveṣu*—amongst the demigods; *vā*—or; *punaḥ*—again; *sattvam*—existence; *prakṛti-jaiḥ*—under the influence of material nature; *muktam*—liberated; *yat*—that; *ebhiḥ*—by this; *syāt*—so becomes; *tribhiḥ*—by three; *guṇaiḥ*—modes of material nature.

TRANSLATION

There is no being existing, either here or among the demigods in the higher planetary systems, which is freed from the three modes of material nature.

PURPORT

The Lord here summarizes the total influence of the three modes of material nature all over the universe.

TEXT 41

ब्राह्मणक्षत्रियविशां शूद्राणां च परंतप ।
कर्माणि प्रविभक्तानि स्वभावप्रभवैर्गुणैः ॥ ४१ ॥

brāhmaṇa-kṣatriya-viśāṁ
śūdrāṇāṁ ca parantapa
karmāṇi pravibhaktāni
svabhāva-prabhavair guṇaiḥ

brāhmaṇa—the *brāhmaṇas*; *kṣatriya*—the *kṣatriyas*; *viśām*—the *vaiśyas*; *śūdrāṇām*—the *śūdras*; *ca*—and; *parantapa*—O subduer of the enemies; *karmāṇi*—activities; *pravibhaktāni*—are divided; *svabhāva*—own nature; *prabhavaiḥ*—born of; *guṇaiḥ*—by the modes of material nature.

TRANSLATION

Brāhmaṇas, kṣatriyas, vaiśyas and śūdras are distinguished by their qualities of work, O chastiser of the enemy, in accordance with the modes of nature.

TEXT 42

शमो दमस्तपः शौचं क्षान्तिरार्जवमेव च ।
ज्ञानं विज्ञानमास्तिक्यं ब्रह्मकर्म स्वभावजम् ॥ ४२ ॥

śamo damas tapaḥ śaucaṁ
kṣāntir ārjavam eva ca
jñānaṁ vijñānam āstikyaṁ
brahma-karma svabhāva-jam

śamaḥ—peacefulness; *damaḥ*—self-control; *tapaḥ*—austerity; *śaucam*—purity; *kṣāntiḥ*—tolerance; *ārjavam*—honesty; *eva*—certainly; *ca*—and; *jñānam*—wisdom; *vijñānam*—knowledge; *āstikyam*—religiousness; *brahma*—of a *brāhmaṇa*; *karma*—duty; *svabhāva-jam*—born of his own nature.

TRANSLATION

Peacefulness, self-control, austerity, purity, tolerance, honesty, wisdom, knowledge, and religiousness—these are the qualities by which the brāhmaṇas work.

TEXT 43

शौर्यं तेजो धृतिर्दाक्ष्यं युद्धे चाप्यपलायनम् ।
दानमीश्वरभावश्च क्षात्रं कर्म स्वभावजम् ॥ ४३ ॥

śauryaṁ tejo dhṛtir dākṣyaṁ
yuddhe cāpy apalāyanam
dānam īśvara-bhāvaś ca
kṣātraṁ karma svabhāva-jam

śauryam—heroism; *tejaḥ*—power; *dhṛtiḥ*—determination; *dākṣyam*—resourcefulness; *yuddhe*—in battle; *ca*—and; *api*—also; *apalāyanam*—not fleeing; *dānam*—generosity; *īśvara*—leadership; *bhāvaḥ*—nature; *ca*—and *kṣātram-kṣatriya*; *karma*—duty; *svabhāva-jam*—born of his own nature.

TRANSLATION

Heroism, power, determination, resourcefulness, courage in battle, generosity, and leadership are the qualities of work for the kṣatriyas.

TEXT 44

कृषिगोरक्ष्यवाणिज्यं वैश्यकर्म स्वभावजम् ।
परिचर्यात्मकं कर्म शूद्रस्यापि स्वभावजम् ॥ ४४ ॥

kṛṣi-go-rakṣya-vāṇijyaṁ
vaiśya-karma svabhāva-jam
paricaryātmakaṁ karma
śūdrasyāpi svabhāva-jam

kṛṣi—ploughing; *go*—cows; *rakṣya*—protection; *vāṇijyam*—trade; *vaiśya*—vaiśya; *karma*—duty; *svabhāva-jam*—born of his own nature; *paricaryā*—service; *ātmakam*—nature; *karma*—duty; *śūdrasya*—of the *śūdra*; *api*—also; *svabhāva-jam*—born of his own nature.

TRANSLATION

Farming, cow protection and business are the qualities of work for the vaiśyas, and for the śūdras there is labor and service to others.

TEXT 45

स्वे स्वे कर्मण्यभिरतः संसिद्धिं लभते नरः ।
स्वकर्मनिरतः सिद्धिं यथा विन्दति तच्छृणु ॥ ४५ ॥

sve sve karmaṇy abhirataḥ
saṁsiddhiṁ labhate naraḥ
sva-karma-nirataḥ siddhiṁ
yathā vindati tac chṛṇu

sve—own; *sve*—own; *karmaṇi*—in work; *abhirataḥ*—following; *saṁsiddhim* —perfection; *labhate*—achieves; *naraḥ*—a man; *svakarma*—by his own duty; *nirataḥ*—engaged; *siddhim*—perfection; *yathā*—as; *vindati*—attains, *tat*—that; *śṛṇu*—listen.

TRANSLATION

By following his qualities of work, every man can become perfect. Now please hear from Me how this can be done.

TEXT 46

यतः प्रवृत्तिर्भूतानां येन सर्वमिदं ततम् ।
स्वकर्मणा तमभ्यर्च्य सिद्धिं विन्दति मानवः ॥ ४६ ॥

yataḥ pravṛttir bhūtānāṁ
yena sarvam idaṁ tatam
sva-karmaṇā tam abhyarcya
siddhiṁ vindati mānavaḥ

yataḥ—from whom; *pravṛttiḥ*—emanation; *bhūtānām*—of all living entities; *yena*—by whom; *sarvam*—all; *idam*—this; *tatam*—is pervaded; *svakarmaṇā*—in his own duties; *tam*—Him; *abhyarcya*—by worshiping; *siddhim*—perfection; *vindati*—achieves; *mānavaḥ*—a man.

TRANSLATION

By worship of the Lord, who is the source of all beings and who is all-pervading, man can, in the performance of his own duty, attain perfection.

PURPORT

As stated in the Fifteenth Chapter, all living beings are fragmental parts and parcels of the Supreme Lord. As such, the Supreme Lord is the beginning of all living entities. This is confirmed in the *Vedānta-sūtra*— *janmādy asya yataḥ*. The Supreme Lord is therefore the beginning of life of every living entity. And the Supreme Lord, by His two energies, His external energy and internal energy, is all-pervading. Therefore one should worship the Supreme Lord with His energies. Generally the Vaiṣṇava devotees worship the Supreme Lord with His internal energy. His external energy is a perverted reflection of the internal energy. The external energy is a background, but the Supreme Lord by the expansion of His plenary portion as Paramātmā is situated everywhere. He is the Supersoul of all demigods, all human beings, all animals, everywhere. One should therefore know that as part and parcel of the Supreme Lord it is his duty to render service unto the Supreme. Everyone should be engaged in devotional service to the Lord in full Kṛṣṇa consciousness. That is recommended in this verse.

Everyone should think that he is engaged in a particular type of occupation by Hṛṣīkeśa, the master of the senses. And, by the result of the work in which one is engaged, the Supreme Personality of Godhead, Śrī Kṛṣṇa, should be worshiped. If one thinks always in this way, in full Kṛṣṇa consciousness, then, by the grace of the Lord, he becomes fully aware of everything. That is the perfection of life. The Lord says in *Bhagavad-gītā*, *teṣām ahaṁ samuddhartā*. The Supreme Lord Himself takes charge of delivering such a devotee. That is the highest perfection of life. In whatever occupation one may be engaged, if he serves the Supreme Lord, he will achieve the highest perfection.

TEXT 47

श्रेयान्स्वधर्मो विगुणः परधर्मात्स्वनुष्ठितात् ।
स्वभावनियतं कर्म कुर्वन्नाप्नोति किल्बिषम् ॥ ४७ ॥

śreyān sva-dharmo viguṇaḥ
para-dharmāt sv-anuṣṭhitāt
svabhāva-niyataṁ karma
kurvan nāpnoti kilbiṣam

śreyān—better; *sva-dharmaḥ*—one's own occupation; *viguṇaḥ*—imperfectly performed; *para-dharmāt*—another's occupation; *svanuṣṭhitāt*—perfectly done; *svabhāva-niyatam*—prescribed duties according to one's nature; *karma*—work; *kurvan*—performing; *na*—never; *āpnoti*—achieve; *kilbiṣam*—sinful reactions.

TRANSLATION

It is better to engage in one's own occupation, even though one may perform it imperfectly, than to accept another's occupation and perform

it perfectly. Prescribed duties, according to one's nature, are never affected by sinful reactions.

PURPORT

One's occupational duty is prescribed in *Bhagavad-gītā.* As already discussed in previous verses, the duties of a *brāhmaṇa, kṣatriya, vaiśya* and *śūdra* are prescribed according to the particular modes of nature. One should not imitate another's duty. A man who is by nature attracted to the kind of work done by *śūdras* should not artificially claim himself to be a *brāhmaṇa,* although he may be born into a *brāhmaṇa* family. In this way one should work according to his own nature; no work is abominable, if performed in the service of the Supreme Lord. The occupational duty of a *brāhmaṇa* is certainly in the mode of goodness, but if a person is not by nature in the mode of goodness, he should not imitate the occupational duty of a *brāhmaṇa.* For a *kṣatriya,* or administrator, there are so many abominable things; a *kṣatriya* has to be violent to kill his enemies, and sometimes a *kṣatriya* has to tell lies for the sake of diplomacy. Such violence and duplicity accompany political affairs, but a *kṣatriya* is not supposed to give up his occupational duty and try to perform the duties of a *brāhmaṇa.*

One should act to satisfy the Supreme Lord. For example, Arjuna was a *kṣatriya.* He was hesitating to fight the other party. But if such fighting is performed for the sake of Kṛṣṇa, the Supreme Personality of Godhead, there need be no fear of degradation. In the business field also, sometimes a merchant has to tell so many lies to make a profit. If he does not do so, there can be no profit. Sometimes a merchant says, "Oh, my dear customer, for you I am making no profit," but one should know that without profit the merchant cannot exist. Therefore it should be taken as a simple lie if a merchant says that he is not making a profit. But the merchant should not think that because he is engaged in an occupation in which the telling of lies is compulsory, he should give up his profession and pursue the profession of a *brāhmaṇa.* That is not recommended. Whether one is a *kṣatriya,* a *vaiśya,* or a *śūdra* doesn't matter, if he serves, by his work, the Supreme Personality of Godhead. Even *brāhmaṇas,* who perform different types of sacrifice, sometimes must kill animals because sometimes animals are sacrificed in such ceremonies. Similarly, if a *kṣatriya* engaged in his own occupation kills an enemy, there is no sin incurred. In the Third Chapter these matters have been clearly and elaborately explained; every man should work for the purpose of *yajña,* or for Viṣṇu, the Supreme

Personality of Godhead. Anything done for personal sense gratification is a cause of bondage. The conclusion is that everyone should be engaged according to the particular mode of nature he has acquired, and he should decide to work only to serve the supreme cause of the Supreme Lord.

TEXT 48

सहजं कर्म कौन्तेय सदोषमपि न त्यजेत् ।
सर्वारम्भा हि दोषेण धूमेनाग्निरिवावृताः ॥ ४८ ॥

saha-jaṁ karma kaunteya
sa-doṣam api na tyajet
sarvārambhā hi doṣeṇa
dhūmenāgnir ivāvṛtāḥ

saha-jam—born simultaneously; *karma*—work; *kaunteya*—O son of Kuntī; *sa-doṣam*—with fault; *api*—although; *na*—never; *tyajet*—to be given up; *sarva-ārambhāḥ*—any venture; *hi*—is certainly; *doṣeṇa*—with fault; *dhūmena*—with smoke; *agniḥ*—fire; *iva*—as; *āvṛtāḥ*—covered.

TRANSLATION

Every endeavor is covered by some sort of fault, just as fire is covered by smoke. Therefore one should not give up the work which is born of his nature, O son of Kuntī, even if such work is full of fault.

PURPORT

In conditioned life, all work is contaminated by the material modes of nature. Even if one is a *brāhmaṇa*, he has to perform sacrifices in which animal killing is necessary. Similarly, a *kṣatriya*, however pious he may be, has to fight enemies. He cannot avoid it. Similarly, a merchant, however pious he may be, must sometimes hide his profit to stay in business, or he may sometimes have to do business on the black market. These things are necessary; one cannot avoid them. Similarly, even though a man is a *śūdra* serving a bad master, he has to carry out the order of the master, even though it should not be done. Despite these flaws, one should continue to carry out his prescribed duties, for they are born out of his own nature.

A very nice example is given herein. Although fire is pure, still there is smoke. Yet smoke does not make the fire impure. Even though there is smoke in the fire, fire is still considered to be the purest of all elements. If one prefers to give up the work of a *kṣatriya* and take up the occupation of a *brāhmaṇa,* he is not assured that in the occupation of a *brāhmaṇa* there are no unpleasant duties. One may then conclude that in the material world no one can be completely free from the contamination of material nature. This example of fire and smoke is very appropriate in this connection. When in wintertime one takes a stone from the fire, sometimes smoke disturbs the eyes and other parts of the body, but still one must make use of the fire despite disturbing conditions. Similarly, one should not give up his natural occupation because there are some disturbing elements. Rather, one should be determined to serve the Supreme Lord by his occupational duty in Kṛṣṇa consciousness. That is the perfectional point. When a particular type of occupation is performed for the satisfaction of the Supreme Lord, all the defects in that particular occupation are purified. When the results of work are purified, when connected with devotional service, one becomes perfect in seeing the self within, and that is self-realization.

TEXT 49

असक्तबुद्धिः सर्वत्र जितात्मा विगतस्पृहः ।
नैष्कर्म्यसिद्धिं परमां संन्यासेनाधिगच्छति ॥ ४९ ॥

asakta-buddhiḥ sarvatra
jitātmā vigata-spṛhaḥ
naiṣkarmya-siddhiṁ paramāṁ
sannyāsenādhigacchati

asakta-buddhiḥ—unattached intelligence; *sarvatra*—everywhere; *jita-ātmā*—control of the mind, *vigata-spṛhaḥ*—without material desires; *naiṣkarmya-siddhim*—perfection of non-reaction; *paramām*—supreme; *sannyāsena*—by the renounced order of life; *adhigacchati*—attains.

TRANSLATION

One can obtain the results of renunciation simply by self-control and by becoming unattached to material things and disregarding material enjoyments. That is the highest perfectional stage of renunciation.

PURPORT

Real renunciation means that one should always think himself part and parcel of the Supreme Lord. Therefore he has no right to enjoy the results of his work. Since he is part and parcel of the Supreme Lord, the results of his work must be enjoyed by the Supreme Lord. This is actually Kṛṣṇa consciousness. The person acting in Kṛṣṇa consciousness is really a *sannyāsī*, one in the renounced order of life. By such mentality, one is satisfied because he is actually acting for the Supreme. Thus he is not attached to anything material; he becomes accustomed to not taking pleasure in anything beyond the transcendental happiness derived from the service of the Lord. A *sannyāsī* is supposed to be free from the reactions of his past activities, but a person who is in Kṛṣṇa consciousness automatically attains this perfection without even accepting the so-called order of renunciation. This state of mind is called *yogārūḍha*, or the perfectional stage of *yoga*, as confirmed in the Third Chapter: *yas tv ātma-ratir eva syāt*. One who is satisfied in himself has no fear of any kind of reaction from his activity.

TEXT 50

सिद्धिं प्राप्तो यथा ब्रह्म तथाप्नोति निबोध मे ।
समासेनैव कौन्तेय निष्ठा ज्ञानस्य या परा ॥ ५० ॥

siddhiṁ prāpto yathā brahma
tathāpnoti nibodha me
samāsenaiva kaunteya
niṣṭhā jñānasya yā parā

siddhim—perfection; *prāptaḥ*—achieving; *yathā*—as; *brahma*—the Supreme; *tathā*—so; *āpnoti*—achieves; *nibodha*—try to understand; *me*—from Me; *samāsena*—summarily; *eva*—certainly; *kaunteya*—O son of Kuntī; *niṣṭhā*—stage; *jñānasya*—of knowledge; *yā*—which; *parā*—transcendental.

TRANSLATION

O son of Kuntī, learn from Me in brief how one can attain to the supreme perfectional stage, Brahman, by acting in the way which I shall now summarize.

PURPORT

The Lord describes for Arjuna how one can achieve the highest perfectional stage simply by being engaged in his occupational duty, performing that duty for the Supreme Personality of Godhead. One attains the supreme stage of Brahman simply by renouncing the result of his work for the satisfaction of the Supreme Lord. That is the process of self-realization. Actual perfection of knowledge is in attaining pure Kṛṣṇa consciousness; that is described in the following verses.

TEXTS 51-53

बुद्ध्या विशुद्धया युक्तो धृत्यात्मानं नियम्य च ।
शब्दादीन्विषयांस्त्यक्त्वा रागद्वेषौ व्युदस्य च ॥ ५१ ॥

विविक्तसेवी लघ्वाशी यतवाक्कायमानसः ।
ध्यानयोगपरो नित्यं वैराग्यं समुपाश्रितः ॥ ५२ ॥

अहङ्कारं बलं दर्पं कामं क्रोधं परिग्रहम् ।
विमुच्य निर्ममः शान्तो ब्रह्मभूयाय कल्पते ॥ ५३ ॥

buddhyā viśuddhayā yukto
dhṛtyātmānaṁ niyamya ca
śabdādīn viṣayāṁs tyaktvā
rāga-dveṣau vyudasya ca

vivikta-sevī laghv-āśī
yata-vāk-kāya-mānasaḥ
dhyāna-yoga-paro nityaṁ
vairāgyaṁ samupāśritaḥ

ahaṅkāraṁ balaṁ darpaṁ
kāmaṁ krodhaṁ parigraham
vimucya nirmamaḥ śānto
brahma-bhūyāya kalpate

buddhyā—by the intelligence; viśuddhayā—fully purified; yuktaḥ—such engagement; dhṛtyā—determination; ātmānam—self; niyamya—regulated; ca—also; śabdādīn—the sense objects, such as sound, etc.; viṣayān—sense objects; tyaktvā—giving up; rāga—attachments; dveṣau—hatred; vyudasya—having laid aside; ca—also; vivikta-sevī—living in a secluded place; laghu-āśī—eating a small quantity; yata-vāk—control of speech; kāya—body; mānasaḥ—control of the mind; dhyāna-yoga-paraḥ—always absorbed in trance; nityam—twenty-four hours a day; vairāgyam—detachment; samupāśritaḥ—taken shelter of; ahaṅkāram—false ego; balam—false strength; darpam—false pride; kāmam—lust; krodham—anger;

Plate 29. Arjuna addressed Kṛṣṇa: "You are the Supreme Brahman, the ultimate, the supreme abode and purifier." (*p. 510*)

Plate 30. "Know that all these beautiful, glorious and mighty creations spring from but a spark of My splendor." (*p. 537*)

Plate 31. The universal form. (*p. 549*)

Plate 32. At last Kṛṣṇa showed Arjuna His two-armed form. *(p. 583)*

Plate 33. Kṛṣṇa delivers His unalloyed devotee from the ocean of birth and death. (*p. 602*)

Plate 34. The three modes of material nature. (*p. 677*)

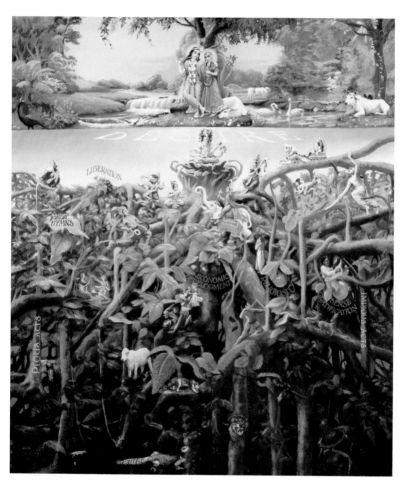

Plate 35. There is a banyan tree which has its roots upward
and its branches down. (*p. 694*)

Plate 36. The spiritual and material worlds. (p. 700)

Plate 37. The living entity in the material world carries his different conceptions of life as the air carries aromas. (*p. 704*)

Plate 38. Bewildered by false ego, strength, pride, lust and anger. *(p. 742)*

Plate 39. Lust, greed and anger are the three gates
leading down to hell. (*p. 745*)

Plate 40. There are three kinds of faith—that in the mode of goodness, that in passion, and that in ignorance. *(p. 755)*

Plate 41. The place of action, the performer, the senses, the endeavor and ultimately the Supersoul. These are the five factors of action. (*p. 790*)

Plate 42. By worship of the Lord, man can, in the performance
of his own duty, become perfect. (*p. 812*)

Plate 43. "Always think of Me and become My devotee.
Worship Me and offer your homage unto Me." *(p. 834)*

Plate 44. "Wherever there is Kṛṣṇa and Arjuna there will certainly be opulence, victory, extraordinary power and morality." (*p. 847*)

parigraham—acceptance of material things; *vimucya*—being delivered; *nirmamaḥ*—without proprietorship; *śāntaḥ*—peaceful; *brahma-bhūyāya*—to become self-realized; *kalpate*—is understood.

TRANSLATION

Being purified by his intelligence and controlling the mind with determination, giving up the objects of sense gratification, being freed from attachment and hatred, one who lives in a secluded place, who eats little and who controls the body and the tongue, and is always in trance and is detached, who is without false ego, false strength, false pride, lust, anger, and who does not accept material things, such a person is certainly elevated to the position of self-realization.

PURPORT

When one is purified by knowledge, he keeps himself in the mode of goodness. Thus one becomes the controller of the mind and is always in trance. Because he is not attached to the objects of sense gratification, he does not eat more than what he requires, and he controls the activities of his body and mind. He has no false ego because he does not accept the body as himself. Nor has he a desire to make the body fat and strong by accepting so many material things. Because he has no bodily concept of life, he is not falsely proud. He is satisfied with everything that is offered to him by the grace of the Lord, and he is never angry in the absence of sense gratification. Nor does he endeavor to acquire sense objects. Thus when he is completely free from false ego, he becomes nonattached to all material things, and that is the stage of self-realization of Brahman. That stage is called the *brahma-bhūta* stage. When one is free from the material conception of life, he becomes peaceful and cannot be agitated.

TEXT 54

ब्रह्मभूतः प्रसन्नात्मा न शोचति न काङ्क्षति ।
समः सर्वेषु भूतेषु मद्भक्तिं लभते पराम् ॥ ५४ ॥

brahma-bhūtaḥ prasannātmā
na śocati na kāṅkṣati
samaḥ sarveṣu bhūteṣu
mad-bhaktiṁ labhate parām

brahma-bhūtaḥ—being one with the Absolute; *prasanna-ātmā*—fully joyful; *na*—never; *śocati*—laments; *na*—never; *kāṅkṣati*—desires; *samaḥ*—equally disposed; *sarveṣu*—all; *bhūteṣu*—living entity; *mat-bhaktim*—My devotional service; *labhate*—gains; *parām*—transcendental.

TRANSLATION

One who is thus transcendentally situated at once realizes the Supreme Brahman. He never laments nor desires to have anything; he is equally disposed to every living entity. In that state he attains pure devotional service unto Me.

PURPORT

To the impersonalist, achieving the *brahma-bhūta* stage, becoming one with the Absolute, is the last word. But for the personalist, or pure devotee, one has to go still further to become engaged in pure devotional service. This means that one who is engaged in pure devotional service to the Supreme Lord is already in a state of liberation, called *brahma-bhūta*, oneness with the Absolute. Without being one with the Supreme, the Absolute, one cannot render service unto Him. In the absolute conception, there is no difference between the served and the servitor; yet the distinction is there, in a higher spiritual sense.

In the material concept of life, when one works for sense gratification, there is misery, but in the absolute world, when one is engaged in pure devotional service, there is no misery. The devotee in Kṛṣṇa consciousness has nothing to lament or desire. Since God is full, a living entity who is engaged in God's service, in Kṛṣṇa consciousness, becomes also full in himself. He is just like a river cleansed of all dirty water. Because a pure devotee has no thought other than Kṛṣṇa, he is naturally always joyful. He does not lament for any material loss or gain because he is full in service of the Lord. He has no desire for material enjoyment because he knows that every living entity is the fragmental part and parcel of the Supreme Lord and therefore eternally a servant. He does not see, in the material world, someone as higher and someone as lower; higher and lower positions are ephemeral, and a devotee has nothing to do with ephemeral appearances or disappearances. For him stone and gold are of equal value. This is the *brahma-bhūta* stage, and this stage is attained very easily by the pure devotee. In that stage of existence, the idea of becoming one with the Supreme Brahman and annihilating one's individuality becomes hellish, and the idea of attaining the heavenly kingdom becomes phantasmagoria, and the senses are like broken serpents' teeth. As there is no fear of a serpent with broken teeth, so there is no fear from the senses when they are automatically controlled. The world is miserable for the materially infected person, but for a devotee the entire world is as good as Vaikuṇṭha, or the spiritual sky. The highest personality in this material universe is no more significant than an ant for a devotee. Such a stage can be achieved by the mercy of Lord Caitanya, who preached pure devotional service in this age.

TEXT 55

भक्त्या मामभिजानाति यावान्यश्चास्मि तत्त्वतः ।
ततो मां तत्त्वतो ज्ञात्वा विशते तदनन्तरम् ॥ ५५ ॥

bhaktyā mām abhijānāti
yāvān yaś cāsmi tattvataḥ
tato māṁ tattvato jñātvā
viśate tad-anantaram

bhaktyā—by pure devotional service; *mām*—Me; *abhijānāti*—one can know; *yāvān*—as much as; *yaḥ ca asmi*—as I am; *tattvataḥ*—in truth; *tataḥ*—thereafter; *mām*—Me; *tattvataḥ*—by truth; *jñātvā*—knowing; *viśate*—enters; *tat*—thereafter; *anantaram*—after

TRANSLATION

One can understand the Supreme Personality as He is only by devotional service. And when one is in full consciousness of the Supreme Lord by such devotion, he can enter into the kingdom of God.

PURPORT

The Supreme Personality of Godhead, Kṛṣṇa, and His plenary portions cannot be understood by mental speculation nor by the nondevotees. If anyone wants to understand the Supreme Personality of Godhead, he has to take to pure devotional service under the guidance of a pure devotee. Otherwise, the truth of the Supreme Personality of Godhead will always be hidden. It is already stated (*nāhaṁ prakāśaḥ*) that He is not revealed to everyone. Everyone cannot understand God simply by erudite scholarship or mental speculation. Only one who is actually engaged in Kṛṣṇa consciousness and devotional service can understand what Kṛṣṇa is. University degrees are not helpful.

One who is fully conversant with the Kṛṣṇa science becomes eligible to enter into the spiritual kingdom, the abode of Kṛṣṇa. Becoming Brahman does not mean that one loses his identity. Devotional service is there, and as long as devotional service exists, there must be God, the devotee, and the process of devotional service. Such knowledge is never vanquished, even after liberation. Liberation involves getting free from the concept of material life; in spiritual life the same distinction is there, the same individuality is there, but in pure Kṛṣṇa consciousness. One should not misunderstand that the word viśate, "enters into Me," supports the monist theory that one becomes homogeneous with the impersonal Brahman. No. Viśate means that one can enter into the abode of the Supreme Lord in his individuality to engage in His association and render service unto Him. For instance, a green bird enters a green tree not to become one with the tree but to enjoy the fruits of the tree. Impersonalists generally give the example of a river flowing into the ocean and merging. This may be a source of happiness for the impersonalist, but the personalist keeps his personal individuality like an aquatic in the ocean. We find so many living entities within the ocean, if we go deep. Surface acquaintance with the ocean is not sufficient; one must have complete knowledge of the aquatics living in the ocean depths.

Because of his pure devotional service, a devotee can understand the transcendental qualities and the opulences of the Supreme Lord in truth. As it is stated in the Eleventh Chapter, only by devotional service can one understand. The same is confirmed here; one can understand the Supreme Personality of Godhead by devotional service and enter into His kingdom.

After attainment of the brahma-bhūta stage of freedom from material conceptions, devotional service begins by one's hearing about the Lord. When one hears about the Supreme Lord, automatically the brahma-bhūta stage develops, and material contamination—greediness and lust for sense enjoyment—disappears. As lust and desires disappear from the heart of a devotee, he becomes more attached to the service of the Lord, and by such attachment he becomes free from material contamination. In that state of life he can understand the Supreme Lord. This is the statement of Śrīmad-Bhāgavatam also. Also after liberation the process of bhakti or transcendental service continues. The Vedānta-sūtra confirms this: āprāyaṇāt tatrāpi hi dṛṣṭam. This means that after liberation the process of devotional service continues. In the Śrīmad-Bhāgavatam, real devotional liberation is defined as the reinstatement of the living entity in his own identity, his own constitutional position. The constitutional position is already explained: every living entity is the part and parcel fragmental portion of the Supreme Lord. Therefore his constitutional position is to serve. After liberation, this service is never stopped. Actual liberation is getting free from misconceptions of life.

TEXT 56

सर्वकर्माण्यपि सदा कुर्वाणो मद्व्यपाश्रयः ।
मत्प्रसादादवाप्नोति शाश्वतं पदमव्ययम् ॥ ५६ ॥

sarva-karmāṇy api sadā
kurvāṇo mad-vyapāśrayaḥ
mat-prasādād avāpnoti
śāśvataṁ padam avyayam

sarva—all; karmāṇi—activities; api—although; sadā—always; kurvāṇaḥ—performing; mat—under My; vyapāśrayaḥ—protection; mat—My; prasādāt—mercy; avāpnoti—achieves; śāśvatam—eternal; padam—abode; avyayam—imperishable.

TRANSLATION

Though engaged in all kinds of activities, My devotee, under My protection, reaches the eternal and imperishable abode by My grace.

PURPORT

The word mad-vyapāśrayaḥ means under the protection of the Supreme Lord. To be free from material contamination, a pure devotee acts under the direction of the Supreme Lord or His representative, the spiritual master. There is no time limitation for a pure devotee. He is always, twenty-four hours, one hundred percent engaged in activities under the direction of the Supreme Lord. To a devotee who is thus engaged in Kṛṣṇa consciousness the Lord is very, very kind. In spite of all difficulties, he is eventually placed in the transcendental abode, or Kṛṣṇaloka. He is guaranteed entrance there; there is no doubt about it. In that supreme abode, there is no change; everything is eternal, imperishable and full of knowledge.

TEXT 57

चेतसा सर्वकर्माणि मयि संन्यस्य मत्परः ।
बुद्धियोगमुपाश्रित्य मच्चित्तः सततं भव ॥ ५७ ॥

cetasā sarva-karmāṇi
mayi sannyasya mat-paraḥ
buddhi-yogam upāśritya
mac-cittaḥ satataṁ bhava

cetasā—by intelligence; *sarva-karmāṇi*—all kinds of activities; *mayi*—unto Me; *sannyasya*—giving up; *mat-paraḥ*—My protection; *buddhi-yogam*—devotional activities; *upāśritya*—taking shelter of; *mat-cittaḥ*—consciousness; *satatam*—twenty-four hours a day; *bhava*—just become.

TRANSLATION

In all activities just depend upon Me and work always under My protection. In such devotional service, be fully conscious of Me.

PURPORT

When one acts in Kṛṣṇa consciousness, he does not act as the master of the world. Just like a servant, one should act fully under the direction of the Supreme Lord. A servant has no individual independence. He acts only on the order of the master. A servant acting on behalf of the supreme master has no affection for profit and loss. He simply discharges his duty faithfully in terms of the order of the Lord. Now, one may argue that Arjuna was acting under the personal direction of Kṛṣṇa, but, when Kṛṣṇa is not present, how should one act? If one acts according to the direction of Kṛṣṇa in this book, as well as under the guidance of the representative of Kṛṣṇa, then the result will be the same. The Sanskrit word *mat-paraḥ* is very important in this verse. It indicates that one has no goal in life save and except acting in Kṛṣṇa consciousness just to satisfy Kṛṣṇa. And, while working in that way, one should think of Kṛṣṇa only: "I have been appointed to discharge this particular duty by Kṛṣṇa." While acting in such a way, one naturally has to think of Kṛṣṇa. This is perfect Kṛṣṇa consciousness. One should, however, note that, after doing something whimsically, he should not offer the result to the Supreme Lord. That sort of duty is not in the devotional service of Kṛṣṇa consciousness. One should act according to the order of Kṛṣṇa. This is a very important point. That order of Kṛṣṇa comes through disciplic succession from the bona fide spiritual master. Therefore the spiritual master's order should be taken as the prime duty of life. If one gets a bona fide spiritual master and acts according to his direction, then his perfection of life in Kṛṣṇa consciousness is guaranteed.

TEXT 58

मच्चित्तः सर्वदुर्गाणि मत्प्रसादात्तरिष्यसि ।
अथ चेत्त्वमहङ्कारान्न श्रोष्यसि विनङ्क्ष्यसि ॥ ५८ ॥

mac-cittaḥ sarva-durgāṇi
mat-prasādāt tariṣyasi
atha cet tvam ahaṅkārān
na śroṣyasi vinaṅkṣyasi

mat—My; *cittaḥ*—consciousness; *sarva*—all; *durgāṇi*—impediments; *mat*—My; *prasādāt*—My mercy; *tariṣyasi*—you will overcome; *atha*—therefore; *cet*—if; *tvam*—you; *ahaṅkārāt*—by false ego; *na*—not; *śroṣyasi*—do not hear; *vinaṅkṣyasi*—then lose yourself.

TRANSLATION

If you become conscious of Me, you will pass over all the obstacles of conditional life by My grace. If, however, you do not work in such consciousness but act through false ego, not hearing Me, you will be lost.

PURPORT

A person in full Kṛṣṇa consciousness is not unduly anxious to execute the duties of his existence. The foolish cannot understand this great freedom from all anxiety. For one who acts in Kṛṣṇa consciousness, Lord Kṛṣṇa becomes the most intimate friend. He always looks after His friend's comfort, and He gives Himself to His friend, who is so devotedly engaged working twenty-four hours a day to please the Lord. Therefore, no one should be carried away by the false ego of the bodily concept of life. One should not falsely think himself independant of the laws of material nature or free to act. He is already under strict material laws. But, as soon as he acts in Kṛṣṇa consciousness, he is liberated, free from the material perplexities. One should note very carefully that one who is not active in Kṛṣṇa consciousness is losing himself in the material whirlpool, in the ocean of birth and death. No conditioned soul actually knows what is to be done and what is not to be done, but a person who acts in Kṛṣṇa consciousness is free to act because everything is prompted by Kṛṣṇa from within and confirmed by the spiritual master.

TEXT 59

यदहङ्कारमाश्रित्य न योत्स्य इति मन्यसे ।
मिथ्यैष व्यवसायस्ते प्रकृतिस्त्वां नियोक्ष्यति ॥ ५९ ॥

yad ahaṅkāram āśritya
na yotsya iti manyase
mithyaiṣa vyavasāyas te
prakṛtis tvāṁ niyokṣyati

yat—therefore; *ahaṅkāram*—false ego; *āśritya*—taking shelter; *na*—not; *yotsya*—shall fight; *iti*—thus; *manyase*—think; *mithyā eṣaḥ*—this is all false; *vyavasāyaḥ te*—your determination; *prakṛtiḥ*—material nature; *tvām*—you; *niyokṣyati*—will engage you.

TRANSLATION

If you do not act according to My direction and do not fight, then you will be falsely directed. By your nature, you will have to be engaged in warfare.

PURPORT

Arjuna was a military man, and born of the nature of the *kṣatriya*. Therefore his natural duty was to fight. But, due to false ego, he was fearing that by killing his teacher, grandfather and friends, there would be sinful reactions. Actually he was considering himself master of his actions, as if he were directing the good and bad results of such work. He forgot that the Supreme Personality of Godhead was present there, instructing him to fight. That is the forgetfulness of the conditioned soul. The Supreme Personality gives directions as to what is good and what is bad, and one simply has to act in Kṛṣṇa consciousness to attain the perfection of life. No one can ascertain his destiny as the Supreme Lord can; therefore the best course is to take direction from the Supreme Lord and act. No one should neglect the order of the Supreme Personality of Godhead or the order of the spiritual master who is the representative of God. One should act unhesitatingly to execute the order of the Supreme Personality of Godhead—that will keep him safe under all circumstances.

TEXT 60

स्वभावजेन कौन्तेय निबद्धः स्वेन कर्मणा ।
कर्तुं नेच्छसि यन्मोहात्करिष्यस्यवशोऽपि तत् ॥ ६० ॥

svabhāva-jena kaunteya
nibaddhaḥ svena karmaṇā
kartuṁ necchasi yan mohāt
kariṣyasy avaśo 'pi tat

sva-bhāva-jena—by one's own nature; kaunteya—O son of Kuntī; nibaddhaḥ—conditioned; svena—by one's own; karmaṇā—activities; kartum—to do; na—not; icchasi—like; yat—that; mohāt—by illusion; kariṣyasi—you will act; avaśaḥ—imperceptibly; api—even; tat—that.

TRANSLATION

Under illusion you are now declining to act according to My direction. But, compelled by your own nature, you will act all the same, O son of Kuntī.

PURPORT

If one refuses to act under the direction of the Supreme Lord, then he is compelled to act by the modes in which he is situated. Everyone is under the spell of a particular combination of the modes of nature and is acting in that way. But anyone who voluntarily engages himself under the direction of the Supreme Lord becomes glorious.

TEXT 61

ईश्वरः सर्वभूतानां हृद्देशेऽर्जुन तिष्ठति ।
भ्रामयन्सर्वभूतानि यन्त्रारूढानि मायया ॥ ६१ ॥

īśvaraḥ sarva-bhūtānāṁ
hṛd-deśe 'rjuna tiṣṭhati
bhrāmayan sarva-bhūtāni
yantrārūḍhāni māyayā

īśvaraḥ—the Supreme Lord; *sarva-bhūtānām*—of all living entities; *hṛd-deśe*—in the location of the heart; *arjuna*—O Arjuna; *tiṣṭhati*—resides; *bhrāmayan*—causing to travel; *sarva-bhūtāni*—all living entities; *yantra*—machine; *ārūḍhāni*—being so placed; *māyayā*—under the spell of material energy.

TRANSLATION

The Supreme Lord is situated in everyone's heart, O Arjuna, and is directing the wanderings of all living entities, who are seated as on a machine, made of the material energy.

PURPORT

Arjuna was not the supreme knower, and his decision to fight or not to fight was confined to his limited discretion. Lord Kṛṣṇa instructed that the individual is not all in all. The Supreme Personality of Godhead, or He Himself, Kṛṣṇa, the localized Supersoul, sits in the heart directing the living being. After changing bodies, the living entity forgets his past deeds, but the Supersoul, as the knower of the past, present and future, remains the witness of all his activities. Therefore all the activities of living entities are directed by this Supersoul. The living entity gets what he deserves and is carried by the material body which is created in the material energy under the direction of the Supersoul. As soon as a living entity is placed in a particular type of body, he has to work under the spell of that bodily situation. A person seated in a high-speed motor car goes faster than one seated in a slower car, though the living entities, the drivers, may be the same. Similarly, by the order of the Supreme Soul, material nature fashions a particular type of body to a particular type of living entity to work according to his past desires. The living entity is not independent. One should not think himself independent of the Supreme Personality of Godhead. The individual is always under His control. Therefore his duty is to surrender, and that is the injunction of the next verse.

TEXT 62

तमेव शरणं गच्छ सर्वभावेन भारत ।
तत्प्रसादात्परां शान्तिं स्थानं प्राप्स्यसि शाश्वतम् ॥ ६२ ॥

tam eva śaraṇaṁ gaccha
sarva-bhāvena bhārata
tat-prasādāt parāṁ śāntiṁ
sthānaṁ prāpsyasi śāśvatam

tam—unto Him; *eva*—certainly; *śaraṇam*—surrender; *gaccha*—go; *sarva-bhāvena*—in all respects; *bhārata*—O son of Bharata; *tat-prasādāt*—by His grace; *parām*—transcendental; *śāntim*—peace; *sthānam*—abode; *prāpsyasi*—you will get; *śāśvatam*—eternal.

TRANSLATION

O scion of Bharata, surrender unto Him utterly. By His grace you will attain transcendental peace and the supreme and eternal abode.

PURPORT

A living entity should therefore surrender unto the Supreme Personality of Godhead who is situated in everyone's heart, and that will relieve him from all kinds of miseries of this material existence. By such surrender, one will not only be released from all miseries in this life, but at the end he will reach the Supreme God. The transcendental world is described in the Vedic literature as *tad viṣṇoḥ paramaṁ padam*. Since all of creation is the kingdom of God, everything material is actually spiritual, but *paramaṁ padam* specifically refers to the eternal abode, which is called the spiritual sky or Vaikuṇṭha.

In the Fifteenth Chapter of *Bhagavad-gītā* it is stated: "*Sarvasya cāham hṛdi sanniviṣṭaḥ.*" The Lord is seated in everyone's heart, so this recommendation that one should surrender unto the Supersoul sitting within means that one should surrender unto the Supreme Personality of Godhead, Kṛṣṇa. Kṛṣṇa has already been accepted by Arjuna as the Supreme. He was accepted in the Tenth Chapter as *paraṁ brahma paraṁ dhāma*. Arjuna has accepted Kṛṣṇa as the Supreme Personality of Godhead and the supreme abode of all living entities, not only because of his personal experience but also because of the evidences of great authorities like Nārada, Asita, Devala and Vyāsa.

TEXT 63

इति ते ज्ञानमाख्यातं गुह्याद्गुह्यतरं मया ।
विमृश्यैतदशेषेण यथेच्छसि तथा कुरु ॥ ६३ ॥

iti te jñānam ākhyātaṁ
guhyād guhyataraṁ mayā
vimṛśyaitad aśeṣeṇa
yathecchasi tathā kuru

iti—thus; *te*—unto you; *jñānam*—knowledge; *ākhyātam*—described; *guhyāt*—confidential; *guhyataram*—still more confidential; *mayā*—by Me; *vimṛśya*—by deliberation; *etat*—that; *aśeṣeṇa*—fully; *yathā*—as you; *icchasi*—you like; *tathā*—that; *kuru*—perform.

TRANSLATION

Thus I have explained to you the most confidential of all knowledge. Deliberate on this fully, and then do what you wish to do.

PURPORT

The Lord has already explained to Arjuna the knowledge of *brahma-bhūta*. One who is in the *brahma-bhūta* condition is joyful; he never laments, nor does he desire anything. That is due to confidential knowledge. Kṛṣṇa also discloses knowledge of the Supersoul. This is also Brahman knowledge, knowledge of Brahman, but it is superior.

Here Lord Kṛṣṇa tells Arjuna that he can do as he chooses. God does not interfere with the little independence of the living entity. In *Bhagavad-gītā*, the Lord has explained in all respects how one can elevate his living condition. The best advice imparted to Arjuna is to surrender unto the Supersoul seated within his heart. By right discrimination, one should agree to act according to the order of the Supersoul. That will help one become situated constantly in Kṛṣṇa consciousness, the highest perfectional stage of human life. Arjuna is being directly ordered by the Personality of Godhead to fight. Surrender to the Supreme Personality of Godhead is in the best interest of the living entities. It is not for the interest of the Supreme. Before surrendering, one is free to deliberate on this subject as far as the intelligence goes; that is the best way to accept the instruction of the Supreme Personality of Godhead. Such instruction comes also through the spiritual master, the bona fide representative of Kṛṣṇa.

TEXT 64

सर्वगुह्यतमं भूयः शृणु मे परमं वचः ।
इष्टोऽसि मे दृढमिति ततो वक्ष्यामि ते हितम् ॥ ६४ ॥

sarva-guhyatamaṁ bhūyaḥ
śṛṇu me paramaṁ vacaḥ
iṣṭo 'si me dṛḍham iti
tato vakṣyāmi te hitam

sarva-guhyatamam—the most confidential; *bhūyaḥ*—again; *śṛṇu*—just hear; *me*—from Me; *paramam*—the supreme; *vacaḥ*—instruction; *iṣṭaḥ asi*—you are very dear to Me; *dṛḍham*—very; *iti*—thus; *tataḥ*—therefore; *vakṣyāmi*—speaking; *te*—for your; *hitam*—benefit.

TRANSLATION

Because you are My very dear friend, I am speaking to you the most confidential part of knowledge. Hear this from Me, for it is for your benefit.

PURPORT

The Lord has given Arjuna confidential knowledge of the Supersoul within everyone's heart, and now He is giving the most confidential part of this knowledge: just surrender unto the Supreme Personality of Godhead. At the end of the Ninth Chapter He has said, "Just always think of Me." The same instruction is repeated here to stress the essence of the teachings of *Bhagavad-gītā.* This essence is not understood by a common man, but by one who is actually very dear to Kṛṣṇa, a pure devotee of Kṛṣṇa. This is the most important instruction in all Vedic literature. What Kṛṣṇa is saying in this connection is the most essential part of knowledge, and it should be carried out not only by Arjuna but by all living entities.

TEXT 65

मन्मना भव मद्भक्तो मद्याजी मां नमस्कुरु ।
मामेवैष्यसि सत्यं ते प्रतिजाने प्रियोऽसि मे ॥ ६५ ॥

man-manā bhava mad-bhakto
mad-yājī māṁ namaskuru
mām evaiṣyasi satyaṁ te
pratijāne priyo 'si me

man-manāḥ—thinking of Me; bhava—just become; mat-bhaktaḥ—My devotee; mat-yājī—My worshiper; mām—unto Me; namaskuru—offer your obeisances; mām—unto Me; eva—certainly; eṣyasi—come; satyam—truly; te—to you; pratijāne—I promise; priyaḥ—dear; asi—you are; me—My.

TRANSLATION

Always think of Me and become My devotee. Worship Me and offer your homage unto Me. Thus you will come to Me without fail. I promise you this because you are My very dear friend.

PURPORT

The most confidential part of knowledge is that one should become a pure devotee of Kṛṣṇa and always think of Him and act for Him. One should not become an official meditator. Life should be so molded that one will always have the chance to think of Kṛṣṇa. One should always act in such a way that all his daily activities are in connection with Kṛṣṇa. He should arrange his life in such a way that throughout the twenty-four hours he cannot but think of Kṛṣṇa. And the Lord's promise is that anyone who is in such pure Kṛṣṇa consciousness will certainly return to the abode of Kṛṣṇa, where he will be engaged in the association of Kṛṣṇa face to face. This most confidential part of knowledge is spoken to Arjuna because he is the dear friend of Kṛṣṇa. Everyone who follows the path of Arjuna can become a dear friend to Kṛṣṇa and obtain the same perfection as Arjuna.

These words stress that one should concentrate his mind upon Kṛṣṇa —the very form with two hands carrying a flute, the bluish boy with a beautiful face and peacock feathers in His hair. There are descriptions of Kṛṣṇa found in the Brahma-saṁhitā and other literatures. One should fix his mind on this original form of Godhead, Kṛṣṇa. He should not even divert his attention to other forms of the Lord. The Lord has multi-forms, as Viṣṇu, Nārāyaṇa, Rāma, Varāha, etc., but a devotee should concentrate his mind on the form that was present before Arjuna. Concentration of the mind on the form of Kṛṣṇa constitutes the most confidential part of knowledge, and this is disclosed to Arjuna because Arjuna is the most dear friend of Kṛṣṇa's.

TEXT 66

सर्वधर्मान्परित्यज्य मामेकं शरणं व्रज ।
अहं त्वां सर्वपापेभ्यो मोक्षयिष्यामि मा शुचः ॥ ६६ ॥

sarva-dharmān parityajya
mām ekaṁ śaraṇaṁ vraja
ahaṁ tvāṁ sarva-pāpebhyo
mokṣayiṣyāmi mā śucaḥ

sarva-dharmān—all varieties of religion; *parityajya*—abandoning; *mām*—unto Me; *ekam*—only; *śaraṇam*—surrender; *vraja*—go; *aham*—I; *tvām*—you; *sarva*—all; *pāpebhyaḥ*—from sinful reactions; *mokṣayiṣyāmi*—deliver; *mā*—not; *śucaḥ*—worry.

TRANSLATION

Abandon all varieties of religion and just surrender unto Me. I shall deliver you from all sinful reaction. Do not fear.

PURPORT

The Lord has described various kinds of knowledge, processes of religion, knowledge of the Supreme Brahman, knowledge of the Supersoul, knowledge of the different types of orders and statuses of social life, knowledge of the renounced order of life, knowledge of nonattachment, sense and mind control, meditation, etc. He has described in so many ways different types of religion. Now, in summarizing *Bhagavad-gītā*, the Lord says that Arjuna should give up all the processes that have been explained to him; he should simply surrender to Kṛṣṇa. That surrender will save him from all kinds of sinful reactions, for the Lord personally promises to protect him.

In the Eighth Chapter it was said that only one who has become free from all sinful reactions can take to the worship of Lord Kṛṣṇa. Thus one may think that unless he is free from all sinful reactions he cannot take to the surrendering process. To such doubts it is here said that even if one is not free from all sinful reactions, simply by the process of surrendering to Śrī Kṛṣṇa he is automatically freed. There is no need of strenuous effort to free oneself from sinful reactions. One should unhesitatingly accept Kṛṣṇa as the supreme savior of all living entities. With faith and love, one should surrender unto Him.

According to the devotional process, one should simply accept such religious principles that will lead ultimately to the devotional service of the Lord. One may perform a particular occupational duty according to his position in the social order, but if by executing his duty one does not come to the point of Kṛṣṇa consciousness, all his activities are in vain.

Anything that does not lead to the perfectional stage of Kṛṣṇa consciousness should be avoided. One should be confident that in all circumstances Kṛṣṇa will protect him from all difficulties. There is no need of thinking how one should keep the body and soul together. Kṛṣṇa will see to that. One should always think himself helpless and should consider Kṛṣṇa the only basis for his progress in life. As soon as one seriously engages himself in devotional service to the Lord in full Kṛṣṇa consciousness, at once he becomes freed from all contamination of material nature. There are different processes of religion and purificatory processes by cultivation of knowledge, meditation in the mystic *yoga* system, etc., but one who surrenders unto Kṛṣṇa does not have to execute so many methods. That simple surrender unto Kṛṣṇa will save him from unnecessarily wasting time. One can thus make all progress at once and be freed from all sinful reaction.

One should be attracted by the beautiful vision of Kṛṣṇa. His name is Kṛṣṇa because He is all-attractive. One who becomes attracted by the beautiful, all-powerful, omnipotent vision of Kṛṣṇa is fortunate. There are different kinds of transcendentalists—some of them are attached to the impersonal Brahman vision, some of them are attracted by the Supersoul feature, etc., but one who is attracted to the personal feature of the Supreme Personality of Godhead, and, above all, one who is attracted by the Supreme Personality of Godhead as Kṛṣṇa Himself, is the most perfect transcendentalist. In other words, devotional service to Kṛṣṇa, in full consciousness, is the most confidential part of knowledge, and this is the essence of the whole *Bhagavad-gītā*. *Karma-yogīs*, empiric philosophers, mystics, and devotees are all called transcendentalists, but one who is a pure devotee is the best of all. The particular words used here, *mā śucaḥ*, "Don't fear, don't hesitate, don't worry," are very significant. One may be perplexed as to how one can give up all kinds of religious forms and simply surrender unto Kṛṣṇa, but such worry is useless.

TEXT 67

इदं ते नातपस्काय नाभक्ताय कदाचन ।
न चाशुश्रूषवे वाच्यं न च मां योऽभ्यसूयति ॥ ६७ ॥

idaṁ te nātapaskāya
nābhaktāya kadācana
na cāśuśrūṣave vācyaṁ
na ca māṁ yo 'bhyasūyati

idam—this; *te*—you; *na*—never; *atapaskāya*—one who is not austere; *na*—never; *abhaktāya*—one who is not a devotee; *kadācana*—at any time; *na*—never; *ca*—also; *aśuśrūṣave*—one who is not engaged in devotional service; *vācyam*—to be spoken; *na*—never; *ca*—also; *mām*—unto Me; *yaḥ*—anyone; *abhyasūyati*—envious.

TRANSLATION

This confidential knowledge may not be explained to those who are not austere, or devoted, or engaged in devotional service, nor to one who is envious of Me.

PURPORT

Persons who have not undergone the austerities of the religious process, who have never attempted devotional service in Kṛṣṇa consciousness, who have not tended a pure devotee, and especially those who are conscious of Kṛṣṇa as a historical personality or who are envious of the greatness of Kṛṣṇa, should not be told this most confidential part of knowledge. It is, however, sometimes found that even demoniac persons who are envious of Kṛṣṇa, worshiping Kṛṣṇa in a different way, take to the profession of explaining *Bhagavad-gītā* in a different way to make business, but anyone who desires actually to understand Kṛṣṇa must avoid such commentaries on *Bhagavad-gītā*. Actually the purpose of *Bhagavad-gītā* is not understandable to those who are sensuous—even if one is not sensuous but is strictly following the disciplines enjoined in the Vedic scripture, if he is not a devotee, he also cannot understand Kṛṣṇa. Even when one poses himself as a devotee of Kṛṣṇa, but is not engaged in Kṛṣṇa conscious activities, he also cannot understand Kṛṣṇa. There are many persons who envy Kṛṣṇa because He has explained in *Bhagavad-gītā* that He is the Supreme and that nothing is above Him or equal to Him. There are many persons who are envious of Kṛṣṇa. Such persons should not be told of *Bhagavad-gītā*, for they cannot understand. There is no possibility of faithless persons' understanding *Bhagavad-gītā* and Kṛṣṇa. Without understanding Kṛṣṇa from the authority of a pure devotee, one should not try to comment upon *Bhagavad-gītā*.

TEXT 68

य इदं परमं गुह्यं मद्भक्तेष्वभिधास्यति ।

भक्तिं मयि परां कृत्वा मामेवैष्यत्यसंशयः ॥ ६८ ॥

ya idaṁ paramaṁ guhyaṁ
mad-bhakteṣv abhidhāsyati
bhaktiṁ mayi parāṁ kṛtvā
mām evaiṣyaty asaṁśayaḥ

yaḥ—anyone; idam—this; paramam—most; guhyam—confidential; mat—
Mine; bhakteṣu—amongst devotees of; abhidhāsyati—explains; bhaktim—
devotional service; mayi—unto Me; parām—transcendental; kṛtvā—having
done; mām—unto Me; eva—certainly; eṣyati—comes; asaṁśayaḥ—without
doubt.

TRANSLATION

For one who explains the supreme secret to the devotees, devotional
service is guaranteed, and at the end he will come back to Me.

PURPORT

Generally it is advised that Bhagavad-gītā be discussed amongst the
devotees only, for those who are not devotees will neither understand
Kṛṣṇa nor Bhagavad-gītā. Those who do not accept Kṛṣṇa as He is and
Bhagavad-gītā as it is should not try to explain Bhagavad-gītā whimsically
and become offenders. Bhagavad-gītā should be explained to persons who
are ready to accept Kṛṣṇa as the Supreme Personality of Godhead. It is a
subject matter for the devotees only and not for philosophical speculators.
Anyone, however, who tries sincerely to present Bhagavad-gītā as it is will
advance in devotional activities and reach the pure devotional state of life.
As a result of such pure devotion, he is sure to go back home, back to
Godhead.

TEXT 69

न च तस्मान्मनुष्येषु कश्चिन्मे प्रियकृत्तमः ।
भविता न च मे तस्मादन्यः प्रियतरो भुवि ॥ ६९ ॥

na ca tasmān manuṣyeṣu
kaścin me priya-kṛttamaḥ
bhavitā na ca me tasmād
anyaḥ priyataro bhuvi

na—never; *ca*—and; *tasmāt*—therefore; *manuṣyeṣu*—among mankind; *kaścit*—anyone; *me*—My; *priya-kṛttamaḥ*—more dear; *bhavitā*—will become; *na*—no; *ca*—and; *me*—My; *tasmāt*—than him; *anyaḥ*—other; *priyataraḥ*—dearer; *bhuvi*—in this world.

TRANSLATION

There is no servant in this world more dear to Me than he, nor will there ever be one more dear.

TEXT 70

अध्येष्यते च य इमं धर्म्यं संवादमावयोः ।
ज्ञानयज्ञेन तेनाहमिष्टः स्यामिति मे मतिः ॥ ७० ॥

adhyeṣyate ca ya imaṁ
dharmyaṁ saṁvādam āvayoḥ
jñāna-yajñena tenāham
iṣṭaḥ syām iti me matiḥ

adhyeṣyate—will study; *ca*—also; *yaḥ*—he; *imam*—this; *dharmyam*—sacred; *saṁvādam*—conversation; *āvayoḥ*—of ours; *jñāna*—knowledge; *yajñena*—by sacrifice; *tena*—by him; *aham*—I; *iṣṭaḥ*—worshiped; *syām*—shall be; *iti*—thus; *me*—My; *matiḥ*—opinion.

TRANSLATION

And I declare that he who studies this sacred conversation worships Me by his intelligence.

TEXT 71

श्रद्धावाननसूयश्च शृणुयादपि यो नरः ।
सोऽपि मुक्तः शुभाँल्लोकान्प्राप्नुयात्पुण्यकर्मणाम् ॥ ७१ ॥

śraddhāvān anasūyaś ca
śṛṇuyād api yo naraḥ
so 'pi muktaḥ śubhāl̐ lokān
prāpnuyāt puṇya-karmaṇām

sraddhāvan—faithful; *anasūyaḥ ca*—and not envious; *śṛṇuyāt*—does hear; *api*—certainly; *yaḥ*—who; *naraḥ*—man; *saḥ api*—he also; *muktaḥ*—being liberated; *śubhān*—auspicious; *lokān*—planets; *prāpnuyāt*—attains; *puṇya-karmaṇām*—of the past.

TRANSLATION

And one who listens with faith and without envy becomes free from sinful reaction and attains to the planets where the pious dwell.

PURPORT

In the 67th verse of this chapter, the Lord explicitly forbade the *Gītā's* being spoken to those who are envious of the Lord. In other words, *Bhagavad-gītā* is for the devotees only, but it so happens that sometimes a devotee of the Lord will hold open class, and in that class all the students are not expected to be devotees. Why do such persons hold open class? It is explained here that although everyone is not a devotee, still there are many men who are not envious of Kṛṣṇa. They have faith in Him as the Supreme Personality of Godhead. If such persons hear from a bona fide devotee about the Lord, the result is that they become at once free from all sinful reactions and after that attain to the planetary system where all righteous persons are situated. Therefore simply by hearing *Bhagavad-gītā*, even a person who does not try to be a pure devotee attains the result of righteous activities. Thus a pure devotee of the Lord gives everyone a chance to become free from all sinful reactions and to become a devotee of the Lord.

Generally those who are free from sinful reaction are righteous. Such persons very easily take to Kṛṣṇa consciousness. The word *puṇya-karmaṇām* is very significant here. This refers to the performance of great sacrifice. Those who are righteous in performing devotional service but who are not pure can attain the planetary system of the polestar, or Dhruvaloka, where Dhruva Mahārāja is presiding. He is a great devotee of the Lord, and he has a special planet which is called the polestar.

TEXT 72

कच्चिदेतच्छुतं पार्थ त्वयैकाग्रेण चेतसा ।
कच्चिदज्ञानसंमोहः प्रनष्टस्ते धनंजय ॥ ७२ ॥

kaccid etac chrutaṁ pārtha
tvayaikāgreṇa cetasā
kaccid ajñāna-sammohaḥ
praṇaṣṭas te dhanañjaya

kaccit—whether; etat—this; śrutam—heard; pārtha—O son of Pṛthā; tvayā—by you; ekāgreṇa—with full attention; cetasā—by the mind; kaccit—whether; ajñāna—ignorant; sammohaḥ—illusion; praṇaṣṭaḥ—dispelled; te—of you; dhanañjaya—O conqueror of wealth (Arjuna).

TRANSLATION

O conqueror of wealth, Arjuna, have you heard this attentively with your mind? And are your illusions and ignorance now dispelled?

PURPORT

The Lord was acting as the spiritual master of Arjuna. Therefore it was His duty to inquire from Arjuna whether he understood the whole Bhagavad-gītā in its proper perspective. If not, the Lord was ready to re-explain any point, or the whole Bhagavad-gītā if so required. Actually, anyone who hears Bhagavad-gītā from a bona fide spiritual master like Kṛṣṇa or His representative will find that all his ignorance is dispelled. Bhagavad-gītā is not an ordinary book written by a poet or fiction writer; it is spoken by the Supreme Personality of Godhead. Any person, if he is fortunate enough to hear these teachings from Kṛṣṇa or from His bona fide spiritual representative, is sure to become a liberated person and get out of the darkness of ignorance.

TEXT 73

अर्जुन उवाच ।
नष्टो मोहः स्मृतिर्लब्धा त्वत्प्रसादान्मयाच्युत ।
स्थितोऽस्मि गतसंदेहः करिष्ये वचनं तव ॥ ७३ ॥

arjuna uvāca
naṣṭo mohaḥ smṛtir labdhā
tvat-prasādān mayācyuta
sthito 'smi gata-sandehaḥ
kariṣye vacanaṁ tava

arjunaḥ uvāca—Arjuna said; naṣṭaḥ—dispelled; mohaḥ—illusion; smṛtiḥ—memory; labdhā—regained; tvat-prasādāt—by Your mercy; mayā—by me; acyuta—O infallible Kṛṣṇa; sthitaḥ—situated; asmi—I am; gata—removed; sandehaḥ—all doubts; kariṣye—I shall execute; vacanam—order; tava—Your.

TRANSLATION

Arjuna said, My dear Kṛṣṇa, O infallible one, my illusion is now gone. I have regained my memory by Your mercy, and I am now firm and free from doubt and am prepared to act according to Your instructions.

PURPORT

The constitutional position of a living entity, represented by Arjuna, is that he has to act according to the order of the Supreme Lord. He is meant for self-discipline. Śrī Caitanya Mahāprabhu says that the actual position of the living entity is that of eternal servant of the Supreme Lord. Forgetting this principle, the living entity becomes conditioned by material nature, but in serving the Supreme Lord, he becomes the liberated servant of God. The living entity's constitutional position is to be servitor; he either has to serve the illusory māyā or the Supreme Lord. If he serves the Supreme Lord, he is in his normal condition, but if he prefers to serve the illusory external energy, then certainly he will be in bondage. In illusion the living entity is serving in this material world. He is bound by his lust and desires, yet he thinks of himself as the master of the world. This is called illusion. When a person is liberated, his illusion is over, and he voluntarily surrenders unto the Supreme to act according to His desires. The last illusion, the last snare of māyā to trap the living entity, is the proposition that he is God. The living entity thinks that he is no longer a conditioned soul, but God. He is so unintelligent that he does not think that if he were God, then how could he be in doubt? That he does not consider. So that is the last snare of illusion. Actually to become free from the illusory energy is to understand Kṛṣṇa, the Supreme Personality of Godhead, and agree to act according to His order. The word mohaḥ is very important in this verse. Mohaḥ refers to that which is opposed to knowledge. Actually real knowledge is the understanding that every living being is eternally servitor of the Lord, but instead of thinking oneself in that position, the living entity thinks that he is not servant, that he is the master of this material world, for he wants to lord it over the material nature. That is his illusion. This illusion can be overcome by the mercy of the Lord or by the mercy of a pure devotee. When that illusion is over, one agrees to act in Kṛṣṇa consciousness.

Kṛṣṇa consciousness is acting according to Kṛṣṇa's order. A conditioned soul illusioned by the external energy of matter does not know that the Supreme Lord is the master who is full of knowledge and who is the proprietor of everything. Whatever He desires He can bestow upon His devotees; He is the friend of everyone, and He is especially inclined to His devotee. He is the controller of this material nature and of all living entities. He is also the controller of inexhaustible time, and He is full of all opulences and all potencies. The Supreme Personality of Godhead can even give Himself to the devotee. One who does not know Him is under the spell of illusion; he does not become a devotee, but a servitor of *māyā*. Arjuna, however, after hearing *Bhagavad-gītā* from the Supreme Personality of Godhead, became free from all illusion. He could understand that Kṛṣṇa was not only his friend, but the Supreme Personality of Godhead. And he understood Kṛṣṇa factually. So to study *Bhagavad-gītā* is to understand Kṛṣṇa factually. When a person is in full knowledge, he naturally surrenders to Kṛṣṇa. When Arjuna understood that it was Kṛṣṇa's plan to reduce the unnecessary increase of population, he agreed to fight according to Kṛṣṇa's desire. He again took up his weapons—his arrows and bow—to fight under the order of the Supreme Personality of Godhead.

TEXT 74

सञ्जय उवाच ।
इत्यहं वासुदेवस्य पार्थस्य च महात्मनः ।
संवादमिममश्रौषमद्भुतं रोमहर्षणम् ॥ ७४ ॥

> *sañjaya uvāca*
> *ity ahaṁ vāsudevasya*
> *pārthasya ca mahātmanaḥ*
> *saṁvādam imam aśrauṣam*
> *adbhutaṁ roma-harṣaṇam*

sañjayaḥ uvāca—Sañjaya said; *iti*—thus; *aham*—I; *vāsudevasya*—of Kṛṣṇa; *pārthasya*—of Arjuna; *ca*—also; *mahātmanaḥ*—two great souls; *saṁvādam*—discussing; *imam*—this; *aśrauṣam*—heard; *adbhutam*—wonder; *roma-harṣaṇam*—hair standing on end.

TRANSLATION

Sañjaya said: Thus have I heard the conversation of two great souls, Kṛṣṇa and Arjuna. And so wonderful is that message that my hair is standing on end.

PURPORT

In the beginning of *Bhagavad-gītā*, Dhṛtarāṣṭra inquired from his secretary Sañjaya, "What happened in the Battlefield of Kurukṣetra?" The entire study was related to the heart of Sañjaya by the grace of his spiritual master, Vyāsa. He thus explained the theme of the battlefield. The conversation was wonderful because such an important conversation between two great souls never took place before and would not take place again. It is wonderful because the Supreme Personality of Godhead is speaking about Himself and His energies to the living entity, Arjuna, a great devotee of the Lord. If we follow in the footsteps of Arjuna to understand Kṛṣṇa, then our life will be happy and successful. Sañjaya realized this, and as he began to understand it, he related the conversation to Dhṛtarāṣṭra. Now it is concluded that wherever there is Kṛṣṇa and Arjuna, there is victory.

TEXT 75

व्यासप्रसादाच्छ्रुतवानेतद्गुह्यमहं परम् ।
योगं योगेश्वरात्कृष्णात्साक्षात्कथयतः स्वयम् ॥ ७५ ॥

vyāsa-prasādāc chrutavān
etad guhyam ahaṁ param
yogaṁ yogeśvarāt kṛṣṇāt
sākṣāt kathayataḥ svayam

vyāsa-prasādāt—by the mercy of Vyāsadeva; *śrutavān*—heard; *etat*—this; *guhyam*—confidential; *aham*—I; *param*—the supreme; *yogam*—mysticism; *yogeśvarāt*—from the master of all mysticism; *kṛṣṇāt*—from Kṛṣṇa; *sākṣāt*—directly; *kathayataḥ*—speaking; *svayam*—personally.

TRANSLATION

By the mercy of Vyāsa, I have heard these most confidential talks directly from the master of all mysticism, Kṛṣṇa, who was speaking personally to Arjuna.

PURPORT

Vyāsa was the spiritual master of Sañjaya, and Sañjaya admits that it was by his mercy that he could understand the Supreme Personality of Godhead. This means that one has to understand Kṛṣṇa not directly but through the medium of the spiritual master. The spiritual master is the transparent medium, although it is true that the experience is direct. This is the mystery of the disciplic succession. When the spiritual master is bona fide, then one can hear Bhagavad-gītā directly, as Arjuna heard it. There are many mystics and yogīs all over the world, but Kṛṣṇa is the master of all yoga systems. Kṛṣṇa's instruction is explicitly stated in Bhagavad-gītā— surrender unto Kṛṣṇa. One who does so is the topmost yogī. This is confirmed in the last verse of the Sixth Chapter. Yoginām api sarveṣām.

Nārada is the direct disciple of Kṛṣṇa and the spiritual master of Vyāsa. Therefore Vyāsa is as bona fide as Arjuna because he comes in the disciplic succession, and Sañjaya is the direct disciple of Vyāsa. Therefore by the grace of Vyāsa, his senses were purified, and he could see and hear Kṛṣṇa directly. One who directly hears Kṛṣṇa can understand this confidential knowledge. If one does not come to the disciplic succession, he cannot hear Kṛṣṇa; therefore his knowledge is always imperfect, at least as far as understanding Bhagavad-gītā is concerned.

In Bhagavad-gītā, all the yoga systems, karma-yoga, jñāna-yoga and bhakti-yoga, are explained. Kṛṣṇa is the master of all such mysticism. It is to be understood, however, that as Arjuna was fortunate enough to understand Kṛṣṇa directly, similarly, by the grace of Vyāsa, Sañjaya was also able to hear Kṛṣṇa directly. Actually there is no difference in hearing directly from Kṛṣṇa or hearing directly from Kṛṣṇa via a bona fide spiritual master like Vyāsa. The spiritual master is the representative of Vyāsadeva also. According to the Vedic system, on the birthday of the spiritual master, the disciples conduct the ceremony called Vyāsa-pūjā.

TEXT 76

राजन्संस्मृत्य संस्मृत्य संवादमिममद्भुतम् ।
केशवार्जुनयोः पुण्यं हृष्यामि च मुहुर्मुहुः ॥ ७६ ॥

rājan saṁsmṛtya saṁsmṛtya
saṁvādam imam adbhutam
keśavārjunayoḥ puṇyaṁ
hṛṣyāmi ca muhur muhuḥ

rājan—O King; *saṁsmṛtya*—remembering; *saṁsmṛtya*—remembering; *saṁvādam*—message; *imam*—this; *adbhutam*—wonderful; *keśava*—Lord Kṛṣṇa; *arjunayoḥ*—and Arjuna; *puṇyam*—pious; *hṛṣyāmi*—taking pleasure; *ca*—also; *muhuḥ muhuḥ*—always, repeatedly.

TRANSLATION

O King, as I repeatedly recall this wondrous and holy dialogue between Kṛṣṇa and Arjuna, I take pleasure, being thrilled at every moment.

PURPORT

The understanding of *Bhagavad-gītā* is so transcendental that anyone who becomes conversant with the topics of Arjuna and Kṛṣṇa becomes righteous, and he cannot forget such talks. This is the transcendental position of spiritual life. In other words, one who hears the *Gītā* from the right source, directly from Kṛṣṇa, attains full Kṛṣṇa consciousness. The result of Kṛṣṇa consciousness is that one becomes increasingly enlightened, and he enjoys life with a thrill, not only for some time, but at every moment.

TEXT 77

तच्च संस्मृत्य संस्मृत्य रूपमत्यद्भुतं हरेः ।
विस्मयो मे महानराजन्हृष्यामि च पुनः पुनः ॥ ७७ ॥

tac ca saṁsmṛtya saṁsmṛtya
rūpam aty-adbhutaṁ hareḥ
vismayo me mahān rājan
hṛṣyāmi ca punaḥ punaḥ

tat—that; *ca*—also; *saṁsmṛtya*—remembering; *saṁsmṛtya*—remembering; *rūpam*—form; *ati*—great; *adbhutam*—wonderful; *hareḥ*—of Lord Kṛṣṇa; *vismayaḥ*—wonder; *me*—my; *mahān*—great; *rājan*—O King, *hṛṣyāmi*—enjoying; *ca*—also; *punaḥ punaḥ*—repeatedly.

TRANSLATION

O King, when I remember the wonderful form of Lord Kṛṣṇa, I am struck with even greater wonder, and I rejoice again and again.

PURPORT

It appears that Sañjaya also, by the grace of Vyāsa, could see the universal form of Kṛṣṇa exhibited to Arjuna. It is, of course, said that Lord Kṛṣṇa never exhibited such a form before. It was exhibited to Arjuna only, yet some great devotees could also see the universal form of Kṛṣṇa when it was shown to Arjuna, and Vyāsa was one of them. He is one of the great devotees of the Lord, and he is considered to be a powerful incarnation of Kṛṣṇa. Vyāsa disclosed this to his disciple, Sañjaya, who remembered that wonderful form of Kṛṣṇa exhibited to Arjuna and enjoyed it repeatedly.

TEXT 78

यत्र योगेश्वरः कृष्णो यत्र पार्थो धनुर्धरः ।
तत्र श्रीर्विजयो भूतिर्ध्रुवा नीतिर्मतिर्मम ॥ ७८ ॥

yatra yogeśvaraḥ kṛṣṇo
yatra pārtho dhanur-dharaḥ
tatra śrīr vijayo bhūtir
dhruvā nītir matir mama

yatra—where; *yogeśvaraḥ*—the master of mysticism; *kṛṣṇaḥ*—Lord Kṛṣṇa; *yatra*—where; *pārthaḥ*—the son of Pṛthā; *dhanur-dharaḥ*—the carrier of the bow and arrow; *tatra*—there; *śrīḥ*—opulence; *vijayaḥ*—victory; *bhūtiḥ*—exceptional power; *dhruvā*—certainly; *nītiḥ*—morality; *matiḥ mama*—is my opinion.

TRANSLATION

Wherever there is Kṛṣṇa, the master of all mystics, and wherever there is Arjuna, the supreme archer, there will also certainly be opulence, victory, extraordinary power, and morality. That is my opinion.

PURPORT

The *Bhagavad-gītā* began with an inquiry of Dhṛtarāṣṭra. He was hopeful of the victory of his sons, assisted by great warriors like Bhīṣma, Droṇa and Karṇa. He was hopeful that the victory would be on his side. But, after describing the scene in the battlefield, Sañjaya told the King, "You are thinking of victory, but my opinion is that where Kṛṣṇa and Arjuna are present, there will be all good fortune." He directly confirmed that Dhṛtarāṣṭra could not expect victory for his side. Victory was certain for the side of Arjuna because Kṛṣṇa was there. Kṛṣṇa's acceptance of the post of charioteer for Arjuna was an exhibition of another opulence. Kṛṣṇa is full of all opulences, and renunciation is one of them. There are many instances of such renunciation, for Kṛṣṇa is also the master of renunciation.

The fight was actually between Duryodhana and Yudhiṣṭhira. Arjuna was fighting on behalf of his elder brother, Yudhiṣṭhira. Because Kṛṣṇa and Arjuna were on the side of Yudhiṣṭhira, Yudhiṣṭhira's victory was certain. The battle was to decide who would rule the world, and Sañjaya predicted that the power would be transferred to Yudhiṣṭhira. It is also predicted here that Yudhiṣṭhira, after gaining victory in this battle, would flourish more and more because he was not only righteous and pious, but he was a strict moralist. He never spoke a lie during his life.

There are many less intelligent persons who take Bhagavad-gītā to be a discussion of topics between two friends in a battlefield. But such a book cannot be scripture. Some may protest that Kṛṣṇa incited Arjuna to fight, which is immoral, but the reality of the situation is clearly stated: Bhagavad-gītā is the supreme instruction in morality. The supreme instruction of morality is stated in the Ninth Chapter, in the thirty-fourth verse: manmanā bhava mad-bhaktaḥ. One must become a devotee of Kṛṣṇa, and the essence of all religion is to surrender unto Kṛṣṇa, as stated, Sarva-dharmān. The instructions of Bhagavad-gītā constitute the supreme process of religion and of morality. All other processes may be purifying and may lead to this process, but the last instruction of the Gītā is the last word in all morality and religion: surrender unto Kṛṣṇa. This is the verdict of the Eighteenth Chapter.

From Bhagavad-gītā we can understand that to realize oneself by philosophical speculation and by meditation is one process, but to fully surrender unto Kṛṣṇa is the highest perfection. This is the essence of the teachings of Bhagavad-gītā. The path of regulative principles according to the orders of social life and according to the different courses of religion may be a confidential path of knowledge in as far as the rituals of religion are confidential, but one is still involved with meditation and cultivation of knowledge. Surrender unto Kṛṣṇa in devotional service in full Kṛṣṇa consciousness is the most confidential instruction and is the essence of the Eighteenth Chapter.

Another feature of Bhagavad-gītā is that the actual truth is the Supreme Personality of Godhead, Kṛṣṇa. Absolute Truth is realized in three features—impersonal Brahman, localized Paramātmā, and the Supreme Personality of Godhead, Kṛṣṇa. Perfect knowledge of the Absolute Truth means perfect knowledge of Kṛṣṇa. If one understands Kṛṣṇa, then all the departments of knowledge are part and parcel of that understanding. Kṛṣṇa is transcendental, for He is always situated in His eternal internal potency. The living entities are manifested and are divided into two classes, eternally conditioned and eternally liberated. Such living entities are innumerable, and they are considered fundamental parts of Kṛṣṇa. Material energy is manifested into twenty-four divisions. The creation is effected by eternal time, and it is created and dissolved by external energy. This manifestation of the cosmic world repeatedly becomes visible and invisible.

In *Bhagavad-gītā* five principal subject matters have been discussed: the Supreme Personality of Godhead, material nature, the living entities, eternal time and all kinds of activities. All of these are dependent on the Supreme Personality of Godhead, Kṛṣṇa. All conceptions of the Absolute Truth, namely, impersonal Brahman, localized Paramātmā, or any other transcendental conception, exist within the category of understanding the Supreme Personality of Godhead. Although superficially the Supreme Personality of Godhead, the living entity, material nature and time appear to be different, nothing is different from the Supreme. But the Supreme is always different from everything. Lord Caitanya's philosophy is that of "inconceivably one and different." This system of philosophy constitutes perfect knowledge of the Absolute Truth.

The living entity in his original position is pure spirit. He is just like an atomic particle of the Supreme Spirit. The conditioned living entity, however, is the marginal energy of the Lord; he tends to be in contact with both the material energy and the spiritual energy. In other words, the living entity is situated between the two energies of the Lord, and because he belongs to the superior energy of the Lord, he has a particle of independence. By proper use of that independence he comes under the direct order of Kṛṣṇa. Thus he attains his normal condition in the pleasure-giving potency.

Thus end the Bhaktivedanta Purports to the Eighteenth Chapter of the Śrīmad-Bhagavad-gītā *in the matter of its Conclusions—the Perfection of Renunciation.*

Appendixes

Picture Index

The illustrations of Bhagavad-gītā As It Is were painted by members of the International Society for Krishna Consciousness working under the personal direction of the author, their spiritual master, In the following descriptive index, the numbers in boldface type which follow each plate number refer to the chapter and verse of the Gītā that the picture illustrates.

Chapter 1

Plate 1   **1.1**   Dhṛtarāṣṭra is on the throne, and Sañjaya, his secretary, is describing what is taking place on the Battlefield of Kurukṣetra. Because of Sañjaya's mystic powers, the discourse on the battlefield between Kṛṣṇa and Aijuna is revealed in his heart.

Plate 2   **1.3**   Dronācārya is seated in his tent, and Duryodhana is pointing to the two armies outside.

Plate 3   **1.3**   A view of the military phalanx on the Battlefield of Kurukṣetra. The chariot of Kṛṣṇa and Arjuna is in the midst of the two armies.

Plate 4   **1.14**   Kṛṣṇa blows His transcendental conchshell to herald the battle. Arjuna is seen in the background.

Plate 5   **1.26-29** Arjuna laments upon seeing his relatives standing opposed to him in battle. Kṛṣṇa, smiling, is ready to console His friend by His transcendental teachings.

Plate 6   1.33-35 Draupadī, the wife of the Pāṇḍava brothers (Arjuna Mahārāja Yudhiṣṭhira, Bhīma, Sahadeva and Nakula), is being disrobed by Duryodhana and Duḥśāsana, two sons of Dhṛtarāṣṭra, after being lost to them in a gambling match. Dhṛtarāṣṭra is sitting on the throne. Kṛṣṇa is becoming Draupadī's infinite robe to save her from being seen naked by the assembly. Because of this incident and other offenses to the Pāṇḍavas, Kṛṣṇa wanted the battle to take place and the miscreants to be killed.

Chapter 2

Plate 7   2.11 A devotee of the Lord comes upon a man lying dead on the ground and beside him two other men in conditions of bodily misery.

Plate 8   2.13 The conditioned spirit soul is seen changing bodies from childhood to youth to old age to death and then into the womb of another mother. Verse 22 is also illustrated by this same picture. Above, a man is changing garments, and below the soul is changing bodies.

Plate 9   2.13 The many, many frames on a reel of movie film, when seen consecutively, appear as one picture on the screen, although there are actually many different pictures. Similarly, we see a man as localized (above), but actually his body is changing at every second. All this is happening without the notice of the viewer. However, the soul within the heart (seen as a sparkling star) does not change; he remains eternally the same.

Plate 10   2.22 The bird on the left is captivated by the fruits of the tree, while the friendly bird on the right acts as witness. Similarly, the embodied living entity enjoys or suffers the fruits of his material activities, while the friendly Supersoul acts as witness and waits for His friend to turn to Him.

Plate 11   2.62-63 The path of destruction of the conditioned soul's intelligence due to the dictation of the senses and mind is portrayed.

Chapter 3

Plate 12   3.10 Lord Caitanya, wearing yellow robes, leads thousands of followers in the congregational chanting of the holy names of Śrī Kṛṣṇa. His four associates are:

    a) Nityānanda Prabhu, wearing purple robes, at Lord Caitanya's immediate right.

    b) Advaita Prabhu, wearing white robes, at Nityānanda's immediate right.

    c) Gadādhara Pandit at Lord Caitanya's immediate left.

    d) Śrīvāsa Pānflit at Gadādhara's immediate left.

Plate 13   **3.12** Devotees are pictured engaging in *saskīrtana-yajña*. Above the clouds are the demigods, and above them the Lord, who is pleased by the singing of His holy names. The demigods are, left to right, Candra (the moon-god), Indra (the god of rain), Vivasvān (the sun-god) and Vāyu (the god of air). At the far right is Lakṣmī, the goddess of fortune.

Plate 14   **3.37-39** The living entity in the center is being enveloped by fiery lust. The analogy in verse 38 is illustrated here. At the top is fire covered by smoke, symbolizing human life. At the bottom left is a mirror covered by dust, symbolizing animal life. At the bottom right is an embryo covered by the womb, symbolizing tree and plant life.

Chapter 4

Plate 15   **4.1** At the top, Kṛṣṇa teaches the science of *Bhagavad-gītā* to Vivasvān, the sun-god. Below, Vivasvān teaches his son, Manu, and in the circle at the right, Manu teaches his son, Ikṣvāku.

Plate 16   **4.7** In the center square, Kṛṣṇa is shown in His original two-handed form, holding a flute. Surrounding Him are ten of His eternal incarnations, pictured in the order in which they appeared in the material world, beginning clockwise from the lower left-hand corner.

    a) Matsya, the fish incarnation, is saving the *Vedas*.

    b) Kūrma, the tortoise incarnation, is holding the hill on His back.

    c) Varāha, the boar incarnation, is fighting with the demon Hiraṇyākṣa.

    d) Nṛsiṁhadeva, the lion incarnation, is killing the demon Hiraṇyakaśipu.

    e) Vāmanadeva, the dwarf incarnation, is begging some land from King Bali.

    f) Paraśurāma is killing the demoniac *kṣatriyas*.

    g) Lord Rāmacandra is going off into exile with His wife, Sītā, and brother, Lakṣmaṇa.

    h) Kṛṣṇa is lifting Govardhana Hill, and beside Him is His brother, Balarāma.

    i) Lord Buddha.

    j) Lord Kalki is riding on His horse, killing all the demons and thus liberating them.

Plate 17   **4.8**   Kṛṣṇa's uncle, Kamsa, is being killed by the Lord. Balarāma, Kṛṣṇa's brother, is standing on Kṛṣṇa's right. Behind Kṛṣṇa are His parents, Devakī and Vasudeva, who were imprisoned by Kamsa but are here freed by their son. This scene takes place in Kamsa's wrestling arena in Mathurā province.

Plate 18   **4.11**   At the top Kṛṣṇa is dancing with His purest devotees as a lover. On the lotus petals the Lord is reciprocating with His devotees as a son, as a friend and as a master. Below left, a devotee in the material world is associating with Kṛṣṇa personally by painting His transcendental form. Next, an impersonalist, by his meditation, is merging with the *brahmajyoti*, the spiritual effulgence emanating from the Lord's body. On the right a mystic *yogi* is walking on the water. On the far right a fruitive worker is receiving the fruits of his labor.

Chapter 5

Plate 19   **5.4-6**   Above, a devotee is engaged in various devotional activities for the Deities (authorized incarnations of the Lord, who comes in this form to accept our service). Below, a *sāṅkhya-yogī* engages in the analytical study of matter and spirit. After some time he realizes the Lord (the forms of Rādhā and Kṛṣṇa include all other forms of the Lord) within his heart, and then he engages in devotional service. The end is the same—devotional service.

Plate 20   **5.18**   A sage sees the Supersoul accompanying the sparklike individual soul in each body.

Chapter 6

Plate 21   **6.11-14**   The goal of *yoga* is seen as Viṣṇu in the *yogī's* heart.

Plate 22   **6.24**   The little sparrow is shown here trying to drink up the ocean to retrieve her eggs. Because of her determination, Lord Visnu has sent Garuḍa, who is standing behind her, to threaten the ocean into giving up the eggs.

Plate 23   6.34   The chariot of the body. The five horses represent the five senses (tongue, eyes, ears, nose and skin). The reins, the driving instrument, symbolize the mind, the driver is the intelligence, and the passenger is the spirit soul.

Plate 24   6.47   Śyāmasundara, the object of the ideal *yogī's* meditation.

Chapter 7

Plate 25   7.4-5   Spirit soul sustains the material universe of earth, water, fire, etc. (represented as the body). The subtle body—mind, intelligence and false ego—is represented by the red dot on the forehead. The soul is seated in the heart of the gross body.

Plate 26   7.15-16   At the top Laksml-Nārāyana are shown in the Lord's transcendental abode. Below are four kinds of miscreants who do not surrender to God and four kinds of pious men who turn to Him in devotional service.

Chapter 8

Plate 27   8.21   Kṛṣṇa brings His thousands of *surabhi* cows back home from the fields at the end of the day.

Chapter 9

Plate 28   9.11   The fools mock the humanlike form of Lord Kṛṣṇa, but the devotee offers his obeisances. Behind Kṛṣṇa are Mahā-Visnu, Garbhodakaśāyī Viṣṇu and the entire cosmic manifestation—all working Under Kṛṣṇa's direction.

Chapter 10

Plate 29   10.12-13   Arjuna offers prayers to Kṛṣṇa.

Plate 30   10.41   A sampling of Kṛṣṇa's infinite manifestations, both in the spiritual and material worlds. Outer circle, clockwise (beginning from the upper left-hand corner): Indra carrying the thunderbolt, the Himalayas, Lord Siva with the Ganges River in his hair, the moon, the horse Ucchaihśravā, the transcendental *om*, Kapila, Rāma, flower-bearing

Spring, Kāmadhuk, Arjuna, Vyāsadeva, Prahlāda, the shark, Vāsuki, Skanda, Varuṇa, Yamarāja, the lion, Kuvera, Agni and Airāvata. Inner circle, clockwise (beginning from four-headed Lord Brahmā sitting on the lotus flower): Brahmā, Nārada, Garuḍa, the sun, the ocean, Lord Viṣṇu, Ananta, and the chanting of the holy names—Hare Kṛṣṇa, Hare Kṛṣṇa, Kṛṣṇa Kṛṣṇa, Hare Hare/ Hare Rāma, Hare Rāma, Rāma Rāma, Hare Hare.

Chapter 11

Plate 31 **11.13** Kṛṣṇa's universal form is displayed to Arjuna. Still the Lord does not lose His original eternal identity. He remains seated on the chariot with Arjuna.

Plate 32 **11.50** After showing Arjuna His universal form, Kṛṣṇa shows him His four-handed Nārāyaṇa form in which He presides over all the spiritual planets. Then He changes to His two-handed form to show everyone that He is the source of the universe and the source of Nārāyaṇa.

Chapter 12

Plate 33 12.6-7 Kṛṣṇa is riding towards the devotee on Garuḍa, His feathered carrier, in order to lift him out of the ocean of birth and death.

Chapter 14

Plate 34 14.14, 15, 18 Life in the higher planetary system, life in the society of human beings and life in the animal kingdom are portrayed.

Chapter 15

Plate 35 **15.1-3** Kṛṣṇa and His eternal consort, Rādhārāṇī, are shown in Their eternal abode, Goloka Vṛndāvana. The upside-down tree below Them is the banyan tree, representing the material world, which is a perverted reflection of the spiritual world. The demigods are on the top branches, the human beings are on the middle branches, and the animals are on the lower branches. On the right, a man is disentangling himself from the tree by cutting it with the weapon of detachment.

Plate 36   15.6   The huge lotus is the original spiritual planet, Goloka Vṛndāvana, the abode of Rādhā and Kṛṣṇa. The spiritual effulgence around this planet is the *brahmajyoti*, which is the ultimate goal of the impersonalists. Within the unlimited *brahmajyoti* are innumerable spiritual planets which are dominated by plenary expansions of Lord Kṛṣṇa and inhabited by ever-liberated living beings. Sometimes a spiritual cloud overtakes a corner of the spiritual sky, and the covered portion is called *mahat-tattva*, or the material sky. The Lord, as Mahā-Viṣṇu, lies down in the water within the *mahat-tattva*, which is called the Causal Ocean. While Lord Viṣṇu sleeps, innumerable universes generate from His breathing and float all over the Causal Ocean. Mahā-Viṣṇu enters each universe as Garbhodakaśāyī Viṣṇu and lies in the Garbha Ocean on the serpentine Śeṣa incarnation. From His navel a lotus stem sprouts, and on the lotus, Brahmā, the lord of the universe, is born. Brahmā creates all the living beings in different shapes in terms of their desires within the universe. He also creates the sun, moon and other demigods.

Plate 37   15.8   Top section: On the left, a boy is dancing before the Deities of Rādhā-Kṛṣṇa. The result of such devotional consciousness is shown on the right, where he is dancing with Kṛṣṇa as a playmate in the Lord's spiritual abode. Second section: On the left a man is offering charity to a *brāhmaṇa*; on the right he has taken the body of a demigod and is enjoying heavenly delights. Third section: A man is eating meat and other abominable foods; in his next life he is seen in the body of a hog who eats anything and everything. Bottom section: A man is approaching a woman with lust. This bestial consciousness carries him to a dog's body.

Chapter 16

Plate 38   16.5, 21   Two men (standing where the stairway makes its turn) are being offered both liberation and bondage. One man looks upward, following the spiritual master who points towards Śrī Rādhā-Kṛṣṇa. The other man embraces the demoniac qualities by accepting the garland offered by Māyā, Kṛṣṇa's illusory energy. Drawn by ropes which are held by the personifications of lust, greed and anger, he follows her down the steps. At the bottom he is reaching for Māyā, and gliding towards hell.

Plate 39   16.10-18   A sample of the demoniac qualities is illustrated here.

Chapter 17

Plate 40   17.4   On the top, three demigods, Vivasvān, Brahmā and Lord Śiva, are being worshiped by their respective devotees. Just below, a man is worshiping a famous mundane personality. At the bottom, women are worshiping a tree which is inhabited by a ghost, and a man is worshiping the tomb of a dead man.

Chapter 18

Plate 41   18.14   Endeavor means energy which is employed. For anything one does there must be some activity; that is the endeavor. The place must be favorable, the activities must be authorized, the doer (the man who is acting) must be expert, the instruments must be fit, and the help from the Supersoul must be adequate. These are the five causes for success, and the opposite are the five factors for failure.

Here a man is conducting business. If he goes to the marketplace it will be very nice, since there are so many customers. Similarly, one looking for spiritual life goes to where there are devotees and associates with them. One must go to a particular type of place for a particular type of activity, and the person acting must be well versed, or expert, just like an expert salesman whose method of business is bona fide. The senses must be in order, to guard against cheating, hear offers, etc. Above all is the help from Supersoul, who dictates in such a way that everything is successful, spiritually or materially. Among the five factors portrayed here, the endeavor is the business which is being conducted.

Plate 42   18.41-46   While engaged in their prescribed duties, these four representatives of the four social orders (*varṇas*) are thinking of Lord Kṛṣṇa and offering Him the results of their work.

Plate 43   18.65   Gopāla Kṛṣṇa, the beautiful original form of the Lord.

Plate 44   18.78   Arjuna's illusion is now gone, and he is acting according to Kṛṣṇa's instructions. Kṛṣṇa, the driver of countless universes, is driving the chariot of Arjuna.

References

The statements of *Bhagavad-gītā As It Is* are all confirmed by standard Vedic authorities. The following authentic scriptures are quoted in *Bhagavad-gītā As It Is* on the pages listed.

Atharva-veda:
503

Bhakti-rasāmṛta-sindhu (Rūpa Gosvāmī):
231, 274, 318, 340, 366, 387, 592

Brahma-saṁhitā:
12-13, 74, 176, 214, 220, 228, 323, 339, 372, 451, 457, 459, 637

Bṛhan-Nāradīya Purāṇa:
320

Caitanya-caritamrta (Kṛṣṇadāsa Kavirāja Gosvāmī):
24, 82, 125, 226, 227

Garga Upaniṣad:
80, 454

Kaṭha Upaniṣad:
86-87, 99, 100, 111, 371

Kūrma Purāṇa:
489

Mādhyandi-nāyana-śruti:
703

Mahābhārata:
215

Mokṣa-dharma:
504

Muṇḍaka Upaniṣad:
95, 102-103

Nārada-pañcarātra:
340

Nārāyaṇīya:
603

Nirukti (Vedic dictionary):
128-129

Padma Purāṇa:
  297, 316, 366
Parāśara-smṛti:
  115
Pauruṣa:
  716
Śrīmad-Bhāgavatam:
  55, 66, 73-74, 95, 120, 124, 131, 136, 147-148, 166, 172, 189, 204,
  208-209, 233, 260, 262, 273, 297, 301, 322, 327, 350-351, 355-356,
  359, 363, 369, 390, 400, 442, 446, 516-517, 519, 611, 634, 756
Svatvata Tantra:
  367
Śvetāśvatara Upaniṣad:
  94, 187, 286, 372, 391, 638, 642
Taittirīya Upaniṣad:
  394, 641
Varāha Purāṇa:
  504, 603
Vedānta-sūtra:
  289, 446, 473, 712, 814, 824
Viṣṇu Purāṇa:
  93, 170-171, 572
Yoga-sūtra (Patañjali):
  330

Glossary

A

Ācārya—a spiritual master who teaches by his own example.

Acintya—inconceivable.

Acintya-bhedābheda-tattva—Lord Caitanya's "simultaneously one and different" doctrine, which establishes the inconceivable simultaneous existence of the Absolute Truth as both personal and impersonal.

Acyuta—(lit., one who never falls down) infallible, an attribute of Kṛṣṇa's.

Adhibhūtam—the physical nature.

Adhidaivatam—the universal form of the Supreme Lord.

Adhiyajña—the Supersoul, the plenary expansion of the Lord in the heart of every living being.

Adhyātma-cetasā—one who depends solely on Kṛṣṇa.

Aditi—the mother of the demigods.

Ādityas—the demigod sons of Aditi.

Advaita—nondual (indicating, when referring to the Lord, that there is no difference between His body and He Himself).

Advaitācārya—one of the four principal associates of Lord Caitanya Mahāprabhu.

Agni—the demigod who controls fire.

Agnihotra-yajña—fire sacrifice.

Ahiṁsā—nonviolence.

Ajam—unborn.

Akarma (naiṣkarma)—action for which one suffers no reaction because it is performed in Kṛṣṇa consciousness.

Ānanda—transcendental bliss.

Ananta—the name of the serpent with unlimited heads on which Viṣṇu rests.

Anantavijaya—name of King Yudiṣṭhira's conchshell.

Aṇu-ātmā—the minute spirit soul, who is part and parcel of Kṛṣṇa.

Apāna-vāyu—one of the internal bodily airs which is controlled by the *aṣṭāṅga-yoga* system. The *apāna-vāyu* travels downwards.

Aparā prakṛti—the inferior, material nature of the Lord.

Apauruṣeya—not made by man (that is, revealed by God).

Arcanā—the process of Deity worship, or engaging all the senses in the service of the Lord.

Arca-vigraha—the incarnation of the Supreme Lord in a form apparently made of matter to facilitate worship by neophyte devotees.

Āryan—one who knows the value of life and has a civilization based on spiritual realization.

Asāṅga—detachment from material consciousness.

Asat—temporary.

Āśrama—one of the four spiritual orders of life—*brahmacārī-āśrama*, or student life; *gṛhasta-āśrama*, or married life; *vanaprastha-āśrama*, or retired life; and *sannyāsa-āśrama*, or the renounced order of life.

Aṣṭāṅga-yoga—(*aṣṭa*—eight + *aṅga*—part) a mystic *yoga* system propounded by Patañjali in his *Yoga-sūtras* and consisting of eight parts—*yama, niyama, āsana, prāṇāyāma, pratyāhāra, dhāraṇā, dhyāna and samādhi.*

Asura—(*a*—not + *sura*—godly) demon, one who does not follow the principles of scripture.

Āsuraṁ bhāvam āśrita—persons who are openly atheistic.

Ātmā—the self (refers sometimes to the body, sometimes to the soul, and sometimes to the senses).

Avatāra—(lit., one who descends) an incarnation of the Lord who descends from the spiritual sky to the material universe with a particular mission described in scriptures.

Avidyā—(*a*—non+*vidyā*—knowledge) nescience, ignorance.

Avyakta—unmanifested.

B

Bhagavān—(*bhaga*—opulence+*van*—possessing) the possessor of all opulences, which are generally six—wealth, strength, fame, beauty, knowledge and renunciation; an epithet of the Supreme Person.

Bhakta—a devotee, or one who practices devotion (*bhakti*).

Bhakti—love of God; purified service of the senses of the Lord by ones own senses.

Bhaktisiddhānta Sarasvatī Gosvāmī Mahārāja Prabhupāda—the spiritual master of His Divine Grace A.C. Bhaktivedanta Swami Prabhupāda.

Bhaktivinode Ṭhākur—the grand-spiritual master of His Divine Grace A.C. Bhaktivedanta Swami Prabhupāda.

Bhakti-yoga—the system of cultivation of *bhakti*, or pure devotional service, which is untinged by sense gratification or philosophical speculation.

Bhāva—the preliminary stage of transcendental love of Godhead.

Bhīma—one of the five Pāṇḍava brothers.

Bhīṣma—a great devotee and senior family member of the Kuru dynasty.

Brahmā—the first created living being.

Brahma-bhūta—state of being freed from material contamination. One in this state is characterized by transcendental happiness, and he engages in the service of the Supreme Lord.

Brahmacārī—celibate student under the care of a bona fide spiritual master.

Brahmacarya—the vow of strict abstinence from sex indulgence.

Brahma-jijñāsā—spiritual inquiry into one's own identity.

Brahmajyoti—(*brahma*—spiritual + *jyoti*—light) the impersonal effulgence emanating from the body of Kṛṣṇa.

Brahmaloka—the abode of Lord Brahmā.

Brahman—(1)the infinitesimal spiritual soul; (2)the all-pervading impersonal aspect of Kṛṣṇa; (3)the Supreme Personality of Godhead; (4)the total material substance.

Brāhmaṇa—the intelligent class of men, according to the system of social and spiritual orders.

Brahma-saṁhitā—a very ancient Sanskrit scripture of the prayers of Brahmā to Govinda, recovered from a temple in South India by Lord Caitanya.

Brahma-sūtra—see *Vedānta-sūtra*.

Buddhi-yoga—(*buddhi*—intelligence + *yoga*—mystic elevation) the practice of devotional service. Action in Kṛṣṇa consciousness is *buddhi-yoga*, for that is the highest intelligence.

C

Caitanya-caritāmṛta—the authoritative scripture by Kṛṣṇadāsa Kavirāja which describes Lord Caitanya's teachings and pastimes.

Caitanya Mahāprabhu—an incarnation of Kṛṣṇa Himself who appeared in the 15th Century at Navadvīpa in Bengal. He was the inaugurator of the congregational chanting of the *mahā-mantra*, Hare Kṛṣṇa, and His life was the most perfect example of the practice of the teachings of *Bhagavad-gītā*.

Caṇḍālas—dog-eaters, the lowest class of human beings.

Candra—the demigod who rules the moon.

Candraloka—the moon.

Caturmasya—a vow of austerity accepted for four months during the year.

Citi-śakti—(*citi*—knowledge+*śakti*—potency) internal or enlightening potency of the Lord.

D

Daśendriya—the ten sense organs: ear, eye, tongue, nose, skin, hands, legs, speech, anus and genitals.

Deva—a demigod or godly person.

Devakī—the mother of Lord Kṛṣṇa. When Kṛṣṇa appears in the material world, He first sends some of His devotees to act as His father, mother, etc.

Devakī-nandana—(Devakī—Kṛṣṇa's mother+*nandana*—joy) Kṛṣṇa, the joy of Devakī.

Dharma—the capacity to render service, which is the essential quality of a living being.

Dharmakṣetra—a holy place of pilgrimage.

Dhīra—one who is undisturbed by the material energy.

Dhṛṣṭadyumna—the son of Drupada who arranged the military phalanx of the Pāṇḍavas on the Battlefield of Kurukṣetra.

Dhṛtarāṣṭra—the father of the Kurus. *Bhagavad-gītā* was related to Dhṛtarāṣṭra by his secretary as it was being spoken on the Battlefield of Kurukṣetra.

Draupadī—daughter of King Drupada and wife of the Pāṇḍavas.

Droṇācārya—the military teacher of Arjuna and the other Pāṇḍavas and the commander-in-chief of the Kurus on the Battlefield of Kurukṣetra.

Drupada—a warrior for the Pāṇḍavas on the Battlefield of Kurukṣetra. His daughter Draupadī was the wife of the Pāṇḍavas, and his son Dhṛṣṭadyumna arranged their military phalanx.

Duryodhana—the chief of the evil-minded sons of Dhṛtarāṣṭra. It was for the sake of establishing Duryodhana as king of the world that the Kurus fought the Battle of Kurukṣetra.

Duṣkṛtam—miscreants who do not surrender to Kṛṣṇa.

Dvāpara-yuga—the third age of the cycle of a *mahā-yuga*. It lasts more than 4,320,000 years.

E

Ekādaśī—a special day for increased remembrance of Kṛṣṇa which devotees observe twice a month by fasting and hearing and chanting the glories of the Lord.

G

Gandharvas—the celestial singers of the heavenly planets.

Gāṇḍiva—the name of Aijuna's bow.

Ganges—the sacred river which runs throughout the entire universe, beginning from the lotus feet of Viṣṇu. One is recommended to bathe in the Ganges for purification.

Garbhodakaśāyī Viṣṇu—the Viṣṇu expansion of the Supreme Lord who enters each universe to create diversity.

Garuḍa—a giant eagle who acts as the carrier of Lord Viṣṇu.

Gāyatrī—a transcendental vibration chanted by the duly qualified twice-born classes for spiritual realization.

Godāsa—servant of the senses.

Goloka—a name of the planet of Kṛṣṇa.

Gosvāmī—(go—senses+svāmī—master) master of the senses.

Govinda—name of Kṛṣṇa. "One who gives pleasure to the land, the cows and the senses."

Gṛhastha—householder stage of life. One who lives in God conscious married life and raises a family in Kṛṣṇa consciousness.

Guṇa—a material quality, of which there are three—ignorance, passion and goodness.

Guṇāvatāras—the three incarnations who control the three modes of material nature. Brahmā controls passion, Viṣṇu goodness, and Śiva ignorance.

Guru—spiritual master.

H

Hanumān—the famous monkey devotee who served the Supreme Lord in His incarnation as Lord Rāmacandra and assisted Him in defeating the demon Rāvaṇa.

Hare Kṛṣṇa, Hare Kṛṣṇa, Kṛṣṇa Kṛṣṇa, Hare Hare/Hare Rāma, Hare Rāma, Rāma Rāma, Hare Hare—the mahā-mantra, or great chant for deliverance. Kṛṣṇa and Rāma are names of the Lord, and Hare addresses the energy of the Lord. These names have been particularly recommended for chanting in this age.

Haridāsa Ṭhākur—a great devotee recommended by Lord Caitanya as nāmācārya (teacher of chanting of the holy name).

Haṭha-yoga—a system of bodily exercises to help control the senses.

Hiraṇyakaśipu—a great atheist killed by Kṛṣṇa in His incarnation as Nṛsiṁhadeva. Hiraṇyakaśipu's son was the great devotee Prahlāda Mahārāja.

Hṛṣīkeśa—a name of Kṛṣṇa, the master of all senses.

I

Ikṣvāku—a son of Manu who received the knowledge of Bhagavad-gītā in the past.

Indra—the King of the heavenly planets.

Indraloka—the planet where Lord Indra resides.

Īśāvāsya—(īśā—the Lord + vāsya—control) the concept that everything is owned and controlled by the Lord and should be used in His service.

Īśvara—a controller. Kṛṣṇa is parameśvara, the supreme controller.

J

Janaka—a great self-realized king and father-in-law of Lord Rāmacandra.

Japa—soft chanting of the holy names of God performed with the aid of 108 prayer beads.

Jīva (jīvātmā)—the soul or atomic living entity.

Jñāna—knowledge. Material jñāna does not go beyond the material body. Transcendental jñāna discriminates between matter and spirit. Perfect jñāna is knowledge of the body, the soul and the Supreme Lord.

Jñāna-kāṇḍa—the division of the Vedas which deals with empirical speculation in pursuit of truth.

Jñāna-yoga—the predominantly empirical process of linking with the Supreme, which is executed when one is still attached to mental speculation.

Jñārī—one who is engaged in the cultivation of knowledge (especially by philosophical speculation). Upon attaining perfection, a jñānī surrenders to Kṛṣṇa.

K

Kaivalyam—the state of realization of one's constitutional position as part and parcel of the Supreme Lord, which is preliminary to manifestation of activities on the platform of devotional service.

Kāla—eternal time.

Kālī—a demigoddess to whom worshipers may offer meat.

Kali-yuga—the age of quarrel, the fourth and last age in the cycle of a mahā-yuga. This is the age in which we are now living. It lasts 432,000 years, of which 5,000 years have already passed.

Kālpa—a day in the time calculation of Lord Brahmā.

Kaṁsa—Kṛṣṇa's uncle, who was always trying to kill Him.

Kapila—an incarnation of Kṛṣṇa who appeared in Satya-yuga as the son of Devahūti and Kardama Muni and expounded the devotional *Sāṅkhya* philosophy. (There is also an atheist named Kapila, but he is not an incarnation of the Lord.)

Kāraṇodakaśāyī Viṣṇu (Mahā-Viṣṇu)—the Viṣṇu expansion of Lord Kṛṣṇa from whom all the material universes emanate.

Karma—(1) material action performed according to scriptural regulations; (2) action pertaining to the development of the material body; (3) any material action which will incur a subsequent reaction; (4) the material reaction one incurs due to fruitive activities.

Karma-kāṇḍa—the division of the *Vedas* which deals with fruitive activities performed for the purpose of gradual purification of the grossly entangled materialist.

Karma-yoga—(1) action in devotional service; (2) action performed by one who knows that the goal of life is Kṛṣṇa but who is addicted to the fruits of his activities.

Karṇa—son of Kuntī and half brother of Arjuna. He fought against the Pāṇḍavas on the Battlefield of Kurukṣetra.

Kaunteya—the son of Kuntī (Arjuna).

Kīrtana—glorification of the Supreme Lord.

Kṛpaṇa—one who is miserly and does not make use of valuable assets; specifically, one who wastes his life by not striving for spiritual realization.

Kṛṣṇa—the original name of the Supreme Lord in His original transcendental form; the Supreme Personality of Godhead, speaker of *Bhagavad-gītā*.

Kṛṣṇadāsa Kavirāja Gosvāmī—the author of *Caitanya-caritāmṛta*.

Kṛṣṇa-karma—doing all work for the sake of Kṛṣṇa.

Kṛṣṇaloka—the planet in the spiritual world where Kṛṣṇa resides.

Kṣara—perishable.

Kṣatriya—the administrative or protective occupation according to the system of four social and spiritual orders.

Kṣetra—field of activities, the body of the conditioned soul.

Kṣetrajña—(*kṣetra*—field or body +*jña*—knowing) one who is conscious of the body. Both the soul and the Supersoul are *kṣetrajña*, for the individual soul is conscious of his own particular body and the Supersoul is conscious of the bodies of all living beings.

Kṣīrodakaśāyī Viṣṇu—the Viṣṇu expansion of the Supreme Lord who enters within each atom and between each atom of the universe and enters the heart of every living entity. He is also called the Supersoul.

Kumāras—four great impersonalist sages, sons of Lord Brahmā, who became great devotees of the Lord and great authorities on devotional service.

Kumbhaka-yoga—complete stoppage of the air currents within the body as part of the eightfold mystic process.

Kuntī—Pṛthā, the mother of Arjuna and aunt of Lord Kṛṣṇa.

Kurukṣetra—name of a place of pilgrimage held sacred since ancient times. It is located near modern New Delhi, India.

Kurus—all of the descendants of King Kuru, but specifically the 100 sons of Dhṛtarāṣṭra. The Pāṇḍavas were also descendants of King Kuru, but Dhṛtarāṣṭra wished to exclude them from the family tradition.

Kuvera—the treasurer of the demigods.

L

Lakṣmī—the goddess of fortune, consort of the Supreme Lord.

Līlā—pastime.

Līlāvatāras—innumerable incarnations, like Matsya, Kūrma, Rāma and Nṛsiṁha, who descend to display the spiritual pastimes of the Personality of Godhead in the material world.

Loka—planet.

Lokāyatikas—a class of philosophers, akin to the Buddhists, who existed when Lord Kṛṣṇa spoke *Bhagavad-gītā* and who accept that life is a product of a mature combination of material elements.

M

Madhusūdana—a name of Kṛṣṇa, "killer of the Madhu demon."

Mahābhārata—great epic poem written by Vyāsadeva and describing the adventures of the Pāṇḍavas. *Bhagavad-gītā* is included within *Mahābhārata*.

Mahābhūta—(*mahā*—great + *bhūta*—element) the five great material elements: earth, water, fire, air and ether.

Mahā-mantra—the great chanting for deliverance: Hare Kṛṣṇa, Hare Kṛṣṇa, Kṛṣṇa Kṛṣṇa, Hare Hare/Hare Rāma, Hare Rāma, Rāma Rāma, Hare Hare.

Mahātmā—a great soul, one who factually understands that Kṛṣṇa is everything and who therefore surrenders unto Him.

Mahat-tattva—the total material energy.

Mahā-Viṣṇu—*See Kāraṇodakaśāyī Viṣṇu.*

Mantra—(*man*—mind+*tra*—deliverance) a pure sound vibration to deliver the mind from its material inclinations.

Manu—the administrative demigod who is the father of mankind.

Manu-saṁhitā—the lawbook for mankind which was written by Manu.

Manvantara-avatāras—the Manu incarnations, fourteen of whom appear in one day of Brahmā.

Māyā—(*mā*—not + *yā*—this) illusion; an energy of Kṛṣṇa's which deludes the living entity into forgetfulness of the Supreme Lord.

Māyāvādī—impersonalist or voidist adhering to the belief that ultimately God is formless and without personality.

Mukti—liberation, freedom from material consciousness.

Mukunda—name of Kṛṣṇa, "giver of liberation."

Muni—a sage or self-realized soul.

N

Naiṣkarma—see Akarma.

Nakula—one of the younger brothers of Arjuna.

Nanda Mahārāja—Lord Kṛṣṇa's foster father.

Nārada Muni—a great devotee of the Supreme Lord who can travel anywhere in the spiritual or material worlds to preach the glories of the Lord.

Narādhama—(lit., "lowest of mankind") those who are socially and politically developed but have no religious principles.

Nārāyaṇa—the four-handed expansion of the Supreme Lord Kṛṣṇa.

Nirguṇa—(*nir*—without + *guṇa*—quality) not possessing attributes (when applied to God, refers to the appearance of material attributes).

Nirmama—consciousness that nothing belongs to oneself.

Nirvāṇa—the end of the process of materialistic life.

Nitya-baddha—eternally conditioned.

Nṛsiṁha—an incarnation of Lord Kṛṣṇa in the form of half-lion, half-man.

O

omkāra—*om,* the transcendental syllable which represents Kṛṣṇa and which is vibrated by transcendentalists for attainment of the Supreme when undertaking sacrifices, charities and penances.

om tat sat—the three transcendental syllables used by *brāhmaṇas* for satisfaction of the Supreme when chanting Vedic hymns or offering sacrifice. They indicate the Supreme Absolute Truth, the Personality of Godhead.

P

Pāñcajanya—the conchshell of Lord Kṛṣṇa.

Pañca-mahābhūta—the five gross elements: earth, water, fire, air and ether.

Pāṇḍavas—the five sons of King Pāṇḍu: Yudhiṣṭhira, Arjuna, Bhīma, Nakula and Sahadeva.

Pāṇḍu—a younger brother of Dhṛtarāṣṭra's who died early, leaving his five young sons, the Pāṇḍavas, under the care of Dhṛtarāṣṭra.

Parag-ātmā—the soul, when attached to sense enjoyment.

Paramahaṁsa—the topmost class of God realized devotees.

Paramātmā—the Supersoul, the localized aspect of the Supreme Lord within the heart of all living entities.

Param Brahman—the Supreme Brahman, the Personality of Godhead, Śrī Kṛṣṇa.

Param dhāma—the eternal planets of the spiritual world.

Paramparā—the disciplic succession through which spiritual knowledge is transmitted.

Parantapaḥ—a name of Arjuna, "chastiser of the enemies."

Parā-prakṛti—the superior, spiritual energy or nature of the Lord.

Parāśara Muni—a great sage, the father of Vyāsadeva.

Parasurāma—an incarnation of Lord Kṛṣṇa who appeared in ancient times to overthrow the warrior class when they had become degraded.

Pārtha-sārathi—Kṛṣṇa, the chariot driver of Arjuna (Pārtha).

Pāṣaṇḍī—an atheist who thinks God and the demigods to be on the same level.

Patañjali—a great authority on the *aṣṭāṅga-yoga* system and author of the *Yoga-sūtra*.

Pavitram—pure.

Pitṛloka-the planet of the departed forefathers.

Prajāpati—(l)a progenitor of living entities; (2)Lord Brahmā.

Prahlāda Mahārāja—a great devotee of Lord Kṛṣṇa who was persecuted by his atheistic father but was always protected by the Lord.

Prakṛti—nature (lit., that which is predominated). There are two *prakṛtis*— *aparā-prakṛti*, the material nature, and *parā-prakṛti*, the spiritual nature (living entities) —which are both predominated over by the Supreme Personality of Godhead.

Prāṇa—the life air.

Pranāva omkāra—*see Omkāra.*

Prāṇāyāma—control of the breathing process (one of the eight parts of the *aṣṭāṅga-yoga* system).

Prasādam—food offered to Kṛṣṇa, which becomes spiritual when offered and which can purify the living entity.

Pratyag-ātmā—the soul, when purified of material attachment.

Pratyāhāra—withdrawal from sensual activities (one of the eight parts of the *aṣṭāṅga-yoga* system).

Premā—real love of God, the highest perfectional stage of life.

Pṛthā—the wife of King Pāṇḍu, mother of the Pāṇḍavas and aunt of Lord Kṛṣṇa.

Pūraka—the stage of equilibrium attained by offering the inhaled breath into the exhaled breath.

Purāṇas—the eighteen very old books which are histories of this and other planets.

Pūrṇam—complete.

Puruṣam—supreme enjoyer.

Puruṣāvatāras—the primary Viṣṇu expansions of Kṛṣṇa who are involved in the creation, maintenance and destruction of the material universe.

R

Rajo-guṇa—the mode of passion of material nature.

Rāma—(1) name of the Absolute Truth as the source of unlimited pleasure for transcendentalists; (2) incarnation of the Supreme Lord as a perfect king (Lord Rāmacandra).

Rasa—relationship between the Lord and the living entities. They are of five principal varieties—neutral relationship (*śānta-rasa*), relationship as servant (*dāsya-rasa*), as friend (*sākhya-rasa*), parent (*vātsalya-rasa*) and conjugal lover (*mādhurya-rasa*).

Rāvaṇa—a powerful demon who wanted to build a staircase to heaven but was killed by Kṛṣṇa in His incarnation as Lord Rāmacandra.

Recaka—the state of equilibrium attained by offering the exhaled breath into the inhaled breath.

Rūpa Gosvāmī—chief of the six great spiritual masters of Vṛndāvana who were authorized by Lord Caitanya Mahāprabhu to establish and distribute the philosophy of Kṛṣṇa consciousness.

S

Śabda-brahma—the injunctions of the *Vedas* and *Upaniṣads.*

Sac-cid-ānanda vigraha—(*sat*—eternal existence+*cit*—knowledge+*ānanda*—
bliss; *vigraha*—form) the eternal form of the Supreme Lord, which
is full of bliss and knowledge; or, the eternal transcendental form
of the living entity.

Sādhaka—one who is a suitable candidate for liberation.

Sādhu—holy man, devotee.

Saguṇa—possessing attributes (when applied to God, refers to spiritual
qualities).

Sahadeva—one of the younger brothers of Arjuna.

Samādhi—trance, absorption in consciousness of God.

Samāna-vāyu—the internal bodily air which adjusts equilibrium. It is one
of the five bodily airs controlled by the breathing exercises of the
aṣṭāṅga-yoga system.

Sanātana—eternal.

Sanātana-dhāma—the eternal abode, the *Vaikuṇṭha* planets in the spiritual
sky.

Sanātana-dhārma—the eternal religion of the living being—to render service
to the Supreme Lord.

Sanātana Gosvāmī—one of the six great spiritual masters of Vṛndāvana
who were authorized by Lord Caitanya Mahāprabhu to establish
and distribute the philosophy of Kṛṣṇa consciousness.

Sanātana-yoga—eternal activities performed by the living entity.

Sañjaya—the secretary of Dhṛtarāṣṭra who related *Bhagavad-gītā* to
Dhṛtarāṣṭra as it was being spoken on the Battlefield of Kurukṣetra.

Śaṅkarācārya—an incarnation of Lord Śiva who appeared in the Eighth
Century to propagate an impersonalist philosophy with the aim of
erasing Buddhism from India and reestablishing the authority of
the *Vedas*.

Sāṅkhya—(1) the devotional *yoga* process described by Lord Kapila in
Śrīmad-Bhāgavatam; (2) analytical understanding of the body and
the soul.

Saṅkīrtana-yajña—the sacrifice prescribed for the age of Kali; that is,
congregational chanting of the name, fame and pastimes of the
Supreme Personality of Godhead.

Sannyāsa—the renounced order of life, which is free from family relationships and in which all activities are completely dedicated to Kṛṣṇa.

Sarasvatī—the demigoddess in charge of learning.

Śāstra—revealed scripture.

Sattva—the mode of goodness of material nature.

Satya-yuga—the first of the four ages of a *mahā-yuga*. Satya-yuga is characterized by virtue, wisdom and religion, and it lasts 1,728,000 years.

Sītā—the wife of Lord Rāmacandra, an incarnation of Kṛṣṇa.

Śiva—the personality in charge of the mode of ignorance and the destruction of the material universe.

Smaraṇam—constant thinking of Kṛṣṇa (one of the nine methods of devotional service).

Smṛti—scriptures compiled by living entities under transcendental direction.

Soma-rasa—a heavenly beverage available on the moon.

Śravaṇam—hearing from an authorized source. (This is the chief of the nine methods of devotional service).

Śrīmad-Bhāgavatam—the scripture composed by Vyāsadeva to describe and explain Kṛṣṇa's pastimes.

Śruti—scriptures received directly from God.

Sthita-dhīra-muni—(*sthita*—steady + *dhīra*—undisturbed + *muni*—sage) one who is always fixed in Kṛṣṇa consciousness and as a result is undisturbed by material nature.

Śūdra—the laborer class of men, according to the system of four social orders and four spiritual orders of life.

Śukadeva Gosvāmī—great devotee who recited the *Śrīmad-Bhāgavatam* to King Parīkṣit during the last seven days of the King's life.

Sukham—happiness or pleasure.

Sukṛtina—pious persons who obey the rules of scripture and are devoted to the Supreme Lord.

Surabhi—the cows in Kṛṣṇaloka. They can give unlimited milk.

Sūryaloka—the sun planet.

Svadharmas—specific duties of a particular body performed in accordance with religious principles in order to achieve liberation.

Svāmī—one who can control his mind and senses.

Svargaloka—the heavenly planets or abodes of the demigods.

Svarūpa—(*sva*—own+*rūpa*—form) the living entity's eternal relationship of service to the Lord, the real form of the soul.

Svarūpa-siddhi—perfection of one's constitutional position.

Śyāmasundara—(*śyāma*—black + *sundara*—very beautiful) a name of the original form of Lord Kṛṣṇa.

T

Tamo-guṇa—the mode of ignorance of material nature.

Tapasya—voluntary acceptance of some material trouble for progress in spiritual life.

Tattvavit—one who knows the Absolute Truth in His three different features.

Tretā-yuga—the second age in the cycle of a *mahā-yuga*. It lasts for 864,000 years.

Tulasī—a great devotee in the form of a plant. This plant is very dear to the Lord, and its leaves are always offered to His lotus feet.

Tyāga—renunciation of activities performed with material consciousness.

U

Uccaiḥśravā—a horse born from nectar and considered to be a representative of Kṛṣṇa.

Udāna-vāyu—bodily air which moves upwards and which is controlled by the breathing exercises of the *aṣṭāṅga-yoga* system.

Upaniṣads—the philosophical portions of the *Vedas*, as *Īśa Upaniṣad, Kena Upaniṣad*, etc. They are 108 in number.

V

Vaibhāṣikas—a class of philosophers, akin to the Buddhists, who existed when Lord Kṛṣṇa spoke *Bhagavad-gītā* and who accept that life is a product of a mature combination of material elements.

Vaikuṇṭhas—(lit., without anxiety) the eternal planets of the spiritual sky.

Vairāgya—detachment from matter and engagement of the mind in spirit.

Vaiṣṇava—a devotee of the Supreme Lord Viṣṇu, or Kṛṣṇa.

Vaiśya—the class of men involved in business and farming, according to the system of four social orders and four spiritual orders.

Vānaprastha—retired life, in which one quits home and travels from holy place to holy place in preparation for the renounced order of life.

Varāha—the incarnation of Lord Kṛṣṇa as a gigantic boar.

Vasudeva—the father of Lord Kṛṣṇa.

Vāsudeva—(1) Lord Kṛṣṇa, "the son of Vasudeva"; (2) the state of pure goodness, which transcends the material modes of nature and in which one can understand the Supreme Lord.

Vedānta-sūtra (Brahma-sūtra)—the philosophical treatise written by Vyāsadeva to give the conclusion of all the *Vedas*.

Vedas—the four Vedic scriptures (*Ṛg, Yajur, Sāma* and *Atharva-Vedas*) and their supplements, the *Purāṇas, Mahābhārata, Vedānta-sūtra*, etc.

Vibhu-ātmā—the Supersoul.

Vibhūti—opulence by which Kṛṣṇa controls the entire material manifestation.

Vidyā—knowledge.

Vijñānam—specific knowledge of spirit soul, his constitutional position and his relationship with the Supreme Soul.

Vikarma—unauthorized or sinful work, performed against the injunctions of revealed scriptures.

Virāṭa-rūpa—see *Viśva-rūpa*.

Viṣṇu—the all-pervading Personality of Godhead (a plenary expansion of Kṛṣṇa) who enters into the material universe before creation.

Viṣṇu-tattva—innumerable primary or Viṣṇu expansions of Kṛṣṇa.

Viśvakośa—an ancient Sanskrit dictionary.

Viśva-rūpa (virāṭa-rūpa)—the universal form of Lord Kṛṣṇa, as described in the Eleventh Chapter of *Bhagavad-gītā*.

Vivasvān—the name of the present sun-god, to whom *Bhagavad-gītā* was instructed at least 120,400,000 years ago.

Vṛndāvana—the site of Kṛṣṇa's transcendental village pastimes, exhibited when He was present on earth about 5,000 years ago.

Vyāna-vāyu—one of the internal bodily airs which is controlled by the *aṣṭāṅga-yoga* system. *The vyāna-vāyu* acts to shrink and expand.

Vyāsadeva—the greatest philosopher of ancient times. He was an incarnation of Viṣṇu empowered for literary activities, and he compiled the *Vedas, Purāṇas, Mahābhārata, Vedānta-sūtra*, etc.

Y

Yajña—sacrifice.

Yajñeśvara—an epithet of Kṛṣṇa, "Lord of sacrifice."

Yamarāja—the demigod who punishes sinful living entities after their deaths.

Yamunācārya—a great spiritual master in the *Śrī-sampradāya*, one of the important disciphc lines.

Yaśodā—Lord Kṛṣṇa's foster mother.

Yaśodā-nandana—the child of Yaśodā, Kṛṣṇa.

Yoga—linking of the consciousness of the infinitesimal living entity with the supreme living entity, Kṛṣṇa.

Yoga-māyā—the internal potency of the Lord, which hides Him from nondevotees.

Yogārūḍha—the highest stage of *yoga*.

Yogārurukṣa—the beginning stage of *yoga*.

Yogeśvara—name of Kṛṣṇa, "the master of all mystic power."

Yudhiṣṭhira—the eldest of the five Pāṇḍava brothers.

Yuga—one of the four ages of the universe, which differ in length and which rotate like calendar months. *See also* Satya-yuga, Tretā-yuga, Dvāpara-yuga and Kali-yuga.

Yugāvatāras—the incarnations of the Lord who appear for each of the four different millenniums to prescribe the appropriate form of spiritual realization for that age.

Sanskrit Pronunciation Guide

Vowels

अ a   आ ā   इ i   ई ī   उ u   ऊ ū   ऋ ṛ   ॠ ṝ

ऌ ḷ   ए e   ऐ ai   ओ o   औ au

ं ṁ *(anusvāra)*   ः ḥ *(visarga)*

Consonants

Gutturals:	क ka	ख kha	ग ga	घ gha	ङ ṅa
Palatals:	च ca	छ cha	ज ja	झ jha	ञ ña
Cerebrals:	ट ṭa	ठ ṭha	ड ḍa	ढ ḍha	ण ṇa
Dentals:	त ta	थ tha	द da	ध dha	न na
Labials:	प pa	फ pha	ब ba	भ bha	म ma
Semivowels:	य ya	र ra	ल la	व va	
Sibilants:	श śa	ष ṣa	स sa		
Aspirate:	ह ha	ऽ =ʼ*(avagraha)* – the apostrophe			

The vowels above should be pronounced as follows:

a – like the *a* in organ or the *u* in but
ā – like the *ā* in far but held twice as long as *a*.

877

i   – like the *i* in p*i*n.
ī   – like the *ī* in p*i*que but held twice as long as *i*.
u   – like the *u* in p*u*sh.
ū   – like the *ū* in r*u*le but held twice as long as *u*.
ṛ   – like the *ri* in *Ri*ta (but more like French *ru*).
ṝ   – same as *ri* but held twice as long.
ḷ   – like *lree* (*lruu*).
e   – like the *e* in th*e*y.
ai – like the *ai* in *ai*sle.
o   – like the *o* in g*o*.
au – like the *ow* in h*ow*.
ṁ *(anusvāra)* – a resonant nasal like the *n* in the French word *bon*.
ḥ *(visarga)* – a final *h*-sound: *aḥ* is pronounced like *aha*; *iḥ* like *ihi*.

The consonants are pronounced as follows:

k	– as in *k*ite	kh –	as in Ec*kh*tart
g	– as in *g*ive	gh –	as in di*g-h*ard
ṅ	– as in si*ng*	c	– as in *ch*air
ch –	as in staun*ch-h*eart	j	– as in *j*oy
jh –	as in he*dg*ehog	ñ	– as in ca*ny*on
ṭ	– as in *t*ub	ṭh –	as in lig*ht-h*eart
ṇ	– as r*n*a (prepare to say	dh –	as in re*d-h*ot
	the *r* and say *na*).	ḍ	– as in *d*ove

Cerebrals are pronounced with tongue to roof of mouth, but the following dentals are pronounced with tongue against teeth:

t   – as in *t*ub but with tongue against teeth.
th – as in lig*ht-h*eart but tongue against teeth.
d   – as in *d*ove but tongue against teeth.
dh– as in re*d-h*ot but with tongue against teeth.
n   – as in *n*ut but with tongue in between teeth.

p	– as in *p*ine	ph–	as in u*p-h*ill (not *f*)
b	– as in *b*ird	bh–	as in ru*b-h*ard
m	– as in *m*other	y	– as in *y*es
r	– as in *r*un	l	– as in *l*ight
v	– as in *v*ine.	s	– as in *s*un

ś (palatal) – as in the *s* in the German word *sprechen*
ṣ (cerebral)– as the *sh* in *sh*ine
h   – as in *h*ome

There is no strong accentuation of syllables in Sanskrit, only a flowing of short and long (twice as long as the short) syllables.

Index of Sanskrit Verses

This index constitutes a complete listing of the first and third lines of each of the Sanskrit verses of Bhagavad-gītā, arranged in English alphabetical order. In the first column the Sanskrit transliteration is given, and in the second and third columns respectively the chapter-verse references and page number for each verse are to be found.

A

abhayaṁ sattva-saṁśuddhir	16.1	721
abhisandhāya tu phalaṁ	17.12	762
abhito brahma-nirvāṇam	5.26	300
abhyāsād ramate yatra	18.36	808
abhyāsa-yoga-yuktena	8.8	417
abhyāsa-yogena tato	12.9	605
abhyāse 'py asamartho 'si	12.10	606
abhyāsena tu kaunteya	6.35	344
abhyutthānam adharmasya	4.7	224
ā-brahma-bhuvanāl lokāḥ	8.16	426
ācaraty ātmanaḥ śreyas	16.22	745
ācāryāḥ pitaraḥ putrās	1.33	58
ācāryam upasaṅgamya	1.2	33
ācāryān mātulān bhrātṝn	1.26	52
ācāryopāsanaṁ śaucam	13.8	628
acchedyo 'yam adāhyo 'yam	2.24	104
adeśa-kāle yad dānam	17.22	771
adharmābhibhavāt kṛṣṇa	1.40	64
adharmaṁ dharmam iti yā	18.32	805
adhaś ca mūlāny anusantatāni	15.2	695
adhaś cordhvaṁ prasṛtās tasya śākhā	15.2	695
adhibhūtaṁ ca kiṁ proktam	8.1	409
adhibhūtaṁ kṣaro bhāvaḥ	8.4	413
adhiṣṭhānaṁ tathā kartā	18.14	790
adhiṣṭhāya manaḥ cāyaṁ	15.9	705
adhiyajñaḥ kathaṁ ko 'tra	8.2	410
adhiyajño 'ham evātra	8.4	413
adhyātma-jñāna-nityatvam	13.12	628
adhyātma-vidyā vidyānāṁ	10.32	528
adhyeṣyate ca ya imaṁ	18.70	839
āḍhyo 'bhijanavān asmi	16.15	737
ādityānām ahaṁ viṣṇur	10.21	519
adṛṣṭa-pūrvaṁ hṛṣito 'smi dṛṣṭvā	11.45	576
adveṣṭā sarva-bhūtānāṁ	12.13	610
ādy-antavantaḥ kaunteya	5.22	296
āgamāpāyino 'nityās	2.14	90
aghāyur indriyārāmo	3.16	180
agnir jyotir ahaḥ śuklaḥ	8.24	434
aham ādir hi devānāṁ	10.2	492
aham ādiś ca madhyaṁ ca	10.20	518
aham ātmā guḍākeśa	10.20	518
aham evākṣayaḥ kālo	10.33	529
ahaṁ hi sarva-yajñānāṁ	9.24	475
ahaṁ kratur ahaṁ yajñaḥ	9.16	467
ahaṁ kṛtsnasya jagataḥ	7.6	370
ahaṁ sarvasya prabhavo	10.8	502
ahaṁ tvāṁ sarva-pāpebhyo	18.66	834
ahaṁ vaiśvānaro bhūtvā	15.14	711
ahaṅkāra itīyaṁ me	7.4	365
ahaṅkāraṁ balaṁ darpaṁ	16.18	741
ahaṅkāraṁ balaṁ darpaṁ	18.53	820
ahaṅkāra-vimūḍhātmā	3.27	192
āhārā rājasasyeṣṭā	17.9	759
āhāras tv api sarvasya	17.7	758
ahiṁsā samatā tuṣṭis	10.5	496
ahiṁsā satyam akrodhas	16.2	721
aho bata mahat pāpaṁ	1.44	68
āhus tvām ṛṣayaḥ sarve	10.13	509
airāvataṁ gajendrāṇāṁ	10.27	524
ajānatā mahimānaṁ tavedaṁ	11.41	572
ajñānaṁ cābhijātasya	16.4	728
ajñānenāvṛtaṁ jñānaṁ	5.15	287
ajñāś cāśraddadhānaś ca	4.40	265
ajo 'pi sann avyayātmā	4.6	222
ajo nityaḥ śāśvato 'yaṁ purāṇo	2.20	98
akarmaṇaś ca boddhavyaṁ	4.17	240
ākhyāhi me ko bhavān ugra-rūpo	11.31	562
akīrtiṁ cāpi bhūtāni	2.34	116
akṣaraṁ brahma paramam	8.3	411
akṣarāṇām a-kāro 'smi	10.33	529

amānitvam adambhitvam | 13.8 | 628
amī ca tvāṁ dhṛtarāṣṭrasya putrāḥ | 11.26 | 559
amī hi tvāṁ sura-saṅghā viśanti | 11.21 | 556
amṛtaṁ caiva mṛtyuś ca | 9.19 | 470
anādi-madhyāntam ananta-vīryam | 11.19 | 554

anādi mat-paraṁ brahma | 13.13 | 635
anāditvān nirguṇatvāt | 13.32 | 657
ananta deveśa jagan-nivāsa | 11.37 | 568
anantaś cāsmi nāgānāṁ | 10.29 | 526
anantavijayaṁ rājā | 1.16 | 45

ananta-vīryāmita-vikramas tvaṁ | 11.40 | 571
ananya-cetāḥ satataṁ | 8.14 | 423
ananyāś cintayanto māṁ | 9.22 | 473
ananyenaiva yogena | 12.6 | 601
anapekṣaḥ śucir dakṣa | 12.16 | 613

anārya-juṣṭam asvargyam | 2.2 | 72
anāśino 'prameyasya | 2.18 | 96
anāśritaḥ karma-phalaṁ | 6.1 | 307
anātmanas tu śatrutve | 6.6 | 313
aneka-bāhūdara-vaktra-netraṁ | 11.16 | 552

aneka-citta-vibhrāntā | 16.16 | 739
aneka-divyābharaṇaṁ | 11.10 | 547
aneka-janma-saṁsiddhas | 6.45 | 356
aneka-vaktra-nayanam | 11.10 | 547
anena prasaviṣyadhvam | 3.10 | 171

anicchann api vārṣṇeya | 3.36 | 202
aniketaḥ sthira-matir | 12.19 | 615
aniṣṭam iṣṭaṁ miśraṁ ca | 18.12 | 789
anityam asukhaṁ lokam | 9.33 | 487
annād bhavanti bhūtāni | 3.14 | 177

anta-kāle ca mām eva | 8.5 | 414
antavanta ime dehā | 2.18 | 96
antavat tu phalaṁ teṣāṁ | 7.23 | 395
anubandhaṁ kṣayaṁ hiṁsām | 18.25 | 799
anudvega-karaṁ vākyaṁ | 17.15 | 765

anye ca bahavaḥ śūrā | 1.9 | 38
anye sāṅkhyena yogena | 13.25 | 650
anye tv evam ajānantaḥ | 13.26 | 651
apāne juhvati prāṇaṁ | 4.29 | 253
aparaṁ bhavato janma | 4.4 | 218

aparaspara-sambhūtaṁ | 16.8 | 732
apare niyatāhārāḥ | 4.29 | 253
apareyam itas tv anyāṁ | 7.5 | 368
aparyāptaṁ tad asmākaṁ | 1.10 | 39
apaśyad deva-devasya | 11.13 | 549

aphalākāṅkṣibhir yajño | 17.11 | 762
aphalākāṅkṣibhir yuktaiḥ | 17.17 | 767
aphala-prepsunā karma | 18.23 | 798
api ced asi pāpebhyaḥ | 4.36 | 262
api cet su-durācāro | 9.30 | 483

api trailokya-rājyasya | 1.35 | 58
aprakāśo 'pravṛttiś ca | 14.13 | 676
aprāpya māṁ nivartante | 9.3 | 448
aprāpya yoga-saṁsiddhiṁ | 6.37 | 346
apratiṣṭho mahā-bāho | 6.38 | 348

āpūryamāṇam acala-pratiṣṭhaṁ | 2.70 | 155
ārto jijñāsur arthārthī | 7.16 | 386
ārurukṣor muner yogaṁ | 6.3 | 310
asad ity ucyate pārtha | 17.28 | 776
asakta-buddhiḥ sarvatra | 18.49 | 818

asaktaṁ sarva-bhṛc caiva | 13.15 | 637
asaktir anabhiṣvaṅgaḥ | 13.10 | 628
asakto hy ācaran karma | 3.19 | 183
asammūḍhaḥ sa martyeṣu | 10.3 | 494
asaṁśayaṁ mahā-bāho | 6.35 | 344

asaṁśayaṁ samagraṁ māṁ | 7.1 | 361
asaṁyatātmanā yogo | 6.36 | 346
āśā-pāśa-śatair baddhāḥ | 16.12 | 736
aśāstra-vihitaṁ ghoraṁ | 17.5 | 757
asat-kṛtam avajñātaṁ | 17.22 | 771

asatyam apratiṣṭhaṁ te | 16.8 | 732
asau mayā hataḥ śatrur | 16.14 | 737
āścarya-vac cainam anyaḥ śṛṇoti | 2.29 | 110
āścarya-vat paśyati kaścid enam | 2.29 | 110
asito devalo vyāsaḥ | 10.13 | 509

asmākaṁ tu viśiṣṭā ye | 1.7 | 36
aśocyān anvaśocas tvam | 2.11 | 85
aśraddadhānāḥ puruṣā | 9.3 | 448
aśraddhayā hutaṁ dattaṁ | 17.28 | 776
āsthitaḥ sa hi yuktātmā | 7.18 | 389

āsurīṁ yonim āpannā | 16.20 | 743
āśvāsayām āsa ca bhītam enaṁ | 11.50 | 583
aśvatthaḥ sarva-vṛkṣāṇāṁ | 10.26 | 523
aśvatthāmā vikarṇaś ca | 1.8 | 37
aśvattham enaṁ su-virūḍha-mūlam | 15.3 | 697

atattvārtha-vad alpaṁ ca | 18.22 | 797
atha cainaṁ nitya-jātaṁ | 2.26 | 106
atha cet tvam ahaṅkārān | 18.58 | 827
atha cet tvam imaṁ dharmyaṁ | 2.33 | 116
atha cittaṁ samādhātuṁ | 12.9 | 605

athaitad apy aśakto 'si 12.11 607
atha kena prayukto 'yaṁ 3.36 202
atha vā bahunaitena 10.42 537
atha vā yoginām eva 6.42 353
atha vyavasthitān dṛṣṭvā 1.20 47

ātmaiva hy ātmano bandhur 6.5 312
ātmany eva ca santuṣṭas 3.17 181
ātmany evātmanā tuṣṭaḥ 2.55 140
ātma-sambhāvitāḥ stabdhā 16.17 740
ātma-saṁsthaṁ manaḥ kṛtvā 6.25 333

ātma-saṁyama-yogāgnau 4.27 251
ātmaupamyena sarvatra 6.32 341
ātmavantaṁ na karmāṇi 4.41 266
ātma-vaśyair vidheyātmā 2.64 151
ato 'smi loke vede ca 15.18 716

atra śūrā maheṣv-āsā 1.4 35
atyeti tat sarvam idaṁ viditvā 8.28 437
avācya-vādāṁś ca bahūn 2.36 118
avajānanti māṁ mūḍhā 9.11 458
avāpya bhūmāv asapatnam ṛddham 2.8 81

avibhaktaṁ ca bhūteṣu 13.17 640
avibhaktaṁ vibhakteṣu 18.20 795
avināśi tu tad viddhi 2.17 94
āvṛtaṁ jñānam etena 3.39 206
avyaktādīni bhūtāni 2.28 109

avyaktād vyaktayaḥ sarvāḥ 8.18 428
avyaktā hi gatir duḥkhaṁ 12.5 599
avyaktaṁ vyaktim āpannaṁ 7.24 397
avyakta-nidhanāny eva 2.28 109
avyakto 'kṣara ity uktas 8.21 431

avyakto 'yam acintyo 'yam 2.25 105
ayaneṣu ca sarveṣu 1.11 40
ayathāvat prajānāti 18.31 804
ayatiḥ śraddhayopeto 6.37 346
āyudhānām ahaṁ vajraṁ 10.28 525

āyuḥ-sattva-balārogya- 17.8 759
ayuktaḥ kāma-kāreṇa 5.12 284
ayuktaḥ prākṛtaḥ stabdhaḥ 18.28 802

B

bahavo jñāna-tapasā 4.10 229
bahir antaś ca bhūtānām 13.16 639
bahūdaraṁ bahu-daṁṣṭrā-karālaṁ 11.23 557
bahūnāṁ janmanām ante 7.19 390
bahūni me vyatītāni 4.5 219

bahūny adṛṣṭa-pūrvāṇi 11.6 544
bahu-śākhā hy anantāś ca 2.41 125
bāhya-sparśeṣv asaktātmā 5.21 295
balaṁ balavatāṁ cāhaṁ 7.11 376
bandhaṁ mokṣaṁ ca yā vetti 18.30 803

bandhur ātmātmanas tasya 6.6 313
bhajanty ananya-manaso 9.13 463
bhaktiṁ mayi parāṁ kṛtvā 18.68 837
bhakto 'si me sakhā ceti 4.3 217
bhaktyā mām abhijānāti 18.55 823

bhaktyā tv ananyayā śakya 11.54 588
bhavāmi na cirāt pārtha 12.7 601
bhavān bhīṣmaś ca karṇaś ca 1.8 37
bhavanti bhāvā bhūtānāṁ 10.5 496
bhavanti sampadaṁ daivīm 16.3 721

bhavāpyayau hi bhūtānāṁ 11.2 540
bhāva-saṁśuddhir ity etat 17.16 766
bhavaty atyāginām pretya 18.12 789
bhaviṣyāṇi ca bhūtāni 7.26 401
bhavitā na ca me tasmād 18.69 838

bhayād raṇād uparataṁ 2.35 117
bhīṣma-droṇa-pramukhataḥ 1.25 51
bhīṣmam evābhirakṣantu 1.11 40
bhīṣmo droṇaḥ sūta-putras tathāsau 11.26 559
bhogaiśvarya-prasaktānāṁ 2.44 128

bhoktāraṁ yajña-tapasāṁ 5.29 303
bhrāmayan sarva-bhūtāni 18.61 829
bhruvor madhye prāṇam āveśya 8.10 420
bhūmir āpo 'nalo vāyuḥ 7.4 365
bhuñjate te tv aghaṁ pāpā 3.13 176

bhūta-bhartṛ ca taj jñeyaṁ 13.17 640
bhūta-bhāvana bhūteśa 10.15 513
bhūta-bhāvodbhava-karo 8.3 411
bhūta-bhṛn na ca bhūta-stho 9.5 451
bhūta-grāmaḥ sa evāyaṁ 8.19 429

bhūta-grāmam imaṁ kṛtsnam 9.8 455
bhūtāni yānti bhūtejyā 9.25 476
bhūta-prakṛti-mokṣaṁ ca 13.35 660
bhūya eva mahā-bāho 10.1 491
bhūyaḥ kathaya tṛptir hi 10.18 516

bījaṁ māṁ sarva-bhūtānāṁ 7.10 375
brahma-bhūtaḥ prasannātmā 18.54 821
brahmacaryam ahiṁsā ca 17.14 764
brahmāgnāv apare yajñaṁ 4.25 248
brahmaiva tena gantavyaṁ 4.24 247

brāhmaṇa-kṣatriya-viśāṁ 18.41 811
brahmāṇam īśaṁ kamalāsana-stham 11.15 551
brāhmaṇās tena vedāś ca 17.23 771
brahmaṇo hi pratiṣṭhāham 14.27 689
brahmaṇy ādhāya karmāṇi 5.10 281

brahmārpaṇaṁ brahma havir 4.24 247
brahma-sūtra-padaiś caiva 13.5 625
bṛhat-sāma tathā sāmnāṁ 10.35 531
buddhau śaraṇam anviccha 2.49 134
buddher bhedaṁ dhṛteś caiva 18.29 803

buddhir buddhimatām asmi 7.10 375
buddhir jñānam asammohaḥ 10.4 496
buddhi-yogam upāśritya 18.57 826
buddhi-yukto jahātīha 2.50 135
buddhyā viśuddhayā yukto 18.51 820
buddhyā yukto yayā pārtha 2.39 120

C

cañcalaṁ hi manaḥ kṛṣṇa 6.34 343
cātur-varṇyaṁ mayā sṛṣṭaṁ 4.13 235
catur-vidhā bhajante māṁ 7.16 386
cetasā sarva-karmāṇi 18.57 826
chandāṁsi yasya parṇāni 15.1 693

chinna-dvaidhā yatātmānaḥ 5.25 299
chittvainaṁ saṁśayaṁ yogam 4.42 267
cintām aparimeyāṁ ca 16.11 736

D

dadāmi buddhi-yogaṁ taṁ 10.10 506
daivam evāpare yajñaṁ 4.25 248
daivī hy eṣā guṇa-mayī 7.14 379
daivī sampad vimokṣāya 16.5 729
daivo vistaraśaḥ prokta 16.6 730

dambhāhaṅkāra-saṁyuktāḥ 17.5 757
dambho darpo 'bhimānaś ca 16.4 728
daṁṣṭrā-karālāni ca te mukhāni 11.25 558
dāna-kriyāś ca vividhāḥ 17.25 774
dānaṁ damaś ca yajñaś ca 16.1 721

dānam īśvara-bhāvaś ca 18.43 812
daṇḍo damayatām asmi 10.38 534
darśayām āsa pārthāya 11.9 547
dātavyam iti yad dānaṁ 17.20 769
dayā bhūteṣv aloluptvaṁ 16.2 721

dehī nityam avadhyo 'yaṁ 2.30 112
dehino 'smin yathā dehe 2.13 88
deśe kāle ca pātre ca 17.20 769

devā apy asya rūpasya 11.52 585
deva-dvija-guru-prājña- 17.14 764
devān bhāvayatānena 3.11 173
devān deva-yajo yānti 7.23 395
dharma-kṣetre kuru-kṣetre 1.1 31

dharma-saṁsthāpanārthāya 4.8 225
dharmāviruddho bhūteṣu 7.11 376
dharme naṣṭe kulaṁ kṛtsnam 1.39 63
dharmyād dhi yuddhāc chreyo 'nyat 2.31 113
dhārtarāṣṭrā raṇe hanyus 1.45 68

dhārtarāṣṭrasya durbuddher 1.23 50
dhṛṣṭadyumno virāṭaś ca 1.17 45
dhṛṣṭaketuś cekitānaḥ 1.5 36
dhṛtyā yayā dhārayate 18.33 806
dhūmenāvriyate vahnir 3.38 205

dhūmo rātris tathā kṛṣṇaḥ 8.25 435
dhyānāt karma-phala-tyāgas 12.12 609
dhyāna-yoga-paro nityaṁ 18.52 820
dhyānenātmani paśyanti 13.25 650
dhyāyato viṣayān puṁsaḥ 2.62 148

diśo na jāne na labhe ca śarma 11.25 558
divi sūrya-sahasrasya 11.12 548
divya-mālyāmbara-dharaṁ 11.11 547
divyaṁ dadāmi te cakṣuḥ 11.8 545
dīyate ca parikliṣṭaṁ 17.21 770

doṣair etaiḥ kula-ghnānāṁ 1.42 66
draṣṭum icchāmi te rūpam 11.3 541
dravya-yajñās tapo-yajñā 4.28 252
droṇaṁ ca bhīṣmaṁ ca jayadrathaṁ ca 11.34 565
dṛṣṭvādbhutaṁ rūpam ugraṁ tavedaṁ 11.20 555

dṛṣṭvā hi tvāṁ pravyathitāntar-ātmā 11.24 558
dṛṣṭvā tu pāṇḍavānīkaṁ 1.2 33
dṛṣṭvedaṁ mānuṣaṁ rūpaṁ 11.51 584
dṛṣṭvemaṁ sva-janaṁ kṛṣṇa 1.28 54
drupado draupadeyāś ca 1.18 45

duḥkham ity eva yat karma 18.8 786
duḥkheṣv anudvigna-manāḥ 2.56 141
dūreṇa hy avaraṁ karma 2.49 134
dvandvair vimuktāḥ sukha-duḥkha 15.5 699
dvau bhūta-sargau loke 'smin 16.6 730

dvāv imau puruṣau loke 15.16 714
dyāv ā-pṛthivyor idam antaraṁ hi 11.20 555
dyūtaṁ chalayatām asmi 10.36 532

E

ekākī yata-cittātmā 6.10 317

ekam apy āsthitaḥ samyag   5.4   275
ekaṁ sāṅkhyaṁ ca yogaṁ ca   5.5   276
ekatvena pṛthaktvena   9.15   465
ekayā yāty anāvṛttim   8.26   436
eko 'tha vāpy acyuta tat-samakṣaṁ   11.42 572

eṣā brāhmī sthitiḥ pārtha   2.72   158
eṣā te 'bhihitā sāṅkhye   2.39   120
eṣa tūddeśataḥ prokto   10.40 535
etac chrutvā vacanaṁ keśavasya   11.35 566
etad buddhvā buddhimān syāt   15.20 719

etad dhi durlabhataraṁ   6.42   353
etad veditum icchāmi   13.1   619
etad-yonīni bhūtāni   7.6   370
etad yo vetti taṁ prāhuḥ   13.2   619
etair vimohayaty eṣa   3.40   207

etair vimuktaḥ kaunteya   16.22 745
etaj jñānam iti proktam   13.12 628
etāṁ dṛṣṭim avaṣṭabhya   16.9   734
etāṁ vibhūtiṁ yogaṁ ca   10.7   501
etan me saṁśayaṁ kṛṣṇa   6.39   349

etān na hantum icchāmi   1.34   58
etāny api tu karmāṇi   18.6   784
etasyāhaṁ na paśyāmi   6.33   342
etat kṣetraṁ samāsena   13.7   626
evaṁ bahu-vidhā yajñā   4.32   257

evaṁ buddheḥ paraṁ buddhvā   3.43   211
evam etad yathāttha tvam   11.3   541
evaṁ jñātvā kṛtaṁ karma   4.15   238
evaṁ paramparā-prāptam   4.2   216
evaṁ pravartitaṁ cakraṁ   3.16   180

evaṁ-rūpaḥ śakya ahaṁ nṛ-loke   11.48 580
evaṁ satata-yuktā ye   12.1   595
evaṁ trayī-dharmam anuprapannā   9.21   472
evam ukto hṛṣīkeśo   1.24   50
evam uktvā hṛṣīkeśaṁ   2.9   83

evam uktvārjunaḥ saṅkhye   1.46   69
evam uktvā tato rājan   11.9   547

G

gacchanty apunar-āvṛttiṁ   5.17   290
gām āviśya ca bhūtāni   15.13 710
gandharvāṇāṁ citrarathaḥ   10.26 523
gandharva-yakṣāsura-siddha-saṅghā   11.22 557
gāṇḍīvaṁ sraṁsate hastāt   1.29   55
gata-saṅgasya muktasya   4.23   246

gatāsūn agatāsūṁś ca   2.11   85
gatir bhartā prabhuḥ sākṣī   9.18   469
gṛhītvaitāni saṁyāti   15.8   704
guṇā guṇeṣu vartanta   3.28   193
guṇān etān atītya trīn   14.20 683

guṇa vartanta ity evaṁ   14.23 685
guṇebhyaś ca paraṁ vetti   14.19 682
gurūn ahatvā hi mahānubhāvān   2.5   77

H

hanta te kathayiṣyāmi   10.19 517
harṣāmarṣa-bhayodvegair   12.15 612
harṣa-śokānvitaḥ kartā   18.27 801
hato vā prāpsyasi svargaṁ   2.37   119
hatvāpi sa imāl lokān   18.17 793

hatvārtha-kāmāṁs tu gurūn ihaiva   2.5   77
hetunānena kaunteya   9.10   457
hṛṣīkeśaṁ tadā vākyam   1.20   47

I

icchā dveṣaḥ sukhaṁ duḥkhaṁ   13.7   626
icchā-dveṣa-samutthena   7.27   402
idam adya mayā labdham   16.13 737
idam astīdam api me   16.13 737
idaṁ jñānam upāśritya   14.2   664

idaṁ śarīraṁ kaunteya   13.2   619
idaṁ te nātapaskāya   18.67 836
idaṁ tu te guhyatamaṁ   9.1   441
idānīm asmi saṁvṛttaḥ   11.51 584
ihaika-sthaṁ jagat kṛtsnaṁ   11.7   545

ihaiva tair jitaḥ sargo   5.19   293
īhante kāma-bhogārtham   16.12 736
ijyate bharata-śreṣṭha   17.12 762
īkṣate yoga-yuktātmā   6.29   337
imaṁ vivasvate yogaṁ   4.1   213

indriyāṇāṁ hi caratāṁ   2.67   153
indriyāṇāṁ manaś cāsmi   10.22 520
indriyāṇi daśaikaṁ ca   13.6   626
indriyāṇi mano buddhir   3.40   207
indriyāṇīndriyārthebhyas   2.58   143

indriyāṇīndriyārthebhyas   2.68   154
indriyāṇīndriyārtheṣu   5.9   280
indriyāṇi parāṇy āhur   3.42   209
indriyāṇi pramāthīni   2.60   145
indriyārthān vimūḍhātmā   3.6   167

indriyārtheṣu vairāgyam   13.9   628
indriyasyendriyasyārthe   3.34   199
iṣṭān bhogān hi vo devā   3.12   174
iṣṭo 'si me dṛḍham iti   18.64   832
iṣubhiḥ pratiyotsyāmi   2.4   76

īśvaraḥ sarva-bhūtānāṁ   18.61   829
īśvaro 'ham ahaṁ bhogī   16.14   737
iti guhyatamaṁ śāstram   15.20   719
iti kṣetraṁ tathā jñānam   13.19   642
iti māṁ yo 'bhijānāti   4.14   236

iti matvā bhajante māṁ   10.8   502
iti te jñānam ākhyātam   18.63   831
ity ahaṁ vāsudevasya   18.74   843
ity arjunaṁ vāsudevas tathoktvā   11.50   583

J

jaghanya-guṇa-vṛtti-sthā   14.18   681
jahi śatruṁ mahā-bāho   3.43   211
janma-bandha-vinirmuktāḥ   2.51   136
janma karma ca me divyam   4.9   227
janma-mṛtyu-jarā-duḥkhair   14.20   683

janma-mṛtyu-jarā-vyādhi-   13.9   628
jarā-maraṇa-mokṣāya   7.29   404
jātasya hi dhruvo mṛtyur   2.27   108
jayo 'smi vyavasāyo 'smi   10.36   532
jhaṣāṇāṁ makaraś cāsmi   10.31   528

jijñāsur api yogasya   6.44   355
jitātmanaḥ praśāntasya   6.7   314
jīva-bhūtāṁ mahā-bāho   7.5   368
jīvanaṁ sarva-bhūteṣu   7.9   374
jñānāgni-dagdha-karmāṇam   4.19   242

jñānāgniḥ sarva-karmāṇi   4.37   263
jñānam āvṛtya tu tamaḥ   14.9   672
jñānaṁ jñeyaṁ jñāna-gamyam   13.18   641
jñānaṁ jñeyaṁ parijñātā   18.18   794
jñānaṁ karma ca kartā ca   18.19   794

jñānaṁ labdhvā parāṁ śāntim   4.39   264
jñānaṁ te 'haṁ sa-vijñānam   7.2   363
jñānaṁ vijñānam āstikyaṁ   18.42   812
jñānaṁ vijñāna-sahitaṁ   9.1   441
jñānaṁ yadā tadā vidyād   14.11   674

jñāna-vijñāna-tṛptātmā   6.8   315
jñāna-yajñena cāpy anye   9.15   465
jñāna-yajñena tenāham   18.70   839
jñāna-yogena sāṅkhyānāṁ   3.3   163
jñānena tu tad ajñānaṁ   5.16   289

jñātuṁ draṣṭuṁ ca tattvena   11.54   588
jñātvā śāstra-vidhānoktaṁ   16.24   747
jñeyaḥ sa nitya-sannyāsī   5.3   274
jñeyaṁ yat tat pravakṣyāmi   13.13   635
joṣayet sarva-karmāṇi   3.26   191
jyāyasī cet karmaṇas te   3.1   161
jyotiṣām api taj jyotis   13.18   641

K

kaccid ajñāna-sammohaḥ   18.72   840
kaccid etac chrutaṁ pārtha   18.72   840
kaccin nobhaya-vibhraṣṭaś   6.38   348
kair liṅgais trīn guṇān etān   14.21   684
kair mayā saha yoddhavyam   1.22   48

kālo 'smi loka-kṣaya-kṛt pravṛddho   11.32   563
kalpa-kṣaye punas tāni   9.7   454
kāma eṣa krodha eṣa   3.37   203
kāmaḥ krodhas tathā lobhas   16.21   744
kāmais tais tair hṛta-jñānāḥ   7.20   391

kāma-krodha-vimuktānāṁ   5.26   300
kāma-krodhodbhavaṁ vegaṁ   5.23   297
kāmam āśritya duṣpūraṁ   16.10   735
kāma-rūpeṇa kaunteya   3.39   206
kāmātmānaḥ svarga-parā   2.43   126

kāmopabhoga-paramā   16.11   736
kāmyānāṁ karmaṇāṁ nyāsaṁ   18.2   781
kāṅkṣantaḥ karmaṇāṁ siddhiṁ   4.12   233
kāraṇaṁ guṇa-saṅgo 'sya   13.22   646
karaṇaṁ karma karteti   18.18   794

karma brahmodbhavaṁ viddhi   3.15   179
karma caiva tad-arthīyaṁ   17.27   774
karma-jaṁ buddhi-yuktā hi   2.51   136
karma-jān viddhi tān sarvān   4.32   257
karmaṇaḥ sukṛtasyāhuḥ   14.16   678

karmaṇaiva hi saṁsiddhim   3.20   184
karmāṇi pravibhaktāni   18.41   811
karmaṇo hy api boddhavyaṁ   4.17   240
karmaṇy abhipravṛtto 'pi   4.20   243
karmaṇy akarma yaḥ paśyed   4.18   241

karmaṇy evādhikāras te   2.47   132
karmendriyaiḥ karma-yogam   3.7   168
karmendriyāṇi saṁyamya   3.6   167
karmibhyaś cādhiko yogī   6.46   357
kārpaṇya-doṣopahata-svabhāvaḥ   2.7   79

karṣayantaḥ śarīra-sthaṁ   17.6   757
kartavyānīti me pārtha   18.6   784

kartuṁ necchasi yan mohāt   18.60 829
kārya-kāraṇa-kartṛtve   13.21 645
kāryam ity eva yat karma   18.9   787
kāryate hy avaśaḥ karma   3.5   165
kasmāc ca te na nameran mahātman   11.37 568

kāśyaś ca parameṣv-āsaḥ   1.17   45
kathaṁ bhīṣmam ahaṁ saṅkhye   2.4   76
katham etad vijānīyāṁ   4.4   218
kathaṁ na jñeyam asmābhiḥ   1.38   62
kathaṁ sa puruṣaḥ pārtha   2.21   100

kathaṁ vidyām ahaṁ yogiṁs   10.17 515
kathayantaś ca māṁ nityam   10.9   504
kaṭv-amla-lavaṇāty-uṣṇa-   17.9   759
kaunteya pratijānīhi   9.31   485
kaviṁ purāṇam anuśāsitāram   8.9   418

kāyena manasā buddhyā   5.11   283
kecid vilagnā daśānāntareṣu   11.27 559
keśavārjunayoḥ puṇyam   18.76 845
keṣu keṣu ca bhāveṣu   10.17 515
kim ācāraḥ kathaṁ caitāṁs   14.21 684

kiṁ karma kim akarmeti   4.16   239
kiṁ no rājyena govinda   1.32   58
kiṁ punar brāhmaṇāḥ puṇyā   9.33   487
kiṁ tad brahma kim adhyātmaṁ   8.1   409
kirīṭinaṁ gadinaṁ cakra-hastam   11.46 577

kirīṭinaṁ gadinaṁ cakriṇaṁ ca   11.17 553
kīrtiḥ śrīr vāk ca nārīṇāṁ   10.34 530
klaibyaṁ mā sma gamaḥ pārtha   2.3   75
kleśo 'dhikataras teṣām   12.5   599
kriyate bahulāyāsaṁ   18.24 799

kriyate tad iha proktaṁ   17.18 767
kriyā-viśeṣa-bahulāṁ   2.43   126
krodhād bhavati sammohaḥ   2.63   149
kṛpayā parayāviṣṭo   1.27   53
kṛṣi-go-rakṣya-vāṇijyaṁ   18.44 813

kṣaraḥ sarvāṇi bhūtāni   15.16 714
kṣetra-jñaṁ cāpi māṁ viddhi   13.3   621
kṣetra-kṣetrajña-saṁyogāt   13.27 653
kṣetra-kṣetrajñayor evam   13.35 660
kṣetra-kṣetrajñayor jñānaṁ   13.3   621

kṣetraṁ kṣetrī tathā kṛtsnaṁ   13.34 659
kṣipāmy ajasram aśubhān   16.19 742
kṣipraṁ bhavati dharmātmā   9.31   488
kṣipraṁ hi mānuṣe loke   4.12   233
kṣudraṁ hṛdaya-daurbalyaṁ   2.3   75

kula-kṣaya-kṛtaṁ doṣam   1.37   62
kula-kṣaya-kṛtaṁ doṣam   1.38   62
kula-kṣaye praṇaśyanti   1.39   63
kuru karmaiva tasmāt tvaṁ   4.15   238
kuryād vidvāṁs tathāsaktaś   3.25   190
kutas tvā kaśmalam idaṁ   2.2   72

L

labhante brahma-nirvāṇam   5.25   299
labhate ca tataḥ kāmān   7.22   394
lelihyase grasamānaḥ samantāl   11.30 562
lipyate na sa pāpena   5.10   281
lobhaḥ pravṛttir ārambhaḥ   14.12 675

loka-saṅgraham evāpi   3.20   184
loke 'smin dvi-vidhā niṣṭhā   3.3   163

M

mac-cittaḥ sarva-durgāṇi   18.58 827
mac-cittā mad-gata-prāṇā   10.9   504
mad-anugrahāya paramaṁ   11.1   539
mad-artham api karmāṇi   12.10 606
mad-bhakta etad vijñāya   13.19 642

mad-bhāvā mānasā jātā   10.6   500
mādhavaḥ pāṇḍavaś caiva   1.14   42
mahā-bhūtāny ahaṅkāro   13.6   626
maharṣayaḥ sapta pūrve   10.6   500
maharṣīṇāṁ bhṛgur ahaṁ   10.25 522

mahāśano mahā-pāpmā   3.37   203
mahātmānas tu māṁ pārtha   9.13   463
mā karma-phala-hetur bhūr   2.47   132
mama dehe guḍākeśa   11.7   545
mamaivāṁśo jīva-loke   15.7   702

māmakāḥ pāṇḍavāś caiva   1.1   31
mām aprāpyaiva kaunteya   16.20 743
mām ātma-para-deheṣu   16.18 741
mama vartmānuvartante   3.23   188
mama vartmānuvartante   4.11   231

mama yonir mahad brahma   14.3   666
māṁ caivāntaḥ śarīra-sthaṁ   17.6   757
māṁ ca yo 'vyabhicāreṇa   14.26 688
mām evaiṣyasi satyaṁ te   18.65 833
mām evaiṣyasi yuktvaivam   9.34   488

mām eva ye prapadyante   7.14   379
māṁ hi pārtha vyapāśritya   9.32   486
mām upetya punar janma   8.15   425
mām upetya tu kaunteya   8.16   426

manaḥ-prasādaḥ saumyatvaṁ	17.16	766
manaḥ saṁyamya mac-citto	6.14	320
manaḥ-ṣaṣṭhānīndriyāṇi	15.7	702
mānāpamānayos tulyas	14.25	685
manasaivendriya-grāmaṁ	6.24	332
manasas tu parā buddhir	3.42	209
man-manā bhava mad-bhakto	9.34	488
man-manā bhava mad-bhakto	18.65	833
mantro 'ham aham evājyam	9.16	467
manuṣyāṇāṁ sahasreṣu	7.3	364
manyase yadi tac chakyaṁ	11.4	542
marīcir marutām asmi	10.21	519
māsānāṁ mārga-śīrṣo 'ham	10.35	531
mā śucaḥ sampadaṁ daivīm	16.5	729
mā te vyathā mā ca vimūḍha-bhāvo	11.49	582
mat-karma-kṛn mat-paramo	11.55	590
mat-prasādād avāpnoti	18.56	825
mātrā-sparśās tu kaunteya	2.14	90
mat-sthāni sarva-bhūtāni	9.4	450
matta eveti tān viddhi	7.12	377
mattaḥ parataraṁ nānyat	7.7	371
mātulāḥ śvaśurāḥ pautrāḥ	1.34	58
maunaṁ caivāsmi guhyānāṁ	10.38	534
mayādhyakṣeṇa prakṛtiḥ	9.10	457
mayā hatāṁs tvaṁ jahi mā vyathiṣṭhā	11.34	565
mayaivaite nihatāḥ pūrvam eva	11.33	564
mayā prasannena tavārjunedam	11.47	578
mayā tatam idaṁ sarvaṁ	9.4	450
māyayāpahṛta-jñānā	7.15	381
mayi cānanya-yogena	13.11	628
mayi sarvam idaṁ protaṁ	7.7	371
mayi sarvāṇi karmāṇi	3.30	195
mayy arpita-mano-buddhir	8.7	416
mayy arpita-mano-buddhir	12.14	610
mayy āsakta-manāḥ pārtha	7.1	361
mayy āveśya mano ye māṁ	12.2	597
mayy eva mana ādhatsva	12.8	604
mithyaiṣa vyavasāyas te	18.59	828
moghāśā mogha-karmāṇo	9.12	462
mohād ārabhyate karma	18.25	799
mohād gṛhītvāsad-grāhān	16.10	735
mohāt tasya parityāgas	18.7	785
mohitaṁ nābhijānāti	7.13	378
mṛgāṇāṁ ca mṛgendro 'haṁ	10.30	527
mṛtyuḥ sarva-haraś cāham	10.34	530
mūḍha-grāheṇātmano yat	17.19	768
mūḍho 'yaṁ nābhijānāti	7.25	399
mukta-saṅgo 'nahaṁ-vādī	18.26	800
munīnām apy ahaṁ vyāsaḥ	10.37	533
mūrdhny ādhāyātmanaḥ prāṇam	8.12	422

N

nabhaḥ-spṛśaṁ dīptam aneka-varṇaṁ	11.24	558
nabhaś ca pṛthivīṁ caiva	1.19	46
nābhinandati na dveṣṭi	2.57	143
na buddhi-bhedaṁ janayed	3.26	191
na cābhāvayataḥ śāntir	2.66	152
na cainaṁ kledayanty āpo	2.23	103
na caitad vidmaḥ kataran no garīyo	2.6	78
na caiva na bhaviṣyāmaḥ	2.12	86
na ca māṁ tāni karmāṇi	9.9	456
na ca mat-sthāni bhūtāni	9.5	451
na ca śaknomy avasthātuṁ	1.30	56
na ca sannyasanād eva	3.4	165
na ca śreyo 'nupaśyāmi	1.31	57
na cāśuśrūṣave vācyaṁ	18.67	836
na cāsya sarva-bhūteṣu	3.18	182
na ca tasmān manuṣyeṣu	18.69	838
na cāti-svapna-śīlasya	6.16	324
nādatte kasyacit pāpaṁ	5.15	287
na dveṣṭi sampravṛttāni	14.22	685
na dveṣṭy akuśalaṁ karma	18.10	788
nāhaṁ prakāśaḥ sarvasya	7.25	399
nāhaṁ vedair na tapasā	11.53	587
na hi deha-bhṛtā śakyaṁ	18.11	788
na hi jñānena sadṛśaṁ	4.38	264
na hi kalyāṇa-kṛt kaścid	6.40	350
na hi kaścit kṣaṇam api	3.5	165
na hinasty ātmanātmānaṁ	13.29	655
na hi prapaśyāmi mamāpanudyād	2.8	81
na hi te bhagavan vyaktiṁ	10.14	512
na hy asannyasta-saṅkalpo	6.2	309
nainaṁ chindanti śastrāṇi	2.23	103
naiṣkarmya-siddhiṁ paramāṁ	18.49	818
naite sṛtī pārtha jānan	8.27	436
naiva kiñcit karomīti	5.8	280
naiva tasya kṛtenārtho	3.18	182
na jāyate mriyate vā kadācin	2.20	98
na kāṅkṣe vijayaṁ kṛṣṇa	1.31	57
na karmaṇām anārambhān	3.4	165

na karma-phala-saṁyogaṁ	5.14	286
na kartṛtvaṁ na karmāṇi	5.14	286
nakulaḥ sahadevaś ca	1.16	45
namaḥ purastād atha pṛṣṭhatas te	11.40	571
na māṁ duṣkṛtino mūḍhāḥ	7.15	381
na māṁ karmāṇi limpanti	4.14	236
namaskṛtvā bhūya evāha kṛṣṇam	11.35	566
namasyantaś ca māṁ bhaktyā	9.14	464
na me pārthāsti kartavyaṁ	3.22	186
na me viduḥ sura-gaṇāḥ	10.2	492
namo namas te 'stu sahasra-kṛtvaḥ	11.39	570
nānā-śastra-praharaṇāḥ	1.9	38
nānavāptam avāptavyaṁ	3.22	186
nānā-vidhāni divyāni	11.5	543
nāntaṁ na madhyaṁ na punas tavādiṁ	11.16	552
nānto 'sti mama divyānāṁ	10.40	535
nānyaṁ guṇebhyaḥ kartāraṁ	14.19	682
nāpnuvanti mahātmānaḥ	8.15	425
na prahṛṣyet priyaṁ prāpya	5.20	294
narake niyataṁ vāso	1.43	67
na rūpam asyeha tathopalabhyate	15.3	697
na sa siddhim avāpnoti	16.23	746
nāsato vidyate bhāvo	2.16	92
na śaucaṁ nāpi cācāro	16.7	731
nāśayāmy ātma-bhāva-stho	10.11	508
nāsti buddhir ayuktasya	2.66	152
naṣṭo mohaḥ smṛtir labdhā	18.73	841
na tad asti pṛthivyāṁ vā	18.40	811
na tad asti vinā yat syān	10.39	535
na tad bhāsayate sūryo	15.6	700
na tu māṁ abhijānanti	9.24	475
na tu māṁ śakyase draṣṭum	11.8	545
na tvat-samo 'sty abhyadhikaḥ	11.43	574
na tv evāhaṁ jātu nāsaṁ	2.12	86
nāty-aśnatas 'tu yogo 'sti	6.16	324
nāty-ucchritaṁ nāti-nīcaṁ	6.11	319
nava-dvāre pure dehī	5.13	285
na veda-yajñādhyayanair na dānair	11.48	580
na vimuñcati durmedhā	18.35	807
nāyakā mama sainyasya	1.7	36
nāyaṁ loko 'sti na paro	4.40	265
nāyaṁ loko 'sty ayajñasya	4.31	256
na yotsya iti govindam	2.9	83
nehābhikrama-nāśo 'sti	2.40	123
nibadhnanti mahā-bāho	14.5	668

nidrālasya-pramādotthaṁ	18.39	810
nihatya dhārtarāṣṭrān naḥ	1.35	58
nimittāni ca paśyāmi	1.30	56
nindantas tava sāmarthyaṁ	2.36	118
nirāśīr nirmamo bhūtvā	3.30	195
nirāśīr yata-cittātmā	4.21	244
nirdoṣaṁ hi samaṁ brahma	5.19	293
nirdvandvo hi mahā-bāho	5.3	274
nirdvandvo nitya-sattva-stho	2.45	129
nirmamo nirahaṅkāraḥ	2.71	157
nirmamo nirahaṅkāraḥ	12.13	610
nirmāṇa-mohā jita-saṅga-doṣā	15.5	699
nirvairaḥ sarva-bhūteṣu	11.55	590
niścayaṁ śṛṇu me tatra	18.4	783
nispṛhaḥ sarva-kāmebhyo	6.18	326
nityaḥ sarva-gataḥ sthāṇur	2.24	104
nityaṁ ca sama-cittatvam	13.10	628
nivasiṣyasi mayy eva	12.8	604
niyataṁ kuru karma tvaṁ	3.8	169
niyataṁ saṅga-rahitam	18.23	798
niyatasya tu sannyāsaḥ	18.7	785
nyāyyaṁ vā viparītaṁ vā	18.15	791

O

oṁ ity ekākṣaraṁ brahma	8.13	423
oṁ tat sad iti nirdeśo	17.23	771

P

pañcaitāni mahā-bāho	18.13	790
pāñcajanyaṁ hṛṣīkeśo	1.15	43
pāpam evāśrayed asmān	1.36	60
pāpmānaṁ prajahi hy enam	3.41	208
paramaṁ puruṣaṁ divyaṁ	8.8	417
paramātmeti cāpy ukto	13.23	648
paraṁ bhāvam ajānanto	7.24	397
paraṁ bhāvam ajānanto	9.11	458
paraṁ bhūyaḥ pravakṣyāmi	14.1	663
paraṁ brahma paraṁ dhāma	10.12	509
parasparaṁ bhāvayantaḥ	3.11	173
paras tasmāt tu bhāvo 'nyo	8.20	430
parasyotsādanārthaṁ vā	17.19	768
paricaryātmakaṁ karma	18.44	813
pariṇāme viṣam iva	18.38	809
paritrāṇāya sādhūnāṁ	4.8	225
pārtha naiveha nāmutra	6.40	350
paryāptaṁ tv idam eteṣāṁ	1.10	39

paśyādityān vasūn rudrān | 11.6 | 544
paśyaitāṁ pāṇḍu-putrāṇām | 1.3 | 34
paśya me pārtha rūpāṇi | 11.5 | 543
paśyāmi devāṁs tava deva dehe | 11.15 | 551
paśyāmi tvāṁ dīpta-hutāśa-vaktraṁ | 11.19 | 554

paśyāmi tvāṁ durnirīkṣyaṁ samantād | 11.17 | 553
paśyañ śṛṇvan spṛśañ jighrann | 5.8 | 280
paśyaty akṛta-buddhitvān | 18.16 | 792
patanti pitaro hy eṣām | 1.41 | 65
patraṁ puṣpaṁ phalaṁ toyam | 9.26 | 477

pauṇḍraṁ dadhmau mahā-śaṅkham | 1.15 | 43
pavanaḥ pavatām asmi | 10.31 | 528
pitāham asya jagato | 9.17 | 468
pitāsi lokasya carācarasya | 11.43 | 574
piteva putrasya sakheva sakhyuḥ | 11.44 | 575

pitṝṇām aryamā cāsmi | 10.29 | 526
prabhavaḥ pralayaḥ sthānaṁ | 9.18 | 469
prabhavanty ugra-karmāṇaḥ | 16.9 | 734
prādhānyataḥ kuru-śreṣṭha | 10.19 | 517
prahlādaś cāsmi daityānām | 10.30 | 527

prajahāti yadā kāmān | 2.55 | 140
prajanaś cāsmi kandarpaḥ | 10.28 | 525
prakāśaṁ ca pravṛttiṁ ca | 14.22 | 685
prakṛteḥ kriyamāṇāni | 3.27 | 192
prakṛter guṇa-sammūḍhāḥ | 3.29 | 194

prakṛtiṁ puruṣaṁ caiva | 13.1 | 619
prakṛtiṁ puruṣaṁ caiva | 13.20 | 643
prakṛtiṁ svām adhiṣṭhāya | 4.6 | 222
prakṛtiṁ svām avaṣṭabhya | 9.8 | 455
prakṛtiṁ yānti bhūtāni | 3.33 | 198

prakṛtyaiva ca karmāṇi | 13.30 | 655
pralapan visṛjan gṛhṇan | 5.9 | 280
pramādālasya-nidrābhis | 14.8 | 671
pramāda-mohau tamaso | 14.17 | 680
praṇamya śirasā devam | 11.14 | 550

prāṇāpāna-gatī ruddhvā | 4.29 | 253
prāṇāpāna-samāyuktaḥ | 15.14 | 711
prāṇāpānau samau kṛtvā | 5.27 | 302
praṇavaḥ sarva-vedeṣu | 7.8 | 373
prāpya puṇya-kṛtāṁ lokān | 6.41 | 352

prasāde sarva-duḥkhānāṁ | 2.65 | 152
prasaktāḥ kāma-bhogeṣu | 16.16 | 739
prasaṅgena phalākāṅkṣī | 18.34 | 806
prasanna-cetaso hy āśu | 2.65 | 152
praśānta-manasaṁ hy enam | 6.27 | 335

praśāntātmā vigata-bhīr | 6.14 | 320
praśaste karmaṇi tathā | 17.26 | 774
pratyakṣāvagamaṁ dharmyam | 9.2 | 443
pravartante vidhānoktāḥ | 17.24 | 773
pravṛtte śastra-sampāte | 1.20 | 47

pravṛttiṁ ca nivṛttiṁ ca | 16.7 | 731
pravṛttiṁ ca nivṛttiṁ ca | 18.30 | 803
prayāṇa-kāle 'pi ca māṁ | 7.30 | 406
prayāṇa-kāle ca kathaṁ | 8.2 | 410
prayāṇa-kāle manasācalena | 8.10 | 420

prayātā yānti taṁ kālaṁ | 8.23 | 433
prayatnād yatamānas tu | 6.45 | 356
pretān bhūta-gaṇāṁś cānye | 17.4 | 755
priyo hi jñānino 'tyartham | 7.17 | 388
procyamānam aśeṣeṇa | 18.29 | 803

procyate guṇa-saṅkhyāne | 18.19 | 794
pṛthaktvena tu yaj jñānam | 18.21 | 796
puṇyo gandhaḥ pṛthivyāṁ ca | 7.9 | 374
purodhasāṁ ca mukhyaṁ māṁ | 10.24 | 522
purujit kuntibhojaś ca | 1.5 | 36

puruṣaḥ prakṛti-stho hi | 13.22 | 646
puruṣaḥ sa paraḥ pārtha | 8.22 | 432
puruṣaḥ sukha-duḥkhānāṁ | 13.21 | 645
puruṣaṁ śāśvataṁ divyam | 10.12 | 509
pūrvābhyāsena tenaiva | 6.44 | 355
puṣṇāmi causadhīḥ sarvāḥ | 15.13 | 710

R

rāga-dveṣa-vimuktais tu | 2.64 | 151
rāgī karma-phala-prepsur | 18.27 | 801
rajaḥ sattvaṁ tamaś caiva | 14.10 | 673
rājan saṁsmṛtya saṁsmṛtya | 18.76 | 845
rajasas tu phalaṁ duḥkham | 14.16 | 678

rajasi pralayaṁ gatvā | 14.15 | 677
rajas tamaś cābhibhūya | 14.10 | 673
rajasy etāni jāyante | 14.12 | 675
rāja-vidyā rāja-guhyaṁ | 9.2 | 443
rajo rāgātmakaṁ viddhi | 14.7 | 670

rakṣāṁsi bhītāni diśo dravanti | 11.36 | 567
rākṣasīm āsurīṁ caiva | 9.12 | 462
rasa-varjaṁ raso 'py asya | 2.59 | 144
raso 'ham apsu kaunteya | 7.8 | 373
rasyāḥ snigdhāḥ sthirā hṛdyā | 17.8 | 759

rātriṁ yuga-sahasrāntāṁ | 8.17 | 427
rātry-āgame pralīyante | 8.18 | 428

rātry-āgame 'vaśaḥ pārtha	8.19	429
ṛṣibhir bahudhā gītaṁ	13.5	625
ṛte 'pi tvāṁ na bhaviṣyanti sarve	11.32	563
rudrādityā vasavo ye ca sādhyā	11.22	557
rudrāṇāṁ śaṅkaraś cāsmi	10.23	521
rūpaṁ mahat te bahu-vaktra-netraṁ	11.23	557

S

śabdādīn viṣayāṁs tyaktvā	18.51	820
śabdādīn viṣayān anya	4.26	250
sa brahma-yoga-yuktātmā	5.21	295
sa buddhimān manuṣyeṣu	4.18	241
sa ca yo yat-prabhāvaś ca	13.4	624
sad-bhāve sādhu-bhāve ca	17.26	774
sādhibhūtādhidaivaṁ māṁ	7.30	406
sādhur eva sa mantavyaḥ	9.30	483
sādhuṣv api ca pāpeṣu	6.9	316
sadṛśaṁ ceṣṭate svasyāḥ	3.33	198
sa evāyaṁ mayā te 'dya	4.3	217
sa ghoṣo dhārtarāṣṭrāṇāṁ	1.19	46
sa guṇān samatītyaitān	14.26	688
saha-jaṁ karma kaunteya	18.48	817
sahasaivābhyahanyanta	1.13	42
sahasra-yuga-paryantam	8.17	427
saha-yajñāḥ prajāḥ sṛṣṭvā	3.10	171
sa kāleneha mahatā	4.2	216
sakheti matvā prasabhaṁ yad uktaṁ	11.41	572
śaknotīhaiva yaḥ soḍhuṁ	5.23	297
sa kṛtvā rājasaṁ tyāgaṁ	18.8	786
saktāḥ karmaṇy avidvāṁso	3.25	190
śakya evaṁ-vidho draṣṭuṁ	11.53	587
samādhāv acalā buddhis	2.53	138
sama-duḥkha-sukhaḥ sva-sthaḥ	14.24	685
sama-duḥkha-sukhaṁ dhīraṁ	2.15	91
samaḥ sarveṣu bhūteṣu	18.54	821
samaḥ śatrau ca mitre ca	12.18	615
samaḥ siddhāv asiddhau ca	4.22	245
samaṁ kāya-śiro-grīvaṁ	6.13	320
samaṁ paśyan hi sarvatra	13.29	655
samaṁ sarveṣu bhūteṣu	13.28	654
samāsenaiva kaunteya	18.50	819
sambhavaḥ sarva-bhūtānāṁ	14.3	666
sambhāvitasya cākīrtir	2.34	116
śamo damas tapaḥ śaucaṁ	18.42	812
samo 'haṁ sarva-bhūteṣu	9.29	482

samprekṣya nāsikāgraṁ svaṁ	6.13	320
saṁvādam imam aśrauṣam	18.74	843
śanaiḥ śanair uparamed	6.25	333
saṅgaṁ tyaktvā phalaṁ caiva	18.9	787
saṅgāt sañjāyate kāmaḥ	2.62	148
sa niścayena yoktavyo	6.24	332
saṅkalpa-prabhavān kāmāṁs	6.24	332
saṅkarasya ca kartā syām	3.24	188
saṅkaro narakāyaiva	1.41	65
sāṅkhya-yogau pṛthag bālāḥ	5.4	275
sāṅkhye kṛtānte proktāni	18.13	790
sanniyamyendriya-grāmaṁ	12.4	598
sannyāsaḥ karma-yogaś ca	5.2	272
sannyāsaṁ karmaṇāṁ kṛṣṇa	5.1	271
sannyāsas tu mahā-bāho	5.6	277
sannyāsasya mahā-bāho	18.1	779
sannyāsa-yoga-yuktātmā	9.28	480
śāntiṁ nirvāṇa-paramāṁ	6.15	322
santuṣṭaḥ satataṁ yogī	12.14	610
sargāṇām ādir antaś ca	10.32	528
sarge 'pi nopajāyante	14.2	664
śārīraṁ kevalaṁ karma	4.21	244
śarīraṁ yad avāpnoti	15.8	704
śarīra-stho 'pi kaunteya	13.32	657
śarīra-vāṅ-manobhir yat	18.15	791
śarīra-yātrāpi ca te	3.8	169
sarva-bhūtāni kaunteya	9.7	454
sarva-bhūtāni sammohaṁ	7.27	402
sarva-bhūta-stham ātmānaṁ	6.29	337
sarva-bhūta-sthitaṁ yo māṁ	6.31	339
sarva-bhūtātma-bhūtātmā	5.7	279
sarva-bhūteṣu yenaikaṁ	18.20	795
sarva-dharmān parityajya	18.66	834
sarva-dvārāṇi saṁyamya	8.12	422
sarva-dvāreṣu dehe 'smin	14.11	674
sarva-guhyatamaṁ bhūyaḥ	18.64	832
sarva-jñāna-vimūḍhāṁs tān	3.32	198
sarva-karmāṇi manasā	5.13	285
sarva-karmāṇy api sadā	18.56	825
sarva-karma-phala-tyāgaṁ	12.11	607
sarva-karma-phala-tyāgaṁ	18.2	781
sarvam etad ṛtaṁ manye	10.14	512
sarvaṁ jñāna-plavenaiva	4.36	262
sarvaṁ karmākhilaṁ pārtha	4.33	258
sarvāṇīndriya-karmāṇi	4.27	251

sarvārambhā hi doṣeṇa	18.48	817
sarvārambha-parityāgī	12.16	613
sarvārambha-parityāgī	14.25	685
sarvārthān viparītāṁś ca	18.32	805
sarva-saṅkalpa-sannyāsī	6.4	311
sarvāścarya-mayaṁ devam	11.11	547
sarvasya cāhaṁ hṛdi sanniviṣṭo	15.15	712
sarvasya dhātāram acintya-rūpam	8.9	418
sarvataḥ pāṇi-pādaṁ tat	13.14	636
sarvataḥ śrutimal loke	13.14	636
sarvathā vartamāno 'pi	6.31	339
sarvathā vartamāno 'pi	13.24	649
sarvatra-gam acintyaṁ ca	12.3	598
sarvatrāvasthito dehe	13.33	658
sarva-yoniṣu kaunteya	14.4	667
sarvendriya-guṇābhāsaṁ	13.15	637
sarve 'py ete yajña-vido	4.30	255
sa sannyāsī ca yogī ca	6.1	307
sa sarva-vid bhajati māṁ	15.19	717
śāśvatasya ca dharmasya	14.27	689
satataṁ kīrtayanto māṁ	9.14	464
sa tayā śraddhayā yuktas	7.22	394
satkāra-māna-pūjārtham	17.18	767
sattvaṁ prakṛti-jair muktaṁ	18.40	811
sattvaṁ rajas tama iti	14.5	668
sattvaṁ sukhe sañjayati	14.9	672
sattvānurūpā sarvasya	17.3	753
sattvāt sañjāyate jñānaṁ	14.17	680
sāttvikī rājasī caiva	17.2	752
saubhadraś ca mahā-bāhuḥ	1.18	45
saubhadro draupadeyāś ca	1.6	36
śauryaṁ tejo dhṛtir dākṣyaṁ	18.43	812
sa yat pramāṇaṁ kurute	3.21	185
sa yogī brahma-nirvāṇaṁ	5.24	298
senānīnām aham skandaḥ	10.24	522
senayor ubhayor madhye	1.21	48
senayor ubhayor madhye	1.24	50
senayor ubhayor madhye	2.10	84
sīdanti mama gātrāṇi	1.28	54
siddhiṁ prāpto yathā brahma	18.50	819
siddhy-asiddhyoḥ samo bhūtvā	2.48	133
siddhy-asiddhyor nirvikāraḥ	18.26	800
siṁha-nādaṁ vinadyoccaiḥ	1.12	41
śītoṣṇa-sukha-duḥkheṣu	6.7	314
śītoṣṇa-sukha-duḥkheṣu	12.18	615
smṛti-bhraṁśād buddhi-nāśo	2.63	149
so 'pi muktaḥ śubhāl lokān	18.71	839
so 'vikalpena yogena	10.7	501
sparśān kṛtvā bahir bāhyāṁś	5.27	302
śraddadhānā mat-paramā	12.20	616
śraddhā-mayo 'yaṁ puruṣo	17.3	753
śraddhāvāl labhate jñānaṁ	4.39	264
śraddhāvān anasūyaś ca	18.71	839
śraddhāvān bhajate yo māṁ	6.47	358
śraddhāvanto 'nasūyanto	3.31	196
śraddhā-virahitaṁ yajñaṁ	17.13	763
śraddhayā parayā taptaṁ	17.17	767
śraddhayā parayopetās	12.2	597
śreyān dravya-mayād yajñāj	4.33	258
śreyān sva-dharmo viguṇaḥ	3.35	201
śreyān sva-dharmo viguṇaḥ	18.47	815
śreyo hi jñānam abhyāsāj	12.12	609
śrotrādīnīndriyāṇy anye	4.26	250
śrotraṁ cakṣuḥ sparśanaṁ ca	15.9	705
śruti-vipratipannā te	2.53	138
sthāne hṛṣīkeśa tava prakīrtyā	11.36	567
sthira-buddhir asammūḍho	5.20	294
sthita-dhīḥ kiṁ prabhāṣeta	2.54	139
sthita-prajñasya kā bhāṣā	2.54	139
sthito 'smi gata-sandehaḥ	18.73	841
sthitvāsyām anta-kāle 'pi	2.72	158
strīṣu duṣṭāsu vārṣṇeya	1.40	64
striyo vaiśyās tathā śūdrās	9.32	486
śubhāśubha-parityāgī	12.17	614
śubhāśubha-phalair evaṁ	9.28	480
śucau deśe pratiṣṭhāpya	6.11	319
śucīnāṁ śrīmatāṁ gehe	6.41	352
su-durdarśam idaṁ rūpaṁ	11.52	585
suhṛdaṁ sarva-bhūtānāṁ	5.29	303
suhṛn-mitrāry-udāsīna-	6.9	316
sukha-duḥkhe same kṛtvā	2.38	119
sukham ātyantikaṁ yat tad	6.21	329
sukhaṁ duḥkhaṁ bhavo 'bhāvo	10.4	496
sukhaṁ tv idānīṁ tri-vidhaṁ	18.36	808
sukhaṁ vā yadi vā duḥkhaṁ	6.32	341
sukha-saṅgena badhnāti	14.6	669
sukhena brahma-saṁsparśam	6.28	336
sukhinaḥ kṣatriyāḥ pārtha	2.32	115
śukla-kṛṣṇe gatī hy ete	8.26	436
sūkṣmatvāt tad avijñeyaṁ	13.16	639
śuni caiva śva-pāke ca	5.18	291
svabhāva-jena kaunteya	18.60	829
svabhāva-niyataṁ karma	18.47	815
sva-dharmam api cāvekṣya	2.31	113

sva-dharme nidhanaṁ śreyaḥ	3.35	201
svādhyāyābhyasanaṁ caiva	17.15	765
svādhyāya-jñāna-yajñāś ca	4.28	252
sva-janaṁ hi kathaṁ hatvā	1.36	60
sva-karmaṇā tam abhyarcya	18.46	814
sva-karma-nirataḥ siddhiṁ	18.45	813
sv-alpam apy asya dharmasya	2.40	123
svastīty uktvā maharṣi-siddha-saṅghāḥ	11.21	556
śvaśurān suhṛdaś caiva	1.26	52
svayam evātmanātmānaṁ	10.15	513
sve sve karmaṇy abhirataḥ	18.45	813

T

tac ca saṁsmṛtya saṁsmṛtya	18.77	846
tadā gantāsi nirvedaṁ	2.52	137
tad ahaṁ bhakty-upahṛtam	9.26	477
tad-arthaṁ karma kaunteya	3.9	170
tad asya harati prajñāṁ	2.67	153
tad-buddhayas tad-ātmānas	5.17	290
tad ekaṁ vada niścitya	3.2	162
tad eva me darśaya deva rūpaṁ	11.45	576
tad ity anabhisandhāya	17.25	774
tadottama-vidāṁ lokān	14.14	676
tadvat kāmā yaṁ praviśanti sarve	2.70	155
tad viddhi praṇipātena	4.34	259
ta ime 'vasthitā yuddhe	1.33	58
tair dattān apradāyaibhyo	3.12	174
tamas tv ajñāna-jaṁ viddhi	14.8	671
tamasy etāni jāyante	14.13	676
tam eva cādyaṁ puruṣaṁ prapadye	15.4	697
tam eva śaraṇaṁ gaccha	18.62	830
taṁ tam evaiti kaunteya	8.6	415
taṁ taṁ niyamam āsthāya	7.20	391
taṁ tathā kṛpayāviṣṭam	2.1	71
tam uvāca hṛṣīkeśaḥ	2.10	84
taṁ vidyād duḥkha-saṁyoga-	6.23	329
tān ahaṁ dviṣataḥ krūrān	16.19	742
tān akṛtsna-vido mandān	3.29	194
tāni sarvāṇi saṁyamya	2.61	147
tan nibadhnāti kaunteya	14.7	670
tān samīkṣya sa kaunteyaḥ	1.27	53
tāny ahaṁ veda sarvāṇi	4.5	219
tapāmy aham ahaṁ varṣaṁ	9.19	470
tapasvibhyo 'dhiko yogī	6.46	357
tāsāṁ brahma mahad yonir	14.4	667
tasmāc chāstraṁ pramāṇaṁ te	16.24	747
tasmād ajñāna-sambhūtaṁ	4.42	267

tasmād aparihārye 'rthe	2.27	108
tasmād asaktaḥ satataṁ	3.19	183
tasmād evaṁ viditvainaṁ	2.25	105
tasmād oṁ ity udāhṛtya	17.24	773
tasmād uttiṣṭha kaunteya	2.37	119
tasmād yasya mahā-bāho	2.68	154
tasmād yogāya yujyasva	2.50	135
tasmān nārhā vayaṁ hantuṁ	1.36	60
tasmāt praṇamya praṇidhāya kāyaṁ	11.44	575
tasmāt sarva-gataṁ brahma	3.15	179
tasmāt sarvāṇi bhūtāni	2.30	112
tasmāt sarveṣu kāleṣu	8.7	416
tasmāt sarveṣu kāleṣu	8.27	436
tasmāt tvam indriyāṇy ādau	3.41	208
tasmāt tvam uttiṣṭha yaśo labhasva	11.33	564
tasyāhaṁ na praṇaśyāmi	6.30	338
tasyāhaṁ nigrahaṁ manye	6.34	343
tasyāhaṁ sulabhaḥ pārtha	8.14	423
tasya kartāram api māṁ	4.13	235
tasya sañjanayan harṣaṁ	1.12	41
tasya tasyācalāṁ śraddhāṁ	7.21	392
tata eva ca vistāraṁ	13.31	656
tataḥ padaṁ tat parimārgitavyaṁ	15.4	697
tataḥ śaṅkhāś ca bheryaś ca	1.13	42
tataḥ sa vismayāviṣṭo	11.14	550
tataḥ sva-dharmaṁ kīrtiṁ ca	2.33	116
tataḥ śvetair hayair yukte	1.14	42
tatas tato niyamyaitad	6.26	334
tathā dehāntara-prāptir	2.13	88
tathaiva nāśāya viśanti lokās	11.29	561
tathāpi tvaṁ mahā-bāho	2.26	106
tathā pralīnas tamasi	14.15	677
tathā śarīrāṇi vihāya jīrṇāny	2.22	101
tathā sarvāṇi bhūtāni	9.6	453
tathā tavāmī nara-loka-vīrā	11.28	560
tat kiṁ karmaṇi ghore māṁ	3.1	161
tat kṣetraṁ yac ca yādṛk ca	13.4	624
tato māṁ tattvato jñātvā	18.55	823
tato yuddhāya yujyasva	2.38	119
tat-prasādāt paraṁ śāntim	18.62	830
tatra cāndramasaṁ jyotir	8.25	435
tatraikāgraṁ manaḥ kṛtvā	6.12	319
tatraika-sthaṁ jagat kṛtsnaṁ	11.13	549
tatraivaṁ sati kartāram	18.16	792
tatrāpaśyat sthitān pārthaḥ	1.26	52
tatra prayātā gacchanti	8.24	434
tatra sattvaṁ nirmalatvāt	14.6	669

tatra śrīr vijayo bhūtir	18.78	847
tatra taṁ buddhi-saṁyogaṁ	6.43	354
tat sukhaṁ sāttvikaṁ proktam	18.37	808
tat svayaṁ yoga-saṁsiddhaḥ	4.38	264
tat tad evāvagaccha tvaṁ	10.41	536
tat te karma pravakṣyāmi	4.16	239
tattva-vit tu mahā-bāho	3.28	193
tāvān sarveṣu vedeṣu	2.46	130
tayor na vaśam āgacchet	3.34	199
tayos tu karma-sannyāsāt	5.2	272
te 'pi cātitaranty eva	13.26	651
te 'pi mām eva kaunteya	9.23	474
te brahma tad viduḥ kṛtsnam	7.29	404
te dvandva-moha-nirmuktā	7.28	403
tejaḥ kṣamā dhṛtiḥ śaucam	16.3	721
tejobhir āpūrya jagat samagraṁ	11.30	562
tejo-mayaṁ viśvam anantam ādyaṁ	11.47	578
tenaiva rūpeṇa catur-bhujena	11.46	577
te prāpnuvanti mām eva	12.4	598
te puṇyam āsādya surendra-lokam	9.20	471
teṣām āditya-vaj jñānaṁ	5.16	289
teṣām ahaṁ samuddhartā	12.7	601
teṣām evānukampārtham	10.11	508
teṣāṁ jñānī nitya-yukta	7.17	388
teṣāṁ niṣṭhā tu kā kṛṣṇa	17.1	751
teṣāṁ nityābhiyuktānāṁ	9.22	473
teṣāṁ satata-yuktānāṁ	10.10	506
te taṁ bhuktvā svarga-lokaṁ viśālaṁ	9.21	472
trai-guṇya-viṣayā vedā	2.45	129
trai-vidyā māṁ soma-pāḥ pūta-pāpā	9.20	471
tribhir guṇa-mayair bhāvair	7.13	378
tri-vidhā bhavati śraddhā	17.2	752
tri-vidhaṁ narakasyedaṁ	16.21	744
tulya-nindā-stutir maunī	12.19	615
tulya-priyāpriyo dhīras	14.24	685
tvad-anyaḥ saṁśayasyāsya	6.39	349
tvam ādi-devaḥ puruṣaḥ purāṇas	11.38	569
tvam akṣaraṁ paramaṁ veditavyaṁ	11.18	553
tvam avyayaḥ śāśvata-dharma-goptā	11.18	553
tvattaḥ kamala-patrākṣa	11.2	540
tyāgasya ca hṛṣīkeśa	18.1	779
tyāgī sattva-samāviṣṭo	18.10	788
tyāgo hi puruṣa-vyāghra	18.4	783
tyājyaṁ doṣa-vad ity eke	18.3	782
tyaktvā dehaṁ punar janma	4.9	227
tyaktvā karma-phalāsaṅgaṁ	4.20	243

U

| ubhau tau na vijānīto | 2.19 | 97 |

ubhayor api dṛṣṭo 'ntas	2.16	92
uccaiḥśravasam aśvānāṁ	10.27	524
ucchiṣṭam api cāmedhyaṁ	17.10	759
udārāḥ sarva evaite	7.18	389
udāsīna-vad āsīnam	9.9	456
udāsīna-vad āsīno	14.23	685
uddhared ātmanātmānaṁ	6.5	312
upadekṣyanti te jñānaṁ	4.34	259
upadraṣṭānumantā ca	13.23	648
upaiti śānta-rajasaṁ	6.27	335
upaviśyāsane yuñjyād	6.12	319
ūrdhvaṁ gacchanti sattva-sthā	14.18	681
ūrdhva-mūlam adhaḥ-śākham	15.1	693
utkrāmantaṁ sthitaṁ vāpi	15.10	706
utsādyante jāti-dharmāḥ	1.42	66
utsanna-kula-dharmāṇāṁ	1.43	67
utsīdeyur ime lokā	3.24	188
uttamaḥ puruṣas tv anyaḥ	15.17	715
uvāca pārtha paśyaitān	1.25	51

V

vaktrāṇi te tvaramāṇā viśanti	11.27	559
vaktum arhasy aśeṣeṇa	10.16	514
vāsāṁsi jīrṇāni yathā vihāya	2.22	101
vaśe hi yasyendriyāṇi	2.61	147
vāsudevaḥ sarvam iti	7.19	390
vasūnāṁ pāvakaś cāsmi	10.23	521
vaśyātmanā tu yatatā	6.36	346
vāyur yamo 'gnir varuṇaḥ śaśāṅkaḥ	11.39	570
vedāhaṁ samatītāni	7.26	401
vedaiś ca sarvair aham eva vedyo	15.15	712
vedānāṁ sāma-vedo 'smi	10.22	520
veda-vāda-ratāḥ pārtha	2.42	126
vedāvināśinaṁ nityaṁ	2.21	100
vedeṣu yajñeṣu tapaḥsu caiva	8.28	437
vedyaṁ pavitram oṁkāra	9.17	468
vepathuś ca śarīre me	1.29	55
vettāsi vedyaṁ ca paraṁ ca dhāma	11.38	569
vetti sarveṣu bhūteṣu	18.21	796
vetti yatra na caivāyaṁ	6.21	329
vidhi-hīnam asṛṣṭānnam	17.13	763
vidyā-vinaya-sampanne	5.18	291
vigatecchā-bhaya-krodho	5.28	302
vihāya kāmān yaḥ sarvān	2.71	157
vijñātum icchāmi bhavantam ādyaṁ	11.31	562
vikārāṁś ca guṇāṁś caiva	13.20	643
vimṛśyaitad aśeṣeṇa	18.63	831
vimucya nirmamaḥ śānto	18.53	820

vimūḍhā nānupaśyanti	15.10	706
vināśam avyayasyāsya	2.17	94
vinaśyatsv avinaśyantaṁ	13.28	654
viṣādī dīrgha-sūtrī ca	18.28	802
viṣayā vinivartante	2.59	144
viṣayendriya-saṁyogād	18.38	809
viṣīdantam idaṁ vākyam	2.1	71
vismayo me mahān rājan	18.77	846
visṛjya sa-śaraṁ cāpaṁ	1.46	69
viṣṭabhyāham idaṁ kṛtsnam	10.42	537
vistareṇātmano yogaṁ	10.18	516
vīta-rāga-bhaya-krodhā	4.10	229
vīta-rāga-bhaya-krodhaḥ	2.56	141
vivasvān manave prāha	4.1	213
vividhāś ca pṛthak ceṣṭā	18.14	790
vivikta-deśa-sevitvam	13.11	628
vivikta-sevī laghv-āśī	18.52	820
vṛṣṇīnāṁ vāsudevo 'smi	10.37	533
vyāmiśreṇeva vākyena	3.2	162
vyapeta-bhīḥ prīta-manāḥ punas tvam	11.49	582
vyāsa-prasādāc chrutavān	18.75	844
vyavasāyātmikā buddhiḥ	2.44	128
vyavasāyātmikā buddhir	2.41	125
vyūḍhāṁ drupada-putreṇa	1.3	34

Y

yābhir vibhūtibhir lokān	10.16	514
yac candramasi yac cāgnau	15.12	708
yac cāpi sarva-bhūtānāṁ	10.39	535
yac cāvahāsārtham asat-kṛto 'si	11.42	572
yac chreya etayor ekaṁ	5.1	271
yac chreyaḥ syān niścitaṁ brūhi tan	2.7	79
yadā bhūta-pṛthag-bhāvam	13.31	656
yad āditya-gataṁ tejo	15.12	708
yad agre cānubandhe ca	18.39	810
yad ahaṅkāram āśritya	18.59	828
yadā hi nendriyārtheṣu	6.4	311
yad akṣaraṁ veda-vido vadanti	8.11	421
yadā saṁharate cāyaṁ	2.58	143
yadā sattve pravṛddhe tu	14.14	676
yadā te moha-kalilaṁ	2.52	137
yadā viniyataṁ cittam	6.18	326
yadā yadā hi dharmasya	4.7	224
yad gatvā na nivartante	15.6	700
yadi bhāḥ sadṛśī sā syād	11.12	548
yad icchanto brahmacaryaṁ caranti	8.11	421
yadi hy ahaṁ na varteyam	3.23	188
yadi mām apratīkāram	1.45	68

yad rājya-sukha-lobhena	1.44	68
yadṛcchā-lābha-santuṣṭo	4.22	245
yadṛcchayā copapannaṁ	2.32	115
yad yad ācarati śreṣṭhas	3.21	185
yad yad vibhūtimat sattvaṁ	10.41	536
yady apy ete na paśyanti	1.37	62
ya enaṁ vetti hantāraṁ	2.19	97
ya evaṁ vetti puruṣaṁ	13.24	649
yaḥ paśyati tathātmānam	13.30	655
yaḥ prayāti sa mad-bhāvaṁ	8.5	414
yaḥ prayāti tyajan dehaṁ	8.13	423
yaḥ sarvatrānabhisnehas	2.57	143
yaḥ sa sarveṣu bhūteṣu	8.20	430
yaḥ śāstra-vidhim utsṛjya	16.23	746
ya idaṁ paramaṁ guhyaṁ	18.68	837
yajante nāma-yajñais te	16.17	740
yajante sāttvikā devān	17.4	755
yaj jñātvā munayaḥ sarve	14.1	663
yaj jñātvā na punar moham	4.35	260
yaj jñātvā neha bhūyo 'nyaj	7.2	363
yajña-dāna-tapaḥ-karma	18.3	782
yajña-dāna-tapaḥ-karma	18.5	783
yajñād bhavati parjanyo	3.14	177
yajñānāṁ japa-yajño 'smi	10.25	522
yajñārthāt karmaṇo 'nyatra	3.9	170
yajña-śiṣṭāmṛta-bhujo	4.30	255
yajña-śiṣṭāśinaḥ santo	3.13	176
yajñas tapas tathā dānaṁ	17.7	758
yajñāyācarataḥ karma	4.23	246
yajñe tapasi dāne ca	17.27	774
yajño dānaṁ tapaś caiva	18.5	783
yakṣye dāsyāmi modiṣya	16.15	737
yaṁ hi na vyathayanty ete	2.15	91
yām imāṁ puṣpitāṁ vācaṁ	2.42	126
yaṁ labdhvā cāparaṁ lābhaṁ	6.22	329
yaṁ prāpya na nivartante	8.21	431
yaṁ sannyāsam iti prāhur	6.2	309
yaṁ yaṁ vāpi smaran bhāvaṁ	8.6	415
yān eva hatvā na jijīviṣāmas	2.6	78
yā niśā sarva-bhūtānāṁ	2.69	154
yānti deva-vratā devān	9.25	476
yasmān nodvijate loko	12.15	612
yasmāt kṣaram atīto 'ham	15.18	716
yasmin sthito na duḥkhena	6.22	329
yaṣṭavyam eveti manaḥ	17.11	762
yas tu karma-phala-tyāgī	18.11	788
yas tv ātma-ratir eva syād	3.17	181

yas tv indriyāṇi manasā	3.7	168
yasyāṁ jāgrati bhūtāni	2.69	154
yasya nāhaṅkṛto bhāvo	18.17	793
yasyāntaḥ-sthāni bhūtāni	8.22	432
yasya sarve samārambhāḥ	4.19	242
yataḥ pravṛttir bhūtānāṁ	18.46	814
yatanto 'py akṛtātmāno	15.11	707
yatanto yoginaś cainaṁ	15.11	707
yatatām api siddhānāṁ	7.3	364
yatate ca tato bhūyaḥ	6.43	354
yatato hy api kaunteya	2.60	145
yāta-yāmaṁ gata-rasaṁ	17.10	759
yatendriya-mano-buddhir	5.28	302
yathā dīpo nivāta-stho	6.19	328
yathaidhāṁsi samiddho 'gnir	4.37	263
yathākāśa-sthito nityaṁ	9.6	453
yathā nadīnāṁ bahavo 'mbu-vegāḥ	11.28	560
yathā pradīptaṁ jvalanaṁ pataṅgā	11.29	561
yathā prakāśayaty ekaḥ	13.34	659
yathā sarva-gataṁ saukṣmyād	13.33	658
yatholbenāvṛto garbhas	3.38	205
yat karoṣi yad aśnāsi	9.27	479
yato yato niścalati	6.26	334
yatra caivātmanātmānaṁ	6.20	329
yatra kāle tv anāvṛttim	8.23	433
yatra yogeśvaraḥ kṛṣṇo	18.78	847
yatroparamate cittaṁ	6.20	329
yat sāṅkhyaiḥ prāpyate sthānaṁ	5.5	276
yat tad agre viṣam iva	18.37	808
yat tapasyasi kaunteya	9.27	479
yat te 'haṁ prīyamāṇāya	10.1	491
yat tu kāmepsunā karma	18.24	799
yat tu kṛtsna-vad ekasmin	18.22	797
yat tu pratyupakārārthaṁ	17.21	770
yat tvayoktaṁ vacas tena	11.1	539
yāvad etān nirīkṣe 'haṁ	1.21	48
yāvān artha udapāne	2.46	130
yāvat sañjāyate kiñcit	13.27	653
yayā dharmam adharmaṁ ca	18.31	804
yayā svapnaṁ bhayaṁ śokaṁ	18.35	807
yayā tu dharma-kāmārthān	18.34	806
ye bhajanti tu māṁ bhaktyā	9.29	482
ye caiva sāttvikā bhāvā	7.12	377
ye cāpy akṣaram avyaktaṁ	12.1	595
ye hi saṁsparśa-jā bhogā	5.22	296
ye me matam idaṁ nityam	3.31	197
yena bhūtāny aśeṣāṇi	4.35	260
ye 'py anya-devatā-bhaktā	9.23	474
yeṣām arthe kāṅkṣitaṁ no	1.32	58
yeṣāṁ ca tvaṁ bahu-mato	2.35	117
yeṣāṁ tv anta-gataṁ pāpaṁ	7.28	403
ye śāstra-vidhim utsṛjya	17.1	751
ye tu dharmāmṛtam idaṁ	12.20	616
ye tu sarvāṇi karmāṇi	12.6	601
ye tv akṣaram anirdeśyam	12.3	598
ye tv etad abhyasūyanto	3.32	198
ye yathā māṁ prapadyante	4.11	231
yogaṁ yogeśvarāt kṛṣṇāt	18.75	844
yogārūḍhasya tasyaiva	6.3	310
yoga-sannyasta-karmāṇaṁ	4.41	266
yoga-sthaḥ kuru karmāṇi	2.48	133
yoga-yukto munir brahma	5.6	277
yoga-yukto viśuddhātmā	5.7	279
yogenāvyabhicāriṇyā	18.33	806
yogeśvara tato me tvaṁ	11.4	542
yoginaḥ karma kurvanti	5.11	283
yoginām api sarveṣāṁ	6.47	358
yogino yata-cittasya	6.19	328
yogī yuñjīta satatam	6.10	317
yo loka-trayam āviśya	15.17	715
yo māṁ ajam anādiṁ ca	10.3	494
yo māṁ evam asammūḍho	15.19	717
yo māṁ paśyati sarvatra	6.30	338
yo na hṛṣyati na dveṣṭi	12.17	614
yo 'ntaḥ-sukho 'ntar-ārāmas	5.24	298
yotsyamānān avekṣe 'haṁ	1.23	50
yo 'yaṁ yogas tvayā proktaḥ	6.33	342
yo yo yāṁ yāṁ tanuṁ bhaktaḥ	7.21	392
yudhāmanyuś ca vikrānta	1.6	36
yuktāhāra-vihārasya	6.17	325
yuktaḥ karma-phalaṁ tyaktvā	5.12	284
yukta ity ucyate yogī	6.8	315
yukta-svapnāvabodhasya	6.17	325
yuñjann evaṁ sadātmānaṁ	6.15	322
yuñjann evaṁ sadātmānaṁ	6.28	336
yuyudhāno virāṭaś ca	1.4	35

General Index

Numerals in boldface type indicate references to translations of the verses of *Bhāgavad-gītā As It Is.*

A

Abhimanyu
  doomed at Kurukṣetra, 46
Abhyāsa-yoga-yuktena cetasā nānya-gāminā
  verses quoted, 26
Abode, Supreme
  See Supreme abode, Spiritual sky, Goloka
    Vṛndāvana
Ābrahma-bhuvanāl lokāḥ punar āvartino 'rjuna.
  quoted, 19
Absolute Truth
  all features realized in Kṛṣṇa, 848-849
  approached by process of knowledge, 630
  as aim of life, 75
  as *ānandamaya*, 399
  as Bhagavān, 73, **634**
  as complete whole, 12
  as goal of *yoga*, 357-358
  as impersonal, 13
  as internal and external, **639**
  as knowing proprietorship of Kṛṣṇa, **261**
  as Kṛṣṇa, 5, 223, 349, 371-372, **510**
  as objective of devotion, **775**
  as personal, 13, 372, 398
  as source of everything, 376
  compared to sun, sunshine, sun-god, 73-74
  covered by *māyā* is called matter, 248
  declared by Kṛṣṇa and *Gītā*, 291
  defeats sense indulgence, 193-194
  ignorance leads to anxiety, 285
  known by self-realized, 294-295
  known by spiritual master, 259-260
  leads to Kṛṣṇa consciousness, 164
  not attained by speculation, 509
  om tat sat indicates, **772-773**
  three features of, 73-74, 194, 513-514
Ācāryas
  accept rules without alteration, 748
  birth in their families fortunate, 353-354
  give rules and regulations, 466
  maintain individuality on spiritual grounds,
    88
  realization by association with, 266, 477

Ācāryas
  reclaim conditioned souls, 16
  teach by example, 186
  (Sec *also* Spiritual master, Teacher)
Ācāryavān puruṣo veda
  quoted, 447
Acintya
  as inconceivable, beyond material world,
    419
Acintya-bheda
  as duality in Kṛṣṇa, 291
  as perfect knowledge of Absolute, 849
  Kṛṣṇa as everything but independent, **377,**
    450-451, 452-453
  Paramātmā divided and yet one, **640**
  philosophy established by Caitanya, 374
Action
  according to order of Kṛṣṇa, 826-829
  according to scripture, 748
  as *karma*, 412, **789**
  as one with inaction, 241
  as symptom of soul, 445
  better than artificial renunciation, 274
  better than inaction, **169**
  burned up by fire of knowledge, **242**
  conditioned soul thinks himself doer, 192-
    193
  entanglement avoided by steadiness, **245**
  equated with functions of senses, 210
  five factors which bring about, **790-793**
  for bare necessities only, **244**
  freedom from, **135, 197**
  free from duality, 246
  fruitive, abandoned by sage, **243**
  in Kṛṣṇa consciousness, 14-15, 184, 191,
    283
  in mode of goodness, **798-799**
  in mode of ignorance, 676, **800**
  in mode of passion, **799**
  in perfection, 184
  intelligent bewildered in determining, **239**
  in the modes and its result, **678-680**
  its bondage overcome by *buddhi-yoga*, 164
  its intricacies hard to understand, **240-241**

Action
    Kṛṣṇa does not aspire to its fruits, **236**
    living entity as cause of, 132
    modes of nature force one to action, **166,
        828-829**
    motivated by knowledge, object and know-
        er, **794**
    not binding on one free of false ego, **793**
    not induced by spirit, **287**
    of great followed by others, 185
    of life determine future state of being, 416
    of soul related to Kṛṣṇa, 277
    one must act at every moment, **166**
    one not entitled to fruits of, **132**
    on spiritual level for liberation, **267, 274,
        275**
    out of love for Kṛṣṇa, 243-244
    renounced, **183, 190, 267, 275, 285**
    senses, work and doer its basis, **794**
    strengthens knowledge, 274
    to be patterned after devotees, 239
    to be performed and avoided, **804**
    (*See also* Activities, *Karma*, Work)
Activities
    according to the three modes, 15, 129,
        377-378
    all initiated by Paramātmā, 712
    all performed by the body, 620-621, **656**
    Arjuna inquires about, **410**
    as conducted by Kṛṣṇa, 269, **456-457**, 575
    as *deva-prakṛti*, transcendental by nature,
        722-723
    as means to spiritual sky, 247-248, **323**
    as oblations to ancestors, 65
    as real life of living entity, 331
    as religion, economics, sense gratification,
        liberation, 694
    as *sadācāra*, purified, 283
    as *sanātana-yoga*, 268
    can be changed, 10
    cease on attainment of *yoga*, 311
    conditioned soul thinks himself the doer of,
        192-193
    defeated without self-understanding, 111
    detachment from, 194
    determine type of body, 22
    directed by three Viṣṇu expansions, 367
    for elevation and degradation, 289
    for senses beget reactions, 120
    for senses perpetuate transmigration, 273-
        274
    impossible to abandon, **789**
    in Kṛṣṇa consciousness, 120, 124, 193, 242

Activities
    in Kṛṣṇa consciousness are alone auspicious,
        134-135, **352**
    in Kṛṣṇa consciousness on absolute plane,
        120, 125, 285
    in material and spiritual worlds, 159
    in relation to birth and death, 108
    known by those who take refuge in Kṛṣṇa,
        405
    leading to devotional service should be
        accepted, 785
    material activities cease in Kṛṣṇa conscious-
        ness, 311
    material activities end with body, 124
    material nature as cause of, 645-646
    neophytes want to retire from, 238
    not created by spirit, 287
    of body and spirit, 443, 445
    of demons and atheists baffled, 462-463
    of devotee transcendental, 11, 327
    of nonregulated never auspicious, 351
    performed as duty, 785
    performed by Janaka as example, 184-185
    prescribed in *Vedas*, 179
    purified as *bhakti*, 10
    reactions burned by fire of knowledge, 263
    renunciation of fruits brings liberation,
        275
    results to be given up, **243, 284**, 781-782
    sinful or pious not assumed by Kṛṣṇa, 288
    some declare they should be abandoned,
        782
    spiritualized by knowledge, 259
    success by contribution to spiritual, 247
    two types for conditioned soul, 484
    welfare activities destroyed, 66
    (*See also* Action, *Karma*, Work)
Acyuta
    Kṛṣṇa addressed as, **842**
    Kṛṣṇa described as, 221
*Ādau śraddhā tataḥ sādhu-saṅgo 'tha bhajana-
    kriyā*
    verses quoted, 231
Adhibhūtam
    physical nature as, 414
Adhidaivatam
    as universal form, 414
Adhiyajña
    as Paramātmā, 414
Adhyātma-cetasā
    as one who depends solely on Kṛṣṇa, 196
Adi-devam
    See Supreme Personality of Godhead

Aditi
> as mother of Āditya devotees, 527

Ādityas
> behold universal form in wonder, 557
> identified, 527
> Kṛṣṇa Viṣṇu amongst, 520
> shown in universal form, 544
> twelve born of Nārāyaṇa, 503

Āditya-varṇam tamasaḥ parastāt
> quoted, 642

Adultery
> provoked by irresponsible men, 64
> religious practice keeps women from, 64

Advaita
> Kṛṣṇa as, 221

Advaitācārya
> in disciplic succession, 29
> obeisances to, 1,2
> quoted, 425

Advaitam acyutam anādim ananta-rūpam
> verses quoted, 220, 228

Āgamāpāyino 'nityās tāṁs titikṣasva bhārata
> quoted, 332

Aggressors
> six types that can be killed, 61

Agni
> donates chariot to Arjuna, 43
> Kṛṣṇa as, 521

Agnihotra yajñas
> fire sacrifices ignored by artificial *sannyāsīs*,
>   308

Aham ādir hi devānām
> quoted, 590

Ahaṁ bhakta-parādhīno-hy asvatantra iva dvija
> verses quoted, 390

Ahaṁ brahmāsmi
> as real identification, 632
> realization of spirit, 405

Ahaṁ sarvasya prabhavaḥ
> quoted, 698

Ahaṁ sarveṣu bhūteṣu bhūtātmāvasthitaḥ sadā
> quoted, 461

Aham tvaṁ ca athānye
> quoted, 625

Āhāra-śuddhau sattva-śuddhiḥ sattva-śuddhau
> verses quoted, 174

*Āhaveṣu mitho 'nyonyaṁ jighāṁsanto mahī-
>   kṣitaḥ*
> verses quoted, 114

Aho bata śvapaco'to garīyān
> verses quoted, 131, 355-356

Āhus tvām ṛṣayaḥ sarve devarṣir nāradas tathā
> verses quoted, 5

Air
> as breath offered as oblation, 251
> as one of eight separated energies, 367-368
> as one of five great elements, 627
> as representation of demigods, 571
> breath suspension described, 254, 302-303
>   422
> compared to soul, 658-659
> generated from ether, generates fire, 110
> Kṛṣṇa as outgoing and incoming, 711-712
> supplied by demigods, 173, 175
> suspended to prolong life in *kumbhaka-
>   yoga*, 254
> ten kinds controlled in *yoga*, 252
> to be fixed between eyebrows at death, 420
> universal form addressed as, 571

Airāvata
> identified, 525
> Kṛṣṇa as, 524-525

Ajam
> *See* Unborn

Ajāmila
> performed duty in Kṛṣṇa consciousness, 124

Ajani ca yanmayaṁ tad avimucya niyantṛ
> verses quoted, 369

*Ajño jantur anīśo 'yam ātmanaḥ sukha-
>   duḥkhayoḥ*
> verses quoted, 289

Ajo nityaḥ śāśvato' yaṁ purāṇo
> verses quoted, 99

Akāmaḥ sarva-kāmo vā mokṣa-kāma udāradhīḥ
> verses quoted, 233

Akāra
> as beginning of sound, 530

Akarma
> as freedom from reaction, 242
> signs of, 244

Akṣobhya
> in disciplic succession, 29

All-pervading
> Arjuna inquires about, 514-516
> as aspect of Supersoul, 636-637
> by diverse energies, 373
> Kṛṣṇa as all-pervading beauty, 510
> Kṛṣṇa as, 5, 432-433, 450-451, 814-815
> living entities as, 105
> universal form as, 570, 572
> Viṣṇu as, 340
> while simultaneously in Vṛndāvana, 461-
>   462
> (*See also* Brahmajyoti, Brahman)

Amara-kośa
> dictionary cited, 518

Ambarīṣa Mahārāja
    cited as example, 153-154
    conquered Durvāsā Muni, 146-147
    engaged all senses in Kṛṣṇa's service, 148
    his transcendental engagements described,
        327
Amṛtam
    narrations about Kṛṣṇa like nectar, 517
Anagha
    Arjuna addressed as sinless, 719-720
Ānanda-cinmaya-rasa
    supreme abode as, 432
Ānandamaya
    Absolute Truth as, 399
    Kṛṣṇa as transcendental to activities, 626
Ānandamaya-cinmaya planets
    See Planets
Ānandamayo 'bhyāsāt, 18, 331, 626
Ananta
    as unlimited energy and influence, 569
    Kṛṣṇa as serpent, 526
Ananta-brahma
    opposed to vijñānaṁ brahma, 636
Anantavijaya
    name of Yudhiṣṭhira's conchshell, 46
Anāsaktasya viṣayān yathārham upayuñjataḥ
    verses quoted, 318
Anger
    Arjuna's fear of acting in, 730
    as cause of delusion, 150, 204
    as demonic quality, 728-729
    as gate leading to hell, 745
    as manifestation of ignorance, 204
    checked by execution of duty, 305
    demons bound by, 737, 742
    develops from lust, 149, 204, 727
    engaged by Hanumān as service, 204
    freedom by breath suspension, meditation,
        302-303
    freedom from, 142, 229-230, 301, 722, 727
    in Kṛṣṇa consciousness becomes a friend,
        205
    living entity overcome by, 403
    must be served if mind not conquered, 314
    pollutes whole body, 727
    surmounted by self-realized, 821
    toleration of, 298
Animals
    do not incur sin by killing, 15
    do not understand being under māyā, 679
    eaten by those in ignorance, 324-325
    eat refuse of food grains, 178

Animals
    family attachment found in, 80
    get human life when sacrificed, 114
    humans generally engaged in their propen-
        sities, 365
    ignorance leads to rebirth amongst 677-678
    no necessity for their killing, 727
    nonregulated humans likened to, 351
        379
    not distinguished from human in realiza-
        tion, 599
    on lower branches of banyan, 696
    sacrificed by brāhmaṇas, 816, 817
    sacrificed to goddess Kālī, 175
    their evolutionary progress should not be
        checked, 727
    their submission compared to devotees', 245
Animal slaughter
    cow killing most vicious, 679
    fat obtainable in milk, 761
    in mode of ignorance, 679
    in sacrificial fire not violence, 114
    karma of, 679
    no necessity for, 98, 727
    prominent amongst demons, 734
    sinful for man, 15
    stopped by Buddha, 225
Aniruddha
    as plenary expansion, 433
    associates with devotees, 23
Anityam asukhaṁ lokam
    quoted, 488
Annamaya
    as depending simply on food for existence,
        626
Aṇor aṇīyān mahato mahīyān
    verses quoted, 100
Antaḥpraviṣṭaḥ śāstā janānām
    quoted, 713
Anta-kāle ca mām eva smaran muktvā kalevaram
    verses quoted, 22
Antavanta ime dehāḥ
    quoted, 110
Anthropology
    based on materialistic philosophy of soul,
        107
Anthropomorphism
    in worship of foolish leaders, 234
Aṇu-ātmā
    as one of two kinds of souls, 100
Ānukūlyasya saṅkalpaḥ prātikūlyasya varjanam
    quoted, 593

Anxiety
  Arjuna exhorted to transcend, 129
  as characteristic of Kali-yuga, 320
  caused by duality, 130, 284-285
  constant for those who do not know future, 498
  demons filled with, 735, 736
  in material existence, 6
  of soul eating the fruits of the body, 103
  one dear to Kṛṣṇa not disturbed by, 103, 612-613
  relieved by work in Kṛṣṇa consciousness, 827
  (See also Miseries, Suffering)

Anyābhilāṣitāśūnyaṁ jñāna-karmādy-anāvṛtam
  verses quoted, 387, 592

Apāna
  as one of five kinds of air, 95
  breathing methods, 254

Apāna-vāyu
  as engaged for realization, 252

Apareyam itas tv anyām
  quoted, 8

Aparimitā dhruvās tanubhṛto yadi sarva-gatās
  verses quoted, 369

Āprāyaṇāt tatrāpi hi dṛṣṭam
  quoted, 824

Arcanā
  as engaging all senses in Kṛṣṇa's service, 328

Arca-mūrti
  See Arca-vigraha

Arca-vigraha
  as incarnation of Supreme Lord, 600
  its worship for realization of Brahman, 405
  not material, 600
  worship discussed, 600
  worship useless without worshiping Supersoul, 461

Arjuna
  accepts all Kṛṣṇa says as truth, 6, 14, 512
  accepts Kṛṣṇa as Supreme, 5-6
  addressed as *anagha*, sinless, 719-720
  addressed as beloved child of Kurus, 125
  addressed as best among men, 92
  addressed as best of Bharatas, 208, 386, 433, 544, 653, 783, 808
  addressed as best of Kurus, 256, 580
  addressed as descendant of Bharata, 96, 112, 224
  addressed as Dhanañjaya, 44, 134, 267, 456, 605, 803, 841
  addressed as Guḍākeśa, 51, 84, 519
  addressed as Lord of the Bhāratas, 377

Arjuna
  addressed as *parantapaḥ*, chastiser of enemies, 83-84
  addressed as Pārtha, 52, 101, 115, 141, 188, 417, 430, 805
  addressed as Savyasācin, 564
  addressed as scion of Bharata, 91, 403, 622, 831
  addressed as son of Bharata, 659, 666, 671, 673, 675, 718, 722
  addressed as son of Kuntī, 90, 119, 170, 296, 345, 373, 427, 454, 457, 475, 480, 620, 667, 670, 745, 817, 819, 829
  addressed as son of Kuru, 354, 676
  addressed as son of Pāṇḍu, 729
  addressed as son of Pṛthā, 75, 121, 186, 232, 258, 362, 375, 424, 464, 486, 543, 602, 728, 730, 775, 785, 804
  addressed as tiger among men, 783
  agrees to fight, regains memory, 15, 539-540, 842-843
  anxious to see with whom he must fight, 49-50
  as always thinking of Kṛṣṇa, 25, 51
  as compassionate and softhearted, 54-55, 60, 69, 72, 118-119
  as disciple and devotee of Kṛṣṇa, 7, 79, 81, 84, 122, 217
  as friend and relative to Kṛṣṇa, 4-5, 76, 84-85, 87, 217
  as ideal disciple of Gītā, 5-6, 23, 32, 81
  as instrument of Kṛṣṇa in battle, 60, 564-565
  as *mahā-bāhu*, mighty-armed, 108
  as representative of atomic soul, 90, 100
  as student of Droṇācārya, 35
  beholds all his friends and relatives on the Battlefield, 53
  blows his transcendental conchshell, 43-44
  cited by Duryodhana as heroic bowman, 36
  compared to eating bird on tree of body, 102
  defeated Śiva and received *pāśupata-astra*, 116
  desires that Kṛṣṇa kill his relatives personally, 60
  disciplic succession reestablished with, 4
  disinterested in seeing four-armed form, 583
  inquires into fate of unsuccessful *yogī*, 347-349
  experiences symptoms of fear, 54-56
  family attachment as root of his problems, 80-81

Arjuna
     favorably influenced by Kurukṣetra, 33
     fears he has offended Kṛṣṇa out of friend-
        ship, 573
     foresees imminent death, 54-55
     forgets Kṛṣṇa's nature, 221
     forgets kṣatriya codes, 57-58
     frightened and bewildered by universal
        form, 558-559, 590
     given military honors by Indra, 116
     Hanumān and Rāma on his chariot, 48
     his chariot capable of conquering in all
        three worlds, 43
     his chariot donated by fire-god Agni, 43
     his delusions and impurities, 14-15, 57-58, 73,
        80-81, 86, 90, 261
     his duty to fight, 63, 98, 101, 113, 115, 116, 157,
        169, 280, 730
     his enlightenment frustrates Dhṛtarāṣṭra,
        84
     his grief overwhelming, 70, 72, 81
     his mind understood by Kṛṣṇa, 52
     his positive attributes, 33, 51, 61, 68, 70, 79,
        343, 729-730
     his prayers and obeisances to universal form,
        550-563, 567-578
     his reluctance and refusal to fight, 49, 56-63,
        69-70, 75, 77-79, 83
     his senses controlled and satisfied by Kṛṣṇa,
        44, 59
     his victory assured, 43, 48, 50
     his wife, Draupadī, daughter of King
        Drupada, 35
     his wife Draupadī's disrobing, 41
     infamy worse for him than death, 117
     inquires on behalf of common people and
        demons, 218-219, 515
     Karṇa identified as his half brother, 38
     Kṛṣṇa as, 533-534
     likened to calf, 28
     not equal to Kṛṣṇa, 90, 104
     one who follows him is not bewildered, 240
     orders Kṛṣṇa to draw chariot between the
        armies, 49
     perplexed by Kṛṣṇa, 272
     petitions Kṛṣṇa's forgiveness and toleration,
        576
     placed in ignorance so Gītā could be spoken,
        7, 11
     present when Gītā was first spoken to sun-
        god, 221
     proclaims yoga system impossible 25
        342-343

Arjuna
     rejects theory of Vaibhāṣikas, 108
     requests to see four-armed Nārāyaṇa form
        577-578
     significance as Pārtha, 52
     significance of his great heritage as
        Kaunteya and Bhārata, 91
     unable to solve problems without spiritual
        master, 81-82
     wants Kṛṣṇa to kill demon of misunder-
        standing, 72
Arrogance
     as demonic quality, 728-729
Arūpam
     impersonalists stress, 372
Aryamā
     Kṛṣṇa as, 526-527
Āryan
     best is one who chants, 131
     defined as spiritual civilization, 75
     has knowledge of liberation from material
        bondage, 75
     scriptural rules followed by, 731
Asamprajñāta-samādhi
     described, 331
Asaṁśayaṁ samagram
     attained by devotion, 363
Āsana
     in aṣṭāṅga-yoga, 303, 305
Asat
     as nonbeing, 6
     characteristic of material body, 22
     sacrifice and charity as, 776-777
Āścaryo vaktā kuśalo 'sya labdhā
     verses quoted, 111
Āsīno dūraṁ vrajati śayāno yāti sarvataḥ
     quoted, 639
Asita
     as learned leader, 382
     influences Arjuna, 831
     proclaims Kṛṣṇa to be Supreme, 5,6
     validates Arjuna's praise, 510
Aṣṭāṅga-yoga
     as inferior method of sense restriction, 145
     as outcome of jñāna-yoga, 359
     automatically practiced in Kṛṣṇa con-
        sciousness, 305
     described by Kṛṣṇa, 302-303
     Kṛṣṇa cannot be understood by, 448
     more difficult than Kṛṣṇa consciousness,
        303
     practiced for perfections, 253
     unnecessary for transfer to other planets, 603

Āsuraṁ bhāvam āśrita
  as class of miscreant, 385-386
Asuras
  behold universal form in wonder, **557**
Aśvattha
  fig tree, often worshiped, 524
  Kṛṣṇa as fig tree, **524**
Aśvatthāmā
  beheld by Arjuna on Battlefield, 53
  cited by Duryodhana as great warrior, 38
  identified as son of Droṇācārya, 38
Aśvins
  behold universal form in wonder, **557**
*Asya mahato bhūtasya naśvasitam etad yad
    ṛg-vedo yajur-vedaḥ sāma-vedo 'tharvaṅ
    girasaḥ*
  quoted, 179
*Ataḥ śrī-kṛṣṇa-nāmādi na bhaved grāhyam
    indriyaiḥ*
  verses quoted, 316, 366
Ātatatvāc ca mātṛtvād ātmā hi paramo hariḥ
  quoted, 337
*Atha puruṣo ha vai nārāyaṇo 'kāmayata prajāḥ
    sṛjeya ity upakramya*
  quoted, 503
Atharva-veda
  as Kṛṣṇa, 469
  as one of four *Vedas*, 581
  emanates from Kṛṣṇa, 179
  quoted, 503
Athāsaktis tato bhāvas tataḥ premābhyudañcati
  verses quoted, 231
Athāto brahma-jijñāsā
  one should inquire into Supreme, 204
Atheists
  as *sāṅkhya* philosophers, 368
  beyond spiritual understanding, 651
  cannot have the divine vision, 580
  cannot understand forms of Kṛṣṇa, 587
  consider Kṛṣṇa as demigod, 234, 538
  demons as, 742
  discussed as *āsuraṁ bhāvam āśrita,* 385-386
  fear universal form, resent praise of Kṛṣṇa, 568
  Kapila and his atheistic *sāṅkhya* philosophy, 122, 123
  may know Kṛṣṇa as superhuman, 219
  one should disassociate from, 592
  reject existence of soul, 109
  their liberation, fruitive activities and knowledge baffled, 462-463

Atheists
  their plans baffled by nature, 382-383
  unnecessary for Kṛṣṇa to destroy them, 226
Ātmā
  denotations of, 312, 410
Ātmānaṁ rathinaṁ viddhi śarīraṁ ratham eva ca
  verses quoted, 344
Attachment
  abandoned and overcome by sages, **133, 142, 190, 243, 283, 821**
  action without, **183, 282, 787-788, 798-799**
  as symptom of passion, **675, 801-802**
  cause of bondage, 133
  defined, 142
  equanimity as freedom from, **499**
  freedom from as requisite for love, 229-230
  of Arjuna for material things, 56-57
  of demons to sense enjoyment, 739-740
  of impersonalists analyzed, 230
  one without attachment fixed in knowledge, 143
  overcome by devotion to Kṛṣṇa, 184, 231
  overcome by regulations, 151
  severe penance performed out of, 757-758
  to activities by ignorant, **190, 194-195**
  to family on basis of skin disease, 80
  to inaction not advised, 132-133
  to Kṛṣṇa by hearing, 345
  to Kṛṣṇa divided in three stages, 450
  to Kṛṣṇa the same as detachment from matter, 277
  to Kṛṣṇa via love, 605-606
  to material world to be severed, **694, 698, 701**
  to sense objects, **149, 698**
A.U.M.
  See Om
Austerity
  according to three modes, **759, 764-769**
  as quality of *brāhmaṇa,* **812**
  demonic when severe, 757-758
  in goodness to please Kṛṣṇa, 767
  in ignorance to destroy self or others, 769
  in passion unstable, 768
  necessary for explanation of knowledge. 837
  not necessary in devotional service, 466
  of speech, 765-766
  of the body, 764-765
  of the mind, 766-767
  of worshiping Kṛṣṇa, *brāhmaṇas,* etc., 764-765
  to be offered to Kṛṣṇa, **480**

Austerity
   useless without faith in Supreme, 776-777
Avajānanti māṁ mūḍhāḥ
   quoted, 359
Avatāra
   See Incarnations
Avyakta
   See Unmanifest
Avyakto kṣara ity uktas tam āhuḥ paramāṁ gatim
   verses quoted, 21
Avyaya
   Kṛṣṇa as inexhaustible, 401
Āyur-vedic śāstra
   cited, 711

B

Bāhlīkas, 38
Bahūnāṁ janmanām ante jñānavān māṁ prapadyate
   quoted, 290, 349
Bahv-īśvara-vādī
   believers in many gods, 249
Baladeva
   appears as son of Vasudeva, 534
Baladeva Vidyābhūṣaṇa
   cited, 434, 436, 624
   in disciplic succession, 29
   quoted, 148, 177
Bālāgra-śata-bhāgasya śatadhā kalpitasya ca
   verses quoted, 94
Bali
   as learned leader, 382
Banyan tree
   material universe likened to, 694-699
   with roots up, branches below, 20
Battlefield of Kurukṣetra
   See Kurukṣetra
Beauty
   Kṛṣṇa as all-pervading, 510
   of Kṛṣṇa described, 431
Behar
   Mithilā subdivision of, 185
Bhagavad-gītā
   as common scripture for whole world, 28
   as essence of *Vedas* and most complete
      scripture, 3, 13, 14, 28, 32, 266
   as knowing Kṛṣṇa factually, 843
   as nectar, 28
   as science of God, 7, 32
   as subject matter for devotees, 4, 88, 838
   as supreme instruction in morality, 848

Bhagavad-gītā
   as the Lord's mercy, 7
   as unique, 844
   based on principles of *Upaniṣads*, 111
   basic subjects and teachings of, 7, 9-11 26, 96,
      135, 159, 632
   benefits derived from, 27-28, 82, 214, 633
   cannot be compared to mundane book, 88
   cannot be explained or understood by the
      envious, 88, 443, 837
   dispels ignorance, 94, 841
   first spoken to sun-god, 4
   for whom it is spoken, 7, 32, 85, 591
   heard by mercy of Vyāsa, 844-845
   higher planets attained by hearing, 840
   imparted by materially uncontaminated, 10
   its history traced, 214-215
   its knowledge super-human, 215
   likened to cow, 28
   likened to Ganges water, 28
   lost when disciplic chain broken, 216, 512-
      513
   main purpose of, 6, 11, 836, 848
   method of hearing and understanding, 1,
      5-7, 14, 26, 29, 32, 81, 215, 216, 268, 439,
      606
   mystery cleared by Arjuna's questions, 163
   not for speculation, 214-215, 229
   original verses as clear as the sun, 585
   part of fifth *Veda*, 130
   related to heart of Sañjaya by Vyāsa, 844
   speaker and spirit of, 3
   study as worship with intelligence, 839
   sung by Kṛṣṇa to dissipate lamentation, 72
   summarized in *Gītā-māhātmya*, 32
   teaching different from Buddhism, 158
   unauthorized commentaries and transla-
      tions, 3, 14, 88, 216-218, 385, 513
   useless if speaker were forgetful, 88, 100
Bhagavān
   as aim of life, 75
   as apellation of Kṛṣṇa throughout *Gītā*,
      73
   as last word in realization of Absolute, 634
   defined and explained, 73-74
   designates Śrī Kṛṣṇa, 3
   His six opulences explained, 74
   realization included in *samādhi*, 139
   sometimes accepted by impersonalists, 514
   understood as reality, 291
Bhāgavata-dharma
   propagated by Caitanya, 385

Bhāgavata Purāṇa
  See Śrīmad-Bhāgavatam
Bhajate
  explained as service, 358-359
Bhakti
  activities may appear ordinary, 10-11
  as *buddhi-yoga*, 123
  as means to freedom and Vaikuṇṭhas, 21, 433
  as sāṅkhya, 123
  continues after liberation, 824
  defined as purified activities, 10
  example of wife and lover, 25
  its path not easy, 365-366
  meaning of, 309
  necessary for seeing universal form, 586
  nine processes, *śravaṇam*, etc., 26
  principles enable attainment of Kṛṣṇa, 27
  (*See also Bhakti-yoga*, Devotional Service,
    service, worship)
Bhakti-rasāmṛta-sindhu
  cited, 442
  quoted, 231, 274, 340, 366, 387, 592
Bhaktir asya bhajanaṁ tadihāmutropādhi, etc
  quoted, 360
Bhaktisiddhānta Sarasvatī
  born in pious family, 354
  cited, 489
  in disciplic succession, 29
Bhaktivedanta Swami Prabhupāda
  born in Vaiṣṇava family, 354
  in disciplic succession, 29
Bhaktivinode Ṭhākur
  his summary of Second Chapter, 159
  in disciplic succession, 29
Bhakti-yoga
  as acting for Kṛṣṇa, Rāma, Nārāyaṇa, 689
  as chanting, 424
  as culmination of all *yoga*, 358-360
  as desiring only Kṛṣṇa, 424
  as highest realization method, 596
  as Kṛṣṇa consciousness, 305
  as means of remembering Kṛṣṇa at death,
    420
  as means to supreme goal, 347, 358, 427
  as means to transcendental pleasure, 331
  as part of *yoga* ladder, 311
  as practical for realization, 634
  as subject of *Gītā*, 159
  defined, 507
  distinguished from *jñāna-yoga*, 600
  dṛḍha-vrata, determined faith, beginning of,
    407

Bhakti-yoga
  five different paths of, 425
  householder allowed sex in, 322
  no impediments to, 331
  regulated principles advised in, 605-606
  severs knot of material affection, 363
  success formula given by Rūpa Gosvāmī,
    333
  (*See also Bhakti*, Devotional Service, Ser-
    vice, Worship)
Bhaktyā tvananyayā śaktaḥ
  quoted, 639
Bharata
  Arjuna addressed as descendant of, **96, 112,
    224**
  Arjuna addressed as scion of, **91, 403, 622,
    831**
  Arjuna addressed as son of, **659, 666, 671,
    673, 675, 718, 722**
  Dhṛtarāṣṭra addressed as descendant, **84**
  significance of name, 91
Bharata Mahārāja
  becomes deer in next life, **416**
  story of his transmigration, 354-355
Bhāratas
  Arjuna addressed as best of, **208, 386, 433,
    544, 783, 808**
  Arjuna addressed as chief of, **653**
  Arjuna addressed as lord of, **377**
Bhāratavarṣa
  earth known among demigods as, 354
Bhāva
  as last stage of devotional life, 231
  as preliminary stage of love of Kṛṣṇa, 231
Bhava-mahādāvāgni-nirvāpaṇam
  as liberation, 330-331
Bhavambudhir vatsa-padaṁ paraṁ padam
  verses quoted, 136
*Bhayaṁ dvitīyābhiniveśataḥ syād īśād apetasya
    viparyayo 'smṛtiḥ*
  quoted, 322
*Bhidyate hṛdaya-granthiś chidyante sarva-saṁ-
    śayāḥ*
  verses quoted, 363
Bhīma
  as performer of Herculean tasks, **44**
  as Vṛkodara, **44**
  blows conchshell, **44**
  cited by Duryodhana as heroic bowman, **36**
  envied by Duryodhana, **40**
  killer of demon Hiḍimba, **44**
  likened to fig before Bhīṣma, **40**

Bhīma
  protects army of Pāṇḍavas, 39-40
Bhīṣma
  as excuse for Arjuna's not fighting, 76, 77,
      113, 730
  beheld by Arjuna on Battlefield, 53
  blows conchshell and gives Duryodhana joy,
      41-42
  cited by Duryodhana as great warrior, 38
  considered worshipable as superior, 77
  described as grandfather of the fighters, 41
  destroyed in mouth of universal form, 560
  did not protest Draupadī's disrobing, 41, 582
  doomed at Kurukṣetra, 46, 566
  forced by finances to side with Duryodhana,
      78
  his conchshell does not disturb Pāṇḍavas,
      47
  his support urged by Duryodhana, 40-41
  knows victory will be on Kṛṣṇa's side, 41-42
  Kṛṣṇa speaks in his presence, 52
  lost respectability as teacher, 78
  no need for lamentation for, 89
  one must follow, 240
  gives protection to the army of Duryodhana,
      39-40
  superior to Bhīma, 40
  supported Kṛṣṇa in assembly of Kurus, 400
  would have spiritual or heavenly body in
      next life, 89
Bhoktā bhogyaṁ preritāram ca matvā sarvaṁ
    proktaṁ trividhaṁ brahmam etat
  quoted, 623
Bhoktāraṁ yajña-tapasām
  quoted, 173
Bhṛgu
  Kṛṣṇa as, 523
Bhūteśa
  as controller of everything, 513-514
Bhuñjate te tv aghaṁ pāpā ye pacanty ātma-kāraṇāt
  quoted, 325
Bhūriśravā
  beheld by Arjuna on Battlefield, 53
  cited by Duryodhana as great warrior, 38
  identified as son of the King of the Bāhlīkas,
      38
Birth
  amongst demonic species, 744
  as one of four principles of material exis-
      tence, 19
  as one of six transformations of body, 99
  Brahman as source of, 666

Birth
  cannot be counteracted by wealth, 82
  cannot be remembered by Arjuna, 220
  caused by Kṛṣṇa, 497, 666-667
  conquered by mind established in equa-
      nimity, 293
  freedom by transcending modes, 684
  fruitive activities for, 127, 134-135
  in family of transcendentalists rare, 353-354
  infant's distress in womb described in
      Bhāgavatam, 632
  its certainty and unity with death, 99, 108
  its cycle according to activities, 108
  its perception as evil, 630
  Kṛṣṇa as deliverer from, 602-604
  Kṛṣṇa can remember all His and Arjuna's
      births, 220-222
  none in spiritual world, 405, 427, 715
  of Kṛṣṇa not ordinary, 223, 495
  overcome by understanding Kṛṣṇa, 324, 642
  present everywhere in material universe,
      137
  repetition of, 137, 426
  soul not subject to, 16, 98-99, 498
  transcended by hearing from authorities,
      652
  transcended by renunciation, 136
  types attained by death in modes, 677-678
  (See also Transmigration)
Body
  See Material body, Spiritual body, Subtle
      body
Bondage
  action without consideration of, 800
  avoided by steadiness, 245
  both good and evil work bind, 171
  causes of, 132, 133, 204, 264, 313, 374
  despite mundane knowledge, 199
  disobedient doomed to, 198
  in struggle for existence, 703
  of demons, 729, 739-740
  overcome by renunciation, knowledge and
      self-realization, 267, 275
  overcome by service to Kṛṣṇa or spiritual
      master, 242, 381
  overcome by work according to duty, 164,
      170, 197
  perpetuated by fruitive activities, 273-274,
      284, 670-671
Brahmā
  annihilation and creation take place at his
      night and day, 429-430, 455

Brahmā
as chief among demigods, 372, 502
as father of Bhṛgu, 523
as first living being in universe, 111
as form of passion, 756
as incarnation of *rājo-guṇa*, cannot liberate,
381
as initiator of Gāyatrī, 532
as innumerable, 428
as learned leader, 382
as part of Kṛṣṇa, 304, 538, **569**, 703
as grandfather, *pitāmaha*, 501
as secondary creator, 529
banyan tree grows from his abode, 694, 695
born from Hiraṇyagarbha, 501
calculation of his lifetime, **427**-428, 455
changes his body, 715
desires to see Kṛṣṇa's two-armed form, 586
destroyed in time, 564
does not possess full opulences, 74
exhibits four, eight, sixteen, etc., heads,
530
exists in Supersoul, 636
his prayers quoted, 214, 440-441
his progeny, 501
in disciplic succession, 14, 29, 224, 503
Kṛṣṇa as father of, 495, 571
Kṛṣṇa as manifold faced, **530**
one must follow, 240
praises Kṛṣṇa's forms and incarnations,
220-221
sitting on lotus flower in universal form,
552
subjected to influence of sense objects, 149,
381
transferred to spiritual universe at annihilation, 427, 428
undergoes thousand year penances to create,
501
uttered *om tat sat*, 773
Vedas originally spoken to him, 224
worshiped in goodness, 756
worships Kṛṣṇa as Supreme, 74, 234
Brahma-bhūta
as freedom from contamination, 336
as joyful, desireless condition, 299, 832
as realization of Brahman, 821
attained by hearing about Kṛṣṇa, 824
attained with devotional service, 822
devotional service begins after, 448
Brahmacārī
controls mind by chanting, 250-251

Brahmacārī
his activities while living with spiritual
master, 438
taught celibacy and *omkāra*, 421-422
Vedic study, austerity and gentleness meant
for, 726
Brahmacarya
as total withdrawal from sex, 322
not possible at moment, 421-422
restricted sex in marriage same as, 322
Brahmaiva san brahmāpyeti
quoted, 689
Brahma-jana
as one who knows Brahman, 500
Brahma-jijñāsā
6, 129
Brahmajyoti
as goal of impersonalists, 22-23, 228, 368,
423, 596
as partial realization, 232, 362
as rays of Kṛṣṇa's body, 19, 248, 360
attained if one dies when fiery god presides,
etc., 435
contains spiritual planets, 19, 22, 701
covered by veil of *māyā*, 248, 641
covers form of Kṛṣṇa, 400
elevation to via *āśramas*, 439
emanates from supreme abode, Kṛṣṇaloka,
19
entered by Supersoul upon leaving body,
716
everything situated in, 248
illuminates spiritual sky, 19, 641
no spiritual diversity in, 368
plant of devotion enters, 506
sunlight emanates from, 374, 709
(*See also* All-pervading, Brahman, Spiritual
sky)
Brahmaloka
attained by death in goodness, 677, 682
contains birth, old age, disease and death, 19,
20
elevated *sannyāsīs* promoted to, 428
its wonders beyond calculation, 682
one subject to fall down from, 427
roots of banyan come from, 697
sacrifice to attain, 427
survives all heavenly planets, 428
(*See also* Planets)
Brahman
Arjuna inquires about, **410**
as a problem for meditation, 596

Brahman

as concentrated transcendental knowledge, 642

as constitutional position of ultimate happiness, 690-691

as form of fire within stomach, 711-712

as Kṛṣṇa's personal effulgence, 248, 261, 318

as mahat-tattva, 666

as object of impersonalist meditation, 278-279, 493-494, 596-597

as object of merging, 22-23, 87, 249-250, 308, 421

as origin of everything, 204

as part of complete whole, 12, 73, 291

as sacrifice, 248

as sat (being) feature, 13

as spirit soul and jīva, 159, 410, 412-413, 623, 635-636

as total material substance, source of birth, 282, 623, 666

as truth behind Viṣṇu, 756

as vijñānaṁ brahma and ananta-brahma, 636

attained by controlling senses, 256

contrasted with Parabrahman, 5, 376, 412-413

Gāyatrī as sound incarnation of, 532

identity with, 295, 405, 824

impregnated by Kṛṣṇa, 666-667

indicated by om tat sat, 772-773

Kṛṣṇa as, 5, 510-511

Kṛṣṇa as basis of, 12, 87, 291, 385, 570, 635-636, 690-691

liberation through identity with, 335-336

likened to ray of sunshine, 12

may be realized by common man, 514

methods of realization, 159, 256, 318, 405 405, 421, 434, 657, 688-689, 819-823

nondifferent from om or Kṛṣṇa, 423

one in modes of nature cannot transcend, 379

one who knows Him dies when fiery god prevails, 434

realization as aham brahmāsmi, 405

realization as svarūpa, 295, 405, 824

realization as vijñānamaya, 626

realization by devotional service, 688-689

realization by worship of arcā, 405

realization included in samādhi, 139

realization of different features, 421

realization takes many births, 349

Brahman

realized when different identities are no longer perceived, 657

sacrifices by yogīs to, 249-250

three conceptions as prakṛti, jīva and controller, 623

work in, 179

(See also All-pervading, Brahmajyoti)

Brāhmaṇa

as division of varṇas, 24, 235-236

as head of body of Supreme, 396

as representative of mode of goodness 379, 669

as spiritual master of varṇas, 679, 723

as worthy recipient of charity, 499-500

attains heavenly planets by sacrifice, 114

born out of energy of Kṛṣṇa, 501

chants Gāyatrī daily, 532

chants om tat sat, 772

distinguished by work in modes, 812

duty unavoidable, 114

his nature and duty compared to kṣatriya's, 202

Kṛṣṇa as well-wisher of, 679

must be given all protection, 679

one should not imitate duty of, 816

Paramātmā in heart of dog and brāhmaṇa, 337

qualities of, 80, 812

rebirth in family of, 124

seen the same as cow, elephant, etc., 292

sometimes must kill animals, 816, 817

status transcended in Kṛṣṇa consciousness, 236

supposed to know about Brahman, 236

unfit as spiritual master unless Vaiṣṇava, 82

unworthy if impious, 76

worshiped as austerity, 764-765

(See also Varṇa)

Brahmaṇaḥ pathi

as path of transcendental realization, 349

Brāhmaṇa vaiṣṇava

unsuccessful yogī born into family of, 353

Brahmaṇi

as Kṛṣṇa consciousness, 282

Brahman-nirvāṇa

attained by Kṛṣṇa consciousness, 158-159, 302, 305

Brahmaṇo pratiṣṭhāham

quoted, 291

Brahmaṇyatīrtha
  in disciplic succession, 29
Brahmaṇyo devakī-putraḥ
  quoted, 504
Brahma-saṁhitā
  accepts Kṛṣṇa as Supreme, 3
  cited, 180, 261, 398, 431, 432, 454, 461, 493,
    520, 575, 578, 584, 586, 594, 639, 710,
    834
  describes Kṛṣṇa as *acyuta*, 221
  describes supreme abode Goloka, 19
  quoted, 12-13, 74, 176, 214, 220, 228, 323, 339,
    372, 451, 457, 459, 637
Brahma-saṁsparśa
  as contact with Supreme, 336
Brahma-sūtra
  cited, 6, 12, 780
Brahmavādī
  as one of three types of transcendentalists,
    22
  his degree of advancement, 73
  (*See also* Impersonalists, Māyāvādī)
Brahma-yoga
  one loses taste for material pleasure in,
    296
Brāhmī sthitiḥ
  as liberation, 159
Bṛhad-Vaiṣṇava mantra
  cited, 463
Bṛhan-Nāradīya Purāṇa
  quoted, 320
Bṛhaspati
  identified, 522
  Kṛṣṇa as, 522
Bṛhat-sāma
  Kṛṣṇa as, 531-532
Buddha
  appeared to stop animal sacrifice, 225
  appeared when materialism rampant, 225
  as principal philosopher, 444
Buddhism
  claims void after life, 158
Buddhists
  view of soul, 107
Buddhi-yoga
  as devotional service, 122-123, 134, 164-
    165
  explained, 507
  frees from bonds of action, 164
  not inaction, 162
  presented unsystematically in Second
    Chapter, 163

C

Caitanya Mahāprabhu
  accepts Kṛṣṇa as Supreme, 3
  advises hearing and chanting, 25, 344, 422,
    652, 748
  as incarnation, 172, 227
  as learned leader, 382
  avoids women, 724
  cited, 503
  considered most munificent, 589
  defines *svarūpa*, 17, 635-636, 842
  delivered saṅkīrtana-yajña, 172, 176
  derided by Prakāśānanda, 508
  described secretly in scriptures, 227
  elevates Haridāsa to *nāmācārya*, 356
  establishes *acintya-bheda* philosophy, 374,
    849
  forbids reading Māyāvādī commentaries on
    Gītā, 88
  gives definition of real fame, 500
  harer nāma verses quoted, 320
  in disciplic succession, 29
  likens devotional service to seed in heart,
    505-506
  more tolerant than tree, humbler than grass,
    415
  obeisances to, 1, 2
  predicts *saṅkīrtana* to be spread all over
    world, 227
  propagates *bhāgavata-dharma*, 385
  quoted, 82, 308-309, 320, 330
  rejects Choṭa Haridāsa for looking at
    woman, 724
  reply to Prakāśānanda why He chants, 131
  taught by example, 186
  took *sannyāsa* early for higher cause, 92
  transcendental stage attained by mercy of,
    823
  wherever He was, there was Vṛndāvana,
    425
Caitanya-caritāmṛta
  cited, 392, 395, 424, 449, 489
  plant of devotional service described in,
    506
  quoted, 24, 82, 125, 226-227
Calmness
  created by Kṛṣṇa, defined, 497-498
Cāṇakya Paṇḍit
  proclaims women generally not intelligent
    or trustworthy, 64
Caṇḍāla
  can be elevated by devotee, 487

Caṇḍāla
    situated on highest platform by chanting,
        131
Candra
    as appointed officer, 178
    worship in goodness, 756
Candraloka
    as goal, 470
Candrāyaṇa
    as austerity, 253
Capital Punishment
    beneficial in absolving karma, 101
    supported by Manu-saṁhitā, 101
Caste System
    See Varṇa
Cāturmāsya
    austerity of fasting and not shaving, 253
Cause
    demonic theory of, 733
    knowing Kṛṣṇa as cause brings surrender,
        390
    Kṛṣṇa as, 12-13, 74, 126, 131, 237, 261,
        367, 370-371, 375-376, 493, 535, 540,
        666-668
    material world nondifferent from, 282
    of result of activities, 132
    of spiritual and material worlds, 503-504
    of universe as Paramātmā, 371
    Paramātmā as ultimate, 791
    universal form as, 569
    when known, nothing remains unknown, 364
Cekitāna
    cited by Duryodhana as great fighter, 36
Ceto-darpaṇa-mārjanam
    clearing mirror of mind, 330
Chandogya Upaniṣad
    436
Chanting
    advocated by Caitanya, 131
    as best means in Kali-yuga, 131, 172-173, 320,
        422
    as devotional process, 424, 505-506, 603, 691
    as engagement of brahmacārī, 251
    as means for pleasure, 446
    as means of pleasing Kṛṣṇa, 603
    as means of reaching supreme destination,
        131, 604
    as means of remembering and under-
        standing Kṛṣṇa, 25, 398, 415, 417-418
    as sign of advanced spiritual life, 356
    by demigods entering universal form, 556
    by demons, 735
    by Haridāsa Ṭhākur, 326, 356

Chanting
    cleanses the mirror of the mind, 205, 265,
        732
    Kṛṣṇa as, 523
    not advised without philosophy, 162
    of Hare Kṛṣṇa for transcendental body 416
    of Kṛṣṇa's glories by mahātmā, 465
    of oṁ tat sat, 772-773
    (See also Saṅkīrtana-yajña)
Charity
    according to three modes, 759, 769-771
    as divine quality, 722, 725
    as dravyamaya-yajña, sacrifice, 253
    as means to purify the mind, 608
    begun with word oṁ, 773
    Caitanya most munificent man of, 589
    created by Kṛṣṇa, 497
    for pleasing Supreme Person, 775
    given in goodness, 499-500, 589, 725, 769-770
    given in ignorance, 771
    given in passion, 673, 770-771
    meant for householders, 725
    purifies even great souls, 784
    should never be abandoned, 782, 784
    tat and sat uttered with, 774-775
    useless without faith in Supreme, 776-777
    will not reveal two-armed form, 587
    will not reveal universal form, 580-581
Chastity
    as means for entering into Brahman, 421
    necessary for spiritual life, 422
    not possible today, 421-422
    of women necessary for good population, 64
Children
    as purpose of sex, 526, 723, 725
    at age of five trained as brahmacārīs, 322
    attachment to, 80, 92
    by-products of body, not of soul, 99
    nonattachment as knowledge, 630, 633
    not given freedom, 732
    require protection, 64
    to be made Kṛṣṇa conscious, 377, 384
Choṭa Haridāsa
    rejected by Caitanya for looking at woman,
        724
Cintāmaṇi-dhāma
    where all desires are fulfilled, 431
Citi-śakti
    as internal transcendental potency, 330-331
Citraratha
    identified, 524
    Kṛṣṇa as, 524

Cleanliness
    as austerity of body, **764**-765
    as divine quality, **722**, 728
    ignored by demons, 731-732
    injunctions for internal and external, 732
Compassion
    Arjuna's compassion befitting non-Āryans,
        75, 118-119
    as divine quality, **722**
    as knowledge, defined, **629**, 631
    for eternal soul, 72
    for the body, 72
    of Kṛṣṇa destroys ignorance, **508**
Complete Whole
    as *pūrṇam*, 14
    constituents, 12
    gives complete facility for complete units, 13
    must possess everything, 13
    not formless, 13
Conceit
    as demonic quality, **728**-729
Conditioned soul
    activities of two types, 484
    allured by modes of nature, 348
    always eager for material enjoyment, 180,
        301
    as divine and demonic, 651, **730**-731
    attracted by bodily relationships, 57
    cause and nature of conditioning, 293, 565,
        644, 842-843
    difference from Supreme, 11
    eternally prone to illusion, 89-90, 104, 380
    fearful due to perverted memory, 322
    forgets his real self-interest, 57
    four defects of, 748
    his program outlined, 172
    ignorance of, 798, 828
    relation to material nature, 172, 180, 620-
        621
    remains compact in body of Viṣṇu, 429
    scriptures meant for, 180, 591
    studies *Vedas* for sense gratification, 192
    the mind is both his friend and enemy, **312**
    thinks himself the doer, **192**-193
    to be delivered by trained mind, 313
    types of, **669**-670
    under laws of material nature, 304, **429**-
        430
    (*See also* Jīvātmā, Living Entity, Soul)
Consciousness
    as basis for peace, **152**
    as subject for Chapter Thirteen, 619-661

Consciousness
    as symptom of soul, 9, **94**-95, 99-100, 106,
        659-660
    cannot come from matter, 9, 10, 521
    conversion of material to spiritual, 182, 248
    definition, 11
    determines material body, 706
    difference between supreme and individual,
        100, 660
    dovetailed to Kṛṣṇa, 10, **147**, **238**
    fixed by experiencing higher taste, **145**
    if divine, one knows he does nothing, **281**
    Kṛṣṇa's never materially affected, 10
    limited to one's own body, 94
    linked to Absolute in *yoga*, 357-358
    obscured by lust and the modes, 205, **206**,
        706
    of devotees pure, 279-280
    of living entity pervertedly reflected, 10
    pervades the body, 94-96, **659**-660
    represented by intelligence, 628
    (*See also* False consciousness, Kṛṣṇa con
        sciousness)
Controller
    cosmos manifested by Kṛṣṇa's will, **455**-459
    Hṛṣīkeśa as, 622-623
    Kṛṣṇa as ultimate, 10, 187, **222**, **455**-459,
        460, 642
    living entity controls his own body, 705
    of energies, nature and soul, 7-8, 460, 623
    position of *īśvaras* superior, 190
Cooperation
    no happiness without, 196
    with the Supreme, 11-12
Cows
    as symbol of most valuable food, 679
    as work of *vaiśyas*, **813**
    dung considered pure, 13
    given pleasure by Govinda, 44, 59
    Kṛṣṇa as well-wisher of, 679
    Kṛṣṇa the *surabhi* amongst, **525**-526
    must be given all protection, **679**
    part of Kṛṣṇa's pastimes, 18
    seen by sage the same as *brāhmaṇa*, 292
    surabhi supply limitless milk, 431
    their slaughter the grossest ignorance, **679**

D

Daityas
    identified, 527
    Kṛṣṇa as Prahlāda amongst, **527**

Daivīm Prakṛti
    divine nature, protects mahātmās, 464
Dāmodara
    as plenary expansion, 433
Darśana-dhyāna-saṁsparśair matsya-kūrma-vi-
        haṅgamāḥ
    verses quoted, 301
Darśa-paurṇamāsī
    as demigod worship, 477
Dāsa-bhūto harer eva nānyasvaiva kadācana
    quoted, 635
Dāsya-bhakta
    service as servant, 425
Dayānidhi
    in disciplic succession, 29
Death
    activities bind one to, 134-135
    as gateway to kingdom of God, 158
    as one of four principles of material
        existence, 19
    as one of six transformations of body, 99
    as purifier on altar and battlefield, 103
    bodies awarded at time of, 22
    Brahmā and Brahmaloka subject to, 428
    called near by imitating Śiva, 190
    created by Kṛṣṇa, 497
    destination according to modes of nature at
        time of, 677-678
    dishonor worse than, 117
    importance of life's thoughts and deeds at,
        411, 416
    inevitability of, 80, 82, 99, 108, 137, 564,
        737
    its cycle according to activities, 108
    its perception as evil, 630
    Kṛṣṇa as deliverer from, 602-604
    Kṛṣṇa as Yama, personification of, 471,
        526-527, 530-531
    methods of transcending, 136, 293, 405,
        642, 652, 684
    no cause for lamentation, 89
    nonexistent in spiritual world, 405, 715
    prāyaścitta system of ablution before, 67
    remembrance and knowledge of Kṛṣṇa at
        time of, 22-23, 324, 406, 415, 420, 437,
        642
    repetition of, 137, 426
    sage callous toward, 332
    soul not subject to, 16, 98, 498
    transmigration at time of, 89, 433-437
Deha-dehi-vibhedo'yaṁ neśvare vidyate kvacit
    quoted, 489

Dehino 'smin yathā
    quoted, 704
Demigods
    Arjuna inquires about, 410
    Arjuna not content with kingdom of 81
    as parts of Kṛṣṇa's body, 173, 233, 394, 552
    born of Prajāpati, 731
    Brahmā, Śiva, Kumāras as chief, 502
    cannot equal Nārāyaṇa, Viṣṇu, Kṛṣṇa, 234
    created by Kṛṣṇa, 495
    do not forget Kṛṣṇa's proprietorship, 394
    five kinds worshiped by impersonalists, 756
    fought by Arjuna, 116
    ignorant of Kṛṣṇa's origin and personality
        366, 493, 512
    Indra as chief of, 411
    Kṛṣṇa as Indra amongst, 521
    Kṛṣṇa as Nārada amongst, 524
    Kṛṣṇa as origin and controller of, 304, 393,
        406, 493, 503, 569, 590
    Kṛṣṇa makes steady worship of, 393-394
    long to see two-handed form, 585-587
    misunderstood to be forms of Kṛṣṇa, 233,
        467
    motives for worship of, 18, 20, 175, 233-234,
        249, 391-393, 395
    necessity of sacrifice to, 173-175, 181
    no obligation due them by devotee of Kṛṣṇa,
        66, 120, 178
    not attractive to pure devotees, 464
    not impersonal, 399
    obey Vedic injunctions, 731
    observe battle from outer space, 568
    on higher branches of banyan, 696
    play songs from Sāma-veda, 531
    sent forth at beginning of creation, 171
    serve Kṛṣṇa, supply necessities, 173-175, 178
    subjected to influence of modes and senses,
        149, 811
    their benefits bestowed by Kṛṣṇa, 394-
        395
    their boons limited and temporary, 234,
        395-396
    their offerings meant for Kṛṣṇa alone, 475
    their relation to universal form, 556-558,
        568
    their worship discouraged, 18, 178, 538
    worshiped by darśa-paurṇamāsī, 477
    worshiped by demons, 741
    worshiped by one in goodness, 755-756
    worshiped by unintelligent, 395-396
    worshiped by yogīs, 249-250

Demigods
  worshipers attain their planets, 395-396, 399, 477
  worshipers never reach Kṛṣṇa, 405
  worship Kṛṣṇa, 187, 237, 580
  vanish at annihilation, 234
Demons
  Arjuna inquires for their sake, 218-219
  as expert in enjoying life's dream, 733
  as subject of Chapter Sixteen, 721-749
  attempt to reach higher planets by machine, 240
  attracted by impermanent and unclean work, 735-736
  believe sense gratification goal of life, 736-737
  blaspheme against religion, 742
  bound by desires, lust and anger, 737
  characteristics of, 730-747
  claim lust as cause of unreal world, 733
  claim to be God themselves, 738-741
  confused about Kṛṣṇa, 219, 221, 397-398, 512,513
  confused by Gītā, 217-218
  destroyed by Kṛṣṇa's agents, 226
  directed to wisdom by spiritual master, 758
  distort Kṛṣṇa and Gītā, 216-217, 219
  engage in horrible works to destroy world, 734-735
  envious of Kṛṣṇa, 742
  fear Kṛṣṇa and flee, 568
  harass devotees, 226
  ignorant of duty, 731-732
  ignorant of Supersoul as witness, 737
  ignore Vedic injunctions, 731
  illusioned by lust, pride, false prestige, 735-736, 742
  Kṛṣṇa expert in killing, 411
  Kṛṣṇa's mercy to, 744
  perform unauthorized sacrifice, 741
  reject sacrifices, 740
  secure money illegally, 737
  sink to abominable species, 743-744
  their liberation, fruitive activities and knowledge baffled, 462-463
  think women should be free, 732
  undergo torturous austerities, 757-758, 769
  Uśanā the spiritual master of, 534
  worshiped by one in passion, 755-756
Designations
  due to lust and desire, 21
  freedom from bodily, 21

Desires
  actions to gratify, 799
  arise from contemplating sense objects, 149
  arise from mental concoction, 141
  as cause of body, 646, 647, 656-657
  as impediments for returning to Godhead, 395
  as life symptoms, 627
  as subtle form of conditioning, 288
  as symptom and basis of passion, 670-671, 675
  banyan tree of material world situated on, 695
  cannot be stopped artificially, 141
  cause surrender to demigods, 391-392
  dissipated by Kṛṣṇa consciousness, 141, 157, 288, 305, 392
  dovetailed by Mahārāja Ambarīṣa to Kṛṣṇa's desire, 148
  eliminated through yoga, 302-303, 311, 317, 327, 332
  for fruitive results deep-rooted, hard to overcome, 301
  for gain discouraged, 196, 275
  fulfilled by Kṛṣṇa, 288, 393, 476
  generate anger, agitate mind, eyes and chest, 298
  greatest enemies of conditioned soul, 211-212
  Kṛṣṇa does not interfere with living entities', 288
  living entity overcome by, 403
  of demons insatiable, 735, 737
  of devotees dovetailed to Kṛṣṇa's, 245
  one free from them eligible for liberation, 301
  peace and happiness achieved if they are tolerated, 156, 157, 298
  senses instruments for gratifying, 646
  their flow likened unto rivers entering ocean, 156
  their quality must be changed, 157
  transcended by Brahman realized, 335, 822
Determination,
  as divine quality, 722, 727-728
  as quality of kṣatriya, 813
  characteristic of mahātmā, 465
  in cutting down banyan tree, 698
  in devotional service, 611-612
  in mode of goodness, 806
  in mode of ignorance, 807-808

Determination
    in mode of passion, 807
    in *yoga* practice, 332-333
    sparrow emptying ocean example of, 333
Devadatta
    name of Arjuna's conchshell, 44
Devahūti
    sāṅkhya explained to her by Kapila, 122
Devakī
    as mother of Kṛṣṇa, 44, 219
    Kṛṣṇa first appeared before her as Nārāyaṇa,
        461, 583, 587
    persecuted by Kaṁsa, 226
Devakī-nandana
    meaning of name, 44
Devala
    as learned leader, 382
    influences Arjuna, 831
    proclaims Kṛṣṇa to be Supreme, 5,6
    validates Arjuna's praise, 510
Devaloka
    See Planets
Devarṣi-bhūtapta-nṛṇāṁ pitṛṇām,
    verses quoted, 66, 120
Deveśa
    as controller of demigods, 569
Devotees
    absorption in Kṛṣṇa, 51, 338-339, 390, 411,
        425, 461
    accepted even when motivated, 389
    activities of Mahārāja Ambarīṣa considered
        pure, 327
    alone only fully realize Kṛṣṇa, 232, 366
    as aid in hearing *Gītā*, 32, 439, 840
    as constant companions of Kṛṣṇa, 221
    as desireless for self-interest, 424
    as friends to all, 279, 341, 593, 612-613
    as highest transcendentalists, 73-74, 318-319,
        836
    as *sādhu* even if uneducated, 226
    association with, 186, 239-241, 333, 362, 388,
        404, 442, 449, 464, 487, 652, 701
    attain liberation, 228, 301
    attain peace, 156, 284-285
    attracted to *saṅkīrtana* movement of
        Caitanya, 227
    automatically have all good qualities, 54-55
    aversion to sense gratification, 322, 634
    bathe twice daily, 613
    can accept all opulences for Kṛṣṇa's service, 60
    can conquer sleep and ignorance, 51
    can create atmosphere of Vṛndāvana, 425

Devotees
    cannot accept pseudo incarnations, 581
    can serve any of the transcendental forms
        424
    characteristics and qualities of, 55, 68,
        140-144, 156, 279-280, 389, 403 505,
        506, 611-617, 651, 821-822
    charity should be given to, 589
    concern for conditioned souls, 404, 516
    considered saintly despite abominable
        actions, 483-485
    contrasted with fruitive *yogīs*, 341-342
    control of action, 10-11, 151, 244-246
    control senses, 44, 144
    could see universal form from other planets,
        579
    defined as demigods, 580
    detachment from money and property, 60,
        245-246, 392, 613, 615-616
    do not desire spiritual planets or liberation,
        424
    do not feel material miseries, 302
    do not need to transfer via *yoga* to spiritual
        sky, 603
    do not retaliate against the wrongdoers, 60
    eager to see Kṛṣṇa in Vṛndāvana, 227
    engaged in serving and satisfying Kṛṣṇa, 49,
        60, 150, 593, 598, 825
    enter supreme abode, 23, 395-396, 423, 825
    exchange opulences with Kṛṣṇa, 691
    four kinds of impure devotees attain
        respective goals, 405
    freed from all obligations by Mukunda, 66
    Gītā especially meant for, 4, 28, 88, 217
    give pleasure to Kṛṣṇa by ordering Him, 49
    indifferent to leaving body, 255, 434-435,
        437
    indifferent to rituals, 138, 481
    knowledge of Kṛṣṇa, 219, 221, 363, 388- 389,
        405, 494, 518, 568, 643
    Kṛṣṇa appears especially to please, 220,
        226-227, 366, 400
    Kṛṣṇa especially inclined to, 62, 482, 843
    Kṛṣṇa supplies their necessities, 156, 474
    Kṛṣṇa tolerates no wrongs to, 60
    love for Kṛṣṇa, 176, 339, 390, 546
    may appear to work as ordinary men, 10-11
    more kind than Kṛṣṇa, 195
    must teach proper action, 185
    Nārada as greatest amongst, 524
    neophyte gives more attention to *arca-
        mūrti*, 461

Devotees
    never go to demigods for needs, 392, 395
    never perish, **485**
    not awarded material benefits, 395
    not confused by misguiding *Gītā* commen-
        taries, 585
    not disturbed by flowery language of *Vedas*,
        139
    not interested in seeing universal form, 581,
        582-583, 590
    often derided by philosophers, 508
    only interested in two-handed Kṛṣṇa, 464,
        582-583, 594
    perform sacrifice in different modes, 176-177
    pleased in discussing Kṛṣṇa's opulences, 518
    process of purification, 387
    never fall down, 490
    relationships with Śrī Kṛṣṇa, 4-5, 23, 232,
        390, 508-509, 551
    released from sin by offering food, **176**
    reside in sacred places, 320
    rewarded according to love, 232
    risk their lives to spread God consciousness,
        195, 593
    sacrifice everything for Kṛṣṇa, 250
    see Kṛṣṇa in everyone, 461
    see the earth as Vaikuṇṭha, 823
    their equality of vision, 337-338, 384, 687-
        688, 822
    their mercy as requisite, 112, 229
    their plans as good as Kṛṣṇa's, 566
    think distresses to be Kṛṣṇa's mercy, 611
    three classes of, 449-450
    transcendental to all attachment, 151
    transcendental to auspicious and inauspi-
        cious, **614-616**
    transcendental to four *varṇas*, 236
    transcendental to three modes of nature,
        11
    (*See also* Sages, Spiritual master, Vaiṣṇavas)
Devotional service
    advocated by Kṛṣṇa, **489**
    as *buddhi-yoga,* 122-123
    as Caitanya's wish birth after birth, 309
    as constitutional position, 137
    as declaration of war against *māyā,* 485
    as disturbance if ignores scriptures, 366
    as eternally existing, 447-448
    as happy process, 447-466
    as knowledge, 70, 264, 444, **630**
    as liberating force, 79, 91, **134**, **136**, 159, **273**,
        279, 381, 701

Devotional service
    as main objective of *Gītā*, 596, 632, 780
    as means of attaining Brahman, **688**-689
    as means of attaining Kṛṣṇa, **424**-425, **432**,
        589, **591**-594, 610
    as method of knowing the Self, **164**
    as only means to see Kṛṣṇa incessantly, 639
    as only way to understand Kṛṣṇa, **588**-590,
        823-824
    as *pavitram uttamam*, the purest, 445
    as process of detachment, 694
    as result of knowing Kṛṣṇa, **502**, **503**-504,
        718
    as spiritual activity, 387, 395, 445-446,
        719-720
    as step toward love of Kṛṣṇa, 231
    as subject for Chapter Nine, 442
    as subject for Chapter Twelve, 595-617
    attained after many births, 357
    attained by Brahman realized, **822**
    automatically develops good qualifications,
        616
    awakens relationship with Kṛṣṇa, 4
    begins with Hare Kṛṣṇa, 472
    brings satisfaction like full meal, 345
    by highest *yogī*, **358**-360
    can alone award peace, 305
    can be rendered by any *āśrama*, 466
    can transform lust into love, 209
    clarifies Kṛṣṇa's pastimes, etc., 439
    continues after liberation, 447-448
    controls senses, 148, 301
    delivers thousands of family members, 65-66
    difficult for sensualists and miscreants, **128**,
        387
    diminishes desire to dominate, 691
    dispels dust of materialism, 509
    does not deprive one of sacrifice, charity,
        etc., **438**
    easier than impersonal path, 600-601
    engaged in by pious free from delusion, **404**
    everything directly perceived through,
        446-447
    five different paths of, 425
    frees one from passion and ignorance, 363
    fulfills all obligations, 66
    guaranteed for one who explains *Gītā*, **838**
    guarantees passage to supreme abode, 433,
        437, **438**-439
    likened to seed in heart, 505-506
    necessary for happiness in renunciation,
        278

Devotional service
  necessary for seeing universal form, 586
  nine processes of, 26, 345, 443, 592, 633, 691-692
  nondifferent from Kṛṣṇa and His abode, 159, 719-720
  nondifferent from sāṅkhya-yoga, 276
  one dear to Kṛṣṇa is determined in, 611
  only absolute path for self-realization, 617
  precludes spiritual processes, 718-719
  removes ignorance, 511
  rendered by four kinds of pious men, 386-388
  rendered by mahātmās, 465-466
  renunciation the same as works in, 277
  requires vanquishing weaknesses of heart, 720
  rids one of good and bad actions, 135, 483-485
  sacrifice in different modes of, 176-177
  strengthened by hearing, 492
  superior to inaction, 168
  superior to renunciation of works, 273
  superior to speculation, 272
  surpasses all rituals, 65, 439
  the wise should encourage the ignorant in, 191-192
  transmigration transcended by faith in, 448-450
  two types of, 609
  vanquishes sin, 445
  (See also Bhakti, Bhakti-yoga, Service, Worship)
Dhanañjaya
  Arjuna addressed as, 134, 267, 456, 605, 803, 841
  meaning of name, 44
Dhāraṇā
  in aṣṭāṅga-yoga, 303, 305
Dharma
  defined, 17
  principles are orders of Kṛṣṇa, 224
  to be abandoned to surrender to Kṛṣṇa, 835-836
  (See also Religion, Sanātana-dharma)
Dharma-Kṣetra
  significance of word, 32, 33
Dharmaṁ hi sākṣāt-bhagavat-praṇītam
  quoted, 224, 240, 260
Dhīra
  defined, 89
Dhṛṣṭadyumna
  blows his conchshell, 46

Dhṛṣṭadyumna
  expertly arranged the Pāṇḍu army, 35
  not an important obstacle to Droṇācārya 36
Dhṛṣṭaketu
  cited by Duryodhana as great fighter, 36
Dhṛtarāṣṭra
  addressed as descendant of Bharata, 84
  Arjuna reluctant to kill his sons, 61, 69
  as father of Kurus, 32
  blind physically and spiritually, 34
  certain his sons could never agree with Pāṇḍavas, 34
  could not expect victory, 847-848
  desirous of usurping kingdom of Pāṇḍavas, 50
  did not want compromise, 32
  doubtful of his sons' victory, 32
  fearful of influence of Kurukṣetra on outcome of battle, 33, 34
  his joy frustrated by Arjuna's enlightenment, 84
  his sons destroyed in mouth of universal form, 560
  his sons disheartened by Pāṇḍava army, 48
  his sons' hearts shattered by conchshells, 47
  his sons religiously blind, 34
  his topics discussed form basic principle of Gītā, 32
  informed by Sañjaya his plans not laudable, 46
  inquires about battle from Sañjaya, 32
  rejoiced to hear Arjuna's refusal to fight, 84
  responsible for catastrophe at Kurukṣetra, 46
  separates sons of Pāṇḍu from family heritage, 33
Dhruva Mahārāja
  attaining his planet, 840
Dhyāna
  in aṣṭāṅga-yoga, 303, 305
Dhyāna-yoga
  as part of yoga ladder, 311
  does not admit householder, 322
  many impediments to, 331
Dhyāyaṁ stuvaṁs tasya yaśas tri-sandhyam
  verses quoted, 126
Digestion
  Kṛṣṇa as fire of, 711-712
Dik-kālādy-anavacchinne kṛṣṇe ceto vidhāya ca
  verses quoted, 340
Disciplic succession
  Arjuna as beginning of, 218, 511-513, 547

Disciplic succession
  as criterion for spiritual master, 259-260
  as means to knowledge, 14, 67, 364
  begins with Brahmā, 14
  begun with sun-god, 4
  broken in course of time, 216
  commentaries by *māyayāpahṛta-jñāna* out-
    side, 385
  from Kṛṣṇa to sun-god to Manu to Ikṣvāku,
    214-215
  Gāyatrī passed down by, 532
  importance in understanding *Gītā*, 32, 216
  must stem from Kṛṣṇa, 574
  one should follow in, 80, 239-240, 266
  outline given, 29
  referred to by Arjuna, 67
  spiritual master in it from time eternal, 268
Disease
  as life symptom, **627**
  cannot be restricted, 633
  cannot be counteracted by wealth, 82
  caused by passionate food, **760-761**
  counteracted by offered food, 178
  due to material body, 645
  its perception as evil, **630**
  none for spiritual body, 405
  one of four principles of material existence,
    19
  present everywhere in material universe, 137
Distress
  for the ignorant, 810-811
  happiness as end of, **808-809**
  nonpermanent, should be tolerated, **90-91**
  not to be considered in fighting, 120
  of birth, old age, disease and death, 632-633
  one dear to Kṛṣṇa equal in, **611, 612**
  one steady in distress is eligible for libera-
    tion, **92**
  result of action in passion, **678-679**
  senses always cause of, 810
Diti
  as mother of Daitya demons, 527
Divyam (transcendental)
  as quality of Kṛṣṇa, 5
Doubt
  arises in heart out of ignorance, **267**
  Arjuna freed from, 510, **842**
  compared to Keśī demon, 781
  destroyed by following *Gītā*, 267
  destroyed by knowledge, **267, 291**
  destroys happiness in this world and next,
    266

Doubt
  freedom from created by Kṛṣṇa, **497**
  impedes God consciousness, **266**
  in Dhṛtarāṣṭra, 32
  only Kṛṣṇa can dispel Arjuna's, **349-350**
  questions of Arjuna arise due to, 411
  removed by association with devotees, 439
  transcended by liberated, **299**
Draupadī
  her disrobing and appeal for justice, 41, 582
Dravyamaya-yajña
  charitable activities, 253
Dṛḍha-vrata
  determined faith, as beginning of *bhakti-
    yoga*, 407
Dream
  always present in all modes, 808
  as natural occurrence, 808
  ignorant determination bound by, **807-808**
  incurred by over-eating, 325
  material body likened to, 110
Droṇa
  addressed by Duryodhana, 35
  Arjuna reluctant to attack, 77, 113, 730
  as teacher of Arjuna and Pāṇḍavas, 35
  awards Arjuna weapon that could kill him,
    116
  beheld by Arjuna on Battlefield, 53
  blows his conchshell, **46**
  cited by Duryodhana as great warrior, **38**
  considered already destroyed, **566**
  considered worshipable as superior, 77
  destined to be killed by son of Drupada, 35
  destroyed in mouth of universal form, **560**
  forced by finances to side with Duryodhana,
    78
  his defects pointed out by Duryodhana, 35
  his great military power not threatened by
    Dhṛṣṭadyumna, 36
  his political quarrel with King Drupada, 35
  his sister married Kṛpa, 38
  imparts military secrets to Dhṛṣṭadyumna,
    35
  Kṛṣṇa speaks in his presence, **52**
  lost respectability as teacher, 78
  no need for lamentation for, 89
  silent during disrobing of Draupadī, **41, 582**
  would have spiritual or heavenly body in
    life, 89
Drupada
  cited by Druyodhana as great fighter, **36**
  father of Draupadī, Arjuna's wife, 35

Drupada
    his sacrifice and benediction, 35
    his son Dhṛṣṭadyumna expertly arranges
        army, 35
Drupadī
    her sons blow their conchshells, 46
    her sons cited by Duryodhana as great
        warriors, 37
Duality
    Arjuna exhorted to transcend, 129
    as cause of anxiety, 284-285
    as simultaneous identity and individuality
        in Kṛṣṇa, 291
    between living entities and Supreme, 623-
        626, 634, 636-637, 648, 716
    difficult for sinful to transcend, 404
    freedom from, 246, 275, 299, 699-700
    Kṛṣṇa transcendental to, 457
    living entity overcome by, 403
    must be tolerated, 130
    not present in Kṛṣṇa's body, 223
    of knowledge and knower rejected by
        monists, 330
    sacrifice unnecessary for those who have
        transcended, 181
    sages free from, 245-246
    transcended by conquered mind, 315
    transcended in Kṛṣṇa consciousness, 120,
        125, 143, 285
Durvāsā Muni
    conquered by Mahārāja Ambarīṣa, 146-147
    could not check his senses out of pride, 147
Duryodhana
    approaches Droṇācārya, 34
    asserts his strength to be immeasurable, 39
    beheld by Arjuna on Battlefield, 53
    Bhīṣma and Droṇa forced to take his side
        for financial reasons, 78
    challenged Arjuna, 63
    compared to unwanted plant, 33
    confident of victory, 39-41
    considers Pāṇḍavas' army limited, 39
    desirous of usurping kingdom of Pāṇḍavas,
        50
    encouraged by Bhīṣma's conchshell, 41
    envies Bhīma who can kill him, 40
    feels fear upon seeing army of Pāṇḍavas 34
    forces Arjuna to fight, 49
    his diplomatic veneer, 34, 35
    his soldiers expert and well equipped, 39
    his soldiers willing to die for his sake, 39
    his victory impossible due to Kṛṣṇa, 42

Duryodhana
    hopes that Bhīṣma's and Droṇācārya's af-
        fection for Pāṇḍavas be abandoned, 41
    mentioned as king, 34
    points out army to Droṇācārya, 35-39
    points out defects of Droṇācārya, 35
    predestined to die at Kurukṣetra, 39
    referred to as evil-minded, 50
    saw some of Kṛṣṇa's universal forms, 579
    urges army to support Bhīṣma, 40
    warns Droṇācārya not to be lenient against
        the Pāṇḍavas, 35
Duṣkṛtina
    as miscreants, four classes discussed, 382-
        386
    (See also Miscreants)
Duty
    action in accord with, 798-799
    action in mode of nature, 132
    Arjuna advised to perform, 170
    as purifier, 169-170, 818
    better one's own, though faulty, than
        another's, 201, 815-817
    demons ignorant of, 731-732
    for different varnas in lieu of meditation,
        609-610
    frees from bondage of action, 197
    gives birth to yajña, 177
    how to discharge, 196-197
    inferior due to lack of knowledge, 194-195
    Janaka attains perfection through, 184
    necessary to control senses, 305
    necessity for performance of, 133, 169, 183,
        351, 785-786
    never affected by sin, 816
    none for Kṛṣṇa, 187
    none for self-realized, 182-183
    not to be abandoned despite difficulties,
        faults, fear, etc., 91, 113, 786-787, 817-
        818
    of kṣatriya, 109, 113, 115
    perfection by performance of, 814-815
    performed in renunciation, 132, 282,
        787-788
    performed with attachment by ignorant,
        190
    prescribed according to one's nature, 201-
        202
    sacrifice according to, 762
    self-illuminated by grace of Kṛṣṇa, 182
    should not be given up without full Kṛṣṇa
        consciousness, 199

Duty
  sin incurred by neglect of, 109, **116**
  spiritualized by liberation, 114
  spiritual master's order as, 201-202, 827
  to be performed in Kṛṣṇa consciousness,
    238, **416-417**, 835
  two types discussed, *svadharmas*, 114
  understood by scriptural regulations, **748**

Dvandvair vimuktāḥ sukha-duḥkha-saṁjñair
  verses quoted, 21

Dvāpara-yuga
  characteristics and duration of, 215, 428
  Kṛṣṇa appears at end of, 224
  (*See also* Yuga)

Dvā suparṇā sayujā sakhāyā
  quoted, 646

Dyāv-āpṛthivyoḥ
  space between heaven and earth, 556

E

Earth
  as one of eight separated energies, 367-368
  as one of five great elements, 627
  generated from water, 110
  Kṛṣṇa as its original fragrance, **374-375**

Ekādaśī
  fasting on, 465-466

Eko devo nitya-līlānurakto bhakta-vyāpī hṛdy
    antarātmā
  quoted, 228

Eko'pi san bahudhā yo'vabhāti
  verses quoted, 340

Eko vai nārāyaṇa āsīn na brahmā na iśāno nāpo
    nāgni samau neme
  verses quoted, 504

Elements
  all-pervading, 432-433, 451, 569, 814-815
  as inconceivable, 400-401, 419
  as means of perceiving Kṛṣṇa, 373-374
  generation of, 110
  twenty-four, 13

Energy
  all manifestations manifested and sustained
    by Kṛṣṇa's, 12, 285, 452, 468-469, 501,
    644
  attracts those hovering on mental plane, 55
  can be ordered by Kṛṣṇa to release condi-
    tioned soul, 381
  described as *prabhā*, 96
  difference and nondifference from ener-
    getic, 93-94

Energy
  distributed as opulences, 518
  divided into three parts, 23
  eight separated material energies, 367-368
  enables planets to float in space, 710
  eternality of, 380, **430**
  from the heart unexplained by scientists,
    102
  inferior energy includes gross and subtle,
    369
  internal and external discussed, 388, 814-
    815
  Kṛṣṇa always in superior, 495
  Kṛṣṇa as controller of, **460**
  Kṛṣṇa as soul of *mahat-tattva*, 519
  Kṛṣṇa its origin and dissolution, 370-371
  living entity as superior, 369-370
  living entity seated on machine made of,
    830
  modes of nature as manifestations of
    Kṛṣṇa's, 377-378
  of Kṛṣṇa as *annamaya, prāṇamaya, jñāna-*
    maya and *vijñānamaya*, 626
  of Kṛṣṇa difficult to overcome, 380-381
  pleasure in discussing Kṛṣṇa's, 518
  relation of living entity to three types of,
    309
  set loose as *mahat-tattva*, 455
  spiritual as basis for material, 371, 831
  spread as a tree spreads roots, 372
  transcendental path as war on illusory,
    347-348
  transferral to spiritual energy at time of
    death, 23
  works as a shadow, 383
  wound up at end of millennium, 455

Enjoyer
  See Puruṣa

Entity, living (*jīva*)
  See Living entity

Envy
  Arjuna never envious of Kṛṣṇa, **442**
  as cause of disregarding teachings, **198**
  as cause of jeering Kṛṣṇa, 463
  as characteristic of materialist, 613
  cause of lower birth, **743**
  disqualifies one to comment on *Gītā*, 443
  eradicated by understanding Supersoul, 599
  freedom from covetousness as divine quality,
    722
  knowledge not to be explained to one
    envious of Kṛṣṇa, **837**

Envy
    Kṛṣṇa envies no one, 482
    none in true yogi, 245, 341
    of Kṛṣṇa and Gītā, 88, 197-198, 385, 403, 742,
        837, 840
    of worker in passion, 801-802
    one dear to Kṛṣṇa not subject to, 611
    teaching should be followed without, 197
Equanimity
    as sign of realization, 293
    created by Kṛṣṇa, 497
    defined as freedom from attachment and
        aversion, 499
    in regarding well-wisher, friend and enemy,
        317
    in viewing pebbles, stones and gold, 316
    mind established in, 293
    of one transcendent to modes of nature,
        687-688
    of one very dear to Kṛṣṇa, 611-612, 615-616
Eṣa u hy eva sādhu karma kārayati taṁ yame-
    bhyo lokebhya unninīṣate
    verses quoted, 288
Eṣo 'nurātmā cetasā veditavyaḥ
    verses quoted, 95
Ete cāṁśa-kalāḥ puṁsaḥ kṛṣṇas tu bhagavān
    svayam
    verses quoted, 74
Eternality
    of both spiritual and material natures, 380
    of devotional service, 16-17, 447-448, 634
    of existent confirmed, 93
    of jīva and spirit world, 15-16
    of Kṛṣṇa and individual soul, 86-88, 98, 105
    of living entity's conditioning, 380
    of Vedas and Kṛṣṇa consciousness, 197
    realized in merging, 601
Ether
    as one of eight separated energies, 367-368
    as one of five great elements, 627
    from it air generates, 110
    Kṛṣṇa as sound in, 373
Evaṁ manaḥ karma vaśaṁ prayuṅkte avidyayāt-
    many upadhīyamāne
    verses quoted, 273
Evaṁ paramparā-prāptam imaṁ rajarṣayo viduḥ,
    verses quoted, 3, 29
Evaṁ prasanna-manaso bhagavad-bhakti-
    yogataḥ,
    verses quoted, 363, 448
Expansions
    See Plenary expansions

F

Faith
    according to position of heart, 754-755
    according to three modes, 753-756
    advised in all Vedic scriptures, 776
    as dṛḍha-vrata, determined, 407
    as quality of highest yogī, 358
    assattva, always comes from goodness, 754
    as subject of Chapter Seventeen, 751-777
    blind faith not elevating, 753
    created by association with devotees, 449
    defined as trust in the sublime, 125
    determines form of sacrifice, 258
    in demigods made steady by Kṛṣṇa, 393-394
    in devotional service, 265, 448-450
    in hearing Gītā, 439, 840
    in ignorance, 764
    in Kṛṣṇa and spiritual master reveals
        knowledge, 360
    in Kṛṣṇa and Vedas, 79, 197, 228, 291,597
    in Kṛṣṇa divided in three stages, 450
    in pure goodness, 754-755
    Kṛṣṇa as, 530
    lacking in demons, 731, 737
    matures to love of God, 777
    necessity of, 265-266, 332-333, 776-777
    of one very dear to Kṛṣṇa, 617
    to perform action, 794
False consciousness
    attempts to be lord of matter, 412
    causes and characteristics of, 11
    conditioned soul thinks himself the doer,
        192-193
    due to dualities of delusion, 403
    in Arjuna, 56-58
    one in it likened to ass, 208
    typical activities of, 195
    (See also False Ego)
False Ego
    acquired due to lusty intelligence, 208
    action according to, 799
    as attachment to bodily designations, 21,
        287, 379
    as binding force, 11, 703
    as constituent of body, 627-628
    as one of eight separated energies, 367-368
    brings ruination, 827
    defined, 11,632
    demons bewildered by, 742
    due to illusion and duality, 370, 403
    freedom from, 196, 283-284, 611, 630, 821

False Ego
in Arjuna, 14-15, 828
includes ten sense organs, 368
makes one forget relationship with Kṛṣṇa,
193
makes one think himself the doer, 193
one is not slayer who is not motivated by,
793
one should abandon desires born of, 332
one who is devoid of it can attain peace, 157
severe penance performed out of, 757-758
work free from, 800-801
(*See also* False consciousness)

Fame
as motivation to religion, 630
created by Kṛṣṇa, defined, 497, 500
equanimity in, 615-616
Kṛṣṇa as, 530

Family
affection for them overwhelms Arjuna with
grief, 84
as nothing but Kṛṣṇa, 468-469
attachment described as skin disease, 80
attachment in passion, 671, 675
connections accepted by ignorant, 195
danger of destroying traditions, 63, 66-67
delivered by one in devotional service,
65-66
difficulty in *sannyāsī's* renouncing, 92
elder members should not be slain, 63
everyone working to maintain, 308
hellish situation created by unwanted
population, 65
ignores oblations to ancestors when corrupt,
65
no obligation due them by devotee of
Mukunda, 66
offering respect to forefathers imperative,
138
process for happiness in, 633
purificatory process in, 63
regulations obeyed by Kṛṣṇa, 188
role in training transcendentalists, 353-354
should be abandoned if spiritual impediment, 633
tradition of helping forefathers by offering
prasādam, 65
women corrupted when irreligion prominent, 64

Fasting
as determined activity, 465-466
demonic when severe, 757-758

Fasting
for political goals condemned, 757-758
how to conduct, 499
should be observed as scriptures recommend, 325

Fear
advancement protects one from most dangerous type of, 124
alleviated by reading *Bhagavad-gītā*, 27
created by Kṛṣṇa, 497
defeated by refuge in Kṛṣṇa, 47
due to materialism, 498, 613
duty not to be abandoned out of, 786
freedom by breath suspension, meditation,
302-303
freedom from as requisite for love, 299-230
generals would think Arjuna motivated by,
118
ignorant determination bound by, 807
in Arjuna upon seeing friends and relatives,
54-56
Kṛṣṇa enjoins Arjuna not to fear, 835-836
of Arjuna of universal form, 577, 590
realized souls free from, 47, 56, 142, 322

Fire
as evidence of Kṛṣṇa's mercy, 709
as one of eight separated energies, 367-368
as one of five great elements, 627
as sacrifice ignored by artificial *sannyāsīs*,
308
compared to living entity, 205
covered by smoke compared to work,
817-818
death during time of, 434-435
does not illumine supreme abode, 701
generated from air, generates water, 110
its splendor comes from Kṛṣṇa, 709
Kṛṣṇa as, 467-468
Kṛṣṇa as Agni, 521
Kṛṣṇa as digestion, 711-712
Kṛṣṇa as its heat, 374-375
living entities found in, 668
lust compared to, 206
needed for digestion, 375
of knowledge burns material reactions, 263
sacrifice to Brahman offered in, 249-250
universal form addressed as, 571
will annihilate everything in time, 530

Food
according to three modes, 15, 759-761
annamaya as dependence on, 626
as method for attaining Kṛṣṇa, 592, 605

Food

    cannot be manufactured by man, 175

    cows as symbol of most valuable, 679

    digested by fire of Kṛṣṇa, 711-712

    eatables in mode of goodness listed, 175

    eating controlled by prasādam, 255

    eating remnants frees one from sin, 65, 176

    four kinds of, 712

    its purpose, 760

    Kṛṣṇa accepts a leaf, flower, fruit or water, 478-479

    made palatable by moon's influence, 711

    not to be renounced, 150, 786

    offerable and unofferable, 324-325, 478-479

    offered only to Kṛṣṇa by devotees, 178

    offered to ancestors, 65

    produced from rain and sacrifice, 177, 257

    purifies existence, refines memory, 174

    sanctified by sacrifice, 174

    scarcity counteracted by saṅkīrtana-yajña, 178

    sinful for sense enjoyment, 176-177, 178

    taken by brahmacārī under spiritual master's orders, 438

    temperance advised, 324-326

    types eaten by humans, 178

    when offered, immunizes body, 178

    (See also Prasādam)

Forgiveness

    as divine quality, 722

    created by Kṛṣṇa, should be practiced, 497

Form (of Kṛṣṇa)

    always fresh like young man, 578

    always manifest to devotees, 220

    appeared at His birth, 495

    as arca-vigraha not material, 600

    as innumerable, 221, 228, 578

    as object of meditation, 22, 27, 51 349 416, 834

    as sac-cid-ānanda, 399

    can be perceived on transcendental platform, 638

    cannot be understood through senses, 316

    compared to sun, 402

    covered by yoga-māyā, 400

    demigods and devotees long to see two-handed form, 582-583, 585-587

    derided by fools, 459-461

    eternally existent, 224

    glorified by mahātmās, 465

    indicated by arūpam, 372

    manifested in material world, 19

Form (of Kṛṣṇa)

    misunderstood as material, 230, 397-399, 463

    proof of its spirituality, 401-402

    saumya-vapuḥ most beautiful, 584

    strikes wonder in Sañjaya, 846-847

    Śyāmasundara most beloved, 594

    the original appears every millennium, 222

    the temporary and eternal discussed, 589-590

    two-armed and four-armed forms discussed, 222-223, 583-584

    two-armed and four-armed forms revealed, 583

    two-armed as origin of all forms, 584, 589-590, 593-594

    two-armed cannot be seen by Vedic study, penance, charity or worship, 587-588

    unlike ordinary living entity, 187

    unmanifested form pervades universe, 450-451

    worship of personal form advised, 597, 598

    (See also Sac-cid-ānanda-vigraha)

Freedom

    from doubt and delusion, created by Kṛṣṇa, 497

    from illusion, prestige, lust, etc., 699-700

    from miseries by samādhi, 330

    of Kṛṣṇa, to act in any way, 224

    only possible by understanding Kṛṣṇa, 381

    women and children should not be given, 732

Friendship

    between Arjuna and Kṛṣṇa, 84-85, 550- 551, 573, 577, 833-834

    between Paramātmā and jīvātmā, 102-103, 649

    Kṛṣṇa friend of all living entities, 153, 469-470

    of devotee with Kṛṣṇa, 4, 482-483

    with Kṛṣṇa attained by following Arjuna, 834

    with Kṛṣṇa conquers sleep and ignorance, 51

    (See also Relationships)

G

Gadādhara, Ācārya

    obeisances to, 2

Gandharvas

    behold universal form in wonder, 557

Gandharvas
Kṛṣṇa as Citraratha amongst, **524**
on higher branches of banyan, 696

Gāṇḍiva
Arjuna's bow slips from his hand, **55**

Ganges
as sacred river, 320
emanates from feet of Kṛṣṇa, 28
its waters compared to *Bhagavad-gītā*, 28
Kṛṣṇa as, **528**

Gāñja (marijuana)
smoked by pseudo-devotees of Śiva, 190

Garbhādhāna-saṁskāra
begetting children in godly atmosphere, 723

Garbhodakaśāyī Viṣṇu
as *puruṣa-avatāra*, 519
Brahmā born from His navel, 569
enters all universes, 367, 456
lies on serpent Vāsuki, 552

Garga Upaniṣad
quoted, 80,454

Garuḍa
Kṛṣṇa as, **527**
Kṛṣṇa rides on him, 603
makes ocean return sparrow's eggs, 333

Gaurakiśora
in disciplic succession, 29

Gāyatrī
discussed, 532
Kṛṣṇa as, **531-532**

Ghosts
forced to remain in subtle bodies, 65
released by offering of *prasādam*, 65
their worshipers may become *rakṣas* or
yakṣas, 477
worshiped by one in ignorance, 755-756
worshiped in conditioned state, 776
worshiped in trees, 756
worshipers of ghosts take birth amongst
ghosts, **477**

Ghrāṇaṁ ga tat-pāda-saroja-saurabhe
verses quoted, 147

Gītā-māhātmya, 32

Godāsa
as servant of senses, 335

Goddess of fortune
hundreds of thousands serve Kṛṣṇa, 431

Goloka eva nivasaty akhilātma-bhūtaḥ
quoted, 19, 323, 637

Goloka Vṛndāvana
all affairs conducted from, 433
as chief Vaikuṇṭha planet, 701

Goloka Vṛndāvana
as original planet, 20
as personal abode, 461-462
as ultimate goal, 592
attained by love of Kṛṣṇa, 439
Brahman-realized persons cannot reach,405
description of, 431-432
devotees enter, 423
devotees do not want to be transferred to,
593
nondifferent from Kṛṣṇa, 432
no return from, 426, 700-701
not illumined by sun, moon, electricity,
700-702
plant of devotion enters, 506
reached by knowing Kṛṣṇa, 323-324, 406
surabhi cows in, 526
(See also Spiritual sky, Supreme abode,
Vṛndāvana)

Goodness
action in, 132, **798-799**
action in the mode purifies, **678**
as manifestation of Kṛṣṇa's energy, 377-378
as mode of nature, 8
as purest form of existence, 677
austerity in mode of, **767**
charity in mode of, **769-770**
charity, sacrifice and penance must be in,
772
conditions one to concept of happiness,
669-670, 672-673
death in the mode leads to higher planets,
677, 681-682
determination in, **806**
enables one to adopt right activities, 10
expected of *brāhmaṇa*, 202
faith in pure goodness, 754-755
food in mode of, **760-761**
happiness in, **809**
illuminating characteristics of mode, **669-
670**
importance of education in mode of, **680-
681**
in pure *vāsudeva* state one can understand
God, 674
knowledge develops from, **680-681**
knowledge in, **796**
manifestations experienced through knowledge, **674-675**
material world not in pure goodness, 754
must be attained to understand Kṛṣṇa, 749
one in the mode worships demigods, **755-756**

Goodness
position steadied by devotional service, 363
renunciation in, 787-788
sacrifice in mode of, 762
sometimes defeats passion, 673-674
transcended by Kṛṣṇa consciousness, 776
transcendental if pure, 754
understanding in, 804
Viṣṇu worshiped by those in mode of, 175
worker in, 800-801
(See also Modes of nature)
Gopāla Bhaṭṭa Gosvāmī
obeisances to, 1
Gosvāmī
as one who controls mind, 335
birth in their families fortunate, 353-354
defined as one who can control senses, 298
knows happiness of transcendental senses, 335
Govardhana Hill
lifted by Kṛṣṇa, 533
one cannot imitate by lifting, 189-190
Govinda
as He appears in Goloka Vṛndāvana, 431-432
as pleasure of senses and cows, 459
as plenary expansion associates with devotees, 23
Kṛṣṇa addressed as, 59, 83
Kṛṣṇa as primeval, 74
living, entity should satisfy His senses, 59-60
meaning of name, 44, 59-60
santas in love with, 176
seen by eyes anointed with love, 339, 451
Grace
Arjuna convinced of Kṛṣṇa's, 540
as means of understanding Kṛṣṇa, 221 543
buddhi-yoga attained by, 122
enables digestion of food, 712
illuminates duty, 182
of Kṛṣṇa can prolong or diminish life, 375
of Kṛṣṇa carries out everything automatically, 617
of Kṛṣṇa enables Arjuna's seeing everything, 552
of Kṛṣṇa enables happiness, 142
of Kṛṣṇa gives opportunities for perfection, 355
of Supersoul enables transmigration, 102
spiritual body attained by, 704
supreme abode attained by, 825, 831

Greed
as gate leading to hell, 745
Gṛhastha
charity, self-control and sacrifice meant for, 725-726
perfection by restriction, 250-251
performs sacrifices for further enlightenment, 438
Guḍākeśa
Arjuna as, 84, 519
meaning of, 51, 519
Guṇa
meaning rope, 380

H

Hanumān
cooperated with Lord Rāma, 48
his wrath engaged as service, 204
on Arjuna's flag, 47-48
Happiness
all living entities search after, 18
arising from sleep, illusion, etc., 810-811
as conditioning concept, 669-670
as enemy of sense enjoyer, 207
as eternal servant of Kṛṣṇa, 141
as life symptom, 627
Brahman as constitutional position of, 690-691
by concentration on Kṛṣṇa, 295, 335-336
by food in the mode of goodness, 760-761
by saṅkīrtana-yajña, 177
by surrender to Kṛṣṇa, 369, 393
cannot be restricted, 633
due to material body, 645
enjoyed by factual experience, 299
enjoyed even in the body, 684
enjoyed in action for Kṛṣṇa, 242
enjoyed when desire to dominate diminishes, 647
flickering when derived from Vedic principles, 473
impossible in this life or next without sacrifice, 256
impossible without peace, 152
in devotional service, not mere renunciation, 278
in Kṛṣṇa, 82, 341
in mode of goodness, 675, 808-809
in mode of ignorance, 810-811
in mode of passion, 679, 809-810
in perceiving self in samādhi, 330

Happiness
    in sense control, **285, 298**
    in spiritual sky, 18, 20, 257, 439
    its worth questioned by Arjuna, 59
    Kṛṣṇa does not desire heavenly, 237
    Kṛṣṇa the cause, 57, 82
    like nectar in beginning, poison at end,
        809-810
    like poison in beginning, nectar at end, **809**
    living entity completely dependent in, 289
    materially sought by fruitive workers, 352
    money cannot bring, **681**
    none in this world or next for doubting soul,
        266
    nonpermanent, arises from sense percep-
        tion, 90-91
    not attained by whimsical action, **746-747**
    not gained by killing kinsmen, **61**
    not possible without faith, 266
    not to be considered in fighting, **120**
    of senses known by *gosvāmī*, 335
    on basis of sense gratification, 121, 208
    one dear to Kṛṣṇa equal in, **611, 612**
    one falls down from it when pious activities
        expire, 83
    one steady in happiness is eligible for
        liberation, 92
    on sensual plane discussed, 128
    process for family, 633
    sacrifice of material, 348
    sages not elated by, **142, 155**
    seems elusive to Arjuna on Battlefield, 57
    should be tolerated, **90-91**, 130
    strange to commit sin to enjoy, **68**
    transcended by conquered mind, **315**
    within for perfect mystic, **299**
Harāv abhaktasya kuto mahad-guṇā
    verses quoted, 55
Hardwar
    as sacred place, 320
Hare Kṛṣṇa
    as best process to make home pleasant, 633
    as best sacrifice, 726
    as devotional service, 265, 424, 472, 505, 606,
        691
    as easy path to elevation, 748
    as engagement of *brahmacārī*, 251
    as escape from creation and destruction,
        429
    as internal potency dancing on the tongue,
        605
    as *mantra* for whole world, 28

Hare Kṛṣṇa
    as means of pleasing Kṛṣṇa, 603
    as means of understanding Kṛṣṇa, 398
    as means to control tongue, 632
    as meditation, 344, 417-418
    as purest representation of Kṛṣṇa, 523
    as remembering process, 415, 417, 425
    chanted for transcendental body, 416, 484
    chanted 300,000 times daily by Haridāsa
        Ṭhākur, 356
    contains *om*, 423
    for internal cleanliness, 265, 631, 732
    for reaching supreme destination, 423, 604
    its chanting the only way in Kali-yuga, 422
    pleasure derived from chanting, 446
    progress by hearing, 652
    promulgated by Caitanya in Benares, 508
    protects devotee from falldowns, 486
    should be chanted without stoppage, 486
Harer nāma harer nāma harer nāmaiva kevalam
    verses quoted, 320
Harer nāmānukīrtanam
    as engagement of *brahmacārī*, 251
Haridāsa Ṭhākur
    elevated to *nāmācārya*, 356
    resists Māyā Devī, 149
    suffered to spread God consciousness, 593
    would not eat until 300,000 names chanted,
        326
Haṭha-yoga
    as childish way to satisfy Supreme, 651
    many impediments to, 331
    meant for controlling five kinds of air, 95
    one must die at suitable time in, 434
    practiced for perfections, 253
    process of *yoga* breathing described, 254
He kṛṣṇa karuṇā-sindho
    prayer, 2
Hiḍimba
    demon killed by Bhīma, 44
Himalayas,
    Kṛṣṇa as, **523**
Hiraṇyagarbha
    Brahmā born out of, 501
Hiraṇyakaśipu
    killed by Kṛṣṇa, 744
    performed penances in ignorance, 769
    persecuted son, 226
    plans baffled by material energy, 383
Hṛṣīkeśa
    as Lord of total senses, 49, 335, 622-623, 815
    as plenary expansion, 433

Hṛṣīkeśa
    as sacred place, 320
    could understand purpose of Arjuna's
        surveying army, 51
    ignorant man forgets, 193
    indicates Kṛṣṇa knows everything, 52
    Kṛṣṇa as, **47, 52**, 84, **780**
    significance of address, 44, **780**-781
    universal form addressed as, **568**
Human life
    as chance to conquer lust, 206
    as most valuable asset, 80
    as regulated and nonregulated, 351
    begins with varṇāśrama-dharma, 114
    can be prolonged or diminished by Kṛṣṇa,
        375
    400,000 human species, 384
    generally engaged in eating, sleeping, de-
        fending, and mating, 365
    guaranteed for one in Kṛṣṇa consciousness,
        124
    love of God its highest perfection, 209
    many forms extant on other planets, 500
    meant for āśramas, not sense gratification,
        250
    meant for realization, 6, 181, 206, 214, 384,
        407
    meant for sacrifice and purification, 175,
        747
    not meant for merely toiling hard, 15
    not properly used by miser, 80
    only loophole out of material life, 256
    perfected in association with Lord, 15-16
Humility
    as knowledge, defined, **629**-630
    as qualification for sannyāsī, **724**-725

I

Ignorance
    all conditioned entities born in, 798
    action in, 676, **678**-679, 800
    Arjuna placed in, 7
    as attachment to results, 127, **190**
    as cause of higher and lower natures, 626
    as cause of sin, bondage and suffering 256,
        264, 287
    as demoniac, **728**-729, **738**, 749
    as manifestation of Kṛṣṇa's energy, **377**-378
    as mode of nature, 8
    as thinking the body to be the self, 195
    austerity in mode of, **769**

Ignorance
    bewilders and covers knowledge, 288
    causes delusion, ends in madness, indolence,
        sleep, 325, **671**-673, **676**, **680**-681
    causes one to try to adjust to world, 136-137
    charity in mode of, **771**
    conquered by Arjuna, 51
    defined as not knowing Kṛṣṇa, **229**
    determination in, **807**-808
    disobedient doomed to, **198**
    dispelled by Gītā, devotion and guru, 93, 94,
        135, 268, 363, **508**-511, 720, 841
    duty abandoned in, 115, **786**
    effects of the mode discussed, **671**-672, **676**
    equated with sleep, 51
    food in mode of, **760**-761
    four signs of, 195
    gives rise to doubts, **267**
    happiness in, **810**-811
    hellish worlds destination of those in, 681-
        682
    impedes realization, **266**, 723
    knowledge in mode of, **797**-798
    lamentation as a sign of, 72
    leads to rebirth in animal kingdom, **677**,
        678
    lust a symbol of, 207
    makes one think Kṛṣṇa responsible, 289
    manifest as wrath, 204
    misguides one in identifying soul and
        Supersoul, 111-112
    one in the mode worships ghosts, **755**-756
    renunciation in mode of, **786**
    sacrifice in mode of, **764**
    Śiva as incarnation of tamo-guṇa, 381
    sometimes defeats goodness and passion,
        673-674
    understanding, in, **805**
    worker in, **802**-803
    (See also Modes of Nature, Nescience, Sleep)
Īhā yasya harer dāsye karmaṇā manasā girā
    verses quoted, 283
Ikṣvāku
    forefather of Raghu dynasty, 215
    instructed via disciplic succession, 4, **214**-
        215, 240
Ilāvartavarṣa
    earth known formerly as, 354
Illusion
    See Māyā
Imaṁ-vivasvate yogaṁ proktavān aham avyayam
    verses quoted, 3

Imitation
    of another's duty dangerous, 201-202
    of Kṛṣṇa discouraged, 189-190
Imperfections
    four basic imperfections of mundaner, 14
    one with the four basic imperfections cannot teach, 88
Impersonalists
    agree on eternality of soul, 93
    as indirectly Kṛṣṇa conscious, 318
    as monopolizers of Vedānta-sūtra, 780
    Brahman their object of meditation, 596
    cannot account for senses, 44
    cannot actually see universal form, 581
    cannot be mahātmās, 465
    cannot enjoy life, 150
    cannot relish transcendental service, 232
    cannot see Kṛṣṇa due to brahmajyoti covering, 400
    cannot understand Kṛṣṇa, 366, 518
    cease activities out of fear, 242
    deride temple worship, 461
    do not even follow Śaṅkarācārya, 398
    for the, Kṛṣṇa cannot eat, 150, 479
    frightened by retained personality, 230
    ignorant of violation of Kṛṣṇa's law, 404
    liberation is Supreme for them, 183
    maintain Brahman takes form of jīva, 413
    maintain Kṛṣṇa has no form, 372, 397-399
    merge into brahmajyoti, 22-23, 230, 232, 249-250, 368, 423, 824
    prefer to vibrate om, 374
    return to material universe, 150, 232
    risk not realizing Absolute, 601
    sacrifice identity by merging, 249-250
    sometimes accept Kṛṣṇa as Bhagavān, 514
    their attachments analyzed, 230
    their degree of advancement, 73
    their leader, Śaṅkarācārya, accepts Kṛṣṇa, 234
    their liberation difficult and temporary, 228
    their renunciation imperfect, 150
    worship five kinds of demigods, 756
    worship themselves as Supreme, 467
    (See also Brahmavādī, Māyāvādī)
Impersonal Realization
    actually no conflict with personalism, 374
    against nature of blissful spiritual self, 601
    as incomplete, 12-13, 318, 362
    as means of attaining Kṛṣṇa, 598-599
    as step to complete realization, 398, 690- 691
    beneficial if there is no pure devotee, 617

Impersonal Realization
    can be attained by senses, 493
    difficult for common man, 599-601
    easier than understanding Kṛṣṇa, 365
    in beginning tendency toward, 390-391
    its degree of advancement, 73
    Kṛṣṇa last word in, 366
    risk of falling from, 691
    supported by Śvetāśvatara Upaniṣad, 372
    theory of merging rejected, 87
    theory of void rejected, 211, 323
    those in modes cannot rise above, 379
    through diverse energies, 373-374
Impregnation
    process of, 413
Inaction
    as cessation of material activities, 310
    discouraged, 132, 162
    inferior to action, 169
    intelligent bewildered in determining, 239
    no freedom from reaction, 165
    one must know it, 240-241
    symptom of ignorance, 671-672, 676
    the intelligent see it as one with action, 241
    the same as work in full knowledge, 272
Incarnations
    appear on schedule, 222-224, 227
    as arca-vigraha, Deity, 600
    as manifestations of internal energy, 460
    as puruṣa manifestations, 519
    as six types of avatāras, 227
    Caitanya advents in Kali-yuga, 227
    can advent anywhere, 225
    cited in Purāṇas, 517
    criterion established by universal form, 542
    descriptions given in Bhāgavatam, 74, 590
    false claims as, 190, 385, 581, 741
    information given in Brahma-saṁhitā, 220-221
    Kṛṣṇa as source of, 74, 227-228, 261, 540, 590
    Kṛṣṇa descends with rise of irreligion, 222, 224
    mission of, 16, 225-226
    named, 360
    of material qualities of Kṛṣṇa, 529
    of rājo-guṇa and tamo-guṇa, 381
    primary and secondary, 225
    should not be accepted if not in scriptures, 225
Independence
    as fragmental quality, 702
    given Arjuna to do as he wishes, 832

Independence
    given to everyone, 393
    Kṛṣṇa does not interfere with living enti-
        ties', 288
    limited to supreme will, 394
    misuse of, 204, 268, 649, 742
    of living entity partial, 204
    proper use of, 849
    to control body, 705
    as eternal fragmental parts, 702-704
Individuality
    essential to bhakti-yoga, 689
    eternality asserted by Kṛṣṇa, 86-88, 104, 121
    its annihilation hellish, 822
    kept even after liberation, 121, 250, 290, 665
    maintained on spiritual grounds, 87-88, 824
    of Kṛṣṇa and living entity, 13, 121, 290, 349
    present in oneness, 714
    sacrificed in fire of Brahman, 249-250
Indra
    as appointed officer, 178
    attainment of his planet, 396
    born from Nārāyaṇa, 503
    chief of administrative demigods, 411
    gives Arjuna military honors, 116
    his priest Bṛhaspati, 522
    his worship discouraged by Kṛṣṇa, 18
    Kṛṣṇa as, 521
    Kṛṣṇa as Bṛhat-sāma sung to, 531-532
    sacrifices for, 249
    worshiped in goodness, 756
Indraloka
    as abode of Indra, 522
    as goal, 470, 472
    soma drinkers take birth on, 472
Indriyāṇi hayānāhur viṣayāṁs teṣu gocarān
    verses quoted, 344
Intelligence
    as constituent of body, 627-628
    as neighbor of spirit soul, 208
    as one of eight separated energies, 367, 368
    as sitting place of lust, 207-208
    compared to driver of car of body, 344
    controlled by meditation and breath sus-
        pension, 302-303
    created by Kṛṣṇa, 497
    defined as power of analyzing things in
        perspective, 497
    frees one from bondage of works, 121
    generally not possessed by women, 64
    given by Kṛṣṇa to understand Vedas, 713
    in buddhi-yoga, 507

Intelligence
    indifference ensues liberation of, 137
    in passion perverse, 805
    Kṛṣṇa as, 375-376, 530
    lost or misdirected by demonic, 383, 734
    necessity of being fixed in Kṛṣṇa, 26, 152,
        154, 291, 416, 604
    need not be highly developed to attain
        Kṛṣṇa, 27
    of Arjuna bewildered, 163
    of irresolute many-branched, 125
    of one dear to Kṛṣṇa agrees with Him, 611
    people in general have little, 127
    perfectly controlled by sage, 244
    self transcendental to, 211
    sometimes overcome by mind, 343-344
    steady when senses restrained, 147, 153, 154
    strengthens mind, 211
    study of Gītā as worship with, 839
    superior to mind, inferior to soul, 210
    to fix one in trance, 334
    two classes of intelligent men, 155
    used only for purification, 283
    vyavasāyātmikā, 125
    when lost, one falls into material pool, 150
Interplanetary Travel
    no mechanical arrangement necessary, 19-
        20
Intoxication
    as demonic pursuit, 736
    as resort of those frustrated in passion, 681
    as shelter of frustrated impersonalists, 230
    for yogī contradictory, 331
    in mode of ignorance, 672
Irreligion
    corrupts women, 64
    developed at death of family elders, 63
    Kṛṣṇa descends when there is rise in, 224
    results from destruction of family tradition,
        63
Īśāvāsya
    as formula for peace, 153, 304
    cited in Īśopaniṣad, 282
    complete renunciation necessitates aware-
        ness of, 274
    everything used for satisfaction of Kṛṣṇa,
        157
    Kṛṣṇa proprietor of universe, 14, 153, 261
Īśāvāsyam idaṁ sarvam
    quoted, 157
Īśopaniṣad
    cited, 282

Īśvara
See Controller
Īśvaraḥ paramaḥ kṛṣṇaḥ sac-cid-ānanda-vigrahaḥ
verses quoted, 12-13, 74, 234, 365, 372, 459
Īśvaraḥ sarva-bhūtāṁ hṛd-deśe 'rjuna tiṣṭhati
quoted, 337
Īśvarāṇāṁ vacaḥ satyaṁ tathaivācaritaṁ kvacit
verses quoted, 189
Īśvara Purī
in disciplic succession, 29

J

Jaḍabharata
as name of Bharata Mahārāja, 355
Jagai
typical narādhama, delivered by
Nityānanda, 384
Jagannātha
in disciplic succession, 29
Jagat-pate
Lord of the universe, 513-514
Janaka
as learned leader, 382
attained perfection through duty, 184
one must follow, 240
self-realized, father of Sītā, 184-185
Janaloka
elevation to, 472
Janārdana
as plenary expansion, 433
Kṛṣṇa addressed as, 62, 162, 516
Janmādyasya yato 'nvayād itarataś ca
quoted, 204, 473, 814
Japa
as best process, 480
as presentation of evidence in logic, 529
Jayadharma
in disciplic succession, 29
Jayadratha
considered already destroyed, 566
willing to die for Duryodhana, 39
Jayatīrtha
in disciplic succession, 29
Jesus Christ
sacrificed his life to spread God consciousness, 593
Jīva
See Conditioned Soul, Jīvātmā, Living
Entity, Soul
Jīva Gosvāmī
in disciplic succession, 29

Jīva Gosvāmī
obeisances to, 1
warns that Kṛṣṇa should be respected in all,
461
Jīvātmā
situated with Paramātmā on tree of body,
100, 102-103
(See also Conditioned Soul, Living Entity,
Soul)
Jñānāgniḥ sarva-karmāṇi
quoted, 290
Jñāna-kāṇḍa
as sacrifice for knowledge, 259
Jñānam
as knowledge of self, 209
Jñānamaya
development to thinking, feeling and willing, 626
Jñānaṁ parama-guhyaṁ me yad-vijñāna-
samanvitam
verses quoted, 209
Jñānasindhu
in disciplic succession, 29
Jñāna-yoga
as difficult path, 331, 600
as means of linking with Absolute Truth,
358
as outcome of karma-yoga, 359
as part of yoga ladder, 311
as subject of Gītā, 159
defined, 507
difference from bhakti-yoga, 600
does not admit householder, 322
leads to bhakti-yoga, 305
one cannot understand Kṛṣṇa by, 448
one must die at suitable time in, 454
third-class devotee's tendency toward, 450
Jñānī
as best of the pious, dear to Kṛṣṇa, 388-389
comes to devotional service when frustrated,
387
confused in attempt to understand Kṛṣṇa,
365
considered to dwell in Kṛṣṇa, 389-390
the supermost, one who thinks of Kṛṣṇa,
26
Juṣṭaṁ yadā paśyaty anyam īśam asya
verses quoted, 103
Jyotīṁṣi viṣṇur bhavanāni viṣṇuḥ
verse quoted, 93
Jyoti-rūpaṁ saṁpadya svena
verses quoted, 716

Jyotiṣṭoma
    Kṛṣṇa as, 468
    sacrifice for higher planets, 127

K

Kaivalyam
    as constitutional position, 330
    as oneness with Supreme, 330
Kāla
    as presiding deity of time, 434
Kālī
    her worship recommended for meat-eaters, 175
Kali-yuga
    Caitanya incarnation for, 227
    chanting as method for, 131, 172-173, 320, 422
    characteristics and duration of, 215, 428
    characteristics of people in, 131, 320
    yoga system difficult in, 308, 342-343
Kalki
    vanquishes demons, 428
Kalpas
    reckoning of, 428
Kalpa-sūtras
    as part of study for sacrifice, 581
Kāmais tais tair hṛt-ajñānāḥ prapadyante 'nya-devatāḥ
    verses quoted, 18
Kāmaṁ ca dāsye na tu kāma-kāmyayā
    verses quoted, 148
Kaṁsa
    always thinking to kill Kṛṣṇa, 489, 593
    killed by Kṛṣṇa, 226, 744
    Kṛṣṇa addressed as enemy of, 138
    persecuted Vasudeva and Devakī, 226
Kaṇāda
    as principal philosopher, 444
Kandarpa
    Kṛṣṇa as god of love, 525-526
Kapila
    as imposter and expostulator of atheistic *sāṅkhya*, 122-123
    as learned leader, 382
    as principal philosopher, 444
    His *sāṅkhya* identical with Kṛṣṇa's, 123
    Kṛṣṇa as, **524**
    one must follow, 240
    the incarnation, expounded true *sāṅkhya* 122-123
Kāraṇodakaśāyī Viṣṇu
    as *puruṣa-avatāra*, 519

Karau harer mandira-mārjanādiṣu
    verses quoted, 147
Karma
    able to be changed, 9, 10
    accrues for those not renounced, **789**
    birth according to, 456, 458, 668, 705
    causes transmigration, 10, 412
    defined as not eternal, 9, 10
    denied by demons, 737, 739
    employing its result for a good cause, 610
    freedom from, 197, 237, 242, **263**, 631
    how one enjoys or suffers, 8-9
    in relation to time and the modes of nature, 8
    meant for *yajña*, 383
    none for acts commanded by Paramātmā, 791
    of killing, 679
    of sin analyzed, 445
    places one in modes of nature, 625-626
    roots of banyan tree bound to, **696**-697
    sinful reactions negated by *Bhagavad-gītā*, 28
    wealth as result of, 739
    (*See also* Action, Activities, Work)
Karma-kāṇḍa
    activities for sense gratification, 130
    as fruitive sacrifice, 259
    portions of *Vedas* discussed, 127-138
    sacrifices as Kṛṣṇa, 468
    to encourage gradual realization, 130
Karmaṇā manasā vācā sarvāvasthāsu sarvadā
    verses quoted, 321
Karma-yoga
    as action in Kṛṣṇa consciousness, subject for Chapter Five, 271-305
    as beginning of path to *bhakti*, 359
    as *buddhi-yoga*, 122-123
    as means of linking with Absolute Truth, 358
    as subject of Chapter Three, 161-212
    as subject of *Gītā*, 159
    better for Kali-yuga than *sāṅkhya-yoga*, 308
    defined, 507
    no impediments to, 331
    nondifferent from *sāṅkhya-yoga*, **276**
    one cannot understand Kṛṣṇa by, 448
    one must die at a suitable time in, 434
    third-class devotee's tendency toward, 450
Karmīs (Fruitive workers)
    as worker in passion, **801**-802
    awarded results by Kṛṣṇa, 232

Karmīs (Fruitive workers)
  come to Kṛṣṇa in time of distress, 387
  determination of, 807
  may be elevated to higher planets, 352
Karṇa
  cited by Duryodhana as great warrior, 38
  considered already destroyed, 566
  destroyed in mouth of universal form, 560
  identified as half brother of Arjuna, 38
  would think Arjuna fearful, 118
Karṣati
  as struggle for existence, 705
Kārttikeya
  born of Śiva and Pārvatī, 149
Kāśirāja
  blows conchshell, 46
  cited by Duryodhana as great fighter, 36
Kaṭha Upaniṣad
  cited, 210, 427, 626, 716
  quoted, 86-87, 99, 100, 111, 371
Kaunteya
  significance of name, 91
Kavis
  as those who think thoroughly, 534
Kena Upaniṣad
  cited, 511
Keśāgra-śata-bhāgasya śatāṁśaḥ sādṛśātmakaḥ
  verses quoted, 95
Keśava
  as plenary expansion, 433
  Kṛṣṇa addressed as, 162
Keśī
  Kṛṣṇa addressed as killer of demon, 56, 780
Keśinisūdana
  significance of address, 780-781
Khaṭvāṅga Mahārāja
  attained Kṛṣṇa consciousness, 158
Kibāvipra, kibā nyāsī, śūdra kene naya
  verses quoted, 82
Kiṁ punar brāhmaṇāḥ puṇyā bhaktā rājarṣayas tathā
  verses quoted, 27
Knowledge
  as destroyer of doubts, 267, 291
  as *jñānam* and *vijñānam*, 209
  as lamp destroying darkness of ignorance, 508-509
  as mature fruit of all mysticism, 264
  as perfection of religion, eternal, and joyful, 444-448
  as purifier leading to love, 229-230
  as quality of *brāhmaṇa*, 812

Knowledge
  as realization, 157-158, 347
  as *śruti*, hearing, 718
  as subject for Chapter Four, 213-269
  as sublime and pure, 264, 444-448
  as superlative in *Gītā*, 13, 32, 215
  as the body, the knowable, *vijñānam*, 643
  as understanding devotional service, 643
  as *vipaścit*, in relation to soul, 99, 126
  as way of perceiving Supersoul, 651
  awarded in *buddhi-yoga*, 122
  Brahman as concentrated, 642
  brings liberation, 79, 91, 228-229, 264
  brings peace, 264, 265
  brings perception and enjoyment of the self, 264, 444-448, 665
  burns up fruitive action, 242-243, 263
  cannot be delivered by one with the four imperfections, 14, 341
  concerning self and Kṛṣṇa, 268, 622-623
  covered by ignorance, 94, 288
  created by Kṛṣṇa, 497, 712-713
  developed in mode of goodness, 669, 680-681, 796
  develops to meditation, 609
  enables sinners to cross ocean of miseries, 262
  equalizes vision, 292
  extraneous endeavors not necessary for, 123
  for understanding transmigration, 89, 706-707
  greater than sacrifice of possessions, 258
  hardly anyone interested in, 365
  imparted by spiritual master through disciplic succession, 14, 67, 259-260, 290, 364
  imparted to Arjuna, 70, 104, 833
  illuminates gates of body in goodness, 674-675
  in mode of darkness, 797-798
  in mode of passion, 797
  in three modes, 665, 798
  its cultivation advised, 609
  its cultivation as divine quality, 722, 724-725
  its detailed constituents, 629-634
  its doors open to all, 27
  jñāna not sufficient for liberation, 274
  Kṛṣṇa as living force, 521
  Kṛṣṇa as object of, 362, 468-469, 834
  Kṛṣṇa knows past, present and future, 401-402

Knowledge
    likened to fire, 243, **263**
    makes sacrifice transcendental, 258-259
    materialistic knowledge, 82, 199, 316, 444
    men of little knowledge attached to *Vedas*,
        127
    more important than religion, 86
    most confidential given to deliberate upon,
        832
    necessary to execute purposes of *Vedas*, 131
    necessity of purification and sense control
        for, 79, 91, **144**, 388-389
    no one knows Kṛṣṇa, 401-402
    not possible in material body, 22
    not to be explained to those not austere,
        devoted, etc., **837**
    of everything, 364, 419
    of Kṛṣṇa as governing principle at time of
        death, 406
    of Kṛṣṇa's opulence, 261, **500**, 502
    of matter and spirit, 86, **364**, 497, 535
    of oneness in quality, difference in quantity,
        275
    of pretenders and atheists, 167, 462-463
    of *sāṅkhya* philosophy discussed, 85-121
    of *yoga* discussed, **121-158**
    one in perfection called *dhīra*, 89
    Paramātmā as knowledge, its object and
        goal, 641-642
    perfection and purpose of, 125-126, 131,
        258-259, 262, 310, 650, 748
    perfect when one is unattached, desireless,
        143, 242
    related to action, 101, 111, 274, 304-305, **794**
    related to surrender, 84, 290, 358, **390-391**
    related to Vedic scriptures, 13-14, **252**, 266
    revealed by faith in Kṛṣṇa and spiritual
        master, 360
    reveals everything like the sun during day,
        289-290
    satisfaction by, **316**
    the most confidential as subject of Chapter
        Nine, 441-490
    useless if selfishness remains, 310
    veiled and destroyed by lust, 207-209
    work merges into, **246, 258**
Kṛpa
    beheld by Arjuna on Battlefield, 53
    cited by Duryodhana as great warrior **38**
    married 's Droṇācārya's sister, 38
Kṛpaṇa (miser)
    as one who enjoys fruits of work, 134

Kṛpaṇa (miser)
    described as not solving problems of life 80
    does not know how to utilize riches, 135
    overly affectionate for family, etc., 80
    thinks he can protect family from death 80
Kṛṣṇa
    as Absolute Truth, 5, 12, 349, 510
    as *acyuta*, 221, **842**
    as *advaita*, 221, 489
    as Agni of Vasus, **521**
    as air, fire, water and moon, **571**
    as air of life, **711-712**
    as all-pervading, 5, 248, 450-451, 510,537-
        538, 555, 570, 572
    as Ananta amongst Nāga serpents, 526
    as Arjuna of the Pāṇḍavas, 533-534
    as Aryamā of departed ancestors, 526-527
    as *aśvattha* fig tree, 524
    as author of *Vedas*, 14, 24, 179-180, 712-714
    as basis of everything, 338, **469-470**
    as beginning, middle and end of all, **519,
        529**
    as benefactor and well-wisher of all, 304
    as beneficiary of all sacrifice, 173, 175,
        177-178
    as Bhagavān, 73-74
    as Bhṛgu the sage, **523**
    as Bhūteśa, 513-514
    as Bṛhaspati the priest, **522**
    as *Bṛhat-sāma*, 531-532
    as butter, fire and offering, 467-468
    as Caitanya, 172
    as cause of all causes, 12-13, 74, 126, 569
    as cause of material happiness, 57
    as Citraratha amongst Gandharvas, 524
    as compiler of *Vedānta*, 712-714
    as complete whole, 12, 14
    as conclusive truth among logicians, 529
    as controller (*īśvara*) of everything, 7-8, 187,
        304, **471**, 571
    as creation and annihilation, 469-470
    as creator, maintainer, annihilator, 122, 171,
        180, **235**, 452-456, 485, 501, 503-504,
        562, 640-641, 666-667
    as creator of Brahmā, Śiva and demigods,
        495
    as death, 471, 526, 530-531, 559
    as deliverer from birth and death, 602-604
    as descendant of Vṛṣṇi, 203
    as Devakī-nandana, 44
    as difficult to know, 6, 219, 365, 366
    as dual word among compounds, 530

Kṛṣṇa

as elephant Airāvata, 524-525
as eternal, 86-88, 555
as far away, yet near to all, 639
as father of Brahmā and all beings, 14, 16, 189, 385, 468-469, 501, 571, 574
as fire of digestion, 711-712
as flower-bearing spring, 531-532
as friend, 76, 300, 469-470
as gambling of cheats, 533
as Ganges River, 528
as Garuḍa bird, 527
as Gāyatrī verse, 531-532
as Govinda, 44, 59-60, 83
as healing herb, 467
as heat of fire, life of all that lives, 374-375
as Himalayas, 523
as Hṛṣīkeśa, 44, 47, 49, 51, 52, 84, 568
as immortality, 471
as impartial, 237, 289, 293, 337, 456-457, 482
as Indra, 521
as inexhaustible, 401
as infallible, 49
as Janārdana, 62, 162, 516
as japa chanting, 523
as Kandarpa, god of love, 525-526
as Kapila the sage, 524
as Keśava, 162
as Keśiniṣūdana, 56, 780-781
as knower of all and object of knowledge, 228, 349, 468-469, 570
as Kuvera, 521
as letter A, 530
as lion among beasts, 527
as Lord of the universe, 513-514
as lotus-eyed, 540-541
as Mādhava, husband of goddess of fortune, 43, 62
as Madhusūdana, 44, 59, 72, 77, 342, 410-411
as mahātmā, 569
as Maheśvara, background of māyā, 380
as maintainer of religion, 33, 554
as maintainer of the people, 67
as manifold faced Brahmā, 530
as mantra, transcendental chant, 467-468
as Marīci of the Maruts, 520
as master of all mysticism, 844-845
as Meru mountain, 521
as mind and living force, 521
as monarch amongst men, 524-525
as morality, 534-535

Kṛṣṇa

as Nārada amongst sages, 524
as nondifferent from His names, 25, 423, 523
as November and December, 531-532
as object and embodiment of realization, 13, 232
as ocean, 522
as om vibration, 373-374, 423, 468-469, 523
as only God for whole world, 28, 576
as original fragrance of earth, 374-375
as original spiritual master, 29, 81, 84, 214-215, 260, 574
as origin of lust, 204
as origin without beginning, middle or end, 555
as Pārtha-sārathi, 44
as pavitram (pure), 5
as penances of all ascetics, 374
as perpetually happy, 18
as pleasure for cows and senses, 18, 44, 59
as Prahlāda, 527
as proprietor, 14, 261, 300
as prowess of powerful men, 373, 375
as purifier, 468-469, 510
as Puruṣottama, Supreme Person, 410, 419, 510, 513-514, 717
as Rāmacandra, 48, 528
as resting place, 337-338, 371, 453-454, 469-471, 570
as ritual and sacrifice, 467-468
as Ṛk, Sāma and Yajur Vedas, 468-469, 521
as rod of chastisement, 534-535
as sac-cid-ānanda-vigrahaḥ, 12-13, 74, 221
as seed-giving father, 667
as seed of all existences, 375-376, 469-470, 530, 535
as Self (Supersoul) in hearts of all, 10, 52, 337-338, 519
as sex life, 377
as shark amongst fishes, 528
as simultaneously one yet different, 233, 337-338, 377, 450-451
as silence, 534-535
as Śiva of Rudras, 521
as Skanda the general, 522
as soul of mahat-tattva, 519
as sound in ether, 373
as source of Brahman, 75, 87, 385
as source of incarnations, 74, 227, 493
as source of Supersoul, Paramātmā, 75, 100, 385

Kṛṣṇa

as speaker of *Gītā*, 32

as spiritual science of Self, 529

as splendor of the splendid, 533

as strength of strong, 377

as superior, 85, 87, 90, 574

as supreme abode, 5, 469-470, 510

as supreme authority, 72, 219

as Supreme Brahman, Parambrahman, 5, 376, 510-511

as supreme enjoyer, 5, 12, 18, 300

as supreme goal, 469-470, 554

as Supreme Personality of Godhead, 3, 6, 73, 510, 554, 570

as supreme transcendental consciousness, 9, 10

as sun and moon, 214, 520, 555, 709

as *surabhi* amongst cows, 525-526

as Śyāmasundara, 19, 360

as taste of water, light of sun and moon, 373-374

as thunderbolt amongst weapons, 525-526

as time, 527, 530, 563

as transcendental to modes, time and space, 11, 14, 219, 236-237, 378-379, 569-570

as Ucchaiḥśravā the horse, 524-525

as unborn, 5, 222, 494

as Uśanā, 533-534

as Varuṇa, god of aquatics, 526

as Vāsudeva or Vṛṣṇi, 44, 533-534

as Vāsuki, chief of serpents, 525

as victory, adventure and strength, 533

as Viṣṇu, 28, 247, 367-368

as Viṣṇu of Ādityas, 520

as Vyāsa, 533-534

as well-wisher of cows and *brāhmaṇas*, 679

as wind, 528

as wisdom of the wise, 534-535

as Yādava, 573

as Yama, lord of death, 526-527

as Yaśodā-nandana, 44

as yogeśvara, 542-543, 847

as young man eternally, 223, 578

being and nonbeing in, 471

blows His conchshell, 43-44

can speak by breathing air, 179-180

characteristics and reasons for advent, 7 16, 18-19, 189, 223, 226

compared to witnessing bird on tree of body, 102

concentration on, 24-27, 51

controls Arjuna's senses, 44

Kṛṣṇa

denied and derided by demons, 19, 733

descriptions of, 431-432, 834

determined to kill miscreants, 60

dissipates lamentation, 72

does not violate scripture, 187

draws up chariot between the armies, 51

engages one in pious and impious activities, 289

enters each planet and keeps it in orbit, 710

everyone follows His path, 232

expansions named and described, 433

extends His hand to accept offerings, 637, 638

forms of, 13, 220-221, 223, 583-585, 836

free to act in any way, 224

had many grandchildren at Battle, 223

His deeds performed as natural sequence, 187

His mind, body and Self are identical, 221, 489

indemnifies all reactions to sin, 28

kills combatants before battle, 60

known only through mercy of pure devotee, 112

likened to *vaidurya* stone, 221

milks the cow of *Bhagavad-gītā*, 28

named according to His activities, 44

never brings misfortune to anyone, 62

never lost to one who sees Him everywhere, 338-339

never manifest to foolish and unintelligent, 400

not a manifestation of universal form or Viṣṇu, 593-594

not responsible for activities of living entities, 237

not subject to illusion, 87, 290

not subject to prescribed work, 186, 456-457

opulences of, 5, 74, 288, 491-538, 543

performed all rules of householder, 188

plays *venu,* His flute, 431

relationships with devotees, 4-5, 25, 49, 171, 232

relation to Arjuna discussed, 84-85

resides eternally in Goloka, 19

reveals Himself to devotees, 366

reveals universal form, 546-547

senses of, 28, 81, 180, 187, 638

sets example by work, 186, 188

should not be imitated, 189-190

Kṛṣṇa
    speaks Gītā for guidance of mankind, 32
    supplies all raw resources, 175
    tolerates no wrong to His devotee, 60
    transcends fallible and infallible, 717
    treats everyone as friend, 292
    uproots the unrighteous at Kurukṣetra, 33
    worshiped as austerity, 764-765
Kṛṣṇa consciousness
    above brāhmaṇa status, 236
    above flowery language of Vedas, 139
    activity and work in, 134-135, 162, 164, 183,
        191, 238, 827-828, 843
    as Absolute Truth, 164
    as best process to make home pleasant, 633
    as best yoga, 133-134, 147, 303, 360
    as Caitanya's requisite for spiritual master,
        82
    as consequence of surrender, 84
    as culmination of knowledge, 258-259
    as duty of everyone, 308
    as fearlessness, 322, 754
    as means to spiritual kingdom, 247-248
    as most direct method of realization, 349
    as only way of understanding Kṛṣṇa, 402
    as peaceful, 83, 153, 264
    as purificatory process, 135, 238, 357
    as purified consciousness, 11, 706
    as samādhi, trance, 51, 139, 143, 340, 422-423,
        471, 593
    as saṅkīrtana-yajña, 172
    as sense control, 145, 201, 212, 318
    as service, 126, 318, 335
    as spiritualizing material world, 305
    as spread by incarnations, 225
    as transcendental to modes, 130, 379, 616,
        680, 682, 776
    as yajña, 170, 180-181
    attained by help of Kṛṣṇa, 474
    attained by nine activities of devotion, 443
    attained upon hearing Gītā, 846
    begins by understanding source of light, 709
    can be attained in a second or a million
        births, 158
    can transform lust into love of God, 209
    characteristics of, 138, 140, 141, 143, 152
    compared to yoga-yajña and svadhyāya-
        yajña, 253
    compared with speculation, 164
    dependent on spiritual master, 126
    different yogas steppingstones to, 362
    difficult for inexperienced, 127

Kṛṣṇa consciousness
    endears one to all, all to one, 279
    faith in, 125, 266
    freedom of action in, 182, 202, 281
    frees one from family, etc., 125
    guarantees higher birth, 124
    in buddhi-yoga, 122-123
    its beginning compared to fire, 205
    its highest perfection, 125, 157
    its jurisdiction extends everywhere, 374
    may appear on sensual plane, 151
    necessary for complete renunciation, 274
    no duality in, 120, 285
    no loss even for the fallen, 166
    path cleared by Arjuna's questions, 163
    revived in next birth, 124, 351, 354-355
    serves aims of jñāna and yoga, 310
    should be learned from beginning of life,
        209
    solves all problems, 257
    spread in India by Caitanya, 227
    three classes of men in, 449-450
    transcends śabda-brahma, 138
    various stages analyzed, 231'
Kṛṣṇadāsa Kavirāja
    in disciplic succession, 29
    mentioned as author, 226
Kṛṣṇaloka
    See Goloka Vṛndāvana, Spiritual sky, Su-
        preme abode
Kṛṣṇas tu bhagavān svayam
    quoted, 3, 590
Kṛṣṇaḥ svayaṁ samabhavat paramaḥ pumān yo
    verses quoted, 220
Kṛṣṇa-varṇaṁ tviṣākṛṣṇaṁ sāṅopāṅgāstra-
        pārṣadam
    verses quoted, 172
Kṛtavarmā
    beheld by Arjuna on Battlefield, 53
    willing to die for Duryodhana, 39
Kṣara
    defined, 89-90
Kṣatriya
    Arjuna deviating from his duties as, 57, 75
    as arms of Supreme, 396
    as varṇa, 24, 108, 235
    attain heavenly planets, 114
    born out of energy of Kṛṣṇa, 501
    cannot attack unarmed or unwilling foe, 69
    cannot engage in any other occupation, 58
    distinguished by work in modes, 812
    duty of, 76, 78, 91, 109, 113-115, 187, 728, 816

Kṣatriya
  eligibility for entering sun, 57-58
  happy with unsought battle, 115
  his fighting transcendental, 730
  his nature and duty compared to
    brāhmaṇa's, 202
  in mode of passion, 379
  Kṛṣṇa performs duty of, 187
  meaning of word, 113-114
  not to lament for gross body, 72
  qualities of, 813
  requires a kingdom for subsistence, 58
  should not be cowardly, 61, 113
  should not refuse battle or gamble, 63, 115
  sun-god as their father, 215
  tradition of tiger-fighting, 114
  (See also Varṇa)
Kṣatriyo hi prajā rakṣan śastra-pāṇiḥ
  verses quoted, 115
Kṣetra
  as field of body, 620, ff.
Kṣetrajña
  as knower of body, 620, ff.
Kṣetrāṇi hi śarīāṇi bījaṁ cāpi śubhāśubhe
  verses quoted, 623
Kṣiṇe puṇye martyalokaṁ viśanti
  verse quoted, 83
Kṣīrodakaśāyī Viṣṇu
  as puruṣa-avatāra, 519
  diffused in all atoms, 367, 456
Kulaśekhara Mahārāja
  quoted, 411
Kumāras,
  as chief demigods, 502
  as learned leaders, 382
  one must follow, 240
  rose from impersonal realization to devo-
    tion, 690-691
Kumbhaka-yoga
  air suspension to prolong life, 254
Kuntī
  Arjuna addressed as son of, 90, 119, 170 296,
    345, 373, 427, 454, 457, 475, 480, 485,
    620, 667, 670, 745, 817, 819, 829
  as mother of Karṇa, 38
  as mother of Yudhiṣṭhira, 46
  her prayers quoted, 400
  significance of Arjuna as her son, 52
Kuntibhoja
  cited by Duryodhana as great fighter, 36
Kūrma Purāṇa
  quoted, 489

Kurukṣetra
  as ancient sacred place of pilgrimage, 32-33
  compared to paddy field where unrighteous
    are uprooted, 33
  envisioned by Sañjaya in Dhṛtarāṣṭra's
    room, 33
  influence on outcome of battle, 33
  no one killed there spiritually, 280
  significance of word, 33
  the battle inevitable by Kṛṣṇa's will, 109
Kurus
  Arjuna addressed as best of, 256, 580
  Arjuna addressed as son of, 125, 354, 676
  Dhṛtarāṣṭra their father, 32
  only Dhṛtarāṣṭra's sons claimed as, 33
  pointed out to Arjuna by Kṛṣṇa, 52
  signs indicate the whole dynasty to be killed,
    46
  their victory dependent on Bhīṣma, 41
Kūṭastha
  describing the soul as steady, 99
Kuvera
  Kṛṣṇa as, 521
  worshiped in conditioned state, 776

                    L

Lakṣmaṇa
  beheld by Arjuna on Battlefield, 53
Lakṣmīpati
  in disciplic succession, 29
Lalitā, Śrī
  obeisances to, 2
Lamentation
  as unnecessary, 72, 87, 89, 97, 106-110, 112
  cannot be driven away by material wealth,
    82-83
  dissipated by Kṛṣṇa, 72, 83, 103, 614
  dissipated by spiritual master, 102-103
  ignorant determination bound by, 807
  transcended by sage, 85-86, 294, 822
  unbecoming to Arjuna, 75, 103
Leaders
  Gītā meant especially for, 214, 216
  king considered representative of God, 525
  lead society into chaos when blind, 66-67
  their refusal to surrender discussed, 382-383
  their responsibilities to teach, 185-186, 214
  what the great does, others follow, 185
  worshiped by foolish, 234
Liberation (mukti)
  all resources should be used for, 175
  as attained by ancient sages, 238

Liberation (*mukti*)
  as *brahmi sthitih*, 159
  as difficult, 228, 380
  as freedom from material energies, 370
  as gateway to eternal life with Kṛṣṇa, 90
  as goal of auspicious activities, 352
  bhakti continues after, 824
  by accepting authority of *Vedas*, 228-229
  by awareness of relationship with Kṛṣṇa, 300
  by being killed by Kṛṣṇa, 593, 744
  by desire to serve Kṛṣṇa, 442
  by equanimity of mind, 245, 293
  by *haṭha-yoga*, 302-303
  by knowing action and inaction, 239, 241
  by knowing Kṛṣṇa's nature, 228-229, 495
  by knowledge, 79, 246, 263-264, 291, 372, 650, 660-661
  by purifying mind, 174, 313, 330-331, 825
  by renounced action, work, 114, 121, 133, 171, 197, 242, 261-262, 273-275, 283-284, 299, 481, 722-723
  by sacrifice, 174, 257-258, 301, 726
  by service to devotees, 404
  by surrender to Kṛṣṇa, 369, 642
  by working in *buddhi-yoga*, 123
  defined, 11, 824-825
  for one who knows the three Viṣṇus, 367
  from death by refuge in Kṛṣṇa, 405
  from material bondage characteristic of Āryans, 75
  frustrated by cycle of activities, 108
  given by Mukunda, 66
  impersonalist theories of, 87, 122, 183, 330
  individuality retained after, 89-90, 104, 121, 290, 331, 824
  in oneness in spiritual world, 715
  jñāna, knowledge, not sufficient for, 274
  necessary for knowing past, present, future, 401
  none for one attached to world, 694-695
  not possible in mode of passion, 671
  of demons and atheists baffled, 462-463
  of devotees, 150, 255, 301
  pure devotee does not hanker for, 424
  qualifications for, 79, 92, 154, 729
  sannyāsa as step to, 92
  Śiva affirms that only Viṣṇu can grant, 381
  soul may remain in *brahmajyoti* or go to Vaikuṇṭha, 105
  spiritual body manifest at, 703
  through identity with Brahman, 335-336

Liberation (*mukti*)
  transcended by love of Kṛṣṇa, 339
  upon reaching spiritual sky, 701
  via love for service to Vāsudeva, 274
  while within material body, 286
Literature
  materialistic, 23-24
  one need read only *Bhagavad-gītā*, 28
  one tires of mundane, 517
Living entity
  accompanied and directed by Supersoul, 10, 100, 654
  all exist in Supersoul, 636
  all sent forth at beginning of creation, 171, 456
  always changing bodies, 10, 89, 621
  as *aṇu*, atomic, 288, 419
  as Brahman, 5, 410, 412-413, 635-636
  as cause of sufferings and enjoyments, 288, 645-646
  as combination of body and its knower, 653
  as consciousness, 9-10, 625-626, 659-660
  as cooperator, 11-12
  as divine and demonic, 730-731
  as eternal, 9, 15, 96, 621, 635, 644
  as individual, 13, 121
  as marginal energy, 309, 412, 649, 849
  as moving and inert, 376
  as part of Kṛṣṇa, 8, 104, 131, 157-158, 204, 261-262, 279, 413, 450-451, 702-704
  as son of Kṛṣṇa, 16, 180, 381
  as subordinate to Kṛṣṇa's control, 78, 90, 94, 196, 289, 369
  as superior energy, 8-9, 23, 93, 261, 309, 337-338, 369-370, 469, 644, 702-703
  as *vijñānam brahma*, 636
  attains immortality in love for Kṛṣṇa, 339
  by nature full of knowledge, 288
  cannot be desireless or senseless, 157
  cannot decide his next body, 22
  carries conceptions from body to body, 704-705
  compared to passenger in machine, 344, 830
  conscious of only one body, 10, 622
  constitutional position (*svarūpa*) as servant, 7, 9, 16-18, 209, 241, 338, 359, 842
  covered by lust, 204-205, 207
  created according to past deeds, 456
  distinguished from Supersoul, 90
  each is an individual soul, 89
  entanglement in modes of nature, 8, 237, 369, 379-380, 647, 668
  equality of all seen by *yogī*, 341

Living entity
  equality to Kṛṣṇa in quality, not quantity,
    7-8, 74, 137, 287, 370
  fallible and infallible, 714-715
  four basic imperfections of, 14
  hankers after pleasure, 12, 18
  highest perfectional stage of, 131
  his consciousness pervertedly reflected, 10, 380
  his faith according to modes, 754-755
  his happiness in service to Kṛṣṇa, 18
  his independence partial, 204
  his memory compared with Kṛṣṇa's, 221
  his senses part of Kṛṣṇa's senses, 44
  Kṛṣṇa benefactor and well-wisher of all, 304
  maintained by Kṛṣṇa, 87, 535, 648
  meets good and evil amongst various species,
    647
  millions of species arise from sensual
    pleasures, 644
  nature of his conditioning, 7-8, 24, 172, 237,
    262, **288-290**, 304, 380, 403, 644, 647
  necessary for growth, 653
  neither the slayer nor is slain, 97-98
  never born and never dies, 16-17
  never supremely conscious, 9
  not proprietor nor controller of body's
    actions, 287, 646
  originally spiritual, pure, 203
  out of thousands one tries for perfection, 365
  overcome by duality of desire and hate 403
  pervades creation, lives in all elements, 105
  process of impregnation, 413
  qualified as light, 97
  responsible for his own acts, 237
  senses satisfied as much as deserved, 60
  six basic changes of, 531, 715
  species number 8,400,000, 384
  spirit the same in all, 645
  struggles hard with senses, 129, **702-704**
  struggles with nature and sustains universe,
    369
  thinks himself lord, 290, 304, 647
  types of conditioned beings, 669-670
  unmanifest, manifest and unmanifest, **109,
    429-430**
  (*See also* Conditioned Soul, *Jīvātmā*, Soul)
Lokāyatikas
  maintain materialistic view of soul, 107
Lokyate vedārtho 'nena
  quoted, 716
Love
  action for Kṛṣṇa out of, 243

Love
  analyzed as *bhāva* and *premā*, 231
  as attachment to Kṛṣṇa, 605-606
  as means of seeing Kṛṣṇa, 339, 451, **507**, 584,
    639
  as necessary for thinking of Kṛṣṇa, 516
  as not doubting Kṛṣṇa's supremacy, 300
  attained through work and service, 607
  exchanged in original form as Kṛṣṇa, 590
  for Kṛṣṇa attained by knowledge, **229-230,
    389-390**
  for Kṛṣṇa dormant in heart, 606
  for Kṛṣṇa in advanced stage, 439
  for service to Vāsudeva for liberation, 274
  Kṛṣṇa accepts love of offering, 447
  Kṛṣṇa as Kandarpa, god of, **525-526**
  matures from faith, 777
  of devotees make them forget Kṛṣṇa is God,
    546
  of Kṛṣṇa as apex of devotion, 506
  of Kṛṣṇa as ultimate goal, 777
  of Kṛṣṇa distributed freely by Caitanya, 589
  of Kṛṣṇa perverted as lust, 209
  of Kṛṣṇa transcends liberation, 339
  relationship not possible with universal
    form, 582-583
  transformed into lust, 204
Lust
  as all-devouring, sinful enemy, **204, 206**
  as cause of demigod worship, 18, 395
  as cause of false ego, 208
  as gate leading to hell, **745**
  as perversion of love for Kṛṣṇa, 204, 209
  as symbol of ignorance, 207
  as symbol of sin, **208**
  born of contact with passion, **204**
  can be conquered in human form, 206
  causes bondage to material world, 204
  causes designations and attachments, 21
  covers living entity, **205**
  covers pure consciousness and knowledge,
    206-209
  demons bound by, **735-737, 742-743**
  demons claim it as cause of world, 733
  develops from attachment to sense objects,
    149
  due to misuse of independence, 204
  freedom from, 205, **208, 211**, 363, 392, **699, 821**
  given vent through senses, 210
  its origin is Kṛṣṇa, 204
  later transformed to wrath, **204**
  must be served if mind not conquered, 314

Lust
    never satisfied, burns like fire, 206
    senses, mind and intelligence its sitting
        places, 207-208
    severe penance performed out of, 757-758
    trees condemned due to, 206

M

Mad-bhaktim labhate parām
    quoted, 336
Mad-bhakti-prabhāvena sarvendriya-vijaya-pūr-
        vikā svātma dṛṣṭiḥ sulabheti bhāvaḥ
    quoted, 148
Madhai
    typical narādhama, delivered by Nityā-
        nanda, 384
Mādhava
    as plenary expansion, 433
    in disciplic succession, 29
    significance of name, 62
Mādhavendra Purī
    in disciplic succession, 29
    quoted, 138
Madhu
    demon killed by Kṛṣṇa, 44, 72, 411
Mādhurya-bhakta
    service as conjugal lover, 425
Madhusūdana
    Kṛṣṇa as, 59, 72, 77, 342, 410-411
    meaning of name, 44, 72
Madhvācārya
    accepts Kṛṣṇa as Supreme, 3
    as learned leader, 382
    in disciplic succession, 29
Mādhyandi-nāyana-ś m ti
    quoted, 703
Mahā-bāhu (mighty-armed)
    meaning of address, 108
Mahābhārata
    as diversion for mind, 767
    contains topics discussed by Dhṛtarāṣṭra
        and Sañjaya, 32
    describes Caitanya, 227
    for less capable people, 24
    Gītā part of, 28, 130, 215
Mahābhūta
    the five great elements, 627-628
Mahā-brahman
    twenty-four elements as, 666
Mahārāja Ambarīṣa
    See Ambarīṣa Mahārāja

Maharloka
    as goal, 470, 472
Mahātmā
    as one who comes to Kṛṣṇa for any purpose,
        389
    cannot be manufactured, 465
    develops through association with devotees,
        464
    fully engaged in devotional service, 464
    Kṛṣṇa addressed as, 569
    never returns to material world, 426
    protected by divine nature, 464
    receives transcendental messages from
        realized devotees, 426
    symptoms of, 426, 464-466
    who surrenders to Kṛṣṇa is very rare, 390
Mahat-tattva
    as cause of cosmos, 644, 666
    covers brahmajyoti in material world, 641,
        701
    created by Mahā-Viṣṇu, 367
    entered by Mahā-Viṣṇu, 455
    Kṛṣṇa as soul of, 519
Mahā-Viṣṇu
    as soul of mahat-tattva, Supersoul, 519
    creates material energy, 367, 529
    does not attract pure devotees, 464
    Kṛṣṇa as cause of, 540, 589
    lies in Causal Ocean and breathes universes,
        455-456
    material nature absorbed in, 644
Mahā-yajña
    Kṛṣṇa as, 468
Maheśvara
    supreme controller, background of may a,
        380
Mā hiṁsyāt sarva bhūtāni
    quoted, 98
Maithunya-āgāra
    the shackles of sex life, 207
Mama yonir mahad brahma
    quoted, 282
Māṁ. hi pārtha vyapāśritya ye 'pi syuḥ pāpa-
        yonayaḥ
    verses quoted, 27
Māṁ tu veda na kaścana
    quoted, 366
Mana eva manuṣyānāṁ kāraṇaṁ bandha-
        mokṣayoḥ
    verses quoted, 313
Maṇipuṣpaka
    name of Sahadeva's conchshell, 46

Manmanā bhava mad-bhaktaḥ
    quoted, 848
Mantra
    Kṛṣṇa as, **467-468**
Manu
    age of the current, 215
    as learned leader, 382
    born out of Kṛṣṇa's mind, 501
    in disciplic succession, **214-215**, 239-240
    instructed by sun-god, 4
    Kṛṣṇa appears in eighth, 224
    one must follow, 240
Manu-saṁhitā
    states women should not be given freedom,
        732
    still followed as lawbook, 186, 732
    supports capital punishment, 101
Mānuṣaṁ rūpam
    Kṛṣṇa originally two-handed, 584
Manu-smṛti
    cited, 206, 384
Marīci
    Kṛṣṇa as, 520
Marriage
    as purificatory ceremony, 784
    as restricted sex life, 200, 251, 257, 322, 765
    as *vivāha-yajña* should be encouraged, 784
    nonattachment to wife as knowledge, **630**,
        633
    now imaginary in society, 732
Maruts
    behold universal form in wonder, 557
    Kṛṣṇa as Marīci of the, 520
Material body
    acquired according to work, 97, 273
    analytical study in Second Chapter, 72
    as *adhibhūtam,* 414
    as cause of action, **656,** 790-791, 830
    as cause of pleasure and pain, 94, 287, 645
    as source of miseries, 22, 137, 287, 300
    as subject for Chapter Thirteen, 619-661
    belongs to Kṛṣṇa, 283-284
    cannot be acquired by ghosts, 65
    cannot know past, present, future, 401
    changes of, 10, 93, 99, **102,** 414, 621, 628, 715
    compared to car driven by intelligence, 344
    contrasted with spiritual body, 230
    destined to die, 86, **96-97**
    determined by consciousness, 706
    difference from soul, 72, 86, 113, 221, **658-661**
    false identification with, 195, 285-286, 600,
        657

Material body
    four demands of, 331-332
    freedom from, 21-22, 110, **283-285,** 294, 511,
        611
    has individual capacity to lord, 623
    immunized by offered food, 178
    its changes do not affect soul, 99
    its constitution, changes, origins, and and
        knower explained, **624,** ff.
    its gates illumined by goodness, **674-675**
    its necessities allowed by rules, 200
    killing of it not encouraged, 98
    known as *kṣetra,* the field, **620,** ff.
    likened to city of nine gates, **285-286**
    likened unto a machine and dream, 110, 656,
        830
    living entity its enjoyer, 644
    maintained by demigods, 173
    materialistic view of its development, 107
    must be maintained by work, 24, **169**
    ext body decided by higher authorities, 22
    not a fixed type, 222
    of twenty-four elements, 627-628, 661
    one forgets when he quits, 713
    one must act in accordance to form of, 646
    one should not grieve for, 72, **106**
    one who knows it called *kṣetrajña,* **620-**
        621, ff.
    perishes at liberation, 703
    plurality does not refer to, 88, 261
    relation to senses, 156, 210, 620-621, 646,
        706
    relation to Supersoul (Paramātmā), 100,
        102-103, **622-624,** 648-649
    relation to the modes, 130, 193, 292, 687
    soul as basis of, **94-97,** 166, 371, 519
    subsists on food grains, **177**
    taken from 8,400,000 species, 412
    theory of oneness with soul, 797
    tortured by demoniac, 757-758
    transmigration of, **89,** 704-705
Material existence
    a source of perplexity for everyone, 80
    by its cessation one attains supreme abode,
        323
    due to sin and ignorance, 256, 351
    envious cast into ocean of, **743**
    four principles of, 19
    its problems cannot be counteracted by
        wealth, 82-83
    likened to forest fire, 80
    likened to tossing ocean, 287

Material existence
    problems solved by *Bhagavad-gītā*, 27-28
    threefold miseries do not exist for devotee, 152
Material nature (*prakṛti*)
    absorbed in Mahā-Viṣṇu, manifest by *mahat-tattva*, 644
    as basis of existence, 653
    as beginningless, 644
    as captivating force, 89-90, 102, 111, 192-193, 203, 369, 380, 818
    as energy of Kṛṣṇa, 9, 23
    as eternally mutable, 9, 414
    as immediate cause of creation, 237, 457-458, 666-668
    as not conscious, 9
    as subject for Chapter Thirteen, 619-661
    can instantly destroy one's wealth, 83
    causes and carries out activities, 192-193, 645-646
    comes from root of banyan tree, 695
    compared to universal form, 544
    complete in itself, 13
    composed of twenty-four elements, 13, 627-628
    consists of three modes, 8, 668
    controlled by Kṛṣṇa, 7-9, 93-94, 304, 367-368, 380, 457-458
    creates 8,400,000 species, 645
    definition, 8-9
    demons claim it as cause of manifestation, 733
    difference from living entity, 9
    fashions body according to desire, 830
    frustrates plans of atheists, 382-383
    impregnated by glance of Kṛṣṇa, 180, 458
    Kālī its ghastly form, 175
    in contact with living entity since time immemorial, 287
    Kṛṣṇa is not subject to, 378
    liberation attained by understanding, 650
    mahātmā not under control of, 464
    not the cause of birth, 667
    punishes those who misuse it, 175
    temporary aspects, 15
    transformations of living entities due to, 644
    working according to plan, 565
Material sky
    See Material universe
Material universe
    all entities fallible in, 714-715
Material universe
    analyzed into twenty-four elements, 651
    Arjuna inquires about, 410
    as chance to return to Godhead, 172
    as combination of *kṣetra* and *kṣetrajña*, 666
    as cosmic form of Kṛṣṇa, 414
    as manifestation of Brahman, 282
    as manifestation of three modes, 282
    as only one quarter of creation, 22
    as reflection of the spiritual, 20, 391, 695, 831
    as temporary energy, 13, 367, 488
    breathed by Mahā-Viṣṇu, 455-456
    called the shackles of sex life, 207
    complete in itself, 13
    contains trillions of planets, suns, etc., 22
    created for sacrifice, 172
    created to fulfill lust, 204
    demonic theories concerning, 733
    develops due to Paramātmā, 371
    different universes in creation, 21, 501, 709
    entered by Garbhodakaśāyī Viṣṇu, 367, 456
    enters Kṛṣṇa's nature at end of millennium, 454-455
    four miseries present everywhere, 19-20, 137, 426-427, 488
    heated by Kṛṣṇa's radiance, 555
    inauspicious aspects of, 20, 136-137, 143, 367, 495
    its connection with Kṛṣṇa discussed, 458
    its contaminations counteracted by *prasādam*, 178
    its duration analyzed in *yugas* and *kalpas*, 428
    Kṛṣṇa as father, mother, support and grandsire of, 468-469
    Kṛṣṇa as governing principle of, 406, 454
    Kṛṣṇa its only sanctuary, 570
    Kṛṣṇa its origin and dissolution, 370-371, 455-456, 503-504
    likened to banyan tree, 20, 694-698
    likened to ocean of nescience and forest fire, 263
    likened unto water in hoofprint of calf, 136
    manifested on basis of spiritual energy, 371
    many thousands seen in body of Kṛṣṇa, 550
    pervaded and supported by Kṛṣṇa, 450-451, 453-454, 537-538
    plant of devotion pierces its covering, 503
    sustained by living entity, 369
    Viṣṇu as the soul within, 276
    worshiped as form of Kṛṣṇa, 467

Mathurā
    as sacred place, 320
Mat-paraḥ
    as under Kṛṣṇa's protection, 826
    significance, 148
Mattaḥ parataraṁ nānyat kiṁcit asti dhanañjaya
    quoted, 291, 590
Māyā
    as bodily difference of living entities, 261
    as contamination of material infection, 331
    Brahmā and Śiva under her influence, 381
    an be escaped by knowledge and devotion,
        91
    cannot cover the Supreme, 402
    causes forgetfulness, 384
    compared to rope binding man, 380-381
    conditioned soul always prone to fall into,
        104
    covers brahmajyoti as material veil, 248
    defined as sense of separated existence from
        Kṛṣṇa, 261, 535
    deludes Arjuna, 90
    difficult to overcome by theoretical know-
        ledge, 199
    disqualifies a teacher, 90
    gives threefold miseries, 749
    her last snare, 122, 842
    illusioned mentality of demons, 738-740
    impersonalists think everything, 398
    indifference ensues extrication from, 137
    its background is the supreme magician 380
    Kṛṣṇa allows living entity to fall into, 393
    living entity's contact with, 305, 403
    manifest in mode of ignorance, 676
    of Arjuna dispelled, 539-540, 842
    separated from soul at time of liberation87
    service either to Kṛṣṇa or, 602
    veils knowledge of self, 209
    Viṣṇu her only master, 381
Māyā devī
    resisted by Haridāsa Ṭhākur, 149
Mayādhyakṣeṇa prakṛtiḥ sūyate sa-carācaram
    quoted, 733
Māyāṁ tu prakṛtim vidyān māyinaṁ tu maheś-
        varam
    quoted, 380
Māyā mugdha jiver nāhi svataḥ kṛṣṇa-jñān
    verses quoted, 24
Māyātita paravyome savāra avasthāna
    verses quoted, 227
Māyāvādī
    argue that individuality is material, 87-88

Māyāvādī
    cannot explain how soul is illusioned, 104
    explanation of Gītā forbidden and mis-
        leading, 88
    quote from Bhāgavatam, 461
    render temporary devotional service, 447
    sannyāsīs compared with Vaiṣṇava sannyā-
        sīs, 278-279
    their renunciation incomplete, 274
    their study of Śrīmad-Bhāgavatam trouble-
        some, 278
    theory of merging not supported by Kṛṣṇa,
        87
    theory of oneness of soul not maintained,
        89
    think Kṛṣṇa loses identity in expansions,
        261
    think Kṛṣṇa's form material, 398
    worship themselves as Supreme, 467
    (See also Brahmavādī, Impersonalists)
Māyayāpahṛta-jñāna
    as class of miscreant, 385
Mayi sannyasya karmāṇi
    quoted, 282
Meditation
    automatic from beginning of Kṛṣṇa con-
        sciousness, 311
    better than knowledge, 609
    for realization of Brahman, 405
    Kṛṣṇa as goal of, 301-302, 321, 417-418
    made possible by nine forms of devotion,
        362
    method of sitting for, 321
    not possible for the disturbed, 320
    of eightfold yoga system considered fruitive,
        311
    on Brahman problematic, 596
    on form and name of Kṛṣṇa 27, 416
    on Supersoul, 328, 340, 651
    on the Supreme Person as knower of all,
        oldest, etc., 419
    on Viṣṇu, not void, advocated, 148, 419
    pretenders make show of, 167-168
    tortoise maintain offspring by, 301
Memory
    change of body makes one forget, 221
    Kṛṣṇa as, 530
    limitations of man's, 222, 322
    of Arjuna regained by Kṛṣṇa's mercy, 842
    of living entity compared with Kṛṣṇa's,
        220-221, 401-402
    refined by sanctified food, 174

Memory
> revived by chanting Hare Kṛṣṇa, 417-418
> (*See also* Remembering process)

Menakā
> misleads Viśvāmitra into sex, 146

Mercy
> action explained out of, 240
> Arjuna questions out of, 516, **576**
> as appearance in original form, 223
> as means for understanding Kṛṣṇa's plan, 566
> enables Arjuna to see everything, 545, **842**
> in Kṛṣṇa's killing demons, 744
> in placing demons in lower species, 744
> Kṛṣṇa known by, 112, 232, 253, 398
> *māyā* overcome by, 842-843
> miscreants delivered by, 227
> miseries accepted as mercy of Kṛṣṇa, 142, 194
> obtained by following regulations, **151**
> of devotee necessary for liberation, 229
> of Kṛṣṇa as deliverer, 381, 603
> of Kṛṣṇa as everything, 391
> of Kṛṣṇa seen in difficulties, 611
> of Kṛṣṇa to devotees, 396-397, 424, 494
> Sañjaya hears *Gītā* by mercy of Vyāsa, **844-845**
> *sannyāsī* dependent on, 723
> shown to speculators, 493
> sun, moon and fire evidence of, 709
> withheld from demoniac, 744

Merging
> as a reward of sacrifice, 256
> as hellish for devotee, 822
> as process of impersonal liberation, 228, 230
> as sacrifice, 249-250
> as spiritual annihilation, 339
> as theory of demonic miscreants, 463
> compared to green bird entering green tree, 824
> eternality but not bliss realized in, 601
> impersonalist conceptions misleading, 824
> into Supreme Brahman, 22-23
> via Patañjali *yoga* system, 253
> with Brahman as self-interest, 308

Meru
> Kṛṣṇa as, **521**
> sometimes movable, not as great as Himalayas, 523

Mīmāṁsā-sūtras
> as part of study for sacrifice, 581

Mind
> as both friend and enemy, **312, 314**

Mind
> as cause of bondage and liberation, 313, 703
> as constituent of body, **627-628**
> as one of eight separated energies, **367-368**
> as restless and unsteady, **27, 335, 342-344**
> as sitting place of lust, **207-208**
> austerities of, **766-767**
> by its control one attains supreme abode, 323
> causes fall of sages, 146
> compared to driving instrument of car of body, 344
> concentration on Kṛṣṇa, 27, **196**, 280, **291**, 327, 335, 344-345, **411**, **416**, 418, **597**, **604**
> control of, 146, 152, 154, **244**, 279-280, 302-303, **317-318**, **321**, 335, 344-346, 418, 766-767, **806, 821**
> does not degrade one who sees Supersoul in all, **655**
> engagement of, 210, **299**, 328
> fixed on lotus feet of Kṛṣṇa, 327, 411
> in equanimity, conquers birth and death, 293
> in relation to senses, **153**, **167-168**, 207-210, 250-251, 332, **706**, 766-767
> in *samādhi*, 26, 128-129, 248, 330
> in *yoga*, 133, 302-303, 312-314, **319-320**, 362
> its mirror cleansed by chanting, 205
> its peace attained through renunciation, 609
> Kṛṣṇa as, 521
> Kṛṣṇa's mind and Self nondifferent, 452
> may be panic-stricken at death, 411
> meditation on Self, **141**, 328, 330, 334-335
> method of fixing it on Kṛṣṇa at death, **420**
> must admit superior dictation, 315
> no goal without Kṛṣṇa consciousness, 153
> not disturbed by flowery language of *Vedas*, 139
> of Arjuna overwhelmed, **56-57, 70**
> of man of discrimination carried off by senses, **146**
> of one dear to Kṛṣṇa agrees with Him, **611**
> purification of, **283**, 608
> uieted by identity with Brahman, 335
> self transcendental to, **211**
> should be used to understand necessity of human life, 498
> sometimes overcomes intelligence, 343-344
> steadiness as *sthīra-buddhi*, 294
> strengthened by intelligence, 211

Mind
    superior to senses, inferior to intelligence,
       210
    Supersoul reached for one who has con-
       quered, 315
    symptoms of sages with steady minds, 142
    when agitated, impersonalists fall down,
       150
    when distorted worships demigods, 391-
       392
Miscreants
    annihilated by Kṛṣṇa, 226
    as duṣkṛtam, lowest of mankind, 226
    cast into demonic wombs, 743
    delivered by mercy of Kṛṣṇa, 227
    devotional service difficult for, 387
    four classes discussed, 382-386
    have no good qualifications, 486
    Kṛṣṇa as their rod of chastisement 534-535
    Kṛṣṇa never manifest to unintelligent, 400
    their false views and frustrations discussed
       462-463
    Yama chief punisher of, 527
Miseries
    accepted as mercy of Kṛṣṇa, 142
    causes of, 22, 57, 296-297, 341, 372, 749
    discussed as perplexities, 80
    even Brahmā not free from, 428
    freedom from, 111, 136, 152, 258, 262 304,
       326, 330, 442, 822, 831
    from the highest planet to the lowest,
       426-427
    in mode of passion, 678-679, 681
    known only to one's own body, 94
    mahātmās never return to, 426
    material universe as temporary and full of
       488
    minimized to lowest by mercy of Kṛṣṇa, 142
    not as severe in mode of goodness, 669
    not felt by devotee, 302
    sages not disturbed by threefold, 142
    undergone if one not purified before death,
       67
    (See also Anxiety, Suffering)
Misers
    See Kṛpaṇa
Mithilā
    Janaka King of, 185
Modes (of nature)
    acquired by soul, 166
    action and activity in relation to, 15, 166,
       285, 287, 678-680, 683, 798-800, 829

Modes (of nature)
    all living entities deluded by, 199, 378-379,
       811
    Arjuna exhorted to transcend them, 129
    as conditioning and binding, 192-195, 664,
       668-673, 691, 795
    as manifestations of Kṛṣṇa's energy, 377-378
    association with, 753
    as subject of Chapter Fourteen, 663-692
    as they apply to varṇas, 235, 379, 487, 812
    austerity according to, 759, 764-769
    charity according to, 759, 569-771
    come from root of banyan tree, 695
    conditioned soul allured by, 348
    contaminate knowledge, 665
    contaminate living entity, 668
    death in, 677-678
    destinations of those situated in, 681-
       682
    determination according to, 806-808
    difficult to overcome, 380-381
    elevation in, 753
    enjoyed by living entity, 647
    faith according to, 753-756
    food according to, 759-761
    happiness according to, 808-811
    interaction of, 673-674
    knowledge according to, 796-798
    Kṛṣṇa transcendental to, 11, 377-378, 570,
       683
    manifest and nourish material world, 282,
       696
    nothing beyond, 683
    Paramātmā their master, 637-638
    process of transcending, 11, 21, 202, 650,
       687-689, 719
    related to material body, 130, 687
    results developing from, 680-681
    sacrifice according to, 175, 759, 762-764
    soul beyond, 658
    Supersoul transcendental, jīva not, 625-626
    symptoms of, 674-676
    understanding according to, 803-805
    unmanifested as pradhāna, 628
    Vedas deal mainly with, 129
    workers according to, 800-803
    work of one unattached to, 246
    (See also Goodness, Ignorance Passion)
Mokṣa-dharma
    quoted, 504
Monism
    as misleading, 369-370

Monism
  as worship of oneself as Supreme, 467
  considered atheistic, 651
  does not accept transcendental pleasure,
    330
  its impersonalist contention untrue, 399
  not supported, 105, 824
  as evidence of Kṛṣṇa's mercy, 709
Moon
  as one of Kṛṣṇa's eyes, 555
  attained by sacrifice and fruitive activities,
    435-436
  does not illumine supreme abode, 700-702
  higher beings on, 436
  its splendor comes from Kṛṣṇa, 709
  Kṛṣṇa as, 520, 710-711
  moves under Kṛṣṇa's order, 454
  nourishes vegetables, 709, 710-711
  Paramātmā source of light in, 641
  positions at times of leaving body, 434-435
  soma-rasa drunk on, 436
  universal form addressed as, 571
Mūdhas
  fools deride Kṛṣṇa's human form, 459-461
  as miscreants discussed, 383-384
Muhyanti yat sūrayaḥ
  quoted, 366
Mukti
  See Liberation
Mukti-pradātā sarveṣāṁ viṣṇur eva na saṁśayaḥ
  quoted, 381
Muktir hitvānyathā rūpaṁ svarūpeṇa vyava-
    sthitiḥ
  quoted, 262
Mukunda
  as giver of mukti, 136
  one who takes shelter of Him has no other
    obligation, 66, 120
  santas in love with, 176
Mukunda-liṅgālaya-darśane dṛśau
  verses quoted, 147, 327
Muṇḍaka Upaniṣad
  cited, 96, 511
  quoted, 95, 102-103
Muni
  See Sages

N

Na dhanaṁ na janaṁ na sundarīṁ kavitāṁ vā
    jagadīśa kāmaye
  verses quoted, 308

Nāga
  Kṛṣṇa as Ananta amongst serpents, 526
Na hi jñānena sadṛśam
  quoted, 290
Naimiṣāraṇya
  sages of, 516
Naitat samācarej jātu manasāpi hy anīśvaraḥ
  verses quoted, 189
Na jāyate mriyate vā vipaścin
  verses quoted, 99, 635
Nakula
  blows his conchshell, 46
Name
  benefits of chanting, 131, 205
  chanted 300,000 times daily by Haridāsa
    Ṭhākur, 326, 356
  chanting as best means in Kali-yuga, 172,
    173, 320
  chanting sign of advanced spiritual life, 356
  glorified by mahātmās, 465
  impersonalists afraid of addressing Kṛṣṇa by,
    374
  of Kṛṣṇa according to His activity, 44
  of Kṛṣṇa and Himself nondifferent, 25, 605
  of Kṛṣṇa cannot be understood through
    senses, 316
  of Kṛṣṇa not sectarian, 18
  of Kṛṣṇa object of concentration, 27, 51
  om tat sat uttered in conjunction with,
    772-773
  should not be chanted without knowing
    philosophy, 162
  to be chanted for transfer to Kṛṣṇaloka, 417
  why chanted by Caitanya, 131
  world becomes joyful upon hearing Kṛṣṇa's,
    568
Namo brahmaṇya-devāya go-brāhmaṇa-hitāya
  verses quoted, 679
Nanda Mahārāja
  discouraged from worshiping Indra, 18
Nandana-kānana
  gardens of sensual delights, 128
Nārada
  as greatest devotee in universe, 524
  as spiritual master of Vyāsa, 350-351, 845
  his entry into devotional service, 446-447
  in disciplic succession, 29
  influences Arjuna, 831
  Kṛṣṇa as, 524
  one must follow, 240
  proclaims Kṛṣṇa to be Supreme, 5, 6, 397
  validates Arjuna's praise, 510-511

Nārada-pañcarātra
    must be obeyed in devotional service, 366
    quoted, 340
Narādhama
    as miscreant, lowest of mankind, discussed, 384-385
    cast into demonic wombs, 743
Nārāyaṇa
    Arjuna requests to see form of, 577-578
    as one of main forms, 578, 834
    associates with devotees, 23
    bhakti-yoga rendered to, 689
    both inside and outside, 639
    demigods born from, 503-504
    demigods cannot be equal to, 234
    does not possess full opulences, 74
    four-handed form is eternal, 589
    four-handed, presides over Vaikuṇṭha planets, 577
    Kṛṣṇa appears before parents as, 223, 583
    one does not become as good as, 165
    supreme enjoyer, expansion, 418, 433
    transcendental to material world, 234
Nārāyaṇād brahmā jāyate, nārāyaṇād prajāpatiḥ prajāyate
    verses quoted, 503
Nārāyaṇaḥ paro devas tasmāj jātaś caturmukhaḥ tasmād rudro 'bhavad devaḥ sa ca sarva-jñatāṁ gataḥ
    quoted, 504
Nārāyaṇīya
    quoted, 603
Narottama
    in disciplic succession, 29
Nāsau munir yasya mataṁ na binnam
    quoted, 142
Naṣṭa-prāyeṣv abhadreṣu nityaṁ bhāgavata-sevayā
    verses quoted, 363
Na tad bhāsayate sūryo na śaśāṅko, etc.
    verses quoted, 19
Na tasmāt kaścid me priyakṛt tamaḥ
    quoted, 341
Na tasya kāryaṁ karaṇaṁ ca vidyate
    verses quoted, 187
Nava-dvāre pure dehī haṁso lelāyate bahiḥ
    verses quoted, 286
Nāyaṁ deho deha-bhājāṁ nṛ-loke
    verses quoted, 297
Nayāmi paramaṁ sthānam arcirādi-gatiṁ vinā
    verses quoted, 603
Nehābhikrama-nāśo 'sti pratyavāyo na vidyate
    verses quoted, 27

Nescience
    destroyed by knowledge, 262-263, 289-290, 313
    driven away by spiritual master, 290
    entraps living entity, 289
    follows everyone like tiger, 7
    how to rescue one fallen in its ocean, 72
    in thinking oneself the doer, 193
    its last snare in thinking oneself God, 290
    Kṛṣṇa not prone to, 290
    (*See also* Ignorance, Sleep)
Nirguṇa
    Kṛṣṇa as, 378, 638
Nikhileṣu avasthāsu jīvanmukta sa ucyate
    quoted, 340
Nimbārka Svāmī
    accepts Kṛṣṇa as Supreme, 3
Nimitta-mātram evāsau sṛjyānāṁ sarga-karmaṇi
    verses quoted, 237
Nirānanda
    See Miseries
Nirmama
    devotee does not identify with body, 611
    nothing is mine, 196
Nirmāṇa-moha
    means to attain spiritual sky, 21
Nirmāna-mohā jita-saṅga-doṣā
    verses quoted, 21
Nirukti
    Vedic dictionary cited, 121-122
    Vedic dictionary quoted, 128-129
Nirvāṇa
    means ending materialistic life, 158
    related to clearing of the mind, 330-331
    spiritual activities after, 331
Nitya-baddha
    as eternally conditioned, 380
Nityānanda
    as incarnation of God as divine master, 384
    delivered Jagai and Madhai, 384
    in disciplic succession, 29
    obeisances to, 1, 2
Nityasyoktāḥ śarīriṇaḥ
    quoted, 110
Nityo nityānāṁ cetanaś cetanānām
    quoted, 13, 87, 234, 371, 716
Niyama
    in *aṣṭāṅga-yoga,* 303, 305
Nonbeing
    See Asat

Nondevotee
approach to *Gītā* compared to bee licking honey bottle, 88
Arjuna inquires for, 218-219
cannot practice *bhakti*, 365-366
cannot understand Kṛṣṇa, 365, 397-398, 823
has no good qualifications, 486
his contamination not washed off, 392
Kṛṣṇa never manifest to unintelligent, 400

Nonviolence
as *ahiṁsā*, defined, 98, 498-499, 727
as austerity of body, 764
as divine quality, 722, 727
as knowledge, defined, 629, 631
as mundane activity, 195
as personal attachment, 184
birth and death do not support war, 108
created by Kṛṣṇa, 497
diplomacy in politics but not principle, 114
expected of *brāhmaṇa*. 202
in sacrifice of Hare Kṛṣṇa, 523
one in knowledge cannot kill or cause killing, 101
principles established by Buddha, 225
should be given up by Arjuna, 76, 115
violence not encouraged, despite soul's immortality, 113

Nṛhari
in disciplic succession, 29

Nṛsiṁha
as expansion, incarnation, 220, 236, 360, 578, 702

Nūnaṁ pramattaḥ kurute vikarma yad-indriya-prītaya āpṛṇoti
verses quoted, 273

O

Old age
cannot be counteracted by wealth, 82
freedom by transcending modes, 684
its perception as evil, 630
Kṛṣṇa never depicted in, 223
liberation by refuge in Kṛṣṇa, 405
none for spiritual body, 405, 715
one of four principles of material existence, 19
present everywhere in material universe, 137

Om
as means for entering into Brahman, 421
as supreme combination of letters, 423

Om
contained in Hare Kṛṣṇa, 423
Kṛṣṇa as, 373-374, 468-469, 523
not different from Brahman and Kṛṣṇa, 423
preferred by impersonalists, 374
sacrifice, charity, penance begun with, 773
used in sacrifice, 772-773
used to indicate Absolute Truth, 772-773

Om ajñāna timirāndhasya
prayer to spiritual master, 1

Om ity etad brahmaṇo nediṣṭaṁ nāma
quoted, 772

Om tad viṣṇoḥ paramaṁ padam
quoted, 772, 773

Omkāra
See Om

Om tat sat
the vibration discussed, 772-775
to perfect all activities, 775

Opulences
displayed wherever there is Kṛṣṇa, 847
full in spiritual world, 702
Kṛṣṇa gives only indication of, 536
Kṛṣṇa owns all wealth and energy, 638
of Kṛṣṇa beget devotion, 502
of Kṛṣṇa exchanged with devotee, 691
of Kṛṣṇa known through *Bhāgavatam* and *Gītā*, 502
of Kṛṣṇa limitless, 517-518, 536
of Kṛṣṇa not understood by impersonalists, 518
of Kṛṣṇa, subject of Chapter Ten, 491-538
pure devotees not interested in Kṛṣṇa's, 546
the six major, 492
whatever is opulent represents Kṛṣṇa's opulence, 537

P

Padam āvyāyām
See Goloka Vṛndāvana, Spiritual sky, Supreme abode

Pādau hareḥ kṣetra-padānusarpaṇe
verses quoted, 148, 327

Padmanābha
as plenary expansion, 433
in disciplic succession, 29

Padma Purāṇa
cited, 445
quoted, 297, 316, 366

Pain
caused by passionate food, 760-761

Pain
    created by Kṛṣṇa, defined, **497-498**
    one dear to Kṛṣṇa free from, **613-614**
Pañcāgni-vidyā
    sacrifice to enter Brahmaloka, 427
Pāñcajanya
    name of Kṛṣṇa's conchshell, **44**
Pañca-mahābhūta
    gross elements come from root of banyan, 695
Pāñcarātrikī
    devotional regulations of Vaiṣṇavas, 278
Pāṇḍavas
    as affectionate students of Droṇācārya, 35
    belong to same family as sons of Dhṛtarāṣṭra, 33
    encouraged by blowing of transcendental conchshells, 44
    guided by direct instruction of Kṛṣṇa, 48
    knew Kṛṣṇa to be Supreme, 400
    Kṛṣṇa as Arjuna amongst, 533-534
    not disturbed by enemy conchshells, 47
    pious since birth, 34
    their army considered limited by Duryodhana, 39
    their confidence in Kṛṣṇa, 47
    their victory assured because of Kṛṣṇa 43
Pāṇḍu
    Arjuna addressed as son of, **47, 429**
    his sons favorably influenced by Kurukṣetra, 33
    his sons' great army pointed out by Duryodhana, **34-35**
    his sons the object of Dhṛtarāṣṭra's inquiry, 32
    his sons separated from the family heritage, 33
    the King married to Kuntī, 38
Parābhavas tāvad abodha-jāto yāvanna jijñāsata ātma tattvam
    verses quoted, 273
Parabrahman
    as personal source of everything, 376
    compared to Brahman, 412-413
Parag-ātmā
    as soul attached to sense enjoyment, 251-252
Paramam
    as one full in six opulences, 492
Paramaṁ padam
    as the eternal abode, 831

Paramaṁ puruṣaṁ (Supreme Person)
    object of meditation, 27
Paramātmā
    appears to be divided but is not, **640**
    as *adhiyajña*, 414
    as cause of action, 712, **790-791**, 792-793
    as companion of living entity, 100, 102-103, 288, 624, 646, **654**, 710
    as enjoyer and proprietor of body, **648**
    as knower in all bodies, **622**-624
    as knowledge and goal of knowledge, 13, 641-642
    as Kṣīrodakaśāyī Viṣṇu, 367, 368
    as localized aspect of Absolute Truth, 73
    as Mahā-Viṣṇu, 519
    as master of modes of nature, 626, 637-638
    as partial realization, 12, 139, 232, 291, 318, 362, 398, 690
    as present in hearts of all entities, 10, 90, 292-293, 321, 337, 340, 394, 402, 414, 815
    as protector of *sannyāsī*, **723**-724
    as smaller than the smallest, 419
    as source of all senses yet without senses, 637-638
    as source of light, beyond darkness, **641**-642
    as support and maintainer of universe, 276, 371, 537-538, 637-638, 648-649, 710, 715-716
    can understand desires of living entity, 288
    demons ignorant of Him as witness, 737
    devours and develops all, **640**
    directs wanderings of all, **830**
    does not cause one to sin, 203
    dwells also within atoms, 232, 710
    enters *brahmajyoti* upon coming out of body, 716
    equal in all, 337, 340, **655**
    fulfills desire of soul as a friend, 102
    His grace enables transmigration, 102
    His hands, legs, eyes, faces, etc., everywhere, **636-637**
    is never destroyed, **654**
    Kṛṣṇa as, 52, 318, **340**, 393, 414
    Kṛṣṇa as source of, 12, 75, 100, 385, 644
    liberation attained by understanding, 650
    methods of perception, 651
    not eternal in spiritual world, 368
    realization of, 349, 514, 599
    realized through *yoga*, 122, 314-**315**, 321, 330, 339
    should be respected in all, 461

Paramātmā
superior to knowledge of Brahman, 832
the misguided think it one with soul, 111-112
theory of reflection applied to, 90
tortured by demoniac, 757-758
ultimate will invested in, 791

Paramātmāvādī,
as indirectly Kṛṣṇa conscious, 318
as one of three types of transcendentalists, 22
his degree of advancement, 73
(See also Yogī)

Param Brahma (Supreme Brahman)
distinguished from Brahman, 5
Kṛṣṇa declared to be, 510-511
(See also Brahman)

Param brahma param dhāma pavitram paramam bhavān
verses quoted, 5, 590, 831

Param dhāma
See Goloka Vṛndāvana, Spiritual sky, Supreme abode

Parameśvaram
interpretations of word, 654

Param padam
no miseries, 136

Paramparā
See Disciplic succession

Parantapaḥ
chastiser of enemies, name of Arjuna, 83-84

Parāśara Muni
explains the word Bhagavān, 74
great authority, father of Vyāsadeva, 74
quoted, 115, 492, 625

Parāśara-smṛti
quote on kṣatriya's duty, 115

Paraśurāma
a brāhmaṇa but acted as kṣatriya, 202

Parāsya śaktir vividhaiva śrūyate
verses quoted, 187

Paratattva
as supreme reality, 291

Pareśānubhūti
as spiritual satisfaction, 345

Parīkṣit Mahārāja
as righteous king, 525

Pārtha
Arjuna addressed as, 52, 101, 115, 141, 188, 417, 430, 805
significance of word, 52

Pārtha-sārathi
meaning of name, 44

Parts
all beings are part of Kṛṣṇa, 261
cooperation with the whole, 11-12
defined as atomic sparks of Kṛṣṇa's rays, 96
difference from whole, 93-94, 275
eternally separated, 714
living entities as eternal fragmental, 702-704
one with Supreme qualitatively, 99
prone to be extinguished when out of fire, 104

Pārvatī
agitates Śiva for sex, 149
Skanda her son, 522

Passion
action in, 670-673, 678-679, 799
as demoniac mode, 749
as impediment to liberation, 723
as manifestation of Kṛṣṇa's energy, 377-378
austerity and penance, in mode of, 757-758, 768
Brahmā as incarnation of rājo-guṇa, 381
cause of lust, 204
charity in mode of, 770-771
determination in, 807
diminished by devotional service, 336, 363
earth destination of those in, 681-682
entire material world in mode of, 671
food in mode of, 760-761
grief develops from, 680-681
happiness in, 809-810
knowledge in, 797
leads to rebirth amongst fruitive workers, 677
must be raised to goodness, 204
quieted by identity with Brahman, 335
renunciation in mode of, 786
sacrifice in mode of, 763
sex as its basis, 670-671
sometimes defeats goodness, 673-674
symptom of attachment, desire, hankering, endeavor, 675
understanding, in, 805
worker in, 801-802
worship in mode of, 755-756

Pastimes
cannot be understood through senses, 316
displayed by Kṛṣṇa on earth are prototypes of those in His abode, 19
exhibited by Kṛṣṇa in Vṛndāvana, 18, 227

Pastimes
    lorified by *mahātmās*, 465
    of Kṛṣṇa always thought of by devotee, 51, 517
Pāśupata-astra
    weapon received by Arjuna, 116
Patañjali
    yoga system discussed, 251-252
    yoga system for merging, 253
Patiṁ patīnāṁ paramaṁ parastād
    verses quoted, 187
Patiṁ viśasyātmeśvaram
    quoted, 172
Patir gatiś cāndhaka-vṛṣṇi-sātvatāṁ
    verses quoted, 172
Patraṁ puṣpaṁ phalam
    quoted, 447, 761
Paundram
    name of Bhīma's conchshell, **44**
Pauruṣa
    quoted, 716
Pavitram
    See Pure
Pavitram Uttamam
    devotional service as, 445
Peace
    as quality of *brāhmaṇa*, 812
    as tranquility, a divine quality, 722
    attained by devotees, 154, **284-285**, 323, 424,
        485
    attainment through control and surrender
        156-157, **265**, 315, **609**, 831
    attainment through Kṛṣṇa consciousness,
        82-83, 87, **152-153**, **304**, 681
    destroyed by Kṛṣṇa's not working, **189**
    enjoyed within self by knowledge, 264
    formula for, 304-305
    impossible in mode of passion, 681
    its basic principle, 157-158
    through identity with Brahman, 335
Penance
    as *candrāyana* and *cāturmāsya*, 253
    as severe austerities for enlightenment, **252**
    as tapas, austerity, a divine quality, 722, 726
    before surrender to Kṛṣṇa, 599
    begun with word *om*, 773
    created by Kṛṣṇa, defined, **497**, 499
    demonic when severe, 757-758
    for pleasing Supreme Person, 775
    for purification recommended, 297
    in goodness, 767
    in ignorance to destroy self or others, **769**
    in passion unstable, **768**

Penance
    in *vānaprastha* life, 438
    Kṛṣṇa as penance of ascetics, **374**
    Kṛṣṇa as purpose and enjoyer of, 153, **304**
    necessary for acceptance of Kṛṣṇa, 112
    not necessary for advanced devotee, 138
    not necessary in devotional service, 466
    of speech, **765-766**
    of the body, **764-765**
    purifies even great souls, **784**
    should never be abandoned, **782**, **784**
    tat and *sat* uttered with, **774-775**
    to be performed according to Vedic prin-
        ciples, 589
    undergone by Brahmā for one thousand
        years, 501
    while studying under spiritual master, 438
    will not reveal two-armed form, **587**
Personality
    as ultimate attribute of Supreme, 13
    confirmed by Kṛṣṇa's memory, 401-402
    Kṛṣṇa as greatest, **715**, **717**
    of Kṛṣṇa not lost in all-pervasiveness, 451,
        541
    of Kṛṣṇa not understood by sages and
        demigods, 493, 512
    of Supreme affirmed, **419**
    retained after liberation frightens imper-
        sonalists, 230
    unintelligent think Kṛṣṇa assumes, 397-399
Personality of Godhead
    See Supreme Personality of Godhead
Pestilence
    caused by unwanted population, 64
Philanthropy
    accepted as step to Kṛṣṇa consciousness,
        608
    as material engagement of Māyāvādī
        sannyāsīs, 278-279
    in mode of passion, 673
    yogī is best philanthropist, 341
Philosophy
    deals with mental activities, not source,
        368
    in modern age no knowledge of, 652
    pretenders speak on, 167
    seven principal philosophers in India, 444
    without religion mental speculation, 164
Piśāca
    as black arts, 477
Pitṛloka
    Kṛṣṇa as offering to, 468

Planets

ānandamaya-cinmaya float in rays of brahmajyoti, 19

Brahmaloka survives all upper systems, 428

cannot be forcibly approached by machine, 83, 682, 740

cannot be made by living entity, 371

described in Vedic literature, 21

disturbed at seeing universal form, 558

divided into three systems, 20

earth belongs to middle system, 20

elevation to higher systems, 20, 105, 114-115, 127, 427, **840**

float in air by Kṛṣṇa's energy, 419

Goloka Vṛndāvana supreme planet in spiritual sky, 20

held in fist of universal form, 710

higher systems sought by drinking soma, 472

if killed, Arjuna would attain heavenly planets, 119

in Kṛṣṇa's body, some made of earth, gold, jewels, etc., 550

innumerable within each universe, 501

in spiritual sky self-illuminated, 19, 323, 701

Kṛṣṇa as controller of, **304**, 454, 710-711

Kṛṣṇa spread throughout, 555

living entities found in all, 667-668

materialists interested in promotion to higher, 348

moon and sun belong to higher system, 20

more in spiritual sky than in material universe, 22

of demigods attained by worshipers, 395-396, 399, 477

of Kṛṣṇa attained by devotees, 23, 395-396, 399

of trees, 526-527

one is subject to fall down from higher, 427

one transferred to hellish planets if not purified, 67

others have other forms of human life, 500

places of misery from highest to lowest, 19, 426-427

ruled by Nārāyaṇa manifestations, 433, 577

sacrifice for elevation to higher, 127-128, 253, 413

sensual comforts on higher systems, 257, 472, 473

unsuccessful yogī born on higher, 352-353

upper systems as head of Kṛṣṇa, 414

(See also Brahmaloka)

Pleasure

all living entities search after, 18

as ultimate goal of yoga, 331

created by Kṛṣṇa, **497**

derived from kingdoms not permanent, 61-62

from chanting Hare Kṛṣṇa, 446

given by Kṛṣṇa to cows and senses, 44

greater in serving, 49

in hearing and glorifying Kṛṣṇa, 59-60, 297, 407, 506, 518

in Pātañjali yoga system, 330

in studying Gītā, 439

known only to one's own body, 94

Kṛṣṇa as the reservoir of, 18

not accepted by monists, 330

not grasped by one dear to Kṛṣṇa, **614-615**

of hard labor available to hogs, 297

of senses have beginning and end, 296-297

of Supreme Self only should be thought of, 334

relished by sage, 155, **295**

sensualists attracted to, 128

should be in that which favors Kṛṣṇa consciousness, 498

Plenary expansions

accept puruṣa incarnations, 519

as Viṣṇu-tattva, 702-703

bhakti-yoga rendered to, 689

devotees associate with, 23

directing material energy, 367-368

Kṛṣṇa does not lose identity in, 261

Kṛṣṇa not different from, 578

Kṛṣṇa origin of all, 74, 93

likened to leaves of tree, 433

millions and millions of four-armed, 433

Paramātmā as, 622

some named, described, 433

Plurality

of individual souls maintained, **86-88**

Population

as varṇa-saṅkara, unwanted, **64-65**, 189

basis for peace when good, 64

considered 99.9 percent narādhama, 384

enough food by sacrifice despite increase, 257

foolish in Kali-yuga, 131

Kṛṣṇa's plan to reduce, 843

rules for peaceful, 189

Potencies

Kṛṣṇa knows Himself by, **513**

Potencies
    of Godhead must be immense, 13
    of Kṛṣṇa cannot be surpassed, 717
    of Kṛṣṇa realized by discussion, 442
Prabhā
    defined as superior energy of Kṛṣṇa, 96
Pradhāna
    as unmanifested modes of nature, 282, 628
Pradhāna-kṣetrajña-patir guṇeśaḥ
    quoted, 635
Pradyumna
    as plenary expansion, 433
    associates with devotees, 23
Prahlāda
    as example of toleration, 631
    as learned leader, 382
    Kṛṣṇa as, 527
    one must follow, 240
    persecuted by father, 226
Prajā-pati
    as Viṣṇu, 172
Prajāpatiṁ ca rudraṁ cāpy aham eva sṛjāmi vai
    tau hi māṁ na vijānīto mama māyā-
    vimohitau
    quoted, 504
Prakāśānanda
    asks Caitanya why He chants, 131
    derided Caitanya, 508
Prakāśaś ca karmaṇy abhyāsāt
    quoted, 446
Prakṛti
    See Material nature
Prakṛtiṁ viddhi me parāṁ jīva bhūtām
    verses quoted, 8
Prāṇa
    as one of five kinds of air, 95
Prāṇaiś cittaṁ sarvam otaṁ prajānām
    verses quoted, 95
Prāṇamaya
    realizing Supreme in life forms, 626
Praṇava
    See Om
Prāṇa-vāyu
    senses as functions of, 252
Prāṇāyāma
    breathing process discussed, 254
    in aṣṭāṅga-yoga, 303, 305
Prāpañcikatayā buddhyā hari-sambandhi-
    vastunaḥ
    verses quoted, 274, 318
Prasādam
    as best type food, 761

Prasādam
    as diet for suffering patient, 345
    as means to control tongue, 632
    as method for attaining Kṛṣṇa, 592
    as principle of bhakti-yoga, 606
    automatically reduces eating, 255
    counteracts contamination of material
        nature, 178
    fitness of foodstuffs discussed, 326
    frees forefathers from ghost bodies, 65
    Kṛṣṇa accepts a leaf, flower, fruit or water,
        478-479
    Nārada freed from sin by taking, 446
    not taken by Haridāsa Ṭhākur until rounds
        chanted, 326
    one should eat only, 325
    palatable long after preparation, 761
    recommended by Caitanya, 748
    taken by devotee, rejected by nondevotee,
        150
    (See also Food)
Pratyag-ātmā
    as withdrawal from activities, 251-252
Pratyāhāra
    as end of sense activity, 334
    as withdrawal of senses from objects, 422
    in aṣṭāṅga-yoga, 303, 305
Prayāg
    as sacred place, 320
Prayāścitta
    system of ablution before death, 67
Predestination
    Kuru dynasty doomed at Kurukṣetra, 39, 46,
        60, 109
    universal form reveals destruction of sol-
        diers, 560-561, 563-566
Premā
    as real love of Kṛṣṇa, 231
Premāñjana-cchurita-bhakti-vilocanena santaḥ
    sadaiva hṛdayeṣu vilokayanti
    quoted, 176, 339
Pretenders
    better to execute duty than become so-
        called yogī, 199
    demoniac as, 729
    deny value of tapasya, austerity, 726,
    do not restrain mind from sense objects,
        167
    inferior to one in controlled life, 168
    Kṛṣṇa did not want Arjuna to become one,
        169
    living at cost of others, 169-170

Pretenders
    make show of meditation, 167
    manufacture own process, 260

Pride
    as demonic quality, 728-729, **735**-736
    as impediment to surrender, 699-700
    demons bewildered by, **742**
    sacrifice performed out of, **763**
    severe penance performed out of, **757**-758

Proprietorship
    false sense of, 700
    freedom from personal possessions, 318-319
    Kṛṣṇa as proprietor of everything, 14, 244,
        261, 341, 622, 701-702
    of body by Paramātmā, **648**
    of Kṛṣṇa as formula for peace, 304
    of Kṛṣṇa cited in *Īśopaniṣad*, 282
    of Kṛṣṇa not forgotten by demigods, 394
    renunciation of, 157, 196, **244**-245, **252**, 274,
        611
    sacrifice of knowledge greater than, **258**

Pṛthā
    Arjuna addressed as son of, **75**, 121, 186,
        232, **258**, 362, 375, 424, 464, 486, 543,
        602, 728, 730, 775, 785, 804-806
    as Kṛṣṇa's aunt, 76
    significance of Arjuna as her son, 52

Pseudo-religions
    based on materialistic philosophy of soul,
        107

Puṇya
    as original, 375

Puṇya-karmaṇām
    as great sacrifice, 840

Pūraka
    as breathing process, 254

Purāṇas
    accept Kṛṣṇa as Supreme, 3
    as diversion for mind, 767
    as historical records, 24, 517
    as part of study for sacrifice, 581
    as representative of Kṛṣṇa, 529
    celebrate glories of Supreme, 713
    cited, 504
    must be obeyed in devotional service, 366
    validate Arjuna's praise, 511

Pure (*pavitram*)
    Kṛṣṇa as, 5

Purification
    as a gradual process, 202
    as aim of human life, 747
    as divine quality, **722**-724, **812**

Purification
    body, mind, intelligence and senses used for,
        283
    by action in Kṛṣṇa consciousness, 169-170,
        274, **278**, 445, 818
    by chanting Hare Kṛṣṇa, 418, 446
    by food in mode of goodness, **760**-761
    by knowledge of Kṛṣṇa, **229**-230
    by Kṛṣṇa of one who hears of Him, 363
    by remembering Kṛṣṇa, 486
    by transcending lust, anger and greed,
        745-746
    Kṛṣṇa as purifier, **468**-469
    marriage for, 784
    necessary before chanting, 356
    necessary before *sannyāsa*, 165
    of dirty things in heart, 238
    of four kinds of pious men, 387-388
    of mind by charity, 608
    of senses via *bhakti-yoga*, 606
    om tat sat vibrated for, 775
    process practiced by *yogī*, **356**-357
    sacrifice for, 184, 782
    via *prāyaścitta* system of ablution, 67

Pūrṇam
    See Complete Whole

Purujit
    cited by Duryodhana as great fighter, **36**

Puruṣa (enjoyer)
    as controller of everything, 367-368, 419
    as Nārāyaṇa, Vāsudeva, 417-418
    as subject for Chapter Thirteen, 619-661
    described as active by Kapila, 122
    incarnations, 519
    Kṛṣṇa as, 5, 11-12,18
    Mahā-Viṣṇu as first *puruṣa* incarnation, 455
    Paramātmā as, **648**

Puruṣārtha
    as religiosity, economics, sense gratification
        and merging, 330

*Puruṣārtha-śūnānāṁ guṇānāṁ pratiprasavaḥ
    kaivalyaṁ svarūpa-pratiṣṭhā vā citi-śak-
    tir iti*
    quoted, 330-331

Purusottama
    as plenary expansion, 433
    in disciplic succession, 29
    Kṛṣṇa as, 410, 513-514

R

Rādhārāṇī, Śrīmatī
    obeisances to, 2

Raghu
  Ikṣvāku the forefather of its dynasty, 215
Raghunātha Bhaṭṭa Gosvāmī
  obeisances to, 1
Raghunātha Gosvāmī
  in disciplic succession, 29
  obeisances to, 1
Rahūgaṇa Mahārāja
  discovers Bharata Mahārāja, 355
Rājendra
  in disciplic succession, 29
Rajo-guṇa
  Brahmā as incarnation of, 381
Rakṣa
  worshipers of ghosts may become, 477
Rakṣasas
  Kṛṣṇa as Kuvera of, **521**
Rāma
  appears in Raghu dynasty, 215
  as expansion of Kṛṣṇa, 48, 236, 578, 702, 834
  as incarnation, 220, 360
  as righteous king, 525
  bhakti-yoga rendered to, 689
  defeated Rāvaṇa, 48, 61, 226, 744
  everyone wanted to live in His kingdom 61
  His servant Hanumān engages his wrath 204
  Janaka His father-in-law, 185
  known also as Personality of Godhead 297
  Kṛṣṇa as, **528**
  never showed cowardice, 61
Ramante yogino'nante satyānanda-cid-ātmani
  verses quoted, 297
Rāmānujācārya
  accepts Kṛṣṇa as Supreme, 3
  as learned leader, 382
  explains words sanātana, 16
  maintains individuality on spiritual grounds, 88
  Yāmunācārya in disciplic succession from, 397
Rasa
  See Friendship, etc., Relationships
Rāsa-līlā
  imitators of, 190
Raso vai saḥ; rasam hy evāyaṁ labdhvānandī
    bhavati
  quoted, 691
Rāvaṇa
  as example of demon, 740
  attempts to build staircase to heaven, 740

Rāvaṇa
  defeated by Rāma, 48, 61, 226
  kidnapped Rāma's wife and chastised, 61
  killed by Kṛṣṇa, 744
  plans baffled by material energy, 383
Reality
  as Paratattva, supreme, 291
  denied by demons, 733
  its eternality confirmed, 93
  understood as Brahman, Paramātmā and Bhagavān, 291
Realization
  aim of human life, 181
  a myth to materialists, 195
  as buddhi-yoga, 162
  as consequence of surrender, 84
  as knowledge, 316, 336, **630**
  attained by chanting, 131, 320
  basis and purpose of, 131, 347
  by controlled senses, 168, 251-252, 298
  by escaping lust, anger and greed, **745-746**
  by speculation and devotion, **164**
  characteristics of, 21, 72, 293, 821
  destroyed by lust, 208-209, 296
  determination for, 92
  difficulty in, 259, 320, **346**
  direct and indirect processes, 610
  gradual development, 130
  happiness conducive to, **809**
  highest perfection as servant of Kṛṣṇa, 139
  Kṛṣṇa as object of, 131, 232
  likened to staircase, 634
  love of Kṛṣṇa beyond, 339
  necessary for spiritual sacrifice, 268
  offered in form of Upaniṣads, 130
  on basis of nonexistence of material body, 110
  out of thousands one tries for, **365**
  preliminary need of desire for, 231
  rogress by following devotees, 186
  senses stumbling blocks to, **200**
  sought by three paths, 347
  taught by analytical study of body and soul, 72
  three stages of, 690
  through purification of work, 818
  undisturbed trance of, **139**
  what happens to one who abandons, **347**
  yoga a ladder for, 310-311
Rebirth
  See Transmigration

Recaka
  as birth process, 254
Reincarnation
  See Transmigration
Relationships
  accepted by Kṛṣṇa, 85
  Arjuna fears he offended Kṛṣṇa out of friendship, 573, 577
  attained by *mahātmās*, 465
  between Arjuna and Kṛṣṇa change from friendship to wonder, 550-551
  between *jīvātmā* and *Paramātmā*, 102-103
  between Kṛṣṇa and devotees, 4-5, 49, 131, 390, 482-483, 573
  characteristics of one dear to Kṛṣṇa, 611-617
  forgetfulness causes change of bodies, 102
  in five different paths of service, 425
  in love for Kṛṣṇa, 339
  Kṛṣṇa as reservoir of all, 551
  Kṛṣṇa may be treated as son, husband, friend, etc., 576
  of cowherd boys with Kṛṣṇa, 546
  to Kṛṣṇa in everything, 391
  to Kṛṣṇa only known through spiritual master, 290
  understanding begets indifference to ritual, 138
  with Kṛṣṇa in spiritual sky, 232
  with Kṛṣṇa remove ignorance, 93
  (*See also* Friendship, etc.)
Religion
  abandon all religion to surrender to Kṛṣṇa, 835-836
  Arjuna advised to sacrifice body for, 97
  Arjuna's arguments based on, 81-82
  as distinguished from *sanātana-dharma*, 16-18
  as quality of *brāhmaṇa*, 812
  cannot be manufactured, 240
  considered irreligion in ignorance, 805
  demons blaspheme, 742
  discussed in terms of time and circumstance, 225
Relationships
  established by Kṛṣṇa, 33, 188, 224, 226, 240, 260
  evolves from types of faith, 755
  ruitive result in, 807
  its principles best cause for fighting, 113
  its principles must be followed for knowledge, 91

Relationships
  keeps women from adultery, 64
  knowledge as perfection of, 444
  Kṛṣṇa as maintainer of, 554
  Kṛṣṇa descends when there is decline in, 224
  not as important as knowledge, 86
  passion misguides one in, 805
  principles enable good population to prevail, 64
  principles in *Vedas*, 224
  solves economic problems, 256-257
  some enter it for fame, 630
  without God is not religion, 384
  without philosophy fanaticism, 164
  (*See also* Dharma, Sanātana-dharma)
Rāmādi mūrttiṣu kalā-niyamena tiṣṭhan
  verses quoted, 220
Remembering process
  at time of death by *yoga*, 415, 420
  chanting Hare Kṛṣṇa for, 415
  comes from Kṛṣṇa, 712-713
  frees one from sinful bondage, 138
  in attaining Kṛṣṇa, 24-26, 417-418, 424-425
  limitations of man's, 222
  not possible for impure, 415
  of lotus feet of Kṛṣṇa, 327
  when bewildered, intelligence is lost, 150
  (*See also* Memory)
Renunciation
  according to three modes, 783, 786-787
  Arjuna inquires into, 272, 780-781
  artificial, 150
  as divine quality, 722
  as incomplete without Kṛṣṇa consciousness, 165, 273-274, 278, 318
  as knowledge, defined, 630-632
  as step to liberation in *sannyāsa*, 92
  as way to attain peace of mind, 609
  better than knowledge and meditation, 609
  by one dear to Kṛṣṇa, 614
  for maintenance not approved, 169-170
  highest perfectional stage, 818-819
  its perfection as subject of Chapter Eighteen, 779-849
  its results obtained by self-control, 818-819
  Kṛṣṇa as master of, 848
  necessitates awareness of *īśāvāsya*, 274
  of action, 136, 267, 275, 285, 781-782
  of work good for liberation, 273
  the same as devotion and *yoga*, 277, 309

Repetition
    necessary for understanding, 106
    symptom of ecstasy, not literary weakness, 555
Ritual
    all surpassed by devotional service, 439
    considered end in itself by ignorant, 195
    devotees indifferent to, 138
    imperative for neophytes, 138
    Kṛṣṇa as, 467-468
    meant for understanding Kṛṣṇa, 191-192
    of Vedas likened unto leaves of banyan, 695
    performed for material motives, 762
    pure devotees not confined to, 192, 355, 481
    useless without faith in Kṛṣṇa, 138, 776-777
Ṛk Veda
    as one of four Vedas, 581
    emanates from Kṛṣṇa, 179
    Kṛṣṇa as, 468-469
Rudra
    came from Brahmā, 501
    Kṛṣṇa as Śiva, 521
    shown in universal form, 544
    the eleven born of Nārāyaṇa, 503
Rūpa Gosvāmī
    cited, 437
    considered Caitanya most munificent, 589
    explains yukta-vairāgya, 481
    in disciplic succession, 29
    prayer and obeisances to, 1
    quoted, 274, 283, 318, 333, 340, 366, 592
    slept only two hours a day, 326

S

Śabda-brahma
    considered attained by Haridāsa Ṭhākur, 356
    transcended by one in Kṛṣṇa consciousness, 138
Śabdādibhyo'ntaḥ pratiṣṭhānāc ca
    quoted, 712
Sac-cid-ānanda-rūpāyam kṛṣṇāya
    quoted, 459
Sac-cid-ānanda-vigraha
    absent in material bodies, 22
    atheists may know, 219
    body attained upon thinking of Kṛṣṇa at death, 22
    body unchangeable, not forgetful, 221
    Kṛṣṇa's body as, 12-13, 22, 74, 399, 459, 638
    Kuntī prays to see, 400

Sac-cid-ānanda-vigraha
    manifested to discourage speculation, 19
    (See also Form of Kṛṣṇa)
Sacrifice
    according to three modes, 176-177, 759, 762-764
    already performed by one chanting, 131, 356
    Arjuna inquires about the Lord of, 410-411
    as Brahman, 248
    as charity, 253
    as divine quality, 722, 726
    as haṭha-yoga breath control, 254
    as impersonal merging, 249-250
    as karma-kāṇḍa and jñāna-kāṇḍa, 259
    as means of attaining moon, 435-436
    as means to higher planets and Vaikuṇṭhas, 114, 127-128, 248, 255-256, 412-413, 427
    as means to Kṛṣṇa consciousness, 112, 181, 191-192, 268, 607-709
    as puṇya-karmaṇām, 840
    as purpose of material universe, 172
    as yajña, Viṣṇu, 170
    as yoga-yajña, 253
    bestows wealth, enjoyment, 171, 178, 181, 256-257
    cycle of, 413
    for purification and sense control, 181, 184, 250, 255-256, 782, 784
    Kṛṣṇa as, 467-468
    Kṛṣṇa as jyotiṣṭoma and mahāyajña, 468
    Kṛṣṇa as ultimate object and enjoyer of, 170-171, 173, 175, 196, 304, 475-476, 775
    marriage as vivāha-yajña, 784
    materially contaminated, 181, 258-259, 268, 763, 776-777, 781-782
    meant for householder, 726
    no happiness in this or next life without, 256
    not easy in Kali-yuga, 173
    of animals, 114, 816, 817
    of comforts, tapomaya-yajña, 253
    of everything for Kṛṣṇa, 250, 633
    of food releases one from sin, 176
    of knowledge greater than of possessions, 258
    of material happiness, 348
    of material possessions, 252
    of studying Vedic literature, 253
    of work culminates in knowledge, 258
    om tat sat uttered during, 772-775
    pañca-mahāyajña for ordinary men, 175

Sacrifice
    produces rain and thus grains, 177
    rejected by demons, 740
    related to work and duty, 170, 177, 247, 249-250, 257, 607-609, 762, 816-817
    saṅkīrtana-yajña as, 173, 726
    sent forth at beginning of creation, 171
    sex as, 251
    should never be abandoned, 782, 784
    sinful not to perform, 180
    spiritualizes atmosphere, 248
    sustained by Kṛṣṇa, 406
    takes different forms according to faith, 258
    to Brahman by yogīs, 249-250
    to demigods discussed, 173-175, 249-250
    to encourage gradual realization, 130-131
    transcendence situated in, 179
    ultimately leads to liberation, 174
    unauthorized, 741-764
    unnecessary for transcendentalists, 138, 181
    will not reveal universal form, 580-581
Sadācāra
    purified activities, 283
Sad eva saumya
    773
Sādhaka
    as candidate for liberation, 154
Sādhu
    See Devotees, Sages, Vaiṣṇavas
Sādhyas
    behold universal form in wonder, 557
Sādvaitaṁ sāvadhūtaṁ parijana-sahitaṁ
    prayer quoted, 1
Sa evāyaṁ mayā te 'dya yogaḥ proktaḥ purā-tanaḥ
    verses quoted, 3
Sages
    action and work of, 183, 199, 238, 243-244
    agree on eternality of soul, 93
    as sādhu if Kṛṣṇa conscious, 226
    as twenty-five patriarchs of the universe, 501
    attain to perfection by supreme wisdom, 664
    cannot equal Kṛṣṇa, 350
    cannot kill or cause killing, 101
    characteristics and symptoms of, 140-144, 155, 183, 194, 294-297, 299, 301, 687-688, 821
    cited by Kṛṣṇa as authority, 625
    conclusions on existent and nonexistent, 93
    debts cancelled to them if surrendered to Kṛṣṇa, 120

Sages
    definition of muni, 142
    do not know Kṛṣṇa's origin or personality, 493
    drink the nectar of Bhagavad-gītā, 28
    even greatest fall, 146
    equality of vision, 292, 316-317
    happiness of, 295, 678
    in full knowledge, 242
    in universal form, 552
    know distinction between body and soul, 85-86
    know Kṛṣṇa as purpose of sacrifice, 304
    know the self slays not nor is slain, 97
    Kṛṣṇa as Bhṛgu amongst, 523
    Kṛṣṇa as Nārada amongst, 524
    Kṛṣṇa the source of, 493
    Nārada develops desire for devotion by association with, 446
    need not observe ritual, 192
    no obligation due them by devotee of Mukunda, 66
    not bewildered by transmigration, 89
    not contradictory to śāstra or spiritual master, 496
    pufiried by devotion, achieve Kṛṣṇa, 278
    seven great born out of Kṛṣṇa's mind, 501
    should set example for ignorant, 190-192, 194-195
    sthita-dhī-muni different from ordinary muni, 142
    take refuge in Kṛṣṇa, 136
    their day is night for all beings, etc., 155
    validate Arjuna's praise, 510
    way of entering into Brahman, 421
    worship Kṛṣṇa knowing Him as source, 503-504"
    (See also Devotees, Spiritual Master, Vaiṣṇavas)
Sahadeva
    blows his conchshell, 46
Śaibya
    cited by Duryodhana as great fighter, 36
Saintliness
    not befitting Arjuna on Battlefield, 61
Sakhya-bhakta
    service as friend, 425
Śakuni
    beheld by Arjuna on Battlefield, 53
Śalya
    beheld by Arjuna on Battlefield, 53
    willing to die for Duryodhana, 39

Samādhi
    activities in Kṛṣṇa consciousness in, 598
    as absorption in Kṛṣṇa, 51, 248, 315, 318
    as beyond influence of dualities, 143
    characteristics described, 330-331
    defined, 128-129
    in *aṣṭāṅga-yoga*, 303, 305
    includes realization of Brahman, Param-
        ātmā and Bhagavān, 139
    Kṛṣṇa consciousness best way to, 422-423
    mind should be fixed in, 334
    not possible for materialists, 129
    of one self-realized, 821
    trance by complete knowledge, 301
    two kinds described, 331
Sa mahātmā sudurlabhaḥ
    quoted, 366
Samāna
    as one of five kinds of air, 95
Samāna-vāyu
    as engaged for realization, 252
Samāne vṛkṣe puruṣo nimagnaḥ
    verses quoted, 103
Samāśrita ye padapallava-plavam
    verses quoted, 136
Sāma veda
    as one of four *Vedas*, 581
    emanates from Kṛṣṇa, 179
    Kṛṣṇa as, 468-469, 521
    rich in beautiful songs, 531
Samprajñāta-samādhi
    described, 331
*Samyag ādhīyate 'sminn ātmatattva-yāthātmy-
    am*
    quoted, 128
Sanaka
    born from Brahmā, 501
Sananda
    born from Brahmā, 501
Sanātana
    born from Brahmā, 501
Sanātana-dhama
    See Goloka Vṛndāvana, Spiritual sky, Su-
        preme abode
Sanātana-dharma
    breaking of its tradition brings chaos, 66-67
    described, 16-18
    distinguished from religion and faith, 16-17
    non-sectarian and unchangeable, 16-18
    of the living entity, 15
    set forth welfare activities, 66-67
    (*See also* Dharma, Religion)

Sanātana Gosvāmī
    in disciplic succession, 29
    inquires about *svarūpa*, 17
    obeisances to, 1
Sanātana-yoga
    as subject of Fourth Chapter, 268
Sanatkumāra
    became devotee by eating *tulasī*, 447
    born from Brahmā, 501
*Sandhyā-vandana bhadram astu bhavato bhoḥ
        snāna tubhyaṁ namo*
    verses quoted, 138
Śāṇḍilya
    as principal philosopher, 444
Sāndīpani *muni*
    teacher of Kṛṣṇa, 77
Sañjaya
    asked about battle by Dhṛtarāṣṭra, 32
    as secretary of Dhṛtarāṣṭra, 32
    by grace of Vyāsa could see universal form,
        549
    could envision Kurukṣetra in Dhṛtarāṣṭra's
        room, 33
    Gītā related to his heart by Vyāsa, 844
    recalls Kṛṣṇa's form with wonder, 846-847
    student of Vyāsa, 33, 845
    thrilled by *Gītā*, **844**, 846
    understands the motives of Dhṛtarāṣṭra's
        inquiries, 34
Śaṅkara
    as Śiva, 521
Śaṅkarācārya
    accepts Kṛṣṇa as Supreme, 3, 365
    accepts *Vedānta-sūtra*, 791
    as author of *Śārīraka-bhāṣya*, 278
    impersonalists do not follow, 398
    maintains Kṛṣṇa is beyond creation, 234
Saṅkarṣaṇa
    as plenary expansion, 433
Sāṅkhya philosophy
    aim of, 276
    analytical knowledge declared completed,
        121
    declares causes of action, **790-791**
    defined by Vedic dictionary, 121
    discussed by Kṛṣṇa, **85-121**
    distinguished from philosophy of atheist
        Kapila, 122-123
    expounded by Lord Kapila, 122-123
    its first process and conclusion, 277
    Kapila's and Kṛṣṇa's identical, 123
    meaning of *sāṅkhya*, 791

Sāṅkhya philosophy
  nondifferent from *karma-yoga* and devotion, 123, **276**
  studied by Māyāvādī *sannyāsīs*, 278
  study as sacrifice, 253
  twenty-four elements the subject of 13, 368
Sāṅkhya-yoga
  as difficult for this age, 347
  as subject matter for Chapter Six, 307-360
  for speculators and philosophers, 164
  inferior to *karma-yoga* in Kali-yuga, 308
  presented unsystematically in Second Chapter, 163
Saṅkīrtana-yajña
  and Kṛṣṇa consciousness go well together, 172
  as easiest and best sacrifice, 173 176, 726
  Caitanya predicts it spread all over world, 227
  inaugurated by Caitanya, 176
  necessary for happiness, 177
  ecommended for Kali-yuga, 172-173
  saves one from food scarcity, 178
  (*See also* Chanting)
Sannyāsa
  abandons fruitive work, 781-782, 788
  accepted upon purification, 165
  Arjuna inquires into purpose of, 780-781
  as disturbance to social order, 165
  as eligible for entering sun, 57-58
  as head of *varṇāśrama* institution, 723
  as painstaking situation, 92
  as spiritual master of *brāhmaṇa*, 723
  as step to realization, 92, 167, 250, 438-439
  as worthy recipient of charity, 500
  begs from door to door, 724-725
  counterfeited by demons, 741
  definition of, 481, 496, 819
  distributes knowledge to householders, 724-725
  duties of, 500, 724-725
  Māyāvādī *sannyasīs* compared with Vaiṣṇava *sannyāsīs*, 278-279
  forbidden relationship with women, 724
  may perform marriage ceremony, 786
  must be convinced of Paramātmā protection, 723-724
  must be fearless, dependent on Kṛṣṇa's mercy, 723-724
  never accepted by *kṣatriyas*, 114
  promoted to Brahmaloka, 428

Sannyāsa
  should not discourage others to marry, 784
  taken by Caitanya for higher cause, 92
  works for whole, not the part, 308
  wrongly ignore fire sacrifices, 308
Sannyāsa-yoga
  meaning of, 309-310
Śānta-bhakta
  service in neutrality, 425
Śāntas
  See Devotees Sarasvatl
  worshiped for education, 393
Śārīraka-bhāṣya
  as commentary on Vedānta-sūtras, 278
Sarva-dharmān parityajya mām ekaṁ śaraṇaṁ vraja
  verses quoted, 28, 604
Sarva-gataḥ
  all-pervasiveness of the living entities, 105
Sarvam etad brahma, tasmād etad brahma nāma-rūpam annaṁ ca jāyate
  quoted, 282
Sarvam etad ṛtam manye yan māṁ vadasi keśava
  verses quoted, 5
Sarvaṁ jñāna-plavena
  quoted, 290
Sarvasya cāhaṁ hṛdi sanniviṣṭaḥ
  quoted, 791, 831
Sarvasya prabhum īśānaṁ sarvasya śaraṇam bṛhat
  quoted, 642
Sarvataḥ pāṇi-pādam
  quoted, 638
Sarvātmanā yaḥ śaraṇaṁ śaraṇyam
  verses quoted, 66, 120
Sarva-yoniṣu... ahaṁ bīja-pradaḥ pita
  quoted, 16
Śāstras
  above four defects of living entity, 748
  as guide to action, 792, 804
  austerities not mentioned in, 757-758
  cited by Kṛṣṇa as authority, 625
  demonic reject, 731, 742, 752
  followed by divine, 730-731, **746-749**, 752
  Gītā best of all, 266
  most confidential part of, **719**
  must be followed by teacher, 186
  not contradicted by spiritual master or sage, 496
  not violated by Kṛṣṇa, 187
  recommend worship to demigods, 393
  sacrifice in defiance of, **764**

Śāstras
    statements should be upheld by, 766
    their injunctions purify the soul, 166
    those who doubt them do not attain Kṛṣṇa
        consciousness, 266
    useless without Kṛṣṇa consciousness, 166
    worker in ignorance works against, 802
Sat
    used in sacrifice to satisfy Supreme, 772-
        773, 775
    used to indicate Absolute Truth, 772-773
Satisfaction
    as characteristic of devotee, 611
    by food in mode of goodness, 760-761
    created by Kṛṣṇa, defined, 497, 499
    of the mind, 766-767
    with anything, 615-616
Ṣaṭ-karma-nipuṇo vipro mantra-tantra-viśāra-
        dah
    verses quoted, 82
Sattvaṁ viśuddhaṁ vāsudeva-śabditam
    quoted, 756
Sātyaki
    blows his conchshell, 46
Satyavatī
    Vyāsadeva the son of, 716
Satya-yuga
    characteristics and duration of, 428
Saumadatti
    another name for Bhūriśravā, 38
Saumya-vapuh
    as most beautiful form, 584
Śaunaka
    cited, 516
Sa vā eṣa brahma-niṣṭha idaṁ śarīraṁ marttyam
        atisṛjya
    quoted, 703
Sa vai manaḥ Kṛṣṇa-padāravindayoḥ
    verses quoted, 147, 324, 327, 336, 344
Savyasācin
    Arjuna addressed as, 564
    meaning of the word, 565
Science of God
    analyzes position of God and His energies,
        367
    can be understood in pure goodness, 674
    explained in Bhagavad-gītā, 7, 32
    instructed via disciplic succession, 214-
        215
    known by one situated in transcendence,
        294
    Kṛṣṇa as, 529

Science of God
    one who has mastered it is spiritual master,
        82
    understood through devotional service,
        363
Scripture
    See Śāstra
Sectarianism
    described as changing of faiths, 17-18
Self
    Arjuna inquires about, 410
    Arjuna exhorted to be established in, 129
    as controller of mind and lower self, 211,
        335
    as eternal nature of living entity, 412
    as sufferer or enjoyer of mind and senses,
        344
    does nothing, 281, 656
    dwelling in body, cannot be slain, 97, 112
    enjoyed by dint of knowledge, 264
    happiness attained by steadiness in, 336
    its pleasure only should be thought of, 334
    known by speculation and devotion, 164
    Kṛṣṇa as Self in hearts of all, 519
    most easily understood through Gītā, 112
    no bondage for one firmly situated in, 267
    no duty for one who takes pleasure in, 182
    perception of, 328, 330, 334, 444
    sacrificed in fire of Brahman, 249-250
    satisfaction in, 141
    transcendental to senses, mind and intelli-
        gence, 211
    two classes of men who realize, 164
Self-control
    as divine quality, 722, 725, 812
    as knowledge, defined, 629, 631
    created by Kṛṣṇa, defined, 497-498
    meant for householders, 725
    results of renunciation obtained by, 818-
        819
Self-interest
    as Viṣṇu, 57
    defined as submission to Kṛṣṇa, 57
    everyone working for, 308
    goal to reach Viṣṇu, 168
    pure devotee has no desire for, 424
Self-realization
    See Realization
Sense gratification
    arises from mental concoction, 141
    Arjuna's not fighting based on, 121
    as activity of material body, 156, 687

Sense gratification
    as cause of work and bondage, 122, 200, 237,
        256, 297, 620
    as demonic engagement, 127-128, 155, 167,
        176, 734, 736-737
    as symptom of attachment, 142
    as vain life, 180
    avoided by sages, 193-194, 295-296, 309,
        311-312
    begets reactions, 120
    can divert devotee, 153
    dangerous even if regulated, 145, 200-201
    destroys peace, 157, 285
    discouraged, 149, 171, 334
    elevation from, 129, 242
    excludes samādhi, 129
    fruitive result in, 807
    full knowledge devoid of, 242
    in mode of passion, 671, 675
    its happiness an enemy, 207
    its spirit current a long time, 200
    people engrossed in, 111, 273
    renounced, 630-632
    restriction of, 145, 250-251, 257
    Vedas studied for, 127, 192
    when finished, realization offered, 130
    work devoid of, 124, 326
    worship of leaders for, 234
Senses
    actually spiritual but exhibited in matter,
        638
    Arjuna had complete control of them, 79
    as basis and cause of action, 790-791, 794
    as cause and constituents of material body,
        627, 646, 706
    as controlled by Mahārāja Ambarīṣa, 147-
        148, 327
    as functions of the prāṇa-vāyu, 252
    as instruments for gratifying desires, 646
    as one of principal gross creations, 368
    as part of banyan tree, 695-696
    as sitting place and outlets of lust, 207- 210
    attraction to, 149, 200, 313
    can carry away the intelligence, 146, 153
    cannot be controlled artificially, 149, 154
    cannot perceive all stars, 21
    cannot perceive or understand Kṛṣṇa, 316,
        366, 451, 518, 542-543, 639
    compared to horses pulling car of body, 344
    control in yoga, 319-320, 422
    control of, 146-148, 151, 164, 168, 254- 255,
        279-280, 301, 332, 599, 632, 806

Senses
    described as strong and impetuous, 146
    engagement of, 26, 144, 149, 151, 153-281,
        327-328, 417
    false ego bewilders due to misuse of, 193
    given pleasure by Kṛṣṇa, 44, 59-60
    happiness derived from, 90-91, 809-810
    how acquired, 208
    knowledge and intelligence through re-
        straint of, 79, 154
    Kṛṣṇa as controller of, 44, 49, 622-623
    likened to serpents, 144, 211, 823
    likened to limbs withdrawn by turtle, 144
    living entities struggle hard with, 702-704
    mind the center of, 207-208
    most people servants of, 144
    most uncontrollable is the tongue, 632
    of Arjuna dried up by grief, 81
    of Kṛṣṇa, 180, 187, 479, 575, 638
    one is happy if he can tolerate urges of,
        298
    one who delights in them lives in vain, 180
    only gratified to keep body fit, 632
    purification via bhakti-yoga, 332, 606
    regulated in marriage, 257
    sacrifice of, 250-252, 255, 256
    satisfied by satisfying Govinda's senses,
        59-60
    self enjoys through transcendental senses,
        330
    self transcendental to, 211, 281
    shutting out objects by trance, 302-303
    Śiva and demigods subjected to influence of,
        149
    stumbling blocks to realization, 200
    subduing them required for peace, 265
    superior to matter, inferior to mind, 210
    their activities temporary, 194
    their contact source of misery, 296-297
    their enjoyment ultimate for demons, 736-
        737
    their forces delineated, 298
    their servant called godāsa, 335
    the Supersoul their source, 637-638
    unaccountable by impersonalists, 44
    used only for purification, 283
    worship of unmanifest beyond, 598-599
Serpents
    as Vāsuki, bed of Garbhodakaśāyī, 552
    in universal form, 552
    Kṛṣṇa as Ananta amongst Nāgas, 526
    Kṛṣṇa as Vāsuki amongst, 525

Service
    as aim of sacrifice, 258
    as *bhajati*, 359
    as *buddhi-yoga*, 134
    as identity, *svarūpa*, 17-18
    as liberation from mode of passion, 336
    as step to love of Kṛṣṇa, 607
    enables approach to supreme abode, 21, 137
    frees one from five causes of work, 281
    if not rendered, one falls down, 359
    in material world for money, 606
    in relationship with Kṛṣṇa, 49
    not to be directed to demigods, 18
    one must become servant of servant, 133-134
    presupposed oneness with Kṛṣṇa, 822
    rendered by Kṛṣṇa to Arjuna and devotee, 49
    rendered by *mahātmās*, 465
    reveals name, form, quality and pastimes of Kṛṣṇa, 316
    to Supreme by *jīva* eternal, 634
    with purified senses called Kṛṣṇa consciousness, 335
    (*See also* Bhakti, Bhakti-yoga, Devotional Service, Worship)
Sex
    allowed only in *bhakti-yoga*, 322
    as attraction of demons, 735-736
    as basis of mode of passion, 670-671
    as center of all activities, 207
    as downfall of Viśvāmitra, 146
    as happiness in passion, 810
    as highest material pleasure, 296
    as Kandarpa, god of love, 526
    as Kṛṣṇa's shackles, 207
    as necessity for conditioned soul, 200
    as worship in ignorance, 756
    celibacy as austerity of the body, 764-765
    contraception condemned, 725
    demons claim it as cause of the world, 733
    discouraged for yogi, 200, 296, 321-322, 327, 331
    for propagation of children, 377, 723, 725
    in household life, 251, 322, 725
    Kṛṣṇa as, 377
    Śiva agitated by Pārvatī, 149
    Yāmunācārya spits at the thought, 146, 295-296
Siddhis
    perfection *for yogīs*, 331

Śikhaṇḍī
    blows his conchshell, 46
Simplicity
    as austerity of body, 764-765
    as austerity of the mind, 766
    as divine quality, 722, 726-727
    as knowledge, defined, 629-631
    for all orders of life, 726-727
Sin
    analyzed in *Padma Purāṇa*, 445
    Arjuna free from, 720
    Arjuna questions why one is impelled to, 203
    Arjuna's fear of incurring, 61-62
    as *vikarma*, 179
    causes of, 68, 133, 180, 203, 256
    cleansed by sacrifice, 103, 255
    freedom through identity with Brahman, 335
    freedom through mode of goodness, 669
    incurred by unoffered food, 65, 176-178, 324-325
    in form of seed and as fructified, 445
    in relation to work and action, 101, 116, 239, 244, 282, 816
    Kṛṣṇa promises to deliver Arjuna from, 835-836
    Kṛṣṇa takes charge of one's past, 604
    liberated free from, 299
    lust as symbol of, 208
    not assumed by Supreme Spirit, 288
    ot due to Supersoul, 203
    not incurred by killing six types of aggressors, 61
    not incurred by one with equanimity, 120
    not the nature of the living entity, 203
    prāyaścitta system of ablution before death, 67
    strange to commit sin for happiness, 68
    transcended by devotional service, 300, 404, 445, 511
    transcended by spiritual knowledge, 138, 262-264, 494-495, 840
Śiśupāla
    spoke against Kṛṣṇa, 400
Śiṣyas te 'haṁ śādhi māṁ tvāṁ prapannam
    quoted, 122
Sītā
    as goddess of fortune, Rāma's eternal consort, 48
    Janaka her father, 185
    kidnapped by Rāvaṇa, 61

Śiva
  affirms that liberation only possible by
      Viṣṇu, 381
  agitated for sex by Pārvatī, 149
  as chief demigod, 502
  as destroyer of total material elements, 529
  as father of Skanda, 522
  as incarnation of tamo-guṇa, Cannot
      liberate, 381
  as learned leader, 382
  as part of Kṛṣṇa, 304, 538, 703
  beholds universal form in wonder, 557
  born of Brahmā, 569
  created by Kṛṣṇa, 495, 504
  defeated by Arjuna, 116
  desires to see Kṛṣṇa's two-armed form, 586
  does not possess full opulences, 74
  drank an ocean of poison, 190, 525
  his wife Ūma worshiped, 393
  in universal form, 552
  Kṛṣṇa as, 521
  one must follow, 240
  should not be imitated, 190
  subjected to influence of sense objects, 149, 381
  worship in goodness, 756
  worships Kṛṣṇa, subservient to Him, 234
Śiva-viriñci-nutam
  quoted, 234
Skanda
  identified, 522
  Kṛṣṇa as, 522
Sleep
  conquered by devotee, 51
  conquered by Guḍākeśa, 519
  equated with ignorance, 51
  happiness from, 810-811
  one in mode of ignorance addicted to, 672
  Rūpa Gosvāmī sets ideal, 326
  six hours sufficient, 325, 672
  temperance advised, 324-326
  (See also Ignorance, Nescience)
Smaraṇam
  as thinking of Kṛṣṇa, 489, 511
Smṛti
  cited, 13, 337, 703
  quoted, 237, 635
Social orders
  See Varṇa
Somadatta
  beheld by Arjuna on Battlefield, 53
  her son Bhuriśravā cited by Duryodhana as
      great warrior, 38

Somarasa
  drunk for immortality, 128
  drunk on moon, 436
  its drinking as indirect worship, 472
Soul
  also called Brahman, 410
  as aṇu-ātmā, minute particle, and vibhu-
      ātmā, Supersoul, 100
  as distinct from Viṣṇu-tattva, 95
  as minute, 94-97, 106
  as pratyag-ātmā and parag-ātmā, 251-252
  bewildered, thinks himself the doer, 192-
      193
  cannot be severed from original Soul, 104
  cannot kill or be killed, 97-98, 101
  can only be understood through Vedas, 106,
      113
  compared to bird on tree of body, 102-103
  compared to sunlight, 96-97
  degraded by lust, anger and greed, 745
  denied by demons, 733
  described as amazing, not understood,
      111-112
  does not create fruits of action, 287
  equated with consciousness, 94-95, 99-100,
      106, 659-660
  eternally fragmental, 89-90, 104
  floats in five kinds of air, 95
  general characteristics of, 89, 98-100,
      104-106, 210, 445, 658, 661
  has no by-products, 99
  has nothing to do with material world, 277
  impregnated into prakṛti by glance of Kṛṣṇa,
      122
  in heart of all, 89, 94-96, 292, 337
  its nature active, 166
  Kṛṣṇa is Soul of all souls, 196, 569
  makes direct contact with Kṛṣṇa, 210-211
  must be understood for solution to miseries,
      111
  of material world is Viṣṇu, Supersoul, 276
  philosophies denying its existence, 107
  plurality of individual souls an eternal fact,
      88
  realizes eternality but not bliss in merging,
      601
  related to intelligence, 208, 210
  relation to material body, 86, 93-94, 96-99,
      102, 110, 166, 208, 210, 285-292-293, 313,
      444-445, 600, 658-659, 796
  relation to Supersoul, 105-106, 330, 622, 637,
      642, 654

Soul
    same quality as Supersoul, 292
    subjected to ten kinds of air, 252
    theory of oneness not maintained, 87, 89
    transmigration explained, **89, 102**
    (*See also* Conditioned Soul, *Jīvātmā*, Living
        Entity)
Space
    compared to Kṛṣṇa's all-pervasiveness, 453-
        454
    Kṛṣṇa different from, 452
    Kṛṣṇa spread throughout, 555-556
    wind and cosmos rest in, **453**
Speculation
    Absolute Truth cannot be attained by, 509
    as engagement of impersonalists, 249, 278
    as inferior process, 212, 260, 272, 718-719
    as method of knowing the Self, **164**
    as philosophy without religion, 164
    as serious sin, 513
    avoidance of those addicted to, 592-593
    cannot manufacture religion, 240
    compared with Kṛṣṇa consciousness, 164
    discouraged, 19, 316, 603-604
    ended for *sthita-dhī-muni*, 142
    gradual path to Kṛṣṇa consciousness, 164
    Kṛṣṇa cannot be known by, 398, 419, 493,
        543, 579, 587-588, **591**, 823
    one on mental plane attracted to material
        energy, 55
    useless in studying *Gītā*, 439
Spirit
    as basic field of creation, 371
    basis of material body, 95, 97
    cannot be cut to pieces, 704
    distinguished from matter, 93
    does not create fruits of action, **287**
    everything related to Kṛṣṇa is spirit, 221
    explained analytically in Second Chapter,
        72
    impersonal, all-pervasive, as Brahman, 73
    its minute size discussed, 94-96
    of living entities the same, 645
    realization as *aham brahmāsmi*, 405
    (*See also* Soul)
Spiritual Body
    attained by remembering process, 26
    attained in spiritual sky, 665
    attained upon thinking of Kṛṣṇa at death,
        22
    beyond conception of materialists, 230
    does not undergo change, 715

Spiritual Body
    enables seeing Kṛṣṇa face to face, 703
    engaged in eternal service, 405
    living entity has only one, 412
    manifested at liberation, 703
    no difference between it and self, 221
    no different from *Viṣṇumūrti*, 703-704
    not affected by material miseries, 405
    of Kṛṣṇa discussed, **222**-223, 459-461, 463,
        575, 586
Spiritual Master
    acceptance as beginning of devotio'nal ser-
        vice, 617, 630
    accepts Kṛṣṇa as Supreme, 3
    as aid in freedom from material concept,
        230-231, 661
    as emerging from *ācārya* or *gosvāmī* family,
        354
    as means to knowledge, 80, **259**-260, 262,
        360, **629**, 631, 683, 758
    as representative of Kṛṣṇa, 100, 290, 829
    as representative of Vyāsa, 845
    as *sannyāsī* and *brāhmaṇa*, 723
    as transparent medium, 845
    Caitanya's prime requisite for, 82
    can be from lower castes if Vaiṣṇava, 82
    can change one's mode of nature, 753
    can solve all problems if totally Kṛṣṇa
        conscious, 82
    dispels ignorance, 290, 841
    does not contradict holy man or scripture,
        496
    does not deviate from Kṛṣṇa's instructions,
        268, 496, 829
    frees one from lamentation, 102-103
    his orders as duty, 126, 139, 201-202, 827
    his satisfaction brings advancement, 260,
        631
    if not superior to student, relation mean-
        ingless, 90
    in discipline succession, 259-260, 268
    initiation as step toward love of God, 231
    Kṛṣṇa as original, 14, 79, 81, 85, 122, 260, **574**
    Kṛṣṇa consciousness best practiced under,
        126
    methods of approaching, 80, **259-260**
    must be consulted for peace and happiness,
        82
    necessary for understanding Kṛṣṇa, 112, 126,
        589
    necessary for understanding purpose of
        Vedas, 727

Spiritual Master
  needed by Arjuna to solve problems, 81-82
  never claims to be God, 290
  one should study *Gītā* under, 268
  only he or Kṛṣṇa can liberate, 381
  paid all the respects of God, 260, 290
  prayers to, 1
  recommended by Vedic literature, 80
  relation with *brahmacārī*, 322, 421, 438
  relation with disciple, 81, 154, 260
  reveals one's relationship to Kṛṣṇa, 290
  Vyāsa-pūjā in his honor, 845
  when he is satisfied, so is God, 126
  worshiped as austerity, 764-765
  (*See also* Ācārya, Devotees, Sages, Vaiṣṇavas)
Spiritual Sky
  all entities infallible in, 714-715
  all planets self-luminous, 323, 701
  as eternal, 15
  as *paramaṁ padam*, 831
  attained by impersonalists, 22-23
  attained by Kṛṣṇa consciousness, 136-137, 247, 423, 439, 591, 603
  attained by one who is *nirmāna-moha*, 21
  attained through sacrifice, 255-256
  body does not change in, 715
  contains actual happiness, 20
  contains innumerable planets, 19, 22
  described as *avyakta*, unmanifested, 21
  diversity manifest in Vaikuṇṭhalokas, 368
  elevation from higher, planetary systems, 427
  entered by one established in equanimity, 293
  free of four principles of material existence, 20
  Goloka Vṛndāvana supreme original planet, 20
  illumined by *brahmajyoti*, 19, 641-642
  its planets controlled by Nārāyaṇa manifestations, 577
  Kṛṣṇa as source of, 503-504
  never lost when once attained, 19, 21
  no creation in, 714
  not illumined by sun, moon, electricity, 700-702
  pure devotees do not hanker for, 424
  variegatedness in, 665, 695
  (*See also* Goloka Vṛndāvana, Supreme abode)
Spiritual universe
  See Spiritual sky

'*Śraddhā*'-*śabde viśvāsa kahe sudṛḍha niścaya*
  verses quoted, 125
Śravaṇam (hearing)
  as hearing Hare Kṛṣṇa, 417-418
  as means of purification, 363
  as one of nine processes, 26
  as process of enlightenment, 442
  brahma-bhūta attained by, 824
  diminishes desire to dominate nature, 647
  importance in devotional service, 362-363, 492, 506
  importance of hearing about Kṛṣṇa, 345
  liberation by, 652
  paramparā necessary for, 845
  śruti, hearing from authorities, 718
  stressed by Caitanya, 385, 652
Śravaṇam, kīrtanam, smaraṇam, arcanam, etc.
  as *yajñas*, sacrifices, 177
Śravaṇaṁ kīrtanaṁ viṣṇoḥ smaraṇaṁ pāda-sevanam
  quoted, 26, 447, 465
Śravaṇāyāpi bahubhiryo na labhyaḥ
  verses quoted, 111
Śrī-caitanya-mano
  prayer to Śrīla Rūpa Gosvāmī, 1
Śrīdhara
  as plenary expansion, 433
Śrī Kṛṣṇa caitanya prabhu nityānanda
  prayer, 2
Śrīmad-Bhāgavatam
  accepts Kṛṣṇa as Supreme, 3, 93
  as representative of Kṛṣṇa, 529
  cited, 141, 186, 188, 194, 223-225, 227, 331, 367, 392, 396, 404, 410, 435, 447-450, 460-461, 465, 484, 486-487, 493, 495-496, 498, 502, 524, 546, 578, 586, 590, 601, 632, 691, 743, 775, 785, 824
  commentation on *Vedānta-sūtra*, 24
  dear to devotees, 506
  defines liberation, 11
  describes Caitanya, 227
  describes important planets, 21
  gives real commentary on *Vedānta-sūtra*, 713
  its study makes family happy, 633
  Māyāvādī study troublesome, 278
  mentions Gāyatrī *mantra*, 532
  must be consulted for peace and happiness, 82

Śrīmad-Bhāgavatam
  quoted, 55, 66, 73-74, 95, 120, 124, 131,
    136, 147-148, 166, 172, 189, 204, 208-
    233, 260, 262, 273, 297, 301, 322, 327,
    350-351, 355-356, 359, 363, 369, 400,
    442, 446, 516-517, 519, 611, 634, 756
  sāṅkhya expounded in, 122-123
  should be accepted, 419
  should be heard constantly from pure devo-
    tee, 606
  studied by the Vaiṣṇava *sannyāsīs*, 278
Śrīvāsa, Ācārya
  obeisances to, 2
Śriyaḥ-patir yajña-patiḥ prajā-patir
  verses quoted, 172
Sṛjāmi
  defined, 224
Śṛnvatāṁ sva-kathāṁ kṛṣṇaḥ puṇya-śravana-kīr-
  tanaḥ
  verses quoted, 363
Sṛṣṭi-hetu yei mūrti prapañce avatare
  verses quoted, 227
Śruti
  as learning by hearing, 718
  as means to understand *Vedas*, 727
  existence of soul cannot be established be-
    yond, 106
Śruti-smṛti-purāṇādi-pañcarātra-vidhiṁ vinā
  verses quoted, 366
Steadiness
  as knowledge, defined, **629, 631**
Sthīra-buddhi
  as steadiness of mind, 294
Sthita-dhī-muni
  difference from ordinary *muni*, 142
Struggle
  with different bodies for existence, 705
  with the senses and mind, **702-703**
Subhadrā
  her son Abhimanyu blows his conchshell,
    46
  her son cited by Duryodhana as great war-
    rior, 37
Submission
  in approaching spiritual master, 259-260
  in understanding *Bhagavad-gītā*, 6
  to Kṛṣṇa's will is real self-interest, 57
  (*See also* Surrender)
Subtle body
  as mind and psychological effects, 661
  carries conceptions from one body to
    another, **704-705**

Subtle body
  creation of material nature, 193
  develops a gross body, 705
  living symptoms as manifestation of, 628
  possessed by ghosts, 65
Śūdra
  as division of social order, 24, 235
  can approach Supreme, **486-487**
  defined as one who laments for gross body,
    72
  distinguished by work in modes, **812**
  in mode of ignorance, 379
  should not claim to be *brāhmaṇa*, 816
  should not expect honor, 728
  work of, **813**
  (*See also* Varṇa)
Suffering
  caused by living entity, **645-646**
  due to body identification, 286-287
  due to forgetfulness of Kṛṣṇa, 300, 593
  in material existence, 6
  māyā as cause of, 305
  transmigration cause of, 89
  (*See also* Anxiety, Miseries)
Sughosa
  name of Nakula's conchshell, **46**
Śukadeva Gosvāmī
  describes the Lord, 172
  one must follow, 240
Sukṛtina
  as four kinds of pious men, 386-387
Sun
  as evidence of Kṛṣṇa's mercy, 709
  as king of planets, 214
  as one of Kṛṣṇa's eyes, 214, 454, 520, **555**
  as origin of all the planets in solar system,
    214
  assumes power and heat from Kṛṣṇa, 214
  compared to Absolute Truth, 73-74
  compared to Kṛṣṇa and clouds to *māyā*, 402
  compared to living entity, **659**
  compared to soul, 99-100
  diseased man recommended to worship, 392,
    393
  does not illumine supreme abode, **700-702**
  eligibility for entering, 57-58
  illuminates solar system, 709
  inhabited by living entities, 105
  its light emanates from *brahmajyoti*, 374,
    709
  its splendor comes from Kṛṣṇa, **709**
  knowledge likened to, **289-290**

Sun
    Kṛṣṇa as, 373-374, **520**
    Kṛṣṇa compared to, **419**, 720
    likened to Kṛṣṇa's appearance and disappearance, 223
    moves under Kṛṣṇa's order, 454
    Paramātmā compared to, 509, 636, 640
    Paramātmā source of light in, 641
    positions of sun at times of leaving body, **434-435**
    thousands of suns likened to universal form, **549, 553**
    verses of *Gītā* compared to, 585
Sun-god
    Arjuna present when *Gītā* first spoken to, 221
    Arjuna to follow in his footsteps, 238-239
    as father of all *kṣatriyas*, 215
    as person perceived through energy, 373
    in disciplic succession, 4, **214**-215, 268
    known as Vivasvān, 214
    Kṛṣṇa recalls instructing, 402
    sacrifices for, 249
    senior by birth to Kṛṣṇa, **218**
    Vivasvān as Kṛṣṇa's first disciple, 214-215, 239
    worship in goodness, 756
Supersoul
    See Paramātmā
Supreme abode
    as *ānanda-cinmaya-rasa*, 432
    as *cintāmaṇi-dhāma*, 431
    as Goloka Vṛndāvana, 19-20
    as Kṛṣṇa, 5, 432, 469-470, 510
    as *sanātana* (eternal), 15
    as self-illu mined, 19, 93, **700-702**
    as unmanifested, infallible, supreme destination, **431**
    attained by cessation of material existence, **323**, **699**-700, **745-746**
    attained by devotion, 21-22, **158**, 228- 229, 231, 323, 591, 823-824
    attained by grace, **825, 831**
    can be approached from this world, 19
    described, 18-19, 431-432
    nondifferent from devotional service, 159
    no rebirth in, **427**
    no return from, **431**, 700-701
    not attained by whimsical action, **746-747**
    transferral at death, **415**
    variegatedness in, 432
    (*See also* Goloka Vṛndāvana, Spiritual sky)

Supreme Absolute Truth
    See Absolute Truth
Supreme Lord
    See Kṛṣṇa
Supreme Personality of Godhead
    above both Brahman and Paramātmā, 12
    always above individual soul, 106
    as Absolute will, 393
    as complete realization, 13, **718**
    as joyful, 626
    as Kṛṣṇa, 5-6, 73-74, 112, 261, **464**
    as only master, 392
    as origin of banyan tree, 698
    as supreme individual person, 87
    as worshipable object, 233, 755
    attained by unalloyed devotion, **432**
    called *sac-cid-ānanda-vigraha*, 12
    described by *Vedas*, 187
    different from parts, 93-94
    expands into *vijñānamaya*, *prāṇamaya*, etc., 626
    expands to increase bliss, 204
    frees one from all obligations, 66
    His six opulences explained, 74
    identical with His many forms, 228
    in heart of all, 87, 286
    last word in Absolute, 291
    manifests *Vedas*, **179**
    no duty for Him, 187
    originally two-handed, 584
    personal attributes discussed, 372-373
    satisfied when spiritual master is, 126
Surabhi
    Kṛṣṇa the *surabhi* amongst cows, **525-526**
Surrender
    after many births and deaths, 122, **390-391**, 599
    as acceptance of Kṛṣṇa's word, 512
    as a result of knowing Kṛṣṇa's opulences, 502
    as direct method of realization, 610
    as highest religious principle, 224-225, 835-836
    as knowledge, 84, 290, 358, 833
    as topmost *yoga*, 845
    as ultimate instruction of *Gītā*, 848
    as way to spiritual world, 380-381, **699**-702, **831**
    choice given to, 832
    erases sin, 511, 835
    follows Kṛṣṇa consciousness, 315
    Khaṭvāṅga Mahārāja's surrender, 158
    Kṛṣṇa directs senses in terms of, 44
    miscreants refuse, 382

Surrender
    of all works to Kṛṣṇa, **196, 282**
    of Arjuna to Kṛṣṇa, **79,** 842-843
    of intelligence, 211
    of learned leaders to Kṛṣṇa's feet, 382
    rewards according to, **232**
    to demigods caused by desires, 391-392
    to devotional service, **134**
    to Kṛṣṇa brings happiness, 393
    to Kṛṣṇa for liberation, 120, 349, 369,464,
        642
    to Kṛṣṇa upon severing banyan tree, **698-**
        699
    to spiritual master, 102-103, 260
    with faith and love, 835
    (See also Submission)
Sūryaloka
    as goal, 470
Sūrya-vaṁśa kṣatriyas
    sun-god father of kṣatriyas, 215
Sūta Gosvāmī
    quoted, 516-517
Svadharmas (specific duties)
    two types discussed, 114
Svādhyāya-yajña
    study as sacrifice, 253
Svalpam apy asya dharmasya trāyate mahato
        bhayāt
    quoted, 165
Svāmī
    controls mind, 335
    controls senses, 298
Svargaloka
    See Planets
Svārtha-gati
    self-interest to reach Viṣṇu, 168
Svarūpa
    as Brahman realization, 295
    as carrying out order of superior, 314
    as eternal servitor, 141, 262, 825
    defined by Caitanya Mahāprabhu, 17
    knowledge and action according to, 309
    lifts one from struggle for existence, 262-263
    not destroyed by liberation, 331
    of all living beings, 5
    of Kṛṣṇa, 222
    of one fully Kṛṣṇa conscious, 775
    represented by Arjuna, 842
Svarūpa
    in disciplic succession, 29
Svarūpa-siddhi
    perfection of one's position, 5

Svarūpeṇa vyavasthitiḥ, 331
Svatvata Tantra
    quoted, 367
Śvetāśvatara Upaniṣad
    asserts Kṛṣṇa to be maintainer of all, 86-
        87
    cited, 716
    compares soul and Supersoul to two birds
        on tree, 102-103
    quoted, 94, 187, 286, 372, 391, 638, 642
Śyāmasundara
    as beloved form for devotees, 339, 594
    His beauty described, 360
    more difficult to see than universal form,
        587
    pastimes in Vṛndāvana, 471

T

Tadā rajas-tamo-bhāvāḥ kāma-lobhādayaś ca ye
    verses quoted, 363
Tadāvadhi bata nārī-saṅgame smaryamāne
    verses quoted, 295
Tadvan na rikta-matayo yatayo niruddha
    verses quoted, 301
Tad viṣṇoḥ paramaṁ padam
    quoted, 831
Taittirīya Upaniṣad
    quoted, 394, 641
Tam akratuḥ paśyati vīta-śokaḥ
    verses quoted, 100
Tam ātmasthaṁ ye 'nupaśyanti dhīrāḥ
    verses quoted, 87
Tam ekaṁ govindam
    quoted, 459
Tam eva viditvātimṛtyumeti nānyaḥ panthā
        vidyate ayanāya
    quoted, 229, 324, 642
Taṁ ha devam ātma-buddhi-prakāśaṁ mumu-
        kṣur vai śaraṇam aham prapadye
    quoted, 642
Tam īśvarāṇāṁ paramaṁ maheśvaram
    verses quoted, 187, 304
Tamo-guṇa
    Śiva as incarnation of, 381
Tapo divyaṁ putrakā yena sattvam
    verses quoted, 297
Tapoloka
    elevation to, 472
Tapomaya-yajña
    as sacrifice of comforts, 253

Tapta-kāñcana-gaurāṅgi
    prayer, 2

Tasmād etad brahma nāma-rūpam annaṁ ca jāyate
    quoted, 666

Tasmāt sarveṣu kāleṣu mām anusmara yudhya ca
    verses quoted, 24

Tat
    used in sacrifice to satisfy Supreme, 772-774
    used to indicate Absolute Truth, 772, 773

Tato yad uttarataraṁ tad arūpam anāmayaṁ ya etad vidur amṛtās te bhavanti athetare duḥkham evāpi yānti
    quoted, 372

Tat te 'nukampāṁ su-samīkṣyamaṇaḥ
    quoted, 611

Tat tu samanvayāt
    quoted, 713

Tattvamasi
    applied to liberation, 228-229

Tattvavit
    as knower of Absolute Truth, 194

Tāvad eṣa samprasādo smāt
    verses quoted, 716

Teacher
    can speak truth to instruct, 765-766
    disqualified by *māyā*, 90
    must be representative of Kṛṣṇa, 574
    must follow principles of *śāstra*, 186
    must teach by example, 186
    when fit to be abandoned, 78
    (*See also* Ācāryas, Spiritual Master)

Temporality
    as law of material world, 15
    causes problems of life, 27
    of happiness and distress, 90-91
    of material body, 93
    of nonexistent confirmed, 93
    of *varṇas* and life, 379

Tepus tapas te juhuvuḥ sasnur āryā
    verses quoted, 131, 356

Teṣām ahaṁ samuddhartā
    quoted, 815

Time
    as form of Kṛṣṇa devouring everything, 593, 640
    as the ultimate killer, 527, 530
    as universal form, destroyer of the worlds, 563-564
    defined, 7-9

Time
    kāla refers to presiding deity of, 434
    Kṛṣṇa as, 527, 530
    universal form subject to, 544

Tolerance
    as characteristic of devotee, 611
    as knowledge, defined, 629, 631
    as quality of *brāhmaṇa*, 812
    Kṛṣṇa tolerates as father, friend, lover, 576
    of happiness and distress, 90-91
    of unpleasant duties, 91

Transcendence
    as formless, beyond materials, 372
    of modes of nature, 129
    materialists not interested in, 348
    sacrifice as means to, 348
    situated in sacrifice, 179
    symptoms of one situated in 294
    unattached work merges into, 246
    yogī situated in, 327

Transcendentalists
    attain to kingdom of God, 323
    birth in their family rare, 353-354
    can understand transmigration, 708
    characteristics of one elevated, 821
    control senses and actions, 297-298, 317, 351
    description of, 299
    discussed as personalists and impersonalists, 596-597, 600
    do not distinguish caste or species, 292
    do not meet with destruction, 350
    even greatest fall, 146
    highest of all, 836
    no worry even if unsuccessful, 351
    reside in sacred places, 320
    sacrifice unnecessary for, 181
    should live alone, secluded, 317-318
    should meditate on Kṛṣṇa, 317-318
    stand above ritualistic principles, 355
    steady in meditation on Self, 328
    their objects of meditation at death, 23
    three classes of, 4, 22, 351-352
    topmost realize Bhagavān, 74
    utter *om* in sacrifice, 773

Transmigration
    as cause of suffering, 89
    as means of rejuvenating energy, 89
    asserted by Kṛṣṇa, 220
    cannot be understood by foolish, 706-707
    caused by *karma*, 273-274, 412
    ceases when one knows Kṛṣṇa's nature, 228-229

Transmigration
conceptions carried from one body to
another, 704-705
denied by demons, 737
due to attachment to material nature, 647
effected by grace of Supersoul, 102
enacted by supreme will, 743
ended for one who attains Kṛṣṇa's abode,
427
explained, 89
from one body to another, 10, 222
higher rebirth in Kṛṣṇa consciousness, 124
likened to changing garments, 102
likened to ferris wheel, 473
none for Kṛṣṇa 495
of envious into demonic wombs, 743-744
of slaughtered animals, 727
process of impregnation, 413
self-realized soul not bewildered by, 89, 708
story of Bharata, 354-355
transcended by devotional service, 448
(See also Birth)
Tretā-yuga
characteristics and duration of, 215, 428
Gītā delivered in, 215
Tretā-yugādau ca tato vivasvān manave dadau
verses quoted, 215
Tri-vedī
as one who studies three Vedas, 472
Trivikrama
as plenary expansion, 433
Truthfulness
as divine quality, 722, 727
created by Kṛṣṇa as presenting facts properly, 497
Tulasī
Sanatkumāra became devotee by tasting,
447
should be cultivated for Kṛṣṇa, 592
tasted by Mahārāja Ambarīṣa, 148, 327
Tvam eva viditvā
quoted, 381
Tyaktvā sva-dharmaṁ caraṇāmbujaṁ harer
verses quoted, 124, 166, 351

U

Ubhe uhaivaiṣa ete taraty amṛtaḥ sādhv-asādhūnī
quoted, 263-264
Uccaiḥśravā
identified, 525
Kṛṣṇa as, 524-525

Udāna
as one of five kinds of air, 95
Udāna-vāyu
as engaged for realization, 252
Ugrasena
grandfather of Kṛṣṇa, 77
Ultimate goal
to return to Kṛṣṇa's abode, 18
Umā
worshiped for good wife, 393
Unborn
freedom from sin by knowing Kṛṣṇa as,
494-495
Kṛṣṇa as, 5, 222-223, 399-401, 510
nature of, 495
within Kṛṣṇa cited as impersonalist object,
81
Understanding
in mode of goodness, 804
in mode of ignorance, 805
in mode of passion, 805
Universal Form
Arjuna fears, 590
Arjuna first to see, 579-580
Arjuna offers obeisances to, 550-563
Arjuna requests to see, 541-542
Arjuna's reasons to see, 540-542, 546-547
as adhidaivatam, 414
as subject of Chapter Eleven, 539-594
as temporary, 544, 589
cannot be seen by impersonalists, 581
cannot be seen by studying Vedas, sacrifice
or charity, 580-581
can only be beheld by spiritual eyes, 546
contains limitless forms, bellies, mouths,
eyes, 553
contemplated by neophyte, 414
devotees not eager to see, 544, 581-583, 590
devours all peoples, scorches the worlds,
561-562
excludes reciprocal love relationship, 582
Kṛṣṇa must give one power to see it, 544
likened to sun, 549, 553, 579
manifested partially to Duryodhana, 579
may be seen by tinge of devotional service,
586
not original form of Kṛṣṇa, 590
perplexes all planetary systems, 555
planets held in fist of, 710
reveals destruction of soldiers at Kurukṣetra, 560-561, 563-566, 582
reveals everything at once, 544-545

Universal Form
    reveals unlimited eyes, mouths, garbs,
        ornaments, **548**
    seen also by Sañjaya, 847
    seen by all who were awake with divine
        vision, 556
    seen by devotees, demigods and Vyāsa,
        557-558, 579, 581, 847
    shown to attract those with no love for
        Kṛṣṇa, 590
    shown to discourage false incarnations, 542,
        589
    shown within material world by internal
        potency, **579**
    unlimited universes seen in one place,
        549-550
    worship of Kṛṣṇa in, **466-467**
Universe
    See Spiritual Sky, Material universe
Unmanifest
    all things unmanifest in their beginning
        and end, **109-110**
    as constituent of body, **627**
    as object of impersonalist meditation,
        596-597
    concentration on discouraged, 601
    realization as difficult path, **599-601**
    spiritual sky described as, 21
    worship of, **598-599**
Upaniṣads
    as means to impersonal realization, 600
    basis for Bhagavad-gītā, 111
    beginning of transcendental life, 130
    celebrate glories of Supreme, 713
    cited, 463, 702, 737
    confirm eternality of individuality, 87
    describe Caitanya, 227
    injunctions impossible in this age, 131
    must be obeyed in devotional service,
        366
    offer realization, 130
    quoted, 454
    study as sacrifice, 253, 581
    transcended by one in Kṛṣṇa consciousness,
        138
    (See also Muṇḍaka Upaniṣad, Śvetāśvatara
        Upaniṣad, etc.)
Ūrdhva-mūlam adhaḥ-śākham aśvatthaṁprāhur
        avyayam
    verses quoted, 20
Uśanā
    Kṛṣṇa as, 533-534

Utsāhān niścayād dhairyāt tat tat karma-
        pravartanāt
    verses quoted, 333
Uttamaujā
    cited by Duryodhana as great warrior, 37

                              V

Vāda
    as final conclusion in logic, 529
Vadanti tat tattva-vidas tattvaṁ yaj jñānam
        advayam
    verses quoted, 73, 634
Vaibhāṣikas
    maintain materialistic view of soul, 107
    their theory rejected by Arjuna, 108
Vaidurya stone
    Kṛṣṇa compared to, 221
Vaikuṇṭha planets
    See Spiritual sky and Planets
Vairāgya
    as detachment from matter and engage-
        ment in spirit, 345
Vaiṣamya-nairghṛnye na sāpekṣatvāt tathā hi
        darśayati
    quoted, 289
Vaiṣṇavas
    as only qualified spiritual masters. 82
    obeisances to, 1-2
    sannyāsīs compared with Māyāvādī sannyāsis,
        278-279
    transcendental to brāhmaṇa status, 236
    worship internal energy, 814-815
    (See also Devotees, Sages, Spiritual master)
Vaiṣṇavera kriyā mudrā vijñe na bujhaya
    quoted, 481
Vaiśvānara
    as principal philosopher, 444
Vaiśya
    as division of social order, 24, 235
    can approach Supreme, though of lower
        birth, **486-487**
    distinguished by work in modes, **812**
    in modes of passion and ignorance, 379
    should not engage in blackmarketing, 728
    work of, **813**
    (See also Varṇa)
Vāmana
    as plenary expansion, 433
Vānaprastha
    accepted after householder life, 726
    helps toward realization, 250
    lives in forests, severe penances, etc., 438

Vāñchā-kalpatarubhyaḥ
  prayer, 2
Vande 'ham
  prayer to spiritual masters, 1
Varāha
  as plenary expansion, 236, 360, 834
Varāha Purāṇa
  describes living entities as parts of Kṛṣṇa,
    104
  quoted, 504, 603
Varṇa
  according to modes of nature, 379, 487
  all orders can attain Kṛṣṇa, 27
  as temporary, 379
  brāhmaṇa as spiritual master, 723
  created by Kṛṣṇa, 235
  created to elevate men from animal level,
    235
  devotees transcendental to, 236
  distinguished by work in modes, 812-813
  four divisions outlined, 24
  in terms of education, not birth, 723
  Kṛṣṇa belongs to none, 235
  no distinction in devotional service, 487
  spiritual master can come from lower castes,
    82
  work should be according to one's nature,
    816
  (See also Brāhmaṇa, Kṣatriya, etc.)
Varṇa-saṅkara
  as unwanted population, 189
Varṇāśrama
  as higher principle of religion, 225
  as method of elevation, 63, 746
  enables good population to prevail, 64
  for satisfying Viṣṇu, 170
  four āśramas discussed, 250-251
  goal to reach Viṣṇu, 168
  progress of āśramas, 438-439
  reformatory ceremonies meant for, 384
  sannyāsa a difficult stage, 92
  sannyāsī as head of, 723
  surpassed by devotional service, 439
  system of ablution before death, 67
  when fails, women prone to adultery, 64
Varṇāśramācāra-vatā puruṣeṇa paraḥ pumān
  verses quoted, 170-171
Varṇāśrama-dharma
  aims to satisfy Viṣṇu, 134, 476
  awakens Kṛṣṇa consciousness, 268
  meant for tapasyā, austerity, 726
  not meant to divide society by birth, 723

Varṇāśrama-dharma
  on bodily platform, 114
  sets forth welfare activities for salvation, 66
Varuṇa
  as appointed officer, 178
  Kṛṣṇa as, 526
Vasudeva
  as father of Kṛṣṇa 52, 76
  Kṛṣṇa first appeared before him as
    Nārāyaṇa, 583, 587
  persecuted by Kaṁsa, 226
Vāsudeva
  Kṛṣṇa as, 418, 433, 533-534
  love for Him leads to liberation, 274
  meaning of name, 44
  root of all causes, 126
  surrender to, 122, 392
  universal vision precipitates full surrender,
    391
  worshiped by one in goodness, 756
Vāsudevḍ sarvam iti sa mdhātmā sudurlabhaḥ
  quoted, 126
Vāsuki
  Kṛṣṇa as serpent, 525
  serpent as bed of Garbhodakaśāyī Viṣṇu,
    552
Vasus
  behold universal form in wonder, 557
  born from Nārāyaṇa, 503
  Kṛṣṇa as Agni of, 521
Vātsalya-bhakta
  service as parent, 425
Vayaṁ tu na vitṛpyāma uttama-śloka-vikrame
  verses quoted, 516
Vedāham etaṁ puruṣaṁ mahāntam āditya-
    varṇaṁ tamasaḥ parastāt
  quoted, 372
Vedaiś ca sarvair aham eva vedyaḥ
  quoted, 172, 191
Vedānta
  Arjuna advised to raise himself to platform
    of, 129
  injunctions impossible in this age, 131
  Kṛṣṇa as compiler of, 131, 712-714
  Kṛṣṇa cannot be understood simply by
    study of, 398
  last word in Vedic wisdom, 131
Vedānta-sūtra
  accepted as ultimate stalk of knowledge, 791
  accepts Kṛṣṇa as origin of all emanations, 93
  ānandamayo'bhyāsāt quote, 18
  as representative of Kṛṣṇa 529

Vedānta-sūtra
  begins with inquiry into one's real position, 204
  Bhāgavatam proper commentary on, 278, 713
  cited, 97, 237, 331, 444, 457, 463, 744, 780
  contents given in summary, 714-715
  describes body and its knower, 625-627
  quoted, 289, 446, 473, 712, 814, 824
  Śārīraka-bhāṣya as commentary on, 278
  stresses devotional service, 780
  study as sacrifice, 253, 581
  summary of all Vedic literature, 24
Vedas
  accept Kapila's explanation of creation,122
  as criterion for action, 179, 748
  as laws of Kṛṣṇa 224, 783
  as representative of Kṛṣṇa, 529
  assert Kṛṣṇa to be maintainer, 86-87
  celebrate Kṛṣṇa as Supreme Person, 717
  cited, 221, 399, 436, 504, 564, 626, 640, 715
  compare soul and Supersoul to two birds on tree, 102-103
  confirm Kṛṣṇa as unborn, 223
  confirm plurality of individual souls, 88
  deal mainly with three modes, 129
  divided into four, 24
  do not approve unrestricted life, 726
  essence of, 130, 197, 444, 718-719, 780
  flowery language of, 127, 139
  followed by both personalists and impersonalists, 748
  for knowing Kṛṣṇa, 131, 172, 191-192, 469, 694-695, 712-714, 748
  gives chance for liberation, 256
  karma-kāṇḍa portions discussed, 127-128
  Kṛṣṇa as knower of, 712-714
  Kṛṣṇa as *om* in, 373
  Kṛṣṇa as the *Sāma-veda*, 521
  manifested from breathing of Kṛṣṇa, 179-180
  meant for formation of character, 438
  not confined to Vedic ritual, 481
  one who knows the banyan tree knows the *Vedas*, 694-695
  only means of understanding soul, 106
  originally spoken by Kṛṣṇa to Brahmā, 224
  prescribe regulated activities, 179
  quoted, 172, 174, 228, 234, 263-264, 282, 304, 324, 340, 344, 364, 376, 380-381, 623, 646, 716

Vedas
  sacrifices recommended in, 127-128, 175, 178, 257, 477
  study of, 192, 252, 438, 472, 580-581, 587-588, 722, 726, 765-766
  their definition of penance, 499
  their sacrifices as Kṛṣṇa, 468
  to be studied under spiritual master, 438, 727
  transcended by one in Kṛṣṇa consciousness, 138
Vedeṣu durlabham adurlabham ātma-bhaktau
  verses quoted, 220, 221
Vedic Knowledge
  See Knowledge
Vedic literature,
  advises approaching a spiritual master, 80
  agrees Kṛṣṇa is source of all demigods, 503
  a limitless stock, 766
  already studied by one chanting, 131
  as best diversion for mind, 767
  as means for understanding Kṛṣṇa, 588-589
  asserts Absolute Truth to be person, 590
  cited, 632, 638-639, 731
  describes body and its knower, 625-626
  enables one to remember Kṛṣṇa at death, 24
  one need read only *Gītā*, 28
  perfection by understanding, 713
  quoted, 635, 641-642, 689
  studied as sacrifice, 253, 581
  validates Arjuna's praise, 511
Veṇum kvaṇantam
  Kṛṣṇa's flute, 431
Vibhu-ātmā
  as one of two kinds of souls, 100
Vibhum
  See All-pervading, *Brahmajyoti*, Brahman
Vibhūti
  as exceptional opulence, 518
Vidyānidhi
  in disciplic succession, 29
Vigata-jvara
  as without lethargy, 197
Vijñānam
  as knowledge of spirit soul, 209
Vijñānamaya
  as distinction between mind and life symptoms, 626
Vijñānaṁ brahma
  opposed to *ananta-brahma*, 636
Vikarma
  as sinful work, 179

Vikarma
  binding on worker, 244
  one must know what it is, 240-241
Vikarṇa
  cited by Duryodhana as great warrior, 38
  identified as brother of Duryodhana, 38
Vipaścit
  as knowledge as a quality of soul, 99
Virāṭa
  blows his conchshell, **46**
  cited by Duryodhana as great fighter, 36
Viśākhā, Śrī
  obeisances to, 2
Viṣayā vinivartante nirāhārasya dehinaḥ
  verses quoted, 322
Viṣṇos tu trīṇi rūpāṇi puruṣākhyāny atho viduḥ
  verses quoted, 367
Viṣṇu
  as aim of life, 66-67, 75
  as aim of *sāṅkhya* and devotional service, 276
  as chief of primal demigods, Brahmā and Śiva, 411
  as deliverer of liberation for everyone, 381
  as Lord of all living entities, 172
  as one's self-interest, 57, 168
  as *prajā-pati*, 172
  as soul of material world, 276, 371
  as Supersoul in heart, 148, 321, 340
  as *yajña*, sacrifice, 170, 173, 175, 476
  burns up all impurities, 148
  compared to sun, one yet omnipresent, 340
  demigods cannot be equal to, 234
  His abode self-luminous, 93
  His conchshell assures victory, 43
  His devotees defined as demigods, 580
  His sacrifices sent forth at beginning of creation, 171
  jīvas remain compact in His body, 429
  Kṛṣṇa as, 28, 247, 324, 340, 590, 703, 834
  Kṛṣṇa as Viṣṇu of Ādityas, 520
  meditation on Him prescribed by *Yoga-sūtra*, 148
  one who knows three Viṣṇus is liberated, 367
  remnants of His food frees one from sin, 65
  the only master of *māyā*, 381
  thousands of forms of, 594
  three Viṣṇus assumed for creation, 367-368
  transcendental to material world, 234
  universal form addressed as, **558**

Viṣṇu
  varṇāśrama-dharma to satisfy, 134
  work as sacrifice for, **170**
  worship of impersonal aspect, 756
Viṣṇu-mantra
  cited, 538
Viṣṇumūrti
  as localized plenary representation of Kṛṣṇa, 321
  as personal expansion, 702
  spiritual body similar to, 703-704
Viṣṇu Purāṇa
  cited, 134
  quoted, 93, 170-171, 572
  total energies of Kṛṣṇa delineated in, 23
Viṣṇu-śakti
  Kṛṣṇa's energies as, 23
Viṣṇu-śaktiḥ parā proktā
  quoted, 23
Viṣṇu-tattva
  as primary expansion, 702-703
  identified with atomic soul by insane, 95
Viśvadevas
  behold universal form in wonder, 557
Viśvakośa Dictionary
  cited, 223
Viśvāmitra
  a *kṣatriya* but acted as *brāhmaṇa*, 202
  misled by Menakā into sex, 146
Viśvanātha Cakravartī Ṭhākur
  in disciplic succession, 29
  quoted, 126
Viśva-rūpa
  See Universal form
Vitaṇḍa
  as attempt to defeat in logic, 529
Vivāha-yajña
  marriage as purificatory ceremony, 784
Vivasvān
  See Sun-god
Vṛkodhara
  meaning of name, 44
Vṛndāvana
  as sacred place, 320
  as scene of supreme pastimes, 18, 44, 471
  devotees can create atmosphere of, 425
  devotees eager to see Kṛṣṇa's pastimes in, 227
  its location, 432
  replica of Goloka Vṛndāvana, 432
  (*See also* Goloka Vṛndāvana)
Vṛṣṇi
  Kṛṣṇa addressed as descendant of, **203**

Vṛṣṇi
    Kṛṣṇa as Vāsudeva among descendants of, 533-534
Vyāna
    as one of five kinds of air, 95
Vyāna-vāyu
    as engaged for realization, 252
Vyāsadeva
    as incarnation of Kṛṣṇa, 713, 847
    as learned leader, 382
    as principal philosopher, 444
    cited, 625
    Gītā heard by his mercy, 844-845
    gives Vedic literatures, 24
    his grace enables Sañjaya to see universal form, 549
    in disciplic succession, 29, 845
    influences Arjuna, 831
    instructed by Nārada Muni, 350-351
    Kṛṣṇa as, 533-534
    proclaims Kṛṣṇa to be Supreme, 5-6, 397
    saw universal form, 847
    son of Parāśara Muni, 74, 716
    teacher of Sañjaya, 33
    validates Arjuna's praise, 510
Vyāsa-Pūjā
    in honor of spiritual master, 845
Vyāsatīrtha
    in disciplic succession, 29
Vyavasāyātmikā
    intelligence as faith in Kṛṣṇa, 125

W

War
    all attempts made to avoid Battle, 185
    caused by unwanted population, 64
    demonic causes of, 739-740
    inevitable to keep law and order, 108-109
    necessary where argument fails, 185
    not supported by cycle of birth and death, 108
    transcendental for kṣatriya, 730
    violence not discouraged in, 113
Water
    as one of eight separated energies, 367-368
    as one of five great elements, 627
    as rain produced by sacrifice, 177
    generated from fire, generates earth, 110
    Kṛṣṇa accepts, 478-479
    Kṛṣṇa as its taste, 373
    Kṛṣṇa as ocean, 522

Water
    living entities found in, 668
    supplied by demigods, 173, 175
    universal form addressed as, 571
Wealth
    as result of karma, 739
    Caitanya does not want to accumulate, 308
    can be instantly destroyed by nature, 83
    cannot counteract problems of material existence, 82
    demons attracted to, 735-736, 738-741
    demons ignorant of causes of, 739
    illegally secured by demons, 737
    Kṛṣṇa as, 530
Weapons
    atomic bomb predicted, 734-735
    cannot harm soul, 104
    different types discussed, 104
    Kṛṣṇa as thunderbolt amongst, 525-526
    pāśupata-astra given Arjuna, 116
Women
    all should be considered as one's mother, 200
    as demonic pursuit, 736
    available in heavenly planets, 127-128
    Caitanya does not want to enjoy, 308-309
    can approach Supreme, 486-487
    corrupted when irreligion prominent, 64
    Kṛṣṇa as the six feminine opulences, 530-531
    methods of protecting, 732
    not very intelligent or trustworthy, 64
    prone to degradation, 64
    sannyāsī forbidden relationships with, 724
    should not be given freedom, 732
    the illumined take no interest in, 182
    their chastity leads to good population, 64
    their morality low today, 732
    Yāmunācārya spits at the thought, 146
Work
    according to modes of nature, 235, 816
    always to be connected to Kṛṣṇa's interest, 326
    Arjuna inquires whether it is to be renounced or not, 272
    as basis of action, 794
    as Kṛṣṇa-karma, 591-592
    as sacrifice, 170-171, 247, 257-258, 816-817
    as vikarma, 179
    as yoga, 121, 135, 310, 607, 651
    better one's own imperfectly than another's perfectly, 815-817

Work
   both good and evil work bind, 171
   capricious, 132, 800
   covered by fault as fire by smoke, 817-818
   determines direction of transmigration, 89,
      97
   for bare necessities only, 244
   for sense gratification condemned, 134, 181,
      297, 608
   for the education and welfare of all, 184,
      299
   honest and independent for devotee, 245
   ignorant should be encouraged to engage in,
      191-192
   in buddhi-yoga, 123, 164
   in full knowledge nonreactive, 272
   in ignorance, 797-798, 802-803
   in Kṛṣṇa consciousness, 24-25, 124, 179,
      193-194, 196, 273, 277-279, 281-282,
      304-305, 507, 591-592, 602-603, 827-828
   in mode of goodness, 800-801
   in mode of passion, 801-802
   its constituents, 794
   Kṛṣṇa not bound by, 186, 236, 456-457
   Kṛṣṇa's engagement in, 186, 188-189
   merges entirely into transcendence, 246
   mūḍhas work hard like asses, 383-384
   necessity for, 24, 124, 169, 305
   no bondage for one firmly situated in, 267
   nonattachment to, 135, 183-184, 236, 308,
      788
   of demons unclean, 735-736
   perfection by following qualities of, 814
   primarily for sense gratification, 237
   process of actualization, 794
   purified by service to Kṛṣṇa, 818
   reactions accumulated since time imme-
      morial, 135
   service to Kṛṣṇa only work for whole world,
      28
   should not be abandoned, 165, 169-170
      817-818
   temperance advised, 325-326
   the highest welfare work, 300
   types of, 132-133
   under Kṛṣṇa's protection, 826
   varṇas distinguished by quality of, 812-813
   worship through, 815
   yields material results quickly, 233
   (See also Action, Activities, Karma)
Worship
   according to three modes, 753-756

Worship
   Arjuna advised to worship Kṛṣṇa, 834
   distinguished from bhajate, 358-359
   for economic motives condemned, 762
   in temple derided by impersonalists, 461
   in temple for progress, 589
   methods cited, 489-490
   of arcā for knowing purport of Brahman, 405
   of arca-vigraha in temple not idol worship,
      600
   of concocted form as Supreme, 467
   of demigods, 175, 178, 234, 249-250, 359,
      391-394, 475, 477, 756
   of ghosts, ancestors and Kṛṣṇa, 477
   of human leaders by foolish, 234
   of Kṛṣṇa by mahātmā, 358-360, 465-466
   of Kṛṣṇa and Supersoul, 340
   of Kṛṣṇa as one without a second, diverse in
      many, 466-467
   of Kṛṣṇa, brāhmaṇas, spiritual master,
      superiors, 764-765
   of Kṛṣṇa by study of Gītā, 839
   of Kṛṣṇa in universal form, 466-467
   of oneself as Supreme Lord, 467
   of sun by diseased, 392,393
   of unmanifest, 598-599
   perfection by, 814-815
   will not reveal two-armed form, 587-588
   (See also Bhakti, Bhakti-yoga, Devotional
      service, Service)

Y

Yac-cakṣur eṣa savitā sakala-grahāṇām
   verses quoted, 214
Yadābadhi mama cetaḥ kṛṣṇa-padāravinde
   verses quoted, 295
Yādava
   Kṛṣṇa addressed as, 573
Ya eṣām puruṣam sākṣād ātma-prabhavam
      īśvaram
   verses quoted, 359
Yajña
   See Sacrifice
Yajña-pati
   purpose of sacrifice is his satisfaction, 173
Yājñavalkya
   as principal philosopher, 444
   quoted, 321-322
Yajñeṣu paśavo brahman hanyante satatam
      dvijaih
   verses quoted, 114

Yajñeśvara, 232
Yajño vai Viṣṇuḥ
    quoted, 170
Yajur-veda
    as one of four Vedas, 581
    emanates from Kṛṣṇa, 179
    Kṛṣṇa as, 468-469
Yakṣas
    behold universal form in wonder, 557
    Kṛṣṇa as Kuvera of, 521
    worshiped in conditioned state, 776
    worshipers of ghosts may become, 447
Yāma
    in aṣṭāṅga-yoga, 303, 305
Yamadūtas
    agents of Kṛṣṇa, 800
Yamarāja
    Kṛṣṇa as, 526-527
    one must follow, 240
Yaṁ śyāmasundaram acintya-guṇa-svarūpam
    verses quoted, 339
Yamunā
    as sacred river, 320
Yamunācārya
    quoted, 146, 149, 295, 386, 397-398
Yaṁ yaṁ vāpi smaran bhāvaṁ tyajaty ante
        kalevaram
    verses quoted, 23
Yānti deva-vratā devān pitṝn yānti pitṛ-vratāḥ
    quoted, 19-20
Yasmin vijñate sarvam eva vijñatam bhavanti
    quoted, 364
Yaśodā
    as childhood guardian of Kṛṣṇa, 44
    Kṛṣṇa descends as son of, 360
Yaśodā-nandana
    meaning of name, 44
Yas tv ātma-ratir eva syāt
    quoted, 819
Yasya brahme ca kṣatram ca ubhe bhavata
        odanaḥ
    verses quoted, 564
Yasya deve parā bhaktir yathā deve tathā gurau
    verses quoted, 369
Yasyājñayā bhramati sambhṛta-kālacakraḥ
    verses quoted, 214
Yasya prasādād bhagavat-prasādaḥ
    verses quoted, 126
Yasyāsti bhaktir bhagavaty akiñcanā
    verses quoted, 55
Yasyātma-buddhiḥ kuṇape tri-dhātuke
    verses quoted, 208

Yataḥ pravṛttir bhūtānām
    quoted, 608-609
Yatanto 'py akṛtātmānaḥ
    as gymnastic yogīs, 708
Yato vā imāni bhūtāni jāyante yena jātāni jīvanti
        yat prayanty abhisaṁviśanti tad brahma tad
        vijijñāsasva
    quoted, 376, 641
Yat-pāda-paṅkaja-palāśa-vilāsa-bhaktyā
    verses quoted, 301
Yatra kvāpi niṣadya yādava-kulottamasya
        kaṁsa-dviṣaḥ
    verses quoted, 138
Yatra kva vābhadram abhūd amuṣya kiṁ
    verses quoted, 124, 166, 351
Yat-tīrtha-buddhiḥ salite na karhicit
    verses quoted, 124, 208
Yā vai sādhana-sampatti-puruṣārtha-catuṣṭaye
    verses quoted, 603
Ye indrādy-aṅga-tayāvasthitaṁ yajñaṁ sarve-
        śvaraṁ viṣṇum, etc.
    quoted, 177
Yeṣāṁ tvanta-gataṁ pāpaṁ janānāṁ puṇya-
        karmaṇām
    verses quoted, 357
Yo brahmāṇaṁ vidadhāti: pūrvaṁ yo vai vedāṁś
        ca gāpayati sma kṛṣṇaḥ
    quoted, 503
Yoga
    Arjuna should arm himself with, 267
    artificial postures do not help, 212
    as control of mind, 133, 312, 346
    as means for linking with Supreme, 310-311,
        357-358
    as means for transferring soul to other
        planets, 603
    as means of knowing Kṛṣṇa in full, 362
    as sanātana-yoga, two divisions discussed, 268
    attained by one situated in Transcendence,
        327
    attained when material desires are re-
        nounced, 311
    blocked by eating, sleeping, defending and
        mating, 326
    cannot be practiced by artificial abstinence,
        325
    compared to ladder, 310-311
    defined by Vedic dictionary, 121
    determination in, 332-333, 806
    eightfold system of, 252, 308, 311, 314, 347,
        352
    following of Kṛṣṇa's orders as, 133-134

Yoga
  for *siddhis*, perfections, 253, 331
  importance at time of death, 420
  impractical and unendurable to Arjuna, 25, 342-343
  Indra and Viṣṇu worshiped by, 411
  in relation to work, 121, 135
  its knowledge discussed, 121-158
  its practice never goes in vain, 355
  its science taught to sun-god, 214-215
  Kṛṣṇa as master of, 844-845
  leading to *samādhi*, 330
  methods of meditation, breath control, 251-252, 302-303, 319-321, 420, 422
  not possible for ordinary man in Kali-yuga, 308, 342-343, 347
  not possible in big cities, 320
  pains mitigated by practice of, 325-326
  Paramātmā realization in, 314, 321
  Patañjali system discussed, 251-252
  perfection in Kṛṣṇa consciousness, 147-148, 322-324, 353, 359-360, 362, 597-598
  religion and philosophy interdependent, 164
  sex to be avoided in, 321-322
  the same as renunciation, 309
  useless if selfishness remains, 310
  (*See also* Bhakti-yoga, Jñāna-yoga, Karma-yoga, etc.)
Yoga-māyā
  Kṛṣṇa covered by, 400, 515-516, 586
Yogārūḍha
  as highest rung of *yoga* ladder, 311
  as perfectional stage of *yoga*, 819
Yogārurukṣa
  as beginning of yoga ladder, 311
Yoga-sūtra
  prescribes meditation on Viṣṇu, 148
  quoted, 330
Yogāt calita-mānasaḥ
  as deviation from transcendental path, 348
Yoga-yajña
  via various systems, 253
Yogeśvara
  Kṛṣṇa as, 542-543, 847
  significance of address, 543
Yogeśvaram
  as mystic power of Kṛṣṇa, 453
Yogī
  acts with body only for purification, 283
  addicted to gymnastics, 708

Yogī
  after many births attains goal, 356-357
  always sees Paramātmā in heart, 148, 339
  Arjuna inquires into fate of unsuccessful 347-349
  as indirectly Kṛṣṇa conscious, 318
  as one who works for whole, not the part 308
  as pretender, 167
  as sincerest friend of all, 341
  attains happiness with mind on Kṛṣṇa, 335
  automatically attracted to yogic principles, 355
  awarded results by Kṛṣṇa, 232
  broadcasts importance of Kṛṣṇa consciousness, 341
  can arrange time to leave body, 435
  cannot be successful without Kṛṣṇa consciousness, 346
  cannot understand Kṛṣṇa, 366
  concentrates on Śyāmasundara, 360
  contrasted with devotees, 341-342
  directions on how to meditate, 319-320
  does not seek improvement in health, 323
  four *āśramas* help one become perfect, 250
  greater than ascetic, empiricist, fruitive worker, 357-358
  his fate if unsuccessful, 352-356
  his liberation difficult and temporary, 228
  Kṛṣṇa addressed as, 515-516
  motivated by personal satisfaction, 308
  must not sleep or eat too much or too little, 324-325
  not attracted to ritualistic principles, 355
  perfection in Kṛṣṇa consciousness, 26, 249, 324, 358-360
  prolongs life by *kumbhaka-yoga*, 254
  qualifications for attaining *yoga*, 327
  resides in sacred place, 320
  satisfied by knowledge, 316
  sees all beings in Kṛṣṇa, Kṛṣṇa in all beings, 337-338, 341
  sees pebbles, stones or gold as same, 316
  sense control by, 144, 297-298, 309, 327, 331
  unhappy because of unfulfilled desires, 156
  wastes time in phantasmagoria, 148
  worships demigods and offers sacrifice, 249-250
  worships Kṛṣṇa and remains in Him, 340
  (*See also* Paramātmāvādī)

Yoginām api sarveṣām mad-gatenāntarātmanā
    verses quoted, 25, 780, 845

Yo'sau sarvair vedair gīyate
    quoted, 713

*Yo vā etad akṣaraṁ gārgy aviditvāsmāl lokāt
    praiti sa kṛpaṇaḥ*
    verse quoted, 80

*Yo 'yaṁ tavāgato deva-samīpaṁ devatā-gaṇaḥ sa
    tvam eva jagat-sraṣṭā yataḥ sarva-gato
    bhavān*
    quoted, 572

*Yo 'yaṁ yogas tvayā proktaḥ sāmyena madhu-
    sūdana*
    verses quoted, 25

Yudhāmanyu
    cited by Duryodhana as great warrior, **37**

Yudhiṣṭhira
    as righteous king, 525
    blows his conchshell, **46**
    heads religious persons to be established by
        Kṛṣṇa, 33
    his victory certain, 848

Yugas
    a thousand is duration of Brahmā's day,
        427-428
    characteristics and durations of, 215, 428

Yukta
    as perfect process for transcendental
        achievement, 328

Yukta-vairāgya
    as renunciation of fruits explained, 481

Yuyudhāna
    cited by Duryodhana as great fighter, **36**

Z

Zoomorphism
    in worship of foolish leaders, 234

BHAGAVAD-GĪTĀ AS IT IS

"No work in all Indian literature is more quoted, because none is better loved, in the West, than the *Bhagavad-gītā*. Translation of such a work demands not only knowledge of Sanskrit, but an inward sympathy with the theme and a verbal artistry. For the poem is a symphony in which God is seen in all things. ...The Swami does a real service for students by investing the beloved Indian epic with fresh meaning. Whatever our outlook may be, we should all be grateful for the labor that has lead to this illuminating work."

Dr. Geddes MacGregor, Emeritus Distinguished Professor of Philosophy University of Southern California

"The *Gītā* can be seen as the main literary support for the great religious civilization of India, the oldest surviving culture in the world. The present translation and commentary is another manifestation of the permanent living importance of the *Gītā*."

Thomas Merton, Theologian

"I am most impressed with A. C. Bhaktivedanta Swami Prabhupāda's scholarly and authoritative edition of *Bhagavad-gītā*. It is a most valuable work for the scholar as well as the layman and is of great utility as a reference book as well as a textbook. I promptly recommend this edition to my students. It is a beautifully done book."

Dr. Samuel D. Atkins Professor of Sanskrit, Princeton University

"...As a successor in direct line from Caitanya, the author of *Bhagavad-gītā As It Is* is entitled, according to Indian custom, to the majestic title of His Divine Grace A. C. Bhaktivedanta Swami Prabhupāda. The great interest that his reading of the *Bhagavad-gītā* holds for us is that it offers us an authorized interpretation according to the principles of the Caitanya tradition."

Olivier Lacombe Professor of Sanskrit and Indology, Sorbonne University, Paris

"I have had the opportunity of examining several volumes published by the Bhaktivedanta Book Trust and have found them to be of excellent quality and of great value for use in college classes on Indian religions. This is particularly true of the BBT edition and translation of the *Bhagavad-gītā*."

Dr. Frederick B. Underwood Professor of Religion, Columbia University

REVIEWS

"...If truth is what works, as Pierce and the pragmatists insist, there must be a kind of truth in the *Bhagavad-gītā As It Is*, since those who follow its teachings display a joyous serenity usually missing in the bleak and strident lives of contemporary people."

> Dr. Elwin H. Powell
> Professor of Sociology
> State University of New York, Buffalo

"There is little question that this edition is one of the best books available on the *Gītā* and devotion. Prabhupāda's translation is an ideal blend of literal accuracy and religious insight."

> Dr. Thomas J. Hopkins
> Professor of Religion, Franklin and Marshall College

"The *Bhagavad-gītā*, one of the great spiritual texts, is not as yet a common part of our cultural milieu. This is probably less because it is alien per se than because we have lacked just the kind of close interpretative commentary upon it that Swami Bhaktivedanta has here provided, a commentary written from not only a scholar's but a practitioner's, a dedicated lifelong devotee's point of view."

> Denise Levertov, Poet

"The increasing numbers of Western readers interested in classical Vedic thought have been done a service by Swami Bhaktivedanta. By bringing us a new and living interpretation of a text already known to many, he has increased our understanding manyfold."

> Dr. Edward C. Dimock, Jr.
> Department of South Asian Languages and Civilization
> University of Chicago

"The scholarly world is again indebted to A. C. Bhaktivedanta Swami Prabhupāda. Although *Bhagavad-gītā* has been translated many times, Prabhupāda adds a translation of singular importance with his commentary..."

> Dr. J. Stillson Judah, Professor of the History of Religions and Director of Libraries
> Graduate Theological Union, Berkeley, California

REVIEWS

"Srila Prabhupāda's edition thus fills a sensitive gap in France, where many hope to become familiar with traditional Indian thought, beyond the commercial East-West hodgepodge that has arisen since the time Europeans first penetrated India.

"Whether the reader be an adept of Indian spiritualism or not, a reading of the *Bhagavad-gītā As It Is* will be extremely profitable. For many this will be the first contact with the true India, the ancient India, the eternal India."

Francois Chenique, Professor of Religious Sciences
Institute of Political Studies, Paris, France

"As a native of India now living in the West, it has given me much grief to see so many of my fellow countrymen coming to the West in the role of *gurus* and spiritual leaders. For this reason, I am very excited to see the publication of *Bhagavad-gītā As It Is* by Sri A. C. Bhaktivedanta Swami Prabhupāda. It will help to stop the terrible cheating of false and unauthorized '*gurus*' and '*yogis*' and will give an opportunity to all people to understand the actual meaning of Oriental culture."

Dr. Kailash Vajpeye, Director of Indian Studies
Center for Oriental Studies, The University of Mexico

"...It is a deeply felt, powerfully conceived and beautifully explained work. I don't know whether to praise more this translation of the *Bhagavad-gītā*, its daring method of explanation, or the endless fertility of its ideas. I have never seen any other work on the *Gīta* with such an important voice and style. ... It will occupy a significant place in the intellectual and ethical life of modern man for a long time to come."

Dr. Shaligram Shukla
Professor of Linguistics, Georgetown University

"I can say that in the *Bhagavad-gītā As It Is* I have found explanations and answers to questions I had always posed regarding the interpretations of this sacred work, whose spiritual discipline I greatly admire. If the aesceticism and ideal of the apostles which form the message of the *Bhagavad-gītā As It Is* were more widespread and more respected, the world in which we live would be transformed into a better, more fraternal place."

Dr. Paul Lesourd, Author
Professeur Honoraire, Catholic University of Paris